Marketing Management

Knowledge and Skills

Eleventh Edition

J. Paul Peter
University of Wisconsin–Madison

James H. Donnelly, Jr.
University of Kentucky

MARKETING MANAGEMENT: KNOWLEDGE AND SKILLS, ELEVENTH EDITION

Published by McGraw-Hill, a business unit of The McGraw-Hill Companies, Inc., 1221 Avenue of the Americas, New York, NY, 10020. Copyright © 2013 by The McGraw-Hill Companies, Inc. All rights reserved. Printed in the United States of America. Previous editions © 2011, 2009, and 2007. No part of this publication may be reproduced or distributed in any form or by any means, or stored in a database or retrieval system, without the prior written consent of The McGraw-Hill Companies, Inc., including, but not limited to, in any network or other electronic storage or transmission, or broadcast for distance learning.

Some ancillaries, including electronic and print components, may not be available to customers outside the United States.

This book is printed on acid-free paper.

5 6 7 8 9 0 DOW/DOW 1 0 9 8 7 6 5

ISBN   978-0-07-786105-6
MHID 0-07-786105-1

Senior Vice President, Products & Markets: *Kurt L. Strand*
Vice President, General Manager, Products & Markets: *Brent Gordon*
Vice President, Content Production & Technology Services: *Kimberly Meriwether David*
Managing Director: *Paul Duchan*
Executive Brand Manager: *Sankha Basu*
Development Editor: *Gabriela Gonzalez*
Marketing Manager: *Donielle Xu*
Director, Content Production: *Terri Schiesl*
Lead Project Manager: *Jane Mohr*
Buyer: *Laura Fuller*
Cover/Interior Designer: *Studio Montage, St. Louis, MO.*
Cover Image: *© Steve Cole/Getty Images*
Media Project Manager: *Prashanthi Nadipalli*
Typeface: *10/12 Times New Roman*
Compositor: *Laserwords Private Limited*
Printer: *RR Donnelley*

All credits appearing on page or at the end of the book are considered to be an extension of the copyright page.

Library of Congress Cataloging-in-Publication Data

Peter, J. Paul.
  Marketing management : knowledge and skills / J. Paul Peter, James H. Donnelly, Jr.—11th ed.
      p. cm.
  ISBN 978-0-07-786105-6 (alk. paper)
  1. Marketing—Management. 2. Marketing—Management—Case studies. I. Donnelly, James H. II. Title.
  HF5415.13.P387 2013
  658.8—dc23

                                                                2012028086

The Internet addresses listed in the text were accurate at the time of publication. The inclusion of a website does not indicate an endorsement by the authors or McGraw-Hill, and McGraw-Hill does not guarantee the accuracy of the information presented at these sites.

www.mhhe.com

To Rose, Angie, and Chelsea

J. Paul Peter

To Gayla

Jim Donnelly

About the Authors

J. Paul Peter

has been a faculty member at the University of Wisconsin since 1981. He was a member of the faculty at Indiana State, Ohio State, and Washington University before joining the Wisconsin faculty. While at Ohio State he was named Outstanding Marketing Professor by the students, and won the John R. Larson Teaching Award at Wisconsin. He has taught a variety of courses including Marketing Management, Marketing Strategy, Consumer Behavior, Marketing Research, and Marketing Theory, among others.

Professor Peter's research has appeared in the *Journal of Marketing,* the *Journal of Marketing Research,* the *Journal of Consumer Research,* the *Journal of Retailing,* and the *Academy of Management Journal,* among others. His article on construct validity won the prestigious William O'Dell Award from the *Journal of Marketing Research,* and he was a finalist for this award on two other occasions. Recently, he was the recipient of the Churchill Award for Lifetime Achievement in Marketing Research, given by the American Marketing Association and the Gaumnitz Distinguished Faculty Award from the School of Business, University of Wisconsin–Madison. He is an author or editor of over 30 books, including *A Preface to Marketing Management,* thirteenth edition; *Marketing Management: Knowledge and Skills,* eleventh edition; *Consumer Behavior and Marketing Strategy,* ninth edition; *Strategic Management: Concepts and Applications,* third edition; and *Marketing: Creating Value for Customers,* second edition. He is one of the most cited authors in the marketing literature.

Professor Peter has served on the review boards of the *Journal of Marketing, Journal of Marketing Research, Journal of Consumer Research,* and *Journal of Business Research* and was measurement editor for *JMR* and professional publications editor for the American Marketing Association. He has taught in a variety of executive programs and consulted for several corporations as well as the Federal Trade Commission.

James H. Donnelly, Jr.

has spent his academic career in the Gatton College of Business and Economics at the University of Kentucky. In 1990 he received the first Chancellor's Award for Outstanding Teaching given at the university. He twice received the UK Alumni Association's Great Teacher Award, an award one can be eligible to receive only every 10 years. He also received two Outstanding Teacher awards from Beta Gamma Sigma, national business honorary. In 1992 he received an Acorn Award recognizing "those who shape the future" from the Kentucky Advocates for Higher Education. In 2001 and 2002 he was selected as "Best University of Kentucky Professor." In 1995 he became one of six charter members elected to the American Bankers Association's Bank Marketing Hall of Fame. He also received a "Distinguished Doctoral Graduate Award" from the University of Maryland.

During his career he has published in the *Journal of Marketing Research, Journal of Marketing, Journal of Retailing, Administrative Science Quarterly, Academy of Management Journal, Journal of Applied Psychology, Personnel Psychology, Journal of Business Research,* and *Operations Research,* among others. He has served on the editorial review board of the *Journal of Marketing,* and is the author of more than a dozen books, which include widely adopted academic texts as well as professional books.

Professor Donnelly is very active in the banking industry where he has served on the board of directors of the Institute of Certified Bankers and the ABA's Marketing Network. He has also served as academic dean of the ABA's School of Bank Marketing and Management.

Preface

The original vision for *Marketing Management: Knowledge and Skills*—to assemble a complete student resource for marketing management education—is as relevant today as it was in earlier editions. Our goal has always been very clear to us: to enhance students' *knowledge* of marketing management and to advance their *skills* in utilizing this knowledge to develop and implement successful marketing strategies. *Knowledge enhancement* and/or *skill development* are the purpose of each section in the book.

We are proud to introduce the 11th edition knowing that our book has been used throughout the world as the main text in courses of marketing management, marketing planning, and marketing strategy. We believe that it has endured because of the options and learning components it offers both instructors and students, and our knowledge and skills framework.

MAXIMUM FLEXIBILITY

Based on our teaching experience we developed this book to provide maximum flexibility for use in a variety of course settings. Three of the most common uses are:

1. in undergraduate programs as the primary text in an integrative, capstone marketing management or marketing strategy course;
2. in MBA programs as the primary text in the required marketing management course or as the primary text in a second, elective course in marketing management; and
3. in Executive MBA programs as the primary text in a required or elective marketing management course.

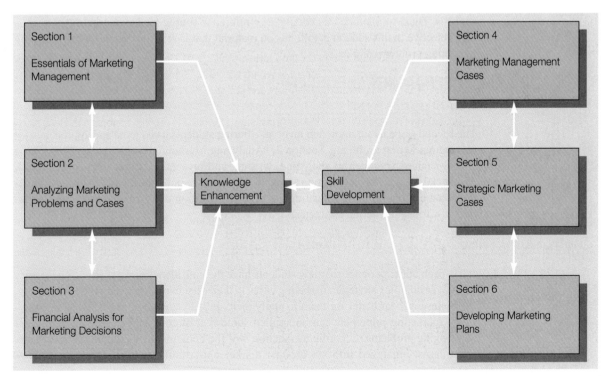

Our book contains six stand-alone sections. Each of them will be discussed in the knowledge enhancement and skill development framework below. Instructors can decide the mix of the six sections that best fulfills their course objectives. We have utilized the book successfully in each of the above three scenarios. We have also found that the knowledge enhancement and skill development framework helps students understand the rationale for the components of the course they are taking. Welcome to our book.

THE STRUCTURE OF THE BOOK

During our years of teaching, we have experimented with many different teaching approaches and philosophies. The structure of this book reflects an evolution from these experiments. Presently, our model includes a five stage learning approach that includes (1) mastering basic marketing principles, (2) learning approaches and tools for performing marketing analyses, (3) analyzing marketing management cases, (4) analyzing strategic marketing cases, and (5) developing marketing plans.

Our five stage learning approach is the focus of the six sections of the book. Each section has as its objective either *knowledge enhancement* or *skill development* or both. The framework and structure of our book is presented in the diagram below and will appear throughout the text to integrate the sections of the book.

STAGE 1: MASTERING BASIC MARKETING PRINCIPLES

It is clearly necessary for students to learn and understand basic definitions, concepts, and marketing logic before they can apply them in the analysis of marketing problems or development of marketing plans. Section 1 of the book contains 13 chapters that present the essentials of marketing management. One problem we continually face in more advanced case-oriented courses is that most students have long ago discarded or sold their basic marketing texts. Consequently, when they are faced with case problems they have nothing to rely on but their memories. We believe this seriously detracts from the usefulness of case analysis. Thus, we include this section as a reference source for key marketing concepts. Our objective in this section is to focus on material that is relevant primarily for analyzing marketing problems and cases.

STAGE 2: LEARNING APPROACHES AND TOOLS FOR PROBLEM ANALYSIS

The second stage in our approach involves offering students basic tools and approaches for solving marketing problems. Section 2, "Analyzing Marketing Problems and Cases," is a widely praised approach to analyzing, writing, and presenting case analyses. Section 3, "Financial Analysis for Marketing Decisions," presents some important financial calculations that can be useful in evaluating the financial position of a firm and the financial impact of various marketing strategies.

STAGE 3: ANALYZING MARKETING MANAGEMENT CASES

It has been our experience that few students have the confidence and experience necessary to analyze complex strategic marketing cases in their first exposure to this type of learning. We believe it is far better for them to apply their skills by analyzing cases for which traditional marketing principles can be applied somewhat directly before they attempt more challenging problems. Accordingly, Section 4 of the book includes 25 marketing management cases, organized into six groups: market opportunity analysis, product strategy, promotion strategy, distribution strategy, pricing strategy, and social and ethical issues in marketing management. Within each group, cases are sequenced so that later cases contain more information and typically require higher levels of marketing management analysis skills than earlier ones.

STAGE 4: ANALYZING STRATEGIC MARKETING CASES

Once students have developed sufficient skills to provide thoughtful analyses of marketing management cases, they are prepared to tackle strategic marketing cases. These cases go beyond traditional marketing principles and focus on the role of marketing in cross-functional business or organization strategies. Section 5 of our book contains 10 such cases. They are sequenced so that the latter cases contain more information and require higher skill levels to analyze them properly.

STAGE 5: DEVELOPING MARKETING PLANS

The final stage in our approach involves the development of an original marketing plan. We believe that after a two-course sequence in marketing management, students should be able to do one thing very well and should know that they can do it well: Students should be able to construct a quality marketing plan for any product or service. Section 6 provides a framework for developing such a plan. Instructors can consult the *Instructor's Manual* that accompanies this book for alternative ways to incorporate this stage into their course.

THE PRESENT EDITION

We continuously revise and update the text chapters in Section 1. Any changes made are based on our own intuition and judgment as well as feedback from students and instructors.

Brand new to this edition, we have added a section of key terms and concepts at the conclusion of each chapter in which they appear where they will be more visible to students and easier to use than as an appendix at the end of the book. More than a glossary, it presents key concepts and terms which can be referred to by students as they master basic marketing principles, develop marketing plans, and analyze marketing cases.

This edition also completes the revision of two important elements of the text chapters. First, "Marketing Insight" features now replace our "Marketing Highlights" feature. We did this to more accurately focus their purpose and content as being a central resource helpful to students in solving marketing problems, analyzing marketing cases, and developing marketing plans. There are approximately 75 "highlights" that are now an integral part of the book and not the "current events" or "news items" often found in other texts.

Second, an "Additional Resources" section now concludes each chapter. The focus of this feature is to provide students current resources which they can utilize in solving marketing problems, analyzing marketing cases, and developing marketing plans. It can also be used to assist in writing assignments and classroom case presentations. As with the new marketing insights, the additional resources reflect our new criteria and focus. Each resource has been selected with students in mind. They contain a mix of academic and professional publications appropriate for advanced MBA students and undergraduate students.

Finally, selecting an appropriate array of cases is always a challenge. We rely heavily on instructor feedback on what cases work well for them and which should be maintained and eliminated. In the end it is our task to find challenging cases for students to analyze. We are fortunate to be able to say that approximately fifty percent of the cases in the recent editions are new. Our array includes domestic and global companies, high-tech and low-tech companies, consumer and organizational products, small and large businesses, product and service organizations, manufacturers and channel members, well-known and not-so-well-known companies, and successful and not-so-successful companies. We believe our selection of cases will continue to meet the needs of instructors and students.

RESOURCES FOR INSTRUCTORS AND STUDENTS

We encourage instructors to go to the website www.mhhe.com/peterdonnelly11e which presents a comprehensive Instructor's Manual and support materials. Your McGraw-Hill representative can also assist in the delivery of additional support materials. The Instructor's Manual includes:

1. A detailed discussion of alternative ways to utilize the book. Because of the importance of student participation and team building, we provide an approach for organizing course projects and team assignments, including project presentation forms for peer evaluations.
2. Outlines for each chapter in the text including Power Point slides that highlight text material.
3. Comprehensive teaching notes for each case. We included the quality of the case teaching notes as a critical selection criterion for a case to be included in the book.
4. In addition to the Instructor's Manual, we offer a test bank of nearly 1,300 multiple-choice, true-false, and brief essay questions for the text chapters.

Finally, we urge instructors to encourage students to view the student section of the Online Learning Center (OLC) at Website www.mhhe.com/peterdonnelly11e which contains a number of useful aids for facilitating learning and supporting student achievement. We believe they will find it a useful resource.

Acknowledgments

It is important that we recognize the many talented people who have contributed to our book in the form of cases and exercises. Our appreciation and thanks go to each of them. Their names and affiliations appear in the Contents and at the point in the book where their contribution appears. Their work will help others better educate marketing students.

We also must thank the users who responded to our survey. Your assistance was needed as we planned this edition, especially in making the hard choices involved in replacing cases, selecting new cases, and deciding which of the "classic" cases to retain. Again, thanks for your assistance.

We also want to acknowledge those colleagues who provided detailed reviews of previous editions:

Sammy G. Amin
Frostburg State University

Amy Beattie
Champlain College

Andrew Bergstein
Pennsylvania State University

David Bourff
Boise State University

Brad Brooks
Queens College

Carol Bruneau
University of Montana

Richard Campbell
California State University–Bakersfield

Daniel P. Chamberlin
Regent University

V. Glenn Chappell
Meredith College

Henry Chen
University of West Florida

Newell Chiesl
Indiana State University

Pravat K. Choudhury
Howard University

Clare Comm
University of Massachusetts–Lowell

John Considine
LeMoyne College

Robert Cosenza
University of Mississippi

Larry Crowson
University of Central Florida

Robert Cutler
Cleveland State University

Mike Dailey
University of Texas–Arlington

Carl Dresden
Coastal Carolina University

Denver D'Rozario
Howard University

Patricia Duncan
Harris-Stowe State College

Adel I. El-Ansary
University of North Florida

Randall Ewing
Ohio Northern University

Renee Foster
Delta State University

John Gauthier
Gateway Technical College

David Griffith
University of Oklahoma

Angela Hausman
University of Texas–Pan American

Jack Healey
Golden State University

JoAnne S. Hooper
Western Carolina University

Jarrett Hudnall
Mississippi University for Women

Patricia Humphrey
Texas A&M University

Arun K. Jain
University at Buffalo

Wesley H. Jones
University of Indianapolis

Benoy Joseph
Cleveland State University

Craig Kelley
California State University

Dee Anne Larson
Mississippi University for Women

Ann Little
High Point University

Brian Little
Marshall University

Anne B. Lowery
University of Mobile

Steven Lysonski
Marquette University

Bill Magrogan
National Louis University & Columbia Union College

Cesar Maloles III
California State University–East Bay

Gregory Martin
University of West Florida

Wendy Martin
Judson College

Mary K. McManamon
Lake Erie College

Donald J. Messmer
College of William & Mary

Elaine Notarantonio
Bryant University

Hudson Nwakanma
Florida A&M University

Alphonso Ogbuehi
Bryant University

Thomas Parkinson
Moravian College

Hatash Sachdev
Eastern Michigan University

Amit Saini
University of Nebraska–Lincoln

Deborah Salvo
University of St. Thomas

Chris Samfilippo
University of Michigan–Dearborn

William F. Schoell
University of Southern Mississippi

Jean Shaneyfelt
Edison Community College

John Shaw
Providence College

Anusorn M. Singhapakdi
Old Dominion University

Charlotte Smedberg
Florida Metropolitan University System

R. Mark Smith
Campbell University

Joseph R. Stasio
Merrimack College

John Stovall
Georgia Southwestern State University

Rodney Stump
Towson University

Albert J. Taylor
Austin Peay State University

Sharon Thach
Tennessee State University

Dillard Tinsley
Austin State University

Mark Toncar
Youngstown State University

Joanne Trotter
Gwynedd-Mercy College

David J. Vachon
California State University–Northridge

Kevin Webb
Drexel University

Paula Welch
Mansfield University

Dale Wilson
Michigan State University

John Wong
Iowa State University

Mark Young
Winona State University

Shaoming Zou
University of Missouri–Columbia

It is always easy to work with a group of professionals. Working with our team of professionals at McGraw-Hill is always enjoyable for us. Sankha Basu, executive editor and Jane Mohr, project manager supported our efforts with this edition and we are very grateful. Special thanks to Gabriela Gonzalez, development editor, for always looking out for us.

Finally, we wish to acknowledge Francois Ortalo-Magné, dean of the School of Business at the University of Wisconsin, and David Blackwell, dean of the Gatton College of Business and Economics at the University of Kentucky, who support our efforts.

J. Paul Peter

James H. Donnelly, Jr.

Contents

Essentials of Marketing Management

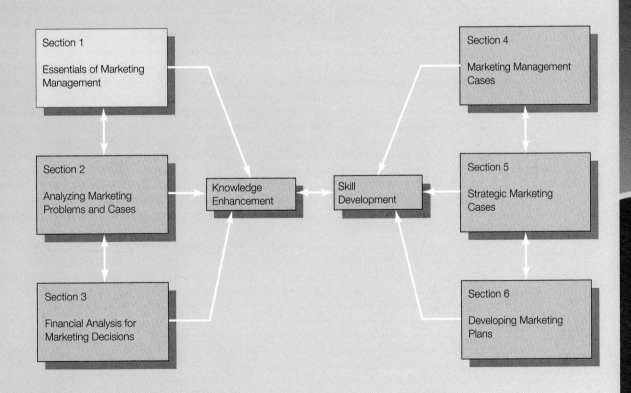

Section 1

Essentials of Marketing
Management

Section 2

Analyzing Marketing
Problems and Cases

Section 3

Financial Analysis for
Marketing Decisions

Knowledge
Enhancement

Skill
Development

Section 4

Marketing Management
Cases

Section 5

Strategic Marketing
Cases

Section 6

Developing Marketing
Plans

Part A

Introduction

1 Strategic Planning and the Marketing Management Process

Chapter 1

Strategic Planning and the Marketing Management Process

The purpose of this introductory chapter is to present the marketing management process and outline what marketing managers must *manage* if they are to be effective. In doing so, it will also present a framework around which the remaining chapters are organized. Our first task is to review the organizational philosophy known as the marketing concept, since it underlies much of the thinking presented in this book. The remainder of this chapter will focus on the process of strategic planning and its relationship to the process of marketing planning.

THE MARKETING CONCEPT

Simply stated, the marketing concept means that *an organization should seek to make a profit by serving the needs of customer groups*. The concept is very straightforward and has a great deal of commonsense validity. Perhaps this is why it is often misunderstood, forgotten, or overlooked.

The purpose of the marketing concept is to rivet the attention of marketing managers on serving broad classes of customer needs (customer orientation), rather than on the firm's current products (production orientation) or on devising methods to attract customers to current products (selling orientation). Thus, effective marketing starts with the recognition of customer needs and then works backward to devise products and services to satisfy these needs. In this way, marketing managers can satisfy customers more efficiently in the present and anticipate changes in customer needs more accurately in the future. This means that organizations should focus on building long-term customer relationships in which the initial sale is viewed as a beginning step in the process, not as an end goal. As a result, the customer will be more satisfied and the firm will be more profitable.

The principal task of the marketing function operating under the marketing concept is not to manipulate customers to do what suits the interests of the firm, but rather to find effective and efficient means of making the business do what suits the interests of customers. This is not to say that all firms practice marketing in this way. Clearly, many firms still emphasize only production and sales. However, effective marketing, as defined in this text, requires that consumer needs come first in organizational decision making.

1. Create customer focus throughout the business.
2. Listen to the customer.
3. Define and nurture your distinctive competence, that is, what your organization does well, better than competitors.
4. Define marketing as market intelligence.
5. Target customers precisely.
6. Manage for profitability, not sales volume.
7. Make customer value the guiding star.
8. Let customers define quality.
9. Measure and manage customer expectations.
10. Build customer relationships and loyalty.
11. Define the business as a service business.
12. Commit to continuous improvement and innovation.
13. Manage the culture of your organization along with strategy and structure.
14. Grow with strategic partners and alliances.
15. Destroy marketing bureaucracy.

Source: See Frederick E. Webster, Jr., "Defining the New Marketing Concept," *Marketing Management 2*, no. 4 (1994), pp. 22–31. For a classic discussion see Robert L. King, "The Marketing Concept: Fact or Intelligent Platitude," *The Marketing Concept in Action,* Proceedings of the 47th National Conference (Chicago, American Marketing Association, 1964), p. 657. Adapted from William O. Bearden, Thomas N. Ingram, and Raymond W. LaForge, *Marketing: Principles and Perspectives,* 5th ed. (Burr Ridge, IL: McGraw-Hill/Irwin, 2007), p. 9.

One qualification to this statement deals with the question of a conflict between consumer wants and societal needs and wants. For example, if society deems clean air and water as necessary for survival, this need may well take precedence over a consumer's want for goods and services that pollute the environment.

WHAT IS MARKETING?

Everyone reading this book has been a customer for most of his or her life. Last evening you stopped at a local supermarket to graze at the salad bar, pick up some bottled water, and a bag of Fritos corn chips. While you were there, you snapped a $1.00 coupon for a new flavor salad dressing out of a dispenser and tasted some new breakfast potatoes being cooked in the back of the store. As you sat down at home to eat your salad, you answered the phone and someone suggested that you need to have your carpets cleaned. Later on in the evening you saw TV commercials for tires, soft drinks, athletic shoes, and the dangers of smoking and drinking during pregnancy. Today when you enrolled in a marketing course, you found that the instructor has decided that you must purchase this book. A friend has already purchased the book on the Internet. All of these activities involve marketing. And each of us knows something about marketing because it has been a part of our life since we had our first dollar to spend.

Since we are all involved in marketing, it may seem strange that one of the persistent problems in the field has been its definition.[1] The American Marketing Association defines marketing as "the activity, set of institutions, and processes for creating, communicating, delivering, and exchanging offerings that have value for customers, clients, partners, and society at large."[2] This definition takes into account all parties involved in the marketing effort: members of the producing organization, resellers of goods and services, and customers or clients. While the broadness of the definition allows the inclusion of nonbusiness

FIGURE 1.1
Major Types of
Marketing

Type	Description	Example
Product	Marketing designed to create exchange for tangible products.	Strategies to sell apple computers.
Service	Marketing designed to create exchanges for intangible products.	Strategies by Allstate to sell insurance.
Person	Marketing designed to create favorable actions toward persons.	Strategies to elect a political candidate.
Place	Marketing designed to attract people to places.	Strategies to get people to vacation in national or state parks.
Cause	Marketing designed to create support for ideas, causes, or issues or to get people to change undesirable behaviors.	Strategies to get pregnant women not to drink alcohol.
Organization	Marketing designed to attract donors, members, participants, or volunteers.	Strategies designed to attract blood donors.

exchange processes, the primary emphasis in this text is on marketing in the business environment. However, this emphasis is not meant to imply that marketing concepts, principles, and techniques cannot be fruitfully employed in other areas of exchange as is clearly illustrated in Figure 1.1.

WHAT IS STRATEGIC PLANNING?

Before a production manager, marketing manager, and personnel manager can develop plans for their individual departments, some larger plan or blueprint for the *entire* organization should exist. Otherwise, on what would the individual departmental plans be based?

In other words, there is a larger context for planning activities. Let us assume that we are dealing with a large business organization that has several business divisions and several product lines within each division (e.g., General Electric, Altria). Before individual divisions or departments can implement any marketing planning, a plan has to be developed for the entire organization.[3] This means that senior managers must look toward the future and evaluate their ability to shape their organization's destiny in the years and decades to come. The output of this process is objectives and strategies designed to give the organization a chance to compete effectively in the future. The objectives and strategies established at the top level provide the context for planning in each of the divisions and departments by divisional and departmental managers.

Strategic Planning and Marketing Management

Some of the most successful business organizations are here today because many years ago they offered the right product at the right time to a rapidly growing market. The same can also be said for nonprofit and governmental organizations. Many of the critical decisions of the past were made without the benefit of strategic thinking or planning. Whether these decisions were based on wisdom or were just luck is not important; they worked for these organizations. However, a worse fate befell countless other organizations. Over three-quarters of the 100 largest U.S. corporations of 70 years ago have fallen from the list. These corporations at one time dominated their markets, controlled vast resources, and had the best-trained workers. In the end, they all made the same critical mistake. Their managements failed to recognize that business strategies need to reflect changing environments

1. It costs a great deal more to acquire a new customer than to keep an old one.
2. Loyal customers buy more from your firm over time.
3. The longer you keep a customer, the more profitable they become over time.
4. It costs less to service loyal customers than new customers.
5. Loyal customers are often excellent referrals for new business.
6. Loyal customers are often willing to pay more for the quality and value they desire.

Source: One of the earliest works on the value of the loyal customer was Frederick F. Reichheld, *The Loyalty Effect,* HBS Press, 1996. Also see Roland T. Rust, Katherine N. Lemon, and Valerie A. Zeithamel, "Return on Marketing: Using Customer Equity to Focus Marketing Strategies," *Journal of Marketing,* January 2004, pp. 76–89, William O. Bearden, Thomas N. Ingram, and Raymond W. LaForge, *Marketing: Principles and Perspectives,* 5th ed. (Burr Ridge, IL: McGraw-Hill/Irwin, 2007), p. 8, and W. D. Perreault, Jr., J. P. Cannon, and E. Jerome McCarthy, *Basic Marketing: A Marketing Strategy Planning Approach,* 18th ed. (Burr Ridge, IL: McGraw-Hill/Irwin, 2011), pp. 18–20.

and emphasis must be placed on developing business systems that allow for continuous improvement. Instead, they attempted to carry on business as usual.

Present-day managers are increasingly recognizing that wisdom and innovation alone are no longer sufficient to guide the destinies of organizations, both large and small. These same managers also realize that the true mission of the organization is to provide value for three key constituencies: customers, employees, and investors. Without this type of outlook, no one, including shareholders, will profit in the long run.

Strategic planning includes all the activities that lead to the development of a clear organizational mission, organizational objectives, and appropriate strategies to achieve the objectives for the entire organization. The form of the process itself has come under criticism in some quarters for being too structured; however, strategic planning, if performed successfully, plays a key role in achieving an equilibrium between the short and the long term by balancing acceptable financial performance with preparation for inevitable changes in markets, technology, and competition, as well as in economic and political arenas. Managing principally for current cash flows, market share gains, and earnings trends can mortgage the firm's future. An intense focus on the near term can produce an aversion to risk that dooms a business to stagnation. Conversely, an overemphasis on the long run is just as inappropriate. Companies that overextend themselves betting on the future may penalize short-term profitability and other operating results to such an extent that the company is vulnerable to takeover and other threatening actions.

The strategic planning process is depicted in Figure 1.2. In the strategic planning process the organization gathers information about the changing elements of its environment. Managers from all functional areas in the organization assist in this information-gathering process. This information is useful in aiding the organization to adapt better to these changes through the process of strategic planning. The strategic plan(s)[4] and supporting plan are then implemented in the environment. The end results of this implementation are fed back as new information so that continuous adaptation and improvement can take place.

The Strategic Planning Process

The output of the strategic planning process is the development of a strategic plan. Figure 1.2 indicates four components of a strategic plan: mission, objectives, strategies, and portfolio plan. Let us carefully examine each one.

Organizational Mission

The organization's environment provides the resources that sustain the organization, whether it is a business, a college or university, or a government agency. In exchange for

FIGURE 1.2 The Strategic Planning Process

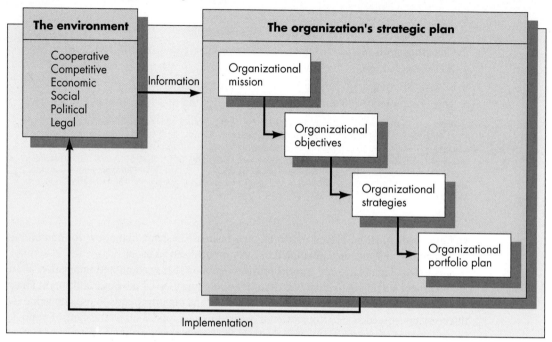

these resources, the organization must supply the environment with quality goods and services at an acceptable price. In other words, every organization exists to accomplish something in the larger environment and that purpose, vision, or mission usually is clear at the organization's inception. As time passes, however, the organization expands and the environment and managerial personnel change. As a result, one or more things are likely to occur. First, the organization's original purpose may become irrelevant as the organization expands into new products, new markets, and even new industries. For example, Levi Strauss began as a manufacturer of work clothes. Second, the original mission may remain relevant, but managers begin to lose interest in it. Finally, changes in the environment may make the original mission inappropriate, as occurred with the March of Dimes when a cure was found for polio. The result of any or all three of these conditions is a "drifting" organization, without a clear mission, vision, or purpose to guide critical decisions. When this occurs, management must search for a purpose or emphatically restate and reinforce the original purpose.

The mission statement, or purpose, of an organization is the description of its reason for existence. It is the long-run vision of what the organization strives to be, the unique aim that differentiates the organization from similar ones, and the means by which this differentiation will take place. In essence, the mission statement defines the direction in which the organization is heading and how it will succeed in reaching its desired goal. While some argue that vision and mission statements differ in their purpose, the perspective we will take is that both reflect the organization's attempt to guide behavior, create a culture, and inspire commitment.[5] However, it is more important that the mission statement comes from the heart and is practical, easy to identify with, and easy to remember so that it will provide direction and significance to all members of the organization regardless of their organizational level.

The basic questions that must be answered when an organization decides to examine and restate its mission are, What is our business? Who is the customer? What do customers

Organization	Mission
Community bank	To help citizens successfully achieve and celebrate important life events with education, information, products, and services.
Skin care products	We will provide luxury skin-care products with therapeutic qualities that make them worth their premium price.
Hotel chain	Grow a worldwide lodging business using total-quality-management (TQM) principles to continuously improve preference and profitability. Our commitment is that *every guest leaves satisfied*.
Mid-size bank	We will become the best bank in the state for medium-size businesses by 2017.

value? and What will our business be?[6] The answers are, in a sense, the assumptions on which the organization is being run and from which future decisions will evolve. While such questions may seem simplistic, they are such difficult and critical ones that the major responsibility for answering them must lie with top management. In fact, the mission statement remains the most widely used management tool in business today. In developing a statement of mission, management must take into account three key elements: the organization's history, its distinctive competencies, and its environment.[7]

1. *The organization's history*. Every organization—large or small, profit or nonprofit—has a history of objectives, accomplishments, mistakes, and policies. In formulating a mission, the critical characteristics and events of the past must be considered.

2. *The organization's distinctive competencies*. While there are many things an organization may be able to do, it should seek to do what it can do best. Distinctive competencies are things that an organization does well—so well in fact that they give it an advantage over similar organizations. For Honeywell, it's their ability to design, manufacture, and distribute a superior line of thermostats.[8] Similarly, Procter & Gamble's distinctive competency is its knowledge of the market for low-priced, repetitively purchased consumer products. No matter how appealing an opportunity may be, to gain advantage over competitors, the organization must formulate strategy based on distinctive competencies.

3. *The organization's environment*. The organization's environment dictates the opportunities, constraints, and threats that must be identified before a mission statement is developed. For example, managers in any industry that is affected by Internet technology breakthroughs should continually be asking, How will the changes in technology affect my customers' behavior and the means by which we need to conduct our business?

However, it is extremely difficult to write a useful and effective mission statement. It is not uncommon for an organization to spend one or two years developing a useful mission statement. When completed, an effective mission statement will be *focused on markets rather than products, achievable, motivating, and specific.*[9]

Focused on Markets Rather than Products The customers or clients of an organization are critical in determining its mission. Traditionally, many organizations defined their business in terms of what they made ("our business is glass"), and in many cases they named the organization for the product or service (e.g., American Tobacco, Hormel Meats, National Cash Register, Harbor View Savings and Loan Association). Many of these organizations have found that, when products and technologies become obsolete, their mission is no longer relevant and the name of the organization may no longer describe what it does. Thus, a more enduring way of defining the mission is needed. In recent years,

1. Incomplete—not specific as to where the company is headed and what kind of company management is trying to create.
2. Vague—does not provide direction to decision makers when faced with product/market choices.
3. Not motivational—does not provide a sense of purpose or commitment to something bigger than the numbers.
4. Not distinctive—not specific to our company.
5. Too reliant on superlatives—too many superlatives such as *#1, recognized leader, most successful.*
6. Too generic—does not specify the business or industry to which it applies.
7. Too broad—does not rule out any opportunity management might wish to pursue.

Source: Adapted from Arthur A. Thomson, Jr., A. J. Strickland III, and John E. Gamble, *Crafting and Executing Strategy,* 18th ed. (Burr Ridge, IL: McGraw-Hill/Irwin, 2012), p. 24.

Examine the mission statements in Marketing Insight 1–3. Do any of the above shortcomings apply to them?

therefore, a key feature of mission statements has been an *external* rather than *internal* focus. In other words, the mission statement should focus on the broad class of needs that the organization is seeking to satisfy (external focus), not on the physical product or service that the organization is offering at present (internal focus). These market-driven firms stand out in their ability to continuously anticipate market opportunities and respond before their competitors. Peter Drucker has clearly stated this principle:

> A business is not defined by the company's name, statutes, or articles of incorporation. It is defined by the want the customer satisfies when he buys a product or service. To satisfy the customer is the mission and purpose of every business. The question "What is our business?" can, therefore, be answered only by looking at the business from the outside, from the point of view of customer and market.[10]

While Drucker was referring to business organizations, the same necessity exists for both nonprofit and governmental organizations. That necessity is to state the mission in terms of serving a particular group of clients or customers and meeting a particular class of need.

Achievable   While the mission statement should stretch the organization toward more effective performance, it should, at the same time, be realistic and achievable. In other words, it should open a vision of new opportunities but should not lead the organization into unrealistic ventures far beyond its competencies.

Motivational   One of the side (but very important) benefits of a well-defined mission is the guidance it provides employees and managers working in geographically dispersed units and on independent tasks. It provides a shared sense of purpose outside the various activities taking place within the organization. Therefore, such end results as sales, patients cared for, students graduated, and reduction in violent crimes can then be viewed as the result of careful pursuit and accomplishment of the mission and not as the mission itself.

Specific   As we mentioned earlier, public relations should not be the primary purpose of a statement of mission. It must be specific to provide direction and guidelines to management when they are choosing between alternative courses of action. In other words, "to produce the highest-quality products at the lowest possible cost" sounds very good, but it does not provide direction for management.

Functions	What They May Want to Deliver	What Marketers May Want Them to Deliver
Research and development	Basic research projects	Products that deliver customer value
	Product features	Customer benefits
	Few projects	Many new products
Production/operations	Long production runs	Short production runs
	Standardized products	Customized products
	No model changes	Frequent model changes
	Long lead times	Short lead times
	Standard orders	Customer orders
	No new products	Many new products
Finance	Rigid budgets	Flexible budgets
	Budgets based on return on investment	Budgets based on need to increase sales
	Low sales commissions	High sales commissions
Accounting	Standardized billing	Custom billing
	Strict payment terms	Flexible payment terms
	Strict credit standards	Flexible credit standards
Human resources	Trainable employees	Skilled employees
	Low salaries	High salaries

Organizational Objectives

Organizational objectives are the end points of an organization's mission and are what it seeks through the ongoing, long-run operations of the organization. The organizational mission is distilled into a finer set of specific and achievable organizational objectives. These objectives must be *specific, measurable, action commitments* by which the mission of the organization is to be achieved.

As with the statement of mission, organizational objectives are more than good intentions. In fact, if formulated properly, they can accomplish the following:

1. They can be converted into specific action.
2. They will provide direction. That is, they can serve as a starting point for more specific and detailed objectives at lower levels in the organization. Each manager will then know how his or her objectives relate to those at higher levels.
3. They can establish long-run priorities for the organization.
4. They can facilitate management control because they serve as standards against which overall organizational performance can be evaluated.

Organizational objectives are necessary in all areas that may influence the performance and long-run survival of the organization. As shown in Figure 1.3 objectives can be established in and across many areas of the organization. The list provided in Figure 1.3 is by no means exhaustive. For example, some organizations are specifying the primary objective as the attainment of a specific level of quality, either in the marketing of a product or the providing of a service. These organizations believe that objectives should reflect an organization's commitment to the customer rather than its own finances. Obviously, during the strategic planning process conflicts are likely to occur between various functional departments in the organization. The important point is that management must translate the

FIGURE 1.3
Sample
Organizational
Objectives
(manufacturing firm)

Area of Performance	Possible Objective
1. Market standing	To make our brands number one in their field in terms of market share.
2. Innovations	To be a leader in introducing new products by spending no less than 7 percent of sales for research and development.
3. Productivity	To manufacture all products efficiently as measured by the productivity of the workforce.
4. Physical and financial resources	To protect and maintain all resources—equipment, buildings, inventory, and funds.
5. Profitability	To achieve an annual rate of return on investment of at least 15 percent.
6. Manager performance and responsibility	To identify critical areas of management depth and succession.
7. Worker performance and attitude	To maintain levels of employee satisfaction consistent with our own and similar industries.
8. Social responsibility	To respond appropriately whenever possible to societal expectations and environmental needs.

organizational mission into specific objectives that support the realization of the mission. The objectives may flow directly from the mission or be considered subordinate necessities for carrying out the mission. As discussed earlier, the objectives are specific, measurable, action commitments on the part of the organization.

Organizational Strategies

Hopefully, when an organization has formulated its mission and developed its objectives, it knows where it wants to go. The next managerial task is to develop a "grand design" to get there. This grand design constitutes the organizational strategies. Strategy involves the choice of major directions the organization will take in pursuing its objectives. Toward this end, it is critical that strategies are consistent with goals and objectives and that top management ensures strategies are implemented effectively. As many as 60 percent of strategic plans have failed because the strategies in them were not well defined and, thus, could not be implemented effectively.[11] What follows is a discussion of various strategies organizations can pursue. We discuss three approaches: (1) strategies based on products and markets, (2) strategies based on competitive advantage, and (3) strategies based on value.

Organizational Strategies Based on Products and Markets   One means to developing organizational strategies is to focus on the directions the organization can take in order to grow. Figure 1.4, which presents the available strategic choices, is a product–market matrix.[12] It indicates that an organization can grow by better managing what it is

FIGURE 1.4
Organizational
Growth Strategies

Products Markets	Present Products	New Products
Present customers	Market penetration	Product development
New customers	Market development	Diversification

1. *The Fit Test*: How well does the strategy fit the company's situation? A strategy must have good *external fit,* which means it will be well matched to industry and competitive conditions, the company's best market opportunities, and other relevant aspects of its business environment. It also must have a good *internal fit,* which means it is tailored to the company's resources and distinctive competencies and be supported by a complementary set of functional capabilities (sales and marketing, production, etc.).

2. *The Competitive Advantage Test*: Can the strategy help the company achieve a sustainable competitive advantage? Strategies that fail this test are unlikely to produce superior performance for more than a brief period of time. A good strategy should enable the organization to achieve a long-term competitive advantage.

3. *The Performance Test*: Is the strategy producing good company performance? Critical performance indicators are (a) profitability and financial strength and (b) competitive strength and market standing. Above average performance in these two areas is an indicator of a winning strategy.

Source: Adapted from Arthur A. Thompson, Margaret A. Peteraf, John E. Gamble, and A. J. Strickland III, *Crafting and Executing Strategy,* 18th ed. (Burr Ridge, IL: McGraw-Hill/Irwin, 2012), pp. 13–14.

presently doing or by finding new things to do. In choosing one or both of these paths, it must also decide whether to concentrate on present customers or to seek new ones. Thus, according to Figure 1.4, there are only four paths an organization can take in order to grow.

Market Penetration Strategies   These strategies focus primarily on increasing the sale of present products to present customers. For example:

- Encouraging present customers to use more of the product: "Orange Juice Isn't Just for Breakfast Anymore."
- Encouraging present customers to purchase more of the product: multiple packages of Pringles, instant winner sweepstakes at a fast-food restaurant.
- Directing programs at current participants: A university directs a fund-raising program at those graduates who already give the most money.

Tactics used to implement a market penetration strategy might include price reductions, advertising that stresses the many benefits of the product (e.g., "Milk Is a Natural"), packaging the product in different-sized packages, or making it available at more locations. Other functional areas of the business could also be involved in implementing the strategy in addition to marketing. A production plan might be developed to produce the product more efficiently. This plan might include increased production runs, the substitution of preassembled components for individual product parts, or the automation of a process that previously was performed manually.

Market Development Strategies   Pursuing growth through market development, an organization would seek to find new customers for its present products. For example:

- Arm & Hammer continues to seek new uses for its baking soda.
- McDonald's continually seeks expansion into overseas markets.
- As the consumption of salt declined, the book *101 Things You Can Do with Salt Besides Eat It* appeared.

Market development strategies involve much, much more than simply getting the product to a new market. Before deciding on marketing techniques such as advertising and packaging, companies often find they must establish a clear position in the market, sometimes spending large sums of money simply to educate consumers as to why they should consider buying the product.

Product Development Strategies   Selecting one of the remaining two strategies means the organization will seek new things to do. With this particular strategy, the new products developed would be directed primarily to present customers. For example:

- Offering a different version of an existing product: mini-Oreos, Ritz with cheese.
- Offering a new and improved version of their product: Gillette's latest improvement in shaving technology.
- Offering a new way to use an existing product: Vaseline's Lip Therapy.

Diversification   This strategy can lead the organization into entirely new and even unrelated businesses. It involves seeking new products (often through acquisitions) for customers not currently being served. For example:

- Altria, originally a manufacturer of cigarettes, is widely diversified in financial services, Post cereals, Sealtest dairy, and Kraft cheese, among others.
- Brown Foreman Distillers acquired Hartmann Luggage, and Sara Lee acquired Coach Leather Products.
- Some universities are establishing corporations to find commercial uses for faculty research.

Organizational Strategies Based on Competitive Advantage   Michael Porter developed a model for formulating organizational strategy that is applicable across a wide variety of industries.[13] The focus of the model is on devising means to gain competitive advantage. Competitive advantage is an ability to outperform competitors in providing something that the market values. Porter suggests that firms should first analyze their industry and then develop either a *cost leadership strategy* or a *strategy based on differentiation.* These general strategies can be used on marketwide bases or in a niche (segment) within the total market.

Using a cost leadership strategy, a firm would focus on being the low-cost company in its industry. They would stress efficiency and offer a standard, no-frills product. They could achieve this through efficiencies in production, product design, manufacturing, distribution, technology, or some other means. The important point is that to succeed, the organization must continually strive to be the cost leader in the industry or market segment it competes in. It must also offer products or services that are acceptable to customers when compared to the competition. Walmart, Southwest Airlines, and Timex Group Ltd. are companies that have succeeded in using a cost leadership strategy.

Using a strategy based on differentiation, a firm seeks to be unique in its industry or market segment along particular dimensions that the customers value. These dimensions might pertain to design, quality, service, variety of offerings, brand name, or some other factor. The important point is that because of uniqueness of the product or service along one or more of these dimensions, the firm can charge a premium price. L. L. Bean, Rolex, Coca-Cola, and Microsoft are companies that have succeeded using a differentiation strategy.

Organizational Strategies Based on Value   As competition increases, the concept of "customer value" has become critical for marketers as well as customers. It can be thought of as an extension of the marketing concept philosophy that focuses on developing and delivering superior value to customers as a way to achieve organizational objectives. Thus, it focuses not only on customer needs but also on the question, How can we create value for them and still achieve our objectives?

It has become pretty clear that in today's competitive environment it is unlikely that a firm will succeed by trying to be all things to all people.[14] Thus, to succeed firms must seek to build long-term relationships with their customers by offering a unique value that only they can offer. It seems that many firms have succeeded by choosing to deliver superior customer value using one of three value strategies—best price, best product, or best service.

Dell Inc., Costco, and Southwest Airlines are among the success stories in offering customers the best price. Rubbermaid, Nike, Starbucks, and Microsoft believe they offer the best products on the market. Airborne Express, Roadway, Cott Corporation, and Lands' End provide superior customer value by providing outstanding service.

Choosing an Appropriate Strategy

On what basis does an organization choose one (or all) of its strategies? Of extreme importance are the directions set by the mission statement. Management should select those strategies consistent with its mission and capitalize on the organization's distinctive competencies that will lead to a sustainable competitive advantage. A sustainable competitive advantage can be based on either the assets or skills of the organization. Technical superiority, low-cost production, customer service/product support, location, financial resources, continuing product innovation, and overall marketing skills are all examples of distinctive competencies that can lead to a sustainable competitive advantage. For example, Honda is known for providing quality automobiles at a reasonable price. Each succeeding generation of Honda automobiles has shown marked quality improvements over previous generations. Likewise, VF Corporation, manufacturer of Wrangler and Lee jeans, has formed "quick response" partnerships with both discounters and department stores to ensure the efficiency of product flow. The key to sustaining a competitive advantage is to continually focus and build on the assets and skills that will lead to long-term performance gains.

Organizational Portfolio Plan

The final phase of the strategic planning process is the formulation of the organizational portfolio plan. In reality, most organizations at a particular time are a portfolio of businesses, that is, product lines, divisions, and schools. To illustrate, an appliance manufacturer may have several product lines (e.g., televisions, washers and dryers, refrigerators, stereos) as well as two divisions, consumer appliances and industrial appliances. A college or university will have numerous schools (e.g., education, business, law, architecture) and several programs within each school. Some widely diversified organizations such as Altria are in numerous unrelated businesses, such as cigarettes, food products, land development, and industrial paper products.

Managing such groups of businesses is made a little easier if resources are plentiful, cash is plentiful, and each is experiencing growth and profits. Unfortunately, providing larger and larger budgets each year to all businesses is seldom feasible. Many are not experiencing growth, and profits and resources (financial and nonfinancial) are becoming more and more scarce. In such a situation, choices must be made, and some method is necessary to help management make the choices. Management must decide which businesses to build, maintain, or eliminate, or which new businesses to add. Indeed, much of the recent activity in corporate restructuring has centered on decisions relating to which groups of businesses management should focus on.

Obviously, the first step in this approach is to identify the various divisions, product lines, and so on that can be considered a "business." When identified, these are referred to as *strategic business units* (SBUs) and have the following characteristics:

- They have a distinct mission.
- They have their own competitors.

- They are a single business or collection of related businesses.
- They can be planned independently of the other businesses of the total organization.

Thus, depending on the type of organization, an SBU could be a single product, product line, or division; a college of business administration; or a state mental health agency. Once the organization has identified and classified all of its SBUs, some method must be established to determine how resources should be allocated among the various SBUs. These methods are known as *portfolio models*. For those readers interested, the appendix of this chapter presents two of the most popular portfolio models, the Boston Consulting Group model and the General Electric model.

The Complete Strategic Plan

Figure 1.2 indicates that at this point the strategic planning process is complete, and the organization has a time-phased blueprint that outlines its mission, objectives, and strategies. Completion of the strategic plan facilitates the development of marketing plans for each product, product line, or division of the organization. The marketing plan serves as a subset of the strategic plan in that it allows for detailed planning at a target market level. This important relationship between strategic planning and marketing planning is the subject of the final section of this chapter.

THE MARKETING MANAGEMENT PROCESS

Marketing management can be defined as "the process of planning and executing the conception, pricing, promotion, and distribution of goods, services, and ideas to create exchanges with target groups that satisfy customer and organizational objectives."[15] It should be noted that this definition is entirely consistent with the marketing concept, since it emphasizes serving target market needs as the key to achieving organizational objectives. The remainder of this section will be devoted to a discussion of the marketing management process according to the model in Figure 1.5.

Situation Analysis

With a clear understanding of organizational objectives and mission, the marketing manager must then analyze and monitor the position of the firm and, specifically, the marketing department, in terms of its past, present, and future situation. Of course, the future situation is of primary concern. However, analyses of past trends and the current situation are most useful for predicting the future situation.

The situation analysis can be divided into six major areas of concern: (1) the cooperative environment; (2) the competitive environment; (3) the economic environment; (4) the social environment; (5) the political environment; and (6) the legal environment. In analyzing each of these environments, the marketing executive must search both for opportunities and for constraints or threats to achieving objectives. Opportunities for profitable marketing often arise from changes in these environments that bring about new sets of needs to be satisfied. Constraints on marketing activities, such as limited supplies of scarce resources, also arise from these environments.

The Cooperative Environment   The cooperative environment includes all firms and individuals who have a vested interest in the firm's accomplishing its objectives. Parties of primary interest to the marketing executive in this environment are (1) suppliers, (2) resellers, (3) other departments in the firm, and (4) subdepartments and employees of the marketing department. Opportunities in this environment are primarily related to methods of increasing efficiency. For example, a company might decide to switch from a competitive bid process of obtaining materials to a single source that is located near the company's plant.

FIGURE 1.5
Strategic Planning
and Marketing
Planning

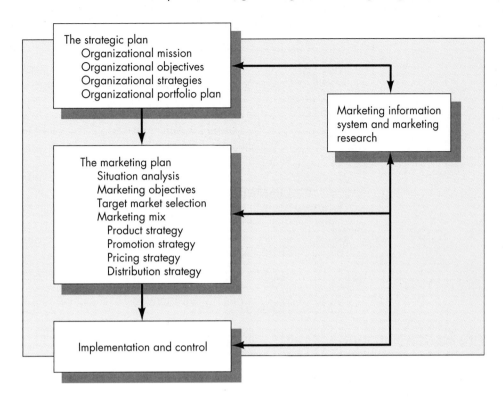

Likewise, members of the marketing, engineering, and manufacturing functions may use a teamwork approach to developing new products versus a sequential approach. Constraints consist of such things as unresolved conflicts and shortages of materials. For example, a company manager may believe that a distributor is doing an insufficient job of promoting and selling the product, or a marketing manager may feel that manufacturing is not taking the steps needed to produce a quality product.

The Competitive Environment The competitive environment includes primarily other firms in the industry that rival the organization for both resources and sales. Opportunities in this environment include such things as (1) acquiring competing firms; (2) offering demonstrably better value to consumers and attracting them away from competitors; and (3) in some cases, driving competitors out of the industry. For example, one airline purchases another airline, a bank offers depositors a free checking account with no minimum balance requirements, or a grocery chain engages in an everyday low-price strategy that competitors can't meet. The primary constraints in these environments are the demand stimulation activities of competing firms and the number of consumers who cannot be lured away from competition.

The Economic Environment The state of the macroeconomy and changes in it also bring about marketing opportunities and constraints. For example, such factors as high inflation and unemployment levels can limit the size of the market that can afford to purchase a firm's top-of-the-line product. At the same time, these factors may offer a profitable opportunity to develop rental services for such products or to develop less-expensive models of the product. In addition, changes in technology can provide significant threats and opportunities. For example, in the communications industry, when technology was developed to a level where it was possible to provide cable television using phone lines, such a system posed a severe threat to the cable industry.

Speed of the Process. There is the problem of either being so slow that the process seems to go on forever or so fast that there is an extreme burst of activity to rush out a plan.

Amount of Data Collected. Sufficient data are needed to properly estimate customer needs and competitive trends. However, the law of diminishing returns quickly sets in on the data-collection process.

Responsibility for Developing the Plan. If planning is delegated to professional planners, valuable line management input may be ignored. If the process is left to line managers, planning may be relegated to secondary status.

Structure. Many executives believe the most important part of planning is not the plan itself but the structure of thought about the strategic issues facing the business. However, the structure should not take precedence over the content so that planning becomes merely filling out forms or crunching numbers.

Length of the Plan. The length of a marketing plan must be balanced between being so long that both staff and line managers ignore it and so brief that it ignores key details.

Frequency of Planning. Too frequent reevaluation of strategies can lead to erratic firm behavior. However, when plans are not revised frequently enough, the business may not adapt quickly enough to environmental changes and thus suffer a deterioration in its competitive position.

Number of Alternative Strategies Considered. Discussing too few alternatives raises the likelihood of failure, whereas discussing too many increases the time and cost of the planning effort.

Cross-Functional Acceptance. A common mistake is to view the plan as the proprietary possession of marketing. Successful implementation requires a broad consensus, including other functional areas.

Using the Plan as a Sales Document. A major but often overlooked purpose of a plan and its presentation is to generate funds from either internal or external sources. Therefore, the better the plan, the better the chance of gaining desired funding.

Senior Management Leadership. Commitment from senior management is essential to the success of a marketing planning effort.

Tying Compensation to Successful Planning Efforts. Management compensation should be oriented toward the achievement of objectives stated in the plan.

Source: Donald R. Lehmann and Russell S. Winer, *Analysis for Marketing Planning*, 7th ed. (Burr Ridge, IL: McGraw-Hill//Irwin, 2008), chap. 1.

The Social Environment   This environment includes general cultural and social traditions, norms, and attitudes. While these values change slowly, such changes often bring about the need for new products and services. For example, a change in values concerning the desirability of large families brought about an opportunity to market better methods of birth control. On the other hand, cultural and social values also place constraints on marketing activities. As a rule, business practices that are contrary to social values become political issues, which are often resolved by legal constraints. For example, public demand for a cleaner environment has caused the government to require that automobile manufacturers' products meet certain average gas mileage and emission standards.

The Political Environment   The political environment includes the attitudes and reactions of the general public, social and business critics, and other organizations, such as the Better Business Bureau. Dissatisfaction with such business and marketing practices as unsafe products, products that waste resources, and unethical sales procedures can have adverse effects on corporation image and customer loyalty. However, adapting business and marketing practices to these attitudes can be an opportunity. For example, these attitudes have brought about markets for such products as unbreakable children's toys, high-efficiency air conditioners, and more economical automobiles.

The Legal Environment   This environment includes a host of federal, state, and local legislation directed at protecting both business competition and consumer rights. In past years, legislation reflected social and political attitudes and has been primarily directed at constraining business practices. Such legislation usually acts as a constraint on business behavior, but again can be viewed as providing opportunities for marketing safer and more efficient products. In recent years, there has been less emphasis on creating new laws for constraining business practices. As an example, deregulation has become more common, as evidenced by events in the airlines, financial services, and telecommunications industries.

Marketing Planning

The previous sections emphasized that (1) marketing activities must be aligned with organizational objectives and (2) marketing opportunities are often found by systematically analyzing situational environments. Once an opportunity is recognized, the marketing executive must then plan an appropriate strategy for taking advantage of the opportunity. This process can be viewed in terms of three interrelated tasks: (1) establishing marketing objectives, (2) selecting the target market, and (3) developing the marketing mix.

Establishing Objectives   Marketing objectives usually are derived from organizational objectives; in some cases where the firm is totally marketing oriented, the two are identical. In either case, objectives must be specified and performance in achieving them should be measurable. Marketing objectives are usually stated as standards of performance (e.g., a certain percentage of market share or sales volume) or as tasks to be achieved by given dates. While such objectives are useful, the marketing concept emphasizes that profits rather than sales should be the overriding objective of the firm and marketing department. In any case, these objectives provide the framework for the marketing plan.

Selecting the Target Market   The success of any marketing plan hinges on how well it can identify customer needs and organize its resources to satisfy them profitably. Thus, a crucial element of the marketing plan is selecting the groups or segments of potential customers the firm is going to serve with each of its products. Four important questions must be answered:

1. What do customers want or need?
2. What must be done to satisfy these wants or needs?
3. What is the size of the market?
4. What is its growth profile?

Present target markets and potential target markets are then ranked according to (1) profitability; (2) present and future sales volume; and (3) the match between what it takes to appeal successfully to the segment and the organization's capabilities. Those that appear to offer the greatest potential are selected. One cautionary note on this process involves the importance of not neglecting present customers when developing market share and sales strategies. A recent study found that for every 10 companies that develop strategies aimed at increasing the number of first-time customers, only four made any serious effort to develop strategies geared toward retaining present customers and increasing their purchases.[16] Chapters 3, 4, and 5 are devoted to discussing consumer behavior, industrial buyers, and market segmentation.

Developing the Marketing Mix   The marketing mix is the set of controllable variables that must be managed to satisfy the target market and achieve organizational objectives.

Poorly Stated Objectives	Well-Stated Objectives
Our objective is to be a leader in the industry in terms of new product development.	Our objective is to spend 12 percent of sales revenue between 2011 and 2013 on research and development in an effort to introduce at least five new products in 2014.
Our objective is to maximize profits.	Our objective is to achieve a 10 percent return on investment during 2012, with a payback on new investments of no longer than four years.
Our objective is to better serve customers.	Our objective is to obtain customer satisfaction ratings of at least 90 percent on the 2012 annual customer satisfaction survey, and to retain at least 85 percent of our 2012 customers as repeat purchasers in 2013.
Our objective is to be the best that we can be.	Our objective is to increase market share from 30 percent to 40 percent in 2012 by increasing promotional expenditures by 14 percent.

Source: Adapted from Charles W. Lamb, Jr., Joseph F. Hair, Jr., and Carl McDaniel, *Marketing*, 10th ed. (Mason, OH: Thomson South-Western Publishing Co., 2008), Chapter 2.

These controllable variables are usually classified according to four major decision areas: product, price, promotion, and place (or channels of distribution). The importance of these decision areas cannot be overstated, and in fact, the major portion of this text is devoted to analyzing them. Chapters 6 and 7 are devoted to product and new product strategies, Chapters 8 and 9 to promotion strategies in terms of both nonpersonal and personal selling, Chapter 10 to distribution strategies, and Chapter 11 to pricing strategies. In addition, marketing mix variables are the focus of analysis in two chapters on marketing in special fields, that is, the marketing of services (Chapter 12) and international marketing (Chapter 13). Thus, it should be clear that the marketing mix is the core of the marketing management process.

The output of the foregoing process is the marketing plan. It is a formal statement of the decisions that have been made on marketing activities; it is a blueprint of the objectives, strategies, and tasks to be performed.

Implementation and Control of the Marketing Plan

Implementing the marketing plan involves putting the plan into action and performing marketing tasks according to the predefined schedule. Even the most carefully developed plans often cannot be executed with perfect timing. Thus, the marketing executive must closely monitor and coordinate implementation of the plan. In some cases, adjustments may have to be made in the basic plan because of changes in any of the situational environments. For example, competitors may introduce a new product. In this event, it may be desirable to speed up or delay implementation of the plan. In almost all cases, some minor adjustments or fine tuning will be necessary in implementation.

Controlling the marketing plan involves three basic steps. First, the results of the implemented marketing plan are measured. Second, these results are compared with objectives. Third, decisions are made on whether the plan is achieving objectives. If serious deviations exist between actual and planned results, adjustments may have to be made to redirect the plan toward achieving objectives.

Marketing Information Systems and Marketing Research

Throughout the marketing management process, current, reliable, and valid information is needed to make effective marketing decisions. Providing this information is the task of the marketing information system and marketing research. These topics are discussed in detail in Chapter 2.

THE STRATEGIC PLAN, THE MARKETING PLAN, AND OTHER FUNCTIONAL AREA PLANS

Strategic planning is clearly a top-management responsibility. In recent years, however, there has been an increasing shift toward more active participation by marketing managers in strategic analysis and planning. This is because, in reality, nearly all strategic planning questions have marketing implications. In fact, the two major strategic planning questions— What products should we make? and What markets should we serve?—are clearly marketing questions. Thus, marketing executives are involved in the strategic planning process in at least two important ways: (1) They influence the process by providing important inputs in the form of information and suggestions relating to customers, products, and middlemen; and (2) they must always be aware of what the process of strategic planning involves as well as the results because everything they do—the marketing objectives and strategies they develop—must be derived from the strategic plan. In fact, the planning done in all functional areas of the organization should be derived from the strategic plan.

Marketing's Role in Cross-Functional Strategic Planning

More and more organizations are rethinking the traditional role of marketing. Rather than dividing work according to function (e.g., production, finance, technology, human resources), they are bringing managers and employees together to participate in *cross-functional teams*. These teams might have responsibility for a particular product, line of products, or group of customers.

Because team members are responsible for all activities involving their products and/or customers, they are responsible for strategic planning. This means that all personnel working in a cross-functional team will participate in creating a strategic plan to serve customers. Rather than making decisions independently, marketing managers work closely with team members from production, finance, human resources, and other areas to devise plans that address all concerns. Thus, if a team member from production says, "That product will be too difficult to produce," or if a team member from finance says, "We'll never make a profit at that price," the team members from marketing must help resolve the problems. This approach requires a high degree of skill at problem solving and gaining cooperation.

Clearly, the greatest advantage of strategic planning with a cross-functional team is the ability of team members to consider a situation from a number of viewpoints. The resulting insights can help the team avoid costly mistakes and poor solutions. Japanese manufacturers are noted for using cross-functional teams to figure out ways to make desirable products at given target costs. In contrast, U.S. manufacturers traditionally have developed products by having one group decide what to make, another calculate production costs, and yet another predict whether enough of the product will sell at a high enough price.

Thus, in well-managed organizations, a direct relationship exists between strategic planning and the planning done by managers at all levels. The focus and time perspectives will, of course, differ. Figure 1.6 illustrates the cross-functional perspective of strategic planning. It indicates very clearly that all functional area plans should be derived from the strategic plan while at the same time contributing to the achievement of it.

FIGURE 1.6   The Cross-Functional Perspective in Planning

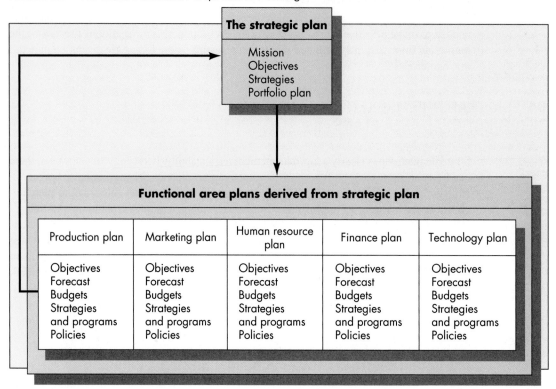

If done properly, strategic planning results in a clearly defined blueprint for management action in all functional areas of the organization. Figure 1.7 clearly illustrates this blueprint using only one organizational objective and two strategies from the strategic plan (above the dotted line) and illustrating how these are translated into elements of the marketing department plan and the production department plan (below the dotted line). Note that in Figure 1.7, all objectives and strategies are related to other objectives and strategies at higher and lower levels in the organization: That is, a hierarchy of objectives and strategies exists. We have illustrated only two possible marketing objectives and two possible production objectives. Obviously, many others could be developed, but our purpose is to illustrate the cross-functional nature of strategic planning and how objectives and strategies from the strategic plan must be translated into objectives and strategies for all functional areas including marketing.

SUMMARY

This chapter has described the marketing management process in the context of the organization's overall strategic plan. Clearly, marketers must understand their cross-functional role in joining the marketing vision for the organization with the financial goals and manufacturing capabilities of the organization. The greater this ability, the better is the likelihood that the organization will be able to achieve and sustain a competitive advantage, the ultimate purpose of the strategic planning process.

At this point, it would be useful to review Figures 1.5, 1.6, and 1.7 as well as the book's table of contents. This review will enable you to better relate the content and progression of the material to follow to the marketing management process.

FIGURE 1.7   A Blueprint for Management Action: Relating the Marketing Plan to the Strategic Plan and the Production Plan

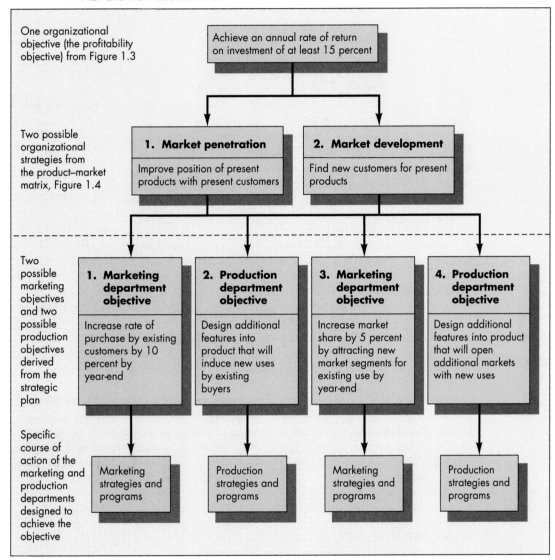

Additional Resources

Charan, Ram. *Leadership in the Era of Economic Uncertainty.* NY: McGraw-Hill, 2009.

Christensen, Clayton, M., Scott Cook, and Tandy Hall. "Marketing Malpractice: The Cause and the Cure." *Harvard Business Review,* December 2005, pp. 74–75.

Dixit, Avinash, K., and Barry J. Noblebuff. *The Art of Strategy.* NY: W.W. Norton and Co., 2009.

Friedman, George. *The Next Decade.* NY: Doubleday, 2011.

Kaplan, Robert S., and David Norton. "How to Implement a New Strategy Without Disrupting Your Organization." *Harvard Business Review,* March 2006, pp. 100–109.

Levitt, Ted. *On Marketing.* Boston: HBS Press, 2006.

London, Ted, and Stuart L. Hart. *Next Generation Business Strategies for the Base of the Pyramid.* Upper Saddle River, NJ: FT Press, 2011.

Markower, Jack. *Strategies for the Green Economy.* NY: McGraw-Hill, 2009.

O'Sullivan, Don, and Andrew W. Abdela. "Marketing Performance Measurement Ability and Performance." *Journal of Marketing,* April 2007, pp. 79–93.

Seiders, Kathleen, and Leonard L. Berry. "Should Business Care about Obesity?" *Sloan Management Review,* Winter 2007, pp. 15–17.

Key Terms and Concepts

Distinctive competencies: Distinctive competencies are things that an organization does so well that they give it an advantage over similar organizations. No matter how appealing an opportunity may be, to gain advantage over competitors, the organization must formulate strategy based on distinctive competencies.

Diversification: An organizational strategy that seeks growth through new products (often through acquisitions) for customers not currently being served.

Market development: An organizational strategy that seeks growth through seeking new customers for present products.

Market penetration: An organizational strategy that seeks growth through increasing the sale of present products to present customers.

Marketing: The activity, set of institutions, and processes for creating, communicating, delivering, and exchanging offerings that have value for customers, clients, partners, and society at large.

Marketing concept: The marketing concept means that an organization should seek to make a profit by serving the needs of customer groups. Its purpose is to rivet the attention of marketing managers on serving broad classes of customer needs (customer orientation), rather than on the firm's products (production orientation) or on devising methods to attract customers to current products (selling orientation).

Marketing information system: Throughout the marketing management process, current, reliable, and valid information is needed to make effective marketing decisions. Providing this information is the task of the marketing information system and marketing research.

Marketing management: Marketing management is the process of planning and executing the conception, pricing, promotion, and distribution of goods, services, and ideas to create exchanges with target groups that satisfy customer and organizational objectives.

Marketing mix: The marketing mix is the set of controllable variables that must be managed to satisfy the target market and achieve organizational objectives. The controllable variables are usually classified according to four major decision areas: product, price, promotion, and place (or channels of distribution).

Marketing planning: The marketing planning process produces three outputs: (1) establishing marketing objectives, (2) selecting the target market, and (3) developing the marketing mix.

Organizational mission: The mission statement, or purpose, of an organization is the description of its reason for existence. It is the long-run vision of what the organization strives to be, the unique aim that differentiates the organization from similar ones and the means by which this differentiation will take place. An effective mission statement will be focused on markets rather than products, achievable, motivating, and specific.

Organizational objectives: Organizational objectives are the end points of an organization's mission and are what it seeks through the ongoing, long-run operation of the organization. The organizational mission is distilled into a finer set of specific, measurable, action commitments by which the mission of the organization is to be achieved.

Organizational portfolio plan: This stage of the strategic plan involves the allocation of resources across the organization's product lines, divisions, or businesses. It involves deciding which ones to build, maintain, or eliminate, or which to add.

Organizational strategies: Organizational strategies are the choice of the major directions the organization will take in pursuing its objectives. There are three major approaches: (1) strategies based on products and markets, (2) strategies based on competitive advantage, and (3) strategies based on value.

Organizational strategies based on competitive advantage: This approach to developing organizational strategy would develop either a cost leadership strategy which focuses on being the lower cost company in the industry or a differentiation strategy which focuses on being unique in the industry or market segment along dimensions that customers value.

Organizational strategies based on products and markets: An approach to developing organizational strategies that focuses on the four paths an organization can grow: market penetration strategies, market development strategies, product development strategies, and diversification strategies.

Organizational strategies based on value: This approach to developing organizational strategy seeks to succeed by choosing to deliver superior customer value using one of three value strategies—best price, best product, or best service.

Product development: An organizational strategy that seeks growth through developing new products primarily for present customers.

Situation analysis: This stage of the marketing planning process involves the analysis of the past, present, and likely future in six major areas of concern: (1) the cooperative environment; (2) the competitive environment; (3) the economic environment; (4) the social environment; (5) the political environment; and (6)) the legal environment. Opportunities for and constraints on marketing activities arise from these environments.

Strategic business units (SBUs): Strategic business units (SBUs) are product lines and divisions that can be considered a "business" for the purpose of the organizational portfolio plan. An SBU must have a distinct mission, have its own competitors, be a single business or collection of related businesses, and be able to be planned independently of the other SBUs.

Strategic planning: Strategic planning provides a blueprint for management actions for the entire organization. It includes all the activities that lead to the development of a clear organizational mission, organizational objectives, and appropriate strategies to achieve the objectives for the entire organization.

Appendix

Portfolio Models

Portfolio models remain a valuable aid to marketing managers in their efforts to develop effective marketing plans. The use of these models can aid managers who face situations that can best be described as "more products, less time, and less money." More specifically, (1) as the number of products a firm produces expands, the time available for developing marketing plans for each product decreases; (2) at a strategic level, management must make resource allocation decisions across lines of products and, in diversified organizations, across different lines of business; and (3) when resources are limited (which they usually are), the process of deciding which strategic business units (SBUs) to emphasize becomes very complex. In such situations, portfolio models can be very useful.

Portfolio analysis is not a new idea. Banks manage loan portfolios seeking to balance risks and yields. Individuals who are serious investors usually have a portfolio of various kinds of investments (common stocks, preferred stocks, bank accounts, and the like), each with different characteristics of risk, growth, and rate of return. The investor seeks to manage the portfolio to maximize whatever objectives he or she might have. Applying this same idea, most organizations have a wide range of products, product lines, and businesses, each with different growth rates and returns. Similar to the investor, managers should seek a desirable balance among alternative SBUs. Specifically, management should seek to develop a business portfolio that will ensure long-run profits and cash flow.

Portfolio models can be used to classify SBUs to determine the future cash contributions that can be expected from each SBU as well as the future resources that each will require. Remember, depending on the organization, an SBU could be a single product, product line, division, or distinct business. While there are many different types of portfolio models, they generally examine the competitive position of the SBU and the chances for improving the SBU's contribution to profitability and cash flow.

There are several portfolio analysis techniques. Two of the most widely used are discussed in this appendix. To truly appreciate the concept of portfolio analysis, however, we must briefly review the development of portfolio theory.

A REVIEW OF PORTFOLIO THEORY

The interest in developing aids for managers in the selection of strategy was spurred by an organization known as the Boston Consulting Group (BCG) over 25 years ago. Its ideas, which will be discussed shortly, and many of those that followed were based on the concept of experience curves.

Experience curves are similar in concept to learning curves. Learning curves were developed to express the idea that the number of labor hours it takes to produce one unit of a particular product declines in a predictable manner as the number of units produced increases. Hence, an accurate estimation of how long it takes to produce the 100th unit is possible if the production times for the 1st and 10th units are known. The concept of experience curves was based on this model.

Experience curves were first widely discussed in the Strategic Planning Institute's ongoing Profit Impact of Marketing Strategies (PIMS) study. The PIMS project studies 150 firms with more than 1,000 individual business units. Its major focus is on determining which environmental and internal firm variables influence the firm's return on investment (ROI) and cash flow. The researchers have concluded that seven categories of variables appear to influence the return on investment: (1) competitive position, (2) industry/market environment, (3) budget allocation, (4) capital structure, (5) production processes, (6) company characteristics, and (7) "change action" factors.[17]

The experience curve includes all costs associated with a product and implies that the per-unit costs of a product should fall, due to cumulative experience, as production volume increases. In a given industry, therefore, the producer with the largest volume and corresponding market share should have the lowest marginal cost. This leader in market share should be able to underprice competitors, discourage entry into the market by potential competitors, and, as a result, achieve an acceptable return on investment. The linkage of experience to cost to price to market share to ROI is exhibited in Figure A.1. The Boston Consulting Group's

FIGURE A.1 **Experience Curve and Resulting Profit**

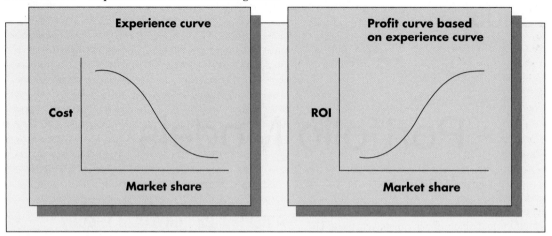

view of the experience curve led the members to develop what has become known as the BCG Portfolio Model.

THE BCG MODEL

The BCG is based on the assumption that profitability and cash flow will be closely related to sales volume. Thus, in this model, SBUs are classified according to their relative market share and the growth rate of the market the SBU is in. Using these dimensions, products are either classified as stars, cash cows, dogs, or question marks. The BCG model is presented in Figure A.2.

- *Stars* are SBUs with a high share of a high-growth market. Because high-growth markets attract competition, such SBUs are usually cash users because they are growing

and because the firm needs to protect their market share position.

- *Cash cows* are often market leaders, but the market they are in is not growing rapidly. Because these SBUs have a high share of a low-growth market, they are cash generators for the firm.
- *Dogs* are SBUs that have a low share of a low-growth market. If the SBU has a very loyal group of customers, it may be a source of profits and cash. Usually, dogs are not large sources of cash.
- *Question marks* are SBUs with a low share of a high-growth market. They have great potential but require great resources if the firm is to successfully build market share.

As you can see, a firm with 10 SBUs will usually have a portfolio that includes some of each of the above. Having

FIGURE A.2
The Boston
Consulting Group
Portfolio Model

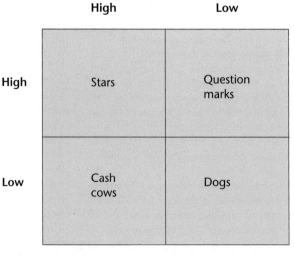

developed this analysis, management must determine what role each SBU should assume. Four basic objectives are possible:

1. *Build share*. This objective sacrifices immediate earnings to improve market share. It is appropriate for promising question marks whose share has to grow if they are ever to become stars.
2. *Hold share*. This objective seeks to preserve the SBU's market share. It is very appropriate for strong cash cows to ensure that they can continue to yield a large cash flow.
3. *Harvest*. Here, the objective seeks to increase the product's short-term cash flow without concern for the long-run impact. It allows market share to decline in order to maximize earnings and cash flow. It is an appropriate objective for weak cash cows, weak question marks, and dogs.
4. *Divest*. This objective involves selling or divesting the SBU because better investment opportunities exist elsewhere. It is very appropriate for dogs and those question marks the firm cannot afford to finance for growth.

There have been several major criticisms of the BCG Portfolio Model, revolving around its focus on market share and market growth as the primary indicators of preference. First, the BCG model assumes that market growth is uncontrollable.[18] As a result, managers can become preoccupied with setting market share objectives instead of trying to grow the market. Second, assumptions regarding market share as a critical factor affecting firm performance may not hold true, especially in international markets.[19] Third, the BCG model assumes that the major source of

SBU financing comes from internal means. Fourth, the BCG matrix does not take into account any interdependencies that may exist between SBUs, such as shared distribution.[20] Fifth, the BCG matrix does not take into account any measures of profits and customer satisfaction.[21] Sixth, and perhaps most important, the thrust of the BCG matrix is based on the underlying assumption that corporate strategy begins with an analysis of competitive position. By its very nature, a strategy developed entirely on competitive analysis will always be a reactive one.[22] While the above criticisms are certainly valid ones, managers (especially of large firms) across all industries continue to find the BCG matrix useful in assessing the strategic position of SBUs.[23]

THE GENERAL ELECTRIC MODEL

Although the BCG model can be useful, it does assume that market share is the sole determinant of an SBU's profitability. Also, in projecting market growth rates, a manager should carefully analyze the factors that influence sales and any opportunities for influencing industry sales.

Some firms have developed alternative portfolio models to incorporate more information about market opportunities and competitive positions. The GE model is one of these. The GE model emphasizes all the potential sources of strength, not just market share, and all of the factors that influence the long-term attractiveness of a market, not just its growth rate. As Figure A.3 indicates, all SBUs are classified according to *business strength* and *industry attractiveness*. Figure A.4 presents a list of items that can be used to position SBUs in the matrix.

FIGURE A.3
The General Electric
Portfolio Model

Business Strength

		Strong	Average	Weak
Industry Attractiveness	**High**	A	A	B
	Medium	A	B	C
	Low	B	C	C

FIGURE A.4
Components
of Industry
Attractiveness
and Business
Strength at GE

Industry Attractiveness	Business Strength
	Market position
Market size	Domestic market share
Market growth	World market share
Profitability	Share growth
Cyclicality	Share compared with leading competitor
Ability to recover from inflation	
World scope	Competitive strengths
	Quality leadership
	Technology
	Marketing
	Relative profitability

Industry attractiveness is a composite index made up of such factors as those listed in Figure A.4. For example: *market size*—the larger the market, the more attractive it will be; *market growth*—high-growth markets are more attractive than low-growth markets; *profitability*—high-profit-margin markets are more attractive than low-profit-margin industries.

Business strength is a composite index made up of such factors as those listed in Figure A.4, such as *market share*—the higher the SBU's share of market, the greater its business strength; *quality leadership*—the higher the SBU's quality compared to competitors, the greater its business strength; *share compared with leading competitor*—the closer the SBU's share to the market leader, the greater its business strength.

Once the SBUs are classified, they are placed on the grid (Figure A.3). Priority "A" SBUs (often called the *green zone*) are those in the three cells at the upper left, indicating that these are SBUs high in both industry attractiveness and business strength, and that the firm should "build share." Priority "B" SBUs (often called *the yellow zone*) are those medium in both industry attractiveness and business strength. The firm will usually decide to "hold share" on these SBUs. Priority "C" SBUs are those in the three cells at the lower right (often called the *red zone*). These SBUs are low in both industry attractiveness and business strength. The firm will usually decide to harvest or divest these SBUs.

Whether the BCG model, the GE model, or a variation of these models is used, some analyses must be made of the firm's current portfolio of SBUs as part of any strategic planning effort. Marketing must get its direction from the organization's strategic plan.

Marketing Information, Research, and Understanding the Target Market

Part B

Section I Essentials of Marketing Management

2

Marketing Research: Process and Systems for Decision Making

Marketing managers require current, reliable, and useful information to make effective decisions. In today's highly competitive global economy, marketers need to exploit opportunities and avoid mistakes if they are to survive and be profitable. Not only is sound marketing research needed, but also a system that gets current, valid information to the marketing decision maker in a timely manner.

This chapter is concerned with the marketing research process and information systems for decision making. It begins by discussing the marketing research process that is used to develop useful information for decision making. Then, marketing information systems are briefly discussed. The chapter is intended to provide a detailed introduction to many of the important topics in the area, but it does not provide a complete explanation of the plethora of marketing research topics.

THE ROLE OF MARKETING RESEARCH

Marketing research is the process by which information about the environment is generated, analyzed, and interpreted for use in marketing decision making.[1] It cannot be overstated that *marketing research is an aid to decision making and not a substitute for it*. In other words, marketing research does not make decisions, but it can substantially increase the chances that good decisions are made. Unfortunately, too many marketing managers view research reports as the final answer to their problems; whatever the research indicates is taken as the appropriate course of action. Instead, marketing managers should recognize that (1) even the most carefully executed research can be fraught with errors; (2) marketing research does not forecast with certainty what will happen in the future; and (3) they should make decisions in light of their own knowledge and experience, since no marketing research study includes all of the factors that could influence the success of a strategy.

Although marketing research does not make decisions, it can reduce the risks associated with managing marketing strategies. For example, it can reduce the risk of introducing new products by evaluating consumer acceptance of them prior to full-scale introduction. Marketing research is also vital for investigating the effects of various marketing strategies after they have been implemented. For example, marketing research can examine the effects of a change in any element of the marketing mix on customer perception and behavior.

At one time, marketing researchers were primarily engaged in the technical aspects of research, but were not heavily involved in the strategic use of research findings. Today, however, many marketing researchers work hand-in-hand with marketing managers throughout the research process and have responsibility for making strategic recommendations based on the research.

THE MARKETING RESEARCH PROCESS

Marketing research can be viewed as systematic processes for obtaining information to aid in decision making. There are many types of marketing research, and the framework illustrated in Figure 2.1 represents a general approach to the process. Each element of this process is discussed next.

Purpose of the Research

The first step in the research process is to determine explicitly why the research is needed and what it is to accomplish. This may be much more difficult than it sounds. Quite often a situation or problem is recognized as needing research, yet the nature of the problem is not clear or well defined nor is the appropriate type of research evident. Thus, managers and researchers need to discuss and clarify the current situation and develop a clear understanding of the problem. At the end of this stage, managers and researchers should agree on (1) the current situation involving the problem to be researched, (2) the nature of the problem, and (3) the specific question or questions the research is designed to investigate. This step is crucial since it influences the type of research to be conducted and the research design.

FIGURE 2.1
The Five Ps of the
Research Process

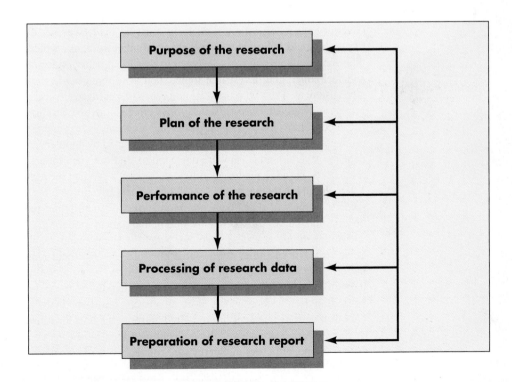

Plan of the Research

Once the specific research question or questions have been agreed on, a research plan can be developed. A research plan spells out the nature of the research to be conducted and includes an explanation of such things as the sample design, measures, and analysis techniques to be used. Three critical issues that influence the research plan are (1) whether primary or secondary data are needed, (2) whether qualitative or quantitative research is needed, and (3) whether the company will do its own research or contract with a marketing research specialist.

Primary versus Secondary Data

Given the information needed and budget constraints, a decision must be made as to whether primary data, secondary data, or some combination of the two is needed. *Primary data* are data collected specifically for the research problem under investigation; *secondary data* are those that have previously been collected for other purposes but can be used for the problem at hand. For example, if a company wanted to know why users of a competitive brand didn't prefer its brand, it may have to collect primary data to find out. On the other hand, if a company wanted to know the population size of key global markets that it might enter, it could find this information from secondary sources. Secondary information has the advantage of usually being cheaper than primary data, although it is not always available for strategy-specific research questions.

There are many sources of secondary data useful for marketing research. Syndicated data providers sell a variety of useful data to companies. Figure 2.2 lists a number of data providers and the type of information they can provide. Government sources, such as the *Statistical Abstracts of the United States* or the *Survey of Current Business,* can provide insights into the economy and industries within it. Trade groups such as the American Medical Association or the National Association of Retail Dealers of America can also be contacted for information relevant to their industries.[2]

Qualitative versus Quantitative Research

Given a research question, a decision must be made whether qualitative or quantitative research would be a better approach. Qualitative research typically involves face-to-face interviews with respondents designed to develop a better understanding of what they think and feel concerning a research topic, such as a brand name, a product, a package, or an advertisement. The two most common types of qualitative research in marketing are focus groups and long interviews. *Focus groups* typically involve discussions among a small number of consumers led by an interviewer and are designed to generate insights and ideas about products and brands. *Long interviews* are conducted by an interviewer with a single respondent for several hours. They are designed to find out such things as the meanings various products or brands have for an individual or how a product influences a person's life.

Quantitative research involves more systematic procedures designed to obtain and analyze numerical data. Four common types of quantitative research in marketing are observation, surveys, experiments, and mathematical modeling.

Observational research involves watching people and recording relevant facts and behaviors. For example, retail stores may use observational research to determine what patterns customers use in walking through stores, how much time they spend in various parts of the store, and how many items of merchandise they examine. This information can be used to design store layouts more effectively. Similarly, many retail marketers do traffic counts at various intersections to help determine the best locations for stores.

Survey research involves the collection of data by means of a questionnaire by mail, phone, online, or in person. Surveys are commonly used in marketing research to investigate

FIGURE 2.2   Some Syndicated Data Providers

Company	Syndicated Service	What it Measures
ACNielsen www.acnielsen.com	Scantrack	Provides sales tracking across grocery, drug, and mass merchandisers.
	Homescan	Provides consumer panel service for tracking retail purchases and motivations.
Yahoo! and ACNielsen www.yahoo.com	Internet Confidence Index	Measures (quarterly) the confidence levels in Internet products and services.
Scarborough Research (a service of Arbitron, Inc., and VNU) www.scarborough.com		Provides a syndicated study to print and electronic media, new media companies, outdoor media, sports teams and leagues, agencies, advertisers, and Yellow Pages on local, regional, and national levels—including local market shopping patterns, demographics, media usage, and lifestyle activities.
Millward Brown www.millwardbrown.com	IntelliQuest www.intelliquest.com	Provides studies enabling clients to understand and improve the position of their technology, brands, products, media, or channels.
Information Resources www.infores.com	BehaviourScan	Collects store tracking data used with consumer panel data to track advertising influence in consumer packaged goods.
Nielsen Media Research www.nielsenmedia.com	National People Meter	Provides audience estimates for all national program sources, including broadcast networks, cable networks, Spanish-language networks, and national syndicators.
NOP World www.nopworld.com	Starch Ad Readership Studies	Provides raw readership scores collected via individual depth interview; records the percent of readers who saw the ad and read the copy. The ad is ranked not only against other ads in the issue but also against other ads in its product category over the last two years.
CSA TMO www.csa-fr.com	OPERBAC	Provides continuous tracking of banking insurance and credit purchases in European markets.
DoubleClick www.doubleclick.com	Diameter	Provides online audience measurement services for Web publishers, advertisers, and agencies.
Nielsen//NetRatings www.nielsen-netratings.com		Measures audience data using actual click-by-click Internet user behavior measured through a comprehensive real-time meter installed on individual computers worldwide (home and work).
Taylor Nelson Sofres Intersearch www.tns-i.com	Global eCommerce	Measures e-commerce activity in 27 countries, providing insights into 37 marketplaces via interviews.
J.D. Power Associates www.jdpower.com	PowerReport, PowerGram, etc.	Publishes in-depth analytical reports on automotive travel, health, and other industries.
MediaMark www.mediamark.com		Supplies multimedia audience research to magazines, television, radio, Internet and other media, leading national advertisers, and over 450 advertising agencies, including 90 of 100 agencies in the U.S.
Simmons (SMRB) www.smrb.com	National	Provides telephone research that covers important markets critical to advertisers, agencies, and media.

Source: Donald R. Cooper and Pamela S. Schindler, *Marketing Research* (Burr Ridge, IL: McGraw-Hill/Irwin, 2006), p. 43.

Qualitative research is commonly used for

- Identifying a business problem or opportunity situation, or establishing information requirements.
- Obtaining preliminary insights into the motivation, emotional, attitudinal, and personality factors that influence marketplace behaviors.
- Building theories and models to explain marketplace behaviors or relationships between two or more marketing variables.
- Developing valid scales for investigating specific market factors, consumer qualities (e.g., attitudes, emotional feelings, preferences, beliefs, perceptions), and behavioral outcomes.
- Determining the preliminary effectiveness of marketing strategies on actual marketplace behaviors.
- Developing new products and services, or repositioning current product or service images.

Quantitative research is commonly used for

- Validating or answering a business problem or information requirements.
- Obtaining detailed descriptions or insights into the motivation, emotional, attitudinal, and personality factors that influence marketplace behaviors.
- Testing theories and models to explain marketplace behaviors or relationships between two or more marketing variables.
- Assessing the reliability and validity of scales for investigating market factors, consumer qualities (e.g., attitudes, emotional feelings, preferences, beliefs, perceptions) and behavioral outcomes.
- Assessing the effectiveness of marketing strategies on marketplace behaviors.
- Examining new-product/service development or repositioning current products or service images.
- Segmenting and/or comparing large or small differences in markets, new products, services, or evaluation and repositioning of current products or service images.

Sources: Joseph F. Hair, Jr., Robert P. Bush, and David J. Ortinau, *Marketing Research,* 4th ed. (Burr Ridge IL: McGraw-Hill/Irwin, 2009), pp.154–155.

customer beliefs, attitudes, satisfaction, and many other issues. Mail surveys are useful for reaching widely dispersed markets but take more time to get responses than telephone surveys; personal surveys involving structured questions are useful but expensive.

Experimental research involves manipulating one variable and examining its impact on other variables. For example, the price of a product could be changed in one test store, while left the same in other stores. Comparing sales in the test store with those in other stores can provide evidence about the likely impact of a price change in the overall market. Experiments are useful for getting a better idea of the causal relationships among variables, but they are often difficult to design and administer effectively in natural settings. Thus, many marketing research experiments are conducted in laboratories or simulated stores to carefully control other variables that could impact results.

Mathematical modeling often involves secondary data, such as scanner data collected and stored in computer files from retail checkout counters. This approach involves the development of equations to model relationships among variables and uses econometric and statistical techniques to investigate the impact of various strategies and tactics on sales and brand choices. Math modeling is useful because it provides an efficient way to study problems with extremely large secondary data sets.

FIGURE 2.3   A Comparison of Data Collection Methods Used in Marketing Research

Method	Advantages	Disadvantages
Focus groups	• Depth of information collected. • Flexibility in use. • Relatively low cost. • Data collected quickly.	• Requires expert moderator. • Questions of group size and acquaintanceships of participants. • Potential for bias from moderator. • Small sample size.
Telephone surveys	• Centralized control of data collection. • More cost-effective than personal interviews. • Data collected quickly.	• Resistance in collecting income, financial data. • Limited depth of response. • Disproportionate coverage of low-income segments. • Abuse of phone by solicitors. • Perceived intrusiveness.
Mail surveys	• Cost-effective per completed response. • Broad geographic dispersion. • Ease of administration. • Data collected quickly.	• Refusal and contact problems with certain segments. • Limited depth of response. • Difficult to estimate nonresponse biases. • Resistance and bias in collecting income, financial data. • Lack of control following mailing.
Personal (in-depth) interviews	• More depth of response than telephone interviews. • Generate substantial number of ideas compared with group methods.	• Easy to transmit biasing cues. • Not-at-homes. • Broad coverage often infeasible. • Cost per contact high. • Data collection time may be excessive.
Mall intercepts	• Flexibility in collecting data, answering questions, probing respondents. • Data collected quickly. • Excellent for concept tests, copy evaluations, other visuals. • Fairly high response rates.	• Limited time. • Sample composition or representativeness is suspect. • Costs depend on incidence rates. • Interviewer supervision difficult.
Internet surveys	• Inexpensive, quickly executed. • Visual stimuli can be evaluated. • Real-time data processing possible. • Can be answered at convenience of respondent.	• Responses must be checked for duplication, bogus responses. • Respondent self-selection bias. • Limited ability to qualify respondents and confirm responses. • Difficulty in generating sample frames for probability sampling.
Projective techniques	• Useful in word association tests of new brand names. • Less threatening to respondents for sensitive topics. • Can identify important motives underlying choices.	• Require trained interviewers. • Cost per interview high.
Observation	• Can collect sensitive data. • Accuracy of measuring overt behaviors. • Different perspective than survey self-reports. • Useful in studies of cross-cultural differences.	• Appropriate only for frequently occurring behaviors. • Unable to assess opinions of attitudes causing behaviors. • May be expensive in data-collection-time costs.

Source: William O. Bearden, Thomas N. Ingram, and Raymond W. LaForge, *Marketing,* 5th ed. (Burr Ridge, IL: McGraw-Hill/Irwin, 2007), p. 134.

Which of these types of research is best for particular research questions requires considerable knowledge of each of them. Often, qualitative research is used in early stages of investigating a topic to get more information and insight about it. Then, quantitative approaches are used to investigate the degree to which the insights hold across a larger sample or population. Figure 2.3 provides a comparison of a variety of qualitative and quantitative data collection methods.

A. Planning
1. Segmentation: What kinds of people buy our products? Where do they live? How much do they earn? How many of them are there?
2. Demand estimation: Are the markets for our products increasing or decreasing? Are there promising markets that we have not yet reached?
3. Environmental assessment: Are the channels of distribution for our products changing? What should our presence on the Internet be?

B. Problem Solving
1. Product
   a. In testing new products and product-line extensions, which product design is likely to be the most successful? What features do consumers value most?
   b. What kind of packaging should we use?
   c. What are the forecasts for the product? How might we reenergize its life cycle?
2. Price
   a. What price should we charge for our products?
   b. How sensitive to price changes are our target segments?
   c. Given the lifetime value assessments of our segments, should we be discounting or charging a premium to our most valued customers?
   d. As production costs decline, should we lower our prices or try to develop higher-quality products?
   e. Do consumers use price as a cue to value or a cue to quality in our industry?
3. Place
   a. Where, and by whom, are our products being sold? Where, and by whom, should our products be sold?
   b. What kinds of incentives should we offer the trade to push our products?
   c. Are our relationships with our suppliers and distributors satisfactory and cooperative?
4. Promotion
   a. How much should we spend on promotion? How should it be allocated to products and to geographic areas?
   b. Which ad copy should we run in our markets? With what frequency and media expenditures?
   c. What combination of media—newspapers, radio, television, magazines, Internet ad banners—should we use?
   d. What is our consumer coupon redemption rate?

C. Control
1. What is our market share overall? In each geographic area? By each customer type?
2. Are customers satisfied with our products? How is our record for service? Are there many returns? Do levels of customer satisfaction vary with market? With segment?
3. Are our employees satisfied? Do they feel well trained and empowered to assist our customers?
4. How does the public perceive our company? What is our reputation with the trade?

Source: Dawn Iacobucci and Gilbert A. Churchill, Jr., *Marketing Research: Methodological Foundations*, 10th ed. (Mason, OH: Thomson South-Western, 2010), p. 6.

Company versus Contract Research

Most large consumer goods companies have marketing research departments that can perform a variety of types of research. In addition many marketing research firms, advertising agencies, and consulting companies do marketing research on a contract basis. Some marketing research suppliers have special expertise in a particular type of research that makes them a better choice than doing the research internally. A decision about

Traditional marketing research typically involves identifying possible drivers and then collecting data: Increasing couponing (the driver) during spring will increase trial by first-time buyers (the result). Marketing researchers then try to collect information to attempt to verify the truth of the relationship.

In contrast, **data mining** is the extraction of hidden predictive information from large databases. The focus is on finding statistical links about consumer purchasing patterns that suggest marketing actions.

Some of these purchase patterns are common sense: You may not need a computer to suspect that peanut butter and grape jelly purchases are linked and that it might be a good idea sometime to run a joint promotion between Skippy peanut butter and Welch's grape jelly. But would you have expected that men buying diapers in the evening sometimes buy a six-pack of beer as well? This is exactly what supermarkets discovered when they mined checkout data from scanners. So they placed diapers and beer near each other, then placed potato chips between them—and increased sales on all three items! On the near horizon: radio-frequency identification (RFID) technology using a "smart tag" microchip on the diapers and beer to tell whether they wind up in the same shopping bag—at 10 in the evening.

Still, the success in data mining ultimately depends on humans—the judgments of the marketing managers and researchers in how to select, analyze, and interpret the information.

Source: Roger A. Kerin, Steven W. Hartley, and William Rudelius, *Marketing,* 10th ed. (Burr Ridge, IL: McGraw-Hill/Irwin, 2011), pp. 210–211.

whether the marketing research department has the ability to do a particular type of research itself or whether all or part of the research should be contracted with a research supplier must be made. In either case, schedules for task completion, the exact responsibilities of all involved parties, and cost need to be considered.

Performance of the Research

Performance of the research involves preparing for data collection and actually collecting them. The tasks at this stage obviously depend on the type of research that has been selected and the type of data needed. If secondary data are to be used, they must be located, prepared for analysis, and possibly paid for. If primary data are to be collected, then observational forms, questionnaires, or other types of measures must be designed, pretested, and validated. Samples must be drawn and interviews must be scheduled or preparations must be made for mailing or phoning selected individuals.

In terms of actual data collection, a cardinal rule is to obtain and record the maximal amount of useful information, subject to the constraints of time, money, and respondent privacy. Failure to obtain and record data clearly can obviously lead to a poor research study, while failure to consider the rights of respondents raises both practical and ethical problems. Thus, both the objectives and constraints of data collection must be closely monitored.

Processing of Research Data

Processing research data includes the preparation of data for analysis and the actual analysis of them. Preparations include such things as editing and structuring data and coding them for analysis. Data sets should be clearly labeled to ensure they are not misinterpreted or misplaced.

The appropriate analysis techniques for collected data depend on the nature of the research question and the design of the research. Qualitative research data consist of interview records that are content analyzed for ideas or themes. Quantitative research data may be analyzed in a variety of ways depending on the objectives of the research.

A critical part of this stage is interpreting and assessing the research results. Seldom, if ever, do marketing research studies obtain findings that are totally unambiguous. Usually, relationships among variables or differences between groups are small to moderate, and judgment and insight are needed to draw appropriate inferences and conclusions. Marketing researchers should always double-check their analysis and avoid overstating the strength of their findings. The implications for developing or changing a marketing strategy should be carefully thought out and tempered with judgment about the overall quality of the study.

Preparation of the Research Report

The research report is a complete statement of everything done in a research project and includes a write-up of each of the previous stages as well as the strategic recommendations from the research. The limitations of the research should be carefully noted. Figure 2.4 illustrates the types of questions marketing researchers and managers should discuss prior to submitting the final research report.

Research reports should be clear and unambiguous with respect to what was done and what recommendations are made. Often research reports must trade off the apparent precision of scientific jargon for everyday language that managers can understand. Researchers should work closely with managers to ensure that the study and its limitations are fully understood.

Limitations of the Research Process

Although the foregoing discussion presented the research process as a set of simple stages, this does not mean that conducting quality marketing research is a simple task. Many problems and difficulties must be overcome if a research study is to provide valuable information for decision making.[3] For example, consider the difficulties in one type of marketing research, *test marketing.*

The major goal of most test marketing is to measure new product sales on a limited basis where competitive retaliation and other factors are allowed to operate freely. In this way, future sales potential can often be estimated reasonably well. Listed below are a number of problems that could invalidate test marketing study results.

1. Test market areas are not representative of the market in general in terms of population characteristics, competition, and distribution outlets.
2. Sample size and design are incorrectly formulated because of budget constraints.
3. Pretest measurements of competitive brand sales are not made or are inaccurate, limiting the meaningfulness of market share estimates.
4. Test stores do not give complete support to the study such that certain package sizes may not be carried or prices may not be held constant during the test period.

FIGURE 2.4
Eight Criteria for
Evaluating Marketing
Research Reports

1. Was the type of research appropriate for the research questions?
2. Was the research well designed?
   a. Was the sample studied appropriate for the research questions?
   b. Were measures well developed, pretested, and validated?
   c. Were the data analysis techniques the best ones for the study?
3. Was there adequate supervision of data collection, editing, and coding?
4. Was the analysis conducted according to standards accepted in the field?
5. Do the findings make sense, given the research question and design, and were they considered in light of previous knowledge and experience?
6. Are the limitations of the study recognized and explained in detail?
7. Are the conclusions appropriately drawn or are they over- or understated?
8. Are the recommendations for marketing strategy clear and appropriate?

Marketing researchers have ethical responsibilities to the respondents who provide primary data, clients for whom they work, and subordinates who work under them. Below are a number of ethical responsibilities to these groups.

RESPONSIBILITIES TO RESPONDENTS

1. *Preserving respondent anonymity.* Marketing researchers should ensure that respondents' identities are safe from invasion of privacy.
2. *Avoiding mental stress for respondents.* Marketing researchers should minimize the mental stress placed on respondents.
3. *Avoiding questions detrimental to respondents.* Marketing researchers should avoid asking questions for which the answers conflict with the self-interest of the respondents.
4. *Avoiding the use of dangerous equipment or techniques.* Physical or reputational harm to respondents based on their participation in marketing research should not occur. Respondents should be informed of any other than minimal risks involved in the research and be free to self-determine their participation.
5. *Avoiding deception of respondents.* Respondents should not be deceived about the purpose of the study in most cases. Many consider deception acceptable in research where it is needed to obtain valid results, there is minimal risk to respondents, and respondents are debriefed explaining the real purpose of the study.
6. *Avoiding coercion of respondents.* Marketing researchers should avoid coercing or harassing people to try to get them to agree to be interviewed or fill out questionnaires.

RESPONSIBILITIES TO CLIENTS

1. *Providing confidentiality.* Marketing researchers are obliged not to reveal information about a client to competitors and should carefully consider when a company should be identified as a client.
2. *Providing technical integrity.* Marketing researchers are obliged to design efficient studies without undue expense or complexity and accurately report results.
3. *Providing administrative integrity.* Marketing researchers are obliged to price their work fairly without hidden charges.
4. *Providing guidance on research usage.* Marketing researchers are obliged to promote the correct usage of research and to prevent the misuse of findings.

RESPONSIBILITIES TO SUBORDINATE EMPLOYEES

1. *Creating an ethical work environment.* Marketing research managers are obliged to create an ethical work environment where unethical behavior is not encouraged or overlooked.
2. *Avoiding opportunities for unethical behavior.* Marketing research managers are obliged to avoid placing subordinates in situations where unethical behavior could be concealed but rewarded.

5. Test-market products are advertised or promoted beyond a profitable level for the market in general.
6. The effects of factors that influence sales, such as the sales force, season, weather conditions, competitive retaliation, shelf space, and so forth, are ignored in the research.
7. The test-market period is too short to determine whether the product will be repurchased by customers.

A list of such problems could be developed for any type of marketing research. However, careful research planning, coordination, implementation, and control can help reduce such problems and increase the value of research for decision making.

MARKETING INFORMATION SYSTEMS

Most marketers use computer-based systems to help them gather, sort, store, and distribute information for marketing decisions.[4] A popular form of marketing information system is the marketing decision support system, which is a coordinated collection of data, tools, and techniques involving both computer hardware and software by which marketers gather and interpret relevant information for decision making. These systems require three types of software:

1. Database management software for sorting and retrieving data from internal and external sources.

FIGURE 2.5 Some Information Sources for Marketing Information Systems

Selected Government Sources

American Factfinder	http://factfinder.census.gov/
Economics Statistics Briefing Room	http://www.whitehouse.gov/fsbr/esbr.html
EDGAR Database of Corporate Information (SEC filings)	http://www.sec.gov/edgar.shtml
FedStats	http://www.fedstats.gov/
GPO Access	http://www.gpoaccess.gov/
Stat-USA	http://www.stat-usa.gov/
U.S. Bureau of Labor Statistics	http://www.bls.gov/
U.S. Bureau of the Census	http://www.census.gov/
U.S. Department of Commerce	http://www.commerce.gov/
U.S. Small Business Administration	http://www.sbaonline.sba.gov/
U.S. Patent and Trademark Office	http://www.uspto.gov/
CBDNet (Commerce Business Daily)—government procurement, sales, and contract awards	http://www.cbdnet.access.gpo.gov

Selected Proprietary Sources (with some free information)

Gallup Poll	http://www.gallup.com/poll/
Harris Poll	http://www.harrisinteractive.com/harris_poll/
The Polling Report	http://www.pollingreport.com/
Public Opinion	http://europa.eu.int/comm./public_opinion/
Public Agenda	http://www.publicagenda.org/
Roper Center for Public Opinion Research	http://www.repercenter.uconn.edu
Poll Question Database	http://www.irss.unc.edu/data_archive/pollsearch.html
Forrester Research Reports	http://forrester.com
Roper Reports	http://www.nopworld.com
JD Power Satisfaction Studies	http://www.jdpower.com
Quirk's Marketing Research Review	http://www.quirks.com
Ad Forum	http://www.adforum.com
BizMiner	http://www.bizminer.com

Selected Nonproprietary Sources

Ad* Access	http://scriptorium.lib.duke.edu/adaccess/
Advertising World (ad industry portal)	http://advertising.utexas.edu/world
American Demographics	http://www.demographics.com
Competia Express (industry portal)	http://www.competia.com/express/
Global Edge	http://www.demographics.com
Kerlins.net Qualitative Research Bibliography	http://kerlins.net/bobbi/research/qualresearch/bibliography/
KnowThis.com Marketing Virtual Library	http://knowthis.com
Marketing and Research Library	http://www.mrlibrary.com/
MarketingPower.com	http://marketingpower.com

Source: Donald R. Cooper and Pamela S. Schindler, *Marketing Research* (Burr Ridge, IL: McGraw-Hill/Irwin, 2006), pp. 122–123.

2. Model base management software that contains routines for manipulating data in ways that are useful for marketing decision making.

3. A dialog system that permits marketers to explore databases and use models to produce information to address their decision-making needs.

Marketing decision support systems are designed to handle information from both internal and external sources. Internal information includes such things as sales records, which can be divided by territory, package size, brand, price, order size, or salesperson; inventory data that can indicate how rapidly various products are selling; or expenditure data on such things as advertising, personal selling, or packaging. Internal information is particularly important for investigating the efficiency and effectiveness of various marketing strategies.

External information is gathered from outside the organization and concerns changes in the environment that could influence marketing strategies. External information is needed concerning changes in global economies and societies, competitors, customers, and technology. Figure 2.5 lists a sample of sources of external information that could be monitored by a marketing information system to help marketers make better decisions. Of course, information from marketing research studies conducted by an organization is also put into marketing information systems to improve marketing strategy development.

SUMMARY

This chapter emphasized the importance of marketing research for making sound marketing strategy decisions. The chapter discussed marketing research as a process involving several stages, which include determining the purpose of the research, designing the plan for the research, performing the research, processing the research data, and preparing the research report. Then, marketing information systems were discussed and one type, the marketing decision support system, was explained. Such systems should provide decision makers with the right information, at the right time in the right way, to make sound marketing decisions.

Additional Resources

Churchill, Gilbert A., Jr.; Tom J. Brown; and Tracy A. Suter. *Basic Marketing Research*. 7th ed. Mason, OH: Thomson South-Western, 2010.

Cooper, Donald R., and Pamela S. Schindler. *Marketing Research*. Burr Ridge, IL: McGraw-Hill/Irwin, 2006.

Hair, Joseph F., Jr.; Robert P. Bush; and David J. Ortinau. *Marketing Research*. 4th ed. Burr Ridge, IL: McGraw-Hill/Irwin, 2009.

Iacobucci, Dawn, and Gilbert A. Churchill, Jr. *Marketing Research: Methodological Foundations*. 10th ed. Mason, OH: Thomson South-Western, 2010.

Molhatra, Naresh K. *Marketing Research*. 6th ed. Upper Saddle River, NJ: Pearson Education, 2010.

Zikmund, William G., and Barry J. Babin. *Exploring Marketing Research*. 10th ed. Mason, OH: Thomson South-Western, 2010.

Zikmund, William G., and Barry J. Babin. *Essentials of Marketing Research*. 4th ed. Mason, OH: Thomson South-Western, 2010.

Key Terms and Concepts

Experimental research: Experimental research involves manipulating one variable and examining its impact on other variables.

Focus groups: A type of qualitative research that typically involves discussions among a small number of consumers led by an interviewer and designed to generate insights and ideas about products and brands.

Long interviews: A type of qualitative research conducted by an interviewer with a single respondent for several hours and designed to find out such things as the meanings various products and brands have for the person or how a product influences the person's life.

Marketing research: Marketing research is the process by which information about the environment is generated, analyzed, and interpreted for use in marketing decision making. Most often consumers or organizational buyers are the subject of the research.

Mathematical modeling: Mathematical modeling involves developing equations to model relationships among variables to investigate the impact of various strategies and tactics on sales and brand choices.

Observational research: Observational research involves watching people and recording relevant facts and behaviors.

Primary data: Primary data are data collected specifically for the research problem under investigation.

Qualitative research: Qualitative research typically involves face-to-face interviews with respondents designed to develop a better understanding of what they think and feel concerning a research topic, such as a brand name, a product, a package, or an advertisement.

Quantitative research: Quantitative research involves systematic procedures designed to obtain and analyze numerical data.

Secondary data: Secondary data are those that have previously been collected for other purposes but can be used for the problem at hand.

Survey research: Survey research involves the collection of data by means of a questionnaire either by mail, phone, online, or in person.

Test marketing: The major goal of most test marketing is to measure new product sales on a limited basis where competitive retaliation and other factors are allowed to operate freely. In this way, future sales potential can often be estimated reasonably well.

Chapter 3

Consumer Behavior

The marketing concept emphasizes that profitable marketing begins with the discovery and understanding of consumer needs and then develops a marketing mix to satisfy these needs. Thus, an understanding of consumers and their needs and purchasing behavior is integral to successful marketing. Unfortunately, there is no single theory of consumer behavior that can totally explain why consumers behave as they do. Instead, there are numerous theories, models, and concepts making up the field. In addition, the majority of these notions have been borrowed from a variety of other disciplines, such as sociology, psychology, anthropology, and economics, and must be integrated to understand consumer behavior.

In this chapter, consumer behavior will be examined in terms of the model in Figure 3.1. The chapter begins by reviewing social, marketing, and situational influences on consumer decision making. These provide information that can influence consumers' thoughts and feelings about purchasing various products and brands. The degree to which this information influences consumers' decisions depends on a number of psychological influences. Two of the most important of these are product knowledge and product involvement, which will then be discussed. The chapter concludes by discussing the consumer decision-making process.

FIGURE 3.1   An Overview of the Buying Process

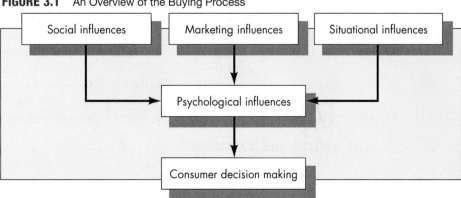

Value	General Features	Relevance to Marketing
Achievement and success activity	Hard work is good; success flows from hard work.	Acts as a justification for acquisition of goods ("You deserve it").
	Keeping busy is healthy and natural.	Stimulates interest in products that are time-savers and enhance leisure time.
Efficiency and practicality	Admiration of things that solve problems (e.g., save time and effort).	Stimulates purchase of products that function well and save time.
	People can improve themselves; tomorrow should be better than today.	Stimulates desire for new products that fulfill unsatisfied needs; ready acceptance of products that claim to be "new" or "improved."
Material comfort	"The good life."	Fosters acceptance of convenience and luxury products that make life more enjoyable.
Individualism	Being oneself (e.g., self-reliance, self-interest, self-esteem).	Stimulates acceptance of customized or unique products that enable a person to "express his or her own personality."
Freedom	Freedom of choice.	Fosters interest in wide product lines and differentiated products.
External conformity	Uniformity of observable behavior; desire for acceptance.	Stimulates interest in products that are used or owned by others in the same social group.
Humanitarianism	Caring for others, particularly the underdog.	Stimulates patronage of firms that compete with market leaders.
Youthfulness	A state of mind that stresses being "young at heart" and having a youthful appearance.	Stimulates acceptance of products that provide the illusion of maintaining or fostering youthfulness.
Fitness and health	Caring about one's body, including the desire to be physically fit and healthy.	Stimulates acceptance of food products, activities, and equipment perceived to maintain or increase physical fitness.

Source: Leon G. Schiffman and Leslie Lazar Kanuck, *Consumer Behavior,* 10th ed., p. 369, 2010. Reprinted by permission of Pearson Prentice Hall, Inc., Upper Saddle River, NJ.

SOCIAL INFLUENCES ON CONSUMER DECISION MAKING

Behavioral scientists have become increasingly aware of the powerful effects of the social environment and personal interactions on human behavior. In terms of consumer behavior, culture, social class, and reference group influences have been related to purchase and consumption decisions. It should be noted that these influences can have both direct and indirect effects on the buying process. By direct effects we mean direct communication between the individual and other members of society concerning a particular decision. By indirect effects we mean the influence of society on an individual's basic values and attitudes as well as the important role that groups play in structuring an individual's personality.

Culture and Subculture

Culture is one of the most basic influences on an individual's needs, wants, and behavior, since all facets of life are carried out against the background of the society in which an individual lives. Cultural antecedents affect everyday behavior, and there is empirical support for the notion that culture is a determinant of certain aspects of consumer behavior.

Cultural values are transmitted through three basic organizations: the family, religious organizations, and educational institutions; and in today's society, educational institutions are playing an increasingly greater role in this regard. Marketing managers should adapt the marketing mix to cultural values and constantly monitor value changes and differences in both domestic and global markets. To illustrate, one of the changing values in America is the increasing emphasis on achievement and career success. This change in values has been recognized by many business firms that have expanded their emphasis on time-saving, convenience-oriented products.

In large nations such as the United States, the population is bound to lose a significant amount of its homogeneity, and thus subcultures arise. In other words, there are subcultures in the American culture where people have more frequent interactions than with the population at large and thus tend to think and act alike in some respects. Subcultures are based on such things as geographic areas, religions, nationalities, ethnic groups, and age. Many subcultural barriers are decreasing because of mass communication, mass transit, and a decline in the influence of religious values. However, age groups, such as the teen market, baby boomers, and the mature market, have become increasingly important for marketing strategy. For example, since baby boomers (those born between 1946 and 1962) make up about a third of the U.S. population and soon will account for about half of discretionary spending, many marketers are repositioning products to serve them. Snickers candy bars, for instance, used to be promoted to children as a treat but are now promoted to adults as a wholesome between-meals snack.

Social Class

While many people like to think of America as a land of equality, a class structure can be observed. Social classes develop on the basis of such things as wealth, skill, and power. The single best indicator of social class is occupation. However, interest at this point is in the influence of social class on the individual's behavior. What is important here is that different social classes tend to have different attitudinal configurations and values that influence the behavior of individual members. For marketing purposes, four different social classes have been identified.[1]

Upper Americans comprise 14 percent of the population and are differentiated mainly by having high incomes. This class remains the group in which quality merchandise is most prized and prestige brands are commonly sought. Spending with good taste is a priority as are products such as theater; books; investments in art; European travel; household help; club memberships for tennis, golf, and swimming; and prestige schooling for children.

The *middle class* comprises 34 percent of the population, and these consumers want to do the right thing and buy what is popular. They are concerned with fashion and buying what experts in the media recommend. Increased earnings have led to spending on more "worthwhile experiences" for children, including winter ski trips, college education, and shopping for better brands of clothes at more expensive stores. Appearance of the home is important. This group emulates the upper Americans, which distinguishes it from the working class.

The *working class* comprises 38 percent of the population, people who are "family folk" who depend heavily on relatives for economic and emotional support. The emphasis on family ties is only one sign of how much more limited and different working-class horizons are socially, psychologically, and geographically compared to those of the middle class. For them, "keeping up with the times" focuses on the mechanical and recreational, and thus, ease of labor and leisure are what they continue to pursue.

Lower Americans comprise 16 percent of the population and are as diverse in values and consumption goals as are other social levels. Some members of this group are homeless and penniless although most work part-time or full-time jobs at low wages. Most receive public housing, food stamps, and Medicaid. The primary demands of this group are food, clothing, and other staples. Given that a number of people in this group have little education or resources, many people feel it is unethical to try to market alcoholic beverages or tobacco products to it.

For the marketing manager, social class offers some insights into consumer behavior and is potentially useful as a market segmentation variable. However, there is considerable controversy as to whether social class is superior to income for the purpose of market segmentation.

Reference Groups and Families

Groups that an individual looks to (uses as a reference) when forming attitudes and opinions are described as *reference groups*.[2] Primary reference groups include family and close friends, while secondary reference groups include fraternal organizations and professional associations. A buyer may also consult a single individual about decisions, and this individual would be considered a reference individual.

A person normally has several reference groups or reference individuals for various subjects or different decisions. For example, a woman may consult one reference group when she is purchasing a car and a different reference group for lingerie. In other words, the nature of the product and the role the individual is playing during the purchasing process influence which reference group will be consulted. Reference group influence is generally considered to be stronger for products that are "public" or conspicuous—that is, products that other people see the individual using, such as clothes or automobiles.

As noted, the family is generally recognized to be an important reference group, and it has been suggested that the household, rather than the individual, is the relevant unit for studying consumer behavior.[3] This is because within a household the purchaser of goods and services is not always the user of these goods and services. Thus, it is important for marketing managers to determine not only who makes the actual purchase but also who makes the decision to purchase. In addition, it has been recognized that the needs, income, assets, debts, and expenditure patterns change over the course of what is called the *family life cycle*. The family life cycle can be divided into a number of stages ranging from single, to married, to married with children of different age groups, to older couples, to solitary survivors. It may also include divorced people, both with and without children. Because the life cycle combines trends in earning power with demands placed on income, it is a useful way of classifying and segmenting individuals and families.[4]

MARKETING INFLUENCES ON CONSUMER DECISION MAKING

Marketing strategies are often designed to influence consumer decision making and lead to profitable exchanges. Each element of the marketing mix (product, price, promotion, place) can affect consumers in various ways.

Product Influences

Many attributes of a company's products, including brand name, quality, newness, and complexity, can affect consumer behavior. The physical appearance of the product, packaging, and labeling information can also influence whether consumers notice a product in-store, examine it, and purchase it. One of the key tasks of marketers is to differentiate their products from those of competitors and create consumer perceptions that the product is worth purchasing.

Price Influences

The price of products and services often influences whether consumers will purchase them at all and, if so, which competitive offering is selected. Stores, such as Walmart, which are perceived to charge the lowest prices, attract many consumers based on this fact alone. For some offerings, higher prices may not deter purchase because consumers believe that the products or services are higher quality or are more prestigious. However,

Marketers know that reference groups can influence both product and brand decisions. They also know that reference group influence varies depending on whether the good is used publicly (a car) or privately (a toothbrush) and whether it is a necessity (a mattress) or a luxury (a sailboat). By examining the nature of products and brands on these two dimensions, the matrix below can be constructed. Marketers could use this matrix to judge how reference group influence should be used in advertising and personal selling efforts. For example, public luxuries could benefit from ads showing owners being admired and complimented for their product and brand selection whereas ads for private necessities might focus more on superior functional performance.

	Necessity	Luxury
Public	**Public necessities** Reference group influence Product: Weak Brand: Strong Examples: Wristwatch, automobile, man's suit	**Public luxuries** Reference group influence Product: Strong Brand: Strong Examples: Golf clubs, snow skis, sailboat, health club
Private	**Private necessities** Reference group influence Product: Weak Brand: Weak Examples: Mattress, floor lamp, refrigerator	**Private luxuries** Reference group influence Product: Strong Brand: Weak Examples: Plasma TV, trash compactor, ice maker

Source: Adapted from William O. Bearden and Michael J. Etzel, "Reference Group Influences on Product and Brand Purchase Decisions," *Journal of Consumer Research,* September 1982, p. 185 as reported in J. Paul Peter and Jerry C. Olson, *Consumer Behavior and Marketing Strategy,* 9th ed. (Burr Ridge, IL: McGraw-Hill/Irwin, 2010), pp. 340–341.

many of today's value-conscious consumers may buy products more on the basis of price than other attributes.

Promotion Influences

Advertising, sales promotions, salespeople, and publicity can influence what consumers think about products, what emotions they experience in purchasing and using them, and what behaviors they perform, including shopping in particular stores and purchasing specific brands. Since consumers receive so much information from marketers and screen out a good deal of it, it is important for marketers to devise communications that (1) offer consistent messages about their products and (2) are placed in media that consumers in the target market are likely to use. Marketing communications play a critical role in informing consumers about products and services, including where they can be purchased, and in creating favorable images and perceptions.

Place Influences

The marketer's strategy for distributing products can influence consumers in several ways. First, products that are convenient to buy in a variety of stores increase the chances of consumers finding and buying them. When consumers are seeking low-involvement products, they are unlikely to engage in extensive search, so ready availability is important. Second, products sold in exclusive outlets such as Nordstrom may be perceived by consumers as having higher quality. In fact, one of the ways marketers create brand equity—that is, favorable

The recession starting in 2008 changed the behavior of consumers and marketers. According to a Gallup Poll, 55 percent of consumers said they cut household spending as a result of lower prices in the stock market and fears about the economy. They said they cut back on travel for the holidays (63 percent), eating out at restaurants (81 percent), entertainment such as going to the movies (72 percent), and household services such as housekeeping and lawn service (37 percent).

Consumers also sold old jewelry and ransacked closets to find "stuff" to put on eBay. According to eBay CEO John Donahoe, Americans typically have about $3,200 worth of goods at home they could sell to raise cash. Coupon usage to trim grocery costs also went up for the first time in 15 years. Rather than use credit cards, many consumers started saving money to buy something they wanted, and layaway plans in which consumers pay in advance for items weekly or monthly also made a comeback. eLayaway, a start-up that handles layaway programs for 1,000 retailers, had its customer base jump from 150 to 3,000 in the fall of the year.

The number of consumers who had both a full-time and a part-time job increased 11 percent over the previous year, according to the Bureau of Labor Statistics. Many of these consumers were trying to increase their income so they could save more to help make up some of the losses in their retirement accounts. Also, sales of Blu-ray high definition disks more than tripled during the year as consumers found watching them at home a lot cheaper than a night at the movies. Finally, 29 percent of consumers said they were buying more store and generic brands to save money.

So what did marketers do to try to keep merchandise moving and the economy from stalling? Most retailers put products on sale at deep discounts and many companies tried to promote the idea that their products provided value to consumers. For example, Procter & Gamble promoted its new Total Care versions of Tide detergent and Downy fabric softener as products that preserved the look of new clothes. In other words, the products would keep clothes looking new longer so consumers wouldn't have to buy clothes as often and could save money. Since consumers were eating more meals at home, Campbell and Kraft banded together to promote a low-cost classic meal: tomato soup and a grilled cheese sandwich. "Warm hearts without stretching budgets" read the copy in the ad that shows a package of Kraft Singles cheese slices and a can of Campbell's tomato soup. Kraft's DiGiorno pizza aired ads that stated that a home-delivered pizza cost twice as much as a DiGiorno.

Gillette ran a series of ads to justify the $20 to $25 price for eight Fusion Power razor blades arguing that "In the world of high performance, what machine can you run for as little as a dollar a week?" Kellogg cereals played up the idea that a bowl of cereal with milk was a meal that cost only 50 cents. It also snatched up paid search terms including "cereal," "breakfast," and "value," on portals such as Google.com to drive budget-conscious consumers to its Web site. When they click on the ad, consumers are linked to a site that plays up the "excellent economic value" of Kellogg's cereal and offers a dollar-off coupon to buy some. Velveeta cheese ads tell shoppers to "forget the cheddar, Velveeta is better," and claim that a package of Velveeta is "twice the size of cheddar, for the same price."

In sum, many consumers tried to find new ways to live within their means and still live comfortably during a difficult economic time. Many marketers tried to convince consumers that their products provided good value for the money, but in a way that did not detract from their high-quality image.

Sources: Jarne O'Donnell and Sandra Block, "Consumers Get Frugal, So Retailers Get Creative," *USA Today*, January 28, 2009, p. B1; Mindy Fetterman, "Americans Are Digging Deep to Save Money," *USA Today*, November 17, 2008, p. 1A+; Laura Petrecca, "Marketers Try to Promote Value Without Cheapening Image," *USA Today*, November 17, 2008, p. 1B+.

consumer perceptions of brands—is by selling them in prestigious outlets. Third, offering products by nonstore methods, such as on the Internet or in catalogs, can create consumer perceptions that the products are innovative, exclusive, or tailored for specific target markets.

SITUATIONAL INFLUENCES ON CONSUMER DECISION MAKING

Situational influences can be defined as all the factors particular to a time and place that have a demonstrable and systematic effect on current behavior. In terms of purchasing situations, five groups of situational influences have been identified.[5] These influences may be perceived either consciously or subconsciously and may have considerable effect on product and brand choice.

1. *Physical features* are the most readily apparent features of a situation. These features include geographical and institutional location, decor, sounds, aromas, lighting, weather, and visible configurations of merchandise or other materials.

2. *Social features* provide additional depth to a description of a situation. These include other persons present, their characteristics, their apparent roles, and interpersonal interactions.

3. *Time* is a dimension of situations that may be specified in units ranging from time of day to season of the year. Time also may be measured relative to some past or future event for the situational participant. This allows such conceptions as time since last purchase, time since or until meals or paydays, and time constraints imposed by prior or standing commitments.

4. *Task features* of a situation include an intent or requirement to select, shop for, or obtain information about a general or specific purchase. In addition, task may reflect different buyer and user roles anticipated by the individual. For instance, a person shopping for a small appliance as a wedding gift for a friend is in a different situation than when shopping for a small appliance for personal use.

5. *Current conditions* make up a final feature that characterizes a situation. These are momentary moods (such as acute anxiety, pleasantness, hostility, and excitation) or momentary conditions (such as cash on hand, fatigue, and illness) rather than chronic individual traits. These conditions are considered to be immediately antecedent to the current situation to distinguish the states the individual brings to the situation from states of the individual resulting from the situation. For instance, people may select a certain motion picture because they feel depressed (an antecedent state and a part of the choice situation), but the fact that the movie causes them to feel happier is a response to the consumption situation. This altered state then may become antecedent for behavior in the next choice situation encountered, such as passing a street vendor on the way out of the theater.

PSYCHOLOGICAL INFLUENCES ON CONSUMER DECISION MAKING

Information from group, marketing, and situational influences affects what consumers think and feel about particular products and brands. However, a number of psychological factors influence how this information is interpreted and used and how it impacts the consumer decision-making process. Two of the most important psychological factors are product knowledge and product involvement.[6]

Product Knowledge

Product knowledge refers to the amount of information a consumer has stored in her or his memory about particular product classes, product forms, brands, models, and ways to purchase them. For example, a consumer may know a lot about coffee (product class), ground versus instant coffee (product form), Folgers versus Maxwell House (brand), and various package sizes (models) and stores that sell it (ways to purchase).

Group, marketing, and situational influences determine the initial level of product knowledge as well as changes in it. For example, a consumer may hear about a new Starbucks opening up from a friend (group influence), see an ad for it in the newspaper (marketing influence), or see the coffee shop on the way to work (situational influence). Any of these increase the amount of product knowledge, in this case, a new source for purchasing the product.

The initial level of product knowledge may influence how much information is sought when deciding to make a purchase. For example, if a consumer already believes that Folgers is the best-tasting coffee, knows where to buy it, and knows how much it costs, little additional information may be sought.

Finally, product knowledge influences how quickly a consumer goes through the decision-making process. For example, when purchasing a new product for which the consumer has little product knowledge, extensive information may be sought and more time may be devoted to the decision.

Product Involvement

Product involvement refers to a consumer's perception of the importance or personal relevance of an item. For example, Harley-Davidson motorcycle owners are generally highly involved in the purchase and use of the product, brand, and accessories. However, a consumer buying a new toothbrush would likely view this as a low-involvement purchase.

Product involvement influences consumer decision making in two ways. First, if the purchase is for a high-involvement product, consumers are likely to develop a high degree of product knowledge so that they can be confident that the item they purchase is just right for them. Second, a high degree of product involvement encourages extensive decision making by consumers, which likely increases the time it takes to go through the decision-making process.

CONSUMER DECISION MAKING

The process by which consumers make decisions to purchase various products and brands is shown in Figure 3.2. In general, consumers recognize a need for a product, search for information about alternatives to meet the need, evaluate the information, make purchases, and evaluate the decision after the purchase. There are three types of decision making, which vary in terms of how complex or expensive a product is and how involved a consumer is in purchasing it.

Extensive decision making requires the most time and effort since the purchase typically involves a highly complex or expensive product that is important to the consumer. For example, the purchase of a car, house, or computer often involves considerable time and effort comparing alternatives and deciding on the right one. In terms of the number of purchases a consumer makes, extensive decision making is relatively rare, but it is critical for marketers of highly complex or expensive products to understand that consumers are willing to process considerable information to make the best choice. Thus, marketers should provide consumers with factual information that highlights competitive advantages for such high-involvement products.

Limited decision making is more moderate but still involves some time and effort searching for and comparing alternatives. For example, when buying shirts or shorts, consumers may shop several stores and compare a number of different brands and styles.

FIGURE 3.2 The Consumer Decision-Making Process

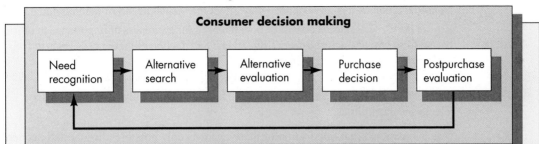

Marketers of products for which consumers usually do limited decision making often use eye-catching advertising and in-store displays to make consumers aware of their products and encourage consumers to consider buying them.

Routine decision making is the most common type and the way consumers purchase most packaged goods. Such products are simple, inexpensive, and familiar; and consumers often have developed favorite brands that they purchase without much deliberation. For example, consumers often make habitual purchases of soft drinks, candy bars, or canned soup without carefully comparing the relative merits of different brands. Marketers of such products need to have them readily available for purchase in a variety of outlets and price them competitively if price is an important criterion to consumers. Marketers of these low-involvement products often use celebrity spokespeople and other non-product-related cues to encourage purchases.

Need Recognition

The starting point in the buying process is the consumer's recognition of an unsatisfied need. Any number of either internal or external stimuli may activate needs or wants and recognition of them. Internal stimuli are such things as feeling hungry and wanting some food, feeling a headache coming on and wanting some Excedrin, or feeling bored and looking for a movie to go to. External stimuli are such things as seeing a McDonald's sign and then feeling hungry or seeing a sale sign for winter parkas and remembering that last year's coat is worn out.

It is the task of marketing managers to find out what needs and wants a particular product can and does satisfy and what unsatisfied needs and wants consumers have for which a new product could be developed. In order to do so, marketing managers should understand what types of needs consumers may have. A well-known classification of needs was developed many years ago by Abraham Maslow and includes five types.[7] Maslow's view is that lower-level needs, starting with physiological and safety needs, must be attended to before higher-level needs can be satisfied. Maslow's hierarchy is described below.

Physiological needs. This category consists of the primary needs of the human body, such as food, water, and sex. Physiological needs will dominate when all needs are unsatisfied. In such a case, none of the other needs will serve as a basis for motivation.

Safety needs. With the physiological needs met, the next higher level assumes importance. Safety needs consist of such things as protection from physical harm, ill health, and economic disaster and avoidance of the unexpected.

Belongingness and love needs. These needs are related to the social and gregarious nature of humans and the need for companionship. This level in the hierarchy is the point of departure from the physical or quasi-physical needs of the two previous levels. Nonsatisfaction of this level of need may affect the mental health of the individual.

Esteem needs. These needs consist of both the need for awareness of importance to others (self-esteem) and actual esteem from others. Satisfaction of these needs leads to feelings of self-confidence and prestige.

Self-actualization needs. These can be defined as the desire to become everything one is capable of becoming. This means that the individual will fully realize her or his talents and capabilities.

Maslow assumed that satisfaction of these needs is only possible after the satisfaction of all the needs lower in the hierarchy. While the hierarchical arrangement of Maslow presents a convenient explanation, it is probably more realistic to assume that the various need categories overlap. Thus, in affluent societies, many products may satisfy more than one of these needs. For example, gourmet foods may satisfy both the basic physiological need of hunger as well as esteem and status needs for those who serve gourmet foods to their guests.

Alternative Search

Once a need is recognized, the individual then searches for alternatives for satisfying the need. The individual can collect information from five basic sources for a particular purchase decision.

1. *Internal sources.* In most cases the individual has had some previous experience in dealing with a particular need. Thus, the individual will usually "search" through whatever stored information and experience is in his or her mind for dealing with the need. If a previously acceptable product for satisfying the need is remembered, the individual may purchase with little or no additional information search or evaluation. This is quite common for routine or habitual purchases.

2. *Group sources.* A common source of information for purchase decisions comes from communication with other people, such as family, friends, neighbors, and acquaintances. Generally, some of these (i.e., relevant others) are selected that the individual views as having particular expertise for the purchase decision. Although it may be quite difficult for the marketing manager to determine the exact nature of this source of information, group sources of information often are considered to be the most powerful influence on purchase decisions.

3. *Marketing sources.* Marketing sources of information include such factors as advertising, salespeople, dealers, packaging, and displays. Generally, this is the primary source of information about a particular product. These sources of information will be discussed in detail in the promotion chapters of this text.

4. *Public sources.* Public sources of information include publicity, such as a newspaper article about the product, and independent ratings of the product, such as *Consumer Reports.* Here, product quality is a highly important marketing management consideration, since such articles and reports often discuss such features as dependability and service requirements.

5. *Experiential sources.* Experiential sources refer to handling, examining, and perhaps trying the product while shopping. This usually requires an actual shopping trip by the individual and may be the final source consulted before purchase.

The consumer then processes information collected from these sources.[8] However, the exact nature of how individuals process information to form evaluations of products is not fully understood. In general, information processing is viewed as a four-step process in which the individual is (1) exposed to information, (2) becomes attentive to the information, (3) understands the information, and (4) retains the information.[9]

The marketing profession has long recognized the need to uphold its integrity, honor, and dignity. Below are the ethical norms established by the American Marketing Association to be used by marketers in dealing with consumers and other stakeholders.

As marketers we must:

1. **Do no harm.** This means consciously avoiding harmful actions or omissions by embodying high ethical standards and adhering to all applicable laws and regulations in the choices we make.
2. **Foster trust in the marketing system.** This means striving for good faith and fair dealing so as to contribute toward the efficacy of the exchange process as well as avoiding deception in product design, pricing, communication, and delivery of distribution.
3. **Embrace ethical values.** This means building relationships and enhancing consumer confidence in the integrity of marketing by affirming these core values: honesty, responsibility, fairness, respect, transparency, and citizenship.

Source: marketingpower.com, March 27, 2011.

Alternative Evaluation

During the process of collecting information or, in some cases, after information is acquired, the consumer evaluates alternatives on the basis of what he or she has learned. One approach to describing the evaluation process is as follows:

1. The consumer has information about a number of brands in a product class.
2. The consumer perceives that at least some of the brands in a product class are viable alternatives for satisfying a recognized need.
3. Each of these brands has a set of attributes (color, quality, size, and so forth).
4. A set of these attributes is relevant to the consumer, and the consumer perceives that different brands vary in how much of each attribute they possess.
5. The brand that is perceived as offering the greatest number of desired attributes in the desired amounts and desired order will be the brand the consumer will like best.
6. The brand the consumer likes best is the brand the consumer will intend to purchase.[10]

Purchase Decision

If no other factors intervene after the consumer has decided on the brand that is intended for purchase, the actual purchase is a common result of search and evaluation. Actually, a purchase involves many decisions, which include product type, brand, model, dealer selection, and method of payment, among other factors. In addition, rather than purchasing, the consumer may make a decision to modify, postpone, or avoid purchase based on an inhibitor to purchase or a perceived risk.

Traditional risk theorists believe that consumers tend to make risk-minimizing decisions based on their *perceived* definition of the particular purchase. The perception of risk is based on the possible consequences and uncertainties involved. Consequences may range from economic loss, to embarrassment if a new food product does not turn out well, to actual physical harm. Perceived risk may be either functional (related to financial and performance considerations) or psychosocial (related to whether the product will further one's self- or reference-group image). The amount of risk a consumer perceives in a particular product depends on such things as the price of the product and whether other people will see the individual using it.

The perceived risk literature emphasizes that consumers generally try to reduce risk in their decision making. This can be done by either reducing the possible negative consequences or by reducing the uncertainty. The possible consequences of a purchase might be minimized by purchasing in small quantities or by lowering the individual's aspiration level to expect less in the way of results from the product. However, this cannot always be done. Thus, reducing risk by attempting to increase the certainty of the purchase outcome may be the more widely used strategy. This can be done by seeking additional information regarding the proposed purchase. In general, the more information the consumer collects prior to purchase, the less likely post-purchase dissonance is to occur.

Postpurchase Evaluation

In general, if the individual finds that a certain response achieves a desired goal or satisfies a need, the success of this cue-response pattern will be remembered. The probability of responding in a like manner to the same or similar situation in the future is increased. In other words, the response has a higher probability of being repeated when the need and cue appear together again, and thus it can be said that learning has taken place. Frequent reinforcement increases the habit potential of the particular response. Likewise, if a response does not satisfy the need adequately, the probability that the same response will be repeated is reduced.

For some marketers this means that if an individual finds that a particular product fulfills the need for which it was purchased, the probability is high that the individual will repurchase the product the next time the need arises. The firm's promotional efforts often act as the cue. If an individual repeatedly purchases a product with favorable results, loyalty may develop toward the particular product or brand. This loyalty can result in habitual purchases, and such habits are often extremely difficult for competing firms to alter.

Although many studies in the area of buyer behavior center on the buyer's attitudes, motives, and behavior before and during the purchase decision, behavior after the purchase has also been studied. Specifically, studies have been undertaken to investigate postpurchase dissonance, as well as postpurchase satisfaction.

The occurrence of postdecision dissonance is related to the concept of *cognitive dissonance*. This theory states that there is often a lack of consistency or harmony among an individual's various cognitions, or attitudes and beliefs, after a decision has been made—that is, the individual has doubts and second thoughts about the choice made. Further, it is more likely that the intensity of the anxiety will be greater when any of the following conditions exist:

1. The decision is an important one psychologically or financially, or both.
2. There are a number of forgone alternatives.
3. The forgone alternatives have many favorable features.

These factors can relate to many buying decisions. For example, postpurchase dissonance might be expected to be present among many purchasers of such products as automobiles, major appliances, and homes. In these cases, the decision to purchase is usually an important one both financially and psychologically, and a number of favorable alternatives are usually available.

These findings have much relevance for marketers. In a buying situation, when a purchaser becomes dissonant, it is reasonable to predict such a person would be highly receptive to advertising and sales promotion that support the purchase decision. Such communication presents favorable aspects of the product and can be useful in reinforcing the buyer's wish to believe that a wise purchase decision was made. For example, purchasers of major appliances

Influencing Factor	Increasing the Influencing Factor Causes the Search to:
I. Market characteristics	
A. Number of alternatives	Increase
B. Price range	Increase
C. Store concentration	Increase
D. Information availability	Increase
1. Advertising	
2. Point-of-purchase	
3. Sales personnel	
4. Packaging	
5. Experienced consumers	
6. Independent sources	
II. Product characteristics	
A. Price	Increase
B. Differentiation	Increase
C. Positive products	Increase
III. Consumer characteristics	
A. Learning and experience	Decrease
B. Shopping orientation	Mixed
C. Social status	Increase
D. Age and household life cycle	Mixed
E. Product involvement	Mixed
F. Perceived risk	Increase
IV. Situational characteristics	
A. Time availability	Increase
B. Purchase for self	Decrease
C. Pleasant surroundings	Increase
D. Social surroundings	Mixed
E. Physical/mental energy	Increase

Source: Del I. Hawkins, David L. Mothersbaugh, and Roger Best, *Consumer Behavior: Building Marketing Strategy*, 11th ed. (Burr Ridge, IL: Irwin/McGraw-Hill, 2010), p. 534.

or automobiles might be given a phone call or sent a letter reassuring them that they have made a wise purchase.

As noted, researchers have also studied postpurchase consumer satisfaction. Much of this work has been based on what is called the *disconfirmation paradigm*. Basically, this approach views satisfaction with products and brands as a result of two other variables. The first variable is the expectations a consumer has about a product before purchase. These expectations concern the beliefs the consumer has about the product's performance.

The second variable is the difference between expectations and postpurchase perceptions of how the product actually performed. If the product performed as well as expected or better than expected, the consumer will be satisfied with the product. If the product performed worse than expected, the consumer will be dissatisfied with it.

One implication of this view for marketers is that care must be taken not to raise prepurchase expectations to such a level that the product cannot possibly meet them. Rather, it is important to create positive expectations consistent with the product's likely performance.[11]

SUMMARY

This chapter presented an overview of consumer behavior. Social, marketing, and situational influences on consumer decision making were discussed first, followed by a discussion of two important psychological factors: product knowledge and product involvement. Consumer decision making, which can be extensive, limited, or routine, was viewed as a series of stages: need recognition, alternative search, alternative evaluation, purchase decision, and postpurchase evaluation. Clearly, understanding consumer behavior is a prerequisite for developing successful marketing strategies.

Additional Resources

Hawkins, Del I., and David L. Mothersbaugh. *Consumer Behavior: Building Marketing Strategy.* 11th ed. Burr Ridge, IL: McGraw-Hill/Irwin, 2010.

Hoyer, Wayne D., and Deborah J. MacInnis. *Consumer Behavior.* 5th ed. Mason, OH: Southwestern, 2010.

Lindguist, Jay, and M. Joseph Sirgy. *Shopper, Buyer, and Consumer Behavior.* 4th ed. Mason, OH: Southwestern, 2009.

Peter, J. Paul, and Jerry C. Olson. *Consumer Behavior and Marketing Strategy.* 9th ed. Burr Ridge, IL: McGraw-Hill/Irwin, 2010.

Schiffman, Leon G., and Leslie Kanuck. *Consumer Behavior.* 10th ed. Upper Saddle River, NJ: Prentice Hall, 2010.

Solomon, Michael R. *Consumer Behavior.* 9th ed. Upper Saddle River, NJ: Prentice Hall, 2011.

Key Terms and Concepts

Belongingness and love needs: According to Maslow, the needs related to the social and gregarious nature of humans and the need for companionship.

Cognitive dissonance: A lack of harmony among a person's thoughts after a decision has been made—that is, the individual has doubts and second thoughts about the choice that was made.

Current conditions: Situational influences such as momentary moods and conditions that influence consumer behavior.

Disconfirmation paradigm: Approach that views consumer satisfaction as the degree to which the actual performance of a product is consistent with expectations a consumer had before purchase. If the product is as good as expected, then the consumer will be satisfied; if not, then the consumer's expectations are disconfirmed.

Esteem needs: According to Maslow, the needs that consist of both the need for awareness of importance to others (self-esteem) and actual esteem from others.

Experiential sources of information: The information a consumer gets from handling, examining, and perhaps trying a product while shopping.

Extensive decision making: Level of decision making that requires the most time and effort since the purchase typically involves a highly complex or expensive product that is important to the consumer.

Family life cycle: Framework that divides the development of a family into a number of stages based on the needs, assets, debts, and expenditures that change as a family begins, grows, and matures.

Group sources of information: A common source of information for purchase decisions that comes from communication with other people such as family, friends, neighbors, and acquaintances.

Internal sources of information: Stored information and experience a consumer has in memory for dealing with a particular need.

Limited decision making: Level of decision making that requires a moderate amount of time and effort to search for and compare alternatives.

Lower Americans: Comprise 16 percent of the population and have the lowest education levels and resources; the bottom of the social class hierarchy.

Marketing sources of information: Include such things as advertising, salespeople, dealers, packaging, and displays offered by marketers to influence consumer decision making and behavior.

Middle class: Middle social class; comprises 34 percent of the population and is concerned with doing the right thing and buying what is popular. This class tends to emulate Upper Americans.

Need recognition: The first step in the consumer decision making process; the recognition by the consumer of a felt need or want.

Physical features of a situation: The geographical and institutional decor, sounds, aromas, lighting, weather, and visible configurations of merchandise or other materials.

Physiological needs: According to Maslow, the primary needs of the human body such as food, water, and sex.

Product knowledge: The amount of information a consumer has stored in her or his memory about particular product classes, product forms, brands, and models, and ways to purchase them.

Public sources of information: Publicity, such as newspaper articles about the product, and independent ratings of the product, such as Consumer Reports.

Reference groups: Groups that an individual looks to (uses as a reference) when forming attitudes and opinions.

Routine decision making: The most common type of decision making, involves little in the way of thinking and deliberation. It is often habitual and is the way consumers commonly purchase packaged goods that are inexpensive, simple, and familiar.

Safety needs: According to Maslow, things such as protection from physical harm, ill health, and economic disaster and avoidance of the unexpected.

Self-actualization needs: According to Maslow, the desire to become everything one can become and fully realize talents and capabilities.

Situational influences: All of the factors particular to a time and place that have a demonstrable and systematic effect on current behavior.

Social features of a situation: Include other persons present in a situation, their characteristics, their apparent roles and interpersonal interactions.

Task features of a situation: Include the intent or requirement to select, shop for, or obtain information about a general or specific purchase.

Time dimension of a situation: The temporal dimension of a situation such as the time of day or season of the year. It can also be relative to other life events such as the time since the last purchase or time until payday.

Upper Americans: Social class that comprises 14 percent of the population and is differentiated mainly by having high incomes. This social class remains the group in which quality merchandise is most prized and prestige brands are commonly sought.

Working class: Social class that comprises 38 percent of the population; "family folk" who depend heavily on relatives for economic and emotional support.

4

Business, Government, and Institutional Buying

In the previous chapter we discussed consumer behavior and the decision-making process used to purchase products and services. However, final consumers are not the only purchasers of products and services. Rather, businesses, government agencies, and other institutions buy products and services to maintain their organizations and achieve their organizational objectives. These organizations are major customers for many marketers. In this chapter we discuss the nature of these organizations and offer a general model of the buying process for them. The chapter begins by discussing four categories of organizational buyers and then presents an overview of the organizational buying process.

CATEGORIES OF ORGANIZATIONAL BUYERS

Organizational buyers can be classified in many ways. For example, the U.S. government classifies organizations in similar lines of business in the North American Industry Classification System (*NAICS*, pronounced "knacks"). NAICS provides information about the number of establishments, sales volume, and number of employees in each industry broken down by geographic area. Information on NAICS codes is available online at www.naics.com. In addition, a commercial source, Dun's Business Locator, provides information on over 10 million U.S. businesses. Both of these can provide useful information for organizational marketers seeking organizational buyers. However, for the purpose of this text, it is useful to classify organizational buyers into four categories: These include producers, intermediaries, government agencies, and other institutions. Taken collectively, marketing to these organizations is called *business-to-business* or *B2B marketing*. Business-to-business marketing has become a topic of increasing interest because it is the major area where Internet marketing has been done profitably.

Producers

These organizational buyers consist of businesses that buy goods and services in order to produce other goods and services for sale. For example, Dell Inc. buys computer chips from Intel in order to make computers to be sold to consumers and other organizations. Producers are engaged in many different industries, ranging from agriculture to manufacturing, from construction to finance. Together they constitute the largest segment of organizational buyers. Producers of goods tend to be larger and more geographically concentrated than producers of services.

Intermediaries

Marketing intermediaries or resellers purchase products to resell at a profit. This group includes a number of types of resellers such as wholesalers (Grainger) and retailers (Walmart) that buy products from manufacturers and distribute them to consumers and other organizational buyers. Intermediaries also purchase products and services to run their own businesses, such as office supplies and maintenance services. Given their importance to marketing, intermediaries will be discussed in detail in Chapter 10.

Government Agencies

In the United States, government agencies operate at the federal, state, and local levels; there are over 86,000 governmental agencies in this country that purchase machinery, equipment, facilities, supplies, and services. Government agencies account for trillions of dollars worth of buying, and over half of this amount represents purchases by the federal government, making it the world's biggest customer. The governments of other countries also are huge customers for marketers. Marketing to government agencies can be complex since they often have strict purchasing policies and regulations.

Other Institutions

Besides businesses and government agencies, marketers also sell products and services to a variety of other institutions, such as hospitals, museums, universities, nursing homes, and churches. Many of these are nonprofit organizations that purchase products and services to maintain their operations and serve their clientele.

THE ORGANIZATIONAL BUYING PROCESS

Regardless of the type of organization, a buying process is needed to ensure that products and services are purchased and received in a timely and efficient manner. In general, organizations develop a buying process to serve their purchasing needs. Figure 4.1 presents a model of organizational buying that represents some of the common influences and stages in the process.

FIGURE 4.1 A Model of the Organizational Buying Process

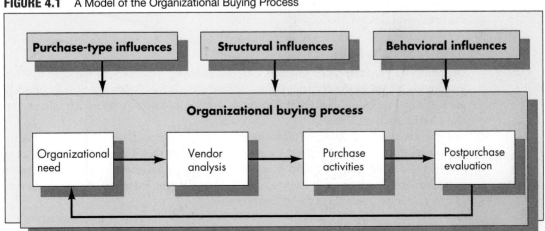

PURCHASE-TYPE INFLUENCES ON ORGANIZATIONAL BUYING

A major consideration that affects the organizational buying process is the complexity of the purchase that is to be made. Three types of organizational purchase based on their degree of complexity include the straight rebuy, modified rebuy, and new task purchase.[1]

Straight Rebuy

The simplest and most common type of purchase is called a *straight rebuy*. This type of purchase involves routinely reordering a product from the same supplier that it had been purchased from in the past. Organizations use a straight rebuy when they are experienced at buying the product, have an ongoing need for it, and have regular suppliers of it. In many cases, organizations have computer systems that automatically reorder certain commonly used products. Organizations use this simple approach to purchasing because it is fast and requires relatively few employees.

Straight rebuys are common among organizations that practice *just-in-time inventory*, which is a system of replenishing parts or goods for resale just before they are needed. Such buyers do not have time to hunt around for potential suppliers and solicit bids. Instead they regularly place their orders with a supplier whose quality and timely delivery can be counted on. If a supplier delivers items that are late or of unacceptable quality, these buyers will not have a reserve in inventory to draw on. Therefore, organizations that use just-in-time inventory tend to favor suppliers with a strong commitment to quality.

To retain customers who use straight rebuys, the marketer needs to maintain high-quality products and reliable service so that the customers will continue to be satisfied with their purchases.

Modified Rebuy

When some aspects of the buying situation are unfamiliar, the organization will use a *modified rebuy*. This type of purchase involves considering a limited number of alternatives before making a selection. Organizational buyers follow this approach rather than a straight rebuy when a routine purchase changes in some way; for example, a supplier discontinues a product or stops satisfying the customer, the price of a usual product rises, or a new product becomes available to meet the same need.

In such situations, the organizational buyer considers the new information and decides what changes to make. If the change proves satisfactory and the product is one needed routinely, the buyer may then make it a straight rebuy. Marketers seek to win new organizational customers by giving them reasons to change from a straight rebuy to a modified rebuy in which the marketer's products are considered.

New Task Purchase

Organizations purchase some products only occasionally, especially in the case of large investments such as machinery, equipment, and real estate. In these cases, the organization may use a *new task purchase*. This type of purchase involves an extensive search for information and a formal decision process.

New task purchases are most often used for big-ticket items, so the cost of a mistake is great. Therefore, a new task purchase is time consuming and involves a relatively large number of decision makers, who may consider many alternatives. This is the type of purchase decision that is most likely to involve joint decision making because many kinds of expertise are required to make the best decision.

A new task purchase is an opportunity for the marketer to learn about the needs of the organizations in its target market and to discuss ways to meet organizational needs, such as

FIGURE 4.2 Marketing Tactics for Reaching Organizational Buyers

Type of Purchase	Marketing Element	Promotional Approach
Straight rebuy	Advertising	Use reminder advertising. Build image for company.
	Promotion	Hospitality events at trade shows.
	Selling	Any personal selling is designed to build relationships. Automate the purchasing process, perhaps through EDI (electronic data exchange).
Modified rebuy	Advertising	Use comparison advertising to show differences between your product and similar products.
	Promotion	Customer site demonstrations, hospitality events at trade shows.
	Selling	Protect relationship with current customers with plant tours, special trade-in pricing, and other offers. Anticipate or respond quickly to changes in customer needs.
New task purchase	Advertising	Detailed, educational ads to try to get users to try product, substitute for old method.
	Promotion	Use demonstrations at trade shows to show how it works. Offer free trials or demonstrations at the customer's site.
	Selling	Heavy emphasis on understanding customers' needs and showing how new product satisfies needs better than old methods.

Source: Based on F. Robert Dwyer and John F. Tanner, Jr., *Business Marketing,* 4th ed. (Burr Ridge, IL: McGraw-Hill/Irwin, 2009), p. 73.

through the use of new products and technology. Figure 4.2 offers some suggestions for reaching organizational buyers for the three types of purchases.

STRUCTURAL INFLUENCES ON ORGANIZATIONAL BUYING

The term *structural influences* refers to the design of the organizational environment and how it affects the purchasing process. Three important structural influences on organizational buying are purchasing roles, organization-specific factors, and purchasing policies and procedures.

Purchasing Roles

It is common in organizational buying for purchases to be made cross-functionally with representatives from different functional departments playing various roles in the process. Taken collectively, these are called the *buying center* and include the following roles:

1. *Initiators,* who start the purchasing process by recognizing a need or problem in the organization. For example, an executive might see a need for faster computers.
2. *Users,* who are the people in the organization who actually use the product, for example, an assistant who would use a new word processor.

How Marketing to Organizational Buyers Differs	Example
Varying buyer-seller relationships	Relationships can be deep and involve several layers of the industry, BASF partners with Gaskell and GM, for example.
Shorter distribution channels	BASF sells fibers *direct* to DuPont for the manufacture of carpet and through distributors to smaller companies.
Greater emphasis on personal selling	BASF salespeople work directly with fire departments to sell the latest fire-fighting chemicals and ensure that they are used properly.
Greater Web integration	BASF uses its *cc-markets* Web site to create a communication space with special customers.
Unique promotional strategies	BASF exhibits at trade shows like Powder Coatings Europe, a show held every January in Amsterdam.
Consumption	Consumption of business products is by organizations who are then dependent on other markets, so how much carpet protectant BASF can sell to DuPont depends on how much carpet DuPont can sell.
Knowledge of customer's customer	BASF has to understand both consumers (of carpet, for example) and manufacturers like DuPont, not just consumers.
Marketing research	In smaller direct markets (such as carpet manufacturers), marketing research techniques tend toward qualitative.

Source: F. Robert Dwyer and John F. Tanner, *Business Marketing,* 4th ed. (Burr Ridge, IL: McGraw-Hill/Irwin, 2009), p. 9.

3. *Influencers,* who affect the buying decision, usually by helping define the specifications for what is needed. For example, an information systems manager would be a key influencer in the purchase of a new computer system.

4. *Buyers,* who have the formal authority and responsibility to select the supplier and negotiate the terms of the contract. For example, in the purchase of ink cartridges, the *purchasing agent* would likely perform this role.

5. *Deciders,* who have the formal or informal power to select or approve the supplier that receives the contract. For important technical purchases, deciders may come from R&D, engineering, or quality control.

6. *Gatekeepers,* who control the flow of information in the buying center. Purchasing personnel, technical experts, and assistants can all keep marketers and their information from reaching people performing the other four roles.[2]

When several persons are involved in the organizational purchase decision, marketers may need to use a variety of means to reach each individual or group. Fortunately, it is often easy to find which individuals in organizations are involved in a purchase because such information is provided to suppliers. Organizations do this because it makes suppliers more knowledgeable about purchasing practices, thus making the purchasing process more efficient.[3] Also, a number of firms have developed closer channel relationships that facilitate these transactions.

Organization-Specific Factors

Three primary organization-specific factors influence the purchasing process: orientation, size, and degree of centralization. First, in terms of orientation, the dominant function in an organization may control purchasing decisions. For example, if the organization is technology oriented, it is likely to be dominated by engineering personnel, who will make buying decisions. Similarly, if the organization is production oriented, production personnel may dominate buying decisions.

Second, the size of the organization may influence the purchasing process. If the organization is large, it will likely have a high degree of joint decision making for other than straight rebuys. Smaller organizations are likely to have more autonomous decision making.

Finally, the degree of centralization of an organization influences whether decisions are made individually or jointly with others. Organizations that are highly centralized are less likely to have joint decision making. Thus, a privately owned, small company with technology or production orientations will tend toward autonomous decision making, while a large-scale public corporation with considerable decentralization will tend to have greater joint decision making.

Purchasing Policies and Procedures

Organizations typically develop a number of policies and procedures for various types of purchases. These policies and procedures are designed to ensure that the appropriate products and services are purchased efficiently and that responsibility for buying is assigned appropriately. Often a purchasing department will be assigned the task of centralized buying for the whole organization, and individuals within this department will have authority to purchase particular types of products and services in a given price range.

A current trend in many organizations is *sole sourcing,* in which all of a particular type of product is purchased from a single supplier. Sole sourcing has become more popular because organizational buyers have become more concerned with quality and timely delivery and less likely to purchase only on the basis of price. Sole sourcing is advantageous for suppliers because it provides them with predictable and profitable demand and allows them to build long-term relationships with organizational buyers. It is advantageous for organizational buyers because it not only increases timely delivery and quality of supplies but also allows the buyers to work more closely with suppliers to develop superior products that meet their needs and those of their customers. The use of sole sourcing also simplifies the buying process and can make what were formerly modified rebuys into simpler straight rebuys.

Of course, many organizational purchases are more complicated and require policies and procedures to direct the buying process. In many cases, organizations will develop a list of approved vendors from which buyers have authorization to purchase particular products. The buyer's responsibility is to select the vendor that will provide the appropriate levels of quality and service at the lowest cost. These policies and procedures also specify what positions in the purchasing department or buying center have authority to make purchases of different types and dollar amounts.

For large one-time projects, such as the construction of a building, organizations may seek competitive bids for part or all of the project. The development of policies and procedures for handling such purchases is usually complex and involves a number of criteria and committees.

BEHAVIORAL INFLUENCES ON ORGANIZATIONAL BUYING

Organizational buyers are influenced by a variety of psychological and social factors. We will discuss two of these, personal motivations and role perceptions.

Personal Motivations

Organizational buyers are, of course, subject to the same personal motives or motivational forces as other individuals. Although these buyers may emphasize nonpersonal motives in their buying activities, it has been found that organizational buyers often are influenced by such personal factors as friendship, professional pride, fear and uncertainty (risk), trust, and personal ambitions in their buying activities.

1. Is the need or problem pressing enough that it must be acted on now? If not, how long can action be deferred?
2. What types of products or services could conceivably be used to solve our need or problem?
3. Should we make the item ourselves?
4. Must a new product be designed, or has a vendor already developed an acceptable product?
5. Should a value analysis be performed?
6. What is the highest price we can afford to pay?
7. What trade-offs are we prepared to make between price and other product/vendor attributes?
8. Which information sources will we rely on?
9. How many vendors should be considered?
10. Which attributes will be stressed in evaluating vendors?
11. Should bids be solicited?
12. Should the item be leased or purchased outright?
13. How far can a given vendor be pushed in negotiations? On what issues will that vendor bend the most?
14. How much inventory should a vendor be willing to keep on hand?
15. Should we split our order among several vendors?
16. Is a long-term contract in our interest?
17. What contractual guarantees will we require?
18. How shall we establish our order routine?
19. After the purchase, how will vendor performance be evaluated?
20. How will we deal with inadequate product or vendor performance?

Source: Michael H. Morris, Leyland F. Pitt, and Earl D. Honeycutt, Jr., *Business-to-Business Marketing,* 3rd ed. (Thousand Oaks, CA: Sage Publications, 2001), p. 74.

For example, professional pride often expresses itself through efforts to attain status in the firm. One way to achieve this might be to initiate or influence the purchase of goods that will demonstrate a buyer's value to the organization. If new materials, equipment, or components result in cost savings or increased profits, the individuals initiating the changes have demonstrated their value at the same time. Fear and uncertainty are strong motivational forces on organizational buyers, and reduction of risk is often important to them. This can have a strong influence on purchase behavior. Marketers should understand the relative strength of personal gain versus risk-reducing motives and emphasize the more important motives when dealing with buyers.

Thus, in examining buyer motivations, it is necessary to consider both personal and nonpersonal motivational forces and to recognize that the relative importance of each is not a fixed quantity. It will vary with the nature of the product, the climate within the organization, and the relative strength of the two forces in the particular buyer.

Role Perceptions

A final factor that influences organizational buyers is their own perception of their role. The manner in which individuals behave depends on their perception of their role, their commitment to what they believe is expected of their role, the "maturity" of the role type, and the extent to which the institution is committed to the role type.

1. Avoid the intent and appearance of unethical or compromising practice in relationships, actions, and communications.

2. Demonstrate loyalty to the employer by diligently following the lawful instructions of the employer, using reasonable care and only the authority granted.

3. Refrain from any private or professional business activity that would create a conflict between personal interests and the interests of the employer.

4. Refrain from soliciting or accepting money, loans, credits, or prejudicial discounts and the acceptance of gifts, entertainment, favors, or services from past or potential suppliers that might influence or appear to influence purchasing decisions.

5. Handle confidential or proprietary information belonging to employers or suppliers with due care and proper consideration of ethical and legal ramifications and government regulations.

6. Promote positive supplier relationships through courtesy and impartiality throughout all phases of the purchasing cycle.

7. Refrain from reciprocal agreements that restrain competition.

8. Know and obey the letter and spirit of laws governing the purchasing function and remain alert to the legal ramifications of purchasing decisions.

9. Encourage all segments of society to participate by demonstrating support for small, disadvantaged, and minority-owned businesses.

10. Discourage purchasing's involvement in employer-sponsored programs of personal purchases that are not business related.

11. Enhance the proficiency and stature of the purchasing profession by acquiring and maintaining current technical knowledge and the highest standards of ethical behavior.

12. Conduct international purchasing in accordance with the laws, customs, and practices of foreign countries, consistent with U.S. laws, your organization's policies, and these Ethical Standards and Guidelines.

Source: Institute for Supply Management as reported in F. Robert Dwyer and John F. Tanner, *Business Marketing*, 4th ed. (Burr Ridge, IL: McGraw-Hill/Irwin, 2009), p. 86.

Different buyers will have different degrees of commitment to their buying role, which will cause variations in role behavior from one buyer to the next. By *commitment* we mean willingness to perform their job in the manner expected by the organization. For example, some buyers seek to take charge in their role as buyer and have little commitment to company expectations. The implication for marketers is that such buyers expect, even demand, that they be kept constantly advised of all new developments to enable them to more effectively shape their own role. On the other hand, other buyers may have no interest in prescribing their role activities and accept their role as given to them. Such a buyer is most concerned with merely implementing prescribed company activities and buying policies with sanctioned products. Thus, some buyers will be highly committed to play the role the firm dictates (i.e., the formal organization's perception of their role), while others might be extremely innovative and uncommitted to the expected role performance. Obviously, roles may be heavily influenced by the organizational climate existing in the particular organization.[4]

Organizations can be divided into three groups based on differences in degree of employee commitment. These groups include innovative, adaptive, and lethargic firms. In an innovative firm, individuals approach their occupational roles with a weak commitment to expected norms of behavior. In an adaptive organization, there is a moderate commitment. In a lethargic organization, individuals express a strong commitment to traditionally accepted behavior and behave accordingly. Thus, a buyer in a lethargic firm would probably be less innovative in order to maintain acceptance and status within the organization and would keep conflict within the firm to a minimum.

Buyers' perception of their role may differ from the perception of their role held by others in the organization. This difference can result in variance in perception of the actual purchase responsibility held by the buyer. One study involving purchasing agents revealed that, in every firm included in the study, the purchasing agents believed they had more responsibility and control over certain decisions than the other influential purchase decision makers in the firm perceived them as having. The decisions were (1) designing the product, (2) setting a cost for the product, (3) determining performance life, (4) naming a specific supplier, (5) assessing the amount of engineering help available from the supplier, and (6) reducing rejects. This variance in role perception held true regardless of the size of the firm or the significance of the item purchased to the overall success of the firm. It is important, therefore, that the marketer be aware that such perceptual differences may exist and to determine as accurately as possible the amount of control and responsibility over purchasing decisions held by each purchase decision influencer in the firm.

STAGES IN THE ORGANIZATIONAL BUYING PROCESS

As with consumer buying, most organizational purchases are made in response to a particular need or problem. Ideally, the products or services purchased will meet the organizational need and improve the organization's efficiency, effectiveness, and profits. The organizational buying process can be analyzed as a series of four stages: organizational need, vendor analysis, purchase activities, and postpurchase evaluation.

Organizational Need

Organizations have many needs for products and services to help them survive and meet their objectives. For example, a manufacturer may need to purchase new machinery to increase its production capacity and meet demand; a retailer may need to purchase services from a marketing research firm to better understand its market; a government agency may need to purchase faster computers to keep up with growing demand for its services; a hospital may need to purchase more comfortable beds for its patients. Recognizing these needs, and a willingness and ability to meet them, often results in organizational purchases. For straight rebuys, the purchase process may involve little more than a phone call or a few clicks on a computer to order products and arrange payment and delivery. For modified rebuys or new task purchases, the process may be much more complex.

Vendor Analysis

Organizational buyers must search for, locate, and evaluate vendors of products and services to meet their needs. Searching for and locating vendors is often easy since they frequently make sales calls on organizations that might need their products. Vendors also advertise in trade magazines or on the Internet and have displays at industry trade shows to increase their visibility to organizational buyers. For products and services that the organization has previously purchased, the organization may already have developed a list of approved vendors.

Organizational buyers often use a vendor analysis to evaluate possible suppliers. A *vendor analysis* is the process by which organizational buyers rate each potential supplier on various performance measures such as product quality, on-time delivery, price, payment terms, and use of modern technology. Figure 4.3 presents a sample vendor analysis form that lists a number of purchase criteria and the weights one organization used to compare potential suppliers.

A formal vendor analysis can be used for at least three purposes. First, it can be used to develop a list of approved vendors, all of which provide acceptable levels of products and services. Organizational buyers can then select any company on the list, simplifying the

FIGURE 4.3   Sample Vendor Analysis Form

	5 Excellent	4 Good	3 Satisfactory	2 Fair	1 Poor	0 N/A
Supplier Name: _____			Type of Product: _____			
Shipping Location: _____			Annual Sales Dollars: _____			
Quality (45%)						
Defect rates	___	___	___	___	___	___
Quality of sample	___	___	___	___	___	___
Conformance with quality program	___	___	___	___	___	___
Responsiveness to quality problems	___	___	___	___	___	___
Overall quality	___	___	___	___	___	___
Delivery (25%)						
Avoidance of late shipments	___	___	___	___	___	___
Ability to expand production	___	___	___	___	___	___
Performance in sample delivery	___	___	___	___	___	___
Response to changes in order size	___	___	___	___	___	___
Overall delivery	___	___	___	___	___	___
Price (20%)						
Price competitiveness	___	___	___	___	___	___
Payment terms	___	___	___	___	___	___
Absorption of costs	___	___	___	___	___	___
Submission of cost savings plans	___	___	___	___	___	___
Overall price	___	___	___	___	___	___
Technology (10%)						
State-of-the-art components	___	___	___	___	___	___
Sharing research & development capability	___	___	___	___	___	___
Ability and willingness to help with design	___	___	___	___	___	___
Responsiveness to engineering problems	___	___	___	___	___	___
Overall technology	___	___	___	___	___	___

Buyer: _____   Date: _____

Comments: _____

purchase process. Second, a vendor analysis could be used to compare competing vendors; the buyers then select the best one on the basis of the ratings. This could help the organization pare down vendors to a single supplier for which a long-term, sole-sourcing relationship could be developed. Third, a vendor analysis can be done both before and after purchases to compare performance on evaluation criteria and evaluate the process of vendor selection.

Purchase Activities

Straight rebuys may involve a quick order to an approved vendor or sole-source supplier. However, other types of organizational purchases can involve long time periods with extensive negotiations on price and terms and formal contracts stating quality, delivery, and service criteria. The complexity of the product or service, the number of suppliers available,

FIGURE 4.4

Functional Areas and
Their Key Concerns in
Organizational Buying

Source: Michael H. Morris,
Leyland F. Pitt, and Earl D.
Honeycutt, Jr., *Business-
to-Business Marketing*, 3rd
ed. (Thousand Oaks, CA:
Sage Publications, 2001),
p. 66.

Functional Areas	Key Concerns
Design and development engineering	Name reputation of vendor; ability of vendors to meet design specifications.
Production	Delivery and reliability of purchases such that interruption of production schedules is minimized.
Sales/marketing	Impact of purchased items on marketability of the company's products.
Maintenance	Degree to which purchased items are compatible with existing facilities and equipment; maintenance service offered by vendor; installation arrangements offered by vendor.
Finance/accounting	Effects of purchases on cash flow, balance sheet, and income statement positions; variances in costs of materials over estimates; feasibility of make-or-buy and lease options to purchasing.
Purchasing	Obtaining lowest possible price at acceptable quality levels; maintaining good relations with vendors.
Quality control	Assurance that purchased items meet prescribed specifications and tolerances, governmental regulations, and customer requirements.

the importance of the product to the buying organization, and pricing all influence the number of purchase activities to be performed and their difficulty. For example, an airline buying a fleet of jumbo jets or a car rental agency buying a fleet of cars may take months or years to negotiate and make purchases. While such buyers may have considerable leverage in negotiating, it should be remembered that these organizations need the products just as badly as the sellers need to sell them. Thus, there is often more collaboration among organizational buyers and sellers than in the consumer market.

Postpurchase Evaluation

Organizational buyers must evaluate both the vendors and the products they purchase to determine whether the products are acceptable for future purchases or whether other sources of supply should be found. A comparison of the performance of the vendor and products with the criteria listed on the prior vendor analysis can be useful for this purpose. If the purchase process goes smoothly and products meet price and quality criteria, then the vendor may be put on the approved list or perhaps further negotiations can be made to sole-source with the supplier.

One problem in judging the acceptability of suppliers and products is that different functional areas may have different evaluation criteria. Figure 4.4 presents several functional areas of a manufacturing company and their common concerns in purchasing. Clearly, these concerns should be considered both prior to purchasing from a particular supplier and after purchasing to ensure that every area's needs are being met as well as possible.

SUMMARY

Organizational buyers include individuals involved in purchasing products and services for businesses, government agencies, and other institutions and agencies. The organizational buying process is influenced by whether the purchase is a straight rebuy, modified rebuy, or new task purchase. It is also influenced by people in various purchasing roles, the orientation, size, and degree of centralization of the organization, the organization's purchasing policies and procedures, and individuals' motivations and perceived roles. The organizational buying process can be viewed as a series of four stages ranging from organizational need, to vendor analysis, to purchase activities, to postpurchase evaluation. It is important that companies marketing to organizations understand the influences and process by which organizations buy products and services so their needs can be met fully and profitably.

<table>
<tr><td>

Additional Resources

</td><td>

Anderson, James C., James A. Narus, and Das Narayandas. *Business Marketing Management.* 3rd ed. Upper Saddle River, NJ: Prentice Hall, 2009.

Brennan, Ross, Louise E. Canning, and Raymond McDowell. *Business-to-Business Marketing.* Thousand Oaks, CA: Sage, 2007.

Dwyer, F. Robert, and John F. Tanner. *Business Marketing.* 4th ed. Burr Ridge, IL: McGraw-Hill/Irwin, 2009.

Hutt, Michael D., and Thomas W. Speh. *Business Marketing Management: B2B.* 10th ed. Mason, OH: Thomson South-Western, 2010.

Vitale, Robert, Waldemar Pfoertsch, and Joseph Giglierano. *Business to Business Marketing.* Upper Saddle River, NJ: Prentice Hall, 2011.

</td></tr>
</table>

Key Terms and Concepts

Business-to-business (B2B) marketing: Marketing products and services to producers, intermediaries, government agencies, and other institutions rather than to consumers.

Buyers: In buying centers, the persons who have formal authority and responsibility to select the supplier and negotiate the terms of the contract.

Buying center: An organizational group formed from different departments which has the responsibility to evaluate and select products for purchase. Different members of the group may play different roles in the process.

Deciders: In a buying center, individuals who have the formal and informal power to select or approve the supplier that receives the contract. For routinely purchased products, the decider is likely to be the buyer but for more complex products, the decider could come from R&D, engineering, or quality control.

Gatekeepers: The people who control the flow of information to a buying center.

Influencers: In buying centers, the people who affect the buying decision usually by helping define the specifications for what is needed.

Initiators: In buying centers, the people who start the buying process by recognizing a need or a problem in the organization.

Modified rebuy: A type of organizational purchase that involves the consideration of a limited number of alternatives before making a selection.

NAICS: The North American Industry Classification System which provides information about the number of establishments, sales volume, and number of employees in each industry broken down by geographic area.

New task purchase: A type of organizational purchase that involves an extensive search for information and a formal decision process.

Sole sourcing: Organizational purchasing in which all of a type of product are obtained from a single supplier.

Straight rebuy: A type of organizational purchase that involves routinely reordering a product from the same supplier that it had been purchased from in the past.

Users: In a buying center, the people in the organization that actually use the product to be purchased.

Vendor analysis: The process by which organizational buyers rate each potential supplier on various performance measures such as product quality, on-time delivery, price, payment terms, and use of modern technology.

Chapter 5

Market Segmentation

Market segmentation is one of the most important concepts in marketing. In fact, a primary reason for studying consumer and organizational buyer behavior is to provide bases for effective segmentation, and a large portion of marketing research is concerned with segmentation. From a marketing management point of view, selection of the appropriate target market is paramount to developing successful marketing programs.

The logic of market segmentation is quite simple and is based on the idea that a single product item can seldom meet the needs and wants of *all* consumers. Typically, consumers vary as to their needs, wants, and preferences for products and services, and successful marketers adapt their marketing programs to fulfill these preference patterns. For example, even a simple product like chewing gum has multiple flavors, package sizes, sugar contents, calories, consistencies (e.g., liquid centers), and colors to meet the preferences of various consumers. While a single product item cannot meet the needs of all consumers, it can almost always serve more than one consumer. Thus, there are usually *groups of consumers* who can be served well by a single item. If a particular group can be served *profitably* by a firm, it is a viable market segment. In other words, the firm should develop a marketing mix to serve the group or market segment.

In this chapter we consider the process of market segmentation. We define *market segmentation* as the process of dividing a market into groups of similar consumers and selecting the most appropriate group(s) for the firm to serve. The group or segment that a company selects to market to is called a *target market*. We break down the process of market segmentation into six steps, as shown in Figure 5.1. While we recognize that the order of these steps may vary, depending on the firm and situation, there are few if any times when market segmentation analysis can be ignored. In fact, even if the final decision is to "mass market" and not segment at all, this decision should be reached only *after* a market segmentation analysis has been conducted. Thus, market segmentation analysis is a cornerstone of sound marketing planning and decision making.

DELINEATE THE FIRM'S CURRENT SITUATION

As emphasized in Chapter 1, a firm must do a complete situational analysis when embarking on a new or modified marketing program. At the marketing planning level, such an analysis aids in determining objectives, opportunities, and constraints to be considered when selecting target markets and developing marketing mixes. In addition, marketing managers must have a clear idea of the amount of financial and other resources that will be available for developing and executing a marketing plan. Thus, the inclusion of this first step in the market segmentation process is intended to be a reminder of tasks to be performed prior to marketing planning.

FIGURE 5.1
A Model of the
Market Segmentation
Process

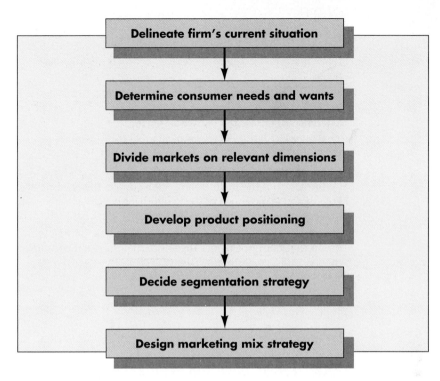

DETERMINE CONSUMER NEEDS AND WANTS

As emphasized throughout this text, successful marketing strategies depend on discovering and satisfying consumer needs and wants. In some cases, this idea is quite operational. To illustrate, suppose a firm has a good deal of venture capital and is seeking to diversify its interest into new markets. A firm in this situation may seek to discover a broad variety of unsatisfied needs. However, in most situations, the industry in which the firm operates specifies the boundaries of a firm's need satisfaction activities. For example, a firm in the communication industry may seek more efficient methods for serving consumers' long-distance telephone needs.

As a practical matter, new technology often brings about an investigation of consumer needs and wants for new or modified products and services. In these situations, the firm is seeking the group of consumers whose needs could best be satisfied by the new or modified product. Further, at a strategic level, consumer needs and wants usually are translated into more operational concepts. For instance, consumer attitudes, preferences, and benefits sought, which are determined through marketing research, are commonly used for segmentation purposes.

DIVIDE MARKETS ON RELEVANT DIMENSIONS

In a narrow sense, this step is often considered to be the whole of market segmentation (i.e., consumers are grouped on the basis of one or more similarities and treated as a homogeneous segment of a heterogeneous total market). Three important questions should be considered here:

1. Should the segmentation be a priori or post hoc?
2. How does one determine the relevant dimensions or bases to use for segmentation?
3. What are some bases for segmenting consumer and organizational buyer markets?

1. Slower rates of market growth, coupled with increased foreign competition, have fostered more competition, increasing the need to identify target markets with unique needs.

2. Social and economic forces, including expanding media, increased educational levels, and general world awareness, have produced customers with more varied and sophisticated needs, tastes, and lifestyles.

3. Technological advances make it possible for marketers to devise marketing programs that focus efficiently on precisely defined segments of the market.

4. Marketers now find that minority buyers do not necessarily adopt the social and economic habits of the mainstream. For example, many Hispanics speak both Spanish and English and retain much of their culture even as they adapt to U.S. lifestyles, while many others remain in Spanish-speaking enclaves in Hispanic states like Texas and California.

5. Roughly 4 in 10 residents in the United States identify with some segment or niche group that does not reflect the white, heterosexual consumer that historically defined the marketing mainstream.

Source: William O. Bearden, Thomas N. Ingram, and Raymond W. LaForge, *Marketing* (Burr Ridge, IL: McGraw-Hill/Irwin, 2007), p. 155.

A Priori versus Post Hoc Segmentation

Real-world segmentation has followed one of two general patterns. An *a priori segmentation* approach is one in which the marketing manager has decided on the appropriate basis for segmentation in advance of doing any research on a market. For example, a manager may decide that a market should be divided on the basis of whether people are nonusers, light users, or heavy users of a particular product. Segmentation research is then conducted to determine the size of each of these groups and their demographic or psychographic profiles.

Post hoc segmentation is an approach in which people are grouped into segments on the basis of research findings. For example, people interviewed concerning their attitudes or benefits sought in a particular product category are grouped according to their responses. The size of each of these groups and their demographic and psychographic profiles are then determined.

Both of these approaches are valuable, and the question of which to use depends in part on how well the firm knows the market for a particular product class. If through previous research and experience a marketing manager has successfully isolated a number of key market dimensions, then an a priori approach based on them may provide more useful information. In the case of segmentation for entirely new products, a post hoc approach may be useful for determining key market dimensions. However, even when using a post hoc approach, some consideration must be given to the variables to be included in the research design. Thus, some consideration must be given to the relevant segmentation dimensions regardless of which approach is used.

Relevance of Segmentation Dimensions

Unfortunately, there is no simple solution for determining the relevant dimensions for segmenting markets. Certainly, managerial expertise and experience are needed for selecting the appropriate dimensions or bases on which to segment particular markets. In most cases, however, at least some initial dimensions can be determined from previous research, purchase trends, and managerial judgment. For instance, suppose we wish to segment the market for all-terrain vehicles. Clearly, several dimensions come to mind for initial consideration, including sex (male), age (18 to 35 years), lifestyle (outdoorsman), and income level (perhaps $30,000 to $80,000). At a minimum, these variables should be included in subsequent segmentation research. Of course, the most market-oriented approach to segmentation is on the basis of what benefits the potential consumer is seeking. Thus, consideration and research of sought benefits are a strongly recommended approach in the marketing literature. This approach will be considered in some detail in the following section.

Bases for Segmentation

A number of useful bases for segmenting consumer and organizational markets are presented in Figure 5.2. This is by no means a complete list of possible segmentation variables but represents some useful bases and categories. Two commonly used approaches for segmenting markets include benefit segmentation and psychographic segmentation. We will discuss these two in some detail. We will also discuss geodemographic segmentation, a recent development with a number of advantages for marketers.

Benefit Segmentation

The belief underlying this segmentation approach is that the benefits people are seeking in consuming a given product are the basic reasons for the existence of true market segments.[1] Thus, this approach attempts to measure consumer value systems and consumer perceptions of various brands in a product class. To illustrate, Russell Haley provided the classic example of a benefit segmentation in terms of the toothpaste market. Haley identified five basic segments, which are presented in Figure 5.3. Haley argued that this segmentation could be very useful for selecting advertising copy, media, commercial length, packaging, and new product design. For example, colorful packages might be appropriate for the sensory segment, perhaps aqua (to indicate fluoride) for the worrier group, and gleaming white for the social segment because of this segment's interest in white teeth.

Calantone and Sawyer also used a benefit segmentation approach to segment the market for bank services.[2] Their research was concerned with the question of whether benefit segments remain stable across time. While they found some stability in segments, there were some differences in attribute importance, size, and demographics at different times. Thus, they argue for ongoing benefit segmentation research to keep track of any changes in a market that might affect marketing strategy.

Benefit segmentation is clearly a market-oriented approach that seeks to identify consumer needs and wants and to satisfy them by providing products and services with the desired benefits. It is clearly very consistent with the approach to marketing suggested by the marketing concept.

Psychographic Segmentation

Whereas benefit segmentation focuses on the benefits sought by the consumer, psychographic segmentation focuses on consumer lifestyles. Consumers are first asked a variety of questions about their lifestyles and then grouped on the basis of the similarity of their responses. Lifestyles are measured by asking consumers about their *activities* (work, hobbies, vacations), *interests* (family, job, community), and *opinions* (about social issues, politics, business). The activity, interest, and opinion (AIO) questions are very general in some studies but in others, at least some of the questions relate to specific products.[3]

FIGURE 5.2 Useful Segmentation Bases for Consumer and Organizational Buyer Markets

Consumer Markets

Segmentation Base	Examples of Market Segments
Geographic:	
Continents	Africa, Asia, Europe, North America, South America
Global regions	Southeast Asia, Mediterranean, Caribbean
Countries	China, Canada, France, United States, Brazil
Country regions	Pacific Northwest, Middle Atlantic, Midwest
City, county, or SMSA size	Under 5,000 people; 5,000–19,999; 20,000–49,999; 50,000–99,999; 100,000–249,999; 250,000–499,999; 500,000–999,999; or over a million
Population density	Urban, suburban, rural
Climate	Tropical, temperate, cold
Demographic:	
Age	Under 6 years old, 6–12, 13–19, 20–29, 30–39, 40–49, 50–59, 60+
Gender	Male, female
Family size	1–2 persons, 3–4 persons, more than 4 persons
Family life cycle	Single, young married, married with children, sole survivor
Income	Under $10,000 per year, $10,000–$19,999, $20,000–$29,999, $30,000–$39,999, $40,000–$49,999, $50,000–$59,999, $60,000–$69,999, $70,000+
Education	Grade school or less, some high school, graduated from high school, some college, graduated from college, some graduate work, graduate degree
Marital status	Single, married, divorced, widowed
Social:	
Culture	American, Hispanic, African, Asian, European
Subculture	
Religion	Jewish, Catholic, Muslim, Mormon, Buddhist
Race	European American, Asian American, African American, Hispanic American
Nationality	French, Malaysian, Australian, Canadian, Japanese
Social class	Upper class, middle class, working class, lower class
Thoughts and feelings:	
Knowledge	Expert, novice
Involvement	High, medium, low
Attitude	Positive, neutral, negative
Benefits sought	Convenience, economy, prestige
Innovativeness	Innovator, early adopter, early majority, late majority, laggards, nonadopter
Readiness stage	Unaware, aware, interested, desirous, plan to purchase
Perceived risk	High, moderate, low
Behavior:	
Media usage	Newspaper, magazine, TV, Internet
Specific media usage	*Sports Illustrated, Cosmopolitan, Ebony*
Payment method	Cash, Visa, MasterCard, American Express, check
Loyalty status	None, some, total
Usage rate	Light, medium, heavy
User status	Nonuser, ex-user, current user, potential user
Usage situation	Work, home, vacation, commuting
Combined approaches:	
Psychographics	Achievers, strivers, strugglers
Person/situation	College students for lunch, executives for business dinner
Geodemography	Money and Brains, American Dreams, Bohemian Mix

Organizational Buyer Markets

Segmentation Base	Examples of Market Segments
Company size	Small, medium, large relative to industry
Purchase quantity	Small, medium, large account
Product application	Production, maintenance, product component
Organization type	Manufacturer, retailer, government agency, hospital
Location	North, south, east, west sales territory
Purchase status	New customer, occasional purchaser, frequent purchaser, nonpurchaser
Attribute importance	Price, service, reliability of supply

FIGURE 5.3   Toothpaste Market Benefit Segments

	Sensory Segment	Sociable Segment	Worrier Segment	Independent Segment
Principal benefit sought	Flavor and product appearance	Brightness of teeth	Decay prevention	Price
Demographic strengths	Children	Teens, young people	Large families	Men
Special behavioral characteristics	Users of spearmint-flavored toothpaste	Smokers	Heavy users	Heavy users
Brands disproportionately favored	Colgate	Macleans, Ultra Brite	Crest	Cheapest brand
Lifestyle characteristics	Hedonistic	Active	Conservative	Value-oriented

The best-known psychographic segmentation is called VALS™, which stands for "values and lifestyles." Originally developed in the 1970s, it has been redone several times to enhance its ability to explain changing lifestyles and predict consumer behavior. Segmentation research based on VALS™ is a product of SRI Consulting Business Intelligence.

As shown in Figure 5.4, the VALS™ framework has eight psychographic groups arranged in a rectangle based on two dimensions. The vertical dimension segments people

FIGURE 5.4   VALS™ Framework and Segments

Source: www.strategicbusinessinsights.com/vals/ustypes.shtml, March 18, 2011.

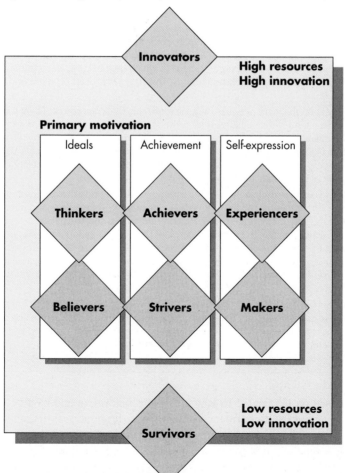

FIGURE 5.4 (continued)

Innovators. Innovators are successful, sophisticated, take-charge people with high self-esteem. Because they have such abundant resources, they exhibit all three primary motivations in varying degrees. They are change leaders and are the most receptive to new ideas and technologies. Innovators are very active consumers, and their purchases reflect cultivated tastes for upscale, niche products and services. Image is important to Innovators, not as evidence of status or power but as an expression of their taste, independence, and personality. Innovators are among the established and emerging leaders in business and government, yet they continue to seek challenges. Their lives are characterized by variety. Their possessions and recreation reflect a cultivated taste for the finer things in life.

Thinkers. Thinkers are motivated by ideals. They are mature, satisfied, comfortable, and reflective people who value order, knowledge, and responsibility. They tend to be well educated and actively seek out information in the decision-making process. They are well-informed about world and national events and are alert to opportunities to broaden their knowledge. Thinkers have a moderate respect for the status quo institutions of authority and social decorum, but are open to consider new ideas. Although their incomes allow them many choices, Thinkers are conservative, practical consumers; they look for durability, functionality, and value in the products they buy.

Achievers. Motivated by the desire for achievement, Achievers have goal-oriented lifestyles and a deep commitment to career and family. Their social lives reflect this focus and are structured around family, their place of worship, and work. Achievers live conventional lives, are politically conservative, and respect authority and the status quo. They value consensus, predictability, and stability over risk, intimacy, and self-discovery. With many wants and needs, Achievers are active in the consumer marketplace. Image is important to Achievers; they favor established, prestige products and services that demonstrate success to their peers. Because of their busy lives, they are often interested in a variety of time-saving devices.

Experiencers. Experiencers are motivated by self-expression. As young, enthusiastic, and impulsive consumers, Experiencers quickly become enthusiastic about new possibilities but are equally quick to cool. They seek variety and excitement, savoring the new, the offbeat, and the risky. Their energy finds an outlet in exercise, sports, outdoor recreation, and social activities. Experiencers are avid consumers and spend a comparatively high proportion of their income on fashion, entertainment, and socializing. Their purchases reflect the emphasis they place on looking good and having "cool" stuff.

Believers. Like Thinkers, Believers are motivated by ideals. They are conservative, conventional people with concrete beliefs based on traditional, established codes: family, religion, community, and the nation. Many Believers express moral codes that are deeply rooted and literally interpreted. They follow established routines, organized in large part around home, family, community, and social or religious organizations to which they belong. As consumers, Believers are predictable; they choose familiar products and established brands. They favor American products and are generally loyal customers.

Strivers. Strivers are trendy and fun loving. Because they are motivated by achievement, Strivers are concerned about the opinions and approval of others. Money defines success for Strivers, who don't have enough of it to meet their desires. They favor stylish products that emulate the purchases of people with greater material wealth. Many see themselves as having a job rather than a career, and a lack of skills and focus often prevents them from moving ahead. Strivers are active consumers because shopping is both a social activity and an opportunity to demonstrate to peers their ability to buy. As consumers, they are as impulsive as their financial circumstance will allow.

Makers. Like Experiencers, Makers are motivated by self-expression. They express themselves and experience the world by working on it—building a house, raising children, fixing a car, or canning vegetables—and have enough skill and energy to carry out their projects successfully. Makers are practical people who have constructive skills and value self-sufficiency. They live within a traditional context of family, practical work, and physical recreation and have little interest in what lies outside that context. Makers are suspicious of new ideas and large institutions such as big business. They are respectful of government authority and organized labor, but resentful of government intrusion on individual rights. They are unimpressed by material possessions other than those with a practical or functional purpose. Because they prefer value to luxury, they buy basic products.

Survivors. Survivors live narrowly focused lives. With few resources with which to cope, they often believe that the world is changing too quickly. They are comfortable with the familiar and are primarily concerned with safety and security. Because they must focus on meeting needs rather than fulfilling desires, Survivors do not show a strong primary motivation. Survivors are cautious consumers. They represent a very modest market for most products and services. They are loyal to favorite brands, especially if they can purchase them at a discount.

based on the degree to which they are innovative and have resources such as income, education, self-confidence, intelligence, leadership skills, and energy. The horizontal dimension represents primary motivations for buying and includes three different types. Consumers driven by knowledge and principles are motivated primarily by *ideals*. These consumers include the Thinkers and Believers groups. Consumers driven by a goal of

You can find your VALS classification by filling out a questionnaire on the Internet. The Web address is www.strategicbusinessinsights.com/vals/surveynew.shtml. The questionnaire takes about 10 minutes to complete, and your lifestyle will take about 10 seconds to compute. You will get a report that includes both your primary and secondary VALS type. The VALS Web site has a lot of information describing the program and different types of VALS segments.

demonstrating success to their peers are motivated primarily by *achievement*. These consumers include Achievers and Strivers. Consumers driven by a desire for social or physical activity, variety, and risk taking are motivated primarily by *self-expression*. These consumers include both the Experiencers and Makers. At the top of the rectangle are the Innovators, who have such high resources that they may express any of the three motivations. At the bottom of the rectangle are the Survivors, who live complacently and within their means without a strong primary motivation of the types listed above. Figure 5.4 gives more details about each of the eight groups.[4]

Marketers can purchase research data that show which VALS™ groups are the primary buyers of specific products and services. This information can be used to better focus elements of the marketing mix, such as promotion, on the best target markets.

Geodemographic Segmentation

One problem with many segmentation approaches is that although they identify types or categories of consumers, they do not identify specific individuals or households within a market. Geodemographic segmentation identifies specific households in a market by focusing on local neighborhood geography (such as zip codes) to create classifications of actual, addressable, mappable neighborhoods where consumers live and shop.[5] One geodemographic system, is called Nielsen PRIZM, which stands for consumers "Potential Ranking Index of ZIP Markets." The system classifies every U.S. neighborhood into one of 14 social groups. Each of these groups is further divided into 3 to 6 segments, with a total of 66 distinct segments in this system. Each group and segment is based on zip codes, demographic information from the U.S. Census, and information on product use, media use, and lifestyle preferences. Figure 5.5 shows a sample group with five segments. The PRIZM® segmentation system includes maps of different areas that rank neighborhoods on their potential to purchase specific products and services. PRIZM segmentation is available on major marketing databases from leading providers.

The PRIZM segmentation system is based on the assumptions that consumers in particular neighborhoods are similar in many respects and that the best prospects are those who actually use a product or other consumers like them. Marketers use PRIZM to better understand consumers in various markets, what they are like, where they live, and how to reach them. These data help marketers with target market selection, direct marketing campaigns, site selection, media selection, and analysis of sales potential in various areas.

DEVELOP PRODUCT POSITIONING

By this time, the firm should have a good idea of the basic segments of the market that could potentially be satisfied with its product. The current step is concerned with positioning the product favorably in the minds of customers relative to competitive products. Several different positioning strategies can be used. First, products can be positioned by focusing on their superiority to competitive products based on one or more attributes. For example, a

FIGURE 5.5   PRIZM Social Group U1—Urban Uptown

Source: Nielsen MyBestSegments (www.mybestsegments.com), March 18, 2011.

Group U1 – Urban Uptown

The five segments in Urban Uptown are home to the nation's wealthiest urban consumers. Members of this social group tend to be affluent to middle class, college educated and ethnically diverse, with above-average concentrations of Asian and Hispanic Americans. Although this group is diverse in terms of housing styles and family sizes, residents share an upscale urban perspective that's reflected in their marketplace choices. Urban Uptown consumers tend to frequent the arts, shop at exclusive retailers, drive luxury imports, travel abroad and spend heavily on computer and wireless technology.

The Urban Uptown group consists of the following segments:

- 04. Young Digerati
- 07. Money and Brains
- 16. Bohemian Mix
- 26. The Cosmopolitans
- 29. American Dreams

04. Young Digerati – Young Digerati are the nation's tech–savvy singles and couples living in fashionable neighborhoods on the urban fringe. Affluent, highly educated and ethnically mixed, Young Digerati communities are typically filled with trendy apartments and condos, fitness clubs and clothing boutiques, casual restaurants and all types of bars–from juice to coffee to microbrew.

07. Money and Brains – The residents of Money & Brains seem to have it all: high incomes, advanced degrees and sophisticated tastes to match their credentials. Many of these citydwellers are married couples with few children who live in fashionable homes on small, manicured lots.

16. Bohemian Mix – A collection of young, mobile urbanites, Bohemian Mix represents the nation's most liberal lifestyles. Its residents are a progressive mix of young singles and couples, students and professionals. In their funky rowhouses and apartments, Bohemian Mixers are the early adopters who are quick to check out the latest movie, nightclub, laptop and microbrew.

26. The Cosmopolitans – Educated, upper-midscale, and ethnically diverse, The Cosmopolitans are urban couples in America's fast-growing cities. Concentrated in a handful of metros-such as Las Vegas, Miami, and Albuquerque-these households feature older, empty-nesting homeowners. A vibrant social scene surrounds their older homes and apartments, and residents love the nightlife and enjoy leisure-intensive lifestyles.

29. American Dreams – American Dreams is a living example of how ethnically diverse the nation has become: just under half of the residents are Hispanic, Asian or African-American. In these multilingual neighborhoods–one in three speaks a language other than English–middle-aged immigrants and their children live in middle-class comfort.

You can find your PRIZM classification by going to www.MyBestSegments.com and clicking on "ZIP Code Look-up." By putting in your zip code (and a security code) you can find out about the segments in your neighborhood. A more detailed explanation of the segments can be found by clicking the "Segments Look-Up" tab.

car could be positioned as less expensive (Hyundai), safer (Volvo), higher quality (Toyota), or more prestigious (Lexus) than other cars. Second, products can be positioned by use or application. For example, Campbell's soup is positioned not only as a lunch item but also for use as a sauce or dip or as an ingredient in main dishes. Third, products can be positioned in terms of particular types of product users. For example, sales for Johnson's Baby Shampoo increased dramatically after the company positioned the product not only for babies but also for active adults who need to wash their hair frequently. Fourth, products can be positioned relative to a product class. For example, Caress soap was positioned by Lever Brothers as a bath oil product rather than as a soap. Finally, products can be positioned directly against particular competitors. For example, Coke and Pepsi and McDonald's and Burger King commonly position directly against each other on various criteria, such as taste. The classic example of positioning is of this last type: Seven-Up positioned itself as a tasty alternative to the dominant soft drink, colas.

One way to investigate how to position a product is by using a *positioning map,* which is a visual depiction of customer perceptions of competitive products, brands, or models. It is constructed by surveying customers about various product attributes and developing dimensions and a graph indicating the relative position of competitors. Figure 5.6 presents a sample positioning map for automobiles that offers marketers a way of assessing whether their brands are positioned appropriately. For example, if Chrysler or Buick wants to be positioned in the minds of consumers as serious competitors to Lexus, then their strategies need to be changed to move up on this dimension. After the new strategies are implemented, a new positioning map could be developed to see if the brands moved up as desired.

FIGURE 5.6
Positioning Map for
Automobiles

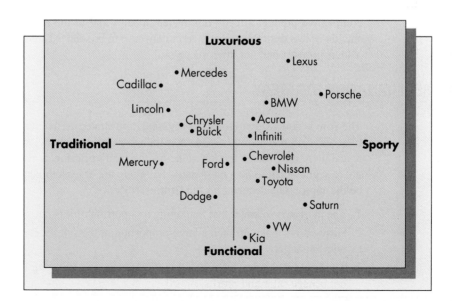

Dividing markets into segments and then selecting the best ones to serve is one of the cornerstones of sound marketing practice. However, there are situations when target marketing has been criticized as being unethical.

- R. J. Reynolds Tobacco Company planned to target African American consumers with a new brand of menthol cigarettes, Uptown. This brand was to be advertised with suggestions of glamour, high fashion, and night life. After criticism for targeting a vulnerable population, the company canceled plans for the brand.
- RJR planned to target white, 18- to 24-year-old "virile" females with a new cigarette brand, Dakota. It was criticized for targeting young, poorly educated, blue-collar women; and although it expanded the market to include males, Dakota failed in test markets and was withdrawn.
- Heileman Brewing Company planned to market a new brand of malt liquor called Power-Master. Malt liquor is disproportionately consumed by African Americans and in low-income neighborhoods. Criticism of this strategy led the brand to be withdrawn.
- The food industry has been criticized for many years for promoting high-fat-content foods to children.

One study suggests that whether targeting a group of consumers is unethical depends on two dimensions. The first is the degree to which the product can harm the consumers, and the second is the vulnerability of the group. Thus, to market harmful products to vulnerable target markets is likely to be considered unethical and could result in boycotts, negative word of mouth, and possibly litigation or legislation.

Source: Kevin Freking, "Marketing to Minors," *Wisconsin State Journal,* July 31, 2008, p. A7; N. Craig Smith and Elizabeth Cooper-Martin, "Ethics and Target Marketing: The Role of Product Harm and Consumer Vulnerability," *Journal of Marketing,* July 1997, pp. 1–20.

Some experts argue that different positioning strategies should be used depending on whether the firm is a market leader or follower and that followers usually should not attempt to position directly against the industry leader.[6] The main point here is that in segmenting markets, some segments might have to be forgone because a market-leading competitive product already dominates in sales and in the minds of customers. Thus, a smaller or less desirable target market may have to be selected since competing with market leaders is costly and not often successful.

DECIDE SEGMENTATION STRATEGY

The firm is now ready to select its segmentation strategy. There are four basic alternatives. First, the firm may decide not to enter the market. For example, analysis to this stage may reveal there is no viable market niche for the firm's offering. Second, the firm may decide not to segment but to be a mass marketer. There are at least three situations when this may be the appropriate decision for the firm:

1. The market is so small that marketing to a portion of it is not profitable.
2. Heavy users make up such a large proportion of the sales volume that they are the only relevant target.
3. The brand is the dominant brand in the market, and targeting to a few segments would not benefit sales and profits.

FIGURE 5.7
Selecting Target
Markets: Some
Questions Marketing
Managers Should
Answer

In order to select the best target markets, marketing managers must evaluate market segments on a number of dimensions. Below is a list of questions managers should answer before selecting target markets.

Measurability Questions

1. What are the appropriate bases for segmenting this market and are these bases readily measurable?
2. Are secondary data available on these bases so that the market segment can be identified and measured inexpensively?
3. If primary data are needed, is there sufficient return on investment to do the research?
4. Are specific names and addresses of people in this market segment needed; or is general knowledge of their existence, number, and geographic location sufficient?
5. Can purchases of people in this market segment be readily measured and tracked?

Meaningfulness Questions

1. How many people are in this market segment and how frequently will they purchase our product?
2. What market share can we expect in this segment?
3. What is the growth potential of this segment?
4. How strong is competition for this market segment and how is it likely to change in the future?
5. How satisfied are customers in this market segment with current product offerings?

Marketability Questions

1. Can this market segment be reached with our current channels of distribution?
2. If new channels are needed, can we establish them efficiently?
3. What specific promotion media do these people read, listen to, or watch?
4. Can we afford to promote to these people in the appropriate media to reach them?
5. Are people in this market segment willing to pay a price that is profitable for the company?
6. Can we produce a product for this market segment and do so profitably?

Third, the firm may decide to market to one segment. And fourth, the firm may decide to market to more than one segment and design a separate marketing mix for each. In any case, the firm must have some criteria on which to base its segmentation strategy decisions. Three important criteria on which to base such decisions are that a viable segment must be (1) measurable, (2) meaningful, and (3) marketable.

1. *Measurable*. For a segment to be selected, the firm must be capable of measuring its size and characteristics. For instance, one of the difficulties with segmenting on the basis of social class is that the concept and its divisions are not clearly defined and measured. Alternatively, income is a much easier concept to measure.
2. *Meaningful*. A meaningful segment is one that is large enough to have sufficient sales and growth potential to offer long-run profits for the firm.
3. *Marketable*. A marketable segment is one that can be reached and served by the firm in an efficient manner.

Figure 5.7 offers a list of questions marketing managers should answer when deciding whether a market segment meets these criteria. Segments that do so are viable target markets for the firm's offering. The firm must now give further attention to completing its marketing mix.

DESIGN MARKETING MIX STRATEGY

The firm is now in a position to complete its marketing plan by finalizing the marketing mix or mixes to be used for each segment. Clearly, selection of the target market and designing the marketing mix go hand in hand, and thus many marketing mix decisions should have already been carefully considered. To illustrate, the target market selected may be price sensitive, so some consideration has already been given to price levels, and clearly product positioning has many implications for promotion and channel decisions. Thus, while we place marketing mix design at the end of the model, many of these decisions are made in *conjunction* with target market selection. In the next six chapters of this text, marketing mix decisions will be discussed in detail.

SUMMARY

The purpose of this chapter was to provide an overview of market segmentation. Market segmentation was defined as the process of dividing a market into groups of similar consumers and selecting the most appropriate group(s) for the firm to serve. Market segmentation was analyzed as a six-stage process: (1) to delineate the firm's current situation, (2) to determine consumer needs and wants, (3) to divide the market on relevant dimensions, (4) to develop product positioning, (5) to decide segmentation strategy, and (6) to design marketing mix strategy.

Additional Resources

Bolton, Ruth N., and Matthew B. Myers."Price-Based Global Market Segmentation for Services." *Journal of Marketing,* July 2003, pp. 108–28.

Dickson, Peter R., and James L. Ginter. "Market Segmentation, Product Differentiation, and Marketing Strategy." *Journal of Marketing,* April 1987, pp. 1–10.

Myers, James H. *Segmentation and Positioning for Strategic Marketing Decisions.* Chicago: American Marketing Association, 1996.

Yankelovich, Daniel, and David Meer. "Rediscovering Market Segmentation." *Harvard Business Review,* February 2006, pp. 122–31.

Key Terms and Concepts

A priori segmentation: Approach in which the marketing manager has decided on the appropriate basis for segmentation in advance of doing any research on the market.

Benefit segmentation: Approach that focuses on satisfying needs and wants by grouping consumers on the basis of the benefits they are seeking in a product.

Geodemographic segmentation: Approach that identifies specific households in a market by focusing on local neighborhood geography (such as zip codes) to create classifications of actual, addressable, mappable neighborhoods where consumers live and shop.

Market segmentation: The process of dividing a market into groups of similar consumers and selecting the most appropriate group(s) for the firm to serve.

Post hoc segmentation: Approach that groups people into segments on the basis of research findings rather than determining the basis prior to any research.

Positioning map: A visual depiction of consumer perceptions of competitive products, brands, or models.

Psychographic segmentation: Approach that focuses on consumer lifestyles as the basis for segmentation. Consumers are asked a variety of questions about their lifestyles (commonly, their activities, interests, and opinions) and then grouped on the basis of the similarity of their responses.

Target market: The group or segment a company selects to serve.

VALS: A product of SRI Consulting Business Intelligence; the best known psychographic approach; stands for "values and lifestyles."

Part C

The Marketing Mix

Chapter

Product and Brand Strategy

Product strategy is a critical element of marketing and business strategy, since it is through the sale of products and services that companies survive and grow. This chapter discusses four important areas of concern in developing product strategies. First, some basic issues are discussed, including product definition, product classification, product quality and value, product mix and product line, branding and brand equity, and packaging. Second, the product life cycle and its implications for product strategy are explained. Third, the product audit is reviewed, and finally, three ways to organize for product management are outlined. These include the marketing manager system, brand manager system, and cross-functional teams.

BASIC ISSUES IN PRODUCT MANAGEMENT

Successful marketing depends on understanding the nature of products and basic decision areas in product management. In this section, we discuss the definition and classification of products, the importance of product quality and value, and the nature of a product mix and product lines. Also considered is the role of branding and packaging.

Product Definition

The way in which the product variable is defined can have important implications for the survival, profitability, and long-run growth of the firm. For example, the same product can be viewed in at least three different ways. First, it can be viewed in terms of the *tangible product*—the physical entity or service that is offered to the buyer. Second, it can be viewed in terms of the *extended product*—the tangible product along with the whole cluster of services that accompany it. For example, a manufacturer of computer software may offer a 24-hour hotline to answer questions users may have or to offer free or reduced-cost software updates, free replacement of damaged software, and a subscription to a newsletter that documents new applications of the software. Third, it can be viewed in terms of the *generic product*—the essential benefits the buyer expects to receive from the product. For example, many personal care products bring to the purchaser feelings of self-enhancement and security in addition to the tangible benefits they offer.

From the standpoint of the marketing manager, to define the product solely in terms of the tangible product is to fall into the error of "marketing myopia." Executives who are guilty of committing this error define their company's product too narrowly, since they overemphasize the physical object itself. The classic example of this mistake can be found in railroad passenger

1. An audit of the firm's actual and potential resources
   a. Financial strength
   b. Access to raw materials
   c. Plant and equipment
   d. Operating personnel
   e. Management
   f. Engineering and technical skills
   g. Patents and licenses
2. Approaches to current markets
   a. More of the same products
   b. Variations of present products in terms of grades, sizes, and packages
   c. New products to replace or supplement current lines
   d. Product deletions
3. Approaches to new or potential markets
   a. Geographical expansion of domestic sales
   b. New socioeconomic or ethnic groups
   c. Overseas markets
   d. New uses of present products
   e. Complementary goods
   f. Mergers and acquisitions
4. State of competition
   a. New entries into the industry
   b. Product imitation
   c. Competitive mergers or acquisitions

service. Although no amount of product improvement could have staved off its decline, if the industry had defined itself as being in the transportation business, rather than the railroad business, it might still be profitable today. On the positive side, toothpaste manufacturers have been willing to exercise flexibility in defining their product. For years, toothpaste was an oral hygiene product in which emphasis was placed solely on fighting tooth decay and bad breath (e.g., Crest with fluoride). More recently, many manufacturers have recognized the need to market toothpaste as a cosmetic item (to clean teeth of stains), as a defense against gum disease (to reduce the buildup of tartar above the gumline), as an aid for denture wearers, and as a breath freshener. As a result, special-purpose brands have been designed to serve these particular needs, such as Ultra Brite, Close-Up, Aqua-Fresh, Aim, Dental Care, and the wide variety of baking soda, tartar-control formula, and gel toothpastes offered under existing brand names.

In line with the marketing concept philosophy, a reasonable definition of product is that it is *the sum of the physical, psychological, and sociological satisfactions the buyer derives from purchase, ownership, and consumption.* From this standpoint, products are customer-satisfying objects that include such things as accessories, packaging, and service.

Product Classification

A product classification scheme can be useful to the marketing manager as an analytical device to assist in planning marketing strategy and programs. A basic assumption underlying such classifications is that products with common attributes can be marketed in a similar fashion. In general, products are classed according to two basic criteria: (1) end use or market, and (2) degree of processing or physical transformation.

1. *Agricultural products and raw materials.* These are goods grown or extracted from the land or sea, such as iron ore, wheat, and sand. In general, these products are fairly homogeneous, sold in large volume, and have low value per unit or in bulk weight.

2. *Organizational goods.* Such products are purchased by business firms for the purpose of producing other goods or for running the business. This category includes the following:
   a. Raw materials and semifinished goods.
   b. Major and minor equipment, such as basic machinery, tools, and other processing facilities.

    c. Parts or components, which become an integral element of some other finished good.

    d. Supplies or items used to operate the business but that do not become part of the final product.

3. *Consumer goods.* Consumer goods can be divided into three classes:

    a. Convenience goods, such as food, which are purchased frequently with minimum effort. Impulse goods would also fall into this category.

    b. Shopping goods, such as appliances, which are purchased after some time and energy are spent comparing the various offerings.

    c. Specialty goods, which are unique in some way so the consumer will make a special purchase effort to obtain them.

In general, the buying motive, buying habits, and character of the market are different for organizational goods vis-à-vis consumer goods. A primary purchasing motive for organizational goods is, of course, profit. As mentioned in a previous chapter, organizational goods are usually purchased as means to an end and not as an end in themselves. This is another way of saying that the demand for organizational goods is a derived demand. Organizational goods are often purchased directly from the original source with few middlemen, because many of these goods can be bought in large quantities; they have high unit value; technical advice on installation and use is required; and the product is ordered according to the user's specifications. Many organizational goods are subject to multiple-purchase influence, and a long period of negotiation is often required.

The market for organizational goods has certain attributes that distinguish it from the consumer goods market. Much of the market is concentrated geographically, as in the case of steel, auto, or shoe manufacturing. Certain products have a limited number of buyers; this is known as a *vertical market,* which means that (1) it is narrow, because customers are restricted to a few industries and (2) it is deep, in that a large percentage of the producers in the market use the product. Some products, such as desktop computers, have a *horizontal market,* which means that the goods are purchased by all types of firms in many different industries. In general, buyers of organizational goods are reasonably well informed. As noted previously, heavy reliance is often placed on price, quality control, and reliability of supply source.

In terms of consumer products, many marketing scholars have found the convenience, shopping, and specialty classification inadequate and have attempted either to refine it or to derive an entirely new typology. None of these attempts appears to have met with complete success. Perhaps there is no best way to deal with this problem. From the standpoint of the marketing manager, product classification is useful to the extent that it assists in providing guidelines for developing an appropriate marketing mix. For example, convenience goods generally require broadcast promotion and long channels of distribution as opposed to shopping goods, which generally require more targeted promotion and somewhat shorter channels of distribution.

Product Quality and Value

Quality can be defined as the degree of excellence or superiority that an organization's product possesses.[1] Quality can encompass both the tangible and intangible aspects of a firm's products or services. In a technical sense, quality can refer to physical traits such as features, performance, reliability, durability, aesthetics, serviceability, and conformance to specifications. Although quality can be evaluated from many perspectives, the customer is the key perceiver of quality because his or her purchase decision determines the success of the organization's product or service and often the fate of the organization itself.

Many organizations have formalized their interest in providing quality products by undertaking total-quality management (TQM) programs. TQM is an organizationwide commitment to satisfying customers by continuously improving every business process involved in delivering products or services. Instead of merely correcting defects when they occur, organizations that practice TQM train and commit employees to continually look for ways to do things better so defects and problems don't arise in the first place. The result of this process is higher-quality products being produced at a lower cost. Indeed, the emphasis on quality has risen to such a level that over 70 countries have adopted the ISO 9000 quality system of standards, a standardized approach for evaluating a supplier's quality system, which can be applied to virtually any business.[2]

The term *quality* is often confused with the concept of value. Value encompasses not only quality but also price. *Value* can be defined as what the customer gets in exchange for what the customer gives. In other words, a customer, in most cases, receives a product in exchange for having paid the supplier for the product. A customer's perception of the value associated with a product is generally based both on the degree to which the product meets his or her specifications and the price that the customer will have to pay to acquire the product. Some organizations are beginning to shift their primary focus from one that solely emphasizes quality to one that also equally encompasses the customer's viewpoint of the price/quality trade-off. Organizations that are successful at this process derive their competitive advantage from the provision of customer value. In other words, they offer goods and services that meet or exceed customer needs at a fair price. Recall that Chapter 1 described various strategies based on value.

Product Mix and Product Line

A firm's *product mix* is the full set of products offered for sale by the organization; a product mix may consist of several *product lines,* or groups of products that share common characteristics, distribution channels, customers, or uses. A firm's product mix is described by its width and depth. *Width* of the product mix refers to the number of product lines handled by the organization. For example, one division of General Mills has a widespread mix consisting of five different product lines: ready-to-eat cereals, convenience foods, snack foods, baking products, and dairy products. *Depth* refers to the average number of products in each line. In its ready-to-eat cereals line, General Mills has eight different products. It has five different products in its line of convenience foods. Thus, the organization has a wide product mix and deep product lines.

An integral component of product line planning revolves around the question of how many product variants should be included in the line.[3] Manufacturing costs are usually minimized through large-volume production runs, and distribution costs tend to be lower if only one product is sold, stocked, and serviced. At a given level of sales, profits will usually be highest if those sales have been achieved with a single product. However, many firms offer many product variants.

Organizations offer varying products within a given product line for three reasons. First, potential customers rarely agree on a single set of specifications regarding their "ideal product," differing greatly in the importance and value they place on specific attributes. For example, in the laundry detergent market, there is a marked split between preferences for powder versus liquid detergent. Second, customers prefer variety. For example, a person may like Italian food but does not want to only eat spaghetti. Therefore, an Italian restaurant will offer the customer a wide variety of Italian dishes to choose from. Third, the dynamics of competition lead to multiproduct lines. As competitors seek to increase market share, they find it advantageous to introduce new products that subsegment an existing market segment by offering benefits more precisely tailored to the specific needs of a portion of that segment. For example, Proctor & Gamble offers Jif peanut butter in a low-salt version to target a specific subsegment of the peanut butter market.

All too often, organizations pursue product line additions with little regard for consequences.[4] However, in reaching a decision on product line additions, organizations need to evaluate whether (1) total profits will decrease or (2) the quality/value associated with current products will suffer. If the answer to either of the above is yes, then the organization

A. CLASSES OF CONSUMER GOODS—SOME CHARACTERISTICS AND MARKETING CONSIDERATIONS

Characteristics and Marketing Considerations	Type of Product		
	Convenience	Shopping	Specialty
Characteristics			
Time and effort devoted by consumer to shopping	Very little	Considerable	Cannot generalize; consumer may go to nearby store and buy with minimum effort or may have to go to distant store and spend much time and effort
Time spent planning the purchase	Very little	Considerable	Considerable
How soon want is satisfied after it arises	Immediately	Relatively long time	Relatively long time
Are price and quality compared?	No	Yes	No
Price	Usually low	High	High
Frequency of purchase	Usually frequent	Infrequent	Infrequent
Importance	Unimportant	Often very important	Cannot generalize
Marketing considerations			
Length of channel	Long	Short	Short to very short
Importance of retailer	Any single store is relatively unimportant	Important	Very important
Number of outlets	As many as possible	Few	Few; often only one in a market
Stock turnover	High	Lower	Lower
Gross margin	Low	High	High
Responsibility for advertising	Producer	Retailer	Joint responsibility
Importance of point-of-purchase display	Very important	Less important	Less important
Brand or store name important	Brand name	Store name	Both
Importance of packaging	Very important	Less important	Less important

Source: Michael J. Etzel, Bruce J. Walker, and William J. Stanton, *Fundamentals of Marketing*, 13th ed. (Burr Ridge, IL: McGraw-Hill/Irwin, 2004), pp. 211, 214.

should not proceed with the addition. Closely related to product line additions are issues associated with branding. These are covered next.

Branding and Brand Equity

For some organizations, the primary focus of strategy development is placed on brand building, developing, and nurturing activities.[5] Factors that serve to increase the strength of a brand include[6] (1) product quality when products do what they do very well (e.g., Windex and Easy-Off); (2) consistent advertising and other marketing communications in which brands tell their story often and well (e.g., Pepsi and Visa); (3) distribution intensity whereby customers see the brand wherever they shop (e.g., Marlboro); and (4) brand personality where the brand stands for something (e.g., Disney). The strength of the Coca-Cola brand, for example, is widely attributed to its universal availability, universal awareness, and trademark protection, which came as a result of strategic actions taken by the parent organization.[7]

B. CLASSES OF ORGANIZATIONAL PRODUCTS—SOME CHARACTERISTICS AND MARKETING CONSIDERATIONS

Characteristics and Marketing Considerations	Type of Product				
	Raw Materials	Fabricating Parts and Materials	Installations	Accessory Equipment	Operating Supplies
Example	Iron ore	Engine blocks	Blast furnaces	Storage racks	Paper clips
Characteristics					
Unit price	Very low	Low	Very high	Medium	Low
Length of life	Very short	Depends on final product	Very long	Long	Short
Quantities purchased	Large	Large	Very small	Small	Small
Frequency of purchase	Frequent delivery; long-term purchase contract	Infrequent purchase, but frequent delivery	Very infrequent	Medium frequency	Frequent
Standardization of competitive products	Very much; grading is important	Very much	Very little; custom made	Little	Much
Quantity of supply	Limited; supply can be increased slowly or not at all	Usually no problem	No problem	Usually no problem	Usually no problem
Marketing considerations					
Nature of channel	Short; no middlemen	Short; middlemen for small buyers	Short; no middlemen	Middlemen used	Middlemen used
Negotiation period	Hard to generalize	Medium	Long	Medium	Short
Price competition	Important	Important	Not important	Not main factor	Important
Presale/postsale service	Not important	Important	Very important	Important	Very little
Promotional activity	Very little	Moderate	Sales people very important	Important	Not too important
Brand preference	None	Generally low	High	High	Low
Advance buying contract	Important; long-term contracts used	Important; long-term contracts used	Not usually used	Not usually used	Not usually used

The brand name is perhaps the single most important element on the package, serving as a unique identifier. Specifically, a *brand* is a name, term, design, symbol, or any other feature that identifies one seller's good or service as distinct from those of other sellers. The legal term for brand is *trademark*.[8] A good brand name can evoke feelings of trust, confidence, security, strength, and many other desirable characteristics.[9] To illustrate, consider the case of Bayer aspirin. Bayer can be sold at up to two times the price of generic aspirin due to the strength of its brand image.

Rank	Previous Rank	Brand	Country of Origin	Sector	Brand Value ($M)
1	1	Coca Cola	US	Beverages	70,452
2	2	IBM	US	Business services	64,727
3	3	Microsoft	US	Computer software	60,895
4	7	Google	US	Internet services	43,557
5	4	GE	US	Diversified	42,808
6	6	McDonalds	US	Restaurants	33,578
7	9	Intel	US	Electronics	32,015
8	5	Nokia	Finland	Electronics	29,495
9	10	Disney	US	Media	28,731
10	11	Hewlett-Packard	US	Electronics	26,867
11	8	Toyota	Japan	Automotive	26,192
12	12	Mercedes-Benz	Germany	Automotive	25,179
13	13	Gillette	US	FMCG	23,298
14	14	Cisco	US	Business services	23,219
15	15	BMW	Germany	Automotive	22,322
16	16	Louis Vuitton	France	Luxury	21,860
17	20	Apple	US	Electronics	21,143
18	17	Marlboro	US	Tobacco	19,961
19	19	Samsung	South Korea	Electronics	19,491
20	18	Honda	Japan	Automotive	18,506

Source: Interbrand, "The Best Global Brands," 2010.

Many companies make use of manufacturer branding strategies in carrying out market and product development strategies. The *line extension* approach uses a brand name to facilitate entry into a new market segment (e.g., Diet Coke and Liquid Tide). An alternative to line extension is brand extension. In *brand extension,* a current brand name is used to enter a completely different product class (e.g., Jello pudding pops, Ivory shampoo).[10]

A third form of branding is *franchise extension* or *family branding,* whereby a company attaches the corporate name to a product to enter either a new market segment or a different product class (e.g., Honda lawnmower, Toyota Lexus). A final type of branding strategy that is becoming more and more common is dual branding. A *dual branding* (also known as joint or cobranding) strategy is one in which two or more branded products are integrated (e.g., Bacardi rum and Coca-Cola, Long John Silver's and A&W Root Beer, Archway cookies and Kellogg cereal, US Airways and Bank of America Visa). The logic behind this strategy is that if one brand name on a product gives a certain signal of quality, then the presence of a second brand name on the product should result in a signal that is at least as powerful as, if not more powerful than, the signal in the case of the single brand name. Each of the preceding four approaches is an attempt by companies to gain a competitive advantage by making use of its or others' established reputation, or both.

Companies may also choose to assign different brand names to each product. This is known as *multibranding* strategy. By doing so, the firm makes a conscious decision to allow the product to succeed or fail on its own merits. Major advantages of using multiple brand names are that (1) the firm can distance products from other offerings it markets; (2) the image of one product (or set of products) is not associated with other products the company markets; (3) the product(s) can be targeted at a specific market segment; and (4) should the product(s) fail, the probability of failure impacting on other company products is minimized.

For example, many consumers are unaware that a number of different brands of laundry detergent are all marketed by Procter & Gamble. The major disadvantage of this strategy is that because new names are assigned, there is no consumer brand awareness and significant amounts of money must be spent familiarizing customers with new brands.

Increasingly, companies are finding that brand names are one of the most valuable assets they possess. Successful extensions of an existing brand can lead to additional loyalty and associated profits. Conversely, a wrong extension can cause damaging associations, as perceptions linked to the brand name are transferred back from one product to the other.[11] *Brand equity* can be viewed as the set of assets (or liabilities) linked to the brand that add (or subtract) value.[12] The value of these assets is dependent upon the consequences or results of the marketplace's relationship with a brand. Figure 6.1 lists the elements of brand equity. Brand equity is determined by the consumer and is the culmination of the consumer's assessment of the product, the company that manufactures and markets the product, and all other variables that impact on the product between manufacture and consumer consumption.

Before leaving the topic of manufacturer brands, it is important to note that, as with consumer products, organizational products also can possess brand equity. However, several differences do exist between the two sectors.[13] First, organizational products are usually branded with firm names. As a result, loyalty (or disloyalty) to the brand tends to be of a more global nature, extending across all the firm's product lines. Second, because firm versus brand loyalty exists, attempts to position new products in a manner differing from existing products may prove to be difficult, if not impossible. Finally, loyalty to organizational products encompasses not only the firm and its products but also the distribution channel members employed to distribute the product. Therefore, attempts to establish or change brand image must also take into account distributor image.

FIGURE 6.1
Elements of Brand Equity

Source: David A. Aaker, *Managing Brand Equity.* © 1991, New York, by David A. Aaker. Reprinted with the permission of Free Press, a division of Simon & Schuster. See David A. Aaker, *Building Strong Brands* (New York: Free Press, 1995), for his seminal work on branding as well as David A. Aaker, *Brand Portfolio Strategy: Creating Relevance, Differentiation, Energy, Leverage, and Clarity* (New York: Free Press, 2004). David A. Aaker, *Strategic Market Management* (Hoboken, NJ: John Wiley, 2008), Chapter 9.

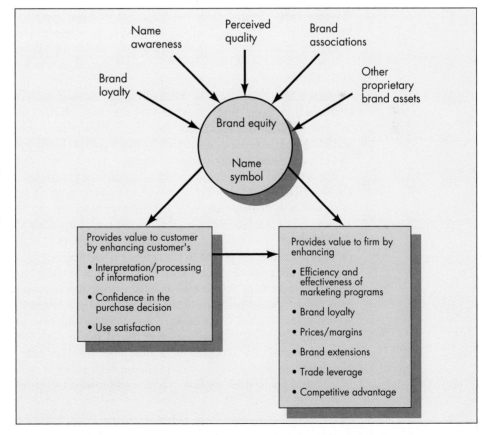

1. The name should suggest the product benefits. Names such as Easy Off (oven cleaner) and PowerBook (laptop computer) clearly suggest the benefits of purchasing the product.
2. The name should be memorable, distinctive, and positive. Many automobiles such as Mustang, Eagle, Firebird, and Bronco have strong names.
3. The name should fit the company or product image. Sharp (audio and video functions), Mustard's Last Stand (hot dogs), and Paddy O'Furniture (patio furniture) are some examples.
4. The name should have no legal restrictions. For example, the U.S. Food and Drug Administration discourages the use of word *heart* in food brand names. Also since brand names often need a corresponding address on the Internet, the choice may be complicated because millions of domain names have already been selected.
5. The name should be simple (such as Bold detergent and Sure deodorant), and emotional (Beautiful, Opium, and Obsession perfumes).

Source: Adapted from Roger A. Kerin, Steven W. Hartley, Eric N. Berkowitz, and William Rudelins, *Marketing,* 10th ed. (Burr Ridge, IL: McGraw-Hill/Irwin 2011), Chapter 11. Also see Kevin Lane Keller, *Strategic Brand Management,* 3rd ed. (Upper Saddle River, NJ: Prentice Hall, 2008), chap. 4.

As a related branding strategy, many retail firms produce or market their products under a so-called private label. For example, Kmart has phased in its own store-brand products to compete with the national brands. There's Nature's Classics, a line of fancy snacks and cookies; Oral Pure, a line of dental care products; Prevail house cleaners; B.E., a Gap-style line of weekend wear; and Benchmark, a line of "made in the U.S.A." tools. Such a strategy is highly important in industries where middlemen have gained control over distribution to the consumer. The growth of the large discount and specialty stores, such as Kmart, Walmart, Target, The Gap, Limited, and others, has accelerated the development of private brands. If a manufacturer refuses to supply certain middlemen with private branded merchandise, the alternative is for these middlemen to go into the manufacturing business, as in the case of Kroger supermarkets.

Private label products differ markedly from the so-called generic products that sport labels such as "beer," "cigarettes," and "potato chips." Today's house brands are packaged in distinctively upscale containers. The quality of the products used as house brands equals and sometimes exceeds those offered by name brands. While generic products were positioned as a means for consumers to struggle through recessionary times, private label brands are being marketed as value brands, products that are equivalent to national brands but are priced much lower. Private brands are rapidly growing in popularity. For example, it only took JCPenney Company, Inc., five years to nurture its private-label jeans, the Arizona brand, into a powerhouse with annual sales surpassing $500 million.

Consolidation within the supermarket industry, growth of super centers, and heightened product marketing are poised to strengthen private brands even further.[14] However, these gains will not come without a fight from national manufacturers who are undertaking aggressive actions to defend their brands' market share. Some have significantly rolled back prices, while others have instituted increased promotional campaigns. The ultimate winner in this ongoing battle between private (store) and manufacturer (national) brands, not surprisingly, should be the consumer who is able to play off these store brands against national brands. By shopping at a mass merchandiser like Walmart or Walgreens, consumers are exposed to and able to choose from a wide array of both national and store brands, thus giving them the best of both worlds: value and variety.

Many different factors work together to make a strong brand. Brand managers often focus on only one or two of these factors. Here is a list of several characteristics shared by the world's strongest brands that can be used to assess the strengths of a brand and to identify points of improvement.

Characteristic	Examples
Delivers benefits desired by customers.	Starbucks offers "coffee house experience," not just coffee beans, and monitors bean selection and roasting to preserve quality.
Stays relevant.	Gillette continuously invests in major product improvements (MACH3), while using a consistent slogan: "The best a man can get."
Prices are based on value.	P&G reduced operating costs and passed on savings as "everyday low pricing," thus growing margins.
Well-positioned relative to competitors.	Saturn competes on excellent customer service, Mercedes on product superiority. Visa stresses being "everywhere you want to be."
Is consistent.	Michelob tried several different positionings and campaigns between 1970 and 1995, while watching sales slip.
The brand portfolio makes sense.	The Gap has Gap, Banana Republic, and Old Navy stores for different market segments; BMW has the 3-, 5-, and 7-series.
Marketing activities are coordinated.	Coca-Cola uses ads, promotions, catalogs, sponsorships, and interactive media.
What the brand means to customers is well understood.	Bic couldn't sell perfume in lighter-shaped bottles; Gillette uses different brand names such as Oral-B for toothbrushes to avoid this problem.
Is supported over the long run.	Coors cut back promotional support in favor of Coors Light and Zima, and lost about 50% of its sales over a four-year period.
Sources of brand equity are monitored.	Disney studies revealed that its characters were becoming "overexposed" and sometimes used inappropriately. It cut back on licensing and other promotional activity as a result.

Source: Kevin Lane Keller, "The Brand Report Card," *Harvard Business Review,* January-February 2000, pp. 147–157. Merle Crawford and Anthony DiBenedetto, *New Product Management,* 10th ed. (Burr Ridge, IL: McGraw-Hill/Irwin, 2011), p. 418.

Opportunity to Add Value	Some Decision Factors	Examples
Promoting	Link product to promotion	The bunny on the Energizer battery package is a reminder that it "keeps going and going."
	Branding at point of purchase or consumption	Coke's logo greets almost everyone each time the refrigerator is opened.
	Product information	Nabisco's nutrition label helps consumers decide which cookie to buy, and a UPC code reduces checkout time and errors.
Protecting	For shipping and storing	Sony's MP3 player is kept safe by Styrofoam inserts.
	From tampering	Tylenol's safety seal prevents tampering.
	From shoplifting	Cardboard hang-tag on Gillette razor blades is too large to hide in hand.
	From spoiling	Kraft's shredded cheese has a resealable zipper package to keep it fresh.
Enhancing product	The environment	Tide detergent bottle can be recycled.
	Convenience in use	Squeezable tube of Yoplait Go-Gurt is easy to eat on the go and in new situations.
	Added product functions	Plastic tub is useful for refrigerator leftovers after the Cool Whip is gone.

Source: William D. Perreault, Jr., Joseph P. Cannon, and E. Jerome McCarthy, *Basic Marketing: A Marketing Strategy Planning Approach,* 18th ed. (Burr Ridge, IL: McGraw-Hill/Irwin, 2011), p. 241.

Packaging

Distinctive or unique packaging is one method of differentiating a relatively homogeneous product. To illustrate, shelf-stable microwave dinners, pumps rather than tubes of toothpaste or bars of soap, and different sizes and designs of tissue packages are attempts to differentiate a product through packaging changes and to satisfy consumer needs at the same time.

In other cases, packaging changes have succeeded in creating new attributes of value in a brand. A growing number of manufacturers are using green labels or packaging their products totally in green wrap to signify low- or no-fat content.[15] Frito-Lay, Quaker Oats, ConAgra, Keebler, Pepperidge Farm, Nabisco, and Sunshine Biscuits are all examples of companies involved in this endeavor.

Finally, packaging changes can make products urgently salable to a targeted segment. For example, the products in the Gillette Series grooming line, including shave cream, razors, aftershave, and skin conditioner, come in ribbed, rounded, metallic-gray shapes, looking at once vaguely sexual and like precision engineering.[16]

Marketing managers must consider both the consumer and costs in making packaging decisions. On one hand, the package must be capable of protecting the product through the channel of distribution to the consumer. In addition, it is desirable for packages to have a convenient size and be easy to open for the consumer. For example, single-serving soups and zip-lock packaging in cereal boxes are attempts by manufacturers to serve consumers better. Hopefully, the package is also attractive and informative, capable of being used as a competitive weapon to project a product's image. However, maximizing these objectives may increase the cost of the product to such an extent that consumers are no longer willing to purchase it. Thus, the marketing manager must determine the optimal protection, convenience, positioning, and promotional strengths of packages, subject to cost constraints.

PRODUCT LIFE CYCLE

A firm's product strategy must take into account the fact that products have a life cycle. Figure 6.2 illustrates this life-cycle concept. Products are introduced, grow, mature, and decline. This cycle varies according to industry, product, technology, and market. Marketing executives need to be aware of the life-cycle concept because it can be a valuable aid in developing marketing strategies.

During the introduction phase of the cycle, there are usually high production and marketing costs, and since sales are only beginning to materialize, profits are low or nonexistent. Profits increase and are positively correlated with sales during the growth stage as the market begins trying and adopting the product. As the product matures, profits for the initiating firm do not keep pace with sales because of competition. Here the seller may be forced to "remarket" the

FIGURE 6.2
The Product Life
Cycle

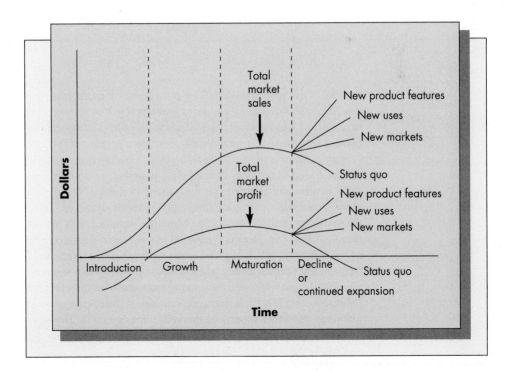

	Life-Cycle Stage			
Strategy Dimension	**Introduction**	**Growth**	**Maturity**	**Decline**
Basic objectives	Establish a market for product type; persuade early adopters to buy	Build sales and market share; develop preference for brand	Defend brand's share of market; seek growth by luring customers from competitors	Limit costs or seek ways to revive sales and profits
Product	Provide high quality; select a good brand; get patent or trademark protection	Provide high quality; add services to enhance value	Improve quality; add features to distinguish brand from competitors' brands	Continue providing high quality to maintain brand's reputation; seek ways to make the product new again
Pricing	Often high to recover development costs; sometimes low to build demand rapidly	Somewhat high because of heavy demand	Low, reflecting heavy competition	Low to sell off remaining inventory or high to serve a niche market
Channels	Limited number of channels	Greater number of channels to meet demand	Greater number of channels and more incentives to resellers	Limited number of channels
Promotion	Aimed at early adopters; messages designed to educate about product type; incentives such as samples and coupons to induce trial	Aimed at wider audience; messages focus on brand benefits; for consumer products, emphasis on advertising	Messages focus on differentiating brand from its competitors' brands; heavy use of incentives such as coupons to induce buyers to switch brands	Minimal, to keep costs down

product, which may involve making price concessions, increasing product quality, or expanding outlays on advertising and sales promotion just to maintain market share. At some point sales decline and the seller must decide whether to (1) drop the product, (2) alter the product, (3) seek new uses for the product, (4) seek new markets, or (5) continue with more of the same.

The usefulness of the product life-cycle concept is primarily that it forces management to take a long-range view of marketing planning. In doing so, it should become clear that shifts in phases of the life cycle correspond to changes in the market situation, competition, and demand. Thus, the astute marketing manager should recognize the necessity of altering the marketing mix to meet these changing conditions. It is possible for managers to undertake strategies that, in effect, can lead to a revitalized product life cycle. For example, past advancements in technology led to the replacement of rotary dial telephones by touch-tone, push-button phones. Today, even newer technology has enabled the cordless and cellular phone to replace the traditional touch-tone, push-button phone. When applied with sound judgment, the life-cycle concept can aid in forecasting, pricing, advertising, product planning, and other aspects of marketing management. However, the marketing manager must also recognize that the life cycle is purely a tool for assisting in strategy development and not let the life cycle dictate strategy development.[17]

As useful as the product life cycle can be to managers, it does have limitations that require it to be used cautiously in developing strategy. For one thing, the length of time a product will remain in each stage is unknown and can't be predicted with accuracy. Thus, while each stage will likely occur for a successful product, marketers can't forecast when one stage will end and another will begin in order to adapt their strategies at the appropriate time. Also, they may misjudge when a stage is ending and implement an inappropriate strategy. For example, marketers who believe their products are ending the maturity stage may cut promotion costs and thus push the product into decline, whereas the product might have continued to sell if promotion had been maintained and altered.

Another limitation is that not all products go through the product life cycle in the same way. For example, many products are failures and do not have anything approaching a complete life cycle. Several variations of the life cycle also exist, two of which are fashions and fads.

Fashions are accepted and popular product styles. Their life cycle involves a distinctiveness stage in which trendsetters adopt the style, followed by an emulation stage in which more customers purchase the style to be the trendsetters. Next is the economic stage, in which the style becomes widely available at mass-market prices. Many fashions, such as skirt length and designer jeans, lose popularity, then regain it and repeat the fashion of cycle. The fashion cycle is clearly visible in clothing, cosmetics, tattoos, and body piercing.

Fads are products that experience an intense but brief period of popularity. Their life cycle resembles the basic product life cycle but in a very compressed form. It is usually so brief that competitors have no chance to capitalize on the fad. Some fads may repeat their popularity after long lapses.

Product Adoption and Diffusion

Obviously not all customers immediately purchase a product in the introductory stage of the product life cycle. The shape of the life-cycle curve indicates that most sales occur after the product has been available for awhile. The spread of a product through the population is known as the diffusion of innovation, as illustrated in Figure 6.3, which presents five adopter categories.

The first category is *innovators,* those who are the first to buy a new product. When innovators are consumers, they tend to be people who are venturesome and willing to take risks. When innovators are organizational buyers, they tend to be organizations that seek to remain at the cutting edge through the use of the latest technology and ideas.

FIGURE 6.3
Adopter Categories

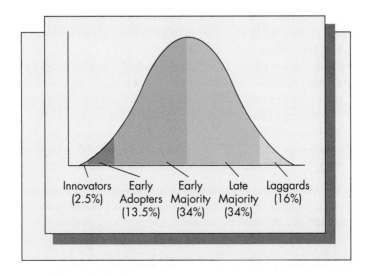

If the experience of innovators is favorable, *early adopters* begin to buy. These buyers, who are respected social leaders and above average in education, influence the next group. Influenced by what early adopters have, the rest of the market begins to get interested in the product. The biggest category of buyers is divided into groups called the early majority and late majority. Members of the *early majority* tend to avoid risk and to make purchases carefully. They also have many informal contacts. Members of the *late majority* not only avoid risks, but are cautious and skeptical about new ideas. Eventually, the product becomes commonplace, and even laggards are ready to buy. *Laggards* are reluctant to make changes and are comfortable with traditional products. They also have a fear of debt, but may eventually purchase a well-established brand.

THE PRODUCT AUDIT

The product audit is a marketing management technique whereby the company's current product offerings are reviewed to ascertain whether each product should be continued as is, improved, modified, or deleted. The audit is a task that should be carried out at regular intervals as a matter of policy. Product audits are the responsibility of the product manager unless specifically delegated to someone else.

Deletions

In today's environment, a growing number of products are being introduced each year that are competing for limited shelf space. This growth is primarily due to (1) new knowledge being applied faster, and (2) the decrease in time between product introductions (by a given organization).[18] In addition, companies are not consistently removing products from the market at the same time they are introducing new products. The result is a situation in which too many products are fighting for too little shelf space. One of the main purposes of the product audit is to detect sick products and then bury them. Rather than let the retailer or distributor decide which products should remain, organizations themselves should take the lead in developing criteria for deciding which products should stay and which should be deleted. Some of the more obvious factors to be considered are

Sales trends. How have sales moved over time? What has happened to market share? Why have sales declined? What changes in sales have occurred in competitive products both in our line and in those of other manufacturers?

Profit contribution. What has been the profit contribution of this product to the company? If profits have declined, how are these tied to price? Have selling, promotion, and distribution costs risen out of proportion to sales? Does the product require excessive management time and effort?

Product life cycle. Has the product reached a level of maturity and saturation in the market? Has new technology been developed that poses a threat to the product? Are more effective substitutes on the market? Has the product outgrown its usefulness? Can the resources used on this product be put to better use?

Customer migration patterns. If the product is deleted, will customers of this product switch to other substitute products marketed by our firm? In total, will profits associated with our line increase due to favorable switching patterns?

The above factors should be used as guidelines for making the final decision to delete a product. Deletion decisions are very difficult to make because of their potential impact on customers and the firm. For example, eliminating a product may force a company to lay off some employees. There are other factors to consider as well, such as keeping consumers supplied with replacement parts and repair service and maintaining the goodwill of distributors who have an inventory of the product. The deletion plan should also provide for clearing out of stock in question.

Product Improvement

One of the other important objectives of the audit is to ascertain whether to alter the product in some way or to leave things as they are. Altering the product means changing one or more of its attributes or marketing dimensions. *Attributes* refer mainly to product features, design, package, and so forth. *Marketing dimensions* refer to such things as price, promotion strategy, and channels of distribution.

It is possible to look at the product audit as a management device for controlling the product strategy. Here, control means feedback on product performance and corrective action in the form of product improvement. Product improvement is a top-level management decision, but the information needed to make the improvement decision may come from the consumer or the middlemen. Advertising agencies or consultants often make suggestions. Reports by the sales force should be structured in a way to provide management with certain types of product information; in fact, these reports can be the firm's most valuable product-improvement tool. Implementing a product improvement decision will often require the coordinated efforts of several specialists, plus some research. For example, product design improvement decisions involve engineering, manufacturing, accounting, and marketing. When a firm becomes aware that a product's design can be improved, it is not always clear how consumers will react to the various alterations. To illustrate, in blind taste tests, the Coca-Cola Company found that consumers overwhelmingly preferred the taste of a reformulated, sweeter new Coke over old Coke. However, when placed on the market in labeled containers, new Coke turned out to be a failure due to consumers' emotional attachments to the classic Coke. Consequently, it is advisable to conduct some market tests in realistic settings.

A discussion of product improvement would not be complete without taking into account the benefits associated with benchmarking, especially as they relate to the notion of the extended product, the tangible product along with the whole cluster of services that accompany it.[19] The formal definition of *benchmarking* is the continuous process of measuring products, services, and practices against those of the toughest competitors or companies renowned as leaders. In other words, benchmarking involves learning about best practices from best-performing companies—how they are achieving strong performance. It is an effective tool organizations use to improve on existing products, activities, functions, or processes. Major corporations such as IBM, AT&T, DuPont, Ford, Eastman Kodak, Miliken, Motorola, and Xerox all have numerous benchmarking studies in progress. Benchmarking can assist companies in many product improvement efforts, including (1) boosting product quality, (2) developing more user-friendly products, (3) improving customer order-processing activities, and (4) shortening delivery lead times. In the case of benchmarking, companies can achieve great success by copying others. Thus, by its very nature, benchmarking becomes an essential element in the ongoing product auditing process.

ORGANIZING FOR PRODUCT MANAGEMENT

Whether managing existing products or developing new products (the subject of the next chapter), organizations that are successful have one factor in common: They actively manage both types. Obviously, if a firm has only one product, it gets everyone's attention. But as the number of products grow and the need to develop new products becomes evident, some rational management system is necessary.

Under a *marketing-manager system,* one person is responsible for overseeing an entire product line with all of the functional areas of marketing such as research, advertising, sales promotion, sales, and product planning. This type of system is popular in organizations with a line or lines of similar products or one dominant product line. Sometimes referred to as category management, the marketing manager system is seen as being superior to a brand manager system because one manager oversees all brands within a particular line, thus avoiding brand competition. Organizations such as PepsiCo, Purex, Eastman Kodak, and Levi Strauss use some form of marketing-manager system.

Under a *brand-manager system,* a manager focuses on a single product or a very small group of new and existing products. Typically, this person is responsible for everything from marketing research and package design to advertising. Often called a product-management system, the brand-manager system has been criticized on several dimensions. First, brand managers often have difficulty because they do not have authority commensurate with their responsibilities. Second, they often pay inadequate attention to new products. Finally, they are often more concerned with their own brand's profitability than with the profitability of all of the organization's brands. These criticisms are not aimed at people but at the system itself, which may force brand managers into the above behaviors. Despite its drawbacks, organizations such as RJR Nabisco and Black & Decker have used this system.

Successful *new* products often come from organizations that try to bring all the capabilities of the organization to bear on the problems of customers. Obviously, this requires the cooperation of all the various functional departments in the organization (see Figure 6.4). Thus, the use of *cross-functional teams* has become an important way to manage the development of new products. A *venture team* is a popular method used in such organizations as Xerox, Polaroid, Exxon, IBM, Monsanto, and Motorola. A venture team is a cross-functional team responsible for all the tasks involved in the development of a new product. Once the new product is already launched, the team may turn over responsibility for managing the product to a brand manager or product manager or it may manage the new product as a separate business.

The use of cross-functional teams in product management and new product development is increasing for a very simple reason: Organizations need the contributions of all functions and therefore require their cooperation. Cross-functional teams operate

FIGURE 6.4

Some Requirements for the Effective Use of Cross-Functional Teams in Product Management and New Product Development

A growing number of organizations have begun using cross-functional teams for product management and new product development. Having representatives from various departments clearly has its advantages, but most important, effective teams must have the nurture and support of management. Some requirements for effective teams are

1. *Commitment of top management and provision of clear goals.* Organizations that successfully use cross-functional teams in product management or development have managers who are deeply committed to the team concept. As a result, high-performance teams have a clear understanding of the product management and development goals of the organization. The importance of these goals encourages individuals to defer their own functional or departmental concerns to team goals.

2. *Trust among members.* For cross-functional teams to work, a high level of trust must exist among members. The climate of trust within a team seems to be highly dependent on members' perception of management's trust of the group as a whole.

3. *Cross-functional cooperation.* If a team is to take responsibility and assume the risk of product development, its members will need detailed information about the overall operation of the organization. It often requires that functional units be willing to share information that previously was not shared with other departments.

4. *Time and training.* Effective cross-functional teams need time to mature. They require massive planning and intense and prompt access to resources, financial and other. Because members have to put aside functional and departmental loyalties and concerns, training is usually necessary.

independently of the organization's functional departments but include members from each function. A team might include a member from engineering, marketing, finance, service, and designers. Some organizations even include important outsiders (e.g., parts suppliers) on cross-functional teams. Figure 6.4 presents some important prerequisites for the use of cross-functional teams in managing existing products and developing new products.

SUMMARY

This chapter has been concerned with a central element of marketing management—product strategy. The first part of the chapter discussed some basic issues in product strategy, including product definition and classification, product quality and value, product mix and product lines, branding and brand equity, and packaging. The product life cycle was discussed as well as the product audit. Finally, three methods of organizing for product management were presented. Although product considerations are extremely important, remember that the product is only one element of the marketing mix. Focusing on product decisions alone, without consideration of the other marketing mix variables, would be an ineffective approach to marketing strategy.

Additional Resources

DeLuca, Luigi M., and Kwaku Atuahene. "Market Knowledge Dimensions and Cross Functional Collaboration: Examining the Different Routes to Product Innovation Performance." *Journal of Marketing,* January 2007, pp. 95–112.

Gladwell, Malcolm. *The Tipping Point.* NY: Book Bag Books, 2006.

Keough, Donald R. *The Ten Commandments of Business Failure.* NY: Portfolio Books, 2008.

Knapp, Duane. *The Brand Promise.* NY: McGraw-Hill, 2008.

Lindstrom, Martin. *Brand Sense: Build Powerful Brands Through Touch, Taste, Smell, Sight, and Sound.* NY: Free Press, 2005.

Pullig, Chris, Carolyn J. Simmons, and Richard G. Netemeyer. "Brand Dilution: When Do New Brands Hurt Existing Brands?" *Journal of Marketing,* April 2006, pp. 52–64.

Rust, Roland, Debra Viana Thompson, and Rebecca Thompson. "Defeating Feature Fatigue." *Harvard Business Review,* February 2006, pp. 98–109.

Key Terms and Concepts

Brand: A name, term, design, symbol, or any other feature that identifies one seller's good or service as distinct from those of other sellers. The legal term for brand is *trademark.*

Brand equity: The set of assets (or liabilities) linked to the brand that add (or subtract) value. The value of these assets is dependent upon the consequences or results of the marketplace's relationship with the brand.

Brand extension: A strategy that uses a current brand name to enter a completely different product class.

Brand-manager system: Type of product management system in which a manager focuses on a single product or a very small group of new and existing products. The brand manager is responsible for everything from marketing research and package design to advertising.

Cross-functional teams: Teams requiring the membership and cooperation of all the various functional departments in the organization to create successful new products.

Dual branding: A strategy in which two or more branded products are integrated. This strategy is sometimes called joint or cobranding.

Extended product: The tangible product along with the whole cluster of services that accompany it; one of the three ways a product can be viewed.

Fads: A product that experiences an intense but often very brief period of popularity. The faster it becomes popular, the faster it will become unpopular. A few fads may repeat their popularity after long absences.

Family branding: Sometimes called franchise extension; an organization's attachment of the corporate name to a product to enter either a new market segment or a different product class.

Fashions: Accepted and popular products that go through a repetitive cycle of popularity, lost popularity, and regained popularity, repeating the cycle again.

Generic product: Product that includes the essential benefits the buyer expects to receive; one of the three ways a product can be viewed.

Horizontal marketing: Market that exists for an organizational product when it is purchased by all types of firms in many different industries.

Marketing-manager system: Type of product management system popular in organizations with a line or lines of similar products or one dominant line. One person is responsible for overseeing an entire product line with all of the functional areas of marketing such as research, advertising, sales promotion, sales, and product planning.

Multibranding: A strategy that assigns different brand names to each product. The organization makes a conscious decision to allow the products to succeed or fail on their own merits.

Product: The sum of the physical, psychological, and sociological satisfactions the buyer derives from purchase, ownership, and consumption. This definition is consistent with the marketing concept.

Product adoption and diffusion: The spread of a product through the population; encompasses five stages of adopters: innovators, early adopters, early majority, late majority, and laggards.

Product life cycle: The concept that many products go through a cycle; that is, they are introduced, grow, mature, and decline. While the cycle varies according to industry, product, technology, and market, it is a valuable aid in developing product and marketing strategies.

Product line: A group of products that share common characteristics, distribution channels, customers, or uses.

Product line extension: A strategy of line extension that uses a well-known brand name to enter into a new market segment.

Product mix: The full set of products offered for sale by an organization; described by its width and depth.

Product mix depth: The average number of products in each product line.

Product mix width: The number of individual product lines offered by the organization.

Quality: The degree of excellence or superiority that an organization's product or service possesses. It can encompass both the tangible and intangible aspects of a product or service. Although quality can be evaluated from many perspectives, the customer's perception of quality is crucial.

Tangible product: The physical entity or service that is offered to the buyer; one of the three ways a product can be viewed.

Value: Encompasses not only quality but also price. Value is what the customer gets for what the customer gives.

Venture team: A cross-functional team responsible for all of the tasks involved in the development of a new product. When the new product is launched, the team usually turns over responsibility for managing the product to a brand manager or product manager or it may manage the new product as a separate business.

Vertical market: Market for organizational products that have a limited number of buyers. A vertical market is narrow because customers are restricted to a few industries and is deep in that a large percentage of the producers in the market use the product.

Chapter 7

New Product Planning and Development

New products are a vital part of a firm's competitive growth strategy. Leaders of successful firms know that it is not enough to develop new products on a sporadic basis. What counts is a climate of product development that leads to one triumph after another. It is commonplace for major companies to have 50 percent or more of their current sales in products introduced within the last 10 years.[1]

Some additional facts about new products are important to remember:

- Many new products are failures. Estimates of new product failures range from 33 percent to 90 percent, depending on industry.
- New product sales grow far more rapidly than sales of current products, potentially providing a surprisingly large boost to a company's growth rate.
- Companies vary widely in the effectiveness of their new product programs.
- A major obstacle to effectively predicting new product demand is limited vision.
- Common elements appear in the management practices that generally distinguish the relative degree of efficiency and success between companies.

In one recent year, almost 22,000 products were introduced in supermarkets, drugstores, mass merchandisers, and health food stores.[2] Of these, only a small percentage (less than 20 percent) met sales goals. The cost of introducing a new brand in some consumer markets can range from $50 million to hundreds of millions of dollars. In addition to the outlay cost of product failures, there are also opportunity costs. These opportunity costs refer not only to the alternative uses of funds spent on product failures but also to the time spent in unprofitable product development.

Product development can take many years. For example, Hills Brothers (now owned by Nestlé) spent 22 years in developing its instant coffee, while it took General Foods (now owned by Altria) 10 years to develop Maxim. However, the success of one new product is no guarantee that additional low-cost brand extensions will be successful. For example, on the positive side, Gillette was able to leverage the research and monies spent on the original Sensor to successfully develop and launch the Sensor razor for women and the Sensor Excel razor. On the negative side, Maxwell House (Altria), Folgers (Procter & Gamble), and Nestlé are still struggling to develop commercially successful lines of fresh whole bean coffee, having been beaten to the punch by smaller companies such as Starbucks, Millstone Coffee, Inc., and Brothers Gourmet Coffees.[3]

Good management, with heavy emphasis on planning, organization, and interaction among the various functional units (e.g., marketing, manufacturing, engineering, R&D), seems to be the key factor contributing to a firm's success in launching new products. The primary reason found for new product failure is an inability on the part of the selling company to match its offerings to the needs of the customer. This inability to satisfy customer needs can be attributed to three main sources: inadequacy of upfront intelligence efforts, failure on the part of the company to stick close to what the company does best, and the inability to provide better value than competing products and technologies.

NEW PRODUCT STRATEGY

When developing new products, the first question must be, In how many ways can a product be new? Authors C. Merle Crawford and Anthony DiBenedetto have developed a useful definition of new products based on the following categories.[4]

1. *New-to-the-world products.* Products that are inventions and create a whole new market. For example, Sony Walkman, Polaroid camera, the Palm Pilot, the laser printer, in-line skates.
2. *New-to-the-firm products.* Products that take the firm into a category new to it but not to the world. Examples are Canon's laser printer, AT&T's Universal Credit Card, Hallmark gift items, P&G's first shampoo.
3. *Additions to existing product lines.* These are products that extend existing product lines to current markets such as Bud Light, Apple's iMac, and Tide's liquid detergent.
4. *Improvements and revisions of existing products.* These are current products that are made better. Virtually every product on the market has been improved, often many times.
5. *Repositionings.* Products that are retargeted for a new use or application. Arm & Hammer baking soda is a classic example, being repositioned as a drain deodorizer, refrigerator freshener, toothpaste, deodorant, and so on. Aspirin has been repositioned as a safeguard against heart attacks.
6. *Cost reductions.* These are new products that simply replace existing products in a line, providing the customer similar performance but at a lower cost.

The new product categories listed above raise the issue of imitation products, strictly me-too or improved versions of existing products. If a firm introduces a form of dry beer that is new to them but is identical or similar to other beers on the market, is it a new product? The answer is yes, because it is new to the firm. Managers should not get the idea that to imitate is bad and to innovate is good, for most of the best-selling products on the market today are improvements over another company's original invention. The best strategy is the one that will maximize company goals. It should be noted that Crawford and DiBenedetto's categories don't encompass variations such as new to a country, new channel of distribution, packaging improvement, and different resources or method of manufacture, which they consider to be variations of the six categories, especially as these variations relate to additions to product lines.

A second broader approach to the new product question is the one developed by H. Igor Ansoff in the form of growth vectors.[5] This is the matrix first introduced in Chapter 1 that indicates the direction in which the organization is moving with respect to its current products and markets. It is shown again in Figure 7.1.

Market penetration denotes a growth direction through the increase in market share for present product markets. *Product development* refers to creating new products to replace existing ones. Firms using either market penetration or product development strategies are attempting to capitalize on existing markets and combat competitive entry and/or further market incursions. *Market development* refers to finding new customers for existing

FIGURE 7.1
Organizational
Growth Strategies

Products Markets	Present	New
Present	Market penetration	Product development
New	Market development	Diversification

products. *Diversification* refers to developing new products and cultivating new markets. Firms using market development and diversification strategies are seeking to establish footholds in new markets or preempt competition in emerging market segments.

As shown in Figure 7.1, market penetration and market development strategies use present products. A goal of these types of strategies is to either increase frequency of consumption or increase the number of customers using the firm's product(s). A strategic focus is placed on altering the breadth and depth of the firm's existing product lines. Product development and diversification can be characterized as product mix strategies. New products, as defined in the growth vector matrix, usually require the firm to make significant investments in research and development and may require major changes in its organizational structure. Firms are not confined to pursuing a single direction. For example, Miller Brewing Co. has decided four key strategies should dictate its activities for the next decade, including (1) building its premium-brand franchises through investment spending, (2) continuing to develop value-added new products with clear consumer benefits, (3) leveraging local markets to build its brand franchise, and (4) building business globally.[6] Success for Miller depends on pursuing strategies that encompass all areas of the growth vector matrix.

It has already been stated that new products are the lifeblood of successful business firms. Thus, the critical product policy question is not whether to develop new products but in what direction to move. One way of dealing with this problem is to formulate standards or norms that new products must meet if they are to be considered candidates for launching. In other words, as part of its new product policy, management must ask itself the basic question, What is the potential contribution of each anticipated new product to the company?

Each company must answer this question in accordance with its long-term goals, corporate mission, resources, and so forth. Unfortunately, some of the reasons commonly given to justify the launching of new products are so general that they become meaningless. Phrases such as *additional profits, increased growth,* or *cyclical stability* must be translated into more specific objectives. For example, one objective may be to reduce manufacturing overhead costs by using plant capacity better. This may be accomplished by using the new product as an off-season filler. Naturally, the new product proposal would also have to include production and accounting data to back up this cost argument.

In every new product proposal some attention must be given to the ultimate economic contribution of each new product candidate. If the argument is that a certain type of product is needed to keep up with competition or to establish leadership in the market, it is fair to ask, Why? To put the question another way, top management can ask: What will be the effect on the firm's long-run profit picture if we do not develop and launch this or that new product? Policy-making criteria on new products should specify (1) a working definition of the profit concept acceptable to top management, (2) a minimum level or floor of profits, (3) the availability and cost of capital to develop a new product, and (4) a specified time period in which the new product must recoup its operating costs and begin contributing to profits.

It is critical that firms not become solely preoccupied with a short-term focus on earnings associated with new products. For example, in some industrial markets, a 20-year

1. A superior differentiated product that is unique by virtue of features, benefits, quality, and value.
2. A market-driven and customer focused new product development process.
3. Predevelopment work prior to beginning the development process.
4. Clear and early product definition.
5. Appropriate internal organizational structure.
6. A product that is familiar to the company's current products and markets.
7. A new product development process that uses profiles of previous product successes.
8. Controls on the new product development process that ensure sound execution.
9. Sound execution rather than speed.
10. Support for the new product through friendly, courteous, prompt, and efficient customer service.

Source: Based on Robert G. Cooper, "What Distinguishes the Top Performing New Products in Financial Services," *Journal of Product Innovation Management,* September 1994, pp. 281–99; and "The New Product System: The Industry Experience," *Journal of Product Innovation Management,* June 1992, pp. 113–27; and William O. Beardon, Thomas N. Ingram, and Raymond W. LaForge, *Marketing: Principles and Perspectives,* 5th ed. (Burr Ridge, IL: McGraw-Hill/Irwin, 2007), p. 219.

spread has been found between the development and wide-spread adoption of products, on average. Indeed, an advantage that some Japanese firms appear to possess is that their management is free from the pressure of steady improvement in earnings per share that plagues American managers who emphasize short-term profits. Japanese managers believe that market share will lead to customer loyalty, which in turn will lead to profits generated from repeat purchases. Through a continual introduction of new products, firms will succeed in building share. This share growth will then ultimately result in earnings growth and profitability that the stock market will support through higher share prices over the long term.

NEW PRODUCT PLANNING AND DEVELOPMENT PROCESS

Ideally, products that generate a maximum dollar profit with a minimum amount of risk should be developed and marketed. However, it is very difficult for planners to implement this idea because of the number and nature of the variables involved. What is needed is a systematic, formalized process for new product planning. Although such a process does not provide management with any magic answers, it can increase the probability of new product success. Initially, the firm must establish some new product policy guidelines that include the product fields of primary interest, organizational responsibilities for managing the various stages in new product development, and criteria for making go-ahead decisions. After these guidelines are established, a process such as the one shown in Figure 7.2 should be useful in new product development.

Idea Generation

Every product starts as an idea. But all new product ideas do not have equal merit or potential for economic or commercial success. Some estimates indicate that as many as 60 or 70 ideas are necessary to yield one successful product. This is an average figure, but it serves to illustrate that new product ideas have a high mortality rate. In terms of money, almost three-fourths of all the dollars of new product expense go to unsuccessful products.

FIGURE 7.2
The New Product
Development Process

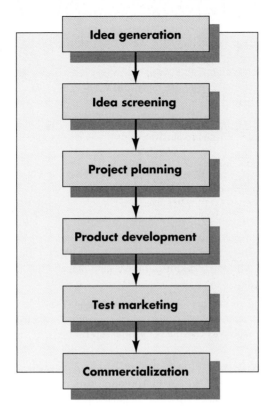

The problem at this stage is to ensure that all new product ideas available to the company at least have a chance to be heard and evaluated. Ideas are the raw materials for product development, and the whole planning process depends on the quality of the idea generation and screening process. Since idea generation is the least costly stage in the new product development process (in terms of investment in funds, time, personnel, and escalation of commitment), it makes sense that an emphasis be placed first on recognizing available sources of new product ideas and then on funneling these ideas to appropriate decision makers for screening.

Top-management support is critical to providing an atmosphere that stimulates new product activity. Many times, great ideas come from some very unusual sources. A top-management structure that is unwilling to take risks will avoid radical new product and other innovation activities and instead concentrate solely on minor areas of improvement such as line extensions. To facilitate top-management support, it is essential that new product development be focused on meeting market needs.

Both technology push and market pull research activities play an important role in new product ideas and development. By taking a broad view of customer needs and wants, basic and applied research (technology push) can lead to ideas that will yield high profits to the firm. For example, Compaq bet millions (and won) on PC network servers in the early 1990s even though business customers said they would never abandon their mainframes. In a similar vein, Chrysler forged ahead with the original minivan despite research showing people disliked the odd-looking vehicle.[7] Marketing, on the other hand, is more responsible for gathering and disseminating information gained from customers and other contacts. This information relates mainly to specific features and functions of the product that can be improved upon or market needs that current products are not satisfying (market pull). For example, product ideas at Rubbermaid often come from employees roaming the aisles at

Marissa Mayer joined Google in early 1999 as a programmer when the workforce totaled 20. By 2007 Google had 5,700 employees and expected sales of $16 billion.

As Director of Consumer Web Products Marissa is a champion of innovation, and she favors new product launches that are early and often.

HOW GOOGLE INNOVATES

The search leader has earned a reputation as one of the most innovative companies in the world of technology. These are illustrative of the ways Google hatches new ideas:

FREE (THINKING) TIME

Google gives all engineers one day a week to develop their own pet projects, no matter how far these projects are from the company's central mission. If work gets in the way of free days for a few weeks, they accumulate. Google News came out of this process.

THE IDEA LIST

Anyone at Google can post thoughts for new technologies of businesses on an ideas mailing list, available companywide for input and vetting. But beware: Newbies who suggest familiar or poorly thought-out ideas can face an intellectual pummeling.

OPEN OFFICE HOURS

Think back to your professors' office hours in college. That's pretty much what key managers, including Mayer, do two or three times a week, to discuss new ideas. One success born of this approach was Google's personalized home page.

BIG BRAINSTORMS

As it has grown, Google has cut back on brainstorming sessions. Mayer still holds them eight times a year, but limits hers to 100 engineers. Six concepts are pitched and discussed for ten minutes each. The goal: To build on the initial idea with at least one complementary idea per minute.

ACQUIRE GOOD IDEAS

Although Google strongly prefers to develop technology in-house, it has also been willing to snap up small companies with interesting initiatives. In 2004 it bought Keyhole, including the technology that let Google offer sophisticated maps with satellite imagery.

Source: "Managing Googles's Idea Factory," *Business Week,* October 3, 2005, pp. 88–90. David Cravens and Nigel F. Piercy, *Strategic Marketing,* 9th ed. (Burr Ridge, IL: McGraw-Hill/Irwin, 2009), p. 240.

hardware stores and conversations with family and friends.[8] Both technology push and market pull approaches are essential to the generation of new product ideas.

Some firms use mechanisms such as "out-rotation," outsider involvement, and rewards to foster cooperation between design engineers and marketers.[9] Out-rotation involves placing employees in positions that require direct contact with customers, competitors, and other key outside groups. For example, Hewlett-Packard regularly rotates design engineers to retail sales positions on a temporary basis. Other organizations actively involve "outsiders" in planning or reward engineers for making external customer contacts. Regardless of the method used, the primary lesson is to keep the communications flow going in all directions throughout the organization.

Idea Screening

The primary function of the idea screening process is twofold: first, to eliminate ideas for new products that could not be profitably marketed by the firm, and second, to expand viable ideas into full product concepts. New product ideas may be eliminated either because they are outside the fields of the firm's interest or because the firm does not have the necessary resources or technology to produce the product at a profit. Generally speaking, the organization has to consider three categories of risk (and its associated risk tolerance) in the idea screening phase prior to reaching a decision:[10]

1. *Strategic risk.* Strategic risk involves the risk of not matching the role or purpose of a new product with a specific strategic need or issue of the organization. If an organization feels it necessary to develop certain types of radical innovations or products new to the company in order to carry out long-term strategies, then management must be willing to dedicate necessary resources and time to pursue these type projects.

2. *Market risk.* Market risk is the risk that a new product won't meet a market need in a value-added, differentiated way. As products are being developed, customer requirements change and new technologies evolve. Management must be willing and able to shift its new product efforts to keep pace with change.

3. *Internal risk.* Internal risk is the risk that a new product won't be developed within the desired time and budget. Up front, management must decide the level of commitment it will extend in terms of time and budgetary expenditures to adequately ensure the completion of specific projects. Concurrently, progress goals must be established so that "proceed" or "do not proceed" decisions can be reached regarding continuation of projects.

In evaluating these risks, firms should not act too hastily in discounting new product ideas solely because of a lack of resources or expertise. Instead, firms should consider forming joint or strategic alliances with other firms. A strategic alliance is a long-term partnership between two organizations designed to accomplish the strategic goals of both parties. Potential benefits to be gained from alliances include (1) increased access to technology, funding, and information; (2) market expansion and greater penetration of current markets; and (3) de-escalated competitive rivalries. Motorola is a company that has prospered by forming numerous joint ventures with both American and foreign companies.[11]

Ideas that appear to have adequate profit potential and offer the firm a competitive advantage in the market should be accepted for further study.

Project Planning

This stage of the process involves several steps. It is here that the new product proposal is evaluated further and responsibility for the project is assigned to a project team. The proposal is analyzed in terms of production, marketing, financial, and competitive factors. A development budget is established, and some preliminary marketing and technical research is undertaken. The product is actually designed in a rough form. Alternative product features and component specifications are outlined. Finally, a project plan is written up, which includes estimates of future development, production, and marketing costs along with capital requirements and manpower needs. A schedule or timetable is also included. Finally, the project proposal is given to top management for a go or no-go decision.

Various alternatives exist for creating and managing the project teams. Two of the better-known methods are the establishment of a *skunkworks,* whereby a project team can work in relative privacy away from the rest of the organization, and a *rugby* or *relay approach,* whereby groups in different areas of the company are simultaneously working on the project.[12] The common tie that binds these and other successful approaches together is the degree of interaction that develops among the marketing, engineering, production, and other critical staff. The earlier in the process that interactive, cooperative efforts begin, the higher is the likelihood that development efforts will be successful. A key component contributing to the success of many companies' product development efforts relates to the emphasis placed on creating *cross-functional teams* early in the development process. Both of the above methods use cross-functional teams. Members from many different departments come together to jointly establish new product development goals and priorities and to develop

1. Customers
   a. Customer requests
   b. Customer complaints/compliments
   c. Market surveys
   d. Focus groups
2. Competitors
   a. Monitoring competitors' developments
   b. Monitoring testing of competitors' products
   c. Monitoring industry movements
3. Distribution channels
   a. Suppliers
   b. Distributors
   c. Retailers
   d. Trade shows
4. Research and engineering
   a. Product testing
   b. Product endorsement
   c. Brainstorming meetings
   d. Accidental discovery
5. Other internal sources
   a. Management
   b. Sales force
   c. Employee suggestions
   d. Innovation group meetings
   e. Stockholders
6. Other external sources
   a. Consultants
   b. Academic journals
   c. Periodicals and other press

new product development schedules. Frequently, marketing and/or sales personnel are called in to lead these teams.[13]

Product Development

At this juncture, the product idea has been evaluated from the standpoint of engineering, manufacturing, finance, and marketing. If it has met all expectations, it is considered a candidate for further research and testing. In the laboratory, the product is converted into a finished good and tested. A development report to management is prepared that spells out in fine detail: (1) results of the studies by the engineering department, (2) required plan design, (3) production facilities design, (4) tooling requirements, (5) marketing test plan, (6) financial program survey, and (7) estimated release date.[14]

Test Marketing

Up until now the product has been a company secret. Now management goes outside the company and submits the product candidate for customer approval. Test-market programs are conducted in line with the general plans for launching the product. Test marketing is a controlled experiment in a limited geographical area to test the new product or in some cases certain aspects of the marketing strategy, such as packaging or advertising.

The main goal of a test market is to evaluate and adjust, as necessary, the general marketing strategy to be used and the appropriate marketing mix. Additionally, producers can use the early interaction with buyers, occurring in test markets, to begin exploration of issues related to the next generation of product development.[15] Especially in cases where new technologies and markets are emerging, firms can benefit greatly from knowledge gained in test markets. Throughout the test market process, findings are being analyzed and forecasts of volume developed. In summary, a well-done test market procedure can reduce the risks that include not only lost marketing and sales dollars but also capital—the expense of installing production lines or building a new factory. Upon completion of a successful test market phase, the marketing plan can be finalized and the product prepared for launch.

Participant*	Activity	Participant*	Activity
1. Project Manager	Leader Integrator Translator Mediator Judge Arbitrator Coordinator	4. Strategist	Longer range Managerial Entire program
2. Product champion	Supporter Spokesperson Pusher Won't concede	5. Inventor	Creative scientist Basement inventor Idea source
3. Sponsor	Senior manager Supporter Endorses Assures hearing Mentor Increases output	6. Rationalist 7. Facilitator	Objectivity Reality Reason Financial Boosts productivity

*The participant role may be either formal or informal.

Source: Merle Crawford and Anthony DiBenedetto, *New Products Management,* 10th ed. (Burr Ridge, IL: McGraw-Hill/Irwin, 2011), p. 348.

Commercialization

This is the launching step in which the firm commits to introducing the product into the marketplace. During this stage, heavy emphasis is placed on the organization structure and management talent needed to implement the marketing strategy. Emphasis is also given to following up on such things as bugs in the design, production costs, quality control, and inventory requirements. Procedures and responsibility for evaluating the success of the new product by comparison with projections are also finalized.

The Importance of Time

Over the course of the last five years, companies have placed an increasing emphasis on shortening their products' time to market. *Time to market* can be defined as the elapsed time between product definition and product availability. It has been well documented that companies that are first in bringing their products to market enjoy a competitive advantage both in terms of profits and market share.[16] Successful time-based innovations can be attributed to the use of short production runs, whereby products can be improved on an incremental basis, and the use of cross-functional teams, decentralized work scheduling and monitoring, and a responsive system for gathering and analyzing customer feedback.

Several U.S. companies, including Procter & Gamble, have taken steps to speed up the new product development cycle by giving managers, at the product class and brand family level, more decision-making power. Increasingly, companies are bypassing time-consuming regional test markets, when feasible, in favor of national launches. It is becoming important, more than ever, that firms do a successful job of developing new products right the first time. To accomplish this, companies must have the right people with the right skills and talents in key positions within the new product framework.

Customer Acceptance Measures	Product Level Performance
Customer acceptance (use)	Product cost
Customer satisfaction	Time to launch
Revenue (dollar sales)	Product performance
Market share	Quality guidelines
Unit volume	
Financial Performance	**Other**
Time to break even	Nonfinancial measures peculiar to the
Margins	new product being launched.
Profitability (IRR, ROI)	Example: competitive effect, image
	change, morale change.

Source: Merle Crawford and Anthony DiBenedetto, *New Products Management,* 10th ed. (Burr Ridge, IL: McGraw-Hill/Irwin, 2011), p. 375.

SOME IMPORTANT NEW PRODUCT DECISIONS

In the development of new products, marketers have several important decisions to make about the characteristics of the product itself. These include quality level, product features, product design, and product safety levels.

Quality Level

Both consumers and organizational buyers consider the level of product quality when making purchase decisions for both new and existing products. At a minimum, buyers want products that will perform the functions they are supposed to and do so reasonably well. Some customers are willing to accept lower quality if product use is not demanding and the price is lower. Some homeowners might prefer Sears brand hand tools over the higher-quality Craftsman brand since they are lower priced and may be used only occasionally. Industrial buyers of nuts and bolts for automobiles seldom use the highest quality used in aircraft since cars are used in less demanding situations.

In designing new products, marketers must consider what criteria potential customers use to determine their perceptions of quality. While these will vary by product, Figure 7.3 presents eight general criteria.

FIGURE 7.3
Some Criteria for Determining Perceptions of Quality

Source: Adopted from David A. Garvin, "Competing on the Eight Dimensions of Quality," *Harvard Business Review,* November–December 1987. For a discussion of some determinants of quality for service businesses, see chapter 12, "The Marketing of Services."

1. *Performance*—How well does the product do what it is supposed to do?
2. *Features*—Does the product have any unique features that are desirable?
3. *Reliability*—Is the product likely to function well and not break down over a reasonable time period?
4. *Conformance*—Does the product conform to established standards for such things as safety?
5. *Durability*—How long will the product last before it will be worn out and have to be replaced?
6. *Serviceability*—How quickly and easily can any problems be corrected?
7. *Aesthetics*—How appealing is the product to the appropriate senses of sight, taste, smell, feel, and/or sound?
8. *Overall Evaluation*—Considering everything about the product, including its physical characteristics, manufacturer, brand image, packaging, and price, how good is this product?

When specialized knowledge is needed to satisfy the needs of customers, cross-functional teams can greatly improve product development success. Such teams bring together complementary skills in one of three areas: technical or functional expertise, problem-solving and decision-making skills, and interpersonal skills.

1. *Technical or functional skills.* It would make little sense for a marketer to design technical specifications for a new type of cellular phone. Likewise, it would make little sense for an engineer to try to guess what features consumers find most important in choosing what type of phone to purchase. In this case, a product development group that consists solely of marketers or engineers would be less likely to succeed than a cross-functional team using the complementary skills of both.

2. *Problem-solving and decision-making skills.* Cross-functional teams possess the ability to identify problems and opportunities the entire organization faces, identify feasible new product alternatives, and make the necessary choices quicker. Most industrial functional units are not able to perform all of these tasks effectively. However, it is likely that the necessary skills are present in a well-chosen cross-functional team and that these skills can be used in the organization's best interests.

3. *Interpersonal skills.* Common understanding and knowledge of problems faced and decisions needed for effective product development cannot arise without effective communication and constructive conflict. What is needed is risk-taking, helpful criticism, objectivity, active listening, support, and recognition of the interests and achievements of others. An effective, cross-functional team is made up of members who, in total, possess all of these skills. Individual members, at various times, will be called on to use their interpersonal skill to move the team forward. The use of the complementary interpersonal skills of team members can lead to extraordinary results for organizations.

An important indicator of a number of the criteria listed in Figure 7.3 is the presence and extent of a new product *warranty*. A warranty is the producer's statement of what it will do to compensate the buyer if the product is defective or does not work properly. In many instances, the courts also hold that businesses have implied warranties or unstated promises to compensate buyers if their products fail to perform up to the basic standards of the industry or to the level promised. Certainly an organization that wants to emphasize high quality will offer customers more than implied warranties enforced by the courts.

Finally, many marketers offer a guarantee instead of or in addition to a warranty on new products. A *guarantee* is an assurance that the product is as represented and will perform properly. Typically if the product fails to perform, the organization making the guarantee replaces the product or refunds the customer's money. Guarantees imply to some buyers that the manufacturer is confident of the new products' quality.

Product Features

A *product feature* is a fact or particular specification about a product (e.g., "less calories than all other soft drinks," "more vitamin C than any other multiple vitamin"). Marketers select new product features by determining what it is that customers want their products to offer. Effective marketers attempt not only to ask potential customers what they want, but to learn what these customers are likely to need. Such marketers may identify a need for new features that target markets have not yet thought of and may not yet even understand.

Product Design

Many well-designed products are easy to use as intended and pleasing to the senses. Designing new products with both ease of use and aesthetic appeal can be difficult, but it can clearly differentiate a new product from competitors. Good design can add great value to a new product. A well-designed product can please customers without necessarily costing more to make. This is especially likely to happen when the organization uses cross-functional teams to develop its products. If employees from engineering, marketing, and manufacturing work together on what the product will look like and how it will operate, they are more likely to create a design that is easy and economical to make as well as use.

Product Safety

Clearly, new products must have a reasonable level of safety. Safety is both an ethical and practical issue. Ethically, customers should not be harmed by using a product as intended. The practical issue is that when users get harmed by a product, they may stop buying, tell others about their experience, or sue the company that made or sold it.

Some products are inherently dangerous and can result in injury to users. However, it may be so expensive to make them safer that buyers could not afford to buy them. Such products include automobiles, farm equipment and other machinery, and guns. Other products such as patented medicines can harm a small portion of users. Hopefully, the benefits such products offer outweigh their risks.

CAUSES OF NEW PRODUCT FAILURE

Many new products with satisfactory potential have failed to make the grade for reasons related to execution and control problems. What follows is a brief list of some of the more important marketing causes of new product failures after the products have been carefully screened, developed, and marketed.[17]

1. No competitive point of difference, unexpected reactions from competitors, or both.
2. Poor positioning.
3. Poor quality of product.
4. Nondelivery of promised benefits of product.
5. Too little marketing support.
6. Poor perceived price/quality (value) relationship.
7. Faulty estimates of market potential and other marketing research mistakes.
8. Faulty estimates of production and marketing costs.
9. Improper channels of distribution selected.
10. Rapid change in the market (economy) after the product was introduced.

Some of these problems are beyond the control of management, but it is clear that successful new product planning requires large amounts of reliable information in diverse areas. Each department assigned functional responsibility for product development automatically becomes an input to the information system that the new product decision maker needs. For example, when a firm is developing a new product, it is wise for both engineers and marketers to consider both the kind of market to be entered (e.g., consumer, organizational, international) and specific target segments. These decisions will be of paramount influence on the design and cost of the finished good, which will, of course, directly influence price, sales, and profits.

1. *Not listening* to the "voice of the customer." Product managers assume they know more than customers or that doing marketing research will not be worth the cost or time.
2. *Skipping steps* in the new product process. (See Figure 7-2.)
3. *Trying to generate* quick revenue by releasing a poorly conceived product to market.
4. *"Groupthink"* in product development committees. This popular problem occurs in groups when members "go along" to "get along" rather than be seen as nay sayers or non-team players.
5. *Not identifying* the lessons from previous failures.

Sources: Adapted from Pierre Loewe and Jennifer Domeniquini, "Overcoming the Barriers to Effective Innovation," *Strategy and Leadership* 34, no. 1 (2006), pp. 24–31; Dan P. Lovallo and Oliver Sibony, "Distortions and Deceptions in Strategic Decisions," *The McKinsey Quarterly,* no. 1 (2006), pp. 19–29; Eyal Biyalogorsky, William Boulding, and Richard Staelin, "Stuck in The Past: Why Managers Persist with New Product Failures," *Journal of Marketing,* April 2006, pp. 108–21; Jena MacGregor, "How Failure Breeds Success," *Business Week,* July 10, 2006, pp. 42–52; and Roger A. Kerin, Steven W. Hartley, and William Rudelius, *Marketing,* 10th ed. (Burr Ridge, IL: McGraw-Hill/Irwin, 2011), pp. 254–55.

Need for Research

In many respects it can be argued that the keystone activity of any new product planning system is research—not just marketing research, but technical research as well. Regardless of the way the new product planning function is organized in the company, top management's new product development decisions require data that provide a base for making more intelligent choices. New product project reports ought to be more than a collection of "expert" opinions. Top management has a responsibility to ask certain questions, and the new product planning team has an obligation to generate answers to these questions based on research that provides marketing, economic, engineering, and production information. This need will be more clearly understood if some of the specific questions commonly raised in evaluating product ideas are examined:

1. What is the anticipated market demand over time? Are the potential applications for the product restricted?
2. Can the item be patented? Are there any antitrust problems?
3. Can the product be sold through present channels and the current sales force? What number of new salespersons will be needed? What additional sales training will be required?
4. At different volume levels, what will be the unit manufacturing costs?
5. What is the most appropriate package to use in terms of color, material, design, and so forth?
6. What is the estimated return on investment?
7. What is the appropriate pricing strategy?

While this list is not intended to be exhaustive, it serves to illustrate the serious need for reliable information. Note also that some of the essential facts required to answer these questions can be obtained only through time-consuming and expensive marketing research studies. Other data can be generated in the engineering laboratories or pulled from accounting records. Certain types of information must be based on assumptions, which may or may not hold true, and on expectations about what will happen in the future, as in the case of anticipated competitive reaction or the projected level of sales.

SUMMARY

This chapter has focused on the nature of new product planning and development. Attention has been given to the management process required to have an effective program for new product development. It should be obvious that this is one of the most important and difficult aspects of marketing management. The problem is so complex that, unless management develops a plan for dealing with the problem, it is likely to operate at a severe competitive disadvantage in the marketplace.

Additional Resources

Bender, Michael. *A Manager's Guide to Project Management.* Upper Saddle River, NJ: FT Press, 2010.

Biyalogorsky, Eyal, William Boulding, and Richard Staelin. "Stuck In The Past: Why Managers Persist in New Product Failures." *Journal of Marketing,* April 2006, pp. 108–122.

Estrin, Judy. *Closing The Innovation Gap.* NY: McGraw-Hill, 2009.

Macintosh, Julie. *Dethroning the King.* NY: John Wiley and Sons, 2011.

Mack, Ben. *Think Two Products Ahead.* NY: John Wiley, 2007.

Moeller, Leslie H., and Edward Landry. *The Four Pillars of Profit Driven Marketing.* NY: McGraw-Hill, 2009.

Key Terms and Concepts

Commercialization: Stage of the new product development process that involves the actual launch of the product and the implementation of the marketing strategy.

Cross-functional teams: Members from many different departments coming together to jointly establish new product development goals and priorities and to develop schedules.

Diversification: A strategy that seeks to develop new products and cultivate new customers. It often leads the organization into new businesses, sometimes through acquisition.

Guarantee: An assurance by the producer that the product is as represented and will perform properly. If not, the organization making the guarantee replaces the product or refunds the customer's money.

Idea generation: Stage of the new product development process at which the goal is to ensure that all new product ideas considered by the organization have the opportunity to be heard and evaluated because the success of the process will depend greatly on the quality of the ideas generated.

Idea screening: Evaluation of an idea based on strategic risk, market risk, and internal risk for the purpose of eliminating ideas that could not be profitably marketed and expanding viable ideas into full product concepts.

Market development: A strategy that seeks to find new customers for existing products. An organization pursuing this strategy seeks to establish footholds in new markets or preempt competition in emerging market segments.

Market penetration: A strategy that denotes a growth direction through the increase in market share of present products in present markets. An organization pursuing this strategy hopes to capitalize on existing markets and combat competitive entry or incursions.

New product development process: Stages include idea generation, idea screening, project planning, product development, test marketing, commercialization.

Product development: A strategy that seeks to create new products to replace existing ones. An organization pursuing this strategy hopes to capitalize on existing markets and combat competitive entry or incursions.

Product development stage: Stage of the new product development process at which the product idea has met all expectations and is considered a candidate for further research and testing. In the laboratory, the product is converted into a finished good and tested.

Project planning: Stage of the new product development process at which the idea is evaluated further and responsibility for the project is assigned to a project team. The idea is evaluated in terms of production, marketing, financial, and competitive factors. A development budget is established, and preliminary marketing and technical research is undertaken.

Rugby or relay: An approach to creating and managing product development teams that involves groups in different areas of the organization working simultaneously on the project.

Skunkworks: An approach to creating and managing product development teams that involves team members working in relative privacy, away from the rest of the organization.

Test marketing: Stage of new product development process at which the product is no longer a company secret. Test marketing is a controlled experiment in a limited geographical area to test the new product as well as elements of the marketing mix.

Time to market: The elapsed time between product definition and product availability. It is important because history has shown that organizations that are first in bringing their product to market often gain a competitive advantage in terms of profits and market share.

Warranty: The statement of the producer of what it will do to compensate the buyer if the product is defective or does not perform properly.

8

Integrated Marketing Communications

Communicating with customers will be the broad subject of the next two chapters that focus on various elements of promotion. To simplify our discussion, the topic has been divided into two basic categories: nonpersonal communication (Chapter 8) and personal communication (Chapter 9). This chapter also discusses the necessity to integrate the various elements of marketing communication.

STRATEGIC GOALS OF MARKETING COMMUNICATION

Marketers seek to communicate with target customers for the obvious goal of increased sales and profits. Accordingly, they seek to accomplish several strategic goals with their marketing communications efforts.

Create Awareness

Obviously, we cannot purchase a product if we are not aware of it. An important strategic goal must be to generate awareness of the firm as well as its products. Marketing communications designed to create awareness are especially important for new products and brands in order to stimulate trial purchases. As an organization expands globally, creating awareness must be a critical goal of marketing communications.

Build Positive Images

When products or brands have distinct images in the minds of customers, the customers better understand the value that is being offered. Positive images can even create value for customers by adding meaning to products. Retail stores and other organizations also use communications to build positive images. A major way marketers create positive and distinct images is through marketing communications.

Identify Prospects

Identifying prospects is becoming an increasingly important goal of marketing communications because modern technology makes information gathering much more practical, even in large consumer markets. Marketers can maintain records of consumers who have

France 26.1 million visitors		Germany 32.6 million visitors		Japan 53.8 million visitors	
1. Google sites	18.2	Google sites	23.0	Yahoo sites	40.7
2. Microsoft sites	16.4	Microsoft sites	17.7	Google sites	32.0
3. France Telecom	14.0	eBay	17.4	Microsoft sites	30.0
4. Illaid/Free.fr	12.9	United-Internet sites	16.2	Rakuten Inc.	28.5
5. Grope Pages Jaunes	11.4	Time Warner Network	14.6	NTT group	24.6
6. eBay	11.4	Wikipedia sites	12.6	FC2 Inc.	24.1
7. Yahoo sites	10.9	T-Online sites	12.1	Nifty Corp.	22.0
8. Skyrock Network	9.5	Yahoo sites	11.2	Wikipedia sites	20.6
9. Groupe PPR	8.9	Otto Grupe	11.1	Livedoor	19.7
10. Wikipedia sites	8.5	Karstadt-Quelle	10.1	Amazon sites	18.4

Source: Philip R. Cateora, Mary C. Gilly, and John I. Graham, *International Marketing,* 15th ed. (Burr Ridge, IL: McGraw-Hill/Irwin, 2011), p. 484.

expressed an interest in a product, then more efficiently direct future communications. Technology now enables marketers to stay very close to their customers. Web sites are used to gather information about prospects, and supermarkets use point-of-sale terminals to dispense coupons selected on the basis of a customer's past purchases.

Build Channel Relationships

An important goal of marketing communications is to build a relationship with the organization's channel members. When producers use marketing communications to generate awareness, they are also helping the retailers who carry the product. Producers may also arrange with retailers to distribute coupons, set up special displays, or hold promotional events in their stores, all of which benefit retailers and wholesalers. Retailers support manufacturers when they feature brands in their ads to attract buyers. Because of such efforts, all members of the channel benefit. Cooperating in these marketing communication efforts can build stronger channel relationships.

Retain Customers

Loyal customers are a major asset for every business. It costs far more to attract a new customer than to retain an existing customer. Marketing communications can support efforts to create value for existing customers. Interactive modes of communication—including salespeople and Web sites—can play an important role in retaining customers. They can serve as sources of information about product usage and new products being developed. They can also gather information from customers about what they value, as well as their experiences using the products. This two-way communication can assist marketers in increasing the value of what they offer to existing customers, which will influence retention.

THE PROMOTION MIX

The promotion mix concept refers to the combination and types of nonpersonal and personal communication the organization puts forth during a specified period.[1] There are five elements of the promotion mix, four of which are nonpersonal forms of communication (advertising, sales promotion, public relations, and direct marketing), and one, personal selling, which is a personal form of communication. Let's briefly examine each one.

1. *Advertising* is a paid form of nonpersonal communications about an organization, its products, or its activities that is transmitted through a mass medium to a target audience. The mass medium might be television, radio, newspapers, Internet, magazines, outdoor displays, car cards, or directories.

2. *Sales promotion* is an activity or material that offers customers, sales personnel, or resellers a direct inducement for purchasing a product. This inducement, which adds value to or incentive for the product, might take the form of a coupon, sweepstakes, refund, or display.

3. *Public relations* is a nonpersonal form of communication that seeks to influence the attitudes, feelings, and opinions of customers, noncustomers, stockholders, suppliers, employees, and political bodies about the organization. A popular form is *publicity,* which is a nonpaid form of nonpersonal communication about the organization and its products that is transmitted through a mass medium in the form of a news story. Obviously, marketers seek positive publicity.

4. *Direct marketing* uses direct forms of communication with customers. It can take the form of direct mail, online marketing, catalogs, telemarketing, and direct response advertising. Similar to personal selling, it may consist of an interactive dialog between the marketer and the customer. Its objective is to generate orders, visits to retail outlets, or requests for further information. Obviously, personal selling is a form of direct marketing, but because it is a very personal form of communication, we place it in its own category.

5. *Personal selling* is face-to-face communication with potential buyers to inform them about and persuade them to buy an organization's product. It will be examined in detail in the next chapter.

Obviously, marketers strive for the right mix of promotional elements to ensure that their product is well received. For example, if the product is a new soft drink, promotional effort is likely to rely more on advertising, sales promotion, and public relations (publicity) in order to (1) make potential buyers aware of the product, (2) inform these buyers about the benefits of the product, (3) convince buyers of the product's value, and (4) entice buyers to purchase the product. If the product is more established but the objective is to stabilize sales during a nonpeak season, the promotion mix will likely contain short-run incentives (sales promotions) for people to buy the product immediately. Finally, if the product is a new complex technology that requires a great deal of explanation, the promotional mix will likely focus heavily on personal selling so that potential buyers can have their questions answered.

As seen by the previous examples, a firm's promotion mix is likely to change over time. The mix must be continually adapted to reflect changes in the market, competition, the product's life cycle, and the adoption of new strategies. In essence, the firm should take into account three basic factors when devising its promotion mix: (1) the role of promotion in the overall marketing mix, (2) the nature of the product, and (3) the nature of the market.

INTEGRATED MARKETING COMMUNICATIONS

In many organizations, elements of the promotion mix are often managed by specialists in different parts of the organization or, in some cases, outside the organization when an advertising agency is used. For example, advertising plans might be developed jointly by

FIGURE 8.1

How Various
Promotion Tools
Might Contribute to
the Purchase of a
Hypothetical Product

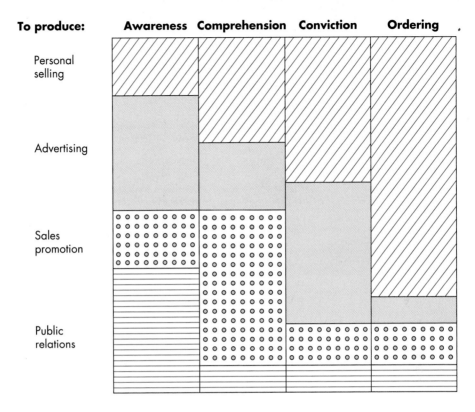

the advertising department and the advertising agency; plans for the sales force might be developed by managers of the sales force; and sales promotions might be developed independently of the advertising and sales plans. Thus, it is not surprising that the concept of *integrated marketing communications* has evolved in recent years.

The idea of integrated marketing communications is easy to understand and certainly has a great deal of commonsense validity. But like so many concepts in marketing, it is difficult to implement. The goal of integrated marketing communications is to develop marketing communications programs that coordinate and integrate all elements of promotion—advertising, sales promotion, personal selling, and publicity—so that the organization presents a consistent message. Integrated marketing communication seeks to manage all sources of brand or company contacts with existing and potential customers.

The concept of integrated marketing communication is illustrated in Figure 8.1. It is generally agreed that potential buyers usually go through a process of (1) *awareness* of the product or service, (2) *comprehension* of what it can do and its important features, (3) *conviction* that it has value for them, and (4) *ordering*. Consequently, the firm's marketing communication tools must encourage and allow the potential buyer to experience the various stages. Figure 8.1 illustrates the role of various marketing communication tools for a hypothetical product.

The goal of integrated marketing communication is an important one, and many believe it is critical for success in today's crowded marketplace. As with many management concepts, implementation is slower than many would like to see. Internal "turf" battles within organizations and the reluctance of some advertising agencies to willingly broaden their role beyond advertising are two factors that are hindering the successful implementation of integrated marketing communication.

These levels demonstrate how Integrated Marketing Communications programs range from narrowly focused corporate monologues to broad, interactive dialogues that result in a corporate culture that permeates an organization and drives everything it does, internally and externally.

Level	Name	Focus	Examples
1	Unified image	One look; one voice; strong brand image focus	3M
2	Consistent voice	Consistent tone and look; coordinated messages to various audiences (customers, suppliers, etc.)	Hallmark, Coca-Cola, Walmart
3	Good listener	Solicits two-way communication, enabling feedback through toll-free numbers, surveys, trade shows, etc.; focus on long-term relationships	Dove, Saturn
4	World-class citizen	Social, environmental consciousness; strong company culture; focus on wider community	Ben and Jerry's, Apple, Google, Honda

Source: Tom Duncan, "Integrated Marketing? It's Synergy," *Advertising Age,* March 8,1993, p. 22; and William F. Arens, Michael F. Weigold, and Christian Arens, *Contemporary Advertising and Integrated Marketing Communications,* 13th ed. (Burr Ridge, IL: McGraw-Hill/Irwin, 2011), p. 274.

ADVERTISING: PLANNING AND STRATEGY

Advertising seeks to promote the seller's product by means of printed and electronic media. This is justified on the grounds that messages can reach large numbers of people and make them aware and persuade and remind them about the firm's offerings.

From a marketing management perspective, advertising is an important strategic device for maintaining a competitive advantage in the marketplace. Advertising budgets represent a large and growing element in the cost of goods and services. In a year it is possible for large multi-product firms to spend $1.5 to $2 billion advertising their products, and it is common to spend $74 to $100 million on one individual brand. Clearly, advertising must be carefully planned.

Objectives of Advertising

There are at least three different viewpoints about the contribution of advertising to the economic health of the firm. The generalist viewpoint is primarily concerned with sales, profits, return on investment, and so forth. At the other extreme, the specialist viewpoint is represented by advertising experts who are primarily concerned with measuring the effects of specific ads or campaigns; here primary attention is given to organizations that offer services that measure different aspects of the effects of advertising such as the Nielsen Index, Starch Reports, Arbitron Index, and Simmons Reports. A middle view, one that might be classified as more of a marketing management approach, understands and appreciates the other two viewpoints but, in addition, sees advertising as a competitive weapon. Emphasis in this approach is given to the strategic aspects of the advertising function.[2]

Building on what was said earlier, objectives for advertising can be assigned that focus on creating *awareness,* aiding *comprehension,* developing *conviction,* and encouraging

Element	Ethical and Legal Concerns
Advertising	• Using deceptive advertising • Reinforcing unfavorable ethnic/racial/sex stereotypes • Encouraging materialism and excessive consumption
Public relations	• Lack of sincerity (paying lip service to worthwhile causes) • Using economic power to gain favorable publicity • Orchestrating news events to present a false appearance of widespread support for the company position
Sales promotion	• Offering misleading consumer promotions • Paying slotting allowances to gain retail shelf space • Using unauthorized mailing lists to reach consumers
Personal selling	• Using high-pressure selling • Failing to disclose product limitations/safety concerns • Misrepresenting product health
Direct marketing communications	• Invading privacy with telemarketing • Using consumer database information without consumers' authorization • Creating economic waste with unwanted direct mail

Source: William O. Bearden, Thomas N. Ingram, and Raymond W. LaForge, *Marketing: Principles and Perspectives,* 5th ed. (Burr Ridge, IL: McGraw-Hill/Irwin, 2007), p. 383.

ordering. Within each category, more specific objectives can be developed that take into account time and degree of success desired. Obviously, compared to the large number of people that advertising makes aware of the product or service, the number actually motivated to purchase is usually quite small.

In the long run and often in the short run, advertising is justified on the basis of the revenue it produces. Revenue in this case may refer to either sales or profits. Economic theory assumes that firms are profit maximizers, and the advertising outlays should be increased in every market and medium up to the point where the additional cost of gaining more business equals the incremental profits. Since most business firms do not have the data required to use the marginal analysis approach, they usually employ less-sophisticated decision-making models. Evidence also shows that many managers advertise to maximize sales on the assumption that higher sales mean more profits (which may or may not be true).

The point to be made here is that the ultimate objective of the business advertiser is to make sales and profits. To achieve this objective, customers must purchase and repurchase the advertised product. Toward this end, an approach to advertising is needed that provides for intelligent decision making. This approach must recognize the need for measuring the results of advertising, and these measurements must be as valid and reliable as possible. Marketing managers must also be aware that advertising not only complements other forms of communication but is subject to the law of diminishing returns. This means that for any advertised product, it can be assumed a point is eventually reached at which additional advertising produces little or no additional sales.

ADVERTISING DECISIONS

In line with what has just been said, the marketing manager must make two key decisions. The first decision deals with determining the size of the advertising budget, and the second deals with how the advertising budget should be allocated. Although these decisions are highly interrelated, we deal with them separately to achieve a better understanding of the problems involved. Today's most successful brands of consumer goods were built by heavy advertising and marketing investment long ago. Many marketers have lost sight of the connection between advertising spending and market share. They practice the art of discounting: cutting ad budgets to fund price promotions or fatten quarterly earnings. Companies employing these tactics may benefit in the short term but may be at a severe competitive disadvantage in the long term.

Marketers at some companies, however, know that brand equity and consumer preference for brands drive market share. They understand the balance of advertising and promotion expenditures needed to build brands and gain share, market by market, regardless of growth trends in the product categories where they compete. For example, Procter & Gamble has built its Jif and Folger's brands from single-digit shares to being among category leaders. In peanut butter and coffee, P&G invests more in advertising and less in discounting than its major competitors. What P&G and other smart marketers such as Kellogg, General Mills, Coke, and PepsiCo hold in common is an awareness of a key factor in advertising: consistent investment spending. They do not raid their ad budgets to increase earnings for a few quarters, nor do they view advertising as a discretionary cost.

The Expenditure Question

Most firms determine how much to spend on advertising by one of the following methods.

Percent of Sales

This is one of the most popular rule-of-thumb methods, and its appeal is found in its simplicity. The firm simply takes a percentage figure and applies it to either past or future sales. For example, suppose next year's sales are estimated to be $1 million. Using the criterion of 2 percent of sales, the ad budget would be $20,000. This approach is usually justified by its advocates in terms of the following argument: (1) Advertising is needed to generate sales; (2) a number of cents (i.e., the percentage used) out of each dollar of sales should be devoted to advertising in order to generate needed sales; and (3) the percentage is easily adjusted and can be readily understood by other executives. The percent-of-sales approach is popular in retailing.

Per-Unit Expenditure

Closely related to the above technique is one in which a fixed monetary amount is spent on advertising for each unit of the product expected to be sold. This method is popular with higher-priced merchandise, such as automobiles or appliances. For instance, if a company is marketing color televisions priced at $500, it may decide that it should spend $30 per set on advertising. Since this $30 is a fixed amount for each unit, this method amounts to the same thing as the percent-of-sales method. The big difference is in the rationale used to justify each of the methods. The per-unit expenditure method attempts to determine the retail price by using production costs as a base. Here the seller realizes that a reasonably competitive price must be established for the product in question and therefore attempts to cost out the gross margin. All this means is that, if the suggested retail price is to be $500 and manufacturing costs are $250, a gross margin of $250 is available to cover certain expenses, such as transportation, personal selling, advertising, and dealer profit. Some of these expense items are flexible, such as advertising, while others are nearly fixed, as in the case of transportation. The basic problem with this method and the percentage-of-sales method is that they view advertising as a function of sales, rather than sales as a function of advertising.

All You Can Afford

Here the advertising budget is established as a predetermined share of profits or financial resources. The availability of current revenues sets the upper limit of the ad budget. The only advantage to this approach is that it sets reasonable limits on the expenditures for advertising. However, from the standpoint of sound marketing practice, this method is undesirable because there is no necessary connection between liquidity and advertising opportunity. Any firm that limits its advertising outlays to the amount of available funds will probably miss opportunities for increasing sales and profits.

Competitive Parity

This approach is often used in conjunction with other approaches, such as the percent-of-sales method. The basic philosophy underlying this approach is that advertising is defensive. Advertising budgets are based on those of competitors or other members of the industry. From a strategy standpoint, this is a "followership" technique that assumes that the other firms in the industry know what they are doing and have similar goals. Competitive parity is not a preferred method, although some executives feel it is a safe approach. This may or may not be true depending in part on the relative market share of competing firms and their growth objectives.

The Research Approach

Here the advertising budget is argued for and presented on the basis of research findings. Advertising media are studied in terms of their productivity by the use of media reports and research studies. Costs are also estimated and compared with study results. A typical experiment is one in which three or more test markets are selected. The first test market is used as a control, either with no advertising or with normal levels of advertising. Advertising with various levels of intensity is used in the other markets, and comparisons are made to see what effect different levels of intensity have. The marketing manager then evaluates the costs and benefits of the different approaches and intensity levels to determine the overall budget. Although the research approach is generally more expensive than some other models, it is a more rational approach to the expenditure decision.

The Task Approach

Well-planned advertising programs usually make use of the task approach, which initially formulates the advertising goals and defines the tasks to accomplish these goals. Once this is done, management determines how much it will cost to accomplish each task and adds up the total. This approach is often in conjunction with the research approach.

The Allocation Question

This question deals with the problem of deciding on the most effective way of spending advertising dollars. A general answer to the question is that management's choice of strategies and objectives determines the media and appeals to be used. In other words, the firm's or product division's overall marketing plan will function as a general guideline for answering the allocation question.

From a practical standpoint, however, the allocation question can be framed in terms of message and media decisions. A successful ad campaign has two related tasks: (1) say the right things in the ads themselves, and (2) use the appropriate media in the right amounts at the right time to reach the target market.

Effective advertising should follow a plan. There is no one best way to go about planning an advertising campaign, but in general, marketers should have good answers to the following eight questions:

1. *The management question:* Who will manage the advertising program?
2. *The money question:* How much should be spent on advertising as opposed to other forms of communication?
3. *The market question:* To whom should the advertising be directed?
4. *The message question:* What should the ads say about the product?
5. *The media question:* What types and combinations of media should be used?
6. *The macroscheduling question:* How long should the advertising campaign be in effect before changing ads or themes?
7. *The microscheduling question:* At what times and dates would it be best for ads to appear during the course of the campaign?
8. *The measurement question:* How will the effectiveness of the advertising campaign be measured and how will the campaign be evaluated and controlled?

Message Strategy

The advertising process involves creating messages with words, ideas, sounds, and other forms of audiovisual stimuli that are designed to affect consumer (or distributor) behavior. It follows that much of advertising is a communication process. To be effective, the advertising message should meet two general criteria: (1) It should take into account the basic principles of communication, and (2) it should be predicated upon a good theory of consumer motivation and behavior.

The basic communication process involves three elements: (1) the sender or source of the communication, (2) the communication or message, and (3) the receiver or audience. Advertising agencies are considered experts in the communications field and are employed by most large firms to create meaningful messages and assist in their dissemination. Translating the product idea or marketing message into an effective ad is termed *encoding*. In advertising, the goal of encoding is to generate ads that the audience understands. For this to occur, the audience must be able to *decode* the message in the ad so that the perceived content of the message is the same as the intended content of the message. From a practical standpoint, all this means is that advertising messages must be sent to consumers in an understandable and meaningful way.

Advertising messages, of course, must be transmitted and carried by particular communication channels commonly known as advertising media. These media or channels vary in efficiency, selectivity, and cost. Some channels are preferred to others because they have less "noise," and thus messages are more easily received and understood. For example, a particular newspaper ad must compete with other ads, pictures, or stories on the same page. In the case of radio or TV, while only one firm's message is usually broadcast at a time, other distractions (noise) can hamper clear communications, such as driving while listening to the radio.

The relationship between advertising and consumer behavior is quite obvious. For many products and services, advertising is an influence that may affect the consumer's decision to purchase a particular product or brand. It is clear that consumers are subjected to many selling influences, and the question arises about how important advertising is or can be. In this case, the advertising expert must operate on some theory of consumer behavior. The reader will recall from the discussion of consumer behavior that the buyer was viewed as progressing through various stages from an unsatisfied need through and beyond a

Newspapers

Advantages

1. Flexible and timely.
2. Intense coverage of local markets.
3. Broad acceptance and use.
4. High believability of printed word.

Disadvantages

1. Short life.
2. Read hastily.
3. Small "pass-along" audience.

Radio

Advantages

1. Mass use (over 25 million radios sold annually).
2. Audience selectivity via station format.
3. Low cost (per unit of time).
4. Geographic flexibility.

Disadvantages

1. Audio presentation only.
2. Less attention than TV.
3. Chaotic buying (nonstandardized rate structures).
4. Short life.

Outdoor

Advantages

1. Flexible.
2. Relative absence of competing advertisements.
3. Repeat exposure.
4. Relatively inexpensive.

Disadvantages

1. Creative limitations.
2. Many distractions for viewer.
3. Public attack (ecological implications).
4. No selectivity of audience.

Television

Advantages

1. Combination of sight, sound, and motion.
2. Appeals to senses.
3. Mass audience coverage.
4. Psychology of attention.

Disadvantages

1. Nonselectivity of audience.
2. Fleeting impressions.
3. Short life.
4. Expensive.

Magazines

Advantages

1. High geographic and demographic selectivity.
2. Psychology of attention.
3. Quality of reproduction.
4. Pass-along readership.

Disadvantages

1. Long closing periods (six to eight weeks prior to publication).
2. Some waste circulation.
3. No guarantee of position (unless premium is paid).

Direct Mail

Advantages

1. Audience selectivity.
2. Flexible.
3. No competition from competing advertisements.
4. Personalized.

Disadvantages

1. Relatively high cost.
2. Consumers often pay little attention and throw it away.

Internet

Advantages

1. Interactive.
2. Low cost per exposure.
3. Ads can be placed in interest sections.
4. Timely.
5. High information content possible.
6. New favorable medium.

Disadvantages

1. Low attention getting.
2. Short message life.
3. Reader selects exposure.
4. May be perceived as intruding.
5. Subject to download speeds.

purchase decision. The end goal of an advertisement and its associated campaign is to move the buyer to a decision to purchase the advertised brand. By doing so, the advertisement will have succeeded in moving the consumer to the trial and repeat purchase stage of the consumer behavior process, which is the end goal of advertising strategy.

The planning of an advertising campaign and the creation of persuasive messages require a mixture of marketing skill and creative know-how. Relative to the dimension of marketing skills, some important pieces of marketing information are needed before launching an ad campaign. Most of this information must be generated by the firm and kept up-to-date. Listed below are some of the critical types of information an advertiser should have.

1. *Who* the firm's customers and potential customers are: their demographic, economic, and psychological characteristics and any other factors affecting their likelihood of buying.
2. *How many* such customers there are.
3. *How much* of the firm's type and brand of product they are currently buying and can reasonably be expected to buy in the short-term and long-term future.
4. *Which* individuals, other than customers and potential customers, *influence* purchasing decisions.
5. *Where* they buy the firm's brand of product.
6. *When* they buy, and frequency of purchase.
7. *Which* competitive brands they buy and frequency of purchase.
8. *How* they use the product.
9. *Why* they buy particular types and brands of products.

Media Mix

Media selection is no easy task. To start with, there are numerous types and combinations of media to choose from. Marketing Insight 8–5 presents a brief summary of the advantages and disadvantages of some of the major advertising media.

In the advertising industry, a common measure of efficiency or productivity is cost per thousand, or CPMs. This figure generally refers to the dollar cost of reaching 1,000 prospects, and its chief advantage lies in its simplicity and allowance for a common base of comparison between differing media types. The major disadvantage of the use of CPMs also relates to its simplicity. For example, the same commercial placed in two different television programs, having the same viewership and the same audience profile, may very well generate different responses depending on the level of viewer involvement. This "positive effects" theory states that the more the viewers are involved in a television program, the stronger they will respond to commercials. In essence, involving programs produce engaged respondents who demonstrate more favorable responses to advertising messages.

Generally, such measures as circulation, audience size, and sets in use per commercial minute are used in the calculation. Of course, different relative rankings of media can occur, depending on the measure used. A related problem deals with what is meant by "effectively reaching" the prospect.[3] *Reach,* in general, is the number of different targeted audience members exposed at least once to the advertiser's message within a predetermined time frame. Just as important as the number of different people exposed (reach) is the number of times, on average, that they are exposed to an advertisement within a given time period. This rate of exposure is called *average frequency.* Since marketers all have budget constraints, they must decide whether to increase reach at the expense of average frequency or average frequency at the expense of reach. In essence, the marketer's dilemma is to develop a media schedule that both (1) exposes a sufficient number of targeted customers (reach) to the firm's product and (2) exposes them enough times (average frequency) to the product to produce the desired effect. The desired effect can come in the

Advertising can be found everywhere these days—even places where we least expect it.

Aerial Banners and Lights

Banners carrying ad messages can be pulled by low-flying planes. After dark, traveling aerial lights can display messages of up to 90 characters. Slow-flying helicopters can carry 40- by 80-foot signs lit by thousands of bulbs.

Blimps

In addition to Goodyear, blimps now carry ads for many companies, including Citibank, Coca-Cola, and Fuji Film, among others. Computer operated lighting systems allow the blimps to advertise at night.

In-Flight Ads

Many airlines' in-flight audio and video entertainment runs ads. The travel industry and advertisers that want to reach business fliers are the primary users.

Newspaper Bags

The protective bags of newspapers are used for full-color advertising and can be enhanced by adding product samples. This method is desirable because it does not have to compete with other advertisers.

Transit Terminal Domination

The latest version of saturation bombing has come to large transit hubs around the country. One advertiser buys up all or most of the message space in one confined site banishing all competition. This greatly increases the chances of being seen even by the most harried passers by.

Electronic Billboards

Most modern sports stadiums and arenas sell ad space on giant electronic displays.

Inflatables

Giant inflatable beer cans, mascots, and even cereal boxes are used for advertising purposes.

Painted Vehicles

Buses, trucks, and cars are completely decorated with larger than life illustrations and messages to attract attention. Some vehicles are 'wrapped' with a material that covers the entire vehicle to present the greatest visual impact.

Reactrix Brand Play

In small theaters and other spaces, Reactrix creates highly entertaining branding displays that respond to the physical movement of the audience.

Trash Receptacles

Uniquely designed and decorated trash bins, boxes, and baskets bear advertising logos and messages. Some major cities now offer advertising space on concrete litter receptacles at major commercial intersections.

Kiosks

Stand-alone kiosks can be painted with eye-catching designs and messages. Unique constructions can be attached to the top and sides to draw attention. Electronic displays running presentation software can show colorful fast-action video clips, slide images, and interactive text. These systems can also play synchronized sounds and music.

Lavatory Advertising

Numerous venues allow advertising in lavatories. Print ads can be found on the inner side of stalls and above urinals in some men's restrooms.

Gobo/Cookie Advertising

The gobo (or cookie) is a piece of metal stenciled with a logo through which light is projected against a wall or other suitable background. This is ideal for huge outdoor or indoor events.

Train Cars

Train cars are wrapped with advertisements instead of graffiti these days. In Chicago an eight-car commuter train was wrapped with Illinois lottery ads.

Grocery Receipts

Today most major supermarket chains print coupons on the back of grocery receipts. The coupons feature discounts at local retailers.

Source: William F. Arens, Michael F. Weigold, and Christian Arens, *Contemporary Advertising*, 13th ed. (Burr Ridge, IL: McGraw-Hill/Irwin, 2011), p. 304.

FIGURE 8.2   Example of Sales Promotion Activities

Source: William D. Perreault, Jr. and E. Jerome McCarthy, *Basic Marketing: A Marketing Strategy Planning Approach,* 18th ed. (Burr Ridge, IL: McGraw-Hill/Irwin, 2011), chap. 14.

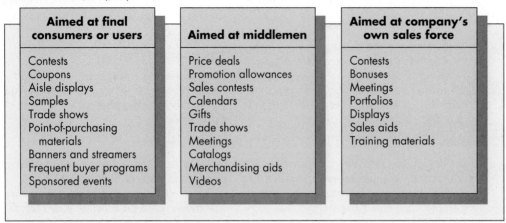

Aimed at final consumers or users	Aimed at middlemen	Aimed at company's own sales force
Contests	Price deals	Contests
Coupons	Promotion allowances	Bonuses
Aisle displays	Sales contests	Meetings
Samples	Calendars	Portfolios
Trade shows	Gifts	Displays
Point-of-purchasing materials	Trade shows	Sales aids
Banners and streamers	Meetings	Training materials
Frequent buyer programs	Catalogs	
Sponsored events	Merchandising aids	
	Videos	

form of reaching goals associated with any or all of the categories of advertising objectives (the prospect becomes aware of the product, takes action, etc.) covered earlier in the chapter.

SALES PROMOTION

Over the past two decades, the popularity of sales promotion has been increasing. Two reasons for this increased popularity are undoubtedly the increased pressure on management for short-term results and the emergence of new purchase tracking technology. For example, many supermarket cash registers are now equipped with a device that dispenses coupons to a customer at the point of purchase. The type, variety, and cash amount of the coupon will vary from customer to customer based on their purchases. In essence, it is now possible for the Coca-Cola Company to dispense coupons only to those customers who purchase Pepsi Cola, thus avoiding spending promotional dollars on already-loyal Coke drinkers. Figure 8.2 presents some popular targets of sales promotion and the methods used.

Push versus Pull Marketing

Push and pull marketing strategies comprise the two options available to marketers interested in getting their product into the hands of customers. They are illustrated in Figure 8.3. *Push strategies* involve aiming promotional efforts at distributors, retailers, and sales personnel to gain their cooperation in ordering, stocking, and accelerating the sales of a product. For example, a local rock band may visit local DJs seeking air play for their record, offer distributors special prices to carry the CD, and offer retailers special allowances for putting up posters or special counter displays. These activities, which are usually in the form of price allowances, distribution allowances, and advertising dollar allowances, are designed to "push" the CD toward the customer.[4]

Pull strategies involve aiming promotional efforts directly at customers to encourage them to ask the retailer for the product. In the past few years drug manufacturers have begun to advertise prescription drugs directly to consumers. Customers are encouraged to "Ask Your Doctor" about Viagra or Paxil. These activities, which can include advertising and sales promotion, are designed to "pull" a product through the channel from manufacturer to buyer.

FIGURE 8.3 Push versus Pull Strategies in Marketing Communications

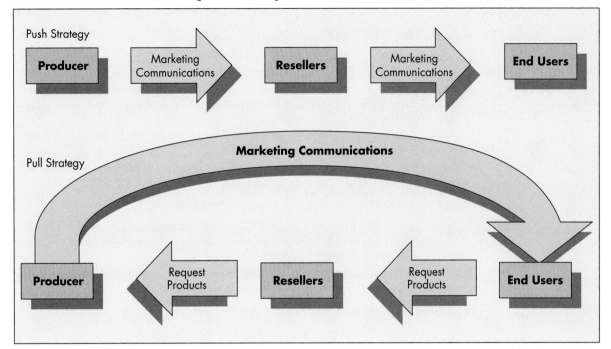

Trade Sales Promotions

Trade promotions are those promotions aimed at distributors and retailers of products who make up the distribution channel. The major objectives of trade promotions are to (1) convince retailers to carry the manufacturer's products, (2) reduce the manufacturer's inventories and increase the distributor's or retailer's inventories, (3) support advertising and consumer sales promotions, (4) encourage retailers either to give the product more favorable shelf space or to place more emphasis on selling the product, and (5) serve as a reward for past sales efforts.

Promotions built around price discounts and advertising or other allowances are likely to have higher distributor/retailer participation levels than other types of promotions because a direct economic incentive is attached to the promotion.[5] The importance attached to individual types of promotions may vary by the size of distributor/retailer. For example, small retailers do not consider contests, sweepstakes, and sales quotas as being important to their decision to participate in promotions; getting the full benefit of such promotions is difficult due to their size. Marketers must keep in mind that not all distributors or retailers will have the same reaction to promotions offered. The manufacturer must carefully consider differences in attitudes when designing and implementing trade promotion programs.

Consumer Promotions

Consumer promotions can fulfill several distinct objectives for the manufacturer. Some of the more commonly sought-after objectives include (1) inducing the consumer to try the product, (2) rewarding the consumer for brand loyalty, (3) encouraging the consumer to trade up or purchase larger sizes of a product, (4) stimulating the consumer to make repeat purchases of the product, (5) reacting to competitor efforts, and (6) reinforcing and serving as a complement to advertising and personal selling efforts.

Procedures for Evaluating Specific Advertisements

1. *Recognition tests.* Estimate the percentage of people claiming to have read a magazine who recognize the ad when it is shown to them (e.g., Starch Message Report Service).
2. *Recall tests.* Estimate the percentage of people claiming to have read a magazine who can (unaided) recall the ad and its contents (e.g., Gallup and Robinson Impact Service, various services for TV ads as well).
3. *Opinion tests.* Potential audience members are asked to rank alternative advertisements as most interesting, most believable, best liked.
4. *Theater tests.* Theater audience is asked for brand preferences before and after an ad is shown in context of a TV show (e.g., Schwerin TV Testing Service).

Procedures for Evaluating Specific Advertising Objectives

1. *Awareness.* Potential buyers are asked to indicate brands that come to mind in a product category. A message used in an ad campaign is given and buyers are asked to identify the brand that was advertised using that message.
2. *Attitude.* Potential buyers are asked to rate competing or individual brands on determinant attributes, benefits, and characterizations using rating scales.

Procedures for Evaluating Motivational Impact

1. *Intention to buy.* Potential buyers are asked to indicate the likelihood they will buy a brand (on a scale from "definitely will not" to "definitely will").
2. *Market test.* Sales changes in different markets are monitored to compare the effects of different messages, budget levels.

Source: Joseph Guiltinan and Gordon Paul, *Marketing Management,* 6th ed., © 1997, New York, McGraw-Hill, Inc., p. 274. Reproduced by permission of The McGraw-Hill Companies.

Figure 8.4 presents a brief description of some of the most commonly used forms of consumer promotion activities.

What Sales Promotion Can and Can't Do

Advocates of sales promotion often point to its growing popularity as a justification for the argument that we don't need advertising; sales promotion itself will suffice. Marketers should bear in mind that sales promotion is only one part of a well-constructed integrated marketing communications program. While sales promotion is proven to be effective in achieving the objectives listed in the previous sections, there are several compelling reasons why it should not be used as the sole promotional tool. These reasons include sales promotion's inability (1) to generate long-term buyer commitment to a brand in many cases; (2) to change, except on a temporary basis, declining sales of a product; (3) to convince buyers to purchase an otherwise unacceptable product; and (4) to make up for a lack of advertising or sales support for a product. In addition, promotions can often fuel the flames of competitive retaliation far more than other marketing activities. When the competition gets drawn into the promotion war, the effect can be a significant slowing of the sharp sales increases predicted by the initiator of the promotion. Worse yet, promotions can often devalue the image of the promoted brand in the consumer's eyes.

FIGURE 8.4
Some Commonly
Used Forms of
Consumer
Promotions

• *Sampling*	Customers are offered regular trial sizes of the product either free or at a nominal price.
• *Price deals*	Customers are offered discounts from the product's regular price.
• *Bonus packs*	Additional amounts of the product are given to buyers when they purchase the product.
• *Rebates and refunds*	Customers are given reimbursements for purchasing the product either on the spot or through the mail.
• *Sweepstakes and contests*	Prizes are available either through chance selection or games of skill.
• *Premiums*	A reward or gift can come from purchasing a product.
• *Coupons*	Probably the most familiar and widely used of all consumer promotions, now often available at point of purchase.

The dilemma marketers face is how to cut back on sales promotions without losing market share to competitors. In an effort to overcome this problem, some consumer products companies are instituting new pricing policies to try to cut back on the amount of sales promotions used. For example, Procter & Gamble and General Mills have instituted everyday low-price strategies for many of their products. The intent of this type of policy is to give retailers a lower list price in exchange for cutting trade promotions. While the net cost of the product to retailers remains unchanged, retailers are losing promotional dollars that they controlled. In many situations, although trade allowances are supposed to be used for encouraging retail sales, it is not uncommon for retailers to take a portion of the trade allowance money as profit. The rationale behind companies' (such as Procter & Gamble and General Mills) efforts to cut back on trade and other promotions is (1) not to force brand-loyal customers to pay unusually high prices when a product isn't on special; (2) to allow consumers to benefit from a lower average shelf price, since retailers will no longer have discretion over the use of allowance dollars; and (3) to improve efficiencies in manufacturing and distribution systems because retailers will lose the incentive to do heavy forward buying of discounted items.

In addition to developing pricing policies to cut back on short-term promotions, some consumer products companies are starting to institute *frequency marketing programs* in which they reward consumers for purchases of products or services over a sustained period of time.[6] These programs are not technically considered sales promotions due to their ongoing nature. Frequency marketing originated in 1981 when American Airlines launched its frequent-flyer program with the intention of securing the loyalty of business travelers.

PUBLIC RELATIONS

As noted earlier in the chapter, public relations is a nonpersonal form of communication that tries to influence the overall image of the organization and its products and services among its various stakeholder groups. Public relations managers prefer to focus on communicating positive news about the organization, but they must also be available to minimize the negative impacts of a crisis or problem. We have already noted that the most popular and frequently used public relations tool is publicity. There are several forms of publicity:

1. *News release.* An announcement regarding changes in the organization or the product line, sometimes called a *press release.* The objective is to inform members of the media of a newsworthy event in the hope that they will convert it into a story.

When Directed at Consumers

1. To obtain the trial of a product.
2. To introduce a new or improved product.
3. To encourage repeat or greater usage by current users.
4. To bring more customers into retail stores.
5. To increase the total number of users of an established product.

When Directed at Salespeople

1. To motivate the sales force.
2. To educate the sales force about product improvements.
3. To stabilize a fluctuating sales pattern.

When Directed at Resellers

1. To increase reseller inventories.
2. To obtain displays and other support for products.
3. To improve product distribution.
4. To obtain more and better shelf space.

2. *News conference.* A meeting held for representatives of the media so that the organization can announce major news events such as new products, technologies, mergers, acquisitions, and special events, or, in the case of a crisis or problem, present its position and plans for dealing with the situation.

3. *Sponsorship.* Providing support for and associating the organization's name with events, programs, or even people such as amateur athletes or teams. Besides publicity, sponsorship can also include advertising and sales promotion activities. Many organizations sponsor sporting events, art festivals, and public radio and television programs.

4. *Public service announcements.* Many nonprofit organizations rely on the media to donate time for advertising for contributions and donors. Many nonprofit organizations cannot afford the cost of advertising or in some cases are prohibited from doing so.

DIRECT MARKETING

We already know that with direct marketing the organization communicates directly with customers either online or through direct mail, catalogs, direct response advertising, or personal selling (the subject of the next chapter).

Direct marketing methods are certainly not new. In fact, several of them will be discussed later in the book as methods of nonstore retailing. What is new is the ability to design and use them more efficiently and effectively because of the availability of computers and databases. Technology has clearly been the catalyst in the tremendous growth in direct marketing activities in the last decade. Because of technology, it is now possible for marketers to customize communication efforts and literally create one-to-one connections and dialogues with customers. This would be especially true for those organizations that have successfully implemented an integrated marketing communications program.

Another obvious catalyst for growth in direct marketing has been consumers' increased use of the Internet for purchasing many types of products. The projected growth rates for online expenditures continue to rise. As growth continues in the number of households with Internet access and in the number of businesses with Web sites and product or service offerings via the Internet, it will likely fuel even greater growth in direct marketing.

For the American consumer facing a "poverty of time," direct marketing offers many benefits. In addition to saving time, consumers often save money, get better service, and enjoy increased privacy; many even find it entertaining. For the marketer, sales revenues are the obvious benefit but not the only one. Direct marketing activities are often very effective in generating sales leads when a customer asks for more information about a product or service and can also increase store traffic when potential buyers are encouraged to visit a dealership or retail store.

SUMMARY

This chapter has been concerned with integrated marketing communications. Remember that advertising and sales promotion are only two of the ways by which sellers can affect the demand for their product. Advertising and sales promotion are only part of the firm's promotion mix, and in turn, the promotion mix is only part of the overall marketing mix. Thus, advertising and sales promotion begin with the marketing plan and not with the advertising and sales promotion plans. Ignoring this point can produce ineffective and expensive promotional programs because of a lack of coordination with other elements of the marketing mix.

Additional Resources

Burns, Brian C., and Tom U. Snyder. *Selling in a New Market Space.* NY: McGraw-Hill, 2010.
Mullin, Jeanniery, and David Daniels. *Email Marketing.* Indianapolis: Wiley Publishers, 2009.
Percival, Sean. *My Space Marketing: Creating a Social Network to Boom Your Business.* Indianapolis: Que Books, 2009.
Postman, Joel. *SocialCorp: Social Media Goes Corporate.* Berkeley, CA: New Riders, 2009.
Reich, Brian, and Don Soloman. *Media Rules: Mastering Today's Technology to Connect With and Keep Your Audience.* Hoboken, NJ: John Wiley and Sons, 2008.
Vollmer, Christopher, and Geoffrey Precourt. *Always On: Advertising and Marketing Media in an Era of Consumer Control.* NY: McGraw-Hill, 2008.

Key Terms and Concepts

Advertising: A paid form of nonpersonal communications about an organization, its product, or its activities that is transmitted through a mass medium to a target audience.

Average frequency: The number of times customers, on average, are exposed to an advertisement within a given time period.

Consumer promotions: Promotions directed at consumers designed to induce the customer to try the product, reward brand loyalty, encourage the consumer to trade-up or purchase larger sizes, stimulate repeat purchases, and reinforce other advertising or personal selling efforts.

Cost per thousand: A common measure of efficiency or productivity in advertising, cost per thousand (CPM) refers to the dollar cost of reaching 1,000 prospects.

Direct marketing: Direct communication with customers through direct mail, online marketing, catalogs, telemarketing, and direct response advertising.

Expenditure question: The methods used to decide how much to spend on advertising, ranging from simple (a percent of sales), to more complex (the task approach which determines goals and how much it will cost to accomplish each goal).

Frequency marketing programs: Programs designed to reward customers for purchases of a product or service over a sustained period of time.

Integrated marketing communications: Marketing communications programs that coordinate and integrate all elements of the promotion mix so that the organization presents a consistent message. It seeks to manage all sources of brand or company contacts with existing and potential customers.

Objectives of advertising: Creating awareness, aiding comprehension, developing conviction, and encouraging ordering. Within each category more specific objectives can be developed that take into account time and degree of success desired.

Personal selling: Face-to-face communication with potential buyers to inform them about and persuade them to purchase an organization's product.

Promotion mix: The combination and types of nonpersonal and personal communication an organization puts forth during a specified period. There are five elements of the promotion mix, four of which are nonpersonal forms of communication (advertising, sales promotion, public relations, and direct marketing), and one, personal selling, which is a personal form of communication.

Public relations: Efforts directed at influencing the attitudes, feelings, and opinions of customers, noncustomers, stockholders, suppliers, employees, and political bodies about the organization. A popular form is publicity.

Pull strategy: Promotional efforts directed at customers to encourage them to ask the retailer for the product. They are designed to "pull" a product through the distribution channel from manufacturer to buyer.

Push strategy: Promotional efforts directed at distributors, retailers, and sales personnel to gain their cooperation in ordering, stocking, and supporting the sales of a product. As such they "push" the product toward the customer.

Reach: The number of targeted audience members exposed at least once to an advertiser's message within a predetermined time frame.

Sales promotion: An activity or material that offers customers, sales personnel, or resellers a direct inducement for purchasing a product.

Trade promotions: Promotions aimed at distributors and retailers of products who make up the distribution channel.

Appendix

Major Federal Agencies Involved in Control of Advertising

Agency	Function
Federal Trade Commission	Regulates commerce between states; controls unfair business practices; takes action on false and deceptive advertising; most important agency in regulation of advertising and promotion.
Food and Drug Administration	Regulatory division of the Department of Health, Education, and Welfare; controls marketing of food, drugs, cosmetics, medical devices, and potentially hazardous consumer products.
Federal Communications Commission	Regulates advertising indirectly, primarily through the power to grant or withdraw broadcasting licenses.
Postal Service	Regulates material that goes through the mails, primarily in areas of obscenity, lottery, and fraud.
Alcohol and Tobacco Tax Division	Part of the Treasury Department; has broad powers to regulate deceptive and misleading advertising of liquor and tobacco.
Grain Division	Unit of the Department of Agriculture responsible for policing seed advertising.
Securities and Exchange Commission	Regulates advertising of securities.

Information Source	Description
Patent Office	Regulates registration of trademarks.
Library of Congress	Controls protection of copyrights.
Department of Justice	Enforces all federal laws through prosecuting cases referred to it by other government agencies.

Personal Selling, Relationship Building, and Sales Management

Personal selling, unlike advertising or sales promotion, involves direct relationships between the seller and the prospect or customer. In a formal sense, personal selling can be defined as a two-way flow of communication between a potential buyer and a salesperson that is designed to accomplish at least three tasks: (1) identify the potential buyer's needs; (2) match those needs to one or more of the firm's products or services; and (3) on the basis of this match, convince the buyer to purchase the product.[1] The personal selling element of the promotion mix can encompass diverse forms of direct interaction between a salesperson and a potential buyer, including face-to-face, telephone, written, and computer communication. The behavioral scientist would most likely characterize personal selling as a type of personal influence. Operationally, it is a complex communication process, one still not fully understood by marketers.

IMPORTANCE OF PERSONAL SELLING

The importance of the personal selling function depends partially on the nature of the product. As a general rule, goods that are new and different, technically complex, or expensive require more personal selling effort. The salesperson plays a key role in providing the consumer with information about such products to reduce the risks involved in purchase and use. Insurance, for example, is a complex and technical product that often needs significant amounts of personal selling. In addition, many organizational products cannot be presold, and the salesperson has a key role to play in finalizing the sale.

It is important to remember that, for many companies, the salesperson represents the customer's main link to the firm. In fact, to some, the salesperson is the company. Therefore, it is imperative that the company take advantage of this unique link. Through the efforts of the successful salesperson, a company can build relationships with customers that continue long beyond the initial sale. It is the salesperson who serves as the conduit through which information regarding product flaws, improvements, applications, or new uses can pass from the customer to the marketing department. To illustrate the importance of using salespeople as an information resource, consider this fact: In some industries, customer information serves as a major source for up to 90 percent of new product and process ideas.

Along with techniques described in the previous chapter, personal selling provides the push needed to get middlemen to carry new products, increase their amount of goods purchased, and devote more effort in merchandising a product or brand.

In summary, personal selling is an integral part of the marketing system, fulfilling two vital duties (in addition to the core sales task itself): one for customers and one for companies.[2] First, the salesperson dispenses knowledge to buyers. Lacking relevant information, customers are likely to make poor buying decisions. For example, computer users would not learn about new equipment and new programming techniques without the assistance of computer sales representatives. Doctors would have difficulty finding out about new drugs and procedures were it not for pharmaceutical salespeople. Second, salespeople act as a source of marketing intelligence for management. Marketing success depends on satisfying customer needs. If present products don't fulfill customer needs, then profitable opportunities may exist for new or improved products. If problems with a company's product exist, then management must be quickly apprised of the fact. In either situation, salespeople are in the best position to act as the intermediary through which valuable information can be passed back and forth between product providers and buyers.

THE SALES PROCESS

Personal selling is as much an art as it is a science. The word *art* is used to describe that portion of the selling process that is highly creative in nature and difficult to explain. This does not mean there is little control over the personal selling element in the promotion mix. It does imply that, all other things equal, the trained salesperson can outsell the untrained one.

Before management selects and trains salespeople, it should have an understanding of the sales process. Obviously, the sales process will differ according to the size of the company, the nature of the product, the market, and so forth, but some elements are common to almost all selling situations. For the purposes of this text, the term *sales process* refers to two basic factors: (1) the objectives the salesperson is trying to achieve while engaged in selling activities; and (2) the sequence of stages or steps the salesperson should follow in trying to achieve the specific objectives (the relationship-building process).

Objectives of the Sales Force

Much like the concepts covered in the previous chapter, personal selling can be viewed as a strategic means to gain competitive advantage in the marketplace. For example, most organizations include service representatives as part of their sales team to ensure that customer concerns with present products are addressed and remedied at the same time new business is being solicited.

In a similar manner, marketing management understands that while, ultimately, personal selling must be justified on the basis of the revenue and profits it produces, other categories of objectives are generally assigned to the personal selling function as part of the overall promotion mix.[3] These objectives are

1. *Information provision.* Especially in the case of new products or customers, the salesperson needs to fully explain all attributes of the product or service, answer any questions, and probe for additional questions.
2. *Persuasion.* Once the initial product or service information is provided, the salesperson needs to focus on the following objectives:
   - Clearly distinguish attributes of the firm's products or services from those of competitors.
   - Maximize the number of sales as a percent of presentations.
   - Convert undecided customers into first-time buyers.

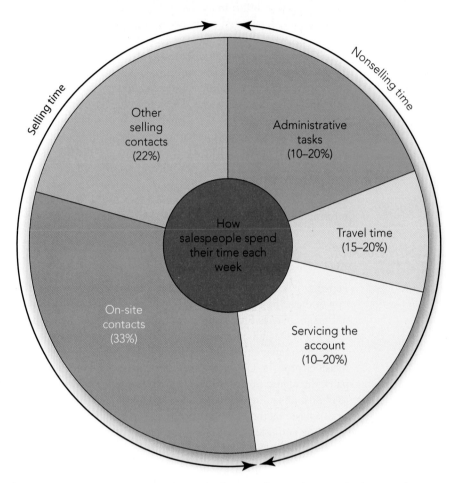

Source: Roger Kerin, Stephen W. Hartley, and William Rudalius, *Marketing,* 10th ed. (Burr Ridge, IL: McGraw-Hill/Irwin, 2011), p. 524.

- Convert first-time customers into repeat purchasers.
- Sell additional or complementary items to repeat customers.
- Tend to the needs of dissatisfied customers.

3. *After-sale service.* Whether the sale represents a first-time or repeat purchase, the salesperson needs to ensure the following objectives are met:
   - Delivery or installation of the product or service that meets or exceeds customer expectations.
   - Immediate follow-up calls and visits to address unresolved or new concerns.
   - Reassurance of product or service superiority through demonstrable actions.
   - Build relationships.

The Sales Relationship-Building Process

For many years, the traditional approach to selling emphasized the first-time sale of a product or service as the culmination of the sales process. As emphasized in Chapter 1, the

FIGURE 9.1
The Sales Relationship-Building Process

Source: Adapted from material discussed in Stephen B. Castleberry and John F. Tanner, *Selling: Building Partnerships,* 8th ed. (Burr Ridge, IL: Irwin/McGraw-Hill, 2011), p. 151.

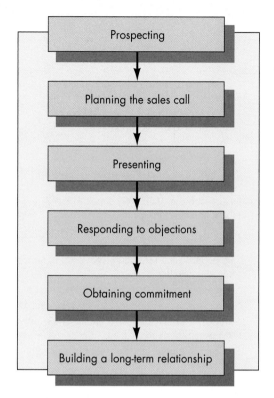

marketing concept and accompanying approach to personal selling view the initial sale as merely the first step in a long-term relationship-building process, not as the end goal. As we shall see later in this chapter, long-term relationships between the buyer and seller can be considered partnerships because the buyer and seller have an ongoing, mutually beneficial affiliation, with each party having concern for the other party's well-being.[4] The relationship-building process, which is designed to meet the objectives listed in the previous section, contains six sequential stages (Figure 9.1). These stages are (1) prospecting, (2) planning the sales call, (3) presentation, (4) responding to objections, (5) obtaining commitment/closing the sale, and (6) building a long-term relationship. What follows is a brief description of each of the stages.

Prospecting

The process of locating potential customers is called *prospecting.* The prospecting activity is critical to the success of organizations in maintaining or increasing sales volume. Continual prospecting is necessary for several reasons, including the fact that customers (1) switch to other suppliers, (2) move out of the organization's market area, (3) go out of business because of bankruptcy, (4) are acquired by another firm, or (5) have only a one-time need for the product or service. In addition, the organization's buying contracts with present customers may be replaced and organizations that wish to grow must increase their customer base. Prospecting in some fields is more important than in others. For example, a stockbroker, real estate agent, or partner in an accounting firm with no effective prospecting plan usually doesn't last long in the business. In these positions, it may take as many as 100 contacts to gain 10 prospects who will listen to presentations from which one to two sales may result. On the other hand, a Procter & Gamble sales representative in a certain geographic area would likely know all the potential retailers for Crest toothpaste.

Source	How Used
Satisfied customers	Current and previous customers are contacted for additional business and leads.
Endless chain	Salesperson attempts to secure at least one additional lead from each person he or she interviews.
Networking	Salesperson uses personal relationships with those who are connected and cooperative to secure leads.
Center of influence	Salesperson cultivates well-known, influential people in the territory who are willing to supply lead information.
The Internet	Salesperson uses Web sites, e-mail, Listservs, bulletin boards, forums, round-tables, and newsgroups to secure leads.
Ads, direct mail, catalogs, and publicity	Salespeople use these forms of promotional activities to generate leads.
Shows, fairs, and merchandise markets	Salespeople use trade shows, conventions, fairs, and merchandise markets for lead generation.
Seminars	Salespeople use seminars for prospects to generate leads.
Lists and directories	Salesperson uses secondary data sources, which can be free or fee-based.
Data mining and CRM systems	Salespeople use sophisticated data analysis software and the company's CRM system to generate leads.
Cold calling	Salesperson tries to generate leads by calling on totally unfamiliar organizations.
Spotters	Salesperson pays someone for lead information.
Telemarketing	Salesperson uses phone and/or telemarketing staff to generate leads.
Sales letters	Salesperson writes personal letters to potential leads.
Other sources	Salesperson uses noncompeting salespeople, people in his or her own firm, friends, and so on, to secure information.

Source: Stephen B. Castleberry and John F. Tanner, Jr., *Selling: Building Partnerships,* 8th ed. (Burr Ridge, IL: McGraw-Hill/Irwin, 2011), p. 155.

The prospecting process usually involves two major activities that are undertaken on a continual, concurrent basis. First, prospects must be located. When names and addresses of prospects are not available, as is usually the case when firms enter new markets or a new salesperson is hired, they can be generated by randomly calling on businesses or households or by employing mass appeals (through advertising). This process, called *random lead generation,* usually requires a high number of contacts to gain a sale. A *lead* is a potential prospect that may or may not have the potential to be a true prospect, a candidate, to whom a sale could be made.

For most professional, experienced salespeople, a more systematic approach to generating leads from predetermined target markets is used. This approach, aptly named *selected-lead generation,* uses existing contacts and knowledge to generate new prospects. In general, the best source of prospects is referrals from satisfied customers. The more satisfied one's customers are, the higher the quality of leads a salesperson will receive from them. Marketing Insight 9–2 lists some common sources of leads and how they are used to generate new contacts.

The second step in the prospecting process involves screening. Once leads are generated, the salesperson must determine whether the prospect is a true prospect. This qualifying process usually entails gathering information, which leads to answering five questions:

1. Does the lead have a want or need that can be satisfied by the purchase of the firm's products or services?
2. Does the lead have the ability to pay?

3. Does the lead have the authority to pay?
4. Can the lead be approached favorably?
5. Is the lead eligible to buy?

Depending on the analysis of answers to these questions, the determination of whether a lead is a true prospect can be made. In seeking and qualifying leads, it is important to recognize that responsibility for these activities should not be totally assumed by individual salespeople. Rather, companies should develop a consistent, organized program, recognizing that the job of developing prospects belongs to the entire company, not just the sales force.

Planning the Sales Call

Salespeople will readily admit that their number one problem is getting through the door for an appointment with a prospect. Customers have become sophisticated in their buying strategies. Consequently, salespeople have to be equally sophisticated in developing their selling strategies.

While a full discussion on the topic of planning sales calls is beyond the scope of this text, what follows are brief descriptions of some key areas of knowledge salespeople should possess prior to embarking on sales calls.

1. They should have thorough knowledge of the company they represent, including its past history. This includes the philosophy of management as well as the firm's basic operating policies.
2. They should have thorough knowledge of their products and/or product lines. This is particularly true when selling organizational products. When selling very technical products, many firms require their salespeople to have training as engineers.
3. They should have good working knowledge of competitors' products. This is a vital requirement because the successful salesperson will have to know the strengths and weaknesses of those products that are in competition for market share.
4. They should have in-depth knowledge of the market for their merchandise. *The market* here refers not only to a particular sales territory but also to the general market, including the economic factors that affect the demand for their goods.
5. They should have accurate knowledge of the buyer or the prospect to whom they are selling. Under the marketing concept, knowledge of the customer is a vital requirement.

Presenting

Successful salespeople have learned the importance of making a good impression. One of the most important ways of improving the buyer's impression is for the salesperson to be well prepared in the knowledge areas discussed above. Some salespeople actually develop a checklist of things to take to the presentation so that nothing is forgotten. Just as important is the development of good interpersonal skills; they are a key ingredient of effective selling. Salespeople who can adapt their selling style to individual buyer needs and styles have a much stronger overall performance than less-flexible counterparts.

Responding to Objections

To assume the buyer will passively listen and positively respond to a sales presentation by placing an immediate order would be unrealistic. Salespeople can expect to hear objections (issues or concerns raised by the buyer) at any time during the presentation and subsequent relationship. Objections can be raised when the salesperson attempts to secure appointments, during the presentation, when the salesperson attempts to obtain commitment, or during the after-sale follow-up.

When sales prospects raise an objection, it is a sign that they are not ready to buy and need an acceptable response to the objection before the buying decision can be made. In response to an objection, the salesperson should not challenge the respondent. Rather, the salesperson's objective should be to present the necessary information so that the prospect is able to make intelligent decisions based on that information.

Obtaining Commitment

At some point, if all objections have been resolved, the salesperson must ask for commitment. It's a rare moment when a customer will ask to buy. Consequently, knowing how and when to close a sale is one of a salesperson's most indispensable skills.

It should be noted that not all sales calls end in commitment, a successful closing. If commitment is not obtained, salespeople should analyze the reasons and determine whether (1) more sales calls are necessary to obtain commitment; or (2) currently, there just does not exist a good match between customer needs and seller offerings. If the salesperson determines that more calls are necessary, then he or she should leave the meeting with a clear action plan, which is agreeable to the customer, for the next visit.

Building a Long-Term Relationship

Focusing on building and maintaining long-term relationships with customers has become an important goal for salespeople. As marketers realize that it can cost five times as much to acquire a new customer than to service an existing one, the importance of customer retention and relationship building has become very clear.[5] Terry Vavra focuses on the value of current customers to the organization and has developed the concept of *aftermarketing,* which focuses the organization's attention on providing continuing satisfaction and reinforcement to individuals or organizations that are past or current customers. The goal of aftermarketing is to build lasting relationships with customers.[6] Successful aftermarketing efforts require that many specific activities be undertaken by the salesperson and others in the organization. These activities include

1. Establishing and maintaining a customer information file.
2. Monitoring order processing.
3. Ensuring initial proper use of the purchased product or service.
4. Providing ongoing guidance and suggestions.
5. Analyzing customer feedback and responding quickly to customer questions and complaints.
6. Continually conducting customer satisfaction research and responding to it.

As seen by the preceding discussion, there are no magic secrets of successful selling. The difference between good salespeople and mediocre ones is often the result of training plus experience. Training is no substitute for experience; the two complement each other. The difficulty with trying to discuss the selling job in terms of basic principles is that experienced, successful salespeople will always be able to find exceptions to these principles.

Relationships Can Lead to Partnerships

When the interaction between a salesperson and a customer does not end with the sale, the beginnings of a relationship are present. Many salespeople are finding that building relationships and even partnering with customers is becoming increasingly important.

When a buyer and a salesperson have a close personal relationship, they both begin to rely on each other and communicate honestly. When each has a problem, they work together to solve it. Such market relationships are known as *functional relationships.* An important trust begins to exist between the parties. As with any relationship, each often

1. *Improved sales productivity.* When the product or system being purchased is for the whole organization, different specialists handle different parts of the job. This usually results in a more effective and efficient sales process.
2. *More flexibility and quicker decisions.* To thrive in today's increasingly competitive markets, buying organizations often require selling organizations to produce small runs of tailored products on a very tight schedule. Cross-functional sales teams enable sellers to be more flexible because all functional units are involved in the sales process, which also enables the seller to make quicker decisions in response to buyer demands.
3. *Better decisions.* In most cases, the use of cross-functional teams composed of individuals with varied backgrounds in the company will lead to more innovative forms of thought and superior decisions than would be the case of an individual acting alone. Improved decisions would benefit both the buyer and the seller.
4. *Increased customer satisfaction.* The ultimate measure of the success of cross-functional sales teams comes with increased customer satisfaction, cemented relationships, and repeat business. The energy, flexibility, and commitment associated with cross-functional sales teams have led many organizations to adopt the approach.

gives and takes when the situation calls for it in order to keep the relationship intact. The reader may have such a relationship with a long-term medical or dental practitioner or hair cutter.

When organizations move beyond functional relationships, they develop *strategic partnerships,* or *strategic alliances.* These are long-term, formal relationships in which both parties make significant commitments and investments in each other in order to pursue mutual goals and to improve the profitability of each other. While a functional relationship is based on trust, a strategic partnership or alliance moves beyond trust. The partners in the relationship actually invest in each other. Obviously, the reasons for forming strategic partnerships vary. Some do it to create joint opportunities (banks, insurance companies, and brokerage firms), to gain access to new markets [United Parcel Service of America (UPS) and Mail Boxes Etc.], to develop new technology or exploit joint opportunities (IBM and Apple), or to gain a marketing advantage over competitors (United Airlines and Starbucks Coffee, American Airlines and Career Track).

People Who Support the Sales Force

In many instances, sales personnel will require some assistance at various stages of the sales process. These support personnel do not seek the order. Their purpose is to focus on the long-term relationship and increase the likelihood of sales in the long run.

Missionary salespeople are used in certain industries such as pharmaceuticals to focus solely on promotion of existing products and introduction of new products. They may call on physicians to convince them to prescribe a new drug or on pharmacies to convince them to promote a new cold remedy with a large display during the cold and flu season.

A *technical sales specialist* supports the sales staff by providing training or other technical assistance to the prospect. This individual may follow up an expression of interest to the salesperson from a prospect, especially when the product is to be used to solve certain technical problems of the buyer. Some organizations will provide training to the front-line staff of the buying organization who will be expected to sell the product to their customers.

1. *Ego strength:* A healthy self-esteem that allows one to bounce back from rejection.
2. *A sense of urgency:* Wanting to get it done now.
3. *Ego drive:* A combination of competitiveness and self-esteem.
4. *Assertiveness:* The ability to be firm, lead the sales process, and get one's point across confidently.
5. *Willingness to take risk:* Willingness to innovate and take a chance.
6. *Sociable:* Outgoing, talkative, friendly, and interested in others.
7. *Abstract reasoning:* Ability to understand concepts and ideas.
8. *Skepticism:* A slight lack of trust and suspicion of others.
9. *Creativity:* The ability to think differently.
10. *Empathy:* The ability to place oneself in someone else's shoes.

Source: Research conducted by Sales and Marketing Management involving 209 salespeople representing 189 companies in 37 industries and reported in George E. Belch and Michael A. Belch, *Advertising and Promotion,* 8th ed. (Burr Ridge, IL: McGraw-Hill/Irwin, 2009), p. 600.

Finally, when the product is extremely high priced and is being sold to the whole organization, *cross-functional sales teams* are often used. Since products increase in technical complexity, and units of the buying organization require specialized knowledge before a buying decision can be made, team selling has increased in popularity. For example, a manufacturer's sales team might be made up of people from sales, engineering, customer service, and finance, depending on the needs of the customer. A bank's sales team might consist of people from the commercial lending, investments, small business, and trust departments.

MANAGING THE SALES AND RELATIONSHIP-BUILDING PROCESS

Every personal sale can be divided into two parts: the part done by the salespeople and the part done for the salespeople by the company. For example, from the standpoint of the product, the company should provide the salesperson with a product skillfully designed, thoroughly tested, attractively packaged, adequately advertised, and priced to compare favorably with competitive products. Salespeople have the responsibility of being thoroughly acquainted with the product, its selling features, and points of superiority and possess a sincere belief in the value of the product. From a sales management standpoint, the company's part of the sale involves the following:

1. Efficient and effective sales tools, including continuous sales training, promotional literature, samples, trade shows, product information, and adequate advertising.
2. An efficient delivery and reorder system to ensure that customers will receive the merchandise as promised.
3. An equitable compensation plan that rewards performance, motivates the salesperson, and promotes company loyalty. It should also reimburse the salesperson for all reasonable expenses incurred while doing the job.
4. Adequate supervision and evaluation of performance as a means of helping salespeople do a better job not only for the company but for themselves as well.

The Sales Management Task

Marketing managers and sales managers must make some very important decisions regarding how the sales force should be organized. Most companies organize their sales efforts either by geography, product, or customer. These are illustrated in Figure 9.2.

In a *geographic structure,* individual salespeople are assigned geographic territories to cover. A salesperson calls on all prospects in the territory and usually represents all of the company's products. A geographic structure provides the practical benefit of limiting the distance each salesperson must travel to see customers and prospects.

In a *product structure,* each salesperson is assigned to prospects and customers for a particular product or product line. A product structure is useful when the sales force must have specific technical knowledge about products in order to sell effectively. However, this structure can result in a duplication of sales efforts because more than one salesperson can call on the same customer. Consequently, it tends to be expensive.

A *customer structure* assigns a salesperson or selling team to serve a single customer or single type of customer. This structure works best when different types of buyers have large or significantly different needs. When this structure involves devoting all of a salesperson's time to a single customer, it is expensive but can result in large sales and satisfied customers.

In a variation of the customer structure, a company may employ *major account management,* or the use of team selling to focus on major customers to establish long-term relationships.[7] Procter & Gamble, whose sales force used to be organized by product, has

FIGURE 9.2

Organizing the Sales Force

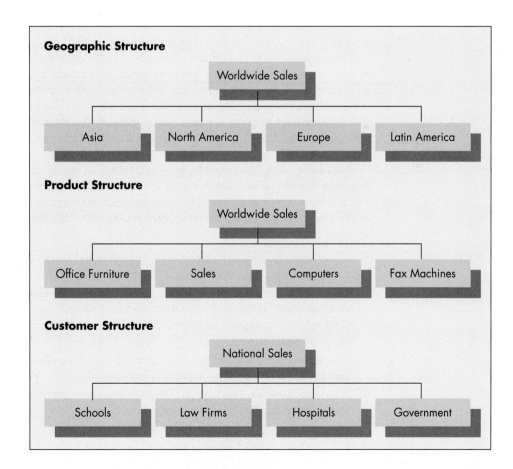

shifted to major account management. Assigning resources to particular customers has proved to be more flexible and customer focused for the company.

The customer-organized structure is well suited for the use of cross-functional teams. However, geographic and product territories can also be effective. The key is that sales management and the sales force must concentrate on learning and meeting customers' wants and needs better than competitors do.

Controlling the Sales Force

There are two obvious reasons why it is critical that the sales force be properly controlled. First, personal selling can be the largest marketing expense component in the final price of the product. Second, unless the sales force is somehow directed, motivated, and audited on a continual basis, it is likely to be less efficient than it is capable of being. Controlling the sales force involves four key functions: (1) forecasting sales, (2) establishing sales territories and quotas, (3) analyzing expenses, and (4) motivating and compensating performance.

Forecasting Sales

Sales planning begins with a forecast of sales for some future period or periods. From a practical standpoint, these forecasts are made on a short-term basis of a year or less, although long-range forecasts of one to five years are made for purposes other than managing the sales force, such as financing, production, and development. Generally speaking, forecasting is the marketing manager's responsibility. In large firms, because of the complexity of the task, it is usually delegated to a specialized unit, such as the marketing research department. Forecast data should be integrated into the firm's marketing information system for use by sales managers and other executives. For many companies, the sales forecast is the key instrument in the planning and control of operations.

The *sales forecast* is an estimate of how much of the company's output, either in dollars or in units, can be sold during a specified future period under a proposed marketing plan and under an assumed set of economic conditions. A sales forecast has several important uses: (1) It is used to establish sales quotas; (2) it is used to plan personal selling efforts as well as other types of promotional activities in the marketing mix; (3) it is used to budget selling expenses; and (4) it is used to plan and coordinate production, logistics, inventories, personnel, and so forth.

Sales forecasting has become very sophisticated in recent years, especially with the increased availability of computer software. It should be mentioned, however, that a forecast is never a substitute for sound business judgment. At the present time no single method of sales forecasting gives uniformly accurate results with infallible precision. Outlined next are some commonly used sales forecasting methods.[8]

1. *Jury of executive opinion method.* This combines and averages the views of top management representing marketing, production, finance, purchasing, and administration.
2. *Sales force composite method.* This is similar to the first method in that it obtains the combined views of the sales force about the future outlook for sales. In some companies all salespeople, or district managers, submit estimates of the future sales in their territory or district.
3. *Customer expectations method.* This approach involves asking customers or product users about the quantity they expect to purchase.
4. *Time-series analysis.* This approach involves analyzing past sales data and the impact of factors that influence sales (long-term growth trends, cyclical fluctuations, seasonal variations).

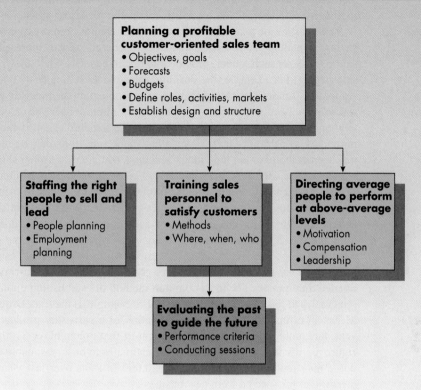

Source: Charles M. Futrell, *Fundamentals of Selling: Customers for Life Through Service,* 12th ed. (Burr Ridge, IL: McGraw-Hill/Irwin, 2011), p. 500.

5. *Correlation analysis.* This involves measuring the relationship between the dependent variable, sales, and one or more independent variables that can explain increases or decreases in sales volumes.

6. *Other quantitative techniques.* Numerous statistical and mathematical techniques can be used to predict or estimate future sales. Two of the more important techniques are (*a*) growth functions, which are mathematical expressions specifying the relationship between demand and time; and (*b*) simulation models, in which a statistical model of the industry is developed and programmed to compute values for the key parameters of the model.

Establishing Sales Territories and Quotas

The establishment of sales territories and sales quotas represents management's need to match personal selling effort with sales potential (or opportunity). Soundly designed sales territories can improve how the market is served.[9] It is much easier to pinpoint customers and prospects and to determine who should call on them when the market is geographically divided than when the market is considered a large aggregate of potential accounts. The geographic segments should represent small clusters of customers or prospects within some physical proximity. Implied here is the notion that there are some distinct economic advantages to dividing the market into smaller segments. Salespeople restricted to a geographic area are likely to get more sales in the territory. Instead of simply servicing the "easy" and larger accounts, they are prone to develop small accounts. Of course, there are criteria other than geography for establishing territories. One important criterion is product specialization. In this case, salespeople are specialists relative to particular product or customer situations.

The question of managing sales territories cannot be discussed meaningfully without saying something about sales quotas. In general, quotas represent goals assigned to salespeople. As such, quotas provide three main benefits. First, they provide incentives for salespeople. For example, the definite objective of selling $500,000 worth of computer equipment is more motivating to most salespeople than the indefinite charge to go out and sell computer equipment. Sales bonuses and commissions based on quotas can also be motivational. Second, quotas provide a quantitative standard against which the performance of individual sales representatives or other marketing units can be measured. They allow management to pinpoint individuals and units that are performing above average and those experiencing difficulty. Third, quotas can be used not only to evaluate salespersons' performances but also to evaluate and control their efforts. As part of their job, salespeople are expected to engage in various activities besides calling on established accounts. These activities might include calling on new accounts, collecting past-due accounts, and planning and developing sales presentations. Activity quotas allow the company to monitor whether salespeople are engaging in these activities to the extent desired.

Sales quotas represent specific sales goals assigned to each territory or unit over a designated time period. The most common method of establishing quotas for territories is to relate sales to forecasted sales potential. For example, if the Ajax Drug Company's territory M has an estimated industry sales potential for a particular product of $400,000 for the year, the quota might be set at 25 percent of that potential, or $100,000. The 25 percent figure represents the market share Ajax estimates to be a reasonable target. This $100,000 quota may represent an increase of $20,000 in sales over last year (assuming constant prices) that is expected from new business.

In establishing sales quotas for its individual territories or sales personnel, management needs to take into account three key factors. First, all territories will not have equal potential and, therefore, compensation must be adjusted accordingly. Second, all salespeople will not have equal ability and assignments may have to be made accordingly. Third, the sales task in each territory may differ from time period to time period. For instance, the nature of some territories may require that salespeople spend more time seeking new accounts, rather than servicing established accounts, especially in the case of so-called new territories. The point to be made here is that quotas can vary, not only by territory but also by assigned tasks. The effective sales manager should assign quotas not only for dollar sales but also for each major selling function. Figure 9.3 is an example of how this is done for the Medi-Test Company, where each activity is assigned a quota and a weight reflecting its relative importance.

Analyzing Expenses

Sales forecasts should include a sales expense budget. In some companies, sales expense budgets are developed from the bottom up. Each territorial or district manager submits estimates of expenses and forecasted sales quotas. These estimates are usually prepared for a period of a year and then broken down into quarters and months. The sales manager then reviews the budget requests from the field offices and from staff departments.

Motivating and Compensating Performance

An important task for the sales manager is motivating and compensating the sales force. These two tasks are major determinants of sales force productivity. Managing people is always a challenge and involves personal interaction with members of the sales force, time in the field visiting customers, free-flowing communication with the sales force, either by e-mail or telephone, and providing feedback on a regular basis as well as coaching and developing incentive programs through which job promotions or increased earnings can be achieved.[10]

MARKETING INSIGHT Effort- and Results-Oriented Measures for Evaluating Salespeople 9–6

EFFORT-ORIENTED MEASURES

1. Number of sales calls made.
2. Number of maintenance-repairs-operations (MRO) calls made.
3. Number of complaints handled.
4. Number of checks on reseller stocks.
5. Uncontrollable lost job time.
6. Number of inquiries followed up.
7. Number of demonstrations completed.

RESULTS-ORIENTED MEASURES

1. Sales volume (total or by product or model).
2. Sales volume as a percentage of quota.
3. Sales profitability (dollar gross margin or contribution).
4. Number of new accounts.
5. Number of stockouts.
6. Number of distributors participating in programs.
7. Number of lost accounts.
8. Percentage volume increase in key accounts.
9. Number of customer complaints.
10. Distributor sales-inventory ratios.

Source: Adapted from Thomas N. Ingram, Raymond W. Laforge, and Charles H. Schwepker, Jr., *Sales Management: Analysis and Decision Making,* 9th ed. (Mason, OH: Thomson Southwestern, 2009), chap. 15; and Thayer C. Taylor, "SFA: The Newest Orthodoxy," *Sales and Marketing Management,* February 1993, pp. 26–28.

There are two basic types of compensation: salary and commission. *Salary* usually refers to a specific amount of monetary compensation at an agreed rate for definite time periods. *Commission* is usually monetary compensation provided for each unit of sales and expressed as a percentage of sales. The base on which commissions are computed may be volume of sales in units of product, gross sales in dollars, net sales after returns,

FIGURE 9.3 Medi-Test Company Sales Activity Evaluation

Territory: Southern
Salesperson: Marsha Smith

Functions	(1) Quota	(2) Actual	(3) Percent (2 ÷ 1)	(4) Weight	(5) Score (3 × 4)
Sales volume					
Old business	$380,000	$300,000	79	0.7	55.3
New business	$ 20,000	$ 20,000	100	0.5	50.0
Calls on prospects					
Doctors	20	15	75	0.2	15.0
Druggists	80	60	75	0.2	15.0
Wholesalers	15	15	100	0.2	20.0
Hospitals	10	10	100	0.2	20.0
				2.0	175.3

Performance index = 175.3

FIGURE 9.4
Types of Sales Force
Incentives and Some
Possible Performance
Outcomes

Source: Some of the
material was adapted from
Gilbert A. Churchill, Jr., Neil
M. Ford, and Orville C.
Walker, *Sales Force
Management,* 5th ed. (Burr
Ridge, IL: Irwin/McGraw-Hill,
1997), p. 490.

Types of Incentives	Some Possible Outcomes
• Positive evaluation feedback.	• Increase in sales volume.
• Company-wide recognition.	• Sale of more profitable products.
• Bonus.	• Attention on selling new products.
• Salary increases.	• Achieving greater market penetration.
• Pay for new product idea.	• Increased number of sales calls.
• Education allowance.	• Larger average orders.
• Time off.	• Attracting new customers.
• Fringe benefits.	• Improved service of existing customers.
• Stock options.	• Reduction in customer turnover.
• Retirement plan.	• Reduction in selling costs.
• Profit sharing.	• Full-line balanced selling.

sales volume in excess of a quota, or net profits. Very often, several compensation approaches are combined. For example, a salesperson might be paid a base salary, a commission on sales exceeding a volume figure, and a percentage share of the company's profits for that year.

In addition to straight dollar compensation, there are numerous other forms of incentives that can be used to motivate the sales force. Some of these types of incentives and their potential performance outcomes are listed in Figure 9.4.

SUMMARY

This chapter has attempted to outline and explain the personal selling aspect of the promotion mix. An emphasis was placed on describing the importance of the relationship-building aspect of the personal selling process. For organizations that wish to continue to grow and prosper, personal selling plays an integral part in the marketing of products and services. As long as production continues to expand through the development of new and highly technical products, personal selling will continue to be an important part of marketing strategy.

Additional Resources

Ash, Mary Kay. *The Mary Kay Way: Timeless Principles from America's Greatest Woman Entrepreneur.* Hoboken, NJ: John Wiley and Sons, 2008.

Gonzalez, Gabriel R., Douglas Hoffman, and Thomas N. Ingram. "Improving Relationship Selling through Failure Analysis and Recovery Efforts: A Framework and Call to Action." *Journal of Personal Selling and Sales Management,* Spring 2005, pp. 24–32.

Hunter, Gary K., and William D. Perreault. "Making Sales Technology Effective." *Journal of Marketing,* January 2007, pp. 16–34.

Pradeep, A. K. *The Buying Brain: Secrets for Selling the Subconscious Mind.* NY: John Wiley and Sons, 2010.

Schroder, Richard M. *From a Good Sales Call to a Great Sales Call.* NY: McGraw-Hill, 2011.

Key Terms and Concepts

After marketing: A concept that focuses attention on the value of current customers to the organization and on providing continuing satisfaction and reinforcement to them as well as past customers. The goal is to build lasting relationships with customers.

Correlation analysis: A method used in sales forecasting that involves measuring the relationship between the dependent variable, sales, and one or more independent variables that can explain increases or decreases in sales volume.

Cross-functional sales teams: A team that might include people from sales, engineering, customer service, and finance, depending on the needs of the customer. When the product is extremely high priced and is being sold to the whole organization, cross-functional sales teams are often used.

Customer organization structure: A structure that assigns a salesperson or team to serve a single customer or type of customer that has large or significant needs.

Geographic organization structure: Structure in which individual salespeople are assigned geographic territories. The salesperson calls on all prospects in the territory and usually represents all of the company's products.

Lead: A prospect that may or may not have the potential to be a true prospect, a candidate, to whom a sale could be made.

Major account organization structure: A variation of the customer organization structure, in which a company may assign a salesperson or a team to focus on major customers to foster long-term relationships.

Missionary salesperson: Used in many industries to focus solely on the promotion of existing products and introduction of new products.

Objectives of the sales force: Ultimately, revenue and sales. Other objectives include information provision, persuasion, and after-sale service.

Product organization structure: Structure in which each salesperson is assigned customers and prospects for a particular product or product line. This structure is useful when the sales force must have specific technical knowledge about products in order to sell effectively.

Prospecting: The process of locating potential customers. The process usually involves random lead generation which usually requires a high number of contacts to gain a sale or selected lead generation which uses existing contacts and knowledge to generate new prospects.

Sales forecast: An estimate of how much of the organization's output, either in dollars or in units, can be sold during a specific period under a proposed marketing plan and under an assumed set of economic conditions. It has many important uses in sales management, marketing planning, and strategic planning.

Sales relationship-building process: Process that views the initial sale as the first step in a long-term relationship-building process, not as the end goal. It contains six sequential stages: (1) prospecting, (2) planning the sales call, (3) presenting, (4) responding to objections, (5) obtaining commitment/closing the sale, and (6) building a long-term relationship.

Strategic alliance: Also called strategic partnership, long-term, formal relationships in which both parties make significant commitments and investments in each other in order to pursue mutual goals and to improve the profitability of each other. The partners in a strategic alliance actually invest in each other.

Technical sales specialist: Often used when the product is to be used to solve technical problems of the buyer. They support the salesperson by providing training or other technical assistance to the prospect.

Time series analyses: A method used in forecasting sales that involves analyzing past sales data and the impact of factors that influence sales (long-term growth trends, cyclical fluctuations, seasonal variations).

10

Distribution Strategy

Channel of distribution decisions involve numerous interrelated variables that must be integrated into the total marketing mix. Because of the time and money required to set up an efficient channel, and since channels are often hard to change once they are set up, these decisions are critical to the success of the firm.

This chapter is concerned with the development and management of channels of distribution and the process of goods distribution in complex, highly competitive, and specialized economies. It should be noted at the outset that channels of distribution provide the ultimate consumer or organizational buyer with time, place, and possession utility. Thus, an efficient channel is one that delivers the product when and where it is wanted at a minimum total cost.

THE NEED FOR MARKETING INTERMEDIARIES

A *channel of distribution* is the combination of institutions through which a seller markets products to organizational buyers or ultimate consumers. The need for other institutions or intermediaries in the delivery of goods is sometimes questioned, particularly since the profits they make are viewed as adding to the cost of the product. However, this reasoning is generally fallacious, since producers use marketing intermediaries because the intermediary can perform functions more cheaply and more efficiently than the producer can. This notion of efficiency is critical when the characteristics of advanced economies are considered.

For example, the U.S. economy is characterized by heterogeneity in terms of both supply and demand. In terms of numbers alone, there are over 7 million establishments with employees comprising the supply segment of the economy, and there are nearly 110 million households making up the demand side. Clearly, if each of these units had to deal on a one-to-one basis to obtain needed goods and services, and there were no intermediaries to collect and disperse assortments of goods, the system would be totally inefficient. Thus, the primary role of intermediaries is to bring supply and demand together in an efficient and orderly fashion.

CLASSIFICATION OF MARKETING INTERMEDIARIES AND FUNCTIONS

There are a great many types of marketing intermediaries, many of which are so specialized by function and industry that they need not be discussed here. Figure 10.1 presents the major types of marketing intermediaries common to many industries. Although there is some overlap in this classification, these categories are based on the marketing

FIGURE 10.1
Major Types
of Marketing
Intermediaries

Source: Based on Peter D. Bennett, ed., *Dictionary of Marketing Terms*, 2d ed. (Chicago: American Marketing Association, 1995).

> **Middleman**—an independent business concern that operates as a link between producers and ultimate consumers or organizational buyers.
>
> **Merchant middleman**—a middleman who buys the goods outright and takes title to them.
>
> **Agent**—a business unit that negotiates purchases, sales, or both but does not take title to the goods in which it deals.
>
> **Wholesaler**—a merchant establishment operated by a concern that is primarily engaged in buying, taking title to, usually storing and physically handling goods in large quantities, and reselling the goods (usually in smaller quantities) to retailers or to organizational buyers.
>
> **Retailer**—a merchant middleman who is engaged primarily in selling to ultimate consumers.
>
> **Broker**—a middleman who serves as a go-between for the buyer or seller. The broker assumes no title risks, does not usually have physical custody of products, and is not looked upon as a permanent representative of either the buyer or the seller.
>
> **Manufacturers' agent**—an agent who generally operates on an extended contractual basis, often sells within an exclusive territory, handles noncompeting but related lines of goods, and possesses limited authority with regard to prices and terms of sale.
>
> **Distributor**—a wholesale middleman especially in lines where selective or exclusive distribution is common at the wholesaler level in which the manufacturer expects strong promotional support; often a synonym for wholesaler.
>
> **Jobber**—a middleman who buys from manufacturers and sells to retailers; a wholesaler.
>
> **Facilitating agent**—a business firm that assists in the performance of distribution tasks other than buying, selling, and transferring title (i.e., transportation companies, warehouses, etc.)

functions performed; that is, various intermediaries perform different marketing functions and to different degrees. Figure 10.2 is a listing of the more common marketing functions performed in the channel.

It should be remembered that whether or not a manufacturer uses intermediaries to perform these functions, the functions have to be performed by someone. In other words, the managerial question is not whether to perform the functions, but who will perform them and to what degree.

FIGURE 10.2
Major Functions
Performed in
Channels of
Distribution

Source: Roger A. Kerin, Steven W. Hartley, and William Rudelius, *Marketing*, 10th ed. (Burr Ridge, IL: McGraw-Hill/Irwin, 2011), p. 381.

> *Transactional Function*
>
> **Buying:** Purchasing products for resale or as an agent for supply of a product.
>
> **Selling:** Contacting potential customers, promoting products, and soliciting orders.
>
> **Risk taking:** Assuming business risks in the ownership of inventory that can become obsolete or deteriorate.
>
> *Logistical Function*
>
> **Assorting:** Creating product assortments from several sources to serve customers.
>
> **Storing:** Assembling and protecting products at a convenient location to offer better customer service.
>
> **Sorting:** Purchasing in large quantities and breaking into smaller amounts desired by customers.
>
> **Transporting:** Physically moving products to customers.
>
> *Facilitating Function*
>
> **Financing:** Extending credit to customers.
>
> **Grading:** Inspecting, testing, or judging products, and assigning them quality grades.
>
> **Marketing information and research:** Providing information to customers and suppliers, including competitive conditions and trends.

CHANNELS OF DISTRIBUTION

As previously noted, a channel of distribution is the combination of institutions through which a seller markets products to the user or ultimate consumer. Some of these links assume the risks of ownership; others do not. The conventional channel of distribution patterns for consumer goods markets are shown in Figure 10.3.

Some manufacturers use *direct channels,* selling directly to a market. For example, Gateway sold computers through the mail without the use of other intermediaries. Using a direct channel, called *direct marketing,* increased in popularity as marketers found that products could be sold directly using a variety of methods. These include direct mail, tele-marketing, direct-action advertising, catalog selling, cable selling, online selling, and direct selling through demonstrations at home or place of work. These will be discussed in more detail later in this chapter.

In other cases, one or more intermediaries may be used in the distribution process. For example, Hewlett-Packard sells its computers and printers through retailers such as Best Buy and Office Max. A common channel for consumer goods is one in which the manufacturer sells through wholesalers and retailers. For instance, a cold remedy manufacturer may sell to drug wholesalers who, in turn, sell a vast array of drug products to various retail outlets. Small manufacturers may also use agents, since they do not have sufficient capital for their own sales forces. Agents are commonly used intermediaries in the jewelry industry. The final channel in Figure 10.3 is used primarily when small wholesalers and retailers are involved. Channels with one or more intermediaries are referred to as *indirect channels.*

In contrast to consumer products, the direct channel is often used in the distribution of organizational goods. The reason for this stems from the structure of most organizational markets, which often have relatively few but extremely large customers. Also, many organizational products, such as computer systems, need a great deal of presale and postsale service. Distributors are used in organizational markets when there is a large number of buyers, but each purchases a small amount of a product. As in the consumer market, agents are used

FIGURE 10.3   Conventional Channels of Distribution of Consumer Goods

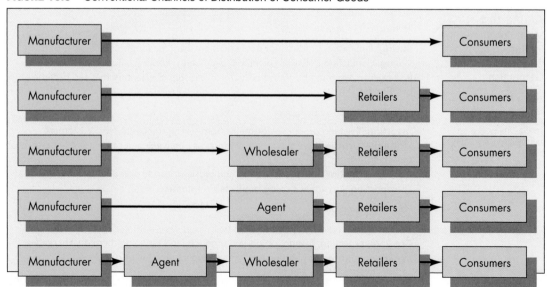

FIGURE 10.4   Conventional Channels of Distribution for Organizational Goods

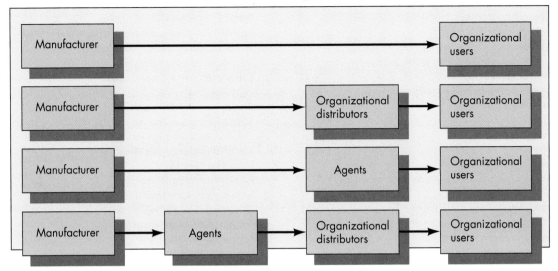

in organizational markets in cases where manufacturers do not wish to have their own sales forces. Such an arrangement may be used by small manufacturers or when the market is geographically dispersed. The final channel arrangement in Figure 10.4 may also be used by a small manufacturer or when the market consists of many small customers. Under such conditions, it may not be economical for sellers to have their own sales organization.

SELECTING CHANNELS OF DISTRIBUTION

Given the numerous types of channel intermediaries and functions that must be performed, the task of selecting and designing a channel of distribution may at first appear to be overwhelming. However, in many industries, channels of distribution have developed over many years and have become somewhat traditional. In such cases, the producer may be limited to this type of channel to operate in the industry. This is not to say that a traditional channel is always the most efficient and that there are no opportunities for innovation. But the fact that such a channel is widely accepted in the industry suggests it is highly efficient. A primary constraint in these cases and in cases where no traditional channel exists is that of availability of the various types of middlemen. All too often in the early stages of channel design, executives map out elaborate channel networks only to find out later that no such independent intermediaries exist for the firm's product in selected geographic areas. Even if they do exist, they may not be willing to accept the seller's products. In general, there are six basic considerations in the initial development of channel strategy. These are outlined in Figure 10.5.

It should be noted that for a particular product any one of these characteristics greatly influences choice of channels. To illustrate, highly perishable products generally require direct channels, or a firm with little financial strength may require intermediaries to perform almost all of the marketing functions.

Specific Considerations

The above characteristics play an important part in framing the channel selection decision. Based on them, the choice of channels can be further refined in terms of

FIGURE 10.5   General Considerations in Channel Planning

1. **Customer characteristics.**
   a. Number.
   b. Geographic dispersion.
   c. Preferred channels and outlets for purchase.
   d. Purchasing patterns.
   e. Use of new channels (e.g., online purchasing).
2. **Product characteristics.**
   a. Unit value.
   b. Perishability.
   c. Bulkiness.
   d. Degree of standardization.
   e. Installation and maintenance services required.
3. **Intermediary characteristics.**
   a. Availability.
   b. Willingness to accept product or product line.
   c. Geographic market served.
   d. Marketing functions performed.
   e. Potential for conflict.
   f. Potential for long-term relationship.
   g. Competitive products sold.
   h. Financial condition.
   i. Other strengths and weaknesses.
4. **Competitor characteristics.**
   a. Number.
   b. Relative size and market share.

   c. Distribution channels and strategy.
   d. Financial condition and estimated marketing budget.
   e. Size of product mix and product lines.
   f. Overall marketing strategy employed.
   g. Other strengths and weaknesses.
5. **Company characteristics.**
   a. Relative size and market share.
   b. Financial condition and marketing budget.
   c. Size of product mix and product lines.
   d. Marketing strategy employed.
   e. Marketing objectives.
   f. Past channel experience.
   g. Marketing functions willing to perform.
   h. Other strengths and weaknesses.
6. **Environmental characteristics.**
   a. Economic conditions.
   b. Legal regulations and restrictions.
   c. Political issues.
   d. Global and domestic cultural differences and changes.
   e. Technological changes.
   f. Other opportunities and threats.

(1) distribution coverage required, (2) degree of control desired, (3) total distribution cost, and (4) channel flexibility.

Distribution Coverage Required

Because of the characteristics of the product, the environment needed to sell the product, and the needs and expectations of the potential buyer, products will vary in the intensity of distribution coverage they require. Distribution coverage can be viewed along a continuum ranging from intensive to selective to exclusive distribution.

Intensive Distribution   Here the manufacturer attempts to gain exposure through as many wholesalers and retailers as possible. Most convenience goods require intensive distribution based on the characteristics of the product (low unit value) and the needs and expectations of the buyer (high frequency of purchase and convenience).

Selective Distribution   Here the manufacturer limits the use of intermediaries to the ones believed to be the best available in a geographic area. This may be based on the service organization available, the sales organization, or the reputation of the intermediary. Thus, appliances, home furnishings, and better clothing are usually distributed selectively. For appliances, the intermediary's service organization could be a key factor, while for better clothing and home furnishings, the intermediary's reputation would be an important consideration.

Exclusive Distribution   Here the manufacturer severely limits distribution, and intermediaries are provided exclusive rights within a particular territory. The characteristics of the product are a determining factor here. Where the product requires certain specialized selling effort or investment in unique facilities or large inventories, this arrangement is usually selected. Retail paint stores are an example of such a distribution arrangement.

THE PERFECT INTERMEDIARY

1. Has access to the market that the manufacturer wants to reach.
2. Carries adequate stocks of the manufacturer's products and a satisfactory assortment of other products.
3. Has an effective promotional program—advertising, personal selling, and product displays. Promotional demands placed on the manufacturer are in line with what the manufacturer intends to do.
4. Provides services to customers—credit, delivery, installation, and product repair—and honors the product warranty conditions.
5. Pays its bills on time and has capable management.

THE PERFECT MANUFACTURER

1. Provides a desirable assortment of products—well designed, properly priced, attractively packaged, and delivered on time and in adequate quantities.
2. Builds product demand for these products by advertising them.
3. Furnishes promotional assistance to its middlemen.
4. Provides managerial assistance for its middlemen.
5. Honors product warranties and provides repair and installation service.

THE PERFECT COMBINATION

1. Probably doesn't exist.

Degree of Control Desired

In selecting channels of distribution, the seller must make decisions concerning the degree of control desired over the marketing of the firm's products. Some manufacturers prefer to keep as much control over their products as possible. Ordinarily, the degree of control achieved by the seller is proportionate to the directness of the channel. One Eastern brewery, for instance, owns its own fleet of trucks and operates a wholly owned delivery system direct to grocery and liquor stores. Its market is very concentrated geographically, with many small buyers, so such a system is economically feasible. However, all other brewers in the area sell through distributors.

When more indirect channels are used, the manufacturer must surrender some control over the marketing of the firm's product. However, attempts are commonly made to maintain a degree of control through some other indirect means, such as sharing promotional expenditures, providing sales training, or other operational aids, such as accounting systems, inventory systems, or marketing research data on the dealer's trading area.

Total Distribution Cost

The total distribution cost concept has developed out of the more general topic of systems theory. The concept suggests that a channel of distribution should be viewed as a total system composed of interdependent subsystems, and that the objective of the system (channel) manager should be to optimize total system performance. In terms of distribution costs, it generally is assumed that the total system should be designed to minimize costs for a given level of service. The following is a representative list of the major distribution costs to be minimized:

1. Transportation.
2. Order processing.

3. Cost of lost business (an opportunity cost due to inability to meet customer demand).
4. Inventory carrying costs, including:
   a. Storage-space charges.
   b. Cost of capital invested.
   c. Taxes.
   d. Insurance.
   e. Obsolescence and deterioration.
5. Packaging.
6. Materials handling.

The important qualification to the total-cost concept is the statement "other things being equal." The purpose of the total-cost concept is to emphasize total system performance to avoid suboptimization. However, other important factors must be considered, not the least of which are level of customer service, sales, profits, and interface with the total marketing mix.

Channel Flexibility

A final consideration relates to the ability of the manufacturer to adapt to changing conditions. To illustrate, much of the population has moved from inner cities to suburbs, and thus buyers make most of their purchases in shopping centers and malls. If a manufacturer had long-term exclusive dealership with retailers in the inner city, the ability to adapt to this population shift could have been severely limited.

MANAGING A CHANNEL OF DISTRIBUTION

Once the seller has decided on the type of channel structure to use and selected the individual members, the entire coalition should operate as a total system. From a behavioral perspective, the system can be viewed as a social system since each member interacts with the others, each member plays a role vis-à-vis the others, and each has certain expectations of the other. Thus, the behavioral perspective views a channel of distribution as more than a series of markets or participants extending from production to consumption.

Relationship Marketing in Channels

For many years in theory and practice, marketing has taken a competitive view of channels of distribution. In other words, since channel members had different goals and strategies, it was believed that the major focus should be on concepts such as power and conflict. Research interests focused on issues concerning bases of power, antecedents and consequences of conflict, and conflict resolution.

More recently, however, a new view of channels has developed. Perhaps because of the success of Japanese companies in the 1980s, it was recognized that much could be gained by developing long-term commitments and harmony among channel members. This view is called *relationship marketing,* which can be defined as "marketing with the conscious aim to develop and manage long-term and/or trusting relationships with customers, distributors, suppliers, or other parties in the marketing environment."[1]

It is well documented in the marketing literature that long-term relationships throughout the channel often lead to higher-quality products with lower costs. These benefits may account for the increased use of vertical marketing systems.[2]

Vertical Marketing Systems

To this point in the chapter the discussion has focused primarily on conventional channels of distribution. In conventional channels, each firm is relatively independent of the other

FIGURE 10.6

Major Types of
Vertical Marketing
Systems

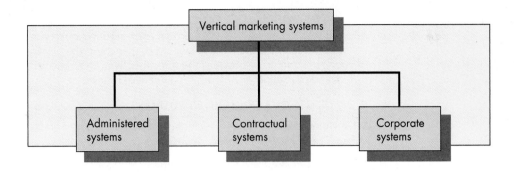

members in the channel. However, one of the important developments in channel management in recent years is the increasing use of vertical marketing systems.

Vertical marketing systems are channels in which members are more dependent on one
another and develop long-term working relationships in order to improve the efficiency
and effectiveness of the system. Figure 10.6 shows the major types of vertical marketing
systems, which include administered, contractual, and corporate systems.[3]

Administered Systems

Administered vertical marketing systems are the most similar to conventional channels.
However, in these systems there is a higher degree of interorganizational planning and
management than in a conventional channel. The dependence in these systems can result
from the existence of a strong channel leader such that other channel members work
closely with this company in order to maintain a long-term relationship. While any level
of channel member may be the leader of an administered system, Walmart, Kmart, and
Sears are excellent examples of retailers that have established administered systems with
many of their suppliers.

Contractual Systems

Contractual vertical marketing systems involve independent production and distribution
companies entering into formal contracts to perform designated marketing functions. Three
major types of contractual vertical marketing systems are the retail cooperative organization, wholesaler-sponsored voluntary chain, and various franchising programs.

In a retail cooperative organization, a group of independent retailers unite and agree
to pool buying and managerial resources to improve competitive position. In a wholesaler-
sponsored voluntary chain, a wholesaler contracts with a number of retailers and performs
channel functions for them. Usually, retailers agree to concentrate a major portion of
their purchasing with the sponsoring wholesaler and to sell advertised products at the
same price. The most visible type of contractual vertical marketing systems involves a
variety of franchise programs. Franchises involve a parent company (the franchisor) and
an independent firm (the franchisee) entering into a contractual relationship to set up and
operate a business in a particular way. Many products and services reach consumers
through franchise systems, including automobiles (Ford), gasoline (Mobil), hotels and
motels (Holiday Inn), restaurants (McDonald's), car rentals (Avis), and soft drinks (Pepsi).
In fact, some analysts predict that within the next 10 years, franchises will account for
50 percent of all retail sales.

Corporate Systems

Corporate vertical marketing systems involve single ownership of two or more levels of a
channel. A manufacturer's purchasing wholesalers or retailers is called *forward integration*.

A franchise is a means by which a producer of products or services achieves a direct channel of distribution without wholly owning or managing the physical facilities in the market.
In effect, the franchisor provides the franchisee with the franchisor's knowledge, manufacturing, and marketing techniques for a financial return.

INGREDIENTS OF A FRANCHISED BUSINESS

Six key ingredients should be included within a well-balanced franchise offered to a franchisee. These are given in order of importance.

- *Technical knowledge* in its practical form is supplied through an intensive course of study.
- *Managerial techniques* based on proven and time-tested programs are imparted to the
  franchisee on a continuing basis, even after the business has been started or taken over
  by the franchisee.
- *Commercial knowledge* involving prescribed methods of buying and selling is explained
  and codified. Most products to be obtained, processed, and sold to the franchisee are
  supplied by the franchisor.
- *Financial instruction* on managing funds and accounts is given to the franchisee during
  the indoctrination period.
- *Accounting controls* are set up by the franchisor for the franchisee.
- *Protective safeguards* are included in the intensive training of the franchisee for employees and customers, including the quality of the product, as well as the safeguards for
  assets through adequate insurance controls.

ELEMENTS OF AN IDEAL FRANCHISE PROGRAM

- *High gross margin.* In order for the franchisee to be able to afford a high franchise fee
  (which the franchisor needs), it is necessary to operate on a high gross margin percentage. This explains the widespread application of franchising in the food and service industries.
- *In-store value added.* Franchising works best in those product categories in which the
  product is at least partially processed in the store. Such environments require constant
  on-site supervision—a chronic problem for company-owned stores using a hired manager. Owners simply are willing to work harder over longer hours.
- *Secret processes.* Concepts, formulas, or products that the franchisee can't duplicate
  without joining the franchise program.
- *Real estate profits.* The franchisor uses income from ownership of property as a significant
  revenue source.
- *Simplicity.* The most successful franchises have been those that operate on automatic
  pilot: All the key decisions have been thought through, and the owner merely implements
  the decisions.

Source: Partially adapted from Philip D. White and Albert D. Bates, "Franchising Will Remain Retailing Fixture,
but Its Salad Days Have Long Since Gone," *Marketing News,* February 17, 1984, p. 14; and Scott Shane and
Chester Spell, "Factors for New Franchise Success," *Sloan Management Review,* Spring 1998, pp. 43–50. Also
see Stephen Spinelli, Jr., Robert M. Rosenberg, and Sue Birley, *Franchising* (Upper Saddle River, NJ: Prentice-
Hall PTR, 2004).

Wholesalers or retailers' purchasing channel members above them is called *backward integration.* Firms may choose to develop corporate vertical marketing systems in order to
compete more effectively with other marketing systems, to obtain scale economies, and to
increase channel cooperation and avoid channel conflict.

WHOLESALING

As noted, wholesalers are merchants that are primarily engaged in buying, taking title to, usually storing and physically handling goods in large quantities, and reselling the goods (usually in smaller quantities) to retailers or to industrial or business users.[4] Wholesalers are also called distributors in some industries, particularly when they have exclusive distribution rights, such as in the beer industry. Other wholesalers that do not take title to goods are called agents, brokers, or manufacturers' representatives in various industries. There are over 890,000 wholesalers in the United States.

Wholesalers create value for suppliers, retailers, and users of goods by performing distribution functions efficiently and effectively. They may transport and warehouse goods, exhibit them at trade shows, and offer advice to retailers concerning which lines of products are selling best in other areas. Producers use wholesalers to reach large markets and extend geographic coverage for their goods. Wholesalers may lower the costs for other channel members by efficiently carrying out such activities as physically moving goods to convenient locations, assuming the risk of managing large inventories of diverse products, and delivering products as needed to replenish retail shelves.

While producers may actively seek out wholesalers for their goods, wholesalers also try to attract producers to use their services. To do so, they may offer to perform all the distribution functions or tailor their services to include only the functions that producers do not have the ability to perform effectively. Naturally, wholesalers especially seek producers of major brands for which sales and profit potential are likely to be the greatest. Wholesalers may compete with other wholesalers to attract producers by offering lower costs for the functions they perform. Wholesalers with excellent track records that do not carry directly competing products and brands, that have appropriate locations and facilities, and that have relationships with major retail customers can more easily attract manufacturers of successful products. Also, wholesalers that serve large markets may be more attractive since producers may be able to reduce the number of wholesalers they deal with and thereby lower their costs. Long-term profitable producer–wholesaler relationships are enhanced by trust, doing a good job for one another, and open communication about problems and opportunities.

Wholesalers also need to attract retailers and organizational customers to buy from them. In many cases, wholesalers have exclusive contracts to distribute products in a particular trading area. For popular products and brands with large market shares, the wholesaler's task is simplified because retailers want to carry them. For example, distributors of Coke and Pepsi can attract retailers easily because the products sell so well and consumers expect to find them in many retail outlets. Retail supermarkets and convenience stores would be at a competitive disadvantage without these brands.

However, for new or small market-share products and brands, particularly those of less well-known manufacturers, wholesalers may have to do considerable marketing to get retailers to stock them. Wholesalers may get placement for such products and brands in retail stores because they have previously developed strong long-term working relationships with them. Alternatively, wholesalers may have to carefully explain the marketing plan for the product, why it should be successful, and why carrying the product will benefit the retailer.

While there are still many successful wholesalers, the share of products they sell is likely to continue to decrease. This is because large retail chains such as Walmart have gained such market power that they can buy directly from manufacturers and bypass wholesalers altogether. The survival of wholesalers depends on their ability to meet the needs of both manufacturers and retailers by performing distribution functions more efficiently and effectively than a channel designed without them.

BENEFITS FOR MANUFACTURERS

- Provide the ability to reach diverse geographic markets cost effectively.
- Provide information about retailers and end users in various markets.
- Reduce costs through greater efficiency and effectiveness in distribution functions performed.
- Reduce potential losses by assuming risks and offering expertise.

BENEFITS FOR RETAILERS

- Provide potentially profitable products otherwise unavailable for resale in retail area.
- Provide information about industries, manufacturers, and other retailers.
- Reduce costs by providing an assortment of goods from different manufacturers.
- Reduce costs through greater efficiency in distribution functions performed.

BENEFITS FOR END USERS

- Increase the product alternatives available in local markets.
- Reduce retail prices by the efficiency and effectiveness contributed to the channel.
- Improve product selection by providing information to retailers about the best products to offer end users.

STORE AND NONSTORE RETAILING

As noted, retailers are merchants who are primarily engaged in selling to ultimate consumers. The more than 1.9 million retailers in the United States can be classified in many ways. For example, they are broken down in the North American Industry Classification System (NAICS) codes into eight general categories and a number of subcategories based on the types of merchandise they sell.[5]

Marketers have a number of decisions to make to determine the best way to retail their products. For example, decisions have to be made about whether to use stores to sell merchandise, and if so, whether to sell through company-owned stores, franchised outlets, or independent stores or chains. Decisions have to be made about whether to sell through nonstore methods, such as the Internet, and if so, which methods of nonstore retailing should be used. Each of these decisions brings about a number of others such as what types of stores to use, how many of them, what locations should be selected, and what specific types of nonstore retailing to use.

Store Retailing

About 90 percent of retail purchases are made through stores. This makes them an appropriate retail method for most types of products and services. Retailers vary not only in the types of merchandise they carry but also in the breadth and depth of their product assortments and the amount of service they provide. In general, *mass merchandisers* carry broad product assortments and compete on two bases. Supermarkets (Kroger) and department stores (Macy's) compete with other retailers on the basis of offering a good selection in a number of different categories, whereas supercenters (Walmart Supercenters), warehouse clubs (Costco), discount stores (Walmart), and off-price retailers (T.J. Maxx) compete more on the basis of offering lower prices on products in their large assortments. Manufacturers of many types of consumer goods must get distribution in one or more types of mass merchandisers to be successful.

Specialty stores handle deep assortments in a limited number of product categories. Specialty stores include limited-line stores that offer a large assortment of a few related product lines (The Gap), single-line stores that emphasize a single product (Batteries Plus), and category killers (Best Buy), which are large, low-priced limited-line retail chains that attempt to dominate a particular product category. If a product type is sold primarily through specialty stores and sales are concentrated in category killer chains, manufacturers may have to sell through them to reach customers.

Convenience stores (7-Eleven) are retailers whose primary advantages to consumers are location convenience, close-in parking, and easy entry and exit. They stock products that consumers want to buy in a hurry, such as milk or soft drinks, and charge higher prices for the purchase convenience. They are an important retail outlet for many types of convenience goods.

In selecting the types of stores and specific stores and chains to resell their products, manufacturers (and wholesalers) have a variety of factors to consider. They want stores and chains that reach their target market and have good reputations with consumers. They want stores and chains that handle distribution functions efficiently and effectively, order large quantities, pay invoices quickly, display their merchandise well, and allow them to make good profits. Selling products in the right stores and chains increases sales, and selling in prestigious stores can increase the equity of a brand and the price that can be charged. The locations of retail stores, the types of people who shop at them, and the professionalism of the salespeople and clerks who work in them all affect the success of the stores and the products they sell. In addition to the merchandise offered, store advertising, and price levels, the characteristics of the store itself—including layout, colors, smells, noises, lights, signs, and shelf space and displays—influence the success of both the stores and the products they offer.

Nonstore Retailing

Although stores dominate sales for most products, there are still opportunities to market products successfully in other ways. Five nonstore methods of retailing include catalogs and direct mail, vending machines, television home shopping, direct sales, and electronic exchanges.[6]

Catalogs and Direct Mail

Catalogs and direct mail dominate nonstore retailing. The advantages of this type of nonstore retailing for marketers are that consumers can be targeted effectively and reached in their homes or at work, overhead costs are decreased, and assortments of specialty merchandise can be presented with attractive pictures and in-depth descriptions of features and benefits. Catalogs can also remain in homes or offices for a lengthy time period, making available potential sales. Catalogs can offer specialty products for unique markets that are geographically dispersed in a cost-effective manner. Although consumers cannot experience products directly as they can in stores, catalog retailers with reputations for quality and generous return policies can reduce consumers' risks. For example, Levenger, which sells pens, desks, and "other tools for serious readers," sends consumers a postage-paid label to return unwanted merchandise. Many consumers enjoy the time savings of catalog shopping and are willing to pay higher prices to use it.

Vending Machines

Vending machines are a relatively limited method of retail merchandising, and most vending machine sales are for beverages, food, and candy. The advantages for marketers include the following: They are available for sales 24 hours a day, they can be placed in a variety of high-traffic locations, and marketers can charge higher prices. While uses of vending machines for such things as airline insurance and concert and game tickets are not unusual, this method has limited potential for most products.

Television Home Shopping

Television home shopping includes cable channels dedicated to shopping, infomercials, and direct-response advertising shown on cable and broadcast networks. Home Shopping Network and QVC are the leaders in this market, and the major products sold are inexpensive jewelry, apparel, cosmetics, and exercise equipment. While this method allows better visual display than catalogs, potential customers must be watching at the time the merchandise is offered; if not, they have no way of knowing about the product or purchasing it.

Direct Sales

Direct sales are made by salespeople to consumers in their homes or offices or by telephone. The most common products purchased this way are cosmetics, fragrances, decorative accessories, vacuum cleaners, home appliances, cooking utensils, kitchenware, jewelry, food and nutritional products, and educational materials. Avon, Mary Kay, and Tupperware are probably the best-known retail users of this channel. Salespeople can demonstrate products effectively and provide detailed feature and benefit information. A limitation of this method is that consumers are often too busy to spend their time this way and do not want to pay the higher prices needed to cover the high costs of this method of retailing.

Electronic Exchanges and Multichannel Marketing

Electronic exchanges or sales made online are the fastest growing method of retailing and in some years, sales have grown 20 to 25 percent per year. Some analysts suggest that in a few years, over 12 percent of all retail sales will be online. Companies like Amazon.com and Priceline.com have created profitable businesses by selling online and both business-to-business and business-to-consumer sales have grown to be profitable for a number of companies.

While the growth of electronic exchanges is partly due to the success of new, entrepreneurial companies, much of the growth can be attributed to large, established companies using a multichannel marketing strategy. *Multichannel marketing* involves the use of both traditional channels and electronic exchanges to better serve customers and build relationships with them. For example, JCPenney offers merchandise and information about it in its brick-and-mortar stores, in its mailed paper catalogs, and online to better serve its customers. In fact, its best customers purchase from all three. Similarly, other companies like Eddie Bauer, Bass Pro Shop, and Cabela's offer customers the opportunity to purchase from its stores, its catalogs, and online.

Figure 10.7 lists some of the advantages and disadvantages of electronic exchanges for marketers. In examining this figure, it is important to recognize that there are some differences in the advantages and disadvantages depending on whether the marketer is a small, entrepreneurial venture or a large, established company. Since electronic exchange offers low-entry barriers, this is an advantage for a small company that wants to get into a market and compete for business with less capital. However, for large, established companies, this

When developing commercial Web sites, it is important to consider what customers experience when searching for information, evaluating alternative products, and purchasing them. Below are some basic questions that Web site designers should consider.

INFORMATION SEARCH

1. Ease of navigation—is it easy to move throughout the Web site?
2. Speed of page downloads—does each page load quickly enough?
3. Effectiveness of search features—are search features returning the information users are looking for?
4. Frequency of product updates—is product information updated often enough to meet user needs?

EVALUATION OF ALTERNATIVES

1. Ease of product comparisons—is it easy to compare different products offered on the Web site?
2. Product descriptions—are product descriptions accurate, clear, and comprehensive enough to allow customers to make informed decisions?
3. Contacting customer service representatives—are customer service phone numbers easy to locate?
4. In-stock status—are out-of-stock products flagged before the customer proceeds to the checkout process?

PURCHASE

1. Security and privacy issues—do users feel comfortable transmitting personal information?
2. Checkout process—are users able to move through the checkout process in a reasonable amount of time?
3. Payment options—are payment options offered that nonbuyers desire?
4. Delivery options—are delivery options offered that nonbuyers desire?
5. Ordering instructions—are ordering instructions easy to understand?

Source: Based on Douglas K. Hoffman and John E. G. Bateson, *Services Marketing: Concepts, Strategies, and Cases,* 3rd ed. (Mason, OH: Thomson South Western, 2006), p. 86.

is less of an advantage since they have the capital to invest; low-entry barriers create more competition for them from smaller companies.

Similarly, large companies with established names and brand equity can more easily market products that customers would ordinarily want to examine before purchase (touch-and-feel products) than can smaller companies with less brand equity. For example, companies like Lands' End, J.C. Penney, and Walmart are more successful in attracting customers electronically because customers know the companies and their offerings better and perceive less risk in purchasing from them than from a new or unknown electronic marketer. This does not mean that newer companies that sell only by electronic means cannot compete for business. Companies such as Amazon.com and Priceline.com have created well-known Web sites and have generated considerable sales and profits.

In sum, electronic exchanges are an established alternative for marketing products and services. They do provide customers with a wealth of product information and large product assortments that are readily available. Many electronic marketers have found ways to deliver superior customer value and become profitable and many others are close to doing so.[7]

FIGURE 10.7
Electronic
Commerce:
Advantages and
Disadvantages for
Marketers

Advantages for Marketers

Reduces the need for stores, paper catalogs, and salespeople; can be cost efficient.

Allows good visual presentation and full description of product features and benefits.

Allows vast assortments of products to be offered efficiently.

Allows strategic elements, such as product offerings, prices, and promotion appeals, to be changed quickly.

Allows products to be offered globally in an efficient manner.

Allows products to be offered 24 hours a day, 365 days a year.

Fosters the development of one-on-one, interactive relationships with customers.

Provides an efficient means for developing a customer database and doing online marketing research.

Disadvantages for Marketers

Strong price competition online often squeezes profit margins.

Low entry barriers lead some e-marketers to overemphasize order-taking and not develop sufficient infrastructure for order fulfillment.

Customers must go to the Web site rather than having marketers seek them out via salespeople and advertising; advertising their Web sites is prohibitively expensive for many small e-marketers.

Limits the market to customers who are willing and able to purchase electronically; many countries still have a small population of computer-literate people.

Not as good for selling touch-and-feel products as opposed to look-and-buy products unless there is strong brand/store/site equity (Dell computers/Walmart/Amazon.com) or the products are homogeneous (books, CDs, plane tickets, etc.).

Often less effective and efficient in business-to-consumer markets than in business-to-business markets.

SUMMARY

This chapter introduced the distribution of goods and services in a complex, highly competitive, highly specialized economy. It emphasized the vital need for marketing intermediaries to bring about exchanges between buyers and sellers in a reasonably efficient manner. The chapter examined various types of intermediaries and the distribution functions they perform as well as topics in the selection and management of distribution channels. Finally, both wholesaling and store and nonstore retailing were discussed.

Additional Resources

Chopra, Sunil, and Peter Meindl. *Supply Chain Management.* 3rd ed. Upper River Saddle, NJ: Prentice Hall, 2007.

Coughlin, Anne T.; Erin Anderson; Louis W. Stern; and Adel I. El-Ansary. *Marketing Channels.* 7th ed. Upper Saddle River, NJ: Prentice Hall, 2006.

Levy, Michael, and Barton A. Weitz. *Retailing Management.* 8th ed. Burr Ridge, IL: Irwin/ McGraw-Hill, 2012.

Rosenbloom, Bert. *Marketing Channels: A Management View.* 8th ed. Mason, OH: Thomson South-Western, 2012.

Simchi-Levi, David; Philip Kaminsky, and Edith Simchi-Levi. *Designing and Managing the Supply Chain.* 3rd ed. Burr Ridge, IL: McGraw-Hill, 2008.

Key Terms and Concepts

Note: For definitions of the major types of marketing intermediaries, see Figure 10.1 and for the major functions performed in channels of distribution, see Figure 10.2 at the beginning of this chapter.

Administered system: A vertical marketing system with a higher degree of interorganizational planning than a conventional channel often brought about by having a strong channel leader.

Backward integration: The purchase by wholesalers or retailers of channel members above them.

Channel of distribution: The combination of institutions through which a seller markets products to organizational buyers or ultimate consumers.

Contractual system: A vertical marketing system that involves independent production and distribution companies entering into formal contracts to perform designated marketing functions.

Convenience stores: Retailers whose primary advantages to consumers are location convenience, close-in parking, and easy entry and exit. They typically stock a limited number of items that consumers want to buy in a hurry, such as milk or soft drinks and include stores like 7-Eleven and PDQ.

Corporate system: A vertical marketing system involving single ownership of two or more levels of a channel such as a manufacturer owning a wholesale operation.

Direct channels: Channels in which the manufacturer sells directly to a market without the use of intermediaries.

Direct marketing: A direct channel in which the seller uses direct mail, telemarketing, direct-action advertising, catalog selling, cable selling, online selling, or direct selling through demonstrations at home or place of work to reach buyers.

Exclusive distribution: An approach to distribution that involves the manufacturer providing exclusive rights to intermediaries in particular territories.

Forward integration: A manufacturer's purchase of wholesalers or retailers who distribute its products.

Indirect channels: Distribution channels with one or more intermediaries.

Intensive distribution: An approach to distribution that involves using as many wholesalers and retailers as possible to get broad distribution. It is commonly used with convenience goods.

Mass merchandisers: Large retailers that carry broad product assortments and compete on the basis of a good selection in a number of different categories (e.g., Macy's, Kroger) or on the basis of lower prices on products in their large assortment (e.g., Walmart, Costco).

Multichannel marketing: The use of traditional channels, such as stores and catalogs, along with electronic exchanges to better serve customers and build relationships with them.

Relationship marketing: Marketing with the conscious aim to develop and manage long-term and/or trusting relationships with customers, distributors, suppliers, or other parties in the marketing environment.

Selective distribution: An approach to distribution in which the manufacturer limits the use of intermediaries to the best available in a geographic area. The intermediaries are commonly selected on the basis of the service or sales organization available or reputation.

Specialty stores: Stores that handle deep assortments in a limited number of product categories, such as The Gap, Batteries Plus, or Best Buy.

Total distribution costs: Concept that suggests that a channel of distribution should be viewed as a total system composed of interdependent subsystems and that the objective of the system (channel) manager should be to optimize total system performance. This typically means the total system should minimize costs for a given level of service.

Vertical marketing systems: Channels in which members are more dependent on one another and develop long-term working relationships in order to improve the efficiency and effectiveness of the system.

Chapter

11

Pricing Strategy

One of the most important and complex decisions a firm has to make relates to pricing its products or services. If consumers or organizational buyers perceive a price to be too high, they may purchase competitive brands or substitute products, leading to a loss of sales and profits for the firm. If the price is too low, sales might increase, but profitability may suffer. Thus, pricing decisions must be given careful consideration when a firm is introducing a new product or planning a short- or long-term price change.

This chapter discusses demand, supply, and environmental influences that affect pricing decisions and emphasizes that all three must be considered for effective pricing. However, as will be discussed in the chapter, many firms price their products without explicitly considering all of these influences.

DEMAND INFLUENCES ON PRICING DECISIONS

Demand influences on pricing decisions concern primarily the nature of the target market and expected reactions of consumers to a given price or change in price. There are three primary considerations here: demographic factors, psychological factors, and price elasticity.

Demographic Factors

In the initial selection of the target market that a firm intends to serve, a number of demographic factors are usually considered. Demographic factors that are particularly important for pricing decisions include the following:

1. Number of potential buyers.
2. Location of potential buyers.
3. Position of potential buyers (organizational buyers or final consumers).
4. Expected consumption rates of potential buyers.
5. Economic strength of potential buyers.

These factors help determine market potential and are useful for estimating expected sales at various price levels.

Psychological Factors

Psychological factors related to pricing concern primarily how consumers will perceive various prices or price changes. For example, marketing managers should be concerned with such questions as these:

1. Will potential buyers use price as an indicator of product quality?
2. Will potential buyers be favorably attracted by odd pricing (e.g., 99¢, $3,999)?

Most analyses of the price of a product focus on the amount of money a buyer must pay to purchase. However, there are other costs involved that can strongly influence purchase decisions. Below are three types of costs marketing analysts should consider when making pricing decisions.

Time Costs. Time is valuable to most people. Time involved in purchasing products often could be used for more pleasant activities. Waiting in a long checkout line or waiting for a pizza to be delivered can be considered a waste of time too. Many people are willing to pay more money to reduce the time they have to wait to get a product. Vending machine sales often depend on buyers who will pay more money to get a product sooner and with less hassle. People who want a product immediately are often willing to finance the purchase on a credit card to reduce the time waiting to get it.

Psychological Costs. The mental energy and stress in making important purchases and accepting the risks of products not performing as expected can make buyers uncomfortable. Purchasing complex or expensive products can involve investigating and evaluating lots of information and worrying about making the right choices. Car dealers that offer "no haggle" sales do so in order to lower buyers' psychological costs of negotiating.

Behavioral Costs. Buying products and services usually requires some level of physical activity. These costs can increase if buyers have to drive a long way to make a purchase, park far away in a large mall parking lot and have to walk to the store, hunt through many aisles looking for products, and stand for long periods waiting to check out. One way buyers reduce this cost is by shopping and buying from catalogs or the Internet even if they have to pay more money because of shipping charges.

If buyers in a target market are sensitive to these costs, it is possible for marketers to get a competitive advantage by reducing them. These strategies include such things as selling through multiple channels, free shipping, fast delivery, in-store credit, no-hassle return policies, and money-back guarantees. Another strategy is to reduce the monetary price of products in order to compensate for higher time, psychological, or behavioral costs. For example, Walmart's lower monetary prices help offset the additional costs to buyers of having to drive longer distances to get to the stores that are located on the outskirts of most markets.

3. Will potential buyers perceive the price as too high relative to the service the product gives them or relative to competition?

4. Are potential buyers prestige oriented and therefore willing to pay higher prices to fulfill this need?

5. How much will potential buyers be willing to pay for the product?

While psychological factors have a significant effect on the success of a pricing strategy and ultimately on marketing strategy, answers to the above questions may require considerable marketing research. In fact, a review of buyers' subjective perceptions of price concluded that very little is known about how price affects buyers' perceptions of alternative purchase offers and how these perceptions affect purchase response.[1] However, some tentative generalizations about how buyers perceive price have been formulated. For example, research has found that persons who choose high-priced items usually perceive large quality variations within product categories and see the consequences of a poor choice as being undesirable. They believe that quality is related to price and see themselves as good judges of product quality. In general, the reverse is true for persons who select low-priced items in the same product categories. Thus, although information on psychological factors involved in purchasing may be difficult to obtain, marketing managers must at least consider the effects of such factors on their desired target market and marketing strategy.[2]

There are three types of psychological pricing strategies. First there is *prestige pricing,* in which a high price is charged to create a signal that the product is exceptionally fine. Prestige pricing is commonly used for some brands of cars, clothing, perfume, jewelry, cosmetics, wine and liquor, and crystal and china. Second, there is *odd pricing,* or odd-even pricing, in which prices are set a few dollars or a few cents below a round number. For example, Frito-Lay's potato chips are priced at 69 cents a bag rather than 70 cents to encourage consumers to think of them as less expensive (60 some-odd cents rather than 70 cents). Hertz economy cars are rented for $129 rather than $130 to appear less expensive. Third, there is *bundle pricing,* in which several products are sold together at a single price to suggest a good value. For example, travel agencies offer vacation packages that include travel, accommodations, and entertainment at a single price to connote value and convenience for customers.

Price Elasticity

Both demographic and psychological factors affect price elasticity. *Price elasticity* is a measure of consumers' price sensitivity, which is estimated by dividing relative changes in the quantity sold by the relative changes in price:

$$e = \frac{\text{Percent change in quantity demanded}}{\text{Percent change in price}}$$

Although price elasticity is difficult to measure, two basic methods are commonly used to estimate it. First, price elasticity can be estimated from historical data or from price/quantity data across different sales districts. Second, price elasticity can be estimated by sampling a group of consumers from the target market and polling them concerning various price/quantity relationships. Both of these approaches provide estimates of price elasticity; but the former approach is limited to the consideration of price changes, whereas the latter is often expensive and there is some question as to the validity of subjects' responses. However, even a crude estimate of price elasticity is a useful input to pricing decisions.[3]

SUPPLY INFLUENCES ON PRICING DECISIONS

For the purpose of this text, supply influences on pricing decisions can be discussed in terms of three basic factors. These factors relate to the objectives, costs, and nature of the product.

Pricing Objectives

Pricing objectives should be derived from overall marketing objectives, which in turn should be derived from corporate objectives. Since it is traditionally assumed that business firms operate to maximize profits in the long run, it is often thought that the basic pricing objective is solely concerned with long-run profits. However, the profit maximization norm does not provide the operating marketing manager with a single, unequivocal guideline for selecting prices. In addition, the marketing manager does not have perfect cost, revenue, and market information to be able to evaluate whether or not this objective is being reached. In practice, then, many other objectives are employed as guidelines for pricing decisions. In some cases, these objectives may be considered as operational approaches to achieve long-run profit maximization.

Research has found that the most common pricing objectives are (1) pricing to achieve a target return on investment, (2) stabilization of price and margin, (3) pricing to achieve a target market share, and (4) pricing to meet or prevent competition.

There are two common pricing strategies at the retail level: EDLP, which stands for "everyday low pricing," and high/low, which means that the retailer charges prices that are sometimes above competitors' but promotes frequent sales that lower prices below them. Four successful U.S. retailers—Home Depot, Walmart, Office Depot, and Toys 'R' Us—have adopted EDLP, while many fashion, grocery, and drug stores use high/low. Below is a list of the advantages of each of these pricing strategies.

ADVANTAGES OF EDLP

- *Assures customers of low prices.* Many customers are skeptical about initial retail prices. They have become conditioned to buying only on sale—the main characteristic of a high/low pricing strategy. The EDLP strategy lets customers know that they will get the same low prices every time they patronize the EDLP retailer. Customers do not have to read the ads and wait for items they want to go on sale.
- *Reduces advertising and operating expenses.* The stable prices caused by EDLP limit the need for the weekly sale advertising used in the high/low strategy. In addition, EDLP retailers do not have to incur the labor costs of changing price tags and signs and putting up sale signs.
- *Reduces stockouts and improves inventory management.* The EDLP approach reduces the large variations in demand caused by frequent sales with large markdowns. As a result, retailers can manage their inventories with more certainty. Fewer stockouts mean more satisfied customers, resulting in higher sales. In addition, a more predictable customer demand pattern enables the retailer to improve inventory turnover by reducing the average inventory needed for special promotions and backup stock.

ADVANTAGES OF HIGH/LOW

- *Increases profits.* High/low pricing allows retailers to charge higher prices to customers who are not price-sensitive and will pay the "high" price and to charge lower prices to price-sensitive customers who will wait for the "low" sale price.
- *Creates excitement.* A "get them while they last" atmosphere often occurs during a sale. Sales draw a lot of customers, and a lot of customers create excitement. Some retailers augment low prices and advertising with special in-store activities, such as product demonstrations, giveaways, and celebrity appearances.
- *Sells merchandise.* Sales allow retailers to get rid of slow-selling merchandise.

Source: Based on Michael Levy and Barton A. Weitz, *Retailing Management,* 8th ed. (Burr Ridge, IL: McGraw-Hill/Irwin, 2012), p. 373.

Cost Considerations in Pricing

The price of a product usually must cover costs of production, promotion, and distribution, plus a profit, for the offering to be of value to the firm. In addition, when products are priced on the basis of costs plus a fair profit, there is an implicit assumption that this sum represents the economic value of the product in the marketplace.

Cost-oriented pricing is the most common approach in practice, and there are at least three basic variations: markup pricing, cost-plus pricing, and rate-of-return pricing. *Markup pricing* is commonly used in retailing: A percentage is added to the retailer's invoice price to determine the final selling price. Closely related to markup pricing is *cost-plus pricing,* in which the costs of producing a product or completing a project are totaled and a profit amount or percentage is added on. Cost-plus pricing is most often used to describe the pricing of jobs that are nonroutine and difficult to "cost" in advance, such as construction and military weapon development.

The following formulas are used to calculate breakeven points in units and in dollars:

$$BEP_{(in\ units)} = \frac{FC}{(SP - VC)}$$

$$BEP_{(in\ dollars)} = \frac{FC}{1 - (VC/SP)}$$

where

FC = Fixed cost

VC = Variable cost

SP = Selling price

If, as is generally the case, a firm wants to know how many units or sales dollars are necessary to generate a given amount of profit, profit (P) is simply added to fixed costs in the formulas. In addition, if the firm has estimates of expected sales and fixed and variable costs, the selling price can be solved for. (A more detailed discussion of breakeven analysis is provided in the financial analysis section of this book.)

Rate-of-return pricing is commonly used by manufacturers. With this method, price is determined by adding a desired rate of return on investment to total costs. Generally, a breakeven analysis is performed for expected production and sales levels and a rate of return is added on. For example, suppose a firm estimated production and sales to be 75,000 units at a total cost of $300,000. If the firm desired a before-tax return of 20 percent, the selling price would be (300,000 + 0.20 × 300,000) ÷ 75,000 = $4.80.

Cost-oriented approaches to pricing have the advantage of simplicity, and many practitioners believe that they generally yield a good price decision. However, such approaches have been criticized for two basic reasons. First, cost approaches give little or no consideration to demand factors. For example, the price determined by markup or cost-plus methods has no necessary relationship to what people will be willing to pay for the product. In the case of rate-of-return pricing, little emphasis is placed on estimating sales volume. Even if it were, rate-of-return pricing involves circular reasoning, since unit cost depends on sales volume but sales volume depends on selling price. Second, cost approaches fail to reflect competition adequately. Only in industries where all firms use this approach and have similar costs and markups can this approach yield similar prices and minimize price competition. Thus, in many industries, cost-oriented pricing could lead to severe price competition, which could eliminate smaller firms. Therefore, although costs are a highly important consideration in price decisions, numerous other factors need to be examined.

Product Considerations in Pricing

Although numerous product characteristics can affect pricing, three of the most important are (1) perishability, (2) distinctiveness, and (3) stage in the product life cycle.

Perishability

Some products, such as fresh meat, bakery goods, and some raw materials are physically perishable and must be priced to sell before they spoil. Typically, this involves discounting the products as they approach being no longer fit for sale. Products can also be perishable in the sense that demand for them is confined to a specific time period. For example, high fashion and fad products lose most of their value when they go out of style and marketers have the difficult task of forecasting demand at specific prices and judging the time period of customer interest. While the time period of interest for other seasonal products, such as winter coats or Christmas trees, is easier to estimate, marketers must still determine the appropriate price and discount structure to maximize profits and avoid inventory losses or carrying costs.

Distinctiveness

Marketers try to distinguish their products from those of competitors and if successful, can often charge higher prices for them. While such things as styling, features, ingredients, and service can be used to try to make a product distinctive, competitors can copy such physical changes. Thus, it is through branding and brand equity that products are commonly made distinctive in customers' minds. For example, prestigious brands like Rolex, Tiffany's, and Lexus can be priced higher in large measure because of brand equity. Of course, higher prices also help create and reinforce the brand equity of prestigious products.

Life Cycle

The stage of the life cycle that a product is in can have important pricing implications. With regard to the life cycle, two approaches to pricing are skimming and penetration price policies. A *skimming policy* is one in which the seller charges a relatively high price on a new product. Generally, this policy is used when the firm has a temporary monopoly and when demand for the product is price inelastic. In later stages of the life cycle, as competition moves in and other market factors change, the price may then be lowered. Flat screen TV's and cell phones are examples of this. A *penetration policy* is one in which the seller charges a relatively low price on a new product. Generally, this policy is used when the firm expects competition to move in rapidly and when demand for the product is, at least in the short run, price elastic. This policy is also used to obtain large economies of scale and as a major instrument for rapid creation of a mass market. A low price and profit margin may also discourage competition. In later stages of the life cycle, the price may have to be altered to meet changes in the market.

ENVIRONMENTAL INFLUENCES ON PRICING DECISIONS

Environmental influences on pricing include variables that the marketing manager cannot control. Two of the most important of these are competition and government regulation.

Competition

In setting or changing prices, the firm must consider its competition and how competition will react to the price of the product. Initially, consideration must be given to such factors as

1. Number of competitors.
2. Market shares, growth, and profitability of competitors.
3. Strengths and weaknesses of competitors.
4. Likely entry of new firms into the industry.
5. Degree of vertical integration of competitors.
6. Number of products sold by competitors.
7. Cost structure of competitors.
8. Historical reaction of competitors to price changes.

These factors help determine whether the firm's selling price should be at, below, or above competition. Pricing a product at competition (i.e., the average price charged by the industry) is called *going-rate pricing* and is popular for homogeneous products, since this approach represents the collective wisdom of the industry and is not disruptive of industry harmony. An example of pricing below competition can be found in *sealed-bid pricing,* in which the firm is bidding directly against competition for project contracts. Although cost and profits are initially calculated, the firm attempts to bid below competitors to obtain the job contract. A firm may price above competition because it has a superior product or because the firm is the price leader in the industry.

Government Regulations

Prices of certain goods and services are regulated by state and federal governments. Public utilities are examples of state regulation of prices. However, for most marketing managers, federal laws that make certain pricing practices illegal are of primary consideration in pricing decisions. The list below is a summary of some of the more important legal constraints on pricing. Of course, since most marketing managers are not trained as lawyers, they usually seek legal counsel when developing pricing strategies to ensure conformity to state and federal legislation.

1. *Price fixing* is illegal per se. Sellers must not make any agreements with competitors or distributors concerning the final price of the goods. The Sherman Antitrust Act is the primary device used to outlaw horizontal price fixing. Section 5 of the Federal Trade Commission Act has been used to outlaw price fixing as an unfair business practice.

2. *Deceptive pricing* practices are outlawed under Section 5 of the Federal Trade Commission Act. An example of deceptive pricing would be to mark merchandise with an exceptionally high price and then claim that the lower selling price actually used represents a legitimate price reduction.

3. *Price discrimination* (the practice of charging different prices to different buyers for goods of like grade and quality) that lessens competition or is deemed injurious to it is outlawed by the Robinson-Patman Act. Price discrimination is not illegal per se, but sellers cannot charge competing buyers different prices for essentially the same products if the effect of such sales is injurious to competition. Price differentials can be legally justified on certain grounds, especially if the price differences reflect cost differences. This is particularly true of quantity discounts.

4. *Predatory pricing* involves charging a very low price for a product with the intent of driving competitors out of business. It is illegal under the Sherman Act and Federal Trade Commission Act.[4]

A GENERAL PRICING MODEL

It should be clear that effective pricing decisions involve considerations of many factors, and different industries may have different pricing practices. Although no single model will fit all pricing decisions, Figure 11.1 presents a general model for developing prices for products and services.[5] While all pricing decisions cannot be made strictly on the basis of this model, it does break pricing strategy into a set of manageable stages that are integrated into the overall marketing strategy.

Set Pricing Objectives

Given a product or service designed for a specific target market, the pricing process begins with a clear statement of the pricing objectives. These objectives guide the pricing strategy and should be designed to support the overall marketing strategy. Because pricing strategy

FIGURE 11.1
A General Pricing
Model

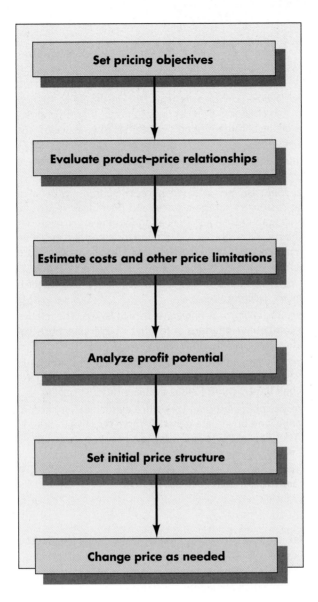

has a direct bearing on demand for a product and the profit obtained, efforts to set prices must be coordinated with other functional areas. For example, production will have to be able to meet demand at a given price, and finance will have to manage funds flowing in and out of the organization at predicted levels of production.

Evaluate Product–Price Relationships

As noted, the distinctiveness, perishability, and stage of the life cycle a product is in all affect pricing. In addition, marketers need to consider what value the product has for customers and how price will influence product positioning. There are three basic value positions. First, a product could be priced relatively high for a product class because it offers value in the form of high quality, special features, or prestige. Second, a product could be priced at about average for the product class because it offers value in the form of good quality for a reasonable price. Third, a product could be priced relatively low for a product class because it offers value in the form of acceptable quality at a low price. A Porsche or

1. *Base pricing strategies on sound research.* Although a recent study found that few companies do serious pricing research, it is a must for sound pricing strategies. Research is needed to understand the factors that influence supply and demand.

2. *Continuously monitor pricing decisions.* Pricing should be treated as a process of developing prices and changing them as needed rather than an annual budgeting exercise. Price decisions define an organization's value image in the eyes of customers and competitors.

3. *Recognize that buyers may have difficulty in computing price differences.* Buyers do not constantly monitor the prices of many products and will not necessarily quickly recognize the value in a price deal.

4. *Recognize that customers evaluate prices comparatively.* Behavioral pricing research suggests that customers compare prices and price deals relative to internal or external reference prices rather than just evaluating them in an absolute sense. An internal reference price is the price a customer has in mind for a product and an external reference price is one the customer has seen in advertising, a catalog, or on a store sign or price tag.

5. *Recognize that buyers typically have a range of acceptable prices.* Buyers often have an upper and lower threshold or range of acceptable prices rather than only one acceptable price they are willing to pay.

6. *Understand the importance of relative price to buyers.* The relative price of a product compared to competitive offerings or to what a buyer previously paid for it may be more important than the absolute price asked.

7. *Understand the importance of price information.* Price information can affect preferences and choices for different models in a product line or for competitive offerings, particularly when buyers cannot easily evaluate product quality.

8. *Recognize that price elasticities vary.* Price elasticities vary according to the direction of a price change, and buyers are generally more sensitive to price increases than to price decreases. Thus, it is easier to lose sales to current customers by increasing prices than it is to gain sales from new buyers by reducing them.

Source: Based on Kent B. Monroe and Jennifer L. Cox, "Pricing Practices That Endanger Profits," *Marketing Management,* September/October 2001, pp. 42–46.

Nike Air Max are examples of the first type of value; a Honda Accord or Keds tennis shoes are examples of the second; and Hyundai cars and private label canvas shoes are examples of the third. Setting prices so that targeted customers will perceive products to offer greater value than competitive offerings is called *value pricing.*

In addition, research is needed to estimate how much of a particular product the target market will purchase at various price levels—price elasticity. This estimate provides valuable information about what the target market thinks about the product and what it is worth to them.

Estimate Costs and Other Price Limitations

The costs to produce and market products provide a lower bound for pricing decisions and a baseline from which to compute profit potential. If a product cannot be produced and marketed at a price to cover its costs and provide reasonable profits in the long run, then it should not be produced in its designed form. One possibility is to redesign the product so that its costs are lower. In fact, some companies first determine the price customers are willing to pay for a product and then design it so that it can be produced and marketed at a cost that allows targeted profits.

Other price limitations that need to be considered are government regulations and the prices that competitors charge for similar and substitute products. Also, likely competitive reactions that could influence the price of a new product or a price change in an existing one need to be considered.

Analyze Profit Potential

Analysis in the preceding stages should result in a range of prices that could be charged. Marketers must then estimate the likely profit in pricing at levels in this range. At this stage, it is important to recognize that it may be necessary to offer channel members quantity discounts, promotional allowances, and slotting allowances to encourage them to actively market the product. *Quantity discounts* are discounts for purchasing a large number of units. *Promotional allowances* are often in the form of price reductions in exchange for the channel member performing various promotional activities, such as featuring the product in store advertising or on in-store displays. *Slotting allowances* are payments to retailers to get them to stock items on their shelves. All of these can not only increase sales but also add marketing cost to the manufacturer and affect profits.

Set Initial Price Structure

Since all of the supply, demand, and environmental factors have been considered, a marketer can now set the initial price structure. The price structure takes into account the price to various channel members, such as wholesalers and retailers, as well as the recommended price to final consumers or organizational buyers.

Change Price as Needed

There are many reasons why an initial price structure may need to be changed. Channel members may bargain for greater margins, competitors may lower their prices, or costs may increase with inflation. In the short term, discounts and allowances may have to be larger or more frequent than planned to get greater marketing effort to increase demand to profitable levels. In the long term, price structures tend to increase for most products as production and marketing costs increase.

SUMMARY

Pricing decisions that integrate the firm's costs with marketing strategy, business conditions, competition, demand, product variables, channels of distribution, and general resources can determine the success or failure of a business. This places a very heavy burden on the price maker. Modern-day marketing managers cannot ignore the complexity or the importance of price management. Pricing strategies must be continually reviewed and must take into account that the firm is a dynamic entity operating in a very competitive environment. There are many ways for money to flow out of a firm in the form of costs, but often there is only one way to bring in revenues and that is by the price-product mechanism.

Additional Resources

Macdivitt, Harry, and Mike Wilkinson. *Value-Based Pricing.* New York: McGraw-Hill, 2012.

Mazumdar, Tridib; S. P. Raj, and Indrajit Sinha. "Reference Price Research: Review and Propositions." *Journal of Marketing,* October 2005, pp. 84–102.

Monroe, Kent B. *Pricing: Making Profitable Decisions.* 3rd ed. New York: McGraw-Hill, 2003.

Nagle, Thomas T.; John Hogan, and Joseph Zale. *The Strategy and Tactics of Pricing.* 5th ed. Englewood Cliffs, NJ: Prentice Hall, 2011.

Smith, Tim. *Pricing Strategy.* Mason, OH: Southwestern, 2012.

Winer, Russell S. *Pricing.* Cambridge, MA: Marketing Science Institute, 2005.

Key Terms and Concepts

Bundle pricing: A form of psychological pricing that involves selling several products together at a single price in order to suggest a good value.

Cost-plus pricing: A cost-oriented pricing approach that involves totaling up the costs of producing a product or completing a project and then adding on a percentage or fixed profit amount. This approach is used when costs are difficult to estimate in advance such as military weapon development.

Deceptive pricing: Illegal under the Federal Trade Commission Act, an approach that involves price deals that mislead the consumer. For example, putting a fake price on a product much higher than the product sells for in the market, crossing it out, and then offering the product at the market price and claiming a price reduction could easily mislead consumers.

Going-rate pricing: Pricing a product at the average charged in the industry.

Markup pricing: A cost-oriented pricing approach that involves adding a percentage to the invoice price in order to determine the final selling price. For example, if a retailer used a 50 percent markup on a product that was bought from a wholesaler for $1, the selling price to the consumer would be $1.50.

Odd pricing: Also called odd-even pricing, a form of psychological pricing in which the prices are set at one or a few cents or dollars below a round number in order to create the perception that the price is low, for example, 99 cents or $129 rather than $1 or $130.

Penetration pricing policy: Approach to pricing in which the seller charges a relatively low price on a new product initially in order to grow a market, gain market share, and discourage competition from entering the market.

Prestige pricing: A form of psychological pricing that involves charging a high price to create a signal that the product is exceptionally fine.

Predatory pricing: Practice that involves charging a very low price for a product with the intent of driving competitors out of business. It is illegal under the Sherman Act and Federal Trade Commission Act.

Price discrimination: The practice of charging different prices to different buyers for goods of like grade and quality which is illegal under the Robinson-Patman Act if it lessens or is deemed injurious to competition.

Price elasticity: A measure of consumers' price sensitivity which is estimated by dividing relative changes in the quantity sold by relative changes in price. If demand is elastic, a slight lowering of price will result in a relatively large increase in quantity demanded.

Price fixing: An unfair business practice outlawed by the Sherman Antitrust Act and the Federal Trade Commission Act that involves competitors in a market colluding to set the final price of a product.

Promotional allowance: Price reduction offered to channel members in exchange for performing various promotional activities such as featuring the product in store advertising or on in-store displays.

Quantity discounts: Discounts offered for purchasing a large number of units.

Rate-of-return pricing: Cost-oriented approach to pricing that involves adding a desired rate of return on investment to total costs. Generally, a breakeven analysis is performed for expected production and sales levels and a rate of return is added on.

Sealed-bid pricing: Bidding process in which each seller submits a sealed bid and attempts to price below competition in order to get the contract. Many large construction and military projects are bid this way.

Skimming pricing policy: Approach to pricing in which the seller charges a relatively high price on a new product initially in order to recover costs and make profits rapidly and then lowers the price at a later date to make sales to more price-sensitive buyers.

Slotting allowances: Payments to retailers to get them to stock items on their shelves, a common tactic for getting new products into stores.

Value pricing: Setting prices so that targeted customers will perceive products to offer greater value than competitive offerings. For existing products, this can be accomplished by offering more product or service while maintaining or decreasing the dollar price.

Part D

Marketing in Special Fields

Section I Essentials of Marketing Management

12

The Marketing of Services

Over the course of the past 40 years, the fastest-growing segment of the American economy has not been the production of tangibles but the performance of services. Spending on services has increased to such an extent that today it captures more than 50 cents of the consumer's dollar. In addition, the service sector in the United States produces a balance-of-trade surplus and is expected to be responsible for all net job growth in the forseeable future.[1] The dominance of the service sector is not limited to the United States. The service sector accounts for more than half the GNP and employs more than half the labor force in most Latin American and Caribbean countries. Over the course of the next decade, the service sector will spawn whole new legions of doctors, nurses, medical technologists, physical therapists, home health aids, and social workers to administer to the needs of an aging population, along with armies of food servers, child care providers, and cleaning people to cater to the wants of two-income families. Also rising to the forefront will be a swelling class of technical workers, including computer engineers, systems analysts, and paralegals.

Many marketing textbooks still devote little attention to program development for the marketing of services, especially those in the rapidly changing areas of health care, finance, and travel. This omission is usually based on the assumption that the marketing of products and services is basically the same, and, therefore, the techniques discussed under products apply as well to the marketing of services. Basically, this assumption is true. Whether selling goods or services, the marketer must be concerned with developing a marketing strategy centered on the four controllable decision variables that comprise the marketing mix: the product (or service), the price, the distribution system, and promotion. In addition, the use of marketing research is as valuable to service marketers as it is to product marketers. However, because services possess certain distinguishing characteristics, the task of determining the marketing mix ingredients for a service marketing strategy may raise different and more difficult problems than those encountered in marketing products.

The purpose of this chapter is fourfold. First, the reader will become acquainted with the special characteristics of services and their strategy implications. Second, key concepts associated with providing quality services will be discussed. Third, obstacles will be described that in the past impeded and still continue to impede development of services marketing. Finally, current trends and strategies of innovation in services marketing will be explored. With this approach, the material in the other chapters of the book can be integrated to give a better understanding of the marketing of services.

Before proceeding, some attention must be given to what we refer to when using the term *services.* Probably the most frustrating aspect of the available literature on services is that the definition of what constitutes a service remains unclear. The fact is that no common definition and boundaries have been developed to delimit the field of services. The American Marketing Association has defined services as follows:[2]

1. *Service products,* such as a bank loan or home security, that are intangible, or at least substantially so. If totally intangible, they are exchanged directly from producer to user, cannot be transported or stored, and are almost instantly perishable. Service products are often difficult to identify, since they come into existence at the same time they are bought and consumed. They are composed of intangible elements that are inseparable; they usually involve customer participation in some important way, cannot be sold in the sense of ownership transfer, and have no title. Today, however, most products are partly tangible and partly intangible, and the dominant form is used to classify them as either goods or services (all are products). These common, hybrid forms, whatever they are called, may or may not have the attributes just given for totally intangible services.

2. *Services,* as a term, is also used to describe activities performed by sellers and others that accompany the sale of a product and that aid in its exchange or its utilization (e.g., shoe fitting, financing, an 800 number). Such services are either presale or postsale and supplement the product but do not comprise it.

The first definition includes what can be considered almost pure services, such as insurance, banking, entertainment, airlines, health care, telecommunications, and hotels; the second definition includes such services as wrapping, financing an automobile, providing warranties on computer equipment, and the like because these services exist in connection with the sale of a product or another service. This suggests that marketers of goods are also marketers of services. For example, one could argue that McDonald's is not in the hamburger business. Its hamburgers are actually not very different from those of the competition. McDonald's is in the service business.

More and more manufacturers are also exploiting their service capabilities as stand-alone revenue producers. For example, General Motors, Ford, and Chrysler all offer financing services. Ford and General Motors have extended their financial services offerings to include a MasterCard, which offers discounts on purchases of their automobiles.

The reader can imagine from his or her own experience that some purchases are very tangible (a coffeemaker) while others are very much intangible (a course in marketing). Others have elements of both (lunch on a flight from New York to Chicago). In other words, in reality there is a goods–service continuum, with many purchases including both tangible goods and intangible services. Figure 12.1 illustrates such a continuum. On the goods side of the continuum, the buyer owns an object after the purchase. On the services side of the continuum, when the transaction is over, the buyer leaves with an experience and a feeling. When the course in marketing is over or the flight from New York to Chicago is completed, the student or passenger leaves with a feeling.

The examples of services on the right side of Figure 12.1 are mostly or entirely intangible. They do not exist in the physical realm. They cannot appeal to the five senses.

FIGURE 12.1
The Goods–Service Continuum

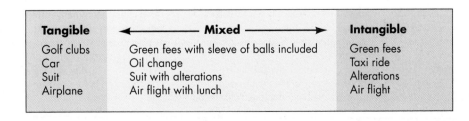

Tangible	←——— Mixed ———→	Intangible
Golf clubs	Green fees with sleeve of balls included	Green fees
Car	Oil change	Taxi ride
Suit	Suit with alterations	Alterations
Airplane	Air flight with lunch	Air flight

IMPORTANT CHARACTERISTICS OF SERVICES

Services possess several unique characteristics that often have a significant impact on marketing program development. These special features of services may cause unique problems and often result in marketing mix decisions that are substantially different from those found in connection with the marketing of goods. Some of the more important of these characteristics are intangibility, inseparability, perishability and fluctuating demand, a client relationship, customer effort, and uniformity. They are presented in Figure 12.2.

Intangibility

The obvious basic difference between goods and services is the intangibility of services, and many of the problems encountered in the marketing of services are due to intangibility. To illustrate, how does an airline make tangible a trip from Philadelphia to San Francisco? These problems are unique to service marketing.

The fact that many services cannot appeal to a buyer's sense of touch, taste, smell, sight, or hearing before purchase places a burden on the marketing organization. For example, hotels that promise a good night's sleep to their customers cannot actually show this service in a tangible way. Obviously, this burden is most heavily felt in a firm's promotional program, but, as will be discussed later, it may affect other areas. Depending on the type of service, the intangibility factor may dictate use of direct channels because of the need for personal contact between the buyer and seller. Since a service firm is actually selling an idea or experience, not a product, it must tell the buyer what the service will do because it is often difficult to illustrate, demonstrate, or display the service in use. For example, the hotel must somehow describe to the consumer how a stay at the hotel will leave the customer feeling well rested and ready to begin a new day.

The above discussion alludes to two strategy elements firms should employ when trying to overcome the problems associated with service intangibility. First, tangible aspects associated with the service should be stressed. For example, advertisements for airlines should emphasize (through text and visuals) the newness of the aircraft, the roominess of the

FIGURE 12.2   Unique Characteristics Distinguishing Services from Goods

Characteristic	Services	Goods
Intangibility	The customer owns only memories, outcomes, or feelings such as an airline flight, greater knowledge, or styled hair.	The customer owns objects that can be used, resold, or given to others.
Inseparability	Services often cannot be separated from the person providing them. They are often produced and consumed at the same time.	Goods are usually produced and sold by different people.
Perishability	Services can be used only at the time they are offered. They cannot be inventoried, stored, or transported.	Goods can be placed in inventory for use at another time.
Client Relationship	Services often involve a long-term personal relationship between buyer and seller.	Goods often involve an impersonal short-term relationship although in many instances relationship strength and duration are increasing.
Customer Effort	Customers are often heavily involved in the production.	Customer's involvement may be limited to buying the completed product and using it.
Uniformity	Because of inseparability and high involvement on the part of the buyer, each service may be unique, with the quality likely to vary.	Variations in quality and variance from standards can be corrected before customers purchase products.

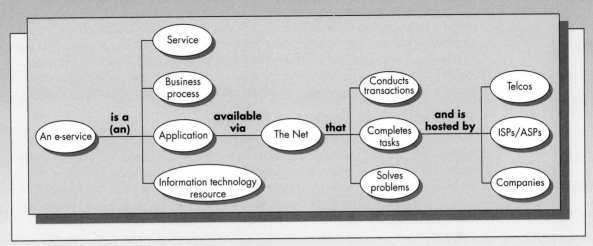

cabin, and the friendliness of the flight attendants. Second, end benefits resulting from completion of the service encounter should be accentuated. In the case of air travel, an individual's ability to make an important meeting or arrive home in time for a special occasion could be the derived benefit.

Inseparability

In many cases, a service cannot be separated from the person of the seller. In other words, the service must often be produced and marketed simultaneously. Because of the simultaneous production and marketing of most services, the main concern of the marketer is usually the creation of time and place utility. For example, the bank teller produces the service of receiving a deposit and markets other appropriate bank services at the same time. Many services, therefore, are tailored and not mass produced. Often, because a company's employees are "the company" at the point of contact, they must be given wide latitude and assistance in determining how best to tailor a specific service to meet customer needs.

The implication of inseparability on issues dealing with the selection of channels of distribution and service quality is quite important. Inseparable services cannot be inventoried, and thus direct sale is the only feasible channel of distribution. Service quality cannot sometimes be completely standardized due to the inability to completely mechanize the service encounter. However, some industries, through innovative uses of technology, have been able to overcome or, at least, alleviate challenges associated with the inseparability characteristic.

For example, in the financial services industry, automated teller machines (ATMs) and home banking, through use of computers and telephones, have contributed greatly to eliminating the need for the customer to directly interact with a bank teller. Further, many banks are developing computer applications to allow tellers and other service representatives to think like expert problem solvers. These applications allow for platform banking, a means of enabling bank representatives in any location to bring up on a screen all the information the bank has about the customer. Every face-to-face contact with a customer can mean an opportunity to make a sale and, more importantly, further the relationship with the customer. Of course, the bank representative is still of critical importance as the one who might recognize by the customer's expression or words that this visit is not the appropriate time to be marketing additional services.

In addition to technology, tangible representations of the service can serve to overcome the inseparability problem. For example, in the insurance industry, a contract serves as the tangible representation of the service. The service itself remains inseparable from the seller (insurance provider), but the buyer has a tangible representation of the service in the form of a policy. This enables the use of intermediaries (agents) in the marketing of insurance. Another example is in the use of a credit card—the card itself is a tangible representation of the service that is being produced and consumed each time the card is being used.

Perishability and Fluctuating Demand

Services are perishable and markets for most services fluctuate either by season (tourism), days (airlines), or time of day (movie theaters). Unused telephone capacity and electrical power; vacant seats on planes, trains, buses, and in stadiums; and time spent by catalog service representatives waiting for customers to reach them all represent business that is lost forever.

The combination of perishability and fluctuating demand has created many problems for marketers of services. Specifically, in the areas of staffing and distribution, avenues must be found to have the services available for peak periods, and new strategies need to be developed to make use of the service during slack periods. Some organizations are attempting to cope with these problems through the use of pricing strategy. *Off-peak pricing* consists of charging different prices during different times or days in order to stimulate demand during slow periods. Discounts given for weekend calling, Saturday night stay-overs, early-bird dinners, or winter cruises are all examples of efforts service providers make to redistribute demand.

Other organizations are dealing with issues related to peak period demand through the use of technology. To illustrate, a well-designed voice mail system allows companies and callers to cut down on missed phone calls, eliminates long waits on hold, and delivers clear, consistent messages. In the catalog industry, automated call routing (ACR) is used to route incoming calls to available service representatives in the order in which they were received. Finally, in the utilities industry, many electric utilities no longer have to generate capacity that will meet peak electrical demand. Instead, they rely on buying unused power from other utilities in other regions of the country.

Client Relationship

In the marketing of a great many services, a client relationship, as opposed to a customer relationship, exists between the buyer and the seller. In other words, the buyer views the seller as someone who has knowledge that is of value. Examples of this type of relationship are the physician–patient, college professor–student, accountant–small business owner, and broker–investor. The buyer, many times, abides by the advice offered or suggestions provided by the seller, and these relationships may be of an ongoing nature. Also, since many service firms are client-serving organizations, they may approach the marketing function in a more professional manner, as seen in health care, finance, legal, governmental, and educational services.

Professionals face at least two marketing challenges. First, in many cases, fear or hostility is brought to the transaction because the customer is uncertain about how genuine the professional's concern for his or her satisfaction is. For example, many unpleasant reasons exist for consulting doctors, lawyers, bankers, or even visiting a college professor. These could include having surgery, being sued, having to take out a loan, or doing poorly on an exam. Second, even high-quality service delivery by the professional can lead to dissatisfied customers. For a physician, the ability to provide high-quality medical care may be overshadowed by a brusque, unfriendly personality. For a college professor, the demand on students to contact or visit him or her only during office hours, coupled with students' own hectic work schedules, can diminish the impact of the professor's classroom presentations. It is vitally important that the professional service provider strive to build long-term positive relationships with clients.

Type of Service	Type of Customer	Principal Expectations
Automobile repair	Consumers	*Be competent.* Fix it right the first time.
		Explain things. Explain why the customer needs the suggested repairs—provide an itemized list.
		Be respectful. "Don't treat me like an idiot."
Automobile insurance	Consumers	*Keep me informed.* "I shouldn't have to learn about insurance law changes from the newspaper."
		Be on my side. "I don't want them to treat me like I am a criminal just because I have a claim."
		Play fair. "Don't drop me when something goes wrong."
		Protect me from catastrophe. "Make sure my estate is covered in the event of a major accident."
		Provide prompt service. "I want a fast settlement of my claims."
Hotel	Consumers	*Provide a clean room.* "Don't have a deep-pile carpet that can't be completely cleaned . . . You can literally see germs down there."
		Provide a secure room. Good deadbolts and a peephole on the door.
		Treat me like a guest. "It is almost like they're looking you over to decide whether or not they're going to let you have a room."
		Keep your promise. "They said the room would be ready at the promised time, but it wasn't."
Property and casualty insurance	Business customers	*Fulfill obligations.* Pay up.
		Learn my business and work with me. "I expect them to know me and my company."
		Protect me from catastrophe. Cover risk exposure so there is no single big loss.
		Provide prompt service. Fast claim service.
Equipment repair	Business customers	*Share my sense of urgency.* Speed of response. "One time I had to buy a second piece of equipment because of the huge downtime with the first piece."
		Be prepared. Have all the parts ready.
Truck and tractor rental/leasing	Business customers	*Keep the equipment running.* Have equipment working all the time—that is the key.
		Be flexible. "The leasing company should have the leasing flexibility to rent us equipment when we need it."
		Provide full service. Get rid of all the paperwork and headaches.

Source: A. Parasuraman, Leonard L. Berry, and Valarie A. Zeithaml, "Understanding Customer Expectations of Service," *Sloan Management Review,* Spring 1991, pp. 39–48.

Customer Effort

Customers are often involved to a relatively great degree in the production of many types of service. In some restaurants you clean your table. You may carry your luggage to a cart parked next to a baggage compartment of the plane. If you wish to enjoy an exhibit at a local art museum, you must walk around the facility and pay careful attention to what is on display. If an organization purchases the services of an advertising agency, employees will have to work with the agency, review its ideas, and make the final selections.

Obviously, not every service requires the same degree of customer effort. Your effort with a credit card service may be little beyond taking it from your wallet to make a purchase and writing a check once a month to pay the bill.

Uniformity

The quality of services can vary more than the quality of goods. Producers of goods have procedures to prevent, identify, and correct defects. If these procedures are working, customers are unlikely to purchase defective products. This is not the case with most services. Because they are often human performances and often customized to the needs of the buyer, quality can vary. Each trip to the bank or airline flight or university course can be a different experience. Many service jobs such as nursing, teaching, and career counseling require a positive attitude; how employees feel influences their performance.

PROVIDING QUALITY SERVICES

In today's increasingly competitive environment, quality service is critical to organizational success. Unlike products in which quality is often measured against standards, service quality is measured against performance.[3] Since services are frequently produced in the presence of a customer, are labor intensive, and are not able to be stored or objectively examined, the definition of what constitutes good service quality can be difficult and, in fact, continually changes in the face of choices.[4] Customers determine the value of service quality in relation to available alternatives and their particular needs. In general, problems in the determination of good service quality are attributable to differences in the expectations, perceptions, and experiences regarding the encounter between the service provider and consumer. These gaps can be classified as follows:

1. The gap between consumer expectations and management perceptions of consumer expectations.
2. The gap between management perceptions of consumer expectations and the firm's service quality specifications.
3. The gap between service quality specifications and actual service quality.
4. The gap between actual service delivery and external communications about the service.

In essence, the customer perceives the level of service quality as being a function of the magnitude and direction of the gap between expected service and perceived service. Management of a company may not even realize that they are delivering poor-quality service due to differences in the way managers and consumers view acceptable quality levels. To overcome this problem and to avoid losing customers, firms must be aware of the determinants of service quality. A brief description of these determinants follows.

1. *Tangibles* include the physical evidence of the service. For example, employees are always visible in a hotel lobby dusting or otherwise cleaning up. Likewise, clean, shiny, up-to-date medical equipment or aircraft are examples of tangible elements.
2. *Reliability* involves the consistency and dependability of the service performance. For example, does a bank or phone company always send out accurate customer statements? Likewise, does the plumber always fix the problem on his or her first visit?
3. *Responsiveness* concerns the willingness or readiness of employees or professionals to provide service. For example, will a physician see patients on the same day they call in to say they are ill? Will a college professor return a student's call the same day?

Throughout this book we have stressed the importance of building long-term relationships in which the initial sale is viewed as a beginning step in a process, not an end or goal. For marketers of services, relationship marketing can present a special set of challenges which require a different new view of the business and a change in strategy.

For decades, most service marketers were concerned with attracting new customers. Promotion programs and convenient locations focused on the acquisition of new customers. During the last two decades, however, service marketers are beginning to think about marketing in a fundamentally new way. The idea is that marketing is about *having customers,* not merely *acquiring customers.* Service marketers now understand that attracting new customers is only the first step in the process, that making existing customers better customers is marketing too. In other words, service marketers understand the importance of relationship marketing. It is fundamentally different from the traditional view of marketing in service organizations.

Traditional Service Marketing	*Relationship Service Marketing*
1. Marketing focuses on attracting new "customers."	1. Marketing focuses on "clients." Customer attraction is a beginning step.
2. Emphasis on selling the service the customer requests.	2. Emphasis on establishing and building a long-term relationship.
3. Need satisfaction is approached from the standpoint of the "part." For example, haircut, checking account, airline ticket.	3. Need satisfaction is approached from the standpoint of the "whole." For example, total hair care, day spa, personal banker, travel management.
4. Primary sales contact is through process driven providers. For example, airline ticket agent, bank teller.	4. Primary sales contact is through a trained marketing professional. For example, travel agent, personal banker.
5. Profitability is assessed on individual services. For example, individual haircut.	5. Profitability is assessed on the total relationship. For example, haircut plus shampoos, conditioners, brushes, combs, dryers, etc.

Source: Based on the work of James H. Donnelly, Jr., Leonard L. Berry, and Thomas W. Thompson.

4. *Assurance* refers to the knowledge and competence of service providers and the ability to convey trust and confidence. This determinant encompasses the provider's name and reputation; possession of necessary skills; and trustworthiness, believability, and honesty. For example, a bank will guarantee same-day loan processing; a doctor is highly trained in a particular specialty.

5. *Empathy* refers to the service provider's efforts to understand the customer's needs and then to provide, as best as possible, individualized service delivery. For example, flight attendants on a customer's regular route learn what type of beverages the customer drinks and what magazines the customer reads.

Each of these determinants plays an important role in how the customer views the service quality of a firm. Turning service quality into a powerful competitive weapon requires continuously striving for service superiority—consistently performing above the adequate service level and capitalizing on opportunities for exceeding the desired service level. Relentless efforts to continually improve service performance may well be rewarded by improvements in customer attitudes toward the firm: from customer frustration to customer preference to customer loyalty. What should be obvious is that to be successful, a service firm must have both an effective means to measure customer satisfaction and dedicated employees to provide high-quality service.

Customer Satisfaction Measurement

As mentioned above, satisfied customers can become loyal customers. Service quality and customer satisfaction are of growing concern to business organizations throughout the world, and research on these topics generally focuses on two key issues: (1) understanding the expectations and requirements of the customer, and (2) determining how well a company and its major competitors are succeeding in satisfying these expectations and requirements.[5]

As such, an organization's approach to measuring service quality through customer satisfaction measurement (CSM) and effectively implementing programs derived from results of such studies can spell the difference between success and failure. Research on market leaders' CSMs found they had the following aspects in common:

1. Marketing and sales employees were primarily responsible (with customer input) for designing CSM programs and questionnaires.
2. Top management and the marketing function championed the programs.
3. Measurement involved a combination of qualitative and quantitative research methods that primarily included mail questionnaires, telephone surveys, and focus groups.
4. Evaluations included both the company's and competitors' satisfaction performance.
5. Results of all research were made available to employees, but not necessarily to customers.
6. Research was performed on a continual basis.
7. Customer satisfaction was incorporated into the strategic focus of the company via the mission statement.
8. There was a commitment to increasing service quality and customer satisfaction from employees at all levels within the organization.

The Importance of Internal Marketing

Properly performed customer satisfaction research can yield a wealth of strategic information about customers, the sponsoring company, and competitors. However, service quality goes beyond the relationship between a customer and a company. Rather, as shown by the last aspect listed, it is the personal relationship between a customer and the particular employee that the customer happens to be dealing with at the time of the service encounter that ultimately determines service quality. The importance of having customer-oriented, frontline people cannot be overstated.[6] If frontline service personnel are unfriendly, unhelpful, uncooperative, or uninterested in the customer, the customer will tend to project that same attitude to the company as a whole. The character and personality of an organization reflects the character and personality of its top management. Management must develop programs that will stimulate employee commitment to customer service. To be successful, these programs must contain five critical components:

1. *A careful selection process in hiring frontline employees.* To do this, management has to clearly define the skills the service person must bring to the job.[7] For example, Fairfield Inn often considers as many as 25 candidates for each housekeeping or front-desk position.[8]
2. *A clear, concrete message* that conveys a particular service strategy that frontline people can begin to act on. People delivering service need to know how their work fits in the broader scheme of business operations.[9] They need to have a cause because servicing others is just too demanding and frustrating to be done well each day without one.[10]
3. *Significant modeling by managers,* that is, managers demonstrating the behavior that they intend to reward employees for performing. For example, some airline executives regularly travel economy class to talk to customers and solicit ideas for improvement.[11]

Practicing relationship marketing is a challenge for service organizations because there are important differences between "customers" and "clients." The notion of "client" is critical for relationship marketing to succeed in a service organization.

Customers	Clients
1. Customers may be nameless.	1. Clients must have names.
2. Customers are served as part of a large mass of people.	2. Clients are served on an individual basis.
3. Customers are statistics; their needs are reflected in market summaries. For example, the most popular ice cream for people over 50 in 2008 was vanilla.	3. Clients are individual entities. Specific information about them is stored in a database. For example, Mr. Smith wants only morning flights, first class seats, vegetarian meals, aisle seats, airport motels, and mid-size rental cars.
4. Customers are served by the first available person. For example, airline ticket agent, bank teller.	4. Clients are served by a trained professional who has been assigned to them. For example, travel agent, personal banker.
5. Customers have no strong reason to feel any loyalty or allegiance to the service provider.	5. Clients often have a strong relationship with the service provider.

Source: Based on the work of James H. Donnelly, Jr., Leonard L. Berry, and Thomas W. Thompson.

4. *An energetic follow-through process,* in which managers provide the training, support, and incentives necessary to give the employees the capability and willingness to provide quality service.[12]

5. *An emphasis on teaching employees to have good attitudes.* This type of training usually focuses on specific social techniques, such as eye contact, smiling, tone of voice, and standards of dress.

However, organizing and implementing such programs will only lead to temporary results unless managers practice a strategy of internal marketing. We define *internal marketing* as the continual process by which managers actively encourage, stimulate, and support employee commitment to the company, the company's goods and services, and the company's customers. Emphasis should be placed on the word *continual.* Managers who consistently pitch in to help when needed, constantly provide encouragement and words of praise to employees, strive to help employees understand the benefits of performing their jobs well, and emphasize the importance of employee actions on both company and employee results are practitioners of internal marketing. In service marketing, successful internal marketing efforts, leading to employee commitment to service quality, are a key to success.

Federal Express serves as a prime example of the benefits accruing to a company that successfully practices internal marketing.[13] Federal Express is the first service organization to win the Malcolm Baldrige National Quality Award. The company's motto is "people, service, and profits." Behind its purple, white, and orange planes and uniforms are self-managing work teams, gainsharing plans, and empowered employees seemingly consumed with providing flexible and creative services to customers with varying needs. Federal

Express is a high-involvement, horizontally coordinated organization that encourages employees to use their judgment above and beyond the rulebook.

OVERCOMING THE OBSTACLES IN SERVICE MARKETING

The factors of intangibility and inseparability, as well as difficulties in coming up with objective definitions of acceptable service quality, make comprehension of service marketing difficult. However, in view of the size and importance of services in our economy, considerable innovation and ingenuity are needed to make high-quality services available at convenient locations for consumers as well as businesspeople. In fact, the area of service marketing probably offers more opportunities for imagination and creative innovation than does goods marketing. Unfortunately, many service firms still lag in the area of creative marketing. Even today, those service firms that have done a relatively good job have been slow in recognizing opportunities in all aspects of their marketing programs. Four reasons, connected to past practices, can be given for the lack of innovative marketing on the part of service marketers: (1) a limited view of marketing, (2) a lack of strong competition, (3) a lack of creative management, and (4) no obsolescence.

Limited View of Marketing

Because of the nature of their service, many firms depended to a great degree on population growth to expand sales. A popular example here is the telephone company, which did not establish a marketing department until 1955. It was then that the company realized it had to be concerned not only with population growth but also with meeting the needs of a growing population. Increases in educational levels and the standard of living also bring about the need for new and diversified services.

Service firms must meet these changing needs by developing new services and new channels and altering existing channels to meet the changing composition and needs of the population. For many service industries, growth has come as a result of finding new channels of distribution. For example, some banks and other financial service companies were able to grow and tap into new markets by establishing limited-service kiosks in malls and supermarkets. Airlines have successfully brought in a whole new class of travelers by offering advance-purchase discounted fares. Traditionally, users of these fares either drove or used other means of transportation to reach their destination.

While many service firms have succeeded in adopting a marketing perspective, others have been slow to respond. It was not until deregulation of the telecommunications industry took place in 1984 that the telephone companies began taking a broadened view of marketing. Even today, critics point to the obsession with inventing new technology versus using current technology in meeting customer needs as a weakness of these companies.

Limited Competition

A second major cause of the lack of innovative marketing in many service industries was the lack of competition. Many service industries such as banking, railroads, and public utilities have, throughout most of their histories, faced very little competition; some have even been regulated monopolies. Obviously, in an environment characterized by little competition, there was not likely to be a great deal of innovative marketing. However, two major forces have changed this situation. First, in the past two decades, banking, financial services, railroad, cable, airline, telecommunications industries, and utilities have all been deregulated in varying degrees. With deregulation has come a need to be able to compete effectively. Second, service marketing has taken on an international focus. Today, many

On the Internet, you cannot have a more convenient location than your competition. Everyone is just a click away. It is critical that it is easy to do business with your company in order to attract and retain customers. Following are some ways to improve e-service.

1. A customer should be able to buy something in seven clicks or less beginning from the home page. Many experts believe the ideal should be four clicks.
2. Images should load quickly. Research shows that eight seconds is the longest people will wait before they move on to another site.
3. From a product section of your site, customers should be able to get from your home page to a product page in that section in one click.
4. Shopping should be easy. Searching, browsing, checking out, returning items, and getting assistance from a live person must be simple.
5. Customers should have the choice to register their personal information (e.g., address and credit card information) or to enter this information each time they purchase.
6. A customer should be able to check out in no more than three steps.
7. Delivery should be on time.

Source: Ron Zemke, *E-Service: 24 Ways to Keep Your Customers—When the Competition Is Just a Click Away* (New York: Amazon, 2001).

foreign companies are competing in domestic service markets. Foreign interests own several banks, many hotels (including Holiday Inn), and shares in major airlines (including Northwest and US Airways). Likewise, American companies are expanding overseas as markets open up. For example, Merrill Lynch & Co. purchased Smith New Court PLC, a large British security firm, to become the world's largest brokerage firm.

Noncreative Management

For many years, the managements of service industries have been criticized for not being progressive and creative. Railroad management has long been criticized for being slow to innovate. More recently, however, railroads have become leading innovators in the field of freight transportation, introducing such innovations as piggyback service and containerization, and in passenger service, introducing luxury overnight accommodations on trains with exotic names such as the Zephyr. Some other service industries, however, have been slow to develop new services or to innovate in the marketing of their existing services. In fact, as a whole, U.S. firms lag behind their Japanese and German competitors not only in collecting customer satisfaction data but also in designing services that address customers' needs.[14]

No Obsolescence

A great advantage for many service industries is the fact that many services, because of their intangibility, are less subject to obsolescence than goods. While this is an obvious advantage, it has also led some service firms to be sluggish in their approach to marketing. Manufacturers of goods may constantly change their marketing plans and seek new and more efficient ways to produce and distribute their products. Since service firms are often not faced with obsolescence, they often failed to recognize the need for change. This failure has led to wholesale changes in many industries as new operators who possessed marketing skills revolutionized the manner in which the service is performed and provided. Many barbershops and hair dressers have gone out of business due to an inability to compete against hairstyling salons. Many accountants have lost clients to tax preparation services, such as H&R Block, that specialize in doing one task well and have used technology, including Internet filing services, to their advantage. Likewise, the old, big movie house has become a relic of the past as entrepreneurs realized the advantages to be gained from building and operating theater complexes that contain several minitheaters in or near suburban malls.

THE SERVICE CHALLENGE

Despite traditional thinking and practices on the part of many marketing managers and writers concerning the similarities between the operation of manufacturing and services organizations, the past decade has seen the growth of many innovative ways of meeting the service challenge. The service challenge is the quest to (1) constantly develop new services that will better meet customer needs, (2) improve on the quality and variety of existing services, and (3) provide and distribute these services in a manner that best serves the customer. This next section illustrates the challenges facing companies in various service industries and examples of marketing strategies they employ to meet the service challenge.

Banking

"Banking is vital to a healthy economy. Banks are not." This is the message that a banking expert delivered to a group of his peers.[15] Needless to say, the days when banking was considered a dead-end career, but one that offered stable employment for marketers, are long gone. Perhaps banking best exemplifies the changes that are taking place as service organizations strive to become practitioners of the "marketing concept." Buy or be bought is the new watchword in the banking industry, which is experiencing the biggest wave of consolidation in its history.

Banking is becoming an increasingly technology-driven business. The main reason is that more and more financial services, from loans to credit cards, are being marketed through computers and telephones instead of through branches. Banks large enough to afford big technology investments can reach customers nationwide even though their physical franchise may be limited. For example, most consumers possess credit cards from banks they have never physically visited. Further, the advent of new electronic delivery systems (via computer) for consumer and small-business banking could, within the next decade, greatly reduce the number of branch banks needed. To prevent a loss of a large portion of their customer base, many of the leading banks, such as Chase Manhattan and Citibank, are aligning themselves with software and hardware manufacturers to develop home banking systems.

Banks have also learned the value of bundling services. Many now offer an account that combines checking, savings, credit card, and auto loan features. Benefits to the customer include free ATM transactions, interest-bearing checking accounts, no-fee credit cards, and the convenience of one-stop banking. In addition, they offer preapproved auto loans and cash-flow statements. Most banks also target some marketing activities toward senior citizens, which may include discount coupons for entertainment, travel newsletters, and lower monthly minimum required balances.

Competition between banks and other financial institutions will continue to intensify. The survivors will be those that have best mastered the art of services marketing.

Health Care

The distribution of health care services is of vital concern. In health care delivery, the inseparability characteristic presents more of a handicap than in other service industries because users (patients) literally place themselves in the hands of the seller. Although direct personal contact between producer and user is often necessary, new and more efficient means of distribution seem to be evolving.

Up until the past few decades, medical care has been traditionally associated with the solo practice, fee-for-service system. Recently, several alternative delivery systems have been developed, most notably the health maintenance organization (HMO). This type of delivery system stresses the creation of group health care clinics using teams of salaried health practitioners (physicians, pharmacists, technicians, and so forth) that serve a specified, enrolled membership on a prepaid basis. The primary benefits to the customer (patient) from membership in an HMO are (1) the ability to have all ailments treated at one facility, (2) payment of a fixed fee for services, and (3) the encouragement of preventive versus remedial treatments. The success of the HMO concept in traditional medical care has inspired similar programs to be developed for dental and eye care.

In the pharmaceutical field, Chronimed of Minnetonka, Minnesota, has focused on providing great customer service as its avenue to success.[16] The company supplies 100,000 patients across the United States with specialized medications that local pharmacies can't afford to stock. Chronimed's skill is twofold. First, it provides needed drugs by mail to organ transplant recipients and patients with diabetes or AIDS. Second, it employs a team of 50 pharmacists and assistants who provide much-needed information about the medications they dispense, such as details about drug interaction and side effects. As evidenced by the above examples, health care companies, regardless of the specific area in which they compete, are becoming more and more market oriented as they try to differentiate their offerings from those of the competition.

Insurance

In recent years, the insurance industry has exploded with new product and service offerings. Not too long ago, customers were faced with limited options in choosing life, hospital, or auto insurance. Now there is a wide array of insurance policies to choose from, including universal life policies, which double as retirement savings; nursing care insurance; reversible mortgages, which allow people to take equity from their house while still living in it; and other offerings aimed at serving an aging population. To illustrate, Prudential Insurance Company offers a program whereby terminally ill policyholders are allowed to withdraw funds against the face value of their policy while still alive. In addition to insurance services, most insurance companies now offer a full range of financial services, including auto loans, mortgages, mutual funds, and certificates of deposit.

Distribution of insurance services has also been growing. The vending machines found in airports for flight insurance have been finding their way into other areas. Travel auto insurance is now available in many motel chains and through the AAA. Group insurance written through employers and labor unions also has been extremely successful. In each instance, the insurance industry has used intermediaries to distribute its services.

Travel

The travel industry, most notably the airlines, has been a leader in the use of technology. Computerized reservation systems allow customers to book plane tickets from home or work. Nearly all airlines are using Internet sites to dispense flight and fare information. Airlines are in the midst of implementing ticketless travel programs in which passengers purchase tickets, select their seats, and pick up boarding passes and luggage tags at machines resembling ATMs.[17] Technology has also allowed airlines to make strategic pricing decisions through the use of yield management. In yield management, certain seats on aircraft are discounted and certain ones aren't. Through the use of elaborate computer programs, managers are able to determine who their customer segments are and who is likely to purchase airline tickets when and to where.

Despite its success in employing technology to attract additional customers and offer added convenience, the airline industry has operated in somewhat dire straits, plagued by

"I'm a nice customer. You all know me. I'm the one who never complains, no matter what kind of service I get.

"I'll go into a restaurant, and I'll sit while the waitress gossips with a friend and never bothers to look to see if my hamburger is ready to go. Sometimes a party who came in after I did gets my hamburger, but I don't say a word in complaint when the waitress tells me, 'Oh, I'm sorry. I'll order another for you.' I just wait.

"It's the same when I go to a bank. I don't throw my weight around. I try to be thoughtful of the other person. If I get poor service I'm as polite as can be. I don't believe rudeness in return is the answer.

"The other day I stopped in at the neighborhood gas station. I waited for almost five minutes before the attendant took care of me. And when he did, he spilled gas and wiped the car windows with an oily rag. I didn't expect him to thank me for stopping by—and he didn't. Naturally, I didn't complain about the service.

"I never kick. I never nag. I never criticize. And I wouldn't dream of making a scene, as I've seen some people do in public places. I think that's uncalled for. No, I'm the nice customer. And I'll tell you what else I am.

"I'm the customer who never comes back!

"In fact, a nice customer like me, multiplied by others of my kind, can just about ruin a business. There are a lot of nice people in the world, just like me. When we get pushed far enough, we go on down the street to another store, another bank, where they're smart enough to hire help who have been trained to appreciate nice customers.

"He laughs loudest, they say, who laughs last. I laugh when I see you frantically spending your money on expensive advertising to get me back, when you could have had me in the first place for a few kind words and a smile and some good services.

"I don't care what business you're in. Maybe you live in a different town; maybe I've never heard of you. But if you're going broke or your business is bad, maybe there are enough people like me, who do know you. I'm your customer who never comes back."

Source: Unknown.

problems associated with overcapacity, high labor costs, and low perceived service quality. The decade of the 90s could be considered the most turbulent ever encountered by U.S. commercial airlines.[18] During this time, some airlines either went out of business (Midway, Eastern, and Pan Am) or were in and out of bankruptcy proceedings (Continental, America West, and TWA); and most others operated at a loss. In the early 2000s, both United Airlines and Delta Airlines faced bankruptcy.

A notable exception to the fate that befell most carriers is Southwest Airlines, which has finally convinced its peers that a carrier can be consistently profitable by offering cheap fares on short-distance routes. Now, big carriers such as Continental and United have created their own Southwest look-alikes to supplement their long-haul, full-service, high-fare operations. Southwest's secret to success (which other airlines may or may not be able to imitate) is the high level of employee morale everyone associated with the company exhibits. This has come as a direct result of upper management's internal marketing efforts.

Implications for Service Marketers

The preceding sections emphasized the use of all components of the marketing mix. Many service industries have been criticized for an overdependence on advertising. The overdependence on one or two elements of the marketing mix is a mistake that service marketers cannot afford. The sum total of the marketing mix elements represents the total impact of the firm's marketing strategy. The slack created by severely restricting one element cannot be compensated by heavier emphasis on another, since each element in the marketing mix is designed to address specific problems and achieve specific objectives.

Services must be made available to prospective users, which implies distribution in the marketing sense of the word. The revised concept of the distribution of services points out that service marketers must distinguish conceptually between the production and distribution of services. The problem of making services more widely available must not be ignored.

The above sections also pointed out the critical role of new service development. In several of the examples described, indirect distribution of the service was made possible because "products" were developed that included a tangible representation of the service. This development facilitates the use of intermediaries, because the service can now be separated from the producer. In addition, the development of new services paves the way for companies to expand and segment their markets. With the use of varying service bundles, new technology, and alternative means of distributing the service, companies are now able to practice targeted marketing.

SUMMARY

This chapter has dealt with the complex topic of service marketing. While the marketing of services has much in common with the marketing of products, unique problems in the area require highly creative marketing management skills. Many of the problems in the service area can be traced to the intangible and inseparable nature of services and the difficulties involved in measuring service quality. However, considerable progress has been made in understanding and reacting to these difficult problems, particularly in the area of distribution. In view of the major role services play in our economy, it is important for marketing practitioners to better understand and appreciate the unique problems of service marketing.

Additional Resources

Berry, Leonard L. *Discovering the Soul of Service.* NY: Free Press, 2000.

Berry, Leonard L., and Kent D. Seltman. *Management Lessons from Mayo Clinic.* NY: McGraw-Hill, 2008.

Collier, Marsha. *The Ultimate Online Customer Service Guide.* NY: John Wiley and Sons, 2011.

Fullerton, Sam. *Sports Marketing.* Burr Ridge, IL: McGraw-Hill/Irwin, 2007.

Gronroos, Christian. *Service Management and Marketing.* 3rd ed. NY: John Wiley and Sons, 2007.

Hoffman, K. Douglas, and John E. G. Bateson. *Service Marketing.* Mason, OH: Thomson Southwestern, 2009.

Keiningham, Timothy, and Terry Vavra. *The Customer Delight Principle.* NY: McGraw-Hill, 2001.

Schultz, Mike, and John E. Doerr. *Professional Service Marketing.* NY: John Wiley and Sons, 2009.

Key Terms and Concepts

Client relationship: Relationship in which the buyer of services views the seller as someone who has knowledge that is of value; may be of an ongoing nature.

Customer effort: For many services, the involvement of customers to some degree in the production of the service (e.g., some restaurants, airline baggage).

Inseparability: An important characteristic of services, the impossibility of separating a service from the person of the seller. In other words, services must often be produced and consumed simultaneously.

Intangibility: An important difference between goods and services is the intangibility of services which means that most services cannot appeal to a buyer's sense of touch, taste, smell, sight, or hearing before purchase, intangibility places a burden on the marketing organization.

Internal marketing: The continual process by which managers actively encourage, stimulate, and support employee commitment to the organization and its customers.

Off-peak pricing: The different prices service marketers charge during different times or days in order to stimulate demand during slow periods and hopefully, smooth out demand for the service.

Perishability and fluctuating demand: Services are perishable which means that unused capacity represents business that is lost forever. The demand for many services also fluctuates by season, day of the week, or time of the day.

Quality service: Customers' perception of quality as a function of (1) *tangibles* which include physical evidence of the service; (2) *reliability* which involves the consistency and dependability of the service performance; (3) *responsiveness* which is the willingness or readiness of employees or professionals to provide service; (4) *assurance* which refers to the knowledge and competence of service providers and the ability to convey trust and confidence; and (5) *empathy* which is the service provider's efforts to understand the customer's needs.

Services: Activities performed by sellers and others that accompany the sale of a product and that aid in its exchange or its utilization (e.g., financing, an 800 number).

Service products: Products that are intangible, or at least substantially so. If totally intangible, they are exchanged directly from producer to user (e.g., hair cut, medical service), cannot be transported or stored, and are almost instantly perishable. Service products are often difficult to identify since they come into existence at the same time they are bought and consumed.

Uniformity: An important characteristic of services is that their quality can vary more than the quality of goods. Because they are often human performances and often customized to the needs of the buyer (e.g., haircut), uniformity is difficult to achieve and quality can vary.

Chapter 13

Global Marketing

A growing number of U.S. corporations have transversed geographical boundaries and become truly multinational in nature. For most other domestic companies, the question is no longer, Should we go international? Instead, the questions relate to when, how, and where the companies should enter the international marketplace. The past 15 years have seen the reality of a truly world market unfold.

Firms invest in foreign countries for the same basic reasons they invest in their own country. These reasons vary from firm to firm but fall under the categories of achieving offensive or defensive goals. Offensive goals are to (1) increase long-term growth and profit prospects, (2) maximize total sales revenue, (3) take advantage of economies of scale, and (4) improve overall market position. As many American markets reach saturation, American firms look to foreign markets as outlets for surplus production capacity, sources of new customers, increased profit margins, and improved returns on investment. For example, the ability to expand the number of locations of McDonald's restaurants in the United States is becoming severely limited. Yet, on any given day, only 0.5 percent of the world's population visits McDonald's. Indeed, in the recent past, of the 50 most profitable McDonald's outlets, 25 were located in Hong Kong. For PepsiCo, the results are similar. Its restaurant division operates over 10,000 Kentucky Fried Chicken, Pizza Hut, and Taco Bell outlets abroad.

Multinational firms also invest in other countries to achieve defensive goals. Chief among these goals are the desire to (1) compete with foreign companies on their own turf instead of in the United States, (2) gain access to technological innovations that are developed in other countries, (3) take advantage of significant differences in operating costs between countries, (4) preempt competitors' global moves, and (5) avoid being locked out of future markets by arriving too late.

Such well-known companies as Zenith, Pillsbury, Shell Oil, CBS Records, and Firestone Tire & Rubber are now owned by non-U.S. interests. Since 1980, the share of the U.S. high-tech market held by foreign products has grown from less than 8 percent to over 50 percent. In such diverse industries as power tools, tractors, television, and banking, U.S. companies have lost the dominant position they once held. By investing solely in domestic operations or not being willing to adapt products to foreign markets, U.S. companies are more susceptible to foreign incursions. For example, there has been a great uproar over Japan's practice of not opening up its domestic automobile market to U.S. companies. However, not too many years ago, a great majority of the American cars shipped to Japan still had the steering wheel located on the left side of the vehicle—the opposite of where it should be for the Japanese market.

In many ways, marketing globally is the same as marketing at home. Regardless of which part of the world the firm sells in, the marketing program must still be built around

Company	Global Revenues (billions)	Percent Revenues from Outside the U.S.
Walmart	$401.1	24.6%
Ford Motor	146.3	51.9
General Electric	182.5	53.7
CitiGroup	52.8	74.8
Hewlett-Packard	118.4	68.2
Boeing	60.9	38.9
Intel	37.6	85.4
Coca-Cola	31.9	77.0
Apple	36.5	46.0
Starbucks	10.4	20.8

Source: Philip R. Cateora, Mary C. Gilly, and John L. Graham, *International Marketing*, 15th ed. (Burr Ridge, IL: McGraw-Hill/Irwin, 2011), p.10.

a sound product or service that is properly priced, promoted, and distributed to a carefully analyzed target market. In other words, the marketing manager has the same controllable decision variables in both domestic and nondomestic markets.

Although the development of a marketing program may be the same in either domestic or nondomestic markets, special problems may be involved in the implementation of marketing programs in nondomestic markets. These problems often arise because of the environmental differences that exist among various countries that marketing managers may be unfamiliar with.

In this chapter, marketing management in a global context will be examined. Methods of organizing global versus domestic markets, global market research tasks, methods of entry strategies into global markets, and potential marketing strategies for a multinational firm will be discussed. In examining each of these areas, the reader will find a common thread—knowledge of the local cultural environment—that appears to be a major prerequisite for success in each area.

With the proper adaptations, many companies have the capabilities and resources needed to compete successfully in the global marketplace. To illustrate, companies as diverse as Kellogg's, Avon, Eli Lilly, and Sun Microsystems all generate a large percentage of their sales from foreign operations. Smaller companies can also be successful. For example, Nemix, Inc., of Bell Gardens, California, is a franchisee of Church's Fried Chicken. Small by world standards, this company has succeeded in developing a fully vertical operation in Poland, doing everything from raising chickens to operating restaurants.[1]

THE COMPETITIVE ADVANTAGE OF NATIONS

As each year passes, it becomes more and more clear that some industries and companies succeed on a global scale while others do not. Harvard Business School professor Michael Porter introduced what he calls the "diamond" of national advantage to explain a nation's competitive advantage and why some companies and industries become global business leaders. Figure 13.1 presents Porter's model. The diamond presents four factors that determine the competitive advantage or disadvantage of a nation.

1. *Factor conditions.* The nation's ability to turn its natural resources, skilled labor, and infrastructure into a competitive advantage.

FIGURE 13.1
Porter's Diamond of
National Advantage

Source: Michael E. Porter,
*The Competitive Advantage
of Nations* (New York: Free
Press, 1990), pp. 577–615.

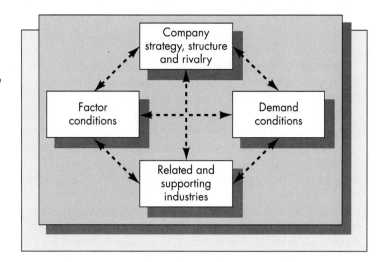

2. *Demand conditions.* The nature of domestic demand and the sophistication of domestic customers for the industry's product or service.

3. *Related and supporting industries.* The existence or absence in the country of supplier and related industries that are also internationally competitive.

4. *Company strategy, structure, and rivalry.* The conditions in the nation that govern how companies are created, organized, and managed, and how intensely they compete domestically.

Before Porter developed his model, he studied companies in more than 100 industries. While the most successful companies differed in many ways and employed different strategies, a very important common theme emerged: A company that succeeds on a global scale, first succeeded in intense domestic competition. His model is a dynamic model and illustrates how over time, a nation can build up and maintain its competitive advantage in any industry.

ORGANIZING FOR GLOBAL MARKETING

When compared with the tasks it faces at home, a firm attempting to establish a global marketing organization faces a much higher degree of risk and uncertainty. In a foreign market, management is often less familiar with the cultural, political, and economic situation. Many of these problems arise as a result of conditions specific to the foreign country. Managers are also faced with the decisions concerning how to organize the multinational company.

Problems with Entering Foreign Markets

While numerous problems could be cited, attention here will focus on those that firms most often face when entering foreign markets.

Cultural Misunderstanding

Differences in the cultural environment of foreign countries may be misunderstood or not even recognized because of the tendency for marketing managers to use their own cultural values and priorities as a frame of reference. Some of the most common areas of difference lie in the way dissimilar cultures perceive time, thought patterns, personal space, material possessions, family roles and relationships, personal achievement, competitiveness, individuality, social behavior, and other interrelated issues.[2] Another important source of misunderstandings is in the perceptions of managers about the people with whom they are dealing. Feelings of superiority can lead to changed communication mannerisms.

American managers must make the necessary efforts to learn, understand, and adapt to the cultural norms of the managers and customers they deal with in other parts of the world. Failure to do so will result in missed market opportunities.

On the other hand, companies should not shy away from attempting to enter global markets because conventional wisdom says that products and service will not succeed in some regions purely due to cultural reasons. For example, PepsiCo's Pepsi division entered into a $500 million offensive to try to grab a larger share of the $6 billion Brazilian soft-drink market.[3] Understanding the dramatic changes that had taken place in Brazil, Pepsi repositioned itself as the choice of a new Brazil. Advertisements for the Pepsi brand feature young people enumerating recent changes in Brazil. Does this campaign sound familiar? It should since it's a takeoff on the popular "Pepsi, the choice of a new generation" theme used in the United States. Actions taken by PepsiCo's Frito-Lay unit serve as another example of a successful adaptation to cultural differences.[4] In China, Frito-Lay introduced its popular Cheetos snack food. The twist to this effort lies in the fact that the Chinese are not big consumers of dairy products. In China, Cheetos are cheeseless, instead consisting of flavors such as "Savory American Cream" and "Zesty Japanese Steak." As a result of these and other adaptations, it's no wonder that PepsiCo ranks among the leaders in the global food and beverage industry.

Political Uncertainty

Governments are unstable in many countries, and social unrest and even armed conflict must sometimes be reckoned with. Other nations are newly emerging and anxious to seek their independence. These and similar problems can greatly hinder a firm seeking to establish its position in foreign markets. For example, at the turn of the century, firms scaled back their investment plans in Russia due to, among other reasons, (1) a business environment plagued by mobsters, (2) politics badly corrupted by the botched invasion of Chechnya, and (3) an economy troubled by runaway inflation and a plummeting ruble.[5] This is not to say investment in Russia is a poor choice. Rather, in situations like this, caution must be used and companies must have a keen understanding of the risks involved in undertaking sizable investments.

Import Restrictions

Tariffs, import quotas, and other types of import restrictions hinder global business. These are usually established to promote self-sufficiency and can be a huge roadblock for the multinational firm. For example, a number of countries, including South Korea, Taiwan, Thailand, and Japan, have placed import restrictions on a variety of goods produced in America, including telecommunications equipment, rice, wood products, automobiles, and produce. In other cases, governments may not impose restrictions that are commonly adhered to in the United States. For example, Chrysler pulled out of a proposed investment deal in China, worth billions of dollars, because the Chinese government refused to protect its right to limit access to technological information.

Exchange Controls and Ownership Restrictions

Some nations establish limits on the amount of earned and invested funds that can be withdrawn from it. These exchange controls are usually established by nations that are experiencing balance-of-payment problems. In addition, many nations have a requirement that the majority ownership of a company operating there be held by nationals. These and other types of currency and ownership regulations are important considerations in the decision

BODY LANGUAGE

- Standing with your hands on your hips is a gesture of defiance in Indonesia.
- Carrying on a conversation with your hands in your pockets makes a poor impression in France, Belgium, Finland, and Sweden.
- Shaking your head from side to side means yes in Bulgaria and Sri Lanka.
- Crossing your legs to expose the sole of your shoe is really taboo in Muslim countries. In fact, to call a person a "shoe" is a deep insult.

PHYSICAL CONTACT

- Patting a child on the head is a grave offense in Thailand or Singapore, since the head is revered as the location of the soul.
- In an Oriental culture, touching another person is considered an invasion of privacy; in Southern European and Arabic countries, it is a sign of warmth and friendship.

PROMPTNESS

- Be on time when invited for dinner in Denmark or in China.
- In Latin countries, your host or business associate would be surprised if you arrived at the appointed hour.

EATING AND COOKING

- It is rude to leave anything on your plate when eating in Norway, Malaysia, or Singapore.
- In Egypt, it is rude *not* to leave something.
- In Italy and Spain, cooking is done with oil.
- In Germany and Great Britain, margarine and butter are used.

OTHER SOCIAL CUSTOMS

- In Sweden, nudity and sexual permissiveness are quite all right, but drinking is really frowned on.
- In Spain, there is a very negative attitude toward life insurance. By receiving insurance benefits, a wife feels that she is profiting from her husband's death.
- In Western European countries, many consumers still are reluctant to buy anything (other than a house) on credit. Even for an automobile, they will pay cash.

Source: William J. Stanton, Michael J. Etzel, and Bruce J. Walker, *Fundamentals of Marketing,* 13th ed. (Burr Ridge, IL: McGraw-Hill/Irwin, 2004), p. 544.

to expand into a foreign market. For example, up until a few years ago, foreign holdings in business ventures in India were limited to a maximum of 40 percent. Once this ban was lifted, numerous global companies such as Sony, Whirlpool, JVC, Grundig, Panasonic, Kellogg's, Levi Strauss, Pizza Hut, and Domino's rushed to invest in this market.[6]

Economic Conditions

As noted earlier, nations' economies are becoming increasingly intertwined, and business cycles tend to follow similar patterns. However, there are differences, mainly due to political upheaval or social changes, and these may be significant. In determining whether to invest, marketers need to perform in-depth analyses of a country's stage of economic development, the buying power of its populace, and the strength of its currency. For example, when the North American Free Trade Agreement (NAFTA) was signed, many American companies rushed to invest in Mexico, building production facilities and retail outlets. These companies assumed that signing the agreement would stabilize Mexico's economy. In the long term, these investments may pay off. However, many companies lost millions of dollars there due to the devaluation of the peso. Indeed, the crash of the peso caused the retail giant Walmart to scale back a $1 billion investment project to open stores throughout Mexico.

Organizing the Multinational Company

There are two kinds of global companies—the multidomestic corporation and the global corporation.[7] The *multidomestic company* pursues different strategies in each of its foreign markets. It could have as many different product variations, brand names, and advertising campaigns as countries in which it operates. Each overseas subsidiary is autonomous. Local managers are given the authority to make the necessary decisions and are held accountable for results. In effect, the company competes on a market-by-market basis. Honeywell and General Foods are U.S. firms that have operated this way.

The *global company,* on the other hand, views the world as one market and pits its resources against the competition in an integrated fashion. It emphasizes cultural similarities across countries and universal consumer needs and wants rather than differences. It standardizes marketing activities when there are cultural similarities and adapts them when the cultures are different. Since there is no one clear-cut way to organize a global company, three alternative structures are normally used: (1) worldwide product divisions, each responsible for selling its own products throughout the world; (2) divisions responsible for all products sold within a geographic region; and (3) a matrix system that combines elements of both of these arrangements. Many organizations, such as IBM, Caterpillar, Timex, General Electric, Siemens, and Mitsubishi, are structured in a global fashion.

Most companies are realizing the need to take a global approach to managing their businesses. However, recognizing the need and actually implementing a truly global approach are two different tasks. For some companies, industry conditions dictate that they take a global perspective. The ability to actually implement a global approach to managing international operations, however, largely depends on factors unique to the company. Globalization, as a competitive strategy, is inherently more vulnerable to risk than a multidomestic or domestic strategy, due to the relative permanence of the organizational structure once established.

In determining whether or not to globalize a particular business, managers should look first at their industry.[8] Market, economic, environmental, and competitive factors all influence the potential gains to be realized by following a global strategy. Factors constituting the external environment that are conducive to a global strategy are:

1. *Market factors.* Homogeneous market needs, global customers, shorter product life cycles, transferable brands and advertising, and the ability to globalize distribution channels.
2. *Economic factors.* Worldwide economies of scale in manufacturing and distribution, steep learning curves, worldwide sourcing efficiencies, rising product development costs, and significant differences in host-country costs.
3. *Environmental factors.* Improving communications, favorable government policies, and the increasing speed of technological change.
4. *Competitive factors.* Competitive interdependencies among countries, global moves of competitors, and opportunities to preempt a competitor's global moves.[9]

Many of the reasons given in the first part of the chapter about why a domestic company should become a multinational can also be used to support the argument that a firm should take a global perspective. This is because the integration of markets is forcing companies that wish to remain successful not only to become multinationals but also to take a global perspective in doing so. In the past, companies had the option of remaining domestic or going multinational due to the separation of markets. This is no longer the case.

Growth in global markets has created opportunities for building global brands. The advantages are many and so are the pitfalls. Here are 10 commandments that marketers can use when planning a global branding campaign.

1. *Understand similarities and differences in the global branding landscape.* The best brands retain consistency of theme and alter specific elements to suit each country.
2. *Don't take shortcuts in brand building.* Build brands in new markets from the "bottom up."
3. *Establish marketing infrastructure.* Most often, firms adopt or invest in foreign partners for manufacturing and distribution.
4. *Embrace integrated marketing communications.* Because advertising opportunities may be more limited, marketers must use other forms of communication such as sponsorship and public relations.
5. *Establish brand partnerships.* Most global brands have marketing partners ranging from joint venture partners to franchisees and distributors who provide access to distribution.
6. *Balance standardization and customization.* Know what to standardize and what to customize.
7. *Balance global and local control.* This is very important in the following areas: organization structure, entry strategies, coordination processes, and mechanisms.
8. *Establish operable guidelines.* Set the rules about how the brand will be positioned and marketed.
9. *Implement a global brand equity measurement system.* The ideal measurement system provides complete, up-to-date information on the brand and on all its competitors to the appropriate decision makers.
10. *Leverage brand elements.* If the meanings of the brand name and all related trademarked identifiers are clear, they can be an invaluable source of brand equity worldwide.

Source: Kevin Lane Keller, "The Ten Commandments of Global Branding," *MBA Bullet Point,* October 3–16, 2000, p. 3, and Kevin Lane Keller, *Strategic Brand Management,* 3rd ed. (Upper Saddle River, NJ: Prentice-Hall, 2008), chap. 14.

Several internal factors can either facilitate or impede a company's efforts to undertake a global approach to marketing strategies. These factors and their underlying dimensions are

1. *Structure.* The ease of installing a centralized global authority and the absence of rifts between present domestic and international divisions or operating units.
2. *Management processes.* The capabilities and resources available to perform global planning, budgeting, and coordination activities, coupled with the ability to conduct global performance reviews and implement global compensation plans.
3. *Culture.* The ability to project a global versus national identity, a worldwide versus domestic commitment to employees, and a willingness to tolerate interdependence among business units.
4. *People.* The availability of employable foreign nationals and the willingness of current employees to commit to multicountry careers, frequent travel, and having foreign superiors.

Overall, whether a company should undertake a multidomestic or global approach to organizing its international operations will largely depend on the nature of the company and its products, how different foreign cultures are from the domestic market, and the company's ability to implement a global perspective. Many large brands have failed in their quest to go global. The primary reason for this failure is rushing the process. Successful global brands carefully stake out their markets, allowing plenty of time to develop their overseas marketing efforts and evolve into global brands.

Indeed, in many cases, firms do not undertake either purely multidomestic or global approaches to marketing. Instead, they develop a hybrid approach whereby these global brands carry with them the same visual identity, the same strategic positioning, and the same advertising. In addition, local characteristics are factored in. Regardless of the approach undertaken, management and organizational skills that emphasize the need to handle diversity are the critical factors that determine the long-term success of any company's endeavors in the global marketplace.

PROGRAMMING FOR GLOBAL MARKETING

In this section of the chapter, the major areas in developing a global marketing program will be examined. As mentioned at the outset, marketing managers must organize the same controllable decision variables that exist in domestic markets. However, many firms that have been extremely successful in marketing in the United States have not been able to duplicate their success in foreign markets.

Global Marketing Research

Because the risks and uncertainties are so high, marketing research is equally important in foreign markets and in domestic markets and probably more so. Many companies encounter losing situations abroad because they do not know enough about the market.[10] They don't know how to get the information or find the cost of collecting the information too high. To be successful, organizations must collect and analyze pertinent information to support the basic go/no-go decision before getting to the issues addressed by conventional market research. Toward this end, in attempting to analyze foreign consumers and markets, at least four organizational issues must be considered.

Population Characteristics

Population characteristics are one of the major components of a market, and significant differences exist between and within foreign countries. If data are available, the marketing manager should be familiar with the total population and with the regional, urban, rural, and interurban distribution. Other demographic variables, such as the number and size of families, education, occupation, and religion, are also important. In many markets, these variables can have a significant impact on the success of a firm's marketing program. For example, in the United States, a cosmetics firm can be reasonably sure that the desire to use cosmetics is common among women of all income classes. However, in Latin America the same firm may be forced to segment its market by upper-, middle-, and lower-income groups, as well as by urban and rural areas. This is because upper-income women want high-quality cosmetics promoted in prestige media and sold through exclusive outlets. In some rural and less prosperous areas, cosmetics must be inexpensive; in other rural areas, women do not accept cosmetics.

Ability to Buy

To assess the ability of consumers in a foreign market to buy, four broad measures should be examined: (1) gross national product or per capita national income, (2) distribution of income, (3) rate of growth in buying power, and (4) extent of available financing. Since each of these vary in different areas of the world, the marketing opportunities available must be examined closely.

Many consumer goods companies have sought growth by expanding into global markets. For U.S. companies, this is sound strategy since 95 percent of the world's population and two-thirds of its purchasing power are located outside their country. The potential for success in global markets is enhanced when companies carefully research and analyze consumers in foreign countries, just as it is in domestic markets. Below are some suggestions for companies seeking to successfully market to global consumers.

- Research the cultural nuances and customs of the market. Be sure that the company and brand name translate favorably in the language of the target country, and if not, consider using an abbreviation or entirely different brand name for the market. Consider using marketing research firms or ad agencies that have detailed knowledge of the culture.

- Determine whether the product can be exported to the foreign country as is or whether it has to be modified to be useful and appealing to targeted consumers. Also, determine what changes need to be made to packaging and labeling to make the product appealing to the market.

- Research the prices of similar products in the target country or region. Determine the necessary retail price to make marketing it profitable in the country, and research whether a sufficient number of consumers would be willing to pay that price. Also, determine what the product has to offer that would make consumers willing to pay a higher price.

- On the basis of research, decide whether the targeted country or region will require a unique marketing strategy or whether the same general strategy can be used in all geographic areas.

- Research the ways consumers purchase similar products in the targeted country or region and whether the company's product can be sold effectively using this method of distribution. Also, determine if a method of distribution not currently being used in the country could create a competitive advantage for the product.

- Pretest integrated marketing communication efforts in the targeted country to ensure not only that messages are translated accurately but also that subtle differences in meaning are not problematic. Also, research the effectiveness of planned communication efforts.

Marketing consumer goods successfully in global markets requires a long-term commitment because it may take time to establish an identity in new markets. However, with improving technology and the evolution of a global economy, both large and small companies have found global marketing both feasible and profitable.

Source: Dom Del Prete, "Winning Strategies Lead to Global Marketing Success," *Marketing News*, August 18, 1997, pp. 1, 2. Also see Philip R. Cateora, Mary C. Gilly, and John L. Graham, *International Marketing*, 15th ed. (Burr Ridge, IL: McGraw-Hill/Irwin, 2011), chap. 8.

Willingness to Buy

The cultural framework of consumer motives and behavior is integral to the understanding of the foreign consumer. If data are available, cultural values and attitudes toward the material culture, social organizations, the supernatural, aesthetics, and language should be analyzed for their possible influence on each of the elements in the firm's marketing program. It is easy to see that such factors as the group's values concerning acquisition of material goods, the role of the family, the positions of men and women in society, and the various age groups and social classes can have an effect on marketing because each can influence consumer behavior.

In some areas tastes and habits seem to be converging, with different cultures becoming more and more integrated into one homogeneous culture, although still separated by national

Procter & Gamble: According to the P&G Web site, P&G products are developed as global R&D projects. P&G has 22 research centers in 13 countries from which they can draw expertise. As a good example of a global product, consider the Swiffer mop. P&G made use of its research centers in the United States and France to conduct market research and testing in support of this new product.

Apple: In the development of the iPod, Apple worked with about ten different firms and independent contractors throughout the world, and did product design and customer requirement definition in both the United States and Japan.

Ikea: The Swedish furniture retailer knows that its target market (middle-class strivers) crosses international and intercontinental lines, so it operates globally in a streamlined fashion. It identifies an unmet customer need (say a certain style of table at a given price point), commissions in-house and outsourced designers to compete for the best design, then its manufacturing partners worldwide compete for the rights to manufacture it. Excellent global logistics complete the value delivery to customers.

Bungie Studios: This boutique software company, now owned by Microsoft, developed the MS Halo gaming software series in the United States, but product-tested it in Europe and Asia. Like Ikea customers in the prior example, gamers are much alike the world over.

Source: Loida Rosario, "Borderless Innovation: The Impact of Globalization on NPD in Three Industries," *Visions*, June 2006. Merle Crawford and Anthony DiBenedetto, *New Products Management*, 10th ed. (Burr Ridge, IL: McGraw-Hill/Irwin, 2011), p. 10.

boundaries. This appears to be the case in Western Europe, where consumers are developing into a mass market. This convergence obviously will simplify the task for a marketer in this region. However, cultural differences still prevail among many areas of the world and strongly influence consumer behavior. Marketing organizations may have to do primary research in many foreign markets to obtain usable information about these issues.

Differences in Research Tasks and Processes

In addition to the dimensions mentioned above, the processes and tasks associated with carrying out the market research program may also differ from country to country. Many market researchers count on census data for in-depth demographic information. However, in foreign countries the market researcher is likely to encounter a variety of problems in using census data. These include[11]

1. *Language.* Some nations publish their census reports in English. Other countries offer census reports only in their native language; some do not take a census.

2. *Data content.* Data contained in a census vary from country to country and often omit items of interest to researchers. For example, most foreign nations do not include an income question on their census. Others do not include such items as marital status or education levels.

3. *Timeliness.* The United States takes a census every 10 years. Japan and Canada conduct one every five years. However, some northern European nations are abandoning the census as a data-collection tool and instead are relying on population registers to account for births, deaths, and changes in marital status or place of residence.

4. *Availability in the United States.* If a researcher requires detailed household demographics on foreign markets, the cost and time required to obtain the data will be significant. Unfortunately, census data for many countries do not exist. For some it will be difficult to obtain, although data about others can be found on the Internet.

Global Product Strategy

Global marketing research can help determine whether (1) there is an unsatisfied need for which a new product could be developed to serve a foreign market or (2) there is an unsatisfied need that could be met with an existing domestic product, either as is or adapted to the foreign market. In either case, product planning is necessary to determine the type of product to be offered and whether there is sufficient demand to warrant entry into a foreign market.

Most U.S. firms would not think of entering a domestic market without extensive product planning. However, some marketers have failed to do adequate product planning when entering foreign markets. An example of such a problem occurred when American manufacturers began to export refrigerators to Europe. The firms exported essentially the same models sold in the United States. However, the refrigerators were the wrong size, shape, and temperature range for some areas and had weak appeal in others—thus failing miserably. Although adaptation of the product to local conditions may have eliminated this failure, this adaptation is easier said than done. For example, even in the domestic market, overproliferation of product varieties and options can dilute economies of scale. This dilution results in higher production costs, which may make the price of serving each market segment with an adapted product prohibitive.

The solution to this problem is not easy. In some cases, changes need not be made at all or, if so, can be accomplished rather inexpensively. In other cases, the sales potential of the particular market may not warrant expensive product changes. For example, Pepsi's Radical Fruit line of juice drinks was introduced without adaptation on three continents. On the other hand, U.S. companies wishing to market software in foreign countries must undertake painstaking and costly efforts to convert the embedded code from English to foreign languages. This undertaking severely limits the potential markets where individual software products can be profitably marketed. In any case, management must examine these product-related problems carefully prior to making foreign market entry decisions.

Global Distribution Strategy

The role of the distribution network in facilitating the transfer of goods and titles and in the demand stimulation process is as important in foreign markets as it is at home. Figure 13.2

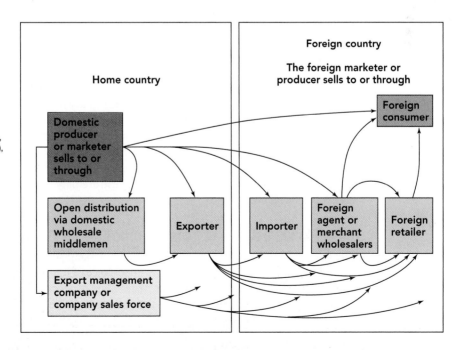

FIGURE 13.2
International Channel-of-Distribution Alternatives

Source: Philip R. Cateora, Mary C. Gilly, and John I. Graham, *International Marketing,* 15th ed. (Burr Ridge, IL: McGraw-Hill/Irwin, 2011), p. 430.

illustrates some of the most common channel arrangements in global marketing. They range from no control to almost complete control of the distribution system by manufacturers.

Global distribution strategy can be extremely challenging because sellers must influence two sets of channels: one in the home country and one in the foreign country. There are many possibilities as the figure clearly illustrates. The arrows indicate to whom the producers and various middlemen might sell in order to move products between countries.

Manufacturers can become more directly involved and, hence, have greater control over distribution, when they select agents and distributors located in foreign markets. Both perform similar functions, except that agents do not assume title to the manufacturers' products, while wholesalers do. If manufacturers should assume the functions of foreign agents or wholesalers and establish their own foreign branch, they greatly increase control over their global distribution system. Manufacturers' effectiveness will then depend on their own administrative organization rather than on independent intermediaries. If the foreign branch sells to other intermediaries, such as wholesalers and retailers, as is the case with most consumer goods, manufacturers again relinquish some control. However, since the manufacturers are located in the market area, they have greater potential to influence these intermediaries. For example, Volkswagen, Anheuser-Busch, and Procter & Gamble have each made substantial investments in building manufacturing facilities in Brazil. These investments allow the companies to begin making direct sales to dealers and retailers in the country.

The channel arrangement that enables manufacturers to exercise a great deal of control is where the manufacturer sells directly to organizational buyers or ultimate consumers. Although this arrangement is most common in the sale of organizational goods, some consumer goods companies have also pursued this arrangement.

Global Pricing Strategy

In domestic markets, pricing is a complex task. The basic approaches used in price determination in foreign markets are the same as those discussed earlier in the chapter on pricing. However, the pricing task is often more complicated in foreign markets because of additional problems associated with tariffs, antidumping laws, taxes, inflation, and currency conversion.

Import duties are probably the major constraint for global marketers and are encountered in many markets. Management must decide whether import duties will be paid by the firm or the foreign consumer, or whether they will be paid by both. This and similar constraints may force the firm to abandon an otherwise desirable pricing strategy or may force the firm out of a market altogether.

Another pricing problem arises because of the rigidity in price structures found in many foreign markets. Many foreign intermediaries are not aggressive in their pricing policies. They often prefer to maintain high unit margins at the expense of low sales volume rather than develop large sales volume by means of lower prices and smaller margins per unit. Many times this rigidity is encouraged by legislation that prevents retailers from cutting prices substantially at their own discretion. These are only a few of the pricing problems foreign marketers encounter.

Global Advertising and Sales Promotion Strategy

When expanding their operations into the world marketplace, most firms are aware of the language barriers that exist and realize the importance of translating their messages into the proper idiom. However, numerous other issues must be resolved as well, such as selecting appropriate media and advertising agencies in foreign markets.

There are many problems in selecting media in foreign markets. Often the media that are traditionally used in the domestic market are not available. For example, it was not until recently that national commercial TV became a reality in the former Soviet Union. If media are available, they may be so only on a limited basis or they may not reach the potential buyers. In addition to the problem of availability, other difficulties arise from the lack of accurate media information. There is no rate and data service or media directory that covers all the media available throughout the world. Where data are available, their accuracy is often questionable.

Another important promotion decision that must be made is the type of agency used to prepare and place the firm's advertisements. Along with the growth in multinational product companies, more multinational advertising agencies are available. Among the top 15 global advertising agencies, less than half are U.S. owned. Alliances and takeovers have stimulated growth in the formation of global agencies. The U.S. company can take either of two major approaches to choosing an agency. The first is to use a purely local agency in each area where the advertisement is to appear. The rationale for this approach is that a purely local agency employing only local nationals can better adapt the firm's message to the local culture.

The other approach is to use either a U.S.-based multinational agency or a multinational agency with U.S. offices to develop and implement the ad campaign. For example, the Coca-Cola Company uses one agency to create ads for the 80 nations in which Diet Coke is marketed. The use of these so-called super agencies is increasing (annual growth rates averaged over 30 percent in the last decade). By using global advertising agencies, companies are able to take advantage of economies of scale and other efficiencies. However, global agencies are not without their critics. Many managers believe that small, local agencies in emerging markets take a more entrepreneurial and fresher approach to advertising than do global agencies. Much discussion has developed over which approach is best, and it appears that both approaches can be used successfully.

The use of sales promotion can also lead to opportunities and problems for marketers in foreign markets. Sales promotions often contain certain characteristics that are more attractive than other elements of the promotion mix.[12] In less-wealthy countries, consumers tend to be even more interested in saving money through price discounts, sampling, or premiums. Sales promotion can also be used as a strategy for bypassing restrictions on advertising placed by some foreign governments. In addition, sales promotion can be an effective means for reaching people who live in rural locations where media support for advertising is virtually nonexistent.

ENTRY AND GROWTH STRATEGIES FOR GLOBAL MARKETING

A major decision facing companies that desire either to enter a foreign market or pursue growth within a specific market relates to the choice of entry or growth strategy. What type of strategy to employ depends on many factors, including the analysis of market opportunities, company capabilities, the degree of marketing involvement and commitment the company is willing to make, and the amount of risk that the company is able to tolerate.[13] A company can decide to (1) make minimal investments of funds and resources by limiting its efforts to exporting, (2) make large initial investments of resources and management effort to try to establish a long-term share of global markets, or (3) take an incremental approach whereby the company starts with a low-risk mode of entry that requires the least financial and other resource commitment and gradually increases its commitment over time. All three approaches can be profitable. In general, a company can initially enter a global market and, subsequently, pursue growth in the global marketplace in six ways:

1. *Exporting.* Exporting occurs when a company produces the product outside the final destination and then ships it there for sale. It is the easiest and most common approach for a company making its first international move. Exporting has two distinct advantages. First, it avoids the cost of establishing manufacturing operations in the host country; second, it may help a firm achieve experience-curve and location economies. By manufacturing the product in a centralized location and exporting it to other national markets, the firm may be able to realize substantial scale economies from its global sales volume. This method is what allowed Sony to dominate the global TV market. The major disadvantages related to exporting include (1) the sometimes higher cost associated with the process, (2) the necessity of the exporting firm to pay import duties or face trade barriers, and (3) the delegation of marketing responsibility for the product to foreign agents who may or may not be dependable.

2. *Licensing.* Companies can grant patent rights, trademark rights, and the right to use technological processes to foreign companies. This is the most common strategy for small and medium-size companies. The major advantage to licensing is that the firm does not have to bear the development costs and risks associated with opening up a foreign market. In addition, licensing can be an attractive option in unfamiliar or politically volatile markets. The major disadvantages are that (1) the firm does not have tight control over manufacturing, marketing, and strategy that is required for realizing economies of scale; and (2) there is the risk that foreign companies may capitalize on the licensed technology. RCA Corporation, for example, once licensed its color TV technology to a number of Japanese firms. These firms quickly assimilated the technology and used it to enter the U.S. market.

3. *Franchising.* Franchising is similar to licensing but tends to involve longer-term commitments. Also, franchising is commonly employed by service firms, as opposed to manufacturing firms. In a franchising agreement, the franchisor sells limited rights to use its brand name in return for a lump sum and share of the franchisee's future profits. In contrast to licensing agreements, the franchisee agrees to abide by strict operating procedures. Advantages and disadvantages associated with franchising are primarily the same as with licensing except to a lesser degree. In many cases, franchising offers an effective mix of centralized and decentralized decision making.

4. *Joint ventures.* A company may decide to share management with one or more collaborating foreign firms. Joint ventures are especially popular in industries that call for large investments, such as natural gas exploration and automobile manufacturing. Control of the joint venture may be split equally, or one party may control decision making. Joint ventures hold several advantages. First, a firm may be able to benefit from a partner's knowledge of the host country's competitive position, culture, language, political systems, and so forth. Second, the firm gains by sharing costs and risks of operating in a foreign market. Third, in many countries, political considerations make joint ventures the only feasible entry mode. Finally, joint ventures allow firms to take advantage of a partner's distribution system, technological know-how, or marketing skills. For example, General Mills teamed up with CPC International in an operation called International Dessert Partners to develop a major baking and dessert-mix business in Latin America. The venture combines General Mills' technology and Betty Crocker dessert products with CPC's marketing and distribution capabilities in Latin America. The major disadvantages associated with joint ventures are that (1) a firm may risk giving up control of proprietary knowledge to its partner, and (2) the firm may lose the tight control over a foreign subsidiary needed to engage in coordinated global attacks against rivals.

5. *Strategic alliances.* Although some consider strategic alliances a form of joint venture, we consider them a distinct entity for two reasons. First, strategic alliances are normally partnerships that two or more firms enter into to gain a competitive advantage on a worldwide versus local basis. Second, strategic alliances are usually of a much longer-term nature than are joint ventures. In strategic alliances, the partners share long-term goals and pledge almost total cooperation. Strategic alliances can be used to reduce manufacturing costs, accelerate technological diffusion and new product development, and overcome legal and trade barriers.[14] The major disadvantage associated with formation of a strategic alliance is the increased risk of competitive conflict between the partners.

6. *Direct ownership.* Some companies prefer to enter or grow in markets either through establishment of a wholly owned subsidiary or through acquisition. In either case, the firm owns 100 percent of the stock. The advantages to direct ownership are that the firm has (1) complete control over its technology and operations, (2) immediate access to foreign markets, (3) instant credibility and gains in the foreign country when acquisitions are the mode of entry or growth, and (4) the ability to install its own management team. Of course, the primary disadvantages of direct ownership are the huge costs and significant risks associated with this strategy. These problems may more than offset the advantages depending upon the country entered.

Regardless of the choice of methods used to gain entry into and grow within a foreign marketplace, companies must somehow integrate their operations. The complexities involved in operating on a worldwide basis dictate that firms decide on operating strategies. A critical decision that marketing managers must make relates to the extent of adaptation of the marketing mix elements for the foreign country in which the company operates. Depending on the area of the world under consideration and the particular product mix, different degrees of standardization/adaptation of the marketing mix elements may take place. As a guideline, standardization of one or more parts of the marketing mix is a function of many factors that individually and collectively affect companies' decision making.[15] It is more likely to succeed under the following conditions:

- When markets are economically similar.
- When worldwide customers, not countries, are the basis for segmenting markets.
- When customer behavior and lifestyles are similar.
- When the product is culturally compatible across the host country.
- When a firm's competitive position is similar in different markets.
- When competing against the same competitors, with similar market shares, in different countries, rather than competing against purely local companies.
- When the product is an organizational and high-technology product rather than a consumer product.
- When there are similarities in the physical, political, and legal environments of home and host countries.
- When the marketing infrastructure in the home and host countries is similar.

The decision to adapt or standardize marketing should be made only after a thorough analysis of the product-market mix has been undertaken. The company's end goal is to develop, manufacture, and market the products best suited to the actual and potential needs of the local (wherever that may be) customer and to the social and economic conditions of the marketplace. There can be subtle differences from country to country and from region to region in the ways a product is used and what customers expect from it.

SUMMARY

The world is truly becoming a global market. Many companies that avoid operating in the global arena are destined for failure. For those willing to undertake the challenges and risks necessary to become multinational organizations, long-term survival and growth are likely outcomes. The purpose of this chapter was to introduce the reader to the opportunities, problems, and challenges involved in global marketing.

Additional Resources

Bahl, Raghaw. *Super Power? The Amazing Race Between China's Hare and India's Tortoise.* NY: Portfolio/Penguin, 2010.

Behravesh, Nariman. *Spin Free Economics: A No-Nonsense Nonpartisan Guide to Today's Global Economic Debates.* NY: McGraw-Hill, 2009.

Friedman, Thomas L. *The World is Flat.* NY: Farrar, Straus, and Giroux, 2005.

McEwen, William, Xiaoguang Fang, Zhang Chuanping, and Richard Bunkholder. "Inside the Mind of the Chinese Consumer." *Harvard Business Review,* March 2006, pp. 66–67.

Milanovic, Branko. *The Haves and the Have Nots.* NY: Basic Books, 2011.

Steenkamp, Jan-Benedict E.M., and Inge Geyskens. "How Country Characteristics Affect the Perceived Value of Web Sites." *Journal of Marketing,* July 2006, pp. 136–150.

Key Terms and Concepts

Diamond of national advantage: Developed by Michael Porter, an explanation of a nation's competitive advantage and why some companies and industries become global business leaders.

Direct ownership: An organization's strategy for entering and growing in global markets either through the establishment of a wholly owned subsidiary or through acquisition where it owns 100 percent of the stock.

Exporting: A strategy for entering global markets where a firm produces the product outside the final destination and then ships it there for sale. It is the easiest and most common approach to entering a foreign market.

Franchising: A market entry strategy that is similar to licensing but usually involves longer-term commitments. The franchisor sells limited rights to use its brand name in return for a lump sum and share of the franchisee's future profits. It is more commonly employed by service organizations than manufacturers.

Global company: A company that views the world as one market and employs its resources against the competition in an integrated fashion. It emphasizes cultural similarities across countries and universal consumer needs and wants rather than differences. It standardizes marketing activities where there are cultural similarities and adapts them when the cultures are different.

Joint venture: An organization's entry into a foreign market by sharing management with one or more collaborating foreign firms. Decision making may be shared equally or controlled by one party.

Licensing: Organization's granting of patent rights, trademark rights, and the right to use technological processes to foreign markets. By licensing, an organization does not have to bear the costs and risks associated with actually locating in a foreign market.

Multidomestic company: A company that pursues different strategies in each of its foreign markets. It could have as many different product variations, brand names, and advertising campaigns as countries in which it operates.

Strategic alliance: Partnerships where two or more firms invest in each other to gain competitive advantages on a worldwide versus local level. They are usually of a much longer-term nature than a joint venture.

Section 2

Analyzing Marketing Problems and Cases

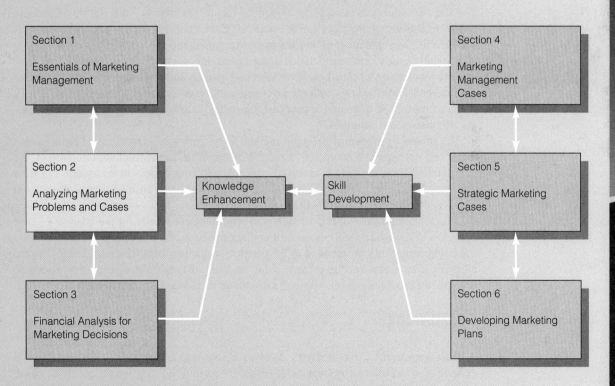

Case studies help bridge the gap between classroom learning and the practice of marketing management. They provide us with an opportunity to develop, sharpen, and test our analytical skills at

- Assessing situations.
- Sorting out and organizing key information.
- Asking the right questions.
- Defining opportunities and problems.
- Identifying and evaluating alternative courses of action.
- Interpreting data.
- Evaluating the results of past strategies.
- Developing and defending new strategies.
- Interacting with other managers.
- Making decisions under conditions of uncertainty.
- Critically evaluating the work of others.
- Responding to criticism.

Source: David W. Cravens, Charles W. Lamb, Jr., and Victoria L. Crittenden, *Strategic Marketing Management Cases,* 7th ed. (Burr Ridge, IL: McGraw-Hill/Irwin, 2002), p. 671.

The use of business cases was developed by faculty members of the Harvard Graduate School of Business Administration in the 1920s. Case studies have been widely accepted as one effective way of exposing students to strategic marketing processes.

Basically, cases represent detailed descriptions or reports of business situations. They are often written by a trained observer who was actually involved in the firm or organization and had some dealings with the problems under consideration. Cases generally entail both qualitative and quantitative data that the student must analyze to determine appropriate alternatives and solutions.

The primary purpose of the case method is to introduce a measure of realism into marketing management education. Rather than emphasizing the teaching of concepts, the case method focuses on application of concepts and sound logic to real-world business problems. In this way, students learn to bridge the gap between abstraction and application and to appreciate the value of both.

The primary purpose of this section is to offer a logical format for the analysis of case problems. Although there is no one format that can be successfully applied to all cases, the following framework is intended to be a logical sequence from which to develop sound analyses. This framework is presented for analysis of comprehensive marketing cases; however, the process should also be useful for shorter marketing cases, incidents, and problems.

A CASE ANALYSIS FRAMEWORK

A basic approach to case analysis involves a four-step process. First, the problem is defined. Second, alternative courses of action are formulated to solve the problem. Third, the alternatives are analyzed in terms of their strengths and weaknesses. And fourth, an alternative is accepted and a course of action is recommended. This basic approach is quite useful for students well versed in case analysis, particularly for shorter cases or incidents. However, for the newcomer, this framework may be oversimplified. Thus, the following expanded framework and checklists are intended to aid students in becoming proficient in case and problem analysis.

1. Analyze and Record the Current Situation

Whether the analysis of a firm's problems is done by a manager, student, or paid business consultant, the first step is to analyze the current situation. This does not mean writing up a history of the firm but entails the type of analysis described below. This approach is useful not only for getting a better grip on the situation but also for discovering both real and potential problems—central concerns of any case analysis.

Phase 1: The Environment

The first phase in analyzing a marketing problem or case is to consider the environment in which the firm is operating. The environment can be broken down into a number of different components such as the economic, social, political, and legal areas. Any of these may contain threats to a firm's success or opportunities for improving a firm's situation.

Phase 2: The Industry

The second phase involves analyzing the industry in which the firm operates. A framework provided by Michael Porter includes five competitive forces that need to be considered to do a complete industry analysis.[1] The framework is shown in Figure 1 and includes rivalry among existing competitors, threat of new entrants, and threat of substitute products. In addition, in this framework, buyers and suppliers are included as competitors because they can threaten the profitability of an industry or firm.

   While rivalry among existing competitors is an issue in most cases, analysis and strategies for dealing with the other forces can also be critical. This is particularly so when a firm is considering entering a new industry and wants to forecast its potential success. Each of the five competitive forces is discussed below.

Rivalry among Existing Competitors   In most cases and business situations a firm needs to consider the current competitors in its industry in order to develop successful strategies. Strategies such as price competition, advertising battles, sales promotion offers, new product

FIGURE 1   Competitive Forces in an Industry

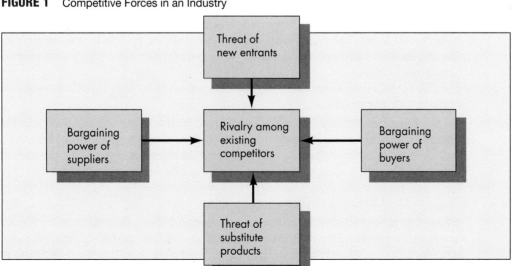

introductions, and increased customer service are commonly used to attract customers from competitors.

To fully analyze existing rivalry, it is important to determine which firms are the major competitors and what are their annual sales, market share, growth profile, and strengths and weaknesses. Also, it is useful to analyze their current and past marketing strategies to try to forecast their likely reactions to a change in a competitive firm's strategy. Finally, it is important to consider any trends or changes in government regulation of an industry or changes in technology that could affect the success of a firm's strategy.

Threat of New Entrants It is always possible for firms in other industries to try to compete in a new industry. New entrants are more likely in industries that have low entry barriers. *Entry barriers* include such things as a need for large financial resources, high brand equity for existing brands in an industry, or economies of scale obtained by existing firms in an industry. Also, existing firms in an industry may benefit from experience curves; that is, their cumulative experience in producing and marketing a product may reduce their per-unit costs below those of inexperienced firms. In general, the higher the entry barriers, the less likely outside firms are to enter an industry. For example, the entry barriers for starting up a new car company are much higher than for starting up an online software company.

Threat of Substitute Products In a broad sense, all firms in an industry compete with industries producing substitute products. For example, in cultures where bicycles are the major means of transportation, bicycle manufacturers compete with substitute products such as motor scooters and automobiles. Substitutes limit the potential return in an industry by placing a ceiling on the prices a firm in the industry can profitably charge. The more attractive the price–performance alternative offered by substitutes, the tighter the lid on industry profits. For example, the price of candy, such as Raisinets chocolate-covered raisins, may limit the price that can be charged for granola bars.

Bargaining Power of Suppliers Suppliers can be a competitive threat in an industry because they can raise the price of raw materials or reduce their quality. Powerful suppliers can reduce the profitability of an industry or firm if companies cannot raise their prices to cover price increases by suppliers. Also, suppliers may be a threat because they may forward-integrate into an industry by purchasing a firm that they supply or other firms in the industry.

Bargaining Power of Buyers Buyers can compete with an industry by forcing prices down, bargaining for higher quality or more services, and playing competitors off against each other. All these tactics can lower the profitability of a firm or industry. For example, because Wal-Mart sells such a large percentage of many companies' products, it can negotiate for lower prices than smaller retailers can. Also, buyers may be a threat because they may backward integrate into an industry by purchasing firms that supply them or other firms in the industry.

Phase 3: The Organization

The third phase involves analysis of the organization itself not only in comparison with the industry and industry averages but also internally in terms of both quantitative and qualitative data. Key areas of concern at this stage are such factors as objectives, constraints, management philosophy, financial condition, and the organizational structure and culture of the firm.

Phase 4: The Marketing Strategy

Although there may be internal personnel or structural problems in the marketing department that need examination, typically an analysis of the current marketing strategy is the next phase. In this phase, the objectives of the marketing department are analyzed in comparison with those of the firm in terms of agreement, soundness, and attainability. Each element of the marketing mix as well as other areas, such as marketing research and

A common criticism of prepared cases goes something like this: "You repeated an awful lot of case material, but you really didn't analyze the case." Yet, at the same time, it is difficult to verbalize exactly what *analysis* means—that is, "I can't explain exactly what it is, but I know it when I see it!"

This is a common problem since the term *analysis* has many definitions and means different things in different contexts. In terms of case analysis, one thing that is clear is that analysis means going beyond simply describing the case information. It includes determining the implications of the case information for developing strategy. This determination may involve careful financial analysis of sales and profit data or thoughtful interpretation of the text of the case.

One way of thinking about analysis involves a series of three steps: synthesis, generalizations, and implications. A brief example of this process follows.

The high growth rate of frozen pizza sales has attracted a number of large food processors, including Pillsbury (Totino's), Quaker Oats (Celeste), American Home Products (Chef Boy-ar-dee), Nestlé (Stouffer's), General Mills (Saluto), and H. J. Heinz (La Pizzeria). The major independents are Jeno's, Tony's, and John's. Jeno's and Totino's are the market leaders, with market shares of about 19 percent each. Celeste and Tony's have about 8 to 9 percent each, and the others have about 5 percent or less.

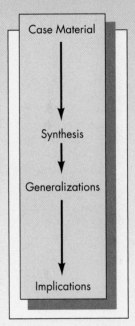

The frozen pizza market is a highly competitive and highly fragmented market.

In markets such as this, attempts to gain market share through lower consumer prices or heavy advertising are likely to be quickly copied by competitors and thus tend not to be very effective.

Lowering consumer prices and spending more on advertising are likely to be poor strategies. Perhaps increasing freezer space in retail outlets could be effective (this might be obtained through trade discounts). A superior product, for example, better-tasting pizza, microwave pizza, or increasing geographic coverage of the market, may be better strategies for obtaining market share.

Note that none of the three analysis steps includes any repetition of the case material. Rather, they all involve abstracting a meaning of the information and, by pairing it with marketing principles, coming up with the strategic implications of the information.

information systems, is analyzed in terms of whether it is internally consistent, synchronized with the goals of the department and firm, and focused on specific target markets. Although cases often are labeled in terms of their primary emphasis, such as "pricing" or "advertising," it is important to analyze the marketing strategy and entire marketing mix, since a change in one element will usually affect the entire marketing program.

In performing the analysis of the current situation, the data should be analyzed carefully to extract the relevant from the superfluous. Many cases contain information that is not relevant to the problem; it is the analyst's job to discard this information to get a clearer picture of the current situation. As the analysis proceeds, a watchful eye must be kept on each phase to determine (1) symptoms of problems, (2) current problems, and (3) potential problems. Symptoms of problems are indicators of a problem but are not problems in and of themselves. For example, a symptom of a problem may be a decline in sales in a particular sales territory. However, the problem is the root cause of the decline in sales—perhaps the field representative quit making sales calls and is relying on phone orders only.

The following is a checklist of the types of questions that should be asked when performing the analysis of the current situation.

Checklist for Analyzing the Current Situation

Phase 1: The Environment

1. What is the state of the economy and are there any trends that could affect the industry, firm, or marketing strategy?
2. What are current trends in cultural and social values and how do these affect the industry, firm, or marketing strategy?
3. What are current political values and trends and how do they affect the industry, firm, or marketing strategy?
4. Is there any current or pending federal, state, or local legislation that could change the industry, firm, or marketing strategy?
5. Overall, are there any threats or opportunities in the environment that could influence the industry, firm, or marketing strategy?

Phase 2: The Industry

1. What industry is the firm in?
2. Which firms are the major competitors in the industry and what are their annual sales, market share, and growth profile?
3. What strategies have competitors in the industry been using and what has been their success with them?
4. What are the relative strengths and weaknesses of competitors in the industry?
5. Is there a threat of new competitors coming into the industry and what are the major entry barriers?
6. Are there any substitute products for the industry and what are their advantages and disadvantages compared to this industry's products?
7. How much bargaining power do suppliers have in this industry and what is its impact on the firm and industry profits?
8. How much bargaining power do buyers have in this industry and what is its impact on the firm and industry profits?

Phase 3: The Organization

1. What are the objectives of the organization? Are they clearly stated? Attainable?
2. What are the strengths of the organization? Managerial expertise? Financial? Copyrights or patents?
3. What are the constraints and weaknesses of the organization?
4. Are there any real or potential sources of dysfunctional conflict in the structure of the organization?
5. How is the marketing department structured in the organization?

Phase 4: The Marketing Strategy

1. What are the objectives of the marketing strategy? Are they clearly stated? Are they consistent with the objectives of the firm? Is the entire marketing mix structured to meet these objectives?
2. What marketing concepts are at issue in the current strategy? Is the marketing strategy well planned and laid out? Is the strategy consistent with sound marketing principles? If the strategy takes exception to marketing principles, is there a good reason for it?

3. To what target market is the strategy directed? Is it well defined? Is the market large enough to be profitably served? Does the market have long-run potential?

4. What competitive advantage does the marketing strategy offer? If none, what can be done to gain a competitive advantage in the marketplace?

5. What products are being sold? What are the width, depth, and consistency of the firm's product lines? Does the firm need new products to fill out its product line? Should any product be deleted? What is the profitability of the various products?

6. What promotion mix is being used? Is promotion consistent with the products and product images? What could be done to improve the promotion mix?

7. What channels of distribution are being used? Do they deliver the product at the right time and right place to meet customer needs? Are the channels typical of those used in the industry? Could channels be made more efficient?

8. What pricing strategies are being used? How do prices compare with similar products of other firms? How are prices determined?

9. Are marketing research and information systematically integrated into the marketing strategy? Is the overall marketing strategy internally consistent?

The relevant information from this preliminary analysis is now formalized and recorded. At this point the analyst must be mindful of the difference between facts and opinions. Facts are objective statements, such as financial data, whereas opinions are subjective interpretations of facts or situations. The analyst must make certain not to place too much emphasis on opinions and to carefully consider any variables that may bias such opinions.

Regardless of how much information is contained in the case or how much additional information is collected, the analyst usually finds that it is impossible to specify a complete framework for the current situation. At this point, assumptions must be made. Clearly, since each analyst may make different assumptions, it is critical that assumptions be explicitly stated. When presenting a case, the analyst may wish to distribute copies of the assumption list to all class members. This avoids confusion about how the analyst perceives the current situation, and others can evaluate the reasonableness and necessity of the assumptions.

2. Analyze and Record Problems and Their Core Elements

After careful analysis, problems and their core elements should be explicitly stated and listed in order of importance. Finding and recording problems and their core elements can be difficult. It is not uncommon when reading a case for the first time for the student to view the case as a description of a situation in which there are no problems. However, careful analysis should reveal symptoms, which lead to problem recognition.

Recognizing and recording problems and their core elements is most critical for a meaningful case analysis. Obviously, if the root problems are not explicitly stated and understood, the remainder of the case analysis has little merit because the true issues are not being dealt with. The following checklist of questions is designed to assist in performing this step of the analysis.

Checklist for Analyzing Problems and Their Core Elements

1. What is the primary problem in the case? What are the secondary problems?

2. What proof exists that these are the central issues? How much of this proof is based on facts? On opinions? On assumptions?

3. What symptoms are there that suggest these are the real problems in the case?

4. How are the problems, as defined, related? Are they independent or are they the result of a deeper problem?

5. What are the ramifications of these problems in the short run? In the long run?

It is possible that a case could describe a company that is doing everything right and there are no serious problems in it. However, most of the time, analysis of a case will reveal one or more important shortcomings in the organization's marketing strategy. Below is a sample list of mistakes that marketers make that could be in a case.

1. The organization failed to offer products that customers want either because it did no research, did poor research, failed to interpret the research appropriately, or failed to react to it appropriately.
2. The organization underestimated the ability of competitors to gain market share and failed to react appropriately to successful competitive strategies.
3. The organization failed to react appropriately to changes in other aspects of the environment such as social, political, or legal changes.
4. The organization failed to keep up with or underestimated the impact of competitors' innovations in production and product development.
5. The organization did not position its products on dimensions that customers care about.
6. The organization overestimated the likely success of new products because of faulty sales forecasts or wishful thinking.
7. The organization expanded too rapidly into new markets or offered its products in too many outlets in existing markets.
8. The organization failed to raise prices when warranted or raised prices too much or too frequently.
9. The organization offered an inconsistent marketing mix that failed to provide a clear image of the product in the minds of customers.
10. The organization relied on promotion to sell an inferior product.
11. The organization failed to use the best channels to reach customers.
12. The organization underestimated the cost of competing effectively in an industry.

3. Formulate, Evaluate, and Record Alternative Courses of Action

This step is concerned with the question of what can be done to resolve the problem defined in the previous step. Generally, a number of alternative courses of action are available that could potentially help alleviate the problem condition. Three to seven are usually a reasonable number of alternatives to work with. Another approach is to brainstorm as many alternatives as possible initially and then reduce the list to a workable number.

Sound logic and reasoning are very important in this step. It is critical to avoid alternatives that could potentially alleviate the problem, but would create a greater new problem or require greater resources than the firm has at its disposal.

After serious analysis and listing of a number of alternatives, the next task is to evaluate them in terms of their costs and benefits. Costs are any output or effort the firm must exert to implement the alternative. Benefits are any input or value received by the firm. Costs to be considered are time, money, other resources, and opportunity costs; benefits are such things as sales, profits, brand equity, and customer satisfaction. The following checklist provides a guideline of questions to be used when performing this phase of the analysis.

Checklist for Formulating and Evaluating Alternative Courses of Action

1. What possible alternatives exist for solving the firm's problems?
2. What limits are there on the possible alternatives? Competence? Resources? Management preference? Ethical responsibility? Legal restrictions?

3. What major alternatives are now available to the firm? What marketing concepts are involved that affect these alternatives?

4. Are the listed alternatives reasonable, given the firm's situation? Are they logical? Are the alternatives consistent with the goals of the marketing program? Are they consistent with the firm's objectives?

5. What are the financial and other costs of each alternative? What are the benefits? What are the advantages and disadvantages of each alternative?

6. Which alternative best solves the problem and minimizes the creation of new problems, given the above constraints?

4. Select and Record the Chosen Alternative and Implementation Details

In light of the previous analysis, the alternative is now selected that best solves the problem with a minimum creation of new problems. It is important to record the logic and reasoning that precipitated the selection of a particular alternative. This includes articulating not only why the alternative was selected but also why the other alternatives were not selected.

No analysis is complete without an action-oriented decision and plan for implementing the decision. The accompanying checklist indicates the type of questions that should be answered in this stage of analysis.

Checklist for Selecting and Implementing the Chosen Alternative

1. What must be done to implement the alternative?
2. What personnel will be involved? What are the responsibilities of each?
3. When and where will the alternative be implemented?
4. What will be the probable outcome?
5. How will the success or failure of the alternative be measured?

PITFALLS TO AVOID IN CASE ANALYSIS

Following is a summary of some of the most common errors analysts make when analyzing cases. When evaluating your analysis or those of others, this list provides a useful guide for spotting potential shortcomings.

1. *Inadequate definition of the problem.* By far the most common error made in case analysis is attempting to recommend courses of action without first adequately defining or understanding the core problems. Whether presented orally or in a written report, a case analysis must begin with a focus on the central issues and problems represented in the case situation. Closely related is the error of analyzing symptoms without determining the root problem.

2. *The search for "the answer."* In case analysis, there are usually no clear-cut solutions. Keep in mind that the objective of case studies is learning through discussion and exploration. There is usually no one "official" or "correct" answer to a case. Rather, there are usually several reasonable alternative solutions.

3. *Not enough information.* Analysts often complain there is not enough information in some cases to make a good decision. However, there is justification for not presenting *all* of the information in a case. As in real life, a marketing manager or consultant seldom has all the information necessary to make an optimal decision. Thus, reasonable assumptions have to be made, and the challenge is to find intelligent solutions in spite of the limited information.

A useful approach to gaining an understanding of the situation an organization is facing at a particular time is called *SWOT analysis*. SWOT stands for the organization's *strengths* and *weaknesses* and the *opportunities* and *threats* it faces in the environment. Below are some issues an analyst should address in performing a SWOT analysis.

POTENTIAL RESOURCE STRENGTHS AND COMPETITIVE CAPABILITIES

- A powerful strategy.
- Core competencies in _____.
- A distinctive competence in _____.
- A product that is strongly differentiated from those of rivals.
- Competencies and capabilities that are well matched to industry key success factors.
- A strong financial condition; ample financial resources to grow the business.
- Strong brand-name image/company reputation.
- An attractive customer base.
- Economy of scale and/or learning and experience curve advantages over rivals.
- Proprietary technology/superior technological skills/important patents.
- Superior intellectual capital relative to key rivals.
- Cost advantages over rivals.
- Strong advertising and promotion.
- Product innovation capabilities.
- Proven capabilities in improving production processes.
- Good supply chain management capabilities.
- Good customer service capabilities.
- Better product quality relative to rivals.
- Wide geographic coverage and/or strong global distribution capability.
- Alliances/joint ventures with other firms that provide access to valuable technology, competencies, and/or attractive geographic markets.

POTENTIAL RESOURCE WEAKNESSES AND COMPETITIVE DEFICIENCIES

- No clear strategic direction.
- Resources that are not well matched to industry key success factors.
- No well-developed or proven core competencies.
- A weak balance sheet; too much debt.
- Higher overall unit costs relative to key competitors.
- Weak or unproven product innovation capabilities.
- A product/service with ho-hum attributes or features inferior to those of rivals.
- Too narrow a product line relative to rivals.
- Weak brand image or reputation.
- Weaker dealer network than key rivals and/or lack of adequate global distribution capability.

4. *Use of generalities.* In analyzing cases, specific recommendations are necessarily not generalities. For example, a suggestion to increase the price is a generality; a suggestion to increase the price by $1.07 is a specific.

5. *A different situation.* Analysts sometimes exert considerable time and effort contending that "If the situation were different, I'd know what course of action to take" or "If the marketing manager hadn't already fouled things up so badly, the firm wouldn't have a problem." Such reasoning ignores the fact that the events in the case have already happened

- Behind on product quality, R&D, and/or technological know-how.
- In the wrong strategic group.
- Losing market share because _____.
- Lack of management depth.
- Inferior intellectual capital relative to leading rivals.
- Subpar profitability because _____.
- Plagued with internal operating problems or obsolete facilities.
- Behind rivals in e-commerce capabilities.
- Short on financial resources to grow the business and pursue promising initiatives.
- Too much underutilized plant capacity.

POTENTIAL MARKET OPPORTUNITIES

- Openings to win market share from rivals.
- Sharply rising buyer demand for the industry's product.
- Serving additional customer groups or market segments.
- Expanding into new geographic markets.
- Expanding the company's product line to meet a broader range of customer needs.
- Utilizing existing company skills or technological know-how to enter new product lines or new businesses.
- Online sales.
- Integrating forward or backward.
- Falling trade barriers in attractive foreign markets.
- Acquiring rival firms or companies with attractive technological expertise or capabilities.
- Entering into alliances or joint ventures that can expand the firm's market coverage or boost its competitive capability.
- Openings to exploit emerging new technologies.

POTENTIAL EXTERNAL THREATS TO A COMPANY'S WELL-BEING

- Increasing intensity of competition among industry rivals—may squeeze profit margins.
- Slowdowns in market growth.
- Likely entry of potent new competitors.
- Loss of sales to substitute products.
- Growing bargaining power of customers or suppliers.
- A shift in buyer needs and tastes away from the industry's product.
- Adverse demographic changes that threaten to curtail demand for the industry's product.
- Vulnerability to industry driving forces.
- Restrictive trade policies on the part of foreign governments.
- Costly new regulatory requirements.

Source: Arthur A. Thompson, Jr., A. J. Strickland III, and John E. Gamble, *Crafting and Executing Strategy,* 16th ed. (Burr Ridge, IL: McGraw-Hill/Irwin, 2008), p. 105.

and cannot be changed. Even though analysis or criticism of past events is necessary in diagnosing the problem, in the end, the present situation must be addressed and decisions must be made based on the given situations.

6. *Narrow vision analysis.* Although cases are often labeled as a specific type of case, such as "pricing," "product," and so forth, this does not mean that other marketing variables should be ignored. Too often analysts ignore the effects that a change in one marketing element will have on the others.

7. *Realism.* Too often analysts become so focused on solving a particular problem that their solutions become totally unrealistic. For instance, suggesting a $1 million advertising program for a firm with a capital structure of $50,000 is an unrealistic solution.

8. *The marketing research solution.* A quite common but unsatisfactory solution to case problems is marketing research; for example, "The firm should do this or that type of marketing research to find a solution to its problem." Although marketing research may be helpful as an intermediary step in some cases, marketing research does not solve problems or make decisions. In cases where marketing research is recommended, the cost and potential benefits should be fully specified in the case analysis.

9. *Rehashing the case material.* Analysts sometimes spend considerable effort rewriting a two- or three-page history of the firm as presented in the case. This is unnecessary since the instructor and other analysts are already familiar with this information.

10. *Premature conclusions.* Analysts sometimes jump to premature conclusions instead of waiting until their analysis is completed. Too many analysts jump to conclusions upon first reading the case and then proceed to interpret everything in the case as justifying their conclusions, even factors logically against it.

COMMUNICATING CASE ANALYSES

The final concern in case analysis deals with communicating the results of the analysis. The most comprehensive analysis has little value if it is not communicated effectively. Case analyses are communicated through two primary media—the written report and the oral presentation.

The Written Report

Since the structure of the written report will vary by the type of case analyzed, the purpose of this section is not to present a "one and only" way of writing up a case; it is to present some useful generalizations to aid analysts in case write-ups.

A good written report starts with an outline that organizes the structure of the analysis in a logical manner. The following is a general outline for a marketing case report.

  I. Title Page
 II. Table of Contents
III. Executive Summary (one- to two-page summary of the analysis and recommendations)
IV. Situation Analysis
    A. *Environment*
      1. Economic conditions and trends
      2. Cultural and social values and trends
      3. Political and legal issues
      4. Summary of environmental opportunities and threats
      5. Implications for strategy development
    B. *Industry*
      1. Classification and definition of industry
      2. Analysis of existing competitors
      3. Analysis of potential new entrants
      4. Analysis of substitute products
      5. Analysis of suppliers
      6. Analysis of buyers
      7. Summary of industry opportunities and threats
      8. Implications for strategy development
    C. *Organization*
      1. Objectives and constraints
      2. Financial condition

1. Read the case quickly to get an overview of the situation.
2. Read the case again thoroughly. Underline relevant information and take notes on potential areas of concern.
3. Review outside sources of information on the environment and the industry. Record relevant information and the source of this information.
4. Perform comparative analysis of the firm with the industry and industry averages.
5. Analyze the firm.
6. Analyze the marketing program.
7. Record the current situation in terms of relevant environmental, industry, firm, and marketing strategy parameters.
8. Make and record necessary assumptions to complete the situational framework.
9. Determine and record the major issues, problems, and their core elements.
10. Record proof that these are the major issues.
11. Record potential courses of action.
12. Evaluate each initially to determine constraints that preclude acceptability.
13. Evaluate remaining alternatives in terms of costs and benefits.
14. Record analysis of alternatives.
15. Select an alternative.
16. Record alternative and defense of its selection.
17. Record the who, what, when, where, how, and why of the alternative and its implementation.

      3. Management philosophy
      4. Organizational structure
      5. Organizational culture
      6. Summary of the firm's strengths and weaknesses
      7. Implications for strategy development
   D. *Marketing strategy*
      1. Objectives and constraints
      2. Analysis of sales, profits, and market share
      3. Analysis of target market(s)
      4. Analysis of marketing mix variables
      5. Summary of marketing strategy's strengths and weaknesses
      6. Implications for strategy development
V. Problems Found in Situation Analysis
   A. *Statement of primary problem(s)*
      1. Evidence of problem(s)
      2. Effects of problem(s)
   B. *Statement of secondary problem(s)*
      1. Evidence of problem(s)
      2. Effects of problem(s)
VI. Strategic Alternatives for Solving Problems
   A. *Description of strategic alternative 1*
      1. Benefits of alternative 1
      2. Costs of alternative 1

B. *Description of strategic alternative 2*
   1. Benefits of alternative 2
   2. Costs of alternative 2
C. *Description of strategic alternative 3*
   1. Benefits of alternative 3
   2. Costs of alternative 3

VII. Selection of Strategic Alternative and Implementation
  A. *Statement of selected strategy*
  B. *Justification for selection of strategy*
  C. *Description of implementation of strategy*

VIII. Summary

IX. Appendices
  A. *Financial analysis*
  B. *Technical analysis*

Writing the case report entails filling out the details of the outline in prose form. Of course, not every case report requires all the headings listed above, and different headings may be required for some cases. Like any other skill, it takes practice to determine the appropriate headings and approach for writing particular cases. However, good case reports flow logically from topic to topic, are clearly written, are based on solid situation analysis, and demonstrate sound strategic thinking.

The Oral Presentation

Case analyses are often presented by an individual or team. As with the written report, a good outline is critical, and it is useful to hand out the outline to each class member. Although there is no best way to present a case or to divide responsibility between team members, simply reading the written report is unacceptable because it encourages boredom and interferes with all-important class discussion.

The use of visual aids can be quite helpful in presenting class analyses. However, simply presenting financial statements contained in the case is a poor use of visual media. On the other hand, graphs of sales and profit curves can be more easily interpreted and can be quite useful for making specific points.

Oral presentation of cases is particularly helpful to analysts for learning the skill of speaking to a group. In particular, the ability to handle objections and disagreements without antagonizing others is a skill worth developing.

CONCLUSION

From the discussion it should be obvious that good case analyses require a major commitment of time and effort. Individuals must be highly motivated and willing to get involved in the analysis and discussion if they expect to learn and succeed in a course where cases are used. Persons with only passive interest who perform "night before" analyses cheat themselves out of valuable learning experiences that can aid them in their careers.

Additional Resources

Aaker, David A. *Strategic Market Management.* 8th ed. Hoboken, NJ: John Wiley, 2008.
Cravens, David W., Charles W. Lamb, Jr., and Victoria L. Crittenden. *Strategic Marketing Management Cases.* 7th ed. Burr Ridge, IL: McGraw-Hill/Irwin, 2002, Appendix B.
Ellet, William. *The Case Study Handbook.* Boston: Harvard Business School Press, 2007.
Kerin, Roger A., and Robert A. Peterson. *Strategic Marketing Problems.* 11th ed. Upper Saddle River, NJ: Prentice Hall, 2007.

Financial Analysis
for Marketing Decisions

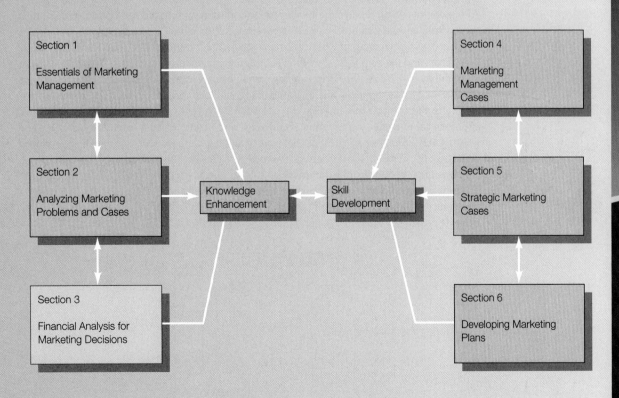

Section 1

Essentials of Marketing
Management

Section 2

Analyzing Marketing
Problems and Cases

Section 3

Financial Analysis for
Marketing Decisions

Knowledge
Enhancement

Skill
Development

Section 4

Marketing
Management
Cases

Section 5

Strategic Marketing
Cases

Section 6

Developing Marketing
Plans

FINANCIAL ANALYSIS

Financial analysis is an important aspect of strategic marketing planning and should be an integral part of marketing problem and case analysis. In this section, we present several financial tools that are useful for analyzing marketing problems and cases. First, we investigate break-even analysis, which is concerned with determining the number of units or dollar sales, or both, necessary to break even on a project or to obtain a given level of profits. Second, we illustrate net present value analysis, which is a somewhat more sophisticated tool for analyzing marketing alternatives. Finally, we investigate ratio analysis, which can be a useful tool for determining the financial condition of the firm, including its ability to invest in a new or modified marketing program.

Break-Even Analysis

Break-even analysis is a common tool for investigating the potential profitability of a marketing alternative. The *break-even point* is that level of sales in either units or sales dollars at which a firm covers all of its costs. In other words, it is the level at which total sales revenue just equals the total costs necessary to achieve these sales.

   To compute the break-even point, an analyst must have or be able to obtain three values. First, the analyst needs to know the selling price per unit of the product (SP). For example, suppose the Ajax Company plans to sell its new electric car through its own dealerships at a retail price of $5,000. Second, the analyst needs to know the level of fixed costs (FC). Fixed costs are all costs relevant to the project that do not change regardless of how many units are produced or sold. For instance, whether Ajax produces and sells 1 or 100,000 cars, Ajax executives will receive their salaries, land must be purchased for a plant, a plant must be constructed, and machinery must be purchased. Other fixed costs include such things as interest, lease payments, and sinking fund payments. Suppose Ajax has totaled all of its fixed costs and the sum is $1.5 million. Third, the analyst must know the variable costs per unit produced (VC). As the name implies, variable costs are those that vary directly with the number of units produced. For example, each car Ajax produces involves costs for raw materials and components to build the car, such as batteries, electric motors, steel bodies, and tires; labor costs for operating employees; and machine costs, such as electricity and welding rods. Suppose Ajax totals these costs and the variable costs for each car produced equal $3,500. With this information, the analyst can now determine the break-even point, which is the number of units that must be sold to just cover the cost of producing the cars. The break-even point is determined by dividing total fixed costs by the *contribution margin*. The contribution margin is simply the difference between the selling price per unit (SP) and variable costs per unit (VC). Algebraically,

$$BEP_{\text{(in units)}} = \frac{\text{Total fixed costs}}{\text{Contribution margin}}$$

$$= \frac{FC}{SP - VC}$$

Substituting the Ajax estimates,

$$BEP_{\text{(in units)}} = \frac{1{,}500{,}000}{5{,}000 - 3{,}500}$$

$$= \frac{1{,}500{,}000}{1{,}500}$$

$$= 1{,}000 \text{ units}$$

In other words, the Ajax Company must sell 1,000 cars to just break even (i.e., for total sales revenue to cover total costs).

Alternatively, the analyst may want to know the break-even point in terms of dollar sales volume. Of course, if the preceding analysis has been done, one could simply multiply the $BEP_{(in\ units)}$ times the selling price to determine the break-even sales volume (i.e., 1,000 units $\times$ \$5,000/unit = \$5 million). However, the $BEP_{(in\ dollars)}$ can be computed directly, using the formula below:

$$BEP_{(in\ dollars)} = \frac{FC}{1 - \dfrac{VC}{SP}}$$

$$= \frac{1,500,000}{1 - \dfrac{3,500}{5,000}}$$

$$= \frac{1,500,000}{1 - .7}$$

$$= \$5,000,000$$

Thus, Ajax must produce and sell 1,000 cars, which equals \$5 million sales, to break even. Of course, firms do not want to just break even but want to make a profit. The logic of break-even analysis can easily be extended to include profits (P). Suppose Ajax decided that a 20 percent return on fixed costs would make the project worth the investment. Thus, Ajax would need 20% $\times$ \$1,500,000 = \$300,000 before-tax profit. To calculate how many units Ajax must sell to achieve this level of profits, the profit figure (P) is added to fixed costs in the above formulas. (We will label the break-even point as BEP' to show that we are now computing unit and sales levels to obtain a given profit level.) In the Ajax example:

$$BEP'_{(in\ units)} = \frac{FC + P}{SP - VC}$$

$$= \frac{1,500,000 + 300,000}{5,000 - 3,500}$$

$$= \frac{1,800,000}{1,500}$$

$$= 1,200\ units$$

In terms of dollars,

$$BEP'_{(in\ dollars)} = \frac{FC + P}{1 - \dfrac{VC}{SP}}$$

$$= \frac{1,500,000 + 300,000}{1 - \dfrac{3,500}{5,000}}$$

$$= \frac{1,800,000}{1 - .7}$$

$$= \$6,000,000$$

Thus, Ajax must produce and sell 1,200 cars (sales volume of $6 million) to obtain a 20 percent return on fixed costs. Analysis must now be directed at determining whether a given marketing plan can be expected to produce sales of at least this level. If the answer is yes, the project would appear to be worth investing in. If not, Ajax should seek other opportunities.

Net Present Value Analysis

The profit-oriented marketing manager must understand that the capital invested in new products has a cost. It is a basic principle in business that whoever wishes to use capital must pay for its use. Dollars invested in new products could be diverted to other uses—to pay off debts, pay dividends to stockholders, or buy U.S. Treasury bonds that would yield economic benefits to the corporation. If, on the other hand, all of the dollars used to finance a new product have to be borrowed from lenders outside the corporation, interest has to be paid on the loan.

One of the best ways to analyze the financial aspects of a marketing alternative is *net present value* analysis. This method employs a discounted cash flow, which takes into account the time value of money and its price to the borrower. The following example will illustrate this method.

To compute the net present value of an investment proposal, the cost of capital must be estimated. The cost of capital can be defined as the required rate of return on an investment that would leave the owners of the firm as well off as if the project was not undertaken. Thus, it is the minimum percentage return on investment that a project must make to be worth undertaking. There are many methods of estimating the cost of capital. However, because these methods are not the concern of this text, we will simply assume that the cost of capital for the Ajax Corporation has been determined to be 10 percent.[1] Again, it should be noted that once the cost of capital is determined, it becomes the minimum rate of return required for an investment—a type of cutoff point. However, some firms in selecting their new product investments select a minimum rate of return that is above the cost of capital figure to allow for errors in judgment or measurement.

The Ajax Corporation is considering a proposal to market instant-developing movie film. After conducting considerable marketing research, sales were projected to be $1 million per year. In addition, the finance department compiled the following information concerning the projects:

New equipment needed	$700,000
Useful life of equipment	10 years
Depreciation	10% per year
Salvage value	$100,000
Cost of goods and expenses	$700,000 per year
Cost of capital	10%
Tax rate	50%

To compute the net present value of this project, the net cash flow for each year of the project must first be determined. This can be done in four steps:

1. Sales − Cost of goods and expenses = Gross income or

$$\$1,000,000 - 700,000 = \$300,000$$

2. Gross income − Depreciation = Taxable income or

$$\$300,000 - (10\% \times 600,000) = \$240,000$$

3. Taxable income − Tax = Net income or

$$\$240,000 - (50\% \times 240,000) = \$120,000$$

4. Net income + Depreciation = Net cash flow or

$$\$120,000 + 60,000 = \$180,000 \text{ per year}$$

Because the cost of capital is 10 percent, this figure is used to discount the net cash flows for each year. To illustrate, the $180,000 received at the end of the first year would be discounted by the factor $1/(1 + 0.10)$, which would be $180,000 \times 0.9091 = \$163,638$; the $180,000 received at the end of the second year would be discounted by the factor $1/(1 + 0.10)^2$, which would be $180,000 \times 0.8264 = \$148,752$, and so on. (Most finance textbooks have present value tables that can be used to simplify the computations.) The table that follows shows the present value computations for the 10-year project. It should be noted that the net cash flow for year 10 is $280,000 because there is an additional $100,000 inflow from salvage value.

Thus, at a discount rate of 10 percent, the present value of the net cash flow from new product investment is greater than the $700,000 outlay required, and so the decision can be considered profitable by this standard. Here the net present value is $444,560, which is the difference between the $700,000 investment outlay and the $1,144,560 discounted cash

Year	Net Cash Flow	0.10 Discount Factor	Present Value
1	$ 180,000	0.9091	$ 163,638
2	180,000	0.8264	148,752
3	180,000	0.7513	135,234
4	180,000	0.6830	122,940
5	180,000	0.6209	111,762
6	180,000	0.5645	101,610
7	180,000	0.5132	92,376
8	180,000	0.4665	83,970
9	180,000	0.4241	76,338
10	280,000	0.3855	107,940
Total	$1,900,000		$1,144,560

flow. The *present value ratio* is nothing more than the present value of the net cash flow divided by the cash investment. If this ratio is 1 or larger than 1, the project would be profitable for the firm to invest in.

There are many other measures of investment worth, but only one additional method will be discussed. It is the very popular and easily understood payback method. *Payback* refers to the amount of time required to pay back the original outlay from the cash flows. Staying with the example, the project is expected to produce a stream of cash proceeds that is constant from year to year, so the payback period can be determined by dividing the investment outlay by this annual cash flow. Dividing $700,000 by $180,000, the payback period is approximately 3.9 years. Firms often set a maximum payback period before a project will be accepted. For example, many firms refuse to take on a project if the payback period exceeds three years.

This example should illustrate the difficulty in evaluating marketing investments from a profitability or economic worth standpoint. The most challenging problem is that of developing accurate cash flow estimates because there are many possible alternatives, such as price of the product and channels of distribution, and the consequences of each alternative

Years	4%	6%	8%	10%	12%	14%
1	.9615	.9434	.9259	.9091	.8929	.8772
2	.9246	.8900	.8573	.8264	.7972	.7695
3	.8890	.8396	.7938	.7513	.7118	.6750
4	.8548	.7941	.7350	.6830	.6355	.5921
5	.8219	.7473	.6806	.6209	.5674	.5194
6	.7903	.7050	.6302	.5645	.5066	.4556
7	.7599	.6651	.5835	.5132	.4523	.3996
8	.7307	.6274	.5403	.4665	.4039	.3506
9	.7026	.5919	.5002	.4241	.3606	.3075
10	.6756	.5584	.4632	.3855	.3220	.2697

must be forecast in terms of sales volumes, selling costs, and other expenses. In spite of all the problems, management must evaluate the economic worth of new product and other decisions, not only to reduce some of the guesswork and ambiguity surrounding marketing strategy development but also to reinforce the objective of making profits.

Ratio Analysis

Firms' income statements and balance sheets provide a wealth of information that is useful for developing marketing strategies. Frequently, this information is included in marketing cases, yet analysts often have no convenient way of interpreting the financial position of the firm to make sound marketing decisions. Ratio analysis provides the analyst an easy and efficient method for investigating a firm's financial position by comparing the firm's ratios across time or with ratios of similar firms in the industry or with industry averages.

Ratio analysis involves four basic steps:

1. Choose the appropriate ratios.
2. Compute the ratios.
3. Compare the ratios.
4. Check for problems or opportunities.

1. Choose the Appropriate Ratios

The five basic types of financial ratios are (1) liquidity ratios, (2) asset management ratios, (3) profitability ratios, (4) debt management ratios, and (5) market value ratios.[2] While calculating ratios of all five types is useful, liquidity, asset management, and profitability ratios provide information that is most directly relevant for marketing decision making. Although many ratios can be calculated in each of these groups, we have selected two of the most commonly used and readily available ratios in each group to illustrate the process.

Liquidity Ratios   One of the first considerations in analyzing a marketing problem is the liquidity of the firm. *Liquidity* refers to the ability of the firm to pay its short-term obligations. If a firm cannot meet its short-term obligations, there is little that can be done until this problem is resolved. Simply stated, recommendations to increase advertising, to do marketing research, or to develop new products are of little value if the firm is about to go bankrupt.

1. http://finance.yahoo.com/. Input the company symbol to receive financial ratios and other useful information. Under the "Company" heading, "Key statistics," "Competitors," and "Industry" are most useful for comparative ratio analyses.
2. *Annual Statement Studies.* Published by Robert Morris Associates, this work includes 11 financial ratios computed annually for over 150 lines of business. Each line of business is divided into four size categories.
3. *Industry Norms and Key Business Ratios.* Published by Dun & Bradstreet, this work provides a variety of industry ratios.
4. *Almanac of Business and Industrial Financial Ratios.* The almanac, published by Prentice Hall, Inc., lists industry averages for 22 financial ratios. Approximately 170 businesses and industries are listed.
5. *Quarterly Financial Report for Manufacturing Corporations.* This work, published jointly by the Federal Trade Commission and the Securities and Exchange Commission, contains balance-sheet and income-statement information by industry groupings and by asset-size categories.
6. Trade associations and individual companies often compute ratios for their industries and make them available to analysts.

The two most commonly used ratios for investigating liquidity are the *current ratio* and the *quick ratio* (or "acid test"). The current ratio is determined by dividing current assets by current liabilities and is a measure of the overall ability of the firm to meet its current obligations. A common rule of thumb is that current ratio should be about 2:1.

The quick ratio is determined by subtracting inventory from current assets and dividing the remainder by current liabilities. Since inventory is the least liquid current asset, the quick ratio deals with assets that are most readily available for meeting short-term (one-year) obligations. A common rule of thumb is that the quick ratio should be at least 1:1.

Asset Management Ratios   Asset management ratios investigate how well the firm handles its assets. For marketing problems, two of the most useful asset management ratios are concerned with *inventory turnover* and *total asset utilization.* The inventory turnover ratio is determined by dividing sales by inventories.[3] If the firm is not turning its inventory over as rapidly as other firms, it suggests that too much money is being tied up in unproductive or obsolete inventory. In addition, if the firm's turnover ratio is decreasing over time, it suggests that there may be a problem in the marketing plan, because inventory is not being sold as rapidly as it had been in the past. One problem with this ratio is that, since sales usually are recorded at market prices and inventory usually is recorded at cost, the ratio may overstate turnover. Thus, some analysts prefer to use cost of sales rather than sales in computing turnover. We will use cost of sales in our analysis.

A second useful asset management ratio is total asset utilization. It is calculated by dividing sales by total assets and is a measure of how productively the firm's assets have been used to generate sales. If this ratio is well below industry figures, it suggests that the firm's marketing strategies are less effective than those of competitors or that some unproductive assets need to be eliminated.

Profitability Ratios   Profitability is a major goal of marketing and is an important measure of the quality of a firm's marketing strategies. Two key profitability ratios are *profit margin on sales* and *return on total assets.* Profit margin on sales is determined by dividing profit before tax by sales. Serious questions about the firm and marketing plan should be raised if profit margin on sales is declining across time or is well below other firms in the industry.

FIGURE 1   Balance Sheet and Income Statement for Ajax Home Computer Company

Ajax Home Computer Company
Balance Sheet
March 31, 2010
(in thousands)

Assets		Liabilities and Stockholders' Equity	
Cash	$ 30	Trade accounts payable	$ 150
Marketable securities	40	Accrued	.25
Accounts receivable	.200	Notes payable	.100
Inventory	.430	Accrued income tax	.40
Total current assets	.700	Total current liabilities	.315
Plant and equipment	.1,000	Bonds	.500
Land	.500	Debentures	. 85
Other investments	.200	Stockholders' equity	.1,500
Total assets	.$2,400	Total liabilities and stockholders' equity	.$2,400

Ajax Home Computer Company
Income Statement
for the 12-Month Period Ending March 31, 2010
(in thousands)

Sales	.$3,600
Cost of sales	
Labor and materials	.2,000
Depreciation	.200
Selling expenses	.500
General and administrative expenses	. . .80
Total cost	.2,780
Net operating income	.820
Less interest expense	
Interest on notes	.20
Interest on debentures	.200
Interest on bonds	. . .300
Total interest	.520
Profit before tax	.300
Federal income tax (@40%)	. . .120
Net profit after tax	.$ 180

Return on total assets is determined by dividing profit before tax by total assets. This ratio is the return on the investment for the entire firm.

2. Compute the Ratios

The next step in ratio analysis is to compute the ratios. Figure 1 presents the balance sheet and income statement for the Ajax Home Computer Company. These six ratios can be calculated from the Ajax balance sheet and income statement as follows:

   Liquidity ratios:

$$\text{Current ratio} = \frac{\text{Current assets}}{\text{Current liabilities}} = \frac{700}{315} = 2.2$$

$$\text{Quick ratio} = \frac{\text{Current assets} - \text{Inventory}}{\text{Current liabilities}} = \frac{270}{315} = .86$$

Asset management ratios:

$$\text{Inventory turnover} = \frac{\text{Cost of sales}}{\text{Inventory}} = \frac{2,780}{430} = 6.5$$

$$\text{Total asset utilization} = \frac{\text{Sales}}{\text{Total assets}} = \frac{3,600}{2,400} = 1.5$$

Profitability ratios:

$$\text{Profit margin on sales} = \frac{\text{Profit before tax}}{\text{Sales}} = \frac{300}{3,600} = 8.3\%$$

$$\text{Return on total assets} = \frac{\text{Profit before tax}}{\text{Total assets}} = \frac{300}{2,400} = 12.5\%$$

3. Compare the Ratios

While rules of thumb are useful for analyzing ratios, it cannot be overstated that comparison of ratios is always the preferred approach. The ratios computed for a firm can be compared in at least three ways. First, they can be compared over time to see if there are any favorable or unfavorable trends in the firm's financial position. Second, they can be compared with the ratios of other firms of similar size in the industry. Third, they can be compared with industry averages to get an overall idea of the firm's relative financial position in the industry.

Figure 2 provides a summary of the ratio analysis. The ratios computed for Ajax are presented along with the median ratios for firms of similar size in the industry and the industry median. The median is often reported in financial sources, rather than the mean, to avoid the strong effect of outliers.[4]

4. Check for Problems or Opportunities

The ratio comparison in Figure 2 suggests that Ajax is in reasonably good shape financially. The current ratio is above the industry figures, although the quick ratio is slightly below them. However, the high inventory turnover ratio suggests that the slightly low quick ratio should not be a problem, since inventory turns over relatively quickly. Total asset utilization is slightly below industry averages and should be monitored closely. This, coupled with the slightly lower return on total assets, suggests that some unproductive assets should be eliminated or that the production process needs to be made more efficient. While the problem could be ineffective marketing, the high profit margin on sales suggests that marketing effort is probably not the problem.

FIGURE 2
Ratio Comparison for Ajax Home Computer Company

	Ajax	Industry Firms Median ($1–10 Million in Assets)	Overall Industry Median
Liquidity ratios			
Current ratio	2.2	1.8	1.8
Quick ratio	.86	.9	1.0
Asset management ratios			
Inventory turnover	6.5	3.2	2.8
Total assets utilization	1.5	1.7	1.6
Profitability ratios			
Profit margin	8.3%	6.7%	8.2%
Return on total assets	12.5%	15.0%	14.7%

CONCLUSION

This section has focused on several aspects of financial analysis that are useful for marketing decision making. The first, break-even analysis, is commonly used in marketing problem and case analysis. The second, net present value analysis, is quite useful for investigating the financial impact of marketing alternatives, such as new product introductions or other long-term strategic changes. The third, ratio analysis, is a useful tool sometimes overlooked in marketing problem solving. Performing a ratio analysis as a regular part of marketing problem and case analysis can increase the understanding of the firm and its problems and opportunities.

Additional Resources

Brealey, Richard A., Stewart C. Myers, and Alan J. Marcus. *Fundamentals of Corporate Finance.* 6th ed. Burr Ridge, IL: McGraw-Hill, 2009.

Cornett, Marcia Millon, Troy Adair, and John Nofsinger. *Finance: Applications and Theory.* Burr Ridge, IL: McGraw-Hill/Irwin, 2009.

Ross, Stephen A., Randolph W. Westerfield, and Bradford D. Jordan. *Fundamentals of Corporate Finance.* 8th ed. Burr Ridge, IL: McGraw-Hill/Irwin, 2008.

Section

4

Marketing
Management Cases

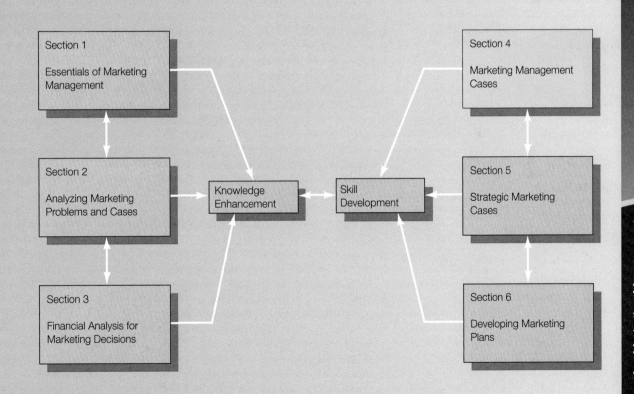

Section 1

Essentials of Marketing
Management

Section 2

Analyzing Marketing
Problems and Cases

Section 3

Financial Analysis for
Marketing Decisions

Knowledge
Enhancement

Skill
Development

Section 4

Marketing Management
Cases

Section 5

Strategic Marketing
Cases

Section 6

Developing Marketing
Plans

NOTE TO THE STUDENT

The primary emphasis of the cases in this section is on marketing as a functional business or organizational area. As such, much of the analysis in these cases involves research and selection of appropriate target markets and the development and management of marketing mix variables.

We have divided these cases into six groups to help focus your analysis. These six groups include cases dealing with market opportunity analysis, product strategy, promotion strategy, distribution strategy, pricing strategy, and selected issues in marketing management. However, keep in mind that regardless of how the case is classified, you should not become too focused on a single issue or marketing mix variable and ignore other elements of marketing strategy.

Case Group A

Market Opportunity Analysis

1

McDonald's Corporation

J. Paul Peter and Ashish Gokhale *University of Wisconsin–Madison*

Jack Greenberg, CEO of McDonald's Corporation, stared into the clear September skies thinking about the "Big Mac Attack." At one time, the term was an advertising slogan referring to a craving for a McDonald's Big Mac burger. However, "Big Mac Attack" now refers to McDonald's earnings declines in the late 1990s and early 2000s. Dynamic market expansion, new products, and special promotional strategies had made McDonald's Corporation a leader of the fast-food industry. However, sales growth in the United States had slowed to below the industry average in recent years. Jack Greenberg was trying to decide on a set of appropriate strategies for the future in order to reverse the declines and to stay ahead of competition.

THE FAST-FOOD INDUSTRY

Years of profit drains and flat sales are driving fast-food chains to find new marketing strategies to compete in a mature market. While McDonald's and most other hamburger chains continue discounting and offering a variety of new products to attract customers, they also seek to shed their "cheap and greasy" image with new store designs. Major competitors in the hamburger segment of the fast-food industry in order of annual sales are McDonald's, Burger King, Wendy's, and Hardee's.

Since these chains recognize the importance of drive-through customers (65 percent of sales), they are all trying to increase the speed of drive-through delivery. Strategies include using timers to encourage employees to prepare and deliver food faster, training employees in faster food preparation methods, having separate kitchens and food preparation facilities for drive-through customers, and even windshield responders that automatically bill customers. Drive-through sales are expected to grow three times faster than on-premise sales. It is estimated that increasing drive-through efficiency by 10 percent increases average fast-food restaurant sales by $54,000. The average fast-food restaurant has sales of about $560,000 per year.

J. Paul Peter was James R. McManus–Bascom Professor in Marketing and Ashish Gokhale was a Project Assistant at the University of Wisconsin–Madison when this case was written.

© Pierre Roussel/Liason/Getty Images

Another segment of the fast-food industry is composed of a number of nonhamburger fast-food restaurants. Major players in this segment include Pizza Hut, KFC (Kentucky Fried Chicken), and Taco Bell. Sales in these restaurants have grown faster than hamburger chains in recent years. A growing trend is the move by customers to nonhamburger sandwiches. Subway dominates the market with more than 13,200 U.S. outlets. Prepared meals and sandwiches available in supermarkets, convenience stores, and gas stations are competitors as are the variety of microwave meals available to consumers.

Another trend is the recognition of the importance of heavy users of fast-food restaurants. It is estimated that heavy users comprise 20 percent of customers but account for 60 percent of all visits. Some of these customers visit fast-food restaurants 20 times per month and spend up to $40 per day in them. Heavy users have been described as single males, under 30 years of age, who have working class jobs, love loud music, don't read much, and hang out with friends.

A major change in the fast-food industry is the increase in the fast-casual segment that includes restaurants like Boston Market, Panera Bread Company, and Atlanta Bread Company. These chains offer deli sandwiches and meals that are more upscale than traditional fast food, served in nicer restaurants with more comfortable surroundings, but faster than in traditional restaurants. It is estimated that the fast-casual sector is growing from 15 percent to 20 percent per year, while growth in the quick service sector is only about 2 percent a year. "People are willing to pay a couple dollars more for a better dining experience, yet don't want to sacrifice the convenience of quick service. Fast-casual combines all the elements for what the on-the-go consumer—which seems to be almost everyone these days—is looking for," said one analyst.[1]

[1]Mitchell Speiser, analyst at Lehman Brothers.

Americans are eating out less often compared to previous years and eating habits are changing.[2] Though recession is a major reason why folks aren't eating out as much at upscale restaurants, it's another story at fast-food restaurants. Many younger consumers are getting tired of fast food and are thinking about their health. There seems to be a growing dissatisfaction with the quality aspect of the McDonald's and Burger Kings of the world. It's not just young adults who are turning away from fast food. Baby boomers are also looking for "better" alternatives and fast food is not as appealing to this large group who frequently eat out.

MCDONALD'S CORPORATION

McDonald's systemwide sales for 2001 were over $40 billion, but net income shrunk 17 percent to $1.64 billion, as shown in the exhibit. McDonald's U.S. market share remained above that of competitors, but grew more slowly. Its share was up 2.2 percent in 2000 compared to 2.7 percent growth for Burger King Corp. and 2.5 percent for Wendy's International.[3]

Looking for hits to reverse earnings declines, McDonald's accelerated plans for "New Tastes Menu" items.[4] Products for limited-time offers included a fried chicken sandwich of tenderloin strips under the Chicken Selects name, a new grilled chicken sandwich, a brownie, a pork tenderloin sandwich, and a Philly cheese steak sandwich. Facing competitors' chicken sandwiches, like Wendy's Spicy Chicken Filet and Burger King's Chicken Whopper, McDonald's put chicken menu items at the forefront of its offerings. The chain also added a chicken-honey biscuit item to its menu. Other entries included a breakfast steak burrito similar to an existing sausage version, hot dog McNuggets for kids, and an Italian-style burger similar to the Chicken Parmesan. The McRib sandwich was reintroduced.

EXHIBIT   McDonald's Corporation Summary of Financial Data 1997–2001

Dollars in Millions, Except per Share Data	2001	2000	1999	1998	1997
Franchised sales	$ 24,838	24,463	23,830	22,330	20,863
Company-operated sales	$ 11,040	10,467	9,512	8,895	8,136
Affiliated sales	$ 4,752	5,251	5,149	4,754	4,639
Total Systemwide Sales	$ 40,630	40,181	38,491	35,979	33,638
Total revenues	$ 14,870	14,243	13,259	12,421	11,409
Operating income	$ 2,697	3,330	3,320	2,762	2,808
Income before taxes	$ 2,330	2,882	2,884	2,307	2,407
Net income	$ 1,637	1,977	1,948	1,550	1,642
Cash provided by operations	$ 2,688	2,751	3,009	2,766	2,442
Capital expenditures	$ 1,906	1,945	1,868	1,879	2,111
Free cash flow	$ 782	806	1,141	887	331
Treasury stock purchases	$ 1,090	2,002	933	1,162	765
Financial position at year end					
Total assets	$ 22,535	21,684	20,983	19,784	18,242
Total debt	$ 8,918	8,474	7,252	7,043	6,463
Total shareholders' equity	$ 9,488	9,204	9,639	9,465	8,852
Shares outstanding IN MILLIONS	1,280.7	1,304.9	1,350.8	1,356.2	1,371.4
Total Systemwide Restaurants	30,093	28,707	26,309	24,513	22,928

[2]Harris Interactive, December 2001.
[3]Kate MacArthur, *Advertising Age,* Mar. 18, 2002.
[4]Bob Sperber, *Brandweek,* Mar. 11, 2002.

McDonald's advertising message focused on tasty and nutritious food, friendly folks, and fun. The company invested heavily in advertising its product and improving its public image. McDonald's annual Charity Christmas Parade in Chicago and its Ronald McDonald House charity provided the company with a positive corporate image. Much of its promotional budget was spent on games, giveaways and deals, including Monopoly II, Scrabble, a Kraft salad dressing give-away, Happy Meals, plush toys, in-store kid videos, and various Big Mac–related deals.

McDonald's opened its first domestic McCafe with the expectation that the gourmet coffee shop would move it closer to its goal of doubling sales at existing U.S. restaurants over the next decade.[5] The 32-seat McCafe occupies a 900-square-foot space that shares an entrance with a traditional McDonald's restaurant. The menu features a selection of specialty drinks, including cappuccinos, lattes, teas, and fruit smoothies served via a limited service front counter. Enhancing the coffee bar is a glass display case filled with a variety of high-end cakes, pastries, cookies and soft pretzels. Customers can place carryout orders that are packaged in disposable containers. If patrons opt to dine in the cafe, all drinks and food items are served on china with stainless steel flatware. McCafe originated in Australia in 1993 and has grown to more than 300 units in 17 countries. The gourmet coffee concept was created to be placed within or adjacent to existing McDonald's restaurants. McDonald's estimates that the new concept will boost sales by 15 percent. At McCafe, cappuccino drinks start at $2.49 featuring a coffee imported from Italy. The drink menu includes specialty coffees, listed as "Caramel Cream Steamer," "French Vanilla" and "Milky Way." The pastries, including tiramisu, cheesecake, apple tart and muffins, range in price from $1.59 to $2.59. Many of the items are baked on-site and the others are prepared daily by various local suppliers. In addition to three on-premise bakers, the cafe has a staff of 15 with about six employees working each shift. Created to enhance an upscale coffee shop environment, the cafe's decor features lace curtains, mahogany accents, a leather couch, an antique mirror, wall sconces, and fresh flowers.

MAJOR COMPETITORS IN THE HAMBURGER SEGMENT

McDonald's has three major competitors in the hamburger segment. These include Burger King, Hardee's and Wendy's. Both Burger King and Wendy's have had small gains in market share while Hardee's lost share.

Burger King Corp.

Burger King Corp., in its ongoing effort to increase sales and market share, offered a new salad line and a permanent array of value-priced offerings, endeavors already under way at its fast-food competitors. The nation's number 2 burger chain, hoping to show signs of a turnaround in order to expedite its pending separation from parent Diageo PLC of London, debuted more than 10 new or improved products, including the Chicken Whopper, which officials said stimulated sales growth. The menu overhaul is one part of a major turnaround strategy engineered by Burger King's chairman and chief executive, John Dasburg, who joined the chain in 2000.

As part of BK's sweeping transformation program, restaurant operators had to make extensive kitchen and drive-through upgrades. The Chicken Whopper, which debuted in 2001, generated "an enormous amount of trial" that led to double-digit same-store-sales growth at restaurants. Burger King is developing a more permanent marketing strategy and moving away from its previous tactical approach, which revolved around the monthly changes in menu items and deals.

[5]*Nation's Restaurant News,* May 14, 2001.

Hardee's

Hardee's parent, CKE Restaurants Inc., owns or franchises 2,784 Hardee's and 112 Taco Bueno restaurants and showed a 15 percent decline in net income in a recent quarter. The chain posted year-to-year quarterly declines of 4.8 percent in company-owned same-store sales. The efforts to reverse slowing but continuing sales erosion at Hardee's, the industry's number 4 burger chain, had dominated management's attention in its conversion of Hardee's to a format called "Star Hardee's."

The company attempted to reverse sliding sales by introducing new items on the menu and joining the price-promotion burger wars. The company tested individual item discounts at most of Hardee's company-owned units. Franchisees in selected markets offered sandwiches bundled with regular-sized French fries and a soft drink for $2.99. Other new Hardee's sales-spiking tactics included its midpriced sandwich option, the Famous Bacon Cheeseburger for $1.59, and a new Croissant Sunrise breakfast sandwich for $1.79. The chain hoped to increase breakfast sales by at least 2 percent; currently, breakfast items account for approximately 10 percent of Hardee's sales.

CKE also owns or franchises 878 upscale fast-food chains, Carl's Jr. It rolled out a premium sandwich product that had first debuted on the Hardee's menu in 1994 and recently was second only to the Carl's Jr.'s $3.99 sirloin steak sandwich in trial markets.

Wendy's International

Wendy's has had the strongest same-store-sales gains of the major burger chains in recent years. Chain officials and Wall Street analysts attributed at least part of the growth to Wendy's line of four upscale salads called "Garden Sensations." The nation's No. 3 burger chain holds an enviable position—analysts consistently rank it ahead of chief rivals in quality, customer satisfaction, innovation, and unit-level sales. Citing Wendy's planned 30 percent boost in media outlays to an estimated $308 million in 2002 and its strong focus on in-store operations, one analyst stated, "This one-two punch looks like a formidable foe for rival chains to face this year."[6] Wendy's same-store sales were expected to grow 3 percent in 2002, eclipsing the 2 percent projections for Tricon Global Restaurants' Taco Bell and KFC, and a 1 percent to 2 percent projection for McDonald's Corp.

Wendy's product line includes four core menu items: burgers, chicken sandwiches, its value menu, and its Garden Sensations salads. The salad line is designed to provide custom taste comparable to salads offered by casual-dining chains and includes the $3.99 Chicken BLT, Taco Supremo, Mandarin Chicken, and $2.99 Spring Mix salads. The Garden Sensations line was expected to contribute 5 percent to total Wendy's sales.[7]

MAJOR COMPETITION IN THE NONHAMBURGER SEGMENT

The gradual shift of consumer preference toward hamburger substitutes has created strong competitors for McDonald's. Three of the major competitors offering nonhamburger fast foods are Pizza Hut, Kentucky Fried Chicken, and Taco Bell.

Pizza Hut

Pizza Hut dominates the pizza segment with 22 percent of all restaurant pizza sales in the country, with Domino's lagging far behind with about 11 percent of sales. Papa John's has steadily expanded to the point where it is the country's fourth largest pizza chain behind Little Caesars.

---

[6]Mark Kalinowski, restaurant analyst for Salomon Smith Barney.
[7]Merrill Lynch analyst Peter Oakes, January 2002.

Pizza Hut is owned by Tricon Global Restaurants, which also owns KFC and Taco Bell. It scored a major success with its P'Zone, a portable, calzone-like item that company officials call "the pizza that actually sold out in test market."[8] The $70 million national product launch featured the P'Zone for $5.99, or two for $10.99. Each pie is made with a 12-inch traditional crust, a layer of sliced mozzarella cheese and a choice of three different ingredient combinations: pepperoni; a mixture of meats that includes pepperoni, sausage, beef and ham; or sausage with green peppers and red onions. The P'Zone exceeded expectations and drove same-store sales up 7 percent to 8 percent. Pizza Hut's latest effort was called "a well-executed, differentiated, yet value-oriented product that would drive traffic and sales over the next several periods"[9] by one industry analyst.

KFC

KFC (Kentucky Fried Chicken) operates 11,000 global outlets of which 5,400 are in the United States. Its recent strategies included a "Kids Lap Top Pack" meal program to attract more kids and families to its food offerings. KFC planned to introduce the meals as part of its new product lineup for 2002.[10] Roughly 80 percent of KFC's domestic stores signed up to offer the kids' meals, which featured more food and variety of choices. The meals are priced at $2.99 and offer 18 different food combinations. The kids' meal containers, designed to open as a laptop computer, featured colorfully illustrated interactive puzzles and games. The idea built upon the latest batch of kids' meals launched previously, which introduced an education theme with crossword puzzles, word searches, and mazes. KFC took away the staple of most kids meals—the plastic toy—after company research found that children, especially older ones, were not interested in them. Instead, the new meals included stickers or a paper-based prize. The chain doesn't expect the new meal to generate substantial returns immediately. "This is about brand building; it's not about building sales today,"[11] said a company spokesperson.

Other new products at KFC for 2002 included a meal of three spicy Blazin' Crispy Strips with a choice of side and a biscuit priced at $2.99 and the Blazin' Buffalo Twister sandwich and a beverage in the price range of $2.29 to $2.79. In fiscal 2001, KFC led its sister brands, Pizza Hut and Taco Bell, in same-store sales at U.S. company-owned stores, posting growth of 3 percent.

Taco Bell

The dramatic rebound in sales at Taco Bell and a 19 percent increase in 2001 profits were due to a strategy shift to higher-priced products, like the Grilled Stuft Burrito and Chicken Quesadilla.[12] Taco Bell's success with high-priced offerings proved that the brand could leverage its strengths to bring up the average meal price, as well as appeal to light and medium users.[13] Taco Bell planned to add more grilled extensions with higher quality tortillas, beef, and beans, and sell them at non discounted prices. Officials said Taco Bell would continue to experiment with ingredients, such as fish and pork, that are unique to fast food.

[8]Amy Zuber, *Nation's Restaurant News,* Feb. 11, 2002.

[9]John Ivankoe of J. P. Morgan Securities in New York.

[10]Cynthia Koplos, KFC's director of marketing.

[11]Cynthia Koplos, KFC's director of marketing.

[12]Amy Zuber, *Nation's Restaurant News,* Feb. 25, 2002.

[13]Salomon Smith Barney analyst Mark Kalinowski.

MCDONALD'S FUTURE

Jack Greenberg recognized the difficult task the company faced in trying to grow sales, market share, and profits in a fiercely competitive industry. He not only recognized the strengths of competitors in the burger segment but also knew that other providers of fast food and other meals were quick to take advantage of changes in customer preferences and tastes. He knew he had to counter attack the "Big Mac Attack" and find market opportunities for McDonald's.

Discussion Questions

1. How are customer tastes changing in the fast-food industry? What impact do these changes have on McDonald's?
2. How well are these changes in customer tastes and preferences being reflected in competitive strategies in the industry?
3. What are McDonald's strengths and weaknesses and what conclusions do you draw about its future?
4. Should McDonald's develop a separate strategy for the heavy user segment of the fast food industry?
5. What should Jack Greenberg do to grow sales, profits, and market share at McDonald's?

Case

2

Southwest Airlines 2011

Andrew C. Inkpen *Thunderbird School of Global Management*

"You are now free to move about the country."™

In 2010, Southwest Airlines (Southwest), the once-scrappy underdog in the U.S. airline industry, carried more domestic passengers than any other U.S. airline. The company, unlike all its major competitors, had been consistently profitable for decades and had weathered energy crises, the September 11 terrorist attacks, and the 2008/09 recession. An insight into Southwest's operating philosophy can be found in the company's 2001 annual report:

> Southwest was well poised, financially, to withstand the potentially devastating hammer blow of September 11. Why? Because for several decades our leadership philosophy has been: we manage in good times so that our Company and our People can be job secure and prosper through bad times. . . . Once again, after September 11, our philosophy of managing in good times so as to do well in bad times proved a marvelous prophylactic for our Employees and our Shareholders.

As Southwest neared its 40th year of service, the company was facing some major challenges. Legacy carriers in the United States had become more efficient, and the recent mega mergers involving Delta/Northwest and Continental/United were shaking up the industry. Smaller companies like JetBlue and Allegiant were pressuring Southwest's cost-advantage and low-fare focus. A major internal challenge for Southwest would be managing its acquisition of AirTran, a deal announced in late 2010. To make the acquisition a success, the company would have to integrate a workforce of more than 8,000 (about 25 percent the size of Southwest), a fleet of aircraft different from the Boeing 737s used by Southwest, and new markets that included non-U.S. destinations.

Case Group A   Market Opportunity Analysis

THE U.S. AIRLINE INDUSTRY

The U.S. commercial airline industry was permanently altered in October 1978 when President Carter signed the Airline Deregulation Act. Before deregulation, the Civil Aeronautics Board regulated airline route entry and exit, passenger fares, mergers and acquisitions, and airline rates of return. Typically, two or three carriers provided service in a given market, although there were routes covered by only one carrier. Cost increases were passed along to customers, and price competition was almost nonexistent. The airlines operated as if there were only two market segments: those who could afford to fly and those who couldn't.

Deregulation sent airline fares tumbling and allowed many new firms to enter the market. The financial impact on both established and new airlines was enormous. The fuel crisis of 1979 and the air-traffic controllers' strike in 1981 contributed to the industry's difficulties, as did the severe recession that hit the United States during the early 1980s. During the first decade of deregulation, more than 150 carriers, many of them start-up airlines, collapsed into bankruptcy. A total of 8 of the 11 major airlines dominating the industry in 1978 ended up filing for bankruptcy, merging with other carriers, or simply disappearing from the radar screen. Collectively, the industry made enough money during this period to buy two Boeing 747s.[1] The three major carriers that survived intact—Delta, United, and American—ended up with 80 percent of all domestic U.S. air traffic and 67 percent of trans-Atlantic business.[2] Appendices A and B provide a summary of the financial data for the major airlines. The rapid growth of Southwest is in stark contrast to the much slower growth of its major competitors.

Competition and lower fares led to greatly expanded demand for airline travel. Controlling for inflation, the average price to fly one domestic mile dropped by more than 50 percent since deregulation. By the mid-1990s, the airlines were having trouble meeting this demand. Travel increased from 200 million travelers in 1974 to 700 million in 2007 in the United States (due to the recession the number decreased in 2008 to 650 million in 2008 and to 620 million in 2009), with increases in runway and airport capacity lagging far behind.

Despite the financial problems experienced by many airlines started after deregulation, new firms continued to enter the market. For example, during the period 1994–2004, 66 new airlines were certified by the FAA. By 2004, 43 had shut down. Most of the new airlines competed with limited route structures and lower fares than the major airlines. The new airlines created a second tier of service providers that saved consumers billions of dollars annually and provided service in markets abandoned or ignored by major carriers.

Although deregulation fostered competition and the growth of new airlines, it also created a regional disparity in ticket prices and adversely affected service to small and remote communities. Airline workers generally suffered, with inflation-adjusted average employee wages falling from $42,928 in 1978 to much lower levels over the subsequent decades. About 20,000 airline industry employees were laid off in the early 1980s, while productivity of the remaining employees rose 43 percent during the same period. In a variety of cases, bankruptcy filings were used to diminish the role of unions and reduce unionized wages. In the most recent round of bankruptcies, airline workers at United, Delta, and other major airlines were forced to accept pay cuts of up to 35 percent.

Industry Economics

About 80 percent of airline operating costs were fixed or semivariable. The only costs that were variable per passenger were travel agency commissions, food costs, and ticketing fees. The operating costs of an airline flight depended primarily on the distance traveled, not the number of passengers on board. For example, the crew and ground staff sizes were

---

[1] P. S. Dempsey, "Transportation Deregulation: On a Collision Course," *Transportation Law Journal,* 13, 1984, p. 329.

[2] W. Goralski, "Deregulation Deja Vu," *Telephony,* June 17, 1996, pp. 32–36.

determined by the type of aircraft, not the passenger load. Therefore, once an airline established its route structure, most of its operating costs were fixed.

Because of this high fixed-cost structure, the airlines developed sophisticated software tools to maximize capacity utilization, known as load factor. Load factor was calculated by dividing RPM (revenue passenger miles—the number of passengers carried multiplied by the distance flown) by ASM (available seat miles—the number of seats available for sale multiplied by the distance flown).

On each flight by one of the major airlines (excluding Southwest and a few other carriers), there were typically a dozen categories of fares. The airlines analyzed historical travel patterns on individual routes to determine how many seats to sell at each fare level. All the major airlines used this type of analysis and flexible pricing practice, known as the "yield management" system. These systems enabled the airlines to manage their seat inventories and the prices paid for those seats. The objective was to sell more seats on each flight at higher yields (total passenger yield was passenger revenue from scheduled operations divided by scheduled RPM). The higher the ticket price, the better the yield.

Although reducing operating costs was a high priority for the airlines, the nature of the cost structure limited cost reduction opportunities. Fuel costs (17 percent of the total operating costs at Southwest in 2004; 30 percent in 2009) were largely beyond the control of the airlines, and many of the larger airlines' restrictive union agreements limited labor flexibility. The airline industry's extremely high fixed costs made it one of the worst net profit margin performers when measured against other industries. Airlines were far outpaced in profitability by industries such as banks, health care, consumer products, and publishing.

In recent years, "a la carte" revenues such as baggage fees and change fees had become increasingly important for most of the airlines. For example, in 2010 US Airways expected to generate about $500 million from a la carte fees, roughly the same as net profit. In contrast to most of its competitors, Southwest did not charge for checked bags.

To manage their route structures, the major airlines (except Southwest) maintained their operations around a "hub-and-spoke" network. The spokes fed passengers from outlying points into a central airport—the hub—where passengers could travel to additional hubs or their final destination. For example, to fly from Phoenix to Boston on Northwest Airlines, a typical route would involve a flight from Phoenix to Northwest's Detroit hub. The passenger would then take a second flight from Detroit to Boston.

Establishing a major hub in a city like Chicago or Atlanta required a huge investment for gate acquisition and terminal construction. JetBlue's new facility at JFK in New York was opened in 2009 and cost about $800 million. Although hubs created inconveniences for travelers, hub systems were an efficient means of distributing services across a wide network. The major airlines were very protective of their so-called "fortress" hubs and used the hubs to control various local markets. For example, Northwest (now Delta) handled about 80 percent of Detroit's passengers and occupied nearly the entire new Detroit terminal that opened in 2002, and Northwest's deal with the local government assured that it would be the only airline that could have a hub in Detroit. When Southwest entered the Detroit market, the only available gates were already leased by Northwest. Northwest subleased gates to Southwest at rates 18 times higher than Northwest's costs. Southwest eventually withdrew from Detroit, and then reentered, one of the only four markets Southwest had abandoned in its history (San Francisco, Denver, and Beaumont, Texas were the other three; Southwest reentered Denver in 2006).

Recent U.S. Airline Industry Performance

Despite the steadily growing customer demand, the airline industry always seemed to be one recession away from crisis. In 2010, the major airlines were on track to be profitable, a marked contrast to the heavy losses of 2009 (with the exception of Southwest). The continuing consolidation in the industry was expected to lead to lower operating costs and higher ticket prices. Exhibits 1–9 provide data on the major U.S. competitors for the period 2002–2009:

- Exhibit 1—operating margins: Southwest has the highest margin in all years except 2007.
- Exhibit 2—average revenue passenger miles (RPM) per passenger: Southwest has the lowest in all years.
- Exhibit 3—passenger yield (passenger revenue per RPM): Southwest is the highest in most years.
- Exhibit 4—load factors: Southwest is the lowest in all years.
- Exhibit 5—unit costs per available seat mile: Southwest is the lowest in all years.
- Exhibit 6—unit costs per available seat mile excluding labor cost: Southwest is the lowest in all years.
- Exhibit 7—labor cost per available seat mile: Southwest moved from the lowest to the second highest.
- Exhibit 8—employees per aircraft: Southwest is the lowest in all years.
- Exhibit 9—net debt: Southwest is the lowest in all years.

After the September 11, 2001, terrorist attacks, domestic airlines lost about $30 billion. The continuing specter of terrorism cast a long shadow on the global airline industry. In the United States, passengers were frustrated by increasingly more invasive security procedures. Fuel costs were a constant uncertainty, and new entrants continued to put pressure on the incumbents.

Other pressures on the industry included the following.

1. **Customer dissatisfaction with airline service.** Service problems were leading to calls for new regulation of airline competitive practices.
2. **Aircraft safety maintenance.** The aging of the general aircraft population meant higher maintenance costs and eventual aircraft replacement. The introduction of stricter government regulations for older planes placed new burdens on operators of older aircraft.
3. **Debt servicing.** The airline industry's debt load exceeded U.S. industry averages.
4. **Air-traffic delays.** Increased air-traffic control delays caused by higher travel demand and related airport congestion were expected to negatively influence customer satisfaction.
5. **Mergers.** Although most U.S. airline mergers had not delivered on their promises, financial pressures were pushing airlines into new merger discussions.
6. **Open Skies Agreement.** Legislation allowing greater access to U.S. markets by non-U.S. carriers was expected to increase competitive pressure.

EXHIBIT 1

Operating Margins for Major U.S. Airlines

Source: Airline Data and Analysis Largest Airlines 2002–2009 by http://AirlineFinancials.com.

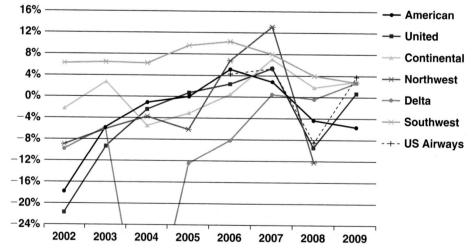

EXHIBIT 2   Average RPM per Passenger (average mileage per passenger flight) for Major U.S. Airlines

Source: Airline Data and Analysis Largest Airlines 2002–2009 by http://AirlineFinancials.com.

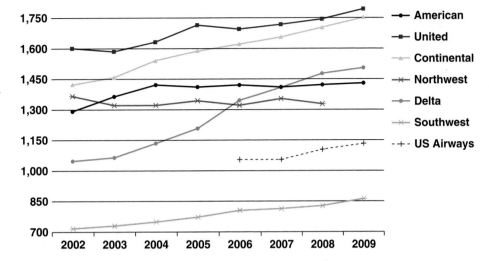

EXHIBIT 3
Passenger Revenue per RPM* 2002–2009 (in cents) for Major U.S. Airlines

*Passenger Revenue Per Revenue Passenger Mile, also known as Passenger Yield, is computed by dividing passenger revenues by revenue passenger miles. Yield—The passenger revenue per RPM in cents

Source: Airline Data and Analysis Largest Airlines 2002–2009 by http://AirlineFinancials.com.

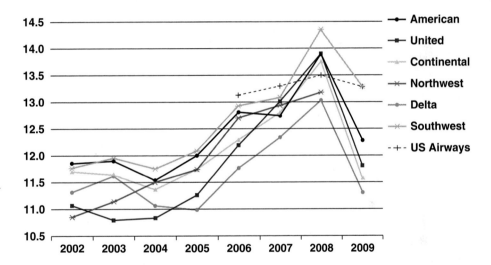

EXHIBIT 4   Load Factors 2002–2009 for Major U.S. Airlines

Source: Airline Data and Analysis Largest Airlines 2002–2009 by http://AirlineFinancials.com.

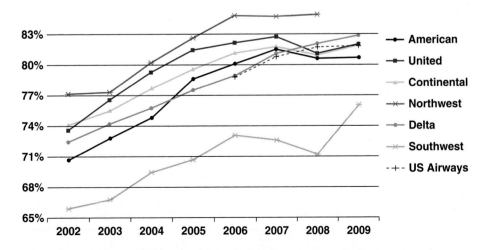

EXHIBIT 5   Unit Cost (CASM) (cents/ASM) for Major U.S. Airlines

Source: Airline Data and Analysis Largest Airlines 2002–2009 by http://AirlineFinancials.com.

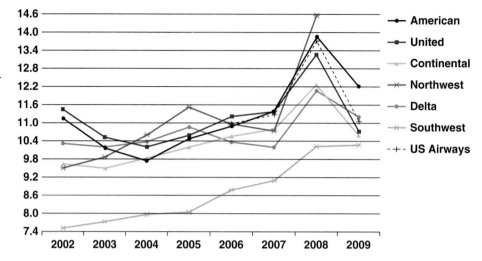

EXHIBIT 6   Unit Costs without Labor (cents/ASM) for Major U.S. Airlines

Source: Airline Data and Analysis Largest Airlines 2002–2009 by http://AirlineFinancials.com.

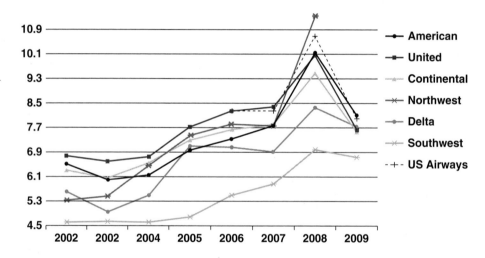

EXHIBIT 7   Total Labor Cost per ASM (cents/ASM) for Major U.S. Airlines

Source: Airline Data and Analysis Largest Airlines 2002–2009 by http://AirlineFinancials.com.

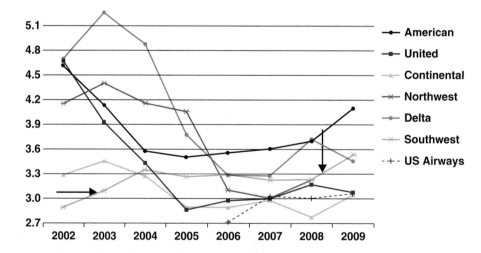

EXHIBIT 8   Average
Employees per
Aircraft (x 10) for
Major U.S. Airlines

Source: Airline Data and Analysis Largest Airlines 2002–2009 by http://AirlineFinancials.com.

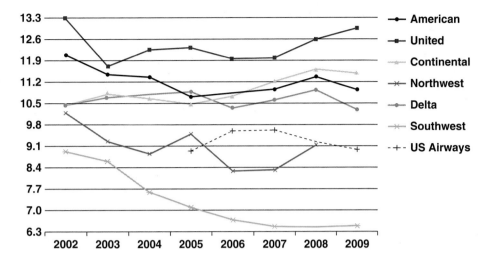

EXHIBIT 9   Net Debt
for Major U.S. Airlines

Source: Airline Data and Analysis Largest Airlines 2002–2009 by http://AirlineFinancials.com.

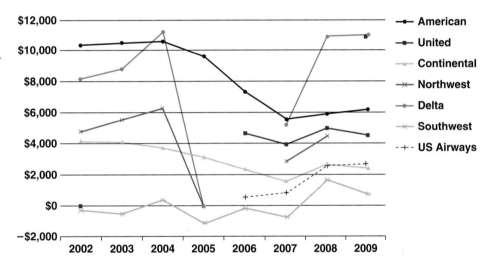

SOUTHWEST AIRLINES BACKGROUND

In 1966, Herb Kelleher was practicing law in San Antonio when a client named Rollin King proposed starting a short-haul airline similar to the California-based Pacific Southwest Airlines. The airline would fly the Golden Triangle of Houston, Dallas, and San Antonio and, by staying within Texas, avoid federal regulations. Kelleher and King incorporated a company, raised initial capital, and filed for regulatory approval from the Texas Aeronautics Commission. Unfortunately, the other Texas-based airlines, namely, Braniff, Continental, and Trans Texas (later called Texas International), opposed the idea and waged a battle to prohibit Southwest from flying. Kelleher argued the company's case before the Texas Supreme Court, which ruled in Southwest's favor. The U.S. Supreme Court refused to hear an appeal filed by the other airlines. In late 1970, it looked as if the company could begin flying.

Southwest began building a management team and the purchase of three surplus Boeing 737s was negotiated. Meanwhile, Braniff and Texas International continued their efforts to prevent Southwest from flying. The underwriters of Southwest's initial public stock offering withdrew and a restraining order against the company was obtained two days before its scheduled inaugural flight. Kelleher again argued his company's case before the Texas Supreme Court, which ruled in Southwest's favor a second time, lifting the restraining order. Southwest Airlines began flying the next day, June 18, 1971.[3]

When Southwest began flying to three Texas cities, the firm had 3 aircraft and 25 employees. Initial flights were out of Dallas' older Love Field airport and Houston's Hobby Airport, both of which were closer to downtown than the major international airports. Flamboyant from the beginning, original flights were staffed by flight attendants in hot pants. By 1996, the flight attendant uniform had evolved to khakis and polo shirts. The "Luv" theme was a staple of the airline from the outset and became the company's ticker symbol on Wall Street.

Southwest management quickly discovered that there were two types of travelers: convenience, time-oriented business travelers and price-sensitive leisure travelers. To cater to both groups, Southwest developed a two-tiered pricing structure. In 1972, Southwest was charging $20 to fly between Houston, Dallas, and San Antonio, undercutting the $28 fares of the other carriers. After an experiment with $10 fares, Southwest decided to sell seats on weekdays until 7:00 P.M. for $26 and after 7:00 P.M. and on weekends for $13.[4] In response, in January 1973, Braniff Airlines began charging $13 for its Dallas–Houston Hobby flights. This resulted in one of Southwest's most famous ads, which had the caption, "Nobody's going to shoot Southwest out of the sky for a lousy $13." Southwest offered travelers the opportunity to pay $13 or $26 and receive a free bottle of liquor. More than 75 percent of the passengers chose the $26 fare and Southwest became the largest distributor of Chivas Regal scotch whiskey in Texas. In 1975, Braniff abandoned the Dallas–Houston Hobby route. When Southwest entered the Cleveland market, the unrestricted one-way fare between Cleveland and Chicago was $310 on other carriers; Southwest's fare was $59.[5] One of Southwest's problems was convincing passengers that its low fares were not just introductory promotions but regular fares.

SOUTHWEST OPERATIONS

Although Southwest became one of the largest airlines in the United States, the firm did not deviate from its initial focus: primarily short-haul (less than 500 miles), point-to-point flights, a fleet consisting only of Boeing 737s, high-frequency flights, low fares, and no international flights. In 2009, the average Southwest one-way fare was $131.82.

Southwest was the only large airline to operate without major hubs, although cities such as Phoenix, Houston, Chicago, Dallas, Denver, and Las Vegas were increasingly becoming important transit points for Southwest trips. For example, daily departures from Chicago, Southwest's second busiest airport, increased to 216 in 2010. With 212 daily flights, Las Vegas was Southwest's top city. Point-to-point service provided maximum convenience for passengers who wanted to fly between two cities, but insufficient demand could make such nonstop flights economically unfeasible. For that reason, the hub-and-spoke approach was generally assumed to generate cost savings for airlines through operational efficiencies. However, Southwest saw it another way: hub-and-spoke arrangements

---

[3] K. Freiberg, and J. Freiberg, *Nuts: Southwest Airlines' Crazy Recipe for Business and Personal Success* (Austin, TX: Bard Press, 1996), p. 14–21.

[4] Ibid., p. 31.

[5] Ibid., p. 55.

resulted in planes spending more time on the ground waiting for customers to arrive from connecting points.

Turnaround time—the time it takes to unload a waiting plane and load it for the next flight—was about 15 minutes for Southwest, compared with the industry average of 45 minutes. This time savings was accomplished with a gate crew 50 percent smaller than other airlines. Pilots sometimes helped unload bags when schedules were tight. Flight attendants regularly assisted in the cleanup of airplanes between flights.

Relative to the other major airlines, Southwest had a "no frills" approach to services: No reserved seating or meals were offered. Seating was first come, first served. As to why the airline did not have assigned seating, Kelleher explained: "It used to be we only had about four people on the whole plane, so the idea of assigned seats just made people laugh. Now the reason is you can turn the airplanes quicker at the gate. And if you can turn an airplane quicker, you can have it fly more routes each day. That generates more revenue, so you can offer lower fares."[6]

Unlike some of the major carriers, Southwest rarely offered delayed customers a hotel room or long-distance telephone calls. Southwest had only a limited participation in computerized reservation systems, preferring to have travel agents and customers book flights through its reservation center. Southwest was the first national carrier to sell seats from an Internet site and was the first airline to create a home page on the Internet. In the first half of 2010, online bookings were 81 percent via http://southwest.com. The company estimated that the online ticketing cost was $1 per booking and $6–8 with a travel agent. Southwest was also one of the first airlines to use ticketless travel, offering the service first in 1995. Southwest was the only major airline with a frequent flyer program based on the number of flights taken by a passenger, not miles flown.

Over the years, Southwest's choice of markets resulted in significant growth in air travel at those locations. In Texas, traffic between the Rio Grande Valley (Harlingen) and the Golden Triangle grew from 123,000 to 325,000 within 11 months of Southwest entering the market.[7] Within a year of Southwest's arrival, the Oakland–Burbank route became the 25th largest passenger market, up from 179th. The Chicago–Louisville market tripled in size 30 days after Southwest began flying that route. Southwest was the dominant carrier in a number of cities, ranking first in market share in more than 50 percent of the largest U.S. city-pair markets. Exhibit 10 shows a comparison of Southwest across several years from 1971 to 2009.

Service Changes in 2007 and 2008/2009

In 2007, Southwest made several changes to its service offering:

- signed deals to participate in the Galileo and Worldspan reservations systems;
- added three new fare categories, including higher-tier fares for business travelers;
- began revamping gate areas that eventually will include television monitors, power ports, and new tables and seats;
- established new boarding processes; for example, travelers could pay extra to board first;
- modified the frequent flyer program to allow high-status customers to board first;
- increased emphasis on corporate sales;
- promoted the two-bags-fly-free campaign aggressively while no one else has such an offer in 2010.

---

[6] Herb Kelleher, @www.iflyswa.com/cgi-bin/imagemap/swagate 530.85.

[7] Freiberg and Freiberg, p. 29.

EXHIBIT 10   Southwest Across the Years

	1971	1999	2007	2009
Size of fleet (end of year)	4	306	515	544
Number of employees	195	29,005	34,378	35,000
Number of passengers carried	108,554	52,600,000	101,947,800	8,600,000
Number of cities served	3	55	64	69
Number of trips flown	6,051	602,578	1,160,699	More than 3,200 per day
Total operating revenues (million $)	2.33	4,736	7,369	10,400
Net income (million $)	−3.8	433	645	99

Sources: Company press releases and Southwest Airlines Fact Sheet at www.southwest.com/about_swa/press/factsheet.html.

The rationale for the 2007 changes was explained by CEO Gary Kelly:

We've always been a business traveler's airline. At the same time, over 37 years we hadn't done much to try to customize the travel experience for the varieties of customer needs that we had. It was one-size-fits-all, and in today's competitive environment we felt that was not the best way to remain on top. We had the desire to improve our overall customer experience for the business traveler.[8]

SOUTHWEST'S PERFORMANCE

Southwest bucked the airline industry trend by earning profit for 38 consecutive years. Since 1987, Southwest ranked first in fewest overall customer complaints as published in the Department of Transportation's Air Travel Consumer Report. In Zagat's 2010 annual traveller's survey, Southwest won awards for top Web site; best consumer on-time estimates—domestic; best check-in experience; best value—domestic; and best luggage policy—domestic.[9] Unfortunately for shareholders, the stock performance over the past few years lagged far behind the performance of the 1980s and 90s.

The average Southwest aircraft trip was 633 miles, with an average duration of about one hour and 52 minutes. This was up from 462 miles in 1999 and 394 in 1996. Southwest had 3,300 flights per day serving 64 cities. Each plane flew about seven flights daily, almost twice the industry average. Planes were used an average of 13 hours a day, about 40 percent more than major carriers like Delta and Northwest. Southwest's cost per available seat mile was the lowest in the industry for the major carriers (Exhibit 1), and the average age of its fleet was nine years, the lowest for the major carriers. Employee cost per available seat mile was much lower than major competitors (but not lower than some smaller carriers like Allegiant).

Southwest accomplished its enviable record by challenging accepted norms and setting competitive thresholds for other airlines to emulate. The company established numerous new industry standards. Southwest flew more passengers per employee than any other major airline while at the same time had the fewest number of employees per aircraft. Southwest maintained a debt-to-equity ratio much lower than the industry average and was one of the few airlines in the world with an investment grade credit rating. The company

[8] "The 25 Most Influential Executives of 2007," *Business Travel News,* February 4, 2008.
[9] Terry Maxon, "Zagat Names Top Airlines in Its Annual Airline Survey," Airline Biz Blog, Nov 29, 2010, http://aviationblog.dallasnews.com/.

had never curtailed service because of a union strike, and no passenger had ever died because of a safety incident.

Southwest had a fleet of 544 Boeing 737s, up from 417 in 2005, 106 in 1990, and 75 in 1987. Of the total fleet, 425 aircraft were owned and the remainder leased.

Herb Kelleher

Herb Kelleher was CEO of Southwest from 1981 to 2001. In 2001, at age 71, Kelleher stepped down as CEO but remained Chairman until 2008 when he resigned from the Board of Directors. Kelleher's leadership style combined flamboyance, fun, and a fresh, unique perspective. Kelleher played Big Daddy-O in one of the company videos, appeared as Elvis Presley in in-flight magazine advertisements, and earned the nickname "High Priest of Ha-Ha" from Fortune.[10] Although Kelleher was unconventional and a maverick in his field, he led his company to consistently new standards for itself and for the industry. Sincerely committed to his employees, Kelleher generated intense loyalty to himself and the company. His ability to remember employees' names and to ask after their families was just one way he earned respect and trust. At one point, Kelleher froze his salary for five years in response to the pilots agreeing to do the same. Often when he flew, Kelleher would help the ground crew unload bags or help the flight crew serve drinks. His humor was legendary and served as an example for his employees to join in the fun of working for Southwest. He was called "a visionary who leads by example—you have to work harder than anybody else to show them you are devoted to the business."[11]

Although Kelleher tried to downplay his personal significance to the company, especially when he gave up the CEO position in 2001, many analysts following Southwest credited the airline's success to Kelleher's unorthodox personality and engaging management style. As one analyst wrote, "The old-fashioned bond of loyalty between employees and company may have vanished elsewhere in corporate America, but it is stronger than ever at Southwest."[12] From October 1 to December 2001, Kelleher, CEO James Parker, and COO Colleen Barrett voluntarily relinquished their salaries. Gary Kelly, Southwest's former CFO, became CEO in 2004.

The Southwest Spirit

Customer service far beyond the norm in the airline industry was not unexpected at Southwest and had its own name—Positively Outrageous Service. Some examples of this service included a gate agent volunteering to watch a dog (a Chihuahua) for two weeks when an Acapulco-bound passenger showed up at the last minute without the required dog crate and an Austin passenger who missed a connection to Houston, where he was to have a kidney transplant operation, was flown there by a Southwest pilot in his private plane. Another passenger, an elderly woman flying to Phoenix for cancer treatment, began crying because she had no family or friends at her destination. The ticket agent invited her into her home and escorted her around Phoenix for two weeks.[13]

Southwest Airlines' customers were often surprised by the Southwest Spirit. On some flights, magazine pictures of gourmet meals were offered for dinner on an evening flight. Flight attendants were encouraged to have fun; songs, jokes, and humorous flight announcements were common. One flight attendant had a habit of popping out of overhead

[10] K. Labich, "Is Herb Kelleher America's Best CEO?" *Fortune,* May 2, 1994, p. 45.
[11] "24th Annual CEO Survey: Herb Kelleher, Flying His Own Course," *IW,* November 20, 1995, p. 23.
[12] Labich, p. 46.
[13] *IW,* p. 23.

luggage compartments as passengers attempted to stow their belongings, until the day she frightened an elderly passenger who called for oxygen.[14] Herb Kelleher once served in-flight snacks dressed as the Easter Bunny.

Intense company communication and camaraderie was highly valued and essential to maintaining the esprit de corps found throughout the firm. The Southwest Spirit, as exhibited by enthusiasm and extroverted personalities, was an important element in employee screening conducted by Southwest's People Department. Employment at Southwest was highly desired. In 2006, a total of 3,363 employees were hired and 284,827 applications were received. Once landed, a job was fairly secure. The airline had not laid off an employee since 1971. Historically, employee turnover hovered around 7 percent, the lowest rate in the industry. In 2011, Southwest had more than 35,000 employees; in 1990, Southwest had 8,600 employees and less than 6,000 in 1987.

During initial training periods, efforts were made to share and instill Southwest's unique culture. New employee orientation, known as the new-hire celebration, have in the past included Southwest's version of the *Wheel of Fortune* game show, scavenger hunts, and company videos including the "Southwest Airlines Shuffle" in which each department introduced itself, rap style, and in which Kelleher appeared as Big Daddy-O. To join the People Department (i.e., Human Resources), employees required frontline customer experience.

Advanced employee training regularly occurred at the University of People at Love Field in Dallas. Various classes were offered, including team building, leadership, and cultural diversity. Newly promoted supervisors and managers attended a three-day class called "Leading with Integrity." Each department also had its own training division focusing on technical aspects of the work. "Walk-a-Mile Day" encouraged employees from different departments to experience firsthand the day-to-day activities of their coworkers. The goal of this program was to promote respect for fellow workers while increasing awareness of the company.[15]

Employee initiative was supported by management and encouraged at all levels. For example, pilots looked for ways to conserve fuel during flights, employees proposed designs for ice storage equipment that reduced time and costs, and baggage handlers learned to place luggage with the handles facing outward to reduce unloading time.

Red hearts and "Luv" were central parts of the internal corporate culture, appearing throughout the company literature. A mentoring program for new hires was called CoHearts. "Heroes of the Heart Awards" were given annually to one behind-the-scenes group of workers, whose department name was painted on a specially designed plane for a year. Other awards honored an employee's big mistake through the "Boner of the Year Award." When employees had a story about exceptional service to share, they were encouraged to fill out a "LUV Report."

Southwest placed great emphasis on maintaining cooperative labor relations: 87 percent of all employees were unionized. Southwest pilots belonged to an independent union and not the Airline Pilots Association, the union that represented more than 60,000 pilots. The company encouraged the unions and their negotiators to conduct employee surveys and to research their most important issues prior to each contract negotiation. At its 1994 contract discussion, the pilots proposed a 10-year contract with stock options in lieu of guaranteed pay increases over the first five years of the contract. In 1974, Southwest was the first airline to introduce employee profit sharing. Through the plan, employees owned about 10 percent of the company's stock.

---

[14] B. O'Brian, "Flying on the Cheap," *Wall Street Journal,* October 26, 1992, p. A1.

[15] A. Malloy, "Counting the Intangibles," *Computerworld,* June 1996, pp. 32–33.

Herb Kelleher summed up the Southwest culture and commitment to employees:

We don t use things like TQM. It's just a lot of people taking pride in what they're doing. . . . You have to recognize that people are still the most important. How you treat them determines how they treat people on the outside . . . I give people the license to be themselves and motivate others in that way. We give people the opportunity to be a maverick. You don't have to fit in a constraining mold at work—you can have a good time. People respond to that.[16]

SOUTHWEST IMITATORS

Southwest's strategy spawned numerous imitators, most of which failed. Two of the more successful start-up firms, Midwest Express and America West, both went through Chapter 11 bankruptcy proceedings. ValuJet was grounded after its May 1996 crash in the Florida Everglades, reemerging a year later as AirTran and JetBlue.

The major airlines tried to compete directly with Southwest. The Shuttle by United, the so-called "airline within an airline," was started in October 1994. United's objective was to create a new airline owned by United with many of the same operational elements as Southwest: a fleet of 737s, low fares, short-haul flights, and less-restrictive union rules. United saturated the West Coast corridor with short-haul flights on routes such as Oakland–Seattle, San Francisco–San Diego, and Sacramento–San Diego. The Shuttle was unable to achieve the same level of productivity as Southwest, and in 2001, United discontinued Shuttle service and folded the remaining flights into its regular service. US Airways did the same with its Metrojet discount service. In 2003, United started a new discount carrier called TED.

Some of the attempts to imitate Southwest were almost comical. Continental Lite (CALite) was an effort by Continental Airlines to develop a low-cost service and revive the company's fortunes after coming out of bankruptcy in April 1993. In March 1994, Continental increased CALite service to 875 daily flights. Continental soon encountered major operational problems with its new strategy.[17] With its fleet of 16 different planes, mechanical delays disrupted turnaround times. Various pricing strategies were unsuccessful. The company was ranked last among the major carriers for on-time service and complaints soared by 40 percent. In January 1995, Continental announced that it would reduce its capacity by 10 percent and eliminate 4,000 jobs. By mid-1995, Continental's CALite service had been largely discontinued. In October 1995, Continental's CEO was ousted.

A SUCCESSFUL START-UP: JETBLUE AIRWAYS

Morris Air, patterned after Southwest, was the only airline Southwest had acquired. Prior to the acquisition, Morris Air flew Boeing 737s on point-to-point routes, operated in a different part of the United States than Southwest, and was profitable. When Morris Air was acquired by Southwest in December 1993, seven new markets were added to Southwest's system. In 1999, Morris Air's former president, David Neeleman, announced plans for JetBlue Airways, a new airline based at New York's JFK Airport. JetBlue had a successful IPO in April 2002, with the stock rising 70 percent on the first day of trading. JetBlue had a geographically diversified flight schedule that included both short-haul and long-haul

[16] H. Lancaster, "Herb Kelleher Has One Main Strategy: Treat Employees Well," *Wall Street Journal,* August 31, 1999, p. B1.
[17] B. O'Brian, "Heavy Going: Continental's CALite Hits Some Turbulence in Battling Southwest," *Wall Street Journal,* January 10, 1995, A1, A16.

routes. Although JetBlue was viewed as a low-fare carrier, the airline emphasized various service attributes, such as leather seats, free LiveTV (a 24-channel satellite TV service with programming provided by DirecTV), and preassigned seating.

In 2011, JetBlue served 63 cities in the domestic United States, Mexico, and the Caribbean. JetBlue had a fleet of 116 Airbus A320 aircraft and 45 Embraer 190 regional jet aircraft. JetBlue's revenue in 2010 was $3.8 billion, 31 percent that of Southwest (up from 26 percent in 2008). A major ice storm that hit New York in early 2007 severely tested the company. More than 1,200 flights were canceled over a six-day period. Not long after, David Neeleman was asked by the Board to step down as CEO. He remained as Chairman.

SOUTHWEST EXPANSION

Southwest grew steadily over the years prior to 2011 but the growth was highly controlled. New airports were carefully selected and only a few new cities were added each year. As Kelleher wrote to his employees in 1993, "Southwest has had more opportunities for growth than it has airplanes. Yet, unlike other airlines, it has avoided the trap of growing beyond its means. Whether you are talking with an officer or a ramp agent, employees just don't seem to be enamored of the idea that bigger is better."[18]

In October 1996, with the initiation of flights to Providence, Rhode Island, Southwest entered the northeast market. The entry into the northeast region of the United States was, in many respects, a logical move for Southwest. The northeast was the most densely populated area of the country and the only major region where Southwest did not compete. New England could provide a valuable source of passengers to Florida's warmer winter climates. Southwest's entry into Florida was exceeding initial estimates.

Despite the large potential market, the northeast offered a new set of challenges for Southwest. Airport congestion and air-traffic control delays could prevent efficient operations, lengthening turnaround time at airport gates and wreaking havoc on frequent flight scheduling. Inclement weather posed additional challenges for both air service and car travel to airports. Nevertheless, Southwest continued to add new northeast cities. A few years later, Southwest was flying to various northeast airports, including Long Island, New Hampshire, and Hartford. In 2004, Southwest began flying to Philadelphia, which was the first major northeast market entry. As of 2011 (excluding AirTran service), Southwest had not entered any markets outside the domestic United States.

THE AIRTRAN DEAL

In September 2010, Southwest announced that it would buy AirTran Airways for $1.4 billion. The acquisition would give Southwest access to more than 30 new markets, including Atlanta and several tourist destinations in Mexico and the Caribbean. The deal strengthened Southwest's position in the Southeast and on the East Coast. AirTran had a lower cost structure than Southwest and integrating AirTran into Southwest's operations and culture could prove challenging. Most of AirTran's fleets were Boeing 717s, whereas Southwest only flew 737s. AirTran had international routes and offered first-class seats. Complicating the integration would be Southwest's limited experience with acquisitions.

Perhaps the most difficult challenge would be ensuring that the acquisition did not change or weaken the Southwest culture. According to Southwest's pilots' union president,

---

[18] Freiberg and Freiberg, p. 61.

"The Achilles' heel of this transaction is how our company will be able to maintain our culture, and keep it alive for the next 40 years."[19]

FUTURE CHALLENGES

Although Southwest was profitable and had a strong financial position, competition was stiff. The newly merged carriers (Delta/Northwest and Continental/United) were expected to become more efficient, and smaller players like JetBlue and Allegiant had lower costs than Southwest. While Southwest's employee productivity remained high, its operating costs were rising. The company had the highest salaries for pilots of narrow-body jets, and salaries for mechanics and flight attendants were among the highest in the industry.

Clearly, the future promised dramatic changes to airline industry structure. Would Southwest be able to maintain its position as America's most prosperous airline? Could Southwest complete the AirTran acquisition and still ensure that customer service and company performance were satisfactory? In 2010, Southwest placed an order for 737-800s to replace older 737-700s, a smaller aircraft. With larger aircraft, would Southwest introduce longer flights to Hawaii and other more distant locations? Would the major airlines finally learn how to compete on cost with companies like Southwest and JetBlue?

According to CEO Gary Kelly, "We still have an underdog mentality. It's not a comfortable country-club environment for us. . . . We're still a maverick."[20]

---

[19] Jad Mouawad, "Pushing 40, Southwest Is Still Playing the Rebel," *New York Times,* November 20, 2010.

[20] Mouawad, *New York Times.*

APPENDIX A   Revenue Passenger Miles (RPM)* 1989–2009 (in billions) for Major U.S. Airlines

	American	America West	Continental	Delta	Northwest	Southwest	Trans World	United	US Airways	Total
2009	122.4		77.8	100.7	62.9	74.6		100.5	57.9	779.9
2008	131.75		80.5	105.7	71.6	73.7		110.0	60.6	823.8
2007	138.4	17.7	81.4	103.3	72.9	72.3		117.4	43.5	646.9
2006	139.4	23.5	76.3	98.8	72.6	67.7		117.2	37.4	632.9
2005	138.4	24.3	68.4	103.7	75.9	60.3		114.3	40.2	625.5
2004	130.2	23.3	63.4	98.3	73.4	53.5		115.2	40.5	597.8
2003	120.3	21.3	57.6	89.4	68.8	48		104.4	37.8	547.6
2002	121.7	19.9	57.3	95.3	72.1	45.5		109.4	40	561.2
2001	106.2	19.1	58.8	97.7	73.3	44.7	20.8	116.6	46	583.2
2000	116.6	19.1	62.4	107.8	79.2	42.4	27.3	126.9	46.9	628.6
1999	110.2	17.7	58	104.8	74.2	36.8	26.1	125.5	41.5	594.8
1998	108.9	16.4	51	102	66.8	31.6	24.5	124.6	41.4	567.2
1997	107	16.2	44.3	99.7	72.1	26.4	25.2	121.4	41.7	554
1996	104.6	15.3	37.6	93.9	68.7	27.3	27.3	116.7	39.2	530.6
1995	102.7	13.3	35.8	85.2	62.6	23.5	25.1	111.8	38.1	498.1
1994	98.8	12.2	38.1	86.4	58.5	19.9	24.8	108.2	38.4	485.3
1993	97.1	11.2	40.1	82.9	58.7	16.9	22.8	101.3	35.5	466.5
1992	97.1	11.8	43.5	80.6	58.7	13.9	29.2	92.7	35.4	462.9

*Revenue Passenger Miles, or RPM, is a measure of the volume of air passenger transportation. A revenue passenger mile is equal to one paying passenger carried one mile.

Source: Bureau of Transportation Statistics Table T1: U.S. Air Carrier Traffic and Capacity Summary by Service Class.

APPENDIX B   Operating Revenues (in millions of dollars) 1992–2009 for Major U.S. Airlines

Year	American	America West	Continental	Delta	Northwest	Southwest	Trans World	United	US Airways	Total
2009	17,886		10,635	22,778		10,350		13,271	8,106	155,049,764
2008	21,210		11,382	15,529	10,903	11,023		17,139	9,365	186,087,333
2007	17,177	2,737	10,615	14,515	9,545	7,369		15,075	6,463	83,496
2006	22,493	3,770	13,010	17,339	12,555	9,086		19,334	8,076	105,663
2005	20,657	3,397	11,108	16,112	12,316	7,584		17,304	7,212	95,690
2004	18,608	2,482	9,851	15,154	11,266	6,530		15,701	7,073	86,665
2003	17,403	2,223	7,333	14,203	9,184	5,937		13,398	6,762	76,443
2002	15,871	2,021	7,353	12,410	9,152	5,522		13,916	6,915	73,160
2001	15,639	2,035	7,972	13,211	9,592	5,555	2,633	16,087	8,253	80,977
2000	18,117	2,309	9,129	15,321	10,957	5,650	3,585	19,331	9,181	93,580
1999	16,090	2,164	8,027	14,901	9,868	4,736	3,309	17,967	8,460	85,522
1998	16,299	1,983	7,299	14,630	8,707	4,164	3,259	17,518	8,556	82,415
1997	15,856	1,887	6,361	14,204	9,984	3,817	3,330	17,335	8,501	81,275
1996	15,136	1,752	5,487	13,318	9,751	3,407	3,554	16,317	7,704	76,426
1995	15,610	1,562	4,919	12,557	8,909	2,873	3,281	14,895	6,985	71,591
1994	14,951	1,414	4,734	12,346	8,929	2,417	3,350	13,887	6,579	68,607
1993	14,737	1,332	5,086	12,376	8,448	2,067	3,094	14,354	6,623	68,117
1992	13,581	1,303	5,210	11,639	7,964	1,685	3,570	12,725	6,236	63,913

Source: Bureau of Transportation Statistics, Air Carrier Financial Reports Table P-12.

South Delaware Coors, Inc.

James E. Nelson and Eric J. Karson *University of Colorado*

Larry Brownlow was just beginning to realize the problem was more complex than he thought. The problem, of course, was giving direction to Manson and Associates regarding which research should be completed by February 20, 1989, to determine market potential of a Coors beer distributorship for a two-county area in southern Delaware. With data from this research, Larry would be able to estimate the feasibility of such an operation before the March 5 application deadline. Larry knew his decision on whether or not to apply for the distributorship was the most important career choice he had ever faced.

LARRY BROWNLOW

Larry was just completing his M.B.A. and, from his standpoint, the Coors announcement of expansion into Delaware could hardly have been better timed. He had long ago decided the best opportunities and rewards were in smaller, self-owned businesses and not in the jungles of corporate giants. Because of a family tragedy some three years ago, Larry found himself in a position to consider small business opportunities such as the Coors distributorship. Approximately $500,000 was held in trust for Larry, to be dispersed when he reached age 30. Until then, Larry and his family lived on an annual trust income of about $40,000. It was on this income that Larry decided to leave his sales engineering job and return to graduate school for his M.B.A.

The decision to complete a graduate program and operate his own business had been easy to make. While he could have retired and lived off investment income, Larry knew such a life would not be to his liking. Working with people and the challenge of making it on his own, Larry thought, were far more preferable to enduring an early retirement.

Larry would be 30 in July, about the time money would actually be needed to start the business. In the meantime, he had access to about $15,000 for feasibility research. While

This case was written by Professor James E. Nelson and doctoral student Eric J. Karson, University of Colorado. This case is intended for use as a basis for class discussion rather than to illustrate either effective or ineffective administrative decision making. Some data are disguised. © by the Business Research Division, College of Business and Administration and the Graduate School of Business Administration, University of Colorado, Boulder, Colorado 80309–0419.

there certainly were other places to spend the money, Larry and his wife agreed the opportunity to acquire the distributorship could not be overlooked.

COORS, INC.

Coors's history dates back to 1873, when Adolph Coors built a small brewery in Golden, Colorado. Since then, the brewery has prospered and become the fourth-largest seller of beer in the country. Coors's operating philosophy could be summed up as "hard work, saving money, devotion to the quality of the product, caring about the environment, and giving people something to believe in." Company operation is consistent with this philosophy. Headquarters and most production facilities are still located in Golden, Colorado, with a new Shenandoah, Virginia, facility aiding in nationwide distribution. Coors is still family operated and controlled. The company issued its first public stock, $127 million worth of nonvoting shares, in 1975. The issue was received enthusiastically by the financial community despite its being offered during a recession.

Coors's unwillingness to compromise on the high quality of its product is well known both to its suppliers and to its consuming public. Coors beer requires constant refrigeration to maintain this quality, and wholesalers' facilities are closely controlled to ensure proper temperatures are maintained. Wholesalers are also required to install and use aluminum can recycling equipment. Coors was one of the first breweries in the industry to recycle its cans.

Larry was aware of Coors's popularity with many consumers in adjacent states. However, Coors's corporate management was seen by some consumers to hold antiunion beliefs (because of a labor disagreement at the brewery some 10 years ago and the brewery's current use of a nonunion labor force). Some other consumers perceived the brewery to be somewhat insensitive to minority issues, primarily in employment and distribution. The result of these attitudes—plus many other aspects of consumer behavior—meant that Coors's sales in Delaware would depend greatly on the efforts of the two wholesalers planned for the state.

MANSON RESEARCH PROPOSAL

Because of the press of his studies, Larry had contacted Manson and Associates in January for their assistance. The firm was a Wilmington-based general research supplier that had conducted other feasibility studies in the south Atlantic region. Manson was well known for the quality of its work, particularly with respect to computer modeling. The firm had developed special expertise in modeling population and employment levels for cities, counties, and other units of area for periods of up to 10 years into the future.

Larry had met John Rome, senior research analyst for Manson, and discussed the Coors opportunity and appropriate research extensively in the January meeting. Rome promised a formal research proposal (Exhibits 1 and 2) for the project, which Larry now held in his hand. It certainly was extensive, Larry thought, and reflected the professionalism he expected. Now came the hard part, choosing the more relevant research from the proposal, because he certainly couldn't afford to pay for it all. Rome had suggested a meeting for Friday, giving Larry only two more days to decide.

Larry was at first overwhelmed. All the research would certainly be useful. He was sure he needed estimates of sales and costs in a form allowing managerial analysis, but what data in what form? Knowledge of competing operations' experience, retailer support, and consumer acceptance also seemed important for feasibility analysis. For example, what if consumers were excited about Coors and retailers indifferent or the other way around? Finally, several of the studies would provide information that could be useful in later

EXHIBIT 1   Manson and Associates Research Proposal

Mr. Larry Brownlow   January 16, 1989
1198 West Lamar
Chester, PA 12345

Dear Larry:

   It was a pleasure meeting you last week and discussing your business and research interests in Coors wholesaling. After further thought and discussion with my colleagues, the Coors opportunity appears even more attractive than when we met.

   Appearances can be deceiving, as you know, and I fully agree some formal research is needed before you make application. Research that we recommend would proceed in two distinct stages and is described below:

Stage One Research Based on Secondary Data and Manson Computer Models:

Study A: National and Delaware per Capita Beer Consumption for 1988–1992.
   Description: Per capita annual consumption of beer for the total population and population aged
      21 and over is provided in gallons.
   Source: Various publications, Manson computer model
   Cost: $1,000

Study B: Population Estimates for 1985–1995 for Two Delaware Counties in Market Area.
   Description: Annual estimates of total population and population aged 21 and over is provided for
      the period 1985–1995.
   Source: U.S. Bureau of Census, Sales Management Annual Survey of Buying Power, Manson
      computer model
   Cost: $1,500

Study C: Coors Market Share Estimates for 1990–1995.
   Description: Coors market share for the two-county market area based on total gallons consumed
      is estimated for each year in the period 1990–1995. This data will be projected from Coors's
      nationwide experience.
   Source: Various publications, Manson computer model
   Cost: $2,000

Study D: Estimated Liquor and Beer Licenses for the Market Area, 1990–1995.
   Description: Projections of the number of on-premise sale operations and off-premise sale
      operations is provided.
   Source: Delaware Department of Revenue, Manson computer model
   Cost: $1,000

Study E: Beer Taxes Paid by Delaware Wholesalers for 1987 and 1988 in the Market Area.
   Description: Beer taxes paid by each of the six presently operating competing beer wholesalers is
      provided. This can be converted to gallons sold by applying the state gallonage tax rate (6 cents
      per gallon).
   Source: Delaware Department of Revenue
   Cost: $200

Study F: Financial Statement Summary of Wine, Liquor, and Beer Wholesalers for Fiscal Year 1986.
   Description: Composite balance sheets, income statements, and relevant measures of performance
      provided for 510 similar wholesaling operations in the United States is provided.
   Source: Robert Morris Associates Annual Statement Studies 1987 ed.
   Cost: $49.50

(continued)

EXHIBIT 1 Manson and Associates Research Proposal *(concluded)*

Stage Two Research Based on Primary Data:

Study G: Consumer Study
     Description: Study G involves focus group interviews and a mail questionnaire to determine
        consumer past experience, acceptance, and intention to buy Coors beer. Three focus
        group interviews would be conducted in the two counties in the market area. From these
        data, a mail questionnaire would be developed and sent to 300 adult residents in the
        market area, utilizing direct questions and semantic differential scale to measure attitudes
        toward Coors beer, competing beers, and an ideal beer.
     Source: Manson and Associates
     Cost: $6,000

Study H: Retailer Study
     Description: Group interviews would be conducted with six potential retailers of Coors beer in
        one county in the market area to determine their past beer sales and experience and their
        intention to stock and sell Coors. From these data, a personal interview questionnaire would
        be developed and executed at all appropriate retailers in the market area to determine
        similar data.
     Source: Manson and Associates
     Cost: $4,800

Study I: Survey of Retail and Wholesale Beer Prices
     Description: Study I involves in-store interviews with a sample of 50 retailers in the market area
        to estimate retail and wholesale prices for Budweiser, Miller Lite, Miller, Busch, Bud Light,
        Old Milwaukee, and Michelob.
     Source: Manson and Associates
     Cost: $2,000

Examples of the form of final report tables are attached [Exhibit 2]. This should give you a better idea of the data you will receive.

  As you can see, the research is extensive and, I might add, not cheap. However, the research as outlined will supply you with sufficient information to make an estimate of the feasibility of a Coors distributorship, the investment for which is substantial.

  I have scheduled 9:00 next Friday as a time to meet with you to discuss the proposal in more detail. Time is short, but we firmly feel the study can be completed by February 20, 1989. If you need more information in the meantime, please feel free to call.

                                            Sincerely,

                                          John

                                          John Rome

                                          Senior Research Analyst

EXHIBIT 2 Examples of Final Research Report Tables

(A) National and Delaware Resident Annual Beer Consumption per Capita, 1988–1992 (Gallons)

Year	U.S. Consumption		Delaware Consumption	
	Based on Entire Population	Based on Population over Age 21	Based on Entire Population	Based on Population over Age 21
1988				
1989				
1990				
1991				
1992				

Source: Study A.

(B) Population Estimates for 1986–1996 for Two Delaware Counties in Market Area

County	Entire Population					
	1986	1988	1990	1992	1994	1996
Kent						
Sussex						

County	Population Age 21 and Over					
	1986	1988	1990	1992	1994	1996
Kent						
Sussex						

Source: Study B.

(C) Coors Market Share Estimates for 1990–1995

Year	Market Share (%)
1990	
1991	
1992	
1993	
1994	
1995	

Source: Study C.

(D) Liquor and Beer License Estimates for Market Area for 1990–1995

Type of License	1990	1991	1992	1993	1994	1995
All beverages						
Retail beer and wine						
Off-premises beer only						
Veterans beer and liquor						
Fraternal						
Resort beer and liquor						

Source: Study D.

(E) Beer Taxes Paid by Beer Wholesalers in the Market Area, 1987 and 1988

Wholesaler	1987 Tax Paid ($)	1988 Tax Paid ($)
A		
B		
C		
D		
E		
F		

Source: Study E.
Note: Delaware beer tax is 6 cents per gallon.

(continued)

EXHIBIT 2   Examples of Final Research Report Tables   *(continued)*

(F) Financial Statement Summary for 510 Wholesalers of Wine, Liquor, and Beer in Fiscal Year 1986

Assets	Percentage
Cash and equivalents	
Accounts and notes receivable net	
Inventory	
All other current	
Total current	
Fixed assets net	
Intangibles net	
All other noncurrent	____
Total	100.0

Ratios
Quick
Current
Debts/worth

Liabilities	Percentage
Notes payable—short-term	
Current maturity long-term debt	
Accounts and notes payable—trade	
Accrued expenses	
All other current	
Total current	
Long-term debt	
All other noncurrent	
Net worth	____
Total liabilities and net worth	100.0
Income Data	
Net sales	100.0
Cost of sales	
Gross profit	
Operating expenses	
Operating profit	
All other expenses net	____
Profit before taxes	

Sales/receivables
Cost sales/inventory
Percentage profit before taxes
  based on total assets

Source: Study F (Robert Morris Associates, © 1987).

Interpretation of Statement Studies Figures

RMA recommends that Statement Studies data be regarded only as general guidelines and not as absolute industry norms. There are several reasons why the data may not be fully representative of a given industry:

1. The financial statements used in the *Statement Studies* are not selected by any random or statistically reliable method. RMA member banks voluntarily submit the raw data they have available each year, with these being the only constraints: (a) The fiscal year-ends of the companies reported may not be from April 1 through June 29, and (b) their total assets must be less than $100 million.

2. Many companies have varied product lines; however, the *Statement Studies* categorize them by their primary product Standard Industrial Classification (SIC) number only.

3. Some of our industry samples are rather small in relation to the total number of firms in a given industry. A relatively small sample can increase the chances that some of our composites do not fully represent an industry.

4. There is the chance that an extreme statement can be present in a sample, causing a disproportionate influence on the industry composite. This is particularly true in a relatively small sample.

5. Companies within the same industry may differ in their method of operations which in turn can directly influence their financial statements. Since they are included in our sample, too, these statements can significantly affect our composite calculations.

6. Other considerations that can result in variations among different companies engaged in the same general line of business are different labor markets; geographical location; different accounting methods; quality of products handled; sources and methods of financing; and terms of sale.

For these reasons, RMA does not recommend the Statement Studies figures be considered as absolute norms for a given industry. Rather the figures should be used only as general guidelines and in addition to the other methods of financial analysis. RMA makes no claim as to the representativeness of the figures printed in this book.

EXHIBIT 2   Examples of Final Research Report Tables   *(continued)*

(G) Consumer Questionnaire Results

	Yes	No		Yes	No
Consumed Coors in the Past:	%	%	**Usually Buy Beer at:**		%

Attitudes toward Coors:	%
Strongly like	
Like	
Indifferent/no opinion	
Dislike	
Strongly dislike	
Total	100.0

Usually Buy Beer at:	%
Liquor stores	
Taverns and bars	
Supermarkets	
Corner grocery	
Total	100.0

Weekly Beer Consumption:	%
Less than 1 can	
1–2 cans	
3–4 cans	
5–6 cans	
7–8 cans	
9 cans and over	
Total	100.0

Features Considered Important When Buying Beer:	%
Taste	
Brand Name	
Price	
Store location	
Advertising	
Carbonation	
Other	
Total	100.0

Intention to Buy Coors:	%
Certainly will	
Maybe will	
Not sure	
Maybe will not	
Certainly will not	
Total	100.0

Semantic Differential Scale—Consumers*

	Extremely	Very	Somewhat	Somewhat	Very	Extremely	
Masculine	___	___	___	___	___	___	Feminine
Healthful	___	___	___	___	___	___	Unhealthful
Cheap	___	___	___	___	___	___	Expensive
Strong	___	___	___	___	___	___	Weak
Old-fashioned	___	___	___	___	___	___	New
Upper-class	___	___	___	___	___	___	Lower-class
Good taste	___	___	___	___	___	___	Bad taste

Source: Study G.
*Profiles would be provided for Coors, three competing beers, and an ideal beer.

(H) Retailer Questionnaire Results

Brands of Beer Carried:	%
Budweiser	
Miller Lite	
Miller	
Busch	
Bud Light	
Old Milwaukee	
Michelob	

Beer Sales:	%
Budweiser	
Miller Lite	
Miller	
Busch	
Bud Light	
Old Milwaukee	
Michelob	
Others	
Total	100.0

(continued)

EXHIBIT 2   Examples of Final Research Report Tables   *(concluded)*

Semantic Differential Scale—Retailers*

	Extremely	Very	Somewhat	Somewhat	Very	Extremely	
Masculine	___	___	___	___	___	___	Feminine
Healthful	___	___	___	___	___	___	Unhealthful
Cheap	___	___	___	___	___	___	Expensive
Strong	___	___	___	___	___	___	Weak
Old-fashioned	___	___	___	___	___	___	New
Upper-class	___	___	___	___	___	___	Lower-class
Good taste	___	___	___	___	___	___	Bad taste

Intention to Sell Coors: ___%___

Certainly will	
Maybe will	
Not sure	
Maybe will not	
Certainly will not	_____
Total	100.0

Source: Study G.

*Profiles would be provided for Coors, three competing beers, and an ideal beer.

(I) Retail and Wholesale Prices for Selected Beers in the Market Area

Beer	Wholesale* Six-Pack Price (dollars)	Retail† Six-Pack Price (dollars)
Budweiser		
Miller Lite		
Miller		
Busch		
Bud Light		
Old Milwaukee		
Michelob		

Source: Study I.
*Price that the wholesaler sold to retailers.
†Price that the retailer sold to consumers.

months of operation in the areas of promotion and pricing, for example. The problem now appeared more difficult than before!

It would have been nice, Larry thought, to have had some time to perform part of the suggested research himself. However, there was just too much in the way of class assignments and other matters to allow him that luxury. Besides, using Manson and Associates would give him research results from an unbiased source.

INVESTING AND OPERATING DATA

Larry was not completely in the dark regarding investment and operating data for the distributorship. In the past two weeks, he had visited two beer wholesalers in his hometown of Chester, Pennsylvania, who handled Anheuser-Busch and Miller beer, to get a feel for their operations and marketing experience. It would have been nice to interview a Coors wholesaler, but Coors management had strictly informed all of their distributors to provide no information to prospective applicants.

While no specific financial data was discussed, general information had been provided in a cordial fashion because of the noncompetitive nature of Larry's plans. Based on his conversations, Larry made the following estimates:

Inventory		$240,000
Equipment		
Delivery trucks	$150,000	
Forklift	20,000	
Recycling and miscellaneous equipment	20,000	
Office equipment	10,000	
Total equipment		200,000
Warehouse		320,000
Land		40,000
Total investment		$800,000

A local banker had reviewed Larry's financial capabilities and saw no problem in extending a line of credit on the order of $400,000. Other sources also might loan as much as $400,000 to the business.

As a rough estimate of fixed expenses, Larry planned on having four route salespeople, a secretary, and a warehouse manager. Salaries for these people and himself would run about $160,000 annually plus some form of incentive compensation he had yet to determine. Other fixed or semifixed expenses were estimated at:

Equipment depreciation	$35,000
Warehouse depreciation	15,000
Utilities and telephone	12,000
Insurance	10,000
Personal property taxes	10,000
Maintenance and janitorial	5,600
Miscellaneous	2,400
	$90,000

According to the wholesalers, beer in bottles and cans outsold keg beer by a three-to-one margin. Keg beer prices at the wholesale level were about 45 percent of prices for beer in bottles and cans.

MEETING

The entire matter deserved much thought. Maybe it was a golden opportunity, maybe not. The only thing certain was that research was needed, Manson and Associates was ready, and Larry needed time to think. Today is Tuesday, Larry thought—only three days until he and John Rome would get together for direction.

Ruth's Chris: The High Stakes of International Expansion

Allen H. Kupetz and Ilan Alon *The University of Western Ontario*

"Well, I was so lucky that I fell into something that I really, really love. And I think that if you ever go into business, you better find something you really love, because you spend so many hours with it . . . it almost becomes your life."

Ruth Fertel, 1927–2002
Founder of Ruth's Chris Steak House

In 2006, Ruth's Chris Steak House (Ruth's Chris) was fresh off a sizzling initial public offering (IPO). Dan Hannah, vice president for business development since June 2004, was responsible for the development of a new business strategy focused on continued growth of franchise and company-operated restaurants. He also oversaw franchisee relations. Now a public company, Ruth's Chris had to meet Wall Street's expectations for revenue growth. Current stores were seeing consistent incremental revenue growth, but new restaurants were critical and Hannah knew that the international opportunities offered a tremendous upside.

With restaurants in just five countries including the United States, the challenge for Hannah was to decide where to go to next. Ruth's Chris regularly received inquiries from would-be franchisees all over the world, but strict criteria—liquid net worth of at least U.S. $1 million, verifiable experience within the hospitality industry, and an ability and desire to develop multiple locations—eliminated many of the prospects. And the cost of a franchise—a U.S. $100,000 per restaurant franchise fee, a 5 percent of gross sales royalty fee, and a 2 percent of gross sales fee as a contribution to the national advertising campaign—eliminated some qualified prospects. All this was coupled with a debate within Ruth's Chris senior management team about the need and desire to grow its international business. So where was Hannah to look for new international franchisees and what countries would be best suited for the fine dining that made Ruth's Chris famous?

THE HOUSE THAT RUTH BUILT

Ruth Fertel, the founder of Ruth's Chris, was born in New Orleans in 1927. She skipped several grades in grammar school and later entered Louisiana State University in Baton Rouge at the age of 15 to pursue degrees in chemistry and physics. After graduation, Fertel landed a job teaching at McNeese State University. The majority of her students were football players who not only towered over her but also were actually older than she was. Fertel taught for two semesters. In 1948, the former Ruth Ann Adstad married Rodney Fertel who lived in Baton Rouge and shared her love of horses. They had two sons, Jerry and Randy. They opened a racing stable in Baton Rouge. Ruth Fertel earned a thoroughbred trainer's license, making her the first female horse trainer in Louisiana. Ruth and Rodney Fertel divorced in 1958.

In 1965, Ruth Fertel spotted an ad in the *New Orleans Times-Picayune* selling a steak house. She mortgaged her home for $22,000 to purchase Chris Steak House, a 60-seat restaurant on the corner of Broad and Ursuline in New Orleans, near the fairgrounds racetrack. In September of 1965, the city of New Orleans was ravaged by Hurricane Betsy just a few months after Fertel purchased Chris Steak House. The restaurant was left without power, so she cooked everything she had and brought it to her brother in devastated Plaquemines Parish to aid in the relief effort.

In 1976, the thriving restaurant was destroyed in a kitchen fire. Fertel bought a new property a few blocks away on Broad Street and soon opened under a new name, "Ruth's Chris Steak House," since her original contract with former owner, Chris Matulich, precluded her from using the name Chris Steak House in a different location. After years of failed attempts, Tom Moran, a regular customer and business owner from Baton Rouge, convinced a hesitant Fertel to let him open the first Ruth's Chris franchise in 1976. It opened on Airline Highway in Baton Rouge. Fertel reluctantly began awarding more and more franchises. In the 1980s, the little corner steak house grew into a global phenomenon with restaurants opening every year in cities around the nation and the world (see Figure 1). Fertel became something of an icon herself and was dubbed by her peers *"The First Lady of American Restaurants."*

Ruth's Chris grew to become the largest fine dining steak house in the United States (see Exhibit 1) with its focus on an unwavering commitment to customer satisfaction and its broad selection of USDA Prime grade steaks (USDA Prime is a meat grade label that refers to evenly distributed marbling that enhances the flavor of the steak). The menu also included premium quality lamb chops, veal chops, fish, chicken, and lobster. Steak and seafood combinations and a vegetable platter were also available at selected restaurants. Dinner entrees were generally priced between $18 to $38. Three company-owned restaurants were open for lunch and offered entrees generally ranging in price from $11 to $24. The Ruth's Chris core menu was similar at all of its restaurants. The company occasionally

FIGURE 1 Ruth's Chris Restaurant Growth by Decade

Source: Ruth's Chris Steak House files.

Decade	New Restaurants (total)	New Restaurants (company-owned)	New Restaurants (franchises)
1965–1969	1	1	0
1970–1979	4	2	2
1980–1989	19	8	11
1990–1999	44	19	25
2000–2005	25	12	13
	93[1]	42	51

introduced new items as specials that allowed the restaurant to offer its guests additional choices, such as items inspired by Ruth's Chris New Orleans heritage.[2]

In 2005, Ruth's Chris enjoyed a significant milestone, completing a successful IPO that raised more than $154 million in new equity capital. In its 2005 annual report, the company said it had plans "to embark on an accelerated development plan and expand our footprint through both company-owned and franchised locations." In 2005, restaurant sales grew to a record $415.8 million from 82 locations in the United States and 10 international locations including Canada (1995, 2003), Hong Kong (1997, 2001), Mexico (1993, 1996, 2001) and Taiwan (1993, 1996, 2001). As of December 2005, 41 of the 92 Ruth's Chris restaurants were company owned and 51 were franchisee owned, including all 10 of the international restaurants (see Exhibit 2).

Ruth's Chris's 51 franchisee-owned restaurants were owned by just 17 franchisees, with five new franchisees having the rights to develop a new restaurant, and the three largest franchisees owning eight, six, and five restaurants. Prior to 2004, each franchisee entered into a 10-year franchise agreement with three 10-year renewal options for each restaurant. Each agreement granted the franchisee territorial protection, with the option to develop a certain number of restaurants in their territory. Ruth's Chris's franchisee agreements generally included termination clauses in the event of nonperformance by the franchisee.[3]

A WORLD OF OPPORTUNITIES

As part of the international market selection process, Hannah considered four standard models (see Figure 2):

1. Product development—new kinds of restaurants in existing markets
2. Diversification—new kinds of restaurants in new markets
3. Penetration—more of the same restaurants in the same market
4. Market development—more of the same restaurants in new markets

The product development model (new kinds of restaurants in existing markets) was never seriously considered by Ruth's Chris. It had built a brand based on fine dining steak houses

---

[1]Due to damage caused by Hurricane Katrina, Ruth's Chris was forced to temporarily close its restaurant in New Orleans, Louisiana.

[2]Ruth's Chris Steak House 2005 Annual Report, p. 7.

[3]Ruth's Chris Steak House 2005 Annual Report, p. 10.

FIGURE 2
Restaurant Growth
Paths*

*This diagram is based on
Ansoff's Product/Market
Matrix, first published in
"Strategies for Diversifica-
tion," *Harvard Business
Review*, 1957.

	Restaurant Brands	
	Existing	**New**
Existing	**Penetration** (more restaurants) *Same market, same product*	**Product development** (new brands) *Same market, new product*
Market **New**	**Market development** (new markets) *New markets, same product*	**Diversification** (new brands for new market) *New product, new market*

and, with only 92 stores, the company saw little need and no value in diversifying with new kinds of restaurants.

The diversification model (new kinds of restaurants in new markets) was also never considered by Ruth's Chris. In only four international markets, Hannah knew that the current fine dining steak house model would work in new markets without the risk of brand dilution or brand confusion.

The penetration model (more of the same restaurants in the same market) was already underway in a small way with new restaurants opening up in Canada. The limiting factor was simply that fine dining establishments would never be as ubiquitous as quick service restaurants (that is, fast food) like McDonald's. Even the largest cities in the world would be unlikely to host more than five to six Ruth's Chris Steak Houses.

The market development model (more of the same restaurants in new markets) appeared the most obvious path to increased revenue. Franchisees in the four international markets—Canada, Hong Kong, Mexico, and Taiwan—were profitable and could offer testimony to would-be franchisees of the value of a Ruth's Chris franchise.

With the management team agreed on a model, the challenge shifted to market selection criteria. The key success factors were well-defined:

- *Beef-eaters:* Ruth's Chris was a steak house (though there were several fish items on the menu) and, thus, its primary customers were people who enjoy beef. According to the World Resources Institute, in 2002 there were 17 countries above the mean per capita of annual beef consumption for high-income countries (93.5 kilograms—see Exhibit 3).[4]

- *Legal to import U.S. beef:* The current Ruth's Chris model used only USDA Prime beef, thus it had to be exportable to the target country. In some cases, Australian beef was able to meet the same high U.S. standard.

- *Population/high urbanization rates:* With the target customer being a well-to-do beef-eater, restaurants needed to be in densely populated areas to have a large enough pool. Most large centers probably met this requirement.

- *High disposable income:* Ruth's Chris is a fine dining experience and the average cost of a meal for a customer ordering an entrée was over $70 at a Ruth's Chris in the United States. While this might seem to eliminate many countries quickly, some

[4]World Resources Institute, "Meat Consumption: Per Capita (1984–2002)," retrieved on June 7, 2006 from http://earthtrends.wri.org/text/agriculture-food/variable-193.html.

countries (e.g., China) have such large populations that even a very small percentage of people with high disposable income could create an appropriate pool of potential customers.

- *Do people go out to eat?:* This was a critical factor. If well-to-do beef-eaters did not go out to eat, these countries had to be removed from the target list.

- *Affinity for U.S. brands:* The name "Ruth's Chris" was uniquely American as was the Ruth Fertel story. Countries that were overtly anti-United States would be eliminated from—or at least pushed down—the target list. One measure of affinity could be the presence of existing U.S. restaurants and successful franchises.

WHAT SHOULD RUTH'S CHRIS DO NEXT?

Hannah had many years of experience in the restaurant franchising business, and thus had both personal preferences and good instincts about where Ruth's Chris should be looking for new markets. "Which markets should we enter first?" he thought to himself. Market entry was critical, but there were other issues too. Should franchising continue to be Ruth's Chris's exclusive international mode of entry? Were there opportunities for joint ventures or company-owned stores in certain markets? How could he identify and evaluate new potential franchisees? Was there an opportunity to find a global partner/brand with which to partner?

Hannah gathered information from several reliable U.S. government and related Web sites and created the table in Exhibit 4. He noted that many of his top prospects currently did not allow the importation of U.S. beef, but he felt that this was a political (rather than a cultural) variable and thus could change quickly under the right circumstances, especially with what he felt was the trend toward ever more free trade. He could not find any data on how often people went out to eat or a measure of their affinity toward U.S. brands. Maybe the success of U.S. casual dining restaurants in a country might be a good indicator of how its citizens felt toward U.S. restaurants. With his spreadsheet open, he went to work on the numbers and began contemplating the future global expansion of the company.

"If you've ever had a filet this good, welcome back."

Ruth Fertel, 1927–2002
Founder of Ruth's Chris Steak House

EXHIBIT 1 Fine Dining Steak Houses by Brand in the United States (2005)

Source: Ruth's Chris Steak House files.

Company Name	Number of Restaurants
Ruth's Chris	92
Morton's	66
Fleming's	32
Palm	28
Capital Grille	22
Shula's	16
Sullivan's	15
Smith & Wollensky	11
Del Frisco	6

EXHIBIT 2   Ruth's Chris Locations in the United States (2005)

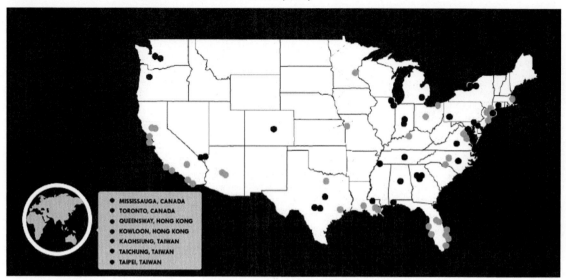

○ Company-owned

● Franchisee-owned

Source: Ruth's Chris Steak House files.

EXHIBIT 3   Meat Consumption per Capita* (in kilograms)

Region/Classification	2002	2001	2000	1999	1998	Growth Rate 1998–2002
World	39.7	38.8	38.6	38.0	37.7	5.31%
Asia (excluding Middle East)	27.8	26.9	26.6	25.7	25.4	9.45
Central America/Caribbean	46.9	45.7	44.8	42.9	41.3	13.56
Europe	74.3	72.5	70.5	70.6	73.1	1.64
Middle East/North Africa	25.7	25.7	26.0	25.1	24.7	4.05
North America	123.2	119.1	120.5	122.2	118.3	4.14
South America	69.7	68.4	69.1	67.6	64.2	8.57
Sub-Saharan Africa	13.0	12.9	13.1	12.8	12.6	3.17
Developed countries	80.0	78.0	77.2	77.3	77.6	3.09
Developing countries	28.9	28.1	28.0	27.1	26.6	8.65
High-income countries	93.5	91.9	92.0	92.2	90.9	2.86
Low-income countries	8.8	8.6	8.4	8.3	8.2	7.32
Middle-income countries	46.1	44.6	43.9	42.7	42.3	8.98

*World Resources Institute, "Meat Consumption: Per Capita (1984–2002)," retrieved on June 7, 2006 from http://earthtrends.wri.org/text/agriculture-food/variable-193.html.

EXHIBIT 4 Data Table

Country	Per Capita Beef Consumption (kg)	Population (1,000s)	Urbanization Rate (%)	Per Capita GDP (PPP in US$)
Argentina	97.6	39,921	90%	$13,100
Bahamas	123.6	303	89	20,200
Belgium	86.1	10,379	97	31,400
Brazil	82.4	188,078	83	8,400
Chile	66.4	16,134	87	11,300
China	52.4	1,313,973	39	6,800
Costa Rica	40.4	4,075	61	11,100
Czech Rep	77.3	10,235	74	19,500
France	101.1	60,876	76	29,900
Germany	82.1	82,422	88	30,400
Greece	78.7	10,688	61	22,200
Hungary	100.7	9,981	65	16,300
Ireland	106.3	4,062	60	41,000
Israel	97.1	6,352	92	24,600
Italy	90.4	58,133	67	29,200
Japan	43.9	127,463	65	31,500
Kuwait	60.2	2,418	96	19,200
Malaysia	50.9	24,385	64	12,100
Netherlands	89.3	16,491	66	30,500
Panama	54.5	3,191	57	7,200
Poland	78.1	38,536	62	13,300
Portugal	91.1	10,605	55	19,300
Russia	51	142,893	73	11,100
Singapore	71.1	4,492	100	28,100
South Africa	39	44,187	57	12,000
South Korea	48	48,846	80	20,400
Spain	118.6	40,397	77	25,500
Switzerland	72.9	7,523	68	32,300
Turkey	19.3	70,413	66	8,200
UAE/Dubai	74.4	2,602	85	43,400
U.K.	79.6	60,609	89	30,300
United States	124.8	298,444	80	41,800
Vietnam	28.6	84,402	26	2,800

Source: World Resources Institute, "Meat Consumption: Per Capita (1984–2002)," retrieved on June 7, 2006 from http://earthtrends.wri.org/text/agriculture-food/variable-193.html and World Bank Key Development Data & Statistics, http://web.worldbank.org/WBSITE/EXTERNAL/DATASTATISTICS/0,,contentMDK:20535285~menuPK:232599~pagePK:64133150~piPK:64133175~theSitePK:239419,00.html, retrieved on June 7, 2006.

Case

5

Coach Inc.: Is Its Advantage in Luxury Handbags Sustainable?

John E. Gamble *University of South Alabama*

In the six years following its October 2000 initial public offering (IPO), Coach Inc.'s net sales had grown at a compounded annual rate of 26 percent and its stock price had increased by 1,400 percent as a result of a strategy keyed to "accessible" luxury. Coach created the "accessible" luxury category in ladies' handbags and leather accessories by matching key luxury rivals on quality and styling, while beating them on price by 50 percent or more. Not only did Coach's $200–$500 handbags appeal to middle-income consumers wanting a taste of luxury, but affluent consumers with the means to spend $2,000 or more on a handbag regularly snapped up its products as well. By 2006, Coach had become the best-selling brand of ladies' luxury handbags and leather accessories in the United States with a 25 percent market share and was the second best-selling brand of such products in Japan with an 8 percent market share. Beyond its winning combination of styling, quality, and pricing, the attractiveness of Coach retail stores and the high levels of customer service provided by its employees contributed to its competitive advantage.

Much of the company's growth in net sales was attributable to its rapid growth in company-owned stores in the United States and Japan. Coach stores ranged from prominent flagship stores on Rodeo Drive and Madison Avenue to factory outlet stores. In fact, Coach's factory stores had achieved higher comparable store growth during 2005 and 2006 than its full-price stores. At year-end 2006, comparable store sales in Coach factory stores had increased by 31.9 percent since year-end 2005, while comparable store sales for Coach full price stores experienced a 12.3 percent year-over-year increase. In 2006, Coach products were sold in 218 full-price company-owned stores, 86 factory stores, 900 U.S. department stores, 118 locations in Japan, and 108 international locations outside Japan.

Going into 2007, the company's executives expected to sustain its impressive growth through monthly introductions of fresh new handbag designs and the addition of retail locations in the United States, Japan, and rapidly growing luxury goods markets in Asia. The company planned to add three to five factory stores per year to eventually reach 105

283

stores in the United States, add 30 full-price stores per year in the United States to reach 300, and add at least 10 stores per year in Japan to reach as many as 180 stores. The company also expected its licensed international distributors to open new locations in Hong Kong and mainland China. Other growth initiatives included strategic alliances to bring the Coach brand to such additional luxury categories as women's knitwear and fragrances. Only time would tell if Coach's growth could be sustained and its advantage would hold in the face of new accessible luxury lines recently launched by such industry elites as Giorgio Armani, Dolce & Gabbana, and Gianni Versace.

COMPANY HISTORY

Coach was founded in 1941 when Miles Cahn, a New York City leather artisan, began producing ladies' handbags. The handbags crafted by Cahn and his family in their SoHo loft were simple in style and extremely resilient to wear and tear. Coach's classic styling and sturdy construction proved popular with discriminating consumers and the company's initial line of 12 unlined leather bags soon developed a loyal following. Over the next 40 years, Coach was able to grow at a steady rate by setting prices about 50 percent lower than those of more luxurious brands, adding new models, and establishing accounts with retailers such as Bloomingdale's and Saks Fifth Avenue. The Cahn family also opened company-owned stores that sold Coach handbags and leather accessories. After 44 years of family management, Coach was sold to the diversified food and consumer goods producer, Sara Lee.

Sara Lee's 1985 acquisition of Coach left the handbag manufacturer's strategy and approach to operations more or less intact. The company continued to build a strong reputation for long-lasting, classic handbags. However, by the mid-1990s, the company's performance began to decline as consumers developed a stronger preference for stylish French and Italian designer brands such as Gucci, Prada, Louis Vuitton, Dolce & Gabbana, and Ferragamo. By 1995, annual sales growth in Coach's best-performing stores fell from 40 percent to 5 percent as the company's traditional leather bags fell out of favor with consumers.

In 1996, Sara Lee made 18-year Coach veteran Lew Frankfort head of its listless handbag division. Frankfort's first move was to hire Reed Krakoff, a top Tommy Hilfiger designer, as Coach's new creative director. Krakoff believed new products should be based upon market research rather than designers' instincts about what would sell. Under Krakoff, Coach conducted extensive consumer surveys and held focus groups to ask customers about styling, comfort, and functionality preferences. The company's research found consumers were looking for edgier styling, softer leathers, and leather-trimmed fabric handbags. Once prototypes had been developed by a team of designers, merchandisers, and sourcing specialists, hundreds of previous customers were asked to rate prototype designs against existing handbags. The prototypes that made it to production were then tested in selected Coach stores for six months before a launch was announced. The design process developed by Krakoff also allowed Coach to launch new collections every month. Prior to his arrival, Coach introduced only two collections per year.

Frankfort's turnaround plan also included a redesign of the company's flagship stores to complement Coach's contemporary new designs. Frankfort abandoned the stores' previous dark, wood paneled interiors in favor of minimalist architectural features that provided a bright and airy ambiance. The company also improved the appearance of its factory stores, which carried test models, discontinued models, and special lines that sold at discounts ranging from 15 percent to 50 percent. Such discounts were made possible by the company's policy of outsourcing production to 40 suppliers in 15 countries. The outsourcing agreements allowed Coach to maintain a sizeable pricing advantage relative to other luxury handbag brands in its full price stores as well. Handbags sold in Coach full-price stores ranged from $200–$500, which was well below the $700–$800 entry-level price charged by other luxury brands.

Coach's attractive pricing enabled it to appeal to consumers who would not normally consider luxury brands, while the quality and styling of its products were sufficient to satisfy traditional luxury consumers. In fact, a *Women's Wear Daily* survey found that Coach's quality, styling, and value mix was so powerful that affluent women in the United States ranked Coach ahead of much more expensive luxury brands such as Hermes, Ralph Lauren, Prada, and Fendi.[1] By 2000, the changes to Coach's strategy and operations allowed the brand to build a sizable lead in the "accessible luxury" segment of the leather handbags and accessories industry and made it a solid performer in Sara Lee's business lineup. With the turnaround successfully executed, Sara Lee management elected to spin off Coach through an IPO in October 2000 as part of a restructuring initiative designed to focus the corporation on food and beverages.

Coach Inc.'s performance proved to be stellar as an independent, public company. The company's annual sales had increased from $500 million in 1999 to more than $2.1 billion in 2006. Its earnings over the same timeframe improved from approximately $16.7 million to $494 million. By late 2006, Coach Inc.'s share price had increased nearly 15 times from the 2000 IPO price. Exhibit 1 presents income statements for Coach Inc. for fiscal 1999 through fiscal 2006. Its balance sheets for fiscal 2005 and fiscal 2006 are presented in Exhibit 2. Coach's market performance between its October 2000 IPO date and December 2006 is presented in Exhibit 3.

OVERVIEW OF THE GLOBAL LUXURY GOODS INDUSTRY IN 2006

The world's most well-to-do consumers spent more than $105 billion on luxury goods such as designer apparel, fine watches and writing instruments, jewelry, and select quality leather goods in 2005. The global luxury goods industry was expected to grow by 7 percent during 2006 to reach $112 billion. Italian luxury goods companies accounted for 27 percent of industry sales in 2005, while French luxury goods companies held a 22 percent share of the market, Swiss companies owned a 19 percent share, and U.S. companies accounted for 14 percent of the luxury goods industry.

Growth in the luxury goods industry had been attributed to increasing incomes and wealth in developing countries in Eastern Europe and Asia and changing buying habits in the United States. Although traditional luxury consumers in the United States ranked in the top 1 percent of wage earners with household incomes of $300,000 or better, a growing percentage of luxury goods consumers earned substantially less, but still aspired to own products with higher levels of quality and styling. The growing desire for luxury goods by middle-income consumers was thought to be a result of a wide range of factors, including effective advertising and television programming that glorified conspicuous consumption. The demanding day-to-day rigor of a two-income household was another suggested factor because it led middle-income consumers to reward themselves with luxuries.

An additional factor contributing to rising sales of luxury goods was the growth of big box discounters such as Wal-Mart and Target. Discounters' low prices on everyday items had facilitated a "Trade up, trade down"[2] shopping strategy, whereby consumers could buy necessities at very low prices and then splurge on indulgences ranging from premium vodka to $4,000 Viking stoves. The combined effect of such factors had allowed spending on luxury goods to grow at four times the rate of overall spending in the United States.

[1]"How Coach Got Hot," *Fortune,* 146, no. 8 (October 28, 2002).
[2]As quoted in "Stores Dancing Chic to Chic," *Houston Chronicle,* May 6, 2006.

EXHIBIT 1 Coach Inc.'s Consolidated Statements of Income, 1999–2006 (in thousands, except share amounts)

	2006	2005	2004	2003	2002	2001	2000	1999
Net sales	$2,111,501	$1,710,423	$1,321,106	$953,226	$719,403	$600,491	$537,694	$500,944
Cost of sales	472,622	399,652	331,024	275,797	236,041	218,507	220,085	226,190
Gross profit	1,638,879	1,310,771	990,082	677,429	483,362	381,984	317,609	274,754
Selling, general and administrative expenses	874,275	738,208	584,778	458,980	362,211	275,727	261,592	248,171
Reorganization costs	—	—	—	—	3,373	4,569	—	7,108
Operating income	764,604	572,563	405,304	218,449	117,778	101,688	56,017	19,475
Interest income (expense), net	32,623	15,760	3,192	1,059	(299)	(2,258)	(387)	(414)
Income before provision for income taxes and minority interest	797,227	588,323	408,496	219,508	117,479	99,430	55,630	19,061
Provision for income taxes	302,950	216,070	152,504	81,219	41,695	35,400	17,027	2,346
Minority interest, net of tax	—	13,641	18,043	7,608	184	—	—	—
Net income	$494,277	$358,612	$237,949	$130,681	$75,600	$64,030	$38,603	$16,715
Net income per share*								
Basic	$1.30	$0.95	$0.64	$0.36	$0.21	$0.20	$0.14	$0.06
Diluted	$1.27	$0.92	$0.62	$0.35	$0.21	$0.19	$0.14	$0.06
Shares used in computing net income per share:								
Basic	379,635	378,670	372,120	359,116	352,192	327,440	280,208	280,208
Diluted	388,495	390,191	385,558	371,684	363,808	337,000	280,208	280,208

*The two-for-one stock splits in April 2005, October 2003 and July 2002 have been retroactively applied to all prior periods.

Source: Coach Inc. 10-Ks.

EXHIBIT 2   Coach Inc.'s Balance Sheets, Fiscal 2005–Fiscal 2006 (in thousands)

ASSETS	July 1, 2006	July 2, 2005
Cash and cash equivalents	$143,388	$154,566
Short-term investments	394,177	228,485
Trade accounts receivable, less allowances of $6,000 and $4,124, respectively	84,361	65,399
Inventories	233,494	184,419
Deferred income taxes	78,019	50,820
Prepaid expenses and other current assets	41,043	25,671
Total current assets	974,482	709,360
Long-term investments		122,065
Property and equipment, net	298,531	203,862
Goodwill	227,811	238,711
Indefinite life intangibles	12,007	12,088
Deferred income taxes	84,077	54,545
Other noncurrent assets	29,612	29,526
Total assets	$1,626,520	$1,370,157
LIABILITIES AND STOCKHOLDERS' EQUITY		
Accounts payable	$79,819	$64,985
Accrued liabilities	261,835	188,234
Revolving credit facility		12,292
Current portion of long-term debt	170	150
Total current liabilities	341,824	265,661
Deferred income taxes	31,655	4,512
Long-term debt	3,100	3,270
Other liabilities	61,207	40,794
Total liabilities	$437,786	$314,237
Stockholders' equity		
Preferred stock: (authorized 25,000,000 shares; $0.01 par value) none issued		
Common stock: (authorized 1,000,000,000 shares; $0.01 par value) issued and outstanding 369,830,906 and 378,429,710 shares, respectively	$3,698	$3,784
Additional paid-in-capital	775,209	566,262
Retained earnings	417,087	484,971
Accumulated other comprehensive (loss) income	(7,260)	903
Total stockholders' equity	$1,188,734	$1,055,920
Total liabilities and stockholders' equity	$1,626,520	$1,370,157

Source: Coach Inc. 2006 10-K.

EXHIBIT 3 Performance of Coach Inc.'s Stock Price, 2000–2006

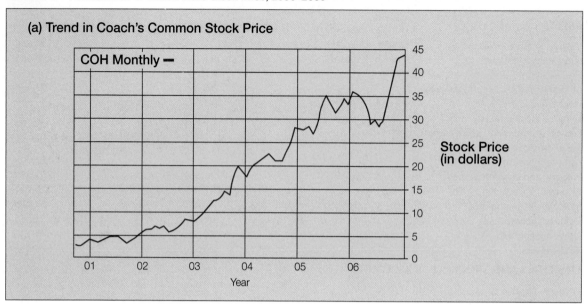

(a) Trend in Coach's Common Stock Price

COH Monthly —

Stock Price (in dollars)

Year

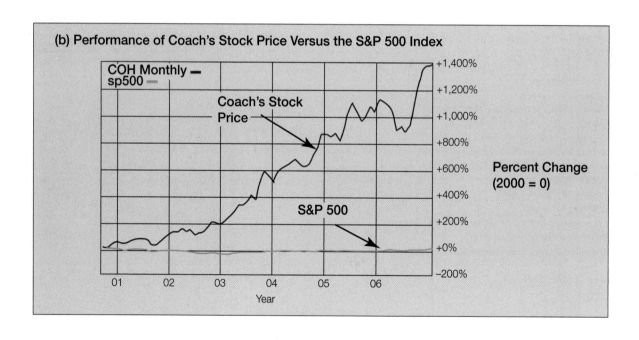

(b) Performance of Coach's Stock Price Versus the S&P 500 Index

COH Monthly —
sp500 —

Coach's Stock Price

S&P 500

Percent Change (2000 = 0)

Year

Both retailers and luxury goods manufacturers had altered their strategies in response to the changing buying preferences of middle-income consumers in the United States. Much of Target's success was linked to its merchandising strategy that focused on relationships with designers such as Philippe Starck, Todd Oldham, Michael Graves, and Isaac Mizrahi. Target's growth had not gone unnoticed by Wal-Mart, which in 2004 began to closely watch haute couture fashion trends for inspiration for new apparel lines. Wal-Mart hosted fashion shows in Manhattan and Miami's South Beach to launch its Metro 7 collection of women's apparel in fall 2005. Exsto was a designer-inspired menswear line that Wal-Mart introduced in summer 2006.

Wal-Mart also had begun to evaluate new store concepts that might appeal to upscale consumers. In 2006, the company was testing a stylish new Supercenter store in Plano, Texas, that stocked gourmet cheeses, organic produce, and 1,200 different wines. The new store also included a Wi-Fi coffee shop and a sushi bar. A Wal-Mart spokesperson explained the company's experimentation by commenting, "We've always been a top choice for the budget-minded customers. What we're trying to do now is expand our product line, and sell products more relevant to folks who are more discerning in their shopping."[3] Like Wal-Mart, other middle market retailers had altered their merchandising strategies to accommodate consumers' desires for luxury. During the 2006 Christmas shopping season, J. Crew offered $1,400 cashmere overcoats and Home Depot stocked $2,800 HDTVs for consumers looking for extraordinary gifts.

Manufacturers of the finest luxury goods sought to exploit middle-income consumers' desire for such products by launching "diffusion lines" that offered "affordable" or "accessible" luxury.[4] In 2006, most leading designer brands had developed subbrands that retained the styling and quality of the marquee brand, but sold at considerably more modest price points. For example, while Dolce & Gabbana dresses might sell at price points between $1,000 and $1,500, very similar appearing dresses under Dolce & Gabbana's "affordable luxury" brand—D&G—were priced at $400 to $600. Giorgio Armani's Emporio Armani line and Gianni Versace's Versus lines typically sold at price points about 50 percent less than similar-looking items carrying the marquee labels. Profit margins on marquee brands approximated 40 percent–50 percent, while most diffusion brands carried profit margins of about 20 percent. Luxury goods manufacturers believed diffusion brands' lower profit margins were offset by the growing size of the "accessible luxury" market and protected margins on such products by sourcing production to low-wage countries.

Growing Demand for Luxury Goods in Emerging Markets

In 2004, the worldwide total number of households with assets of at least $1 million increased by 7 percent to reach 8.3 million. The number of millionaires was expected to increase another 23 percent by 2009 to reach 10.2 million. With much of the increase in new wealth occurring in Asia and the Eastern Europe, demand for luxury goods in emerging markets was projected to grow at annual rates approaching 10 percent. Rising incomes and new wealth had allowed Chinese consumers to account for 11 percent of all luxury goods purchases in 2004. The Chinese market for luxury goods was predicted to increase to 24 percent of global revenues by 2014, which would make it the world's largest market for luxury goods. In 2006, a number of prestigious Western retailers such as Saks Fifth Avenue had opened retail stores in China to build a first mover advantage in the growing market. Similarly, most luxury goods companies had opened stores in China's largest cities with Louis Vuitton operating 12 stores in 10 cities in 2006.

---

[3]Ibid.

[4]"Some Fashion Houses Bolster Lower Priced Lines," *The Wall Street Journal,* September 25, 2006.

Luxury goods producers were also opening retail stores in India, which was another rapidly growing market for luxury goods. In 2005, approximately 50,000 households earned more than 10 million rupees (approximately $250,000) and were the backbone of India's $500 million luxury goods market. The number of households in India with annual incomes over 10 million rupees was expected to double by 2010. As of 2006, Versace, Louis Vuitton, Dior, Chanel, Hugo Boss, and Tommy Hilfiger had opened retail locations in India. Gucci and Giorgio Armani had announced plans to open flagship stores in India by 2008. LVMH, which was the parent company of Louis Vuitton, Givenchy, Fendi, and others, planned to expand its network of 50 stores in 18 Indian cities to 100 luxury stores in 23 cities by 2008.

Counterfeiting

In 2006, more than $500 billion worth of counterfeit goods were sold in countries throughout the world. European and American companies that produced highly sought after branded products were most vulnerable to counterfeiting, with fakes plaguing almost every industry. Fake Rolex watches or Ralph Lauren Polo shirts had long been a problem, but by the mid-2000s, counterfeiters were even making knockoffs of branded auto parts and prescription drugs. Counterfeiting had become so prevalent that the Global Congress on Combating Counterfeiting estimated that 9 percent of all goods sold worldwide were not genuine. The European Union's trade commission categorized the problem as "nothing short of an economic crisis."[5] Interpol believed in 2005 that terrorist organizations such as al Qaeda commonly used counterfeiting to fund their activities since fake brands were as profitable as drugs and because there was very little risk of being prosecuted if caught. About two-thirds of all counterfeit goods were produced by manufacturers in China.

One problem in combating counterfeiting was the demand for knockoffs. In the United States, China, and Europe, vendors and consumers who traded in outdoor street markets knowingly bought and sold fakes and had little reservations about doing so. Using Great Britain as an illustration of the problem, experts estimated that 100 million fake luxury goods were sold in Britain in 2005 and that one in eight adult Britons had purchased a fake in the past year. The European Union and the Chinese government took a step toward combating piracy in 2005 with the signing of an agreement that would fine owners of outdoor bazaars in China if vendors were caught selling counterfeit goods. In addition, the agreement called for landlords to terminate the lease of any vendor caught selling counterfeit goods a second time. The Chinese government convicted more than 5,500 individuals of intellectual property rights crimes in 2005. However, many piracy and counterfeiting experts believed the problem would not subside until the Chinese government adopted a zero tolerance policy against fakes.

COACH'S STRATEGY AND INDUSTRY POSITIONING

In 2006, Coach Inc. designed and marketed ladies handbags, leather accessories such as key fobs, belts, electronics accessories, and cosmetics cases, and outerwear such as gloves, hats, and scarves. Coach also designed and marketed leather business cases and luggage. The company entered into a licensing agreement with the Movado Group in 1998 to make Coach-branded watches available in Coach retail stores. Coach entered into a similar agreement with the Jimlar Corporation in 1999 that gave Jimlar the right to manufacture and market Coach-branded ladies footwear. In 2006, Coach footwear was available in 500

---

[5]As quoted in "Gumshoe's Intuition: Spotting Counterfeits at Port of Antwerp," *The Wall Street Journal*, December 14, 2006, A1.

locations in the United States, including department stores and Coach retail stores. Marchon Eyewear became a licensee for Coach branded eyewear and sunglasses in 2003. Coach sunglasses were sold in Coach retail stores, department stores, and specialty eyewear stores. Coach frames for prescription glasses were sold through Marchon's network of optical retailers.

Handbags accounted for 67 percent of Coach's 2006 sales, while women's accessories accounted for 23 percent of the company's sales, men's accessories accounted for 2 percent of sales, and outerwear made up 2 percent of 2006 net sales. Business cases and luggage each accounted for 1 percent of company 2006 revenues. Royalties from Coach's licensing agreements with Movado, Jimlar, and Marchon accounted for 1 percent, 2 percent, and 1 percent of the company's 2006 net sales, respectively.

Coach held a 25 percent share of the U.S. luxury handbag market and was the second best-selling brand of luxury handbags in Japan with an 8 percent market share. Through 2006, Coach had focused on Japan and the United States since those two countries ranked numbers 1 and 2, respectively, in global luxury goods spending. Coach's sales in Japan had increased from $144 million in 2002 to more than $420 million in 2006, while the company's market share in the United States had more than doubled from the 12 percent it held in 2002.

Approach to Differentiation

The market research design process developed by Executive Creative Director Reed Krakoff provided the basis of Coach's differentiated product line, but the company's procurement process that selected only the highest quality leathers and its sourcing agreements with quality offshore manufacturers were additional contributors to the company's reputation for high quality. Monthly product launches enhanced the company's voguish image and gave consumers reason to make purchases on a regular basis. The company's market research found its best customers visited a Coach store once every two months and made a purchase every seven months. In 2006, the average Coach customer purchased four handbags per year, which had doubled since 2002. Lew Frankfort said the increase was attributable to monthly product launches that "increase the frequency of consumer visits" and women's changing style preference of "using bags to complement their wardrobes in the same way they used to use shoes."[6] A retail analyst agreed with Frankfort's assessment of the importance of frequent product introductions, calling it "a huge driver of traffic and sales [that] has enabled them to capture the . . . customer who wants the newest items and fashions."[7] Seventy percent of Coach's 2006 sales came from products introduced within the fiscal year.

The aesthetic attractiveness of Coach's full price stores, which were designed by an in-house architectural group under the direction of Krakoff, further enhanced the company's luxury image. A 2006 survey of 2,000 wealthy shoppers by the Luxury Group ranked Coach store environments tenth among luxury brands. The surveyed shoppers found little differences among the 10 highest-rated store atmospheres, with number 1 Louis Vuitton scoring 88.1 out of 100, number 2 Hermes scoring 87.9, Armani and Gucci scoring 86, Versace, Ferragamo, and Prada all scoring 85, and Burberry and Coach tying at 84 out of 100.

Coach sought to make customer service experiences an additional differentiating aspect of the brand. Coach had agreed since its founding to refurbish or replace damaged handbags, regardless of the age of the bag. In 2006, the company provided store employees with regular customer service training programs and scheduled additional personnel during peak

[6]As quoted in "Fashions Keep Retailer Busy," *Investor's Business Daily*, February 10, 2005, p. A4.
[7]Ibid.

shopping periods to ensure that all customers were attended to satisfactorily. Through the company's Special Request service, customers were allowed to order merchandise for home delivery if the particular handbag or color wasn't available during a visit to a Coach store.

Retail Distribution

Coach channels of distribution included direct-to-consumer channels and indirect channels. Direct-to-consumer channels included full price stores in the United States, factory stores in the United States, Internet sales, catalog sales, and stores in Japan. Wholesale accounts with department stores in the United States and in international markets outside Japan represented the company's indirect sales. Exhibit 4 provides selected financial data for Coach Inc. by channel of distribution.

EXHIBIT 4   Selected Financial Data for Coach Inc. by Channel of Distribution, Fiscal 2004–Fiscal 2006 (in thousands)

FISCAL 2006

	Direct-to-Consumer	Indirect	Corporate Unallocated*	Total
Net sales	$1,610,691	$500,810		$2,111,501
Operating income (loss)	717,326	313,689	(266,411)	764,604
Income (loss) before provision for income taxes and minority interest	717,326	313,689	(233,788)	797,227
Depreciation and amortization expense	43,177	5,506	16,432	65,115
Total assets	$743,034	$91,247	792,239	$1,626,520
Additions to long-lived assets	$70,440	$6,036	57,400	$133,876

FISCAL 2005

	Direct-to-Consumer	Indirect	Corporate Unallocated*	Total
Net sales	$1,307,425	$402,998		$1,710,423
Operating income (loss)	548,520	243,276	(219,233)	572,563
Income (loss) before provision for income taxes and minority interest	548,520	243,276	(203,473)	588,323
Depreciation and amortization expense	37,275	4,362	8,763	50,400
Total assets	$646,788	$69,569	$653,800	$1,370,157
Additions to long-lived assets	$70,801	$4,778	$19,013	$94,592

FISCAL 2004

	Direct-to-Consumer	Indirect	Corporate Unallocated*	Total
Net sales	$1,002,737	$318,369		$1,321,106
Operating income (loss)	403,884	178,390	(176,970)	405,304
Income (loss) before provision for income taxes and minority interest	403,884	178,390	(173,778)	408,496
Depreciation and amortization expense	30,054	3,509	6,537	40,100
Total assets	$328,530	$64,770	$666,979	$1,060,279
Additions to long-lived assets	$57,589	$3,884	$12,186	$73,659

Breakdown of Coach Inc.'s Unallocated Corporate Expenses, 2004–2006 (in thousands)

	Fiscal Year Ended		
	July 1, 2006	July 2, 2005	July 3, 2004
Production variances	$14,659	$11,028	$12,581
Advertising, marketing and design	(91,443)	(70,234)	(56,714)
Administration and information systems	(148,846)	(125,217)	(102,682)
Distribution and customer service	(40,781)	(34,810)	(30,155)
Total corporate unallocated	($266,411)	($219,233)	($176,970)

Source: Coach Inc. 2006 10-K.

In the United States, Coach products could be found in approximately 900 department stores, 218 Coach full price stores, and 86 Coach factory outlet stores. U.S. consumers could also order Coach products through either the company's Web site or its printed catalog. The company mailed about 4.1 million catalogs to strategically selected households in the United States during 2006 and placed another 3.5 million catalogs in Coach retail stores for customers to pick up during a store visit. Sales from catalogs were incidental since the catalogs were primarily used to build brand awareness, promote store traffic, and help shoppers evaluate styles before visiting a Coach retail store. Coach's Web site accomplished the same goals as its catalogs, but had become a significant contributor to overall sales. In 2006, the Web site had 40 million unique visitors and generated $54 million in net sales. The company also sent promotional e-mails to 55 million selected customers in 2006.

Full Price Stores

Coach's full price U.S. retail stores accounted for 54 percent of Coach's 2006 net sales. Beginning in 2003, full price stores were divided into three categories—core locations, fashion locations, and flagship stores. Under Coach's tiered merchandising strategy, the company's flagship stores carried the most sophisticated and highest-priced items, while core stores carried widely demanded lines. The company's fashion locations tended to stock a blend of Coach's best-selling lines and chic specialty bags. By 2006, the company had successfully graduated many core locations to fashion locations. Management believed Coach had remaining opportunities in the United States to move core stores to fashion stores and fashion stores to flagship stores.

Coach's site selection process placed its core and fashion stores in upscale shopping centers and downtown shopping areas, while flagship stores were restricted to high-profile fashion districts in cities such as New York, Chicago, Beverly Hills, and San Francisco. Even though flagship stores were "a beacon for the brand"[8] as Frankfort described them, the company had been very prudent in the number of flagship stores it operated since such stores, by definition, were required to be located on the world's most expensive parcels of real estate.

Factory Stores

Coach's factory stores in the United States were generally located 50 or more miles from its full price stores and made up about 19 percent of the company's 2006 net sales. About 75 percent of factory store inventory was produced specifically for Coach's factory stores, while the remaining 25 percent was made up of overstocked items and discontinued models. Coach's 10 percent to 50 percent discounts offered in factory stores allowed the company to maintain a year-round full-price policy in full price stores. Coach CEO Lew Frankfort believed discounted prices were critical to success in retailing since 80 percent of women's apparel sold in the United States was bought on sale or in a discount store. "Women in the U.S. have been trained to expect to be able to find a bargain if they either go through the hunt . . . or are willing to buy something after the season," said Frankfort.[9]

Coach had found that there was very little overlap between shoppers in full-price stores and factory stores. The company's market research found the typical full-price store shopper was a 35-year-old, college-educated, single or newly married working woman. The typical factory store shopper was a 45-year-old, college-educated, married, professional woman with children. The average annual spending in a Coach store by full-price shoppers was $1,100. Factory store shoppers spent about $770 annually on Coach products, with 80 percent spent in factory stores and 20 percent spent in a full-price store. The 80:20 ratio of spending also

---

[8]As quoted in "Coach's Split Personality," *BusinessWeek*, November 7, 2005.
[9]As quoted in "Coach Sales Strategy Is in the Bag," *Financial Times*, April 18, 2006, p. 22.

applied to full-price store customers. A retail analyst characterized the difference between the two types of Coach customers as "one wants fashion first and the other is a discount shopper. . . . There is no question it is a very different mindset."[10] Coach had found that its full-price customers and factory store customers were equally brand loyal.

Coach's factory stores had outperformed full-price stores in terms of comparable store sales growth during 2005 and 2006, with comparable factory store sales increasing by 31.9 percent during 2006 and comparable full price store sales increasing by 12.3 percent during the year. The company's impressive overall growth in comparable store sales was attributable, to some degree, to its policy of charting sales for every store and every type of merchandise on a daily basis. During holiday shopping periods, management received sales updates two or three times per day. The frequent updates allowed management to shift production to the hottest selling items to avoid stockouts.

The company's top-performing factory store during 2005 was its Woodbury Common outlet store located about 50 miles outside New York City. The store's 2005 sales of $20 million and estimated 2006 sales of $25 million made it as productive as the company's Madison Avenue flagship store. Some degree of Coach's success with its outlet stores resulted from its strategy that valued factory stores as much as full-price stores. The company was committed to providing factory store customers with service and quality equal to that provided to full-price customers. A May 2006 *Consumer Reports* review of outlet stores rated Coach number 1 in terms of merchandise quality and customer service.

At year-end 2006, Lew Frankfort stated that the company would add three to five factory stores per year until it reached 105 and 30 full-price stores per year to reach 300. Long-term, Frankfort believed North America could support 400 full-price Coach stores. Frankfort did not want factory outlet stores to grow too rapidly since "Our destiny lies in our ability to grow full-price stores."[11] Some analysts were worried that Coach's highly successful factory stores might someday dilute its image. A Luxury Institute analyst described the dilemma faced by Coach and luxury diffusion brands by commenting "To be unique and exclusive you cannot be ubiquitous."[12] Exhibit 5 shows Coach's growth in retail stores by type and geographic region between 2001 and 2006.

U.S. Wholesale

Wholesale sales of Coach products to U.S. department stores increased by 23 percent during 2006 to reach $232 million. Department stores were becoming less relevant in U.S. retailing with the average consumer spending less time in malls and shopping in fewer stores during visits to malls. The share of the U.S. retail market held by department stores declined from about 30 percent in 1990 to approximately 20 percent in 2000. However, handbags and accessories remained a better performing product category for such retailers. Coach had eliminated 500 department store accounts between 2002 and 2006. Macy's, Bloomingdale's, Lord and Taylor, Marshall Fields, Filene's, Dillards, Nordstrom, Saks Fifth Avenue, and Parisian were the highest-volume department store sellers of Coach merchandise in 2006.

International Markets

International Wholesale

Coach's wholesale distribution in international markets involved department stores, free-standing retail locations, shop-in-shop locations, and specialty retailers in 18 countries. The company's largest international wholesale accounts were the DFS Group,

---

[10]Ibid.

[11]As quoted in "Coach's Split Personality."

[12]As quoted in "Expansion into U.S.: Extending the Reach of the Exclusive Lifestyle Brands," *Financial Times*, July 8, 2006, p. 17.

EXHIBIT 5   Coach Inc.'s Retail Stores by Geographic Region, Fiscal 2001–Fiscal 2006

NORTH AMERICA

	2006	2005	2004	2003	2002	2001
Full-price company-owned stores	218	193	174	156	138	121
Net increase vs. prior year	25	19	18	18	17	15
Percentage increase vs. prior year	11.5%	9.8%	10.3%	11.5%	12.3%	12.4%
Retail square footage	562,553	490,925	431,617	363,310	301,501	251,136
Net increase vs. prior year	71,628	59,308	68,307	61,809	50,365	42,077
Percentage increase vs. prior year	12.7%	12.1%	15.8%	17.0%	16.7%	16.8%
Average square footage	2,581	2,544	2,481	2,329	2,185	2,076
Factory stores	86	82	76	76	74	68
Net increase vs. prior year	4	6	0	2	6	5
Percentage increase vs. prior year	4.7%	7.3%	0.0%	2.6%	8.1%	7.4%
Factory square footage	281,787	252,279	231,355	232,898	219,507	198,924
Net increase vs. prior year	29,508	20,924	(1,543)	13,391	20,583	16,414
Percentage increase vs. prior year	10.5%	8.3%	(0)	5.7%	9.4%	8.3%
Average square footage	3,277	3,077	3,044	3,064	2,966	2,925

COACH JAPAN

	2006	2005	2004	2003	2002	2001
Total locations	118	103	100	93	83	76
Net increase vs. prior year	15	3	7	10	7	6
Percentage increase vs. prior year	12.7%	2.9%	7.0%	10.8%	8.4%	7.9%
Total square footage	194,375	161,632	119,291	102,242	76,975	63,371
Net increase vs. prior year	32,743	42,341	17,049	25,267	13,604	7,229
Percentage increase vs. prior year	16.8%	26.2%	14.3%	24.7%	17.7%	11.4%
Average square footage	1,647	1,569	1,193	1,099	927	834

OTHER INTERNATIONAL

	2006	2005	2004	2003	2002	2001
International freestanding stores	21	14	18	n.a.	n.a.	n.a.
International department store locations	63	58	70	n.a.	n.a.	n.a.
Other international locations	24	22	27	n.a.	n.a.	n.a.
Total international wholesale locations	108	94	115	n.a.	n.a.	n.a.

n.a. Not available
Source: Coach Inc. 10-Ks.

EXHIBIT 6 Coach Inc.'s Net Sales and Assets by Geographic Region, Fiscal 2004–Fiscal 2006 (in thousands)

Source: Coach Inc. 2006 10-K.

	United States	Japan	Other International	Total
FISCAL 2006				
Net sales	$1,574,285	$420,509	$116,707	$2,111,501
Long-lived assets	266,190	298,087	3,684	567,961
FISCAL 2005				
Net sales	$1,253,170	$372,326	$84,927	$1,710,423
Long-lived assets	314,919	288,338	2,995	606,252
FISCAL 2004				
Net sales	$982,668	$278,011	$60,427	1,321,106
Long-lived assets	280,938	55,487	2,384	338,809

Lotte Group, Shila Group, Tasa Meng Corporation, and Imaginex. The largest portion of sales by these companies was to traveling Japanese consumers. Coach's largest wholesale country markets were Korea, Hong Kong, Taiwan, Singapore, Japan, Saudi Arabia, Australia, Mexico, Thailand, Malaysia, the Caribbean, China, New Zealand, and France. In 2006, international wholesale accounts amounted to $147 million.

Coach Japan

Coach products in Japan were sold in shop-in-shop department store locations, full-price Coach stores, and Coach factory stores. The company had 118 retail locations in Japan in 2006 although company managers believed Japan could support as many as 180 retail outlets. Coach's expansion plan for Japan called for at least 10 new stores annually, which would more than double its number of flagship stores to 15. Coach management believed the increase in stores would allow the company to increase its market share in Japan to 15 percent. The number of Coach retail locations in Japan and other international markets for 2001 through 2006 is presented in Exhibit 5. Coach Inc.'s sales and assets by geographic region are provided in Exhibit 6.

COACH'S STRATEGIC OPTIONS IN 2007

Going into 2007, Lew Frankfort's key growth initiatives involved store expansion in the United States, Japan, Hong Kong, and mainland China, increasing sales to existing customers to drive comparable store growth, and creating alliances to exploit the Coach brand in additional luxury categories. The company's managers believed there was an opportunity to double the number of full-price retail stores in North America and increase the number of North American factory stores by a third. Also the company believed Japan could support approximately 70 additional Coach stores. Licensed distributors in Hong Kong operated 13 locations there and planned to open at least 10 locations on mainland China by 2007.

The company's second growth initiative was to increase same-store sales through continued development of new styles, the development of new usage collections, and the exploitation of gift-giving opportunities. The company had recently begun to prewrap items during holiday shopping periods and had created a new section of its Web site for gift-givers. Coach.com's gift guide recommended items that might appeal to women based upon their needs. For example, the Web site recommended handbags preferred by professional women, handbags for formal events, items for fashion-oriented teens, and essential handbags.

During late 2006, Coach launched a women's knitwear collection through a strategic alliance with Lutz & Patmos. The leather and fur trimmed cashmere and wool knits ranged from $300 to $1,500. The company also entered into an agreement with a division of the Estee Lauder Company for the development of a fragrance that would be sold in Coach stores beginning in spring 2007.

For the first quarter of fiscal 2007, Coach's comparable store sales for full price stores increased by 16 percent relative to the same period in 2006. Coach factory stores achieved year-over-year comparable store sales growth of 27.1 percent. The company's indirect sales improved by 11 percent between the first quarter of 2006 and the first quarter of fiscal 2007. Operating income during the first quarter of 2007 increased by 36 percent, while operating margins improved by 340 basis points to reach 35.7 percent. Lew Frankfort attributed the company's continuing sales and profit growth to 19 new store openings in the United States, new handbag collections such as Coach Signature Stripe, Chelsea, Hamptons silhouettes, and Legacy lifestyle, and the increased assortment of gifts under $100 geared to price-sensitive holiday shoppers. The company's stock provided nearly a 35 percent return to shareholders during the 2006 calendar year. The challenge for Lew Frankfort and other key Coach executives was to defend against competitive attack from French and Italian luxury goods makers and sustain the impressive growth rate the company had achieved since its 2000 IPO.

Case

6

Panera Bread Company

Arthur A. Thompson, Jr. *University of Alabama*

As Panera Bread Company headed into 2007, it was continuing to expand its market presence swiftly. The company's strategic intent was to make great bread broadly available to consumers across the United States. It had opened 155 new company-owned and franchised bakery-cafés in 2006, bringing its total to 1,027 units in 36 states. Plans were in place to open another 170 to 180 café locations in 2007 and to have nearly 2,000 Panera Bread bakery-cafés open by the end of 2010. Management was confident that Panera Bread's attractive menu and the dining ambience of its bakery-cafés provided significant growth opportunity, despite the fiercely competitive nature of the restaurant industry.

Already Panera Bread was widely recognized as the nationwide leader in the specialty bread segment. In 2003, Panera Bread scored the highest level of customer loyalty among quick-casual restaurants, according to a study conducted by TNS Intersearch.[1] J. D. Power and Associates' 2004 restaurant satisfaction study of 55,000 customers ranked Panera Bread highest among quick-service restaurants in the Midwest and Northeast regions of the United States in all categories, which included environment, meal, service, and cost. In 2005, for the fourth consecutive year, Panera Bread was rated among the best of 121 competitors in the Sandleman & Associates national customer satisfaction survey of more than 62,000 consumers. Panera Bread had also won "best of" awards in nearly every market across 36 states.

COMPANY BACKGROUND

In 1981, Louis Kane and Ron Shaich founded a bakery-café enterprise named Au Bon Pain Company Inc. Units were opened in malls, shopping centers, and airports along the East Coast of the United States and internationally throughout the 1980s and 1990s; the company prospered and became the dominant operator within the bakery-café category. In 1993, Au Bon Pain Company purchased Saint Louis Bread Company, a chain of 20 bakery-cafés located in the St. Louis, Missouri, area. Ron Shaich and a team of Au Bon Pain managers then spent considerable time in 1994 and 1995 traveling the country and studying the market for fast-food and quick-service meals. They concluded that many patrons of fast-food chains like McDonald's, Wendy's, Burger King, Subway, Taco Bell, Pizza Hut, and

[1]According to information in Panera Bread's press kit; the results of the study were reported in a 2003 *Wall Street Journal* article.

KFC could be attracted to a higher-quality, quick-dining experience. Top management at Au Bon Pain then instituted a comprehensive overhaul of the newly acquired Saint Louis Bread locations, altering the menu and the dining atmosphere. The vision was to create a specialty café anchored by an authentic, fresh-dough artisan bakery and upscale quick-service menu selections. Between 1993 and 1997, average unit volumes at the revamped Saint Louis Bread units increased by 75 percent, and over 100 additional Saint Louis Bread units were opened. In 1997, the Saint Louis Bread bakery-cafés were renamed Panera Bread in all markets outside St. Louis.

By 1998, it was clear that the reconceived Panera Bread units had connected with consumers. Au Bon Pain management concluded the Panera Bread format had broad market appeal and could be rolled out nationwide. Ron Shaich believed that Panera Bread had the potential to become one of the leading fast-casual restaurant chains in the nation. Shaich also believed that growing Panera Bread into a national chain required significantly more management attention and financial resources than the company could marshal if it continued to pursue expansion of both the Au Bon Pain and Panera Bread chains. He convinced Au Bon Pain's board of directors that the best course of action was for the company to go exclusively with the Panera Bread concept and divest the Au Bon Pain cafés. In August 1998, the company announced the sale of its Au Bon Pain bakery-café division for $73 million in cash to ABP Corporation; the transaction was completed in May 1999. With the sale of the Au Bon Pain division, the company changed its name to Panera Bread Company. The restructured company had 180 Saint Louis Bread and Panera Bread bakery-cafés and a debt-free balance sheet.

Between January 1999 and December 2006, close to 850 additional Panera Bread bakery-cafés were opened, some company-owned and some franchised. Panera Bread reported sales of $829.0 million and net income of $58.8 million in 2006. Sales at franchise-operated Panera Bread bakery-cafés totaled $1.2 billion in 2006. A summary of Panera Bread's recent financial performance is shown in Exhibit 1.

THE PANERA BREAD CONCEPT AND STRATEGY

The driving concept behind Panera Bread was to provide a premium specialty bakery and café experience to urban workers and suburban dwellers. Its artisan sourdough breads made with a craftsman's attention to quality and detail and its award-winning bakery expertise formed the core of the menu offerings. Panera Bread specialized in fresh baked goods, made-to-order sandwiches on freshly baked breads, soups, salads, custom roasted coffees, and other café beverages. Panera's target market was urban workers and suburban dwellers looking for a quick-service meal and a more aesthetically pleasing dining experience than that offered by traditional fast-food restaurants.

In his letter to shareholders in the company's 2005 annual report, Panera chairman and CEO Ron Shaich said:

> We think our continued commitment to providing crave-able food that people trust, served in a warm, community gathering place by associates who make our guests feel comfortable, really matters. When this is rooted in our commitment to the traditions of hand-crafted, artisan bread, something special is created. As we say here at Panera, it's our Product, Environment, and Great Service (PEGS) that we count on to deliver our success—year in and year out.

Panera Bread's distinctive menu, signature café design, inviting ambience, operating systems, and unit location strategy allowed it to compete successfully in five submarkets of the food-away-from-home industry: breakfast, lunch, daytime "chill out" (the time between breakfast and lunch and between lunch and dinner when customers visited its bakery-cafés

EXHIBIT 1   Selected Consolidated Financial Data for Panera Bread, 2002–2006 ($ in millions, except for per share amounts)

	2006	2005	2004	2003	2002
INCOME STATEMENT DATA					
Revenues:					
Bakery-café sales	$666,141	$499,422	$362,121	$265,933	$212,645
Franchise royalties and fees	61,531	54,309	44,449	36,245	27,892
Fresh dough sales to franchisees	101,299	86,544	72,569	61,524	41,688
Total revenues	828,971	640,275	479,139	363,702	282,225
Bakery café expenses:					
Food and paper products	197,182	142,675	101,832	73,885	63,370
Labor	204,956	151,524	110,790	81,152	63,172
Occupancy	48,602	37,389	26,730	18,981	15,408
Other operating expenses	92,176	70,003	51,044	36,804	27,971
Total bakery café expenses	542,916	401,591	290,396	210,822	169,921
Fresh dough costs of sales to franchisees	85,618	75,036	65,627	54,967	38,432
Depreciation and amortization	44,166	33,011	25,298	18,304	13,794
General and administrative expenses	59,306	46,301	33,338	28,140	24,986
Preopening expenses	6,173	3,241	2,642	1,531	1,051
Total costs and expenses	738,179	559,180	417,301	313,764	248,184
Operating profit	90,792	81,095	61,838	49,938	34,041
Interest expense	92	50	18	48	32
Other (income) expense, net	(1,976)	(1,133)	1,065	1,592	467
Provision for income taxes	33,827	29,995	22,175	17,629	12,242
Net income	$ 58,849	$ 52,183	$ 38,430*	$ 30,669	$ 21,300
Earnings per share					
Basic	$1.88	$1.69	$1.28	$1.02	$0.74
Diluted	1.84	1.65	1.25	1.00	0.71
Weighted average shares outstanding					
Basic	31,313	30,871	30,154	29,733	28,923
Diluted	32,044	31,651	30,768	30,423	29,891
BALANCE-SHEET DATA					
Cash and cash equivalents	$ 52,097	$ 24,451	$ 29,639	$ 42,402	$ 29,924
Investments in government securities	20,025	46,308	28,415	9,019	9,149
Current assets	127,618	102,774	58,220	70,871	59,262
Total assets	542,609	437,667	324,672	256,835	195,431
Current liabilities	109,610	86,865	55,705	44,792	32,325
Total liabilities	144,943	120,689	83,309	46,235	32,587
Stockholders' equity	397,666	316,978	241,363	193,805	151,503
CASH FLOW DATA					
Net cash provided by operating activities	$104,895	$110,628	$ 84,284	$ 73,102	$ 46,323
Net cash used in investing activities	(90,917)	(129,640)	(102,291)	(66,856)	(40,115)
Net cash provided by financing activities	13,668	13,824	5,244	6,232	5,664
Net (decrease) increase in cash and cash equivalents	27,646	(5,188)	(12,763)	12,478	11,872

*After adjustment of $239,000 for cumulative effect of accounting change.
Sources: 2006 10-K report, pp. 36–38; 2005 10-K report, pp. 16–17; 2003 10-K report, pp. 29–31; and company press release, February 8, 2007.

to take a break from their daily activities), light evening fare for eat-in or take-out, and take-home bread. In 2006, Panera began enhancing its menu in ways that would attract more diners during the evening meal hours. Management's long-term objective and strategic intent was to make Panera Bread a nationally recognized brand name and to be the dominant

EXHIBIT 2   Selected Operating Statistics, Panera Bread Company, 2000–2006

	2006	2005	2004	2003	2002	2001	2000
Revenues at company-operated stores (in millions)	$ 666.1	$ 499.4	$ 362.1	$ 265.9	$ 212.6	$ 157.7	$ 125.5
Revenues at franchised stores (in millions)	$1,245.5	$1,097.2	$ 879.1	$ 711.0	$ 542.6	$ 371.7	$ 199.4
Systemwide store revenues (in millions)	$1,911.6	$1,596.6	$1,241.2	$ 976.9	$ 755.2	$ 529.4	$ 324.9
Average annualized revenues per company-operated bakery-café (in millions)	$ 1.967	$ 1.942	$ 1.852	$ 1.830	$ 1.764	$ 1.636	$ 1.473
Average annualized revenues per franchised bakery-café (in millions)	$ 2.074	$ 2.016	$ 1.881	$ 1.860	$ 1.872	$ 1.800	$ 1.707
Average weekly sales, company-owned cafés	$ 37.833	$ 37,348	$ 35,620	$35,198	$33,924	$31,460	$28,325
Average weekly sales, franchised cafés	$ 39,894	$ 38,777	$ 36,171	$35,777	$35,997	$34,607	$32.832
Comparable bakery-café sales percentage increases*							
Company-owned	3.9%	7.4%	2.9%	1.7%	4.1%	5.8%	8.1%
Franchised	4.1%	8.0%	2.6%	(0.4)%	6.1%	5.8%	10.3%
Systemwide	4.1%	7.8%	2.7%	0.2%	5.5%	5.8%	9.1%
Company-owned bakery-cafés open at year-end	391	311	226	173	132	110	90
Franchised bakery-cafés open at year-end	636	566	515	429	346	259	172
Total bakery-cafés open	1,027	877	741	602	478	369	262

*The percentages for comparable store sales are based on annual changes at stores open at least 18 months.
Sources: Company 10-K reports 2000, 2001, 2003, 2005, and 2006; company press releases, January 4, 2007, and February 8, 2007.

restaurant operator in the specialty bakery-café segment. According to Scott Davis, Panera's senior vice president and chief concept officer, the company was trying to succeed by "being better than the guys across the street" and making the experience of dining at Panera so attractive that customers would be willing to pass by the outlets of other fast-casual restaurant competitors to dine at a nearby Panera Bread bakery-café.[2] Davis maintained that the question about Panera Bread's future was not *if* it would be successful but *by how much*.

Management believed that its concept afforded growth potential in suburban markets sufficient to expand the number of Panera Bread locations by 17 percent annually through 2010 (see Exhibits 3 and 4) and to achieve earnings per share growth of 25 percent annually. Panera Bread's growth strategy was to capitalize on Panera's market potential by opening both company-owned and franchised Panera Bread locations as fast as was prudent. So far, franchising had been a key component of the company's efforts to broaden its market penetration. Panera Bread had organized its business around company-owned bakery-café operations, the franchise operations, and fresh dough operations; the fresh bread unit supplied dough to all Panera Bread stores, both company-owned and franchised.

[2]As stated in a presentation to securities analysts, May 5, 2006.

EXHIBIT 3   Areas of High and Low Market Penetration of Panera Bread Bakery-Cafés, 2006

High Penetration Markets			Low Penetration Markets		
Area	Number of Panera Bread Units	Population per Bakery-Café	Area	Number of Panera Bread Units	Population per Bakery-Café
St. Louis	40	67,000	Los Angeles	17	1,183,000
Columbus, OH	19	83,000	Miami	2	1,126,000
Jacksonville	12	98,000	Northern California	10	1,110,000
Omaha	12	101,000	Seattle	5	860,000
Cincinnati	26	108,000	Dallas/Fort Worth	10	590,000
Pittsburgh	25	142,000	Houston	12	335,000
Washington, D.C./Northern Virginia	26	152,000	Philadelphia	25	278,000

UNTAPPED MARKETS

New York City	Phoenix	Austin
Salt Lake City	Tucson	San Antonio
Memphis	District of Columbia	Green Bay/Appleton
New Orleans	Spokane	Shreveport
Atlantic City	Baton Rouge	Toronto
Albuquerque	Little Rock	Vancouver

Source: Panera Bread management presentation to securities analysts, May 5, 2006.

EXHIBIT 4   Comparative U.S. Market Penetration of Selected Restaurant Chains, 2006

Restaurant Chain	Number of Locations	Population per Location
Subway	19,965	15,000
McDonald's	13,727	22,000
Starbucks Coffee	7,700	39,000
Applebee's	1,800	166,000
Panera Bread	910	330,000

Note: Management believed that a 17 percent annual rate of expansion of Panera Bread locations through 2010 would result in 1 café per 160,000 people.
Source: Panera Bread management presentation to securities analysts, May 5, 2006.

PANERA BREAD'S PRODUCT OFFERINGS AND MENU

Panera Bread's signature product was artisan bread made from four ingredients—water, natural yeast, flour, and salt; no preservatives or chemicals were used. Carefully trained bakers shaped every step of the process, from mixing the ingredients, to kneading the dough, to placing the loaves on hot stone slabs to bake in a traditional European-style stone deck bakery oven. Exhibit 5 shows Panera's lineup of breads.

The Panera Bread menu was designed to provide target customers with products built on the company's bakery expertise, particularly its 20-plus varieties of bread baked fresh throughout the day at each café location. The key menu groups were fresh baked goods, made-to-order sandwiches and salads, soups, light entrées, and café beverages. Exhibit 6 shows a sampling of the items on a typical Panera Bread menu.

The menu offerings were regularly reviewed and revised to sustain the interest of regular customers, satisfy changing consumer preferences, and be responsive to various seasons of the year. The soup lineup, for example, changed seasonally. Product development was

EXHIBIT 5   Panera's Lineup of Bread Varieties, 2006

Sourdough

Panera's signature sourdough bread that featured a golden, crackled crust and firm, moderately structured crumb with a satisfying, tangy flavor. *Available in Baguette, Loaf, XL Loaf, Roll and Bread Bowl.*

Asiago Cheese

Chunks of Asiago cheese were added to the standard sourdough recipe and baked right in, with more Asiago cheese sprinkled on top. *Available in Demi and Loaf.*

Focaccia

A traditional Italian flatbread made with Panera's artisan starter dough, olive oil, and chunks of Asiago cheese. *Available in three varieties—Asiago Cheese, Rosemary & Onion and Basil Pesto.*

Nine Grain

Made with cracked whole wheat, rye, corn meal, oats, rice flour, soy grits, barley flakes, millet, and flaxseed plus molasses for a semisweet taste. *Available in Loaf.*

Tomato Basil

A sourdough-based bread made with tomatoes and basil, topped with sweet walnut streusel. *Available in XL Loaf.*

Cinnamon Raisin

A light raisin bread with a swirl of cinnamon, sugar and molasses. *Available in Loaf.*

Artisan Sesame Semolina

Made with enriched durum and semolina flours to create a golden yellow crumb, topped with sesame seeds. *Available in Loaf and Miche.*

Artisan Multigrain

Nine grains and sesame, poppy and fennel seeds blended with molasses, topped with rolled oats. *Available in Loaf.*

Artisan French

Made with Panera's artisan starter to create a nutty flavor with a wine-like aroma. *Available in Baguette and Miche.*

Whole Grain

A moist, hearty mixture of whole spelt flour, millet, flaxseed and other wheat flours and grains, sweetened with honey and topped with rolled oats. *Available in Loaf, Miche and Baguette.*

White Whole Grain

A new bread created especially for Panera Kids sandwiches; a sweeter alternative to the whole grain bread with a thin, caramelized crust sweetened with honey and molasses. *Available in Loaf.*

French

A classic French bread characterized by a thin, crackly crust, slightly sweet taste and a lighter crumb than our sourdough. *Available in Baguette, Loaf, XL Loaf and Roll.*

Ciabatta

A flat, oval-shaped loaf with a delicate flavor and soft texture; made with Panera's artisan starter and a touch of olive oil. *Available in Loaf.*

Honey Wheat

A mild wheat bread with tastes of honey and molasses; the soft crust and crumb made it great for sandwiches. *Available in Loaf.*

Rye

Special nature leavening, unbleached flour, and chopped rye kernels were used to create a delicate rye flavor. *Available in Loaf.*

Sunflower

Made with honey, lemon peel, and raw sunflower seeds and topped with sesame and honey-roasted sunflower seeds. *Available in Loaf.*

Artisan Three Seed

The addition of sesame, poppy, and fennel seeds created a sweet, nutty, anise-flavored bread. *Available in Demi.*

Artisan Three Cheese

Made with Parmesan, Romano, and Asiago cheeses and durum and semolina flours. *Available in Demi, Loaf and Miche.*

Artisan Stone-Milled Rye

Made with Panera's artisan starter, chopped rye kernels, and caraway seeds, topped with more caraway seeds. *Available in Loaf and Miche.*

Artisan Country

Made from artisan starter with a crisp crust and nutty flavor. *Available in Loaf, Miche and Demi.*

Lower-Carb Pumpkin Seed

Made from Panera's artisan starter dough, pumpkin seeds and flax meal to create a subtle, nutty flavor. *Available in Loaf.*

Lower-Carb Italian Herb

Made from Panera's artisan starter dough, roasted garlic, dried herbs and sesame seed topping. *Available in Loaf.*

Source: www.panerabread.com (accessed July 28, 2006).

EXHIBIT 6   Sample Menu Selections, Panera Bread Company, 2006

Bakery
Loaves of Bread (22 varieties)
Bagels (11 varieties)
Cookies (5 varieties)
Scones (5 varieties)
Cinnamon Rolls, Pecan Rolls
Croissants
Coffee Cakes
Muffins (5 varieties)
Artisan and Specialty Pastries (8 varieties)
Brownies (3 varieties)
Mini-Bundt Cakes (3 varieties)

Signature Sandwiches
Pepperblue Steak
Garden Veggie
Tuscan Chicken
Asiago Roast Beef
Italian Combo
Bacon Turkey Bravo
Sierra Turkey
Turkey Romesco
Mediterranean Veggie

Café Sandwiches
Smoked Turkey Breast
Chicken Salad
Tuna Salad
Smoked Ham and Cheese

Hot Panini Sandwiches
Turkey Artichoke
Frontega Chicken
Smokehouse Turkey
Portobello and Mozzarella

Baked Egg Souffles
Four Cheese
Spinach and Artichoke
Spinach and Bacon

Soups
Broccoli Cheddar
French Onion
Baked Potato
Low Fat Chicken Noodle
Cream of Chicken and Wild Rice
Boston Clam Chowder
Low Fat Vegetarian Garden Vegetable
Low Fat Vegetarian Black Bean
Vegetarian Roasted Red Pepper and Lentil
Tuscan Chicken and Ditalini
Tuscan Vegetable Ditalini

Hand Tossed Salads
Asian Sesame Chicken
Fandango
Greek
Caesar
Grilled Chicken Caesar
Bistro Steak
Classic Café
California Mission Chicken
Fuji Apple Chicken
Strawberry Poppyseed and Chicken
Grilled Salmon Salad

Side Choices
Portion of French Baguette
Portion of Whole Grain Baguette
Kettle-cooked or Baked Chips
Apple

Panera Kids
Grilled Cheese
Peanut Butter and Jelly
Kids Deli

Beverages
Coffee
Hot and Iced Teas
Sodas
Bottled Water
Juice
Organic Milk
Organic Chocolate Milk
Hot Chocolate
Orange Juice
Organic Apple Juice
Espresso
Cappuccino
Lattes
Mango Raspberry Smoothie

Source: Sample menu posted at www.panerabread.com (accessed July 29, 2006).

focused on providing food that customers would crave and trust to be tasty. New menu items were developed in test kitchens and then introduced in a limited number of the bakery-cafés to determine customer response and verify that preparation and operating procedures resulted in product consistency and high quality standards. If successful, they were then rolled out systemwide. New product rollouts were integrated into periodic or seasonal menu rotations, which Panera referred to as "Celebrations."

Panera recognized in late 2004 that significantly more customers were conscious about eating "good" carbohydrates, prompting the introduction of whole grain breads. In 2005, several important menu changes were made. Panera introduced a new line of artisan sweet goods made with gourmet European butter, fresh fruit toppings, and appealing fillings; these new artisan pastries represented a significantly higher level of taste and upgraded quality. To expand its breakfast offerings and help boost morning-hour sales, Panera introduced egg soufflés baked in a flaked pastry shell. And, in another health-related move, Panera switched to the use of natural, antibiotic-free chicken in all of its chicken-related sandwiches and salads. During 2006, the chief menu changes involved the addition of light entrées to jump-start dinner appeal; one such menu addition was crispani (a pizzalike topping on a thin crust). In 2006, evening-hour sales represented 20 percent of Panera's business.

PANERA FRESH CATERING

In 2004–2005, Panera Bread introduced a catering program to extend its market reach into the workplace, schools, parties, and gatherings held in homes. Panera saw catering as an opportunity to grow lunch and dinner sales with making capital investments in additional physical facilities. By the end of 2005, catering was generating an additional $80 million in sales for Panera Bread. Management foresaw considerable opportunity for future growth of Panera's catering operation.

MARKETING

Panera's marketing strategy was to compete on the basis of providing an entire dining experience rather than by attracting customers on the basis of price only. The objective was for customers to view dining at Panera as being a good value—meaning high-quality food at reasonable prices—so as to encourage frequent visits. Panera Bread performed extensive market research, including the use of focus groups, to determine customer food and drink preferences and price points. The company tried to grow sales at existing Panera locations through menu development, product merchandising, promotions at everyday prices, and sponsorship of local community charitable events.

Historically, marketing had played only a small role in Panera's success. Brand awareness had been built on customers' satisfaction with their dining experience at Panera and their tendency to share their positive experiences with friends and neighbors. About 85 percent of consumers who were aware that there was a Panera Bread bakery-café in their community or neighborhood had dined at Panera on at least one occasion.[3] The company's marketing research indicated that 57 percent of consumers who had "ever tried" dining at Panera Bread had been customers in the past 30 days. This high proportion of trial customers to repeat customers had convinced management that getting more first-time diners into Panera Bread cafés was a potent way to boost store traffic and average weekly sales per store.

---

[3]As cited in Panera Bread's presentation to securities analysts on May 5, 2006.

Panera's research also showed that people who dined at Panera Bread very frequently or moderately frequently typically did so for only one part of the day. Yet 81 percent indicated "considerable willingness" to try dining at Panera Bread at other parts of the day.[4]

Franchise-operated bakery-cafés were required to contribute 0.7 percent of their sales to a national advertising fund and 0.4 percent of their sales as a marketing administration fee and were also required to spend 2.0 percent of their sales in their local markets on advertising. Panera contributed similar amounts from company-owned bakery-cafés toward the national advertising fund and marketing administration. The national advertising fund contribution of 0.7 percent had been increased from 0.4 percent starting in 2006. Beginning in fiscal 2006, national advertising fund contributions were raised to 0.7 percent of sales, and Panera could opt to raise the national advertising fund contributions as high as 2.6 percent of sales.

In 2006, Panera Bread's marketing strategy had several elements. One element aimed at raising the quality of awareness about Panera by continuing to feature the caliber and appeal of its breads and baked goods, by hammering the theme "food you crave, food you can trust," and by enhancing the appeal of its bakery-cafés as a neighborhood gathering place. A second marketing initiative was to raise awareness and boost trial of dining at Panera Bread at multiple meal times (breakfast, lunch, "chill out" times, and dinner). Panera avoided hard-sell or in-your-face marketing approaches, preferring instead to employ a range of ways to softly drop the Panera Bread name into the midst of consumers as they moved through their lives and let them "gently collide" with the brand; the idea was to let consumers "discover" Panera Bread and then convert them into loyal customers by providing a very satisfying dining experience. The third marketing initiative was to increase perception of Panera Bread as a viable evening meal option and to drive early trials of Panera for dinner (particularly among existing Panera lunch customers).

FRANCHISE OPERATIONS

Opening additional franchised bakery-cafés was a core element of Panera Bread's strategy and management's initiative to achieve the company's growth targets. Panera Bread did not grant single-unit franchises, so a prospective franchisee could not open just one bakery-café. Rather, Panera Bread's franchising strategy was to enter into franchise agreements that required the franchise developer to open a number of units, typically 15 bakery-cafés in six years. Franchisee candidates had to be well capitalized, have a proven track record as excellent multiunit restaurant operators, and agree to meet an aggressive development schedule. Applicants had to meet eight stringent criteria to gain consideration for a Panera Bread franchise:

- Experience as a multiunit restaurant operator.
- Recognition as a top restaurant operator.
- Net worth of $7.5 million.
- Liquid assets of $3 million.
- Infrastructure and resources to meet Panera's development schedule for the market area the franchisee was applying to develop.
- Real estate experience in the market to be developed.
- Total commitment to the development of the Panera Bread brand.
- Cultural fit and a passion for fresh bread.

[4]Ibid.

The franchise agreement typically required the payment of a franchise fee of $35,000 per bakery-café (broken down into $5,000 at the signing of the area development agreement and $30,000 at or before a bakery-café opened) and continuing royalties of 4–5 percent on sales from each bakery-café. Franchise-operated bakery-cafés followed the same in-store operating standards for product quality, menu, site selection, and bakery-café construction as did company-owned bakery-cafés. Franchisees were required to purchase all of their dough products from sources approved by Panera Bread. Panera's fresh dough facility system supplied fresh dough products to substantially all franchise-operated bakery-cafés. Panera did not finance franchisee construction or area development agreement payments or hold an equity interest in any of the franchise-operated bakery-cafés. All area development agreements executed after March 2003 included a clause allowing Panera Bread the right to purchase all bakery-cafés opened by the franchisee at a defined purchase price, at any time five years after the execution of the franchise agreement.

Exhibit 7 shows estimated costs of opening a new franchised Panera Bread bakery-café. As of 2006, the typical franchise-operated bakery-café averaged somewhat higher average weekly and annual sales volumes than company-operated cafés (see Exhibit 2), was equal to or slightly more profitable, and produced a slightly higher return on equity investment than company-operated cafés (partly because many franchisees made greater use of debt in financing their operations than did Panera, which had no long-term debt at all).[5] During the 2003–2006 period, in four unrelated transactions, Panera purchased 38 bakery-cafés from franchisees.

Panera provided its franchisees with market analysis and site selection assistance, lease review, design services and new store opening assistance, a comprehensive 10-week initial training program, a training program for hourly employees, manager and baker certification, bakery-café certification, continuing education classes, benchmarking data regarding costs and profit margins, access to company-developed marketing and advertising programs, neighborhood marketing assistance, and calendar planning assistance. Panera's

EXHIBIT 7   Estimated Initial Investment for a Panera Bread Bakery-Café, 2007

Investment Category	Actual or Estimated Amount	To Whom Paid
Franchise fee	$35,000	Panera
Real property	Varies according to site and local real estate market conditions	
Leasehold improvements	$350,000 to $1,250,000	Contractors
Equipment	$250,000 to $300,000	Equipment vendors, Panera
Fixtures	$60,000 to $90,000	Vendors
Furniture	$50,000 to $70,000	Vendors
Consultant fees and municipal impact fees (if any)	$20,000 to $120,000	Architect, engineer, expeditor, others
Supplies and inventory	$19,000 to $24,175	Panera, other suppliers
Smallwares	$24,000 to $29,000	Suppliers
Signage	$20,000 to $72,000	Suppliers
Additional funds (for working capital and general operating expenses for 3 months)	$175,000 to $245,000	Vendors, suppliers, employees, utilities, landlord, others
Total	$1,003,000 to $2,235,175, plus real estate and related costs	

Source: www.panerabread.com (accessed February 9, 2007).

[5]Ibid.

surveys of its franchisees indicated high satisfaction with the Panera Bread concept, the overall support received from Panera Bread, and the company's leadership. The biggest franchisee issue was the desire for more territory. In turn, Panera management expressed satisfaction with the quality of franchisee operations, the pace and quality of new bakery-café openings, and franchisees' adoption of Panera Bread initiatives.[6]

As of April 2006, Panera had entered into area development agreements with 42 franchisee groups covering 54 markets in 34 states; these franchisees had commitments to open 423 additional franchise-operated bakery-cafés. If a franchisee failed to develop bakery-cafés on schedule, Panera had the right to terminate the franchise agreement and develop its own company-operated locations or develop locations through new area developers in that market. As of mid-2006, Panera Bread did not have any international franchise development agreements but was considering entering into franchise agreements for several Canadian locations (Toronto and Vancouver).

SITE SELECTION AND CAFÉ ENVIRONMENT

Bakery-cafés were typically located in suburban, strip mall, and regional mall locations. In evaluating a potential location, Panera studied the surrounding trade area, demographic information within that area, and information on competitors. Based on analysis of this information, including the use of predictive modeling using proprietary software, Panera developed projections of sales and return on investment for candidate sites. Cafés had proved successful as freestanding units, as both in-line and end-cap locations in strip malls, and in large regional malls.

The average Panera bakery-café was approximately 4,600 square feet. The great majority of the locations were leased. Lease terms were typically for 10 years with one, two, or three 5-year renewal option periods thereafter. Leases typically entailed charges for minimum base occupancy, a proportionate share of building and common-area operating expenses and real estate taxes, and a contingent percentage rent based on sales above a stipulated sales level. The average construction, equipment, furniture and fixture, and signage cost for the 66 company-owned bakery-cafés opened in 2005 was $920,000 per bakery-café after landlord allowances.

Each bakery-café sought to provide a distinctive and engaging environment (what management referred to as "Panera Warmth"), in many cases using fixtures and materials complementary to the neighborhood location of the bakery-café. In 2005–2006, the company had introduced a new G2 café design aimed at further refining and enhancing the appeal of Panera bakery-cafés as a warm and appealing neighborhood gathering place (a strategy that Starbucks had used with great success). The G2 design incorporated higher-quality furniture, cozier seating areas and groupings, and a brighter, more open display case. Many locations had fireplaces to further create an alluring and hospitable atmosphere that patrons would flock to on a regular basis, sometimes for a meal, sometimes to meet friends and acquaintances for a meal, sometimes to take a break for a light snack or beverage, and sometimes to just hang out with friends and acquaintances. Many of Panera's bakery-cafés had outdoor seating, and virtually all cafés featured free wireless high-speed (Wi-Fi) Internet access—Panera considered free Wi-Fi part of its commitment to making its bakery-cafés open community gathering places where people could catch up on some work, hang out with friends, read the paper, or just relax. All Panera cafés used real china and stainless silverware instead of paper plates and plastic utensils.

[6]Ibid.

BAKERY-CAFÉ SUPPLY CHAIN

Panera had invested about $52 million in a network of 17 regional fresh dough facilities (16 company-owned and one franchise-operated) to supply fresh dough daily to both company-owned and franchised bakery-cafés. These facilities, totaling some 313,000 square feet, employed about 830 people who were largely engaged in preparing the fresh doughs, a process that took about 48 hours. The dough-making process began with the preparation and mixing of Panera's all-natural starter dough, which then was given time to rise; other all-natural ingredients were then added to create the different bread and bagel varieties (no chemicals or preservatives were used). Another period of rising then took place. Next the dough was cut into pieces, shaped into loaves or bagels, and readied for shipment in fresh dough form. There was no freezing of the dough, and no partial baking was done at the fresh dough facilities. Each bakery-café did all of the baking itself, using the fresh doughs delivered daily. The fresh dough facilities manufactured about 50 different products, with 11 more rotated throughout the year.

Distribution of the fresh bread and bagel doughs was accomplished through a leased fleet of about 140 temperature-controlled trucks operated by Panera personnel. Trucks on average delivered dough to six bakery-cafés, with trips averaging about 300 miles (but in some cases extending to as much as 500 miles—management believed the optimal trip length was about 300 miles). The fresh dough was sold to both company-owned and franchised bakery-cafés at a delivered cost not to exceed 27 percent of the retail value of the product. Exhibit 8 provides financial data relating to each of Panera's three business segments: company-operated bakery-cafés, franchise operations, and fresh dough facilities. The sales and operating profits associated with the fresh doughs supplied to company-operated bakery cafés are included in the revenues and operating profits of the company-owned bakery-café segment. The sales and operating profits of the fresh dough facilities segment shown in Exhibit 8 all represent transactions with franchised bakery-cafés.

Management claimed that the company's fresh-dough-making capability provided a competitive advantage by ensuring consistent quality and dough-making efficiency. It was more economical to concentrate the dough-making operations in a few facilities dedicated to that function than it was to have each bakery-café equipped and staffed to do all of its baking from scratch.

Panera obtained ingredients for its doughs and other products manufactured at the fresh dough facilities from a variety of suppliers. While some ingredients used at the fresh dough facilities were sourced from a single supplier, there were numerous suppliers of each ingredient and Panera could obtain ingredients from another supplier when necessary. Panera contracted externally for the supply of sweet goods to its bakery-cafés. In November 2002, it entered into a cost-plus agreement with Dawn Food Products Inc. to provide sweet goods for the period 2003–2007. Sweet goods were completed at each bakery-café by professionally trained bakers—completion entailed finishing with fresh toppings and other ingredients and baking to established artisan standards.

Panera had arrangements with independent distributors to handle the delivery of sweet goods and other materials to bakery-cafés. Virtually all other food products and supplies for retail operations, including paper goods, coffee, and smallwares, were contracted for by Panera and delivered by the vendors to the designated distributors for delivery to the bakery-cafés. Individual bakery-cafés placed orders for the needed supplies directly from a distributor two to three times per week. Franchise-operated bakery-cafés operate under individual contracts with one of Panera's three primary independent distributors or other regional distributors.

EXHIBIT 8   Business Segment Information, Panera Bread Company, 2003–2006 ($ in thousands)

	2006	2005	2004	2003
Segment revenues				
Company bakery-café operations	$666,141	$499,422	$362,121	$265,933
Franchise operations	61,531	54,309	44,449	36,245
Fresh dough operations	159,050	128,422	103,786	93,874
Intercompany sales eliminations	(57,751)	(41,878)	(31,217)	(32,350)
Total revenues	$828,971	$640,275	$479,139	$363,702
Segment operating profit				
Company bakery-café operations	$123,225	$ 97,831	$ 71,725	$ 55,111
Franchise operations	54,160	47,652	39,149	32,132
Fresh dough operations	15,681	11,508	6,942	6,557
Total segment operating profit	$193,066	$156,991	$117,816	$ 93,800
Depreciation and amortization				
Company bakery-café operations	$ 32,741	$ 23,345	$ 17,786	$ 12,256
Fresh dough operations	7,097	6,016	4,356	3,298
Corporate administration	4,328	3,650	3,156	2,750
Total	$ 44,166	$ 33,011	$ 25,298	$ 18,304
Capital expenditures				
Company bakery-café operations	$ 86,743	$ 67,554	$ 67,374	$ 33,670
Fresh dough operations	15,120	9,082	9,445	8,370
Corporate administration	7,433	5,420	3,610	3,721
Total capital expenditures	$109,296	$ 82,056	$ 80,429	$ 45,761
Segment assets				
Company bakery-café operations	$374,795	$301,517	$204,295	$147,920
Franchise operations	3,740	2,969	1,778	1,117
Fresh dough operations	59,919	37,567	39,968	33,442
Other assets	104,155	95,614	78,631	74,356
Total assets	$542,609	$437,667	$324,672	$256,835

Sources: Company 10-K reports, 2004, 2005, and 2006.

COMPETITION

According to the National Restaurant Association, sales at the 925,000 food service locations in the United States were forecast to be about $511 billion in 2006 (up from $308 billion in 1996), and account for 47.5 percent of consumers' food dollars (up from 25 percent in 1955). Commercial eating places accounted for about $345 billion of the projected $511 billion in total food service sales, with the remainder divided among drinking places, lodging establishments with restaurants, managed food service locations, and other types of retail, vending, recreational, and mobile operations with food service capability. The U.S. restaurant industry had about 12.5 million employees in 2006, served about 70 billion meals and snack occasions, and was growing about 5 percent annually.[7] Just over 7 out of 10 eating and drinking places in the United States were independent single-unit establishments with fewer than 20 employees.

Even though the average U.S. consumer ate 76 percent of meals at home, on a typical day, about 130 million U.S. consumers were food service patrons at an eating establishment—sales at commercial eating places averaged close to $1 billion daily. Average household expenditures for food away from home in 2004 were $2,434, or $974 per person. In 2003, unit sales averaged $755,000 at full-service restaurants and $606,000 at

[7]Information posted at www.restaurant.org (accessed August 1, 2006).

limited-service restaurants; however, very popular restaurant locations achieved annual sales volumes in the $2.5 million to $5 million range. The profitability of a restaurant location ranged from exceptional to good to average to marginal to money-losing.

The restaurant business was labor-intensive, extremely competitive, and risky. Industry members pursued differentiation strategies of one variety or another, seeking to set themselves apart from rivals via pricing, food quality, menu theme, signature menu selections, dining ambience and atmosphere, service, convenience, and location. To further enhance their appeal, some restaurants tried to promote greater customer traffic via happy hours, lunch and dinner specials, children's menus, innovative or trendy dishes, diet-conscious menu selections, and beverage/appetizer specials during televised sporting events (important at restaurants/bars with big screen TVs). Most restaurants were quick to adapt their menu offerings to changing consumer tastes and eating preferences, frequently featuring heart-healthy, vegetarian, organic, low-calorie, and/or low-carb items on their menus. It was the norm at many restaurants to rotate some menu selections seasonally and to periodically introduce creative dishes in an effort to keep regular patrons coming back, attract more patrons, and remain competitive.

Consumers (especially those who ate out often) were prone to give newly opened eating establishments a trial, and if they were pleased with their experience to return, sometimes frequently—loyalty to existing restaurants was low when consumers perceived there were better dining alternatives. It was also common for a once-hot restaurant to lose favor and confront the stark realities of a dwindling clientele, forcing it to either reconceive its menu and dining environment or go out of business. Many restaurants had fairly short lives; there were multiple causes for a restaurant's failure—a lack of enthusiasm for the menu or dining experience, inconsistent food quality, poor service, a bad location, meal prices that patrons deemed too high, and superior competition by rivals with comparable menu offerings.

While Panera Bread competed with specialty food, casual dining, and quick-service restaurant retailers—including national, regional, and locally owned restaurants—its closest competitors were restaurants in the so-called fast-casual restaurant category. Fast-casual restaurants filled the gap between fast-food and casual, full-table-service dining. A fast-casual restaurant provided quick-service dining (much like fast-food enterprises) but were distinguished by enticing menus, higher food quality, and more inviting dining environments; typical meal costs per guest were in the $7–$12 range. Some fast-casual restaurants had limited table service and some were self-service (like fast-food establishments). Exhibit 9 provides information on prominent national and regional chains that were competitors of Panera Bread.

EXHIBIT 9   Representative Fast-Casual Restaurant Chains and Selected Full-Service Restaurant Chains in the United States, 2006

Company	Number of Locations, 2005–2006	Select 2005 Financial Data	Key Menu Categories
Atlanta Bread Company	160 bakery-cafés in 27 states	Not available (privately held company)	Fresh-baked breads, waffles, salads, sandwiches, soups, wood-fired pizza and pasta (select locations only), baked goods, desserts
Applebee's Neighborhood Grill and Bar	1,730+ locations in 49 states, plus some 70 locations in 16 other countries	2005 revenues of $1.2 billion; average annual sales of $2.5 million per location; alcoholic beverages accounted for about 12 percent of sales	Beef, chicken, pork, seafood, and pasta entrées plus appetizers, salads, sandwiches, a selection of Weight Watchers branded menu alternatives, desserts, and alcoholic beverages

(continued)

EXHIBIT 9 Representative Fast-Casual Restaurant Chains and Selected Full-Service Restaurant Chains in the United States, 2006 *(continued)*

Company	Number of Locations, 2005–2006	Select 2005 Financial Data	Key Menu Categories
Au Bon Pain	190 company-owned and franchised bakery-cafés in 23 states; 222 locations internationally	Systemwide sales of about $245 million in 2005	Baked goods (with a focus on croissants and bagels), soups, salads, sandwiches and wraps, and coffee drinks
Baja Fresh	300+ locations across the United States	A subsidiary of Wendy's International	Tacos, burritos, quesadillas, fajitas, salads, soups, sides, and catering services
Bruegger's	260 bakery-cafés in 17 states	2005 revenues of $155.2 million; 3,500 full-time employees	Several varieties of bagels and muffins, sandwiches, salads, and soups
California Pizza Kitchen*	190+ locations in 27 states and 5 other countries	2005 revenues of $480 million; average annual sales of $3.2 million per location	Signature California-style hearth-baked pizzas; creative salads, pastas, soups and sandwiches; appetizers; desserts, beer, wine, coffees, teas, and assorted beverages
Chili's Grill and Bar* (a subsidiary of Brinker International**)	1,074 locations in 49 states and 23 countries	Average revenue per meal of ≈12.00; average capital investment of $2.4 million per location	Chicken, beef, and seafood entrées, steaks, appetizers, salads, sandwiches, desserts, and alcoholic beverages (13.6 percent of sales)
Chipotle Mexican Grill	500+ locations (all company-owned)	2005 sales of $628 million; 13,000 employees	A selection of gourmet burritos and tacos
Corner Bakery Café (a subsidiary of Brinker International**)	90 locations in 8 states and District of Columbia	Average revenue per meal of ≈ $7.44; average capital investment of $1.7 million per location	Breakfast selections (egg scramblers, pastries, mixed berry parfaits); lunch/dinner selections (hot and cold sandwiches, salads, soups, and desserts); catering (≈ 21 percent of sales)
Cracker Barrel	527 combination retail stores and restaurants in 42 states	Restaurant sales of $2.1 billion in 2005; average restaurant sales of $3.3 million	Two menus (breakfast and lunch/dinner); named "Best Family Dining Chain" for 15 consecutive years
Culver's	330 locations in 16 states	Not available (a privately held company)	Signature hamburgers served on buttered buns, fried battered cheese curds, value dinners (chicken, shrimp, cod with potato and slaw), salads, frozen custard, milk shakes, sundaes, and fountain drinks
Fazoli's	380 locations in 32 states	Not available (a privately held company)	Spaghetti and meatballs, fettuccine Alfredo, lasagna, ravioli, submarinos and panini sandwiches, salads, and breadsticks
Fuddruckers	200+ locations in the United States and 6 Middle Eastern countries	Not available (a privately held company)	Exotic hamburgers (the feature menu item), chicken and fish sandwiches, French fries and other sides, soups, salads, desserts
Jason's Deli	150 locations in 20 states	Not available (a privately held company)	Sandwiches, extensive salad bar, soups, loaded potatoes, desserts; catering services, party trays, and box lunches
McAlister's Deli	200+ locations in 18 states	Not available (a privately held company)	Deli sandwiches, loaded baked potatoes, soups, salads, and desserts, plus sandwich trays and lunch boxes

(continued)

EXHIBIT 9   Representative Fast-Casual Restaurant Chains and Selected Full-Service Restaurant Chains in the United States, 2006   *(concluded)*

Company	Number of Locations, 2005–2006	Select 2005 Financial Data	Key Menu Categories
Moe's Southwest Grill	200+ location in 35 states	Not available (a privately held company)	Tex-Mex foods prepared fresh—tacos, burritos, fajitas, quesadillas, nachos, salads, chips and salsa
Noodles & Company	120+ urban and suburban locations in 16 states	Not available (a privately held company)	Asian, Mediterranean and American noodle/pasta entrées, soups and salads
Nothing But Noodles	39 locations in 20 states	Not available (a privately held company)	Starters, a wide selection of American and Italian pastas, Asian dishes with noodles, pasta-less entrées, soups, salads, and desserts
Qdoba Mexican Grill	280+ locations in 40 states	A subsidiary of Jack in the Box, Inc.; Jack in the Box had 2005 revenues of $2.5 billion, 2,300+ Jack in the Box and Qdoba locations, and 44,600 employees	Signature burritos, a "Naked Burrito" (a burrito served in a bowl without the tortilla), nontraditional taco salads, three-cheese nachos, five signature salsas, and a Q-to-Go Hot Taco Bar catering alternative
Rubio's Fresh Mexican Grill	150 locations in 5 western states	2005 revenues of $141 million; average sales of $960,000 per location	Signature fish tacos; chicken, beef, and pork tacos; burritos and quesadillas; salads; proprietary salsas; sides; and domestic and imported beers
Starbucks	7,500+ company-operated and licensed locations in the United States, plus ≈3,000 international locations	2005 revenues of $6.4 billion; estimated retail sales of $1.1 million per company-operated location	Italian-style espresso beverages, teas, sodas, juices, assorted pastries and confections; some locations offer sandwiches and salads

*Denotes a full-service restaurant.
**Brinker International was a multiconcept restaurant operator with over 1,500 restaurants including Chili's Grill & Bar, Chili's Too, Corner Bakery Café, Romano's Macaroni Grill, On the Border Mexican Grill & Cantina, and Maggiano's Little Italy. Brinker had 2005 sales of $3.9 billion.
Sources: Company Web sites and en.wikipedia.org/wiki/Fast_casual_restaurant (accessed August 2, 2006).

Case Group B

Product Strategy

Starbucks

J. Paul Peter *University of Wisconsin–Madison*

© Davis Barber/Photo Edit

Starbucks Corporation is the world's largest coffee retailer and has continued its phenomenal success into 2008. The company has won a variety of awards for its work in setting coffee-buying guidelines that are environmentally, socially, and economically responsible and for being one of the most admired companies in the United States. In one recent year, it donated over $36 million in cash and products and nearly 400,000 hours of community volunteer work. Exhibit 1 summarizes its growth in revenues, earning, and stores in recent years. However, the company made some serious strategic errors and faced increasingly strong competition, causing its stock price to fall from $36 to $18 per share in early 2008.

Starbucks was started in Seattle, Washington, in 1971 when three young men decided to try their hand at selling gourmet coffee. They were betting that consumers would pay $1.50

J. Paul Peter was James R. McManus–Bascom Professor in Marketing at the University of Wisconsin–Madison. All information in this case is taken from public sources including starbucks.com.

EXHIBIT 1   Starbucks Growth in Revenue, Earnings, and Number of Stores

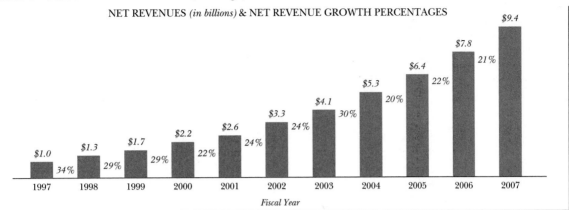

NET REVENUES *(in billions)* & NET REVENUE GROWTH PERCENTAGES

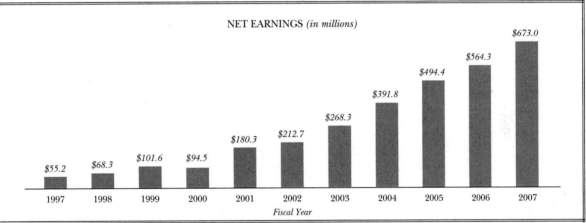

NET EARNINGS *(in millions)*

STORES OPEN AT YEAR END
(Company-operated and licensed stores)

Source: www.Starbucks.com.

for a cup of their coffee compared to 40 cents for a generic coffee offered elsewhere. By 2008, there were more than 15,000 Starbucks coffeehouses in 44 countries worldwide. Starbucks' long-term goal is to have 30,000 stores worldwide. Store locations are selected for high traffic and high visibility. Over 33 million customers visit a Starbucks coffeehouse each week worldwide.

A recent study found that there are over 166 million coffee drinkers in the United States, and the number of them has increased steadily since the mid-1990s. A significant trend in U.S. coffee drinking has been the increase in the amount of coffee drinking in the out-of-home segment. For example, coffee drinkers aged 25–29 increased their out-of-home coffee consumption from 42 to 66 percent in a recent year and 30–59-year-olds from 33 to 46 percent. Coffee drinkers 60 and older increased their out-of-home consumption from 14 to 20 percent in the same year. Of the out-of-home segment, the biggest increase was among those who drink their coffee at work. However, while more consumers are drinking coffee in the workplace, they are increasingly getting their coffee from outside the office. This means the percentage of at-work coffee being sourced from within the workplace has declined dramatically.

Starbucks has made coffee drinking a social phenomenon by offering consumers a comfortable atmosphere in which to drink a premium beverage while either chatting with friends, reading a newspaper or magazine, or working on their laptops. Howard Schultz, chairman of Starbucks, believes that the company has created a "third place" between home and work where people can go for personal time out or to relax with friends. While many of these people previously would have stopped in a bar for a beer, they now frequent Starbucks for coffee.

Schultz also attributes the company's success to the 172,000 employees working worldwide. Starbucks' employee training program churns out "baristas" by educating classes of 300 to 400 in courses such as "Brewing the Perfect Cup at Home" and "Coffee Knowledge." They are taught to remind customers who buy Starbucks coffee beans to brew at home to purchase new beans weekly and that tap water might not be sufficient for brewing really good coffee. They are also encouraged to share their feelings about working at Starbucks. Employees are given guidelines for maintaining and enhancing self-esteem, learning how to listen and acknowledge customer comments, and knowing when to ask for help. If the annual barista turnover of 60 percent compared to 140 percent for hourly wage earners in the fast-food industry is any indication of the quality of its training programs, Starbucks seems to have made progress in developing employee loyalty. Most of Starbucks' employees have some education beyond high school, and their average age is 26. Eligible employees qualify for a comprehensive benefits package, including stock options and health, medical, dental, and vision coverage. Concern for employees is one of Starbucks' guiding principles, as shown in Exhibit 2.

EXHIBIT 2   Starbucks' Mission Statement and Guiding Principles

Establish Starbucks as the premier purveyor of the finest coffee in the world while maintaining our uncompromising principles while we grow.
The following six guiding principles will help us measure the appropriateness of our decisions:
–Provide a great work environment and treat each other with respect and dignity.
–Embrace diversity as an essential component in the way we do business.
–Apply the highest standards of excellence to the purchasing, roasting and fresh delivery of our coffee.
–Develop enthusiastically satisfied customers all of the time.
–Contribute positively to our communities and our environment.
–Recognize that profitability is essential to our future success.

Environmental Mission Statement

Starbucks is committed to a role of environmental leadership in all facets of our business.
We fulfill this mission by a commitment to:
–Understanding of environmental issues and sharing information with our partners.
–Developing innovative and flexible solutions to bring about change.
–Striving to buy, sell and use environmentally friendly products.
–Recognizing that fiscal responsibility is essential to our environmental future.
–Instilling environmental responsibility as a corporate value.
–Measuring and monitoring our progress for each project.
–Encouraging all partners to share in our mission.

Source: www.Starbucks.com.

Starbucks' product line includes more than 30 blends and single-origin coffees, handcrafted espresso and blended beverages, Tazo teas, a line of bottled Frappuccino coffee drinks and Starbucks DoubleShot. In addition, it offers an exclusive line of Starbucks Barista home espresso machines, coffee brewers and grinders, freshly baked pastries, a line of super-premium ice cream, a line of premium chocolate, sandwiches, salad, coffee mugs and coffee accessories, compact discs, and assorted gift items. It also offers a highly successful Starbucks Card, a reloadable stored-value card, which allows consumers to prepay the purchase of Starbucks products. The card can then be used and reloaded with funds when needed either at a Starbucks store or at Starbucks.com. This card has been hugely successful with over 27 million cards in use and over $400 million in sales in the first quarter of 2008 alone. The card is so successful that it is being launched internationally with initial rollouts in Japan and Greece. The card provides convenience to customers but does not offer any discount for prepayment. In fact, Starbucks does not discount any of its products or offer special prices or sales.

Starbucks also has licensing agreements for its products with a number of other companies. For example, it has an agreement with Pepsi-Cola Company to produce and distribute bottled Starbucks products and one with Kraft Foods, Inc., to distribute Starbucks coffee beans and ground coffees and packaged tea products in grocery and warehouse club stores. It has an agreement with Dreyer's Grand Ice Cream, Inc., to develop and distribute Starbucks' line of superpremium ice cream and one with Jim Beam Brands Inc. to manufacture and market a Starbucks premium liqueur product. It has an alliance with SYSCO Corporation to distribute its coffee and tea products to institutional food services for health care accounts, office coffee distributors, hotels, restaurants, airlines, and other retailers.

Starbucks Corporation is a very successful company. However, its stock price recently dropped, which can be attributed to a variety of factors. First, the success of Starbucks encouraged competitors to focus on coffee products and new restaurants. For example, McDonald's Corporation has greatly improved its sales and profits by putting increased emphasis on the quality of its coffee. The growth in the number of café-style coffeehouses and restaurants, like Panera Bread, also hurt Starbucks' same-store sales.

Second, while growing the number of stores rapidly has fueled growth in revenue and earnings, it also makes Starbucks so available that it may not be as special to consumers as it once was. Not too long ago, the arrival of a Starbucks store was a major event, a recognition that a town or neighborhood was worthy of the chic Seattle-based chain. However, in recent years, every street corner, airport concourse, and roadside rest stop in America seemed to attract a Starbucks. Recognition of the over-saturation problem is one reason why Starbucks decided to place its emphasis on store growth in international markets where its business remains robust. It also closed 100 underperforming locations in the United States.

Finally, in its attempts to be more efficient, Starbucks may have reduced the quality of the purchase and use experience. For example, by using flavor-locked packaging for its coffees, the fresh-ground-coffee aroma was lost, not to mention the sound of beans being scooped and ground onsite. By adding hot sandwiches and bakery products to compete with McDonald's, Starbucks became more of a fast-food restaurant than a coffeehouse in the minds of some consumers. By trading comfy, stuffed chairs for plastic and selling a variety of games and other products, the quality of the coffee-drinking experience was reduced for many consumers. By adding drive-through windows and speeding up service, many consumers may have started to view Starbucks coffee as a commodity rather than something special and its employees as order-takers rather than knowledgeable coffee experts.

Discussion Questions

1. What is Starbucks' product?
2. What advantages does McDonald's have in competing with Starbucks for coffee sales?

3. What changes in society helped Starbucks become successful?

4. What strategic factors account for Starbucks' long-term success in building brand equity?

5. What are the advantages of the Starbucks Card to the company and to customers?

6. What recommendations do you have to improve Starbucks' competitive position?

7. Evaluate Starbucks' mission statement and guiding principles. What do they suggest about the company?

Case 8

IVEY

Richard Ivey School of Business
The University of Western Ontario

Your Home Is a Good Place, Inc.

Professors Kevin Coulson and Zane Swanson wrote this case solely to provide material for class discussion. The authors do not intend to illustrate either effective or ineffective handling of a managerial situation. The authors may have disguised certain names and other identifying information to protect confidentiality.

Ivey Management Services prohibits any form of reproduction, storage or transmittal without its written permission. Reproduction of this material is not covered under authorization by any reproduction rights organization. To order copies or request permission to reproduce materials, contact Ivey Publishing, Ivey Management Services, c/o Richard Ivey School of Business, The University of Western Ontario, London, Ontario, Canada, N6A 3K7; phone (519) 661-3208; fax (519) 661-3882; e-mail cases@ivey.uwo.ca.

Copyright © 2009, Ivey Management Services   Version: (A) 2009-09-17

INTRODUCTION

In 2006, Bill Norwalk, a 50-something entrepreneur with a decidedly independent streak, was at the cusp of a major change in his business. Norwalk's background in marketing started with a bachelor's degree in business and a marketing major. He had taken his marketing training to heart and developed a novel way of satisfying homeowner customer needs, one which had the potential to launch a new industry. Like many entrepreneurs with a good idea, Norwalk was confronting the issues of implementation and the attainment of critical mass. Should the business expand and attract new customers as well as contractors, suppliers, and other facilitators, and how? How could the business increase the number of affiliates and draw from an appropriate customer base? Norwalk concluded that the best thing to do when you do not know what to do is get outside help. He decided to hire a consultant to prepare a situational analysis (SWOT) and a marketing plan for the business.

BACKGROUND

Bill Norwalk grew up in Ohio, one of three children in a middle class family. He spent his formative years playing ball, going to Scouts, and being a member of his local church. Norwalk went to college at Miami University, where he got a bachelor's degree in business. After graduation he worked construction and eventually started his own business as a DJ at bars and at wedding receptions.

All through his life he displayed an independent streak, doing things his way. When he was 40, his customers and friends convinced him to start installing music systems as a sideline. His experience and taste in matching sound equipment made him the perfect entrepreneur, someone who knew what he wanted and was sufficiently risk-prone to be willing to work for it.

In 2006, Norwalk was tired of working for someone else and searched for a way to use his entrepreneurial talents. He realized that his success would necessitate doing business his way. Norwalk's construction experience had taught him that traditional home improvement was an iffy proposition for both contractors and for the homeowners. Because home improvement was frustrating for homeowners, the more well-to-do homeowner might be willing to pay for alleviating that pain! Contractors were good at building but conducting anything like business-solicitation took away from their time on task. However, most of them were not good at developing customers. In fact, most of them hated it.

Norwalk developed a way to increase small contractor productivity by locating new customers and handling the up-front details. In exchange, contractors were willing to pay for that service. The added benefit was that customers needed and were willing to pay for the facilitation of their home improvement as well.

Home-owning customers who sought improvements did not always know exactly what they wanted, nor did they know what was within the range of possibilities or who could make their dreams come true. Norwalk knew he could bring together (1) the designers and architects; (2) the contractors and their labour supply; and (3) the financiers, insurers and other project resources. Norwalk acted as an intermediary between the supply side and the demand side, so that all parties had the entire mess simplified. Thus was born Your Home Is a Good Place, Inc. (YHGP).

Your Home Is a Good Place, Inc., was a novel channel intermediary that employed convenience as a strategic marketing variable. It differed from traditional home improvement by providing the well-to-do homeowner with a one-stop shopping experience. Gone was the need to search out an architect or design firm and get plans. Gone was the need to then locate one or more independent contractors and put up with their continual mess while the constructive destruction processes took place. Instead, people with incomes of $100,000 or more came to the suite of showrooms at YHGP. There, on the model site, end-users could glimpse a vision of how their homes could be transformed into a luxurious playground.

Home improvement is all about making one's personal environment more comfortable, and at the upper levels of consumption, making it uniquely different from what the neighbors own. As such, it includes much more than basic bathroom, bedroom and/or kitchen design. Unfortunately, consumers do not have the time or, in the majority of cases, the talent to visualize the elements that would make their place both tasteful and unique.

Customers could walk the site visiting showroom kitchens, living rooms, bedrooms, game rooms, libraries, entertainment home theaters, pool areas, and even home putting greens for the avid golfer. If you could dream it, Norwalk could get it built. If you could not, Norwalk could locate people to dream it up for you.

For example, there was an indoor driving range simulator and an outdoor putting green for the golf enthusiast. In the bath area, there were complete luxury bath spaces. No more visits to the lumber yard or home store to examine a bathtub in one place, sink in another, and shower in another space with the faucets in yet another. The consumer could see the complete package with wall treatments and lighting, and Norwalk could put clients together with all the people needed to accomplish their dreams. Luxury bedrooms, kitchens, and home theaters were also provided for viewing.

At YHGP the consumer could literally see how different wall or floor finishes and construction techniques came together to produce an extremely unique and satisfying life-improving living space, hence the name Your Home Is a Good Place, Inc. The ease of selection was just the beginning. Once a design concept was born in the consumer's mind, YHGP personnel would take charge of the details of preparing the construction plans, obtaining and contracting with construction contractors, dealing with financing agencies, obtaining building permits, and finalizing the contracts. YHGP would arrange for coordination between the various participants and see that the contractors minimized the mess they created and that they cleaned up their work spaces before they left at the end of the day, so that there would be no more mess for the homeowner.

YHGP differed in concept from the typical home store/hardware store or design center. These businesses exist as a ready-made industry in place to cater to the do-it-yourself (DIY) consumer in terms of providing the tools and components. However, most DIY projects tend to be relatively small and are undertaken by people whose primary objective is to save money. Norwalk realized that his niche was elsewhere.

Consumers who have large amounts of disposable income and who want to undertake a major redesign of their space have to overcome these problems: (1) design and architectural changes including permits and safety inspections; (2) sourcing of appliances and components for the projects, e.g., faucets for baths and speakers for home theaters; (3) provision of professional contracting labour; (4) financing for the project; and (5) dealing with the uncertainty during construction.

Customers could see the central theme of the YHGP concept at a pavilion located in central Michiana on a leased site. Berrien and Cass counties in Michigan as well as Elkhart, La Porte, Marshall, St. Joseph and Starke in Indiana made up the market area. Local organizations and their statistical reporting recognized a larger 15-county area as the expanded Michiana area, though Norwalk felt it was too large to serve effectively and efficiently.

YHGP differed from traditional businesses because it required little of the entrepreneur's cash up front. Norwalk convinced local contractors, landscapers, designers, architects, appliance suppliers and others to donate their work or products to develop a series of showcase rooms on the leased site. Each model environment was chock-full of design ideas to spur the creative juices of potential clients.

THE SUPPLY SIDE

In return for donations of labour and material, the contractors and other facilitators (including local advertising outlets, which provided the publicity/advertising) got to showcase their wares in the "whole enchilada" pavilion. The supply-side participants got a ready source of potential clients, access through YHGP-coordinated job scheduling and help with obtaining building permits and inspections. Some of the suppliers of labour and contracting as well as components included painters and wallpaper hangers, rough-in carpenters, finish carpenters and cabinet makers, masons, electrical contractors, plumbers, landscapers, faux finishers, sound design engineers, roofing contractors, welders and other certified tradespeople. Additional players were land surveyors, movers, HVAC contractors, insulation contractors, and solar/wind/alternative energy designers and installers.

Not everyone who provided home remodeling services in the Michiana area was allied with Norwalk. A significant number were direct competitors, though they did not have the advantages provided by YHGP.

THE DEMAND SIDE

YHGP was located in the town of Mishawaka, Indiana, in the middle of the Michiana area. While not officially recognized by the U.S. government (thus no official metropolitan statistics), the Michiana area had two associations of area government agencies. MACOG, the Michiana Area Council of Governments, representing four of the seven counties, was located in Indiana. The Southwest Michigan Planning Commission, SWMPC, represented the remaining three counties in Michigan (http://swmpc.org and www.macog.com).

U.S. census data is available for the seven counties in Michiana (2000 and 2006 data were combined) (see Exhibit 1). Cass, Marshall and Starke (Michigan) and Elkhart, La Porte,

EXHIBIT 1
U.S. Census Data for Michiana

Census Descriptor	Value	Census Descriptor	Value
Total population	856,755	HOUSING OCCUPANCY	
SEX AND AGE		Total housing units	366,470
Male	389,096	Built 2000 or later	21,984
Female	433,050	Built 1990 to 1999	48,107
		Built 1980 to 1989	34,995
Under 5 years	54,990	Built 1970 to 1979	55,761
5 to 9 years	58,892	Built 1960 to 1969	42,340
10 to 14 years	63,460	Built 1950 to 1959	53,625
15 to 19 years	61,785	Built 1940 to 1949	38,309
20 to 24 years	58,217	Built 1939 or earlier	66,379
25 to 34 years	104,390		
35 to 44 years	119,079	Occupied housing units	319,373
45 to 54 years	125,590	Owner-occupied	224,583
55 to 59 years	58,744		
60 to 64 years	38,573	VALUE (Owner-occupied units)	
65 to 74 years	52,164	Less than $50,000	16,609
75 to 84 years	41,705	$50,000 to $99,999	69,403
85 years and over	17,271	$100,000 to $149,999	65,051
		$150,000 to $199,999	33,258
18 years and over	597,108	$200,000 to $299,999	19,780
Male	295,056	$300,000 to $499,999	8,773
Female	304,224	$500,000 to $999,999	5,512
		$1,000,000 or more	0
65 years and over	100,848		
Male	41,363	EDUCATIONAL ATTAINMENT	
Female	127,467	Population 25 years and over	555,402
		Less than 9th grade	30,504
EMPLOYMENT STATUS		9th to 12th grade, no diploma	64,031
Population 16 years and over	662,062	High school graduate (includes equivalency)	202,811
In labor force	439,766	Some college, no degree	111,000
Civilian labor force	439,507	Associate's degree	35,900
Employed	408,854	Bachelor's degree	70,478
Unemployed	29,023	Graduate or professional degree	38,654
Armed Forces	71,379		
Not in labor force	150,917		
Females 16 years and over	338,912		
In labor force	205,518		
Civilian labor force	205,467		
Employed	190,700		
INCOME AND BENEFITS (2000)			
Total households	319,290		
Less than $10,000	21,753		
$10,000 to $14,999	19,015		
$15,000 to $24,999	41,095		
$25,000 to $34,999	38,195		
$35,000 to $49,999	55,525		
$50,000 to $74,999	69,157		
$75,000 to $99,999	35,080		
$100,000 to $149,999	22,586		
$150,000 to $199,999	5,561		
$200,000 or more	5,206		

St. Joseph and Berrien counties (Indiana) had approximately 856,000 residents. The median household income in Michiana's counties varied over a range of $37,000 to $57,000.

The entrepreneur's vision for YHGP was to serve only private individual customers whose household income exceeded $100,000 and whose project cost averaged $10,000. Norwalk felt that anyone who had an income below this level would be most likely to use the DIY process to serve their needs. Norwalk had not considered other options for customers.

Although Norwalk considered any private individual with an income above $100,000 as a potential consumer of his services, there were limits on even this. For example, renters and people living in new homes were less likely to purchase upgrades than were others. Additionally, Norwalk wondered if age or other demographic factors might have an impact on those who might purchase.

THE INTERSECTION OF SUPPLY AND DEMAND

Norwalk's concept went beyond the idea of a general contractor who subcontracted out portions of a job. YHGP coordinated projects from start to finish. In the beginning, when a customer was considering an environmental improvement, Norwalk showed them what could be done. YHGP arranged for complete plans to be drawn up, for the permits for construction, and for the financing.

During construction, Norwalk worked with the contractors to see that proper building site "etiquette" was maintained. That meant that each day's mess was contained to the extent possible, with the work stopped and the debris cleaned up before the crews quit for the day. Homeowners had a less stressful experience because of this.

As such, customers were more likely to pay the bills which were submitted by Norwalk on time. YHGP's billing schedule billed for work on a percentage of work completed. This improved Norwalk's and the contractors' cash flows.

THE STAFF

Norwalk had six employees on staff. Norwalk was worried that he did not have the right mix of employees. Some skills were needed that his employees did not have and some dysfunctional behavior was present. For example, the chief of operations, David, was the business manager who made things happen, but stifled initiative in the process.

Rory served as project manager in charge of scheduling and service calls. He was a compliant type who wanted everyone to be happy, but could not discipline workers. David had to step in when work was not progressing.

Priscilla did sales and estimating. She was aggressive and probably was that way from a background in radio station sales management. Sam also did sales and was very good at nurturing clients. Even though he was a self-starter, he could not initiate a sale with a new client.

Rowdy was an installer and gopher (as in "Go for coffee!") who did what was needed, but exhibited no initiative. The bookkeeper, Johanna, was a classic pencil pusher. She would start at the top of a stack of paper and work down in order, never deviating from one item until the work was done.

NORWALK'S THOUGHTS

Because YHGP had few employees and relied instead on partnerships with independent contractors, expansion, in Norwalk's opinion, was as easy as bringing on a firm that wasn't currently employed by YHGP. Additionally, in harder times, Norwalk would not have to furlough employees.

Norwalk felt that his primary contacts in the customer market were women. Women wanted a complete packaged solution rather than a piecemeal approach. Some would come to the firm after viewing one of the TV home remodeling shows and want to duplicate those concepts.

Since YHGP was new, it had yet to develop a well-known image in consumers' minds. Often a new concept is slow to catch fire with consumers. Norwalk was worried about building a brand identity in Michiana.

YHGP got paid a flat percentage of the bill, typically 10 percent. Since Norwalk's staff arranged all of the details with both buyer and supplier, and tied everything up in a neat package, consumers were not aware of the facilitating charge. The various subcontractors negotiated with Norwalk or his staff beforehand, and because they were guaranteed their cut when the contract was signed, they did not object to the fee either. At this point, Norwalk could personally oversee all contracts. However, he worried that at some point in the future, he would need one or more project supervisors to maintain quality. Norwalk felt that if he could gain five customers a month at a minimum total bill of $10,000 each, YHGP would be successful.

CURRENT MARKETING ENDEAVORS

One element of Norwalk's plan was demonstrated in his promotional endeavors. Large home improvement purchases are often facilitated by the availability of credit and almost never occur without some form of promotion. He worked with banks and credit unions, realtors, radio stations and regional automobile dealers to develop promotions that used these facilitators' money and resources to attract business for the supply-side participants.

For example, he would put together a deal with a local car dealer, a bank and a radio station. The bank would offer financing, the car dealer a one-year lease on a new car and the radio station would promote a package where a Your Home Is a Good Place, Inc., client could receive the whole package as an incentive. Each business participant got the enhanced promotional effects and Norwalk's business got a cut of the overall price of the development package up front for no cash outlay. These monies were used to pay YHGP staffers and for daily operations.

Other promotional events revolved around social meetings of regional groups of professionals like doctors. A catered dinner would be provided (at the caterer's expense in exchange for the publicity and an introduction to the group) at the YHGP showrooms. Before and after the dinner, the invited guests would have access to architects, bankers and other professionals who might be involved in the transactions, and to the model showrooms demonstrating possible changes to their living spaces. The networking opportunities provided convenience for all parties and usually resulted in new contracts. YHGP got no direct income from these events.

THE CONSULTANT'S TASK

The consultant's task was to develop (a) a strength, weakness, opportunity and threat (SWOT) analysis and (b) a marketing plan for YHGP which included major implementation details for that plan. The following were the criteria for the consultant's task:

1. It should provide details of who would (or would not) be *competitors* for YHGP's niche.

2. It should consider that Norwalk's idea was one of channel integration wherein he brought together both supply and demand sides, and he needed to expand his business.

   a. YHGP must attract partners (contractors, etc.) to participate in this endeavor. How could Norwalk attract appropriate independent contractors (and others) and get them, in effect, to work for him?

      i.   Provide information on what types of functionaries he should partner with and how he should accomplish this.

      ii. Note the types of business that might otherwise be involved in this endeavor but that should not be sought out to partner with YHGP. (Why?)

      iii. What types of employees (skill sets) should Norwalk bring within the boundaries of his firm and what could he afford to obtain from his suppliers?

   b. Who would (or would not) be in Norwalk's target market as a part of this process? How could Norwalk influence the demand side to patronize YHGP? Use the demographic data provided to identify demand potential.

   c. Had Norwalk fully identified appropriate demand segments in the marketplace? Was he missing viable customer groups?

3. How could YHGP successfully expand Norwalk's promotional ideas to minimize his firm's cash outlays while still attracting new business?

4. Given Norwalk's independent streak and his reluctance to accept ideas which were not originally his own, how could advice be positioned to Norwalk?

easyCar.com

John J. Lawrence *University of Idaho*

Luis Solis *University of Idaho Instituto de Empresa*

> At easyCar we aim to offer you outstanding value for money. To us value for money means a reliable service at a low price. We achieve this by simplifying the product we offer, and passing on the benefits to you in the form of lower prices.[1]

This was the stated mission of car rental company easyCar.com. EasyCar was a member of the easyGroup family of companies, founded by the flamboyant Greek entrepreneur Stelios Haji-Ioannou, who was known simply as Stelios to most. Stelios founded low-cost air carrier easyJet.com in 1995 after convincing his father, a Greek shipping billionaire, to loan him the £5 million (note: in January 2003, £1 = €1.52 = U.S.$1.61) needed to start the business.[2] EasyJet was one of the early low-cost, no-frills air carriers in the European market. It was built upon a foundation of simple point-to-point flights, booked over the Internet, and the aggressive use of yield management policies to maximize the revenues it derived from its assets. The company proved highly successful, and as a result Stelios had expanded this business model to industries with similar characteristics as the airline industry. EasyCar, founded in 2000 on a £10 million investment on the part of Stelios, was one of these efforts.

EasyCar's approach, built on the easyJet model, was quite different from the approaches used by the traditional rental car companies. EasyCar rented only a single vehicle type at each location it operated, while most of its competitors rented a wide variety of vehicle types.

EasyCar did not work with agents—over 95 percent of its bookings were made through the company's Web site, with the remainder of bookings being made directly through the company's phone reservation system (at a cost to the customer of €0.95 per minute for the call). Most rental car companies worked with a variety of intermediaries, with their own Web sites accounting for less than 10 percent of their total booking.[3] And like easyJet, easyCar managed prices in an attempt to have its fleet rented out 100 percent of the time and to generate the maximum revenue from its rentals. EasyCar's information system constantly evaluated projected demand and expected utilization at each site, and adjusted price accordingly. Because of its aggressive pricing, easyCar was able to achieve a fleet utilization

---

This case was prepared by John J. Lawrence of the University of Idaho and Luis Solis of the Instituto de Empresa as a basis for class discussion.

[1]EasyCar.com Web site.

[2]"The Big Picture—An Interview with Stelios," *Sunday Herald* (UK), March 16, 2003.

[3]"Click to Fly," *Economist,* 13 May 2004.

rate in excess of 90 percent[4]—much higher than other major rental car companies. Industry leader Avis Europe, for example, had a fleet utilization rate of 68 percent.[5]

It was January 2003. EasyCar had broken even in the fiscal year ending September 2002[6] on revenues of £27 million.[7] This represented a significant improvement over 2001, when easyCar had lost £7.5 million on revenues of £18.5 million.[8] While pleased that the company had broken even in only its third year of operation, Stelios set aggressive financial goals for easyCar for the next two years. Plans called for quadrupling revenues in the next two years in preparation for a planned initial public offering in the second half of 2004. EasyCar's goal was to reach £100 million in revenue and £10 million in profit for the year 2004. The £100 million revenue goal and £10 million profit goal were felt necessary to obtain the desired return from an IPO. It was thought that with this level of performance, the company might be worth about £250 million.[9] In order to achieve these financial goals, the company was pushing to open an average of two new sites a week through 2003 and 2004 to reach a total of 180 sites by the end of 2004.[10]

THE RENTAL CAR INDUSTRY IN WESTERN EUROPE

The Western European rental car industry consisted of many different national markets that were only semi-integrated. While there were many companies that competed within this European rental car industry, a handful of companies held dominant positions, either across a number of national markets or within one or a few national markets. Industry experts saw the sector as ripe for consolidation.[11] Several international companies—notably Avis, Europcar, and Hertz—had strong positions across most major European markets. Within most countries, there was also a primarily national or regional company that had a strong position in its home market and perhaps moderate market share in neighboring markets. Sixt was the market leader in Germany, for example, while Atesa (in partnership with National) was the market leader in Spain. Generally, these major players accounted for more than half of the market. In Germany, for example, Sixt, Europcar, Avis and Hertz had a combined 60 percent of the €2.5 billion German rental car market.[12] In Spain, the top five firms accounted for 60 percent of the €920 million Spanish rental car market. Generally, these top firms targeted both business and vacation travelers and offered a wide range of vehicles for rent. Exhibit 1 provides basic information on these market-leading companies.

In addition to these major companies, many smaller rental companies operated in each market. In Germany, for example, there were over 700 smaller companies,[13] while in Spain there were more than 1,600 smaller companies. Many of these smaller companies operated at only one or a few locations and were particularly prevalent in tourist locations. A number of brokers also operated in the sector, like Holiday Autos. Brokerage companies did not

---

[4]E. Simpkins, "Stelios Isn't Taking It Easy," *Sunday Telegraph* (UK), December 15, 2002.

[5]Avis Europe PLC 2002 annual report, p. 10, at ir.avis-europe.com/avis/reports on August 16, 2004.

[6]E. Simpkins, "Stelios Isn't Taking It Easy."

[7]"Marketing: Former eBay UK Chief Lands Top easyCar Position," *Financial Times Information Limited,* January 9, 2003.

[8]T. Burt, "EasyCar Agrees Deal with Vauxhall," *Financial Times,* April 30, 2002, p. 24.

[9]N. Hodgson, "Stelios Plans easyCar Float," *Liverpool Echo,* September 24, 2002.

[10]E. Simpkins, "Stelios Isn't Taking It Easy."

[11]"Marketing Week: Don't Write off the Car Rental Industry," *Financial Times Information Limited,* September 26, 2002.

[12]"EasyCar Set to Shake up German Car Rental Market," European Intelligence Wire, February 22, 2002.

[13]Ibid.

EXHIBIT 1 Information on easyCar's Major European Competitors

	easyCar	Avis Europe	Europcar	Hertz	Sixt
Number of rental outlets	46	3,100	2,650	7,000	1,250
2002 fleet size	7,000	120,000	220,000	700,000	46,700
Number of countries	5	107	118	150	50
Largest market	UK	France	France	U.S.	Germany
Who owns company	EasyGroup/ Stelios Haji-Ioannou	D'Ieteren (Belgium) is majority shareholder	Volkswagen AG	Ford Motor Company	Publicly traded
European revenues	€41 million	€1.25 billion	€1.12 billion	€910 million	€600 million
Company Web site	www.easycar.com	www.avis-europe.com	www.europcar.com	www.hertz.com	ag.sixt.com

Source: Information in this table came from each company's Web site and online annual reports. European revenues are for vehicle rental in Europe and are estimated based on market share estimates for 2001 from Avis Europe's Web site.

own their own fleet of cars but basically managed the excess inventory of other companies and matched customers with rental companies with excess fleet capacity.

Overall, the rental car market could be thought of as composed of two broad segments: a business segment and a tourist/leisure segment. Depending on the market, the leisure segment represented somewhere between 45 and 65 percent of the overall market, and a large part of this segment was very price conscious. The business segment made up the remaining 35 to 55 percent of the market. It was less price sensitive than the tourist segment and more concerned about service quality, convenience, and flexibility.

THE GROWTH OF EASYCAR

EasyCar opened its first location in London, on April 20, 2000, under the name EasyRentacar. In the same week, easyCar opened locations in Glasgow and Barcelona. All three locations were popular easyJet destinations. Vehicles initially could be rented for as low as €15 per day plus a one-time car preparation fee of €8. Each of these locations had a fleet consisting entirely of Mercedes A-class vehicles. It was the only vehicle that easyCar rented at the time.

EasyCar had signed a deal with Mercedes, amidst much fanfare, at the Geneva Motor Show earlier in the year to purchase a total of 5,000 A-class vehicles. The vehicles, which came with guaranteed buy back terms, cost easyCar's parent company a little over £6 million.[14] Many in the car rental industry were surprised by the choice, expecting easyCar to rely on less expensive models.[15] In describing the acquisition of the 5,000 Mercedes vehicles, Stelios had said:

> The choice of Mercedes reflects the easyGroup brand. EasyRentacar will use brand new Mercedes cars in the same way that easyJet uses brand new Boeing aircraft. We do not compromise on the hardware, we just use innovation to substantially reduces costs. The car hire industry is where the airline industry was five years ago, a cartel feeding off the corporate client. EasyRentacar will provide a choice for consumers who pay out of their own pockets and who will not be ripped off for traveling mid-week.[16]

EasyCar quickly expanded to other locations, focusing first on those locations that were popular with easyJet customers, including Amsterdam, Geneva, Nice, and Malaga. By July 2001, a little over a year after its initial launch, easyCar had fleets of Mercedes A-class vehicles in 14 locations in the UK, Spain, France, and the Netherlands. At this point, easyCar

[14]N. Hodgson, "Stelios Plans easyCar Float."
[15]A. Felsted, "EasyCar Courts Clio for Rental Fleet," *Financial Times*, February 11, 2002, p. 26.
[16]EasyCar.com Web site news release, March 1, 2000.

secured £27 million from a consortium of Bank of Scotland Corporate Banking and NBGI Private Equity to further expand its operations. The package consisted of a combination of equity and loan stock.

While easyCar added a few sites in the second half of 2001 and early 2002, volatile demand in the wake of the September 11 attacks forced easyCar to roll out new rental locations somewhat slower than originally expected.[17] Growth accelerated, however, in spring 2002. Between May 2002 and January 2003, easyCar opened 30 new locations, going from 18 sites to a total of 48 sites. This acceleration in growth also coincided with a change in easyCar's policy regarding the makeup of its fleet. By May 2002, easyCar's fleet consisted of 6,000 Mercedes A-class vehicles across 18 sites. Beginning in May, however, easyCar began to stock its fleet with other types of vehicles. It still maintained its policy of only offering a single vehicle at each location, but now the vehicle the customer received depended on the location. The first new vehicle easyCar introduced was the Vauxhall Corsa. According to Stelios,

> Vauxhall Corsas cost easyCar £2 a day less than Mercedes A-Class so we can pass this saving on to customers. Customers themselves will decide if they want to pay a premium for a Mercedes. EasyGroup companies benefit from economies of scale where relevant but we also want to create contestable markets among our suppliers so that we can keep the cost to our customers as low as possible.[18]

By January 2003, easyCar was also using Ford Focuses (four locations), Renault Clios (three locations), Toyota Yarises (three locations), and Mercedes Smart cars (two locations), in addition to the Vauxhall Corsas (seven locations) and the Mercedes A-class vehicles (28 locations). Plans called for a further expansion of the fleet, from the 7,000 vehicles that easyCar had in January to 24,000 vehicles across 180 rental sites by the end of 2004.[19]

In addition to making vehicles available at more locations, easyCar had also changed its policies for 2003 to allow rentals for as little as one hour, and with as little as one hour's notice of rental. By making this change, Stelios felt that easyCar could be a serious competitor to local taxis, buses, trains, and even car ownership. EasyCar expected that if it made car rental simple enough and cheap enough, some people living in traffic-congested European cities who only use their car occasionally would give up the costs and hassles of car ownership and simply hire an easyCar when they needed a vehicle. Tapping into this broader transportation market would help the company reach its ambitious future sales goals.

FACILITIES

EasyCar had facilities in a total of 17 cities in five European countries, as shown in Exhibit 2. It primarily located its facilities near bus and train stations in the major European cities, seeking out sites that offered lower lease costs. It generally avoided prime airport locations, as the cost for space at and, in some cases, near airports was significantly higher than most other locations. When easyCar did locate near an airport, it generally chose sites off the airport, in order to reduce the cost of the lease. Airport locations also tended to require longer hours to satisfy customers arriving on late flights or departing on very early flights. EasyCar kept its airport locations open 24 hours a day, whereas its other locations were generally only open from 7 A.M. to 11 P.M.

The physical facilities at all locations were kept to a minimum. In many locations, easyCar leased space in an existing parking garage. Employees worked out of a small, self-contained

---

[17]T. Burt, "EasyCar Agrees Deal with Vauxhall."

[18]EasyCar.com Web site news release, May 2, 2002.

[19]"Marketing Week: EasyCar Appoints Head of European Marketing," *Financial Times Information Limited,* January 9, 2003.

EXHIBIT 2
EasyCar Locations in
January 2003

Source: EasyCar.com
Web site January 2003.

Country	City	Number	Number Near an Airport
France	Nice	1	1
France	Paris	8	0
Netherlands	Amsterdam	3	1
Spain	Barcelona	2	0
Spain	Madrid	2	0
Spain	Majorca	1	1
Spain	Malaga	1	1
Switzerland	Geneva	1	1
UK	Birmingham	2	0
UK	Bromley	1	0
UK	Croydon	1	1
UK	Glasgow	2	1
UK	Kingston-Upon-Thames	1	0
UK	Liverpool	2	1
UK	London	15	0
UK	Manchester	2	1
UK	Waterford	1	0
Total	5 Countries, 17 Cities	46	9

cubicle within the garage. The cubicle, depending on the location, might be no more than 15 square meters, and included little more than a small counter and a couple of computers at which staff processed customers as they came to pick up or return their vehicles. EasyCar also leased a number of spaces within the garage for its fleet of cars. However, because easyCar's vehicles were rented 90 percent of the time, the number of spaces required at an average site, which had a fleet of about 150 cars, was only 15–20 spaces.[20] To speed up the opening of new sites, easyCar had equipped a number of vans with all the needed computer and telephone equipment to run a site.[21] From an operational perspective, it could open a new location by simply leasing 20 or so spaces in a parking garage, hiring a small staff, driving a van to the location, and adding the location to the company's Web site. Depending on the fleet size at a location, easyCar typically had only one or two people working at a site at a time.

VEHICLE PICKUP AND RETURN PROCESSES

Customers arrived at a site to pick up a vehicle within a prearranged one-hour time period. Each customer selected this time slot when he or she booked the vehicles. EasyCar adjusted the first day's rental price based on the pickup time. Customers who picked their cars up earlier in the day or at popular times were charged more compared to customers picking up their cars later in the day or at less busy times. Customers were required to bring a printed copy of their contract, along with the credit card they used to make the booking and identification. Given the low staffing levels, customers occasionally had to wait 30 minutes or more to be processed and receive their vehicles, particularly at peak times of the day. Processing a customer began with the employee accessing the customer's contract online. If the customer was a new easyCar customer to the site, the basic policies and possible additional charges were briefly explained. The employee then made copies of the customer's identification and credit card and took a digital photo of the customer. The customer was charged an €80 refundable deposit, signed the contract, and was on the way.

[20]E. Simpkins, "Stelios Isn't Taking It Easy."
[21]Ibid.

All vehicles were rented with more or less empty fuel tanks with the exact level dependent on how much gasoline was left in the vehicle when the previous renter returned it. Customers were provided with a small map of the immediate area around the rental site, showing the location and hours of nearby gas stations. Customers could return vehicles with any amount of gas in them as long as the "low-fuel" indicator light in the vehicle was not on. Customers who returned vehicles with the low-fuel indicator light on were charged a fueling fee of €16.

Customers were also expected to return the vehicle within a prearranged one-hour period, which they also selected at the time of booking. While customers did not have to worry about refueling the car before returning it, they were expected to thoroughly clean the car. This clean car policy had been implemented in May 2002 as a way to further reduce the price customers could pay for their vehicle. Prior to this change, all customers paid a fixed preparation fee of €11 each time they rented a vehicle (up from the €8 preparation fee when the company started operations in 2000). The new policy reduced this up-front preparation fee to €4 but required customers to either return the vehicle clean or pay an additional cleaning fee of €16. In order to avoid any misunderstanding about what it meant by a clean car, easyCar provided customers with an explicit description of what constituted a clean car, both for the interior and the exterior of the car. This included that it had to be apparent that the exterior of the car had been washed prior to returning the vehicle. The map that customers were provided when they picked up their cars that showed nearby gas stations also showed nearby car washes where they could clean the car before returning it. While easyCar had received some bad press in relation to the policy,[22] 85 percent of customers returned their vehicles clean as a result of the policy.

When a customer returned the vehicle, an easyCar employee would check to make sure that the vehicle was clean, undamaged, and that the low-fuel indicator light was not on. The employee would also check the kilometers driven. The customer would then be notified of any additional charges. These charges would be subtracted from the €80 deposit and the difference refunded to the customer's credit card (or, if additional charges exceeded the €80 deposit, the customer's credit card would be charged the difference).

PRICING

EasyCar clearly differentiated itself from its competitors with its low price. In addition, pricing also played a key role in easyCar's efforts to achieve high utilization of its fleet of cars. EasyCar advertised prices as low as €5 per day plus a per-rental preparation fee of €4. Prices, however, varied by the location and dates of the rental, when the booking was made, and what time the car was to be picked up and returned. EasyCar's systems constantly evaluated projected demand and expected utilization at each site and adjusted price accordingly. Achieving the €5 per day rate usually required customers to book well in advance, and these rates were typically only available on weekdays. Weekend rates, when booked well in advance, typically started a few euros higher than the weekday rates. As a given rental date approached, however, the price typically went up significantly as easyCar approached 100 percent fleet utilization for that day. Rates could literally triple overnight if there was sufficient booking activity. Generally, however, easyCar's price was less than half that of its major competitors. EasyCar, unlike most other rental car companies, required customers to pay in full at the time of booking, and once a booking was made, it was nonrefundable.

EasyCar's base price covered only the core rental of the vehicle—the total price customers paid was in many cases much higher and depended on how the customer reserved, paid for,

[22]J. Hyde, "Travel View: Clearing up on the Extras," *The Observer* (UK), July 7, 2002.

used, and returned the vehicle. EasyCar's price was based on customers booking through the company's Web site and paying for their rental with their easyMoney credit card. EasyMoney was the easyGroup's credit and financial services company. Customers who chose to book through the company's phone reservation system were charged an additional €0.95 a minute for the call, and those who used other credit cards were charged €5 extra. All vehicles had to be paid for by a credit or debit card—cash was not accepted. The base rental price allowed customers to drive vehicles 100 kilometers per day—additional kilometers were charged at a rate of €0.12 per kilometer. In addition, customers were expected to return their cars clean and on time. Customers who returned cars that did not meet easyCar's standards for cleanness were charged a €16 cleaning fee. Those who returned their cars late were immediately charged €120 and subsequently charged an additional €120 for each 24-hour period in which the car was not returned. EasyCar explained the high late fee as representing the cost that it would likely incur in providing another vehicle to the next customer. Customers wishing to make any changes to their bookings were also charged a change fee of €16. Changes could be made either before the rental started or during the rental period but were limited to changing the dates, times, and location of the rental and were subject to the prices and vehicle availability at the time the change was being made. If the change resulted in an overall lower price for the rental, however, no refund was provided for the difference.

Beginning in 2003, all customers were also required to purchase loss/damage insurance for an additional charge of €4 a day that eliminated the customer's liability for loss or damage to the vehicle (excluding damage to the tires or windshield of the vehicle). Through 2002, customers were able to choose whether or not to purchase additional insurance from easyCar to eliminate any financial liability in the event that the rental vehicle was damaged. The cost of this insurance had been €6 a day, and approximately 60 percent of easyCar's customers purchased this optional insurance. Those not purchasing this insurance had either assumed the liability for the first €800 in damages personally, or had their own insurance through some other means (e.g., some credit card companies provide this insurance to their cardholders at no additional charge for short-term rentals paid for with the credit card).

EasyCar's Web site attempted to make all these additional charges clear to customers at the time of their booking. EasyCar had received a fair amount of bad press when it first opened for business after many renters complained about having to pay undisclosed charges when they returned their cars.[23] In response, easyCar had revamped its Web site in an effort to make these charges more transparent to customers and to explain the logic behind many of these charges.

PROMOTION

EasyCar's promotional efforts had through 2002 focused primarily on posters and press advertising. Posters were particularly prevalent in metro systems and bus and train stations in cities where easyCar had operations. All this advertising focused on easyCar's low price. According to founder Stelios:

> You will never see an advert for an easy company offering an experience—it's about price. If you create expectations you can't live up to then you will ultimately suffer as a result.[24]

In 2002, easyCar spent £1.43 million on such advertising.[25]

EasyCar also promoted itself by displaying its name, phone number, and Web site address prominently on the doors and rear window of its entire fleet of vehicles, and took advantage

---

[23]J. Stanton, "The Empire That's Easy Money," *Edinburgh Evening News,* November 26, 2002.
[24]"The big picture—an interview with Stelios."
[25]"Marketing Week: EasyCar Appoints Head of European Marketing."

of free publicity when the opportunity presented itself. An example of seeking out such publicity occurred when Hertz complained that easyCar's comparative advertising campaign in the Netherlands that featured the line "The best reason to use easyCar.com can be found at hertz.nl" violated Dutch law that required comparative advertising to be exact, not general. In response, Stelios and a group of easyCar employees, dressed in orange boiler suits and with a fleet of easyCar vehicles, protested outside the Hertz Amsterdam office with signs asking "What is Hertz frightened of?"[26]

In an effort to help reach its goal of quadrupling sales in the next two years, easyCar had hired Jennifer Mowat for the new position of commercial director to take over responsibility for easyCar's European marketing. Mowat had previously been eBay's UK country manager and had recently completed an MBA in Switzerland. Previously, Stelios and easyCar's managing director, Andrew Fitzmaurice, had handled the marketing function themselves.[27] As part of this stepped-up marketing effort, easyCar also planned to double its advertising budget for 2003, to £3 million, and to begin to advertise on television. The television advertising campaign was to feature easyCar's founder, Stelios.[28]

LEGAL CHALLENGES

EasyCar faced several challenges to its approaches. The most significant dealt with a November 2002 ruling made by the Office of Fair Trading (OFT) that easyCar had to grant customers seven days from the time they made a booking to cancel their booking and receive a full refund. The OFT was a UK governmental agency that was responsible for protecting UK consumers from unfair and/or anticompetitive business practices. The ruling against easyCar was based on the 2000 Consumer Protection Distance Selling Regulations. These regulations stipulated that companies that sell at a distance (e.g., by Internet, phone) must provide customers with a seven-day cooling-off period, during which time customers can cancel their contracts with the company and receive a full refund. The law exempted accommodation, transportation, catering, and leisure service companies from this requirement. The OFT's ruling concluded that easyCar did not qualify as a transportation service company because the consumers had to drive themselves, and as such they were not receiving a transport service, just a car.[29]

EasyCar had appealed the OFT's decision to the UK High Court on the grounds that it was indeed a transportation service company and was entitled to an exemption from this requirement. EasyCar was hopeful that it would eventually win this legal challenge. EasyCar had argued that this ruling would destroy the company's book-early-pay-less philosophy and could lead to a tripling of prices.[30] Chairman Stelios was quoted as saying:

> It is very serious. My fear is that as soon as we put in the seven-day cooling-off periods our utilization rate will fall from 90 percent to 65 percent. That's the difference between a profitable company and an unprofitable one.[31]

EasyCar was also concerned that prolonged legal action on this point could interfere with its plans for a 2004 IPO.

---

[26]EasyCar.com Web site news release, April 22, 2002.

[27]"Marketing Week: EasyCar Appoints Head of European Marketing."

[28]"Campaigning: EasyGroup Appoints Publicist for easyCar TV Advertising Brief," *Financial Times Information Limited,* January 31, 2003.

[29]J. Macintosh, "EasyCar Sues OFT Amid Threat to Planned Flotation," *Financial Times,* November 22, 2002, p. 4.

[30]"Marketing Week: EasyCar Appoints Head of European Marketing."

[31]J. Mackintosh, "EasyCar Sues OFT Amid Threat to Planned Flotation."

OFT, for its part, had also applied to the UK High Court for an injunction to make the company comply with the ruling. Other rental car companies were generally unconcerned about the ruling, as few offered big discounts for early bookings or nonrefundable bookings.[32]

EasyCar's new policy of posting the pictures of customers whose cars were 15 days or more overdue was also drawing legal criticism. EasyCar had recently received public warnings from lawyers that this new policy might violate data protection, libel, privacy, confidentiality, and human rights laws.[33] Of particular concern to some lawyers was the possibility that easyCar might post the wrong person's picture, given the large number of customers the company dealt with.[34] Such a mistake could open the company to costly libel suits. The policy of posting the pictures of overdue customers on the easyCar Web site, initiated in November 2002, was designed to reduce the losses associated with customers renting a vehicle and never returning it. The costs were significant, according to Stelios:

> These cars are expensive, £15,000 each, and we have 6,000 of them. At any given time we are looking for as many as twenty or thirty, which are overdue. If we don't get one back, it's a write-off. We are writing off an entire car, and its uninsurable.[35]

Stelios was also convinced of the legality of the new policy. In a letter to the editor responding to the legal concerns raised in the press, Stelios said:

> From a legal perspective, we have been entirely factual and objective and are merely reporting the details of the overdue car and the person who collected it. In addition, our policy is made very clear in our terms and conditions and the photo is taken both overtly and with the consent of the customer. . . . I estimate the total cost of overdue cars to be 5 percent of total easyCar costs, or 50p on every car rental day for all customers. In 2004, when I intend to float easyCar, this cost will amount to £5 million unless we can reduce our quantity of overdue cars.[36]

In the past, easyCar had simply provided pictures to police when a rental was 15 or more days overdue. It was hoped that posting the picture would both discourage drivers from not returning vehicles and shame those drivers who currently had overdue cars into returning them. In fact, the first person who easyCar posted to its Web site did indeed return his car two days later. The vehicle was 29 days late.[37]

THE FUTURE

At the end of 2002, Stelios had stepped down as the CEO of easyJet so that he could devote more of his time to the other easyGroup companies, including easyCar. He had three priorities for the new year. One was to turn around a money-losing easyInternetCafe business, which Stelios had described as "the worst mistake of my career."[38] The 22-store chain had lost £80 million in the last two years. The second was to oversee the planned launch of another new easyGroup business, easyCinema, in spring 2003. And the third was to oversee the rapid expansion of the easyCar chain, so that it would be ready for an initial public offering in the second half of 2004.

[32]Ibid.

[33]B. Sherwood & A. Wendlandt, "EasyCar May Be in Difficulty over Naming Ploy," *Financial Times,* November 14, 2002, p. 2.

[34]Ibid.

[35]"e-business: Internet Fraudsters Fail to Steal Potter Movie's Magic & Other News," *Financial Times Information Limited,* November 19, 2002.

[36]S. Haji-Ioannou, "Letters to the Editor: Costly Effect of Late Car Return," *Financial Times,* November 16, 2002, p. 10.

[37]M. Hookham, "How Stelios Nets Return of His Cars," *Daily Post* (Liverpool, UK), November 14, 2002.

[38]S. Bentley, "The Worst Mistake of My Career, By Stelios," *Financial Times,* December 24, 2002.

Case

10

The Lego Group: Building Strategy

Paul Bigus and Darren Meister *University of Western Ontario*

On February 15, 2011, world-famous toy maker the LEGO Group (LEGO) assembled an internal management team to create a strategic report on LEGO's different product lines and business operations. Over the past two years, numerous threats had emerged against LEGO in the toy industry: The acquisition of Marvel Entertainment by The Walt Disney Company created major implications for valuable toy license agreement. LEGO had lost a long legal battle with major competitor MEGA Brands—maker of MEGA Bloks—with a European Union court decision that removed the LEGO brick trademark; new competition was preparing to enter the marketplace from Hasbro—the second-largest toy maker in the world—with the company launching a new rival product line called Kre-O. It was critical for the management team to identify where to expand LEGO's product lines and business operations in order to develop a competitive strategy to continue the organization's financial success and dominance in the building toy market.

COMPANY HISTORY[1]

LEGO was founded during the Great Depression in 1932, when Danish carpenter Ole Kirk Kristiansen and his sons started making wooden toys after the demand for building houses and furniture declined. Some of the first toys they made included yo-yos, wooden blocks,

[1]Daniel Lipkowitz, *The LEGO Book* (NY: Dorley Kindersley Publishing, 2009), pp. 10–49.

pull-along animals, and wooden vehicles. Kristiansen believed that "only the best is good enough" in manufacturing children's toys; this motto was so important to him that it was carved on a sign and hung on the workshop wall to serve as a reminder to always produce top-quality products. He used the highest quality materials and workmanship to produce toys that were designed to last through years of play. In 1934, the company name LEGO was created when Kristiansen held a friendly competition among the workshop employees to help name the company, with a bottle of wine as the prize. Kristiansen won the competition himself by creatively combining the first two letters of the Danish words *leg* and *godt,* meaning "play well," to form the name LEGO, which also meant "I put together" in Latin. In 1942, disaster hit the small company of only 12 employees as the entire workshop burned to the ground. Not willing to quit, Kristiansen rebuilt the factory and painstakingly remade all lost designs from memory in order to keep the company going.

After World War II, LEGO became the first company in Denmark to purchase a plastic injection molding machine in 1947; however, the new machine came at a high cost, requiring the company to risk a large portion of revenues and face the additional financial risk of plastic toys being expensive to manufacture. With the acquisition of the new machine, one of the first plastic toys to be created by LEGO was a baby rattle that was shaped like a fish. It did not take long before the investment in the machine proved to be a success, as LEGO quickly expanded its business operations to produce over 200 varieties of plastic and wooden toys. Using the new technology, the first plastic LEGO bricks—named Automatic Binding Bricks—were created and sold in sets in 1949; however, this name did not last long as it was changed to LEGO Bricks in 1953, with the LEGO name being molded onto every brick manufactured.

Godtfred Kirk Christiansen, one of Kristiansen's sons, had grown up with the family company and eventually became the junior managing director of LEGO. On returning from a toy fair in 1954, Godtfred and a coworker had a conversation during which they realized that no system existed to connect different products or items in the toy industry. To Godtfred, this represented a key opportunity to design a new structured system of toy products, selecting the LEGO brick as the best company product with which to create what he referred to as the "LEGO System of Play." The idea behind the LEGO System of Play was that each and every LEGO brick should connect to each other—not just within one set but across multiple sets. A 'Town Plan' series with 28 building sets and 8 vehicle sets was developed and released. The strategy was simple but important: Each additional LEGO set obtained by a child increased the amount of LEGO bricks that the child had available to build with, thus more sets equaled more creative opportunities. The different Town Plan models included LEGO bricks as well as various plastic people, trees, vehicles, and road signs. In order to help market the product to children and parents, the sets were creatively designed in collaboration with the Danish Road Safety Council to help teach children about traffic safety. Godtfred commented on the LEGO System of Play: "Our idea is to create a toy that prepares the child for life, appeals to the imagination and develops the creative urge and joy of creation that are the driving force in every human being."[2]

The development of the LEGO System of Play led Godtfred to realize that improvements were needed in the LEGO brick design so that bricks could lock together firmly yet come apart easily: He referred to this as the brick's 'clutch power.' Finding the correct clutch power would allow for more stable and secure LEGO brick models that would not easily fall apart. With such a brick design and building capability, Godtfred believed that it would be possible to create anything out of LEGO bricks. In attempting to find such a design, LEGO experimented with different plastic injection molding designs that included various shapes and connection methods before finally selecting a brick design that added

[2]Daniel Lipkowitz, *The LEGO Book* (NY: Dorley Kindersley Publishing, 2009), p. 18.

hollow connection tubes to the bottom of the existing LEGO brick design. With the improved design, when two bricks were placed directly on top of each other, the hollow tubes on the underside of the top brick connected firmly between the existing circular studs on the top of the bottom brick, providing the perfect amount of clutch power. Pleased with the results, Godtfred submitted an application in Denmark on January 28, 1958, to officially patent the improved LEGO brick design. This year signified a historical event for LEGO; unfortunately, it also represented a major loss with the death of LEGO founder Kristiansen. This left Godtfred in charge of the company, which had grown to 140 employees.

The 1960s

During the 1960s, LEGO had experienced rapid success with the new brick design, expanding sales to many European countries as well as new markets in the United States, Canada, Japan, and Australia. After another fire destroyed the workshop where LEGO wooden toys were made, the company decided to stop selling wooden toys altogether and focus completely on the LEGO brick and System of Play. By 1967, more than 18 million LEGO sets had been sold in 42 different countries, with LEGO employing over 600 people. The company had also expanded the LEGO brick design to include over 200 different shapes such as wheels, flat bricks, train tracks, windows, doors, and flags; this added further detail and allowed more creative possibilities to the System of Play sets. In an effort to help children and parents with the variety of bricks and the increased complexity of building sets, LEGO introduced building instructions as a standard feature of each building set. The increased success and popularity of LEGO around the world led to the development of the first LEGOLAND theme park, opening in LEGO's home country of Denmark in 1968. In the same year, LEGO continued to experiment with new products, introducing a brick called DUPLO that was eight times the size of an original LEGO brick and safe for children under five.

The 1970s

By 1975, LEGO had grown to over 2,500 employees and continued to develop new innovative sets that included a series for girls involving doll houses and furniture, ships made out of LEGO that could float in water, and a LEGO Technic series that created models with mechanical moving parts. In 1978, LEGO continued to transform the building toy industry by introducing the first miniature figures with painted faces and movable arms and legs. LEGO incorporated the minifigures into the launch of three new play themes: LEGO Castle featuring medieval knights and castle sets, LEGO Town featuring city characters and modern buildings, and LEGO Space featuring astronauts and spacecraft. The company changed leadership again in 1979, when third-generation Kjeld Kirk Kristiansen, Godtfred's son, became the president and chief executive officer (CEO) of LEGO.

The 1980s

With LEGO celebrating its 50th anniversary in 1982, the company continued to expand operations, launching an educational line for schools as well as a DUPLO Baby series. Over the years, LEGO continued to experiment by combining LEGO bricks with technology, introducing a Light & Sound series in addition to a LEGO Technic series—which allowed motors to be controlled by a computer—in 1986. Success of the LEGO play themes continued with new Castle, City, and Space sets being released each year, in addition to a new LEGO Pirates theme being launched. With many children building their own LEGO creations without instructions, buckets full of assorted LEGO bricks were also made available to purchase for creative building. LEGO had become established around the world as the building toy of choice, with many fan clubs being created and building competitions taking place. To stay connected to the ever-growing market, a LEGO magazine was also made available in many countries to keep members up to date on new product information and creative building ideas.

The 1990s

LEGO had grown to become one of the top 10 largest toy manufactures in the world by 1990. Global operations employed over 7,000 people and included over 1,000 injection molding machines in five LEGO factories. LEGO utilized its strong brand image by opening LEGO stores to exclusively sell LEGO products and merchandise. The use of television advertising also helped the company to build a familiar "LEGO Maniac" slogan. With the increase of home computer use and the rise of the Internet, LEGO launched the official LEGO website (www.LEGO.com) in 1996. Soon after, in 1997, LEGO expanded into a new business area with the release of the first-ever LEGO computer game. The combination of LEGO and computers continued with the LEGO MINDSTORMS line, which allowed users to build and control complex sets with the use of desktop computers and remote controls.

LEGO also diversified its product line by launching many new creative play themes such as LEGO Western, LEGO Adventurers, LEGO Aquazone, LEGO Iceplanet, LEGO Time Cruisers, and LEGO Space Insectoids. The company had even created a LEGO brick vacuum device to help children do their least-favorite LEGO activity—picking up the bricks. LEGO advanced again in 1999, as for the first time the company acquired the licensed rights to famous movies and children themes, which led to the launch of LEGO Star Wars and DUPLO Winnie the Pooh product lines. Combining Star Wars licensed property with LEGO bricks allowed for constructible sets to be created, featuring various well-known characters and vehicles from the widely popular franchise films. The LEGO Star Wars theme was a huge success, quickly developing into one of LEGO's most profitable product lines.

2000 and Beyond

Following the success of LEGO Star Wars, other popular licensed rights were obtained for new product lines. Harry Potter, Spiderman, Batman, Indiana Jones, and SpongeBob SquarePants were all developed into LEGO series sets. Licensed rights were also obtained for DUPLO sets including Bob the Builder, Dora the Explorer, and Disney themes. The licensed agreements did not stop there as LEGO viewed professional sports as new opportunities, subsequently launching series sets with LEGO NBA Basketball, LEGO NHL Hockey, and LEGO Soccer. Lego also continued to develop products internally, offering new play themes such as LEGO Knights' Kingdom, LEGO Alpha Team, LEGO Bionicle, LEGO Discovery, LEGO Clikits Jewelry, LEGO Studios, LEGO Mars Mission, and LEGO Exo-Force. As LEGO was also popular with many adults, special edition sets were created for advanced LEGO builders and collectors, featuring famous structures such as the Statue of Liberty, Taj Mahal, Eiffel Tower, and the Star Wars Death Star. Some sets proved to be more successful than others; as a result, some product lines were only sold for a few years before being discontinued in order to free valuable shelf space, production, and advertising resources to produce LEGO sets that were in high demand.

With the successful acquisition of many licensed rights, LEGO partnered with video game design companies to develop video games for both computers and video game consoles: This resulted in over 30 LEGO video games being released between 1997 and 2009, featuring the popular LEGO licensed product lines of Harry Potter, Batman, Indiana Jones, and Star Wars. LEGO had also developed video games based on its own successful product lines and themes. Overall, many of the video games were highly popular with both children and adult age groups, as they featured LEGO characters and famous movie storylines to play and explore in LEGO-designed environments. At a time when many video games were seen as too violent—with content inappropriate for children—LEGO provided nonviolent video games with content that parents could trust.

LEGO continued to expand beyond traditional video games to develop a virtual online LEGO Universe in 2010. After paying online to register, players could design their own personalized LEGO minifigures to be used to explore online environments and interact with other online players. LEGO was also constantly updating and improving the LEGO website, which was receiving over 4 million visitors per month from over 200 countries by 2003. All LEGO items were made available for online purchase, and the website also provided interactive games, animated videos, and comics. One of the most popular additions to the LEGO website was the introduction of software called LEGO Digital Designer: This allowed a user to design a LEGO set online, using the enormous catalog of LEGO bricks available. After users finished building their own personal designs, the site would automatically calculate the cost for the materials, providing users with the option to buy their unique creations. If purchased, LEGO would package the physical bricks needed to build the online design and ship them directly to the user's home. Users could also share their designs online, with contests taking place from which winning designs were turned into official LEGO sets.

THE FIRST TIME MANAGEMENT SAVED THE COMPANY[3]

The threats in the toy industry did not represent the first time LEGO management had faced serious issues. Between 1998 and 2004, the company lost money in four years. Revenues had dropped 30 percent in 2003, and fell another 10 percent in 2004. Problems existed not with the LEGO products but behind the scenes in how the company manufactured and distributed LEGO around the world. Years of continuous growth added layers of complexity to LEGO's operations. Knowing that the company needed to change directions, Kjeld stepped down as company CEO in 2004. He was replaced by Jorgen Vig Knudstorp, who had started at LEGO as the director of strategic development in 2001. In his first actions as CEO, Knudstorp assembled a leadership team of senior executives and managers to start analyzing every part of LEGO's supply chain operations as a whole: This included everything from new product development to materials sourcing, production, and distribution.

The leadership team discovered that over the years, as new products represented a larger amount of annual revenues, newer-generation LEGO sets had become more elaborate while providing less profit in return. Product designers were creating new sets without giving full consideration to the costs of materials or production: This resulted in LEGO dealing with over 11,000 suppliers, as designers often selected their own vendors. Not considering production costs resulted in serious waste. If a designer created a new brick or selected a rare color, manufacturing would often be left with extra materials or costly resin colors that would never be used again. Inefficiencies were also revealed from the poor organization of LEGO's plastic-injection molding machines, with each one capable of producing every type of LEGO brick: This required costly retooling and created long downtimes, translating into production facilities only operating at 70 percent of capacity. On producing a finished product, the leadership team traced additional high costs to distribution operations. Logistics represented a web of 26 different providers that shipped products from multileveled distribution networks: This created a backlog of orders and inefficiencies in inventory levels. The leadership team continued to uncover damaging business practices at the final

---

[3]Keith Oliver, Edouard Samakh, and Peter Heckmann, "Rebuilding Lego, Brick by Brick," *Strategy and Business,* August 29, 2007, www.strategy-business.com/article/07306?gko=99ab7, accessed on August 27, 2011.

retail level. Overall, LEGO was spending the same amount of time dealing with thousands of smaller independent stores that represented one-third of revenues as it did with 200 larger chain and big box stores that generated two-thirds of revenues. Smaller stores also added extra costs for LEGO in shipping, labor, and inventory, as they often ordered less than a full carton of product. In turn, the disproportionate amount of time with chain and big box stores equaled inaccurate forecasting and inventory shortages that decreased sales.

In order to make LEGO profitable again, the leadership team introduced numerous changes across the organization. Cost-saving measures were found by cutting the selection of LEGO brick colors in half while also reducing the number of different minifigures available. The production cost for each individual LEGO brick shape helped identify and reduce expensive items: This resulted in an 80 percent reduction in the amount of suppliers needed. With better production costs, designers could be shown the impact of using existing brick shapes compared to creating new molds and colors. Further down the supply chain, the leadership team increased production capacity by assigning certain machines to make only specific LEGO bricks on scheduled production cycles: This reduced the amount of downtime and costly retooling for each machine. The leadership team also realized that revenue could increase by moving more inventory; therefore, using greater economies of scale they reduced the number of logistic suppliers from 26 to 4, improving structure and communication. Smaller distribution centers were replaced by larger hub centers that were strategically located closer to retailers, providing better control over inventory and fewer stock shortages. Owing to the contrast in revenue between small and large retailers, changes were introduced to create value and optimize sales: Discounts were offered to smaller stores in exchange for placing orders early, and LEGO would no longer ship cartons that were not full. In order to maximize business opportunities with large chain stores and big-box retailers, LEGO worked closely to provide joint forecasting, inventory management, and marketing support.

The significant changes to design, production, distribution, and sales resulted in LEGO increasing its inventory turnover by 12 percent in 2005, earning a profit of $72 million. This continued with an inventory turnover increase of 11 percent in 2006, as well as profits increasing by 240 percent. Knudstorp's leadership had successfully modernized LEGO's business operations while placing his mark on the company. He commented on the company's progress: "It has allowed us to again focus on developing the business."

LEGO IN 2010

As of 2010, LEGO remained a privately held company by the Kirk Kristiansen family. Annual sales reached an all-time high at DKK16.014 billion (Danish kroner), equaling over US$3.7 billion (see Exhibit 1).[4] Overall, the company's strongest-selling product lines were LEGO Star Wars, LEGO City, and LEGO DUPLO. The high sales figures translated into seven LEGO sets being sold each second around the world.

With over 9,000 employees, LEGO had grown to become the fourth-largest toy manufacturer in the world.[5] The company had developed a global brand that spread across numerous business operations (see Exhibit 2). As a household name and icon in the toy

[4]Andrew Couts, "Lego Systems' sales surpassed $1 billion mark in 2010," *Digital Trends,* February 14, 2011, www.digitaltrends.com/gaming/lego-systems-sales-surpassed-1-billion-mark-in-2010/, accessed on August 27, 2011.

[5]"LEGO 2010 Annual Report," *LEGO,* 2011, http://cache.lego.com/upload/contentTemplating/AboutUsFactsAndFiguresContent/otherfiles/downloadE994290D230BFB0E2A914F4DC3B6531C.pdf, accessed on August 27, 2011.

EXHIBIT 1

Financial Highlights
(in millions of DKK)

Source: The Lego Group:
Annual Report 2010," LEGO
2011, http://cache.lego.com/
upload/contentTemplating/
AboutUsFactsAndFigures
Content/otherfiles/download
E994290D230BFB0E2A914F
4DC3B6531C.pdf, accessed
on August 27, 2011.

	2010	2009	2008	2007	2006
Income Statement:					
Revenue	16,014	11,661	9,526	8,027	7,798
Expenses	(10,899)	(8,659)	(7,522)	(6,556)	(6,393)
Operating profit before special items	5,115	3,002	2,004	1,471	1,405
Special items	(142)	(100)	96	(22)	(80)
Financial income and expenses	(84)	(15)	(248)	(35)	(44)
Profit before income tax	4,889	2,887	1,852	1,414	1,281
Net profit for the year	3,718	2,204	1,352	1,028	1,290
Balance Sheet:					
Total assets	10,972	7,788	6,496	6,009	6,907
Equity	5,473	3,291	2,066	1,679	1,191
Liabilities	5,499	4,497	4,430	4,330	5,716
Cash Flow Statement:					
Cash flows from operating activities	3,744	2,712	1,954	1,033	1,157
Investment in property, plant and equipment	1,077	1,042	368	399	316
Investment in intangible assets	123	216	75	34	-
Cash flows from financing activities	(3,477)	(906)	(1,682)	(467)	597
Total cash flows	(871)	558	128	592	1,925
Employees:					
Average number (full-time)	8,365	7,286	5,388	4,199	4,908
Financial ratios (in %):					
Gross margin	72.5	70.3	66.8	65.0	64.9
Operating margin (ROS)	31.1	24.9	22.0	18.1	17.0
Net profit margin	23.2	18.9	14.2	12.8	16.5
Return on equity (ROE)	84.8	82.3	72.2	71.6	147.1
Return on invested capital (ROIC I)	161.2	139.5	101.8	69.7	63.6
Return on invested capital (ROIC II)	157.9	138.0	113.8	77.1	67.4
Equity ratio	49.9	42.3	31.8	27.9	17.2
Equity ratio	49.9	42.3	39.5	46.2	33.2

industry, LEGO had received the distinction of being named 'Toy of the Century' by the British Association for Toy Retailers.[6] Since first starting to manufacture LEGO bricks back in 1949, the company had produced over 400 billion bricks, with 19 billion new bricks being made each year—translating to over 2 million bricks made every hour, or 36,000 each minute.[7] Starting with one patented brick design in 1958, over the span of 50 years, LEGO had developed over 2,400 different brick shapes, which were available in 53 different colors.

The LEGO mission stated, "Our ultimate purpose is to inspire and develop children to think creatively, reason systematically and release the potential to shape their own future—experiencing the endless human possibility";[8] such a vision could be started with a handful

[6]Daniel Lipkowitz, *The LEGO Book* (NY: Dorley Kindersley Publishing, 2009), p. 30.

[7]Jesus Diaz, "LEGO Brick Timeline: 50 Years of Building Frenzy and Curiosities," *Gizmodo,* January 28, 2008, http://gizmodo.com/349509/lego-brick-timeline-50-years-of-building-frenzy-and-curiosities, accessed on August 27, 2011.

[8]"Mission and Vision," *LEGO,* 2011, http://aboutus.lego.com/en-us/group/vision.aspx, accessed on August 27, 2011.

EXHIBIT 2
Business
Operations (2010)

Source: *LEGO*, 2011, www.
lego.com/en-us/default.aspx,
accessed on August 27, 2011.

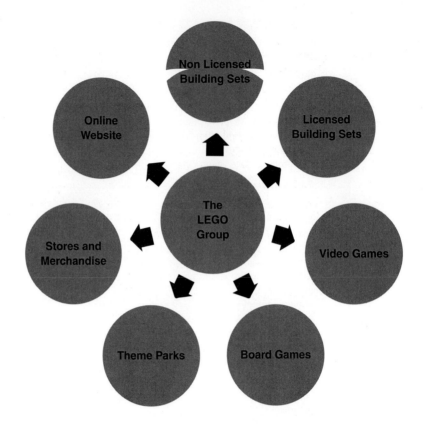

of LEGO, requiring just six original shaped LEGO bricks to build over 915 million different creations.[9]

COMPETITION

Selling plastic bricks over a span of 50 years, LEGO had faced a variety of competitors, as other companies entered the building toy market hoping to capitalize on LEGO's success. Some companies introduced products based on their own unique design: One example was introduced by the toy company Fisher Price, with a plastic construction toy called Construx. It used plastic beams and connector nuts to form different structures, but only lasted in production from 1983 to 1988.[10] Another attempt was seen as a new company entered the building toy market in 1992, introducing a product called K'NEX that used flat plastic gear shapes and thin straw-shaped beams to build different designs.[11]

Some companies introduced plastic brick products that were compatible with the LEGO brick design: This meant that competitors' bricks could be fitted together and be built with LEGO bricks. Toy manufacturer TYCO introduced TYCO Super Blocks in 1984, with a plastic brick design that was almost identical to that of LEGO bricks.[12] In addition, TYCO also made reference to LEGO in its advertising, communicating to consumers that TYCO

[9]Daniel Lipkowitz, *The LEGO Book* (NY: Dorley Kindersley Publishing, 2009), p. 7.

[10]"Construx Main Index," *This Old Toy,* 2007, www.thisoldtoy.com/fisher-price/dept-7-playsets/f-construx/a-construx-index.html, accessed on August 27, 2011.

[11]"About K'NEX," *K'NEX,* 2011, www.knex.com/About_KNEX/, accessed on August 27, 2011.

[12]"TYCO Super Blocks Resource," *Tony Cook's HQ-Scale Trains Resource,* 2011, www.ho-scaletrains.net/tycosuperblocks/index.html, accessed on August 27, 2011.

Super Blocks connected to LEGO, providing slogans such as, "If you can't tell the difference, why pay the difference."[13] In response, LEGO launched a lawsuit that lasted four years (1984–1988); the outcome was that LEGO was successful in forcing the removal of the advertisements and product reference; however, the US Supreme Court denied LEGO's claim on the building block design as the LEGO patent expired in 1988.[14]

On expiry of the LEGO plastic brick design patent in 1988, the barriers of competition were lowered in the building toy market.[15] In 1991, Canadian toy manufacturer MEGA Brands, which had been selling plastic brick building products called MEGA Bloks since 1984, introduced a smaller-sized line of MEGA Bloks that were compatible with LEGO bricks.[16] By 2003, MEGA Bloks had seen 17 straight years of sales growth with an annual revenue of over US$188 million to become the world's second-largest building toy producer behind LEGO.[17] MEGA Bloks continued to quickly expand to different countries around the world. In 2010, MEGA Bloks had developed successful product lines that included license agreements with the popular HALO video game franchise, Marvel Comics, Disney, Thomas the Train, Hello Kitty, Nickleodeon, and Caterpillar Construction Equipment.[18] Although MEGA Bloks had significantly smaller sales with an annual revenue of over US$368 million, it represented the largest competition to LEGO.[19] It had also proved that other companies could carve out a percentage of the building toy market, with MEGA Bloks management estimating that the company had a 25 percent share of the North American building toy market and a 12 percent share of the international building toy market.[20]

NEW BUSINESS THREATS

Over the past two years LEGO has faced new threats emerging in the toy industry from company acquisitions, court battles, and new product competition.

Company Acquisitions

In a strategic move to strengthen its position in the global entertainment industry, the Walt Disney Company (Disney) acquired Marvel Entertainment (Marvel) for US$4 billion in 2009.[21] This provided Disney with control over Marvel's vast catalogue of over 5,000 comic book characters to be used in future publishing, movie production, and licensing

---

[13]Barbara Demick, "Judge Blocks Tyco Ads Claiming Blocks Are Like Lego's," *The Philadelphia Inquirer,* September 2, 1987, http://articles.philly.com/1987-09-02/business/26207754_1_tyco-toys-lego-systems-plastic-bricks, accessed on August 27, 2011.

[14]"Tyco wins lawsuit over Lego," *HighBeam Research,* May 6, 1988, www.highbeam.com/doc/1G1-6653339.html, accessed on August 27, 2011.

[15]"Patents that changed the world: Lego," *New Legal Review,* June 23, 2010, www.cpaglobal.com/newlegalreview/widgets/notes_quotes/more/3123/patents_that_changed_the_world_lego, accessed on August 27, 2011.

[16]"Mega Bloks, Inc.," *Funding Universe,* 2011, www.fundinguniverse.com/company-histories/Mega-Bloks-Inc-Company-History.html, accessed on August 27, 2011.

[17]Ibid.

[18]"Shop," *MEGA Bloks,* 2011, www.megabloks.com/Shop/MEGA_Bloks/, accessed on August 27, 2011.

[19]"MEGA Brands Inc.: Consolidated Financial Statements December 31, 2010 and 2009," a PricewaterhouseCoopers report, March 16, 2011, *MEGA Brands,* www.megabrands.com/media/pdf/corpo/en/reports/Financial_Statements_2010-2009.pdf, accessed on August 27, 2011.

[20]"MEGA Bloks Inc.," *Industry Today,* 2010, www.usitoday.com/article_view.asp?ArticleID=1495, accessed on August 27, 2011.

[21]"Disney Completes Marvel Acquisition," *Marvel,* December 31, 2009, http://marvel.com/news/story/10809/disney_completes_marvel_acquisition, accessed on August 27, 2011.

operations. Movies based on comic book characters had been proved to be extremely successful and profitable in the film industry, with Spider-Man earning over US$821 million in 2002[22] and The Dark Knight earning over US$1 billion in 2008.[23] Apart from producing massive revenues in the movie industry, comic book characters also generated huge revenues in the toy industry with the Spider-Man film generating over US$100 million in related toy sales in 2002.[24] Mattel and Hasbro were the two largest toy manufactures in the world. Mattel had the highest revenue of any toy company with US$5.8 billion in 2010.[25] It manufactured popular products such as Hot Wheels and Barbie, as well as a large selection of toys based on licensed rights. Behind Mattel, but still significant in size, Hasbro operated as the world's second-largest toy maker with a revenue of US$4 billion in 2010.[26] The company produced many long-running successful toy products including Transformers, Mr. Potato Head, Play-Doh, and Board Games, in addition to licensed toy products.

Although licensing arrangements often varied, many involved a foundation in which the licensee toy company paid the licensor a large advance of money. This advance guaranteed the licensor a large profit regardless of the licensee successfully selling its product; however, the licensee would often also be required to pay the licensor a percentage of the net sales for a licensed product, called a royalty. Licensing agreements also specified numerous details including the amount of time a licensee could produce a product, the type of products to be created, and in which countries the products could be sold. The acquisition of Marvel by Disney represented a significant move, as it placed a large amount of entertainment licensing under the control of one organization.

Mattel, Hasbro, and LEGO all had individual licensing agreements with Disney to produce toys; however, Disney had a long and favorable history of licensing toys with Mattel. Hasbro on the other hand had an existing license agreement to produce Marvel toys and games until 2017.[27] This created speculation in the toy industry as to which direction Disney would proceed in with future toy licensing agreements. Disney Chief Financial Officer Tom Staggs commented on this topic to the media: "As many of these deals conclude over time, we will have the flexibility to either bring them in-house or pursue third-party licensing agreements depending on how we feel we can create the most value."[28]

Court Battle

LEGO had also been facing competition in the courtroom. In 1999, LEGO registered its classic eight-stud plastic brick shape as a trademark with the European Union, causing objection from rival competitor MEGA Brands. LEGO argued that its brick shape was distinctive and that consumers were often misled, believing that they were purchasing a LEGO product even when viewing a different company name on the box. The result was an 11-year court battle that came to a final decision in September 2010. The European Court

---

[22]"Box Office History for Spider-Man Movies," *The Numbers,* 2011, http://www.the-numbers.com/movies/series/SpiderMan.phpit , accessed on August 27, 2011.

[23]"The Dark Knight," *The Numbers,* 2011, http:/www.the-numbers.com/movies/2008/BATM2.php, accessed on August 27, 2011.

[24]"Box Office History for Spider-Man Movies," *The Numbers,* 2011, http://www.the-numbers.com/movies/series/SpiderMan.php, accessed on August 27, 2011.

[25]"Mattel 2010 Annual Report," *Mattel,* 2011, http://corporate.mattel.com/annualreport2010/pdfs/2010%20Mattel%20Annual%20Report(Bookmarked).pdf, accessed on August 27, 2011.

[26]"Hasbro Annual Report 2010," *Hasbro,* 2011, http://investor.hasbro.com/annuals.cfm, accessed on August 27, 2011.

[27]Aarthi Sivaraman, "Disney-Marvel deal casts web of issues for toymakers," *Reuters,* August 31, 2009, www.reuters.com/article/2009/08/31/us-hasbro-analysis-sb-idUSTRE57U63C20090831, accessed on August 27, 2011.

[28]Ibid.

of Justice ruled in favor of MEGA Brands, stating that shapes used for a technical result did not qualify for a trademark, thus revoking the LEGO brick trademark.[29] This decision represented a major loss for LEGO. The company still held trademarks with the LEGO logo and popular minifigure, but opportunities and business conditions existed for competition to increase.

New Competition

In 2011, new competition was set to emerge as Hasbro was planning to launch a new building block line called Kre-O that would be compatible with LEGO bricks. Although many different plastic brick building toys had been launched to compete with LEGO over the past 50 years, most did not succeed and were eventually discontinued; however, this product had serious threat potential because of the size and brand power of Hasbro. The new Kre-O line was set to be released in the spring of 2011, with the introductory Kre-O product line featuring the popular Transformers characters. Each set would include two sets of instructions that would allow builders to create a vehicle and a robot with the same building pieces. The launch was designed to take advantage of the release of the third installment in the blockbuster Transformers movie franchise, *Transformers: Dark of the Moon.* Hasbro was hoping to tap into a licensed theme in the building toy market that had not been used before. The Transformers Kre-O line was scheduled to launch with 12 sets, with Hasbro planning to release additional product lines soon after.[30]

FUTURE STRATEGY

The global toy sales represented over US$83.3 billion in 2010.[31] One of the fastest-growing categories was building sets, with an increase of 13 percent in 2010.[32] The future in the building toy market held both opportunity and uncertainty, with new threats emerging from increased control over licensing agreements, loss of trademark protection, and competition from new and existing sources. It was important for the LEGO management team to identify where to expand current product lines in order to help the company formulate a strategy to ensure that LEGO maintained dominance in the building toy market and financial success in the years ahead.

[29]Sean Farrell, "Lego loses 11-year trademark battle," *The Telegraph,* September 14, 2010, www.telegmph.co.uk/finance/newsbysector/retailandconsumer/8002268/Lego-loses-11-year-trademark-battle.html, accessed on August 27, 2011.

[30]Mark Lennihan, "Hasbro pushes into Lego's land with new blocks," *USA TODAY,* February 12, 2011, http://www.usatoday.com/money/companies/2011-02-12-hasbro-transformers_N.htm, accessed on August 27, 2011.

[31]"Global Toy Sales in 2010 Increased by Nearly 5%, NPD Reports," International Council of Toy industries, June 27, 2011. http://www.toy-icti.org/news/globaltoysalesin2010.html, accessed on August 27, 2011.

[32]Mae Anderson, "Hasbro to challenge Legos with 'Transformers,'" *Msnbc.com,* February 13, 2011, www.msnbc.msn.com/id/41561886/ns/business-consumer_news/t/hasbro-challenge-legos-transformers/, accessed on August 27, 2011.

Case

11

The Launch of the Sony PlayStation 3[1]

David Wesley and Gloria Barczak *Northeastern University*

"The PlayStation 3 was the most successful launch in Sony's history."

—Jack Tretton, president and chief executive officer
of Sony Computer Entertainment of America[2]

In the days leading up to the November 17, 2006, launch of the PlayStation 3 (PS3), enthusiasts lined city blocks for the privilege of spending $600 for the most powerful video game console ever created. Its predecessor, the acclaimed PlayStation 2 (PS2), had already become the world's best selling video game console with more than 100 million units sold. The unprecedented display of enthusiasm for the PS3 suggested that Sony had another winner on its hands.[3] The company projected sales of six million PS3 consoles worldwide by March 2007,[4] a level that the PS2 took almost a year to reach.[5]

[1]This case has been written on the basis of published sources only. Consequently, the interpretation and perspectives presented in this case are not necessarily those of Sony Computer Entertainment of America or any of its employees.

[2]"Battle Station," *Electronic Gaming Monthly,* March 2007, p. 64.

[3]"PS3 'To Win Console War'," *Personal Computer World,* January 25, 2007.

[4]"Sony Ships 1 Million PS3s in Japan, Seen Missing Target," *EWeek,* January 16, 2007.

[5]"Cumulative Production Shipments of Hardware/PlayStation 2," Sony Computer Entertainment Inc. Business Data, www.scei.co.jp/corporate/data/bizdataps2_e.html, accessed April 18, 2007.

At the core of the PS3 was an IBM "cell" processor, touted by Sony as a "supercomputer on a chip."[6] "The Cell outperforms many of the latest PC processors and delivers up to ten times the performance of a typical home computer," stated a company press release.

> In terms of real-world application, it means incredibly detailed and interactive environments, more enemies, larger battles, and hyper-realistic game play. The increased processing power of the Cell also means developers for the first time can create games closer to actual intelligence instead of artificial intelligence, giving them the ability to closely mimic human reasoning and movement.[7]

Sony's initial euphoria was short-lived, however. By February 2007, more than a third of PS3 consoles remained unsold, and some retailers reported a higher number of returns than sales.[8] Consumers said they felt let down by Sony. The PS3 looked no better than Microsoft's Xbox 360, they complained, even though the Xbox 360 had already been on the market for more than a year, and sold for $200 less than the PS3. Customers also lamented the PS3's lack of interesting games, spotty support for PlayStation 2 games, and uninspiring online capabilities. Meanwhile, Nintendo's inexpensive and quirky Wii console had become all the rage, despite its underpowered processor and comparatively basic graphics.

COMPANY BACKGROUND

Sony Corporation was founded in Tokyo, in 1945, as the Tokyo Telecommunications Engineering Corporation. After building Japan's first tape recorder, the company convinced Bell Laboratories to license its new transistor technology. At a time when transistors were used primarily in military applications, Sony was one of the first companies to successfully apply the technology to consumer radios. By the late 1950s, Sony had become one of the world's leading producers of radios. The company later expanded into televisions, stereos, and other home entertainment products. In 2006, Sony had an annual net income of $1 billion on $64.5 billion in revenues.

Product Innovation

Sony had a long history of product innovation that had resulted in well-known brands, such as Betamax, Trinitron, and Walkman. The company was also very protective of its intellectual property and was therefore reluctant to license its technologies to competitors. As a result, Sony products often lost market share to inferior technologies offered by competitors.

The Betamax videotape format was the one of the more infamous examples of a superior product that failed to win consumer acceptance. Introduced in 1975, Betamax tapes were smaller and provided higher definition video than the competing VHS format introduced by JVC the following year. However, Sony was unwilling to adapt the technology to accommodate longer play times because doing so would degrade the video quality. Consumers, however, preferred longer recording times over higher definition images. Moreover, Sony Betamax players were significantly more expensive than the VHS players being produced by third-party manufacturers under license from JVC. In 1988, Sony abandoned the format and began manufacturing VHS players.[9]

---

[6]John C. Dvorak, "Sony's New PlayStation 3 Game Machine Will Use an Advanced 2-teraflop CPU Being Developed Jointly by IBM, Sony, and Toshiba," *PC Magazine,* March 22, 2005, p. 53.

[7]"Cell Broadband Engine Fact Sheet," *Sony Computer Entertainment Inc. Press Release,* October 23, 2006.

[8]"Battle Station," *Electronic Gaming Monthly,* March 2007, p. 70.

[9]Marc Wielage, "The Rise and Fall of Beta," *Videofax,* Spring 1988, pp. 28–29.

A more celebrated brand was the Walkman portable music player, which Sony introduced in 1979. The Walkman was a portable music player that played standard audio cassettes and was capable of sound reproduction on par with much larger players. The brand dominated the portable music market in the 1980s and for much of the 1990s. By the mid-1990s, portable music had moved from cassettes to CDs. The digital technology used in music CDs reproduced sounds with higher quality at lower cost. As a result, Sony's competitors were able to introduce a large number of inexpensive portable CD players. Nevertheless, the Sony CD Walkman continued to enjoy strong market share.

When digital music became popular in the late 1990s, Sony opted to promote its own proprietary ATRAC format over the more popular mp3 standard.[10] In early 2005, Ken Kutaragi, chairman and chief executive officer (CEO) of Sony Computer Entertainment, admitted that Sony employees were frustrated by the company's unwillingness to support other formats.[11] All the same, Sony continued to promote ATRAC for its Walkman and other Sony electronics products. The decision allowed Sony's rivals to capture most of the portable music market.

The iPod, introduced by Apple in 2001, became the fastest selling portable music player in history with 100 million units sold by 2007. The Walkman, by comparison, took a decade to reach the 100 million mark.[12] The iPod supported at least seven different audio formats, including standard mp3 and Microsoft WAV, in addition to video and data. Apple also provided its easy-to-use iTunes music software as a free download for users of both Macintosh and Windows computers.[13]

Although iTunes was originally developed as an interface for the iPod, anyone could use it to organize, purchase, and play music, as well as to copy and burn music CDs. By early 2007, Apple had sold more than 2.5 billion songs, 50 million television shows and 1.3 million movies through its iTunes music store.[14] Lastly, iTunes acted both as an interface for the free distribution of audio files, known as Podcasts, and as a conduit for online radio stations.

To counter the trend toward lower fidelity digital music, Sony launched its Super Audio Compact Disc (SACD), an audio format that greatly improved the sound fidelity of recorded music and, through proprietary copy protection technologies, prevented unauthorized copying of music content. However, Sony's copy protection schemes significantly added to manufacturing costs and made SACD systems incompatible with most stereos.[15] In the end, Sony found few electronics manufacturers willing to accept its restrictive licensing terms, and few consumers willing to invest in expensive proprietary stereo equipment. In 2004, after being on the market for four years, SACD had a market share of less than 0.5 percent of U.S. music sales.[16] The following year, sales of lower fidelity online music more than tripled to $1.1 billion, representing a market share of 6 percent of total U.S. music sales.[17]

[10]"Sony PSP: How Well Does the PlayStation Portable Play Music?" www.about.com, accessed March 16, 2007.

[11]"Proprietary Worries Delayed New Sony Products, Top Executive Admits," *The Globe and Mail,* January 21, 2005, p. B12.

[12]"100 Million iPods Sold Since 2001," *San Francisco Chronicle,* April 10, 2007, p. C1.

[13]www.apple.com/ipod, accessed April 9, 2007.

[14]"Apple Sells 100 Million iPods," *eWeek,* April 9, 2007.

[15]"SACD Is Dead," ultraaudio.com/opinion/20050401.htm, April 1, 2005, accessed April 5, 2007.

[16]"DVD-Audio Sales Five Times Higher Than SACD Sales," highfidelityreview.com/news/news.asp?newsnumber=18483611, April 22, 2004, accessed April 5, 2007.

[17]"Digital Music Sales Triple in 2005," *PC World,* January 20, 2006, p. 8.

In 2005, Sony's copy protection schemes resulted in one of the most notorious scandals to hit the music industry. Without informing its customers, Sony installed what was known as a rootkit on many of its music CDs. When the CD was inserted into a drive on a Windows computer, the rootkit software installed itself on the computer. The software not only disabled the owner's ability to copy music, it also opened the computer to a number of serious security risks and in some cases allowed Sony to remotely monitor the user's actions.

Sony was later found to be in violation of the laws of the United States and several other countries. In early 2007, Sony settled charges by the U.S. Federal Trade Commission after it agreed to provide compensation and remedies to consumers.[18] However, the scandal became a lightning rod for the growing movement against proprietary and protected media and caused irreparable harm to Sony's reputation within the music industry. Nevertheless, Sony continued to seek new ways to prevent consumers from copying digital media. For example, in early 2007, the company distributed 25 million DVDs with a new copy protection technology, known as the Advanced Regional Copy Control Operating Solution (ARccOS). However, ARccOS unintentionally prevented movies from being played on many DVD players, including at least one Sony-branded player. This time, Sony immediately offered to send free replacement discs to affected consumers.[19]

One of Sony's most successful brands was Trinitron, a superior television technology patented by Sony in the 1960s. Trinitron's ability to produce higher quality color images quickly established Sony as the category leader. As a result, consumers were often willing to pay a premium for Trinitron-branded televisions. More importantly, Trinitron televisions were capable of displaying every standard video format, including over-the-air broadcasts, digital and analog cable, standard and progressive scan DVD, VHS, computers and, more recently, both Blu-ray and HD-DVD high-definition video disc formats. Later, Trinitron became one of the most popular technologies used in computer CRT monitors. It was sold under license by most major computer manufacturers, including Apple, Dell, and IBM.[20]

Sony continued to enjoy strong market share in Trinitron televisions and monitors well after its patent expired in 1996. In 2006, Sony continued to lead the market in televisions. "Sony's leadership position in television has been consistent over the past few years," noted Steve Baker of NPD, a market research firm. "What makes this performance impressive is the number of competitors in the TV space continues to grow at a staggering pace."[21]

To meet the growing demand for high-definition video content, Sony developed a high-capacity proprietary DVD player, known as Blu-ray. Blu-ray was one of two competing technologies that offered a much higher definition than standard DVDs. The other was HD-DVD, a format developed by Toshiba. PlayStation 3 consoles had built-in support for Blu-ray content, in contrast to Microsoft's Xbox 360, which supported HD-DVD through an optional external drive. Although Blu-ray discs had a higher capacity than HD-DVD, the video quality was comparable. However, Blu-ray players were more costly to manufacture and sold for nearly twice the price of comparable HD-DVD players. Yet, most major movie studios supported either Blu-ray or both formats.[22]

[18]"Sony BMG Settles FTC Charges," *Federal Trade Commission News Release,* ftc.gov/opa/2007/01/sony.shtm, January 30, 2007, accessed April 5, 2007.

[19]"Sony Replaces Some Copy-Protected DVDs," blogs.pcworld.com/staffblog/archives/004150.html, April 18, 2007, accessed June 28, 2007.

[20]"Superior Quality of Trinitron TV Screens Leads to Computer Display Applications," www.sony.net/Fun/SH/1-25/h1.html, accessed April 3, 2007.

[21]"Sony Takes TV Market Share Lead," *TWICE (This Week in Consumer Electronics),* January 12, 2007.

[22]"Universal Backs Out of Blu-ray," *PC Magazine,* September 19, 2006.

VIDEO GAMING

In the 1980s and early 1990s, the video game market was dominated by Nintendo and Atari. Sony entered the market originally as a supplier of components for the Nintendo Entertainment System (NES) home console. However, when Nintendo failed to introduce new technologies that would considerably improve the gaming experience, Sony decide to seize the opportunity.

When Sony launched its $299 PlayStation console in 1995, it was one of the first to use 32-bit three-dimensional graphics.[23] Sony offered developers a number of incentives, including higher margins and advanced development tools. Even before the console was launched, Sony entered into development partnerships with 164 Japanese software companies.[24] By 2005, the PlayStation had become the most popular console in history with sales of more than 100 million units and a library of more than 7,000 games.[25]

Sony launched the PlayStation 2 (PS2) in 2000 with a price of $299. Not only could the PS2 play existing PlayStation games, newly developed games were able to take advantage of the console's more advanced graphical and processing capabilities as well as its ability to deliver enhanced content through a built-in DVD drive. The "emotion engine" processor was specifically designed to enhance 3-D full-motion video, and it was several times more powerful than processors used in most personal computers at the time.[26] Although production delays marred the initial launch, once production caught up with demand, sales remained solid. By 2007, the PS2 had surpassed the original PlayStation as the best selling console in history.[27]

In 2003, Sony introduced a handheld gaming device known as the PlayStation Portable (PSP). In true Sony fashion, the PSP was the most advanced portable console on the market, in terms of both graphics and processing power. It also supported playback of full-length movies and digital music.[28] The PSP proved less successful than Sony's home consoles. In addition to costing nearly twice as much as competing handheld devices from Nintendo, the PSP had a limited number of innovative game titles. Many were games that had been ported from home consoles, and few took advantage of the unique capabilities of portable gaming. In contrast, the $129 Nintendo DS had two screens and a touch pen that allowed gamers to interact with the console in unique ways. The PSP fared just as poorly as a music player. Its built-in memory could not hold even one album in mp3 format, and purchasing additional proprietary memory from Sony proved just as expensive as purchasing a new Apple iPod.

[23]The first console to offer these capabilities was the 3DO Player, launched in 1993 by the 3DO Company of California. The 3DO also played music, video, and karaoke CDs, and could serve as home computer with Internet capabilities. However, the $700 unit was deemed too expensive by consumers who saw its primary function as a video game machine. By 1996, 3DO was forced out of the market. 3DO Interactive Multiplayer FAQ, classicgaming.com/museum/faqs/3dofaq.shtml, June 10, 2000, accessed June 26, 2007.

[24]"Sony Has Some Very Scary Monsters in the Works," *BusinessWeek,* May 23, 1994, p. 116.

[25]www.scei.co.jp/corporate/data/bizdataps2_e.html, accessed March 9, 2007.

[26]"The Sony Emotion Engine: Will PlayStation2 Replace Your PC?" archives.cnn.com/2000/TECH/computing/02/01/emotion.engine.idg/, February 1, 2000, accessed June 28, 2007.

[27]"Cumulative Production Shipments of PlayStation2," *Sony Computer Entertainment Inc. Business Data,* available at www.scei.co.jp/corporate/data/bizdataps2_e.html, accessed April 10, 2007.

[28]"From Sony, a Hand-Held Entertainment Center," *The New York Times,* May 13, 2004, p. 7.

The PlayStation 3

As early as 2005, Ken Kutaragi, chairman and CEO of Sony Computer Entertainment, pledged to deliver a machine with twice the processing power of the PS3's nearest competitor, Microsoft's Xbox 360.[29] Like the Xbox 360, the target market for the PlayStation 3 was 18- to 35-year-old male gamers with above-average education and a high degree of comfort with new technology.[30]

Technical problems related to the console's built-in Blu-ray drive caused Sony to delay manufacturing and push back the initial launch from spring 2006 to fall 2006.[31] Despite the delayed release, Sony was unable to manufacture the anticipated one million consoles needed to meet market demand.[32] By the time the PS3 was launched in North America on November 17, 2006, retailers had fewer than 200,000 units to distribute. Kaz Hirai, president and group chief operating officer (COO) of Sony Computer Entertainment, recognized the problem, but tried to downplay its importance over the longer term:

> We are going to ramp up production and try to get as many units into the hands of consumers as possible for the launch. That is also why we strategically decided to delay the European launch [until Spring 2007], so that we could concentrate more on the Japanese and North American markets. But the most important thing for us is providing compelling software for the long term, so that six or seven years from now we can have a platform that consumers can embrace and enjoy.[33]

Sony attempted to mitigate the shortage by air freighting consoles directly from Japan. "We will continue to utilize airfreight delivery for the PlayStation 3 to assure a steady stream of systems for North American consumers through the end of the year," Sony assured retailers in an official statement.

> And while initial day-one launch shipment goals weren't achievable due to early manufacturing issues, those problems have been resolved and we do remain focused on having one million PS3s in the pipeline by December 31, 2006.[34]

Sony supported the launch of the PS3 with a $150 million advertising campaign that aimed to convince potential customers to hold off purchasing a new system until after the holiday season instead of purchasing an Xbox 360 or Wii. The slogan "Play Beyond," originally developed for the Electronic Entertainment Expo (E3) 2006 trade show by Sony's advertising agency TBWA, continued to be used throughout the prelaunch period. However, it quickly became the target of popular Internet spoofs by gamers protesting the high cost of the console. One spoof, titled "Pay Beyond" became widely circulated on the Internet (see Exhibit 1). TBWA campaign director Rob Schwartz expressed concern over the negativity surrounding the upcoming launch. "Sometimes I feel like a character in a video game, like everybody's shooting at me," he joked.[35]

In New York City, Sony celebrated the launch with free food and live performances by Ludacris, Charles Q. Murphy, and other well-known performers.[36] Elsewhere, enthusiastic

[29]"Sony Claims PlayStation 3 Performance Edge," *Electronic Engineering Times,* May 23, 2005, p. 33.

[30]"Sony Gets Its Game On," *Daily Variety,* May 10, 2006, p. 1.

[31]"It's a Gaming Console! It's an Entertainment Hub!" *Fast Company,* December 2005, p. 41.

[32]"'06 Had Sony Singing the Blues," *Electronic Engineering Times,* December 28, 2006, p. 8.

[33]"Interview with Kaz Hirai," available at games.kikizo.com/news/200610/009_p2.asp, October 3, 2006, accessed April 9, 2007.

[34]"Sony Responds to NPD Figures," 1up.com/do/newsStory?cId=3155762, December 8, 2006, accessed April 9, 2007.

[35]"Sony Needs a Home Run with the PS3," *Fortune,* money.cnn.com/magazines/fortune/ fortune_archive/2006/11/13/8393083/index.htm, October 31, 2006, accessed June 28, 2007.

[36]"Wii Got Game in Console Face-off," *The New York Post,* November 16, 2006.

EXHIBIT 1   Sony Billboard and "Pay Beyond" Spoof

Source: www.Kotaku.com, accessed June 8, 2007.

gamers camped out for as long as several days in front of retail stores in an often futile attempt to secure one of the few consoles allocated to each retail store. Many stores stayed open past midnight, and lines often stretched around city blocks. Across the United States, extra police had to be called in to control unruly crowds that had gathered in front of shops.[37] In the days that followed, consoles sold for well over $2,000 on eBay.

When Sony launched the European PlayStation 3 in March 2007, it experienced none of the problems encountered during the North American release. Instead, it was plagued by a different problem, namely lack of demand. In the United Kingdom alone, retailers canceled more than $20 million worth of orders in the days leading up to the launch. In an attempt to generate positive publicity, on launch day, Sony gave a free high-definition television valued at more than $4,000 to the first 125 people to purchase a PS3.[38] "People knew that we have a huge level of stock and that meant that there wasn't the usual level of hysteria that you get with a stock shortage," explained Alan Duncan, marketing director for Sony Computer Entertainment UK. "For us, we just wanted to say to the people who did make the effort, 'Thank you very much.'"[39]

Pricing

The Sony PlayStation 3 was the most expensive console ever launched, with a price tag of $600, or $500 for a stripped-down version with a smaller hard drive and no wireless module. Nevertheless, Sony lost between $240 and $306 on each console sold (see Exhibit 2). In fact, the basic console cost Sony almost as much to make as the premium model. Sony saved only $11 by using a smaller hard drive and $15.50 by eliminating the wireless adaptor.[40] Microsoft had also initially lost $126 on each Xbox 360 it sold. However, by the end of 2006, lower component costs and operational efficiencies helped bring the console's cost to $323, earning Microsoft a gross margin of $76 on each unit sold.[41]

Despite Sony's willingness to subsidize each console purchase, many users complained that the PS3 cost $200 more than the Xbox 360. Some also criticized Sony's decision to not include the video cables needed to take advantage of the console's graphics capabilities and to eliminate rumble (a vibration feedback feature).[42] According to Sony, eliminating rumble was a "strategic decision" aimed at reducing costs. "The issue is trying to isolate the vibration feature from the motion sensors," Hirai claimed.

> It is a balancing act to be able to present the controller to the consumer at an affordable price. We have one controller in the box, but many consumers will want to go out and get an extra controller. If isolating the vibration from the sensing means that the controllers are going to be expensive, then we're doing the consumer a huge disservice.[43]

Skeptics, however, claimed that the decision had more to do with a lawsuit in which Sony was found guilty of infringing on a rumble patent registered by Immersion Corporation and

[37]"PlayStation Craze: Lucky Few Got Game," *The Boston Herald,* November 18, 2006, p. 5.

[38]"Sony PS3 Hit by £10m in Cancellations," *Brand Republic Daily News,* brandrepublic.com/BrandRepublicNews/News/646182/Sony-PS3-hit-10m-cancellations/, March 27, 2007, accessed June 28, 2007.

[39]"Q&A: Sony UK's Alan Duncan," gamespot.com/news/6168115.htm, March 30, 2007, accessed April 12, 2007.

[40]"Sony Taking Big Hit on Each PS3 Sold; Xbox 360 in the Black," arstechnica.com/news.ars/post/20061116-8239.html, November 16, 2006, accessed March 21, 2007.

[41]Ibid.

[42]"Battle Station," *Electronic Gaming Monthly,* March 2007, p. 67.

[43]"Hirai: Motion Sensing Beats Rumble," games.kikizo.com/news/200610/009.asp, October 3, 2006, accessed June 13, 2007.

EXHIBIT 2

Sony PlayStation 3
Manufacturing Cost
(60 Gb Model)

Source: "Sony Taking Big Hit
on Each PS3 Sold; Xbox 360
in the Black," www.
arstechnica.com/news.ars/
post/20061116-8239.html,
November 16, 2006,
accessed March 21, 2007.

Miscellaneous Manufacturing Components	$148.00
Reality Synthesizer	129.00
Blu-ray Drive	125.00
Cell CPU	89.00
I/O Bridge Controller	59.00
SATA Hard Drive	54.00
XDR RAM	48.00
Power Supply	37.50
Case	33.00
Emotion Engine/Graphics Synthesizer	27.00
Motherboard and Cooling	22.00
Wireless Module	15.50
Memory Board	5.00
Bluetooth	4.10
Other Miscellaneous Components	4.75
Manufacturing Expense	40.00
Total Cost	840.85

ordered to pay $90.7 million in damages. Immersion Corporation also challenged Sony's claim that it would be costly to isolate the vibration and motion sensors. "The two signals can be differentiated using filtering and other techniques," it noted.[44] For example, Nintendo spent approximately $5 on each controller to include both rumble and motion-sensing features.[45]

Tretton defended the console's higher cost relative to competitors. "I would point out a couple of things," he said.

> Historically our platforms have staying power. Not three years, not five years, but 10 years. So are you making an investment for the next 45 days, the next year, the next five years, or 10 years? The PS3 has the best gaming experience of any platform that's ever shipped, with great gaming, free online play, Blu-ray movie playback, the ability to go online and surf the Internet, the ability to download your pictures and videos and the ability to rip your music.[46]

> I think the consumers that get their hands on a PlayStation 3 clearly see the value and not only want to buy one for $599, in some instances they're willing to pay ridiculous prices to buy one on eBay.[47]

Although consoles did indeed sell for more than $2,000 on eBay during the first few days of the U.S. launch, prices quickly plummeted to just over $1,000. By early 2007, auction prices for new PS3 consoles were near or below suggested retail. With the end of the holiday rush, retail stores began to report an excess build-up of stock. "Customers are disappointed," one retailer complained.

> They are telling us that too many of the launch games are also available on the Xbox 360, and first-party titles aren't innovative enough for them. We have 24 PS3s in stock right now and we're getting more returns than we are selling systems.[48]

[44]"Immersion Offers to Rumble PS3," ps3.ign.com/articles/713/713259p1.html, June 19, 2006.

[45]"The Motion Sensing Accelerometer and the Rumble Pack Cost Nintendo Approximately $2.50 Each: Wii Will Rock You," *Fortune,* June 11, 2007, pp. 82–92.

[46]"Battle Station," *Electronic Gaming Monthly,* March 2007.

[47]"SCEA CEO Says PS3 Will Be 'Difficult to Cost Reduce'," dailytech.com/article.aspx?newsid=5810, January 23, 2007, accessed March 7, 2007.

[48]"Battle Station," *Electronic Gaming Monthly,* March 2007, p. 70.

With stand-alone Blu-ray players costing as much or more than the PS3, some felt that Blu-ray capability alone justified the extra cost. Others were not so sure. "The decision to make the PS3 a Trojan horse for Sony's high-def Blu-ray disc technology could be backfiring," one analyst suggested. "Unless you convince consumers that this extra feature is something they truly want, they'll only view it as an added expense."[49]

Pundits took opposite sides in the debate over whether Microsoft or Sony had the best strategy. On one side, the release of the Xbox 360 a year in advance of Sony would give Microsoft a considerable head start over its rival. Microsoft could then attract core gamers who were unwilling to wait for the PlayStation 3 and build up a library of quality titles. Conversely, Sony would have a year to learn from Microsoft's mistakes and adapt its console more to the needs of customers.

"Content Is King"

Every console manufacturer understood that one of the keys to success was having a library of quality game titles to offer consumers. Consider the Sega Dreamcast. When the Sega console was launched in 1999, it was far ahead of its time. Hardcore gamers were so enthusiastic, that for several months after its release, the Dreamcast was almost impossible to find on store shelves. Yet, the Dreamcast proved a failure and eventually had to be withdrawn from the market. In the book *Smartbomb,* video games journalists Heather Chaplin and Aaron Ruby reflected on the Dreamcast's demise. The Dreamcast was "awesome," they observed, "and many gamers still refer to it as one of the best consoles ever built."

> There are a dozen stories about consoles that were ahead of their time. . . . The Dreamcast was discontinued after only two years, because Sega simply couldn't get enough machines into people's homes and couldn't establish a library of games quickly enough.[50]

The lessons of the Dreamcast and other consoles were not lost on Hirai. "Compelling entertainment content" was the most important feature of any entertainment device, he explained a few weeks before the launch of the PS3:

> We all know—it's a cliché but it's a truism—that content is king. The most important thing for us is being able to provide a platform for content creators to really get excited about, so that they can take full advantage of what we bring to them in terms of a technological palette. The PlayStation 3 really brings so much more in terms of the raw processing power and so much more in terms of storage capacity with the Blu-ray drive.[51]

Nevertheless, the PlayStation 3 launched with only 15 titles, the majority of which were franchise games that had previously been available for the Xbox 360. Among the handful of exclusive titles, *Resistance: Fall of Man* quickly became the console's best selling title. It was also its most violent, garnering a "mature" rating from the Entertainment Software Review Board (ESRB) for intense violence, blood and gore, and strong language.[52]

Although Sony praised *Resistance* as its highest-ranking and best selling title, users were less enthusiastic. Professional reviewers called it "mostly unoriginal," a first-person shooting game that borrowed heavily from previously successful games for other platforms.[53] In

---

[49]Ibid.

[50]Heather Chaplin and Aaron Ruby, *Smartbomb: The Quest for Art, Entertainment, and Big Bucks in the Videogame Revolution,* Algonquin, Chapel Hill, NC, 2005, p. 225.

[51]"Interview with Kaz Hirai," games.kikizo.com/news/200610/009_p2.asp, October 3, 2006, accessed February 21, 2007.

[52]Mature-rated games were considered suitable for ages 17 and older.

[53]"Review of Resistance: Fall of Man," gamespot.com/ps3/action/insomniacshooter/ review.html?om_act=convert&om_clk=gssummary&tag=summary;review, November 15, 2006, accessed February 20, 2007.

EXHIBIT 3   Sony Press Release

PLAYSTATION®3 system
FACT SHEET

Building on its more than 10 years as the leader and innovator in the gaming industry, Sony Computer Entertainment ushers in a new era in gaming and home entertainment with the launch of the PLAYSTATION®3 (PS3™) system. This revolutionary computer entertainment system will serve as a platform for consumers to enjoy next generation entertainment in the home for years to come.

The PS3™ system is powered by the Cell Broadband Engine™, a revolutionary microprocessor that leapfrogs the performance of existing processors giving the PS3 system supercomputer-like power and performance that up until now, game developers have only dreamt about. Every PS3 system is equipped with a built-in Blue-ray™ Disc player so users can enjoy high-definition gaming and movies. Blue-ray offers developers unprecedented storage capacity so they can fully express their creativity and pristine picture quality at 1080p, the highest-definition resolution available today. The PS3 system supports a broad range of displays from conventional or standard TVs to the latest full HD (1080i/1080p) flat panel displays.

The PS3 system also comes standard with Giga-bit Ethernet and a pre-installed upgradeable Hard Disk Drive (HDD) so users can download a variety of content as well as access on-line games and services over the network.

The PS3 system features the new SIXAXIS™ wireless controller which was built by refining the popular PlayStation® controller, the de facto standard in gaming with several hundred million units sold worldwide. The new SIXAXIS controller features breakthrough technology and a highly sensitive motion-sensing system so users are able to maneuver the controller as a natural extension of their bodies in real-time and with high-precision.

The PS3 system is backwards compatible so users can still enjoy virtually their entire PS one™ and PlayStation®2 computer entertainment system games as well as their CDs and DVDs.

Source: Sony Computer Entertainment of America, December 18, 2006.

contrast, the Xbox 360 boasted 12 titles that were ranked higher than *Resistance,* including several similar style shooting games. Even the Nintendo Wii, a console which had been on the market for about as long as the PS3, had higher ranking titles.[54]

Tretton defended Sony's lineup of launch titles. In his opinion, the company's track record for best selling titles spoke for itself:

> Take a look back at the debuts of all the past consoles to compare launch lineups. We have published thousands of great games for all our PlayStation platforms over the years, selling billions of units. That won't suddenly change for the PS3. You can expect a steady flow of exceptional titles for the PS3 for years to come.[55]

Sony advertised that the PS3 would be "backward compatible" with virtually all of the "thousands of great games" (see Exhibit 3). In reality, only a few titles worked properly on

[54]www.gamespot.com, accessed February 20, 2007.
[55]"Battle Station," *Electronic Gaming Monthly,* March 2007.

the system. Sony eventually provided an update that resolved most compatibility issues, but not soon enough for many consumers who believed that the company should have been more upfront about compatibility issues.[56]

Software Development

The complexity of the advanced graphics engines and processors utilized in the Xbox 360 and PS3 significantly increased the burden on software developers who sought to take advantage of these features. Development cycles stretched from 12 months for the previous generation consoles to up to 36 months for Xbox 360 and PS3 titles.[57] As a result, fewer game developers were willing to stake their future on a single platform, preferring instead to spread their development costs over several platforms. For some developers, there was no other option. "When companies try to create these vast games that consumers really want," explained Shigeru Miyamoto, director and general manager of Nintendo Entertainment Analysis and Development, "they try and use every last bit of technology to create really incredible games." Miyamoto, an industry veteran who famously developed the original Donkey Kong, Mario Brothers, and Zelda games, believed that "the development cost is going to be so high that they'll never be able to recoup it from sales."[58] Cross-platform licensing was one way to reduce that risk.

Microsoft's solution was to create a core set of developer tools, known as XNA, that allowed code to be shared across different Microsoft platforms.[59] As a result, games developed for personal computers, such as *Final Fantasy XI* by Square Enix, could be more easily ported to the Xbox 360. Whereas *Final Fantasy* took about six months to port to the Xbox 360, Square Enix estimated that it could take up to three years and cost several million dollars to completely rewrite the code for the PS3.[60]

When Microsoft created the original Xbox, it too was similar to Microsoft personal computers (PCs), and for this reason some developers believed it "would kill the PlayStation 2." The simplicity of the Xbox, they contended, made it a console "that gamers and game developers would die for," while the PlayStation 2, with its proprietary processor and unique operating system, created programming challenges that would take years to sort through. Instead, most developers chose the PS2 over the Xbox despite the technical challenges.[61] By 2006, the PS2 had a library of approximately 8,000 titles worldwide and a market share of 51 percent, compared to 34 percent for the Xbox and 15 percent for the Nintendo Gamecube.[62]

Average unit costs could be broken into several categories (see Exhibit 4). Art, design and programming accounted for nearly half of the total retail cost of a next generation video game, while the remainder went to marketing, distribution and retail markup. Increasingly detailed computer-generated graphics and animation, much of which mirrored the special effects work normally associated with Hollywood studios, had the most impact

[56]"PS3 Updated to 1.50," *IGN News* (ps3.ign.com/articles/758/758306p1.html), January 24, 2007, accessed April 12, 2007.

[57]"Product Development," *THQ 2006 Annual Report,* June 7, 2006.

[58]From an interview published on N-Europe (n-europe.com/news.php?nid=4563), May 22, 2003, accessed March 20, 2007.

[59]"Sony and Microsoft Take the Next-Gen Battle to the Japanese Front," *Electronic Gaming Monthly,* October 1, 2005, p. 18.

[60]"Square Enix Working on PS3, Vista MMORPG," gamespot.com/news/6147946.html, April 19, 2006, accessed March 5, 2007.

[61]Chaplin and Ruby, *Smartbomb,* p. 231.

[62]"Microsoft Bets Console Can Draw in Non-gamers," *USA Today* (usatoday.com/tech/gaming/2005-11-12-xbox360-ambition_x.htm), November 12, 2005, accessed June 28, 2007.

EXHIBIT 4
Video Game per Unit
Cost Next Generation
Console Estimates

Source: Forbes.com.

Art and design	$15	25%
Programming and engineering	12	20
Retail markup	12	20
Console license fee	7	12
Marketing	4	7
Market development fund	3	5
Manufacturing and packaging	3	5
Third-party licensing	3	5
Publisher profit	1	2
Total Retail Cost	$60	100%

on development costs. Programming costs, which included basic game play, artificial intelligence and online services, also increased.[63]

Retail markup on a $60 title was about $12. Of this, *Forbes* estimated a net earnings contribution of only $1 per title sold at large retailers, such as Best Buy and Circuit City.

The Nintendo Wii, on the other hand, was a much simpler system. Development costs were likewise lower. Brian Farrell, CEO of THQ Inc., one of the world's leading game developers, noted:

> One of the things we like about the Wii is that development costs are nowhere near what they are on the PS3 and Xbox 360. It wasn't a whole new programming environment. So we had a lot of tools and tech that work in that environment. Costs could be as little as a third of the high-end next-generation titles. Maybe the range is a quarter to a half.[64]

As a result, Nintendo was able to boast a number of exclusive titles for the launch of the Wii, including highly rated games, such as *Zelda: Twilight Princess* and *WarioWare: Smooth Moves*. It also allowed Nintendo to include its popular *Wii Sports* title free with each console.

Better Looking Games?

Although Hirai recognized the challenges of having the same content released on multiple platforms, he felt the PS3 offered advantages over other consoles.

> When you compare the PlayStation 3 version of a game to any other version of the same game, it's a completely different entertainment experience. It is an exclusive entertainment experience for consumers enjoying a game on the PS3 as compared to any other console.[65]

In his opinion, the PS3's photorealistic graphics and advanced processing ability would revolutionize gaming in ways never before seen. Therefore, when the console failed to live up to those expectations, many consumers turned their backs on Sony. By early 2007, returns outstripped sales, and store shelves became overstocked with unsold consoles.

Sony was dismayed by the amount of negative press the PS3 had received (see Exhibit 5). Some blamed Sony for delivering a console that did not live up to the prelaunch hype. Even the editors of the *Official PlayStation Magazine*, a periodical that normally advocated on

---

[63]"Why Gears of War Costs $60," *Forbes* (www.forbes.com/2006/12/19/ps3-xbox360-costs-tech-cx_rr_game06_1219expensivegames.html), December 19, 2006, accessed June 28, 2007.

[64]"Wii Dev Costs Fraction of PS3's, 360's," gamespot.com/wii/driving/cars/news.html?sid=6149154, May 5, 2006, accessed February 20, 2007.

[65]"Interview with Kaz Hirai," games.kikizo.com/news/200610/009_p2.asp, October 3, 2006, accessed February 21, 2007.

EXHIBIT 5   News Headlines

"Sony's PlayStation 3 Is Not Worth the Hype"
The PlayStation 3 goes on sale in the U.S. today, but I wouldn't recommend buying one, not even for the regular price, which is plenty expensive without the import markup.

Time, November 17, 2006

"Enthusiasts Warn Masses, Don't Believe the Hype"
Is Sony's new PlayStation 3 worth getting pumped full of lead? The answer: not likely, since software programmers for the new gaming system want to fire a few rounds into the machine themselves.

Boston Herald, November 18, 2006

"Will PlayStation 3 Be the New Betamax?"
Sony's Blu-ray technology is hot stuff. But, as it found out back in the 1980s, technical superiority doesn't always guarantee success.

The Independent (UK), November 26, 2006

"Glitches a New-tech Byproduct"
The race to get first-generation concepts to market often means they're available before all the bugs have been worked out. Tyson J. Carter slept through a hailstorm as he camped outside a Target store to nab a PlayStation 3 last month. But the deluge of woe began when he got Sony Corp.'s $600 video game console home.

Los Angeles Times, December 18, 2006

"The HD War Wages On"
Blu-ray vs. HD DVD is more than PlayStation 3 vs. Xbox 360. Why? Because people would rather play with their Wii.

Toronto Sun (Canada), January 7, 2007

"Sony Ships 1 Million PS3s in Japan, Seen Missing Target"
Japan's Sony said it has shipped 1 million PlayStation 3 game consoles in Japan, but speculation is rising that the company would fall far short of its 6 million global shipment target by March.

EWeek, January 16, 2007

"Hobbled by Disappointing Sales and a Loss at the Game Unit, Sony's Profit Drops 5%"
The dip in Sony's quarterly earnings released early Tuesday underscores what many analysts call the biggest single challenge now facing the recovering Japanese electronics conglomerate: the shaky start of its long-awaited PlayStation 3 game console.

The New York Times, January 31, 2007

Sony's behalf, said they felt let down by Sony's "promises for better looking games." In their view, the PS3 offered few advantages over the Xbox 360:

> Blu-ray. The Cell Processor. The RSX graphics chip. The PS3 was supposed to be the most insanely advanced gaming machine ever created. It was supposed to be able to deliver visuals well beyond anything capable on console or PC. According to Sony, the next generation wasn't supposed to begin until PS3 arrived. So why is it, then, that all these PS3 games look just the same as they do on the Xbox 360?[66]

Tretton believed that many journalists simply did not understand the needs of gamers. Instead, they targeted Sony because of its undisputed position as the market leader. "Because we're in that leadership position, there are a lot of expectations thrust upon us, and some of them are a little unrealistic," he asserted:

> I did an interview with *Time* magazine, and the guy did his first interview ever on the games industry, and touched his first machine two days before that. I would argue that *Time* magazine may not be plugged in to the consumer or the gamer. All I can talk to is the people that we've attempted to sell PlayStation 3s to, and we've attempted to sell PlayStation 3s to a million people, and they have bought them as quickly as we can get them out to them. . . . I'll look at what gets written in the press for just what it is: an attempt to try to create headlines and sell newspapers.[67]

[66]"What the Cell Is Going On?" *The Official Sony PlayStation Magazine* (1up.com/do/feature?cId=3155393), November 28, 2006, accessed June 28, 2007.
[67]"Battle Station," *Electronic Gaming Monthly*, March 2007, p. 66.

Product Sales

Although initial sales were promising, by early 2007, the PS3 had dropped to fourth place in the United States (see Exhibit 6). Worldwide, the Nintendo Wii outsold the PS3 by a ratio of two to one, and total global PS3s sales through to March 2007 numbered 1.5 million units, compared to 5 million units of the Nintendo Wii and more than 10 million units of the Xbox 360.[68]

Most games analysts believed that the success of the PS3 would ultimately depend more on Sony's ability to bring quality game titles to the platform than on raw performance. "The real issue for Sony is whether they can get back the momentum they had with PS2," declared one. "The only thing that is going to drive that is the number of titles available."[69] At the end of the day, the PlayStation was "still the world's most successful gaming brand ever."[70] In the minds of some experts, that would be enough for the PS3 to eventually surpass its competitors.

Tretton blamed "society" and its penchant to support underdogs for the PS3's problems. If the console were to fall to third place, "people would have a warm spot in their hearts for the good old days of PlayStation," he asserted.

> I think in time we'll be able to migrate the vast majority of the audience we've established with PlayStation 2 to PlayStation 3.[71]

EXHIBIT 6
Monthly U.S. Sales of Video Game Hardware

Source: NPD Funworld. Cited in "NPD: $1.25B in US Game Sales Kick off '07," gamespot.com/wii/action/ thelegendofzelda/ news.html?sid=6166199, February 21, 2007, accessed March 16, 2007.

Company	Platform	Units Sold		
		November 2006	December 2006	January 2007
Nintendo	Wii	476,000	604,200	435,503
Sony	PlayStation 2	664,000	1,400,000	299,352
Microsoft	Xbox 360	511,000	1,100,000	294,000
Sony	PlayStation 3	197,000	490,700	243,554
Nintendo	DS	918,000	1,600,000	239,000
Sony	PSP	412,000	953,200	211,000
Nintendo	Game Boy Advance	641,000	850,000	179,000
Nintendo	Game Cube	70,000	64,000	24,000

[68]"Sony PS3 Hit by £10m in Cancellations," *Brand Republic Daily News,* brandrepublic.com/ BrandRepublicNews/News/646182/Sony-PS3-hit-10m-cancellations/, March 27, 2007, accessed June 28, 2007.

[69]"Gamers Get Set for PlayStation 3," *BBC News,* March 22, 2007.

[70]"PlayStation 3 Launched in Europe," *BBC News,* March 23, 2007.

[71]"Battle Station," *Electronic Gaming Monthly,* March 2007, p. 66.

Case Group C

Promotion Strategy

12

Mountain Dew: Selecting New Creative

Douglas B. Holt *Oxford University*

Standing at the front of a PepsiCo conference room, Bill Bruce gestured enthusiastically, pointing to the sketches at his side. Bruce, a copywriter and executive creative director, headed up the creative team on the Mountain Dew account for PepsiCo's advertising agency, BBDO New York. In fact, it was Bruce who devised the famous "Do the Dew" campaign that had catapulted Mountain Dew to the number 3 position in its category. With his partner, art director Doris Cassar, Bruce had developed 10 new creative concepts for Mountain Dew's 2000 advertising to present to PepsiCo management. Gathered in the room to support Bruce and Cassar were BBDO senior executives Jeff Mordos (chief operating officer), Cathy Israelevitz (senior account director), and Ted Sann (chief creative officer). Each of the three executives had over a decade of experience working on Mountain Dew. Representing PepsiCo were Scott Moffitt (Marketing Director, Mountain Dew), Dawn Hudson (chief marketing officer, and a former senior ad agency executive), and Gary Rodkin (chief executive officer, Pepsi-Cola North America).

Scott Moffitt scribbled notes as he listened to Bruce speak. Moffitt and the brand managers under him were charged with day-to-day oversight of Mountain Dew marketing. These responsibilities included brand strategy, consumer and sales promotions, packaging, line extensions, product changes, and sponsorships. But for Moffitt and the senior managers above him, the most important decisions of the year were made in conference rooms with BBDO creatives. Each of the ads would cost over a million dollars to produce. But the production costs were minor compared to the $55 million media budget that would be committed to air these spots. Historically, PepsiCo management had learned that selecting the right creative was one of the most critical decisions they made in terms of impact on sales and profits.

Mountain Dew had carried PepsiCo's soft drink revenues during the 1990s as cola brands struggled. But now the "*Do the Dew*" campaign was entering its eighth year, a long stretch by any consumer goods baseline. Many other brands were now sponsoring the same alternative sports that Mountain Dew had relied upon to boost its image. And teens were gravitating to new activities and new music that Dew's competitors had successfully exploited in their branding activities. Figuring out how to keep the campaign working hard to maintain the brand's relevance with its target consumers had become a chief preoccupation of senior management at both PepsiCo and BBDO. At the same time, key competitors were raising their ad budgets as competition in both the carbonated soft drink (CSD) and noncarbonated drinks categories was heating up, sending Dew sales below targets. Choosing the right ads to maximize the impact of Mountain Dew's relatively small media budget was a make-or-break decision.

PEPSICO AND BBDO

PepsiCo was widely considered to be one of the most sophisticated and aggressive marketing companies in the world. In North America, the company had three divisions, each with category-leading brands. Pepsi and Mountain Dew were the number 2 and 3 soft drinks. Frito-Lay dominated the salty-snack category with Ruffles, Lay's, Doritos, and Cheetos. And the company had recently acquired Tropicana, the leading juice brand. In 2000, PepsiCo had acquired the SoBe line of teas and "functional" drinks from South Beach Beverages, which it operated as a stand-alone subsidiary.

BBDO was one of the 10 largest ad agencies in the world, with worldwide billings of about $15 billion. Of the largest full-service agencies, BBDO was particularly renowned for the quality of its creative work. The roster of the New York office, BBDO New York, included many high-powered clients such as General Electric, Visa, M&M/Mars, Charles Schwab, and FedEx. Their top 10 accounts had been BBDO clients for an average of 32 years. BBDO's relationship with PepsiCo dated to breakthrough campaigns for Pepsi in the 1960s. BBDO took over Mountain Dew from Ogilvy & Mather in 1974 and had held the account ever since. In 1998, PepsiCo hired Uniworld, the largest African-American owned ad agency in the United States, to develop a separate Mountain Dew campaign targeted to African Americans.

THE CARBONATED SOFT DRINKS CATEGORY

As in most other countries, in the United States soft drink consumption was ubiquitous. And, until recently, soft drinks had meant cola. The retail carbonated soft drinks (CSD) category had long been dominated by the two cola giants, Coke and Pepsi. In the so-called cola wars of the 1960s and 70s, Pepsi directly attacked Coke with taste tests and with advertising designed to make Pepsi the hipper and more stylish "choice of the new generation," implying that Coke was a drink for older and less "with it" people. The soft drink category, and colas in particular, boomed throughout the 1970s and 1980s as people substituted away from coffee to soft drinks as a source of caffeine. The industry also consolidated as once-important brands (RC Cola, Orange Crush, A&W Root Beer) faded into the background. By the 1990s, three companies controlled all of the major national brands: The Coca-Cola Company (Coke, Diet Coke, Sprite), PepsiCo (Pepsi, Diet Pepsi, Mountain Dew), and Cadbury-Schweppes (Dr Pepper and 7-UP).

CSDs were a promotion-intensive category. In most grocery stores, Coke and Pepsi controlled a great deal of shelf space and displays. They had so much clout that their bottlers were able to choose how to stock the shelves and what to display. Impulse purchase displays had become an important source of incremental volume. A substantial and increasing share of volume came from convenience stores, where most purchases were of single servings purchased for immediate consumption. The major brands ran seasonal promotions, such as "under the cap" games in which every tenth bottle had a free bottle give-away written under the cap. More junior brand managers spent considerable time developing and implementing these promotions.

Product, promotion, packaging, and pricing innovations were constant though usually incremental, quickly diffusing throughout the category. In the last decade, one of the major innovations in the category had been the 20-ounce single serve bottle, usually priced at \$.99 and sold as an impulse purchase. The margins on this bottle were higher than the 12-packs or 2-liter bottles. Also, all of the large brands introduced 24-pack cases sold to heavy users. Brand managers worked to keep package design contemporary. For example, at PepsiCo, both Pepsi and Mountain Dew had substantial make overs in the 1990s resulting in richer and more vibrant colors and simplified graphics. Other brands, including 7-UP and Sprite, also executed similar packaging redesigns.

For most of the twentieth century, PepsiCo and The Coca-Cola Company competed fiercely, each responding in tit-for-tat fashion to the other's successes. Pepsi rolled out lemon-lime Slice in the 1980s to compete against Sprite, but soon withdrew support for that brand. Recently it was rumored that the company was plotting yet another new lemon-lime introduction. In the 1970s, Coca-Cola introduced Mr. Pibb to attack Dr Pepper and Mello-Yello as a me-too competitor against Mountain Dew. With Mountain Dew's national success in the 1990s, Coca-Cola launched a second frontal assault, introducing another copy-cat brand called Surge. In addition, both companies had launched other new products without much success: Coke had flopped with OK Cola (the cynical retro cola), and Fruitopia (the neo-hippie fruit beverage). PepsiCo had similar problems with the introduction of Crystal Pepsi (the clear crisp cola), although it was able to establish Pepsi One as a niche brand.

In the 1990s, cola growth slowed and the "flavor" CSDs did very well. Sprite, Mountain Dew, and Dr Pepper all enjoyed great success, although 7-UP continued to struggle (see Exhibit 1). In 1999, however, all CSD sales suffered as a result of customers' sticker shock to a category-wide 5 percent retail price increase, and also a trend toward experimentation with noncarbonated drinks and bottled water as substitutes for soft drinks. Sports drinks were led by Gatorade, tea and juice blends by Snapple, Arizona, and SoBe, and the highly caffeinated "energy" drinks by Red Bull. These drinks, sometimes termed "functional" or "alternative," often included a stimulant (caffeine or similar substance) and plant extracts reputed to have medicinal value (ginkgo, guarana, St. Johns Wort, ginseng). Many of these drinks were launched by small companies with grass-roots marketing efforts focused on music and sports sponsorships, on-site promotions, and nontraditional distribution (e.g., sandwich shops for Snapple, record stores for Red Bull). Industry rumors were circulating that Coca-Cola, Anheuser-Busch, PepsiCo, and Cadbury-Schweppes were working aggressively to develop functional drinks to tap into this growing segment.

ADVERTISING AND BRANDING

Over many decades, Coca-Cola had become "America's drink" (and later the preferred drink in many countries around the world) through advertising that conveyed that Coke served as a social elixir. Coke promoted the idea that the drink brought people together in friendship around ideas that people in the nation cared about. From 1995 onward, Coke had struggled as it experimented with a variety of new branding ideas. Pepsi rose to the rank of Coke's loyal opposition in the 1960s with the successful "The Pepsi Generation" ad campaign, in which the brand harnessed the ideas and passions of the 1960s counterculture.

EXHIBIT 1 CSD Sales/Share (Million cases/Percent market)

	1990		1991		1992		1993		1994		1995		1996		1997		1998		1999 (Est.)	
	Sales	Share	Sales	Share	Sales	Share	Sales	Share	Sales	Share	Sales	Share	Sales	Share	Sales	Share	Sales	Share	Sales	Share
Coke	1,565.5	20.1	1,597.9	20.1	1,613.9	20.1	1,680.4	20.2	1,776.7	20.4	1,868.6	20.8	1,929.2	20.8	1,978.2	20.6	2,037.5	20.6	2,018.0	20.3
Pepsi	1,370.0	17.6	1,338.0	16.9	1,327.3	16.5	1,305.9	15.7	1,310.0	15.0	1,344.3	15.0	1,384.6	14.9	1,391.5	14.5	1,399.8	14.2	1,371.8	13.8
Diet Coke	726.9	9.3	741.2	9.3	732.6	9.1	740.6	8.9	767.6	8.8	793.0	8.8	811.4	8.7	819.0	8.5	851.8	8.6	843.0	8.5
Diet Pepsi	490.0	6.3	500.0	6.3	509.5	6.4	491.5	5.9	511.2	5.9	521.4	5.8	541.5	5.8	523.5	5.5	529.7	5.4	503.0	5.1
Sprite	295.0	3.8	313.1	3.9	328.1	4.1	357.6	4.3	396.3	4.5	460.3	5.1	529.8	5.7	598.0	6.2	651.8	6.6	671.5	6.8
Dr Pepper	364.8	4.7	385.3	4.9	414.0	5.2	445.6	5.4	485.1	5.6	515.0	5.7	536.8	5.8	566.8	5.9	599.4	6.1	630.0	6.3
Mountain Dew	300.0	3.9	327.5	4.1	351.1	4.4	387.6	4.7	455.0	5.2	509.6	5.7	535.6	5.8	605.2	6.3	665.1	6.7	705.0	7.1
7-UP	211.5	2.7	207.7	2.6	211.3	2.6	209.9	2.5	221.5	2.5	219.9	2.5	217.7	2.3	216.7	2.3	210.9	2.1	204.9	2.1
Surge															69.0		51.8		26.7	
Mello-Yello	42.9		49.5		59.5		64.0		64.6		61.6		59.0		46.6		42.4		41.6	

Source: Maxwell Report.

EXHIBIT 2 Advertising Spending: Television Media
(Major CSDs, $MM)

	1990	1991	1992	1993	1994	1995	1996	1997	1998	1999	2000 (Est.)
Coke	$157.4	$139.9	$168.1	$131.1	$161.5	$124.7	$199.8	$156.8	$140.4	$167.7	$208.3
Pepsi	129.8	141.3	137.8	144.0	120.6	133.1	98.1	133.1	140.5	165.9	159.6
Mountain Dew	12.9	20.0	25.9	29.1	30.3	38.3	40.4	43.1	50.3	45.0	55.9
Sprite	32.0	36.1	27.5	26.9	36.0	54.6	57.9	60.6	56.2	69.9	87.7
Dr Pepper	32.2	49.3	50.1	52.8	61.5	65.4	67.9	81.0	86.8	102.4	106.8
7-UP	38.8	37.4	23.7	29.4	27.3	23.2	33.1	38.7	27.0	38.7	45.1
Surge	0.0	0.0	0.0	0.0	0.0	0.0	0.0	15.5	21.0	19.6	0.2

Source: Competitive Media Reports.

More recently, Pepsi used celebrities—particularly musicians such as Michael Jackson, Madonna, Faith Hill, Ricky Martin, and Mary J. Blige—to convey the idea that Pepsi was an expression of youth attitudes. Nonetheless, the Pepsi brand also had struggled to maintain sales in the 1990s.

7-UP was successful in the 1970s branding against the colas as the "uncola" in ads that used a charismatic Jamaican actor to describe the purity and naturalness of 7-UP in a tropical setting. Similarly, the sweet cherry-cola concoction Dr Pepper challenged the audience to "be a Pepper" with well-received dance numbers that encouraged consumers to do their own thing rather than follow the masses in drinking cola. From the late 1980s onward, 7-UP faded as the brand was used as a cash cow with ever-shrinking media investments. Meanwhile, Mountain Dew rose from its regional status to become a major "flavor" brand. The three major flavor brands dominated different geographic areas: Dr Pepper dominated Texas and the rest of the deep South, Mountain Dew dominated rural areas, particularly in the Midwest and Southeast, and Sprite dominated urban-ethnic areas.

Category advertising spending exceeded $650 million (see Exhibit 2). PepsiCo spent substantially less as a percentage of sales than its competitors. Instead, the company relied on exceptional creativity to make the advertising work harder for less cost. PepsiCo viewed the creative development process as a key organizational competency, a strategic weapon that was central to their financial success.

MOUNTAIN DEW BRAND HISTORY

Mountain Dew was invented by the Hartman Beverage Company in Knoxville, Tennessee, in the late 1940s. The bright yellow-green drink in the green bottle packed a powerful citrus flavor, more sugar and more caffeine than other soft drinks, and less carbonation so that it could be drunk quickly. The drink became a favorite on the Eastern seaboard, through Kentucky, Tennessee, and eventually spread up through the Great Lakes states (skirting the big cities) and into the Northern Plains of Minnesota and the Dakotas. PepsiCo, amazed by Dew's success in what brand managers would come to call the "NASCAR belt" (the stock car racing circuit that drew rural men as its primary audience), and in need of a "flavor" soft-drink to round out its line-up, purchased Mountain Dew in 1964.

PepsiCo originally assigned Mountain Dew to the Ogilvy & Mather ad agency. The strategy for the new brand extrapolated from Dew's origins and existing packaging. The beverage's heart-pumping caffeine and sugar rush were linked to its backwoods heritage to produce the idea of a comic "hillbilly" character named Willie who drank Mountain Dew to "get high" on the soft drink equivalent of moonshine liquor. The tagline, "Yahoo! Mountain Dew!" was accompanied by "Thar's a bang in ever' bottle."

In 1973 PepsiCo assigned the brand to BBDO, its agency of record for Pepsi. For two decades client and agency worked to expand the brand's reach from America's hinterlands into the suburbs and cities of the major metropolitan areas. The major campaign of the 1970s—"Hello Sunshine"—sought to tie Mountain Dew's distinctive product characteristics to a set of backcountry recreational images. The yellow-green product and strong citrus flavor are represented over and over by the gleaming sun sparkling in beautiful natural settings. The product name is represented in virtually every ad by mountains, dew drops reflecting in the sun, and condensed drops on cans to represent dew. The energizing effects of the caffeine and sugar are toned down and now are a refreshing part of an active outdoor lifestyle. Often the ads featured casual coed athletic activities that always ended in a plunge into a rural pond or creek.

This campaign pulled the Mountain Dew brand into more contemporary terrain, but it was still too rural to get much traction in the suburbs. So in the 1980s, PepsiCo directly targeted suburban teenagers with a new campaign called "Country Cool." The creative idea was to marry the popular athletic endeavors of suburban kids (cool) with Mountain Dew's active rural lifestyle (country), all punctuated by the refreshing Dew plunge. Ads featured male teens performing on skateboards, mountain bikes, and BMX bikes. A new tune was crafted for the occasion: "Being cool you'll find is a state of mind. Your refreshing attitude. Things get hot. Cool is all you got. Dewin' it country cool. So chill on out; when the heat comes on. With a cool, smooth Mountain Dew. Dewin' it Country Cool. Mountain Dew. Dewin' it Country Cool."

BBDO jettisoned the "country" component of the campaign in 1991 to build an entire campaign around athletic stunts. This advertising departed dramatically from anything that BBDO had produced in the previous 16 years. The spots featured daredevil maneuvers of sports like windsurfing, rollerblading, motocross cycling, and paragliding. The closely framed shots, which put the viewer in the middle of the action, also suggested excitement and energy. The spots were set to aggressive rock music rather than studio jingles. In 1992, a new song called "Get Vertical" was introduced with the lyrics "Ain't no doubt about the power of dew, got the airborne thrust of rocket fuel."

CULTURAL TRENDS

PepsiCo and BBDO managers paid close attention to cultural trends. They were particularly focused on track music and sports trends since these activities were so central to youth culture.

Music

Three musical trends dominated the airwaves in the 1990s. Rap music exploded to become the most popular genre in the country. At first, gangsta rap, which flaunted misogynistic and violent lyrics, was said to represent the reality of life in the "hood" (the American ghetto). From 1992 onward, gangsta rap broke out with a lighter sound and slightly less aggressive lyrics, sometimes called gangsta-lite, that made the music much more accessible while maintaining the forbidding connotations. By 1993, media coverage of the travails of celebrity rappers like Snoop Doggy Dog and Tupac Shakur ruled not only the music magazines but also *People* and *Newsweek*. Rap music, and the hip-hop lifestyle of which it was a part, permeated teen life. MTV's program *Yo! MTV Raps* and specialty magazines like *The Source* and *Vibe* became mainstream cultural venues. By 1999, rap remained very popular among male teens, especially in urban areas, although its Top 40 appeal had subsided somewhat.

At roughly the same time, the alternative rock music scene, which throughout the 1980s existed as a small subcultural scene found mostly on college campuses, also exploded. Two Seattle bands—Nirvana and Pearl Jam—put CDs at the top of the charts with aggressive and emotive music that combined equal parts punk and heavy metal. The media tagged this music "grunge" and anointed Seattle as grunge headquarters. Grunge was marketed heavily by the culture industries—music labels put out dozens of grunge bands, films that displayed the grunge attitude appeared, and fashion runways and J.C. Penney's stores were clogged with flannel shirts and clothes that had the look of the vintage Salvation Army gear that was the uniform of the grunge scene. Grunge faded in its influence in part due to the death of its most talented lead actor when Nirvana's Kurt Cobain committed suicide in 1995.

Later in the 1990s, techno music began making significant inroads into American youth culture. Invented in the 1980s as "house music" in low-budget studios of Chicago and Detroit, this beat-driven dance music became the lifeblood of dance parties called "raves" in places like London and the Spanish island of Ibiza. Raves quickly spread throughout continental Europe and beyond. Raves were all-night dancing marathons often set up in warehouses, exotic outdoor locales, and other improvised spaces. Raves attracted young people, mostly teens, who danced for hours at a time, not in pairs, but in free-form groups. The highly rhythmic music and long-winded dancing combined to produce for some fans an ecstatic trance-like state. The music was produced almost entirely by disk jockeys sampling records with tape loops and other electronic tricks. Many subgenres have since emerged that mix and match musical styles from around the world. Part of the scene was a drug called ecstasy, a drug that induces promiscuous affection, sensory overload, and euphoria. And, to keep the energy flowing all night, the dancers demanded energizing drinks. In particular, an enterprising Austrian company marketed Red Bull, a drink that was once an Asian hangover cure, as a rave stimulant. Either straight or mixed with vodka, Red Bull became the rave drink of choice. Raves diffused rather late to the United States, but proved to be most popular in the major metropolitan areas.

Sports

The so-called "alternative sports" took off in the early 1990s. Teen enthusiasts transformed casual hobby activities—mountain biking, skateboarding, paragliding, BMX biking, and inline skating—into highly technical, creative, and often dangerous sports. Snowboarding became an overnight hit with teens. Bungee jumping was a fad that disappeared quickly. As these sports became increasingly risky and creative, they began to attract spectators. So-called extreme sports—skiing down extremely steep terrain or jumping off tall buildings with a parachute—were covered by ESPN. ESPN also aggressively promoted circuits and tournaments to professionalize these new sports, which culminated in the Extreme Games in 1994, a nontraditional Olympics of sorts. Mountain Dew was one of the founding lead sponsors of the Extreme Games, which later became the X Games. Later, NBC followed with the Gravity Games, and MTV also began to cover these sports. Grunge music, more aggressive styles of rap, and various hybrids were prominent aural expressions of these sports.

GenX Ethos

During the 1990s, teens and young adults evinced a growing cynicism toward the dominant work-oriented values of the previous generation and toward corporations more generally. They found that working hard to get ahead in terms of salary and occupational prestige was harder to swallow in an era of corporate reengineering. Their cynicism also extended to corporations themselves and their marketing efforts. As this cohort became increasingly knowledgeable about how marketing worked and increasingly jaded about why brands were popular, they were not interested in listening to "sales messages" that tried to persuade them into believing a particular brand of soft drink or beer was cool. Instead, these youth adopted a campy interest in non-trendy products, television programs, and music of previous eras.

As these odd new tastes became commercialized in programming like Nickelodeon cable channel's "Nick at Nite" series—which featured less-than-notable programming from the 1950s–1970s—"retro" was born.

THE DO THE DEW CAMPAIGN

In 1992, senior management at PepsiCo sensed an opportunity to increase business on Diet Mountain Dew. Diet Mountain Dew's distribution was limited mostly to the rural regions where the brand was strongest, even though regular Dew was now a national brand. Diet Mountain Dew performed very well on product tests versus other diet drinks in the category because the heavy citrus flavor did a better job of masking the undesirable taste of the artificial sweetener. So PepsiCo allocated money for incremental advertising to support an effort to expand Diet Mountain Dew distribution. Bill Bruce, then a junior copywriter working on several brands, was assigned to the project. The strategy statements that guided the initial creative idea and subsequent spots in the campaign are reported in Exhibit 3. Bruce came up with the "Do Diet Dew" tag line (which soon evolved into "Do the Dew" to support the entire brand) and several new ideas to embellish what BBDO had begun with the Get Vertical campaign.

The first breakthrough ad of the new campaign, *Done That,* features a hair-raising shot of a guy jumping off the edge of a cliff to take a free-fall toward the narrow canyon's river bottom, set to throbbing grunge music. This was the first ad to feature the "Dew Dudes"—four young guys who are witnessing the daredevil stunts presented in the ad and commenting on them. *Done That* became a huge hit, capturing the country's imagination. The ad was widely parodied and the phrase "been there, done that" entered the vernacular. For 1994 and 1995, BBDO produced three carbon-copy "pool-outs"[1] of *Done That.* By 1995, after two years of these ads, consumer interest in the creative was fading fast. According to Jeff Mordos, if the creative hadn't moved to another idea that year, consumers' flagging interest and the potential of a revolt by PepsiCo bottlers likely would have forced PepsiCo to develop an entirely new campaign.

For 1995, three of four spots produced relied upon different creative ideas. One of these spots, *Mel Torme,* became the second hit of the campaign. The spot was a parody featuring the aging Vegas lounge singer Mel Torme, tuxedo-clad atop a Vegas hotel crooning "I Get a Kick out of You," with lyrics altered to incorporate Mountain Dew references. He impresses the Dew Dudes with a base jump of his own. Similar ads followed. In *007,* a teenage James Bond engages in a frenetic pursuit scene with typical Bond stunts, accompanied by the familiar Bond theme music. The Dew Dudes are not impressed until Bond comes upon a Mountain Dew vending machine. In *Training,* brash tennis star Andre Agassi performs extreme stunts as training exercises, and then plays an extreme game of tennis with the Dew Dudes as his coaches.

In 1997, BBDO came up with two breakthrough spots. The director of Nirvana's classic music video "Smells Like Teen Spirit" was hired to direct *Thank Heaven,* which mimics a music video. The spot stars the lead singer of an alternative rock band called Ruby. She sings a punked-up version of the classic song "Thank Heaven for Little Girls," in which the grunge style suggests the "little girls" of old have been replaced by the feminine brand of

---

[1]The noun *pool-out* is derived from a verb that is particular to the advertising business—"to pool out." The idea is to develop a pool of ads that are all closely related derivations from the same creative idea. Some advertisers feel that pools deliver a more consistent campaign while others feel that the ads become too formulaic when they are so similar. Regardless, there is a great temptation when an ad breaks through and becomes a hit to develop pool-outs to extend the popularity.

EXHIBIT 3 Mountain Dew Brand Communications Strategies (1993–1999)

	Objective	Strategy	Target	Executional Direction
1993–94	Increase awareness and trial of Mountain Dew	You can have the most thrilling, exciting, daring experience but it will never compete with the experience of a Mt. Dew	Male teens/young adults	• Distinct campaign with Dew equity consistency • Leverage "full tilt taste" and "rush" as point of difference
1995	Distinguish Mt. Dew within the competitive environment through contemporary communication of the trademark's distinct, historical positioning	You can have the most thrilling, exciting, daring experience but it will never compete with the experience of a Mt. Dew	Bull's eye: 18 yr. old leading-edge male Broad: 12–29 year olds	• Shift to a unified trademark focus modeled after "Do Diet Dew" • Explore outdoor settings • Predominant male, mid-20's casting • Preserve balance between "outlandish" and "realistic" actions/sports
1996	Optimize Dew's positioning equity among the target in a highly relevant and contemporary manner	(You can have the most thrilling, exciting, daring experience but . . .) there's nothing more intense than slamming a Mt. Dew	Bull's eye: 18 yr. old leading-edge male Broad: 12–29 year olds	• Bring "Do the Dew" trademark campaign to the next level
1997	Optimize Dew's positioning equity among the target in a highly relevant and contemporary manner • Strengthen brand perceptions among AA • Encourage product trial where familiarity is low	(You can have the most thrilling, exciting, daring experience but . . .) there's nothing more intense than slamming a Mt. Dew	Bull's eye: 18 yr. old leading-edge male Broad: 12–29 year olds	• Continue "Do the Dew" trademark campaign and encompass the Mt. Dew experience
1998	Build badge value and authentic, true Icon status for Mt. Dew in the world of youth-targeted consumer goods	Associate Mt. Dew with thrilling and exhilarating adventures in a light-hearted manner	Bull's eye: 18 yr. old leading-edge male Broad: 12–29 male/female	• Evolve the "Do the Dew" campaign against core target with fresh and relevant copy • Develop ethnically-targeted "cross-appeal" spot • Enhance product perception • Develop pool of "Do the Dew" executions • Explore other metaphors beyond alternative sports to express "exhilarating intensity" • One execution should have AA/urban relevance • Communicate quenching • Inclusion of water-greenery elements not mandatory
1999	Optimize relevance of Dew's positioning among the target	Associate Mt. Dew with the exhilarating intensity of life's most exciting, fun adventures	Male Teens (16 yr. old epicenter) • Invite teen girls while continuing as male CSD • Maintain cross-over appeal among 20–39 year olds	

Source: PepsiCo.

aggressiveness presented in the ad. *Jackie Chan* deploys the Hong Kong movie star's patented martial arts with humorous stunts into the campaign's jaded, "seen it already" motif. The ad begins in the midst of what seems like a classic chase scene from a Chan film with lots of harrowing action. When Chan faces down his enemy, the Dew Dudes magically appear as Confucian wisemen who assist Chan with cans of Mountain Dew.

Other ads produced were significantly less effective. *Scream,* a high-speed amalgam of extreme sports shots that are organized to answer the lead-in question—"What is a Mountain Dew?"—did not fare well. And *Michael Johnson,* a spot developed to broaden Dew's appeal in the African-American community, did not meet the company's expectations.

By 1998, PepsiCo managers worried that the advertising was becoming too predictable. In particular, they were concerned that the use of alternative sports was becoming less impactful due to oversaturation. Many other brands, including companies like Bagel Bites, AT&T, Gillette Extreme Deodorant, and Slim Jims beef jerky snacks, were now major sponsors of alternative sports. To keep the campaign fresh, they needed to find alternative ways to express Mountain Dew's distinctive features. *Parking Attendant,* produced in 1999, was a solid effort at advancing toward an alternative expression. The spot features a parking attendant who takes liberties when parking a BMW handed off by a stuffy businessman. The kid drives as if in a police chase, flying from one building to another, accompanied by a frenetic surf instrumental that had been featured in Quentin Tarantino's *Pulp Fiction* a few years prior.

MOUNTAIN DEW MARKET RESEARCH

Mountain Dew's distinctive demographic profile reflected the brand's historic popularity in the NASCAR belt (see the Brand Development Index Map in Exhibit 4 and lifestyle analysis in Exhibit 5a). And Mountain Dew had much lower penetration of the total population than its major competitors. But its consumers were the most loyal in the category. Mountain Dew had the highest "gatekeeping" rating of all CSDs—it was the drink that mothers tried the hardest to keep out of the stomachs of their children. Periodically, the PepsiCo research department fielded a major study to assess the "health" of the brand, and to direct any fine-tuning. A 1997 "brand fitness" study profiled the status of the Dew brand versus its major competitors (Exhibits 6a–d).

PepsiCo monitored both the effectiveness of individual ads, as well as the cumulative impact of advertising on the overall health of the Mountain Dew brand. The contribution made by a single ad toward building brand equity was notoriously challenging to measure. Both quantitative and qualitative research provided data from which managers make useful inferences. But Pepsi managers had yet to find a research method that was accurate enough to rely upon to provide definitive judgments on ad effectiveness. PepsiCo routinely gathered a wide variety of data that hinted at an ad's impact. In addition to formal research, managers monitored "talk value" or "buzz"—the extent to which the ad has been picked up by the mass media. In particular, *The Tonight Show* and David Letterman were useful barometers. Feedback from the Mountain Dew Web site, unofficial Web sites, and the brand's 800 number were important gauges as well. In addition, PepsiCo carefully monitored how the salesforce and bottlers responded to the ads, since they were getting direct feedback from their customers. PepsiCo managers used all these data as filters. But, ultimately, the evaluation of advertising rested on managerial judgement. Based on their past experience with the brand and with advertising across many brands, managers made a reasoned evaluation.

However, PepsiCo managers did rely on market research to assess the cumulative impact of advertising on the brand. Because many other factors—especially pricing and retail display activity—had an immediate short-term impact on sales, it was often difficult to draw causal relationships between advertising and sales. But advertising campaigns do directly

EXHIBIT 4 Mountain Dew Brand Development Index Map

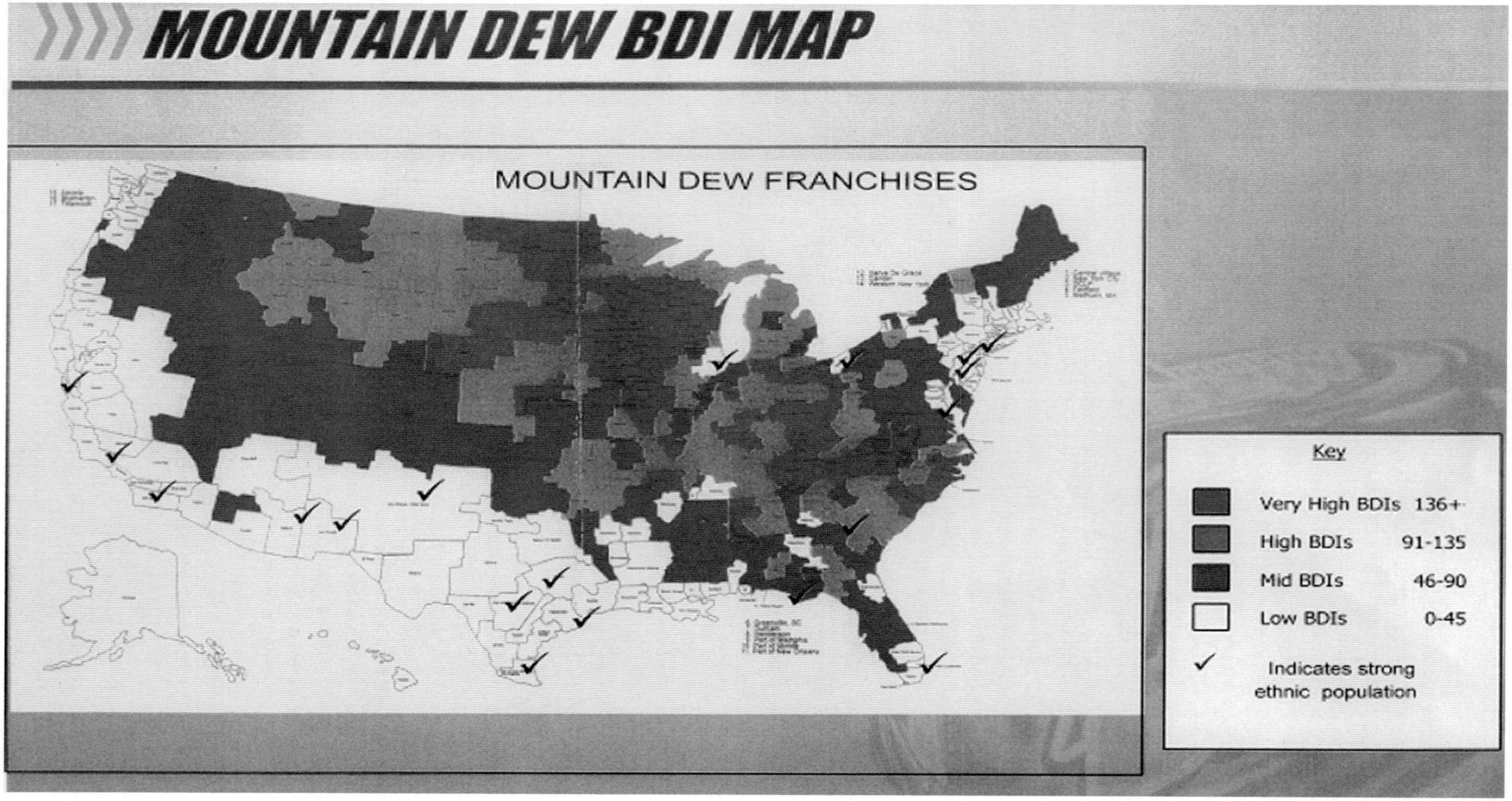

MOUNTAIN DEW BDI MAP

MOUNTAIN DEW FRANCHISES

Key

Very High BDIs 136+

High BDIs 91–135

Mid BDIs 46–90

Low BDIs 0–45

Indicates strong ethnic population

Source: BBDO New York.

EXHIBIT 5A   Spectra Lifestyle Analysis

MOUNTAIN DEW CONSUMPTION INDEX

Lifestage

Spectra Lifestyle	18–34 W/Kids	18–34 W/O Kids	35–54 W/Kids	35–54 W/O Kids	55–64	65+	Total Lifestyle
Upscale Suburbs	82	77	101	56	45	13	64
Traditional Families	118	121	160	79	42	35	96
Mid Upscale Suburbs	101–	111	108	71	64	18	66
Metro Elite	139	85	141	47	47	21	72
Working Class Towns	237	139	242	121	67	42	139
Rural Towns & Farms	225	153	212	141	91	39	140
Mid Urban Melting Pot	148	104	97	52	49	31	74
Downscale Rural	309	142	291	127	87	43	158
Downscale Urban	99	98	107	73	55	32	76
Total Lifestage	171	112	165	83	61	31	100

Source: AC Nielsen Product Library 11/97 to 11/99.

impact how the brand is perceived. And these perceptions, in turn, drive sales. So PepsiCo had assembled a set of what they termed key performance indicators (KPIs), intermediate measures that were directly impacted by advertising and that had been proven to significantly impact sales. Managers tracked KPIs, also referred to as *brand health* measures, both for teens and for 20–39 year olds. But managers were particularly concerned with brand health amongst teens because at this age soft drink consumers often moved from experimenting with a variety of drinks to becoming loyal lifetime drinkers of a single soda. The latest study, conducted in the spring of 1999, reported Mountain Dew's teen KPIs. Dew improved 6 points on "Dew Tastes Better" (to 48 percent versus a year ago). Unaided brand awareness had dropped 5 points (to 39 percent). "For someone like me" had increased 5 points (to 53 percent). And "Dew Drinkers are Cool" increased 5 points (to 64 percent).

2000 PLANNING

In 1999, Mountain Dew became the third largest carbonated soft drink at retail, overtaking Diet Coke. However, part of this success in gaining share had to do with the sustained weakness of Pepsi and Coke. In 1999, the problems that the colas were facing seemed to be spreading to Mountain Dew, Sprite, and Dr Pepper. All of the leading CSDs began to show real weakness as alternative noncarbonated drinks began to attract a great deal of trial, especially amongst teens. While Mountain Dew sales began to lag, all of the "brand health" indicators remained strong. And the advertising continued to significantly outperform competition. In planning for 2000, Moffitt and his senior management were particularly concerned with two dilemmas:

- How to keep the "Do the Dew" campaign working hard to build the brand given that extreme sports were becoming overexposed.
- How to respond to the growing threat of non-CSDs, especially Gatorade and the new highly caffeinated and sugary energy drinks like Red Bull.

A detailed strategy statement was developed by Moffitt's team at Pepsi-Cola North America, in conjunction with the account team at BBDO New York led by Cathy Israelevitz. This strategy was boiled down to a single sentence to focus the development of new

EXHIBIT 5B   Lifestyle Glossary

UPSCALE SUBURBS

"The American Dream," a nice house in a nice suburban neighborhood. College-educated executives and professionals who index high on travel, eating out, playing golf, going to health clubs, buying imported cars, watching/reading business and news. Low African American and Hispanic. High income.

TRADITIONAL FAMILIES

Like Upscale Suburbs, but lower socioeconomic level. Mix of lower level administrators and professionals with well-paid blue-collar. Index high on gardening, DIY home improvement, driving SUVs, camping, classic rock, sports radio. Low African American and Hispanic. Mid-high income.

MID/UPSCALE SUBURBS

Live in first-generation suburbs that are now part of the urban fringe. Lower income than Traditional Families, but more college-educated and white collar. Index high on baseball fans, casino gambling using Internet, attending live theater, reading science and technology, listening/watching news. Low African American and Hispanic. Mid-high income.

METRO ELITE

Younger and more urban, college-educated, ethnically diverse. Very attuned to new fashions. Geographically mobile. Index high on health clubs, bars and night clubs, fashion magazines, VH-1, music, film, computers. Middle income.

WORKING CLASS TOWNS

Well-paid blue collar families living in suburbs of smaller cities. Index high on auto racing, fishing, hunting, country music, camping, televised sports. Own trucks or minivans. Low African American and Hispanic. Middle income.

RURAL TOWNS & FARMS

Small towns mostly in the middle of the country, dominated by blue-collar and agricultural work. Index high on rodeos, fishing, woodworking, chewing tobacco, wrestling, camping, country music, TV movies, USA and TNN channels. Don't read magazines and newspapers. Low African American. Lower income.

MID-URBAN MELTING POT

Urban multiethnic neighborhoods. Old European ethnic enclaves and new Asian immigrants, mixed with African-American and Hispanic neighborhoods. Index high on menthol cigarettes, dance music, boxing, pro basketball, lottery, Home Shopping Network, heavy TV viewing, urban contemporary radio. Lower income, low college, service industries.

DOWNSCALE RURAL

Poor rural areas in Appalachia, throughout the South, and the Plains States. This socially conservative and religious area is sometimes called "the Bible belt." While indexing high African American, these are very segregated neighborhoods with little racial mixing. Lowest on education, occupation, income, housing. Index high on trucks, chewing tobacco, belonging to veteran's club, target shooting, tractor pulls, country music, fishing and hunting, daytime drama TV programs.

DOWNSCALE URBAN

Same socioeconomic profile as Downscale Rural but very different cultural profile, more similar to Mid-Urban Melting Pot. Mostly African-American and Hispanic urban neighborhoods.

Source: AC Nielsen Product Library 11/97 to 11/99.

creative: *Symbolize that drinking Mountain Dew is an exhilarating experience.* This document was used to brief Bruce and his creative team (Exhibit 7).

Super Bowl

In addition to these strategic issues, Moffitt had to consider carefully where these ads would be broadcast. Mountain Dew's national media plan focused on a younger audience. Typical buys would include MTV, *The Simpsons,* and ESPN during alternative sports broadcasts. However, with its long run of sales increases in the 1990s, Mountain Dew was becoming less of a niche brand. Partly in recognition of this expanding customer base and partly to celebrate within the company Dew's arrival as the third most popular CSD, top management decided to feature Mountain Dew rather than Pepsi during the Super Bowl.

EXHIBIT 6A
Brand Imagery—
Mountain Dew

Source: BBDO New York.

User Imagery (54%)

Product Imagery

*Too sweet
Most entertaining ads
Fun to drink
Intense experience
Lots of flavor

When need energy boost
In mood for something different
*At a sporting event

Psychographic Imagery

Adventurous
Wild
Active
Daring
*Courageous
Exciting
Free-spirited
Rebellious
Spontaneous
Athletic
Youthful
Cool
Hip
*Out-going

EXHIBIT 6B
Brand Imagery—
Surge

Source: BBDO New York.

User Imagery (49%)

Product Imagery

*Can't relate to ads
*Low quality product
*Not always available
Unique
Intense experience
*Tastes artificial

When need energy boost
In mood for something
   different

Psychographic Imagery

Wild
Rebellious
Daring
Adventurous
Active
Up-to-date
Athletic
*Trendy
Youthful
*Leading-edge
Exciting
Spontaneous
Individualistic
*Powerful
Hip
In style

EXHIBIT 6C
Brand Imagery—7-UP

Source: BBDO New York.

Product Imagery

*Least fattening
Lowest calories
Low in sodium
*Too little flavor
*Not sweet enough
*Not filling
*Healthy/good for you
Most refreshing

User Imagery (48%)

Psychographic Imagery

Sensitive
Relaxed
Peaceful
*Healthy
Feminine
Kind
*Nurturing

(Nice)
(Loyal)
(Cooperative)

EXHIBIT 6D
Brand Imagery—
Sprite

Source: BBDO New York.

Product Imagery

Lowest calories
Most refreshing
*Thirst quenching
*Goes down easy
Low in sodium

In a nice restaurant
*After exercise/sports

(In the evening)
(In the morning)

User Imagery (56%)

Psychographic Imagery

Feminine
Sensitive
Peaceful
*Nice
Relaxed
Free-spirited
*Cooperative
*Friendly
*Happy
Kind

(Innovative)

EXHIBIT 7

Mountain Dew FY
2000 Brand
Communications
Strategy

Source: PepsiCo.

Objective: Expand appeal of Mountain Dew to new users while reinforcing it among current users

Positioning: To 18-year-old males, who embrace excitement, adventure and fun, Mountain Dew is the great tasting carbonated soft drink that exhilarates like no other because it is energizing, thirst-quenching, and has a one-of-a-kind citrus flavor.

Communication Strategy: Symbolize that drinking Mountain Dew is an exhilarating experience.

Target: Male Teens—18-year-old epicenter

- Ensure appeal amongst 20–39-year-olds (current users)
- Drive universal appeal (white, African-American, Hispanic, and other ethnic)

Product Benefits	Emotional Benefits	Personality
Energizing	Exhilaration	Irreverent
Quenching	Excitement	Daring
Great Taste		Fun

The Super Bowl had for decades been a hugely influential event for advertisers. The game drew the biggest audience of the year and the ads received an amazing amount of attention. In recent years, the frenzy around the advertising had grown disproportionately to the game itself. The media paid almost as much attention to the ads shown as to the teams and players. The networks interviewed the advertisers and the stars of the ads, and even replayed the ads on their programs. So a Super Bowl ad now had a huge ripple effect in free public relations. In addition, the Super Bowl was an extremely important contest for advertisers and especially for ad agencies. To "win" the Super Bowl (to be voted the top ad in the *USA Today* Ad Meter poll reported in the newspaper the following day) was a prestigious honor within the industry. Finally, Super Bowl ads provided a powerful sales tool to motivate retailers and distributors. PepsiCo and other grocery products advertisers used their annual Super Bowl advertising to sell in retail displays.

Super Bowl advertising, as a result, had become a distinctive genre within advertising. The demographically diverse audience demanded advertising with hooks that were easily understood. Insider humor did not work. While MTV ads could talk in a colloquial language to teens, Super Bowl ads could not afford this luxury. Second, the heated competition to win the affection of the audience had led to "big" productions that would stand out against an ever-more impressive set of competitors.

THE NEW CREATIVE

Bruce and Cassar had just finished presenting 10 new ad concepts for PepsiCo to evaluate. For each concept, PepsiCo managers were given a "storyboard"—a script and a set of rough pencil sketches that depicted the most important scenes. Bruce and Cassar talked through each storyboard to help the client imagine how the ad would look if it were produced. The storyboard served as the skeletal outline of the ad. The creatives put flesh on these bones by describing in detail the characters, the action, how the scene is depicted, and the music. Of the 10 new concepts, Moffitt and his senior managers hoped to select three ads to produce. The two best ads would run on the Super Bowl and then all three ads would be broadcast throughout 2000. It was already October, so there was barely enough time to produce the ads presented to get them on the Super Bowl. Asking Bruce to try again was not an option. The 10 initial concepts were quickly whittled down to five finalists.

1. *Labor of Love.* A humorous spot about the birth of a Dew drinker. The doctor in the delivery room calls out "code green" and retreats to catch with a baseball mitt the baby as it shoots out of its mother like a cannon.

2. *Cheetah.* One of the Dew Dudes chases down a cheetah on a mountain bike. The cheetah, running on the African plain, has stolen his Dew and he wants it back. He tackles the cat, pulls the can out of the cat's stomach, but finds that it's empty and full of holes.

3. *Dew or Die.* The Dew Dudes are called in to foil the plot of an evil villain who is threatening to blow up the planet. Performing daredevil maneuvers down a mountain, they get sidetracked in a ski lodge with some girls, but accidentally save the world anyway, powered by a spilled can of Dew.

4. *Mock Opera.* A parody of the Queen song *Bohemian Rhapsody* sung by the Dew Dudes who mock the cover of the original Queen album. The ad portrays the story of the altered lyrics: alternative sports action in which the athletes just miss cans of Dew as they shoot by.

5. *Showstopper.* A take-off on an extravagantly choreographed production number that mimics a Buzby Berkeley musical/dance film from the 1930s. The dancers are silver-clad BMX riders and skateboarders who perform for the Dew Dudes posing as directors.

PepsiCo viewed the evaluation of new creative as the most challenging aspect of brand management. Unlike decisions on new product ideas, consumer promotions, or product improvements, there was no market research or marketplace data to guide the decision. Junior managers typically did not sit in the agency presentations as they were not yet seasoned enough to judge creative work. PepsiCo believed that managers first had to gain knowledge of how advertising worked to build brands through years of seasoning and tutorials on several of the company's brands. So Scott Moffitt was the most junior person in the room. The skills and judgment that he demonstrated would be key to moving up the ladder at PepsiCo.

Bill Bruce finished presenting his last storyboard and scanned the room to lock eyes with the PepsiCo executives who would be deciding the fate of his ideas. Scott Moffitt didn't return the gaze. Instead he looked anxiously at his superiors, knowing that the spotlight would next focus on him. This was his chance to prove himself not only to PepsiCo senior management, but also to BBDO. BBDO's senior managers had become influential advisors, whom PepsiCo's top marketing executives routinely relied upon to help guide branding decisions. With six years of experience under his belt, this was Moffitt's chance to earn their respect as a contributing member to these critical discussions. Moffitt was eager to make a strong impression with nuanced and well-reasoned evaluations. Following long-standing protocol in packaged goods companies, the junior manager at the table gets the first crack at evaluating the creative. Moffitt cleared his throat, complimented Bruce on the high quality of the new work he had presented, and began his evaluation.

Case

13

Red Bull

**Richard R. Johnson, Jordan Mitchell, Paul W. Farris,
and Ervin Shames** *University of Virginia*

"We don't bring the product to the people. We bring the people to the product."[1]
—Dietrich Mateschitz, Founder, Red Bull GmbH

By any measure, Red Bull was a runaway success. Sales of Red Bull, a nonalcoholic, carbonated energy drink, reached 1.9 billion cans in 120 countries in 2004.[2] Red Bull had been a forerunner in establishing the worldwide energy-drink category estimated at more than $4.7 billion,[3] enjoying approximately half of the worldwide market share.[4] Since the company's 1997 U.S. debut, Red Bull had emerged as the seventh-leading carbonated soft drink company in terms of market share, growing by 45 percent to achieve sales of 30 million cases (see Table 1).[5] Hundreds of companies had entered the segment in hopes that they would rush the "Bull" and grab a piece of the lucrative market. Only a handful of enterprises such as Hansen Natural, with their drink called Monster, and Rockstar with a beverage of the same name, were able to challenge Red Bull's dominant market position by offering double the size at the same price. Along with small upstarts, Coca-Cola and Pepsi were eager to increase their lagging positions in the energy-drink sphere. Coca-Cola had entered the category in 2000 with its brand KMX, but it had failed to win over consumers. In early 2005, Coca-Cola launched a new energy-drink brand called Full Throttle

This case was written from public sources by Richard R. Johnson and revised by Jordan Mitchell under the supervision of Paul W. Farris, Landmark Communications Professor of Business Administration, and Ervin Shames, Visiting Lecturer in Business Administration. It was written as a basis for class discussion rather than to illustrate effective or ineffective handling of an administrative situation. Copyright © 2002 by the University of Virginia Darden School Foundation, Charlottesville, VA. All rights reserved. *To order copies, send an e-mail to sales@dardenbusinesspublishing.com. No part of this publication may be reproduced, stored in a retrieval system, used in a spreadsheet, or transmitted in any form or by any means—electronic, mechanical, photocopying, recording, or otherwise—without the permission of the Darden School Foundation.* Rev. 07/05.

[1]"Selling Energy—Red Bull," *Economist,* May 11, 2002.
[2]"Canada Prepares for Energy Drink Surge," *Globe and Mail,* March 24, 2005.
[3]"The World Market for Soft Drinks," *Euromonitor,* September 2004, Table 2, p. 39.
[4]"Hansen Natural Analyst Report," Adams Harkness, May 4, 2005, p. 4.
[5]"Beverage Digest," www.beveragedigest.com (accessed June 30, 2005).

TABLE 1
Top 10 U.S. Carbonated Soft Drink Companies, 2004

Source: "Maxwell Ranks Soft Drink Industry for 2004," *Beverage Digest.*

Company	2004 Market Share	2004 Cases (millions)	Volume % Change
Coca-Cola Co.	43.1	4414.8	−1.0%
Pepsi-Cola Co.	31.7	3241.7	+0.4%
Cadbury-Schweppes	14.5	1485.9	+2.3%
Cott Corp.	5.5	564.9	+18.2%
National Beverage	2.4	249.4	+2.2%
Big Red	0.4	41.5	−0.5%
Red Bull	0.3	30.0	+45.0%
Hansen Natural	0.2	20.2	+56.6%
Monarch Co.	0.1	9.8	+7.6%
Rockstar	0.1	9.7	+154.5%
Private Label/Other	1.7	171.5	−11.2%
Total	100.0	10,239.4	+1.0%

to fight back. Pepsi had purchased the South Beach Beverage Company (SoBe) and had launched Amp under the Mountain Dew brand to etch out a competitive position.

It looked as though the energy-drink segment would continue growing, with some analysts predicting the U.S. market to double at $3.5 to $4 billion by 2009. Some also predicted that Coca-Cola and Pepsi would force consolidation. How could Red Bull maintain its leadership position in a maturing category? Could the company survive the onslaught of competition, or was Red Bull a sitting duck?

BACKGROUND

While touring Thailand in the early 1980s, Austrian businessman Dietrich Mateschitz took note of a Thai energy drink called Krating Daeng (or "red bull") that had become a popular pick-me-up or stimulant, especially amongst blue-collar workers. Believing that such a drink would be popular in Europe, Mateschitz made a deal with TC Pharmaceuticals, owners of Krating Daeng, that gave him the international rights to the drink in exchange for a 51 percent share in his Red Bull company.[6] Mateschitz adapted the taste of the drink to suit the western palate, and replaced the Thai bottle with a slim silver 250 ml. (8.3 oz.) can featuring a logo with two red bulls about to collide head-on in the foreground, and a yellow sun in the background. Beneath the logo appeared the words "energy drink."

As the name implies, energy drinks were designed to give the body a jolt of energy. Red Bull alleged that its product contained several energy-boosting ingredients, including taurine, glucoronolactone, and caffeine. Taurine is an amino acid occurring naturally in the body that acts as a metabolic transmitter with detoxifying qualities, but whose levels can drop as a result in situations of high stress or physical exertion. Glucoronolactone, like taurine, also has a detoxifying effect and can help eliminate harmful substances from the body. Caffeine, a known stimulant, acts on the brain and circulatory system, and a single 250 ml. can of Red Bull contained 80 milligrams, a level of caffeine equivalent to a cup of coffee. Coca-Cola had 34 milligrams in each 12-ounce can.[7] The combination

[6]Acharn Terry Fredrickson, "About Business," *Bangkok Post,* October 18, 2000, http://www.bangkokpost.net/education/site2000/bcoc1800.htm (accessed September 12, 2002).
[7]Kerry A. Dolan, "The Soda with Buzz," *Forbes,* March 28, 2005.

A Red Bull Flügtag participant prepares to launch a
homemade chicken-craft into an Austrian lake

of these ingredients, along with carbohydrates in the form of glucose and sucrose as well as various vitamins, formed a beverage that, according to Red Bull, created the following effects:

- Increased physical endurance.
- Improved reaction speed and concentration.
- Increased mental alertness (to stay awake).
- Improved overall feeling of well-being.
- Stimulated metabolism and increased stamina.

The company captured these attributes in the phrase "Red Bull stimulates body and mind."[8]

PRODUCT INTRODUCTION IN AUSTRIA

Red Bull faced challenges even before the product debuted. The company's ability to make claims regarding Red Bull's performance benefits was restricted under Austria's laws for "traditional foods." Arguing that its product contained characteristics from all three of Austria's food and drug categories—traditional, dietary, and pharmaceutical—but did not belong in any one, Red Bull successfully lobbied the government to create a new classification, "functional foods." This category required extensive documentation to support health-benefit claims, which created a significant entry barrier that had the effect of keeping away competitors for five years following Red Bull's launch.[9]

Red Bull finally debuted in 1987 in Mateschitz's home country of Austria. The product was positioned not for specific occasions, but rather for a range of occasions. With the flexible brand positioning "Revitalizes Body and Mind," Red Bull touted itself as suitable for such occasions as these:

- When a long day is over, and a long night starts.
- On long sleep-inducing motorways.
- During intensive working days when the date planner is filling up, and your energy reserves are emptying out.

[8]Red Bull Web site: http://www.redbull.com/faq/index.html (accessed September 12, 2002).
[9]Kevin Lane Keller, "Red Bull: Branding Brand Equity in New Ways," *Strategic Brand Management and Best Practice in Branding Cases* (Upper Saddle River: Prentice Hall, 2003), 53–72.

- Prior to demanding athletic activities, or in a performance drop during a game . . . [along with water].
- Before tests and exams, when there's no time to sleep.
- Or as first-aid after a long party night.[10]

Red Bull provided tips for the best use of its product during athletic events lasting more than an hour: "The best way to achieve the full effect of Red Bull is to drink 1–2 cans about 30–45 minutes before the end of the competition, for example, before the final spurt phase of bike racing or long distance running, at halftime in soccer, rugby, basketball, and volleyball matches, and before the final set in tennis, squash, or table tennis."[11]

Early adopters of Red Bull included people attending clubs and rave parties, as well as truckers and students. Norbert Kraihamer, the company's global director of marketing and sales, explained:

> There are five user categories: students, drivers, clubbers, business people, and sports people. Forget about age, where do they shop and when do they use it? Well, drivers use it on petrol forecourts. Clubbers use it in pubs and clubs, students use it in pubs and clubs and around campuses. We say we only have two dimensions: people who are mentally fatigued and people who are physically fatigued, or both. . . . I find loyal customers as soon as I can convince them that the product works. If they experience that the product keeps them awake, in a good mood, focused, vigilant, then they'll buy again. That's one of our secrets. If you do it right, you'll be getting up to 75 percent or even 80 percent re-purchase rate.[12]

In nightspots, Red Bull was often used as a mixer. A common combination was Red Bull and vodka, sometimes called a Smirnoff Bull. Another combination, called a shambles, featured Red Bull and champagne. Other mixers included gin, whisky, or, in southern Germany, beer. Kraihamer clarified that the company was not opposed to its product being used as a mixer, but that "over time we must make sure that the product is regarded as much more than a mixer. This is not a drink for a restaurant, this is a nutritional item."[13]

In line with selling Red Bull as a nutritional item, the company charged up to four times more per ounce than average soft drink prices, or $1.99 to $3 per 250 ml. can, and deliberately set prices at least 10 percent above competing energy drinks to maintain a premium image. Kraihamer noted, "We are much more expensive than [cola]. This is OK because ours is an efficiency product, so we can charge this price premium, which is the secret of its success."[14]

Red Bull's strategy for market entry relied heavily on word-of-mouth and "seeding." The company targeted a select handful of hip and trendy clubs, bars, and stores, allowing trendsetters the first opportunity to sample its product in hopes that they would become influencers and generate buzz. The company limited availability of the product during the seeding process. After six months of seeding, Red Bull introduced its product to locations surrounding the "in" seeding locations, thus making it easier for the consumer to purchase the brand. The final step was to enter supermarkets, thus reaching the mass market.[15]

Red Bull also targeted specific celebrities, including sports figures and entertainers, and sponsored sporting events ranging from Formula One racing to extreme skiing to soapbox races to the "Flügtag," where participants launched homemade flying objects off of a ramp

[10]Red Bull Web site: http://www.redbull.com/product/ingredients/index.html (accessed September 17, 2002).

[11]Claire Phoenix, "Red Bull—Fact and Function," *Softdrinksworld,* February 2001, pp. 26–35.

[12]Phoenix, "Red Bull."

[13]Ibid.

[14]Dolan, "The Soda with Buzz."

[15]Keller, "Red Bull."

into a lake. In late 2004, the company purchased the Jaguar Formula One racing team, renaming it after the Red Bull brand. With estimates that the team would cost $100 million per year to run while only bringing in $70 million in revenues,[16] some industry savants questioned Red Bull's move. Mateschitz explained:

> As the CEO of Red Bull I have hard responsibilities. I cannot spend any marketing money, any budgets, any sponsorship by Red Bull on behalf of my personal passions, likes, or dislikes. So the decision to be involved in motor sports is all good for the brand, a good marketing decision. If you then in addition gain personal satisfaction, all the better. But the underlying decision has to be a purely rational rather than an emotional decision.[17]

Unlike any other major beverage company's marketing plan, Red Bull bought its traditional advertising last. Their approach was to plan a media push only when the market had matured, thus reinforcing, rather than introducing, the brand. As Red Bull's vice president of marketing noted, "Media is not a tool that we use to establish the market. It is a critical part. It's just later in the development."[18] Red Bull invested 65 percent of sales in its early days in marketing, and entering 2005, continued to spend 30 percent of sales on marketing.[19]

Red Bull employed the slogan "Red Bull Verleiht Flüüügel" ("Red Bull Gives You Wiiings") in its advertising. With the assistance of a colleague, Mateschitz created Red Bull's "adult cartoon" advertisement, which featured one character with an energy deficiency and another with a solution: Red Bull. One ad featured a dentist and Count Dracula. The dentist tells Dracula that he'll have to remove the Count's teeth, to which Dracula replies that without his teeth he will not be able to drink blood: "But without fresh blood my body will wither and my mind will fade." The dentist proposes a solution: "One revitalizing Red Bull and you'll be prince of the night again." A picture of the Red Bull can appears, along with the copy, "Red Bull Energy Drink. Vitalizes Body and Mind." The dentist then samples the drink, delivers the punchline, "You know, Red Bull gives you *wiiings,*" then sprouts wings and flies away. The animated spots transcended specific target groups, enabling the company to establish a wide consumer base.[20]

RED BULL MYSTIQUE

Several experts argued that Red Bull achieved its cult following in part due to the rumors surrounding the product. One false rumor suggested that taurine, a key ingredient in Red Bull, was derived from bull testicles. Another falsity claimed that the drink was an aphrodisiac. Yet amongst the outright falsehoods circulated about Red Bull were a few grains of truth, including the partially correct rumor that Red Bull was banned in Europe. The drinks were banned in Denmark, Norway, Sweden, and France after health officials believed that the consumption of Red Bull was linked to deaths.[21] Cans of Red Bull in several countries bore labels warning against mixing the drink with alcohol. Across the Atlantic, sales of Red Bull were not permitted in Canada for several years, leading to cross-border smuggling of the product.[22] However, in 2004, health officials in Canada approved the sale of energy drinks with warning labels recommending that quantities should not surpass 500 ml. (16.6 oz.) per day.

[16]Dolan, "The Soda with Buzz."

[17]Alan Henry, "Motor Racing: Red Bull Puts Fizz Back into the Grid. . . .," *The Guardian,* March 1, 2005, p. 29.

[18]Kenneth Hein, "A Bull's Market," *Brandweek,* May 28, 2001, p. 21.

[19]Phoenix, "Red Bull."

[20]Keller, "Red Bull."

[21]"Canada Prepares for Energy Drink Surge," *Globe and Mail,* March 24, 2005.

[22]Ibid.

A research team from the Loughborough University Sleep Research Centre conducted a study to verify Red Bull's controversial claims of its product's ability to increase concentration, reaction time, and endurance. They tested the product on fatigued drivers. Their results indicated that one can of Red Bull was effective in reducing sleepiness and that two cans of Red Bull could eliminate fatigue altogether for 90 minutes.[23]

MISSTEPS IN THE U.K. MARKET

Red Bull faced a challenge when considering expansion in Europe in the mid-1990s. Most countries within what is now the European Union, of which Austria was not yet a member, had a list of allowable food ingredients, and taurine was not on the list. However, Red Bull was able to enter through Scotland and then the United Kingdom, as Scotland only maintained a list of ingredients *not* approved for use in food, and taurine was not on that list. This entry point enabled access to certain other European markets (see Table 2).[24]

The U.K. sports and energy market consisted of two segments at the time of Red Bull's entry in 1995. The first segment consisted of refreshment energy drinks. Market leader Lucozade, originally launched in 1927, offered several variants and sizes, and had built a reputation for offering energy through glucose. The second segment, sports drinks, was created by the introduction of Lucozade Sport in 1990. This segment consisted of isotonic drinks designed to enhance physical performance and provide rapid replenishment by boosting absorption of fluid, minerals, and sugar.[25]

Red Bull changed its traditional market-entry strategy as it launched its product in the United Kingdom. First, the company marketed Red Bull as a sports drink instead of as a stimulation drink as in Austria. This was a significant decision considering Lucozade's domination of the sports-drink market and consumers' preestablished notions of what a sports drink should be. Second, rather than pursuing the word-of-mouth strategy, Red Bull sold its product immediately through mass-market channels, such as chain stores, in hopes that consumers would choose Red Bull over the other products on the shelf. Kraihamer commented, "The U.K. team started from the wrong end . . . they were wrong, they totally misunderstood how to create a customer base." Third, the marketing mix used in Austria,

TABLE 2

Red Bull Early Market Entries

Source: Claire Phoenix.

1987	Austria	1996	Belgium
1992	Hungary		Greece
1993	Scotland		New Zealand
1994	Germany		Portugal
	Slovenia		Romania
1995	Baltic States		Spain
	Czech Republic		Sweden
	Netherlands	1997	Ireland
	Poland		South Africa
	Russia		U.S.A.
	Slovakia	1998	Brazil
	Switzerland		Finland
	U.K.		Italy
		1999	Australia

[23]Phoenix, "Red Bull."

[24]Keller, "Red Bull."

[25]"UK Energy and Sports Drinks—Space . . . The Final Frontier," *Softdrinksworld,* February 2001, pp. 36–43.

including the ironic advertising with the cartoon commercial and the sporting-event links, was ignored in favor of a billboard-focused campaign in the United Kingdom. The company chose a new slogan for the U.K. campaign: "You should never underestimate what Red Bull can do for you."[26] By the end of 1996, Red Bull's share of the sports- and energy-drink market stood at less than 2 percent.[27] One industry expert referred to Red Bull's U.K. experience as "an expensive disaster."[28]

The U.K. management team was replaced following this disappointing showing. The new management team repositioned Red Bull as a functional energy (or stimulation) drink, thus creating a new third segment in the U.K. sports- and energy-drink market. They also returned to the company's traditional method of building markets through word-of-mouth. Further, they replaced the U.K. slogan with what had worked in Austria. As Kraihamer explained of the U.K. slogan, "'You should never underestimate what Red Bull can do for you,' was far too long and misunderstood, whereas the 'It gives you wiiings' slogan as we now know works at all levels and on a worldwide scale."[29]

FROM FAILURE TO SUCCESS IN THE UNITED KINGDOM

Following these changes, Red Bull was positioned for success in the United Kingdom. Red Bull's volume tripled in 1998, and then quadrupled in 1999 to sales of 170 million cans—and then climbed another 50 percent in 2000 to 260 million cans.[30] By 2004, Red Bull had become the third-leading soft drink by value in the United Kingdom, trailing only Coca-Cola and Pepsi. The brand held a 62 percent share of the growing "functional-energy" segment of the sports- and energy-drink market.[31] Red Bull achieved significant market penetration among the 14–19 and 20–29 year old age groups (see Figure 1). Red Bull proved popular for social occasions, with 32 percent saying that they drank Red Bull in pubs and bars at night, and 13 percent indicating that Red Bull was their favorite drink during that time.

Kraihamer credited Red Bull's premium price as part of the brand's success in the United Kingdom.

If you have a product and the consumer recognizes the benefit, you are going to create a large consumer base. . . . If the product doesn't do anything and is eight times, five times, whatever

FIGURE 1
Red Bull Market
Penetration, 2000

Source: Red Bull College:
Kevin Lane Keller.

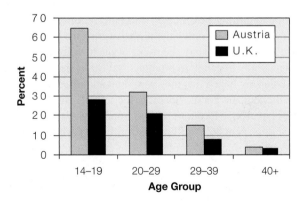

[26]Phoenix, "Red Bull."

[27]Keller, "Red Bull."

[28]Phoenix, "Red Bull."

[29]Ibid.

[30]Ibid.

[31]"The European Market for Energy & Sports Drinks to 2006," Mindbranch.com (accessed June 30, 2005).

more expensive than a normal soft drink, what will people say? Very often I have the impression that all of our so-called competitors have never understood that. They think it is a fashion thing or that it is all a hype issue—which it is not.

Kraihamer continued, "We need people to hate us. As soon as we run out of haters, we have to create a foundation for haters because we lose our sharp image."[32]

AMERICA: A BULL MARKET?

Red Bull was introduced to the U.S. market in 1997. The company launched the product in a handful of targeted geographic areas, or "cells," instead of launching nationwide. As Kraihamer described:

> Our intention was never to go to the States and say "We are launching Red Bull. . . ." We chose small market cells. Santa Cruz was the first test market. Then we went to parts of San Francisco. After that we went to Santa Monica—our home base in the U.S. Our concept works better, the smaller the community we go into, because we are word-of-mouth people. In a huge area nobody hears you. In a small area you get the message across quite quickly. So we worked in the United States with the principle of healthy cells. When one small cell became a success story, we moved on to the next cell. . . . [T]hese cells are becoming bigger and bigger. But initially it was towns or parts of towns.[33]

Red Bull maintained its strategy of appearing first in trendy on-premise locations. Markus Pichler, executive vice president of Strategic Planning for Red Bull North America, explained, "We go to on-premise accounts [versus retailers] first, because the product gets a lot of visibility and attention. It goes faster to deal with individual accounts, not big chains and their authorization process. In clubs, people are open to new things."[34] A distributor commented, "They only select five accounts in an area instead of all of them. It could be a boards-and-blades store or an underage disco. . . . If a [bar next door asks for it], they'll say, 'You can't have it yet.'"[35]

In addition to its emphasis on sampling events at hip nightspots, Red Bull sponsored several dozen alterna-athletes, and underwrote many extreme sports competitions. One such event was the Red Bull Huckfest ski and snowboard competition in Utah. Said Pichler, "We find consumers there, early adopters."[36] Other events included cliff diving in Hawaii, street luge in San Francisco, paragliding in Chicago, and hang gliding in Aspen. The fourth Red Bull Music Academy, held in New York City in 2001, featured a collection of 60 club deejays from around the world gathered to learn the tricks of the turntable trade from master deejays. The deejays were under no obligation to promote Red Bull when they returned to their respective clubs, but the company hoped that they would mention Red Bull when telling others of their trip, and credit the company for its support of the scene.[37] The Red Bull Music Academy toured around the world in diverse locations such as London, Sao Paulo, Cape Town, and Rome.

In total, Red Bull spent $600 million on worldwide advertising and marketing, which represented 30 percent of sales. In contrast, Coca-Cola spent 9 percent on advertising, albeit on sales of $20 billion.[38] Some industry observers believed that measured media accounting for only about 18 percent of Red Bull's total marketing.[39] A Red Bull spokesperson, disputing

[32]Phoenix, "Red Bull."

[33]Ibid.

[34]Hein, "A Bull's Market."

[35]Kenneth Hein, "Red Bull Charging Ahead," *Brandweek,* October 15, 2001, p. 438.

[36]Ibid.

[37]Ibid.

[38]Dolan, "The Soda with Buzz."

[39]Hein, "A Bull's Market."

the figure, admitted that, "the perception that these events don't cost much to produce is good for us. We don't want to be seen as having lots of money to spend. But it's not as easy and inexpensive as people think."[40] Giving insight into Red Bull's strategy of highly specific use of electronic media, Kraihamer commented, "After 11 o'clock, we are much more likely to find our target audience. With cinema, we never just buy a media plan; we always choose to go with certain films—extreme action films or highly sophisticated cult films. . . ."[41]

THE SOFT DRINK AND FUNCTIONAL DRINKS MARKET

The global soft-drink market was estimated at nearly U.S. $300 billion and accounted for approximately 11 trillion U.S. fluid ounces.[42] The soft-drink market generally included the following classifications: carbonated soft drinks (40 percent of market), bottled water (35 percent), fruit/vegetable juice (12 percent), ready-to-drink tea (4.5 percent), ready-to-drink coffee (0.9 percent), Asian specialty drinks (2.7 percent), concentrates (0.8 percent), and functional drinks (3 percent). Exhibit 1 shows the growth of each segment within the global soft-drink market.

Functional drinks encompassed three main rubrics: sports drinks, energy drinks, and elixirs (a beverage with curing properties). Led by Pepsi's Gatorade[43] and Coca-Cola's Aquarius, the sports-drink category grew at a compound annual growth rate of 9.5 percent over the past five years, and dominated the functional drinks sector representing 77 percent of the volume. The sports-drink segment was considered to be relatively more mature than other functional drinks such as energy drinks and elixirs. Gatorade, for example, had been on the U.S. market since the 1960s, but continued to grow through product development and aggressive marketing. Euromonitor estimated that sports drinks would grow at an average rate of 5 percent on a global basis until 2008.[44] Some industry observers believed that sports drinks and elixirs containing healthier ingredients such as vitamins and electrolytes would outperform energy drinks, as consumers demanded more healthy alternatives.

EXHIBIT 1 Global Volume of Soft Drinks Market by Category

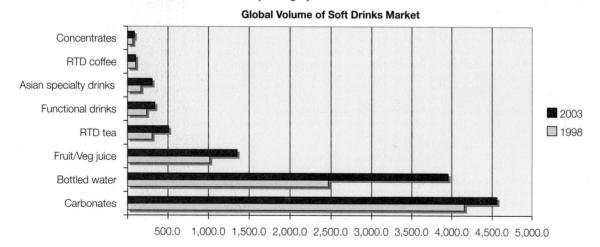

40Ibid.
41Phoenix, "Red Bull."
42"The World Market for Soft Drinks," *Euromonitor,* September 2004, Table 80, p. 39.
43Gatorade was developed by Quaker Oats. Pepsi purchased Quaker Oats in 2001.
44"The World Market for Soft Drinks," *Euromonitor,* September 2004, Table 95, p. 43.

COMPETITION ABOUNDS

By 2001, Red Bull had captured 65 percent of the $275 million new energy-drink market that it helped to create.[45] Around that time, Anheuser-Busch launched 180, Coke introduced KMX, and Pepsi brought to market both Mountain Dew Amp and SoBe Adrenaline Rush, all as competitors to Red Bull. Other entrants included Snapple Venom, Arizona Extreme Energy, Blue Ox, Bomba Energy, Dark Dog, Red Alert, Deezel, Power Horse USA, Go-Go Energy, and Hemp Soda.[46] Still, Red Bull maintained its position as the leader of the pack.[47] Kraihamer, speaking of Red Bull's competitors at the time, commented:

> I think they perceive it all as a micro-market thing. . . . This is peanuts. It's keeping some marketing people busy, but they don't realize the true potential. They might become competitors in time, but I think it is to our advantage that we are small.[48]

By 2005, the landscape for energy drinks had changed significantly. The U.S. energy-drink market was estimated between $1.6 and $2.0 billion in 2004 with growth hovering between 58 percent and 73 percent.[49] Red Bull's U.S. overall market share (including all points of distribution) had dropped from 75 percent in 1998 to 47 percent in 2005.[50] Several competitors had been successful in growing their distribution networks and appealing to consumers through innovative communication. Exhibit 2 shows key competitors' volumes in the U.S. energy-drinks market.

EXHIBIT 2   Top Energy Brands in the United States

Top 12 Energy Brands In U.S. Food, Drug and Mass Channels-Period Ending Dec 2004						
Brand	Sales $	YoY Change	Share $	*Volume Sales oz.*	YoY Change	Share %
Red Bull	$ 155,728,144	71.0%	60.3%	*700,026,495*	73.5%	49.6%
Rockstar	$ 22,797,562	125.4%	8.8%	*189,600,224*	127.2%	13.4%
Monster (Hansen)	$ 16,268,929	223.1%	6.3%	*139,289,344*	228.0%	9.9%
SoBe Adrenaline Rush (Pepsi)	$ 15,231,377	15.7%	5.9%	*67,769,376*	15.3%	4.8%
Amp (Mountain Dew)	$ 14,191,741	14.7%	5.5%	*63,349,544*	13.6%	4.5%
SoBe No Fear (Pepsi)	$ 10,108,871	190.3%	3.9%	*79,767,944*	187.0%	5.6%
Hansen (Hansen Energy)	$ 3,130,313	−13.1%	1.2%	*15,669,595*	−3.7%	1.1%
KMX (Coca-Cola)	$ 1,917,185	−63.7%	0.7%	*8,985,793*	−64.8%	0.6%
EAS Piranha (Abbot Labs)	$ 1,555,390	100.7%	0.6%	*7,821,674*	60.0%	0.6%
Lost (Hansen)	$ 1,401,335	n/a	0.5%	*11,765,080*	n/a	0.8%
Rush (Monarch)	$ 1,245,518	202.1%	0.5%	*9,480,658*	282.2%	0.7%
Fuze Omega	$ 1,207,002	629.9%	0.5%	*10,910,017*	684.3%	0.8%
Other	$ 13,459,817		5.2%	*107,986,527*		7.6%
Energy Category	$ 258,243,184	61.1%	100.0%	*1,412,422,272*	70.0%	100.0%

Source: Information Resources Inc. as cited in Hansen Natural Analyst Report, Adams Harkness, May 4, 2005, p. 7. Data is for food, drug and mass only and excludes Wal-Mart, club, food service, bar and convenience-store channels.
NOTE: These volumes likely represent between 15 and 25% of the overall volume sold in the U.S. in the energy drinks sector.

[45]Ibid.

[46]Kenneth Hein, "Necessity and Invention," *Brandweek,* February 19, 2001, p. 22.

[47]Ibid.

[48]Phoenix, "Red Bull."

[49]Adams Harkness; Scott Leith, "The Buzz on Energy Drinks: Coke, Pepsi, and Tiny Firms Vie for Sip of Caffeine-Packed Beverage Market," *Atlanta Journal-Constitution,* April 8, 2005, p. F-1.

[50]Dolan, "The Soda with Buzz."

HANSEN NATURAL

A Red Bull alterna-athlete competes in the 2000 X Games in San Francisco

California's Hansen Natural had first competed against Red Bull in 1997 in the United States when the company launched Hansen Energy drink. Lacking targeted advertising to energy-drink consumers such as sports enthusiasts, college students, and truckers, Hansen's energy product did not make a dent in the Red Bull-dominated market. In 2002, the company came back with Monster, packaged in black cans with neon-accented claw marks.

The cans were double the volume of Red Bull's cans and were offered to distributors for a comparable price, resulting in a $1.99 price to the final consumer.[51] The company also used its own staff to assist the 300 independent distributors restock the product in convenience-store refrigerators.[52]

Hansen supported the launch with its slogan "Unleash the Beast," and sent out teams of Monster "ambassadors" to distribute samples at motocross, surfing, and skateboarding competitions as well as concerts and beach parties. The company was a sponsor of the Vans Warped music tour and in 2005, the company created the "Monster Army," a sponsored group of professional athletes.

Largely driven by the success of the Monster brand, Hansen experienced sales increases of 162 percent in 2004. This propelled Monster to second place, capturing an 18 percent market share of the energy-drinks segment. Hansen's CEO Rodney Sacks bubbled over with enthusiasm at the results, "These are the new soft drinks of the world."[53]

Hansen had a slew of new product releases, such as Joker, exclusively for Circle-K stores; Rumba, a juice with high caffeine content, and Lost, a name that Hansen had licensed from a leading skateboarding, surfing, and snowboarding apparel brand.[54]

OTHER UPSTARTS

A number of other entrepreneurial ventures had challenged Red Bull's leadership. Rockstar, based in Las Vegas, launched its energy beverage in 2001, and occupied third place in the U.S. market with 16 percent share. Rockstar's primary consumers were teenage males. The company promoted its brand through associations with celebrities and music events. In 2005, the company inked a deal with Coca-Cola whereby Rockstar would pay fees for Coca-Cola to distribute the product throughout the United States.[55]

It was estimated that more than 1,000 products from hundreds of different small enterprises had attempted to break through the noise by launching their own energy drinks, often focusing on a specific subset of consumers. For instance, extreme sports enthusiasts were targeted by not only Red Bull and Monster but also Go Fast! and Fuze, whereas video game junkies were targeted by BAWLS and Guarana. Three brands—Crunk!!!, Pimp Juice, and DefCon 3—were focused on the hip-hop market, and consumers interested in Jewish

[51]Christopher Palmeri, "Hansen Natural; Charging at Red Bull with a Brawny Energy Brew," *BusinessWeek,* June 6, 2005, p. 74.

[52]Ibid.

[53]Ibid.

[54]Harkness, "Hansen Natural."

[55]"Food Brief—Coca-Cola Co. Deal Is Reached to Distribute another Firm's Energy Drink," *The Wall Street Journal,* April 29, 2005, p. A-11.

mysticism were singled out with the product Kaballah energy drink.[56] Kaballah even signed pop-icon Madonna to endorse the product.[57]

THE TWO GIANTS: COCA-COLA AND PEPSI

In early 2005, Coca-Cola released Full Throttle, its second energy drink, after its first energy brand KMX captured only 0.9 percent of the U.S. market.[58] Full Throttle was marketed in 16 oz. black cans with bright lettering set to a backdrop of dramatic flames. Coca-Cola planned on using its wide distribution system, supported by promotions such as giveaways at Monster Truck Jams and motorcycles shows. A Coca-Cola spokesperson explained that the target for Full Throttle was different from that of the club-goers and extreme-sports people who typically consumed energy drinks: "We are speaking to the guy's guy."[59] A Red Bull spokesperson seemed unconcerned: "Movement by the bigger players onto the scene really just validates the category."[60]

Pepsi's position was distinct from Coca-Cola's as they had gained more market share with Mountain Dew Amp and two SoBe products called No Fear and Adrenaline Rush. SoBe, a short form for South Beach Beverage Company, was founded in 1996 and was purchased by Pepsi in 2001 for an estimated $400 million.[61] To spur on sales, SoBe had partnered with the national convenience store 7-11 for a cobranded SoBe Slurpee.

THE CANNED-COFFEE CATEGORY: A THREAT?

Regular coffee served hot was a mainstay throughout the world with an estimated 500 billion cups served each year. In the United States, per capita consumption was about seven pounds a year, whereas Scandinavian countries topped the worldwide list, consuming more than 20 pounds per capita per year.[62] More than half of Americans were estimated to drink coffee daily, consuming an average of 3.4 cups per day.[63]

Several packaged-goods companies were looking to offer innovative ready-to-drink cold-coffee products. Pepsi, for example, had introduced the coffee-flavored Pepsi Kona as a test product in the mid-1990s, but never launched it due to lackluster results. Later, Pepsi teamed up with Starbucks to introduce Mazagran, a carbonated coffee-based drink that was sold at select Starbucks locations, but Mazagran was never released nationally. The Pepsi–Starbucks partnership continued, and together the companies launched Starbucks Frappuccino iced coffee and Starbucks DoubleShot espresso drink, which held 90 percent of the noncarbonated, ready-to-drink coffee segment as of 2005.[64]

In other countries, companies were experimenting with a fusion of coffee, milk, and energy drinks. Backed by a Nestlé venture-capital fund, an Austrian executive who helped introduce

[56]Burt Helm, "The Sport of Extreme Marketing," *BusinessWeek,* March 14, 2005, p. 14.

[57]Adam Hellinker, "Madonna to Give Cult Drink a Boost," *Express on Sunday,* February 6, 2005, p. 17.

[58]Gillian Wee, "Coca-Cola Seeks Swig of Revved-Up Energy Drink Market," *Knight Ridder/Tribune Business News,* February 5, 2005.

[59]Ibid.

[60]Ibid.

[61]Hoovers Company Capsule, www.hoovers.com (accessed June 29, 2005).

[62]Nation Master Statistics, www.nationmaster.com (accessed July 7, 2005).

[63]Roast and Post Coffee Company, www.realcoffee.co.uk (accessed July 7, 2005).

[64]Christina Cheddar Berk, "Coca-Cola Seeks to Refresh Product Line with New Items," *Dow Jones Newswires,* January 11, 2005.

Red Bull to the United States was launching his own brand called Returnity in Europe—a milk-based product deemed to be a "brain shake."[65] In Australia, the milk brand Dare launched a coffee, guarana, and milk drink with the appeal that it could be used to replace real coffee or energy drinks. A representative commented on the approach to the end consumers, "[We want to] touch them through their passion points—reach out through credible links to music, entertainment, fashion, sports, technology, and sex. The entire marketing mix will drive the brand's outlaw personality and encapsulate the 24–7, nonstop living theme."[66]

Even Red Bull Beverages Co. in Thailand (the producer of Red Bull) was preparing for the Thai relaunch of a canned-coffee version of Krating Daeng in the summer of 2005.[67]

LOOKING AHEAD

Red Bull estimated it would sell 1 billion cans in the United States in 2005. Based on per-capita consumption, many believed that there was room for Red Bull to grow. Kraihamer had explained the per-capita targets as Red Bull was growing:

> In the best markets today, we can achieve a potential of 10 per person—ten cans per head, per year. We don't know if we can achieve a potential 15 or 20 per person, but I believe so.[68]

It was estimated that in the United States, Red Bull had moved from 0.4 of a can per person in 2001 to 2.5 cans per person in 2004. While further growth opportunities appeared significant since the energy-drinks segment was still growing rapidly, Red Bull needed to overcome several challenges. One analyst gave this view of the competitive situation:

> Market-leader Red Bull is also a very strong competitor, but focused on the 8 oz. can category (particularly in liquor establishments), while Hansen and Rockstar focus their energy efforts on 16 oz. cans at retail. While Coke and Pepsi are obviously the dominant beverage players in the U.S. and have had some success in energy (more so Pepsi than Coke) with their respective Full Throttle and SoBe brands, we doubt that their success has met internal expectations. Coke's first effort under the KMX brand was clearly a failure. If brands such as Monster and Rockstar continue to grow north of $100 million each with strong sales per point of distribution, we would expect the big players to consolidate the fast-growing brands.[69]

Analysts with *BevNet.com,* a Web site and industry newsletter tracking the entire beverage industry, shared their opinion of how Red Bull fits into the market as of 2005:

> Red Bull faces some potential bumps in the road in the coming 24 months. First, the product has completely oversaturated the market—Red Bull is in just about anywhere that you can fit a mini-cooler, as well as mass merchandisers, bike shops, bars, etc., etc., etc. This could result in Red Bull becoming passé by removing the "cool" factor that made the brand so successful. Second, while other companies are improving formulations, flavors, and packaging, Red Bull stays the same. Will consumers find something that truly works better? Third, from our point of view Red Bull has a less-than-stellar industry reputation—and many people are praying for their demise as a result. Finally, given that Red Bull is a one-trick pony (compared to others such as Coke and Pepsi), the party is in serious jeopardy if sales start to slump, a price war starts, or over-energy-drink health concerns start to proliferate. Overall, tremendous brand power right now, but does it have true staying power to last another five years as number one?

[65]Dagmar Mussey, "Nestle Introduces European 'Brain Shake,'" *Advertising Age,* June 6, 2005, p. 20.
[66]"Dare Shoots into Energy Drinks Market with a New Coffee Product," *B&T Weekly,* February 3, 2005.
[67]"Thailand: Red Bull Changes Aim to Coffee Drinks," *Thai News Service,* June 20, 2005.
[68]Phoenix, "Red Bull."
[69]Harkness, "Hansen Natural."

In response to extending the brand's reach, Red Bull was testing an herbal tea drink named Carpe Diem in Los Angeles and was considering using the name to launch an international fast-food concept served in edible potato containers. As well, the company was about to release a quarterly magazine touching upon the key themes of the Red Bull lifestyle such as extreme sports, the clubbing life, and music.[70]

"We have the next hundred years in front of us,"[71] stated Mateschitz about the brand's future. He then offered up his opinion on why consumers would continue drinking Red Bull: "We created the market. If you appreciate the product, you want the real one, the original. Nobody wants to have a Rolex made in Taiwan or Hong Kong."[72]

[70]Dolan, "The Soda with Buzz."
[71]Ibid.
[72]Ibid.

14

IVEY

Richard Ivey School of Business
The University of Western Ontario

"Hips Feel Good"— Dove's Campaign for Real Beauty

David Wesley *Northeastern University*

Kerstin Dunleavy, brand manager for Unilever's Dove line, was both excited and concerned about her meeting the next morning with Unilever's senior management. She was about to make one of the most important presentations of her career, one that involved taking the successful relaunch of Dove beauty products to the next level.

Dunleavy had already helped mastermind the original turnaround of Unilever's Dove line, which some believed had already been a career-maker for her. She, however, knew that the real test would come as phase two became operational. Only then would she truly be able to establish her reputation as a premier brand manager in the ultra-competitive beauty industry.

Without doubt, Unilever had placed a heavy load on Dunleavy's shoulders. As she gathered her thoughts, she wondered what the next month would hold as Dove rolled out the second phase of the relaunch in September 2006. She placed a call to her assistant executive brand manager and marketing advisor, Michael B. Allen. "Tomorrow I will be laying out the specifics of phase two of the relaunch," she reminded him.

> Things are looking good right now. The self-esteem issues we have focused on have resonated with our target audience. I want it to continue, but I am not so sure about our next move. I want it to continue in the right way.
>
> If the competition copies our strategy, we will just become one of them. Remember that a difference that doesn't stand out is not a difference. Let's go over what has happened in the past two years one more time to make sure we understand how we got here.

Allen agreed that societal marketing had both benefited the brand and helped customers feel good about themselves. He replied,

> Our business has been to sell products, not to satisfy our customers or cure society's ills. But now we know that we can do both. As long as we keep listening to customers, there is no reason why we can't continue to stand out and distinguish ourselves from our competitors.

BACKGROUND

Unilever was one of the largest consumer products companies in the world with annual revenues of approximately $50 billion and a staff of 250,000. The company's product lines were organized into four main areas: Cooking and Eating, Beauty and Style, Healthy Living, and Around the House.

Unilever employed a global marketing strategy that was adapted to suit individual cultures and the unique requirements of its subsidiaries. The company's branding policies had been considerably modified in recent years. In 2004, its "Path to Growth" strategy reduced the number of products from 1,600 to 400. The company's brand strategy was also modified to emphasize product brand names, while a newly designed Unilever logo adorned its packages (see Exhibit 1).

EXHIBIT 1   Unilever Logo and Symbols

SUN

Our primary natural resource. All life begins with the sun—the ultimate symbol of vitality. It evokes Unilever's origins in Port Sunlight and can represent a number of our brands. Flora, Slim Fast and Omo all use radiance to communicate their benefits.

HAND

A symbol of sensitivity, care and need. It represents both skin and touch. The flower represents fragrance. When seen with the hand, it represents moisturizers or cream.

BEE

Represents creation, pollination, hard work and bio-diversity. Bees symbolize both environmental challenges and opportunities.

DNA

The double helix, the genetic blueprint of life and a symbol of bio-science. It is the key to a healthy life. The sun is the biggest ingredient of life, and DNA the smallest.

HAIR

A symbol of beauty and looking good. Placed next to the flower it evokes cleanliness and fragrance; placed near the hand it suggests softness.   (*continued*)

EXHIBIT 1   Unilever Logo and Symbols   *(continued)*

PALM TREE

A nurtured resource. It produces palm oil as well as many fruits—coconuts and dates—and also symbolizes paradise.

SAUCES OR SPREADS

Represents mixing or stirring. It suggests blending in flavors and adding taste.

BOWL

A bowl of delicious-smelling food. It can also represent a ready meal, hot drink or soup.

SPOON

A symbol of nutrition, tasting and cooking.

SPICE & FLAVORS

Represents chili or fresh ingredients.

FISH

Represents food, sea or fresh water.

SPARKLE

Clean, healthy and sparkling with energy.

BIRD

A symbol of freedom. It suggests a relief from daily chores, and getting more out of life.

TEA

A plant or an extract of a plant, such as tea. Also a symbol of growing and farming.

LIPS

Represent beauty, looking good and taste.

ICE CREAM

A treat, pleasure and enjoyment.

(continued)

EXHIBIT 1   Unilever Logo and Symbols   *(concluded)*

RECYCLE

Part of our commitment to sustainability.

PARTICLES

A reference to science, bubbles and fizz.

FROZEN

The plant is a symbol of freshness, the snowflake represents freezing. A transformational symbol.

CONTAINER

Symbolizes packaging–a pot of cream associated with personal care.

HEART

A symbol of love, care and health.

CLOTHES

Represent fresh laundry and looking good.

WAVE & LIQUID

Symbolizes cleanliness, freshness and vigor. A reference to clean.

Along with the new public image came a new corporate mission. Titled "Vitality," it proclaimed:

We meet everyday needs for nutrition, hygiene, and personal care with brands that help people feel good, look good and get more out of life.[1]

DEVELOPMENT OF DOVE

Dove was originally developed in the United States as a nonirritating skin cleaner for pretreatment use on burns and wounds during World War II. In 1957, the basic Dove bar was reformulated as a beauty soap bar. It was the first beauty soap to use mild nonsoap ingredients plus moisturizing cream to avoid drying the skin, the way soap can.

[1]"Vitality," *Unilever Magazine,* 132 (2004) p. 19.

In the 1970s, an independent clinical study found Dove to be milder than 17 leading bar soaps. Based on the results of that study, the company launched a promotional campaign that highlighted the soap's mildness.

Between 1990 and 2004, Dove expanded its product line to include body wash, facial cleansers, moisturizers, deodorants, and hair care products. In 2005, revenues from Unilever's Dove product line reached $3 billion.

COMPETITION

The beauty industry was highly competitive with many well-supported brands and products. There were few secrets within the industry, and products were in many ways similar. As such, marketing and communications were as critical to a product's success as new product development. For example, the Body Shop line of beauty care products emphasized social and environmental responsibility as well as all-natural products, thereby appealing to the psyche of the emotionally influenced buyer. As the importance of situational influences increased, marketers began to shift their emphasis from product-related variables to consumer-related variables.[2]

Modernizing the Brand Image

In 2003, the management of Unilever met to discuss the future of the Dove brand. Even though the company's growing product line was available in 40 countries, sales of its flagship Dove brand were in decline since market share was being lost to competitors.

To understand the reasons for the decline, the company undertook a focused brand analysis under the direction of the Ernest Dichter Institute, a Zürich-based market research firm. The result of the brand audit was revealing. Consumers appreciated Dove both for its natural ingredients and its reliability as a moisturizer. However, on a more emotional level, the brand felt dated and old-fashioned.

Although Dove's brand image did not resonate with consumers, those who used it recognized the quality of the products. For Unilever, it was clear that the Dove brand needed a new image, and to that end, management laid out the following targets:

- Increase market share through improvement of the brand image.
- Develop an outstanding marketing campaign.
- Retain the functional strengths of the brand.

Dove needed to evolve into a modern and desirable brand, while at the same time standing out against the myriad other products offered by Unilever's competitors (see Exhibit 2). With that goal in mind, Unilever created a global team under the direction of Kerstin Dunleavy, global brand manager for Dove, to develop a new brand strategy for Dove beauty care products.

The Dove Research Study

Before setting out to design a new marketing strategy, Dunleavy's team sought to first understand the relationship of women to beauty, without specifically focusing on beauty care products. They wanted to answer four basic questions:

- What do women mean by beauty?
- How happy are they with their own beauty?

[2]A *situational influence* is a temporary force that influences behavior, usually associated with the immediate purchasing environment. Dimensions of situational influence include the time when purchases are made, the physical surroundings, and the emotional state or mood of the purchaser. Where consumers buy are the physical surroundings. How consumers buy refers to the terms of the purchase. Conditions under which consumers buy relate to states and moods.

EXHIBIT 2   Examples of Competitor Advertisements

Sources: Garnier, Nivea and Jergens (Center for Interactive Advertising, University of Texas, Austin), L'Oreal Communication.

- How does a woman's sense of her own beauty affect her well-being?
- What influence does mass media and pop culture have on the perception of ideal beauty?

To find answers to these questions, the company turned to StrategyOne, a global research firm that worked with experts from Massachusetts General Hospital, the Harvard University Program in Aesthetics and Well Being, and the London School of Economics.

Between February and June 2004, StrategyOne surveyed 3,200 women from Argentina, Brazil, Canada, France, Italy, Japan, the Netherlands, Portugal, Spain, the United Kingdom and the United States. The results of the survey were presented in a paper titled, "The Real Truth about Beauty: A Global Report."[3] The report showed a wide disparity between the ideal of beauty portrayed in the media and the perception of beauty as understood by women themselves. The following were the most notable observations.

- Only 2 percent of women described themselves as beautiful.
- 47 percent said they were overweight—a trend that increases with age.
- 68 percent believed that the media and advertising set an unrealistic standard of beauty that most women can never achieve.
- 75 percent wished that the media would portray more diverse measures of physical attractiveness, such as size, shape, and age.
- 77 percent said that beauty could be achieved through attitude, spirit, and other attributes that have nothing to do with physical appearance.
- 48 percent strongly agreed with the statement: "When I feel less beautiful, I feel worse about myself in general."
- 45 percent believed that women who are more beautiful have greater opportunities in life.
- 26 percent have considered plastic surgery, a result that varied considerably by country. For example, 54 percent of Brazilian participants have considered cosmetic surgery.

Aside from the perceived need for cosmetic surgery, the results were remarkably consistent from country to country. For Susie Orbach, a feminist psychotherapist and writer who coauthored the report, the problem was clear. She explained:

> Most of the images we see of women bear little relationship to reality. Overwhelmingly, beauty is defined as tall, thin and young. It is a very limited definition that is presented as the norm, although it is anything but—it excludes most women and encourages them to be unnecessarily self-critical as most of us fall far short of the images of perfection that we are bombarded with daily.[4]

Based on the results of the report, Dunleavy's team perceived an opportunity to redefine beauty in a way that Unilever's competitors had ignored. The team presented its findings to Unilever's executive board along with a strategy to relaunch Dove using new and unconventional ideals of beauty. True beauty could be found in many forms, sizes, and ages, they explained. Dove had to integrate this idea in its own brand image and spark discussions by attention-seeking campaigns. The team wanted to choose "real" women for the ensuing advertising campaigns, women who were not "treated" via retouching, the type of women one might encounter every day.

---

[3]Nancy Etcoff et al., "The Real Truth about Beauty: A Global Report: Findings of the Global Study on Women, Beauty and Well-Being," September 2004, available at www.campaignforrealbeauty.com/uploadedfiles/dove_white_paper_final.pdf.

[4]"Vitality," *Unilever Magazine*, 132 (2004), p. 9.

The functional advantages of a high-quality product were to be retained. At the same time, it was considered essential to differ significantly in the emotional positioning from Unilever's main competitors. In contrast to competitors such as Nivea, L'Oreal, and Garnier, emphasis was not to be placed on perfect looks of top models but on the ethical aspect of beauty. The moral concern was to boost the self-confidence of women. The products were to be derived from this starting point. According to Dunleavy, the brand and not the single products were to be in the foreground. The emotional ties to the target group needed to be strengthened.

Some members of the executive board expressed concern that taking such an unconventional approach to beauty might expose the company to unnecessary risk. After all, if portraying regular women in beauty advertising was such a good idea, why hadn't anyone tried it? Eventually the board decided to support the effort noting that the risk was outweighed by the need to turn around the flagging Dove brand. In Dunleavy's mind, it was the strength of the supporting data presented in the StrategyOne report that finally swayed the vote of the more reticent board members in favor of the real women campaign.

THE CAMPAIGN FOR REAL BEAUTY

The campaign was launched with a mandate from Unilever to increase revenues by a lofty 80 percent, an undertaking that would be supported by an advertising budget of approximately $27 million in Europe alone. Unilever worked closely with the advertising firm Ogilvy & Mather to rebrand Dove.

The "Campaign for Real Beauty" began in earnest in September 2004, with the launch of the Web site campaignforrealbeauty.com. Women went online to cast their votes and join the beauty debate in chat rooms. Confessions, philosophical questions, and rants showed that nerves were being struck.[5] Statements such as "My mommy taught me to believe in myself and to feel good about who I am" were prominently displayed on the site, along with opportunities for potential customers to share their views about the concept of beauty (see Exhibit 3).

The main target group was 30- to 39-year-old women, who had not yet tried any skin-firming products. Although the broader target group included any women who used body lotions and creams, Dove expected to experience significant gains among women over age 30, a time when signs of age appear, skin is increasingly less firm, and cellulite forms.

Based on the results of the StrategyOne research, the Dove team believed that beauty could be reflected in different shapes, sizes, and ages, and that "real beauty can be genuinely stunning." Dunleavy explained:

> With the Dove beauty philosophy, we're not saying that the stereotypical Claudia Schiffer view of beauty isn't great—it is—we simply want to broaden the definition of beauty.

That definition was reflected in a new brand mission statement, "to make more women feel beautiful every day, by widening today's stereotypical view of beauty and inspiring women to take great care of themselves."

The Advertising Campaign: What Is Beauty?

When Unilever launched its ground-breaking advertising campaign in Europe, the core message stated, "No models—but firm curves." Ads featured a group of women of different ages, shapes, and racial backgrounds, dressed only in bras and knickers, animated and laughing among themselves and clearly happy to be themselves. Models for the ads were chosen by well-trained assistants in a "street casting" in order to achieve a great acceptance

[5]"Dove's Flight of Fancy," *Marketing Magazine* (Ireland), April 2006, www.marketing.ie, accessed April 16, 2007.

EXHIBIT 3   Campaign for Real Beauty Online Discussion Forum

| share your views | in the news | inside the campaign | dove self-esteem fund | ◀ campaignforrealbeauty | Dove. |

Campaign For Real Beauty   a⁻ A⁺

Other Discussion Boards   **Register Login Discussion Standards Help**

Please register to participate in the Campaign for Real Beauty Discussion Forums.

Self Esteem Forum

Forum Name: Self Esteem Forum
Forum Summary: Share your opinion about the issue of low self-esteem among young girls. And tell them how beautiful they really are.

‹‹ | 426 | 427 | 428 | 429 | 430 | 431 | 432 | Previous | Next | ›› |

☐ 08/18/2006 02:37 AM

Ann_4396

Posts 1
Member Since
08/18/2006

Thank you for executing such a positive image for girls. I'm a youth leader and it saddens me to see how kids are growing up these days. I'm only 3-4 older than these girls & already I see the dramatic effect of the media's perception of the "pefect body." I am exposed to girls confession of being fat and ugly. "I make my hair dramatic, so that people would not focus on my face" is something that I hear. It's because of your campaign that I see hope in changing the image. Years ago it was wrong to marry someone from another race. Today it is common. Norms can be changed! It's possible. Keep up the progress!

Reply : Quote Original : Top : Bottom

☐ 08/18/2006 02:42 AM

Tiffini

Posts 1
Member Since
08/18/2006

I think what you are doing is extremely kewl!! I'm sixteen and have struggled with low self asteem for a long time now. I want to do modeling but I don't think that they would except me for who I am..I would love to model for something like this if I ever got the chance to.

Reply : Quote Original : Top : Bottom

☐ 08/18/2006 03:33 AM

123

Posts 1
Member Since
08/18/2006

that video makes me cry so much every time i see it. i thoguht i was the only one but i guess im not. i live with rich and gorgeous people. im neither. i get called ugly by guys, people, my sister. and all i ever wanted was for them to except me. idc if they dont like me fine
but people i dont even know hate me. my school has so many rich and gorgeous people i feel like an ugly duckling. i havent told anyone this ever. i hate the way i look. but i hate how i feel also. i cry basically every night because i cant live up to peoples expectations and i can have a good enough house for my friends and i dont have cute clothes like my friends and im not pretty like my friends. i never want to go anywehre do anything. i wasted my summer staying home because i thought i could be pretty tht way. no matter how hard i try they wont except me.

Reply : Quote Original : Top : Bottom

☐ 08/18/2006 04:55 PM

Nina_7348

Posts 1
Member Since
08/18/2006

That clip also makes me cry because I know how hard it is on young girls with everyone else being so judgemental. People dont even know how to be true to themselves anymore, its all about pleasing everyone else. Im sorry that you have to go through all that because I know how it is. As a kid I always wanted to fit in and have nice things but I never did either. There were times when I just wanted to run away and hide and never face anyone again. Then someone told me that in order for others to accept me, I must accept myself first and stop being so hard on myself.It took a while to realize that if im always comparing myself to others, I will always fall short. You are beautiful, so dont let anyone make you feel otherwise. Please dont compare yourself with other people because you are who God made you to be. If other people cant accept that then its their loss. But Im sure there are people around you that care for you and just love it when you smile. Keep smiling and looking up because I know God has something great planned for you. I love you and will be praying for you! Take care

Reply : Quote Original : Top : Bottom

Source: www.campaignforrealbeauty.com, accessed February 26, 2007.

EXHIBIT 4   Tick Box ADS

☐ 44 and hot?
☐ 44 and not?

Can women be hotter at 40 than 20? Join the beauty debate.

campaignforrealbeauty.com 🐦 | *Dove*

☐ grey?
☐ gorgeous?

Why can't more women feel glad to be grey? Join the beauty debate.

campaignforrealbeauty.com 🐦 | *Dove*

Source: Unilever.

among the observers. When the campaign was later rolled out in other countries, different models were chosen to reflect local cultural differences.

Some ads asked viewers to make a choice. For example, one featured a 96-year-old woman named Irene and asked "wrinkled or wonderful?" followed by the question "Will society ever accept the beauty of old age?" Another ad featured a heavy-set woman named Tabatha, and asked "oversized or outstanding?" followed by the question, "Does true beauty only squeeze into a size 6?" (See Exhibit 4 for two other ads in the series.) At the campaignforrealbeauty Web site, Internet users could cast votes for the ads or join online debates in the forums section.

The company supplemented traditional television and magazine-based beauty advertising with outdoor advertising, such as billboards, posters and signs. Billboards specifically provided a presence that made it easy for journalists to report about the campaign (see Exhibit 5). When the campaign was later rolled out in the United States, an electronic billboard was erected in Times Square that asked bystanders to text message their responses to a beauty question posed by the Dove ads and see their votes counted instantly in the debate. It was the first-ever outdoor mobile marketing event in the United States.

The promotional mix was supported by an unprecedented amount of public relations that built as Ogilvy & Mather coaxed the news media to cover the launch of the campaign and to create debate around Western society's concepts of beauty. The objective was to provoke public attention with a controversial message. To foster discussion, Unilever partnered with American Women in Radio and Television, a nonprofit organization that sought to advance the impact of women in the electronic media by educating, advocating, and acting as a resource to its members. "It was to be the talk of town," noted Sebastian Munden, managing director for Home and Personal Care of Unilever.

The Results

Early results were dramatic. Massive media coverage that included as many as 800 newspaper and magazine articles, many of which featured high-profile debates, helped to nearly quadruple sales of Dove-branded products. Market share increased in six European core markets from an average of 7.4 percent in 2003 to 13.5 percent by the end of 2004.[6] Traffic on the company Web site quickly reached 4,000 visitors a day.

In 2005, a new brand audit by Millward Brown, a market research company, showed a significant image shift. The brand gained attributes such as "open," "active" and "self-confident," and existing characteristics for the skin-firming series, such as "fun," "energetic" and "confident," strengthened further (see Exhibit 6). The turnaround was no less than remarkable. Dove was seen not only as a top-quality brand but also as an industry expert in cosmetics and beauty. Moreover, for the first time, the brand was able to break into the premium segment of the market. For its part, Ogilvy & Mather won the Grand Effie Award from the New York American Marketing Association in 2006, for the "most significant achievement in marketing communications."[7]

Realbeauty

Many girls developed low self-esteem from insecurities about their looks. As a direct result, some failed to reach their full potential later in life. To help these girls, Dove simultaneously established a "Self-Esteem Fund" to support local initiatives. "We've made it mandatory that every country launching the campaign links up with an association that's in line with the Dove Self-Esteem Fund," explained Dunleavy.[8] For example, one program titled "uniquely ME!" partnered with U.S. Girl Scout troops to help build self-confidence in girls aged 8 to 14, largely in economically disadvantaged communities.

Unilever also sought to address eating disorders in young females, which research had shown to be directly linked to low self-esteem. The company focused on girls between the ages of 8 and 17. Unilever hired Ogilvy & Mather to develop a 45-second commercial for the 2006 Super Bowl football championship, considered by many to be the most important television advertising event of the year. The commercial suggested ways adults could make a difference in how girls felt about themselves. "All throughout the spot, the voices for the

---

[6]"Medaillenflut für deutsche Agenturen," *Horizont*, October 6, 2005, p. 34.

[7]"Dove's 'The Campaign for Real Beauty,' Created by Ogilvy & Mather Wins the 2006 Grand Effie Award," Company Press Release, June 8, 2006.

[8]"Vitality," *Unilever Magazine,* 132 (2004), p. 11.

EXHIBIT 5 Outdoor Advertising

Source: Unilever.

EXHIBIT 6
Brand Audit 2005 by
Millward Brown

Note: Pre-Ads were
surveyed from November to
December 2003. During/
After Ads were surveyed
from March to July 2004.

Source: Millward Brown
International Research,
Agreeing Before and After
Dove Communications
Strategy, "Firming Lotion."

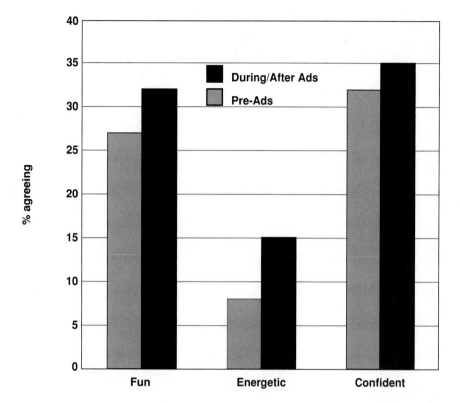

members of the Girl Scouts of Nassau County Chorus from Long Island, New York, can be heard singing a version of True Colors."[9]

In Canada and Germany, similar projects were launched under the name "Body Talk," "a program to inform and educate young schoolgirls about perceptions of beauty, helping boost their self-esteem."[10] Further ideas for projects were collected in seminars with teachers in order to include Body Talk messages effectively into teaching subjects.

Another activity was a mother–daughter workbook, designed by the U.S. Girl Scouts, in cooperation with the team that developed the original "Real Truth about Beauty" report. The free workbook could be used together by mother and daughter, and it supported mothers in their efforts to encourage communication in the family and to help their daughters improve their self-esteem.

Finally, Unilever needed to improve communication about Dove products so that statements in advertisements appeared more sincere.

Next Steps

Dunleavy's mind was working at warp speed. The more she thought, the more questions she had. While the first steps of the relaunch were clearly successful, she knew it would not be enough to satisfy Unilever. She sincerely believed that customer-based marketing was paramount. Unilever had quality, well-positioned products. Keeping them there would be the real test.

[9]"Super Bowl Spot Launches Multi-Tiered Effort Encouraging Girls to Feel More Confident, Recognize Their Unique Beauty," Campaignforrealbeauty.com, January 27, 2006, available at http://sev.prnewswire.com/advertising/20060127/NYF01927012006-1.html, accessed August 28, 2006.
[10]"How Real Curves Can Grow Your Brand," *Viewpoint Online Magazine,* Ogilvy.com, April 2005, available at http://www.ogilvy.com/uploads/koviewpoint/dove.pdf, accessed August 28, 2006.

The next step of the relaunch was set to commence in September. Dunleavy wondered how to maintain the brand's momentum while continuing to take advantage of the stubborn portrayal of flawless beauty by competitors. She also wondered whether the competition would try to imitate Dove's success by launching similar campaigns. In the world of marketing, the reward for success is typically more and better competition. What should Dove do to prepare for the next phase?

CONCLUSION

Dunleavy and Allen joked about how much was riding on their next series of strategic moves. "I believe we are doing what needs to be done," noted Allen.

> Our customers are our customers. That may sound a little silly, but I know that we are making a difference beyond just making good products. We make good products and we sell them in a manner that is fair and honest. Our promotional work has been cutting edge and I believe it has changed the industry's approach to the portrayal of what is real beauty. Let's listen to the research and combine it with what we have learned in the past two years.

"Tomorrow morning I am going to be asking for some substantial resources to keep this thing going," Dunleavy added.

> We need to be aware of what we need and why we need it. Do me a favor. Be ready with specifics as we lay out the plan. You can brief me later.

Case Group D

Distribution Strategy

15

IKEA's Global Strategy: Furnishing the World

Paul Kolesa

IKEA is a furniture manufacturer and retailer, well known throughout the world for its knockdown furniture. Its large retail stores in the blue-and-yellow colors of the Swedish flag are located on the outskirts of major cities, attracting shoppers who are looking for modern designs at good value. The low-cost operation relies on buyers with automobiles to carry the disassembled furniture in packaged kits and assemble the pieces at home.

The IKEA case is interesting because it shows how even retailers can go global once the key competitive advantages of the offering are standardized. The case focuses on the American entry, which posed barriers IKEA had not encountered before and which forced adaptation of some features.

IKEA, the Swedish furniture store chain virtually unknown outside of Scandinavia 25 years ago, has drawn large opening crowds to its stores as it has pushed into Europe, Asia, and North America. Along the way it has built something of a cult following, especially among young and price-conscious consumers. But the expansion was not always smooth and easy, for example, in Germany and Canada, and it was particularly difficult in the United States.

COMPANY BACKGROUND

IKEA was founded in 1943 by Ingvar Kamprad to serve price-conscious neighbors in the province of Smaland in southern Sweden. Early on, the young entrepreneur hit upon a winning formula, contracting with independent furniture makers and suppliers to design furniture that could be sold as a kit and assembled in the consumer's home. In return for favorable and guaranteed orders from IKEA, the suppliers were prohibited from selling to other stores. Developing innovative modular designs whose components could be mass produced and venturing early into eastern Europe to build a dedicated supplier network, IKEA could offer quality furniture in modern Scandinavian designs at very low prices. By investing profits in new stores, the company expanded throughout Scandinavia in the 1950s.

This case was prepared by Paul Kolesa for class analysis and discussion.

Throughout the following years, the IKEA store design and layout remained the same; IKEA was basically a warehouse store. Because the ready-to-assemble "knockdown" kits could be stacked conveniently on racks, inventory was always large, and instead of waiting for the store to deliver the furniture, IKEA's customers could pick it up themselves. Stores were therefore located outside of the big cities, with ample parking space for automobiles. Inside, an assembled version of the furniture was displayed in settings along with other IKEA furniture. The purchaser could decide on what to buy, obtain the inventory tag number, and then either find the kit on the rack, or, in the case of larger pieces, have the kit delivered through the back door to the waiting car.

This simple formula meant that there were relatively few sales clerks on the floor to help customers sort through the more than 10,000 products stocked. The sales job consisted mainly of making sure that the assembled pieces were attractively displayed, that clear instructions were given as to where the kits could be found, and that customers did not have to wait too long at the checkout lines. IKEA's was a classic "cash-and-carry" approach, except that credit cards were accepted.

This approach, which trims costs to a minimum, is dependent on IKEA's global sourcing network of more than 2,300 suppliers in 67 countries. Because IKEA's designers work closely with suppliers, savings are built into all its products from the outset. Also since the same furniture is sold all around the world, IKEA reaps huge economies of scale from the size of its stores and the big production runs necessary to stock them. Therefore, IKEA is able to match rivals on quality while undercutting them up to 30 percent on price.

To draw the customers to the distant stores, the company relies on word-of-mouth, limited advertising, and its catalogs. These catalogs are delivered free of charge in the mailboxes of potential customers living in the towns and cities within reach of a store. The catalogs depict the merchandise not only as independent pieces of furniture but also together in actual settings of a living room, bedroom, children's room, and so on. This enables the company to demonstrate its philosophy of creating a "living space," not just selling furniture. It also helps the potential buyer visualize a complete room and simplifies the planning of furnishing a home. It also shows how IKEA's various components are stylistically integrated into a complete and beautiful whole. Even though furniture is hardly high-tech, the philosophy is reminiscent of the way high-tech producers, such as mobile phone makers, attempt to develop add-on features that fit their particular brand and not others.

As the company has grown, the catalog has increased in volume and in circulation. By 2003, the worldwide circulation of the 360-page catalog reached over 130 million, making it the world's largest printed publication distributed for free. In 2003, the catalog was distributed in 36 countries and 28 languages, showing more than 3,000 items from storage solutions and kitchen renovation ideas to office furniture and bedroom furnishings.

Sales totaled about 12.2 billion U.S. dollars in 2003, with a net profit margin around 6–7 percent. Of this, Europe accounted for over 80 percent of revenues, with Asia accounting for 3 percent, and North America 15 percent. The huge stores are relatively few in number—only 175 worldwide but growing rapidly—and the company employs about 76,000 people around the world (see Exhibits 1 and 2). Many of the stores have only one expatriate Swedish manager at the top, sufficient to instill the lean Ingvar Kamprad and IKEA ethos in the local organization.

Although the firm remains private, it continues to innovate and reorganize itself. For instance, fast decision making is aided by a management structure that is as flat as the firm's knockdown furniture kits, with only four layers separating IKEA's chief executive from its checkout workers. In 1992, IKEA abolished internal budgets, and now each region must merely keep below a fixed ratio of costs to turnover.

EXHIBIT 1
IKEA Sales Data

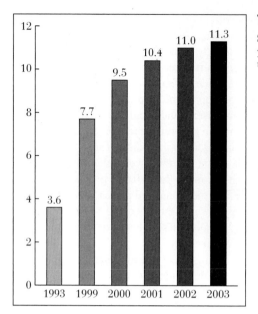

Turnover for the IKEA Group:

Sales for the IKEA Group for the financial year 2003 (1 September 2002–31 August 2003) totaled 11.3 billion euro (12.2 billion USD).

EUROPEAN EXPANSION

In the 1960s and 70s, as modern Scandinavian design became increasingly popular, expansion into Europe became a logical next step. The company first entered the German-speaking regions of Switzerland, thereby testing itself in a small region similar to Scandinavia. Yet expansion so far away from Sweden made it necessary to develop new suppliers, which meant that Kamprad traveled extensively, visiting potential suppliers and convincing them to become exclusive IKEA suppliers. Once the supply chain was established, the formula of consumer-assembled furniture could be used. After some resistance from independent furniture retailers who claimed that the furniture was not really "Swedish," since much of it came from other countries, IKEA's quality/price advantage proved irresistible even to fastidious Swiss consumers.

The next logical target was Germany, much bigger than Switzerland, but also culturally close to IKEA's roots. In Germany, well-established and large furniture chains were formidable foes opposed to the competitive entry and there were several regulatory obstacles. The opening birthday celebration of the first store in 1974 outside Cologne was criticized because in German culture birthdays should be celebrated only every 25 years. The use of the Swedish flag and the blue-yellow colors was challenged because the IKEA subsidiary was an incorporated German company (IKEA GmbH). The celebratory breakfast was mistitled because no eggs were served. Despite these rearguard actions from the established German retailers, IKEA GmbH became very successful, and was thus accepted, being voted German marketer of the year in 1979. The acceptance of IKEA's way of doing business was helped by the fact that IKEA had enlarged the entire market by its low prices, and some of the established retailers adopted the same formula in their own operations.

To get the stores abroad started, Kamprad usually sent a team of three or four managers who could speak the local language and had experience in an existing IKEA store. This team hired and trained the sales employees, organized the store layout, and established the sales and ordering routines. Although the tasks were relatively simple and straightforward, IKEA's lean organizational strategies meant that individual employees were assigned

EXHIBIT 2
IKEA Retail
Operations

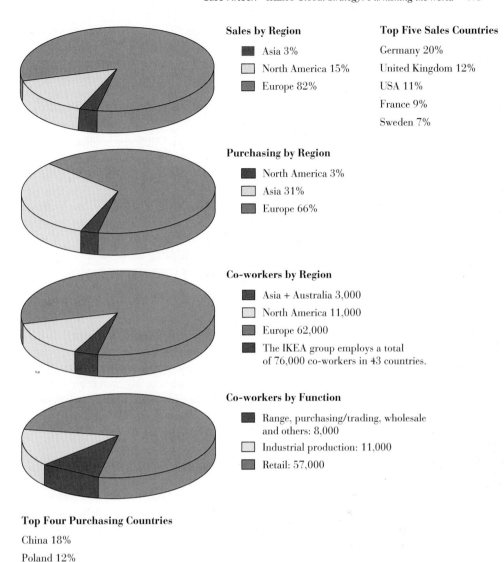

Sales by Region

- ■ Asia 3%
- ☐ North America 15%
- ▨ Europe 82%

Top Five Sales Countries

Germany 20%

United Kingdom 12%

USA 11%

France 9%

Sweden 7%

Purchasing by Region

- ■ North America 3%
- ☐ Asia 31%
- ▨ Europe 66%

Co-workers by Region

- ■ Asia + Australia 3,000
- ☐ North America 11,000
- ▨ Europe 62,000
- ■ The IKEA group employs a total of 76,000 co-workers in 43 countries.

Co-workers by Function

- ■ Range, purchasing/trading, wholesale and others: 8,000
- ☐ Industrial production: 11,000
- ▨ Retail: 57,000

Top Four Purchasing Countries

China 18%

Poland 12%

Sweden 9%

Italy 7%

greater responsibilities and more freedom than usual in more traditional retail stores. Although this was not a problem in Europe and Japan (where its Japanese-sounding name also was an advantage), it was a problem in the United States.

CANADIAN ENTRY

To prepare for eventual entry into the United States, IKEA first expanded into Canada. The Canadian market was close to the U.S. market, and creating the supply network for Canada would lay the foundation for what was needed for the much larger U.S. market. Drawing upon a successful advertising campaign and positive word-of-mouth, and by combining newly recruited local suppliers with imports from existing European suppliers, the Canadian entry was soon a success. The advertising campaign was centered around the slogan, "IKEA: The impossible furniture store from Sweden," which was supported by a cartoon drawing of a moose's head, complete with antlers. The moose symbol had played very well in Germany, creating natural associations "with the north," and also creating an image of fun and games that played well in the younger segments the company targeted. The Canadians responded equally well to the slogan and the moose, as well as to IKEA's humorous cartoonlike ads poking fun at its Swedish heritage ("How many Swedes does it take to screw in a lightbulb? Two—one to screw in the lightbulb, and one to park the Volvo"), which became often-heard jokes.

The United States presented a much different challenge, as it offered a much larger market with a dispersed population, great cultural diversity, and strong domestic competition. The initial problems centered around which part of the United States to attack first. While the east coast seemed more natural, with its closer ties to Europe, the California market on the west coast was demographically more attractive. But trafficking supplies to California would be a headache, and competition seemed stronger there, with the presence of established retailers of Scandinavian designs.

Then, there was the issue of managing the stores. In Canada, the European management style had been severely tested. The unusually great independence and authority of each individual employee in the IKEA system had been welcomed, but the individuals often asked for more direction and specific guidance. For example, the Swedish start-up team would say to an employee, "You are in charge of the layout of the office furniture section of the store," and consider this a perfectly actionable and complete job description. This seemed to go against the training and predisposition of some employees, who came back with questions such as, "How should this piece of furniture be displayed?" IKEA's expansion team suspected that the situation would be possibly even more difficult in the United States. The team also wondered if the same slogan and the moose symbol would be as effective in the United States as it had been in Germany and Canada.

ENTRY HURDLES IN THE UNITED STATES

From the outset IKEA had succeeded despite breaking many of the standard rules of international retailing: enter a market only after exhaustive study; cater to local tastes as much as possible; and tap into local expertise through acquisitions, joint ventures, or franchising. Although breaking these rules had not hurt IKEA in Europe, the firm got into some trouble in America with its initial seven stores: six on the east coast and one in California. Many people visited the stores, looked at the furniture, and left empty-handed, citing long queues and nonavailable stock as chief complaints.

IKEA managers believed that their most pressing problem in entering the U.S. market was the creation of a stable supply chain. By taking an incremental approach, starting with a few stores on the east coast including an initial one outside Philadelphia, IKEA managers believed that they had ensured a smooth transition from the eastern United States, with its relative proximity to European suppliers, and its Canadian beachhead. Although the store in southern California was much farther away, its large market and customer demographics—young and active—favored IKEA's modern designs and assemble-it-yourself strategy. The California entry was also precipitated by the emergence of a local imitator, "Stør," which had opened ahead of IKEA, capitalizing on the word-of-mouth generated by IKEA's new concept.

IKEA's early effort had problems because of less adaptation to the American market than customers desired. For example, IKEA decided not to reconfigure its bedroom furniture to the different dimensions used in the American market. As a result, the European-style beds sold by IKEA were slightly narrower and longer than standard American beds, and customers' existing mattresses and sheets did not fit the beds. Even though IKEA stocked

European-sized sheets in the stores, bed sales remained very slow. IKEA ended up re-designing about a fifth of its American product range and sales immediately increased by around 30–40 percent.

The American suppliers, whom IKEA gradually recruited to reduce the dependence on imports, also proved in need of upgrading and instruction in IKEA's way of producing furniture. IKEA sent its people to the suppliers' plants, providing technical tips about more efficient methods and helping the suppliers shop around for better-quality or lower-price materials. Now IKEA produces about 45 percent of the furniture sold in its American stores locally, up from 15 percent just a few years earlier. In turn this has helped the firm cut prices in its American stores for three years running. The American difficulties also highlighted how growth could lead to quality problems in managing its increasingly complex global supply chain, so IKEA began conducting random checks.

Other adaptations to the American market proved just as successful. For instance, new cash registers were installed to speed throughput by 20 percent, with the goal of eliminating long checkout lines. Store layout was altered to conform more with American aesthetics and shopping styles. A more generous return policy than in Europe was instituted and a next-day delivery service was implemented.

PROMOTION

While some managers helped establish the supply side of the stores, IKEA's marketing staff was busy with the promotional side of the business. Store locations had generally disadvantaged IKEA relative to competitors. Because of the huge size of the stores (typically around 200,000 square feet), the need to keep a large inventory so that customers could get the purchased furniture immediately, and the amount of land needed for parking around each store, most stores were located in out-of-the-way places—next to the airport in New Jersey in one case and in a shopping mall 20 miles south of Washington, DC, in another. Thus, advertising was needed to make potential customers aware of store locations. It was thought that lower prices and selection would do the rest—positive word-of-mouth had proven the best advertising in most other markets.

But in the United States' competitive retail climate IKEA found that more focused media advertising was needed. As one manager stated: "In Europe you advertise to gain business; in the United States you advertise to stay in business." The diversity of the consumers made word-of-mouth less powerful than in ethnically more homogeneous countries. Management decided that a strong slogan and unique advertising message were going to be necessary to really bring awareness close to the levels in other countries.

The Moose symbol of IKEA (see Exhibit 3), although successful in Germany and Canada, was considered strange and too provincial for the U.S. market and would project the wrong image especially in California. Instead IKEA, in collaboration with its New York–based advertising agency Deutsch, developed a striking slogan that combined the down-home touch of the company philosophy with the humorous touch of the Moose: "It's a big country. Someone's got to furnish it" (see Exhibit 4).

Following the success of this advertising strategy, the company ventured further to establish itself as a pioneering store and to attract new kinds of customers. IKEA and Deutsch developed a series of eight TV advertising spots that featured people at different transitional stages in their lives, when they were most likely to be in the market for furniture. One spot featured a young family who had just bought a new house, another a couple whose children had just left home, and so on. IKEA even developed one spot that featured a homosexual couple, two men talking about furnishing their home. It was a daring step, applauded by

EXHIBIT 3

EXHIBIT 4

It's a big country.
Someone's got to furnish it.

most advertising experts and impartial observers. The campaign had a positive impact on IKEA's image—and on IKEA's sales. The company has continued the trend. One 30-second TV spot showed a divorced woman buying furniture for the first time on her own.

The privately held company won't reveal income figures, but it is successful in each of the market areas where it has located its U.S. stores. It is credited with being partly responsible for a shift in furniture buying behavior in the United States. Choosing furniture has become a matter of personality, lifestyle, and emotions in addition to functionality. IKEA's managers like that—they want IKEA to be associated with the "warmest, most emotional furniture in the world."

Discussion Questions

1. What are IKEA's firm-specific advantages? Country-specific advantages?

2. What are the cultural factors that make expansion abroad in retailing difficult? What has made it possible in IKEA's case?

3. Describe how IKEA's expansion has reenergized mature markets around the world and changed the competitive situation.

4. How does the TV advertising campaign initiated by IKEA overcome the entry barrier of high advertising expenditures?

5. Should IKEA expand further in the United States or focus on other countries?

Sources: Case compiled by Paul Kolesa from Rita Martenson, "Innovations in International Retailing," University of Gothenburg, Sweden: Liber, 1981; "Furnishing the World," *The Economist,* November 19, 1994, pp. 79–80; Richard Stevenson, "IKEA's New Realities: Recession and Aging Consumers," *The New York Times,* April 25, 1993, p. F4; Kate Fitzgerald, "IKEA Dares to Reveal Gays Buy Tables Too," *Advertising Age,* March 12, 1994, pp. 3, 41; Vito Pilieci, "The IKEA Catalogue: Swedish for Massive Circulation," *Calgary Herald,* August 27, 2003, p. C1.

16

IVEY

Richard Ivey School of Business
The University of Western Ontario

Pets.com Inc.: Rise and Decline of a Pet Supply Retailer[1]

Version: (A) 2009-09-15

THE BIRTH OF PETS.COM

In 1994, Pasadena-based entrepreneur Greg McLemore registered the Pets.com name.[2] Although McLemore's commercial intentions for the Pets.com address were not clear from the start,[3] they became apparent in 1998, when he set up an online pet shop with colleague Eva Woodsmall and relocated to San Francisco shortly afterward.[4] In February 1999, Pets.com, Inc., was incorporated as an online retailer of pet products, and the Pets.com Web site was also launched.[5] Greg McLemore, aged 31, was best known for his prior start-up, Toys.com, which had recently been sold to eToys. McLemore still owned approximately 750,000 shares of eToys, which had filed for an initial public offering (IPO).[6]

By January 1999, the world was on the threshold of a new era in which companies would increasingly interact with customers through the virtual space of the Internet, and

---

[1]This case has been written on the basis of published sources only. Consequently, the interpretation and perspectives presented in this case are not necessarily those of Pets.com or any of it employees.

[2]Brad Stone, "Amazon's Pet Projects," *Newsweek,* June 21, 1999.

[3]Note that during this time, people often registered domain names with no intention of using them for business purposes, but simply to sell them to interested parties at a later date. This practice was particularly true for "generic" names, such as Pets.com. See Matt Haig, *Brand Failures: The Truth about the 100 Biggest Branding Mistakes of All Times,* Kogan Page, London, 2003.

[4]Tim Clark, "Amazon Invests in Online Pet Store," *CNET News,* March 29, 1999, available at http://news.cnet.com/Amazon-invests-in-online-pet-store/2100-1017_3-223621.html, accessed June 20, 2009.

[5]John M. Coulter and Thomas J. Vogel, "Pets.com, Inc.: Assessing Financial Performance and Risks in the e-Commerce Industry," *Issues in Accounting Education,* November 2004.

[6]Clark, "Amazon Invests in Online Pet Store," March 29, 1999.

businesses would undergo a transformation on the scale of the Industrial Revolution.[7] This was the "information revolution," and it had captured the imagination of investors and entrepreneurs who wanted a piece of the cake. Although the Internet had created the opportunity of a new distribution channel for established companies, it also opened the possibility for new companies to enter into established industries without a huge capital investment in a retail distribution channel.

The company leading the dot-com race was Amazon.com. Despite initial skepticism by some industry observers, the company's stock performance was outstanding: by February 1, 1999, its share price had increased to $58 per share from its IPO offer price of $18 per share in May 1997. Moreover, Amazon.com had successfully defined the business model of the dot-com age. According to an observer:

> Amazon.com has been a darling of Wall Street, albeit a rather unusual one. In five quarters as a public company, Amazon.com has not come close to posting a profit. But the company that makes it easy to order books and music online has seen its stock soar astoundingly as investors see Amazon.com as a leader in Internet commerce.[8]

Amazon.com's growth strategy had become an example for all subsequent companies to follow: when choosing between profits and growth, a start-up should opt for growth because substantial growth in revenue and subscribers ensures investor confidence and portrays market leadership.

After the success of Amazon.com, the case for selling pet supplies online mirrored that of online bookstores. If Amazon.com could successfully sell books online within the $12 billion U.S. retail book industry, surely a portion of pet supplies could be sold online, given a total domestic industry size almost twice as large.[9]

Pets.com was an exciting business concept that was guaranteed to be a success.[10] By 2004, Forrester Research had forecast online pet product sales to be more than $4.5 billion,[11] and Pets.com was positioning itself to capture a large part of that market. Pets.com's prospects looked so favorable that even outsiders became fans of the company.[12]

In March 1999, McLemore succeeded in his first-round attempts to secure funding for Pets.com, receiving $2 million from a premier venture capital fund, Hummer Winblad Venture Partners (Hummer Winblad).[13] The Silicon-Valley-based Hummer Winblad, which focused exclusively on software and Internet investing, had more than $500 million under management. Hummer Winblad's investments included PowerSoft Corporation and Arbor Software, as well as Internet companies Net Perceptions, AdForce, HomeGrocer and Employease.[14]

Pets.com named Julie Wainwright as chief executive officer (CEO), a post she took over in March 1999.[15] Her previous job had been CEO of the online video store Reel.com, which Amazon.com had recently surpassed as the Internet's top video outlet for non-adult

[7]Barua et al., *Measuring the Internet Economy,* June 1999.

[8]Greg Heberlein, "Amazon.Com Loss Is Less than Forecast: Though Red Ink Grows, Sales Skyrocket, New Accounts Rise," *Seattle Times Business Reporter,* July 23, 1998.

[9]"Pet Quarters, Inc.," SECinfo, December 22, 1999, available at www.secinfo.com/dsvrp.6B38.htm, accessed June 17, 2009.

[10]Matt Haig, *Brand Failures: The Truth about the 100 Biggest Branding Mistakes of All Times,* Kogan Page, London, 2003.

[11]Dana Blankenhorn, "Pet Sites Prove It's a Dog-Eat-Dog World," *Interactive Week* from *ZDWire,* August 27, 2000.

[12]"Death of a Spokespup," *Adweek,* New England Edition, December 2000.

[13]Stone, "Amazon's Pet Projects," June 21, 1999.

[14]"Pets.com Raises $35 Million Third Round of Funding; Most Recent Round of Funding Raises Online Pet Site's Total Capital to Nearly $100 Million," *Business Wire,* November 3, 1999.

[15]"Reading List," *BusinessWeek,* 2000, available at www.businessweek.com/bschools/books/recommenders/wainwright.htm, accessed June 19, 2009.

titles.[16] When Wainwright was approached to be the top executive for Pets.com, she didn't even read the proposal:

> I did research instead and found the market for pet products is extremely fragmented. . . . Sales go through multiple stores—mass merchants, independent pet stores, supermarkets.
> There isn't one monopolistic figure out there that owns the pet world. . . . I knew it was an opportunity to aggregate products.[17]

Wainwright's team consisted of a handful of well-regarded, experienced managers, including a former Procter & Gamble marketing executive, John Hommeyer, who was Pets.com's new vice-president of marketing.[18]

THE PET INDUSTRY

In 1998, the pet industry was large and growing, consisting of a US$53-billion-a-year global marketplace.[19] Americans spent nearly $23 billion on their pets annually, according to the Pet Industry Joint Advisory Council,[20] and this number was growing at a rate of $1 billion per year.[21] To put this industry in context, each year, Americans spent approximately $21 billion on toys, $13 billion on music recordings and $12 billion on retail books.[22] Some experts predicted that, by 2001, the pet product and services industry would total more than $28 billion.[23]

Pet Ownership in the United States

Pets were an integral part of American family life, evidenced by the 60 percent of all U.S. households that owned a pet[24] and the 40 percent of all households that owned more than one pet.[25] In particular, dogs and cats drove pet industry sales.[26] As of 1996, Americans reportedly owned 53 million dogs and 59 million cats, with four million more households owning dogs than cats.[27] Pet ownership break-down in 1999 is set out in Exhibit 1.[28]

Americans simply loved to spend money spoiling their pets. According to a 1999 American Animal Hospital Association survey, 30 percent of pet owners admitted to cooking special meals for their pets, 25 percent of pet owners bought their pets gifts and five percent gave their pets greeting cards.[29]

Favorable demographic trends indicated continued growth of the already recession-resistant industry of pet products and services. Families with children between the ages of 5 and 15 were most likely to own pets. Meanwhile, projections suggested the number of

---

[16]Clark, "Amazon Invests in Online Pet Store," March 29, 1999.

[17]Connie Guglielmo, "Category Killer: Pets.com," *Interactive Week* from *ZDWire,* May 31, 1999.

[18]Ibid.

[19]Barry Janoff, "Reigning Cats and Dogs," *Progressive Grocer,* June 2000.

[20]"Amazon.com Announces Investment in Pets.com," *PR Newswire,* March 29, 1999.

[21]Pet Products Manufacturers Association (APPMA), Greenwich, CT.

[22]"Pet Quarters, Inc.," December 22, 1999.

[23]Ibid.

[24]Joanna Sabatini, "Best of Breed," *Adweek,* Eastern Edition, November 22, 1999, p. 56.

[25]John Fetto and Jennifer Lach, "Pets Can Drive," *American Demographics,* March 2000, p. 10.

[26]"Pet Quarters, Inc.," December 22, 1999.

[27]"U.S. Pet Ownership & Demographics Sourcebook," Center for Information Management, American Veterinary Medical Association, Schaumburg, IL, 1997.

[28]"Pet Quarters, Inc.," December 22, 1999.

[29]John Fetto and Jennifer Lach, "Pets Can Drive," *American Demographics,* March 2000, p. 10.

EXHIBIT 1   Pet Ownership in the United States by Pet Type, 1999

Pet Type	Total # of Pets (millions)	% of Total Number of Pets	# of Households (millions)	% of Total Number of Households
Cats	59	30	32	33
Dogs	53	27	36	37
Fish	56	28	6	6
Birds	14	7	5	5
Rabbits/Ferrets	6	3	2	2
Rodents	5	3	2	2
Reptiles	4	2	1	1

Source: American Veterinary Medical Association in "Pet Quarters, Inc.," SECinfo, December 22, 1999, available at www.secinfo.com/dsvrp.6B38.htm, accessed June 17, 2009.

families with children younger than 18 years of age would grow steadily over the next several years.[30]

Furthermore, pet-owning households tended to be wealthier than average and, thus, were able to afford to spend more on pet products. According to the American Veterinarian Medical Association, nearly 65 percent of households earning $60,000 or more were pet owners (see Exhibit 2).[31]

Consumer Spending on Pets

Of the total pet products and services industry, approximately half was accounted for by the pet food category.[32] This category could be divided into non-premium supermarket brands and premium brands. Historically, non-premium supermarket brands, such as Alpo, Kal Kan and Purina, dominated sales, comprising nearly 55 percent of all pet food supplies. These non-premium brands, which were primarily sold through grocery and convenience stores, as well as through other mass merchant outlets, featured slow annual growth rates, small gross margins and low nutrient levels compared with their premium counterparts.[33]

After the pet food industry became accustomed to the low competition that characterized the 1980s, by the mid-1990s, supermarket pet food brands began losing market share amid growing concern for animal welfare and nutrition. Healthy diet recommendations from veterinarians and breeders increased the popularity of premium brands, such as Iams, Nutro and Science Diet. These and other premium pet food brands became increasingly available and offered wider varieties, despite typically restricted distribution, which led to only a few supermarkets or mass merchants carrying these premium lines. From 1994 to

EXHIBIT 2

Pet Ownership in the United States by Income, 1999

Source: American Veterinary Medical Association in "Pet Quarters, Inc.," SECinfo, December 22, 1999, available at www.secinfo.com/dsvrp.6B38.htm, accessed June 17, 2009.

Household Income	% Owning a Pet
Less than $12,500	47.8
$12,500 to $24,999	55.6
$25,000 to $39,000	60.7
$40,000 to $59,999	64.8
$60,000 or more	64.6

[30]"Pet Quarters, Inc.," December 22, 1999.

[31]Ibid.

[32]Barry Janoff, "Reigning Cats and Dogs," June 2000.

[33]"Pet Quarters, Inc.," December 22, 1999.

1999, premium brand sales grew at an annual growth rate of approximately 18 percent, until capturing approximately 25 percent of the total pet food market in 1999.[34]

Consumers bought many pet products on impulse during their regular shopping trips to purchase pet food, cat litter or items for flea control. Typically, consumer demand was less price-sensitive for such impulse buys compared with staples such as pet food and other bulk products. Thus, non bulk, non food pet products required fewer discounts and yielded higher gross margins, attracting strong interest from supermarkets that were looking to stock their shelves with profitable goods. However, because of space constraints, supermarkets could carry only limited basic pet supplies, such as collars, dog chews, leashes, flea collars and toys. Conversely, pet supply stores could stock a wider variety of items, including grooming products, pet carriers, cat furniture, doghouses, vitamins, treats and veterinary products.[35] Despite the higher margins on non-bulk items, pet product profit margins on the whole were still low: in the bricks-and-mortar world, they ranged between two percent and four percent.[36]

The pet services category—i.e., veterinary, boarding, grooming, and training services—yielded higher margins, though typically only large, experienced specialty retailers had both the skill and insurance to offer these services. Most pet owners sought veterinary care at least once a year, including approximately 92 percent of households with dogs and 78 percent of households with cats. From 1991 to 1999, U.S. veterinary expenditures grew 9.5 percent annually.[37]

In 1999, the pet industry appeared to potential online retailers as an attractive and growing sector. Analysts were optimistic because the Internet had already been proven to be a successful distribution channel for software, music, and books.

Internet and Retail e-Commerce Trends

At the end of 1998, International Data Corporation (IDC) estimated 97 million people were using the Internet worldwide, with projections of 320 million users by the end of 2002.[38] Moreover, in 1998, nearly 60 percent of all Internet-connected households went online at least once a day, compared with only 35 percent the previous year. Not only was the number of users increasing but also the frequency and duration of users' online time. Experts predicted this trend would only strengthen, as more people sourced information and conducted market transactions online.[39]

Internet usage boomed among a wide range of age groups and demographic profiles, as a result of e-mail, online information and virtual commerce becoming a part of daily American life.[40] The majority of Internet access occurred through personal computers (PCs). However, IntelliQuest (which measured the media habits and purchase behavior of people involved in technology-related purchasing decisions and usage) predicted alternative technologies, such as handheld computers and WebTV, would further drive Internet growth by 2000.[41]

---

[34]Ibid.

[35]Ibid.

[36]Pui-Wing Tam and Mylene Mangalindan, "Pets.com's Demise: Too Much Litter, Too Few Funds—Pet-Supply Site Sought Money but Couldn't Find Backers; 'It's Sad,' Says the Founder," *The Wall Street Journal*, November 8, 2000.

[37]"Pet Quarters, Inc.," December 22, 1999.

[38]"Drilling Down into Computer and Web Trends," *LearnFrame,* 2001, available at www.learnframe.com/aboutelearning/page16.asp, accessed June 19, 2009.

[39]"New IDC Study Predicts 23 Percent of All Households Online by 1998; Reveals Increasing Popularity of Business-to-Business Commerce Solutions," *PR Newswire,* March 30, 1998.

[40]"Drilling Down into Computer and Web Trends," 2001.

[41]Michael Pastore, "More People Online Without PCs," *ClickZ,* April 20, 1999, available at www.clickz.com/150271, accessed June 18, 2009.

In 1998, according to the Texas Centre for Research in Electronic Commerce, the Internet economy generated U.S. revenues of $301.4 billion. Internet commerce accounted for approximately one-third of total revenues, or $101.9 billion. Growth nearly doubled between 1995 and 1998, with the Internet economy increasing by 174.5 percent, compared with a global average economic growth rate of 3.8 percent during the same period. Moreover, transfer of existing economic activity to the Internet, rather than newly created Internet activities, drove a significant proportion of Internet growth.[42] Finally, the globalization of e-commerce brought further opportunities for e-retailers prepared to transact beyond U.S. borders. The International Data Corporation predicted that, by 2001, international shoppers would outspend their U.S. counterparts $277 billion to $248 billion.[43]

Other factors influencing the growing Internet usage and e-commerce included a growing base of home and workplace computers; improved network security, infrastructure and bandwidth; faster modems and PCs; cheaper, more reliable Internet access and increased consumer adoption of online commerce.[44]

Pets Products Online

NPD Online Research's October 1999 online pet store survey, which was based on 2,009 individual responses, suggested the Internet had yet to capture the attention of most Internet-using pet owners. However, present online pet store shoppers reported high levels of satisfaction. Of the nearly 30 percent of Internet users who had purchased from an online pet store, more than half reported being very satisfied with their buying experience, and many intended to shop online again. The survey also revealed that females were the majority of buyers of online pet supplies. Women comprised 68 percent of all online sales and spent nearly double the online pet supply purchases of men. The study also found that most pet owners discovered online pet stores by browsing the Internet.[45]

Toys were the most popular Internet pet store purchase, despite wide-ranging available items. Forty percent of polled consumers bought toys for their pets online, compared with approximately 30 percent of consumers who bought food or treats online; 26 percent who purchased non food accessories online and 17 percent who bought health products online. Nearly half of all buyers spent up to $25 during an average visit, whereas 37 percent spent between $25 and $50.[46]

According to NPD, convenience was the top reason for making an online pet supplies purchase. Other rationale reflected the time savings, flexible hours and reduced effort of Internet purchasing (see Exhibit 3).[47] However, some experts believed such benefits were

EXHIBIT 3
Most Frequent
Reasons for Buying
From Online Pet
Stores

Source: "Online Pet Stores
Poised for Success, Reports
NPD Online Research,"
Business Wire, October 12,
1999.

Reason for Buying	% of Respondents
24-hour shopping	54
Orders delivered to front door	48
Low prices	47
Online discount promotions	35
No waiting or standing in line	34

[42]Barua et al., *Measuring the Internet Economy,* June 1999.

[43]Ann Sullivan, "E-comm's Biggest Mistakes," *Network World,* February 26, 2001, available at www.networkworld.com/ecomm2001/mistakes/mistakes.html, accessed June 17, 2009.

[44]"Drilling Down into Computer and Web Trends," 2001.

[45]"Online Pet Stores Poised for Success, Reports NPD Online Research," *Business Wire,* October 12, 1999.

[46]Ibid.

[47]Ibid.

limited to a small market and, in the long run, would be outweighed by higher costs and longer waits. For example, Matt Stamski of Gomez Advisors, an e-commerce consultancy, claimed that pet supplies were not a natural e-tail market and, instead, believed that pet owners were less likely than others to shop online. Thus, one of the key challenges of online pet shops was to convince the public of the superior value of online shopping compared with regular shopping trips. The online competitors needed to be quick to establish a clear identity in the market and to communicate their unique value proposition.[48]

THE COMPETITION: READY FOR A CAT FIGHT

Wainwright acknowledged the attractiveness of the pet industry, which was appealing to a large number of competitors:

> I've never seen so many companies in a category, and they may all get funded. I don't think there's room for two. It'll be a bloodbath with huge cash outlays and low margins. It's a tough business.[49]

In 1999, a *Fortune* magazine article observed:

> In the beginning there were books. Then came CDs and videos. Travel vacations, toys, and prescription drugs followed. The latest e-commerce market to hit the Net? Pets. Until now pet owners haven't had a Web site that will answer questions, quell concerns, and sell chewy toys for Fido and Fluffie. Now get ready for the pet portal wars.[50]

With at least six major online pet competitors, Silicon Valley venture capitalists studied the largest pet portals to determine the next lucrative "Amazon or eBay of the animal kingdom."[51]

Of the dozens of competitors that were being set up at the same time as Pets.com, or shortly after, the most noteworthy were Petopia.com, PetSmart.com and PetStore.com.[52] Each claimed superior advantages, predicting that other sites were likely to fold first; yet, at various times, all had also talked about merging with competitors. In the meantime, predicting which company would emerge as top dog was nearly impossible.[53]

Petopia.com

The bricks-and-mortar pet chain Petco, with 465 stores nationwide and 100 international stores, hired banker Morgan Stanley to create its own online strategy.[54] Petopia.com, a San Francisco-based company, caught Petco's attention because it had just secured $9 million from Technology Crossover, a high-profile venture capital firm, that believed in the pet market's online potential.[55] The name Petopia was the brainchild of Catchword,

[48]Troy Wolverton, "Pets.com Latest High-Profile Dot-com Disaster," *CNET News,* November 7, 2000, available at http://news.cnet.com/2100-1017-248230.html, accessed June 20, 2009.

[49]Clark, "Amazon Invests in Online Pet Store," March 29, 1999.

[50]Melanie Warner, "The Latest Fad in Portals: Your Pet," *Fortune,* May 10, 1999.

[51]Ibid.

[52]Joelle Tessler, "San Francisco-Based Online Pet Store Will Close," *Knight Ridder Tribune Business News,* November 8, 2000.

[53]Kara Swisher, "E-Commerce (A Special Report): The Industries—A Web Surfer's Best Friend? Sites Battle to Be the Online Store for Pet Owners; A Guide to Their Strategies—and Their Chances of Success," *The Wall Street Journal,* July 12, 1999.

[54]Stone, "Amazon's Pet Projects," June 21, 1999.

[55]Guglielmo, "Category Killer: Pets.com," May, 31 1999.

a brand-development firm. Burt Alper, Catchword's co-founder and strategy director, commented on the name:

> When we evaluated the competitive landscape, it became clear that we needed a name that would stand out from the crowd without distancing the consumer. Petopia, coined from the words "pet" and "utopia," meaning "an ideally perfect place," communicates a terrific shopping experience for pet owners, in a playful, yet sophisticated way.[56]

In 1999, Petco decided to back Petopia.com. Petco's brand name was well known for its quality products and its commitment to animal care.[57] Andrea Reisman, Petopia.com's co-founder and CEO commented:

> We're changing the way pet owners think about shopping for pet supplies. By extending the "bricks-and-mortar" pet business to the online marketplace, Petopia.com is able to create a place to go, a virtual park of sorts, where owners can research information about their pet's needs, shop for pet food and supplies, and interact in a warm community with other owners who share the same interests.[58]

The Petco portion of the deal involved a strategic partnership in which the two companies could cross-promote each other and leverage both their assets.[59] For example, with Petco as a partner, Petopia.com had access to world-class purchasing and distribution capabilities.[60]

A further source of funding for Petopia was found in Groupe Arnault, a new venture capital arm of the European consumer products giant LVMH Moet Hennessey Louis Vuitton. The deal opened the door to potential international expansion at a later stage.[61]

In total, Petopia.com had managed to secure $66 million in investment, one of the largest sums ever for an Internet start-up; however, Petopia joined Pets.com in an already crowded market. When asked how Petopia differentiated itself from the competition, chair and co-founder Andrea Reisman responded with an answer that foreshadowed the spending spree the industry was just about to witness: "We're the best funded."[62]

PetSmart.com

One of Petco's main bricks-and-mortar competitors, PetSmart, also wanted a piece of the action. PetSmart launched its online presence, PetSmart.com, in 1999. PetSmart, a Phoenix-based discounter of pet products, with nearly 500 stores nationwide and 100 international stores, generated $2 billion a year in sales. In 1999, PetSmart entered into a joint venture with e-commerce entrepreneur Bill Gross of Idealab.[63] A July 1999 article in the *Wall Street*

[56]"Catchword Names Petopia.com, New Online Pet Supply and Service Firm," *Business Wire*, May 26, 1999.

[57]"PETCO Announces Strategic Partnership with Petopia.com to Launch the Premier Online Pet Commerce Site," *Business Wire*, July 13, 1999.

[58]"Petopia.com Announces $9 Million Equity Investment from Technology Crossover Ventures; Company Changes Name From paw.net to Petopia.com," *PR Newswire*, May 10, 1999.

[59]Andrea Orr, "Online Pet Store Raises $66 Million in Funding," *Reuters News,* July 14, 1999.

[60]"Petopia.com Unleashes the Internet Pet Paradise; The Virtual Animal Park Blending Commerce, Content and Community with Individual Customization," *Business Wire,* August 2, 1999.

[61]Orr, "Online Pet Store Raises $66 Million in Funding," July 14, 1999.

[62]Ibid.

[63]"Discounter PetSmart, Entrepreneur to Merge Pet-Products Web Sites," *Dow Jones Business News,* May 13, 1999.

Journal reported: "PetSmart.com presents to Pets.com the same kind of challenge that Amazon.com has been fighting off from Barnesandnoble.com."[64]

According to PetSmart officials, the two partners invested $5 million each in the PetSmart.com venture based in Pasadena, California. PetSmart CEO Phil Francis said PetSmart's strong brand name, marketing clout, close vendor relationships and efficient catalog order fulfillment systems would greatly benefit the Web site. Referring to bricks-and-mortar stores that had seen intense competition from Web competitors, Francis commented:

> Usually, the story is how the online retailer attacks the big box. Now it's big box and e-commerce retailers combining . . . this is a template for the future.[65]

Tom McGovern, CEO of the joint venture, thought a fast-moving traditional retailer with a substantial Internet presence could dominate the nascent online pet market. According to McGovern, PetSmart.com's advantages included a strong back-end warehouse and delivery systems, purchasing power, vendor relationships, national advertising and brand name.[66] Many analysts agreed that PetSmart was ahead of the pack because it had already developed brand recognition. Indeed, McGovern did not expect to lose to Pets.com when the new Web site went online in 1999:

> They are not the Goliath in this situation. I don't discount any of the [competitors], but each one is going to have to struggle through the basic blocking and tackling that we have done already.[67]

Petstore.com

Pets.com's third main competitor was another California-based start-up, Petstore.com. This company's initial round of funding yielded $10.5 million, mainly supplied by Battery Ventures, a national venture capital firm.[68] As Petstore.com co-founder and vice-president of Marketing, Bruce Gallaher, put it, "In e-commerce, a leadership position can quickly be established with 'the category killer' domain name, innovative marketing and a superior customer experience." Joshua Newman, co-founder and CEO of Petstore.com, agreed:

> Amazon's recent purchase of a major stake in Drugstore.com validates the strength of names like Petstore.com. Both Drugstore.com and Petstore.com will spend millions promoting their brands, and both are sure to benefit.[69]

Newman was also not put off by PetSmart's effort, considering the combination of an old-line retailer with a new media company problematic: "I think there will be a lot of marriage counseling there," he said.[70]

---

[64]Swisher, "E-Commerce (A Special Report): The Industries—A Web Surfer's Best Friend? Sites Battle to Be the Online Store for Pet Owners; A Guide to Their Strategies—and Their Chances of Success," July 12, 1999.

[65]Kara Swisher, "Discounter PetSmart Scampers Online in Venture with E-Commerce Incubator," *The Wall Street Journal,* May 13, 1999.

[66]Swisher, "E-Commerce (A Special Report): The Industries—A Web Surfer's Best Friend? Sites Battle to Be the Online Store for Pet Owners; A Guide to Their Strategies—and Their Chances of Success," July 12, 1999.

[67]Ibid.

[68]"Petstore.com Announces $10.5 Million Financing Round; Petstore.com Rapidly Dominating the Online Market for Pet Supplies," *Business Wire,* April 13, 1999.

[69]"Petstore.com Acquired by Truepet, Inc.: Petstore.com Brand to Dominate the Online Market for Pet Supplies and Services," *Business Wire,* March 29, 1999.

[70]Swisher, "E-Commerce (A Special Report): The Industries—A Web Surfer's Best Friend? Sites Battle to Be the Online Store for Pet Owners; A Guide to Their Strategies—And Their Chances of Success," July 12, 1999.

Petstore.com was the first to have a warehouse in operation. The company focused heavily on advertising (for example, it signed an advertising agreement with Yahoo), capitalized on both its name and its exclusive relationship with 12,000 veterinarians with membership in the American Animal Hospital Association and targeted its marketing efforts to drawing users to the site's content.[71] Late in 1999, Petstore.com secured a further investment of $97 million from Discovery Communications Inc., the parent company of the Animal Planet cable network.[72]

PETS.COM'S STRATEGY

Wainwright had been hired by the board of Pets.com Inc. to lead the company and establish it as the market leader of the online pet supplies category. Soon after joining, she wondered whether Amazon.com, which had established itself as the leader in selling books and music online, would also be looking to enter the pet supplies category. Consequently, she decided to offer shares of Pets.com to Amazon.com. Indeed, despite all the competitive activity, the competitor Wainwright had feared most was Amazon.com. "The opportunity just got significantly less risky with Amazon in as a partner, not a competitor," she noted.[73]

In June 1999, $50 million was invested in Pets.com. Jeff Bezos, CEO and founder of Amazon.com, purchased 54 percent of the shares, and a second round of funding came from Hummer Winblad Venture Partners.[74] The investment by Amazon.com in Pets.com followed its recent similar deal with Drugstore.com, a newly launched online pharmacy of which Amazon.com now owned 46 percent.[75] Bezos said:

> We invest only in companies that share our passion for customers. [Pets.com's] proven management team is dedicated to a great customer experience, whether it's making a product like a ferret hammock easy to find, or help in locating a pet-friendly hotel.[76]

In addition to receiving cash, Pets.com obtained a link on Amazon.com's home page, and Amazon.com took a seat on Pets.com's board. Behind the scenes, Amazon also offered a buddy system, whereby every Pets.com employee could turn to his or her counterpart at Amazon for guidance on any kind of business issue. The investment would also help Pets.com recruit top talent and, crucially, raise more money.[77]

Wainwright commented on the Amazon.com/Pets.com deal:

> This is a marriage made in heaven and clearly positions us as the online category leader. The successful track record represented by Amazon.com and Hummer Winblad really makes this a CEO's dream team.[78]

The partnership with Amazon.com was an early success for Wainwright because it had eliminated a strong potential competitor and enabled Pets.com to use the experience and strategic assets of Amazon.com to build a competitive advantage. Wainwright's strategy was to partner with the industry leader, hire the best people, bring in the best advertising

[71]Ibid.

[72]"Petstore.com, Discovery Communications in Financing, Marketing Pact," *Dow Jones News Service,* November 3, 1999.

[73]Clark, "Amazon Invests in Online Pet Store," March 29, 1999.

[74]Laurie Freeman, "Pets.com Socks It to Competitors," *Advertising Age,* November 29, 1999.

[75]Stone, "Amazon's Pet Projects," June 21, 1999.

[76]Clark, "Amazon Invests in Online Pet Store," March 29, 1999.

[77]Stone, "Amazon's Pet Projects," June 21, 1999.

[78]Haig, *Brand Failures: The Truth about the 100 Biggest Branding Mistakes of All Times,* 2003.

talent and focus on a business model that had worked for Amazon.com. The following is an extract from an interview with FDCH Nightly Business Report:

REPORTER: Can the market support four major players in this particular marketplace? Wall Street is skeptical of that. Can the market support it?

WAINWRIGHT: Absolutely not. Absolutely not.

REPORTER: So you have to drive one of your competitors out of business?

WAINWRIGHT: Oh, actually, you know, I have to tell you. They will, the business to consumer market right now as we speak is not exactly the hottest market. Therefore, it will translate into a shortage of venture capital. Every one of our competitors actually is backed by venture capitalists. I would have believed around now they're probably running out of money. So, you know, I don't have to drive them out. The market dynamics will drive them out.

REPORTER: So it was very important for you to be first to market with your idea?

WAINWRIGHT: Absolutely, absolutely. But, you know, I've got to tell you, we wouldn't have done it. It was important. It was a really strategy but we wouldn't have done it if we hadn't had the people, the infrastructure and the brand that we thought was saleable.[79]

Wainwright clearly wanted Pets.com to build market share as quickly as possible: "We're simply going to be able to pull out of the pack faster, because there is no room for four of us," she said in another interview.[80] "Pulling out of the pack faster" was as much a strategy decision as a survival guide for Pets.com. According to Wainwright, an aggressive marketing strategy was crucial, or the company would not have had enough money to sustain it through the launch phase. For investors to have confidence in the company, Pets.com needed to be seen as the leader of the online pet supplies industry, in the same way as Amazon.com was seen as the leader of the online books industry. Investors had confidence in Amazon.com because of consecutive quarters of high revenue and subscriber growth despite losses that exceeded the expectations of Wall Street.

Being seen as the number-one company in the online pet products category espoused among investors a confidence that was critical for providing the funding required for survival. Wainwright seemed to believe that such funding could only come through rapid growth in revenues, by adopting an aggressive marketing strategy. Typically, such an aggressive growth strategy presupposed that the market was large enough, or would grow quickly enough that revenue would provide a profit before the seed money ran out. Such a strategy also assumed that the company would be able to retain the customers that it had acquired profitably through a unique selling proposition and meaningful sources of differentiation. As Jupiter analyst Ken Cessar pointed out, Pets.com's cost model would have worked if the company had achieved a very high level of sales, and if it had accessed sufficient resources to sustain itself until the requisite level of sales could be reached.[81] Such an aggressive strategy was often risky, but if well thought-out and well executed, it could be very successful.

[79]Paul Kangas and Susie Gharib, "Pets.com: Chairman and CEO," *Nightly Business Report,* March 20, 2000.

[80]Swisher, "E-Commerce (A Special Report): The Industries—A Web Surfer's Best Friend? Sites Battle to Be the Online Store for Pet Owners; A Guide to Their Strategies—And Their Chances of Success," July 12, 1999.

[81]Pui-Wing Tam and Mylene Mangalindan, "Scarcity of Backers Forces Pets.com to Close Its Doors: Company Will Sell the Majority of Its Assets," *The Asian Wall Street Journal,* November 9, 2000.

Pets.com's significant investments in building market share through promotion and infrastructure development resulted in the company needing a very large critical mass of customers to be profitable. On the basis of optimistic estimations of Internet shopping trends, pet owners' online shopping behavior and projected demand curves, management believed that a revenue target of nearly $300 million would be needed to break even, and this target would take a minimum of five years to attain.[82]

THE MARKETING MIX

According to the Pets.com Web site:

> Pets.com is committed to serving pets and their owners with the best care possible through products, information, and service. Pets.com is an online retailer of pet products, information, and resources. Offering a broad product selection and expert advice from a staff of pet-industry experts and veterinarians, Pets.com believes that it gives consumers the confidence that they are providing their pets with the best possible care.[83]

The selection of products at Pets.com was indeed fairly broad, offering many different pet products for cats, dogs and fish, in more stock keeping units (SKUs) than any other supplier. Pets.com went a step further in 2000, when it launched its private label of cat and dog food, dog biscuits and cat litter, marketed under the Petsplete and Pets brand names.[84]

Pets.com was "designed to become a pet portal," said co-founder Eva Woodsmall. It relied heavily on chat areas for pet owners, editorial content on pets, a monthly "Pet Lawyer" column, pet-health-related information and searchable databases that provided listings on hotels that welcomed animals and access to other topics, such as veterinarians, dog breeders and boarding facilities.[85]

Additionally, several strategic alliances allowed Pets.com to offer animal health insurance and to also become the featured pet store on Yahoo![86]

Pets.com relied on two critical elements of the marketing mix to achieve its strategic objectives: an unprecedentedly aggressive communication strategy and a penetration pricing policy.

A large amount of resources was devoted to marketing communication (see Exhibit 4). The huge budget was immediately put to work, and the Pets.com site design was well received, garnering several advertising awards.[87] The company also launched an advertising campaign that relied mainly on TV, print, radio and, eventually, a Pets.com magazine.[88] The five-city advertising campaign expanded rapidly, reaching 10 cities by December 1999. In January 2000, Pets.com showed its first national commercial, a $1.2 million Super Bowl advertisement,[89] which introduced the country to Pets.com's tongue-in-cheek advertising slogan: "Because pets can't drive."[90]

---

[82]Nate Lanxon, "The Greatest Defunct Web Sites and Dotcom Disasters," *CNET UK,* June 5, 2008, available at http://crave.cnet.co.uk/gadgets/0,39029552,49296926-8,00.htm, accessed June 25, 2009.

[83]Erika Matulich and Karen Squires, "What a Dog Fight! TKO: Pets.com," *Journal of Business Case Studies,* May 2008.

[84]Ibid.

[85]Clark, "Amazon Invests in Online Pet Store," March 29, 1999.

[86]Matulich and Squires, "What a Dog Fight! TKO: Pets.com," May 2008.

[87]Jennifer Owens, "Pets.com," *Adweek,* June 5, 2000.

[88]Charlie Fletcher, "Pets.com Publishes Print Magazine," *Catalog Age,* June 2000.

[89]"The Sock Puppet," Tribble Ad Agency, March 26, 2007, available at www.tribbleagency.com/?p=195, accessed June 20, 2009.

[90]Matulich and Squires, "What a Dog Fight! TKO: Pets.com," May 2008.

EXHIBIT 4   Pets.com Financial Data

STATEMENT OF FINANCIAL OPERATIONS (IN 000S)				
	Quarter ended June 30, 1999	Quarter ended Sept 30, 1999	Quarter ended Dec 31, 1999	Feb 17, 1999* to Dec 31, 1999
Net Sales	39	568	5,168	5,787
Cost of goods sold	76	1,766	11,570	13,412
Gross margin	(37)	(1,198)	(6,402)	(7,625)
Operating expenses				
Marketing and sales	1,122	10,693	30,676	42,491
Product development	1,624	2,194	2,646	6,481
General and administrative	838	1,205	2,211	4,254
Amort. of stock-based comp.	—	1,139	979	2,118
Total operating expenses	3,584	15,231	36,512	55,344
Operating loss	(3,621)	(16,429)	(42,914)	(62,969)
Interest income	123	577	491	1,191
Net loss	(3,498)	(15,852)	(42,423)	(61,778)

Source: John M. Coulter and Thomas J. Vogel, "Pets.com, Inc.: Assessing Financial Performance and Risks in the e-Commerce Industry," *Issues in Accounting Education,* November 2004. This data also available at http://ipoalerts.edgaronline.com/EFX_dll/EDGARpro.dll?FetchFilingHTML1?ID=in_1091153&SessionID=ohNCWAxkZ304H8Y, accessed June 29, 2009.

John Hommeyer, the vice-president of marketing at Pets.com, was known for his sharp relationship marketing skills honed during his former position as director of baby care products at Procter and Gamble. In developing an early marketing strategy for the pet retailer, Hommeyer ensured that thorough research was conducted in homes and at dog parks to discern the likes and dislikes of pet owners. Working with leading advertising agency, TBWA\Chiat\Day, Hommeyer created a sock puppet that would serve as a brand icon for the company. This character would be the central feature in promotional campaigns, akin to Kellogg's Tony the Tiger and the pink Energizer bunny.[91] The sock puppet was launched in the autumn of 1999 in an impressive promotional campaign, which, within a few months, was successful at both ingraining the sock puppet in the public consciousness and making consumers more aware of the availability of online pet products.[92]

In the coming months, the marketing team worked hard to promote the sock puppet, which quickly became a celebrity. It appeared in 13 TV spots, on "Nightline," "Good Morning America" and "Access Hollywood." It received exposure in such magazines as *Entertainment Weekly, Time* and *People.* It was also featured in Macy's Thanksgiving Day Parade in New York and was the star of its own line of merchandise.[93] Wainwright was clearly impressed with the success of the sock puppet and observed: "People love the sock puppet. We have gotten over 10,000 letters of love, professing love for the sock puppet."[94] Naturally, all of these promotional efforts did come at a high cost, and eventually the cost per customer acquisition grew from approximately $80 per customer[95] to $400 per customer.[96]

After heavy promotional efforts, aggressive pricing was the second key element of Pets.com's marketing mix. The company ran numerous product specials, and its prices were

[91]Adrienne Mand, "A Sock's Best Friend," *Brandweek,* June 5, 2000.

[92]Fletcher, "Pets.com Publishes Print Magazine," June 2000.

[93]"Death of a Spokespup," December 11, 2000.

[94]Kangas and Gharib, "Pets.com—Chairman & CEO," March 20, 2000.

[95]Haig, *Brand Failures: The Truth about the 100 Biggest Branding Mistakes of All Times,* 2003.

[96]Chris Bucholtz, "Poor Product Choices Doom E-tailer E-failures," *VARBusiness,* November 17, 2000.

low across the board, particularly compared with bricks-and-mortar pet shops. In an attempt to grow revenue quickly, the company even decided to sell some of its merchandise at prices below cost.[97] In the online world, this strategy is often justified on the basis of low overheads and efficiency. In addition, profit were made from incidentals, such as inflated shipping charges, renting out customer lists, online advertising and other charges.[98] However, low initial demand and fierce competition forced Pets.com to slash its shipping charges regularly, and on numerous occasions the company offered free shipping promotions to entice customers to place orders.[99] However, the lack of a warehouse on the east coast put pressure on Pets.com's margins because many orders had to be shipped by expensive air freight.[100]

Although some of Pets.com's competitors were eager to expand their market quickly (for example, by shipping internationally), Pets.com decided against shipping products even to Canada, choosing instead to concentrate on building market share in the United States.

EPILOGUE

By the middle of 2000, many observers believed that the online pet market needed to consolidate to deal with the razor-thin margins, increasing competition and company names that carried few differences.[101] In February 2000, Pets.com raised $82.5 million in an initial public offering and four months later bought its rival, Petstore.com.[102] Wainwright said, "By acquiring these key assets and strategic relationships, we expect to reap the benefits of consolidation and thus strengthen our position as the online pet category leader."[103] Retail analyst Matt Stamski wasn't surprised that Petstore.com was closing its business, especially given the company's failure to forge a retail partnership similar to its rivals.[104]

Nevertheless, some observers believed that the Petstore.com acquisition was not enough. As a June 2000 article in the *Wall Street Journal* noted:

> The pet-supply business is a $23 billion industry, much of which is food that is often discounted. Even with the demise of Petstore.com, Pets.com must compete against Petopia Inc., PetSmart.com and about 100 other online pet retailers.[105]

Faced with large outlays of money just to attract traffic to the Web site, Pets.com eventually had to pursue cost-cutting activities. In September 2000, it announced plans to move some of its staff and, notably, its customer service call center, to Indiana to cut

[97]Arlene Weintraub and Robert D. Hof, "For Online Pet Stores, It's Dog-Eat-Dog," *BusinessWeek,* March 6, 2000.

[98]Jacques R. Chevron, "Name Least of Pets.com's Woes: Blame Poor Management, not Generic Moniker," *Advertising Age,* January 22, 2001.

[99]Bob Tedeschi, "The Pet Supply Business Is Finding That a Site May Serve Mostly to Guide Shoppers to Stores and Catalogs," *The New York Times,* October 28, 2002.

[100]Weintraub and Hof, "For Online Pet Stores, It's Dog-Eat-Dog," March 6, 2000.

[101]Stefanie Olsen, "Pets.com to Buy Assets of Rival Petstore.com," *CNET News,* June 13, 2000, available at http://news.cnet.com/Pets.com-to-buy-assets-of-rival-Petstore.com/2100-1017_3-241823.html, accessed June 22, 2009.

[102]Wolverton, "Pets.com Latest High-Profile Dot-com Disaster," November 7, 2000.

[103]Olsen, "Pets.com to Buy Assets of Rival Petstore.com," June 13, 2000.

[104]Khanh T. L. Tran, "Pets.com to Buy Petstore.com Assets," *The Wall Street Journal Europe,* June 15, 2000.

[105]Khanh T. L. Tran, "Pets.com Will Buy Assets of Online Rival Petstore.com: Consolidation of Web Retailers Continues," *The Asian Wall Street Journal,* June 15, 2000.

EXHIBIT 5
Pets.com's Share
Price

Source: Compiled from
NASDAQ data.

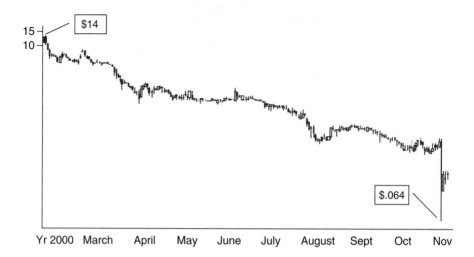

costs. The company also sought new revenue sources. For example, in April 2000, the company attempted to diversify and capitalize on the popularity of its mascot by licensing sock puppet merchandise.[106]

Despite these moves, the company's stock price continued to drop (see Exhibit 5). After an $11 per share price at the time of the IPO, and a 52-week high of $14 per share on the same day, the share value steadily fell over the next 10 months, as investors demanded rapid returns. Suddenly, according to a former Pets.com employee, "spending millions on advertising and selling products at a loss merely to add to Pets.com's list of 475,000 customers became folly," and the company started a steep slide.[107] Pets.com's lowest stock price of 2000 valued the entire company at $6.4 million. A month before going public, Pets.com had spent nearly one-fifth of that on a 30-second Super Bowl commercial.[108]

Carlotta Mast, managing editor of the Pets.com magazine, said of these tough times:

> Managers accustomed to spending whatever was necessary to keep Pets.com growing were told to conserve cash while the CEO and CFO [chief financial officer] scrambled to refill the company's shrinking reserves. I knew Pets.com was one sick puppy at the end of October, when management pulled the plug on our print magazine.[109]

After only nine months as a public firm, it looked like Pets.com had come to the end of its nine lives.

Dr. Omar Merlo is an assistant professor at the Judge Business School, University of Cambridge.

---

[106]Tan and Mangalindan, "Pets.com's Demise: Too Much Litter, Too Few Funds—Pet-Supply Site Sought Money but Couldn't Find Backers; 'It's Sad,' Says the Founder," November 8, 2000.

[107]Carlotta Mast, "Living Through the Death of a Dot-Com," *BusinessWeek*, December 13, 2000, available at www.businessweek.com/careers/content/dec2000/ca20001213_830.htm, accessed June 18, 2009.

[108]Wolverton, "Pets.com Latest High-Profile Dot-Com Disaster," November 7, 2000.

[109]Mast, "Living Through the Death of a Dot-Com," December 13, 2000.

Case

17

organicKidz: Marketing Strategy

Ken Mark and Matthew Thomson *University of Western Ontario*

INTRODUCTION

"I was prepared to handle inquiries from two different retail groups," thought Jane Walter, founder of organicKidz, a Calgary-based firm marketing the world's first stainless steel baby bottles. Walter was standing outside her booth at the All Baby & Child Kids Expo in Las Vegas on September 13, 2009. It had been a year and a half since Walter had started her company, and she had been pleased with the response to her new products. But as Walter began to list her products with specialty and mass merchandiser accounts, she started to think about the types of product and promotional choices she would be asked to make. She wanted to define her marketing strategy for the next few years.

Walter expected several dozen buyers and category managers to come by her booth in the next four days. "I've decided to sell my higher end bottles—the narrow-necked ones—to specialty stores, and the entry level bottles—the wide-mouthed ones—to big-box stores. I think that having two product lines is the right strategy." Walter had heard that specialty stores and big-box stores tended to earn gross margins of about 50 percent and 30 percent, respectively.

"But this morning, a buyer from Costco, a warehouse club, wanted to know whether we would sell our bottles to them," Walter continued. Costco tended to price its merchandise to generate gross margins of under 10 percent. Walter weighed the potential for large volume against the potential pressure on prices with her current accounts. She wondered how to respond to the Costco buyer's request.

The Infant Feeding Industry

The global baby-care supplies industry was considered a mature market, with about $9 billion in sales in 2006.[1] There were five main categories in the market: disposable diapers, wipes or moist towelettes, baby body-care products, pacifiers and teethers, and feeding accessories. Feeding accessories generated about $500 million in sales and included products such as baby bottles, baby bottle liners, breast pumps, and pads.

At the start of 2008, 95 percent of baby bottles sold in the United States were made from polycarbonate, a rigid plastic.[2] The baby bottle market was considered mature, with top brands growing by taking market share from each other. The three leaders in the baby bottle market were Playtex, Novartis (with its Gerber brand), and Avent. Each company had its own line of baby bottles that had essentially remained unchanged for the past decade. Bottles were, on an average, priced between $6 and $12, depending on the features each one carried. One key development in this market had been the introduction of bottle liners, which were disposable plastic sleeves that lined the bottle. These liners were primarily meant to reduce the incidence of colic when feeding babies: Milk was poured into the sleeve and, as the baby consumed the milk, the sleeve contracted.

Manufacturers marketed their baby bottles by advertising in baby-focused magazines, sponsoring events or shows in the infant industry, and investing in trade promotions at the store level. In the United States, an annual marketing budget for one of the three leaders might be $5 million.

Large mass merchandisers generally purchased bottles directly from manufacturers, selecting three to four key brands to merchandise. These mass merchandisers typically sold a full range of consumer products—about 100,000 individual stock-keeping units (SKUs)—and carried baby products as part of their store's assortment. They operated on gross margins of about 30 percent, with the objective of being a "one-stop shop" for consumers. The mass merchandisers were chain stores, with a few hundred to several thousand locations across the country. Baby bottles that were sold at mass merchandisers ranged from entry level $3 bottles to mid-range $8 bottles.

Specialty stores focused on selling higher-end infant and toddler products, such as furniture, strollers, clothing, and accessories. These stores—at about one-tenth the size of a typical big-box store—usually stocked merchandise that was higher in price and quality compared to what was available at mass merchandisers. Staff members were usually very knowledgeable about products. There were perhaps 2,000 specialty stores across the United States, most of which were owner-operated. They worked on typical gross margins of 50 percent and focused on providing top-notch service. Baby bottles that were sold at specialty stores were usually a manufacturer's higher-end bottles and retailed for $10–$15.

Warehouse clubs—for example, Costco—tended to stock and sell merchandise in bulk. Their targets were the small business owners who would resell products in their stores. Warehouse clubs usually stacked their merchandise on wooden pallets in a large unadorned warehouse. They worked on gross margins of perhaps 8 percent to 10 percent, earning their profits from investing cash that was available because of the difference between when the stores collected funds (most consumers used debit cards or cash, which was available to warehouse clubs almost immediately) and when the payables were due (typical terms for suppliers were 45–60 days).

---

[1]Matthias Grossmann, Sarah Steimet, Austin Boyle, "Philips," WestLB Equity Research, 30 June 2006, p. 9.
[2]JPMA press release.

The baby bottle market changed dramatically in April 2008, when Canada banned the sale of polycarbonate bottles. Research had shown that a chemical, bisphenol-A (BPA), was leaching from polycarbonate bottles when they were heated. BPA is known as an endocrine disrupter that, in large amounts, can be harmful to humans.

As soon as the ban was announced, Canadian retailers were forced to clear their retail shelves of any baby bottles made of polycarbonate. Retail buyers, already on the alert for BPA-free bottles, started taking calls from nontraditional manufacturers who were offering BPA-free alternatives.

organicKidz

Walter's new business idea—stainless steel BPA-free baby bottles—came to her when she was on a shopping trip in preparation for a family visit. She wanted to give BPA-free baby bottles as gifts for her nieces and nephews, and when she could not find any on the store shelves, she started thinking about the opportunity to launch a new company. Since Walter came from a family of entrepreneurs, she was able to get a referral to a relative's connections at a Chinese factory that had the capability of producing steel bottles. She recalled, "I wanted to make the safest baby bottles in the world. They would be BPA-free and they would be shatterproof. I thought—what material is safer than stainless steel?"

Walter sketched out bottle designs, paid for molds to be built, and produced prototypes. In the early days, she worked through several setbacks as she tweaked the design of the bottles. Looking to promote her products, Walter signed up for the ABC Kids Expo in Las Vegas but was told that she was too late—the show was full. Determined to get into the show, she called repeatedly and finally secured a slot when another manufacturer cancelled. She shipped the bottles to the show but arrived to find that her samples were stuck in customs. Undeterred, she started the show with nothing more than a stand and some brochures. Walter's narrow-necked bottles, examples of which can be seen in Exhibit 1, retailed for $19.99 to $24.99. They came in different colors, such as pink, green, and blue. Walter's contribution rate was about $11.25 per bottle.

Walter was unprepared for the huge response that her products received; there was a frenzy of activity at her booth at all times. Buyers who were desperate for a BPA-free alternative were crowding her booth, even though she did not have any samples until two days into the event. All the major retailers—Target, WalMart, Kmart—came by, along with dozens of specialty stores. Distributors representing specialty stores from half a dozen different countries visited her booth as well.

Walter was glad to see the overwhelming response to her products, taking orders for $2,000 worth of bottles during the show alone. Walter elected to start marketing her products at specialty retailers. She signed with five distributors for sales in Europe and Asia, and she handled the North American orders on her own. She decided not to offer the same narrow-necked bottles to the mass merchandisers and hence declined their orders, stating that she would develop a different line of products for them.

From late 2008 to mid-2009, Walter sold approximately $15,000 worth of stainless steel bottles and expanded her distribution to 12 countries from 5. Her sales climbed from month to month, even as the global economy slipped into a recession. While she began operations by shipping all bottles from Calgary, by March 2009, she located a US warehouse from which she could ship bottles to US specialty stores.

By September 2009, Walter had upgraded her website (see Exhibit 2), won several industry awards, and sold a total of about 6,000 bottles for $65,000 in sales. At this rate, Walter was on track to reach $100,000 in sales by the end of 2009. To promote her bottles, she worked to be included in articles in baby magazines and attended consumer and retailer trade shows. Two of these shows were celebrity gifting shows, where she provided free product to celebrities.

Exhibit 1
organicKidz — Products

4 oz Durable single-hulled dark blue stainless steel baby bottle. The unique bottle design allows for easy heating and cooling of liquids. The lid is a 2 oz durable stainless steel design providing a built-in measuring cup. BPA, PVC, and phthalate free. Compatible with most narrow-necked nipples.

4 oz Dark Blue Baby Bottle #0048
US$19.99

7 oz Durable single-hulled green dots Stainless steel baby bottle. The unique bottle design allows for easy heating and cooling of liquids. The lid is 2 oz durable stainless steel design providing a built-in measuring cup. BPA, PVC, and phthalate free. Compatible with most narrow-necked nipples.

7 oz Green Dots Baby Bottle #0352
US$21.99

9 oz Durable vacuum-insulated Raspberry stainless steel baby bottle. The double-hulled bottle design **keeps liquids cool for 5-6 hours**. The lid is a 2 oz durable stainless steel design that doubles as a measuring cup. BPA, PVC, and phthalate free. Compatible with most narrow-necked nipples.

9 oz Raspberry Baby Bottle #0154
US$24.99

4 oz Wide-mouthed baby bottle. The unique bottle design allows for easy heating and cooling of liquids. The lid has a durable stainless steel design. BPA, PVC, and phthalate free. Compatible with most wide-mouthed nipples.

Available in 4 colours!

4 oz Wide-Mouthed Baby Bottles

9 oz Wide-mouthed red baby bottle.
The unique bottle design allows for easy heating and cooling of liquids. The lid has a durable stainless steel design. BPA, PVC, and phthalate free. Compatible with most wide mouthed nipples.

9 oz Red Wide-Mouthed Baby Bottle #0543

Your **organicKidz™** baby bottle can grow with your child! Turn your **organicKidz™** narrow-necked baby bottle into a sippy cup!

Sippy Spouts and Handles are available in all 6 **organicKidz™** colours and fit all 4, 7, and 9 oz **organicKidz™** Narrow Necked Baby Bottles.

Sippy Cu   Conversion

Source: Company files

Exhibit 2
organicKidz — Website

Organic Kidz

BROWSE BY CATEGORIES

-→ 4oz Narrow Necked Baby Bottles
-→ 7oz Narrow Necked Baby Bottles
-→ 9oz Narrow Necked Baby Bottles
-→ Wide Mouthed Baby Bottles
-→ Accessories
-→ **Shopping Cart**

INFORMATION

- **About Us**
- **Retail Sales**
- **FAQ's**
- **organicKidz™ on YouTube**
- **Our Friends**
- **Where We Are**
- **Stainless Steel & BPA**
- **facebook**
- **Our Brochure**
- **Baby Bottle Care Guide**

Welcome To organicKidz™!

Our Stainless Steel Baby Bottles are a safe and practical alternative to plastic, aluminum and glass drinking containers. Made with kids and parents in mind, they are easy to hold and hard to damage.

organicKidz™ Stainless Steel Baby Bottles:

- 4 and 7oz Narrow Necked single hulled bottles for easy warming
- 9oz Narrow Necked vacuum insulated bottles so liquids keep cold for 5-6 hours
- 4oz and 9oz Wide Mouthed single hulled bottles available
- 2oz lid for easy measuring
- BPA, PVC and Phthalate free
- Compatible with most narrow necked nipples
- Light weight and dishwasher safe
- Unbreakable and dent resistant
- Our products are packaged in environmentally friendly, recyclable cardboard

Our goal is to provide you with healthy and safe choices that are flexible and do not impact your lifestyle.

Source: http://www.organickidz.ca/index.php

Walter invested another $5,000 in molds and design work to develop a second line of baby bottles—wide-mouthed versions (see Exhibit 1)—to be sold at mass merchandisers. The wide-mouthed bottles had the same margin structure as the narrow-necked versions, but they retailed for $15 to $18. At that price range, Walter's contribution would average $9.45 per bottle. She was excited about the prospects of generating high growth from her two lines of products.

One issue that Walter had to address concerned her inventory levels. As orders increased, she wondered how much inventory of each stock keeping unit (SKU) she should be holding in her Canadian and US warehouses. Adding a second line would definitely increase the amount of product being stockpiled, and Walter wondered whether it would make sense to hold a few hundred or even a few thousand bottles at any given time. There were about eight different styles per SKU.

In addition to working on organicKidz, Walter had designed a line of children's jackets, and she was thinking of starting her own distribution firm to place unique products at North American specialty stores.

At the ABC Kids Expo in September 2009, Walter announced the launch of her second line of bottles. Retailer interest remained very high, and Walter took orders for about $10,000 worth of wide-mouthed bottles. On September 13, 2009, the buyer for Costco dropped by the booth, wanting to know whether Walter would sell her baby bottles in a selection of Costco's 413 US warehouse stores. The initial order could be for $20,000 to $40,000.

Walter's Dilemma

At first, Walter was delighted by the Costco offer since it had the potential of vaulting her company's sales to a different level. While the buyer did not state an amount for the purchase order, Walter could guess that if the initial order sold well, a subsequent order could be for as many as 45,000 bottles—or nearly $400,000 in sales to organicKidz. This would be more than twice her cumulative sales since starting the company. Consistent orders from Costco would mean that Walter could invest in her product lineup, pay off loans, and put in place an advertising strategy that would involve the development of web- or TV-ready commercials, a magazine advertising budget, and perhaps even a few event sponsorships. She could start to hire a staff to manage details such as billing and shipping. Two or three consecutive sales to Costco could result in a large return for organicKidz.

On the other hand, Walter thought about the 100 different specialty stores and five mass-merchandiser accounts that currently sold her merchandise. A sale to Costco would draw negative reactions from her existing customer base since Costco would likely price even the lower-end bottle at about $10 or less. Managing the backlash could be difficult, and there was also the potential of being delisted.

Walter wondered whether Costco's offer to purchase her bottles was a one-time deal or whether it suggested that Costco might be willing to feature her items regularly. If the product did well at the store level, there was a high possibility that Costco could reorder. If this was a one-time purchase, however, Walter was worried that the negative reaction from her existing clients would outweigh any monetary benefits to be gained. How should she respond to the Costco buyer?

18

The Challenges Facing eBay in 2008: Time for a Change in Strategy?

Louis Marino *University of Alabama*

Patrick Kreiser *Ohio University*

On January 23, 2008, eBay announced that Meg Whitman would step down as president and CEO as of March 31, 2008. When Whitman joined eBay in 1998, the company had revenues of $86 million and employed just 30 people. After a decade of impressive growth fueled by international expansion, acquisition of new businesses, and internal growth, by 2008 eBay employed 15,000 people and had revenues of over $5.9 billion. Despite this growth, eBay's new president and CEO, John Donahoe, faced several significant challenges.

The most significant challenge facing Donahoe was the slowing growth in eBay's core business of online auctions. Donahoe had served as president of eBay Marketplaces, the division that includes online auctions and eBay's other e-commerce businesses, since 2005. In that time, despite several acquisitions such as StubHub.com, an online ticket marketplace, that diversified eBay's revenues in its Marketplaces division, the percentage of eBay's total revenues that came from this key division fell from 72 to 56 percent. This slowing growth in the company's core division was highlighted by a 1 percent decrease in gross merchandise volume, a measure of total sales, in the third quarter of 2008 as compared to sales in the third quarter of 2007 and a declining growth rate in the number of registered users, as can be seen in Exhibit 1.

There was also a significant concern that eBay's 2006 acquisition of Skype, an online communications service, had not produced the intended results. Specifically, although Skype's considerable revenue growth had contributed to eBay's ability to reach its revenue targets, eBay had never been able to meaningfully integrate Skype into is core operations and to capture the synergies that had provided the original justification for acquisition. Additionally, in late 2007 eBay had to take a $900 million writedown in the value of Skype,

EXHIBIT 1　Selected Indicators of eBay's Growth, 1998–2007 (all figures are in millions)

	2000	2001	2002	2003	2004	2005	2006	2007	2008 Partial Year[†]
Registered users	22.0	42.4	61.7	94.9	135.5	180.6	221.6	276.3	370.2
Active users*	NA	18.0	27.7	41.2	56.1	71.8	81.8	83.2	85.7
Gross merchandise sales	$5,400	$9,300	$14,900	$24,000	$34,200	$44,299	$52,474	$59,353	$46,004
Number of auctions listed	264	423	638	971	1,412.6	1,876.8	2,365.3	2,340.5	2,015

*Defined as a user who has bid on, bought, or listed an item during the most recent 12-month period.
[†]Totals as of September 30, 2008, based on third-quarter results, as posted in third-quarter report.

indicating that the company had significantly overpaid in the 2005 acquisition. When asked about Skype's fit with eBay's business model, eBay's newly appointed president, John Donahoe, said, "What we're about this year are the synergies. If the synergies are strong, we'll keep it in our portfolio, if not, we'll reassess it."[1]

Finally, heading into the holiday season of 2008, traditionally eBay's strongest quarter, net transaction revenues in eBay's core Marketplaces division, which included online auctions, were down 6 percent from the second quarter of 2007. Company executives predicted that this weakness would continue and that the fourth quarter of 2008 was likely to be the weakest quarter of the year. Donahoe attributed this poor performance to weakness in key economies across the globe, but some analysts and eBay customers believed it was indicative of deeper problems, including an erosion of eBay's core customer base and a loss of the company's innovative capabilities. In response to a series of changes eBay made between 2007 and 2008, one seller who had been with eBay since 2001 stated, "They've forgotten the base of their operation—the sellers. . . . It's not a fair selling venue anymore."[2] Additionally, analysts were concerned that the company's innovative culture, one of the keys to the company's early success, had eroded to the extent that some eBay employees were referring to the company as "the IBM of Silicon Valley"—an uncomplimentary reference to the stifling bureaucracy that now permeated the company. In describing how eBay would go about sustaining its growth and profitability, Donahoe said, "We will continue to stay focused on connecting consumers on our various e-commerce platforms, maintaining financial discipline, and capitalizing on new opportunities for growth."

However, analysts were not convinced that eBay could recover its dominance in the online auction industry given the projected weakness in the global economy. Further, a report by David Joseph, an investment analyst from Morgan Stanley, reported that eBay's share of the U.S. e-commerce market had fallen from 19 percent to 17 percent between 2006 and 2008, while Amazon.com's share rose from 3.7 percent to 5.3 percent over the same time period. As a reflection of these concerns, between November 2007 and November 2008, eBay's stock price dropped by more than 50 percent from its 52-week high of $35.98 to close at $15.01 on November 3, 2008. Additionally, there were significant concerns as to whether Donahoe was suited to lead eBay's turnaround. Following an announcement that eBay would lay off 10 percent of its workforce, Donahoe's CEO approval rating on Glassdoor.com, a Web site that allows employees to rate their CEOs, fell to 22 percent. Whitman's was 75 percent

[1]Richard Waters, "eBay ready to Sell Skype If Strong Synergies Prove Elusive," *Financial Times,* April 18, 2008, www.ft.com/cms/s/0/13482a26-0ce1-11dd-86df-0000779fd2ac.html?nclick_check=1 (accessed November 1, 2008).

[2]E. Maltby, "Has eBay Hit Its Twilight?" Money.cnn.com, October 17, 2008 (accessed October 28, 2008).

when she retired, with one employee saying, "Donahoe has made eBay a miserable debacle and it's getting worse every day. . . . I never thought I would say this, but I miss Meg! Come back Meg!!!!!"[3]

THE GROWTH OF E-COMMERCE AND ONLINE AUCTIONS

The fundamental concepts underlying the Internet were first conceived in the 1960s, but it wasn't until the 1990s that the Internet garnered widespread use and became a part of everyday life. The International Data Corporation (IDC), a leading Internet analysis firm, estimated that in 2008 there were approximately 1.4 billion Internet users worldwide and that that number would grow to 1.9 billion users worldwide by 2012. Additionally, it was predicted that almost half of Internet users would make online purchases in 2008. Internationally, Asia had the most Internet users, with more than 550 million in 2008, followed by Europe with more than 380 million, and North America with approximately 250 million. It was estimated that the United States alone accounted for approximately 220 million Internet users and that over 70 percent of the U.S. population used the Internet. However, the highest areas of Internet usage growth were expected to be in developing countries where Internet penetration was currently low, such as Asia, Latin America, and Eastern Europe due to increasing access through new technologies such as Web-enabled cell phones. Further, IDC predicted that by 2012 the number of users accessing the Internet from mobile devices such as phones would surpass the number accessing it from personal computers.

In 2007, according to Forrester Research, online retail sales in the United States increased by 21 percent over 2006, to $175 billion. Forrester predicted that the growth rate in online retail sales would continue to slow, dropping from 17 percent in 2008 to 11 percent in 2012; Forrester's forecast called for online sales in the U.S. to grow about $30 billion annually and reach a total of $335 billion by 2012. Internationally, IDC estimated that roughly 1.4 billion people used the Internet regularly, and the number of Internet users was expected to grow to 30 percent of the world's population, or 1.9 billion, by 2012. Further, IDC predicted that nearly 1 billion of these users would make purchases online in 2012 for a total of $1.2 trillion. However, it was estimated that business-to-business e-commerce would be 10 times larger, for a total of $12.4 trillion in 2012.

KEY SUCCESS FACTORS IN ONLINE RETAILING

While it was relatively easy to create a Web site that functioned like a retail store, the more significant challenge was for an online retailer to generate traffic to the site in the form of both new and returning customers. To reach new customers some online retailers partnered with shopping search engines (such as www.google.com, www.mysimon.com, or www.streetprices.com) that allowed customers to compare prices for a given product from many retailers. Other tactics employed to build traffic included direct e-mail, online advertising at portals and content-related sites, and some traditional advertising such as print and television. Most online retailers endeavored to set up their Web site so as to provide customers with extensive product information, include pictures of the merchandise, make the site easily navigable, and have enough new things happening at the site to keep customers coming back. (A site's ability to generate repeat visitors was known as "stickiness.") Retailers also had to overcome new Internet users' nervousness about using the Internet

[3]Blog poster "Software Engineer in San Jose," GlassDoor.com, http://blog.glassdoor.com/2008/10/07/ebay-layoffs-%e2%80%93-is-donahoe-next/ (accessed on November 4, 2008).

itself to shop for items they generally bought in stores. Web sites had to appease concerns regarding entering credit card numbers over the Internet and the possible sale of personal information to marketing firms. Online retailing had severe limitations in the case of those goods and services people wanted to see in person to verify their quality. From the retailer's perspective, there was the issue of collecting payment from buyers who wanted to use checks or money orders instead of credit cards.

ONLINE AUCTIONS

The first known auctions in history were held in Babylon around 500 BC. In AD 193, the entire Roman Empire was put up for auction after the emperor Pertinax was executed. Didius Julianus bid 6,250 drachmas per royal guard and was immediately named emperor of Rome. However, Julianus was executed only two months later, suggesting that he may have been the first-ever victim of the winner's curse (bidding more than the good would cost in a non-auction setting).

Auctions have endured throughout history for several reasons. First, they give sellers a convenient way to find a buyer for something they would like to dispose of. Second, auctions are an excellent way for people to collect difficult-to-find items, such as Beanie Babies or historical memorabilia that have a high value to them personally. Finally, auctions are one of the "purest" markets that exist for goods, in that they bring buyers and sellers into contact to arrive at a mutually agreeable price. As technological advances led to the advent and widespread adoption of the Internet, this ancient form of trade found a new medium.

Online auctions worked in essentially the same way as traditional auctions, the difference being that the auction process occurred over the Internet rather than at a specific geographic location with buyers and sellers physically present. There were three basic categories of online auctions:

1. Business-to-business auctions, typically involving equipment and surplus merchandise.
2. Business-to-consumer auctions, in which businesses sold goods and services to consumers via the Internet. Many such auctions involved companies interested in selling used or discontinued goods, or liquidating unwanted inventory.
3. Person-to-person auctions, which gave interested sellers and buyers the opportunity to engage in competitive bidding.

Online auction operators could generate revenue in four principal ways:

1. Charging sellers for listing their good or service.
2. Charging a commission on all sales.
3. Selling advertising on their Web sites.
4. Selling their own new or used merchandise via the online auction format.

More recently, however, the new revenue-generation option that was growing the most quickly was one that allowed buyers to purchase the desired good without waiting for an auction to close:

5. Selling their own goods or allowing other sellers to offer their goods in a fixed-price format.

Most sites charged sellers either a fee or a commission and sold advertising to companies interested in promoting their goods or services to users of the auction site.

Online Auction Users

Participants in online auctions could be grouped into six categories: (1) bargain hunters, (2) hobbyist/collector buyers, (3) professional buyers, (4) casual sellers, (5) hobbyist/collector sellers, and (6) corporate and power sellers.

Bargain Hunters

Bargain hunters viewed online auctions primarily as a form of entertainment; their objective usually was to find a great deal. Bargain hunters were thought to make up only 8 percent of active online users but 52 percent of eBay visitors. To attract repeat visits from bargain hunters, industry observers said sites must appeal to them on both rational and emotional levels, satisfying their need for competitive pricing, the excitement of the search, and the desire for community.

Hobbyist/Collector Buyers

Hobbyists and collectors used auctions to search for specific goods that had a high value to them personally. They were very concerned with both price and quality. Collectors prized eBay for its wide variety of product offerings.

Professional Buyers

As the legitimacy of online auctions grew, a new type of buyer began to emerge: the professional buyer. Professional buyers covered a broad range of purchasers, from purchasing managers acquiring office supplies to antique and gun dealers purchasing inventory. Like bargain hunters, professional buyers were looking for a way to help contain costs; also, like hobbyists and collectors, some professional buyers were seeking unique items to supplement their inventory. The primary difference between professional buyers and other types, however, was their affiliation with commercial enterprises. With the growth of online auction sites dedicated to business-to-business auctions, professional buyers were becoming an increasingly important element of the online auction landscape.

Casual Sellers

Casual sellers included individuals who used eBay as a substitute for a classified ad listing or a garage sale to dispose of items they no longer wanted. While many casual sellers listed only a few items, some used eBay to raise money for some new project.

Hobbyist/Collector Sellers

Sellers who were hobbyists or collectors typically dealt in a limited category of goods and looked to eBay as a way to sell selected items in their collections to others who might want them. Items ranged from classic television collectibles, to hand-sewn dolls, to coins and stamps. The hobbyists and collectors used a range of traditional and online outlets to reach their target markets. A number of the sellers used auctions to supplement their retail operations, while others sold exclusively through online auctions and on fixed-price sites such as Half.com.

Corporate and Power Sellers

Corporate and power sellers were typically individuals and small to medium-sized businesses that favored eBay as a primary distribution channel for their goods and often sold tens of thousands of dollars' worth of goods every month on the site. To achieve "PowerSeller" status on eBay, an individual had to meet minimum average sales requirements ($1,000 a month for 3 months or 100 items a month, or $12,000 a year or 1,200 items for the prior 12 months), have a feedback rating of at least 100 (98 percent of which had to be positive), and continue to maintain the minimum average monthly sales volume requirements. Some estimates indicated that PowerSellers accounted for over 80 percent of eBay's total business. Individuals who were PowerSellers could often make a full-time job of the endeavor.

As with the evolution of buyers, commercial enterprises were becoming an increasingly important part of the online auction industry. These commercial enterprises generally achieved PowerSeller status relatively rapidly. On eBay, for example, some of the new PowerSellers were familiar names such as IBM, Compaq, and the U.S. Post Office (which sells undeliverable items on eBay under the user name "usps-mrc").

PIERRE OMIDYAR AND THE FOUNDING OF EBAY

Pierre Omidyar was born in Paris, France, to parents who had left Iran decades earlier. The family emigrated to the United States when Pierre's father began a residency at Johns Hopkins University Medical Center. Pierre Omidyar attended Tufts University, where he met his future wife, Pamela Wesley, who came to Tufts from Hawaii to get a degree in biology. Upon graduating in 1988, the couple moved to California, where Omidyar, who had earned a bachelor's degree in computer science, joined Claris, an Apple Computer subsidiary in Silicon Valley, and wrote a widely used graphics application, MacDraw. In 1991, Omidyar left Claris and co-founded Ink Development (later renamed eShop), which became a pioneer in online shopping and was eventually sold to Microsoft in 1996. In 1994, Omidyar joined General Magic as a developer services engineer and remained there until mid-1996, when he left to pursue full-time development of eBay.

Internet folklore has it that eBay was founded solely to allow Pamela to trade Pez dispensers with other collectors. While Pamela was certainly a driving force in launching the initial Web site, Pierre had long been interested in how one could establish a marketplace to bring together a fragmented market. In 1995, he launched the first online auction under the name of Auctionwatch at the domain name of www.eBay.com with the intention of creating a person-to-person trading community based on a democratized, efficient market where everyone could have equal access through the same medium, the Internet. The name *eBay* stood for "electronic Bay area," coined because Pierre's initial concept was to attract neighbors and other interested San Francisco Bay area residents to the site to buy and sell items of mutual interest. The first auctions charged no fees to either buyers or sellers and contained mostly computer equipment (and no Pez dispensers). Pierre's fledgling venture generated $1,000 in revenue the first month and an additional $2,000 the second. Traffic grew rapidly, however, as word about the site spread in the Bay area, a community of collectors emerged, using the site to trade and chat—there were even some marriages that resulted from exchanges in eBay chat rooms.[4]

By February 1996, the traffic at Pierre Omidyar's site had grown so much that his Internet service provider informed him that he would have to upgrade his service. When Omidyar compensated for this by charging a listing fee for the auction, and saw no decrease in the number of items listed, he knew he was on to something. Although he was still working out of his home, Omidyar began looking for a partner and in May asked his friend Jeffrey Skoll to join him in the venture. While Skoll had never cared much about money, his Stanford MBA degree provided the firm with the business background that Omidyar lacked. With Omidyar as the visionary and Skoll as the strategist, the company embarked on a mission to "help people trade practically anything on earth." Their concept for eBay was to "create a place where people could do business just like in the old days—when everyone got to know each other personally, and we all felt we were dealing on a one-to-one basis with individuals we could trust."

[4]Quentin Hardy, "The Radical Philanthropist," *Forbes,* May 1, 2000, p. 118.

In eBay's early days, Pierre Omidyar and Jeff Skoll ran the operation alone, using a single computer to serve all of the pages. Omidyar served as CEO, chief financial officer, and president, while Skoll functioned as co-president and director. It was not long until the partners grew the company to a size that forced them to move out of Pierre's living room, due to the objections of Pamela, and into Jeff's living room. Shortly thereafter, the operations moved into the facilities of a Silicon Valley business incubator for a time until the company settled in its current facilities in San Jose, California. Exhibits 2 and 3 present eBay's recent financial statements.

EBAY'S TRANSITION TO PROFESSIONAL MANAGEMENT

From the beginning, Pierre Omidyar intended to hire a professional manager to serve as the president of eBay: "[I would] let him or her run the company so . . . [I could] go play."[5] In 1997, both Omidyar and Skoll agreed that it was time to locate an experienced professional to function as CEO and president. In late 1997, eBay's headhunters came up with a candidate for the job: Margaret (Meg) Whitman, then general manager for Hasbro Inc.'s preschool division. Whitman had received her BA in economics from Princeton and her MBA from the Harvard Business School; her first job was in brand management at Procter & Gamble. Her experience also included serving as the president and CEO of FTD, as the president of Stride Rite Corporation's Stride Rite Division, and as the senior vice president of marketing for the Walt Disney Company's consumer products division.

When first approached by eBay, Whitman was not especially interested in joining a company that had fewer than 40 employees and less than $6 million in revenues the previous year. It was only after repeated pleas that Whitman agreed to meet with Omidyar in Silicon Valley. After a second meeting, Whitman realized the company's enormous growth potential and agreed to give eBay a try. According to Omidyar, Meg Whitman's experience in global marketing with Hasbro's Teletubbies, Playskool, and Mr. Potato Head brands made her "the ideal choice to build upon eBay's leadership position in the one-to-one online trading market without sacrificing the quality and personal touch our users have grown to expect."[6] In addition to convincing Whitman to head eBay's operations, Omidyar had been instrumental in helping bring in other talented senior executives and in assembling a capable board of directors. Notable members of eBay's board of directors included Scott Cook, the founder of Intuit, a highly successful financial software company, and Fred D. Anderson, executive vice president and chief financial officer of Apple.

On January 23, 2008, with slowing growth in eBay's core auction division, the company announced that, after a decade as CEO, Meg Whitman would step down but would remain on the company's board of directors. Whitman was succeeded by John Donahoe, who had joined eBay in 2005 from the consulting firm Bain & Co., where he had worked with Whitman. Since joining the firm in 2005, Donahoe had served as president of eBay's Marketplaces division and had been instrumental in a number of major initiatives that were helping eBay transition from a simple auction business to a portfolio of retail sites. These initiatives included the acquisition of StubHub; the launch of eBay Express, a site featuring new merchandise; and the introduction of online advertising through partnerships with Yahoo and Google. In taking the helm of the company, Donahoe noted that he

---

[5]"Billionaires of the Web," *Business 2.0,* June 1999.
[6]eBay press release, May 7, 1998.

EXHIBIT 2 eBay's Income Statements, 2000–2007 ($ in thousands, except per share figures)

	2000	2001	2002	2003	2004	2005	2006	2007
Net revenues	$431,424	$748,821	$1,214,100	$2,165,096	$3,271,309	$4,552,401	$5,969,741	$7,672,329
Cost of net revenues	95,453	134,816	213,876	416,058	614,415	818,104	1,256,792	1,762,972
Gross profit	335,971	614,005	1,000,224	1,749,038	2,656,894	3,734,297	4,712,949	5,909,357
Operating expenses:								
Sales and marketing	166,767	253,474	349,650	567,565	857,874	1,185,929	1,619,857	1,925,393
Product development	55,863	75,288	104,636	159,315	240,647	328,191	494,695	619,727
General and administrative	73,027	105,784	171,785	304,703	415,725	649,529	978,363	1,156,015
Patent litigation expense	—	—	—	29,965	17,479	—	—	—
Payroll taxes on stock options	2,337	2,442	4,015	9,590				
Amortization of acquired intangibles	1,443	36,591	15,941	50,659	65,927	128,941	197,078	204,104
Impairment of goodwill								1,390,938
Merger related costs	1,550	—	—					
Total operating expenses	300,977	473,579	646,027	1,119,797	1,597,652	2,292,590	3,289,993	5,296,177
Income (loss) from operations	34,994	140,426	354,197	629,241	1,059,242	1,441,707	1,422,956	613,180
Interest and other income (expense), net	46,337	41,613	49,209	37,803	77,867	111,099	130,017	154,271
Interest expense	(3,374)	(2,851)	(1,492)	(4,314)	(8,879)	(3,478)	(5,916)	(16,600)
Impairment of certain equity investments	0	(16,245)	(3,781)	(1,230)	—	—	—	—
Income before income taxes and minority interest	77,957	162,943	398,133	661,500	1,128,230	1,549,328	1,547,057	750,851
Provision for income taxes	(32,725)	(80,009)	(145,946)	(206,738)	(343,885)	(467,285)	(421,418)	(402,600)
Minority interests in consolidated companies	3,062	7,514	(2,296)	(7,578)	(6,122)	—	—	—
Net income	$ 48,294	$ 90,448	$ 249,891	$ 447,184	$ 778,223	$ 1,082,043	$1,125,639	$ 348,251
Net income per share:								
Basic	$0.19	$0.34	$0.43	$0.69	$0.59	$0.79	$0.80	$0.26
Diluted	$0.17	0.32	$0.43	$0.67	$0.57	$0.78	$0.79	$0.25
Weighted average shares:								
Basic	251,776	268,971	574,992	638,288	1,319,458	1,361,708	1,399,251	1,358,797
Diluted	280,346	280,595	585,640	656,657	1,367,720	1,393,875	1,425,472	1,376,174

Source: Company financial documents.

EXHIBIT 3 eBay's Consolidated Balance Sheets, 2000–2007 ($ in thousands)

	12/31/00	12/31/01	12/31/02	12/31/03	12/31/04	12/31/05	12/31/06	12/31/07
ASSETS								
Current assets:								
Cash and cash equivalents	$ 201,873	$ 523,969	$1,109,313	$1,381,513	$1,330,045	$2,180,598	$ 2,662,792	$ 4,221,191
Short-term investments	354,166	199,450	89,690	340,576	682,004	888,783	554,841	676,264
Accounts receivable, net	67,163	101,703	131,453	225,871	240,856	274,238	393,195	480,557
Funds receivable	—	—	41,014	79,893	123,424	210,593	399,297	427,337
Other current assets	52,262	58,683	96,988	118,029	534,820	436,781	960,461	1,317,156
Total current assets	675,464	883,805	1,468,458	2,145,882	2,911,149	3,990,993	4,970,586	7,122,505
Long-term investments	—	286,998	470,227	934,171	1,266,289	827,191	277,853	138,237
Restricted cash and investments	—	129,614	134,644	127,432	1,418	—	—	—
Property and equipment, net	125,161	142,349	218,028	601,785	709,773	762,413	998,196	1,120,452
Goodwill	—	187,829	1,456,024	1,719,311	2,709,794	3,529,895	6,544,278	6,257,153
Investments	—	—	—	—	—	—	—	—
Deferred tax assets	—	21,540	84,218	—	—	—	—	—
Intangible and other assets, net	23,299	26,394	292,845	291,553	392,628	515,551	682,977	596,038
	$1,182,403	$1,678,529	$4,040,226	$5,820,134	$7,991,051	$9,626,043	$13,494,011	$15,366,037
LIABILITIES AND SHAREHOLDERS' EQUITY								
Current liabilities:								
Accounts payable	$ 31,725	$ 33,235	$ 47,424	$ 64,633	$ 37,958	$ 42,726	$ 83,392	$ 156,613
Funds payable and amounts due to customers	—	—	50,396	106,568	331,805	517,309	1,159,952	1,513,578
Accrued expenses and other current liabilities	60,882	94,593	199,323	356,491	421,969	523,584	681,669	1,151,139
Deferred revenue and customer advances	12,656	15,583	18,846	28,874	50,439	44,222	128,964	166,495
Debt and leases, current portion	15,272	16,111	2,970	2,840	124,272	—	—	—
Income taxes payable	11,092	20,617	67,265	87,870	118,427	138,951	464,418	111,754
Deferred tax liabilities, current	—	—	—	—	—	—	—	—
Other current liabilities	5,815	—	—	—	—	—	—	—
Total current liabilities	137,442	180,139	386,224	647,276	1,084,870	1,266,792	2,518,395	3,099,579
Debt and leases, long-term portion	11,404	12,008	13,798	124,476	75	—	—	—
Deferred tax liabilities, long-term	—	3,629	27,625	79,238	135,971	298,197	31,784	510,557
Other liabilities	6,549	15,864	22,874	33,494	37,698	33,690	39,200	51,299
Minority interests	—	37,751	33,232	39,408	4,096	—	—	—
Total liabilities	168,643	249,391	483,753	923,892	1,262,710	1,598,679	2,589,379	3,661,435
Total stockholders' equity	1,013,760	1,429,138	3,556,473	4,896,242	6,728,341	8,027,364	10,904,632	11,704,602
	$1,182,403	$1,678,529	$4,124,444	$5,820,134	$7,991,051	$9,626,043	$13,494,011	$15,366,037

Source: Company financial documents.

was "a big fan of breaking patterns,"[7] and one of the first initiatives he announced was an effort to leverage the internal data eBay had from its auctions and from its PayPal transactions to enhance the precision of eBay's internal search engine to help buyers locate items more efficiently. Perhaps more striking and controversial was Donahoe's introduction of a fee structure that shifted the cost from the initial listing to a fee based on the final value of the item sold and a fundamental change in eBay's feedback system that would no longer allow sellers to leave negative, or even neutral, feedback for buyers.

HOW AN EBAY AUCTION WORKED

The mission of eBay was to make it very simple for people to buy and sell goods. In order to sell or bid on goods, users first had to register at the site. Once they registered, users selected both a user name and a password. Unregistered users were able to browse the Web site but were not permitted to bid on any goods or list any items for auction.

On the Web site, search engines helped customers determine what goods were currently available. When registered users found an item they desired, they could choose to enter a single bid or to use automatic bidding (called proxy bidding). In automatic bidding, the customer entered an initial bid sufficient to become the high bidder; the bid would be automatically increased as others bid for the same object until the auction ended and either the bidder won or another bidder surpassed the original customer's maximum specified bid. Regardless of which bidding method they chose, users could check bids at any time and either bid again, if they had been outbid, or increase their maximum amount in the automatic bid. Users could choose to receive e-mail notification if they were outbid.

Once the auction had ended, the buyer and seller were each notified of the winning bid and were given each other's e-mail address. The parties to the auction would then privately arrange for payment and delivery of the good and in doing so were encouraged to use eBay's payment processing division, PayPal, and to ship their goods through partnerships eBay had with the U.S. Postal Service and major shipping companies. To encourage sellers to use eBay's ancillary services, the company offered an automated checkout service to help expedite communication, payment, and delivery between buyers and sellers.

Under the terms of eBay's user agreement, if a seller received one or more bids above the stated minimum, or reserve, price, the seller was obligated to complete the transaction, although eBay had no enforcement power beyond suspending a noncompliant buyer or seller from using eBay's service. In the event that the buyer and seller were unable to complete the transaction, the seller notified eBay, which then credited the seller the amount of the final value fee.

Fees and Procedures for Sellers

Buyers on eBay were not charged a fee for bidding on items on the site, but the total fee paid by sellers included an insertion fee and a "final value" fee; sellers could also elect to pay additional fees to promote their listing. Listing, or insertion, fees differed depending on the selling format (auction or fixed-price) and the type of merchandise being sold; fees were lower for books, music, DVDs and movies, and video games than for other items. Insertion fees ranged from \$0.10 for auctions with opening bids, minimum values, or reserve prices of between \$0.01 and \$0.99, to \$4.00 for auctions with opening bids, minimum values, or reserve prices of \$500 and up.

---

[7]Brad Stone, "Ebay President Is 'A Big Fan of Breaking Patterns,'" *International Herald Tribune*, February 20, 2007.

Final value fees were computed according to a graduated fee schedule in which the percentage fell as the final sales price rose:

Value of Auction	Final Value Fee
Below $25.00	8.75 percent
Between $25.01 and $1,000	8.75 percent of the first $25.00 plus 3.5 percent of the amount between $25.01 and $1,000.00
Over $1,000	8.75 percent of the first $25.00, plus 3.5 percent of the amount between $25.01 and $1,000 plus 1.5 percent of the amount over $1,000

As an example, in a basic auction with no promotion, if the item had a starting price of $500.00 and eventually sold for $1,500, the total fee paid by the seller would be $47.81—the $4.00 insertion fee plus $43.81. This amount was based on a fee structure of 8.75 percent of the first $25 (or $2.19), 3.5 percent of the additional amount between $25.01 and $1,000 (or $34.12), and 1.5 percent of the additional amount between $1,000.01 and $1,500 (or $7.50).

Auction fees varied for special categories of goods. For example, passenger vehicles in eBay Motors were charged a $125 transaction fee when the first successful bid was placed but only $10.00 for power sports vehicles under 50 cc, and a $100 insertion fee for residential and commercial vehicles. In real estate, timeshare properties were charged an insertion fee of $35.00 for auction-style listings or fixed-price listings of up to 10 days and a final value fee of $35.00, while residential and commercial real estate was charged an insertion fee of between $100 and $300 based on the auction style and duration, but no final value fee was charged. For fixed-price sales, a format that allowed sellers to set a specific price for their goods similar to a more traditional retail format, the insertion fees were lower than those for the auction format, capping out at $0.35, but the percentages for final value fees were generally higher, ranging from 6 percent for the first $50 of computers and networking equipment to 15 percent for the first $50 of books, music, DVDs, and video games.

Sellers could also customize items by adding photographs and featuring their item in a gallery. Sellers could upload a photograph to include in the item's description, and items could be showcased in the Gallery section with a catalog of pictures rather than text. Sellers could either include a Gallery picture at no cost, pay an additional $24.95 to ensure that their auction would be listed on the first page of search results, or have their auction featured on eBay's home page for $59.95. The cost to list real estate on the Real Estate home page was also $59.95, but listing a vehicle on eBay Motors' home page cost $99.95.

To make doing business on eBay more attractive to potential sellers, eBay introduced several features. To ensure receiving a minimum price for an auction, the seller could specify an opening bid or set a reserve price. If the bidding did not top the reserve price, the seller was under no obligation to sell the item to the highest bidder and could relist the item free. For items with a reserve price between $0.01 and $199.99, the fee was $2.00; for items over $200, the fee was 1 percent of the reserve price, up to $50. If sellers wished, they could also set a "Buy It Now" price that allowed bidders to pay a set amount for a listed item. The fee for this service ranged from $0.05 for goods with a Buy It Now price for $1.00–$9.99 to $0.25 for a Buy It Now price of over $50. If the Buy It Now price was met, the auction would end immediately.

To register at eBay, sellers were required to provide both a credit card number and bank account information. While eBay acknowledged that these requirements were extreme, the company argued that they helped protect everyone in the community against fraudulent sellers and ensured that sellers were of legal age and were serious about listing the item on eBay.

Fostering Community Affinity

From its founding, eBay considered developing a loyal, vivacious trading community to be a cornerstone of its business model. This community was nurtured through open and honest communication and was built on five basic values that eBay expected its members to honor:

> We believe people are basically good.
>
> We believe everyone has something to contribute.
>
> We believe that an honest, open environment can bring out the best in people.
>
> We recognize and respect everyone as a unique individual.
>
> We encourage you to treat others the way that you want to be treated.[8]

The company recognized that these values could not be imposed by fiat. According to Omidyar, "As much as we at eBay talk about the values and encourage people to live by those values, that's not going to work unless people actually adopt those values. The values are communicated not because somebody reads the Web site and says, 'Hey, this is how we want to treat each other, so I'll just start treating people that way.' The values are communicated because that's how they're treated when they first arrive. Each member is passing those values on to the next member. It's little things, like you receive a note that says, 'Thanks for your business.'"[9] Consistent with eBay's desire to stay in touch with its customers and be responsive to their needs, the company flies in 10 new sellers every few months to hold group meetings known as Voice of the Customer. Another indication of eBay's responsiveness is that 75–80 percent of new features are originally suggested by community members.

To foster a sense of community among eBay users, the company employed tools and tactics designed to promote both business and personal interactions between consumers, to foster trust between bidders and sellers, and to instill a sense of security among traders. Interactions between community members were facilitated through the creation of chat rooms based on personal interests. These chat rooms allowed individuals to learn about their chosen collectibles and to exchange information about items they collected.

To manage the flow of information in the chat rooms, eBay employees went to trade shows and conventions to seek out individuals who had knowledge about and a passion for either a specific collectible or a category of goods. These enthusiasts would act as group leaders or ambassadors.

Feedback Forum

Although personal communication between members fostered a sense of community, as eBay's community grew from "the size of a small village to a large city" additional measures were necessary to ensure a continued sense of trust and honesty among users.[10] One of eBay's primary trust-building mechanisms was the Feedback Forum. The Feedback Forum was designed to build trust among buyers and sellers and to facilitate the establishment of reputations within its community. Feedback Forum encouraged individuals to record comments about their trading partners. From the time the Feedback Forum was originally implemented in 1996 until May 2008, both the buyer and seller were allowed to leave positive, negative, or neutral comments about each other. Individuals could dispute feedback left about them by annotating comments in question, or buyers and sellers could negotiate with each other to resolve problems and to have negative feedback removed from an account.

---

[8]eBay.com, http://pages.ebay.com/community/people/values.html, November, 11, 2008.

[9]"Q&A with eBay's Meg Whitman," *BusinessWeek E.Biz*, December 3, 2001.

[10]Claire Tristram, "'Amazoning' Amazon," Contextmag.com, November 1999.

Users who received a sufficiently negative net feedback rating (typically a −4) had their registrations suspended and were thus unable to bid on or list items for sale. Users could review a person's feedback profile before deciding to bid on an item listed by that person or before choosing payment and delivery methods. Sellers with the highest positive feedback ratings could receive discounts on selling fees. As of November 2008, the seller with the highest feedback rating was Eforcity, which had a feedback rating of over 1 million.

The company believed its Feedback Forum was extremely useful in overcoming users' initial hesitancy about trading over the Internet, since it reduced the uncertainty of dealing with an unknown trading partner. However, there was growing concern among sellers and bidders that feedback could be positively skewed, as many eBayers were afraid to leave negative feedback for fear of unfounded retribution that could damage their carefully built reputations. This concern was heightened by the fact that buyers and sellers could agree to mutually withdraw negative feedback and thus expunge evidence of a failed transaction as if it never occurred.

In response to concerns about the feedback system, in May 2008, in a somewhat controversial move, Donahoe made a significant change to the feedback system so that sellers could no longer leave negative or neutral feedback for buyers. According to Donahoe, the change was intended to enhance honesty in the feedback system and to increase buyer participation on eBay since internal research indicated that receiving negative feedback discouraged buyers from purchasing goods on eBay. However, some smaller sellers felt that this change had essentially robbed them of their voice and made them more vulnerable to buyer fraud. One disgruntled eBay seller voiced these concerns by writing, "I am now open to threats and extortion and unethical pressure from buyers. I have absolutely no viable recourse if a buyer chooses to give me negative feedback and it is unjustified. The feedback system worked when it went both ways, there were mutual pressures to work out any difficulties. Now it is totally one-sided, and the seller can be targeted with unethical behavior by unscrupulous buyers."[11]

Unfortunately, eBay's Feedback Forum was not always sufficient to ensure honesty and integrity among traders. The company estimated that far less than 1 percent of the millions of auctions completed on the site involved some sort of fraud or illegal activity but some users, like Clay Monroe, disagreed. Monroe, a Seattle-area trader of computer equipment, estimated that "ninety percent of the time everybody is on the up and up [but] . . . ten percent of the time you get some jerk who wants to cheat you." Fraudulent or illegal acts perpetrated by sellers included misrepresentation of goods; trading in counterfeit goods or pirated goods that infringed on others' intellectual property rights; failure to deliver goods paid for by buyers; and shill bidding, whereby sellers would use a false bidder to artificially drive up the price of a good. Buyers could manipulate bids by placing an unrealistically high bid on a good to discourage other bidders and then withdraw their bid at the last moment to allow an ally to win the auction at a bargain price. Buyers could also fail to deliver payment on a completed auction.

EBAY'S BUSINESS MODEL

According to eBay's former CEO, Meg Whitman, the company could best be described as a dynamic, self-regulating economy. Its business model was based on creating and maintaining a person-to-person trading community where buyers and sellers from around the

---

[11]Ed Foster, "Negative Feedback on eBay's Feedback Changes," www.gripe2ed.com/scoop/story/2008/5/23/91215/5053 (accessed November 11, 2008).

globe could readily and conveniently exchange information and goods. The Web site functioned as a value-added facilitator of buyer-seller transactions by providing a supportive infrastructure that enabled buyers and sellers to come together in an efficient and effective manner. Success depended not only on the quality of eBay's infrastructure but also on the quality and quantity of buyers and sellers attracted to the site; in management's view, this entailed maintaining a compelling trading environment, a number of trust and safety programs, a cost-effective and convenient trading experience, and strong community affinity. By developing the eBay brand name and increasing the customer base, eBay endeavored to attract a sufficient number of high-quality buyers and sellers necessary to meet the organization's goals. Each of the segments in eBay's business model was designed to carry zero inventories and could thus operate a marketplace without the need for a traditional sales force.

The eBay business model was built around three operating segments: Marketplaces, Payments, and Communications. As of December 31, 2007, the Marketplaces segment, representing 69.91 percent of eBay's net revenues, was focused on online commerce platforms: eBay.com, considered the core platform of the Marketplaces segment; Rent.com; Shopping.com; StubHub.com; and classified ad Web sites Kijiji, Gumtree.com, LoQUo.com, OpusForum, Marktplaats.nl, and Mobile.de. The Payments segment consisted of eBay's PayPal operations and represented 25.11 percent of eBay's total net revenues. Finally, eBay's Communications segment was comprised of Skype and represented 6.78 percent of eBay's total net revenue (see Exhibit 4). In terms of geography, as of December 31, 2007, only 48.78 percent of eBay's net revenues were derived from the United States (see Exhibit 5).

Marketplaces

The Marketplaces segment was comprised of a diverse set of online commerce platforms that were designed to bring together buyers and sellers on a local, national, and international basis. The largest platform in this segment was the one most people thought of when they heard the name *eBay:* eBay.com. This segment operated with localized Web sites in 28 countries and included both auction-style listings, which represented 60 percent of gross merchandise value in 2007, as well as fixed-price formats including Buy It Now and eBay Stores.

In the second quarter of 2008, 667 million new listings were added to eBay.com worldwide, with more than 7 million listings added each day. Users could trade in more than

EXHIBIT 4
eBay's Net Revenues by Segment
(in thousands)

	2005	2006	2007
Marketplaces	$3,499,137	$4,334,290	$5,363,891
Payments	1,028,455	1,440,530	1,926,616
Communications	24,809	194,921	381,822
Total	$4,552,401	$5,969,741	$7,672,329

EXHIBIT 5
eBay's Net Revenues by Geography
(in thousands)

	2005	2006	2007
U.S.	$2,471,273	$3,108,968	$3,742,670
International	2,081,128	2,860,773	3,929,659
	$4,552,401	$5,969,741	$7,672,329

50,0000 categories. In the second quarter of 2008, the 10 largest categories and their annualized gross merchandise value totals were as follows:

Category	Annualized Gross Merchandise Value ($ in billions)
eBay Motors	$18.9
Clothing & Accessories	5.3
Consumer Electronics	5.2
Home & Garden	4.2
Computers	3.7
Sports	3.2
Books/Music/Movies	3.0
Collectibles	2.5
Business & Industrial	2.5
Jewelry & Watches	2.2

Despite impressive statistics regarding the sheer size of eBay's online commerce platform, there was evidence to suggest that growth in this key business unit was slowing. In the third quarter of 2008, one key metric, gross merchandise volume, fell for the first time in eBay's history, down 1 percent from the same quarter in 2007 and down 9 percent from the second quarter of 2008. Additionally, while eBay's net transaction revenues, excluding revenues from marketing services and other revenues, in the third quarter were up 1 percent to $1.16 billion from the same quarter in the previous year, this represented a 3 percent decline from the second quarter of 2008. Finally, while the number of eBay stores increased 3 percent, to 534,000, from the third quarter of 2007, this was a decrease of 3 percent from the second quarter of 2008.

Company executives had recognized the eventual maturation of their core segment as early as 2004, when they began expanding the variety of online commerce platforms within the Marketplaces segment. Accordingly the company expanded its offerings to include other classified ad Web sites, Rent.com, Shopping.com, and StubHub.

- *Other classified ad Web sites*—eBay realized that the classifieds market was a potential source of revenue generation for the company. In August 2004, eBay acquired a minority share in Craigs-list, a leading provider of online classifieds and forums. However, eBay was particularly concerned about penetrating international markets with classified listings. In February 2005, eBay launched online classified ad Web sites in select international markets. The international Web site was launched under the brand name *Kijiji,* which means "village" in Swahili. As of March 2005, Kijiji was available in more than 50 cities in Canada, China, France, Germany, Italy, and Japan. Other acquisitions eBay made to supplement the global reach of its online classified operations included Gumtree.com, LoQUo.com, OpusForum, Marktplaats.nl, and Mobile.de.

- *Rent.com*—eBay acquired Rent.com, a leader in the online listing of apartment and rental houses, in the first quarter of 2005. The company viewed this acquisition as a natural extension of its online real estate market. It earned its revenues in this segment from landlords who paid eBay a fee for renters who located their apartments through Rent.com.

- *Shopping.com*—In the second quarter of 2005, eBay completed the acquisition of Shopping.com. Shopping.com, which had more than 50 million unique visitors per month in the United States, the United Kingdom, and France, was the world's third largest Internet shopping destination. In 2008, Shopping.com was a leading company in online comparison shopping and consumer reviews. Retailers paid a fee to eBay for shoppers that were directed to their sites from Shopping.com.

- StubHub—In 2007, eBay acquired StubHub, a leading online marketplace for sports and concert tickets. StubHub was seen as a strong fit with eBay's existing tickets business.

These businesses had proved to be successful additions to eBay's Marketplaces segment and were recognized as key to the company's future growth. The growth strategy for the Marketplaces segment was focused on increasing the gross merchandise value on eBay.com and expanding into additional adjacent markets as had been done with the acquisition of StubHub.com. Executives planned to increase traffic to the site through advertising and promotions while investing in the site to enhance the buyer experience and seller economics; improve customer support and the company's Trust and Safety initiatives; expand product offerings into new geographies, formats, and categories; and test new buyer retention and seller pricing strategies.

Payments

The Payments segment included PayPal and Bill Me Later. Acquired in 2002 to facilitate person-to-person credit card payments, PayPal allowed eBay to make credit card payment a "seamless and integrated part of the trading experience."[12] By 2008, PayPal had expanded its original business model to include payments throughout the businesses in eBay's Marketplaces division, as well as facilitating payments for any online merchant, and had more than 57 million active, registered accounts, up from 41 million accounts in 2005. In expanding its business model, PayPal also expanded its geographic reach: individuals and businesses in more than 190 markets worldwide could make and receive payments through the service.

PayPal offered three types of accounts—Personal, Business, and Premier. Buyers benefited from PayPal as it allowed them to make payments without disclosing personal financial information to individual online merchants. Additionally, PayPal offered a Buyer Protection Program for certain qualified purchases on eBay that would reimburse buyers who were victims of fraudulent transactions. Sellers benefited from PayPal by having the ability to process online transactions without having to make a significant investment in software and by paying lower fees relative to other merchant accounts. Also, PayPal's Seller Protection Program could reduce the risks associated with unauthorized credit card use and fraudulent chargebacks.

PayPal earned revenue in several ways, including receiving fees from business and premier account holders who received funds, merchants who used PayPal's online payment processing services, users who withdrew money to non-U.S. bank accounts, and users who converted funds to foreign currencies. Additionally PayPal generated revenues through the PayPal Buyer Credit Program, operated in conjunction with GE Money Bank; PayPal ATM/debit cards; and the PayPal Plus credit card and eBay MasterCard issued by GE Money Bank. As of the third quarter of 2008, the majority of PayPal revenues were earned from payments associated with eBay Marketplaces transactions, but PayPal president Scott Thompson estimated that by the end of 2009, the company would derive more of its total payment volume from its merchant services than from eBay transactions.

The revenue growth in the Payments segment had been strong from 2005 to 2007, with the unit experiencing 40 percent growth from 2005 to 2006 and an additional 34 percent from 2006 to 2007. The merchant services operations within the Payments segment were especially rapidly growing, experiencing 59 percent growth from 2006 to 2007 and growing from 35 percent of the Payments segment's total payment volume in 2006 to 42 percent

---

[12]Company press release, May 18, 1999.

in 2007. The percentage of segment revenues derived from international sources was growing as well, with an increase from 36 percent of total net transaction revenues in 2005 to 42 percent in 2007. The company planned to continue to grow PayPal's user base and revenues by continuing to expand the usage of PayPal on Marketplaces transactions, including those on eBay and in adjacent markets; continuing to build a global network of merchants who used PayPal for the payment processing; and expanding the breadth of financial products offered.

Recognizing the growing potential of the financial services and payment processing operations, eBay expanded its presence in this market by purchasing Bill Me Later, a provider of instant credit to e-commerce customers, for $945 million in October 2008. Interestingly, one of the early investors in Bill Me Later was Amazon.com, one of eBay's primary rivals. Bill Me Later used a proprietary credit algorithm based on criteria including an individual's credit score, credit outstanding, and status with credit agencies to determine, in less than three seconds, whether to grant credit to that individual for a specific purchase. The purchase of Bill Me Later allowed eBay to expand its operations into consumer credit, rather than merely offering credit through partners. In 2008, Bill Me Later had more than 4 million customers, serving a diverse range of stores from Amazon.com to the Apple Store online to Zappos.com and was expected to finance over $1 billion in online purchases, resulting in $125 million in revenues, with a projected growth rate of 20 percent in 2009. However, Bill Me Later was not expected to be profitable on a net income basis until the end of 2009, at the earliest.

Despite the rapid growth of PayPal, some of the company's safety policies had been drawing increasing criticism from eBay and PayPal users. One of the policies announced in February 2008 that sellers found particularly troubling was that eBay would hold payments associated with high-risk transactions for up to 21 days. The factors that would determine whether a transaction was high-risk included the length of time a seller had been on eBay, the seller's feedback score, and the amount of the transaction. The company felt that its transaction hold policy would enhance security by making it easier for the company to issue refunds in case of fraudulent transactions. PayPal estimated that this new policy would affect less than 5 percent of eBay transactions and that the impact would largely be on new or untested sellers. Specifically, PayPal stated that sellers with a dissatisfied buyer rate of less than 5 percent who had been on eBay for more than six months and had a feedback score of higher than 100 would never have their funds held. If PayPal did freeze a transaction, the funds would be released after the buyer left positive feedback, three days after the item's confirmed delivery, or 21 days after the transaction if there were no disputes filed. Another policy that was troubling to sellers was that eBay required new sellers in some categories to have a PayPal account or a merchant credit card account to sell on eBay. While many eBay sellers understood these policies, some, such as Bob Lee, who ran Power-SellersUnite, felt that the new policies were helpful for buyers but not sellers. Lee said, "A seller is at risk of being taken advantage of by the buyer. Not having access to revenue, and having to wait for a buyer to leave positive feedback, leaves sellers in the lurch. PayPal and eBay are not allowing sellers to play on a level playing field."[13]

Communications

The Communications segment was based on Skype. In September 2005, eBay had acquired Skype Technologies, a global Internet communications company, for $3.1 billion in an effort to increase the company's global presence and, according to Meg Whitman, to facilitate communication between buyers and sellers on the eBay.com platform. Skype allowed

[13]Kathleen Ryan O'Connor, "eBay's PayPal Funds Freeze Plan Draws Fire," Money.com, February 11, 2008 (accessed November 13, 2008).

users to make free Skype-to-Skype voice and video calls and to send instant messages. Skype earned revenues by charging users to place calls from Skype to landline and mobile phones, and by charging for services such as text messaging, voice mail, and call forwarding. Users could purchase a subscription plan that would provide them with an unlimited number of calls.

At the time of the acquisition, Skype had 54 million members in more than 225 countries and eBay believed that this move would allow the company to develop an enhanced global marketplace and payments platform.[14] In 2007, Skype sought to expand its user base by forming an agreement with Wal-Mart stores in the United States to sell Skype-certified handsets and prepaid cards, forming an agreement with MySpace, a popular social networking site, and further integrating Skype with PayPal by launching Skype Send Money, which allowed users to send and receive funds using PayPal through the Skype platform. These growth initiatives proved successful. In the third quarter of 2008, Skype added 32 million registered users, for a global total of 370 million users, and reported revenue growth of 46 percent over the same quarter the previous year.

The growth strategy eBay planned for Skype was keyed on securing new users and encouraging users to upgrade to premium services and subscriptions. The company also intended to continue to encourage users of the eBay.com marketplace to use Skype for communicating between buyers and sellers in an effort to enhance the speed of communication between these parties and thereby reduce friction in online shopping.

Despite Skype's impressive growth and the potential benefits that eBay felt could be gained through further integration of Skype and the eBay trading platform, Skype's future with eBay was unclear heading into 2009. A number of analysts felt that eBay had never been able to capture the synergies Whitman hoped Skype would generate with eBay and pointed to eBay's 2007 writedown of $1.4 billion of the value of Skype as evidence of the company's inability to maximize Skype's potential. When Donahoe replaced Whitman in 2008, he added additional fuel to the speculation regarding Skype's future when he stated that the company's ownership of Skype would be evaluated. Analysts who supported the potential sale of Skype speculated that Microsoft or Google would be likely buyers.

HOW EBAY COMPARED WITH RIVALS

Auction sites varied in a number of respects, including their inventory, the bidding process, extra services and fees, technical support, functionality, and sense of community. Since its inception, eBay had gone to great lengths to make its Web site intuitive, easy to use by both buyers and sellers, and reliable. Efforts to ensure ease of use ranged from narrowly defining categories (to allow users to quickly locate desired products) to introducing services designed to personalize a user's eBay experience, such as My eBay. My eBay gave users centralized access to confidential, current information regarding their trading activities. From their My eBay page, users could view information pertaining to their current account balances with eBay, their feedback rating, the status of any auctions in which they were participating (as either buyer or seller), and auctions in favorite categories.

Among the most important competitive factors in both the online auction and the general e-commerce industries were the ability to attract buyers, the volume of transactions, the selection of goods, customer service and security, and brand recognition. In positioning its offerings vis-à-vis competitors, eBay's advertising campaigns ranged from focusing on the expansive amount of product variety offered by the company to the thrill shoppers could get

---

[14]Company press release, September 12, 2005.

from winning an auction for a hard-to-find item. In addition to factors such as variety and brand image, eBay was also attempting to differentiate itself from its competition along several other dimensions: sense of community, system reliability, reliability of delivery and payment, Web site convenience and accessibility, low levels of service fees, and efficient information exchange.

Early in its history, eBay's main rivals could be considered classified ads in newspapers, garage sales, flea markets, collectibles shows, local auction houses, and liquidators. As eBay's product mix and selling techniques evolved, the company's range of competitors did as well. The broadening of eBay's product mix beyond collectibles to include practical household items, office equipment, toys, and so on brought the company into more direct competition with brick-and-mortar retailers, import/export companies, and catalog and mail order companies. Further, with the acquisition of Half.com, the introduction of eBay stores, and the growing percentage of fixed-price and Buy It Now sales as a percentage of eBay's revenue, eBay considered itself to be competing in a broad sense with a number of other on-line retailers, such as Wal-Mart, Kmart, Target, Sears, JCPenney, and Office Depot. In competing with these larger sellers, eBay began to adopt some of their tools, such as the use of gift certificates. The company also felt that it was competing with a number of specialty retailers, such as Christie's (antiques), KB Toys (toys), Blockbuster (movies), Dell (computers), Foot Locker (sporting goods), Ticketmaster (tickets), and Home Depot (tools).[15] Exhibit 6 displays eBay's customer service rankings as compared to a variety of rivals.

Management at eBay saw traditional brick-and-mortar competitors as inefficient because their fragmented local and regional nature made it expensive and time-consuming for

EXHIBIT 6   Comparative Customer Service Rankings, Selected Web Sites (scores out of 100)

Company/Sector	2000	2001	2002	2003	2004	2005	2006	2007
INTERNET RETAIL	**78**	**77**	**83**	**84**	**80**	**81**	**83**	**83**
1-800-Flowers.com	69	76	78	76	79	77	77	NA
Amazon.com	84	84	88	88	84	87	87	88
Barnesandnoble.com	77	82	87	86	87	87	87	88
Buy.com	78	78	80	80	80	81	80	81
eBay	80	82	82	84	80	81	80	81
Priceline.com*	66	69	71	71	73	72	72	73
uBid.com	NM	67	69	70	73	73	73	74
DEPARTMENT AND DISCOUNT STORES	**72**	**75**	**74**	**76**	**74**	**75**	**74**	**73**
Dillards	72	75	75	75	77	76	75	76
Kmart	67	74	70	70	67	70	70	NA
Macy's	69	69	71	71	74	74	71	75
Sears	71	73	76	75	73	74	73	73
Target	73	77	78	77	75	75	78	77
Wal-Mart	73	75	74	75	73	72	72	68
SPECIALTY RETAIL STORES	**76**	**73**	**74**	**74**	**75**	**74**	**75**	**75**
Best Buy	NM	NM	NM	72	72	71	76	74
Circuit City	NM	NM	NM	73	72	70	69	71

*Priceline.com is included in the ACSI in the Internet Travel industry.
Source: American Customer Satisfaction Index, www.theacsi.org.

[15]eBay, 2001 annual report.

buyers and sellers to meet, exchange information, and complete transactions. Moreover, they suffered from three other deficiencies: (1) they tended to offer limited variety and breadth of selection as compared to the millions of items available on eBay, (2) they often had high transactions costs, and (3) they were information-inefficient in the sense that buyers and sellers lacked a reliable and convenient means of setting prices for sales or purchases. Management saw eBay's online auction format as competitively superior to these rivals because (1) it facilitated buyers and sellers meeting, exchanging information, and conducting transactions; (2) it allowed buyers and sellers to bypass traditional intermediaries and trade directly, thus lowering costs; (3) eBay provided global reach to a greater selection and a broader base of participants; (4) the eBay format permitted trading at all hours and provided continuously updated information; and (5) it fostered a sense of community among individuals with mutual interests.

Competitors for eBay's services ranged from brick-and-mortar discount retailers such as Wal-Mart to auction houses such as Christie's; however, many analysts agreed that the most significant competitors to eBay included e-tailers such as Amazon.com and Overstock.com as well as auction sites such as uBid.com.

Amazon.com

Amazon.com's business strategy was to "Offer Earth's Biggest Selection and seek to be Earth's most customer-centric company for three primary customer sets: consumer customers, seller customers and developer customers."[16] With its customer base of 35 million users in more than 220 countries and a very well-known brand name, Amazon.com was considered the closest overall competitive threat to eBay, especially as eBay expanded its business model beyond its traditional auction services. Amazon was created in July 1995 as an online bookseller and rapidly transitioned into a full-line, one-stop-shopping retailer with a product offering that included books, music, toys, electronics, tools and hardware, lawn and patio products, video games, software, and a mall of boutiques (called z-shops). Amazon was the Internet's number one music, video, and book retailer; as of the third quarter of 2008, media represented 62 percent of Amazon's sales. Additionally, in 2008 Amazon had Web sites in seven countries, including the United States, the United Kingdom, Germany, Canada, France, Japan, and China, with international revenues representing approximately 45 percent of the company's net sales in 2007, a percentage that had been relatively stable since 2005. One of the distinctive features customers appreciated about Amazon.com was the extensive reviews available for each item. These product reviews were written both by professionals and by regular users who had purchased a specific product. The company's 2007 net income was more than $476 million, which was an increase of over 250 percent from 2006 (as seen in Exhibit 7). Exhibit 8 shows Amazon's balance-sheet data.

Amazon's strategy was centered on servicing customers by providing them with a broad selection of merchandise, low prices, and convenience. While many companies made similar claims, Amazon consistently invested in developing new products, partnerships, and service offerings to support the basic tenets of its strategy. To increase the selection of products available to customers, Amazon offered merchandise in a broad array of categories, hosted Web stores for sellers such as Target, operated specialty Web sites such as Shopbop.com and Endless.com (fashion Web sites) and operated the Amazon Marketplace. To help keep prices low, Amazon regularly offered free or low-cost shipping deals; allowed customers to use Amazon Prime, which provided free two-day shipping on millions of items in the United States, for a nominal fee of $79 annually; and allowed sellers to offer used merchandise through the Marketplace. Finally, to expand its product offerings and enhance customer convenience, Amazon had developed a number of service

---

[16]Amazon.com, 2007 annual report, p. 11.

EXHIBIT 7   Amazon.com's Income Statement, 2005–2007 ($ in millions)

	2005	2006	2007
Net sales	$8,490	$10,711	$14,835
Cost of sales	6,451	8,255	11,482
Gross profit	2,039	2,456	3,353
Operating expenses:			
Fulfillment	745	937	1,292
Marketing	198	263	344
Technology and content	451	662	818
General and administrative	166	195	235
Other operating expense, net	47	10	9
Total operating expenses	1,607	2,067	2,698
Income from operations	432	389	655
Interest income	44	59	90
Interest expense	(92)	(78)	(77)
Other income (expense), net	2	(4)	(1)
Remeasurements and other	42	11	(7)
Total non-operating income (expense)	(4)	(12)	5
Income before income taxes	428	377	660
Provision for income taxes	95	187	184
Income before cumulative effect of change in accounting principle	333	190	476
Cumulative effect of change in accounting principle	26	—	—
Net income	$ 359	$ 190	$ 476

Source: Amazon.com, 2007 annual report, p. 11.

offerings, including the ability for customers to download books through Amazon's Kindle device or Audible.com (acquired in 2008), as well as music and videos.

Amazon's Marketplace was the most direct competitor to eBay, as it allowed individuals and companies to list their new and used goods alongside those offered by Amazon for any given product; customers could choose to buy new from Amazon or to buy new or used from another seller. Amazon did not charge sellers a listing fee but did charge a transaction fee that ranged from $0.80 to $1.35, which was waived for Pro Merchant Subscribers, who paid $39.99 a month, and a commission called a referral fee based on the type of good sold. Referral fees ranged from 6 percent for computers to 20 percent for jewelry and other items. In return for these relatively high commissions, Amazon took care of order and payment processing and after-sale service. If sellers chose, they could even store their merchandise in one of Amazon's 19 fulfillment centers located worldwide, and, for a fee, Amazon would pack and ship their orders directly to their customers. As on eBay, buyers were able to rate sellers. Sellers who did not maintain a sufficient rating, and those who had customer service problems (e.g., having to issue an excessive amount of refunds) or who had guarantee claims filed against them, could be charged higher fees or no longer allowed to sell on Amazon. Despite these higher fees, there was evidence that Amazon was luring sellers away from eBay, especially in the wake of increasing seller dissatisfaction with changes in eBay's policies and fees. In August 2008, Gene Munster, an analyst for Piper Jaffray, estimated that third parties had sold $6 billion in goods on Amazon over the last 12 months. While this was only one-tenth the value of goods sold on eBay, Munster predicted that if Amazon was willing to cut its fees, it could capture more market share from eBay.[17]

[17]Larry Dignan, "Amazon: Still Trailing eBay in Third Party Sales, But . . . ," www.zdnet.com, August 11, 2008 (accessed November 5, 2008).

EXHIBIT 8
Amazon.com's
Balance Sheet,
2005–2007 ($ in
millions)

Source: Amazon.com, 2007
annual report, p. 11.

	2006	2007
ASSETS		
Current assets:		
Cash and cash equivalents	$1,022	$2,539
Marketable securities	997	573
Inventories	877	1,200
Accounts receivable, net and other	399	705
Deferred tax assets	78	147
Total current assets	3,373	5,164
Fixed assets, net	457	543
Deferred tax assets	199	260
Goodwill	195	222
Other assets	139	296
Total assets	$4,363	$6,485
LIABILITIES AND STOCKHOLDERS' EQUITY		
Current liabilities:		
Accounts payable	$1,816	$2,795
Accrued expenses and other	716	919
Total current liabilities	2,532	3,714
Long-term debt	1,247	1,282
Other long-term liabilities	153	292
Outstanding shares 416 and 414	4	4
Treasury stock, at cost	(252)	(500)
Additional paid-in capital	2,517	3,063
Accumulated other comprehensive income (loss)	(1)	5
Accumulated deficit	(1,837)	(1,375)
Total stockholders' equity	431	1,197
Total liabilities and stockholders' equity	$4,363	$6,485

Overstock.com

Overstock.com was another competitor that was beginning to compete more directly with eBay, especially as the latter increasingly focused on fixed-price selling. Founded in 1999 in Salt Lake City, the company was conceived as an online outlet mall where customers could find brand-name merchandise at deep discounts and sellers could liquidate their excess inventory. In 1999, Overstock offered fewer than 100 products, but by 2008 the company offered a total of 783,000 products (720,000 in the books, music, movies, and games [BMMG] category and 63,000 in non-BMMG). Over 99 percent of the company's sales were made in the United States, and Overstock earned revenues from two main sources: direct sales (those fulfilled from Overstock's own warehouse) and fulfillment partner sales (which involved third parties selling their merchandise on Overstock's Web sites). As can be seen in Exhibit 9, despite the company's growth efforts, total revenue had declined from 2005–2007 as the company struggled with its net income. Overstock's balance for 2006 and 2007 is shown in Exhibit 10.

In an attempt to build revenue growth, Overstock had expanded its business model several times. In 2004, Overstock launched an auction site to compete with eBay. As on eBay, sellers listed the opening bid price, the duration of the auction, and the Make It Mine price (which was optional) and were charged a listing fee (ranging from $0.10 to $3.15) and a closing fee (3 percent for $0.01–$25.00, $0.75 plus 2 percent of the value over $25.01 for auctions closing with a value of between $25.01 and $1,000, and $20.25 plus 1 percent of

EXHIBIT 9   Overstock.com's Income Statement, 2005–2007 ($ in thousands)

	2005	2006	2007
REVENUE			
Direct revenue	$324,875	$ 303,202	$195,622
Fulfillment partner revenue	474,441	484,948	564,539
Total revenue	799,316	788,150	760,161
Cost of goods sold			
Direct	282,383	284,943	164,368
Fulfillment partner	400,057	408,407	468,222
Total cost of goods sold	682,440	693,350	632,590
Gross profit	$116,876	$ 94,800	$127,571
OPERATING EXPENSES			
Sales and marketing	$ 77,155	$ 70,897	$ 55,458
Technology	27,901	65,158	59,453
General and administrative	33,043	46,837	41,976
Restructuring	—	5,674	12,283
Total operating expenses	138,099	188,566	169,170
Operating loss	(21,223)	(93,766)	(41,599)
Interest income, net	(270)	3,566	4,788
Interest expense	(5,582)	(4,765)	(4,188)
Other (expense) income, net	4,728	81	(92)
Loss from continuing operations	(22,347)	(94,884)	(41,091)
Discontinued operations:			
Loss from discontinued operations	(2,571)	(6,882)	(3,924)
Net loss	$(24,918)	$(101,766)	$ (45,015)

Source: Overstock.com, 2007 annual report.

the value over $1,000.01 for auctions closing with a value over $1,000). Sellers could pay additional fees if they wanted a reserve price auction or could upgrade their listing with options such as a bold or highlighted font.

In 2007, the company launched an automobile marketplace named Overstock Cars. Overstock Cars served as an intermediary that connected customers to local dealers and provided them with a fixed, no-haggle price. The site also used a proprietary search function named Clearance Lot, to help bargain hunters identify cars offered at the greatest discount. In 2008, Overstock expanded this business model to real estate; like Overstock Cars, Overstock Real Estate connected potential buyers with realtors in their local areas and used a proprietary algorithm to help buyers locate properties that might represent an especially good value.

uBid.com

Founded in April 1997, uBid.com launched an initial public offering on the NASDAQ in December 1998. The company's mission statement was to "be the most recognized and trusted business-to-consumer marketplace, consistently delivering exceptional value and service to its customers and supplier partners."[18] As of 2005, uBid believed that its core values of integrity, agility, execution, caring, and innovation would allow the company to deliver competitive success in the online auction industry and to build valuable relationships

[18]uBid.com, www.ubid.com/about/companyinfo.asp, December 18, 2005.

EXHIBIT 10
Overstock.com's
Balance Sheet,
2006–2007 ($ in
thousands)

Source: Overstock.com,
2007 annual report.

	2006	2007
ASSETS		
Current assets:		
Cash and cash equivalents	$126,965	$101,394
Marketable securities	—	46,000
Cash, cash equivalents and marketable securities	126,965	147,394
Accounts receivable, net	11,638	12,304
Note receivable	6,702	1,506
Inventories, net	20,274	25,933
Prepaid inventory	2,241	3,572
Prepaid expense	7,473	7,572
Current assets of held for sale subsidiary	4,718	—
Total current assets	180,011	198,281
Property and equipment, net	56,198	27,197
Goodwill	2,784	2,784
Other long-term assets, net	578	86
Notes receivable	—	4,181
Long-term assets of held for sale subsidiary	16,594	—
Total assets	$256,165	$232,529
LIABILITIES AND STOCKHOLDERS' EQUITY		
Current liabilities:		
Accounts payable	$ 66,039	$ 70,648
Accrued liabilities	40,142	52,598
Capital lease obligations, current	5,074	3,796
Current liabilities of held for sale subsidiary	3,684	—
Total current liabilities	114,939	127,042
Capital lease obligations, non-current	3,983	—
Other long-term liabilities	—	3,034
Convertible senior notes	75,279	75,623
Total liabilities	194,201	205,699
Total stockholders' equity	61,964	26,830
Total liabilities and stockholders' equity	$256,165	$232,529

with its customers, employees, and suppliers.[19] As such, uBid considered itself to be in direct competition with eBay, although the company had difficulty denting the portion of eBay's business that was derived from large corporations and smaller companies wanting to sell their products through an auction format. As a company, uBid had experienced increased revenues almost every year since its inception, but it had never captured the share of the auction market that its founders hoped was possible, although it at one time had a 14.7 percent share of revenues in the online auction market. In mid-2000, uBid was sold to CGMI Networks, and then it was sold again to Petters Group Worldwide in 2003. With each sale, the number of workers employed by uBid fell and the product mix was changed in an attempt to find a niche market that would insulate the company from the competitive power of eBay.

Despite the company's challenges, in 2007 uBid claimed to have more than 3,500 certified merchants who sold to more than 6 million registered uBid users. The company's business model centered on offering brand-name merchandise (often refurbished and closeout goods) at a deep discount in a relatively broad range of categories from leading brand-name

[19]Ibid.

manufacturers such as Sony, Hewlett-Packard, IBM, Compaq, AMD, Minolta, and 1,000-plus additional suppliers. Categories included Computer and Office; Consumer Electronics; Music, Movies & Games; Jewelry & Gifts; Travel & Events; Home & Garden; Sports; Toys & Hobbies; Apparel; Collectibles; and Everything Else. The merchandise was offered in both an online auction format (in which prices started at $1.00) and through uBid's fixed-price superstore. The merchandise was sourced from corporate partners and from uBid's own operations, which included a 400,000-square-foot warehouse and refurbishment center; from parent company Petters Group Worldwide; and from small and medium-sized companies that were members of uBid's Certified Merchant Program.

In 2008, uBid.com launched a site to compete directly with Overstock.com. Similar to Overstock.com, uBid's site, named RedTag.com, worked with manufacturers, distributors, and retailers of brand-name products to provide an outlet for their excess merchandise. RedTag planned to distinguish its offerings from rivals by offering $1.95 shipping and by providing a 30-day money back guarantee on purchases.

EBAY'S NEW CHALLENGES

Throughout its history, eBay faced each new challenge with an eye on its founding values and an ear for community members. As Pierre Omidyar stated in 2001, "What we do have to be cautious of, as we grow, is that our core is the personal trade, because the values are communicated person-to-person. It can be easy for a big company to start to believe that it's responsible for its success. Our success is really based on our members' success. They're the ones who have created this, and they're the ones who will create it in the future. If we lose sight of that, then we're in big trouble."[20] The company had historically applied this perspective in response to significant customer concerns regarding the growing presence of corporate sellers on eBay.

Omidyar and Whitman recognized the importance of eBay's culture and were aware of the potential impact rapid growth and the evolution of the product line could have on this valued asset. When asked about the importance of the culture, Omidyar said, "If we lose that, we've pretty much lost everything."[21] Whitman agreed with the importance of eBay's culture, but she did not see the influx of larger retailers and liquidators as a significant problem. Even as these sellers grew to account for 5 percent of eBay's total business in 2004 (from 1 percent in 2001), these large sellers received no favorable treatment; Whitman stated, "There are no special deals. I am passionate about creating this level playing field."[22]

However, there was significant doubt among the eBay community as to whether eBay's newest CEO, John Donahoe, shared these values or whether he would focus on improving internal efficiencies at the expense of the company's culture. One eBay staffer admitted that employees feared for eBay's culture since, when Meg Whitman was leading the company, employees regularly bought and sold products on eBay and discussed this as a badge of honor. However, in the holiday season of 2007, eBay's mailroom was reportedly receiving a dismaying number of packages from Amazon.com.

Heading into the 2008 holiday season, eBay faced two fundamental questions:

1. As eBay's business model evolved to include more fixed-price sales in an effort to combat the saturation of its domestic market, how could the company transfer its competitive advantage in the online auction industry to the more general area of online retail?

---

[20]"Q&A with eBay's Pierre Omidyar," *BusinessWeek E.Biz,* December 3, 2001.

[21]"The People's Company," *BusinessWeek E.Biz,* December 3, 2001.

[22]"Queen of the Online Flea Market," Economist.com, December 30, 2003.

EXHIBIT 11 eBay's Stock Price Performance, December 2007–November 2008

eBay's stock price

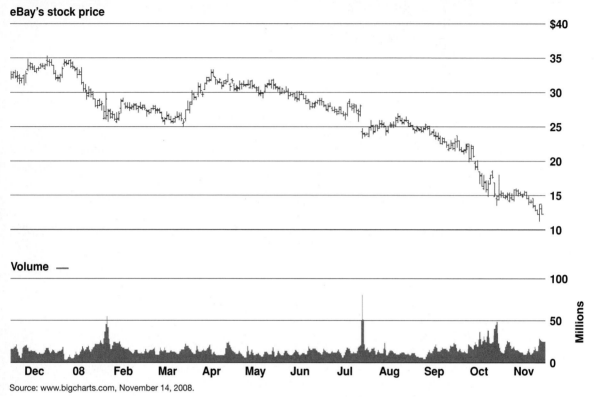

Source: www.bigcharts.com, November 14, 2008.

2. How could the company reinvigorate growth in its core market, especially in the face of a global economic slowdown and growing dissatisfaction among smaller eBay sellers? Given the slowing growth in the company's core market, should the company be concerned with the growing dissatisfaction among smaller eBay sellers? If so, what could it do to remedy this without alienating the larger sellers?

Downgrades of eBay's stock seemed to indicate that analysts were not as optimistic about eBay's future growth potential as they once had been, and some questioned whether eBay could extend its dominance to the general online retailing segment. While some industry experts predicted that eBay could make the transition, others suggested that eBay might consider selling its online auction operations and focusing its attentions on PayPal. Donahoe emphatically rejected this potential course of action, but when the company announced that it would lay off more than 1,000 employees in 2008, it was becoming increasingly clear that something had to change. These concerns were clearly reflected in eBay's stock price, as can be seen in Exhibit 11.

Case

19

Wal-Mart Stores Inc. in 2008: Management's Initiatives to Transform the Company and Curtail Wal-Mart Bashing

Arthur A. Thompson, Jr. *University of Alabama*

In June 2008, Wal-Mart's CEO, H. Lee Scott, presented a glowing report to the estimated 16,000 shareholders attending the company's annual shareholder meeting held at the 19,000-seat Bud Walton Arena on the University of Arkansas campus, located a few miles from Wal-Mart's headquarters in Bentonville, Arkansas. In the tradition of prior annual meetings of Wal-Mart shareholders, the 2008 meeting was an elaborate event lasting most of the day; the meeting included not only a series of presentations by company executives but also entertainment by Tim McGraw, David Cook (who had been named the 2008 American Idol a few weeks earlier), British singer Joss Stone, and Oscar winner and Idol finalist Jennifer Hudson. Scott said he was quite pleased with the results of the transformation process that top management had initiated in 2006 to provide customers with a more satisfying shopping experience, better fulfill the company's new mission, and do a better job of getting Wal-Mart's 2.1 million employees worldwide to understand and practice the cultural values and business principles espoused by the company's esteemed founder, Sam Walton.

Scott explained to shareholders why transformation had become essential to the company's continued growth and success even though in 2006 Wal-Mart's traditional business model of driving costs out of its supply chain, constantly implementing ways to operate more cost-efficiently, offering customers worldwide a broad range of merchandise at appealingly low prices, and opening stores in more and more places to serve an ever-growing customer base had served the company well:

> It would be easy to take comfort in the success we have had in our business. . . . If you know that something works, why not just replicate it and replicate it and replicate it? Well, we have done that before. For several years, we did what we knew worked. And we did it very well. We grew beyond expectations. Our stock price went up. And we felt good about it. And we had every right to.
>
> But, in time, the world changed. People's expectations of us—and of corporations in general—changed. And we found ourselves playing catch-up. We can never let that happen again. Not only must we never fall behind . . . we must always push ourselves to stay ahead.
>
> We must continue to ask fundamental questions that alter perspectives and ultimately behavior. Questions like: How do you persuade someone in a successful organization that real change is needed and can be achieved in a way that is consistent with their core beliefs? How do you get a leadership team to step back and ask what success means not just in their own business, but in the larger context of the company as a whole? How do you take the trends of the future and put them into the business, so a company is relevant to today's consumers and well positioned for tomorrow's consumers?
>
> These are not easy questions to ask. They are not easy questions to answer. But we have to keep asking them. And when necessary make difficult decisions.
>
> Your Wal-Mart has an opportunity to be a leader in the retail industry for more ethical and environmentally friendly sourcing. Your Wal-Mart can play a role in reducing the world's dependence on oil and other high-carbon sources of energy. Your Wal-Mart can bring even greater value to customers who need and deserve to save on everyday needs.
>
> And there are things we need to do inside our company—such as making your Wal-Mart more diverse and creating a more inclusive environment. I am confident that if we put diversity and inclusion into our business and really commit to it, we can make real progress. I am determined Wal-Mart will do this. It is essential to attracting and keeping the best possible people and staying relevant to our customers. [In 2008, as Scott delivered his remarks, Wal-Mart was already a decidedly diverse employer. Its workforce included more than 154,000 Hispanics; 237,000 African Americans; 41,000 Asian Americans; 15,000 Native Americans; 826,000 women; and 256,000 people age 55 or older.]
>
> But I also urge you to think about what we can do—and what the world will expect us to do in the future. There are very clear trends that the retail industry and the world will have to confront—the aging of the global population, a multi-polar balance of power, income inequality, the disruptive power of technology, increased demand for energy, to name a few.
>
> Think about these trends, the strengths of your Wal-Mart and our model of "Saving Money" and "Living Better." We have the best global footprint to serve millions worldwide who will want the opportunity to lift themselves up into the middle class. Our leadership in sustainability will give customers and suppliers everywhere the ability to be more energy efficient and therefore more energy independent. An older global population will need us to help them stretch their money and maintain their quality of life while living on a fixed income. Here's the bottom line for our business and the larger role we can play. . . . Your Wal-Mart is uniquely positioned to succeed not just in this economy, but in these times. And among retailers, we are the best positioned to lead in the world of tomorrow.
>
> So how do we continue to turn our position of strength into leadership for the future? I want to repeat a quote from Sam [Walton] that I shared on this stage two years ago: "You can't just keep doing what works one time. Everything around you is always changing. To succeed, stay out in front of that change."
>
> The world has become too complex and changes too rapidly for a company of our size to just replicate. I am not saying that we have to constantly reinvent ourselves. We do not. And we should not. We have a culture, a mission, and core values that are timeless and universal.

But we have to constantly look at how we apply those things to the changing world around us. The challenge ahead is that we must continue to challenge ourselves.

I am confident that your Wal-Mart will continue to transform. And I am confident we will continue to succeed.[1]

Scott's leadership of the transformation process under way at Wal-Mart included a number of initiatives:

- *Recasting the company's mission as one of "Saving People Money So They Can Live Better."* "Saving money" had always been a fundamental component of what Wal-Mart was all about—for decades, the front of every Wal-Mart store had signage touting "We Sell for Less" and its everyday low prices were unmatched by any other retailer. But the new "Live Better" piece of Wal-Mart's mission was, in Scott's view, a way to "unlock the full potential of Wal-Mart" and "strengthen our ability not only to do well as a business . . . but also to do good in the world."[2]

- *Revising Wal-Mart's logo* to better mirror the company's shift in emphasis away from "Always low prices. Always." and "We Sell for Less" to the broader mission of "Saving People Money So They Can Live Better."

- *Making a special effort to convince Wal-Mart's 2.1 million associates why the company's new mission was more than a hollow statement* and a reflection of the company's new marketing campaign tied to the theme "Save Money. Live Better." Scott and Wal-Mart's other senior executives believed the new mission would not have the desired transformational effect unless it led to better operating practices and a cultural energy that actually delivered added value to customers and touched the communities in which Wal-Mart operated.

- *Broadening Wal-Mart's appeal to existing customers and attracting new customers to shop at Wal-Mart, updating merchandise offerings, instituting faster checkout procedures, and revising the layout and decor of Wal-Mart stores to enhance store ambience and better present merchandise offerings in a manner calculated to spur sales.* A sizable number of the company's apparel lines were upgraded to better appeal to shoppers looking for a bit more upscale and stylish clothing. Stores were redecorated, aisles were widened, skylights were added to improve lighting, clutter was reduced, cleanliness was improved, and inventory on shelving that was out of reach to shoppers was eliminated. Store managers and regional managers were given more authority to stock their stores with merchandise that was particularly appealing to the local population—the objective was for each store's merchandise offerings to be "locally and regionally correct." For instance, most Wal-Mart stores stocked sports apparel and merchandise of locally popular teams, along with products that were made locally or had local appeal. Numerous Wal-Mart Supercenters began stocking locally grown produce. According to Scott, who along with other Wal-Mart executives toured Wal-Mart stores every week, in 2008 the company's 6,800 stores "look better . . . they feel better and are friendlier too."

- *Initiating a flat $4 price for the generic versions of some 200 common prescription drugs.* In 2008, this program was extended to provide a 90-day supply of certain prescription medicines for $10. Wal-Mart estimated that its $4 prescription program had saved customers $1.1 billion in the first 20 months of the program's existence. The company also lowered the prices of some 1,000 over-the-counter drugs.

---

[1]Presentation to attendees at the 2008 annual meeting of Wal-Mart shareholders on June 6, 2008; Scott's remarks were posted in the news section at www.walmart.com (accessed June 9, 2008).

[2]H. Lee Scott's remarks at Wal-Mart's 2008 shareholders meeting, www.wal-mart.com (accessed on June 9, 2008).

- *Increasing "green" merchandise offerings and promoting their use to customers.* One such effort entailed helping customers live better by promoting the use of superefficient compact fluorescent light bulbs. When the program was initiated in November 2006, Wal-Mart announced the goal of selling 100 million bulbs; by early 2008, it had sold 192 million bulbs, estimated to save customers $6 billion in electricity costs and eliminate the need to build the equivalent of 3 power plants (which in turn promoted a cleaner environment and reduced carbon dioxide emissions that were said to contribute to global warming). Another effort involved stocking a wider selection of organic foods, which were all grown using sustainable agricultural methods that did not include the use of pesticides and chemical fertilizers. Wal-Mart's tracking of customers' decisions to purchase five key eco-friendly products showed that sales increased 66 percent between April 2007 and April 2008.[3] These and other "green" initiatives being pursued by Wal-Mart were follow-ons to Scott's public commitment in October 2005 that Wal-Mart would henceforth take a leadership position in promoting environmental sustainability via efforts to operate all aspects of its business in a manner calculated to promote sustainability and make the earth a better place. To make the sustainability commitment a reality, Scott had appointed several new top executives to spearhead Wal-Mart's campaign to be a good steward of the environment.

- *Launching a multifaceted "Zero Waste" campaign.* Through its Kids Recycling Challenge, Wal-Mart worked with elementary schools in 12 states to begin recycling plastic bags—each school received $5 for each 60-gallon collection bag that students brought to their local Wal-Mart store. In October 2007, Wal-Mart introduced reusable shopping bags inscribed with "Paper or Plastic? Neither"; management estimated that a reusable bag could eliminate the use of 100 disposable plastic bags and, by May 2008, Wal-Mart had sold enough of the reusable shopping bags to eliminate the need for 400 million plastic bags. In April 2008, as part of Earth Month, Wal-Mart gave away 1 million reusable bags. Wal-Mart partnered with its laundry detergent suppliers to introduce concentrated liquid laundry detergents in smaller containers and thereby save on packaging; in May 2008, Wal-Mart announced that it had achieved its goal of selling only concentrated detergents in its U.S. and Canadian stores, estimating that over a three-year period its actions would save more than 400 million gallons of water, more than 95 million pounds of plastic resin, and more than 125 million pounds of cardboard—approximately 25 percent of the liquid laundry detergent sold in the United States was at Wal-Mart stores. Wal-Mart began pushing its suppliers to use biodegradable packaging; it made the use of biodegradable packaging a part of its standards for suppliers and actively began working with its 66,000 suppliers to develop more eco-friendly packaging. Wal-Mart was engaged in both internal efforts and efforts with the trucking industry to double the fuel efficiency of its fleet of 7,200 trucks, which logged some 850 million miles annually—since 2005, efficiency had been improved by 20 percent.

- *Instituting ways to make Wal-Mart stores both more energy efficient and supplied by 100 percent renewable energy.* Wal-Mart began working with architects, engineers, contractors, and landscape designers to begin a long-term effort to build new stores that would reduce energy usage, reduce pollution, and conserve natural resources. Two experimental stores were built to serve as living laboratories for testing new technologies and products—in 2008, one such new technology, LED lighting, was in the process of being incorporated in Wal-Mart stores across the United States. In 2007, Wal-Mart opened three high-efficiency stores that used 20 percent less energy than a typical Supercenter, were constructed with recycled building materials, and had motion-sensing LED lighting,

---

[3]"Wal-Mart Live Better Index Shows Improvement in Acceptance of Green Products," Datamonitor NewsWire, April 22, 2008, www.walmart.com (accessed June 10, 2008).

low-flow bathroom faucets, reflective white roofs, and a 100-percent integrated water-source heating, cooling, and refrigeration system. In January 2008, the first of four ultra-high-efficiency stores with additional energy-saving and environment friendly building features was opened. Pilot projects for solar-powered stores were under way at 22 stores in California and Hawaii. In March 2008, Wal-Mart announced that it would begin building a series of still more efficient prototype stores that were designed for specific climates and that could make use of energy-saving innovations specific to those climates. Wal-Mart was open to sharing its learning and experiences with all its new energy-saving stores so as to help drive energy-saving innovations in building design worldwide.

- *Making Wal-Mart an even better place to work.* Efforts here included making every full-time and part-time Wal-Mart associate (and their children) eligible for health insurance, improving the affordability of the various health insurance options (in terms of both monthly premiums and co-pay amounts), and revising the health insurance coverage to include security from catastrophic medical expenses (after one year of eligibility, there was no lifetime maximum for most types of expenses). Going into 2008, some 92.7 percent of Wal-Mart's associates had some form of health insurance, up from 90.4 percent in 2006. Senior management was sensitive to the importance of providing good jobs with competitive pay and benefits. The average hourly wage for full-time Wal-Mart associates was $10.83 in early 2008; the hourly averages were in the $11–$12 range in urban areas and states like California. A sizable fraction of the jobs at Wal-Mart, particularly those in its retail stores, were considered entry-level jobs that required minimal skills and education. While the majority of Wal-Mart's associates were full-time employees (defined as working 34–40 hours per week), many were students who wanted work experience and seniors looking for part-time jobs to supplement their retirement income. In January 2006, some 25,000 people applied for 325 available jobs at a new store in the Chicago area; in March 2007, there were more than 11,000 applicants for 300 job openings at a new store in Maryland; and in March 2008, there were more than 12,000 applications for 450 jobs at a new store in Decatur, Georgia. For decades, Wal-Mart had offered company personnel good opportunities for advancement owing to an ongoing stream of new store openings and a policy of promoting from within—more than 75 percent of the managerial personnel at Wal-Mart's stores had joined the company as hourly associates.

- *Driving growth in the company's international operations via both acquisitions of foreign retailers* (whose operations could later be converted to Wal-Mart stores) and opening newly constructed stores. This strategic thrust was aimed at transforming Wal-Mart into an increasingly global retailer with more and more stores in more and more countries.

- *Making a positive contribution to the quality of life in every community in which the company conducted business.* Following the Katrina disaster, the company established nine disaster distribution centers strategically located across the United States that were stocked with relief supplies needed to assist communities recover in the event of a disaster. Health clinics to treat common ailments were opened in numerous Wal-Mart stores as a means of helping bring affordable and accessible health care to low-income people—between 30 and 40 percent of the patients at these clinics were uninsured. Wal-Mart expected to have 400 "Clinic at Wal-Mart" outlets by 2010; all the clinics were leased to and operated by local, certified health care professionals, not Wal-Mart personnel. Wal-Mart was the biggest corporate cash donor in the United States, giving some $296 million to 4,000+ communities in 2007. It donated $1 million or more annually to such charitable organizations as the National Fish and Wildlife Foundation, the Special Olympics, Boys & Girls Clubs of America, the United Negro College Fund, and the Muscular Dystrophy Association.

RECENT WAL-MART BASHING: THE REASON FOR SCOTT'S TRANSFORMATION INITIATIVES

H. Lee Scott's sweeping effort to transform Wal-Mart was, to a large degree, a thoughtfully and carefully crafted response to a loud and growing chorus of Wal-Mart critics and a series of embarrassing incidents. During the 2003–2005 period, numerous journalists, union leaders, community activists, and so-called cultural progressives had united in a campaign to bash Wal-Mart on a variety of fronts and turn public opinion against Wal-Mart and its seemingly virtuous business model of relentlessly wringing cost efficiencies out of its supply chain and providing customers with everyday low prices. At the center of the crusade to cast Wal-Mart in a bad light were Wal-Mart Watch and Wake Up Wal-Mart.[4] Wal-Mart Watch was founded by Andrew Stern, president of the Service Employees International Union (SEIU). Wake Up Wal-Mart was a project of the United Food and Commercial Workers International Union (UFCW). Wal-Mart Watch had an e-mail utility that visitors could use to direct the recipient to anti-Wal-Mart stories; the e-mail carried a prewritten header: "I thought you might enjoy this story from Wal-Mart Watch, a group who is starting to expose Wal-Mart for their bad labor standards, political corruptness and overall bad citizenship. It's getting a lot of attention in the press. Take a look."[5] The SEIU and the UFCW, along with most other unions, had for decades voiced their displeasure with Wal-Mart's conduct on a variety of fronts.

The biggest complaint of critics was that Wal-Mart's zealous pursuit of low costs had resulted in substandard wages and insufficient medical benefits for Wal-Mart's U.S. employees. Others complained that Wal-Mart sourced too much of its merchandise from Chinese suppliers, thus costing jobs for American workers and hastening the decline of the U.S. manufacturing sector. Some said the "Beast of Bentonville" was too big and too powerful. Community activists in California, New York, Vermont, Massachusetts, and several other areas were vigorously opposing the company's attempts to open big-box stores in their locales, claiming that they were unsightly and detracted from the small merchant atmosphere they wanted to preserve. Wal-Mart's low prices tended to attract customers away from locally owned apparel shops, general stores, pharmacies, sporting goods stores, shoe stores, hardware stores, supermarkets, and convenience stores. It was common for a number of local businesses that carried merchandise similar to Wal-Mart's lines to fail within a year or two of Wal-Mart's arrival—this phenomenon, known as the "Wal-Mart effect," was so potent that it had spawned sometimes fierce local resistance to the entry of a new Wal-Mart among both local merchants and area residents wanting to preserve the economic vitality of their downtown areas.

Union leaders at the UFCW, which represented workers at many supermarket chains, were adamant in their opposition to the opening of Wal-Mart Supercenters that had a full-sized supermarket in addition to the usual merchandise selection. The UFCW and its Wake Up Wal-Mart organization were exerting all the pressure they could to force Wal-Mart to raise its wages and benefits for associates to levels that would be comparable to union wages and benefits at unionized supermarket chains. A UFCW spokesperson said:

> Their productivity is becoming a model for taking advantage of workers, and our society is doomed if we think the answer is to lower our standards to Wal-Mart's level. What we need to do is to raise Wal-Mart to the standard we have set using the supermarket industry as an example so that Wal-Mart does not destroy our society community by community.[6]

[4]Kevin Haslett, "Unions Wage Vicious, Misguided War on Wal-Mart," December 19, 2005, www.bloomberg.com (accessed December 20, 2005).

[5]www.walmartwatch.com (accessed December 20, 2005).

[6]As quoted in Lorrie Grant, "Retail Giant Wal-Mart Faces Challenges on Many Fronts," *USA Today,* November 11, 2003, p. B2.

Wal-Mart's labor costs were said to be 20 percent less than those at unionized super-markets.[7] In Dallas, 20 supermarkets had closed once Wal-Mart had saturated the area with its Supercenters. According to one source, for every Wal-Mart Supercenter opened in the next five years, two other supermarkets would be forced to close.[8] A trade publication had estimated that Wal-Mart's opening of more than 1,000 Supercenters in the United States in the 2004–2008 period would boost Wal-Mart's grocery and related revenues from $82 billion to $162 billion, thus increasing its market share in groceries from 19 percent to 35 percent and its share of pharmacy and drugstore-related sales from 15 percent to 25 percent.[9]

Wal-Mart's public image took a hit in late 2003 when federal agents arrested nearly 250 illegal immigrants who worked for companies that had contracts to clean some 61 Wal-Mart stores in 21 states. Agents had searched a manager's office at Wal-Mart's Bentonville head-quarters and taken 18 boxes of documents relating to cleaning contractors dating back to March 2000.[10] Federal officials reportedly had wiretaps showing that Wal-Mart officials knew the company's janitorial contractors were using illegal cleaning crews. Wal-Mart, however, was indignant about the charges, saying that its managers had cooperated with federal authorities in the investigations for almost three years, helped agents tape conversations between some of its store managers and employees of the cleaning contractors suspected of using illegal immigrants, and revised its cleaning contracts in 2002 to include language that janitorial contractors comply with all federal, state, and local employment laws (because of the information developed in 2001), and begun bringing all janitorial work in-house because outsourcing was more expensive—at the time of the arrests, fewer than 700 Wal-Mart stores used outside cleaning contractors, down from almost half in 2000. In March 2005, Wal-Mart settled the charges with the Justice Department.

But Wal-Mart was battling a class action discrimination lawsuit filed in 2003 by six female employees claiming that management systematically discriminated against women in pay, promotions, training, and job assignments at Wal-Mart's U.S. stores. According to data from various sources, while two-thirds of Wal-Mart's hourly employees were women, less than 15 percent of management positions were held by women. There were also indications of pay gaps of 5–6 percent between male and female employees doing similar jobs and with similar experience levels; the pay gap allegedly widened higher up the management ladder. Female management trainees allegedly made an average of $22,371 a year, compared with $23,175 for male trainees. A second lawsuit claimed that some Wal-Mart store managers forced employees to work beyond their shifts without pay whenever employees were unable to complete assigned tasks.

And there had been several other incidents that had resulted in unflattering publicity and hits to Wal-Mart's public persona:

- In December 2005, Wal-Mart became the subject of a criminal investigation in Los Angeles over how it handled merchandise classified as hazardous waste. Wal-Mart apparently transported the materials from stores in California via a return center in Las Vegas before dumping them at a disposal site. But federal prosecutors said that violated the U.S. Resource Conservation and Recovery Act. Instead of stopping by the return center in Vegas, the materials should have gone straight to the disposal site.

- Wal-Mart was ordered to compensate a number of former employees in Canada after it was ruled that the retail giant closed a store as a reprisal against unionization attempts.

---

[7]Anthony Bianco and Wendy Zellner, "Is Wal-Mart Too Powerful?" *BusinessWeek,* October 6, 2003, p. 103.

[8]Ibid.

[9]Ibid., p. 108.

[10]Ann Zimmerman, "After Huge Raid on Illegals, Wal-Mart Fires back at U.S.," *Wall Street Journal,* December 19, 2003, pp. A1, A10.

In Colorado, the UFCW had accused Wal-Mart of harassing workers to keep them from joining its local in Denver and elsewhere; the number of such complaints had grown in recent years.

- A Wal-Mart board member, a high-level executive, and two Wal-Mart associates were dismissed following an internal investigation of improper expense account charges, improper payment of third-party invoices, and improper use of gift cards (some of which, according to critics, entailed efforts to finance anti-union activities and defeat unionization efforts at various Wal-Mart stores).

- Wal-Mart had to temporarily stop selling guns at its 118 stores across California following what California's attorney general said were hundreds of violations of state laws. Investigations by California authorities revealed that six Wal-Mart stores had released guns before the required 10-day waiting period, failed to verify buyers' identity properly, sold illegally to felons, and allowed other violations. Wal-Mart cooperated with government officials and agreed to immediately suspend firearm sales until correction action could be taken and store associates properly trained on state firearms laws.

- In New York State, Wal-Mart had run afoul of a 1988 toy weapons law. The toy guns Wal-Mart sold had an orange cap at the end of the barrel but otherwise looked real, thus violating New York laws banning toy guns with realistic colors such as black or aluminum and not complying with New York's requirement that toy guns have unremovable orange stripes along the barrel. Investigators from the state attorney general's office shopped 10 Wal-Marts in New York state from Buffalo to Long Island and purchased toy guns that violated the law at each of them. Wal-Mart had sold more than 42,000 toy guns in the state.

- Critics had slammed the company for refusing to stock CDs or DVDs with parental warning stickers (mostly profanity-laced hip-hop music) and for either pulling certain racy magazines (*Maxim, Stuff,* and *FHM*) from its shelves or obscuring their covers. They contended that Wal-Mart made no effort to survey shoppers about how they felt about such products but rather that it responded in ad hoc fashion to complaints lodged by a relative handful of customers and by conservative outside groups.[11] Wal-Mart had also been the only one of the top 10 drugstore chains to refuse to stock Preven, a morning-after contraceptive introduced in 1999, because company executives did not want its pharmacists to have to grapple with the moral dilemma of abortion. Moreover, Wal-Mart's high profile had made it a lightning rod for lawsuits, including one that it discriminated against female employees.

- A 98-minute feature-length documentary entitled *Wal-Mart: The High Cost of Low Price* premiered in November 2005 and bashed the company for destroying once-thriving downtowns, running local merchants out of business, paying meager wages, selling goods produced in sweatshops in third world countries, and assorted other corporate sins. The film included testimony from ex-employees describing seedy practices as well as clips of individuals, families, and communities that had struggled to fight the company on various issues. Canadian unions had urged their 340,000 members to take time to see the documentary and, where possible, to arrange screenings at local meetings and other union events. Anti-Wal-Mart journalists had praised the documentary. The *San Francisco Bay Guardian* said the movie "will make you fear and loathe it even more. The unscrupulous megaretailer is exposed from every angle: its devastating effect on small businesses and communities; its inadequate health care plans; its rabid antiunion stance; the racism and sexism sprinkled throughout its ranks; its blatant disregard for environmental issues; its practice of importing nearly all of its goods (churned from company

---

[11]Bianco and Zellner, "Is Wal-Mart Too Powerful?" pp. 104, 106.

sweatshops in countries like China, Bangladesh, and Honduras); and—perhaps most offensively—its faux-homespun television advertisements, which cast a golden glow on a corporation that clearly cares not for human beings, but for cold, hard cash."[12]

Initially, H. Lee Scott and other top Wal-Mart executives shrugged off the bad publicity and criticism and concentrated their full attention on running the business and expanding the company's operations into more countries and more communities—as Scott put it, "We would put up the sandbags and get out the machine guns."[13] But in 2004–2005, Scott started to see that all the Wal-Mart bashing was taking a toll on the company's sales growth and throwing up roadblocks to its expansion plans. He initiated an in-depth review of the company's legal and public relations woes and concluded that Wal-Mart ought to reach out to its critics, examine whether their concerns had merit, and seriously consider whether Wal-Mart ought to alter some of its practices without abandoning doing things that were the keys to its success.[14] Over the next several months, he met with an assortment of environmentalists and company critics to better understand their views, learn how companies could promote environmental sustainability, and solicit their suggestions about how the company could improve. The comprehensive transformation program initiated by Scott in 2005–2006 was his response.

COMPANY BACKGROUND

Wal-Mart's journey from humble beginnings in the 1960s as a folksy discount retailer in the boondocks of Arkansas to a global retailing juggernaut in 2008 was unprecedented among the companies of the world:

Fiscal Year	Sales	Profits	Stores
1962	$1.4 million	$112,000	9
1970	$31 million	$1.2 million	32
1980	$1.2 billion	$41 million	276
1990	$26 billion	$1 billion	1,528
2000	$153 billion	$5.3 billion	3,884
2008	$375 billion	$12.7 billion	7,262

Sales were expected to exceed $400 billion in fiscal 2009. Wal-Mart was the largest retailer in the United States, Canada, and Mexico, as well as the world as a whole. In 2007, Wal-Mart's sales revenues were bigger than the combined revenues of The Home Depot, Kroger, Costco, Target, and Sears and about 2.7 times the revenues of the world's second biggest retailer, France-based Carrefour. In calendar year 2006–2007, Wal-Mart's sales grew by more than Target's total 2007 sales. A 2003 report by the prominent Boston Consulting Group concluded that "the world has never known a company with such ambition, capability, and momentum."

Just as unprecedented was Wal-Mart's impact on general merchandise retailing and the attraction its stores had to shoppers in locations where it had stores. In 2008, nearly 180 million people per week shopped Wal-Mart's stores in 14 countries; in the United States, the numbers averaged 127 million per week. Since the early 1990s, the company had gone from dabbling in supermarket sales to being number one in grocery retailing worldwide. In the

---

[12]*San Francisco Bay Guardian* 40, no. 8 (November 23–29, 2005), www.sfbg.com (accessed December 20, 2005).

[13]As quoted in Marc Gunter, "The Green Machine," *Fortune,* August 7, 2006, p. 48.

[14]As quoted in "Can Wal-Mart Fit into a White Hat?" *BusinessWeek,* October 3, 2005, p. 94.

United States, Wal-Mart was the biggest employer in 21 states. As of June 2008, the company employed about 2.1 million people worldwide and was expanding its workforce by about 120,000 members annually.[15]

Wal-Mart's performance and prominence in the retailing industry had resulted in numerous awards. It had been named "Retailer of the Century" by *Discount Store News,* made the *Fortune* magazine lists of "Most Admired Companies in America" (it was ranked first in 2003 and 2004 and fourth in 2005) and "100 Best Companies to Work for in America," and been included on *Financial Times'* "Most Respected in the World" list. In 2005, Wal-Mart was ranked second on *Fortune*'s "Global Most Admired Companies" list. Wal-Mart was number one on both the Fortune 500 list of the largest U.S. corporations and *Fortune*'s Global 500 list every year from 2002 through 2007. Wal-Mart received the 2002 Ron Brown Award, the highest presidential award recognizing outstanding achievement in employee relations and community initiatives. In 2003, American Veterans Awards gave Wal-Mart its Corporate Patriotism Award. Three Wal-Mart executives were named to *Fortune*'s 2006 "50 Most Powerful Women in Business" list.

Exhibit 1 provides a summary of Wal-Mart's financial and operating performance for the 2000–2008 fiscal years. Wal-Mart's success had made the Walton family (Sam Walton's heirs and relatives) exceptionally wealthy—in 2008, various family members controlled more than 1.7 billion shares of Wal-Mart stock worth over $100 billion. Increases in the value of Wal-Mart's stock over the years had made hundreds of Wal-Mart employees, retirees, and shareholders millionaires or multimillionaires. Since 1970, when Wal-Mart shares were first issued to the public, the company's stock had split 11 times. A 100-share investment in Wal-Mart stock in 1970 at the initial offer price of $16.50 equated to 204,800 shares worth $12.1 million as of June 2008.

Sam Walton, Founder of Wal-Mart

Sam Walton graduated from the University of Missouri in 1940 with a degree in economics and took a job as a management trainee at J. C. Penney Co. His career with Penney's ended with a call to military duty in World War II. When the war was over, Walton decided to purchase a franchise and open a Ben Franklin retail variety store in Newport, Arkansas, rather than return to Penney's. Five years later, when the lease on the Newport building was lost, Walton decided to relocate his business to Bentonville, Arkansas, where he bought a building and opened Walton's 5 & 10 as a Ben-Franklin–affiliated store. By 1960 Walton was the largest Ben Franklin franchisee, with nine stores. But Walton was becoming concerned about the long-term competitive threat to variety stores posed by the emerging popularity of giant supermarkets and discounters. An avid pilot, he took off in his plane on a cross-country tour studying the changes in stores and retailing trends, then put together a plan for a discount store of his own because he believed deeply in the retailing concept of offering significant price discounts to expand sales volumes and increase overall profits. Walton went to Chicago to try to interest Ben Franklin executives in expanding into discount retailing; when they turned him down, he decided to go forward on his own.

The first Wal-Mart Discount City opened July 2, 1962, in Rogers, Arkansas. The store was successful, and Walton quickly began to look for opportunities to open stores in other small towns and to attract talented people with retailing experience to help him grow the business. Although he started out as a seat-of-the-pants merchant, he had great instincts, was quick to learn from other retailers' successes and failures, and was adept at garnering ideas for improvements from employees and promptly trying them out. Sam Walton incorporated his business as Wal-Mart Stores in 1969, with headquarters in obscure Bentonville,

---

[15]Jerry Useem, "One Nation Under Wal-Mart," *Fortune,* March 3, 2003, p. 66.

EXHIBIT 1   Financial and Operating Summary, Wal-Mart Stores, Fiscal Years 2000–2008 ($ in billions, except earnings per share data)

	Fiscal Years Ending January 31					
	2008	2007	2006	2004	2002	2000
FINANCIAL AND OPERATING DATA						
Net sales	$374.5	$345.0	$308.9	$252.8	$202.2	$156.2
Net sales increase	8.6%	11.7%	9.8%	11.6%	13.0%	18.7%
Comparable store sales increase in the United States*	2%	2%	3%	4%	6%	8%
Cost of sales	286.5	264.2	237.6	195.9	156.8	119.5
Operating, selling, general, and administrative expenses	70.3	64.0	55.7	43.9	34.3	25.2
Interest costs, net	1.8	1.5	1.2	.8	1.2	.8
Net income	12.7	11.3	11.2	9.1	6.6	5.3
Earnings per share of common stock (diluted)	$ 3.13	$ 2.71	$ 2.68	$ 2.07	$ 1.47	$ 1.19
BALANCE-SHEET DATA						
Current assets	$ 47.6	$ 47.0	$ 43.8	$ 34.2	$ 25.9	$ 23.0
Net property, plant, equipment, and capital leases	97.0	88.4	77.9	55.2	44.2	34.6
Total assets	163.5	151.6	136.2	104.9	79.3	67.3
Current liabilities	58.5	52.1	49.0	37.4	26.3	25.1
Long-term debt	29.8	27.2	26.4	17.5	15.6	13.7
Long-term obligations under capital leases	3.6	3.5	3.7	3.0	3.0	2.9
Shareholders' equity	64.6	61.6	53.2	43.6	35.2	25.9
FINANCIAL RATIOS						
Current ratio	0.8	0.9	0.9	0.9	1.0	0.9
Return on assets	8.4%	8.8%	9.3%	9.7%	9.0%	10.1%
Return on shareholders' equity	21.1%	22.0%	22.9%	22.4%	20.7%	24.5%
OTHER YEAR-END DATA						
Number of Wal-Mart discount stores in the United States	971	1,075	1,209	1,478	1,647	1,801
Number of Wal-Mart Supercenters in the United States	2,447	2,256	1,980	1,471	1,066	721
Number of Sam's Clubs in the United States	591	579	567	538	500	463
Number of Neighborhood Markets in the United States	132	112	100	64	31	7
Number of stores outside the United States	3,121	2,757	2,181	1,248	1,050	892

*Based on sales at stores open a full year that have not been expanded or relocated in the past 12 months.
Source: Wal-Mart annual report for 2008.

Arkansas—in 2005, the Wal-Mart-related traffic into and out of Bentonville was sufficient to support daily nonstop flights from New York City and Chicago. When the company went public in 1970, it had 38 stores and sales of $44.2 million. In 1979, with 276 stores, 21,000 employees, and operations in 11 states, Wal-Mart became the first company to reach $1 billion in sales in such a short time.

As the company grew, Sam Walton proved an effective and visionary leader. His folksy demeanor, and his talent for motivating people, combined with a very hands-on management style and an obvious talent for discount retailing, produced a culture and a set of values and beliefs that kept Wal-Mart on a path of continuous innovation and rapid expansion. Moreover, Wal-Mart's success and Walton's personable style of leadership generated numerous stories in the media that cast the company and its founder in a positive light. As Wal-Mart emerged as the premier discount retailer in the United States in the 1980s, an uncommonly large cross-section of the American public came to know who Sam Walton was and to associate his name with Wal-Mart. Regarded by many as "the entrepreneur of the century" and "a genuine American folk hero," he enjoyed a reputation as being community-spirited, a devoted family man who showed concern for his employees, demonstrated the virtues of hard work, and epitomized the American Dream. People inside and outside the company held him in high esteem.

Just before Walton's death in 1992, his vision was for Wal-Mart to become a $125 billion company by 2000. But his handpicked successor, David D. Glass, beat that target by almost two years. Under Glass's leadership (1988–2000), Wal-Mart's sales grew at an average annual compound rate of 19 percent, pushing revenues up from $20.6 billion to $156 billion. When Glass retired in January 2000, H. Lee Scott was chosen as Wal-Mart's third president and CEO. In the eight years that Scott had been CEO, Wal-Mart's sales had grown to $218 billion, more than double the revenue level the company achieved in its first 30 years.

WAL-MART'S STRATEGY

The hallmarks of Wal-Mart's strategy were a deeply ingrained dedication to cost-efficient operations, everyday low prices, multiple store formats, wide selection, a mix of both name-brand and private-label merchandise, a customer-friendly store environment, astute merchandising, limited advertising, customer satisfaction, disciplined expansion into new geographic markets, and the use of acquisitions to enter foreign country markets. Several of these elements merit further discussion.

Cost-Efficient Operations and Everyday Low Prices

From its earliest days and continuing to the present, top executives at Wal-Mart had vigorously and successfully pursued a low-cost leadership strategy. None of the world's major retailers could match Wal-Mart's zeal and competence in ferreting out cost savings and finding new and better ways to operate cost-efficiently. Wal-Mart's emphasis on achieving low costs extended to each and every value chain activity—starting with all the activities related to obtaining the desired merchandise from suppliers and then proceeding to all the logistical and distribution-related activities associated with managing inventory levels and stocking the shelves of its retail stores, all the activities involving the construction and operation of its retail stores, and keeping a tight rein on the costs of selling, general, and administrative activities. The company's competencies and capabilities in keeping its costs low allowed it to sell its merchandise at or near rock-bottom prices.

While Wal-Mart had not invented the concept of everyday low pricing, it had done a better job than any other discount retailer in executing the concept. The company was widely seen by consumers as being the general merchandise retailer with the lowest everyday prices, and its pricing strategy spilled over to cause other discount retailers to keep their prices lower than they otherwise might when one of their stores had to compete with a nearby Wal-Mart store. An independently certified study showed that Wal-Mart saved the average U.S. household more than $2,500 annually, counting both the direct effect on the purchases made by Wal-Mart shoppers and the indirect effect stemming from lower prices on the part of nearby retailers to better compete with Wal-Mart.[16] A second independent

[16]Business Planning Solutions, Global Insight Advisory Services Division, "The Price Impact of Wal-Mart: An Update Through 2006," September 4, 2007, www.livebetterindex.com (accessed June 11, 2008).

study showed that prices of grocery items at Wal-Mart Supercenters were 5 to 48 percent below such leading supermarket chain competitors as Kroger (which used the City Market brand in the states west of the Mississippi), Safeway, and Albertson's, after making allowances for specials and loyalty cards.[17] On average, Wal-Mart offered many identical food items at prices averaging 15 to 25 percent lower than traditional supermarkets. Warren Buffet said, "You add it all up and they have contributed to the financial well-being of the American public more than any other institution I can think of."[18]

Multiple Store Formats

In 2008, Wal-Mart employed four different retail concepts in the United States and Canada to attract and satisfy customers' needs: Wal-Mart discount stores, Supercenters, Neighborhood Markets, and Sam's Clubs:

- *Discount stores*—These stores ranged from 30,000 to 224,000 square feet (the average was 108,000 square feet), employed an average of 150 people, and offered as many as 80,000 different items, including family apparel, automotive products, health and beauty aids, home furnishings, electronics, hardware, toys, sporting goods, lawn and garden items, pet supplies, jewelry, housewares, prescription drugs, and packaged grocery items. Annual sales at a Wal-Mart discount store normally ran in the $40 to $60 million range. Wal-Mart was phasing down the number of discount stores; since 2000, the company had expanded or relocated and converted anywhere from 100 to 170 of its discount stores to the Supercenter format annually.

- *Supercenters*—*Supercenters*, which Wal-Mart started opening in 1988 to meet a demand for one-stop family shopping, joined the concept of a general merchandise discount store with that of a full-line supermarket. They ranged from 98,000 to 246,000 square feet (the average was 187,000 square feet), employed between 200 and 500 associates, had about 36 general merchandise departments, and offered up to 150,000 different items, at least 30,000 of which were grocery products. In addition to the value-priced merchandise offered at discount stores and a large supermarket section with 30,000+ items, Supercenters contained such specialty shops as vision centers, tire and lube express centers, a fast-food restaurant, portrait studios, one-hour photo centers, hair salons, banking, and employment agencies. Typical Supercenters had annual sales in the $70–$100 million range.

- *Sam's Clubs*—A store format that Wal-Mart launched in 1983, Sam's was a cash-and-carry, members-only warehouse that carried about 4,000 frequently used, mostly brand-name items in bulk quantities along with some big-ticket merchandise. The product lineup included fresh, frozen, and canned food products; candy and snack items; office supplies; janitorial and household cleaning supplies and paper products; apparel; CDs and DVDs; and an assortment of big-ticket items (TVs, tires, large and small appliances, watches, jewelry, computers, camcorders, and other electronic equipment). Stores ranged from 71,000 to 190,000 square feet (the average was 132,000 square feet), with most goods displayed in the original cartons stacked in wooden racks or on wooden pallets. Many items stocked were sold in bulk (five-gallon containers, bundles of a dozen or more, and economy-size boxes). Prices tended to be 10–15 percent below the prices of the company's discount stores and Supercenters since merchandising costs and store

[17]See Jerry Hausman and Ephraim Leibtag, "Consumer Benefits from Increased Competition in Shopping Outlets: Measuring the Effect of Wal-Mart" paper presented at the Economic Impact Research Conference: An In-Depth Look at Wal-Mart and Society, held in Washington, D.C., on November 4, 2005.

[18]As quoted in Useem, "One Nation Under Wal-Mart," p. 68.

operation costs were lower. Sam's was intended to serve small businesses, churches and religious organizations, beauty salons and barber shops, motels, restaurants, offices, schools, families, and individuals looking for great prices on large-volume quantities or big-ticket items. Annual member fees were $35 for businesses and $40 for individuals—there were more than 47 million members in 2008. Sam's stores employed about 125 people and had annual sales averaging $75 million. A number of Sam's stores were located adjacent to a Supercenter or discount store.

- *Neighborhood Markets*—Neighborhood markets, the company's newest store format, launched in 1998, were designed to appeal to customers who just needed groceries, pharmaceuticals, and general merchandise. They were always located in markets with Wal-Mart Supercenters so as to be readily accessible to Wal-Mart's food distribution network. Neighborhood Markets ranged from 37,000 to 56,000 square feet (the average was 42,000 square feet), employed 80–120 people, and had a full-line supermarket and a limited assortment of general merchandise.

U.S. and Canadian customers could also purchase a broad assortment of merchandise and services online at www.walmart.com.

During 2008 and 2009, Wal-Mart expected to open about 310 new Supercenters, 50 new Neighborhood Markets, and 50 new Sam's Clubs in the United States. Internationally, Wal-Mart planned to spend more than $10 billion to add about 50 million square feet of retail space in 2008 and 2009. A major initiative to enter the retailing market in India was under way. Wal-Mart expected that its international growth would outpace its domestic growth in the years to come.

Exhibit 2 shows the number of Wal-Mart stores by country as of January 31, 2008. A number of locations in the United States were underserved by Wal-Mart stores. Inner-city sections of New York City had no Wal-Mart stores of any kind because ample space with plenty of parking was unavailable at a reasonable price. Wal-Mart's first Supercenter in all of California opened in March 2004, and the whole state had just 31 Supercenters in early 2008. There were only 6 Supercenters in Massachusetts, 1 in New Jersey, and 5 in Connecticut (versus 289 in Texas, 152 in Florida, 119 in Georgia, 99 in Tennessee, 87 in Alabama, and 86 in Missouri).

Wide Product Selection and a Mix of Name-Brand and Private-Label Merchandise

A core element of Wal-Mart's strategy was to provide customers with such a wide assortment of products that they could obtain much of what they needed at affordable prices in one convenient place. Supercenters, which carried a broad lineup of general merchandise as well as a full selection of supermarket items, were very much a one-stop shopping experience for many consumers.

A significant portion of the merchandise that Wal-Mart stocked consisted of name-brand, nationally advertised products. But it also marketed merchandise under some 20 private-label brands and, in addition, such licensed brands as General Electric, Disney, McDonald's, and Better Homes and Gardens.

Customer-Friendly Store Environment

In all Wal-Mart stores, efforts were made to present merchandise in easy-to-shop shelving and displays. Floors in the apparel section were carpeted to make the department feel homier and to make shopping seem easier on customers' feet. Lighting was designed to create a soft, warm impression. Signage indicating the location of various departments was prominent. Store layouts were constantly scrutinized to improve shopping convenience and make it easier for customers to find items. Store associates wore blue vests with the tag line

EXHIBIT 2 Wal-Mart's Store Count, January 31, 2008

Country	Discount Stores	Supercenters	Sam's Clubs	Neighborhood Markets
United States	971 (all states except Nebraska, South Dakota, and Wyoming)	2,447 (all states except Hawaii and Vermont)	591 (all states except Oregon and Vermont)	132 (in 15 states)

	Number of Stores	Store Formats and Brand Names		
Argentina	21	20 Supercenters and 1 combination discount and grocery store (Changomas)		
Brazil	313	29 Supercenters; 21 Sam's Clubs; 70 hypermarkets (Hiper Bompreco, Big); 158 supermarkets (Bompreco, Mercadorama, Nacional); 13 cash-and-carry stores (Maxxi Alacado); 21 combination discount and grocery stores (Todo Dia); and 1 general merchandise store (Magazine)		
Canada	305	31 Supercenters, 268 discount stores, 6 Sam's Clubs		
China	202	96 Supercenters, 2 Neighborhood Markets, 3 Sam's Clubs, 101 hypermarkets (Trust-Mart)		
Costa Rica	154	6 hypermarkets (Hiper Mas), 28 supermarkets (Más por Menos), 9 warehouse stores (Maxi Bodega), and 111 discount stores (Despensa Familiar)		
El Salvador	70	2 hypermarkets (Hiper Piaz), 32 supermarkets (La Despensa de Don Juan), and 36 discount stores (Despensa Familiar)		
Guatemala	145	6 hypermarkets (Hiper Piaz), 28 supermarkets (Piaz), 12 warehouse stores (Maxi Bodega), 2 membership clubs (Club Co), and 97 discount stores (Despensa Familiar)		
Honduras	47	1 hypermarket (Hiper Piaz), 7 supermarkets (Piaz), 7 warehouse stores (Maxi Bodega), and 32 discount stores (Despensa Familiar)		
Japan	394	114 hypermarkets (Livin, Seiyu), 276 supermarkets (Seiyu, Sunny), and 4 general merchandise stores (Seiyu)		
Mexico	1,023	136 Supercenters; 83 Sam's Clubs; 129 supermarkets (Superama, Mi Bodega); 246 combination discount and grocery stores (Bodega); 76 department stores (Suburbia); 349 restaurants; and 4 discount stores (Mi Bodega Express)		
Nicaragua	46	6 supermarkets (La Unión) and 40 discount stores (Pali)		
Puerto Rico	54	6 Supercenters, 8 discount stores, 9 Sam's Clubs, and 31 supermarkets (Amigo)		
United Kingdom	352	29 Supercenters (Asda); 298 supermarkets (Asda, Asda Small Town); 13 general merchandise stores (Asda Living); and 12 apparel stores (George)—the apparel stores were scheduled to be closed in 2008		

Source: Wal-Mart's 2008 annual report, p. 51.

"How May I Help You?" on the back to make it easier for customers to pick them out from a distance. Yet nothing about the decor conflicted with Wal-Mart's low-price image; retailing consultants considered Wal-Mart as being adept at sending out an effective mix of vibes and signals concerning customer service, low prices, quality merchandise, and friendly shopping environment. Wal-Mart's management believed that the attention paid to all the details of making the stores more user-friendly and inviting caused shoppers to view Wal-Mart in a more positive light.

Astute Merchandising

Wal-Mart was unusually active in testing and experimenting with new merchandising techniques. From the beginning, Sam Walton had been quick to imitate good ideas and merchandising practices employed by other retailers. According to the founder of Kmart, Sam Walton "not only copied our concepts; he strengthened them. Sam just took the ball and ran with it."[19] Wal-Mart prided itself on its "low threshold for change," and much of

[19]As quoted in Bill Saporito, "What Sam Walton Taught America," *Fortune,* May 4, 1992, p. 105.

management's time was spent talking to vendors, employees, and customers to get ideas for how Wal-Mart could improve. Suggestions were actively solicited from employees. Most any reasonable idea was tried; if it worked well in stores where it was first tested, then it was quickly implemented in other stores. Experiments in store layout, merchandise displays, store color schemes, merchandise selection (whether to add more upscale lines or shift to a different mix of items), and sales promotion techniques were always under way. Wal-Mart was regarded as an industry leader in testing, adapting, and applying a wide range of cutting-edge merchandising approaches. In 2005–2006, Wal-Mart began upgrading the caliber of the merchandise it stocked in certain departments so as to be more competitive with Target, its major rival in discount retailing.

Limited Advertising

Wal-Mart relied less on advertising than most other discount chains. The company distributed only one or two circulars per month and ran occasional TV ads, relying primarily on its widely known reputation and word of mouth to generate store traffic. Wal-Mart's advertising expenditures ran about 0.3 percent of sales revenues, versus around 1.5 percent for Kmart and 2.3 percent for Target. Wal-Mart's spending for radio and TV advertising was said to be so low that it didn't register on national ratings scales. Most Wal-Mart broadcast ads appeared on local TV and local cable channels. The company often allowed charities to use its parking lots for their fund-raising activities. Wal-Mart did little or no advertising for its Sam's Club stores; however, in 2008, Wal-Mart did put a four-page color brochure insert in local newspapers that included a printed invitation giving anyone (including nonmembers) the ability to shop at their local Sam's Club during Sam's special 25th Anniversary Open House celebration on April 18–20.

Disciplined Expansion into New Geographic Markets

One of the most distinctive features of Wal-Mart's domestic strategy in its early years was the manner in which it expanded into new geographic areas. Whereas many chain retailers achieved regional and national coverage quickly by entering the largest metropolitan centers before trying to penetrate less populated markets, Wal-Mart always expanded into adjoining geographic areas, saturating each area with stores before moving into new territory. New stores were usually clustered within 200 miles of an existing distribution center so that deliveries could be made cost-effectively on a daily basis; new distribution centers were added as needed to support store expansion into additional areas. In the United States, the really unique feature of Wal-Mart's geographic strategy had involved opening stores in small towns surrounding a targeted metropolitan area before moving into the metropolitan area itself—an approach Sam Walton had termed "backward expansion." Wal-Mart management believed that any town with a shopping area population of 15,000 or more was big enough to support a Wal-Mart discount store and that towns of 25,000 could support a Supercenter. Once stores were opened in towns around the most populous city, Wal-Mart would locate one or more stores in the metropolitan area and begin major market advertising. By clustering new stores in a relatively small geographic area, the company's advertising expenses for breaking into a new market could be shared across all the area stores, a tactic Wal-Mart used to keep its advertising costs under 1 percent of sales.

The Use of Acquisitions to Expand into Foreign Markets

In recent years, Wal-Mart had been driving hard to expand its geographic base of stores outside the United States largely through acquisition and partly through new store construction. Wal-Mart's entry into Canada, Mexico, Brazil, Japan, Puerto Rico, China, Germany, South Korea, and Great Britain had been accomplished by acquiring existing general merchandise or supermarket chains. Many of the acquired stores still operated under their former names (see Exhibit 2), and in most countries Wal-Mart was being cautious in rebranding them as Wal-Mart stores. In August 2007, Wal-Mart and India-based Bharti Enterprises announced a joint venture to conduct wholesale cash-and-carry and back-end supply chain management operations in India, the world's second most populous country; the first wholesale facility was scheduled to open in late 2008. Wal-Mart's international strategy was to "remain local" in terms of the goods it merchandised, its use of local suppliers where feasible, and in some of the ways it operated. Management strived to adapt Wal-Mart's "standard" operating practices to be responsive to local communities and cultures, the needs and merchandise preferences of local customers, and local suppliers. Most store managers and senior managers in its foreign operations were natives of the countries where Wal-Mart operated; many had begun their careers as hourly employees. Wal-Mart did, however, have a program where stores in different countries exchanged best practices.

Wal-Mart's international division had fiscal 2008 sales of $90.6 billion (up 17.5 percent over fiscal 2007) and operating profits of $4.8 billion (up 21.7 percent). International sales accounted for 24.2 percent of total sales—this percentage had been rising steadily since 2000 and was expected to continue to rise in coming years. Sales at Wal-Mart's international stores averaged about $29 million in sales per store in fiscal 2008; Wal-Mart had more than 620,000 employees in its international operations.

WAL-MART'S COMPETITORS

Discount retailing was an intensely competitive business. Competition among discount retailers centered around pricing, store location, variations in store format and merchandise mix, store size, shopping atmosphere, and image with shoppers. Wal-Mart's primary competitors were Kmart and Target. Like Wal-Mart, Kmart and Target had stores that stocked only general merchandise as well as superstores (Super Target and Super Kmart) that included a full-line supermarket on one side of the store. Wal-Mart also competed against category retailers like Best Buy and Circuit City in electronics; Toy "R" Us in toys; Kohl's and Goody's in apparel; and Bed, Bath, and Beyond in household goods.

Wal-Mart's rapid climb to become the largest supermarket retailer via its Supercenters had intensified competition in the supermarket industry in the United States and Canada. Virtually all supermarkets located in communities with a Supercenter were scrambling to cut costs, narrow the price gap with Wal-Mart, and otherwise differentiate themselves so as to retain their customer base and grow revenues. Continuing increases in the number of Wal-Mart Supercenters meant that the majority of rival supermarkets in the United States would be within 10 miles of a Supercenter by 2010. Wal-Mart had recently concluded that it took fewer area residents to support a Supercenter than originally thought—sales data indicated that Supercenters in sizable urban areas could be as little as four miles apart and still attract sufficient store traffic.

The two largest competitors in the warehouse club segment were Costco Wholesale and Sam's Clubs; BJ's Wholesale Club, a smaller East Coast chain, was the only other major U.S. player in this segment. In 2007, Costco had sales of $63.1 billion at 499 stores versus $44.4 billion at 591 stores for Sam's. The average Costco store generated annual revenues of $126 million, about 68 percent more than the $75 million average at Sam's. Costco, which had 52.6 million members as of May 2008, catered to affluent households with upscale tastes and located its stores in mostly urban areas. Costco was the United States' biggest retailer of fine wines ($500 million annually) and roasted chickens (100,000 a day). While its product line included food and household items, sporting goods, vitamins, and various other merchandise, its main attraction was big-ticket luxury items (diamonds and big-screen TVs) and the latest gadgets at bargain prices (Costco capped its markups at

14 percent). Costco had beaten Sam's in being the first to sell fresh meat and produce (1986 versus 1989), to introduce private-label items (1995 versus 1998), and to sell gasoline (1995 versus 1997).[20] Costco offered its workers good wages and fringe benefits: full-time hourly workers made about $40,000 a year after four years.

Internationally, Wal-Mart's biggest competitor was Carrefour, a France-based retailer with 2007 sales of €92.2 million and nearly 15,000 stores of varying formats and sizes across much of Europe and in such emerging markets as Argentina, Brazil, Colombia, China, Indonesia, South Korea, and Taiwan. Both Wal-Mart and Carrefour were expanding aggressively in Brazil and China, going head-to-head in an increasing number of locations. Going into 2008, Carrefour had 1,615 stores (500 of which were hypermarkets) in Asia and Latin America, with sales approximating €15.8 million.

WAL-MART'S APPROACHES TO STRATEGY EXECUTION

To profitably execute its everyday low price strategy, Wal-Mart put heavy emphasis on getting the lowest possible prices from its suppliers, forging close working relationships with key suppliers in order to capture win–win cost savings throughout its supply chain, keeping its internal operations lean and efficient, paying attention to even the tiniest details in store layouts and merchandising, making efficient use of state-of-the art technology, and nurturing a culture that thrived on pleasing customers, hard work, constant improvement, and passing cost-savings on to customers in the form of low prices.

Relationships with Suppliers

Wal-Mart was far and away the biggest customer of virtually all of its 66,000 suppliers. Wal-Mart's scale of operation (see Exhibit 3) allowed it to bargain hard with suppliers and get their bottom prices. In 2005, Wal-Mart's requirements for personal computers for the holiday sales season were so big that Hewlett-Packard devoted 3 of its 10 plants operated

EXHIBIT 3   The Scale of Wal-Mart's Purchases from Selected Suppliers and Its Market Shares in Selected Product Categories, 2002–2003

Supplier	Percent of Total Sales to Wal-Mart	Product Category	Wal-Mart's U.S. Market Share*
Tandy Brands Accessories	39%	Dog food	36%
Dial	28	Disposable diapers	32
Del Monte Foods	24	Photographic film	30
Clorox	23	Shampoo	30
Revlon	20–23	Paper towels	30
RJR Tobacco	20	Toothpaste	26
Procter & Gamble	17	Pain remedies	21
		CDs, DVDs, and videos	15–20
		Single-copy sales of magazines	15

Although sales percentages were not available, Wal-Mart was also the biggest customer of Disney, Campbell Soup, Kraft, and Gillette.	Although market shares were not available, Wal-Mart was also the biggest seller of toys, guns, detergent, video games, socks, and bedding.

*Based on sales through food, drug, and mass merchandisers.
Sources: Jerry Useem, "One Nation Under Wal-Mart," *Fortune*, March 3, 2003, p. 66, and Anthony Bianco and Wendy Zellner, "Is Wal-Mart Too Powerful?" *BusinessWeek*, October 6, 2003, p. 102.

[20]John Helyar, "The Only Company Wal-Mart Fears," *Fortune*, November 24, 2003, pp. 158–166.

by contract manufacturers to turning out products solely for Wal-Mart. Wal-Mart looked for suppliers who were dominant in their category (thus providing strong brand-name recognition), who could grow with the company, who had full product lines (so that Wal-Mart buyers could both cherry-pick and get some sort of limited exclusivity on the products it chose to carry), who had the long-term commitment to R&D to bring new and better products to retail shelves, and who had the ability to become more efficient in producing and delivering what they supplied. But it also dealt with thousands of small suppliers (mom-and-pop companies, small farmers, and minority businesses) who could furnish particular items for stores in a certain geographical area. Many Wal-Mart stores had a "Store of the Community" section that showcased local products from local producers; in addition, Wal-Mart had set up an export office in the United States to help small and medium-sized businesses export their American-made products (especially to Wal-Mart stores in foreign countries).

Wal-Mart buyers literally shopped the world for merchandise suitable for the company's stores—it purchased from 61,000 U.S. suppliers and some 5,000 foreign suppliers in 40 countries in 2007; purchases from U.S. suppliers totaled $200 billion in 2005 and supported more than 3 million American jobs. Procurement personnel spent a lot of time meeting with vendors and understanding their cost structure. By making the negotiation process transparent, Wal-Mart buyers soon learned whether a vendor was doing all it could to cut down its costs and quote Wal-Mart an attractively low price. Wal-Mart's purchasing agents were dedicated to getting the lowest prices they could, and they did not accept invitations to be wined or dined by suppliers. The marketing vice president of a major vendor told *Fortune* magazine:

> They are very, very focused people, and they use their buying power more forcefully than anybody else in America. All the normal mating rituals are verboten. Their highest priority is making sure everybody at all times in all cases knows who's in charge, and it's Wal-Mart. They talk softly, but they have piranha hearts, and if you aren't totally prepared when you go in there, you'll have your ass handed to you.[21]

All vendors were expected to offer their best price without exception; one consultant that helped manufacturers sell to retailers observed, "No one would dare come in with a half-ass price."[22] Even though Wal-Mart was tough in negotiating for absolute rock-bottom prices, the price quotes it got were still typically high enough to allow suppliers to earn a profit. Being a Wal-Mart supplier generally meant having a stable, dependable sales base that allowed the supplier to operate production facilities cost-effectively. Moreover, once it decided to source from a vendor, then Wal-Mart worked closely with the vendor to find *mutually beneficial* ways to squeeze costs out of the supply chain. Every aspect of a supplier's operation got scrutinized—how products got developed, what they were made of, how costs might be reduced, what data Wal-Mart could supply that would be useful, how sharing of data online could prove beneficial, and so on. Nearly always, as they went through the process with Wal-Mart personnel, suppliers saw ways to prune costs or otherwise streamline operations to enhance profit margins.

In 1989, Wal-Mart became the first major retailer to embark on a program urging vendors to develop products and packaging that would not harm the environment. In addition, Wal-Mart expected its vendors to contribute ideas about how to make its stores more fun insofar as their products were concerned. Those suppliers that were selected as "category managers" for such product groupings as lingerie, pet food, and school supplies were expected to educate Wal-Mart on everything that was happening in their respective product category.

---

[21]As quoted in *Fortune,* January 30, 1989, p. 53.
[22]As quoted in Useem, "One Nation Under Wal-Mart," p. 68.

Some 200 vendors had established offices in Bentonville to work closely with Wal-Mart on a continuing basis—most were in an area referred to locally as "Vendorville." Vendors were encouraged to voice any problems in their relationship with Wal-Mart and to become involved in Wal-Mart's future plans. Top-priority projects ranged from using more recyclable packaging to working with Wal-Mart on merchandise displays and product mix to tweaking the just-in-time ordering and delivery system to instituting automatic reordering arrangements to coming up with new products with high customer appeal. Most recently, one of Wal-Mart's priorities was working with vendors to figure out how to localize the items carried in particular stores and thereby accommodate varying tastes and preferences of shoppers in different areas where Wal-Mart had stores. Most vendor personnel based in Bentonville spent considerable time focusing on which items in their product line were best for Wal-Mart, where they ought to be placed in the stores, how they could be better displayed, what new products ought to be introduced, and which ones ought to be rotated out.

A 2007 survey conducted by Cannondale Associates found that manufacturers believed Wal-Mart was the overall best retailer with which to do business—the ninth straight year in which Wal-Mart was ranked number one.[23] Target was ranked second, and Costco was ranked third. The criteria for the ranking included such factors as clearest company strategy, store branding, best buying teams, most innovative consumer marketing/merchandising, best supply chain management practices, overall business fundamentals, and best practice management of individual product categories. One retailing consultant said, "I think most [suppliers] would say Wal-Mart is their most profitable account."[24] While this might seem surprising because of Wal-Mart's enormous bargaining clout, the potentially greater profitability of selling to Wal-Mart stemmed from the practices of most other retailers to demand that suppliers pay sometimes steep slotting fees to win shelf space and their frequent insistence on supplier payment of such "extras" as in-store displays, damage allowances, handling charges, penalties for late deliveries, rebates of one kind or another, allowances for advertising, and special allowances on slow-moving merchandise that had to be cleared out with deep price discounts. Further, most major retailers expected to be courted with Super Bowl tickets, trips to the Masters Golf tournament, fancy dinners at conventions and trade shows, or other perks in return for their business. All of these extras represented costs that suppliers had to build into their prices. At Wal-Mart, everything was boiled down to one price number and no "funny-money" extras ever entered into the deal.[25]

Most suppliers viewed Wal-Mart's single bottom-line price and its expectation of close coordination as a win–win proposition, not only because of the benefits of cutting out all the funny-money costs and solidifying their relationship with a major customer but also because what they learned from the collaborative efforts and mutual data sharing often had considerable benefit in the rest of their operations. Many suppliers, including Procter & Gamble, liked Wal-Mart's supply chain business model so well that they had pushed their other customers to adopt similar practices.[26]

Wal-Mart's Standards for Suppliers

In 1992 Wal-Mart began establishing standards for its suppliers, with particular emphasis on suppliers located in foreign countries that had a history of problematic wages and working conditions. Management believed that the manner in which suppliers conducted their

[23]Cannondale Associates, "2005 PoweRanking Results," press release, November 2, 2005, www.cannondaleassoc.com (accessed December 15, 2005).

[24]As quoted in Useem, "One Nation Under Wal-Mart," p. 74.

[25]Ibid.

[26]Ibid.

business regarding the hours of work required of workers daily and weekly, the use of child labor, discrimination based on race or religion or other factors, and workplace safety and whether suppliers complied with local laws and regulations could be attributed to Wal-Mart and affect its reputation with customers and shareholders. To mitigate the potential for Wal-Mart to be adversely affected by the manner in which its suppliers conducted their business, Wal-Mart had established a set of supplier standards and set up an internal group to see that suppliers were conforming to the ethical standards and business practices stated in its published standards. The company's supplier standards had been through a number of changes as the concerns of Wal-Mart management evolved over time.

In February 2003, Wal-Mart took direct control of foreign factory audits; factory certification teams based in China, Singapore, India, United Arab Emirates, and Honduras were staffed with more than 200 Wal-Mart employees dedicated to monitoring foreign factory compliance with the company's supplier standards. Training and compliance sessions were held regularly with foreign suppliers at various locations around the world. All suppliers were asked to sign a document certifying their compliance with the standards and were required to post a version of the supplier standards in both English and the local language in each production facility servicing Wal-Mart. In 2006, Wal-Mart conducted 16,700 audits at 8,873 plants of suppliers; 26 percent of the audits conducted were unannounced. Wal-Mart worked closely with suppliers to correct any violations; supplier factories that failed to correct serious violations were permanently banned from producing merchandise sold by Wal-Mart (0.2 percent of the foreign factories failed Wal-Mart's auditing of their operations in both 2005 and 2006 and were permanently banned; an additional 2.1 percent in 2006 and 0.1 percent in 2005 were banned for one year after re-audits found insufficient progress in correcting prior audit violations that were deemed significant).

Wal-Mart's Use of Cutting-Edge Technology

Wal-Mart's approach to technology was to be on the offense—probing, testing, and then deploying the newest equipment, retailing techniques, computer software programs, and related technological advances to increase productivity and drive costs down. Wal-Mart was typically a first-mover among retailers in upgrading and improving its capabilities as new technology was introduced. The company's technological goal was to provide employees with the tools to do their jobs more efficiently and to make better decisions.

Wal-Mart began using computers to maintain inventory control on an item basis in distribution centers and in its stores in 1974. In 1981, Wal-Mart began testing point-of-sale scanners and then committed to systemwide use of scanning bar codes in 1983—a move that resulted in 25–30 percent faster checkout of customers. In 1984, Wal-Mart developed a computer-assisted merchandising system that allowed the product mix in each store to be tailored to its own market circumstances and sales patterns. Between 1985 and 1987, Wal-Mart installed the nation's largest private satellite communication network, which allowed two-way voice and data transmission between headquarters, the distribution centers, and the stores and one-way video transmission from Bentonville's corporate offices to distribution centers and to the stores; the system was less expensive than the previously used telephone network. The video system was used regularly by company officials to speak directly to all employees at once.

In 1989, Wal-Mart established direct satellite links with about 1,700 vendors supplying close to 80 percent of the goods sold by Wal-Mart; this link-up allowed the use of electronic purchase orders and instant data exchanges. Wal-Mart had also used the satellite system's capabilities to develop a credit card authorization procedure that took 5 seconds, on average, to authorize a purchase, speeding up credit checkout by 25 percent compared to the prior manual system. In the early 1990s, through pioneering collaboration with Procter & Gamble, it instituted an automated reordering system that notified suppliers as their items moved though store checkout lanes; this allowed suppliers to track sales and inventories of their products (so they could plan production and schedule shipments accordingly).

By 2003, the company had developed and deployed sophisticated information technology (IT) systems and online capability that not only gave it real-time access to detailed figures on most any aspect of its operations but also made it a leader in cost-effective supply chain management. It could track the movement of goods through its entire value chain—from the sale of items at the cash register backward to stock on store shelves, in-store backup inventory, distribution center inventory, and shipments en route. Moreover, Wal-Mart had collaborated with its suppliers to develop data-sharing capabilities aimed at streamlining the supply of its stores, avoiding both stock-outs and excess inventories, identifying slow-selling items that might warrant replacement, and spotting ways to squeeze costs out of the supply chain. The company's Retail Link system allowed 30,000 suppliers to track their wares through Wal-Mart's value chain, get hourly sales figures for each item, and monitor gross margins on each of their products (Wal-Mart's actual selling price less what it paid the supplier).

In mid-2003, in another of its trend-setting moves, Wal-Mart informed its suppliers that they had to convert to electronic product code (EPC) technology based on radio frequency identification (RFID) systems. Electronic product codes involved embedding every single item that rolled off a manufacturing line with an electronic tag containing a unique number. EPC tags could be read by radio frequency scanners when brought into range of a tag reader, thus providing the ability to locate and track items throughout the supply chain in real time. With EPC and RFID capability, every single can of soup or DVD or screwdriver in Wal-Mart's supply chain network or on its store shelves could be traced back to when it was made, where and when a case or pallet of goods arrived, and where and when an item was sold or turned up missing. Further, EPC codes linked to an online database provided a secure way of sharing product-specific information with supply chain partners. Wal-Mart management believed EPC technology, in conjunction with the expanding production of RFID capable printers/encoders, had the potential to revolutionize the supply chain by providing more accurate information about product movement, stock rotation, and inventory levels; it was also seen as a significant tool for preventing theft and dealing with product recalls. An IBM study indicated that EPC tagging would reduce out-of-stocks by 33 percent, while an Accenture study showed that EPC/RFID technology could boost worker productivity by 5 percent and shrink working capital and fixed capital requirements by 5 to 30 percent. In 2005, EPC/RFID technology implementation was under way for Wal-Mart's top 200 suppliers, with some 20,000 suppliers to be involved in some way by the end of 2006 and virtually all suppliers to have RFID capabilities by 2010.

In 2008, Wal-Mart's data center was tracking more than 700 million stock-keeping units (SKUs) weekly. The company had more than 88,000 associates engaged in logistics and information systems activities. The attention Wal-Mart management placed on using cutting-edge technology and the astuteness with which it deployed this technology along its value chain to enhance store operations and continuously drive down costs had, over the years, resulted in Wal-Mart being widely regarded as having the most cost-effective, data-rich IT systems of any major retailer in the world. It spent less than 1 percent of revenues on IT (far less than other retailers) and had stronger capabilities. According to Linda Dillman, Wal-Mart's chief information officer, "The strength of this division is, we are doers and do things faster than lightning. We can implement things faster than anyone could with a third party. We run the entire world out of facilities in this area [Bentonville] at a cost that no one can touch. We'd be nuts to outsource."[27] Wal-Mart rarely used commercial software, preferring to develop its own IT systems. So powerful had Wal-Mart's

---

[27]As quoted in "Wal-Mart's Way," *Information Week,* September 27, 2004.

influence been on retail supply chain efficiency that its competitors (and many other retailers as well) had found it essential to follow Wal-Mart's lead and pursue "Wal-Martification" of their retail supply chains.[28]

Distribution Center Operations

In 2008, Wal-Mart had 112 distribution centers. A distribution center served 75–100 stores (usually within a 250-mile radius) and employed anywhere from 500 to 1,000 associates. Distribution centers had as much as five miles of conveyor belts and the capability to move hundreds of thousands of cases through the center each day.

Over the past three decades, Wal-Mart had pursued a host of efficiency-increasing actions at its distribution centers. It had been a global leader in adopting the latest technology to automate most all of the labor-intensive tasks at its distribution centers, gradually creating an ever-more-sophisticated and cost-efficient system of conveyors, bar coders, handheld computers, and other devices with the capability to quickly sort incoming shipments from manufacturers into smaller, store-specific quantities and route them to waiting trucks to be sent to stores to replenish sold merchandise. Prior to automation, bulk cases received from manufacturers had to be opened by distribution center employees and perhaps stored in bins, then picked and repacked in quantities needed for specific stores and loaded onto trucks for delivery to Wal-Mart stores—a manual process that was error-prone and sometimes slow in filling store orders. Often, incoming goods from manufacturers being unloaded at one section of the warehouse were immediately sorted into store-specific amounts and conveyed directly onto waiting Wal-Mart trucks headed for those particular stores—a large portion of the incoming inventory was in a Wal-Mart distribution center an average of only 12 hours. Distribution center employees had access to real-time information regarding the inventory levels of all items in the center and used the different barcodes for pallets, bins, and shelves to pick up items for store orders. Handheld computers also enabled the packaging department to get accurate information about which items to pack for which store and what loading dock to have packages conveyed. Wal-Mart's trendsetting use of cutting-edge retailing technologies and its best-practices leadership in logistical activities had given it operating advantages and raised the bar for not only its competitors but most other retailers as well.

The company's latest initiatives to enhance distribution and logistical efficiency were to (1) achieve full implementation of RFID systems from suppliers to distribution systems to store operations and (2) double the fuel efficiency of its truck fleet. In early 2008, because some 15,000 suppliers were deemed to be dragging their heels in implementing RFID, Wal-Mart announced it would begin charging its Sam's Club suppliers a $2 fee for each pallet delivered without RFID tagging to select distribution centers, with the fee applying to progressively more distribution centers in upcoming periods; Wal-Mart also said the $2 fee would gradually be increased to $3 and that RFID tagging would in upcoming months begin applying to cases and selling-unit packages on pallets.

Truck Fleet Operations

Wal-Mart had a fleet of 7,200+ company-owned trucks and a force of 8,000+ drivers that it used to transport goods from its 112 distribution centers to its stores. Wal-Mart hired only experienced drivers who had driven more than 300,000 accident-free miles with no major traffic violations. Distribution centers had facilities where drivers could shower, sleep, eat, or do personal business while waiting for their truck to be loaded. A truck dispatch coordinator

---

[28]Paul Lightfoot, "Wal-Martification," *Operations and Fulfillment,* June 1, 2003, www.opsandfulfillment.com.

scheduled the dispatch of all trucks based on the available time of drivers and estimated driving time between the distribution center and the designated store. Drivers were expected to pull their truck up to the store dock at the scheduled time (usually late afternoon or early evening) even if they arrived early; trucks were unloaded by store personnel during nighttime hours, with a two-hour gap between each new truck delivery (if more than one was scheduled for the same night).

In instances where it was economical, Wal-Mart trucks were dispatched directly to a manufacturer's facilities, picked up goods for one or more stores, and delivered them directly, bypassing the distribution center entirely. Manufacturers that supplied certain high-volume items or even a number of different items sometimes delivered their products in truckload lots directly to some or many of Wal-Mart's stores.

Store Construction and Maintenance

Wal-Mart management worked at getting more mileage out of its capital expenditures for new stores, store renovations, and store fixtures. Ideas and suggestions were solicited from vendors regarding store layout, aisle width, the design of fixtures, and space needed for effective displays. Wal-Mart's store designs had open-air offices for management personnel that could be furnished economically and featured a maximum of display space that could be rearranged and refurbished easily. Because Wal-Mart insisted on a high degree of uniformity in the new stores it built, the architectural firm Wal-Mart employed was able to use computer modeling techniques to turn out complete specifications for 12 or more new stores a week. Moreover, the stores were designed to permit quick, inexpensive construction as well as to allow for high energy efficiency and low-cost maintenance and renovation. All stores were renovated and redecorated at least once every seven years. If a given store location was rendered obsolete by the construction of new roads and highways and the opening of new shopping locations, then the old store was abandoned in favor of a new store at a more desirable site.

In keeping with the low-cost theme for facilities, Wal-Mart's distribution centers and corporate offices were also built economically and furnished simply. The offices of top executives were modest and unpretentious. The lighting, heating, and air-conditioning controls at all Wal-Mart stores were connected via computer to Bentonville headquarters, allowing cost-saving energy management practices to be implemented centrally and freeing store managers from the time and worry of trying to hold down utility costs. Wal-Mart mass-produced a lot of its displays in-house, not only saving money but also cutting the time to roll out a new display concept to as little as 30 days. It also had a group that disposed of used fixtures and equipment that could not be used at other stores via auctions at the store sites where the surplus existed—a calendar of upcoming auctions was posted on the company's Web site.

Wal-Mart's Approach to Customer Service and Creating a Pleasant Shopping Experience

Wal-Mart tried to put some organization muscle behind its pledge of "Satisfaction Guaranteed" and do things that would make customers' shopping experience at Wal-Mart pleasant. Store managers challenged store associates to practice what Sam Walton called "aggressive hospitality." A "greeter" was stationed at store entrances to welcome customers with a smile, thank them for shopping at Wal-Mart, assist them in getting a shopping cart, and answer questions about where items were located. Clerks and checkout workers were trained to be courteous and helpful to customers and to exhibit a "friendly, folksy attitude." Store associates were expected to adhere to the "10-foot rule": "I promise that when I come within 10 feet of a customer, I will look them in the eye, greet them, and ask if I can be of help." Wal-Mart management believed that friendly, helpful store associates were a strong contributor to getting customers to shop frequently at Wal-Mart.

At the same time, Wal-Mart worked at continuously improving customers' shopping experience. H. Lee Scott's transformation program featured a major initiative to boost the appeal of shopping at Wal-Mart's stores. In 2005, Scott appointed Eduardo Castro-Wright, the head of Wal-Mart Mexico, as the new chief executive of Wal-Mart's U.S. stores division and charged him with upgrading the customer experience. Castro-Wright immediately put together a three-year plan to improve store atmosphere and make shopping at Wal-Mart more appealing. He was particularly concerned about slow checkout lines and what he saw as cluttered merchandising tactics. His campaign included replacing high shelves to reduce shelf clutter and improve sight lines throughout the stores, widening the aisles, improving navigational signs in the stores so shoppers could find things more easily, boosting efforts to keep the store environment clean and attractive (which included a more upscale store decor), and investing in technology that speeded the checkout process. Castro-Wright, together with Wal-Mart's buyers, also shifted their thinking about customer choice, concluding that good customer choice went beyond just providing low prices and broad selection; the new theme was to place more attention on carefully selecting products and brands that shoppers cared about. Three of the biggest merchandising mix and product choice changes involved stocking more items in faster-growing categories such as consumer electronics, including more of the biggest and best brand names in select product categories (to broaden Wal-Mart's appeal to more upscale customers), and localizing product selection to better accommodate variations in shopper tastes and preferences from one area to another.

The Culture at Wal-Mart in 2008

Wal-Mart's culture in 2008 continued to be deeply rooted in Sam Walton's business philosophy and leadership style. Mr. Sam, as he was fondly referred to, was not only Wal-Mart's founder and patriarch but also its spiritual leader—and still was in many respects. Four key core values and business principles underpinned Sam Walton's approach to managing:[29]

- Treat employees as partners, sharing both the good and bad about the company so they will strive to excel and participate in the rewards. (Wal-Mart fostered the concept of partnership by referring to all employees as "associates," a term Sam Walton had insisted upon from the company's beginnings because it denoted a partner-like relationship.)
- Build for the future, rather than just immediate gains, by continuing to study the changing concepts that are a mark of the retailing industry and be ready to test and experiment with new ideas.
- Recognize that the road to success includes failing, which is part of the learning process rather than a personal or corporate defect or failing. Always challenge the obvious.
- Involve associates at all levels in the total decision making process.

Walton practiced these principles diligently in his own actions and insisted that other Wal-Mart managers do the same. Up until his health failed badly in 1991, he spent several days a week visiting the stores, gauging the moods of shoppers, listening to employees discuss what was on their minds, learning what was or was not selling, gathering ideas about how things could be done better, complimenting workers on their efforts, and challenging them to come up with good ideas.

[29]Sam Walton with John Huey, *Sam Walton: Made in America* (New York: Doubleday, 1992), p. 12.

The values, beliefs, and practices that Sam Walton instilled in Wal-Mart's culture and that still carried over in 2008 were reflected in statements made in his autobiography:

Everytime Wal-Mart spends one dollar foolishly, it comes right out of our customers' pockets. Everytime we save a dollar, that puts us one more step ahead of the competition—which is where we always plan to be.

One person seeking glory doesn't accomplish much; at Wal-Mart, everything we've done has been the result of people pulling together to meet one common goal. . . .

I have always been driven to buck the system, to innovate, to take things beyond where they've been.

We paid absolutely no attention whatsoever to the way things were supposed to be done, you know, the way the rules of retail said it had to be done.

. . . I'm more of a manager by walking and flying around, and in the process I stick my fingers into everything I can to see how it's coming along. . . . My appreciation for numbers has kept me close to our operational statements, and to all the other information we have pouring in from so many different places. . . .

. . . The more you share profit with your associates—whether it's in salaries or incentives or bonuses or stock discounts—the more profit will accrue to your company. Why? Because the way management treats the associates is exactly how the associates will then treat the customers. And if the associates treat the customers well, the customers will return again and again. . . .

. . . There's no better way to keep someone doing things the right way than by letting him or her know how much you appreciate their performance.

The bigger we get as a company, the more important it becomes for us to shift responsibility and authority toward the front lines, toward that department manager who's stocking the shelves and talking to the customer.

We give our department heads the opportunity to become real merchants at a very early stage of the game. . . . We make our department heads the managers of their own businesses. . . . We share everything with them: the costs of their goods, the freight costs, the profit margins. We let them see how their store ranks with every other store in the company on a constant, running basis, and we give them incentives to want to win.

We're always looking for new ways to encourage our associates out in the stores to push their ideas up through the system. . . . Great ideas come from everywhere if you just listen and look for them. You never know who's going to have a great idea.

. . . A lot of bureaucracy is really the product of some empire builder's ego. . . . We don't need any of that at Wal-Mart. If you're not serving the customers, or supporting the folks who do, we don't need you.

You can't just keep doing what works one time, because everything around you is always changing. To succeed, you have to stay out in front of that change.[30]

Walton's success flowed from his cheerleading management style, his ability to instill the principles and management philosophies he preached into Wal-Mart's culture, the close watch he kept on costs, his relentless insistence on continuous improvement, and his habit of staying in close touch with both shoppers and associates. It was common practice for Walton to lead cheers at annual shareholder meetings, store visits, managers' meetings, and company events. His favorite was the Wal-Mart cheer:

Give me a W!

Give me an A!

Give me an L!

Give me a squiggly! (Here, everybody sort of does the twist.)

[30]Ibid., pp. 10, 12, 47, 63, 115, 128, 135, 140, 213, 226–29, 233, 246, 249–54, and 256.

Give me an M!

Give me an A!

Give me an R!

Give me a T!

What's that spell?

Wal-Mart!

Whose Wal-Mart is it?

My Wal-Mart!

Who's number one?

The customer! Always!

In 2008, the Wal-Mart cheer was still a core part of the Wal-Mart culture and was used throughout the company at meetings of store employees, managers, and corporate gatherings in Bentonville to create a "whistle while you work" atmosphere, loosen everyone up, inject fun and enthusiasm, and get sessions started on a stimulating note. While the cheer seemed corny to outsiders, once they saw the cheer in action at Wal-Mart they came to realize its cultural power and significance. And much of Sam Walton's cultural legacy remained intact in 2008, most especially among the company's top decision makers and longtime managers. As a *Fortune* writer put it:

> Spend enough time inside the company—where nothing backs up a point better than a quotation from Walton scripture—and it's easy to get the impression that the founder is orchestrating his creation from the beyond.[31]

The Three Basic Beliefs Underlying the Wal-Mart Culture in 2008

Wal-Mart top management stressed three basic beliefs that Sam Walton had preached since 1962:[32]

1. *Respect for the individual*—Management consistently drummed the theme that dedicated, hardworking, ordinary people who teamed together and who treated each other with respect and dignity could accomplish extraordinary things. Throughout company literature, comments could be found referring to Wal-Mart's "concern for the individual." Such expressions as "Our people make the difference," "We care about people," and "People helping people" were used repeatedly by Wal-Mart executives and store managers to create and nurture a family-oriented atmosphere among store associates.

2. *Service to our customers*—Management always stressed that the company was nothing without its customers. To satisfy customers and keep them coming back again and again, management emphasized that the company had to offer quality merchandise at the lowest prices and do it with the best customer service possible. Customers had to trust in Wal-Mart's pricing philosophy and to always be able to find the lowest prices with the best possible service. One of the standard Wal-Mart mantras preached to all associates was that the customer was number one and that the customer was boss. Associates in stores were urged to observe the "10-foot rule."

[31]Useem, "One Nation Under Wal-Mart," p. 72.

[32]Information posted at www.walmartstores.com (accessed June 18, 2008).

3. *Strive for excellence*—The concept of striving for excellence stemmed from Sam Walton's conviction that prices were seldom as low as they needed to be and that product quality was seldom as high as customers deserved and expected. The thesis at Wal-Mart was that new ideas and ambitious goals made the company reach further and try harder—the process of finding new and innovative ways to push boundaries and constantly improve made the company better at what it did and contributed to higher levels of customer satisfaction. Wal-Mart managers at all levels spent much time and effort motivating associates to offer ideas for improvement, and to function as partners. It was reiterated that every cost counted and that every worker had a responsibility to be involved.

Wal-Mart's culture had unusually deep roots at the headquarters complex in Bentonville and mirrored Sam Walton's 10 rules for building a business—see Exhibit 4. The numerous journalists and business executives who had been to Bentonville and spent much time at Wal-Mart's corporate offices uniformly reported being impressed with the breadth, depth, and pervasive power of the company's culture. Jack Welsh, former CEO of General Electric and a potent culture builder in his own right, noted that "the place vibrated" with cultural energy. There was little evidence that the culture in Bentonville was any weaker in 2008 than it had been 17 years earlier when Sam Walton personally led the culture-building, culture-nurturing effort and infused the company with unparalleled dedication to frugality, wringing every penny out of costs, and passing the savings on to customers in the form of low prices. Not only were there tireless efforts to achieve cost savings in product design, materials, packaging, labor, transportation, store construction, and store operations but Wal-Mart associates, including executives, also flew coach, shared hotel rooms, and emptied their own trash. The philosophy was expressed as follows: "If we can go without something to save money, we do. It's the cornerstone of our culture to pass on our savings. Every penny we save is a penny in our customers' pockets."[33] But in 2008, a new cultural trait was evident in the Bentonville headquarters: the "Living Better" element of the company's new mission statement was fast becoming a core value at Wal-Mart and an integral part of its culture and operating practices. While saving money was still the dominant value and a pervasive cultural trait, much energy and effort at headquarters was being devoted to modifying Wal-Mart's priorities and conducting the company's business in a manner that produced "Living Better" outcomes.

But Wal-Mart executives nonetheless were currently facing a formidable challenge in instilling a vibrant, resourceful, and dedicated Bentonville-like culture in the company's distribution centers and most especially in its stores. Annual turnover rates at Wal-Mart stores ran as high as 40 percent in 2002–2008 and had run as high as 70 percent in 1999, when the economy was booming and the labor market was tight. Such high rates of turnover in a workforce that numbered 2.1 million people in 2008, coupled with net workforce increases of about 120,000 associates annually, made it a Herculean task to maintain a deeply ingrained, values-driven culture—indeed, no other company in all of business history had been confronted with having to culturally indoctrinate so many new employees in so many locations in such a relatively short time. Even though Wal-Mart's distribution centers had lower turnover and fewer new employees to culturally train and absorb annually than the company's retail stores, Wal-Mart's culture was much less deeply rooted in its distribution centers than in Bentonville. And the cultural traits so evident in Bentonville were shared by relatively few of the associates at Wal-Mart's retail stores, partly or even mostly because so many store associates chose not to make a career of working at Wal-Mart.

[33]Quote taken from the section on Wal-Mart Culture, www.walmartstores.com (accessed December 19, 2005).

EXHIBIT 4 Sam Walton's Rules for Building a Business

Rule 1: Commit to your business. Believe in it more than anybody else. I think I overcame every single one of my personal shortcomings by the sheer passion I brought to my work. I don't know if you're born with this kind of passion, or if you can learn it. But I do know you need it. If you love your work, you'll be out there every day trying to do it the best you possibly can, and pretty soon everybody around will catch the passion from you—like a fever.

Rule 2: Share your profits with all your Associates, and treat them as partners. In turn, they will treat you as a partner, and together you will all perform beyond your wildest expectations. Remain a corporation and retain control if you like, but behave as a servant leader in a partnership. Encourage your Associates to hold a stake in the company. Offer discounted stock, and grant them stock for their retirement. It's the single best thing we ever did.

Rule 3: Motivate your partners. Money and ownership alone aren't enough. Constantly, day-by-day, think of new and more interesting ways to motivate and challenge your partners. Set high goals, encourage competition, and then keep score. Make bets with outrageous payoffs. If things get stale, cross-pollinate; have managers switch jobs with one another to stay challenged. Keep everybody guessing as to what your next trick is going to be. Don't become too predictable.

Rule 4: Communicate everything you possibly can to your partners. The more they know, the more they'll understand. The more they understand, the more they'll care. Once they care, there's no stopping them. If you don't trust your Associates to know what's going on, they'll know you don't really consider them partners. Information is power, and the gain you get from empowering your Associates more than offsets the risk of informing your competitors.

Rule 5: Appreciate everything your Associates do for the business. A paycheck and a stock option will buy one kind of loyalty. But all of us like to be told how much somebody appreciates what we do for them. We like to hear it often, and especially when we have done something we're really proud of. Nothing else can quite substitute for a few well-chosen, well-timed, sincere words of praise. They're absolutely free—and worth a fortune.

Rule 6: Celebrate your successes. Find some humor in your failures. Don't take yourself so seriously. Loosen up, and everybody around you will loosen up. Have fun. Show enthusiasm—always. When all else fails, put on a costume and sing a silly song. Then make everybody else sing with you. Don't do a hula on Wall Street. It's been done. Think up your own stunt. All of this is more important, and more fun, than you think, and it really fools the competition. "Why should we take those cornballs at Wal-Mart seriously?"

Rule 7: Listen to everyone in your company. And figure out ways to get them talking. The folks on the front lines—the ones who actually talk to the customer—are the only ones who really know what's going on out there. You'd better find out what they know. This really is what total quality is all about. To push responsibility down in your organization, and to force good ideas to bubble up within it, you must listen to what your Associates are trying to tell you.

Rule 8: Exceed your customers' expectations. If you do, they'll come back over and over. Give them what they want—and a little more. Let them know you appreciate them. Make good on all your mistakes, and don't make excuses—apologize. Stand behind everything you do. The two most important words I ever wrote were on that first Wal-Mart sign, "Satisfaction Guaranteed." They're still up there, and they have made all the difference.

Rule 9: Control your expenses better than your competition. This is where you can always find the competitive advantage. For 25 years running—long before Wal-Mart was known as the nation's largest retailer—we ranked No. 1 in our industry for the lowest ratio of expenses to sales. You can make a lot of different mistakes and still recover if you run an efficient operation. Or you can be brilliant and still go out of business if you're too inefficient.

Rule 10: Swim upstream. Go the other way. Ignore the conventional wisdom. If everybody else is doing it one way, there's a good chance you can find your niche by going in exactly the opposite direction. But be prepared for a lot of folks to wave you down and tell you you're headed the wrong way. I guess in all my years, what I heard more often than anything was: a town of less than 50,000 population cannot support a discount store for very long.

Source: www.walmartstores.com (accessed December 19, 2005).

Soliciting Ideas from Associates

Associates at all levels were expected to be an integral part of the process of making the company better. Wal-Mart store managers usually spent a portion of each day walking around the store checking on how well things were going in each department, listening to associates, soliciting suggestions and discussing how improvements could be made, and praising associates who were doing a good job. Store managers frequently asked associates what needed to be done better in their department and what could be changed to improve store operations. Associates who believed a policy or procedure detracted from operations were encouraged to challenge and change it. Task forces to evaluate ideas and plan out future actions to implement them were common, and it was not unusual for the person who developed the idea to be appointed the leader of the group.

Listening to employees was a very important part of each manager's job. All of Wal-Mart's top executives relied on management by walking around (MBWA); they visited stores, distribution centers, and support facilities regularly, staying on top of what was happening and listening to what employees had to say about how things were going. Senior managers at Wal-Mart's Bentonville headquarters believed that visiting stores and listening to associates was time well spent because a number of the company's best ideas had come from Wal-Mart associates—Wal-Mart's use of people greeters at store entrances was one of those ideas.

Compensation and Benefits

In 2007, Wal-Mart's average hourly wage for regular full-time associates in the United States was $10.83, up from $9.68 an hour in 2005 (the federal minimum wage was raised from $5.15 to $5.85 beginning July 24, 2007; existing legislation called for the hourly minimum to increase to $6.55 beginning July 24, 2008, and to $7.25 beginning July 24, 2009). Wal-Mart's average pay was higher in certain urban areas; for example, average hourly wages in Chicago were $11.18; in Atlanta, $11.27; and in Boston, $11.98.[34] Store clerks generally earned the lowest wage; workers who unloaded trucks and stocked store shelves could earn anywhere from $25,000 to $50,000. Part-time jobs at Wal-Mart were most common among sales clerks and checkout personnel in the stores where customer traffic varied appreciably during days of the week and months of the year.

New hourly associates in the United States were paid anywhere from $1 to $6 above the minimum wage, depending on the type of job, and could expect to receive a raise within the first year at one or both of the semiannual job evaluations. Typically, at least one raise was guaranteed in the first year if Wal-Mart planned to keep the individual on the staff. The other raise depended on how well the associate worked and improved during the year. In addition, every store associate was eligible to receive performance bonuses based on the performance of their store, and every hourly associate with 20 or more years of service was awarded an extra week of pay—in fiscal 2008, Wal-Mart awarded more than $636 million in performance bonuses to its U.S. hourly associates. At the store level, only the store manager and assistant manager were salaried; all other associates, including the department managers, were considered hourly employees. Store managers generally had six-figure incomes.

A majority of Wal-Mart's hourly store associates in the United States worked full time—at most U.S. retailers, the percentage of employees that worked full time ranged between 20 and 40 percent.

Improving Health Care Benefits

In 2005, about 48 percent of Wal-Mart's associates in the United States had signed up for health insurance coverage in a Wal-Mart-sponsored plan (compared with an average of 72 percent for the whole retailing industry). Many Wal-Mart associates did not sign up for health coverage because another household member already had family coverage at his or her place of employment. New full-time and part-time associates became eligible for health care benefits, after a six-month wait and a one-year exclusion for preexisting conditions. Worker premiums for coverage were as little as $11 per month for individuals and 30 cents per day for children (no matter how many children an associate had). There were several plans that workers could choose from; usually, the lower the premium, the higher the annual deductible. There were no lifetime maximums for most expenses (a feature offered by fewer than 50 percent of employers). The health benefit package covered 100 percent of most major medical expenses above $1,750 in employee out-of-pocket expenses and entailed no lifetime cap on medical cost coverage (a feature offered by fewer than 50 percent of

---

[34]Information posted at www.walmartstores.com (accessed June 10, 2008).

employers).[35] The company's health benefits in 2005 also included dental coverage, short- and long-term disability, an illness protection plan, and business travel accident insurance. But to help control its health costs for associates, Wal-Mart's health care plan did not pay for flu shots, eye exams, child vaccinations, chiropractic services, and certain other treatments allowed in the plans of many companies; further, Wal-Mart did not pay any health care costs for retirees.

However, during 2004–2006, critics assailed Wal-Mart's health care offering on grounds that the coverage was skimpier than that of many employers and that far too few Wal-Mart employees were eligible for coverage. For example, until 2005, Wal-Mart's health insurance plan did not cover the cost of vaccinations for routine childhood diseases and part-time employees had to work for two years before becoming eligible for coverage for themselves (family coverage was not available to part-time employees). According to 2005 data, 5 percent of Wal-Mart associates were on Medicaid, compared to an average for national employers of 4 percent, and 27 percent of associates' children were on such programs, compared to a national average of 22 percent. In total, 46 percent of associates' children were either on Medicaid or were uninsured.[36]

Wal-Mart recognized that its critics had made valid points regarding the shortcomings of the company's health care offering. Starting in January 2006, Wal-Mart began providing health insurance to more than 1 million of its 1.7 million associates and offering up to 18 different plans. As of 2008, further improvements had been made in Wal-Mart's health care benefits. Every associate who worked in the United States could become eligible for individual health coverage costing as little as $5 per month in some areas and as little as $8 per month nationwide; full-time employees were eligible for coverage after 6 months, and the two-year waiting period for part-time associates was reduced to one year. As soon as an associate became eligible for benefits, his or her spouse and children became eligible too. Associates had more than 50 ways to customize their health coverage. In the $5-per-month plan, Wal-Mart gave each employee or family a grant of $100 to $500 to defray health expenses; an $8-per-month plan entailed a $100 health care credit and a deductible of $2,000 before medical expense coverage kicked in. In still another plan, an associate paid premiums of up to $79 a month, received a health care credit of $100, and paid a deductible of $500. Most options paid for 80 percent of eligible medical expenses incurred after the deductible was reached; however, once an associate's out-of-pocket medical expenses reached $5,000, the plans paid 100 percent of eligible charges. Some 2,400 generic drugs were available for $4; brand-name drugs cost $30 to $50. There were no lifetime maximums on most health care expenses.

Other Benefits

Wal-Mart's package of fringe benefits for full-time employees (and some part-time employees) also included the following:

- Vacation and personal time.
- Holiday pay.
- Jury duty pay.
- Medical and bereavement leave.
- Military leave.
- Maternity/paternity leave.

[35]Bernard Wysocki and Ann Zimmerman, "Wal-Mart Cost-Cutting Finds Big Target in Health Benefits," *Wall Street Journal,* September 30, 2003, pp. A1, A16.

[36]Based on an internal memo by Susan Chambers to Wal-Mart's board of directors that was leaked to Wal-Mart Watch and posted at www.walmartwatch.com (accessed December 20, 2005).

- Confidential counseling services for associates and their families.
- Child care discounts for associates with children (through four national providers).
- GED reimbursement/scholarships for associates and their spouses.
- 10 percent discounts on regularly priced merchandise, fresh fruits and vegetables, and eyewear purchased at Wal-Mart Vision Centers. (Sam's Club associates received a Sam's membership card at no cost. In fiscal 2008, Wal-Mart contributed $420 million in discounted merchandise to hourly associates and family members.)

Profit-Sharing and Retirement Plans

Wal-Mart maintained a profit-sharing plan for full-time and part-time associates in the United States; individuals were eligible after one year and 1,000 hours of service. Annual contributions to the plan were tied to the company's profitability and were made at the sole discretion of management and the board of directors. Employees could contribute up to 15 percent of their earnings to their 401(k) accounts. Wal-Mart's contribution to each associate's profit-sharing account became vested at the rate of 20 percent per year beginning the third year of participation in the plan. After seven years of continuous employment the company's contribution became fully vested; however, if the associate left the company prior to that time, the unvested portions were redistributed to all remaining employees.

The plan was funded entirely by Wal-Mart and most of the profit-sharing contributions were invested in Wal-Mart's common stock. In recent years, the company's contribution to profit sharing and the 401(k) plan had averaged 4 percent of a U.S. associate's eligible pay, with total contributions amounting to $945 million in fiscal 2008, $890 million in fiscal 2007, and $827 million in fiscal 2006. Wal-Mart's contributions to the profit-sharing and retirement plans of foreign associates totaled $267 million in fiscal 2008, $274 million in fiscal 2007, and $244 million in fiscal 2006. Associates could begin withdrawals from their account upon retirement or disability, with the balance paid to family members upon death.

Stock Purchase and Stock Option Plans

A stock purchase plan was adopted in 1972 to allow eligible employees a means of purchasing shares of common stock through regular payroll deduction or annual lump-sum contribution. Prior to 1990, the yearly maximum under this program was $1,500 per eligible employee; starting in 1990, the maximum was increased to $1,800 annually. The company contributed an amount equal to 15 percent of each participating associate's contribution. Long-time employees who had started participating in the early years of the program had accumulated stock worth over $100,000. About one-fourth of Wal-Mart's employees participated in the stock purchase plan in 1993, but this percentage had since declined, as many new employees opted not to participate. In fiscal 2008, Wal-Mart contributed $50.1 million to the stock purchases of some 764,000 associates.

In addition to regular stock purchases, certain employees qualified to participate in stock option plans; options expired 10 years from the date of the grant and could be exercised in nine annual installments. Share-based compensation of executives and associates totaled $276 million in fiscal 2008 and $271 million in fiscal 2007.

Overall Benefit Costs

In fiscal 2005, Wal-Mart spent $4.2 billion on benefits for its associates (equal to 1.9 percent of revenues), up from $2.8 billion in 2002 (1.5 percent of revenues). The company's benefit expenses were growing 15 percent annually due to a combination of factors: growing workforce size, increased age and average tenure of associates, and rising cost trends for benefits, particularly health care. Top management and the board of directors were actively looking at strategies to contain the rising costs of the company's fringe benefit package, while at the same time preserving employee satisfaction with the benefit package and avoiding outcries from critics. Recent surveys of associates indicated overall satisfaction with the current benefit package (although this varied by benefit and associate demographics), but there was opposition to higher deductibles. Interestingly, the least healthy, least productive employees tended to be the most satisfied with their benefits and expressed interest in longer careers with Wal-Mart.

Training

Top management was committed to providing all associates state-of-the-art training resources and development time to help achieve career objectives. The company had a number of training tools in place, including classroom courses, computer-based learning, distance learning, corporate intranet sites, mentor programs, satellite broadcasts, and skills assessments. In November 1985, the Walton Institute of Retailing was opened in affiliation with the University of Arkansas. Within a year of its inception, every Wal-Mart manager from the stores, the distribution facilities, and the general office was expected to take part in special programs at the Walton Institute to strengthen and develop the company's managerial capabilities.

Management Training

Wal-Mart store managers were hired in one of three ways. Hourly associates could move up through the ranks from sales to department manager to manager of the checkout lanes to store manager—more than 65 percent of Wal-Mart's managers had started out as hourly associates. Second, people with outstanding merchandising skills at other retail companies were recruited to join the ranks of Wal-Mart managers. And third, Wal-Mart recruited college graduates to enter the company's training program. Store management trainees went through an intensive on-the-job training program of almost 20 weeks and then were given responsibility for an area of the store. Trainees who progressed satisfactorily and showed leadership and job knowledge were promoted to an assistant manager, which included further training in various aspects of retailing and store operations. Given Wal-Mart's continued store growth, above-average trainees could progress to store manager within five years. Through bonuses for sales increases above projected amounts and company stock options, the highest-performing store managers earned well into six figures annually.

Associate Training

Wal-Mart did not provide a specialized training course for its hourly associates. Upon being hired, an associate was immediately placed in a position for on-the-job training. From time to time, training films were shown in associates' meetings. Store managers and department managers were expected to train and supervise the associates under them in whatever ways were needed. As one associate put it, "Mostly you learn by doing. They tell you a lot; but you learn your job every day."

Special programs had been put in place to ensure that the company had an adequate talent pool of women and minorities who were well prepared for management positions. If company officers did not meet their individual diversity goals, their bonuses were cut 15 percent.

Wal-Mart's Use of Meetings: A Time for Rapid Action

The company used meetings both as a communication device and as a culture-building exercise. Store managers had several regularly scheduled meetings with store associates daily. In Bentonville, there were Thursday-afternoon meetings dealing with store operations, Friday-morning management meetings, Friday-noon merchandising meetings, and Saturday-morning meetings covering a range of topics. Almost every meeting began and ended with the Wal-Mart cheer.

Store and Distribution Center Meetings

Each Wal-Mart store had a 15-minute shift-change meeting when a new group of cashiers, stockers, and supervisors arrived. Managers reviewed sales numbers for the previous day, making a point to single out (1) displays that were effective and those that needed attention and (2) products that were selling particularly well and those whose sales were lagging.[37] An assistant department manager who reported big sales of particular items was likely to receive supportive applause and cheering. Associates were nearly always asked for their suggestions about how to spur sales and improve customers' shopping experience. They quickly learned that a key to advancement at Wal-Mart was to be a frequent and thoughtful contributor of ideas and suggestions at these meetings (as well as in conversations with their department manager and when assistant store managers and the store manager were touring their part of the store). Good ideas and suggestions were acted on immediately, with the associate responsible for the suggestion having a lead implementation role when it involved something he or she could undertake. When appropriate, store managers relayed the best ideas and suggestions on up the chain to regional vice presidents (VPs), who had responsibility over 100 or so stores and who visited each store about 6 times annually. The regional VPs decided which ideas and suggestions bubbling up from the stores to bring up at one of the weekly meetings in Bentonville.

The same kind of meeting cycles and solicitation of ideas from associates occurred in Wal-Mart's 110+ distribution centers, in the Sam's Club division, and in Wal-Mart's stores in countries outside the United States.

The Meetings in Bentonville

The weekly Thursday-afternoon store operations meeting, attended by about 70 people, dealt with the nuts and bolts of making the stores operate smoothly. Attendees remained standing—a tactic that kept the meeting from dragging on and prompted those speaking to make their point quickly; topics ranged from inventory management to store staffing issues to new-store real estate planning.[38] The weekly management meetings held at 7:00 a.m. on Fridays included the top 200 people in the company; outsiders were not permitted to attend, since the sometimes spirited discussions and debates involved sensitive strategic and competitive issues.[39] At both meetings, the information sharing and the ensuing discussions led to decisions about what actions needed to be taken; very rarely were issues left open for further debate and resolution at an upcoming meeting.

The weekly Friday merchandising meeting was an hour-and-a-half noontime session involving about 300 people—Wal-Mart's buyers and merchandising staff headquartered in Bentonville and the regional vice presidents who directed store operations and were fresh back from tours of Wal-Mart stores and, frequently, visits to the stores of the company's two closest competitors, Kmart and Target, earlier in the week. The merchandising meeting had two purposes: (1) to give the buyers a direct sense of what was and was not selling well in the stores and why and (2) to give the regional VPs a means to get instant action to resolve merchandising issues in their stores.[40] Considerable time was usually devoted to merchandising errors—having too much of a product (which prompted markdowns) and not having enough of a hot-selling item. It was also normal for the regional VPs to report on instances when they found that Wal-Mart's prices for particular items were higher that those at either Kmart or Target and when they believed that Wal-Mart was missing out on a hot-selling

---

[37]Brent Schlender, "Wal-Mart's $288 Billion Meeting," *Fortune,* April 18, 2005, p. 102.
[38]Ibid.
[39]Ibid.
[40]Ibid.

product. On one occasion, a regional VP reported that a Kmart store he had just visited was selling a $9.99 poker table cover and chip set that was a much better value than a comparable item Wal-Mart was selling—he pulled the poker set Kmart was selling out of a Kmart bag and showed it to the group.[41] Wal-Mart's divisional merchandising manager responded by saying, "We've got a pretty nice poker set in our stores, but I will check with our sources and get back to you." The discussion then moved to another regional VP complaining about a series of shortages of bedding and kitchen items at her stores. Then the divisional merchandising manager reported to the group that he had arranged for the poker sets sold at Kmart to be acquired and that they would be on Wal-Mart trucks for delivery to stores the upcoming week—attendees cheered. David Glass, Wal-Mart's former CEO, recalled what took place at the Friday merchandise meetings during his tenure:

> In retailing, there has always been a traditional, head-to-head confrontation between operations and merchandising. You know, the operations guys say, "Why in the world would anybody buy this? It's a dog, and we'll never sell it." Then the merchandising folks say, "There's nothing wrong with that item. If you guys were smart enough to display it well and promote it properly, it would blow out the doors." So we sit all these folks down together every Friday at the same table and just have at it.
>
> We get into some of the doggonedest, knock-down drag-outs you have ever seen. But we have a rule. We never leave an item hanging. We will make a decision in that meeting even if it's wrong, and sometimes it is. But when the people come out of that room, you would be hard-pressed to tell which ones oppose it and which ones are for it. And once we've made that decision on Friday, we expect it to be acted on in all the stores on Saturday. What we guard against around here is people saying, "Let's think about it." We make a decision. Then we act on it.[42]

Shortly after the conclusion of the Friday merchandise meetings, the "priorities were culled from the meeting, and buyers and regional VPs were sent a priority e-mail outlining perhaps a dozen follow-on assignments to complete by the end of the day."[43]

The Saturday-morning meetings, a Wal-Mart ritual since 1961, were held 52 weeks a year at 7:00 a.m. sharp. Top officers and as many as 600 other people (including relatives of Wal-Mart personnel attending the meeting and special VIP guests, frequently including celebrities with a role on the program) gathered in a 400-seat stageless auditorium and an adjoining cafeteria for a two-and-a-half-hour session that was a combination pep rally, talk show, financial report, town-hall forum, gripe session, idea exchange, business update, merchandising lesson, decision-making meeting, and morale booster.[44] Each week's agenda was deliberately designed to be interesting and important enough to cause attendees to want to be there despite the early hour. Typically, the meeting began with CEO H. Lee Scott or honored guests leading the Wal-Mart cheer, with other attendees standing, clapping their hands, and joining in enthusiastically. The business part of the meeting featured presentations concerning how well things were going, a new company initiative, a review of the week's sales, ideas and suggestions that originated in the stores and distribution centers, new product launches and special promotion items, store construction and new store openings, distribution centers, transportation, supply chain activities, and the like. Management described the nature and purpose of the Saturday meetings as follows:

> Created with a sense of the unpredictable and intended to entertain as well as inform, the Saturday morning meeting lets everyone know what the rest of the company is up to.

[41]Ibid.
[42]Walton with Huey, *Sam Walton,* pp. 225–26.
[43]Schlender, "Wal-Mart's $288 Billion Meeting," pp. 102, 104.
[44]Ibid.

The agenda constantly changes, so each meeting has an element of spontaneity. Sometimes we'll bring associates from the field in to Bentonville to praise them in front of the whole meeting. Other mornings, an associate may get a standing ovation as he receives a 20-year service award.

On any given Saturday, we may invite special guests to promote product launches or just to share insights. We've had CEOs of other Fortune 500 companies, musicians, actors, journalists, authors, athletes, politicians, and children's characters. . . . That kind of unpredictability keeps things interesting.

But beyond focusing on giving good news, entertaining special guests, and having a good time, we use that valuable time to critique our business. We review what we could do better and encourage suggestions about correcting those weaknesses. If the solution is obvious, we can order changes right then and carry them out over the weekend, while almost everyone else in retail business is off.

The meeting is where we discuss and debate management philosophy and strategy. It's the focal point of our communication efforts, where we share ideas. We look at what our competition is doing well and look for ways to improve upon their successes in our own business. Often, it's the place where we decide to try things that seem unattainable, and instead of shooting those ideas down, we try to figure out how to make them work.

The Saturday morning meeting remains the pulse of our culture.

As at the Friday merchandise meetings, decisions were made at the Saturday-morning meetings about what actions needed to be taken. According to former CEO David Glass, "The rule of thumb was that by noon we wanted all the corrections made in the stores. Noon on Saturday."[45]

The store meetings and the Thursday-Friday-Saturday meetings in Bentonville, along with the in-the-field visits by Wal-Mart management, created a strong bias for action. A *Fortune* reporter observed, "Managers suck in information from Monday to Thursday, exchange ideas on Friday and Saturday, and implement decisions in the stores on Monday."[46]

Wal-Mart's Environmental Sustainability Campaign

In 2008, Wal-Mart was fast emerging as the world's greenest retailer and a model of how companies could promote environmental sustainability by conducting their business in an eco-friendly manner. The environmental commitment at Wal-Mart was a by-product of H. Lee Scott's efforts to combat the bad press the company was receiving in 2004–2005. In June 2004, Scott had an informal meeting with two officials from Conservation International with whom he had recently become acquainted and another environmentally oriented individual; all three argued that Wal-Mart could improve its image, motivate employees, and save money by going green. Scott was intrigued. Shortly thereafter, he decided to hire Conservation International to measure Wal-Mart's environmental impact. Rather quickly, Conservation International spotted ways that Wal-Mart could cut waste, reduce excessive packaging, and improve energy efficiency—and save tens of millions of dollars in the process. Another influential consulting firm that advocated green operating practices was brought in to study how Wal-Mart could wring more energy efficiency out of its trucking fleet. Because going green held the promise of reducing Wal-Mart's operating costs—something always cherished at Wal-Mart—Scott and other senior executives very quickly began pulling eco-friendly ideas from everywhere, including prominent environmental advocates, suppliers, regulators, and other eco-friendly companies like Starbucks, Patagonia, and Whole Foods.[47] Wal-Mart set up meetings with suppliers, environmental groups, and regulators every few months to share ideas, set goals, and monitor progress. Al Gore was

[45]Ibid.
[46]Saporito, "What Sam Walton Taught America," p. 105.
[47]Gunter, "The Green Machine," p. 48.

invited to speak at a Saturday-morning meeting, following the showing of his movie An Inconvenient Truth; Gore's parting thought was that there need not be any conflict between the environment and the economy.[48]

Over a period of 12–14 months, Scott came to the conclusion that Wal-Mart should be an engaged, difference-making contributor to environmental sustainability. He told a *Fortune* reporter:

> To me, there can't be anything good about putting all these chemicals in the air. There can't be anything good about the smog you see in cities. There can't be anything good about putting chemicals in these rivers in Third World countries so that somebody can buy something for less money in a developed country. Those things are just inherently wrong whether you are an environmentalist or not.
>
> Some people say this is foreign to what Sam Walton believed. . . . What people forget is that there was nobody more willing to change. Sam Walton did what was right for his time. Sam loved the outdoors. And he loved the idea of building a company that would endure. I think Sam Walton would, in fact, embrace Wal-Mart's efforts to improve the quality of life for our customers and our associates by doing what we need to do in sustainability.[49]

In October 2005, Scott gave a speech titled "Twenty-First Century Leadership" in which he committed Wal-Mart to achieving three long-term objectives:

1. To be 100 percent supplied by renewable energy.
2. To create zero waste.
3. To sell products that sustained natural resources and the environment.

Then in a speech broadcast to all Wal-Mart facilities in November 2005, Scott announced that Wal-Mart would be pursuing three specific short-term objectives:

- Increase the efficiency of its truck fleet by 25 percent within three years and by 100 percent in 10 years.
- Reduce solid waste in U.S. stores by 25 percent in three years.
- Reduce energy usage in stores by 30 percent.

Scott also said the company would invest $500 million in sustainability projects. A senior vice president for sustainability was appointed to spearhead and oversee Wal-Mart's environmental sustainability strategies. A number of Wal-Mart's critics—union leaders, environmental extremists, and ideological elites—were unimpressed. The union-funded Wal-Mart Watch labeled Wal-Mart's environmental push as a "high-priced green-washing campaign."[50]

But Scott's resolve was unshaken. What began as a defensive strategy soon became something of a crusade. Pursuing ways to save money was a company strength. And Wal-Mart was adept at getting suppliers to do things that served the company's long-term interests. Company personnel warmed quickly to the idea of being a far better steward of the environment, and ideas for how Wal-Mart could further the cause of environmental sustainability began to blossom and take root across the company. Wal-Mart's buyers, already responding to growing buyer interest in organic food products, began contracting to buy the products of organic foods producers. In many instances, Wal-Mart made a point of buying organic produce locally, which had the effect of increasing freshness, reducing the shipping costs of food products, and providing local organic farmers with a market for their crops.

[48]Ibid, p. 44.
[49]Ibid.
[50]Ibid., p. 45.

In February 2006, Wal-Mart announced that over the next three to five years it would purchase all of its wild-caught seafood from fisheries that had been certified as sustainable by the Marine Stewardship Council, an independent nonprofit organization.

After a ladies' apparel buyer for Sam's Club ordered 190,000 units of a yoga outfit made of organic cotton that quickly sold in 10 weeks, Wal-Mart buyers visited organic cotton farms, learned about the environmental benefits of organically grown cotton as opposed to conventionally grown cotton, and began purchasing a range of organic cotton products for Wal-Mart and Sam's Club stores, despite their higher cost.[51] Going into 2007, Wal-Mart was the organic cotton industry's biggest customer, using more than 8 million metric tons; the company made a verbal commitment to buy organic cotton for at least five years, giving organic cotton farmers assurance of a market for their crops.

Wal-Mart began working with suppliers to explore ways to cut packaging costs, promote recycling, and boost energy efficiency. H. Lee Scott spoke personally with the CEO at General Electric about superefficient LED lighting for Wal-Mart stores and a campaign to promote compact fluorescent bulbs, with the CEO of Kimberly-Clark about compressing toilet paper and paper towels into package-saving megarolls, with the CEO of PepsiCo about a contest to recycle plastic bottles of Aquafina water and other PepsiCo beverages, and with the CEOs at Procter & Gamble and Unilever about selling concentrated laundry detergent in slimmed-down plastic bottles. In all these instances, Scott indicated that Wal-Mart would put its marketing muscle behind the efforts to win greater consumer acceptance of green products. Scott's efforts had paid off. As of May 2008, all laundry detergent sold at Wal-Mart was concentrated and packaged in smaller containers. Also in 2008, Wal-Mart was selling packs of 6 Charmin megarolls that contained the same amount of toilet paper as a regular Charmin 24-roll pack—selling twice as many packs of Charmin allowed Wal-Mart to ship twice as many units on its trucks, eliminate 89.5 million cardboard roll cores, eliminate 360,087 pounds of plastic wrapping, and reduce diesel fuel consumption by 53,966 gallons.

In 2007 and 2008, Wal-Mart's environmental sustainability campaign became increasingly sweeping and comprehensive. This was mirrored by a statement on the company's Web site: "Our opportunity is to become a better company by looking at every facet of our business—from the products we offer to the energy we use—through the lens of sustainability."[52] Eighteen environmental sustainability initiatives were launched, including those relating to reduction of greenhouse gases, alternative fuels, protection of wildlife habitat, the use of chemical intensive products, sustainable agriculture and seafood, reusable bags, and eco-friendly textiles and apparel. In November 2007, Wal-Mart issued a comprehensive report detailing its sustainability initiatives and the results being achieved.

WAL-MART'S FUTURE

Sam Walton had engineered the development and rapid ascendancy of Wal-Mart to the forefront of the retailing industry—the discount stores and Sam's Clubs were strategic moves that he directed. His handpicked successor, David Glass, had directed the hugely successful move into Supercenters and grocery retailing, as well as presiding over the company's growth into the world's largest retailing enterprise; the Neighborhood Market store format also came into being during his tenure as CEO. H. Lee Scott, Wal-Mart's third CEO, had the challenge of sustaining the company's growth, globalizing Wal-Mart operations, continuing the long-term process of saturating the U.S. market with Supercenters, overseeing Wal-Mart's ever-larger business operations, and, most recently, figuring out how to

[51]Ibid., p. 54.

[52]Information posted at www.walmart.com (accessed August 18, 2008).

counteract the efforts of the company's critics and adversaries to portray Wal-Mart as a corporate villain.

In 2008, Scott had reason to believe that his transformation plan was producing the desired results. Company morale was decidedly improved, partly because Wal-Mart's far-reaching efforts to adopt business practices that were better for the environment had energized company personnel, triggered a burst of innovative thinking, and made associates feel good about their jobs and the company. There had been a noticeable falloff in the Wal-Mart bashing that had taken place in 2004–2006. Time would tell whether Scott's transformation initiatives would eventually restore the luster to Wal-Mart's image, spur the company's sales revenues, and reduce community resistance to opening new Supercenters.

But Wal-Mart was beginning to fight back. It had hired a public relations firm, which had put a staff of seven professionals in Bentonville to assist Wal-Mart's own public relations staff to get the company's story out and respond within hours to any new blast of criticism.[53] Since mid-2004, Lee Scott had done nine interviews on TV, met with the editorial boards of the *Wall Street Journal* and *The Washington Post,* been interviewed by numerous newspaper journalists, and spoken to business and community leaders in Chicago, Los Angeles, Istanbul, and Paris. The company was striving to build relationships with congressional delegations, governors, mayors, community leaders, and activists in key locations. It had run ads in more than 100 newspapers. And it created a Web site (www.walmartfacts.com) to help set the record straight about what Wal-Mart did and did not do.

Wal-Mart had received favorable publicity in the media following Hurricane Katrina, when its quick response with food, supplies, and cash assistance was praised for being faster than the U.S. government's effort; Wal-Mart had also donated $15 million to the Katrina relief effort. Also, there was growing interest on the part of academic researchers over whether Wal-Mart had a positive or negative effect on the economy. A New York University economist reported that a Wal-Mart store opening in Glendale, Arizona, received 8,000 applicants for 525 jobs. A University of Missouri economist in an article published in the prestigious *Review of Economics and Statistics* found that the entry of a Wal-Mart store increased a county's retail employment by 100 jobs in the first year and over time led to the elimination of 50 jobs at less-efficient retailers. Studies also showed that new businesses quickly sprang up near Wal-Mart stores; both new and existing stores along the routes leading to a Wal-Mart tended to flourish because of the heavy traffic flow to and from the company's stores.

But heading into 2009, there continued to be occasional stories in the media that were critical of Wal-Mart's operating practices and of the company in general. It was unclear whether the company's transformation initiatives were having the desired impact on public opinion and whether Wal-Mart's growth and profitability would be adversely affected by its critics and adversaries.

Nonetheless, the economic slowdown that began in early 2008, followed by the global financial crisis and even sharper economic downturn that transpired in Fall 2008, had resulted in significant increases in customer traffic and purchases at Wal-Mart's stores. Many consumers—already feeling the pinch of recessionary forces or else anxious about the prospects of being laid off—were shopping at Wal-Mart more frequently and Wal-Mart's average sales per customer checkout were above prior-year levels, due in part to steep declines in gasoline prices in September–November 2008 which made a trip to Wal-Mart cheaper and gave consumers more discretionary income to spend at Wal-Mart. Sales at Wal-Mart stores open at least a year rose a robust 3.4 percent for the 43-week period ending November 28, 2008 (versus just 1.4 percent for the same period in 2007). Wal-Mart executives believed that in tough economic times Wal-Mart was the best destination for shoppers to save money.

[53]Robert Berner, "Can Wal-Mart Fit into a White Hat?" *BusinessWeek,* October 3, 2005, p. 94.

Case Group E

Pricing Strategy

20

Schwinn Bicycles

J. Paul Peter *University of Wisconsin–Madison*

Inside a plain, brown building in Boulder, Colorado, is a shrine to an American icon: the Schwinn bicycle. Some mud-caked from daily use, some shiny museum pieces—dozens of bikes stand atop file cabinets and lean against cubicles. Amid the spokes and handlebars, a group of zealots is working to pull off the turnaround of the century in the bike business. Brimming with energy, they're determined to resurrect the best known brand on two wheels. But as Schwinn celebrates its 100th anniversary, its management team faces a long uphill climb. Just two years ago, once-mighty Schwinn had a near-death experience in bankruptcy court. Now it's trying to rise to the top of the crowded mountain bike market.

For years, Schwinn was the top U.S. brand with as much as 25 percent of the market. Now, it has less than 5 percent of the $2.5 billion annual retail bike market. The new Schwinn will sell about 400,000 redesigned bikes—many of them Asian-made models—that sell for $200 to $400 retail, the lower end of the adult bike market. Those models are catching on. But the turnaround won't be a success unless Schwinn persuades cyclists to fork over $700 or more for its newer bikes. Below are market shares of manufacturers for bikes retail-priced $400 and up:

Trek	24%
Cannondale	12%
Specialized	12%
Schwinn	7%
Giant	6%
Diamondback	6%
GT	6%
Scott	4%
Mongoose	3%
Pro Flex	3%

This case prepared by J. Paul Peter of the University of Wisconsin–Madison.

Source: Patrick McGeehan, "Biking Icon Wants to Lose Training Wheels," *USA Today,* August 8, 1995, pp. 1B, 2B; "Hard Pedaling Powers Schwinn Uphill in Sales, Toward Profits," *Chicago Tribune,* June 22, 1995, p. 2N; " 'New Schwinn' Bike Has Gone Full Cycle," *Chicago Tribune,* May 16, 1995, p. 3N.

The mass market for low-priced bikes and those made for children is dominated by three U.S. manufacturers: Huffy, Murray, and Roadmaster. The mass market accounts for about 8.5 million of the 12 million bikes sold in the nation annually.

Schwinn's history as a maker of sturdy, low-cost bikes is no longer the asset it once was. Many under-30 cyclists see Schwinns as the bikes their parents rode. They prefer trendier mountain bikes, with their padded seats, upright handlebars, fat tires, and additional gears for climbing.

"We have an image challenge," admits Schwinn Marketing Director Gregg Bagni. That's clear from a walk around the University of Colorado campus a half-mile away. Outside dorms and classrooms, racks are filled with bikes made by Trek Bicycle, Specialized Bicycle Components, Cannondale and Giant. Waterloo, Wisconsin-based Trek, is the leader. This year it expects about $300 million in revenue on sales of more than 900,000 bikes.

"When I was a kid, if you had a Schwinn, you were the luckiest kid in the world," says Scott Montgomery, a Cannondale marketing chief. "Ask a college kid now and they'll say, 'Oh, Schwinn? They're toast.'"

For decades, the Schwinn brand, synonymous with durability, ruled the road. Generations of kids clamored for the company's Excelsiors, Phantoms, Sting-Rays and 10-speed Varsitys. "Schwinn used to be number one and you could hardly find number two," says industry consultant Bill Fields. But in the late 1970s and early 1980s, cyclists veered off the road into the woods and mountains. Schwinn ignored the mountain bike craze for most of the 1980s. By 1992, two-thirds of bikes sold were mountain bikes and Schwinn was in bankruptcy court. Unable to pay lenders or suppliers, the descendants of company founder Ignaz Schwinn sold the company to the Zell/Chilmark Investment fund for $43 million. Zell/Chilmark appointed new management and funded the company, Scott Sports Group, with an additional $7 million.

So far, the Schwinn turnaround is being attempted on a shoestring. Schwinn's workforce shrank from 300 employees to about 180 when the company was reorganized and moved from Chicago to Boulder. The move west was calculated to attract young workers plugged into the mountain-biking community. Once assembled, the managers focused on product design. They had inherited a Schwinn line whose only mountain bikes were priced at the low end of the bike-shop range, between $200 and $400.

"Previous management wouldn't believe anybody would buy a $1,500 mountain bike with the Schwinn name on it," one Schwinn executive stated. Now, Schwinn is emblazoned on everything from $100 kids' bikes to $2,500 mountain bikes. Its top-of-the-line, American-made Homegrown model starts at $1,750. One of its hottest products is a decidedly low-tech, retro-style, one-speed Cruiser with a wide seat and balloon tires. It's selling fast in Sunbelt states for up to $250. The Cruiser appeals to retirees and snowbirds in beach communities and to college students who call them "bar bikes" because they are ridden to bars and back.

"They want to position this company as high-end, high-tech," says Cannondale's Montgomery. "And what they've got is this traditional, old-fashioned Harley-Davidson type of product. That's their greatest marketing challenge."

Today's bike business is quite different from the one Schwinn dominated so long ago. Exclusive dealerships like Schwinn uses are disappearing, being replaced by independent bike shops. The typical bike shop carries four brands, so Schwinn bikes are subjected to side-by-side comparisons with competing products. Some of the other brands, such as Trek and Cannondale, have built reputations for cutting-edge technology. Cannondale makes aluminum-frame bikes in U.S. plants, and Trek, a pioneer in carbon fiber frames, is moving production back from Taiwan. All but a few thousand Schwinns are made in Asia.

"Handmade in the USA is a tremendous marketing feature," says Brett Hahn, manager of Yeti Cycles in Durango, Colorado. "Bottom line: Mountain biking is a U.S. sport." Yeti makes hundreds of frames for Schwinn's top-of-the-line Homegrown models. Schwinn is considering buying Yeti or another U.S. manufacturer.

Discussion Questions

1. What are the strengths and weaknesses of Schwinn?
2. What opportunities and threats does the company face?
3. How important is it for mountain bikes to be made in America?
4. Evaluate Schwinn's strategy of selling bikes for prices from $100 to $2,500.
5. Evaluate Zell/Chilmark's decision to invest $50 million in Schwinn. What did it get for its money? Calculate the breakeven point and the payback period for this investment given the following assumptions: Schwinn has 4 percent of the retail bike market; Schwinn bikes are marked up an average of 20 percent at retail; Schwinn has a 25 percent profit margin on its bikes.
6. Noting that 80 percent of Trek's sales are for bikes priced $400 and over, how many bikes does Schwinn sell in this category?

Case

21

Cowgirl Chocolates

John J. Lawrence, Linda J. Morris, and Joseph J. Geiger *University of Idaho*

Marilyn looked at the advertisement—a beautiful woman wearing a cowboy hat in a watering trough full of hot and spicy Cowgirl Chocolates' truffles (see Exhibit 1). The ad would appear next month in the March/April edition of *Chile Pepper* magazine, the leading magazine for people who like fiery foods. The ad, the first ever for the business, cost $3,000 to run and Marilyn wondered if it would be her big mistake for 2001. Marilyn allowed herself one $3,000–$6,000 mistake a year in trying to get her now four-year-old business to profitability. Two years ago, it was the pursuit of an opportunity to get her product into Great Britain on the recommendation of the owner of a British biscuit company who loved her chocolates. Despite significant effort and expense, she could not convince anyone in Great Britain to carry her chocolates. Last year, it was her attempt to use a distributor for the first time. It was a small, regional distributor, and she had provided $5,000 worth of product and had never gotten paid. She eventually got half her product back, but by the time she did it had limited remaining shelf life and she already had enough new stock on hand to cover demand. She ended up giving most of what she got back away.

Marilyn knew it took time to make money at something. She was now an internationally celebrated ceramicist, but it had taken 20 years for her ceramic art to turn a profit. She also knew, however, that she could not wait 20 years for her foray into chocolates to make money, especially not at the rate that she was currently losing money. Last year, despite not paying herself a salary and occasionally bartering her art for services, the small business's revenues of $30,000 did not come close to covering her $50,000+ in expenses. While her art for a long time did not make money, it did not lose that kind of money either. Her savings account was slowly being depleted as she loaned the company money. She knew that the product was excellent—it had won numerous awards from the two main fiery food competitions in the United States—and her packaging was also excellent and had won awards itself. She just was not sure how to turn her award-winning products into a profitable business.

This case was prepared by the authors for the sole purpose of providing material for class discussion. It is not intended to illustrate either effective or ineffective handling of a managerial situation. The authors thank Marilyn Lysohir for her cooperation and assistance with this project.

Reprinted by permission from the *Case Research Journal*, 22, no 1. Copyright 2002 by John L. Lawrence, Linda J. Morris, Joseph J. Geiger, and the North American Case Research Association. All rights reserved.

EXHIBIT 1   Cowgirl Chocolates' Ad to Appear in *Chile Pepper* Magazine

spicy chocolate truffles and more • www.cowgirlchocolates.com • toll free 888.882.4098

COMPANY HISTORY

Cowgirl Chocolates was started in Moscow, Idaho, in 1997 by Marilyn Lysohir and her husband, Ross Coates. Marilyn and Ross were both artists. Marilyn was an internationally known ceramicist and lecturer; Ross was also a sculptor and a professor of fine arts at a nearby university. They had started publishing a once-a-year arts magazine in 1995 called *High Ground. High Ground* was really a multimedia product—each edition contained more than simply printed words and pictures. For example, past editions had included such things as vials of Mount St. Helen's ash, cassette tapes, seeds, fabric art, and chocolate bunnies in addition to articles and stories. One edition was even packaged in a motion picture canister. With a total production of about 600 copies, however, *High Ground* simply would not pay for itself. But the magazine was a labor of love for Marilyn and Ross, and so they sought creative ways to fund the endeavor. One of the ways they tried was selling hot and spicy chocolate truffles.

The fact that Marilyn and Ross turned to chocolate was no random event. Marilyn's first job, at age 16, was at Daffin's Candies in Sharon, Pennsylvania. The business's owner, Pete Daffin, had been an early mentor of Marilyn's and had encouraged her creativity. He even let her carve a set of animals, including an 8-foot-tall chocolate bunny, for display. Her sculptures proved irresistible to visiting youngsters, who would take small bites out of the sculptures. It was at this point that Marilyn realized the power of chocolate.

In addition to loving chocolate, Marilyn loved things hot and spicy. She also was aware that cayenne and other chilies had wonderful health properties for the heart. But it was her brother who originally gave her the idea of combining hot and spicy with chocolate. Marilyn considered her brother's idea for a while, and could see it had possibilities, so she started experimenting in her kitchen. She recruited neighbors, friends, and acquaintances to try out her creations. While a few people who tried those early chocolates were not so sure that combining hot and spicy with chocolate made sense, many thought the chocolates were great. Encouraged, and still searching for funding for *High Ground,* Marilyn found a local candy company to produce the chocolates in quantity, and she and her husband established Cowgirl Chocolates.

The name itself came from one friend's reaction the first time she tasted the chocolates—the friend exclaimed "these are cowboy chocolates!" Marilyn agreed that there was a certain ruggedness to the concept of hot and spicy chocolates that matched the cowboy image, but thought that *Cowgirl* Chocolates was a more appropriate name for her company. Marilyn found the picture of May Lillie that would become the Cowgirl Chocolates' logo in a book about cowgirls. May Lillie was a turn of the century, pistol-packing cowgirl, and Marilyn loved the picture of May looking down the barrel of a pistol because May looked so tough. And it certainly was not hard to envision May adopting the Cowgirl Chocolates' motto—Sissies Stay Away. That motto had come to Marilyn when a group of friends told her that they really did not like her hot and spicy chocolates. Marilyn was a little disappointed and hurt, and thought to herself "well, sissies stay away, if you don't like them, don't eat them."

THE PRODUCT

Cowgirl Chocolates sold its hot and spicy creations in three basic forms: individually wrapped truffles, chocolate bars, and a hot caramel dessert sauce. The individually wrapped truffles were available in a variety of packaging options, with most of the packaging designed to set Cowgirl Chocolates apart. The truffles could be purchased in gift boxes, in drawstring muslin bags, and in a collectible tin. According to Marilyn, this packaging made them "more than a candy—they become an idea, an experience, a gift." The truffles were also available in a plain plastic bag over Cowgirl Chocolates' Web site for customers who just wanted the chocolate and did not care about the fancy packaging. The chocolate bars and truffles were offered in several flavors. The chocolate bars were available in either orange espresso or lime tequila crunch. The truffles were available in plain chocolate, mint, orange, lime tequila, and espresso. The plain chocolate, mint, and orange truffles were packaged in gold wrappers, while the lime tequila truffles were packaged in green wrappers. The espresso truffles were the hottest, about twice as hot as the other varieties, and were wrapped in a special red foil to give customers some clue that these were extra hot. Cowgirl Chocolates' full line of product offerings are described in Exhibit 2 and are shown in Exhibit 3.

EXHIBIT 2   Cowgirl Chocolates Product Offerings with Price and Cost Figures

Item	Approximate Percentage of Total Revenues	Suggested Retail Price[1]	Wholesale Price[1]	Total Item Cost (a + b)	Cost of Chocolate or Sauce (a)	Cost of Product Packaging[2] (b)
Spicy Chocolate Truffle Bars (available in 2 flavors: orange-espresso or lime tequila crunch)	50%	$ 2.99	$ 1.50	$ 1.16	$ 1.04	$0.12
1/4-pound Muslin Bag (13 truffles in a drawstring muslin bag—available in 3 flavors: assorted hot, lime-tequila, and mild-mannered)	16%	$ 6.95	$ 3.50	$ 2.35	$ 1.69	$0.66
1/2-pound Tin (assorted hot & spicy truffles in a collectible tin)	12%	$14.95	$ 7.50	$ 4.78[3]	$ 3.25	$1.53
Hot Caramel Dessert Sauce (9.5 oz. Jar)	10%	$ 5.95	$ 3.50	$ 2.50	$ 2.00	$0.50
Sampler Bag (4 assorted hot truffles in a small drawstring muslin bag)	7%	$ 2.95	$ 1.50	$ 0.97	$ 0.52	$0.45
1/4-pound Gift Box (assorted hot truffles or mild-mannered truffles in a fancy gift box with gift card)	~ 1%	$ 8.95	$ 4.50	$ 2.95	$ 1.69	$1.26
1-pound Gift Box (assorted hot truffles or mild-mannered truffles in a fancy gift box with gift card)	~ 1%	$24.95	$12.95	$ 9.05	$ 6.37	$2.68
Gift Bucket (tin bucket containing 1/4-pound gift box, 2 truffle bars and 1 jar of caramel sauce)	~ 1%	$39.95	$20.95	$11.02	$ 5.77	$5.25
Gift Basket (made of wire and branches and containing 1/2-pound tin, 2 truffle bars, 1 jar of caramel sauce and a T-shirt)	~ 1%	$59.95	$30.95	$23.06	$15.29[3]	$7.77
Nothing Fancy (1-pound assorted hot truffles or mild-mannered truffles in a plastic bag)	~ 1%	$19.50	N.A.	$ 7.42	$ 6.37	$1.05

[1]Approximately 1/3 of sales were retail over the Cowgirl Chocolates' Web site, the remaining 2/3 of sales were to wholesale accounts (i.e., to other retailers).
[2]Packaging cost includes costs of container (bags, tins, or boxes), labels, and individual truffle wrapping. Packaging cost assumes Marilyn packs the items and does not include the packing & labeling fee charged by Seattle Chocolates if they do the packing ($1.00 per 1/2 pound tin or 1 pound box; $0.75 per 1/4 pound box; $0.25 per 1/4 pound bag; $0.20 per sampler bag).
[3]This cost includes the cost of the T-shirt.

EXHIBIT 3
Picture of Cowgirl
Chocolates Products
& Packaging

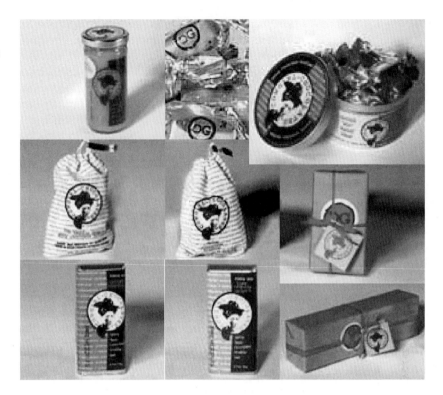

Marilyn was also in the process of introducing "mild-mannered" truffles. Mild-mannered truffles were simply the same fine German chocolate that Marilyn started with to produce all of her chocolates, but without the spice. Marilyn had chosen silver as the wrapper color for the mild-mannered truffles. While she took kidding from friends about how this did not fit with the company's motto—Sissies Stay Away—which was integrated into the company's logo and printed on the back of company t-shirts and hats, she had decided that even the sissies deserved excellent chocolate. Further, she thought that having the mild-mannered chocolate might allow her to get her product placed in retail locations that had previously rejected her chocolates as being too spicy. Marilyn was the first to admit that her chocolates packed a pretty good kick that not everybody found to their liking. She had developed the hot and spicy chocolates based primarily on her own tastes and the input of friends and acquaintances. She had observed many peoples' reactions upon trying her hot and spicy chocolates at trade shows and at new retail locations, and while many people liked her chocolates, the majority found at least some of the varieties to be too hot. In general, men tended to like the hotter truffles much more than women did. Marilyn knew her observations were consistent with what information was available on the fiery foods industry— only approximately 15 percent of American consumers were currently eating hot and spicy foods and men were much more inclined to eat hot and spicy foods than were women. In addition to introducing "mild-mannered" chocolates, Marilyn was also thinking about introducing a chocolate with a calcium supplement aimed at woman concerned about their calcium intake.

All of Cowgirl Chocolates' chocolate products were sourced from Seattle Chocolates, a Seattle-based company that specialized in producing European-style chocolate confections wrapped in an elegant package fit for gift giving. Seattle Chocolates obtained all of its raw chocolate from world-renowned chocolate producer Schokinag of Germany. Seattle Chocolates sold its own retail brand plus provided private label chocolate products for a variety of companies including upscale retailers like Nieman Marcus and Nordstrom. Seattle Chocolates was, at least relative to Cowgirl Chocolates, a large company with annual sales in excess of $5 million. Seattle Chocolates took Cowgirl Chocolates on as a private label customer because they liked and were intrigued by the company's product and owners, and they had made some efforts to help Cowgirl Chocolates along the way. Seattle Chocolates provided Cowgirl Chocolates with a small amount of its table space at several important trade shows and produced in half batches for them. A half batch still consisted of 150 pounds of a given variety of chocolate, which was enough to last Cowgirl Chocolates for six months at 2000 sales rates. Marilyn hoped that she could one day convince Seattle Chocolates to manage the wholesale side of Cowgirl Chocolates, but Seattle Chocolates simply was not interested in taking this on at the present time, at least in part because they were not really sure where the market was for the product. Marilyn also knew she would need to grow sales significantly before Seattle Chocolates would seriously consider such an arrangement, although she was not sure exactly how much she would have to grow sales before such an arrangement would become attractive to Seattle Chocolates.

The chocolate bars themselves cost Cowgirl Chocolates $1.04 per bar while the individual chocolate truffles cost $0.13 per piece. Seattle Chocolates also performed the wrapping and packing of the product. The chocolate bar wrappers cost $0.06 per bar. The wrapper design of the bars had recently been changed to incorporate dietary and nutritional information. While such information was not required, Marilyn felt it helped convey a better image of her chocolates. The change had cost $35 to prepare the new printing plates. Including the materials, wrapping the individual truffles cost $0.02 per piece.

The distinctive muslin bags, collector tins, and gift boxes also added to the final product cost. The muslin bags cost $0.35 each for the quarter-pound size and $0.32 each for the sampler size. The tamperproof seals for the bags cost an additional $0.05/bag. The minimum bag order was 500 bags. As with the chocolate bar wrappers, Cowgirl Chocolates had to buy the printing plates to print the bags. The plates to print the bags, however, cost $250 per plate. Each color of each design required a separate plate. Each of her three quarter-pound bag styles (assorted, lime-tequila, and mild-mannered) had a three-color design. One plate that was used to produce the background design was common to all three styles of bags, but each bag required two additional unique plates. There was also a separate plate for printing the sampler bags. Marilyn was planning to discontinue the separate lime-tequila bag, and just include lime-tequila truffles in the assorted bag as a way to cut packaging costs. The lime-tequila bags had been introduced a year ago, and while they sold reasonably well, they also appeared to mostly cannibalize sales of the assorted bags.

The collectible tins cost $0.80 each, and the labels for these tins cost $0.19 per tin. The tape used to seal the tins cost $0.04 per tin. The minimum order for the tins was for 800 units. The company that produced the tins had recently modified the tin design slightly to reduce the chance that someone might cut themselves on the edge of the can. Unfortunately, this change had resulted in a very small change to the height of the can, which left Cowgirl Chocolates with labels too big for the can. Each label currently had to be trimmed slightly to fit on the can. The alternative to this was to switch to a smaller label. This would require purchasing a new printing plate at a cost of about $35 and might require the purchase of a new printing die (the die holds the label while it is printed), which would cost $360. Marilyn also had hopes of one day being able to get her designs printed directly on the tins. It would make for even nicer tins and save the step of having to adhere the labels to the tins. The minimum order for such tins, however, was 15,000 units.

The gift boxes, including all of the associated wrapping, ribbon, and labels, cost about $1.70 per box. The gift boxes did not sell nearly as well as the tins or bags and were available primarily through Cowgirl Chocolates' Web site. Marilyn was still using and had a reasonable inventory of boxes from a box order she had placed three years ago.

Marilyn currently had more packaging in inventory than she normally would because she had ordered $5,000 worth in anticipation of the possibility of having her product placed in military PX stores at the end of 2000. Seattle Chocolates had been negotiating to get its product into these stores, and there had been some interest on the part of the PX stores in also having Cowgirl Chocolates' products. Given the six- to eight-week lead time on packaging, Marilyn had wanted to be positioned to quickly take advantage of this opportunity if it materialized. While Marilyn was still hopeful this deal might come about, she was less optimistic than she had been at the time she placed the packaging order.

Marilyn was concerned that the actual packing step was not always performed with the care it should be. In particular, she was concerned that not enough or too many truffles ended up in the bags and tins, and that the seals on these containers, which made the packages more tamper resistant, were not always applied correctly. Each quarter-pound bag and gift box was supposed to contain 13 individual truffles, each half-pound tin was supposed to contain 25 individual truffles, and each one-pound gift box was supposed to contain 49 individual truffles. The tins, in particular, had to be packed pretty tightly to get 25 truffles into them. Marilyn had done some of the packing herself at times, and wondered if she would not be better off hiring local college or high school students to do the packing for her to insure that the job was done to her satisfaction. It could also save her some money, as Seattle Chocolates charged her extra for packing the tins and bags. The tins, in particular, were expensive because of the time it took to apply the labels to the top and side of the tin and because of the extra care it took to get all 25 truffles into the tin. Seattle Chocolates charged $1.00 per tin for this step.

Marilyn made the caramel sauce herself with the help of the staff in a commercial kitchen in Sandpoint, Idaho, about a 2½-hour drive north of Moscow. She could make 21 cases of 12 jars each in one day, but including the drive it took all day to do. As with the chocolate, she used only the best ingredients, including fresh cream from a local Moscow dairy. Marilyn figured her costs for the caramel sauce at about $2.50 per jar, which included the cost of the ingredients, the jars, the labeling and the cost of using the Sandpoint kitchen. That figure did not include any allowance for the time it took her to make the sauce or put the labels on the jars. She was considering dropping the caramel sauce from her product line because it was a lot of work to produce and she was not sure she really made any money on it after her own time was factored in. She had sold 70 cases of the sauce in 2000, however, so she knew there was some demand for the product. She was considering the possibility of only offering it at Christmas time as a special seasonal product. She was also looking into the possibility of having a sauce company in Montana make it for her. The company produced caramel, chocolate, and chocolate-caramel sauces that had won awards from the fancy food industry trade association. Marilyn thought the sauces were quite good, although she did not like their caramel sauce as much as her own. The company would sell her 11 oz. jars of any of the sauces, spiced up to Marilyn's standards, for $2.75 per jar. Marilyn would have to provide the labels, for which she would need to have new label designs made to match the jar style the company was set up for, and she would also have to pay a shipping cost of $70–$90 per delivery. The company requested a minimum order size of 72 cases, although the company's owner had hinted that they might be willing to produce in half batches initially.

All of Cowgirl Chocolates' products had won awards, either in the annual Fiery Food Challenges sponsored by *Chile Pepper* magazine or the Scovie Award Competitions sponsored by *Fiery Foods* magazine (the Scovie awards are named after the Scovie measure of heat). All in all, Cowgirl Chocolates had won 11 awards in these two annual competitions. Further, the truffles had won first place in the latest Fiery Food Challenge and the caramel sauce won first place in the latest Scovie competition. The packaging, as distinctive as the chocolate itself, had also won several awards, including the 2000 Award for Excellence for Package Design from American Corporate Identity.

DISTRIBUTION AND PRICING

Marilyn's attempts to get her chocolates into the retail market had met with varying degrees of success. She clearly had been very successful in placing her product in her hometown of Moscow, Idaho. The Moscow Food Co-op was her single best wholesale customer, accounting for 10 percent–15 percent of her annual sales. The Co-op sold a wide variety of natural and/or organic products and produce. Many of its products, like Cowgirl Chocolates, were made or grown locally. The Co-op did a nice job of placing her product in a visible shelf location and generally priced her product lower than any other retail outlet. The Co-op sold primarily the chocolate bars, which it priced at $2.35, and the quarter-pound muslin bags of truffles, which it priced at $5.50. This compared to the suggested retail prices of $2.99 for the bars and $6.99 for the bags. The product was also available at three other locations in downtown Moscow: Wild Women Traders, a store that described itself as a "lifestyle outfitter" and that sold high-end women's clothing and antiques; Northwest Showcase, a store that sold locally produced arts and crafts; and Bookpeople, an independent bookstore that catered to customers who liked to spend time browsing an eclectic offering of books and drinking espresso before making a book purchase.

Marilyn was unsure how many of these local sales were to repeat purchasers who really liked the product and how many were to individuals who wanted to buy a locally made product to give as a gift. She was also unsure how much the Co-op's lower prices boosted the sales of her product at that location. At the Co-op, her product was displayed with other premium chocolates from several competitors, including Seattle Chocolates' own branded chocolate bars, which were priced at $2.99. Marilyn knew the Seattle Chocolates bars were clearly comparable in chocolate quality (although without the spice and cowgirl image). Some of the other competitors' comparably sized bars were priced lower, at $1.99, and some smaller bars were priced at $1.49. While these products were clearly higher in quality than the inexpensive chocolate bars sold in vending machines and at the average supermarket checkout aisle, they were made with a less expensive chocolate than she used and were simply not as good as her chocolates. Marilyn wondered how the price and size of the chocolate bar affected the consumer's purchase decision, and how consumers evaluated the quality of each of the competing chocolate bars when making their purchase.

Outside of Moscow, Marilyn had a harder time getting her product placed onto store shelves and getting her product to move through these locations. One other Co-op, the Boise Food Co-op, carried her products, and they sold pretty well there. Boise was the capital of Idaho and the state's largest city. The Boise Museum of Fine Arts gift shop also carried her product in Boise, although the product did not turn over at this location nearly as well as it did at the Boise Co-op. Other fine art museums, gift shops in places like Missoula, Montana, Portland, Oregon, and Columbus, Ohio, carried Cowgirl Chocolates and Marilyn liked having her product in these outlets. She felt that her reputation as an artist helped her get her product placed in such locations, and the product generally sold well in these locations. She thought her biggest distribution coup was getting her product sold in the world-renowned Whitney Museum in New York City. She felt that the fact that it was sold there added to the product's panache. Unfortunately, the product did not sell there particularly well and it was dropped by the museum. The museum buyer had told Marilyn that she simply thought it was too hot for their customers. Another location in New York City, the Kitchen Market, did much better. The Kitchen Market was an upscale restaurant and gourmet food take-out business. The Kitchen Market was probably her steadiest wholesale customer other than the Moscow Co-op. The product also sold pretty well at the few similar gourmet markets where she had gotten her product placed, like Rainbow Groceries in Seattle and the Culinary Institute of America in San Francisco.

Marilyn had also gotten her product placed in a handful of specialty food stores that focused on hot and spicy foods. Surprisingly, she found, the product had never sold well in these locations. Despite the fact that the product had won the major fiery food awards, customers in these shops did not seem to be willing to pay the premium price for her product. She had concluded that if her product was located with similarly priced goods, like at the Kitchen Market in New York City, it would sell, but that if it stood out in price then it did not sell as well. Marilyn was not sure, however, just how similarly her product needed to be priced compared to other products the store sold. It seemed clear to her that her $14.95 half-pound tins were standing out in price too much in the hot and spicy specialty stores that thrived on selling jars of hot sauce that typically retailed for $2.99 to $5.99. Marilyn wondered how her product might do at department stores that often sold half-pound boxes of "premium" chocolates for as little as $9.95. She knew her half-pound tins contained better chocolate, offered more unique packaging and logo design, and did not give that "empty feeling" that the competitor's oversized boxes did, but wondered if her product would stand out too much in price in such retail locations.

Several online retailers also carried Cowgirl Chocolates, including companies like Salmon River Specialty Foods and Sam McGee's Hot Sauces, although sales from such sites were not very significant. Marilyn had also had her product available through Amazon.com for a short time, but few customers purchased her product from this site during the time it was listed. Marilyn concluded that customers searching the site for music or books simply were not finding her product, and those who did simply were not shopping for chocolates.

Marilyn also sold her products retail through her own Web site. The Web site accounted for about one-third of her sales. She liked Web-based sales, despite the extra work of having to process all the small orders, because she was able to capture both the wholesale and retail profits associated with the sale. She also liked the direct contact with the retail customers, and frequently tossed a few extra truffles into a customer's order and enclosed a note that said "a little extra bonus from the head cowgirl." Marilyn allowed customers to return the chocolate for a full refund if they found it not to their liking. Most of her sales growth from 1999 to 2000 had come from her Web site.

The Web site itself was created and maintained for her by a small local Internet service provider. It was a fairly simple site. It had pages that described the company and its products and allowed customers to place orders. It did not have any of the sophisticated features that would allow her to use it to capture information to track customers. Although she did not know for sure, she suspected that many of her Internet sales were from repeat customers who were familiar with her product. She included her Web site address on all of her packaging and had listed her site on several other sites, such as saucemall.com and worldmall.com, that would link shoppers at these sites to her site. Listing on some of these sites, such as saucemall.com, was free. Listing on some other sites cost a small monthly fee—for the worldmall.com listing, for example, she paid $25/month. Some sites simply provided links to her site on their own. For example, one customer had told her she had found the Cowgirl Chocolates' site at an upscale shopping site called Style365.com. She was not sure how much traffic these various sites were generating on her site, and was unsure how best to attract new customers to her Web site aside from these efforts.

Marilyn had attempted to get her product into a number of bigger name, upscale retailers, like Dean & Delucca and Coldwater Creek. Dean and Delucca was known for its high-end specialty foods, and the buyers for the company had seemed interested in carrying Cowgirl Chocolates, but the owner had nixed the idea because he found the chocolates too spicy. One of the buyers had also told Marilyn that the owner was more of a chocolate purist or traditionalist who did not really like the idea of adding cayenne pepper to chocolate. Marilyn had also tried hard to get her product sold through Coldwater Creek, one of the largest catalog and online retailers in the country that sold high-end women's apparel and gifts for the home. Coldwater Creek was headquartered just a couple of hours north of Moscow in Sandpoint, Idaho. Like Dean & Delucca, Coldwater Creek had decided that the chocolate was too spicy. Coldwater Creek had also expressed some reservations about carrying food products other than at its retail outlet in Sandpoint. Marilyn hoped that the introduction of mild-mannered Cowgirl Chocolates would help get her product into sites like these two.

PROMOTION

Marilyn was unsure how best to promote her product to potential customers given her limited resources. The ad that would appear in *Chile Pepper* magazine was her first attempt at really advertising her product. The ad itself was designed to grab readers' attention and pique their curiosity about Cowgirl Chocolates. Most of the ads in the magazine were fairly standard in format. They provided a lot of information and images of the product packed into a fairly small space. Her ad was different—it had very little product information and utilized the single image of the woman in the watering trough. It was to appear in a special section of the magazine that focused on celebrity musicians like Willie Nelson and The Dixie Chicks.

Other than the upcoming ad, Marilyn's promotional efforts were focused on trade shows and creating publicity opportunities. She attended a handful of trade shows each year. Some of these were focused on the hot and spicy food market, and it was at these events that she had won all of her awards. Other trade shows were more in the gourmet food market, and she typically shared table space at these events with Seattle Chocolates. She always gave away a lot of product samples at these trade shows, and had clearly won over some fans to her chocolate. But while these shows occasionally had led to placement of her product in retail locations, at least on a trial basis, they had as yet failed to land her what she would consider to be a really high volume wholesale account.

Marilyn also sought ways to generate publicity for her company and products. Several local newspapers had carried stories on her company in the last couple of years, and each time something like that would happen, she would see a brief jump in sales on her Web site. *The New York Times* had also carried a short article about her and her company. The day after that article ran, she generated sales of $1,000 through her Web site. More publicity like *The New York Times* article would clearly help. The recently released movie *Chocolat* about a woman who brings spicy chocolate with somewhat magical powers to a small French town was also generating some interest in her product. A number of customers had inquired if she used the same pepper in her chocolates as was used in the movie. Marilyn wondered how she might best capitalize on the interest the movie was creating in spicy chocolates. She thought that perhaps she could convince specialty magazines like *Art & Antiques* or regional magazines like *Sunset Magazine* or even national magazines like *Good Housekeeping* to run stories on her, her art, and her chocolates. But she only had so much time to divide between her various efforts. She had looked into hiring a public relations firm, but had discovered that this would cost something on the order of $2,000/month. She did not expect that any publicity a public relations firm could create would generate sufficient sales to offset this cost, particularly given the limited number of locations where people could buy her chocolates. Marilyn was considering trying to write a cookbook as a way to generate greater publicity for Cowgirl Chocolates. She always talked a little about Cowgirl Chocolates when she gave seminars and presentations about her art, and thought that promoting a cookbook would create similar opportunities. The cookbook would also feature several recipes using Cowgirl Chocolates' products.

In addition to being unsure how best to promote her product to potential customers, Marilyn also wondered what she should do to better tap into the seasonal opportunities that presented themselves to sellers of chocolate. Demand for her product was somewhat seasonal, with peak retail demand being at Christmas and Valentine's Day. But she was clearly not seeing the Christmas and Valentine sales of other chocolate companies. Seattle Chocolates, for example, had around three-quarters of its annual sales in the fourth quarter, whereas Cowgirl Chocolates' sales in the second half of 2000 were actually less than in the first half. Likewise, while Cowgirl Chocolates experienced a small increase in demand around Valentine's Day, it was nowhere near the increase in demand that other chocolate companies experienced. Marilyn did sell some gift buckets and baskets through her Web site, and these were more popular at Christmas and Valentine's Day. The Moscow Co-op had also sold some of these gift baskets and buckets during the 2000 Christmas season. Marilyn knew that the gift basket industry in the United States was pretty large, and that the industry even had its own trade publication called the *Gift Basket Review.* But she was not sure if gift baskets were the best way to generate sales at these two big holidays and thought that she could probably be doing more. One other approach to spur these seasonal sales that she was planning to try was to buy lists of e-mail addresses, that would allow her to send out several e-mails promoting her products right before Valentine's Day and Christmas. She had talked to the owners of a jewelry store about sharing the expense of this endeavor and they had tentative plans to purchase 10,000 e-mail addresses for $300.

WHAT NEXT?

Marilyn looked again at the advertisement that would be appearing soon in *Chile Pepper* magazine. The same friend who had helped her with her award winning package design had helped produce the ad. It would clearly grab people's attention, but would it bring customers to her products in the numbers she needed?

Next to the ad sat the folder with what financial information she had. Despite having little training in small business accounting and financial management, Marilyn knew it was important to keep good records. She had kept track of revenues and expenses for the year, and she had summarized these in a table (see Exhibit 4). Marilyn had shared this revenue and cost information with a friend with some experience in small business financial management, and the result was an estimated income statement for the year 2000 based upon the unaudited information in Exhibit 4. The estimated income statement, shown in Exhibit 5, revealed that Cowgirl had lost approximately $6,175 on operations before taxes. Combining the information in Exhibits 4 and 5, it appeared that the inventory had built up to approximately $16,848 by December 31, 2000. Marilyn had initially guessed she had $10,000 worth of product and packaging inventory, about twice her normal level of inventory, between what was stored in her garage turned art studio turned chocolate warehouse and what was stored for her at Seattle Chocolates. But the financial analysis indicated that she either had more inventory than she thought or that she had given away more product than she originally thought. Either way, this represented a significant additional drain on her resources—in effect cash expended to cover both the operational loss and the inventory buildup was approximately $23,000 in total (see note 3 of Exhibit 4 for a more detailed explanation). When Marilyn looked at the exhibits, she could see better why she had to loan the firm money. She also recognized that the bottom line was that the numbers did not look good, and she wondered if the ad would help turn things around for 2001.

If the ad did not have its desired affect, she wondered what she should do next. She clearly had limited resources to work with. She had already pretty much decided that if this ad did not work, she would not run another one in the near future. She was also pretty wary of working with distributors. In addition to her own bad experience, she knew of others in the industry that had bad experiences with distributors, and she did not think she could afford to take another gamble on a distributor. She wondered if she should focus

EXHIBIT 4
Summary of 2000
Financial Information
(Unaudited)

REVENUES:	
Product Sales	$ 26,000
Revenue from Shipping	4,046 (see Note 1)
Total Revenues	**$ 30,046**

EXPENSES: (RELATED TO COST OF SALES)	
Chocolate (raw material)	$ 16,508
Caramel (raw material)	2,647
Packaging (bags, boxes, tins)	9,120
Printing (labels, cards, etc.)	3,148
Subtotal	$ 31,423 (see Note 2)

OTHER EXPENSES	
Shipping and Postage	$ 4,046
Brokers	540
Travel (airfare, lodging, meals, gas)	5,786
Trade Shows (promotions, etc.)	6,423
Web site	1,390
Phone	981
Office Supplies	759
Photography	356
Insurance, Lawyers, Memberships	437
Charitable Contributions	200
Miscellaneous Other Expenses	1,071
State Taxes	35
Subtotal	$ 22,024
Total Expenses	**$ 53,447**
Cash needed to sustain operations	**$ 23,023** (see Note 3)

ESTIMATED YEAR-END INVENTORY (12/31/00):	
Product Inventory	$ 9,848
Extra Packaging and Labels	7,000
Total Inventory	**$ 16,848**

Notes (1) The $4,046 Revenue from Shipping represents income received from customers who are charged shipping and postage up front as part of the order. Cowgirl then pays the shipping and postage when the order is delivered. The offsetting operating expense is noted in "Other Expenses."
(2) Of this amount, $14,575 is attributed to product actually sold and shipped. The remaining $16,848 represents leftover inventory and related supplies (i.e., $16,848 + $14,575 = $31,423).
(3) Marilyn made a personal loan to the firm in the year 2000 for approximately $23,000 to sustain the business's operations.

more attention on her online retail sales or on expanding her wholesale business to include more retailers. If she focused more on her own online sales, what exactly should she do? If she focused on expanding her wholesale business, where should she put her emphasis? Should she continue to pursue retailers that specialized in hot and spicy foods, try to get her product placed in more co-ops, expand her efforts to get the product positioned as a gift in museum gift shops and similar outlets, or focus her efforts on large, high-end retailers like Coldwater Creek and Dean & Delucca now that she had a nonspicy chocolate in her product mix? Or should she try to do something else entirely new? And what more should she do to create publicity for her product? Was the cookbook idea worth pursuing? As she thought about it, she began to wonder if things were beginning to spin out of control. Here she was, contemplating writing a cookbook to generate publicity for her chocolate company that she started to raise money to publish her arts magazine. Where would this end?

EXHIBIT 5   Cowgirl Chocolates Income Statement (Accountant's unaudited estimate for Year 2000)

			% of Sales
REVENUES:			
Product Sales	$26,000		
Miscellaneous Income	$ 4,046		
Total Net Sales		**$30,046**	100%
Cost of Sales (shipped portion of chocolate, caramel, packaging, and printing)		$14,197	47%
Gross Margin		**$15,849**	53%
OPERATING EXPENSES:			
Advertising & Promotions:			
Trade Shows	6,423		
Web site	1,390		
Charitable Contributions	200		
Subtotal		8,013	27%
Travel		5,786	19%
Miscellaneous		1,071	4%
Payroll Expense/Benefits @ 20%	(no personnel charges)	—	0%
Depreciation on Plant and Equipment	(no current owner-ship of PPE)	—	0%
Continuing Inventory (finished and unfinished)	(not included in income statement)	—	
Shipping & Postage		4,046	13%
Insurance, Lawyers, Professional			
Memberships		437	1.5%
Brokers		540	1.8%
Office Expenses (phone, supplies, photography, taxes)		2,131	7%
Total Operating Expenses		**22,024**	
Grand Total: All Expenses		**$36,221**	
Profit before Interest & Taxes		**($6,175) [see note]**	
Interest Expense (short term)		—	
Interest Expense (long term)		—	
Taxes Incurred (Credit @ 18%, approximate tax rate)		($1,124)	
Net Profit after Taxes		**($5,051.15)**	
Net Profit after Taxes/Sales			−17%

Note: The ($6,175) loss plus the $16,848 in inventory build-up approximates the cash needed ($23,023—see Exhibit 4) to cover the total expenses for year 2000.

22

Clearwater Technologies

Susan F. Sieloff and Raymond M. Kinnunen *Northeastern University*

At 9:00 AM on Monday, May 2004, Rob Erickson, QTX Product Manager; Hillary Hanson, Financial Analyst; and Brian James, District Sales Manager; were preparing for a meeting with Mark Jefferies, Vice President of Marketing, at Clearwater Technologies. The meeting's objective was to establish the end-user pricing for a capacity upgrade to the QTX servers Clearwater offered.

No one was looking forward to the meeting because company pricing debates were traditionally long and drawn out. Because there had already been several meetings, everyone knew that there was no consensus on how to determine the appropriate price, but company policy insisted on agreement. Only one price proposal went forward, and it had to represent something everyone could accept.

When Jefferies called the meeting, he commented:

> We've struggled with this pricing issue for several months. We can't seem to all agree on the right price. Finance wants the price as high as possible to generate revenue. Sales wants it low to sell volume. Product management wants the price to be consistent with the current product margin model. We've debated this for quite a while, but we need to finalize the third quarter price book update before June in order to get it into print and out to the sales force. We need to get this done.

CLEARWATER TECHNOLOGIES, INC. HISTORY

Clearwater Technologies, Inc. was a small, publicly traded technology firm outside Boston. It was the market share leader in customer relationship management (CRM) servers for sales staffs of small- to medium-sized companies. Four MIT graduates had founded the company when they saw an opportunity to meet a market need that larger firms ignored. Unlike the CRM systems from Oracle or SAP, Clearwater customized the QTX for companies with sales forces of 10 to 30 people. Clearwater had been first to market in this particular segment, and QTX sales represented $45 million of its $80 million sales in 2004.

The QTX product line represented Clearwater's core franchise. Clearwater's premium-priced products were renowned for high reliability in performance supported by free lifetime technical support. The QTX line held 70 percent of its mature market. To date, competition in this market had been minimal, because no competitor had been able to match Clearwater's general functionality, and Clearwater held a U.S. patent on a popular feature that directed faxed documents to a specific salesperson's e-mail rather than a central fax machine.

Since 1999, Clearwater had used the cash generated by the QTX line to support engineering-intensive internal product development and to buy four other companies. None of these other businesses had achieved a dominant market position or profitability, so maximizing the QTX cash flow remained a priority.

THE QTX PRODUCT

QTX was a sales support server that allowed multiple users to simultaneously maintain their sales account databases. These databases covered contact information, quote histories, copies of all communications, and links to the customer's corporate database for shipping records. The basic QTX package consisted of a processor, chassis, hard drive, and network interface, with a manufacturing cost of $500. The package provided simultaneous access for 10 users to the system, referred to as 10 "seats." Each seat represented one accessing employee. The product line consisted of 10-, 20-, and 30-seat capacity QTX servers. Each incremental 10 seats required $200 of additional manufacturing cost. Yearly sales were at the rate of 4,000 units across all sizes. In initial sales, approximately 30 percent of customers bought the 30-seat unit, 40 percent bought the 20-seat unit, and 30 percent bought the 10-seat unit. Customers who needed more than 30 seats typically went to competitors servicing the medium-to-large company market segment.

Clearwater set a per-seat manufacturer's suggested retail price (MSRP) that decreased with higher quantity seat purchases, reflecting the customer perception of declining manufacturing cost per seat. Clearwater also saw this as advantageous because it encouraged customers to maximize their initial seat purchase.

Clearwater typically sold its products through value-added resellers (VARs). A VAR was typically a small local firm that provided sales and support to end users. The value added by these resellers was that they provided a complete solution to the end user/customer from a single point of purchase and had multiple information technology products available from various vendors. Using VARs reduced Clearwater's sales and service expense significantly and increased its market coverage.

These intermediaries operated in several steps. First, the VAR combined the QTX from Clearwater with database software from other suppliers to form a turnkey customer solution. Second, the VAR loaded the software with customer-specific information and linked it to the customer's existing sales history databases. Finally, the VAR installed the product at the customer's site and trained the customer on its use. Clearwater sold the QTX to resellers at a 50 percent discount from the MSRP, allowing the VARs to sell to the end user at or below the MSRP. The discount allowed the VARs room to negotiate with the customer and still achieve a profit (Table 1).

TABLE 1

Number of Seats	MSRP to End User	VAR Price	Unit Cost*	Uni Margin**
10	$ 8,000	$4,000	$500	87.5%
20	$14,000	$7,000	$700	90.0%
30	$17,250	$8,625	$900	89.6%

*Unit cost reflects additional $200 for memory capability for each additional 10 seats.

**Margin $= \dfrac{\text{VAR Price} - \text{Unit Cost}}{\text{VAR Price}}$

TABLE 2

Number of Seats	Original Unit Cost	Original Unit Margin	Actual Unit Cost	Actual Unit Margin
10	$500	87.5%	$900	77.5%
20	$700	90.0%	$900	87.1%
30	$900	89.6%	$900	89.6%

THE UPGRADE

Initially, the expectation had been that the 30-seat unit would be the largest volume seller. In order to gain economies of scale in manufacturing, reduce inventory configurations, and reduce engineering design and testing expense to a single assembly, Clearwater decided to manufacture only the 30-seat server with the appropriate number of seats "enabled" for the buyer. Clearwater was effectively "giving away" extra memory and absorbing the higher cost rather than manufacturing the various sizes. If a customer wanted a 10-seat server, the company shipped a 30-seat capable unit, with only the requested 10 seats enabled through software configuration. The proposed upgrade was, in reality, allowing customers to access capability already built into the product (Table 2).

Clearwater knew that many original customers were ready to use the additional capacity in the QTX. Some customers had added seats by buying a second box, but because the original product contained the capability to expand by accessing the disabled seats, Clearwater saw an opportunity to expand the product line and increase sales to a captive customer base. Customers could double or triple their seat capacity by purchasing either a 10- or a 20-seat upgrade and getting an access code to enable the additional number of seats. No other competitor offered the possibility of an upgrade. To gain additional seats from the competitor, the customer purchased and installed an additional box. Because customers performed a significant amount of acceptance testing, which they would have to repeat before switching brands, the likelihood of changing brands to add capacity was low.

The objective of this morning's meeting was to set the price for the two upgrades.

As QTX product manager Rob Erickson stopped to collect his most recent notes from his desk, he reflected:

> What a way to start the week. Every time we have one of these meetings, senior management only looks at margins. I spent the whole weekend cranking numbers and I'm going in there using the highest margin we've got today. How can anybody say that's too low?

He grabbed his notes, calculator, and coffee and headed down the hall.

From the other wing of the building, financial analyst Hillary Hanson was crossing the lobby toward the conference room. She was thinking about the conversation she had late Friday afternoon with her boss, Alicia Fisher, Clearwater's CFO. They had been discussing this upcoming meeting and Alicia had given Hillary very clear instructions.

> I want you to go in and argue for the highest price possible. We should absolutely maximize the profitability on the upgrade. The customers are already committed to us and they

have no alternative for an upgrade but with us. The switching costs to change at this point are too high since they've already been trained in our system and software. Let's go for it. Besides, we really need to show some serious revenue generation for the year-end report to the stockholders.

Hillary had not actually finalized a number. She figured she could see what the others proposed and then argue for a significant premium over that. She had the CFO's backing so she could keep pushing for more.

From the parking lot, Brian James, the district sales manager, headed for the rear entrance. He, too, was thinking about the upcoming meeting and anticipating a long morning.

I wish marketing would realize that when they come up with some grandiose number for a new product, sales takes the hit in the field. It's a killer to have to explain to customers that they have to pay big bucks for something that's essentially built in. It's gonna be even tougher to justify on this upgrade. At least with the QTX, we have something the buyer can see. It's hardware. With the upgrade, there isn't even a physical product. We're just giving customers a code to access the capability that's already built into the machine. Telling customers that they have to pay several thousand dollars never makes you popular. If you think about it, that's a lot of money for an access code, but you won't hear me say that out loud. Maybe I can get them to agree to something reasonable this time. I spent the weekend working this one out, and I think my logic is pretty solid.

PRICE PROPOSALS

Once everyone was settled in the conference room, Rob spoke first:

I know we have to come up with prices for both the 10-seat and 20-seat upgrades, but to keep things manageable, let's discuss the 20-seat price first. Once that number is set, the 10-seat price should be simple. Because the margin on the 30-seat unit is the highest in the line, I think we should use that as the basis to the price for the upgrade.

He went to a whiteboard to show an example:

If a customer is upgrading from a 10-seat unit to a 30-seat unit, they are adding two steps of capacity costing $200 each to us, or $400. $400/1-0.90 = $4,000 to the reseller, and $8,000 to the end user. We keep the margin structure in place at the highest point in the line. The customer gets additional capacity, and we keep our margins consistent.

He sat down feeling pleased. He had fired the first shot, had been consistent with the existing margin structure, and had rounded up the highest margin point in the line.

Brian looked at Rob's calculations and commented:

I think that's going to be hard for the customer to see without us giving away information about our margins, and we don't want to do that, since they are pretty aggressive to begin with. However, I think I have solved this one for us. I've finally come up with a simple, fair solution to pricing the upgrade that works for us and the customers.

He walked over to a whiteboard and grabbed a marker:

If we assume an existing 10-seat customer has decided to upgrade to 30-seat capability, we should charge that customer the difference between what the buyer has already paid and the price of the new capacity. So . . .

New 30-seat unit	$17,250
Original 10-seat unit	$ 8,000
Price for 20-seat upgrade	$ 9,250

It's consistent with our current pricing for the QTX. It's fair to the customer. It's easy for the customer to understand and it still makes wads of money for us. It also is easy for the customer to see that we're being good to them. If they bought a 20-seat box in addition to the 10-seat box they already have, it would be costing them more.

He wrote:

> New 20-seat unit $14,000

A new unit provides customers with redundancy by having two boxes, which they might want in the event of product failure, but the cost is pretty stiff. Upgrading becomes the logical and affordable option.

Hillary looked at the numbers and knew just what she was going to do.

That all looks very logical, but I don't see that either of you has the company's best interests at heart. Brian, you just want a simple sale that your sales people and the customers will buy into, and Rob, you are charging even less than Brian. We need to consider the revenue issue as well. These people have already bought from us; are trained on our hardware and software and don't want to have to repeat the process with someone else. It would take too long. They've got no desire to make a change and that means we've got them. The sky is really the limit on how much we can charge them because they have no real alternative. We should take this opportunity to really go for the gold, say $15,000 or even $20,000. We can and should be as aggressive as possible.

All three continued to argue the relative merits of their pricing positions, without notable success. Jefferies listened to each of them and after they finished, he turned to a clean whiteboard and took the marker.

I've done some more thinking on this. In order to meet the needs of all three departments, there are three very important points that the price structure for these upgrades must accomplish:

1. The pricing for the upgrades shouldn't undercut the existing pricing for the 30-seat QTX.
2. We want to motivate our buyers to purchase the maximum number of seats at the initial purchase. A dollar now is better than a potential dollar later. We never know for sure that they will make that second purchase. If we don't do this right, we're going to encourage customers to reduce their initial purchase. They'll figure they can add capacity whenever, so why buy it if they don't need it. That would kill upfront sales of the QTX.
3. We don't want to leave any revenue on the table when buyers decide to buy more capacity. They are already committed to us and our technology and we should capitalize on that, without totally ripping them off. Therefore, while Hillary says "the sky's the limit," I think there is a limit and we need to determine what it is and how close we can come to it.

If we assume that those are the objectives, none of the prices you've put together thus far answers all three of those criteria. Some come close, but each one fails. See if you can put your heads together and come to a consensus price that satisfies all three objectives. OK?

Heads nodded and with that, Jefferies left the conference room. The three remaining occupants looked at one another. Brian got up to wipe the previous numbers off the whiteboards and said:

OK, one more time. If our numbers don't work, why not and what is the right price for the 20-seat upgrade?

Case Group F

Social and Ethical Issues in Marketing Management

Case

23

E. & J. Gallo Winery

Marion Armstrong *University of Alabama*

Taylor Green *University of Alabama*

A. J. Strickland III *University of Alabama*

In 2006, wine in the United States represented a $28 billion industry, with 716 million gallons sold, of which about 92 million gallons were dessert wines.[1,2] Included within the dessert wine category was a group of cheap, low-grade, and highly controversial high-proof, or "fortified," wines that contained added alcohol to increase their potency and additional sugar or sweetener to enhance their taste—see Exhibit 1. Most natural wine products had only about 8–12 percent alcohol by volume, since the yeasts that were used in the fermentation process were killed by higher alcohol concentrations. Many of the cheap fortified wine products were deliberately made and sold at the highest potency because they were the low-cost alcoholic beverage favored by people with low incomes and budget-constrained teenagers and college students who were looking for something "relatively strong, inexpensive, and pleasant tasting."[3]

Wild Irish Rose and Cisco were two fortified wines that together made their parent company, Canandaigua, the number one seller in the fortified wine market, with about 70 percent of the industry's business in 1996,[4] followed by Gallo's Thunderbird brand and Mogen David Wine's MD 20/20. Canandaigua's Cisco wine cooler, known as "liquid cocaine" on the streets, had the fourth leading market share in the dessert wine segment. For several decades, low-end dessert and fortified wines had been a profitable, high-volume market segment that winemakers had targeted. *The Wall Street Journal* reported in 1988 that, of all the wine brands sold in America, Richard's Wild Irish Rose (named after the founder's son,

[1]Wine Institute, "Wine Consumption in the U.S.," www.wineinstitute.org/resources/statistics/article86.

[2]National Association for Business Economics, "Economics of the U.S. Wine Industry," www.nabe.com/publib/news/07/10/05.html.

[3]American Alcohol & Drug Information Foundation,"High Potency and Other Alcoholic Beverage Consumption Among Adolescents," 2005, www.thefreelibrary.com/High+potency+and+other+alcoholic+beverage+consumption+among. . .-a0142871709.

[4]"The Bottom of the Barrel," *San Francisco Chronicle,* www.sfgate.com/cgi-bin/article.cgi?f=/c/a/1996/07/07/sc22167.dtl&hw=Thunderbird+Wine&sn=002&sc=926.

EXHIBIT 1   Examples of Low-end Fortified Wines That Had Attracted Criticism

Richard Sands, who had been Canandaigua's president until 1999) was 6th in volume of sales, Thunderbird was 10th, and MD 20/20 was 16th.

Originally, fortified wines were made by adding brandy (distilled wine) to wine to raise the alcohol content so as to help prevent spoilage during shipping and to extend the shelf life—the higher alcohol content killed off bacteria and other organisms. Port and sherry wines were good examples of high-quality fortified wines. However, the makers of low-grade fortified wines often used cheaper grain alcohol to raise the alcohol content to 14 to 20 percent and thus make their products more appealing to buyers looking to get drunk cheap. Low-grade fortified wines like Richard's Wild Irish Rose, Thunderbird, Night Train (another Gallo product), and Boone's Farm are generally sold for less than $3.50 per 750 ml bottle and for between $1 and $2 per 375 ml bottle (about 12.5 ounces). These low prices made them a favorite of low-income drinkers, skid-row alcoholics, and young adults since they produced more intoxication for less money than just about any other type of alcoholic beverage. The dose of alcohol in a typical 12.5-ounce Cisco wine cooler or a pint of Thunderbird was five times the dose of alcohol in a 12-ounce can of beer, a 4- to 5-ounce serving of wine, or a 1.25-ounce shot of bourbon—see Exhibit 2.

Typical of the critics of fortified wines was Mark Dalton, a social worker for Washington State's Division of Alcohol and Substance Abuse; Dalton said, "Fortified wines and cheap strong beer are packaged and marketed to alcoholics, and the corner stores who sell them are making profits while contributing to a cycle of addiction as well as a public nuisance."[5] Addiction professionals had dubbed cheap fortified wine "the most seriously abused drug in this country."[6] It was common for people who were charged with trying to help the chronic alcoholics who drank cheap fortified wines to express the view that manufacturing and selling such products was unethical, even bordering on being criminal; they often

[5]Kelly Payne, "Drying Up the Square," www.realchangenews.org/pastarticles/features/articles/new_dec_Boozeban.html.
[6]"Banning the Saturday Night Special of Booze," *Newsweek,* March 10, 1986.

EXHIBIT 2
Alcohol Content of
Selected Alcoholic
Beverages

Source: William J. Bailey,
"Factline on High Potency
Alcoholic Beverages,"
Indiana Prevention Resource
Center, Indiana University,
www.drugs.indiana.edu/
publications/iprc/factline/
high_potency.html.

Alcoholic Beverage	Alcohol Content
12 ounces of 4% beer	0.48 ounces
5 ounces of 10% wine	0.50 ounces
1.25 ounces of 40% vodka (80 proof)	0.50 ounces
1.25 ounces of 43% whiskey (86 proof)	0.52 ounces
40 ounce bottle of 8% malt liquor	3.20 ounces
1.25 ounce shot of 151 proof rum	0.94 ounces
12.5 ounce bottle of 6% wine cooler	0.75 ounces
12.5 ounce bottle of 20% fortified wine cooler	2.50 ounces

EXAMPLES OF HIGH-POTENCY ALCOHOLIC BEVERAGES

- Fortified wines (most low-cost brands were sold at or near 20% alcohol by volume)
- Wine coolers (most were about 6% alcohol by volume, 1.5 times more potent than typical beer)
- Specialty wine coolers, such as Cisco (up to 20% alcohol by volume)
- Malt liquors (up to 8% alcohol by volume, nearly twice the potency of typical American beer)
- Neutral grain spirits, such as Everclear (95% alcohol by volume)
- High-proof liquors, such as 151 Rum (75.5% alcohol by volume, about twice the potency of other rums)

charged that the providers (wineries and licensed retail stores) had no conscience and that their actions were repulsive. A drug and alcohol counselor from Mountain View Hospital in Gadsden, Alabama, told of crack addicts' stories about buying Mad Dog (the street name for MD 20/20) to help them come off their crack high; according to the counselor, addicts said they chose Mad Dog because it was "cheap and strong." The president of one winery said, "Fortified wines lack any socially redeeming values." In a 1988 *Wall Street Journal* article, Paul Gillette, publisher of *Wine Investor,* said, "Makers of skid-row wines are the dope-pushers of the wine industry. And these companies are the largest producers and appear the most successful wineries."[7]

In many states, fortified wines were effectively limited to a maximum of 20 percent alcohol content by tax and licensing laws. For example, Indiana law defined *wine* as a beverage "that does not contain 21 percent or more alcohol." This meant that a wine with higher alcohol content could not be sold in grocery and convenience stores (which were typically licensed to sell only beer and wine); wines with more than the legal alcohol content limit were taxed at the much higher rates for distilled spirits. Federal taxes also jumped up for wines with alcohol content above 20 percent.

The major producers and marketers of low-end dessert and fortified wines defended their products and disputed the critics' characterization of the buyers of fortified wines. Sid Abrams of the Wine Institute, which represented California vintners, said, "There are a lot of people who just like the flavor. And some older people buy inexpensive sherry because they can't afford the more expensive product."[8] The problem of street alcoholics presents a dilemma, Abrams said, "but I don't think you can blame the manufacturers." Another defense was that since it was legal to produce and market cheap fortified wines, there was nothing wrong with winemakers and store retailers pursuing the market opportunities that existed. However, the producers of the top-selling fortified wines distanced themselves from their fortified wine product offerings by leaving their corporate names off the labels—an

---

[7]Alix Freedman, "Market Misery—Winos and Thunderbird Are a Subject Gallo Doesn't Like to Discuss," *Wall Street Journal,* February 25, 1988, pp. 1, 18.

[8]As quoted in Warren King, "Ethics of Manufacturing Profits from Drunks," *Seattle Times,* January 20, 1998.

omission that critics interpreted as being deliberately intended to obscure the producer's link to these brands. While vintners claimed that "indistinct labeling is a common industry practice that reserves a vintner's name only for its most expensive products," critics of the industry segment were not convinced, claiming hypocrisy on the part of the manufacturers. Gallo manufactured wines for a number of different price ranges under various labels and listed all of those wines as a part of its family of brands. But while this list included Gallo's lower-end labels such as Boone's Farm and Bartles & Jaymes, noticeably absent from the list was Thunderbird, even though it was still sold in low-income areas across the United States.

THE E. & J. GALLO WINERY

The Early Years

The E. & J. Gallo Winery, the largest wine producer in the world, was founded by Ernest and Julio Gallo in 1933. The Gallo brothers got their start in the wine business working during their spare time in their father's vineyard near Modesto, California. Their father, Joseph Gallo Sr., had immigrated from the Piedmont region in northwest Italy and was a small-time grape grower and shipper of California wine. He survived Prohibition because the government permitted the personal production of no more than 100 gallons of wine per year; many Californians made wine in amounts under this limit if they could get the grapes. This loophole allowed the elder Gallo to sell grapes in bulk shipments to private brewers. But the Depression was tough, and Gallo's company almost went under and during the spring of 1933 the family was scarred by tragedy when Joseph Gallo Sr. and his wife were found dead in an apparent murder/suicide.

Following his parents' deaths, Ernest Gallo became head of the family and the business. The Gallo brothers, both in their early 20s, decided it would be a good idea to integrate forward into making wine even though neither knew anything about the process. Ernest and Julio found two thin pamphlets on winemaking in the Modesto Public Library and, with $5,900 to their names, began to invest in winemaking capability. Julio oversaw the vineyards and the winemaking operation, while Ernest handled marketing and distribution; their youngest brother, Joseph Gallo Jr., was an employee. Ernest pushed to build the company, aiming at a broad national market and envisioning E. & J. Gallo as becoming the "Campbell Soup company of the wine industry." He drove himself and his employees hard, sometimes working 16-hour days and taking long trips around the country by car to make sales calls and learn about consumers' wine-drinking preferences and habits. It was his practice to study the company's markets and customers very carefully and base the winery's marketing strategy on detailed market research concerning buyer behavior and preferences.

With the end of Prohibition, the Gallo brothers set out to become market leaders in what was then a relatively small and mostly downscale American wine market. Ernest effectively marketed cheap, fortified wines like White Port and lemon-flavored Thunderbird in inner-city markets. There were stories, which Gallo denied, that the winery got the idea for citrus-flavored Thunderbird from reports that liquor stores in Oakland, California, were catering to the tastes of certain customers by attaching packages of lemon Kool-Aid to bottles of white wine to be mixed at home. Thunderbird, introduced in the late 1950s and named after the ritzy Thunderbird Hotel in Las Vegas, Nevada, became Gallo's first phenomenal success. A catchy radio jingle helped send Thunderbird to the top of the sales charts in many inner-city and low-income neighborhoods across the United States:

What's the word?

Thunderbird

How's it sold?

Good and cold

What's the jive?

Bird's alive

What's the price?

Thirty twice.

According to author Ellen Hawkes, who wrote an unauthorized history of the Gallo family called *Blood and Wine,* Ernest later delighted in telling the story of driving through a tough inner-city neighborhood and, upon seeing a man walking down the sidewalk, pulling alongside, rolling down his window, and calling out, "What's the word?" The man's immediate answer was "Thunderbird."

The Gallos began researching varietal grapes in 1946, planting more than 400 varieties in experimental vineyards during the 1950s and 1960s and testing each variety in the different grape-growing regions of California for its ability to produce fine table wines. Their greatest difficulty was to persuade growers to convert from common grape varieties to the delicate, thin-skinned varietals because it took at least four years for a vine to begin bearing and perhaps two more years to develop typical varietal characteristics. As an incentive, in 1967, Gallo offered long-term contracts to growers, guaranteeing the prices for their grapes every year, provided they met Gallo quality standards. With a guaranteed long-term buyer for their crops, growers were able to borrow the needed capital to finance the costly replanting, and the winery's staff of skilled viticulturists provided technical assistance to aid contract growers.

While most California wineries concentrated on production and sold their wines through wholesale distributors, Gallo pursued a vertical integration strategy and participated in every aspect from growing grapes to making wine to sales and marketing to owning and operating its wine distributorships. E. & J. Gallo Winery owned the wholesale distributors of Gallo wines in about 10 geographic markets and probably would have bought many of the more than 300 independent distributors handling its wines if laws in most states had not prohibited it. The entrepreneurial freedom that came with private ownership, the wise stewardship of Ernest and Julio Gallo, low-cost mass production, and strong distribution were the major competitive advantages contributing to Gallo's success. Since the company was family-owned, the Gallo brothers could use low prices and paper-thin margins to win market share from higher-cost rivals and could absorb occasional losses in introducing new brands and widening the winery's geographic reach, whereas wineries that were publicly held had to appease earnings-minded stockholders. While Gallo bought about 95 percent of its grapes, it virtually controlled its 1,500 growers through long-term contracts. Gallo's trucking company, Fairbanks, hauled wine out of Modesto and brought raw materials in. Gallo was the only winery that manufactured its own bottles (2 million a day) and screw-top caps.

Gallo's Gradual Shift to More Upscale Wines

Gallo's major competitive weakness over the years had always been its reputation as a maker of low-end wines in screw-top bottles—an image that flowed partly from its Thunderbird and Night Train brands. This was not so much a liability in the company's early days, when wine sales in the United States were heavily concentrated in the low end of the market, but Gallo's low-end image became an increasing liability in the 1980s as wine consumers began to purchase better-quality table wines in increasing numbers and as wine became a favored beverage at cocktail parties. As the company grew over the years, first becoming the largest winemaker in the United States and then the largest in the world, the Gallo brothers initiated a series of moves to shed the winery's image as a maker of low-end wines sold in screw-top bottles and jugs. Gallo's new strategy was to distance itself from the Thunderbird and Night Train brands and begin the long-range task of repositioning itself as a maker of better quality, moderately priced table wines and then later as a maker of truly fine wines.

From 1985 to 2000, the company spent hundreds of millions in advertising aimed at boosting consumer perceptions of Gallo wines and cultivating a clientele for its new, more upscale wines.[9] At the same time, the company invested in production facilities to make more upscale table wines under a variety of labels, some of which were created internally and some of which were acquired. Ernest Gallo studied the markets the company targeted and the tastes and wine-drinking habits of consumers very carefully—from the high end to the low end of the price/quality scale. Under his watchful eye, Gallo's marketing strategy was always based on detailed market research concerning buyer behavior and preferences. By the mid-1990s, the company had been reasonably successful in attracting more upscale wine drinkers to try its newly introduced wines and wine brands. In 1998, one of the company's estate-bottled premium Chardonnay wines was rated 94 points on *Wine Spectator*'s 100-point scale.[10] In 1998 and again in 2001, Gallo won the Premio Gran VinItaly at the International Wine and Distilled Fair in Verona, Italy, making Gallo the only foreign winery to win twice in the history of the award. As of 2001, the company had more than 75 brands in its product lineup and was exporting wines to countries all over the world.

While Ernest and Julio Gallo were pouring their money and efforts into introducing new, higher quality wines with the goal of improving the company's overall image, they not only tried to distance themselves from their earlier all-star labels but also began to phase out the production of these products altogether. In 1993, Gallo was selling roughly 3 million cases of Thunderbird a year. The company had quit advertising the product altogether by 2003 and sold only 300,000 cases that year.[11] This decrease in focus on Thunderbird was more than likely a result of the changing tastes of American wine consumers as well as the social pressures the company began to face in the late 1980s. In August 1989, Gallo stopped distributing its two lower-end wines (Thunderbird and Night Train) and instructed retailers not to sell these brands anymore. Whatever good intentions it demonstrated, this ban didn't last: Thunderbird returned to inner cities and skid-row areas less than six months later.[12]

Ernest and Julio Gallo were active contributors to political campaigns, with Ernest contributing largely to Democrats and Julio giving more to Republicans. Over the years, the Gallos reportedly contributed $381,000 to Senator Robert Dole and about $900,000 to foundations with which Dole was connected.[13] In 1998, Ernest Gallo helped bring in $100,000 for a Bill Clinton fund-raising lunch in San Francisco only weeks after the *Los Angeles Times* reported that he had met privately with President Clinton to discuss Chilean wine imports (which had recently been gaining market share in the low-priced end of the U.S. wine market). Shortly after Ernest's meeting with the president, Congress delayed any action to authorize increases in Chilean wine imports and also passed increased funding for

[9] *Standard Directory of Advertisers,* 2000.

[10] Jeff Morgan, "Gallo of Sonoma," *Wine Spectator Online,* June 30, 1999.

[11] "Last Call for Thunderbird," *L.A. Times,* http://pqasb.pqarchiver.com/latimes/access/275328361 .html?dids=275328361:275328361&FMT=ABS&FMTS=ABS:FT&type=current&date=Jan+8%2C+ 2003&author=Corie+Brown&pub=Los+Angeles+Times&edition+&startpage=F.7&desc=Last+call+for+ Thunderbird.

[12] "Cheap Wine Returns to the Tenderloin," *San Francisco Chronicle,* www.winefiles.org/results.cgi? boolean=thunderbird+wine&f=simple&start=1.

[13] "So You Want to Buy a President," *Frontline,* www.pbs.org/wgbh/pages/frontline/president/ players/gallo.html.

a wine promotion program that funneled millions of dollars to Gallo to promote its wines overseas. A bipartisan group of senators included this program in a 1998 listing of a "dirty dozen" examples of corporate welfare.

E. & J. Gallo Winery in 2007

In 2007, the E. & J. Gallo Winery was continuing to operate as a privately owned and family-operated corporation. Second-generation family members Joseph and Robert Gallo, along with Julio's son-in-law James Coleman, were serving as co presidents of the company in 2007. Julio died in a 1993 car accident, and Ernest passed away in 2007 in his Modesto home at the age of 97. Julio's grandchildren Matt and Gina had by this time become important members of the company's winemaking team. Gina Gallo studied winemaking at the University of California–Davis and crafted her first wine in 1993.[14] Her views on winemaking were featured at the company's Web site:

> For me, wine is a pleasure. It has to be beautiful to look at and smell and astonishing to taste. But I don't want to make obvious wines. I want depth and a little mystery, and I want some "wow" in there too. Along with the rest of my family, I was very proud when Gallo of Sonoma was named Winery of the Year in 1996, 1998 and again in 2001. As a winemaker, however, I've never forgotten a secret that my grandpa once told me. The true test of a wine, he said, happens in the face of someone when they drink it for the first time. If they smile before their eyes meet yours, then the wine is a success. They have already told you so, without ever saying a word.[15]   .

At another point, Gina Gallo wrote:

> Our guiding principle remains the same as it was for our grandparents: Make each vintage better than the last. This philosophy has helped us create wines that continue to receive international recognition.[16]

Matt Gallo commented on the company's grape-growing practices and technological advances in how Gallo's vineyards in California's Sonoma wine region were now being managed:

> Many of the vineyards I look after today were planted by my grandfather, Julio. He was an early pioneer of sustainable agriculture in this county. At a time when farmers took what they could get from the land, Julio was conserving the soil, the water and the natural environment. Only half of the property we own in Sonoma is actually cultivated, thanks to the 50/50 Give Back Program he created. Julio didn't just believe in the land—he showed people that redwoods and vineyards could thrive together.
>
> From my father, Bob Gallo, I learned how to focus my efforts on the fruit. He was forever experimenting with new rootstock, trellising techniques and better ways of harvesting the grapes. As a result, every vine at Gallo of Sonoma is "touched" at least six times prior to harvest to ensure the growing conditions are optimal.
>
> Fortunately, I have access to new technologies—tools Dad and Grandpa didn't have—that can help. For instance, I can pinpoint weather conditions in a certain section of a vineyard using the latest technology. The accuracy is unbelievable, especially when you cross-reference it with soil and crop data. Does that mean less time in the vine rows, tasting grapes and touching the soil? Not by a long shot. Computers have memory, but farmers have a feeling for the land—a feeling that someday I hope to hand down to my kids.

In April 2001, Ernest Gallo received the Lifetime Achievement Award from the prestigious James Beard Foundation; in presenting the award, Charles Osgood spoke about "the power and persistence of the Gallo mission to make not just the most, but the best

[14]California Farm Bureau Federation, "Growing Up Gallo," www.cfbf.com/magazine/MagazineStory.cfm?ID=42&ck=A1D0C6E83F027327D8461063F4AC58A6.

[15]Posted at www.gallo.com, December 11, 2001.

[16]Posted at www.gallosonoma.com, April 8, 2008.

wines possible."[17] John Deluca, chairman of the Wine Institute, further elaborated on Ernest Gallo and the Gallo legacy: "He has really created the modern wine industry in America. . . . The Gallo brothers have been the most important force in the positive transformation of the California wine industry this last century." Marvin Shanken, publisher of *Wine Spectator,* said, "All Americans who drink wine at their dinner table today are in his debt." But what always seemed to go unsaid was that, despite the company's industry prominence and the growing market success and quality of Gallo table wines, the cheap bottles of Thunderbird and Night Train still continued to be among the best-selling and most notorious wines that E. & J. Gallo Winery produced and marketed. In 2008, the company's Web site featured many of its award-winning wines and highlighted the care and attention paid by the company's winemakers to making quality wines—but there was no mention of Thunderbird.

Exhibit 3 shows the 10 largest U.S. wineries. In 2006, the E. & J. Gallo Winery produced more than one-fifth of the total volume of wine in the United States (20.6 percent).[18]

EXHIBIT 3   The 10 Largest U.S. Wineries Based on Sales Volume, 2006

Winery	Brands	Sales Volume (cases)
E. & J. Gallo	Gallo, Turning Leaf, Carlo Rossi, Thunderbird, Red Bicyclette, Sonoma County, Barelli Creek, Stefani, Laguna, Frei, New Russian River, Reserve, and others	62,000,000
Constellation Brands	Includes labels under Canandaigua (Wild Irish Rose), Franciscan Estates, Hardy Wine Company, Nobilo Wine Group, Pacific Wine Partners, and others	57,000,000
The Wine Group	Franzia Bros., Mogen David, Tribuno, Edgewood Estate, Monthaven, Summerfield, The Big House, bulk wines, and others	42,000,000
		22,000,000
Bronco Wine Company	Forestville, Estrella, Charles Shaw Montpellier, Grand Cru, Silver Ridge, Rutherford Vintners, Fox Hollow, Napa Ridge, and others	
Foster's Wine Estates	Lindemans, Rosemount, Little Penguin, Beringer, Etude, Stags' Leap, St. Clement, Jean, Asti, Meridian, and others	16,000,000
Trinchero Family Estates	Sutter Home, alcohol-free Fre, Trinchero, Montevina, Trinity Oaks, Ménage a Trois, and others	10,000,000
Brown-Forman Wines	Virgin Wines, Gala Rouge, Little Black Dress, Fetzer, and others	6,600,000
Diageo Chateau & Estate Wines	Beaulieu Vineyard, Sterling Vineyards, Sterling Vintner's Collection, Solaris, Century Cellars, Monterey Vineyard, and others	5,500,000
Jackson Family Wines	Kendall-Jackson, White Rocket, Vintner's Reserve, Cambria, Hartford Family Wines, and others	5,000,000
St. Michelle Wine Estates	Chateau Ste. Michelle, Columbia Crest, Snoqualmie, NorthStar, Stimson Estate Cellars, Red Diamond, and others	4,200,000

Source: The Wine Institute, Gomberg, Fredrikson & Associates.

[17]www.gallo.com/UK/html/ernestaward.htm.
[18]"Wine Industry Market Share Summary," Goliath Business Knowledge on Demand, http://goliath.ecnext.com/comsite5/bin/comsite5.pl.

The company sold about 70 million cases of wine in domestic and international markets in 2007, resulting in about $3.5 billion in sales revenues.[19] Constellation, the second leading winery based on volume, produced 20.5 percent of U.S. wine. Constellation was the parent company of Canandaigua, a New York–based winery and producer of Richard's Wild Irish Rose. Constellation showed approximately $4.6 billion in 2007 sales revenues, but that figure included the sale of beer and spirits.[20]

As E. & J. Gallo approached its 75th anniversary, the company had a lot of things to be proud of. Gallo had more than 60 different wine brands visible in many segments of the industry, in 90 different countries, and they were growing. In 2007, Gallo purchased more than 325 acres in the Napa Valley reportedly to "keep pace with growing consumer demand worldwide."[21] Gallo also recently appointed the Swedish company Spendrups Vin as a new importer to handle the distribution of its products in Sweden.[22]

In addition to its expansive growth, E. & J. Gallo Winery continued to position itself as a maker of high-end fine wines. According to *Wine Spectator,* Gallo was the "largest-selling global brand." Gallo produced the top-selling (by unit volume) red and white table wines in the United States. Its Blush Chablis became the best-selling blush-style wine within the first year of its national introduction. Gallo's award-winning vertical wines were among the top sellers in their classification. During 1999 and 2000, Gallo's Carlo Rossi and Livingston Cellars brands outsold all other popular-priced wines except Franzia. Gallo's Andre Champagne brand was by far the best-selling champagne in the United States, and E&J Brandy outsold the number two and three brands combined. Gallo's line of wine coolers, produced under the brand name of Bartles & Jaymes, had been a leader in the wine cooler segment since its introduction in the 1980s and was the top-ranking seller in 2000. VinItaly named Gallo of Sonoma the International Winery of the year in 1998, 2001, and 2002, making Gallo the first (and to date only) American company to win three times. In 2006, Gallo received the Gold and Best of Class awards at the San Francisco Wine Competition and won individual awards for its cabernet sauvignon and its chardonnay. In 2007, Gallo partnered with Martha Stewart to market a special edition premium wine.[23]

So why, after winning so many awards and apparently having done so well in other parts of the wine market, did Gallo still produce the skid-row wines?

THE U.S. WINE INDUSTRY

Sales of all types of wines in the United States grew from about 90 million gallons in 1940 to 587 million gallons in 1986. Over the next 7 years, wine sales declined annually and totaled 449 million gallons in 1993. But a resurgence of consumer interest in wine began, pushing wine sales up steadily each year. Total sales reached 745 million gallons in 2007—see Exhibit 4. Exhibit 5 shows trends in per capita wine consumption in the United States. In 2006, wine accounted for 16.6 percent of the total alcohol consumed in the United States, up from 15.7 in 2000.[24] The United States was the world's fourth leading wine

[19]"At 75, Wine Giant Gallo Is Refining Its Palate," *L.A. Times,* www.latimes.com/business/la-fi-gallo4apr04,1,3429722.story.

[20]Constellation annual reports, www.cbrands.com/CBI/constellationbrands/AboutUs/AnnualReport/FY06_Annual_Report.pdf.

[21]E. & J. Gallo press release, www.gallo.com/PDFs/WilliamHillNewsRelease.pdf.

[22]"E & J Gallo Winery," *BusinessWeek,* http://investing.businessweek.com/research/stocks/private/snapshot.asp?privcapId=162756.

[23]E. & J. Gallo press release, www.gallo.com/PDFs/MarthaStewartVintageRelease.pdf.

[24]"Wine Industry Table Database Articles," Goliath Business Knowledge on Demand, http://goliath.ecnext.com/comsite5/bin/comsite5.pl.

EXHIBIT 4
Wine Consumption
in the United States,
1940–2007

Source: The Wine Institute,
Gomberg, Fredrikson &
Associates.

Year	Total Consumption, All Types of Wines* (in millions of gallons)	Total Consumption, Table Wines Only (in millions of gallons)
2007	745	650
2006	717	628
2005	692	609
2004	665	589
2003	639	570
2002	617	552
2001	574	512
2000	568	507
1995	464	404
1990	509	423
1985	580	478
1980	480	360
1970	267	133
1960	163	53
1950	140	36
1940	90	27

*Includes table wines, sparkling wines, dessert wines, vermouth, and all other still wines not over 14 percent alcohol.

EXHIBIT 5
Per Capita Wine
Consumption in the
United States,
1935–2007

Source: The Wine Institute,
Gomberg; Fredrikson &
Associates.

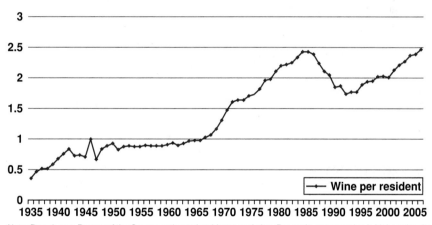

Note: Based upon Bureau of the Census estimated resident population. Per capita consumption is higher when based only on legal drinking age population.

producer, in terms of volume, behind France, Italy, and Spain. Retail wine sales in the United States exceeded $28 billion in 2006.

Per capita consumption of wine in the United States was relatively low prior to the 1970s because wine was perceived as a drink either for the very wealthy or for skid-row winos. Fortified dessert wines were the top-selling wines of the 1935–1970 period. The first surge in wine consumption in the late 1960s was the result of the introduction of inexpensive "pop" wines such as Boone's Farm, Cold Duck, and various brands of sangria. These wines were bought by baby boomers, who were then college-aged young adults; sweet pop wines with a kick were better suited to the high-energy party atmosphere in which they were consumed than were the more pricey table wines. By the mid-1970s, pop wine drinkers began moving up to Lambrusco and trendy wine spritzers. The introduction of wine coolers helped drive several years of rising consumption in the 1984–1988 period; by 1987 sales of wine coolers totaled 72.6 million nine-liter cases, with Gallo's Bartles & Jaymes brand rising quickly to a market-leading position. Some of the slowdown in wine consumption in the 1985–1995 period was attributed to the national obsession with fitness, increases in the legal drinking age from 18 to 21, and crackdowns on drunk driving.

During the 1990s, consumer interest in the United States began to grow in better-quality and premium-quality table wines; interest in red wines had increased considerably because of medical reports that a glass of red wine was healthy owing to its ability to reduce the risk of heart disease. In addition, the booming stock market of the 1990s and busy lifestyles contributed to more dining out and, thus, an increase in the sale of wine in restaurants. Although more than half of the U.S. adult population enjoyed wine occasionally in 2007, research indicated that by global standards most Americans were still infrequent wine drinkers. Per capita consumption in the United States was only about 2.5 gallons per year in 2007, compared to about 18 gallons in France and Italy, where drinking wine with meals was part of the local culture.

The Dessert and Fortified Wine Segment

During the 1980s, dessert wine sales totaled about 55 million gallons annually (about 10 percent of total wine sales based on volume); sales of low-end brands accounted for 43 million gallons (nearly 80 percent of all dessert wines). Approximately 50 percent of the low-end fortified dessert wines were sold in half pints; buyers of high-proof dessert wines were said to like half-pint bottles because they fit well in the back pocket of a pair of pants and gave skid-row drinkers a more secure feeling. However, dessert wine volume had trended down in the 1990s, to around 32 million gallons in 2000 (Exhibit 4), the majority of which continued to be low-end fortified wines. Whereas dessert wines accounted for almost 10 percent of total wine sales (based on volume) in the late 1980s, by 2000 the dessert wine category accounted for just 5.7 percent of total volume—the percentage drop was chiefly attributable to a decline in the popularity of wine coolers. By 2005, fortified dessert wines accounted for only 7.03 percent of the wine sold in the United States (see Exhibits 6 and 7).

The dessert wine category was typically a profitable market segment for low-end wine producers to pursue because many of the wines in this category were made with less expensive ingredients, packaged in less expensive containers, and could be sold with little or no marketing and promotion. Canandaigua estimated that profit margins in this category were as much as 10 percent higher than those of ordinary table wines. Gallo said this was not true for its products, but did not reveal its figures.

EXHIBIT 6

Wine Sales, by Category, 2005

Sources:
www.commerce.gov,
www.ita.doc.gov/td/ocg/
outlook 05_wine.pdf.

Category	Millions of Gallons	Percentage of Sales
Table wine	591	88.47%
Dessert wine	47	7.03
Sparkling wine	30	4.49

EXHIBIT 7

Consumer Wine Purchases by Price Category, 2006

Source: Goliath Business Knowledge on Demand, http://goliath.ecnext.com/ comsite5/bin/comsite5.pl.

Price Category	Volume Share
Up to $3	12.0%
$3 to $6	25.1%
$6 up to $9	24.6%
$9 up to $15	27.2%
$15 and over	10.8%

According wine industry analysts, local wine distributors were anxious to handle the low-end dessert and fortified wines because the margins were relatively large and it was generally easy to convince food retailers in low-income neighborhoods to stock them. As one distributor said, "All you have to do is to put it on the shelf in the right zip codes and it sells itself." Little or no advertising or sales promotion was needed—although in 1988 one magazine reported that Gallo sales representatives, in attempting to gain customers in newly entered markets, had on occasion gone so far as to trash the streets with empty bottles of Thunderbird and Night Train as a way to advertise to winos. Since distributors owned by Gallo were restricted by law from handling spirits (bourbon, vodka, scotch, gin, etc.), they were anxious to stock and distribute low-end wines because the sizable volumes and good profit margins were a major contributor to covering fixed costs and ensuring decent profitability.

A sales representative for an Alabama distributor of Gallo wines indicated that his company distributed Thunderbird and other high-proof wines to retail outlets in ethnic and low-income neighborhoods, with bottle sizes varying according to the time of the month. The representative indicated that it was the distributor's practice at the first of the month, when many people in poorer ethnic neighborhoods were cashing their government checks, to stock area retailers' shelves with larger containers of wines (jugs and 1.5-liter bottles). Then toward the middle and end of the month, when customers were likely to have less cash in their pockets, the wine distributor made sure that retailers' shelves were amply stocked with pint bottles that retailed anywhere from $0.99 to $1.49 per bottle.

Low-End Fortified Wines and Pop Culture

Cheap fortified wines had, over the years, found their way into the pop culture in the United States, often coming to symbolize the plight of the poor and less fortunate. Such wines were what people drank when they were sad, miserable, or just wanted to get drunk. Gallo's Night Train Express, an apple-flavored wine known as the Pocket Rocket and popular with both street alcoholics and teenagers, was alluded to in Guns N' Roses' debut album, *Appetite for Destruction,* on which Axl Rose sang "Nightrain":

Loaded like a freight train

flying like an aeroplane

Speeding like a space brain

one more time tonight

I'm on a Nightrain

bottoms up

I'm on a Nightrain

fill my cup

I'm on the Nightrain

I love that stuff,

I'm on the Nightrain

I can never get enough.

Wild Irish Rose was the inspiration for a song written and sung by Neil Diamond. On a 1970 trip to an Indian reservation in Canada where there were many more men than women, Diamond observed men leaving without a date on Saturday night and making wine their "woman for the night." He decided to compose "Cracklin' Rosie" to characterize the relationship of a lonely wine drinker and his bottle of Richard's Wild Irish Rose:

Cracklin' Rosie, make me a smile

God if it lasts for an hour, that's alright

We got all night

To set the world right

Find us a dream that don't ask no questions, yeah

Oh, I love my Rosie child

You got the way to make me happy

You and me, we go in style

Cracklin Rosie, you're a store-bought woman

You make me sing like a guitar hummin'

So hang on to me, girl

Our song keeps runnin' on.

Product Reviews of Low-End Fortified Wines

By and large, low-end fortified wines did not fare well in product reviews, even when the reviewers were members of the target clientele and experienced drinkers. Adam Martin, a college-age writer for a Web site in California called West Oakland Wine Tasting, offered his take on the appeal of low-end wines to the college crowd and presented colorful ratings of five brands:

> We live in one of the great wine producing regions of the world and it's a crying shame that nobody around here gives a #@&%. I know I don't. We could be in France, taking all kinds of wine baths and I would still be craving Pabst Blue Ribbon and Milwaukee's Best. As a young, unrefined student on a budget, I simply can't afford to be a wine aficionado. I couldn't, that is, until last Friday, when, along with a panel of experts (namely Wrath and the Reverend, my good-for-nothing-except-drinking-cheap-wine-when-I-buy-it roommates), I ventured out into my neighborhood to see what good old Grand Foods had to offer for the sacred palate. The following review focuses on five wines popular in West Oakland and the surrounding areas (North Oakland and East Oakland). Wines are rated on packaging, taste, alcohol content, and some other stuff.

> **Night Train Express 17.5% apv, $3.49 for 750 ml.**

> This bottle looks foreboding at first because of the spooky-ass train on the front. It's all dark, done in deep maroons and yellows. There's a heavy fog and the train is probably loaded with all kinds of dangerous cargo and people. Wrath points out, however, that although it's scary at first, if you look close you can see how the windows on the front of the engine make bright little eyes, the single headlight a perfect button nose, and the rim of the tank right above the cow-catcher a wide, welcoming grin. "I'm not nearly as afraid to drink it any more," he proclaimed, and fell to it. We also liked the ornate cursive writing at the bottom of the label explaining how it's a product of Modesto, and the instruction to "serve very cold."

> Night Train is thick, heavy, syrupy stuff, but for some reason it still tastes pretty bad. It's sort of like sucking on a rotten lollipop or something. We decided that, while Brussels sprouts taste good, and chocolate tastes good, you wouldn't want a chocolate Brussels sprout,

and that's what this is. It's strong, though, and one bottle will get you very drunk. Night Train is the classic hobo wine, celebrated in story and song, so get a bottle if for no other reason than to celebrate our American heritage.

Thunderbird 17.5% apv, $3.49 for 750 ml.

Thunderbird is by far the burliest wine we tasted, and we are still afraid to say anything bad about it for fear it will come hunt us down and kill us in our sleep. I dare you to drink a whole bottle. Seriously, I dare you. Even looking at it makes me shiver. The word "Thunderbird" is written in a boldly slanted, straight lined typeface in white on a red background with a gold border. Directly under that word is the instruction to "Serve Cold," and under that is written "The American Classic." Then there is this . . . logo of an eagle wearing a crown. It looks like a state seal or something—the state of being all drunk and mean.

Wrath thought this was the most likely to give you whiskey face, and once we finished it I agreed with all three of him. Drink this wine if you want to get in a fight. But make sure the other person has also drunk a bottle of T-bird, too, or you'll get beat up. Thunderbird doesn't help you once you're in the fight. It just helps you get started. Even though it has the same amount of alcohol as Night Train and slightly less than Wild Irish Rose, it will still kick both of their asses and then yours. Watch it, punk.

Carlo Rossi California Sangria 10% apv, $4.00 per 1.5 liter bottle

While Burgundy is generally the favorite in Carlo Rossi's circles, the California Sangria definitely wins, as far as we were concerned. For starters, it has that classic "moonshine jug" shape that can't be beat, with the round bottle, and little finger loop on the neck. The proper way to take a slug of Carlo Rossi is to hook your finger through the loop and rest the bottle on the outside of your elbow while you drink it over your shoulder. . . .

The flavor of Carlo Rossi is better than the others because it's spicy as well as sweet. It has a nice light flavor with a little kick to it, and you can definitely nurse it for a while. Sure, you could nurse a bottle of the burgundy for a while too, but the sangria won't turn your mouth all purple and make you throw up. Compared to the other wines we tasted, this is the easiest to drink. It also has the most pretensions toward serious winehood, although this may be a strike against its image.

Wild Irish Rose 18% apv, $3.49 for 750 ml.

Wild Irish Rose has a simple, understated bottle with a picture of a rose above its name, and the accurate (if vague) description "100% pure grape wine." What's nice about this bottle is that it kind of knows it's being treated more like a liquor than a wine. The bottle is flat on the sides and kind of rectangular which makes it look more like a bottle of gin. This may be why it needs to say the word "wine" at least three times on the bottle. For a fun party game, see who can find all three the fastest. If you're drinking alone, see how fast you can find them and then try to break that record.

Taste wise, Wild Irish Rose is surprisingly agreeable. . . . We thought it was the best value for the money because it was the strongest and still really cheap. Also, even though it still had the same "death" aftertaste as Night Train and Thunderbird, it wasn't as prominent. We licked our lips and howled at the moon after Wild Irish Rose. Try it. It's a winner.

Boone's Farm Kiwi-Strawberry 8% apv, $2.90 for 750 ml.

This crap needs to stay on the store shelf. It's weak, bubbly and sweet in just the wrong ways. Both bottle and drink are bland as hell. The label just has this boring old picture of some farm-house (presumably Boone's) and nothing else really eye-catching. It tastes like weak strawberry soda, but . . . you could drink Vintage soda for about a third of the price and still get just as loaded. Unless you're a sixteen-year-old girl, don't bother with the stuff.[25]

[25]Adam Martin, "What to Do When You've Only Got $5.22 and a Serious Liquor Monkey on Your Back," West Oakland Wine Tasting, www.readsatellite.com/culture/2.4/wine.martin.2.4.1.htm.

Brian Gnatt, another college reviewer writing for the *Michigan Daily Online* at the University of Michigan, had the following to say about low-end fortified wines and their appeal to younger consumers of alcoholic beverages:

> For those who don't care for the taste of beer or hard alcohol, those who can't afford to buy quality alcohol, or for those who simply like the taste and effects of drinking cheap wine, usually out of a bottle with a screw-off cap, there's a line of alcoholic beverages just for you that adds a splash of color to liquor store shelves everywhere. Best of all, the bottles come in various shapes, sizes and colors; the wine comes in different flavors and most important, various strengths so everyone can find one to their liking.
>
> From the bright rainbow colors of MD 20/20 (a.k.a. Mad Dog) to the lighter, pastels of Boone's, ghetto wines look quite similar to wine coolers or even Kool-Aid. But don't be deceived—their punch is stronger than Bartles & Jaymes or the Kool-Aid Man. Ranging from about 5 percent alcohol (similar to beer) to 18 percent (about half of hard alcohol), cheap wines offer easy, economical and colorful ways to get drunk.
>
> The fact that the wines are cheap, easy and appealing are some of the reasons many young people enjoy drinking the less-than-tasty beverages. When I first started drinking, Mad Dog was my drink of choice. And I thought it was great; memories of skipping high school and watching reruns of "Alf" with friends and a bottle of Wild Berry 20/20—life didn't get much better. But as I got older, and my taste buds refined a bit, I realized Mad Dog and Thunderbird weren't the best drinks in the world, but that they're not all that bad either.
>
> Years later, the occasional bottle of wine still hits the spot. Now, however, it usually includes ridicule by friends and other onlookers who respond with the customary "Mad Dog? Yuck!" Nevertheless, cheap wine will always have a place in my heart, even though I have moved on to some finer forms of fermented fruit drinks, like Franzia, a.k.a. "wine in a box."
>
> While all wino-wines may get a bad rap for being a little pungent, there still are better cheap wines. The Michigan Daily taste-tested a number of the area's top-selling rot-gut wines to find which ones are the best bargains in the cheap wine market.

The Test

> Finding cheap wine isn't a problem in Ann Arbor. Just about every beer, wine and liquor store sells some variation of the drink, most for less than $4. While all of our selections aren't available at every store, they are all available within walking distance of campus. . . .
>
> For the taste test, we gathered 11 different bottles of wine: five of Mad Dog (Hawaiian Blue, Lightning Creek, Pink Grapefruit, Red Grape Wine and Wild Berry), two Boone's (Snow Creek Berry and Strawberry Hill), two Wild Irish Rose varieties (regular and White Label), a bottle of Thunderbird and a bottle of Night Train. Then we tasted. Here's the findings:
>
> Out of the 11 samples, Boone's Snow Creek Berry was the best tasting of all the samples, but to no surprise. The lightly carbonated drink is only about five percent alcohol, while many of the other samples had more than three times that amount. It was sweet, fruity and fresh, and the taste of alcohol was almost non-existent.
>
> Boone's Strawberry Hill variety ranked No. 2 on the list, weighing in at 7.5 percent alcohol. The alcohol was a bit more prevalent and the wine had a bit of a sharp taste—drinkable, yet not as enjoyable as the Snow Creek Berry. Again though, the relatively small amount of alcohol almost nullifies Boone's from the contest, and forces it to stand alone in its own lightweight wine category.
>
> The Mad Dog flavors were the next most successful in the taste test, with the Pink Grapefruit flavor ranking No. 3, after the weaker Boone's. At 13.5 percent alcohol, Pink Grapefruit was fairly smooth and had less of a church-wine taste than the rest of the MD 20/20 flavors. It was tangy and not too sweet, for a somewhat refreshing flavor.
>
> Wild Berry Mad Dog (13.5 percent alcohol) was the next best, but was quite sweet and sharp and had a lasting aftertaste. Mad Dog's Red Grape Wine (18 percent alcohol) followed at No. 5, the first drink to ever make me hurl. The wine was quite sweet, a bit dry and very grapey, but still drinkable. At No. 6 was Lightning Creek (17 percent alcohol), the clear

variety of Mad Dog for all of you who don't like artificial colors in your food. The smell of rubbing alcohol and a taste of watered-down alcohol made this selection the turning point in the tasting, and the wines went downhill from here.

Next in line was the potent Thunderbird (18 percent alcohol)—with "An American Classic" as the slogan on the bottle. With its strong alcohol flavor, Thunderbird is strong at first taste, but it doesn't linger on the palate as much as some of the other selections, mainly the Wild Irish Rose and the Hawaiian Blue Mad Dog, which followed Thunderbird for a No. 8 ranking. With its 2,000 Flushes aqua blue color, alcohol flavor and a hint of coconut, Hawaiian Blue coats your system like a good bathtub scum, with its only redeeming quality being it's a pretty color.

Wild Irish Rose Wine (18 percent) ranked in at No. 9, with its red color, hint of grape flavor and plain taste. Not very tasty, to say the least. The infamous Night Train (18 percent) pulled into the station at No. 10, pushing a train wreck for anyone who could top off the entire bottle of wine. It had a rather nasty, pungent and incarcerating taste and side effects to back up its poor reputation.

Coming in last was Wild Irish Rose's White Label (18 percent alcohol), a harsh, sharp and brutal wine without any flavor whatsoever. The White Label produced breath of fire, and left nothing to be desired.

For all it's worth, cheap wine still has its virtues, even if it doesn't have a very desirable taste. All but the Boone's could probably get you drunk for less than the price of the average beer at the average bar. So if drunk's what you want, and $3 is all you've got, a not-so-good bottle of wine is all you need to cure those sobriety blues.[26]

ATTEMPTS TO CONTROL EXCESSIVE CONSUMPTION OF HIGH-PROOF WINES

Public drunkenness in inner cities and low-income neighborhoods, alcoholism, and binge drinking on college campuses had provoked concerns among various citizens groups, community organizations, churches, government agencies, makers of alcoholic beverages, and wine companies. In June 1989, Gallo conducted an experiment whereby it stopped distributing Thunderbird and Night Train wines in the Tenderloin District of San Francisco for six months. Canandaigua Wine Company indicated it would cooperate in the experiment by pulling Wild Irish Rose from the shelves, but it failed to follow through during the trial period because it said the ultimate decision to halt sales was up to its local distributors. But there was reportedly little beneficial impact; as local winos said, "You can't get it in one store, you get it in another . . . or you just drink something else." The minimal impact of pulling Gallo's Thunderbird and Night Train wines off retailer shelves in San Francisco was taken as validation of the oft-stated views within the wine industry (and elsewhere as well) that alcoholics, if deprived of one source, would simply seek out alternatives to satisfy their desires for alcohol.

In addition to Gallo's mostly independent effort in San Francisco, several cities had experimented with ways to remove cheap fortified wines from inner-city stores as a means of defeating the efforts of people looking for a cheap way to get drunk. Salt Lake City and Portland tried imposing bans on the sales of such wines, with somewhat conflicting results. Both cities reported substitute alcohol sales up. However, while Salt Lake City reported a decline in public drunkenness, in Portland the conclusion was that winos just drank something else.

Banning Cisco, one of the most potent fortified wine coolers, became a cause célèbre during the early 1990s, because its packaging was deceptively similar to that of normal wine coolers and because it was shelved in the same beverage cases in convenience stores

[26]Brian A. Gnatt, "A Touch of Underclass: Cheap Wine, an Alternative, Proletariat Potable," *Michigan Daily Online,* www.pub.umich.edu/daily/1997/apr/04-10-97/arts/art3.html.

and supermarkets. Cisco's very sweet flavorings made it a favorite target of adolescent shoplifters. Former U.S. surgeon general Antonio Novello referred to heavily fortified wine coolers as "wine foolers"—innocent-looking bottles of wine and sugared fruit juices that looked like a regular wine cooler but packed more than three times the punch (Exhibit 2).

One defense of winemakers who were profiting from producing and marketing cheap, fortified wines to skid-row alcoholics was offered by Professor Edward Freeman, a nationally prominent ethicist at the University of Virginia's Darden Graduate School of Business Administration: "There is a long tradition of freedom of contract in our country. People are free to make their own mistakes."[27] Freeman emphasized that the problem of street alcoholics was far more complex than just the sale of the products. The root issue, he claimed, was the underlying social conditions that helped push alcoholics into their disease. "Not selling this stuff is like moving the deck chairs on the Titanic," he said. "The question is, do you really want to be a company associated with these products that are so abused? In our system, we let the companies decide."

[27]As quoted in Warren King, "Ethics of Manufacturing Profits from Drunks," *Seattle Times,* January 20, 1998.

24

Abercrombie & Fitch: An Upscale Sporting Goods Retailer Becomes a Leader in Trendy Apparel

Janet Rovenpor *Manhattan College*

On November 10, 2005, Abercrombie & Fitch (A&F) celebrated the opening of a new 36,000 square-foot, four-level flagship store on Fifth Avenue and 56th Street in Manhattan. The timing was perfect—right ahead of the busy Christmas shopping season during which the retailer hoped to sell large quantities of cashmere sweaters, Henley long-sleeved fleeces, hand-knit wool sweaters, polo shirts, and jeans. The Fifth Avenue store, considered a prototype for other flagship stores, featured dark interiors, oak columns, bronze fixtures and a central staircase with frosted glass-block flooring. A mural of muscular, skin-showing rope climbers in a setting from the 1930s by the artist Mark Beard, was prominently displayed. "We're really excited to be back on Fifth Avenue. We're really trying to build the character of the brand. We had a little store in Trump Tower that closed in 1986, and we have been looking on Fifth Avenue for a few years. This is a prestige location and great for the positioning of the brand," commented CEO Michael Jeffries.[1]

In an attempt to gauge customer reaction to the opening of the new store, *New York Magazine* surveyed 75 teenagers asking them what the A&F brand meant to them. Answers were varied: "It's gross"; "It's overpriced"; "It's stylish and sleek"; "It's very logotistical"; "It projects the typical image of the perfect American male—good at school and masculine;" "It

[1]J.E. Palmierie and D. Moin, "A&F Hits Fifth Avenue Fray," *DNR* 35 (November 14, 2005), p. 4. Retrieved April 19, 2006, from ABI/Inform (ProQuest) database.

Case Group F Social and Ethical Issues in Marketing Management

was cool up until we were 16. Then it got this dumb-jock-meathead image."[2] Perhaps such contradictory statements were just what A&F's senior executives wanted. Consumers either loved or hated the company, its products and its image. Part of the trendy retailer's competitive strategy, in fact, was to stir up controversy, go against convention and appeal emotionally to its youthful customers.

A&F's 5th Avenue store symbolized the values the retailer held: sensuality, a youthful lifestyle, a love for the outdoors and fun with friends. It was the culmination of the retailer's creative endeavors to design and implement an exciting store format that drew shoppers in and captivated them. The loud music, appealing visuals, and perfumed interiors encouraged teenagers to "hang out" and "browse." A&F had come a long way from its early beginnings in 1892. Back then, A&F was considered a luxury sporting goods retailer with conservative tastes that appealed to affluent clients, including adventurers, hunters, presidents, and heads of royal families. President Theodore Roosevelt, for example, purchased snake-proof sleeping bags for a 1908 African safari at an Abercrombie store. Admiral Richard Byrd bought equipment for his 1950s expedition to Antarctica.

A&F's competitive strategies seemed to be working. By February 2007, the retailer operated 944 stores in 49 states, the District of Columbia and Canada. It had 8,500 full-time and 77,900 part-time employees (including temporary staff hired during peak periods such as the back-to-school and holiday seasons). Its fiscal 2006 revenues were $3.32 billion and its net income was $422.2 million. It opened its first European store, in London, in March 2007. It expected to open a store in Tokyo in late 2009. *Apparel Magazine* ranked A&F number 3 in terms of profitability (net income as a percentage of sales) among apparel retailers in 2007 (up from number 4 in 2006).[3] In March 2007, A&F joined the S&P 500 stock index (replacing Univision Communications, Inc. which had been acquired by an investor group).

At the same time, questions existed regarding the retailer's long-term success. Would teenagers, A&F's primary target market, remain loyal to the company and its products? Could A&F bring back some of the shoppers it had alienated because of its treatment of minority employees and its racy slogans on its T-shirts? Would A&F be able to maintain its competitive advantage in a fragmented industry in which new entrants from both the U.S. as well as from overseas markets were intent on imitating A&F's strategies? Should CEO Jeffries be concerned with the exodus of talented senior executives from his top management team? Who would eventually succeed Jeffries? Would the retailer's new corporate governance and diversity initiatives pay off?

THE U.S. SPECIALTY APPAREL INDUSTRY

A&F was considered a "specialty retailer." Retailers in this category sold products in specific merchandise categories—apparel, footwear, office supplies, home furnishings, books, jewelry, or toys, among others. Numerous small to midsized firms existed. They survived by catering to local tastes and preferences. Sometimes, their financial performance was adversely affected when a competitor entered their niche or when the preferences, life-styles, and demographics of their target markets changed. As young people became interested in electronics and began spending more and more time playing video games, for example, the fortunes of retailers like Best Buy rose at the expense of retailers like Toys "R" Us.[4]

---

[2] D. Penny, "The Abercrombie Report," *New York* 38 (November 21, 2005), p. 6. Retrieved April 19, 2006, from ABI/Inform (ProQuest) database.

[3] "The Apparel Top 50," *Apparel Magazine* 48, no. 11 (July 2007), pp. 12–20. Retrieved September 13, 2007, from EBSCOhost database.

[4] M. Souers and M. Normand, "Specialty Retailers Demonstrate Resilience in Face of Adversity," *Standard & Poor's Industry Surveys: Retailing: Specialty*, January 12, 2006.

Specialty apparel retailers opened stores in shopping malls and constructed free-standing units along major roadways. The firms enhanced their capabilities to sell products via direct mailings of catalogs and through Web sites equipped with shopping cart technologies. To compete with mass merchandiser and department stores, they tried to maintain high prices and high quality merchandise, cultivate customer loyalty through various membership programs, and promote their own private-label brands. J. Crew, for example, offered high-end, limited edition items (e.g., crocodile sling-backs and silk wedding dresses), which created excitement and enticed consumers to buy early at full prices. Chico's FAS Inc. offered a customer loyalty program, Passport Club, which gave customers discounts and other benefits when their purchases exceeded $500.

In 2007, consumer spending tightened as the economy slowed. Individuals spent more on gasoline and food and began to cut back on other purchases amid lower consumer confidence and a slump in the housing market. Retailers saw declines in customer traffic and sales in July, the start of the usually brisk back-to-school shopping season.[5] July same-store sales (that is, sales dollars generated by stores that have been open more than one year) at A&F, American Eagle Outfitters (AEOS), and the Gap fell 4 percent, 6 percent, and 7 percent, respectively.

Demographics began to shift; the children of the "baby boom" generation were getting older. Those specialty apparel retailers who appealed mostly to teenagers realized that they needed to hold on to their consumers as they entered their 20s. A&F, AEOS, and even the Gap began to open, with varying degrees of success, stores that targeted an older demographic. Rivals who already catered to an older consumer group, such as Ann Taylor Loft and Express LLC, were equally eager to lure such young adults away.[6] Specialty apparel retailers also faced increased competition from such department store chains as JC Penney and Kohl's which started offering more fashionable and exclusive private labeled goods.

There was some threat of being an acquisition target. Many private equity transactions were completed in 2007. Apollo Management LP acquired Claire's Stores Incorporated (a teen accessory retailer) for $3.1 billion; Golden Gate Capital acquired a 67 percent stake in The Limited's Express clothing chain. Private equity firms saw an opportunity to turn around struggling businesses and get them ready for resale. When retailers went private, they no longer had to report comparable same store sales or quarterly earnings to investors; they could concentrate on improving their business operations.[7]

Believing that "trend transcends age," A&F catered to cool, attractive, fashion-conscious consumers offering products to meet their needs through different life stages—from elementary school to postcollege.[8] The retailer managed four brands:

- A&F: a brand that was repositioned in 1992. It offered apparel that reflected the youthful lifestyle of the East Coast and Ivy League traditions for 18–22-year-old college students. In February 2007, there were 360 A&F brand stores in the United States (close to its capacity of 400 stores).
- abercrombie: a brand that was launched in 1998. It targeted customers aged 7–14 with fashions similar to the A&F line. There were 177 stores in early 2007.

[5]J. Covert, "Shoppers Held Back in July; Retailers' Weak Sales Show Impact of Tumult in the Housing Market," *The Wall Street Journal,* August 10, 2007, p. A2. Retrieved September 6, 2007, from ABI/Inform (ProQuest) database.

[6]M. Souers & J. DeFoe, "Specialty Retailers Experience Mixed Results in 2007," *Standard & Poor's Industry Surveys: Retailing: Specialty,* August 2, 2007.

[7]Ibid.

[8]A&F, 10-K; J. Sheban, "Oh, Canada!" *Knight Ridder Tribune Business News,* February 26, 2006, p. 1. Retrieved April 18, 2006, from ABI/Inform (ProQuest) database.

- Hollister Company: a brand that was launched in 2000. It targeted 14–18-year-old high school students with lower priced casual apparel, personal care products, and accessories. It promoted the laid-back, California surf lifestyle. There were 393 stores in early 2007 (with potential for many more).

- Ruehl: a brand that was launched in 2004. It sold casual sportswear, trendy apparel, and leather goods to postcollege consumers aged 22–35 years. Its line of clothing was inspired by the lifestyle of New York City's Greenwich Village. The merchandise was more upscale and more expensive than the A&F line. There were 14 stores in early 2007.

A fifth store concept was on its way. A&F refused to reveal details, although Jeffries remarked that accessories—hats, totes, fragrances, and jewelry—were a growing and important part of the business.[9] Rumors circulated that the retailer would launch either an accessories brand or an intimate apparel line with its own store locations.

A&F had three main competitors. Two were publicly held firms—American Eagle Outfitters, Incorporated (AEOS), and Gap Incorporated. A third firm, J. Crew Group, had been a privately held firm until June 2006. For basic comparative financial data, see Exhibit 1 (five-year data for JC are not reported because the retailer had operated at a loss when it was privately held; ratios, such as return on revenues and return on equity, are not meaningful).

Based in Warrendale, Pennsylvania, AEOS sold lower-priced casual apparel and accessories to men and women aged 15–25. The Schottenstein family (who held interests in Value City Department and Furniture Stores) owned 14 percent of the retailer. AEOS operated over 900 stores in the US and Canada with approximately 40 percent of its stores located west of the Mississippi River. Revenues in fiscal 2006 were $2.8 billion (an increase of 21 percent from fiscal 2005); net income reached $387 million (an increase of 31.9 percent from fiscal 2005).

AEOS launched two new store concepts in 2006. Martin + Osa was a clothing store selling denim and active sportswear targeting men and women aged 24–40. It did not perform as well as expected. Efforts were underway in 2007 to make the women's merchandise more feminine, less outdoorsy, less expensive, and of better quality. AEOS hired a former Liz Claiborne executive to become president of Martin + Osa (who replaced the previous president). Aerie was an intimate apparel subbrand that was launched adjacent to existing AEOS stores and as stand-alone stores. It was successful and plans were in place to expand upon its merchandise with fragrance and personal care items.

JC operated 227 retail and outlet stores in the United States. With a joint venture partner, it also had 45 stores in Japan. Millard "Mickey" Drexler, former CEO of the Gap, headed the retailer. He promised that JC would "be the best, not the biggest."[10] Revenues in fiscal 2006 were $1.15 billion (up 20.9 percent from fiscal 2005). Net income (applicable to common shareholders) in fiscal 2006 was $71.6 million (or $1.49 a diluted share) compared to a net loss of $9.7 million (or a loss of 39 cents a diluted share) in fiscal 2005. JC launched Madewell, a casual clothing store for women which sold merchandise at prices that were 20 percent to 30 percent lower than JC merchandise. Its initial public offering of common stock in June 2006 raised $402.8 million. At the time, this was the third largest apparel retailing IPO in history.

Whereas JC was the smallest of A&F's direct competitors, the Gap was the largest with 3,000 stores worldwide. The Gap sold basic casual clothing and accessories for children, men and women. Revenues in fiscal 2006 were $15.9 billion (a decrease of 0.5 percent

[9]J. Sheban, "Abercrombie & Fitch Plans Fifth Concept," *Knight Ridder Tribune Business News*, November 18, 2006, p. 1. Retrieved September 6, 2007, from ABI/Inform (ProQuest) database.

[10]D. Molin, "J. Crew Mission: Being Best, Not Biggest," *WWD* 193, no. 125 (June 13, 2007), p. 2. Retrieved September 13, 2007, from ABI/Inform (ProQuest) database.

EXHIBIT 1 Basic Comparative Financial Information for Abercrombie & Fitch (A&F), American Eagle Outfitters (AEOS), and the Gap

	A&F					AEOS					GAP				
	2006	2005	2004	2003	2002	2006	2005	2004	2003	2002	2006	2005	2004	2003	2002
Operating revenues (in millions $)	3,318.2	2,784.7	2,021.3	1,707.8	1,595.8	2,794.4	2,309.4	1,881.2	1,520.0	1,463.1	15,943.0	16,023.0	16,267.0	15,854.0	14,454.7
Net income (in millions $)	422.2	334.0	216.4	204.8	194.8	387.4	293.7	224.2	60.0	88.7	778.0	1,113.0	1,150.0	1,030.0	477.5
Return on revenues (%)	12.7	12.0	10.7	12.0	12.2	13.9	12.7	11.9	3.9	6.1	4.9	6.9	7.1	6.5	3.3
Return on assets (%)	20.9	21.3	15.8	17.2	22.1	21.6	20.3	20.8	7.5	12.6	9.0	11.8	11.3	10.2	5.4
Return on equity (%)	35.2	40.1	28.3	25.5	29	30.1	27.7	27.9	9.8	16.4	14.7	21.5	23.7	24.4	14.3
Current ratio	2.1	1.9	1.6	2.4	2.8	2.6	3.0	3.3	2.8	3.0	2.2	2.7	2.8	2.7	2.1
Debt/capital ratio (%)	0	0	0	0	0	0	0	0	2.1	2.8	3.5	8.6	27.6	34.2	44.2
Debt as a % of net working capital	0	0	0	0	0	0	0	0	4.1	5.7	6.8	15.6	46.4	59.3	96.1
Price/earnings ratio (high-low)	17-10	19-12	20-10	16-10	17-8	19-9	18-10	15-5	28-16	25-8	23-17	18-13	20-14	20-10	31-15
Earnings per share—basic ($)	4.79	3.83	2.33	2.12	1.99	1.74	1.29	1.03	.28	.41	.94	1.26	1.29	1.15	.55
Share price (high-low, $)	79.42-49.98	74.10-44.17	47.45-23.07	33.65-20.65	33.85-14.97	33.01-14.83	22.69-12.97	15.92-5.28	7.79-4.40	10.15-3.25	21.39-15.91	22.70-15.90	25.72-18.12	23.47-12.01	17.14-8.35

Sources: Standard & Poor's Industry Surveys: Retailing Specialty; August 2007.

from fiscal 2005); net income was $778 million (a decrease of 30.1 percent from fiscal 2005). It operated Banana Republic (high quality, fashionable apparel) and Old Navy (low-priced trendy clothing). Its most recent entry, Forth&Towne (stylish apparel for women over 35), was open for 18 months before being shut down.

The Gap was struggling to turn around its performance which began to decline in 2000 when it overexpanded, assumed too much debt, and made a few fashion-related miscalculations. Under pressure from the board of directors, CEO Paul Pressler resigned in January 2007. Glenn Murphy, who had been the CEO of a large Canadian drug store chain, was hired to replace him. The firm also hired Goldman Sachs to explore strategic options for the retailer. Rumors circulated that the company intended to put itself up for sale or to spin off one of its divisions, most likely Banana Republic.

A&F'S EARLY BEGINNINGS

A&F was founded in 1892 by David T. Abercrombie (see Exhibit 2 for key milestones in A&F's history). Abercrombie was a civil engineer, topographer, and colonel in the Officers Reserve Corps. He was also an avid hunter and fisherman. The first store was located on Water Street in lower Manhattan. Ezra Fitch, a lawyer and one of Abercrombie's best customers, became a partner in 1900. The two men frequently argued. Fitch continued to run the company after Abercrombie resigned in 1907.

EXHIBIT 2

Key Milestones in A&F's Early History

1892:	A&F was founded by David T. Abercrombie, an engineer, topographer, outdoorsman and colonel.
1900:	Ezra Fitch, a lawyer from Kingston, NY, became Abercrombie's business partner.
1907:	Abercrombie resigned from the company.
1917:	A&F's 12-story building on Madison Avenue and 45th Street opened.
1928:	Ezra Fitch resigned as president. He was succeeded by James S. Cobb.
1929:	A&F acquired an interest in Von Lengerke & Detmold, a gun, camp, and fishing chain based in Chicago.
1935:	A&F earned a net profit of $148,123, up from $123,424 in the previous year.
1940:	Otis Guernsey was elected president and CEO.
1943:	A&F earned a net profit of $286,694.
1958:	A store in San Francisco opened.
1961:	John H. Ewing became president and CEO, succeeding Guernsey. Earl Angstadt became the president and CEO in the mid-1960s.
1962:	A&F opened a store in Colorado Springs, CO.
1963:	A&F opened a store in Short Hills, NJ.
1967:	A&F acquired the Crow's Nest, a nautical supply store with a national mail order business.
1968:	Sales peaked at $28 million and net income rose to $866,000.
1970:	Angstadt resigned. He was replaced by William Humphreys. Henry Haskell, a major shareholder, soon replaced Humphreys as CEO. A&F lost money every year until 1977.
1972:	A store in a Chicago suburb opened.
1977:	A&F declared bankruptcy.
1978:	A&F was acquired by Oshman's Sporting Goods Incorporated.
1988:	The Limited acquired A&F from Oshman's.
1989:	Sally Frame-Kasaks was named president and chief executive of A&F. She left in 1992.
1992:	Michael Jeffries became president and chief executive of A&F.
1996:	A&F was spun off from the Limited.
1999:	A&F ran 186 A&F stores and 13 abercrombie stores.
2001:	A&F opened a new 260,000 square foot corporate office and a 700,000 square foot distribution center in New Albany, Ohio. It cost $130 million.

A&F's 12-story building on Madison Avenue and 45th Street opened in 1917. It featured a log cabin and casting pool on the roof and a rifle range in the basement. The store's location was excellent. By 1923, Madison Avenue and 45th Street had become the "heart" of the "specialized shop trade."[11] Near A&F's flagship store were Brooks Brothers, Tiffany Studios, Eastman Kodak, and Maillard's. The Roosevelt Hotel was just undergoing construction. Abercrombie died in 1931 at the age of 64; Fitch died of a stroke aboard his yacht in Santa Barbara, California, in 1930 at the age of 65.

A&F's managers promoted it as "The Finest Sporting Goods Store in the World." An early advertisement announcing the opening of a new store on 36th Street appears in Exhibit 3. A&F was known for its expensive and exotic goods as well as for its affluent clientele. It was possible to buy an antique miniature cannon for $300, a custom-made rifle for $6,000 or a Yukon dog sled for $1,188. Presidents William Taft and Warren Harding purchased golf clubs at A&F. President Dwight Eisenhower bought hunting boots for $55 for his walks in the woods at Camp David. Other famous customers included Amelia Earhart, Greta Garbo, Charles Lindbergh, Clark Gable, the Duke of Windsor, Howard Hughes, and Ernest Hemmingway.

A&F was not just a place to purchase sporting goods and rugged apparel. It was also a place where individuals could learn new skills and get involved in the community. In 1923, the Adirondack Club held its annual meeting in A&F's log cabin. Its members discussed whether or not an open season should be declared on beavers whose dam-building activities were causing floods which damaged timber and ruined trout streams. In 1966, A&F held a lecture on how to capture a musk ox bare-handed without harming it. In 1967, A&F ran a fishing clinic in which experts discussed tackle, knot tying, and trout angling techniques. In 1973, A&F served flambé quail, prepared in the log cabin's fireplace, in celebration of a talking cookbook it had produced. The cookbook contained two 40-minute cassettes and a booklet of recipes printed on waterproof and grease-proof plastic.

Throughout its early history, A&F did a good job keeping up with its customers and with changing fashions. During World War II, when activities such as parlor skeet and military board games were popular, A&F sold a wooden box that could be filled with water and used to blow sailboats from side to side. In the 1940s, barbeque picnics in fields outside country homes became the latest fad arriving from the West. A&F sold high quality BBQ equipment and insulated canvas bags to keep drinks cold. In 1964, A&F made a splash when it developed the capacity to produce a cashmere sweater with a lifelike reproduction of a color photograph of one's pet embroidered on it. It sold resort wear with a fruit motif in the 1940s and Bermuda length culottes in the 1960s. A&F had a clearly defined target market. CEO Anstadt said, "We aren't out for the teenage business. Our customers are on the go and have the time and the money to enjoy travel and sport."[12]

A&F had its share of problems. Some were typical of all retailers throughout the decades, and some were atypical. During the early 1940s, A&F stores were low on inventory. Commerce had been disrupted by the war effort. It was difficult to import goods from abroad. Manufacturers were busy making binoculars, field glasses, saddles, and marine clocks for use by the army and navy. A&F wrote to its customers, asking them if they would like to sell optical or sporting goods in satisfactory condition back to the retailer so that the items could be refurbished and resold to new customers. One year, the Office of Price Administration placed limitations on civilian consumption of rubber products. This caused a rush on golf balls sold by A&F. A&F joined other retailers in asking customers to do their

EXHIBIT 3
An Early A&F
Advertisement in
The New York Times
from 1912

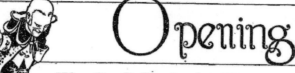

Opening

We Cordially Invite You to Inspect Our New Store

We maintain at this address, the finest Sporting Goods Store in the world. We want you to visit the establishment—we are proud of it, and we are proud of the stock we have to show you. It comprises everything for the Great Out of Doors, each article the BEST for its purpose and most of them exclusive. You can't get them elsewhere.

For a good many years, this concern, The Abercrombie & Fitch Co., occupied a small, exclusive store at 57 Reade Street, in the dingy downtown district where buyers came only because they HAD to—because they could not buy elsewhere the things they bought from us. We have been known the world over not only as the one place where the big Nimrods, Explorers, Hunters, Trappers, Fishermen,—the whole Out-of-Door Brotherhood were outfitted, but as a sort of informal clearing house of information for them. We outfitted Col. Roosevelt for his trip into Africa—Stewart Edward White speaks of our outfits in his textbooks—our peculiar specialty of having the RIGHT thing, the CORRECT thing and finally the EXCLUSIVE thing was recognized by the adept many years ago. Our business grew by word of mouth—by talks over camp fires and at club tables, because when once a man or woman found us, they had found the ONLY one there was and took a pride in passing on the good news. We outgrew our store—we outgrew the building—and now we have our own building on 36th Street. So long as we

had to move, we moved to a place where you could get at us—right in the centre of your shopping district.

We have the finest store of its kind in the world. We have not merely the finest stock of our sort in the world, but we carry the ONLY correct things for the purpose. We have broadened our business and to bring this about, we have manufactured in quantities impossible before because of the restrictions of space in our old quarters. All the economies due to manufacturing and buying on a wholesale plan are reflected in the very low prices of the goods we offer you.

We want you to see our Out-of-Door Clothing for Men and Women and for Boys. We want you to see our complete outfits for camping, for canoeing, for fishermen, for golfers, for every one of the sports. We want you to see to what lengths we have gone to provide not only the best, but the exactly RIGHT and the EXCLUSIVE thing for your favorite sport, the thing you have always wanted but couldn't get elsewhere because it didn't EXIST elsewhere.

EZRA H. FITCH, President

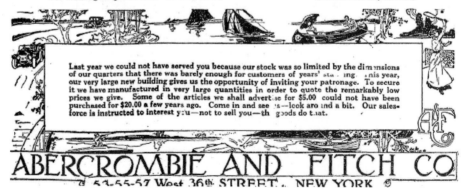

Last year we could not have served you because our stock was so limited by the dimensions of our quarters that there was barely enough for customers of years' standing. This year, our very large new building gives us the opportunity of inviting your patronage. To secure it we have manufactured in very large quantities in order to quote the remarkably low prices we give. Some of the articles we shall advertise for $5.00 could not have been purchased for $20.00 a few years ago. Come in and see us—look around a bit. Our salesforce is instructed to interest you—not to sell you—th goods do that.

ABERCROMBIE AND FITCH CO

53-55-57 West 36th STREET, NEW YORK

Christmas shopping early—in November. A lack of manpower had overwhelmed the postal services and caused delays.

At least twice in A&F's history, a customer used one of the guns on display in an A&F shop to commit suicide. The first shooting occurred in 1932, when the son of a famous horse breeder killed himself. The second shooting occurred in 1968 when an immigrant from Czechoslovakia killed himself. Subsequently, extra care was taken to ensure that every gun was fitted with a trigger lock and kept in locked show cases. Customers were no longer handed guns or ammunition over the counter; upon purchase, the firearms were delivered to their homes.

Employee theft and shoplifting occurred. In 1915, for example, Gustave Touchard, Jr., a champion tennis player, was charged with stealing 48 dozen golf balls worth $288 from an A&F store on 36th Street. He had worked at the store as a manager of its sporting department. In 1923, a well-dressed woman was caught with 21 yards of Scotch tweed cloth hidden in the ulster (a bulky overcoat) she was wearing. The theft occurred a few weeks after two sisters who shopped at Macy's while carrying small dogs in their arms were caught with stolen items in their wide sleeves. In 1969, inventory shrinkage (from bookkeeping errors, internal theft and shoplifting) totaled $1 million (up from between $600,000 and $700,000 the previous year). This contributed to the retailer's pretax loss for the year.[13]

Between 1970 and 1976, A&F continued to incur financial losses. In the fiscal year ending January 31, 1976, A&F incurred a net loss of $1 million on sales of $23.8 million.[14] The loss followed annual deficits ranging from $287,000 to $540,000 every year since 1970.[15] A&F's best year had been in 1968 when it reported pretax earnings of $866,000 on sales of $28 million.[16] Managers began to search for a possible buyer of the firm. No one was seriously interested.

In August 1976, A&F filed for bankruptcy. It held a sale to liquidate its inventory of $8.5 million. A sign in the retailer's Madison Avenue store read: "They say we're stuffy so we're moving the stuff out at tremendous reductions on all floors."[17] After the sale, the stores were closed. A&F's difficulties were attributed to competition from mass marketers (e.g., Hermann's World of Sporting Goods) that sold discounted merchandise, the lack of professional managers and leadership turnover (the retailer had three different CEOs in its last six years), high overhead costs, and fewer customers who could afford its exotic, high-priced items.

In 1978, Oshman's Sporting Goods, Incorporated of Houston acquired A&F's name, trademark, and mailing list for $1.5 million. A&F's slogan was changed from "The Finest Sporting Goods Store in the World" to "The Adventure Goes On." The new owners had studied A&F's business model for two years. According to president Nanna, "We examined the original business, took it apart and retained the good qualities. We also retained some of the legendary old products that Abercrombie had and expanded their variety. But we dropped most of the tailored clothing that proved to be a drain."[18] The owners believed that they could bring A&F up-to-date to the styles of the 1980s. The chain expanded to 12 stores; sales of $20 million were expected in 1982.

In 1988, The Limited Incorporated acquired 25 A&F stores and its catalogue business for $47 million from Oshman's. Two additional stores were closed. At the time, the Limited operated a chain of 3,100 stores that sold women's apparel. In 1992, Michael Jeffries

[13]"Changes Weighed for Abercrombie," *The New York Times*, September, 1970, p. 73. Retrieved April 21, 2006, from ProQuest Historical Newspapers database.

[14]"Abercrombie Reports Loss of $1 Million in Fiscal Year," *The New York Times*, August 26, 1976, p. 68. Retrieved April 21, 2006, from ProQuest Historical Newspapers database.

[15]R. Hanley, "Abercrombie & Fitch Put Up for Sale," *The New York Times*, July 20, 1976. Retrieved April 21, 2006, from ProQuest Historical Newspapers database.

[16]I. Barmash, "Abercrombie & Fitch in Bankruptcy Step," *The New York Times*, August 7, 1976, p. 47. Retrieved April 21, 2006, from ProQuest Historical Newspapers database.

[17]C. G. Fraser, "'Stuffy' Abercrombie's Gets Sale Relief," *The New York Times*, August 29, 1976, p. 47. Retrieved April 21, 2006, from ProQuest Historical Newspapers database.

[18]I. Barmash, "New Guise for Abercrombie's," *The New York Times*, November 9, 1982, p. D1. Retrieved April 21, 2006, from ProQuest Historical Newspapers database.

became president and chief executive of A&F, a retailing unit of the Limited. A new format was introduced. The chain began to carry casual, classic American clothes for 20-year-old men and women. A&F became one of the Limited's fastest growing divisions. The number of stores grew from 40 in 1992 to 113 in 1996. Its sales increased at a compounded annual rate of 40.3 percent during those same years.[19] In 1996, the Limited spun off A&F. Jeffries stayed on as CEO.

SENIOR EXECUTIVES AND CORPORATE GOVERNANCE

Michael Jeffries got his start in retailing at an early age when he helped his father select the toys that were sold in the family's chain of party supply stores. He also enjoyed organizing and designing the window and counter displays. Born in 1944, Jeffries received a BA in economics from Claremont McKenna College and an MBA from Columbia University. He entered the management training program of Abraham & Straus (a New York department store that belonged to Federated) in 1968. From there, he went on to start a women's clothing store, Alcott & Andrews, which later failed. He worked in merchandising at Paul Harris, which also went bankrupt.[20]

In his flip-flops, polo shirt, and torn jeans, Jeffries embodied the casual look of A&F more than anyone else. He made sure that A&F's apparel reflected the life styles of college students. Teams of designers, merchandisers, and marketers visited college campuses once a month to talk to students and find out what they liked and how they spent their time. On one of those visits in 1998, Jeffries saw someone wearing nylon wind pants. A&F was quick to make its own version of the pants. Tom Lennox, A&F's director of corporate communications and investor relations once said, "We just believe that it is our job to position Abercrombie and Fitch as the coolest brand, the brand with the greatest quality, the aspirational brand of college students."[21]

A&F's success did not make Jeffries complacent. He was quoted as saying, "Every morning I'm scared. I'm superstitious. I come in every morning being afraid to look at yesterday's figures, and I want everyone else to have that same kind of fear."[22] He worked hard and constantly traveled from store to store. He was always thinking of ways to extend the A&F brand. Jeffries had a few eccentric habits. He went through revolving doors twice, parked his black Porsche at an odd angle in the company's parking lot and wore the same lucky shoes when he reviewed financial reports.[23] It was almost as if he felt that his firm's good fortune could change at any time. Perhaps he realized that his primary target audience—teenagers—was fickle and that trendy apparel quickly became outdated.

Between 2003 and 2006, A&F had three different chief financial officers and two different chief operating officers. The latter position remained unfilled. In July 2003, Wesley McDonald, who had been A&F's CFO for four years, left to become CFO of Kohl's Corporation. He was replaced in February 2004 by Susan Riley who had held CFO positions at Mount Sinai Medical Center, Dial Corporation, and Tambrands Incorporated. In August 2005, Riley resigned for family reasons and returned to her home in New York City.

[19]D. Canedy, "After Unbuttoning Its Image, A Retail Legend Comes to Market," *The New York Times*, September 1996, p. F3. Retrieved April 21, 2006, from ProQuest Historical Newspapers database.

[20]R. Berner, "Flip-Flops, Torn Jeans—And Control," *BusinessWeek*, May 30, 2005, p. 68. Retrieved December 12, 2005, from ABI/Inform (ProQuest) database.

[21]M. Cole, "Facing a Brave New World," *Apparel* 45 (July 2004), p. 22. Retrieved April 20, 2006, from ProQuest Historical Newspapers database.

[22]M. Pledger, "Abercrombie & Fitch Focuses on American College Audience," *The Plain Dealer*, June 22, 1999, p. 2S. Retrieved April 19, 2006, from Lexis/Nexis Academic database.

[23]Berner, "Flip-Flops."

Michael Kramer became A&F's new CFO. He had been the CFO of the retail unit of Apple Incorporated. He also had retail experience working for Gateway Inc., The Limited, and Pizza Hut. He had a BA in Business Administration and Accounting from Kansas State University and was a certified public accountant.

Seth Johnson was A&F's COO between 2000 and 2004. Before that, he had been its CFO. Johnson was credited with keeping costs down by reducing payroll and travel expenses. He was responsible for installing computer systems to help A&F's distribution system run more efficiently. He had aspired to a CEO position and was offered such an opportunity at Pacific Sunwear of California, Inc. Robert Singer, a former executive at Gucci, became the next president and COO in 2004. After 15 months on the job, Singer resigned to become the CEO of Barilla Holding SpA. Disagreements about international expansion were cited as the reason for his departure. Singer's duties were divided between John Lough (executive vice president of logistics and store operations) and Michael Kramer (CFO). Search for a replacement began.

Unlike other retailers, A&F did not have division presidents for its brands. Merchants from different businesses reported directly to the CEO. They did not work within a particular brand. Instead, they led categories—for example, denim or outerwear. They were responsible for these brands across each of the company's divisions. That way, their expertise and knowledge could best be leveraged and exploited.

A&F encountered criticism from shareholders regarding executive compensation and the composition of its board of directors. In February 2005, shareholders charged A&F directors with wasting corporate assets by paying CEO Jeffries $22.9 million in salary, bonus, and stock options. The company settled the lawsuit and Jeffries agreed to reduce his $12 million bonus to $6 million and to forgo new stock options for two years. The bonus was contingent on meeting specific earnings targets. Jeffries would receive the full $6 million bonus if A&F's earnings per share increased by 13.5 percent between February 1, 2005 to January 31, 2009.[24]

Shareholders also expressed concern over the independence of A&F's board of directors. John W. Kessler, chair of the compensation committee, had financial ties to the retailer. As chair of a real estate development firm owned by the Limited's CEO Wexner (Jeffries' former boss), Kessler sold the land upon which A&F built its headquarters in 1999. He received a fee for finding the site. Kessler's son-in-law, Thomas D. Lennox, was A&F's director of investor relations and communications. Samuel Shahid, president and creative director of the advertising agency that received $2 million a year from A&F for its services, was a board member until May 2005. He was replaced by Allan A. Tuttle, an attorney for the luxury goods maker, Gucci Group. While Tuttle did not have financial ties to A&F, he was a friend of Robert Singer, who at the time was A&F's president and COO.

A&F denied wrongdoing and settled the lawsuits to "avoid the uncertainty, harm and expense of litigation."[25] As part of its agreement with shareholders, A&F promised to provide more public information about executive compensation and to add independent members to its board and compensation committee.

A&F faced a formal investigation by the U.S. Securities and Exchange Commission regarding insider selling of stock. In June and July of 2005, when A&F's stock price was high, Jeffries sold 1.6 million shares worth $120 million. In August, share prices declined after the company announced it would miss Wall Street expectations regarding its second quarter earnings. A&F was also sued for making false and misleading statements of monthly and quarterly sales figures and for failing to disclose that profit margins were

[24]"Abercrombie CEO Benefits Settlement OKd," *Los Angeles Times*, June 15, 2005. Retrieved May 18, 2006, from ABI/Inform (ProQuest) database.

[25]"Abercrombie CEO Benefits."

declining and inventory rising. The company announced that it was cooperating with the SEC and that the shareholder lawsuit had no merit.

STORE CONCEPT AND MARKETING STRATEGIES

When customers walked into an original A&F clothing store in a local mall, they were often greeted by a young, handsome salesperson wearing the latest fashion in casual attire. The store's lights were dimmed and posters of attractive models wearing its trademark cargo pants and polo shirts adorned the walls. In some stores, chandeliers made of fake deer antlers or whitewashed moose antlers hung from the ceilings. Apparel was neatly folded and placed on long wooden tables. The retailer's hip, trendy, and "All-American" look was reinforced by loud dance music and sprays of men's cologne. The intent was to provide a sensual experience that appealed to a shopper's sense of sight, smell, and sound. According to marketing expert, Pam Danziger, "Shoppers are rejecting the old concept of 'hunting and gathering' shopping in favor of a more involved, interesting, dynamic retail experience."[26] A&F was able to successfully implement an exciting store format.

Every A&F store was designed according to one of several specific models created at company headquarters. The retailer wanted to maintain complete control over its brand and to communicate a consistent message in all stores across the nation. Jeffries himself made sure the model stores were "perfect."[27] The prototypes were photographed and sent to the store managers of the individual outlets for replication. Jeffries was known for paying attention to every detail. He visited stores and made sure that the clothes were folded correctly. He approved of the background music to be played in the stores and selected the appropriate volume level for all locations. He even gave suggestions on how mannequins could be made to look more rugged and masculine.

A&F's Web site (www.abercrombie.com) was created to match the feel and aura of its stores as much as possible. It featured striking black and white images of young people in outdoor settings. A&F's low rise jeans for men and women were advertised. Was that shirtless young man lying on the grass placing his hand in a sexually suggestive position (see Exhibit 4)? The photograph appeared on the store locator Web page. Through its "A&F Lifestyle" link, Web surfers could download screen savers or send e-postcards to one another. According to *Forbes* magazine, the Web site's best feature is the photo gallery showing images of the models that made A&F famous. Its worst feature was that its line of clothing was not shown by the models.[28]

A&F extended its successful store concept and marketing ideas to its newer brand name stores, Hollister Company and Ruehl. Hollister stores were designed to look like beach houses with faux porches and house style layouts. The name came from a span of gated coastal property north of Santa Barbara where surfers liked to hang out. Surfboards leaned against the store walls. Fans blew constantly to mimic the breeze coming in from the ocean. Shoppers could sit in comfortable chairs and read surfing, skateboarding, and snowboarding magazines.

Ruehl (rhymes with "cool") stores imitated the architecture of Greenwich Village with red-brick facades, iron fences, flowerboxes, and small windows. They looked like brownstones. Ruehl was the name of a fictitious German family who had come to America in the

[26]M. Wilson, "The 'Pop' Factor," *Chain Store Age* 82 (April 2006), p. 78. Retrieved May 18, 2006, from ABI/Inform (ProQuest) database.

[27]Denizet-Lewis, "The Man."

[28]"Web Site Reviews: Abercrombie & Fitch," Forbes.com. Retrieved May 1, 2006, from http://www.forbes.com/bow/b2c/review. jhtml?id=6833.

EXHIBIT 4
A Photograph from
A&F's Web Site

1850s and opened a leather-goods shop in Greenwich Village. Couches and armchairs were available for lounging. Copies of the *Village Voice* and *The New York Times* are found on coffee tables. The music playing was jazz. Signs were not posted outside. The shopper was expected to stumble upon the store just as if he or she were walking in a city neighborhood; the great "find" would be spread via word-of-mouth.[29] Experts reported that young people want to be part of a brand story.[30]

A&F had an enviable target market. It catered to teenagers, whose population in the United States was expanding. In 2003, 32 million teens lived in the United States. This number was expected to rise to 35 million by 2010. Moreover, teens spent approximately $170 billion on goods and services in 2002, with one-third going towards apparel.[31] Spending in 2005 was lower—$159 billion.[32] Teen retailing was considered to be somewhat recession-proof. Although teens worked for low wages, they had multiple revenue streams—babysitting, paper routes, part-time jobs, and assistance from parents.[33] They usually did not have financial obligations (no mortgages or bills to pay.) Parents, too, were more likely to spend money on their children than on themselves.

[29]J. Verdon, "Abercrombie Targets 20-Somethings with Coffeehouse-Style Store in Paramus, N.J.," *Knight Ridder Tribune Business News*, September 17, 2004, p. 1. Retrieved April 20, 2006, from ABI/Inform (ProQuest) database.

[30]C. Collins, "Status of U.S. Brands Slips Globally Among Teens," *Christian Science Monitor*, February 16, 2006, p. 13. Retrieved June 11, 2006, from ABI/Inform (ProQuest) database.

[31]J. Ablan, "Trend Setter," *Barron's* 83 (March 31, 2003), p. 21. Retrieved April 20, 2006, from ABI/Inform (ProQuest) database.

[32]P.B. Erikson, "Companies Focus on Youthful Influence for Prosperity," *Knight Ridder Tribune Business News*, April 16, 2006, p. 1. Retrieved April 21, 2006, from ABI/Inform (ProQuest) database.

[33]Ablan, "Trend Setter."

A&F's busy seasons were spring and fall. Forty percent of its sales were realized in the spring and 60 percent in the fall (during the back to school and holiday season periods). It hired extra employees during those times. A&F was able to maintain its high prices without resorting to sales and discounts. It was afraid that cutting prices for a big sale would cheapen its brand. A&F saved money on promotions, relying frequently on word of mouth advertising. The retailer claimed that it spent less than 2 percent of net sales on marketing in 2004.[34] It also kept down its administrative expenses and negotiated lower fees from its suppliers. High prices and low costs comprised a formula that clearly worked.

In its A&F stores, the retailer tried to introduce two or three new items in its stores every week. It launched a new men's line, "Ezra Fitch," which featured high-quality apparel made from cashmere, velvet, and leather. A&F cultivated brand loyalty. Shoppers could join Hollister's Club Cali and receive gift cards based on how much they spent. Invitations to after-hours parties with new bands at the stores were also available. Instead of marking down items the day after Thanksgiving in 2004 (the start of the busy Christmas shopping season), preferred customers who spent $1,000 a year or more were invited to a live concert given by Ryan Cabrera. The concert was also shown on big screen televisions in 50 other Hollister stores around the nation.

A&F generated controversy. Adults often reacted negatively to its catalogs, revealing clothes, and racy slogans (see Exhibit 5 for some of its t-shirts). Some teenagers, however, might have responded positively to its advertising in a show of rebellion against the traditional values and lifestyles of their parents. Teens were reluctant to shop in the same stores as their parents. Some observers believed that A&F purposely created controversy and engaged in risky practices to attract attention, draw in shoppers, and sell more products. As an analyst with Midwest Research in Cleveland remarked, "Abercrombie is not a company that really cares about backing away from controversy. They use controversy as a free advertising gig and are successful in driving traffic into the stores."[35]

Here is a list of A&F's controversial moves:

- In July 1998, a story entitled, "Drinking 101," appeared in an A&F Fall back-to-school catalog. It featured recipes for alcoholic beverages and a game for helping students decide which drink to mix. After being criticized by Mothers Against Drunk Driving (MADD), A&F deleted the story and sent postcards to students who received the publication by mail reminding them to "be responsible, be 21, and don't ever drink and drive."[36]

- In April 2002, A&F sold a line of T-shirts with Asian cartoon characters and matching ethnic slogans: "Wong Brothers Laundry Service, Two Wongs Can Make it White"; "Wok-N-Bowl"; "Buddha Bash, Get Your Buddha on the Floor." The retailer took the T-shirts off store shelves after protests from college students from campuses around the country. A&F's spokesperson, Hampton Carney apologized, saying "It is not, and never has been, our intention to offend anyone. These were designed to add humor and levity to our fashion line. Since some of our customers were offended by these T-shirts, we removed them from all our stores."[37]

[34]Presentation at the Merrill Lynch Retailing Leaders & Household Products & Cosmetics Conference, March 25, 2005. Retrieved April 22, 2006, from the World Wide Web: http://www.abercrombie.com.

[35]T. Turner, "Retailer Abercrombie & Fitch Angers West Virginia Residents with New T-Shirt," *Knight Ridder Tribune Business News*, March 24, 2004, p. 1. Retrieved November 8, 2004, from ABI/Inform (ProQuest) database.

[36]"Abercrombie & Fitch Plans to Delete Drinking Section," *The Wall Street Journal*, July 30, 1998, p. 1. Retrieved November 8, 2004, from ABI/Inform (ProQuest) database.

[37]G. Kim, "Racism Doesn't Belong on T-shirts," *Knight Ridder Tribune Business News*, April 28, 2002, p. 1. Retrieved April 21, 2006, from ABI/Inform (ProQuest) database.

EXHIBIT 5
A&F's Controversial
T-Shirt Slogans

Source: http://www.click2houston.com/ money/3683643/detail.html

Source: http://news.bbc.co.uk/.../newsid_1938000/1938914.st

Source: http://www.80-20initiative.net/tshirts.html

- In May 2002, A&F sold thong underwear for girls 10 years and over with sexual phrases such as "eye candy" and "wink, wink" printed on the front. Family-advocacy groups and Christian organizations protested. The line was recalled in Washington, DC area stores.[38]

[38]D. DeMarco, "Abercrombie & Fitch Pulls Children's Thong," *Knight Ridder Tribune Business News,* May 23, 2002, p. 1. Retrieved November 8, 2004, from ABI/Inform (ProQuest) database.

- In December 2003, under heavy criticism from parents and consumer groups, A&F decided to stop publishing its provocative catalog, *A&F Quarterly*. Its holiday issue featured nude models and articles about group sex and masturbation.[39]
- In March 2004, Bob Wise, Governor of West Virginia asked A&F to pull from its shelves T-shirts with the slogan, "It's All Relative in West Virginia." Wise explained that the slogan was offensive because it referred to a stereotype that West Virginia was a state that condoned incest.[40]
- In October 2004, officials of USA Gymnastics sought the immediate removal of a T-shirt depicting a male gymnast performing on the still rings alongside the phrase, "L is for Loser." They wrote a letter to Jeffries saying its members would be encouraged to withdraw their support of the chain.[41]
- In May 2005, A&F quietly pulled a line of T-shirts from its stores with slogans that read: "I Brews Easily," "Candy is Dandy but Liquor is Quicker," and "Don't Bother I'm Not Drunk Yet." The company was criticized for glorifying underage drinking and promoting a lifestyle that was illegal for its target audience. Pressure came from the International Institute for Alcohol Awareness, a public advocacy group that worked to reduce underage drinking. This time, A&F responded to criticism before the issue was reported in national newspapers.[42]
- In November 2005, 24 participants in the Allegheny County Girls as Grantmakers program, organized a "girlcott" of A&F stores to protest its "attitude T-shirts" which featured such slogans as: "Who needs brains when you have these?"; "Blondes are Adored, Brunettes Are Ignored;" "All Men Like Tig Old Bitties." Other groups, such as Peace Project, an antidiscrimination student club in Norwalk, Connecticut, and the Women & Girls Foundation of Southwestern Pennsylvania, joined in. A&F pulled two of the more offensive T-shirts and its executives agreed to meet with several of the protestors. The girls suggested that the retailer print more appropriate slogans such as: "All This and Brains to Match" and "Your Future Boss." They hoped the firm would launch such a line and donate a portion of revenues to groups like theirs.[43]

LOGISTICS AND SUPPLY CHAIN MANAGEMENT

A&F operated solely as a retailer. It assumed responsibility for creating and managing its brands. Unlike other businesses, A&F did not distribute its apparel and accessories through wholesale channels, through licensing or through franchising. Abercrombie clothing could not be purchased in department stores or in discount stores. It could, however, be purchased online via A&F's Web site. E-commerce transactions generated over $100 million in business a year.[44]

[39] J. Caggiano, "Abercrombie & Fitch Drops Racy Publication," *Knight Ridder Tribune Business News,* December 11, 2003, p. 1. Retrieved November 8, 2004, from ABI/Inform (ProQuest) database.

[40] T. Turner, "Retailer Abercrombie & Fitch Angers West Virginia Residents with New T-Shirt."

[41] "USA Gymnastics Upset with Abercrombie & Fitch," *The Washington Post*, October 8, 2004, p. D2. Retrieved November 8, 2004, from ABI/Inform (ProQuest) database.

[42] K.S. Shalett, "Shamed off Shelves," *Times-Picayune*, May 20, 2005, p. 1. Retrieved December 12, 2005, from ABI/Inform (ProQuest) database.

[43] M. Haynes, "'Girlcott' Organizers Meet with Abercrombie & Fitch Execs over T-shirts," *Knight Ridder Tribune Business News*, December 6, 2005, p. 1. Retrieved December 12, 2005, from ABI/Inform (ProQuest) database.

[44] "Abercrombie & Fitch Co. at Banc of America Securities Consumer Conference," *Fair Disclosure Wire*, March 17, 2005. Retrieved May 24, 2006, from ABI/Inform (ProQuest) database.

During 2005, A&F purchased merchandise from approximately 246 factories and suppliers located around the globe, primarily in Southeast Asia and Central and South America. It did not source more than 50 percent of its apparel from any single factory or supplier. The design and development process for a garment took between six weeks to three months.[45] Retailers struggled to reduce this time so as not to get stuck with inventory of merchandise that had lost its fashion appeal. A&F made the process more efficient by centralizing its design services at its New Albany headquarters, which reduced overseas travel of executives.

A&F also operated a distribution center in New Albany, Ohio. Merchandise was received and inspected and then distributed to stores via contract carriers. It was here that concepts for new divisions were created and prototypes for new stores were constructed. The new formats were kept secret until their launch dates.

A&F launched an anticounterfeiting program in an effort to protect its brand and prevent low-cost manufacturers in Asian factories from making imitations of its products. Local authorities seized 300,000 pairs of fake Abercrombie jeans (worth $20 million) in a raid of a Chinese warehouse in 2006. The retailer hired a former FBI agent to head a 10-person department to conduct investigations overseas and to work with foreign authorities.[46]

A&F began experimenting with radio frequency identification (RFID) technology in its Ruehl stores which sold higher priced and higher quality merchandise. Tags that could be monitored electronically were sewn into the seams of garments. The location of the garments could be tracked, enabling an employee to quickly return to the shelves garments that had been left in dressing rooms or placed in the wrong spots on the floor. The technology could be used to prevent theft and to differentiate between authentic products and counterfeit goods.

A&F'S FINANCIAL PERFORMANCE

In fiscal 2006, A&F achieved revenues of $3.32 billion, an increase of 19 percent from fiscal 2005. Its net income rose to $422.2 million, an increase of 26.4 percent from fiscal 2005 (see Exhibit 6). Earnings per share rose to $4.59 from $3.66. A&F opened 93 new stores and added 11,000 employees to its payroll. It had no long-term debt. It repurchased 1.8 million shares of common stock for $103.3 million in fiscal 2005, but it did not make additional purchases in fiscal 2006. It paid dividends of 70 cents a share for a total of $61.6 million.

Managers at the retailer considered Abercrombie & Fitch to be a maturing brand with opportunities for expansion in prime locations in the United States and with greater potential overseas. The Abercrombie brand might grow to 250 stores and seek locations in Canada. Hollister was seen as the fastest growing brand while Ruehl was building a strong customer base but still needed to prove itself (see Exhibit 7 for sales by brand).[47]

[45]K. Showalter, "A&F Readies $10 Million Expansion," *Business First of Columbus*, March 11, 2005. Retrieved April 29, 2006, from the World Wide Web: http://columbus.bizjournals.com/columbus/stories/ 2005/03/14/story5.html.

[46]J. Sheban, "Fighting Fakes: Abercrombie Enlists Expert to Help it Combat Counterfeiting," *Knight Ridder Tribune Business News*, February 3, 2006, p. 1. Retrieved April 23, 2006, from ABI/Inform (ProQuest) database.

[47]A&F 10-K, 2006, p. 31.

EXHIBIT 6

Five Year Summary of
A&F's Financial
Performance

Source: A&F 10-K.

	2006*	2005	2004	2003	2002
Operating revenues (in thousands)	$3,318,158	$2,784,711	$2,021,253	$1,707,810	$1,595,757
Gross profit (in thousands)	$2,209,006	$1,851,416	$1,341,224	$1,083,170	$ 980,555
Operating income (in thousands)	$ 658,090	$ 542,738	$ 347,635	$ 331,180	$ 312,315
Net income (in thousands)	$ 422,186	$ 333,986	$ 216,376	$ 204,830	$ 194,754
Earnings per share—diluted	$ 4.59	$ 3.66	$ 2.28	$ 2.06	$ 1.94
Dividends declared per share	$ .70	$ .60	$ .50	0	0
Total assets (in thousands)	$2,248,067	$1,789,718	$1,386,791	$1,401,369	$1,190,615
Capital expenditures (in thousands)	$ 403,476	$ 256,422	$ 185,065	$ 159,777	$ 145,662
Long-term debt (in thousands)	0	0	0	0	0
Shareholder's equity (in thousands)	$1,405,297	$ 995,117	$ 669,326	$ 857,764	$736,307
Number of stores	944	851	788	700	597
Gross square feet	6,693,000	6,025,000	5,590,000	5,016,000	4,358,000
Number of employees (average)	80,100	69,100	48,500	30,200	22,000

*Fiscal 2006 is a 53-week year.

EXHIBIT 7

Three Year Summary
of A&F's Financial
Performance by
Brand

Source: A&F 10-K.

	2006*	2005	2004
Net Sales by Brand (in thousands)	**$3,318,158**	**$2,784,711**	**$2,021,253**
Abercrombie & Fitch	$1,515,123	$1,424,013	$1,210,222
abercrombie	$ 405,820	$ 344,938	$ 227,204
Hollister	$1,363,233	$ 999,212	$ 579,687
RUEHL**	$ 33,982	$ 16,548	$ 4,140

	2006*	2005	2004
Increase (Decrease) in Comparable Store Sales * **	2%	26%	2%
Abercrombie & Fitch	(4)%	18%	(1)%
abercrombie	10%	54%	1%
Hollister	5%	29%	13%
RUEHL**	14%	N/A	N/A

	2006*	2005	2004
Net Retail Sales Per Average Store (in thousands)	$ 3,533	$ 3,284	$ 2,569
Abercrombie & Fitch	$ 3,945	$ 3,784	$ 3,103
abercrombie	$ 2,251	$ 1,957	$ 1,241
Hollister	$ 3,732	$ 3,442	$ 2,740
RUEHL**	$ 3,248	$ 2,903	$ 1,255

*Fiscal 2006 is a 53-week year.
**Data for RUEHL reflect the activity of 14 stores open in fiscal 2006, 8 stores open in fiscal 2005, and 4 stores open in fiscal 2004. Year to year comparisons may not be meaningful.
***A store is included in comparable store sales when it has been open as the same brand at least one year and its square footage has not been expanded or reduced by more than 20 percent within the past year.

A&F'S SOCIALLY RESPONSIBLE PRACTICES

A&F held fund-raising activities that benefited local charities and communities. Every Christmas holiday season, shoppers were invited into its stores to have their picture taken with its models. The fee was $1, which the retailer matched. The proceeds were donated to foundations such as Toys for Tots or the Juvenile Diabetes Research Foundation. It held the "A&F Challenge," an action-packed outdoor event, at its headquarters in New Albany, Ohio. Participants, who paid an entry fee of $25, went on a 20-mile cycling tour, a 5K in-line skating tour and a 5K run. They heard live music from a band, enjoyed food and drinks, and received a T-shirt. All proceeds went to the Center for Child and Family Advocacy in Columbus, Ohio. Its largest donation—$10 million—went to a Children's Hospital in Columbus, in June 2006. The hospital's new trauma center would bear the A&F name.

A&F also sometimes got involved in issues at the supplier end of its business. In 2004, it joined a boycott of Australian merino wool in an effort to force ranchers to end a cruel procedure that protected lambs from flies, mulesing. Even though A&F did not purchase much Australian wool, wool producers feared that the retailer would set a precedent and that other retailers would soon join the boycott. They agreed to end the practice of mulesing by 2010 or sooner.[48]

ORGANIZATIONAL CULTURE AND HUMAN RESOURCE MANAGEMENT

A&F's core corporate values were: "nature, friendships and having fun."[49] The values were reflected in everything from the decor of the retailer's stores and the casual attire of its employees to the layout of A&F's headquarters in New Albany, Ohio, and to the firm's advertising messages. If there were no customers to serve, employees might throw a football to one another in the store. The retailer's home page on the World Wide Web featured a tree house that could be downloaded as wallpaper.

A&F's headquarters, built in 2001, was situated in the woods along Blacklick Creek in New Albany, Ohio. Its campus-like setting served as a continual reminder to employees that the firm's target audience was college students. It was also designed to encourage team work and creativity. Instead of using desks in individual cubicles, employees engaged in collaborative work situated at long tables in doorless conference rooms. Employees could walk along paths in the woods to relax, think, or seek inspiration for a new idea. There was no executive suite. Jeffries had no desk or office. He worked in a conference room with a view of the grounds from large windows.

Employees enjoyed healthy meals that included roast chicken, international dishes, salads, fruit juices, and gourmet coffees in the full-service cafeteria. They traveled from building to building on scooters and were allowed to bring their skateboards. A bonfire pit provided the atmosphere of an outdoors summer camp. Employees worked out in the gym. One of the architects said, "A&F wants to give back to the people who work there. That's why they can go to that rusty barn the first thing in the morning, or get sweaty in the gym and then go to work, have a great meal and then go back to work again. It reinforces the idea that this is community."[50]

[48]J. Sheban, "Abercrombie & Fitch's Wool Boycott Helps End 'Mulesing' Practice," *Knight Ridder Tribune Business News*, November 12, 2004, p. 1. Retrieved April 19, 2006, from ABI/Inform (ProQuest) database.

[49]D. Gebolys, "Inside Abercrombie & Fitch," *Columbus Dispatch*, May 24, 2001, p. 1F. Retrieved April 19, 2006, from LexisNexis Academic database.

[50]K. Showalter, "Abercrombie & Fitch: Campus Reflects the True Nature of New Albany Firm's Culture," *Business First of Columbus*, August 24, 2001. Retrieved April 29, 2006, from http://columbus.bizjournals.com/columbus/stories/2001/08/27/focus1.html?page=3.

Store managers visited nearby fraternities and sororities to recruit salespeople or "brand representatives." They were encouraged to ask attractive shoppers in their stores if they wanted to apply for a sales position. Lennox, A&F's investor relations and communications director, acknowledged that the firm liked to hire job candidates who looked great. "Brand representatives are ambassadors to the brand. We want to hire brand representatives that will represent the Abercrombie & Fitch brand with natural classic American style, look great while exhibiting individuality, project the brand and themselves with energy and enthusiasm, and make the store a warm, inviting place that provides a social experience for the customer," he said.[51] The company ran a manager-in-training program for seniors and graduates. Promotion to store manager could occur one year after completing the training.

Brand representatives were expected to adhere to a dress code outlined in an Abercrombie Associate's Handbook. Hair was to be neatly combed and attractive; makeup was to be worn to enhance natural features and create a fresh, natural appearance; fingernails were not to extend more than 1/4 inch beyond the tip of the finger and nail polish was to be a natural color; mustaches, goatees, and beards were unacceptable; jewelry was to be simple and classic (only women were allowed to wear earrings as long as they wore no more than two earrings in each ear and each earring was no larger than a dime and did not dangle).[52]

In 2000, the California Department of Industrial Relations received complaints from several A&F employees who said that they were forced to buy and wear the company's clothes on the job. One woman, in another part of the country, later claimed that she spent more on clothes for work than she earned at the store. Such company policy might have violated a state work uniform law which required employees to supply the clothing when they wanted workers to wear specific apparel. In 2003, A&F settled the lawsuit in California for $2.2 million without admitting wrongdoing. Employees received reimbursements ranging from $180 to $490 depending on their job status and the amount of money spent on clothing.[53] The case spurred other similar lawsuits across the state and the rest of the nation against The Limited, The Gap, Chico's, and Polo Ralph Lauren. In some states, lawyers used the federal Fair Labor Standards Act that required employers to pay minimum wage to argue that sales associates ended up with less than minimum wage after spending their earnings on store clothing.

A&F's legal problems were only just beginning. In July 2003, two former A&F employees filed a lawsuit accusing the company of failing to pay overtime wages when they were required to work 50–60 hours a week. The plaintiffs claim that they were sales associates, with no management responsibilities, but were classified as managers so that the retailer could avoid paying overtime. According to the Federal Fair Labor Standards Act and the Ohio Minimum Fair Wage Standards Act, nonexempt employees must be paid time and a half for work in excess of 40 hours a week.

In June 2003, lawyers for nine plaintiffs filed a lawsuit against the retailer for discriminating against minorities in its hiring practices and job placement. It allegedly cultivated an "overwhelmingly white work force" and steered minority applicants into less visible jobs.[54] Former A&F employees appeared on CBS's television program *60 Minutes* and said that A&F was interested in hiring employees who fit a certain look. Anthony Ocampo worked

---

[51]S. Greenhouse, "Going for the Look, But Risking Discrimination," *The New York Times*, July 13, 2003, p. 12. Retrieved November 9, 2004, from ABI/Inform (ProQuest) database.

[52]B. Paynter, "Don't Hate Me Because I'm Beautiful," *Kansas City Pitch Weekly*, September 4, 2003. Retrieved February 12, 2005, from LexusNexis Academic database.

[53]"Abercrombie & Fitch Settles Dress Code Case," *Houston Chronicle*, June 25, 2003, p. 2. Retrieved November 4, 2004, from ABI/Inform (ProQuest) database.

[54]T. Turner, "Cincinnati Suit Charges Abercrombie & Fitch with Failing to Pay Overtime," *Knight Ridder Tribune Business News*, July 9, 2003, p. 1.

at an Abercrombie store during his Christmas break from Stanford University. When he returned to get a summer job, he was told that he could not be rehired because the store already had too many Filipinos working there. Eduardo Gonzalez, another Stanford University student who was Latino, was told that he could only work in the store's stock room or as part of the overnight crew. At Banana Republic, he was asked if he was applying for a management position. Carla Grubb, an African-American student at California State University at Bakersfield, felt she was not treated fairly because she was scheduled to work only during closing times and was asked to wash the front windows, vacuum, and clean the mannequins.

In November 2003, another lawsuit was filed against A&F on behalf of a New Jersey woman who claimed that her application for a sales associate position was denied because she was African-American. A&F denied that it discriminated against minorities. It claimed that minorities represented 13 percent of all its store associates (which exceeded national averages). The U.S. Equal Employment Opportunity Commission also initiated a lawsuit, claiming that A&F violated parts of the Civil Rights Act of 1964 (see Exhibit 8 for a summary of relevant laws and legal procedures). Store managers reported that they were instructed to discard job applications if the candidates did not possess the right look.

In November 2004, A&F paid $50 million (including legal fees) to settle the discrimination lawsuits. It agreed to hire a vice president of diversity, provide training in diversity and inclusion to its employees and managers, increase the number of minority employees in sales and store management positions, enhance its compliance and oversight processes, and use more minority models in its advertising. The retailer promised that within two years its sales force would be 9 percent African Americans, 9 percent Latinos, its current percentage of Asians, and 53 percent women.[55] A&F was told to stop recruiting from predominantly white fraternities and sororities. It agreed to hire 25 full-time diversity recruiters who would seek new hires from historically black colleges, minority job fairs,

---

EXHIBIT 8

Summary of Workplace Discrimination Acts in the United States

Source: D. Kolber, "Knowledge of Discrimination Laws Vital," *Atlanta Business Chronicle*, May 27, 2005. Retrieved June 10, 2005, from http://atlanta .bizjournals.com/atlanta/ stories /2005/05/30/ smallb7.html. For more information, go to: http://www.eeoc.gov/.

a. Title VII of the Civil Rights Act of 1964 makes discrimination based on race, color, religion, sex, and natural origin, illegal. It applies to employers with 15 or more employees. Before a plaintiff can file a lawsuit, he or she must file a charge with the Equal Employment Opportunity Commission within 180 days of the discriminatory act. The EEOC will conduct an initial investigation and will attempt to reconcile the parties. If the EEOC decides not to sue, it will issue a right-to-sue letter, giving the complaining party 90 days to file a lawsuit on her own. A charging party can request the EEOC to issue a right-to-sue letter 180 days after filing the charge with the EEOC.

b. The Americans with Disabilities Act of 1990 prohibits discrimination against the disabled. It applies to employers with 15 or more employees. "Disability" is broadly defined. The same EEOC procedures must be followed under this Act as with a Title VII action as discussed above.

c. The Age Discrimination in Employment Act of 1967 prohibits discrimination against employees who are more than 40 years old. It pertains to employers with 20 or more employees. The complainant must file a charge with the EEOC but can file a lawsuit after waiting only 60 days after filing with the EEOC.

d. The Civil Rights Act of 1866, 42 U.S.C. Section 1981, protects against racial discrimination. This statute does not require any filing with the EEOC and applies to all employers, regardless of number of employees. An employer's practice is illegal if it treats one protected group of employees more harshly than others, unless the employer can prove the practice was justified because of "business necessity." This Act allows for unlimited compensatory and punitive damages as well as reimbursement of legal expenses.

---

[55]J. Sheban, "Abercrombie & Fitch: The Face of Change," *Columbus Dispatch*, July 31, 2005, p. F1. Retrieved April 19, 2006, from ABI/Inform (ProQuest) database.

and minority recruiting events. Michael Jeffries issued a statement: "We have, and always have had, no tolerance for discrimination. We decided to settle this suit because we felt that a long, drawn-out dispute would have been harmful to the company and distracting to management."[56]

Todd Corley became A&F's new vice president of diversity. Due to his efforts, A&F established a $300,000 grant for scholarships for the United Negro College Fund, became a sponsor of the Organization of Chinese Americans' College Leadership Summit, became a sponsor of the National Black MBA Association, and offered internships for minority college juniors seeking retail-management careers through Inroads, Incorporated.

A&F'S FUTURE

Looking ahead, A&F was likely to face increased competition. One of its direct rivals, American Eagle Outfitters, was able to outperform A&F in terms of profitability and assume the number 1 rank (compared to A&F's third rank) among U.S. publicly traded apparel companies in 2007 as listed by *Apparel Magazine*. Newcomers to the specialty apparel industry, as well as large department stores, sought to imitate A&F's product offerings. Metropark, for example, a West Coast chain for 20- to 35-year-old shoppers, opened its 15th store in Atlanta, Georgia. It planned to open an additional 50 stores by 2007. The retailer sold brand name casual apparel made by such designers as True Religion and Joe's Jeans. It also tried to create a night club-like atmosphere in its stores with flat screen televisions playing music videos and a lounge offering energy drinks and magazines.

Department stores, too, began to diversify their lines by stocking merchandise from new suppliers and by promoting their own in-house labels. Oved Apparel launched Company 81 in 2005 as "an Abercrombie for department stores."[57] It began to sell distressed denim, chinos, shorts, golf jackets, blazers, and graphic T-shirts at the wholesale level. It provided department stores with in-store signage and imagery from its advertising campaign to complement its merchandise. Federated Department stores, which operated Macy's and Bloomingdales, created an in-house label called, "American Rag." Its merchandise was similar in style to A&F's but priced more moderately.

As if sensing the encroachment of competitors, A&F began an unusual effort to improve its customer service. In the past, brand representatives acted more like models than salespeople. They were known for their snobbish disregard of shoppers. They did not talk to customers until they were within five feet of each other.[58] Some customers felt intimidated. Under COO Singer, store greeters were positioned in the entrance to each store and salespeople were posted in every section. A vice president of training was hired to work with store staff. The number of employees was increased and hours of store operations were extended. The added attention helped reduce shrink of merchandise.[59] Nonetheless, progress in customer service may have been derailed by the departure of Singer from the company.

A&F also needed to be ever vigilant regarding the needs and preferences of its target markets. Teenagers were perceived as being fickle. According to experts on the reactions of millenials to pop culture, they were difficult to influence because they thought more

---

[56]S. Greenhouse, "Abercrombie & Fitch Bias Case is Settled," *The New York Times*, November 17, 2004, p. A16. Retrieved May 24, 2006, from ABI/Inform (ProQuest) database.

[57]L. Bailey, "The New South: Young Men's & Streetwear," *DNR* 35 (August 22, 2005), p. 94. Retrieved June 1, 2006, from ABI/Inform (ProQuest) database.

[58]Paynter, "Don't Hate."

[59]S. Kang, "Style and Substance: Abercrombie & Fitch Tries to Be Less Haughty," *The Wall Street Journal*, June 17, 2005, p. B1. Retrieved June 23, 2005, from ABI/Inform (ProQuest) database.

independently and changed their minds more frequently than previous generations. They would find the "emphasis on the physicality of models" in A&F advertisements unappealing.[60] The emerging trend towards ethical consumption was also something to be watched. Young people began to purchase food products and clothing with "Fair Trade" labels. They were committed, for example, to purchasing coffee that was organically grown from suppliers who paid bean pickers higher wages than the going rate. They bought T-shirts that were not made in overseas sweatshops.

The challenges for A&F executives in 2007 and beyond were to anticipate competitor moves, to improve customer service, and to maintain consumer loyalty. They needed to hire talented top managers who could work well alongside CEO Jeffries. These domestic imperatives came at a critical time for the retailer. It was about to expand further into the European and Asian markets by opening stores in Italy, France, Germany, Spain, Denmark, Sweden and Japan. Pamela Quintiliano, a WR Hambrecht retail analyst, gave the expansion plan a nod of approval: "Abercrombie is an incredibly strong brand name, and there's a hunger for American brands around the world."[61]

[60]V. Seckler, "Brands' Challenge: Bridging Gap with Young People," *WWD* 77 (April 12, 2006). Retrieved June 1, 2006, from ABI/Inform (ProQuest) database.
[61]Sheban, "Oh Canada!"

Strategic
Marketing Cases

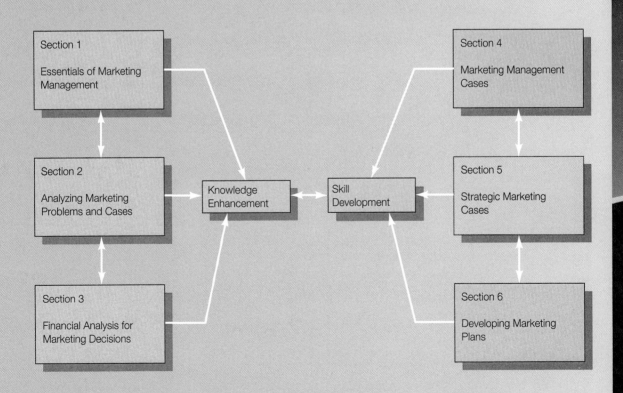

NOTE TO THE STUDENT

The cases in this section emphasize the role of marketing in developing successful business or organizational strategies. While marketing is critical in these cases, successful analysis and strategy formulation will often involve other areas in the organization as well.

The knowledge and skills you've developed in the analysis of the cases in the previous section provide a useful foundation for analyzing the cases in this section. However, these cases are intended to broaden your knowledge of marketing and your skills at analyzing various strategic problems.

Case 1

Yum! Brands, Pizza Hut, and KFC

Jeffrey A. Krug *Appalachian State University*

Yum! Brands, Inc., was the world's largest fast-food company in 2004. It operated more than 33,000 KFC, Pizza Hut, Taco Bell, Long John Silver's, and A&W restaurants worldwide. It was the market leader in the chicken, pizza, Mexican, and seafood segments of the U.S. fast-food industry. Yum! Brands also operated more than 12,000 restaurants outside the United States. KFC and Pizza Hut accounted for more than 96 percent of the company's international restaurant base and managed restaurants in 116 countries. Among the first fast-food chains to go international in the late 1950s and 1960s, KFC and Pizza Hut were two of the world's most recognizable brands. Both KFC and Pizza Hut expanded through the 1990s by growing their restaurants into as many countries as possible. However, Yum! Brands realized that different countries offered different opportunities to contribute to the company's worldwide operating profits.

By 2004 Yum! Brands began to focus more attention on portfolio management in individual countries. It increasingly focused its international strategy on developing strong market share positions in a small number of high-growth markets such as Japan, Canada, the United Kingdom, China, Australia, Korea, and Mexico. It also hoped to build strong positions in continental Europe, Brazil, and India. Consumer awareness in these markets, however, was still low and neither KFC nor Pizza Hut had strong operating capabilities there. China and India were appealing markets because of their large populations. From a regional point-of-view, Latin America was appealing because of its close proximity to the United States, language and cultural similarities, and the potential for a future World Free Trade Area of the Americas, which would eliminate tariffs on trade within North and South America. The most important long-term challenge for Yum! Brands was to strengthen its position in a set of core international markets while also developing new markets where consumer awareness and operating capabilities were weak.

COMPANY HISTORY

Kentucky Fried Chicken Corporation

Fast-food franchising was still in its infancy in 1952 when Harland Sanders began his travels across the United States to speak with prospective franchisees about his "Colonel Sanders Recipe Kentucky Fried Chicken." By 1960, "Colonel" Sanders had granted Kentucky Fried Chicken (KFC) franchises to more than 200 take-home retail outlets and restaurants across the United States. Four years later, at the age of 74, he sold KFC to two Louisville businessmen for $2 million. In 1966 KFC went public and was listed on the New York Stock Exchange. In 1971 Heublein, Inc., a distributor of wine and alcoholic beverages, successfully approached KFC with an offer and merged KFC into a subsidiary. Eleven years later, R.J. Reynolds Industries, Inc., (RJR) acquired Heublein and merged it into a wholly owned subsidiary. The acquisition of Heublein was part of RJR's corporate strategy of diversifying into unrelated businesses such as energy, transportation, food, and restaurants to reduce its dependence on the tobacco industry. In 1985 RJR acquired Nabisco Corporation in an attempt to redefine RJR as a world leader in the consumer foods industry. As RJR refocused its strategy on processed foods, it decided to exit the restaurant industry. It sold KFC to PepsiCo, Inc., one year later.

Pizza Hut

In 1958, two students at Wichita State University—Frank and Dan Carney—decided to open a pizza restaurant in an old building at a busy intersection in downtown Wichita. To finance their new business, they borrowed $500 from their mother. They called the restaurant the "Pizza Hut," a reference to the old tavern beside the market that they renovated to open the new business. They opened four more restaurants during the next two years. The Pizza Hut concept was so well received by consumers that they were soon licensing the concept to franchises. By 1972, the Carneys had opened 1,000 restaurants and listed the firm on the New York Stock Exchange. In less than 15 years, Pizza Hut had become the number 1 pizza restaurant chain in the world in terms of sales and number of units. Internationally, Pizza Hut opened its first restaurant in Canada in 1968 and soon established franchises in Mexico, Germany, Australia, Costa Rica, Japan, and the United Kingdom. In 1977 it sold the business to PepsiCo, Inc. Pizza Hut's headquarters remained in Wichita and Frank Carney served as Pizza Hut's president until 1980. (It is interesting to note that Frank opened a Papa John's Pizza franchise in 1994. Today he is one of Papa John's largest franchisees.)

PepsiCo, Inc.

PepsiCo believed the restaurant business complemented its consumer product orientation. The marketing of fast food followed many of the same patterns as soft drinks and snack foods. Pepsi-Cola and Pizza Hut pizza, for example, could be marketed in the same television and radio segments, which provided higher returns for each advertising dollar. Restaurant chains also provided an additional outlet for the sale of Pepsi soft drinks. In 1978, PepsiCo acquired Taco Bell. After acquiring KFC in 1986, PepsiCo controlled the leading brands in the pizza, Mexican, and chicken segments of the fast-food industry. PepsiCo's strategy of diversifying into three distinct but related markets created one of the world's largest food companies.

In the early 1990s, PepsiCo's sales grew at an annual rate of more than 10 percent. Its rapid growth, however, masked troubles in its fast-food businesses. Operating margins at Pepsi-Cola and PepsiCo's Frito-Lay division averaged 12 and 17 percent, respectively. Margins at KFC, Pizza Hut, and Taco Bell, however, fell from an average of 8 percent in 1990 to 4 percent in 1996. Declining margins reflected increasing maturity in the U.S. fast-food industry, intense competition, and the aging of KFC and Pizza Hut restaurants. PepsiCo's restaurant chains absorbed nearly one-half of PepsiCo's annual capital spending but generated less than one-third of its cash flows. Cash had to be diverted from PepsiCo's soft drink and snack food businesses to its restaurant businesses. This reduced PepsiCo's corporate return on assets, made it more difficult to compete effectively with Coca-Cola, and hurt its stock price. In 1997 PepsiCo decided to spin off its restaurant businesses into a new company called Tricon Global Restaurants, Inc.

Yum! Brands, Inc.

The spin-off created a new, independent, publicly traded company that managed the KFC, Pizza Hut, and Taco Bell franchises. David Novak became Tricon's new CEO. He moved quickly to create a new culture within the company. One of his primary objectives was to reverse the long-standing friction between management and franchisees that was created under PepsiCo ownership. Novak announced that PepsiCo's top-down management system would be replaced by a new management emphasis on providing support to the firm's franchise base. Franchises would have greater independence, resources, and technical support. Novak symbolically changed the name on the corporate headquarters building in Louisville to "KFC Support Center" to drive home his new philosophy.

The firm's new emphasis on franchise support had an immediate effect on morale. In 1997, the year of the divestiture, the company recorded a loss of $111 million in net income. In 2003, it recorded a net income of $617 million on sales of $7.4 billion, a return on sales of 8.3 percent. In 2002, Tricon acquired Long John Silver's and A&W All-American Food Restaurants. The acquisitions increased Tricon's worldwide system to almost 33,000 units. One week later, shareholders approved a corporate name change to Yum! Brands, Inc. (Exhibit 1). The acquisitions signaled a shift in the company's strategy from a focus on individual to multibranded units. Multibranding combined two brands in a single

EXHIBIT 1   Yum! Brands, Inc.: Organizational Chart, 2004

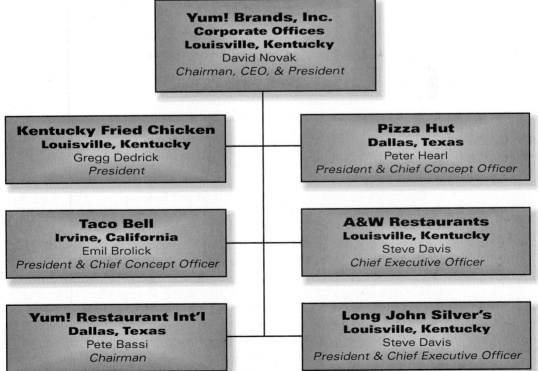

restaurant such as KFC and Taco Bell, KFC and A&W, Pizza Hut and Taco Bell, and Pizza Hut and Long John Silver's. Multibranded units attracted a larger consumer base by offering them a broader menu selection in one location. By 2004 the company was operating more than 2,400 multibrand restaurants in the United States.

FAST-FOOD INDUSTRY

The National Restaurant Association (NRA) estimated that U.S. food service sales increased by 3.3 percent to $422 billion in 2003. More than 858,000 restaurants made up the U.S. restaurant industry and employed 12 million people. Sales were highest in the full-service, sit-down sector, which grew 3.3 percent to $151 billion. Fast-food sales rose at a slower rate, 2.7 percent to $119 billion. The fast-food sector was increasingly viewed as a mature market. As U.S. incomes rose during the late 1990s and early 2000s, more consumers frequented sit-down restaurants that offered better service and a more comfortable dining experience. Together, the full-service and fast-food segments made up about 64 percent of all U.S. food service sales.

Major Fast-Food Segments

Eight major segments made up the fast-food segment of the restaurant industry: sandwich chains, pizza chains, family restaurants, grill buffet chains, dinner houses, chicken chains, nondinner concepts, and other chains. Sales data for the leading chains in each segment are shown in Exhibit 2. Most striking is the dominance of McDonald's, which had sales of more than $22 billion in 2003. McDonald's accounted for 14 percent of the sales of the top 100 chains. To put McDonald's dominance in perspective, the second largest chain—Burger King—held less than a 5 percent share of the market.

Sandwich chains made up the largest segment of the fast-food market. McDonald's controlled 35 percent of this segment, while Burger King ran a distant second with a 12 percent share. Sandwich chains struggled through early 2003 as the U.S. recession lowered demand and the war in Iraq increased consumer uncertainty. U.S. consumers were also trending away from the traditional hamburger, fries, and soft drink combinations and demanding more healthy food items and better service. Many chains attempted to attract new customers through price discounting. Instead of drawing in new customers, however, discounting merely lowered profit margins. By mid-2003 most chains had abandoned price discounting and began to focus on improved service and product quality. McDonald's, Taco Bell, and Hardee's were particularly successful. They slowed new restaurant development, improved drive-through service, and introduced a variety of new menu items. McDonald's and Hardee's, for example, introduced larger, higher-priced hamburgers to increase value perceptions and ticket prices. The shift from price discounting to new product introductions increased average ticket sales and helped sandwich chains improve profitability in 2004.

Dinner houses made up the second-largest and fastest-growing fast-food segment. Segment sales increased by almost 9.0 percent in 2003, surpassing the average increase of 5.5 percent in the other segments. Much of the growth in dinner houses came from new unit construction in suburban areas and small towns. Applebee's, Chili's, Outback Steakhouse, Red Lobster, and Olive Garden dominated the segment. Each chain generated sales of more than $2 billion in 2003. The fastest-growing dinner houses, however, were newer chains generating less than $700 million in sales, such as P. F. Chang's China Bistro, the Cheesecake Factory, Carrabba's Italian Grill, and LongHorn Steakhouse. Each chain was increasing sales at a 20 percent annual rate. Dinner houses continued to benefit from rising household incomes in the United States. As incomes rose, families were able to move up from quick-service restaurants to more upscale, higher-priced dinner houses. In addition, higher incomes enabled many professionals to purchase more expensive homes in new

EXHIBIT 2 Top U.S. Fast-Food Restaurants (Ranked by 2003 sales, $ millions)

Sandwich Chains	Sales	Change	Dinner Houses	Sales	Change
McDonald's	$22,121	8.9%	Applebee's	$ 3,520	10.6%
Burger King	7,680	−2.8	Chili's	2,505	11.8
Wendy's	7,315	5.2	Outback Steakhouse	2,456	7.1
Subway	5,690	8.8	Red Lobster	2,315	−1.9
Taco Bell	5,346	2.8	Olive Garden	2,165	11.6
Arby's	2,710	0.6	TGI Friday's	1,791	2.6
Jack in the Box	2,360	5.4	Ruby Tuesday	1,450	14.8
Sonic Drive-In	2,359	7.0	Romano's	699	9.4
Dairy Queen	2,165	−1.1	Cheesecake Factory	689	20.6
Hardee's	1,662	−2.3	Hooter's	670	6.5
Other Chains	3,934	9.4	Other Chains	5,277	10.7
Total Segment	**$63,342**	**5.2%**	**Total Segment**	**$23,537**	**8.8%**
Pizza Chains			**Chicken Chains**		
Pizza Hut	$ 5,033	−1.3%	KFC	$ 4,936	2.8%
Domino's	3,003	2.6	Chick-fil-A	1,534	11.8
Papa John's	1,719	−2.4	Popeyes	1,274	1.6
Little Caesars	1,200	4.3	Church's	700	−2.5
Chuck E. Cheese's	476	3.5	Boston Market	646	0.8
CiCi's Pizza	380	13.9	El Pollo Loco	396	8.7
Round Table Pizza	378	1.1	Bojangles'	375	8.0
Total Segment	**$12,189**	**0.7%**	**Total Segment**	**$ 9,861**	**3.8%**
Family Restaurants			**Other Dinner Chains**		
Denny's	$ 2,132	0.6%	Panera Bread	$ 908	32.0%
IHOP	1,676	14.7	Long John Silver's	777	2.8
Cracker Barrel	1,480	5.3	Disney Theme Parks	707	0.4
Bob Evans	954	9.0	Old Country Buffet	548	−4.5
Waffle House	789	2.7	Captain D's Seafood	506	1.7
Perkins	787	−1.3	**Total Segment**	**$ 3,446**	**7.0%**
Other Chains	2,162	1.2	**Nondinner Concepts**		
Total Segment	**$ 9,980**	**4.3%**	Starbucks	$ 3,118	25.8%
Grill Buffet Chains			Dunkin' Donuts	2,975	10.2
Golden Corral	$ 1,247	7.8%	7-Eleven	1,410	5.6
Ryan's	814	0.2	Krispy Kreme	957	24.0
Ponderosa	537	−2.1	Baskin-Robbins	510	−2.5
Total Segment	**$ 2,598**	**3.2%**	**Total Segment**	**$ 8,970**	**14.9%**

Source: *Nation's Restaurant News*. Sales rankings for contract and hotel chains not included.

suburban developments, thereby providing additional opportunities for dinner houses to build new restaurants in unsaturated areas.

Increased growth among dinner houses came at the expense of sandwich chains, pizza and chicken chains, grill buffet chains, and family restaurants. "Too many restaurants chasing the same customers" was responsible for much of the slower growth in these other fast-food categories. Sales growth within each segment, however, differed from one chain to another. In the family segment, for example, Denny's (the segment leader in sales), Shoney's, Perkins, and Big Boy shut down poorly performing restaurants. At the same time, IHOP, Bob Evans, and Cracker Barrel expanded their bases. The hardest-hit segment was grill buffet chains. Declining sales caused both Sizzlin' and Western Sizzlin' to drop out of the list of Top 100 chains, leaving only three chains in the Top 100 (Golden Corral, Ryan's,

EXHIBIT 3

Leading Pizza, Chicken, and Sandwich Chains, 2003

Source: *Nation's Restaurant News.*

PIZZA CHAINS	Sales ($ millions)	Growth Rate (%)	Units	Growth Rate (%)	Sales per Unit ($000s)
Pizza Hut	$ 5,033.0	(1.3)%	7,523	(1.0)%	$ 665.7
Domino's Pizza	3,003.4	2.6	4,904	1.2	616.0
Papa John's Pizza	1,718.5	(2.4)	3,035	(0.4)	661.5
Little Caesars Pizza	1,200.0	4.4	2,593	(0.2)	395.1
Chuck E. Cheese's	476.2	3.5	485	5.1	1,070.1
CiCi's Pizza	380.4	13.9	465	11.5	862.6
Round Table Pizza	378.4	1.1	456	(5.6)	757.6
Total	$12,189.9	3.1%	19,461	1.5%	$718.3
CHICKEN CHAINS					
KFC	$ 4,936.0	2.8%	5,524	1.0%	$ 897.8
Chick-fil-A	1,534.4	11.8	1,235	4.9	1,394.3
Popeyes Chicken	1,274.0	1.6	1,447	3.8	896.9
Church's Chicken	700.0	(2.5)	1,235	(1.0)	564.1
Boston Market	646.0	0.8	630	(3.1)	1,009.4
El Pollo Loco	395.7	8.7	314	2.6	1,276.5
Bojangles'	374.8	8.0	320	9.6	1,224.8
Total	$ 9,860.9	4.5%	10,705	2.6%	$1,037.7
SANDWICH CHAINS					
McDonald's	$22,121.4	8.9%	13,609	0.9%	$1,632.6
Burger King	7,680.0	(2.8)	7,656	(3.1)	987.1
Wendy's	7,315.0	5.2	5,761	3.8	1,293.5
Subway	5,690.0	8.8	16,499	13.6	366.8
Taco Bell	5,346.0	2.8	5,989	(2.9)	879.7
Arby's	2,710.0	0.6	3,303	1.6	827.1
Jack in the Box	2,360.0	5.4	1,947	4.6	1,239.2
Total	$53,222.4	4.1%	54,764	2.6%	$1,032.3
Long John Silver's	777.0	2.8	1,204	(1.4)	640.8
A&W Restaurants	200.0	NA	576	(13.4)	NA
Yum! Brands Total	16,292.0	NA	20,822	(1.4)	NA

Note: Sales per unit are calculated based on a mathematical equation of annual systemwide sales growth and changes in the number of operating units.

and Ponderosa). Each of these three chains shut down restaurants in 2003. Dinner houses, because of their more upscale atmosphere and higher-ticket items, were better positioned to take advantage of the aging and wealthier U.S. population.

Yum! Brands: Brand Leadership

Exhibit 3 shows sales and restaurant data for the pizza, chicken, and sandwich segments. Yum! Brands generated U.S. sales of $16.3 billion across its five brands. It operated close to 21,000 U.S. and 12,000 non-U.S. restaurants, or more than 33,000 restaurants worldwide. Four of its brands—Pizza Hut (pizza), KFC (chicken), Taco Bell (Mexican), and Long John Silver's (seafood)—were the market leaders in their segments. Taco Bell was the third most profitable restaurant concept behind McDonald's and Starbucks. Profitability at McDonald's was primarily driven by volume; each McDonald's restaurant generated an annual average of $1.6 million in sales compared to an industrywide average of $1.0 million. Starbucks, in contrast, generated less revenue per store—about $660 million each year—but premium pricing for its specialty coffee drinks drove high profit margins. Taco Bell was able to generate greater overall profits because of its lower operating costs. Products such as tacos, burritos, gorditas, and chalupas used similar ingredients. In addition, cooking machinery was simpler, less costly, and required less space than pizza ovens or chicken broilers.

Pizza Hut controlled the pizza segment with a 41 percent share, followed by Domino's (25 percent) and Papa John's (14 percent). As the pizza segment became increasingly mature, the traditional pizza chains were forced to close old or underperforming restaurants. Only relatively new pizza chain concepts such as CiCi's Pizza, which offered an inexpensive all-you-can-eat salad and pizza buffet, and Chuck E. Cheese's, which focused on family entertainment, were able to significantly grow their restaurant bases during 2003. Most chains could no longer rely on new restaurant construction to drive sales. Another problem was the proliferation of new diets. Many Americans were eating pizza less often as they pursued the Atkins Diet (low carbohydrates), "The Zone" (balanced meals containing equal parts of carbohydrates, protein, and unsaturated fat), or a traditional low-fat diet. Each diet discouraged users from eating pizza, which was high in both fat and carbohydrates.

Operating costs were also rising because of higher cheese and gasoline prices. Pizza chains were forced to develop unique strategies that attracted more customers but protected profit margins. Some chains raised pizza prices to offset higher-priced ingredients or raised home delivery charges to offset higher gasoline costs. Most chains, however, responded with new product introductions. Pizza Hut introduced a low-fat "Fit 'n Delicious" pizza that used one-half the cheese of normal pizzas and toppings with lower fat content. It also introduced a "4forAll" pizza that contained four individually topped six-inch square pizzas in the same box. Domino's introduced a Philly cheese steak pizza, its first new product introduction since 2000. Papa John's introduced a new barbeque chicken and bacon pizza. In addition, it began a campaign that allowed customers to choose one of three free DVDs with the purchase of a large pizza. By matching pizza and movies, Papa John's hoped to encourage customers to eat pizza more often. Pizza Hut quickly responded with its own offer for a free DVD with the purchase of any pizza at the regular price.

KFC continued to dominate the chicken segment with sales of $4.9 billion in 2003, more than 50 percent of sales in the chicken segment. Its nearest competitor, Chick-fil-A, ran a distant second with sales of $1.5 billion. KFC's leadership in the U.S. market was so extensive that it had fewer opportunities to expand its U.S. restaurant base. Despite its dominance, KFC was slowly losing market share as other chicken chains increased sales at a faster rate. Sales data indicated that KFC's share of the chicken segment fell from a high of 64 percent in 1993, a 10-year drop of 14 percent. During the same period, Chick-fil-A and Boston Market increased their combined share by 11 percent. On the surface, it appeared that these market share gains came by taking customers away from KFC. The growth in sales at KFC restaurants, however, had generally remained steady during the last two decades. In reality, the three chains competed for different market groups. Boston Market, for example, appealed to professionals with higher incomes and health-conscious consumers who didn't regularly frequent KFC. It expanded the chicken segment by offering healthy, "home-style" alternatives to nonfried chicken in a setting resembling an upscale deli. Chick-fil-A concentrated on chicken sandwiches rather than fried chicken and most of its restaurants were still located in shopping mall food courts.

The maturity of the U.S. fast-food industry intensified competition within the chicken segment. As in the pizza segment, chicken chains could not rely on new restaurant construction to build new sales. In addition, chicken costs, which represented about one-half of total food costs, increased dramatically in 2004. A boneless chicken breast, which cost $1.20 per pound in early 2001, cost $2.50 per pound in 2004, an increase of more than 100 percent. Profit margins were being squeezed from both the revenue and cost sides. All chains focused on very different strategies. KFC added new menu boards and introduced new products such as oven roasted strips and roasted twister sandwich wraps. Boston Market experimented with home delivery and began to sell through supermarkets. Chick-fil-A continued to build freestanding restaurants to expand beyond shopping malls. Church's focused on adding drive-through service. The intensity of competition led chicken chains to implement very different strategies for differentiating their product and brand.

TRENDS IN THE RESTAURANT INDUSTRY

A number of demographic and societal trends influenced the demand for food eaten outside the home. Rising income, greater affluence among a larger percentage of American households, higher divorce rates, and the marriage of people later in life contributed to the rising number of single households and the demand for fast food. More than 50 percent of women worked outside the home, a dramatic increase since 1970. This number was expected to rise to 65 percent by 2010. Double-income households contributed to rising household incomes and increased the number of times families ate out. Less time to prepare meals inside the home added to this trend. Countering these trends, however, was the slower growth rate of the U.S. population and a proliferation of fast-food chains that increased consumer alternatives and intensified competition.

Baby boomers (ages 35 to 50) constituted the largest consumer group for fast-food restaurants. Generation Xers (ages 25 to 34) and the "mature" category (ages 51 to 64) made up the second and third largest groups, respectively. As consumers aged, they became less enamored of fast food and were more likely to trade up to more expensive restaurants such as dinner houses and full-service restaurants. Sales for many Mexican restaurants, which were extremely popular during the 1980s, began to slow as Japanese, Indian, and Vietnamese restaurants became more fashionable. Ethnic foods were rising in popularity as U.S. immigrants, who constituted 13 percent of the U.S. population in 2004, looked for establishments that sold their native foods.

Labor was the top operational challenge of U.S. restaurant chains. Restaurants relied heavily on teenagers and college-age workers. Twenty percent of all employed teenagers worked in food service, compared to only 4 percent of all employed men over the age of 18 and 6 percent of all employed women over age 18. As the U.S. population aged, fewer young workers were available to fill food service jobs. The short supply of high school and college students meant they had greater work opportunities outside food service. Turnover rates were notoriously high. The National Restaurant Association estimated that about 96 percent of all fast-food workers quit within a year, compared to about 84 percent of employees in full-service restaurants.

Labor costs made up about 30 percent of a fast-food chain's total costs, second only to food and beverage costs. To deal with the decreased supply of employees in the age 16 to 24 category, many restaurants were forced to hire less reliable workers. This affected service and restaurant cleanliness. To improve quality and service, restaurants hired elderly employees who wanted to return to the workforce. To attract more workers, especially the elderly, restaurants offered health insurance, noncontributory pension plans, and profit-sharing benefits. To combat high turnover rates, restaurants turned to training programs and mentoring systems that paired new employees with experienced ones. Mentoring systems were particularly helpful in increasing the learning curve of new workers and providing better camaraderie among employees.

THE GLOBAL FAST-FOOD INDUSTRY

As the U.S. market matured, more restaurants turned to international markets to expand sales. Foreign markets were attractive because of their large customer bases and comparatively little competition. McDonald's, for example, operated 48 restaurants for every one million U.S. residents. Outside the United States, it operated only one restaurant for every

EXHIBIT 4   The World's 35 Largest Fast-Food Chains in 2004

Franchise	Corporate Headquarters	Home Country	Number of Countries with Operations
1. McDonald's	Oak Brook, Illinois	U.S.	121
2. KFC	Louisville, Kentucky	U.S.	99
3. Pizza Hut	Dallas, Texas	U.S.	92
4. Subway Sandwiches	Milford, Connecticut	U.S.	74
5. TCBY	Little Rock, Arkansas	U.S.	67
6. Domino's Pizza	Ann Arbor, Michigan	U.S.	65
7. Burger King	Miami, Florida	U.S.	58
8. TGI Friday's	Dallas, Texas	U.S.	53
9. Baskin-Robbins	Glendale, California	U.S.	52
10. Dunkin' Donuts	Randolph, Massachusetts	U.S.	40
11. Wendy's	Dublin, Ohio	U.S.	34
12. Chili's Grill & Bar	Dallas, Texas	U.S.	22
13. Dairy Queen	Edina, Minnesota	U.S.	22
14. Little Caesars Pizza	Detroit, Michigan	U.S.	22
15. Popeyes	Atlanta, Georgia	U.S.	22
16. Outback Steakhouse	Tampa, Florida	U.S.	20
17. A&W Restaurants	Lexington, Kentucky	U.S.	17
18. PizzaExpress	London	U.K.	16
19. Carl's Jr.	Anaheim, California	U.S.	14
20. Church's Chicken	Atlanta, Georgia	U.S.	12
21. Taco Bell	Irvine, California	U.S.	12
22. Hardee's	Rocky Mount, North Carolina	U.S.	11
23. Applebee's	Overland Park, Kansas	U.S.	9
24. Sizzler	Los Angeles, California	U.S.	9
25. Arby's	Ft. Lauderdale, Florida	U.S.	7
26. Denny's	Spartanburg, South Carolina	U.S.	7
27. Skylark	Tokyo	Japan	7
28. Lotteria	Seoul	Korea	5
29. Taco Time	Eugene, Oregon	U.S.	5
30. Mos Burger	Tokyo	Japan	4
31. Orange Julius	Edina, Minnesota	U.S.	4
32. Yoshinoya	Tokyo	Japan	4
33. IHOP	Glendale, California	U.S.	3
34. Quick Restaurants	Brussels	Belgium	3
35. Red Lobster	Orlando, Florida	U.S.	3

Source: Case author's research.

five million residents. McDonald's, Pizza Hut, KFC, and Burger King were the earliest and most aggressive chains to expand abroad beginning in the 1960s. This made them formidable competitors for chains investing abroad for the first time. Subway, TCBY, and Domino's were more recent global competitors. By 2004 each was operating in more than 65 countries. Exhibit 4 lists the world's 35 largest restaurant chains.

The global fast-food industry had a distinctly American flavor. Twenty-eight chains (80 percent of the total) were headquartered in the United States. U.S. chains had the advantage of a large domestic market and ready acceptance by the American consumer. European firms had less success developing the fast-food concept because Europeans were more inclined to frequent midscale restaurants where they spent several hours enjoying multicourse meals in a formal setting. KFC had trouble breaking into the German market during the 1970s and 1980s because Germans were not accustomed to buying takeout or

EXHIBIT 5

Yum! Brands, Inc.—
Largest International
Markets, 2004

Source: Yum! Brands, Inc.

	KFC	Pizza Hut	Taco Bell	Long John Silver's	A&W	Yum! Brands
			Number of Restaurants			
United States	5,524	7,523	5,989	1,207	579	20,822
International	7,354	4,560	249	31	183	12,377
Worldwide	12,878	12,083	6,238	1,238	762	33,199
International Total (%)	57.1%	37.7%	4.0%	2.5%	24.0%	37.3%
TOP FOREIGN MARKETS						
1. Japan	1,167	327	24			1,518
2. Canada	733	353	84			1,170
3. U.K.	591	556				1,147
4. China	979	127	1			1,107
5. Australia	516	319	7			842
6. Korea	209	299				508
7. Malaysia	329	106	32	6	26	499
8. Mexico	309	180	1		1	491
9. Thailand	299	77	28		28	432
10. Indonesia	198	85	69		74	426
11. South Africa	360	3				363
12. Philippines	128	113	6		6	253
OTHER LATIN AMERICA						
Puerto Rico	95	60	32			187
Ecuador	45	20	4			69
Costa Rica	15	41	11			67
Brazil	3	63				66
Chile	30	28				58
OTHER ASIA						
Taiwan	132	111				242
Singapore	73	34	24	24		155
OTHER SELECTED MARKETS						
France	24	126				150
Germany	45	77				122
Saudi Arabia	50	92	9		9	160
India	2	65				67

ordering food over the counter. McDonald's had greater success in Germany because it made changes to its menu and operating procedures to appeal to German tastes. German beer, for example, was served in all of McDonald's restaurants in Germany. In France, McDonald's used a different sauce that appealed to the French palate on its Big Mac sandwich. KFC had more success in Asia and Latin America where chicken was a traditional dish.

Yum! Brands operated more than 12,000 restaurants outside the United States (see Exhibit 5). The early international experience of KFC and Pizza Hut put them in a strong position to exploit the globalization trend in the industry. A separate subsidiary in Dallas— Yum! Brands International—managed the international activities of all five brands. As a result, the firm had significant international experience concentrated in one location and a well-established worldwide distribution network. KFC and Pizza Hut accounted for almost all of the firm's international restaurants. Yum! Brands planned to open 1,000 new KFC and

Pizza Hut restaurants outside the United States each year, well into the future. This came at a time when both KFC and Pizza Hut were closing units in the mature U.S. market.

Of the KFC and Pizza Hut restaurants located outside the United States, 77 percent were owned by local franchisees or joint venture partners who had a deep understanding of local language, culture, customs, law, financial markets, and marketing characteristics. Franchising allowed firms to expand more quickly, minimize capital expenditures, and maximize return on invested capital. It was also a good strategy for establishing a presence in smaller markets like Grenada, Bermuda, and Suriname where the small number of consumers only allowed for a single restaurant. The costs of operating company-owned restaurants were prohibitively high in these markets. In larger markets such as China, Canada, Australia, and Mexico, there was a stronger emphasis on building company-owned restaurants. Fixed costs could be spread over a larger number of units and the company could coordinate purchasing, recruiting, training, financing, and advertising. This reduced per unit costs. Company-owned restaurants also allowed the company to maintain tighter control over product quality and customer service.

COUNTRY EVALUATION AND RISK ASSESSMENT

International Business Risk

Worldwide demand for fast food was expected to grow rapidly during the next two decades as rising per capita income made eating out more affordable for greater numbers of consumers. International business, however, carried a variety of risks not present in the domestic market. Long distances between headquarters and foreign franchises made it more difficult to control the quality of individual restaurants. Large distances also caused servicing and support problems, and transportation and other resource costs were higher. In addition, time, cultural, and language differences increased communication problems and made it more difficult to get timely and accurate information.

During the 1970s and 1980s, KFC and Pizza Hut attempted to expand their restaurant bases into as many countries as possible—the greater the number of countries, the greater the indicator of success. By the early years of the 21st century, however, it became apparent that serving a large number of markets with a small number of restaurants was a costly business. If a large number of restaurants could be established in a single market or region, then significant economies of scale could be achieved by spreading fixed costs of purchasing, advertising, and distribution across a larger restaurant base. Higher market share, as a result, was typically associated with greater cash flow and higher profitability.

Country analysis was an important part of the strategic decision-making process. Few companies had sufficient resources to invest everywhere simultaneously. Choices had to be made about when and where to invest scarce capital. Country selection models typically assessed countries on the basis of market size, growth rates, the number and type of competitors, government regulations, and economic and political stability. In an industry such as fast food, however, an analysis of economic and political variables was insufficient. As mentioned earlier, KFC had trouble establishing a presence in Germany because many consumers there didn't accept the fast-food concept. An analysis of Germany's large, stable economy would otherwise have indicated a potentially profitable market.

An important challenge for multinational firms was to accurately assess the risks of doing business in different countries and regions in order to make good choices about where to invest. A useful framework for analyzing international business risk was to separate risk into factors of country, industry, and firm. Country factors, for example, included risks associated with changes in a country's political and economic environment. These included political risk (e.g., war, revolution, changes in government, price controls, tariffs, and government regulations), economic risk (e.g., inflation, high interest rates, foreign exchange rate volatility, balance of trade movements, social unrest, riots, and terrorism), and natural risk (e.g., rainfall, hurricanes, earthquakes, and volcanic activity).

Industry factors addressed changes in industry structure that inhibited a firm's ability to compete successfully in its industry. These included supplier risk (e.g., changes in supplier quality and supplier power), product market risk (e.g., consumer tastes and the availability of substitute products), and competitive risk (e.g., rivalry among competitors, new market entrants, and new product innovations).

Last, firm factors examined a firm's ability to control its internal operations. They included labor risk (e.g., labor unrest, absenteeism, employee turnover, and labor strikes), supplier risk (e.g., raw material shortages and unpredictable price changes), trade secret risk (e.g., protection of trade secrets and intangible assets), credit risk (e.g., problems in collecting receivables), and behavioral risk (e.g., control over franchise operations, product quality and consistency, service quality, and restaurant cleanliness). Each of these factors—country, industry, and firm—had to be analyzed simultaneously to fully understand the costs and benefits of international investment.[1]

Country Risk Assessment in Latin America

Latin America is comprised of some 50 countries, island nations, and principalities that were settled by the Spanish, Portuguese, French, Dutch, and British during the 1500s and 1600s. Spanish is spoken in most countries, the most notable exception being Brazil where the official language is Portuguese. Despite commonalities in language, religion, and history, however, political and economic policies differ significantly from one country to another.

Mexico

Many U.S. companies considered Mexico to be one of the most attractive investment locations in Latin America in the 1990s. Its population of 105 million was more than one-third as large as the United States, and three times larger than Canada's population of 32 million. Prior to 1994, Mexico levied high tariffs on many goods imported from the United States. As a result, many U.S. consumers purchased less expensive products from Asia or Europe. In 1994 the North American Free Trade Agreement (NAFTA) was signed. NAFTA eliminated tariffs on goods traded between the United States, Canada, and Mexico. It created a trading bloc with a larger population and gross domestic product than the European Union. The elimination of tariffs led to an immediate increase in trade between Mexico and the United States. By 2004, 85 percent of Mexico's exports were purchased by U.S. consumers. In turn, 68 percent of Mexico's total imports came from the United States.

Most Mexicans (70 percent) lived in urban areas such as Mexico City, Guadalajara, and Monterrey. Mexico City's population of 18 million made it one of the most populated areas in Latin America. Many U.S. firms had operations in or around Mexico City. The fast-food industry was well developed in Mexico's cities. The leading U.S. fast-food chains already had significant restaurant bases in Mexico, most importantly KFC (274 restaurants), McDonald's (261), Pizza Hut (174), Burger King (154), and Subway (71). Mexican consumers readily accepted the fast-food concept. Chicken was also a staple product in Mexico and helped explain KFC's wide popularity. Mexico's large population and ready acceptance of fast-food represented a significant opportunity for fast-food chains. Competition, however, was intense.

---

[1]For an in-depth discussion of international business risk, see Kent D. Miller, "A Framework for Integrated Risk Management in International Business," *Journal of International Business Studies*, 21 (2): (1992), pp. 311–31.

Brazil

Brazil, with a population of 182 million, was the largest country in Latin America and the fifth largest country in the world. Its land base was almost as large as the United States and bordered 10 countries. It was the world's largest coffee producer and largest exporter of sugar and tobacco. In addition to its abundant natural resources and strong export position in agriculture, Brazil was a strong industrial power. Its major exports were airplanes, automobiles, and chemicals. Its gross domestic product of $1.3 trillion was larger than Mexico's and the largest in Latin America (see Exhibit 6). Some firms viewed Brazil as one of the most important emerging markets, along with China and India.

The fast-food industry in Brazil was less developed than in Mexico or the Caribbean. This was partly the result of the structure of the fast-food industry that was dominated by U.S. restaurant chains. U.S. chains expanded further away from their home base as they gained experience operating in Latin America. As firms gained a foothold in Mexico and Central America, it was a natural progression to move into South America. McDonald's understood the importance of Brazil. It opened its first restaurant in 1979 and by 2004 was operating 1,200 restaurants, ice-cream kiosks, and McCafés there. Many restaurant chains such as Burger King, Pizza Hut, and KFC built restaurants in Brazil in the early- to mid-1990s but eventually closed them because of poor sales. Like Germany, many Brazilians were not quick to accept the fast-food concept.

One problem facing U.S. fast-food chains was eating customs. Brazilians ate their big meal in the early afternoon. In the evening, it was customary to have a light meal such as soup or a small plate of pasta. Brazilians rarely ate food with their hands, preferring to eat with a knife and fork. This included food like pizza, which Americans typically ate with their hands. They also were not accustomed to eating sandwiches; if they did eat sandwiches, they wrapped the sandwich in a napkin. U.S. fast-food chains catered to a different kind of customer who wanted more than soup but less than a full sit-down meal. U.S. fast-food chains were more popular in larger cities such as São Paulo and Rio de Janeiro where business people were in a hurry. Food courts were well developed in Brazil's shopping malls but included sit-down as well as fast-food restaurants. U.S. restaurant chains were, therefore, faced with the challenge of changing the eating habits of Brazilians or convincing Brazilians of the attractiveness of fast-food, American style.

RISKS AND OPPORTUNITIES

Yum! Brands faced difficult decisions surrounding the design and implementation of an effective international strategy over the next 20 years. Its top seven markets generated more than 70 percent of its international profits. As a result, it planned to continue its aggressive investments in its primary markets. It was also important, however, to improve brand equity in other regions of the world such as continental Europe, Brazil, and India where consumer acceptance of fast food was still weak and the company had limited operational capabilities. Latin America as a region was of particular interest because of its geographic proximity to the United States, cultural similarities, and NAFTA. The company needed to sustain its leadership position in Mexico and the Caribbean but also looked to strengthen its position in countries such as Brazil, Venezuela, and Argentina. Limited resources and cash flow limited KFC's ability to aggressively expand in all countries simultaneously. Country evaluation and risk assessment would be an important tool for developing and implementing an effective international strategy.

EXHIBIT 6 Latin America: Selected Economic and Demographic Data

	United States	Canada	Mexico	Colombia	Venezuela	Peru	Brazil	Argentina	Chile
Population (millions)	290.3	32.2	104.9	41.7	24.7	28.4	182.0	38.7	15.7
Growth rate (%)	0.9%	0.9%	1.4%	1.6%	1.5%	1.6%	1.5%	1.1%	1.1%
Population Data: Origin									
European (non-French origin)	65.1%	43.0%	9.0%	20.0%	21.0%	15.0%	55.0%	97.0%	95.0%
European (French origin)		23.0%							
African	12.9%			4.0%	10.0%		6.0%		
Mixed African and European				14.0%		37.0%	38.0%		
Latin American (Hispanic)	12.0%								
Asian	4.2%	6.0%							
Amerindian or Alaskan native	1.5%	2.0%	30.0%	1.0%	2.0%	45.0%			3.0%
Mixed Amerindian and Spanish			60.0%	58.0%	67.0%				
Mixed African and Amerindian				3.0%					
Other	4.3%	26.0%	1.0%			3.0%	1.0%	3.0%	2.0%
Total	100.0%	100.0%	100.0%	100.0%	100.0%	100.0%	100.0%	100.0%	100.0%
GDP ($ billions)	$10,400	$ 923	$ 900	$ 268	$ 133	$ 132	$1,340	$ 391	$ 151
Per capita income (US$)	$37,600	$29,400	$9,000	$6,500	$5,500	$4,800	$7,600	$10,200	$10,000
Real GDP growth rate	2.5%	3.4%	1.0%	2.0%	–8.9%	4.8%	1.0%	–14.7%	1.8%
Inflation rate	1.6%	2.2%	6.4%	6.2%	31.2%	0.2%	8.3%	41.0%	2.5%
Unemployment rate	5.8%	7.6%	3.0%	17.4%	17.0%	9.4%	6.4%	21.5%	9.2%
Literacy rate	97.0%	97.0%	92.2%	92.5%	93.4%	90.9%	86.4%	97.0%	96.2%

Source: U.S. Central Intelligence Agency, *The World Factbook*, 2002. Demographic data is 2003 estimate; economic data as of year-end 2002.

Case

2

Apple Inc. in 2010

Lou Marino *The University of Alabama*

John E. Gamble *University of South Alabama*

Despite the effects of ongoing poor economic conditions in the United States, Apple Inc. celebrated record quarterly revenues and unit sales of computers during its third quarter of 2010. In addition, the company's newly released iPad tablet computer had sold 3.3 million units between its April 3, 2010, launch and the June 26, 2010, quarter end. The company also sold 8.4 million iPhones during the quarter. Most of the smartphone units sold during the third quarter of 2010 were iPhone 3GS models since the new iPhone 4 was launched only four days before the close of the quarter. Although there had been some criticism of the antenna design of the iPhone 4, more than 3 million iPhone 4 units had been purchased by July 16, 2010, with only 1.7 percent being returned by dissatisfied customers. By comparison, the iPhone 3GS had a 6 percent return rate.

Apple's Chief Executive Officer, Tim Cook, commented to the *Wall Street Journal* that the company was selling iPads and iPhones "as fast as we can make them" and was "working around the clock to try to get supply and demand in balance."[1] Some analysts were projecting that Apple would sell nearly 12 million iPad tablet computers by year-end 2010. However, others were concerned that once Apple aficionados had purchased an iPad to complement their iPhone, iPod, or Mac, further sales growth might be difficult to achieve. A former Apple executive commented, "The first five million will be sold in a heartbeat. But let's see: you can't make a phone call with it, you can't take a picture with it, and you have to buy content that before now you were not willing to pay for. That seems tough to me."[2]

Analysts were also concerned with the general decline in iPod unit sales and worried that Apple might have to struggle to sustain its growth in the smartphone market. The iPod had been important in the company's resurgence in the past decade, but sustained growth in iPhone sales were critical to the company's financial performance, since iPhone sales accounted for $5.33 billion of the company's third-quarter 2010 revenues of $15.7 billion. Research in Motion (RIM) had been known for innovative smartphones since it was introduced by BlackBerry in 1999, but Google's development of the Android operating system

[1]Quoted in "New Gadgets Power Apple Sales," Wall Street Journal Online, July 21, 2010.

[2]Quoted in "Doing the iPad Math: Utility 1 Price 1 Desire," New York Times, April 2, 2010, p. B1.

for smartphones had allowed HTC, LG, Nokia, and Samsung to introduce smartphones that matched many of the iPhone's best features. In addition, Microsoft's Windows Mobile 7 operating system, planned for a late-2010 launch, was expected to surpass some of the capabilities of the iPhone operating system. Google was also a growing threat to Apple, since many computer makers were developing new tablet computers similar to the iPad that would run the Android operating system; the two companies seemed to be headed for a future battle in mobile ads.

COMPANY HISTORY AND FINANCIAL PERFORMANCE

Steven Wozniak and Steven Jobs founded Apple Computer in 1976 when they began selling a crudely designed personal computer called the Apple I to Silicon Valley computer enthusiasts. Two years later, the partners introduced the first mass-produced personal computer (PC), the Apple II. The Apple II boasted the first color display and eventually sold more than 10,000 units. While the Apple II was relatively successful, the next revision of the product line, the Macintosh (Mac), would dramatically change personal computing through its user-friendly graphical user interface (GUT), which allowed users to interact with screen images rather than merely type text commands.

The Macintosh that was introduced in 1984 was hailed as a breakthrough in personal computing, but it did not have the speed, power, or software availability to compete with the PC that IBM had introduced in 1981. One of the reasons the Macintosh lacked the necessary software was that Apple put very strict restrictions on the Apple Certified Developer Program, which made it difficult for software developers to obtain Macs at a discount and receive informational materials about the operating system.

With the Mac faring poorly in the market, founder Steve Jobs became highly critical of the company's president and CEO, John Sculley, who had been hired by the board in 1983. Finally, in 1985, as Sculley was preparing to visit China, Jobs devised a boardroom coup to replace him. Sculley found out about the plan and canceled his trip. After Apple's board voted unanimously to keep Sculley in his position, Jobs, who was retained as chairman of the company but stripped of all decision-making authority, soon resigned. During the remainder of 1985, Apple continued to encounter problems and laid off one-fifth of its employees while posting its first ever quarterly loss.

Despite these setbacks, Apple kept bringing innovative products to the market, while closely guarding the secrets behind its technology. In 1987, Apple released a revamped Macintosh computer that proved to be a favorite in K–12 schools and with graphic artists and other users needing excellent graphics capabilities. However, by 1990, PCs running Windows 3.0 and Word for Windows were preferred by businesses and consumers and held a commanding 97+ percent share of the market for PCs.

In 1991, Apple released its first-generation notebook computer, the PowerBook and, in 1993, Apple's board of directors opted to remove Sculley from the position of CEO. The board chose to place the chief operating officer, Michael Spindler, in the vacated spot. Under Spindler, Apple released the PowerMac family of PCs in 1994, the first Macs to incorporate the PowerPC chip, a very fast processor codeveloped with Motorola and IBM. Even though the PowerMac family received excellent reviews by technology analysts, Microsoft's Windows 95 matched many of the capabilities of the Mac OS and prevented the PowerMac from gaining significant market share. In January 1996, Apple asked Spindler to resign and chose Gil Amelio, former president of National Semiconductor, to take his place.

During his first 100 days in office, Amelio announced many sweeping changes for the company. He split Apple into seven distinct divisions, each responsible for its own profit or loss, and he tried to better inform the developers and consumers of Apple's products and projects. Amelio acquired NeXT, the company Steve Jobs had founded on his resignation from Apple in 1985. Steve Jobs was rehired by Apple as part of the acquisition. In 1997, after recording additional quarterly losses, Apple's board terminated Amelio's employment with the company and named Steve Jobs interim CEO.

Apple introduced the limited-feature iMac in 1998 and the company's iBook line of notebook computers in 1999. The company was profitable in every quarter during 1998 and 1999, and its share price reached an all-time high in the upper $70 range. Jobs was named permanent CEO of Apple in 2000 and, in 2001, oversaw the release of the iPod. The iPod recorded modest sales until the 2003 launch of iTunes—the online retail store where consumers could legally purchase individual songs. By July 2004, 100 million songs had been sold and iTunes had a 70 percent market share among all legal online music download services. The tremendous success of the iPod helped transform Apple from a struggling computer company into a powerful consumer electronics company.

By 2005, consumers' satisfaction with the iPod had helped renew interest in Apple computers, with its market share in personal computers growing from a negligible share to 4 percent. The company also exploited consumer loyalty and satisfaction with the iPod to enter the market for smartphones with the 2007 launch of the iPhone. Much of Apple's turnaround could be credited to Steve Jobs, who had idea after idea for how to improve the company and turn its performance around. He not only consistently pushed for innovative new ideas and products but also enforced several structural changes, including ridding the company of unprofitable segments and divisions.

The success of the turnaround could also be attributed to the efforts of Tim Cook, Apple's chief operating officer. While Jobs provided the vision for the organization, Cook and the other members of the executive staff and the board of directors were responsible for ensuring that all operations of Apple ran efficiently and smoothly. Between mid-2008 and mid-2009, when Steve Jobs took a leave of absence to receive a liver transplant, Cook took on the role of acting CEO.

A summary of Apple's financial performance for fiscal years 2005 through 2009 is provided in Exhibit 1. The company's net sales by operating segment and product line and unit sales by product line for 2005 through 2009 are provided in Exhibit 2.

OVERVIEW OF THE PERSONAL COMPUTER INDUSTRY

The PC industry was relatively consolidated, with five sellers accounting for 78.5 percent of the US shipments and 60.3 percent of worldwide shipments in 2009—see Exhibit 3. Before the onset of the recession in 2008, the PC industry was expected to grow at a rate of 5–6 percent, to reach $354 billion by 2012. However, the effects of the recession caused a dramatic decline in industry revenues in 2008 and 2009.

PC industry shipments grew by a healthy 22.4 percent during the second quarter of 2010 as businesses were forced to replace aging computers. The sharp spike in shipments was not expected to continue throughout the year, with analysts expecting a 12.6 percent increase in worldwide shipments for the full year 2010. PC shipments in emerging markets were expected to grow at 18.5 percent to allow demand in emerging markets to overtake demand for PCs in developed countries by the end of 2010. Shipments of PCs in developed countries were expected to increase by only 7.2 percent in 2010 and were not expected to reach double-digit rates until 2011. Industry revenues were projected to grow more slowly than shipments because average selling prices had declined steadily since 2008.

EXHIBIT 1 Summary of Apple, Inc.'s Financial Performance, 2005–2009 ($ millions, except share amounts)

Income Statement Data	2009	2008	2007	2006	2005
Net Sales					
Domestic	$ 19,870	$ 18,469	$ 14,128	$ 11,486	$ 8,334
International	16,667	14,010	9,878	7,829	5,597
Total net sales	36,537	32,479	24,006	19,315	13,931
Costs and Expenses					
Cost of sales	23,397	21,334	15,852	13,717	9,889
Research and development (R&D)	1,333	1,109	782	712	535
Selling, general and administrative (SG&A)	4,149	3,761	2,963	2,433	1,864
Total operating expenses	5,482	4,870	3,745	3,145	2,399
Operating income	7,658	6,275	4,409	2,453	1,643
Other income and expense	326	620	599	365	165
Income before provision for income taxes	7,984	6,895	5,008	2,818	1,808
Provision for income taxes	2,280	2,061	1,512	829	480
Net income	$ 5,704	$ 4,834	$ 3,496	$ 1,989	$ 1,328
Earnings per common share—diluted	$6.29	$5.36	$3.93	$2.27	$1.55
Shares used in computing earnings per share—diluted (in thousands)	907,005	902,139	889,292	877,526	856,878
Balance Sheet Data (as of September 30)					
Cash, cash equivalents, and short-term investments	$ 23,464	$ 24,490	$ 15,386	$ 10,110	$ 8,261
Accounts receivable, net	3,361	2,422	1,637	1,252	895
Inventories	455	509	346	270	165
Property, plant, and equipment, net	2,954	2,455	1,832	1,281	817
Total assets	53,851	39,572	25,347	17,205	11,516
Current liabilities	19,284	14,092	9,299	6,443	3,487
Noncurrent liabilities	6,737	4,450	1,516	778	601
Shareholders' equity	$ 27,832	$ 21,030	$ 14,532	$ 9,984	$ 7,428

Source: Apple Inc., 2007 and 2009 10-K reports.

Both businesses and consumers were tending to replace desktop PCs with portable PCs such as laptops and netbooks. Total shipments of portable PCs grew by 18.4 percent in 2009, with consumer purchases of portable PCs growing by 38 percent during the year. Low-end laptops and netbooks accounted for the majority of consumer portable PC sales in 2009. The sale of desktop computers was expected to decline in markets of all countries except emerging markets in Asia, which would allow portable PCs to make up 70 percent of industry shipments by 2012.

APPLE'S COMPETITIVE POSITION IN THE PERSONAL COMPUTER INDUSTRY

Even though a larger percentage of Apple's revenues were increasingly coming from non-computer products, the company still saw computers as its core business. Apple's proprietary operating system and strong graphics-handling capabilities differentiated Macs from PCs, but many consumers and business users who owned PCs were hesitant to purchase a Mac because of Apple's premium pricing and because of the learning curve involved with mastering its proprietary operating system. The company's market share in the United States had improved from 4 percent in 2005 to 8 percent in 2009 primarily because of the success of the iPod and iPhone. These products created a halo effect whereby

EXHIBIT 2   Apple, Inc.'s Net Sales by Operating Segment, Net Sales by Product, and Unit Sales by Product, 2005–2009 ($ millions)

	2009	2008	2007	2006	2005
Net Sales by Operating Segment					
Americas net sales	$16,142	$14,573	$11,596	$ 9,415	$ 6,950
Europe net sales	9,365	7,622	5,460	4,096	3,073
Japan net sales	1,831	1,509	1,082	1,211	920
Retail net sales	6,574	6,315	4,115	3,246	2,350
Other Segments net sales*	2,625	2,460	1,753	1,347	998
Total net sales	$36,537	$32,479	$24,006	$19,315	$13,931
Net Sales by Product					
Desktops**	$ 4,308	$ 5,603	$ 4,020	$ 3,319	$ 3,436
Portables***	9,472	8,673	6,294	4,056	2,839
Total Macintosh net sales	$13,780	$14,276	10,314	7,375	6,275
iPod	8,091	9,153	8,305	7,375	4,540
Other music related products and services[†]	4,036	3,340	2,496	1,885	899
iPhone and related products and services[‡]	6,754	1,844	123	—	—
Peripherals and other hardware[a]	1,470	1,659	1,260	1,100	1,126
Software, service, and other sales[b]	2,406	2,207	1,508	1,279	1,091
Total net sales	$36,537	$32,479	$24,006	$19,315	$13,931
Unit Sales by Product:					
Desktops**	3,182	3,712	2,714	2,434	2,520
Portables***	7,214	6,003	4,337	2,869	2,014
Total Macintosh unit sales	10,396	9,715	7,051	5,303	4,534
Net sales per Macintosh unit sold[c]	$ 1,326	$ 1,469	$ 1,463	$ 1,391	$ 1,384
iPod unit sales	54,132	54,828	51,630	39,409	22,497
Net sales per iPod unit sold[d]	$149	$167	$161	$195	$202
iPhone unit sales	20,731	11,627	1,389	—	—

*Other segments include Asia Pacific and FileMaker.
**Includes iMac, eMac, Mac mini, Power Mac, and Xserve product lines.
***Includes MacBook, MacBook Pro, iBook, and PowerBook product lines.
[†]Consists of iTunes Music Store sales, iPod services, and Apple-branded and third-party iPod accessories.
[‡]Derived from handset sales, carrier agreements, and Apple-branded and third-party iPhone accessories.
[a]Includes sales of Apple-branded and third-party displays, wireless connectivity and networking solutions, and other hardware accessories.
[b]Includes sales of Apple-branded operating system, application software, third-party software, AppleCare, and Internet services.
[c]Derived by dividing total Macintosh net sales by total Macintosh unit sales.
[d]Derived by dividing total iPod net sales by total iPod unit sales.
Source: Apple Inc., 2007 and 2009 10-K reports.

some consumers (but not business users) switched to Apple computers after purchasing an iPod or iPhone.

Apple's computer product line consisted of several models in various configurations. Its desktop lines included the Mac Pro (aimed at professional and business users), the iMac (targeted toward consumer, educational, and business use); and Mac mini (made specifically for consumer use). Apple had three notebook product lines as well: MacBook Pro (for professional and advanced consumer users), the MacBook (designed for education users and consumers), and the MacBook Air (designed for professional and consumer users).

The MacBook Air was Apple's most recent notebook introduction. The MacBook Air was designed to target users who valued both portability and power. The notebook featured a 13.3-inch screen, a full-size keyboard, a built-in video camera, and cutting-edge wireless connectivity. This sleek notebook measured only 0.76 inches at its maximum height when closed and weighed only 3 lb. The MacBook Air had won critical acclaim for both its design

EXHIBIT 3 US and Global Market Shares of Leading PC Vendors, 2000 and 2005–2009

A. U.S. Market Shares of the Leading PC Vendors 2000 and 2005–2009

	Vendor	2009		2008		2007		2006		2005		2000	
		Shipments (in 000s)	Market Share	Shipments (in 000s)	Market Share	Shipments (in 000s)	Market Share	Shipments (in 000s)	Market Share	Shipments (in 000s)	Market Share	Shipments (in 000s)	Market Share
1	Hewlett-Packard*	18,781	26.9%	16,218	24.7%	16,759	23.9%	11,600	21.5%	12,456	19.5%	5,630	11.5%
2	Dell	17,099	24.5	19,276	29.4	19,645	28.0	20,472	31.2	21,466	33.6	9,645	19.7
	Compaq*	—		—								7,761	15.9
3	Acer*	7,983	11.4	6,106	9.3	3,860	5.5	1,421	2.2	n.a.	n.a.	n.a.	n.a.
4	Apple	5,579	8.0	5,158	7.9	4,081	5.8	3,109	4.7	2,555	4.0	n.a.	n.a.
5	Toshiba	5,379	7.7	3,788	5.8	3,509	5.0	2,843	4.3	2,372	3.6	n.a.	n.a
	Others	15,008	21.5	15,026	22.9	22,235	31.7	23,350	35.7	25,070	39.2	18,959	38.8
	All vendors	69,829	100.0%	65,571	100.0%	70,088	100.0%	65,481	100.0%	63,874	100.0%	48,900	100.0%

B. Worldwide Market Shares of the Leading PC Vendors 2000 and 2005–2009

2003 Rank	Vendor	2009		2008		2007		2006		2005		2000	
		Shipments (in 000s)	Market Share	Shipments (in 000s)	Market Share	Shipments (in 000s)	Market Share	Shipments (in 000s)	Market Share	Shipments (in 000s)	Market Share	Shipments (in 000s)	Market Share
1	Hewlett-Packard[1]	59,942	20.3%	54,293	18.9%	50,526	18.8%	38,838	16.5%	32,575	15.7%	10,327	7.4
2	Dell	38,416	13.1	42,388	14.7	39,993	14.9	39,094	16.6	37,755	18.2	14,801	10.6%
	Compaq[1]	—				—						17,399	12.5
3	Acer[2]	38,377	13.0	31,377	10.9	21,206	7.9	13,594	5.8	9,845	4.7	n.a.	n.a.
4	Lenovo/IBM[3]	24,887	8.5	21,870	7.6	20,224	7.5	16,609	7.1	12,979	6.2	9,308	6.7
5	Toshiba	15,878	5.4	13,727	4.8	10,936	4.1	9,292	3.9	7,234	3.5	n.a.	n.a.
	Others	116,709	39.7	123,910	43.1	126,075	46.9	117,971	50.1	107,450	51.7	80,640	58
	All Vendors	294,208	100.0%	287,566	100.0%	268,960	100.0%	235,397	100.0%	207,837	100.0%	139,057	100.0%

n.a. = not available; sales and market shares for these companies in the years where n.a. appears are included in the "Others" category because the company was not in the top 5 in shipments or market share.

*Compaq was acquired by Hewlett-Packard in May 2002.

**Acer acquired Gateway in 2007 and Packard Bell in 2008. Data for Acer includes shipments for Gateway starting in Q4 2007 and shipments for Packard Bell starting in Q1 2008, and only Acer data for prior periods.

***Lenovo, a Chinese computer company, completed the acquisition of IBM's PC business in 2005. The numbers for Lenovo/IBM for 2000 reflect sales of IBM branded PCs only; the numbers for 2005–2009 reflect their combined sales beginning in the second quarter of 2005. In 2007, Lenovo rebranded all IBM PCs as Lenovo.

Source: International Data Corp.

and its ease of use and was one of the products helping Apple gain ground in the competitive computer industry. All Apple computers were priced at a steep premium compared to PCs and laptops offered by Dell, HP, and other rivals. The company lowered the prices of all its computer models by 10 percent or more in June 2009, with the price of the MacBook Pro falling to $1,199 and the MacBook Air getting a $300 price cut, to $1,499.

APPLE'S RIVALS IN THE PERSONAL COMPUTER INDUSTRY

Hewlett-Packard

Hewlett-Packard (HP) was broadly diversified across segments of the computer industry with business divisions focused on information technology consulting services, large enterprise systems, software, PCs, printers and other imaging devices, and financial services. The company's Personal Systems Group (PSG), which manufactured and marketed HP and Compaq desktop computers and portable computers, was its largest division, accounting for revenues of $35.3 billion in 2009. HP recorded total net revenues of $114.6 billion in 2009, with information technology services contributing nearly $34.7 billion, imaging and printing devices contributing $24 billion, and enterprise systems accounting for about $15.4 billion. The company's financial services and software business units accounted for sales of about $6 billion in 2009.

HP's sales of personal computers declined by 16.5 percent between 2008 and 2009 as the recession forced consumers and businesses to reduce expenditures and capital investments. Handheld computers and workstations were affected most by the recession, with sales declining by 52.2 percent and 33.7 percent, respectively, during 2009. The company's sales of desktop computers were affected not only by the recession but also by business users' and consumers' growing preference for portable computers over desktop models. HP portable computers were harmed least by the recession, with a 10.8 percent decline in sales between 2008 and 2009. HP did sustain some growth in emerging markets despite the recession in developed countries. Exhibit 4 provides the revenue contribution by PSG product line for 2005 through 2009.

Dell Inc.

Dell Inc. was the world's second-largest seller of PCs, with revenues of $52.9 billion for the fiscal year ending January 29, 2010. Exhibit 5 presents Dell's revenues by product category for fiscal 2008 through fiscal 2010. The recession significantly affected Dell's financial performance in late 2008, when its fourth-quarter sales declined by 48 percent from the same period in the previous year. The revenue decline was a result of an overall decline in unit sales and strong price competition in both desktop PCs and portables. In addition,

EXHIBIT 4   Hewlett-Packard Personal Systems Group, Net Revenue ($ millions)

Product	2009	2008	2007	2006	2005
Notebooks	$20,210	$22,657	$17,650	$12,005	$ 9,763
Desktop PCs	12,864	16,626	15,889	14,641	14,406
Workstations	1,261	1,902	1,721	1,368	1,195
Handhelds	172	360	531	650	836
Other	798	750	618	502	541
Total	$35,305	$42,295	$36,409	$29,166	$26,741

Source: Hewlett-Packard, 2007 and 2008 10-K reports.

EXHIBIT 5   Dell's Revenues by Product Category, Fiscal 2008–Fiscal 2010 ($ millions)

Fiscal Year Ended	January 29, 2010		January 30, 2009		February 1, 2008	
	Dollars	% of Revenue	Dollars	% of Revenue	Dollars	% of Revenue
Servers and networking	$ 6,032	11	$ 6,512	11	$ 6,486	11
Storage	2,192	4	2,667	4	2,429	4
Services	5,622	11	5,351	9	4,980	8
Software and peripherals	9,499	18	10,603	17	9,927	16
Mobility	16,610	31	18,604	30	17,961	29
Desktop PCs	12,947	25	17,364	29	19,350	32
Totals	$52,902	100%	$61,101	100%	$61,133	100%

Source: Dell Inc., 2010 10-K report.

Dell's net earnings fell from $2.9 billion in fiscal 2008 to $2.5 billion in fiscal 2009 to $1.4 billion in fiscal 2010. The company offered a wide range of desktop computers and portables, ranging from low-end low-priced models to state-of-the-art high-priced models. The company also offered servers; workstations; peripherals such as printers, monitors, and projectors; and Wi-Fi products.

Acer

Taiwan-based Acer was the world's second-largest portable computer provider and third-largest desktop computer manufacturer in 2010. Acer's 2009 consolidated revenues rose by approximately 13 percent from the previous year to reach $18.3 billion, while operating income increased by 17 percent to reach $488 million. Its 40.5 percent annual growth in global PC shipments between 2005 and 2009 ranked first among the industry's leading sellers. The company's largest and one of its fastest-growing geographic segments was the Europe/Middle East/Africa segment, which accounted for 52 percent of the company's PC, desktop, and notebook sales. A summary of the company's financial performance between 2006 and 2009 is presented in Exhibit 6.

Acer's multibrand strategy—which positioned Acer, Gateway, eMachines, and Packard Bell at distinct price points in the market for PCs—had helped it become one of the fastest-growing vendors in the United States. The company based its competitive strategy on its four pillars of success: a winning business model, competitive products, an innovative marketing strategy, and an efficient operation model. The company's computer offering included desktop and mobile PCs, LCD monitors, servers and storage, and high-definition TVs and projectors. In 2009, the company entered the market for smartphones with the launch of its liquid line of stylish high-end smartphones, which used Google's Android operating system.

EXHIBIT 6   Financial Summary for Acer Incorporated, 2006–2009 ($ thousands)

	2009	2008	2007	2006
Revenue	$18,264,125	$16,186,102	$15,252,801	$10,577,113
Gross profit	1,855,993	1,697,374	1,565,278	1,150,865
Operating income	488,102	416,962	336,211	224,993
Operating margin	2.7%	2.6%	2.2%	2.1%
Income before income taxes	476,759	438,723	498,736	408,481
Net income	$361,248	$347,919	$427,774	$308,080

Source: Acer Incorporated Financial Snapshot, http://www.acer-group.com/public/Investor_Relations/financial_snapshot.htm.

APPLE'S COMPETITIVE POSITION IN THE PERSONAL MEDIA PLAYER INDUSTRY

Although Apple did not introduce the first portable digital music player, the company held a 73 percent market share of digital music players in 2010 and the name iPod had become a generic term used to describe digital media players. When Apple launched its first iPod, many critics did not give the product much of a chance for success, given its fairly hefty price tag of $399. However, the iPod's sleek styling, ease of use, and eventual price decreases allowed it to develop such high levels of customer satisfaction and loyalty that rivals found it difficult to gain traction in the marketplace.

The most popular portable players in 2010 played music and could also be connected to Wi-Fi networks to play videos, access the Internet, view photos, or listen to FM high-definition radio. The iPod Touch was the best-selling media player in 2010, but electronics sector reviewers generally agreed that Microsoft's Zune, Archos's Vision models, and Sony's X-series media players compared quite favorably to the iPod Touch. In addition, electronics reviewers found that inexpensive MP3 music players offered by SanDisk, Creative, iRiver, and others generally performed as well as Apple's more basic iPod models. However, none of Apple's key rivals in the media player industry had been able to achieve a market share greater than 5 percent in 2010. Most consumers did not find many convincing reasons to consider any brand of media player other than Apple.

In 2010, Apple offered four basic styles in the iPod product line:

- *The iPod Shuffle*—a basic flash-based player with no screen, FM radio, or voice recorder. The 4 gigabyte (GB) model was capable of storing 1,000 songs, and its rechargeable lithium polymer battery provided up to 10 hours of playback time.

- *The iPod Nano*—a multimedia player offered in 8 GB (8 hours of video or 2,000 songs) and 16 GB (16 hours of video or 4,000 songs) sizes that used a click wheel interface to navigate the player's controls. It allowed users to view photos and videos as well as to listen to music in Apple's Advanced Audio Coding (AAC) format, and it provided up to 24 hours of music playback and 5 hours of video playback on a single charge.

- *The iPod Classic*—a hard-drive-based click-wheel-controlled multimedia player offered with a 160 GB hard drive that, similar to the smaller Nano, played music in Apple's AAC format and showed videos and photos. The 160 GB player held up to 40,000 songs or 200 hours of video and provided up to 36 hours of audio playback or 6 hours of video playback on a single charge.

- *The iPod Touch*—a multimedia flash memory player controlled though an innovative touch screen interface that was a feature of the iPhone. It was offered in 8 GB (1,750 songs, 10 hours of video), 32 GB (7,000 songs, 40 hours of video), and 64 GB (14,000 songs, 80 hours of video) sizes and provided up to 30 hours of music playback and 6 hours of video playback on a single charge. This multimedia player featured a wide 3.5-inch screen and built-in Wi-Fi, which allowed users to connect to the Internet and access e-mail, buy music from the iTunes store, and surf the Web from wireless hotspots. Touch users also had access to maps, the weather, and stocks, and the ability to write notes to themselves. The Touch featured an accelerometer that detected when the Touch rotated and automatically changed the display from portrait to landscape.

iTunes

Aside from the iPod's stylish design and ease of use, another factor that contributed to the popularity of the iPod was Apple's iPod/iTunes combination. In 2010, more than 50 million customers visited the iTunes Store to purchase and download music, videos, movies, and television shows that could be played on iPods, iPhones, or Apple TV devices. (Apple TV was a device that allowed users to play iTunes content on televisions.) Also in 2010, Apple's iTunes Store recorded its 10-billionth download since its launch in 2003. In addition, iTunes was the world's most popular online movie store, with customers purchasing and renting more than 50,000 movies each day. Apple did not offer an iTunes subscription service, although a July 2010 survey by research firm NPD Group found that 7–8 million iPod owners would have a strong interest in subscribing to a service that would allow them to stream iTunes music and videos.

The success of the iPod/iTunes combination gave iTunes a 69 percent share of the US digital music market in 2010. Since downloads accounted for about 40 percent of all music sales in the United States, iTunes' commanding share of the digital music sales also gave it a 27 percent share of total US music sales. Amazon.com was the second-largest seller of digital music in the United States, with an 8 percent share of the market. Amazon.com and Walmart were tied for second in total US music sales, with 12 percent market shares.

APPLE'S COMPETITIVE POSITION IN THE MOBILE PHONE INDUSTRY

The first version of the iPhone was released on June 29, 2007, and had a multitouch screen with a virtual keyboard, a camera, and a portable media player (equivalent to the iPod) in addition to text messaging and visual voice mail. It also offered Internet services including e-mail, web browsing (using access to Apple's Safari Web browser), and local Wi-Fi connectivity. More than 270,000 first-generation iPhones were sold during the first 30 hours of the product's launch. The iPhone was named Time magazine's Invention of the Year in 2007. The iPhone 3G was released in 70 countries on July 11, 2008, and was available in the United States exclusively through AT&T Mobility. The iPhone 3G combined the functionality of a wireless phone and an iPod, and allowed users to access the Internet wirelessly at twice the speed of the previous version of the iPhone. Apple's new phone also featured a built-in global positioning system (GPS) and, in an effort to increase adoption by corporate users, was compatible with Microsoft Exchange.

The iPhone 3GS was introduced on June 19, 2009, and included all features of the iPhone 3G and could also launch applications and render Web pages twice as fast as the iPhone 3G. The iPhone 3GS also featured a 3-MP camera, video recording, voice control, and up to 32 GB of flash memory. The iPhone 4 was launched on June 24, 2010, with the 16 GB model priced at $199 on a two-year AT&T contract and the 32 GB model priced at $299 on a two-year AT&T contract. Upgrades over the 3GS included video-calling capabilities (only over a Wi-Fi network), a higher resolution display, a 5-MP camera including flash and zoom, 720p video recording, a longer-lasting battery, and a gyroscopic motion sensor to enable an improved gaming experience. More than 1.7 million units of iPhone 4 were sold within three days of its launch.

Similar to the iTunes/iPod partnership, Apple launched the App Store for the iPhone. The App Store allowed developers to build applications for the iPhone and to offer them either for free or for a fee. In January 2010, more than 3 billion apps had been downloaded by iPhone and iPod Touch users. Both Apple and Google had begun to embed ads into mobile apps to both create additional revenue sources and to allow app developers to earn revenues from apps that could be downloaded free of charge.

While worldwide shipments of mobile phones declined from 1.19 billion in 2008 to 1.27 billion in 2009 because of poor economic conditions in the United States and many other major country markets, worldwide sales of mobile phones grew by 21.7 percent during the first quarter of 2010 as economies in most countries began to improve. However, industry

EXHIBIT 7   Worldwide Market Shares of Leading Mobile Phone Vendors, 2000 and 2005–2009

Q1 2010 Rank	Vendor	Q1 2010		2009		2008		2007	
		Shipments (in millions)	Market Share	Shipments (in millions)	Market Share	Shipments (in millions)	Market Share	Shipments (in millions)	Market Share
1	Nokia	107.8	36.6%	431.8	38.3%	468.4	39.4%	437.1	38.3%
2	Samsung	64.3	21.8	227.2	20.1	196.8	16.5	161.1	14.1
3	LG	27.1	9.2	117.9	10.5	100.8	8.5	80.5	7.1
4	RIM	10.6	3.6	n.a.	n.a.	n.a.	n.a.	n.a.	n.a.
5	Sony Ericsson	10.5	3.6	57.0	5.1	96.6	8.1	103.4	9.1
	Others	74.6	25.3	293.8	26.0	327.7	27.5	358.8	31.4
	All vendors	294.9	100.0%	1,127.8	100.0%	1,190.1	100.0%	1,140.9	100.0%

n.a. = not available; sales and market shares for these companies in the years where n.a. appears are included in the "Others" category because the company was not in the top 5 in shipments or market share.

Source: International Data Corp.

analysts did not expect the 21.7 percent year-over-year sales increase during the first quarter of 2010 to continue throughout the year and projected annual sales growth of about 11 percent for 2010. The growth in shipments of smartphones during the first quarter of 2010 outpaced the growth in basic-feature phone shipments by a considerable margin. The shipments of smartphones grew by 56.7 percent during the first quarter of 2010, while shipments of basic-feature phones increased by 18.8 percent between the first quarter of 2009 and the first quarter of 2010. The rapid growth in demand for smartphones during early 2010 allowed RIM to become the first company producing only smartphones to become a Top 5 vendor in the industry—see Exhibit 7.

Developing countries such as China not only offered the greatest growth opportunities but also presented challenges to smartphone producers. For example, there were 700 million mobile phone users in China, but popular-selling models were quickly counterfeited, it was difficult to develop keyboards that included the thousands of commonly used characters in the Chinese language, and most consumers preferred inexpensive feature phones over smartphones. Nevertheless, many analysts expected China to account for 10 percent of worldwide smartphone shipments within the near term. Apple planned to begin selling the iPhone in China in 2010 through a network of 25 flagship stores located in the country's largest cities. The iPhone would be available in 80 countries by year-end 2010.

With the market for smartphones growing rapidly and supporting high average selling prices, competition was becoming more heated. Google's entry into the market with its Android operating system had allowed vendors such as HTC, Motorola, Acer, and Samsung to offer models that matched many of the features of the iPhone. In addition, Microsoft's Windows Mobile 7, which was planned for a late-2010 launch, was expected to exceed the capabilities of the iPhone operating system with live tiles of rotating pictures, e-mail messages, and social-networking feeds. In addition, smartphones operating on Windows Mobile 7 would have all functionality of a Zune media player just as the iPhone included all functionality of the iPod Touch. While iPhones and Android phones primarily targeted consumers enthralled with clever and helpful web apps, RIM had built a number one position in the smartphone market by appealing to businesspeople who needed the ability to check e-mail, maintain appointment calendars; receive fax transmissions; and open, edit, and save Microsoft Office and Adobe PDF files. Hewlett-Packard entered the market for smartphones in May 2010 with its $1.2 billion acquisition of Palm. However, Palm had lost its edge in innovation years before and was primarily popular with users who had purchased

EXHIBIT 8   US Smartphone Platform Market Share Rankings, Selected Periods, September 2009

Smartphone Platform	Share of Smartphone Subscribers			
	September 2009	December 2009	February 2010	May 2010
RIM (BlackBerry)	42.6%	41.6%	42.1%	41.7%
Apple iPhone	24.1	25.3	25.4	24.4
Microsoft Windows Mobile	19.0	18.0	15.1	13.2
Google Android	2.5	5.2	9.0	13.0
Palm	8.3	6.1	5.4	4.8
Others	3.5	3.8	3.0	2.9
Total	100.0%	100.0%	100.0%	100.0%

Source: ComScore.com.

Palm Pilots in the company's heyday. Exhibit 8 presents market shares for the leading smartphone brands between 2006 and the first quarter of 2010.

APPLE'S ENTRY INTO THE MARKET FOR TABLET COMPUTERS

Apple entered the market for tablet computers with its April 3, 2010, launch of the iPad. Tablet computers such as the iPad allowed users to access the Internet, read and send e-mail, view photos, watch videos, listen to music, read e-books, and play video games. In addition, Apple's iPad could run 11,000 apps developed specifically for the iPad and most of the 225,000-plus apps developed for the iPhone and iPod Touch. Apple sold more than 3 million iPads within the first 90 days the product was on the market. Industry analysts expected that 13 million tablet computers would be sold in 2010, with Apple accounting for almost all shipments of tablet computers. The market for tablet computers was expected to increase to 46 million units by 2014. By comparison, the market for portable PCs was expected to grow to 398 million units by 2014.

Tablet computers had been on the market since the late 1990s, but only Apple's version had gained any significant interest from consumers and business users. Previous-generation tablet computers required the use of a stylus to launch applications and enter information. Most users found the stylus interface to be an annoyance and preferred to use a smartphone or laptop when portability was required. Dell, Acer, Hewlett-Packard, and Nokia were all racing to get touch-screen tablet computers to market but were unable to do so until very late 2010 or early 2011 because of the technological differences between tablet computers and PCs. Tablet computers were technologically similar to smartphones and shared almost no components with PCs. The primary reason tablet computers could not use PC components was that the small size of tablet computers limited battery size. The small battery size prevented the use of energy-hungry PC components and required that tablet computers run the limited-capability microprocessors and operating systems found in smartphones. This minimal processing capability made tablet computers suitable only for viewing information and prevented the devices from running applications such as Microsoft Word, Excel, or PowerPoint.

Intel's new Atom microprocessor and Microsoft's Windows Mobile 7 would both be suitable for use in tablet computers and were expected to arrive to market in late 2010. PC manufacturers unwilling to wait for the development of the Atom and Windows Mobile 7 were designing tablet computers that used smartphone microprocessors and Google's Android operating system. Analysts believed that HP's 2010 acquisition of Palm was motivated more by the desire to use the Palm operating system in HP tablet computers than the company's interest in entering the smartphone market. Smartphone manufacturer Archos was the only vendor offering a viable competing product to the iPad in mid-2010. E-readers such as Amazon's Kindle were not considered direct competitors to the iPad since dedicated reading devices could not browse the Internet, view videos, play music, or perform other media tasks. In addition, e-readers carried prices in the $99 to $189 range, which was considerably lower than the $499 to $829 range charged by Apple for various iPad models.

APPLE'S PERFORMANCE GOING INTO THE FOURTH QUARTER OF 2010

Apple set a number of records with its third quarter 2010 performance. The company's quarterly revenue of 15.7 billion was its highest-ever quarterly sales figure, and the company set a new record for quarterly shipments of computers, with 3.47 million Macs shipped during the quarter. The company also sold 3.3 million iPads by the June 26, 2010, close of the quarter. By comparison, it took the first iPod 20 months to reach 1 million units in sales—the iPad hit the 1-million-unit mark within 30 days of its April 3, 2010, launch. In addition, Apple sold 8.4 million iPhones during the third quarter of 2010, which was 61 percent more than what was sold during the same period in 2009. The increase in iPhone sales came primarily from sales of iPhone 3GS models since the iPhone 4 was launched only four days before the quarter end. Unit sales for the iPod declined by 8.6 percent between the third quarter of 2009 and the third quarter of 2010, although iPod revenues increased by 4 percent to reach $1.5 billion as consumers purchased a higher percentage of iPod Touch models rather than lower-priced iPod Shuffle, iPod Nano, and iPod Classic models.

However, the company did face some concerns going into the fourth quarter of 2010. The US Justice Department had launched a preliminary inquiry into the company's tactics in the digital music industry. Specifically, the government was investigating reports that Apple had discouraged music labels from participating in an Amazon promotion by threatening to withdraw marketing support for songs included in Amazon's promotion that were also sold by the iTunes Store. Also, Steve Jobs was called upon to personally intervene in a flap involving the antenna design of the iPhone 4. Shortly after the iPhone 4 launch, the media widely reported that the iPhone 4's antenna design caused calls to be dropped if users touched the lower edged of the phone. The company reported that it had received fewer returns of iPhone 4s than iPhone 3GS models at its launch. To calm the media frenzy that he dubbed "Antennagate," Steve Jobs called a press conference to announce that the company would provide free bumper cases to iPhone 4 buyers concerned with reception problems caused by touching the metal edge of the phone.

Case

3

EMR Innovations

Kay M. Palan *Iowa State University*

Eric Reynolds stood inside the door to his RV repair shop and surveyed the activities. He and his wife Mary were avid RVers and had combined their love of RVing with business by starting an RV repair business out of their home in 1995. In 1999, the business was large enough to allow them to open their own shop in Amana, Iowa. By 2002, the business had steadily grown, but he and Mary wanted more—they wanted to be "the" supplier of innovative RV products. To that end, they had developed their first product, the Lock-Awn antibillow device for RV patio awnings. In fact, Eric mused, he and Mary had invested about $10,000 of their own money to develop a prototype product. They had even sought assistance from an industry research center located at a nearby university with respect to developing the prototype. Now, in late fall 2003, Eric and Mary had a working prototype, and preliminary feedback from some of their RV repair customers who had seen the product was very positive.

However, even though potential customers seemed to like it, Eric and Mary were unsure about whether or not the Lock-Awn product would be successful. In the last several months, they had become aware of a potential competitor selling a similar product. While Eric and Mary believed the Lock-Awn was superior to the competitor's product, they were uncertain if potential customers would feel the same way. Money was too tight for the Reynolds to risk market entry without a better grasp of the Lock-Awn's market viability.

Mary, who did the bookkeeping for the RV repair shop in between caring for their three children, looked up from her desk and saw Eric. She walked over to him and placed her hand on his shoulder. "What are you thinking about?" she asked.

Eric turned and said, "I just wish I knew for certain if investing more money in the Lock-Awn is the right thing to do. I think we need to know more about how we would actually market it before we can seek additional funding. That manufacturing consultant we've talked with said the next step was to decide on a marketing strategy."

Mary nodded her agreement, stating, "I've been thinking the same thing. I know you've got your hands full with the shop right now, so I'll start reviewing the information we have about customers and competitors and start thinking about how we would market the Lock-Awn. Hopefully, in a few weeks we can make sense of it all and decide on a marketing strategy."

EXHIBIT 1
Estimated Breakdown
of RV Ownership

Type of RV	Estimated Ownership[1] (Percent)	Estimated Number in U.S.[2]
Folding camper trailers	24	1,800,000
Truck campers	5	375,000
Travel trailer (includes fifth-wheel trailers)	47	3,525,000
Class C motorhomes	8	600,000
Class A motorhomes	16	1,200,000

[1]Estimated from data taken from 2001 RVIA industry survey.
[2]Based on 7.5 million estimated households owning RVs in 2002.

THE RV INDUSTRY

Recreational vehicles (RVs) were vehicles that combined transportation and temporary living quarters for recreation, camping, and travel. According to Web sites that Mary found (RV Central and RV Hotline Canada), interest in RVs dated back to the early 1900s when nature enthusiasts customized their own vehicles with such accessories as bunks, storage lockers, and cooking capabilities, in order to see the country. When roads began to improve in the 1920s, RV enthusiasm grew and did not diminish during the Depression. After World War II, the RV industry flourished. Enthusiasts could build their own RVs with home kits or could purchase ready-made motor homes. However, it wasn't until the 1960s that the term *RV* was coined as a marketing tool.

By 2000, the RV industry consisted of 135 RV manufacturers and more than 200 suppliers of component parts and services. There were two main RV categories—motorhomes (motorized) and towables (towed behind the family car, van, or pickup). Purchased new, towables were the least expensive. Towables included folding camping trailers, ranging from $5,000 to $10,000, and truck campers, affixed to the bed or chassis of a truck, at an average sticker price of $10,500. Conventional travel trailers, which were also towed, cost about $13,000, while fifth-wheel trailers (towed by a vehicle equipped with a device known as a fifth-wheel hitch) ranged from $25,000 to over $80,000. Motorhomes were considerably more expensive than towables, ranging from $35,000 for Class C motorhomes (built on a van cutaway chassis) to over $500,000 for the most luxurious Class A motorhomes (built on a specially designed motor vehicle chassis).

According to the Recreational Vehicle Industry Association (RVIA), nearly 7.5 million households in the U.S. owned an RV in 2002, and RV sales were expected to hit a 25-year high in 2003. RV shipments, shown in Exhibit 1, had steadily grown, although there were occasional decreases in shipped units that tended to coincide with increases in gasoline prices. Although it was difficult to find hard-and-fast numbers detailing exactly how many of which types of RVs were owned by U.S. households, data from a 2001 survey suggested the breakdown of RV ownership, illustrated in Exhibit 2.

Nonetheless, the economic forecast for the RV industry was positive. There was renewed interest in domestic ground travel in the United States, resulting in more people taking driving vacations than ever before. The aging baby boom generation, which had greater buying power relative to previous generations, was buying more RVs as it neared retirement. Moreover, low interest rates since 2001 encouraged Americans to purchase big-ticket, leisure items.

THE RV CULTURE

According to a 2001 University of Michigan study commissioned by the RVIA, RV enthusiasts were growing in numbers. In 2001, nearly 7 million U.S. households owned an RV, which translated to almost one RV in every 12 households, although the RVIA estimated

EXHIBIT 2

Total RV Shipments:
1986–2002 (Units in
Thousands)

Source: Recreation Vehicle
Industry Association (RVIA),
RVIA Facts, RV Shipments
Data, http://www.rvia.org/
media/ShipmentsData.htm

Year	Shipped Units
1986	189.8
1987	211.7
1988	215.8
1989	187.9
1990	173.1
1991	163.3
1992	203.4
1993	227.8
1994	259.2
1995	247.0
1996	247.5
1997	254.5
1998	292.7
1999	321.2
2000	300.1
2001	256.8
2002	311.0

that there were as many as 30 million RV enthusiasts in the U.S., which included RV renters. Although people of all ages owned RVs, the largest segment was the 55 and older crowd, with about 10 percent of the RVs, closely followed by the 35–54-year-olds, who owned 8.9 percent of the nation's RVs. The fastest growing segment of the RV market was the Baby Boomers. By 2010, the RVIA projected that there would be 8.5 million RV-owning households.

The same University of Michigan study identified the typical RV owner as 49 years old, married, owning his/her own home, and having an annual household income of $56,000. RV owners spent their disposable income on traveling an average of 4,500 miles and 28–35 days annually. The RVIA further noted several reasons why people chose RVs as a way to travel:

- Convenience, flexibility, and freedom to go where they wanted, when they wanted, without having to plan in advance.
- Comfort and amenities of home while on the road or at a campground.
- Enjoyment of traveling together as a family.
- Affordability—even factoring in RV ownership, a family of four spent up to 70 percent less when traveling by RV (according to a cost-comparison study conducted in 2000 by PKF Consulting).
- Accessibility to enjoying outdoor getaways—the beach, mountains, parks, tourist attractions.
- Versatility of vehicle—in addition to traveling, the RV was used for shopping, tailgating, and pursuing special hobbies.

Two-thirds of RV owners purchased a previously owned vehicle. RV owners tended to keep their RVs a long time—nearly 25 percent owned their RVs for 10 or more years. The average age of used RVs when purchased was 11.6 years.

RVers were an adventuresome group. From their own experience in the RV business, Mary knew that some RVers lived full-time on the road, traveling from place to place, absorbing the sights and sounds wherever they happened to be. Many of these people were retired couples who wanted to see the country. Others traveled for part of the year; for example, it was common for retirees in the Midwest to spend spring/summer in the Midwest and fall/winter in warmer climates. They would use their RV as their residence during the fall and winter months. Still others took a week or two here or there for short vacations. In 2003, Workamper News, an RV publication, estimated that approximately 750,000 Americans lived and worked out of travel trailers, truck campers, or motor homes full-time—it called these people "workampers," individuals motivated to earn a living but without being tied down to either one address or to an employer.

RVers were well connected through a variety of networking groups and forums. In her research, Mary found countless Web sites devoted to members of RV clubs. Members formed clubs based on type of RV ownership (e.g., Gulf Streamers International RV Club), travel and leisure interests (e.g., Happy Camper Club), geographic location (e.g., Carolina Cruisers), or other demographics (e.g., The Handicapped Travel Club). Numerous Web sites were devoted to answering RVers' questions and also featured chat rooms, which encouraged informal networking among RVers.

Regardless of how many months of the year RVers lived on the road or what their specific purpose was, all of them wanted their accommodations to be as comfortable as possible and, Mary knew, were willing to spend money on products that improved their RVs. Dozens of companies manufactured and sold RV gadgets and accessories like auxiliary fuel tanks, power booster equipment, and antisway trailer hitches (RV-Info). Some RVers invented their own gadgets to improve RVs, and then peddled these inventions to other RVers they met on the road. In some instances, this led to substantive businesses. One such RVer, Richard Dahl of Roseburg, Oregon, invented a water filter for RV plumbing systems and subsequently sold the $30 filter, which he manufactured himself, at trailer parks, campgrounds, and motor-home shows. Eventually he expanded his product line to 300 items, created The RV Water Filter Store, and made more than enough to pay for his and his wife's travels, plus $30,000 or so left over each year for fun (Henricks 2003). What Dahl discovered was that RVers were more than willing to purchase accessories like his water filter when they appreciated the benefits.

EMR INNOVATIONS

Eric and Mary Reynolds hoped to be as successful as Richard Dahl had been. Being acquainted with RVs through both personal experience and through their repair business, Eric and Mary discovered that most RVs suffered from design flaws. Some were minor inconveniences, but others were dangerous.

One such problem was with patio awnings, which were standard equipment on virtually all RVs, including motor homes, fifth-wheel trailers, and travel trailers. A very small percentage of RVs had motorized awnings, but most RVs had manually operated awnings, which had a propensity to become unwound while the RV was in motion or parked. The awnings, which were 8 feet wide and up to 22 feet long, could billow in the wind, either startling the driver or causing the driver to lose control and cause accidents (Siuru, RV Awning Care). In fact, although Eric could not find specific numbers on exactly how many accidents the billowing problem had caused, he had found several RV Internet forums and chat rooms where the string of discussion focused on the awning billowing problem. Many RVers reported trying to fix the problem with things like duct tape and Velcro. Eric saw an opportunity to create a permanent and practical fix for the many RV owners who still had to deal with the awning problem.

Thus began the idea for EMR Innovations. Eric believed that he could design a product that would lock awnings in place and be affordable. Moreover, he readily identified several other RV design flaws that EMR Innovations could address: sewer hookups, a battery fluid indicator cap, an all-in-one tow tester, an RV essentials toolkit, and a streamlined brake control device. Some of these devices Eric had already designed for use on his own RV while others were just ideas. However, he was certain there was a market for all these products.

Both Eric and Mary thought that the best product to introduce first to the market was the Lock-Awn device. Given RVers' concerns about this problem, it made sense that the product would sell. They had invested $10,000 so far to design and perfect a prototype. In addition, they had invested a lot of their time. However, if they proceeded to introduce the product, they needed an infusion of cash, either from an investor or through a bank loan. Although they did not have a well-formulated business or marketing plan, they roughly estimated that they needed about $200,000 to begin production, distribution and promotion. The local bank estimated that the Reynolds' RV repair business was worth $800,000 to $900,000, so Eric and Mary planned to use that as collateral for a loan if necessary. Their credit history with the bank was excellent, and they had no outstanding debt other than their house mortgage. If they borrowed $200,000 from the bank, Eric and Mary wanted to repay the loan within two years, even though the bank would be willing to give them anywhere from three to seven years, because they just didn't want any debt hanging over their heads any longer than necessary.

Eric and Mary had talked with a nearby manufacturer about producing the Lock-Awn, although they had not formalized any agreement. To begin, they planned to manage EMR Innovations themselves with part-time workers to help with production—Mary would manage inventory and shipping, and Eric would manage sales. However, they thought that eventually, as the business grew, they would hire a full-time office manager and additional help for shipping. This would permit them to focus on marketing and sales, and would free up some of Eric's time to develop new products. However, they knew this would not happen right away. For the first year or two at least, they did not think they would need to hire additional help. The profits from the RV repair business, while not large, were sufficient to maintain their current modest lifestyle and support their involvement in EMR Innovations. EMR Innovations was just an idea—it was not formalized into any type of organization (e.g., sole proprietorship or subchapter S corporation).

Now in their mid-30s, neither Eric nor Mary had attended college or taken business courses. High-school sweethearts, they had married and started their family when they were young. Eric trained and worked as a mechanic and, given his love for RVs, had found it natural to begin an RV repair business. Mary had always been a stay-at-home mom, but had helped Eric by taking on the bookkeeping responsibilities. Now that their youngest child had started kindergarten, Mary found herself with more time to devote to beginning EMR Innovations. What Eric and Mary knew about business was what they had learned by owning the RV repair business, so they felt challenged by all of the details necessary to develop, manufacture, and sell a new product. Mary appreciated that they didn't know everything there was to know about operating a business, but she knew that both she and Eric had common sense, a strong work ethic, and the desire to succeed.

THE LOCK-AWN ANTIBILLOW DEVICE

Manually operated patio awnings on RVs consisted of a long aluminum roller tube with two spring-loaded end-cap assemblies, the awning fabric, a locking cam or ratchet on the front spring, two vertical awning arms, and an awning rod. The awning rod or wand, separately stored, disengaged the awning's locking mechanism. The user pulled a strap attached to the awning fabric to extend the awning for use. In windy conditions, when the awning was stored or retracted, the force of the wind could cause the locking cam mechanism to fail by

EXHIBIT 3   Components of the Lock-Awn Antibillowing Device

Figure A.
A catch that attaches to
the awning arm.

Figure B.
A lock rod with spring-loaded
handle.

Figure C.
A two-piece roller tube collar.

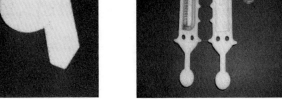

Source: Eric and Mary Reynolds.

overcoming the spring tension. This, in turn, could cause the aluminum cam to break. The aluminum teeth could also become so worn that they no longer held. Or, the lock could break. Any of these scenarios caused the fabric roller tube to come loose, allowing the awning fabric to release and billow in the wind.

The Lock-Awn antibillow device consisted of three main components—a catch that attached to the awning arm, a lock rod with a spring-loaded handle, and a two-piece roller tube collar, shown in Exhibit 3. Eric had designed the spring-loaded handle to keep constant tension on the awning roller tube to minimize friction wear from the wind and road rattle; thus, the Lock-Awn would protect the internal awning mechanisms from wear and tear *and* would prevent billowing. Mary was especially excited because the Lock-Awn replaced the awning rod, which she (and all the RVers she knew) found to be very inconvenient to use and store. The Lock-Awn would operate the awning lock and pull the awning strap when extending the awning for use.

Eric had put great thought and care into designing and developing the Lock-Awn. The device had the following features:

- Heavy-duty injection molded U.V. and weather-resistant collar and handle.
- Nickel-plated steel lock rod.
- Ergonomically designed handle.
- Heavy-duty spring and rivet components.
- A 30-day, 100 percent satisfaction guarantee and a 90-day limited warranty against defects in parts or workmanship.
- Embossed company and product logo on the formed handle with contact information.

Moreover, the Lock-Awn took only a few minutes to install, would work on either the right or left spring assembly of RV awnings, and did not detract from the RV's appearance, as shown in Exhibit 4.

Production costs for the Lock-Awn included a one-time investment of $40,000 for the mold and tooling. In addition, material cost for each unit was $5.95, packaging cost per unit, $0.75, and labor cost per unit, $5.90. Labor cost was calculated by dividing monthly projected part-time payroll costs, including wages and taxes, for part-time production workers by estimated Lock-Awn units produced per month. Eric and Mary thought of this as a variable cost because the workers' hours would fluctuate with demand. There would also be costs for packaging and assembly equipment ($3,500), office equipment ($1,000),

EXHIBIT 4 The Lock-Awn Antibillowing Device Installed on an RV

Source: Eric and Mary Reynolds.

product liability insurance ($5,000/year), building lease ($1,500/month), utilities (estimated to be $400/month), and standard commercial insurance ($1,000/year). Eric and Mary's time was also worth something, although that was more difficult for them to quantify. Mary figured she would eventually devote about half of her workweek (20 hours) to EMR, and to replace her would cost roughly $300/week. Mary further assumed that Eric would also put in about 20 hours a week into marketing the Lock-Awn, and to replace his time in the RV repair business would be about $600/week.

Eric had considered and rejected patenting the Lock-Awn because he didn't think patent protection was worth the $10,000 investment. He believed they could better protect their competitive advantage by penetrating the market.

COMPETITORS

There were many do-it-yourself homemade versions of awning locks—Eric and Mary found many described on RV Internet chat sites, and they had seen some themselves on their RV travels. As one might expect, the homemade versions varied in sophistication, level of function, attractiveness, and ease of use. The most common homemade "fix" was to use rope to tie up the awning, which people did when their awnings had already been damaged by billowing. More sophisticated versions utilized dog-collar metal-strap devices to secure the awning. Although some of these homemade devices provided protection, in Eric and Mary's opinion all of the do-it-yourself devices were lacking in some way, either in appearance, ease of installation, or ease of operation.

Eric found one commercial product designed to prevent billowing, the "AwningSaver" which a small company in Texas sold by mail order. The company had first offered the AwningSaver in 2001, but did not distribute it widely. However, some of the RV Internet chatters mentioned they had purchased the product. According to the company's materials, the AwningSaver worked by locking the awning roller tube to the awning arm. The device, shown in Exhibit 5, was permanently clamped to the awning arm, and a brake clamp gripped the roller tube end securely, preventing rotation of the tube. The user opened the brake clamp with the standard awning wand.

Neither Eric nor Mary believed the AwningSaver was a credible threat to the Lock-Awn. After examining one of the AwningSaver devices themselves, they believed that the product would prevent billowing. But, they found it difficult to operate, contrary to the company's claims, and they thought the AwningSaver had a "homemade" look to it when installed, which Eric and Mary found unappealing. As Mary said, "why would you want to put something that looks cheap on a motor home that cost $100,000?" In addition, Eric and Mary thought the AwningSaver was overpriced—it retailed at $59.95 plus $7.50 for shipping, for an assortment of bolts, nuts, washers, and clamps that could be purchased for under $5 from any hardware store.

MARKETING AND DISTRIBUTION OF THE LOCK-AWN

When Mary finished collecting information about RVers and competitors, she began to research information she could use to develop a marketing mix. Mary thought there were three viable distribution channels. First, they could sell the Lock-Awn as a mail-order product, much as the AwningSaver, passing the shipping costs on to the buyer. This would require a good Web site and knowledge about how to get the Web site highly ranked on search engines. Neither Eric nor Mary had that knowledge, but Mary thought that perhaps they could use the plethora of RV-related Web sites to direct Internet traffic to a Lock-Awn Web site. Mary contacted a regional company well known for its Web site

EXHIBIT 5
The Awning Saver

Source: www.awningsaver
.com

design and management and discovered that a basic five-page Web site design and hosting would cost $600, while search engine optimization would cost a minimum of $1,795 per year. If they wanted customized features on their Web site, the cost could go as high as $2,000–$3,000.

A second possibility was to attract individual dealers from the Workampers group. This group, at 70,000 members, lived full time in their RVs and looked for business opportunities they could conduct from their RVs. "Who better to sell the Lock-Awn to RVers than people who live in their RVs all the time?" thought Mary. They could recruit Workampers through the Workamper publication and Web site (a one-time ad cost $100). They would advance qualified applicants 10 Lock-Awn units on 30-day net terms. EMR would also provide promotional materials and one free display unit for the dealers to install on their own awnings. Workampers would earn a 25 percent margin (a 25 percent discount off the retail price) on each Lock-Awn unit they sold. Mary thought that Workamper dealers could not only make money by selling the Lock-Awn devices, but they could also charge to install the Lock-Awn to earn some additional income. Dealers also had the option to sell the product to retail distributors, such as RV repair shops or campground stores.

A third distribution method was to use an established distributor that already sold RV accessories, such as Camping World. Camping World was the largest RV after-market retailer in the United States. Mary thought that without a strong sales record, it would be difficult to get Camping World to sell the Lock-Awn. Still, she recognized it as a possibility, if not right away, then at least in the future. Mary was not sure what kind of margin Camping World required, but she assumed that the distributor would dictate the terms, not the Reynolds.

As she considered the distribution options, Mary figured that she and Eric would probably use some combination of direct selling and the Workampers (indirect selling). She also

EXHIBIT 6 EMR Sales Projections in Units—Years 1 and 2

					Year 1								
Month	**1**	**2**	**3**	**4**	**5**	**6**	**7**	**8**	**9**	**10**	**11**	**12**	**Total Unit Sales**
Direct Sales	0	0	0	100	300	400	500	500	600	600	600	600	4,200
Indirect Sales	0	0	0	20	40	100	300	350	500	500	500	500	2,810
Total Sales	0	0	0	120	340	500	800	850	1,100	1,100	1,100	1,100	7,010
					Year 2								
Month	**1**	**2**	**3**	**4**	**5**	**6**	**7**	**8**	**9**	**10**	**11**	**12**	**Total Unit Sales**
Direct Sales	650	650	650	650	650	675	675	675	675	675	675	675	7,975
Indirect Sales	550	550	550	550	550	575	575	575	575	575	575	575	6,775
Total Sales	1,200	1,200	1,200	1,200	1,200	1,250	1,250	1,250	1,250	1,250	1,250	1,250	14,750

Source: Eric and Mary Reynolds.

assumed that for the first few months EMR Innovations was officially open, there would be no sales, as they implemented their distribution systems. Mary quickly projected what the sales of the Lock-Awn might be for the first couple of years (Exhibit 6), given that it would take a few months to establish the sales channels and that EMR Innovations was a small company. These projections were very modest, amounting to only 0.02 percent of the entire U.S. RV market (7.5 million households) by the end of the second year. Mary had no idea how many Lock-Awns would be returned under the 30-day satisfaction guarantee or 90-day warranty, but to be safe, she thought maybe a 0.5 percent return rate was a reasonable expectation.

To support selling efforts, Mary knew it was important to increase awareness for the Lock-Awn. She researched several different ways to do this:

- Advertise in popular RV magazines, such as *Motor Home* and *Trailer Life*. The combined circulation of these two publications was 1.5 million. A ⅓ page, black-and-white ad inserted four times would cost $25,000.

- Advertise on RV-related Web sites. Some would include links to other Web sites. Some would include ads on their sites for minimal or no cost.

- Develop promotional brochures detailing the awning billowing problem and the benefits of the Lock-Awn in addressing this problem. They would make the brochures available to dealers and RV parts distributors throughout the country. For high-quality 4-color brochures, design and printing costs would be about $1,500 for 10,000 brochures, according to some printing Web sites Mary consulted.

- Promote and demonstrate the Lock-Awn at RV shows and rallies. These types of shows attracted RV enthusiasts either for the purpose of learning more about RVs or for social gathering (traveling) with other RVers. Virtually every state had an RV show every year, and numerous rallies were sponsored throughout the company by RV clubs and organizations. Mary estimated that registration and travel costs for each show would be approximately $1,800, and that they could go to four regional shows annually.

- Ask RV trade publications to evaluate and feature the Lock-Awn in new product spotlight columns.

- Generate discussion about the Lock-Awn in RV chat rooms.

- Use the networking systems of RV clubs to spread information about the Lock-Awn device.

CONCLUSION

Eric and Mary carved some time out of their busy schedules a few weeks later to look at the marketing information Mary had put together. As she summarized her findings, she explained, "We need to decide which RVers are most likely to buy the Lock-Awn. And we have to decide how much we want to charge and how to distribute it. Once we've done that, we should be able to have a better idea about whether or not we can make money selling the Lock-Awn."

Eric was quiet for a moment, sighed, and then replied, "I know the Lock-Awn is a good product, and I think all RV owners should install it on their RVs, but I guess we can't build a business on what I think. So, let's really look at this information and consider our options with respect to how we would market the Lock-Awn."

"Yes," Mary said, "we have to. Otherwise we can't really know if we should do this or not."

Focused on their decision-making task, Mary and Eric began to review the market data piece by piece. Both knew the future of EMR Innovations depended on what the data told them.

REFERENCES

AwningSaver, retrieved from http://www.awningsaver.com, January 4, 2006.

Henricks, Mark, "RV-Based Businesses Can Be 'Going Concerns,'" *WSJ.com Startup Journal,* October 31, 2003, retrieved from http://www.startupjournal.com/ startuplifestyle/20030910-lifestyle.html.

Recreation Vehicle Industry Association, *2001 National Survey of Recreation Vehicle Owners,* 2001, conducted by Dr. Richard Curtin, University of Michigan.

Recreation Vehicle Industry Association (RVIA) RVIA Facts, http://www.rvia.org/ media/fastfacts.htm.

Recreation Vehicle Industry Association (RVIA) RVIA Facts, http://www.rvia.org/ media/shipmentsdata.htm.

RV Central, RV History, retrieved from http://www.rvcentral.com/rv_history.htm, June 2, 2005.

RVHotlineCanada.com—From Past to Present, retrieved from http://www. rvhotlinecanada.com/rvhistory.asp, June 2, 2005.

RV-Info: Your RV News and Information Portal, RV gadgets and accessories, retrieved from http://www.rv-info.net/rvgadgets.html, February 26, 2006.

Siuru, William D., Jr., "RV Awning Care: Protect this Expensive Investment," *Woman Motorist,* retrieved from http://www.womanmotorist.com/index.php/news/man/3062/ event=view, January 4, 2006.

4

Gap Inc. in 2010: Is the Turnaround Strategy Working?

Annette Lohman *California State University, Long Beach*

In the 1990s, Gap Inc. appeared to be in perfect sync with American pop culture and tastes. The brands represented affordable style, and just about everyone—from well-known celebrities to typical American families—was wearing Gap clothing. Many people had to have the latest pair of khakis or a cardigan from Gap. In addition, the annual revenues of the company's Old Navy clothing stores had reached $1 billion in 1997 and its Banana Republic chain hit the $1 billion sales mark in 1998. However, the company's rapid expansion during the late 1990s was accompanied by the addition of long-term debt of nearly $3 billion, decline in the quality of clothing, and the waning of popularity of its styling. Despite being so perfectly attuned to American fashion and tastes in the 1990s, Gap began a decline in 2000 that had yet to be fully resolved by 2010.

The company had brought in a new CEO in 2002 and then again in 2007, both with turnaround strategies that produced some level of positive results. The 2002 turnaround strategy had successfully eliminated all long-term debt by 2007, while the company's turnaround strategy launched in 2007 was directed at expanding internationally and improving Gap's quality, styling, and overall image. By 2008, Gap had opened dozens of franchised stores in the Middle East and Asia and hired the well-known designer Patrick Robinson to develop more stylish and fashionable lines for its clothing stores.

Even though the company's profitability had improved through year-end 2009, its annual revenues continued the decline that began in 2005. Particularly disturbing was its rapid decline in comparable-store sales. Comparable-store sales for US and international Gap, Banana Republic, and Old Navy Stores declined on average by 5 percent in 2005, 7 percent in 2006, 4 percent in 2007, 12 percent in 2008, and 3 percent in 2009. Comparable-store sales had improved slightly during the first quarter of 2010, with Gap stores experiencing a 2 percent quarter-over-quarter improvement in comparable-store sales, Banana Republic comparable-store sales improving by 5 percent between the first quarter of 2009 and the first quarter of 2010, and Old Navy comparable-store sales in the first quarter of 2010 improving by 7 percent over the same quarter in 2009. International sales remained unchanged from the first quarter of 2009 to the first quarter of 2010. It was yet to be determined if the slight improvement in comparable-store sales was a signal that Gap's latest turnaround strategy was working as planned or was a result of the gradually improving US economy, which had been in a deep recession since 2008 and grew by 2.7 percent during the first quarter of 2010. Gap's consolidated statements of income for fiscal 2005 through fiscal 2009 are presented in Exhibit 1. Exhibit 2 presents the company's consolidated balance sheets for fiscal 2007 through fiscal 2009.

COMPANY HISTORY AND OVERVIEW

The Gap was founded as a San Francisco blue jeans retailer in 1969 by Doris and Don Fisher. The Fishers' vision was to "make it simple to find a pair of jeans," and stocked a wide variety of sizes and styles that appealed primarily to San Francisco's teenagers. The Fishers expanded their product line during the 1970s by adding active wear appealing to a

EXHIBIT 1   Gap Inc. Consolidated Statements of Earnings, Fiscal 2005–Fiscal 2009 ($ millions, except per share amounts)

	Fiscal Year Ending				
	Jan. 30, 2010	Jan. 31, 2009	Feb. 2, 2008	Feb. 3, 2009	Jan. 28, 2006
Net sales	$14,197	$14,526	$15,763	$15,923	16,023
Cost of goods sold and occupancy expenses	8,473	9.079	10,071	10,266	10,154
Gross profit	5,724	5,447	5,692	5,657	5,869
Operating expenses	3,909	3,899	4,377	4,432	4,124
Operating income	1,815	1,548	1,315	1,225	1,745
Interest expense	6	1	26	41	45
Interest income	(7)	(37)	(117)	(131)	(93)
Earnings from continuing operations before income taxes	1,816	1,584	1,406	1,315	1,793
Income taxes	714	617	539	506	680
Earnings from discontinued operations, net of income tax benefit	—	—	(34)	(31)	??—
Net earnings	$ 1,102	$ 967	$ 833	$ 778	1,113
Weighted-average number of shares—basic*	694	716	791	831	881
Weighted-average number of shares—diluted*	699	719	794	836	902
Earnings from continuing operations, net of income taxes	$ 1.59	$ 1.35	$ 1.10	$ 0.97	$1.26
Loss from discontinued operation, net of income tax benefit	—	—	(0.05)	(0.03)	—
Net earnings per share	$ 1.59	$ 1.35	$ 1.05	$ 0.94	$1.26
Diluted earnings per share:					
Earnings from continuing operations, net of income taxes	$ 1.58	$ 1.34	$ 1.09	$ 0.97	$1.24
Loss from discontinued operation, net of income tax benefit	—	—	(0.04)	(0.04)	—
Net earnings per share	$ 1.58	$ 1.34	$ 1.05	$ 0.93	$1.24

*In millions.

Source: Gap Inc., 2009, 2008, and 2006 annual reports.

EXHIBIT 2   Gap Inc. Consolidated Balance Sheets, Fiscal 2007–Fiscal 2009 ($ millions except par value)

	January 30, 2010	January 31, 2009	February 2, 2008
ASSETS			
Current assets			
Cash and cash equivalents	$2,348	$1,715	$1,724
Short-term investments	225	—	177
Restricted cash	18	41	38
Merchandise inventory	1,477	1,506	1,575
Other current assets	596	743	572
Total current assets	4,664	4,004	4,086
Property and equipment, net	2,628	2,933	3,267
Other long-term assets	693	626	485
Total assets	$7,985	$7,564	$7,838
LIABILITIES AND STOCKHOLDERS' EQUITY			
Current liabilities			
Current maturities of long-term debt	$ —	$50	$138
Accounts payable	1,027	975	1,006
Accrued expenses and other current liabilities	1,063	1,076	1,259
Income taxes payable	41	57	30
Total current liabilities	$2,131	$2,158	$2,433
Long-term liabilities			
Long-term debt	—	—	50
Lease incentives and other long-term liabilities	963	1,019	1,081
Total long-term liabilities	963	1,019	1,131
Commitments and contingencies*			
Stockholders' equity			
Common stock $0.05 par value	55	55	55
Authorized 2,300 shares: Issued 1,105 and 1,100 shares			
Outstanding 694 and 734 shares			
Additional paid-in capital	2,935	2,895	2,783
Retained earnings	10,815	9,447	9,223
Accumulated other comprehensive earnings	155	123	125
Treasury stock, at cost (411 and 366 shares)	(9,069)	(8,633)	(7,912)
Total stockholders' equity	4,891	4,387	4,274
Total liabilities and stockholders' equity	$7,985	$7,564	$7,838

*Gap Inc. leases most of its facilities and distribution centers. Most are five-year renewable leases that come due at staggered intervals. The company also leases much of its equipment. Total lease commitments are valued at $4,694.

Source: Gap Inc. 2008, 2009, and 2010 annual reports.

broader range of customers. The company went public in 1976 and began a rapid expansion strategy after the consummate retailer Millard "Mickey" Drexler was hired as the company's president in 1983. Through a combination of acquisitions, new ventures, and strategies designed to produce organic growth, Drexler transformed Gap from a company with annual revenues of $400 million and 450 stores in 1983 to a retailing giant with annual revenues of $14 billion and more than 2,000 stores in 2002. Drexler was largely credited with creating Gap's hip image and making its preppy product line cool, with memorable print ads such as the ones depicting iconic photos of Ernest Hemingway, Humphrey Bogart, Jack Kerouac, and Marilyn Monroe wearing khakis similar to those sold by Gap. Under Drexler, Gap also acquired the Banana Republic chain in 1983, opened its first GapKids store in 1986, expanded internationally in 1989, became the second-largest apparel brand in the world in 1992, and launched Old Navy in 1994. Drexler was fired from his position as CEO in 2002 after Gap's comparable-store sales declined by double digits every quarter between 2000 and 2002.

Paul Pressler replaced Drexler as Gap's CEO in 2002. Pressler launched the Internet-only retailer Piperlime.com and expanded into new markets in Asia and the Middle East in 2006. He resigned in 2007 and was replaced by Glen Murphy. Murphy began franchising Gap and Banana Republic stores in countries located in the Middle East and Asia and acquired the women's activewear company Athleta in 2008. Also, under Murphy, Gap.com was reconfigured to allow Internet customers to shop for Gap, Old Navy, Banana Republic, Piperlime, or Athleta apparel using a single shopping cart. The following list presents an overview of Gap's five brands in 2010.

- *Gap*—Gap offered an extensive selection of "classically styled, high quality casual apparel at moderate price points. Products ranged from wardrobe basics such as khakis and T-shirts to fashion apparel, accessories and personal care products for men and women."[1] GapKids and babyGap brands offered casual apparel for infants and children through preteen. Gap stores also offered a line of maternity apparel and women's underwear, sleepwear, loungewear, and sports and active apparel.
- *Old Navy*—The Old Navy clothing store brand targeted customers seeking value-priced casual family apparel, shoes, and accessories. Old Navy stores also offered a line of maternity wear and personal care items.
- *Banana Republic*—The Banana Republic clothing store brand carried more sophisticated casual and tailored apparel, shoes, accessories, and personal care products at price points higher than those at Gap.
- *Athleta*—Athleta offered "stylish and functional high-quality apparel for women for a variety of sports, including running, skiing, snowboarding, surfing and yoga."[2] Advertised as athletic apparel, "designed by women athletes for women athletes" in 2010, this brand was only sold through the company's website and a catalog.
- *Piperlime*—Piperlime.com offered men, women, and children over 200 leading footwear brands from casual to high fashion and nearly 40 handbag brands. Gap Inc. controlled all aspects of the Piperlime.com except product design.

OVERVIEW OF THE US FAMILY CLOTHING STORES INDUSTRY

Gap Inc. was one of the four largest retailers in the US family clothing store industry in 2010. The family clothing store industry was one of six industries that made up the broader US clothing stores sector, which in 2009 accounted for approximately $156 billion in revenues. Sales for the US clothing store sector had declined from $164 billion in 2008, due in large part to the severe worldwide recession that began in 2008. As the largest industry within the sector, the US family clothing store industry accounted for sales of $84.4 billion in 2009, representing more than 54 percent of clothing store sector sales during the year. The remaining 46 percent of clothing store sector sales were made by retailers in the department store industry, the men's clothing store industry, the women's clothing store industry, the children's and infant's clothing store industry, and the lingerie, swimwear, uniform, and bridal store industry. Sales in all industry segments of the clothing store sector were highly seasonal, with the 13 weeks during the back-to-school (August) and

---

[1]Gap, 2008 annual report, p. 4.

[2]Gap, www.gapinc.com/public/Media/Press_Releases/med_pr_Athleta041709.shtml, accessed April 24, 2009.

EXHIBIT 3   Selected Industry Statistics for the US Family Clothing Stores Industry, 2006–2010

	2006	2007	2008	2009*	2010*
Industry Data					
Industry revenue ($ millions)	$88,154	$89,256	$86,410	$83,950	$84,400
Industry gross product ($ millions)	$14,208	$14,999	$12,584	$12,280	$13,166
Number of establishments (units)	35,929	36,595	34,564	32,741	33,760
Number of enterprises (units)	18,398	18,664	17,628	16,063	16,880
Quantity of clothing items (thousands)	573,000	583,737	582,482	543,650	547,104
Annual Percent Change					
Industry revenue	2.6%	1.3%	−3.2%	−2.8%	0.5%
Industry gross product	4.1	5.6	−16.1	−2.4	7.2
Number of establishments	2.4	1.9	−5.5	−5.3	3.1
Number of enterprises	0.8	1.4	−5.6	−8.9	5.1
Quantity of clothing	3.1	1.9	−0.2	−6.7	0.6

*All numbers are estimates.

Source: IBISWorld Inc., "Family Clothing Stores in the US: 44814. Recession Update: January 12, 2009 and Industry Report," January 2010.

holiday (November through December) periods accounting for a substantial proportion of most clothing retailers' business. Exhibit 3 presents selected industry statistics for the US family clothing store industry.[3]

GLOBALIZATION

The level of globalization in the US family clothing stores industry was relatively low. In 2010, the industry was made up of a large number of small local companies and the major companies selling in the US market were domestically owned. The larger industry rivals such as Gap and TJX Stores generated between 10 and 20 percent of their sales from international operations. However, there had been some entry into the US clothing store market by international companies such as Uniqlo from Japan, H&M from Sweden, and Zara from Spain. This group of new entrants focused their market penetration efforts on the youth demographic (people aged 18 to 24), which was particularly well-suited to these companies because of their access to low-cost contract manufacturers and a distinctive competence in developing new designs to cater to minitrends in as few as two weeks.

Foreign entrants and domestic-based clothing stores both relied on independent third parties to manufacture the majority of their products, with most suppliers located in Asia, the Middle East, and South America. Overseas factories placed retailers at risk for exposure to negative publicity through sourcing partners' illegal or unethical operations, such as using child labor or sweatshop working conditions and low pay. Many companies had developed procedures to monitor and train their partners to minimize these risks. Risk also came from potential shortages of apparel or materials. If significant increases in demand for a product occurred or a company lost a vendor, there was the likelihood that retailers would not have the products needed to meet demand in their stores. Other risks associated with overseas manufacturing included shipment delays and interruptions in supply because of foreign government action.

[3]IBISWorld, "Family Clothing Stores in the US: 44814. Recession Update: January 12, 2009," industry report, January 2010.

INDUSTRY SEGMENTATION

The US clothing store industry could be segmented by gender, age, size, and price considerations. Women traditionally spent more on clothes than men did, with women's wear accounting for 50 percent of the product share in this industry, men's wear 37 percent, and children's wear 13 percent.[4] The plus-sized segment had become a $27 billion segment within the industry by 2010, as the number of obese adults aged 20 and over had grown to 34 percent of the population by 2008. US government statistics indicated that 18 percent of adolescents aged 12 to 19 could be considered obese. The demand for plus-size garments had increased for both genders and consumers of all ages.

The industry was also segmented by price point, with value-priced clothing lines accounting for about 65 percent of industry sales. The remaining 35 percent of industry sales were made up of higher-priced items, which carried higher margins. In the family clothing stores industry, the majority of stores—such as Ross Stores, TJX Companies, and Stein—all targeted price-conscious consumers who still wanted name brands but at a discount and were willing to purchase styles off-season or from the previous year. Fashion- and brand-conscious consumers who shopped at retailers such as Gap and Abercrombie & Fitch tended to be emotionally driven in their purchasing behavior and were influenced by marketing efforts that showcased a store's latest and greatest offerings.[5] The discount segment had withstood the effects of the 2008–2009 recessionary period somewhat better than premium-priced stores as consumers at almost all income levels placed a greater focus on value.[6]

COST/PROFIT STRUCTURE OF THE INDUSTRY

The average cost/profit structure of retailers in the US family clothing store industry, as estimated by IBISWorld, followed the chain of value-adding activities and was made up as follows:

- *Purchases of clothing:* Purchases of clothing from contract manufacturers primarily located offshore made up approximately 68.9 percent of industry revenues. Purchases of clothing were often affected by exchange-rate fluctuations and trade restrictions. Perhaps the most important trade policy affecting US family clothing stores was the World Trade Organization (WTO) agreement on textiles and clothing. Implemented in 1974, the internationally negotiated Multi-Fiber Arrangement (MFA) created a system of quotas that limited the amount of textiles and apparel that could be exported from developing countries to developed ones. This agreement was intended to be a short-term solution that would allow manufacturers of textiles and apparel in developed countries time to adjust to imports from underdeveloped countries.[7] The unintended outcome of these restrictions was a practice known as "chasing quota," in which clothing buyers would satisfy their production needs by scattering orders over numerous countries. On many occasions, this practice created garment industries in countries that otherwise lacked the proximity, infrastructure, workforce, or cost base to compete effectively in the open market.
  - With the ending of the MFA on January 1, 2005, US family clothing stores industry participants anticipated the ability to develop supply chains with fewer artificial

---

[4]Ibid.
[5]Reuters, "(2007) Retail (Apparel): Overview."
[6]IBISWorld, "Family Clothing Stores."
[7]Wikipedia, "Multi Fibre Agreement," http://accessed March 30, 2009.

restrictions than they had previously experienced.[8] However, because the United States and China, which in 2008 provided about 37 percent of women's and girls' apparel, agreed to continue with certain restrictions on apparel and textiles through December 2008, there was concern that some restrictions might continue beyond this point.[9] However, as China's minimum wage had increased, imported clothing had become sourced from the Philippines and Vietnam, where labor remained cheap. Industry analysts anticipated that American wholesalers would seek additional contract manufacturing sources from Indonesia, India, and Cambodia.[10]

- The extensive use of off-shore sourcing had another unintended consequence—the growing bargaining power and leverage of low-cost foreign clothing manufacturers when negotiating with US clothing stores. In response, retail family clothing store companies had tended toward using a "portfolio approach to sourcing," which involved sourcing from various global regions. The portfolio approach allowed companies to diminish some of the risk associated with conducting business with only one or very few suppliers.[11]

- *Wages:* Industry wages in 2009 were estimated at 9.8 percent of US clothing stores' industry sales. Retailing industries were labor-intensive, with staff needed to serve store customers and maintain store inventory levels. While some chains achieved lower labor costs through lower wages and fewer personnel, others used higher-quality personnel and more employees in the stores to make customer service a differentiating feature of the chain. Most retailers used a combination of full- and part-time employees to meet light and peak store traffic requirements. In addition, seasonal factors—particularly summer and holiday sales—required the use of part-time personnel.

- *Other expenses:* Typical other expenses included rent (5 percent), advertising (1.5 percent), depreciation (1.5 percent), and others (10.3 percent).

- *Before-tax profits:* After all expenses, IBISWorld estimated, average before-tax profits for the US clothing store industry were 3.0 percent in 2009—IBISWorld estimated the industry's before-tax profit margin at 3.4 percent in 2008.[12]

FACTORS DETERMINING COMPETITIVE SUCCESS IN THE FAMILY CLOTHING STORE INDUSTRY

Of the competitive elements directly affecting the prosperity of companies in the branded segment of the US family clothing industry, none was more important than the ability to successfully develop new product lines that reflected the latest fashion trends and then quickly bring them to market. Consumer purchasing decisions were also affected by the number of similar stores in the buyer's immediate shopping environment, although strong brand loyalty could cause buyers to extend their shopping range. However, it was generally important for clothing store chains to have a broad network of retail stores located in prime real estate locations. The growth of Internet retailing had made it easier for consumers to find sought-after items if a store was not nearby or if a store was out of stock,

---

[8]Ibid.

[9]Gap, 2007 annual report.

[10]IBISWorld, "Family Clothing Stores."

[11]S. Kusterbeck, "China Appeals to U.S. Buyers with 'Supply Chain Cities,'" *Apparel 46* (August 2005), pp. 24–28.

[12]IBISWorld, "Family Clothing Stores."

but many consumers preferred to visually inspect or try on clothing items that they were unfamiliar with.

It was also critical for rivals in the US family clothing stores industry to build brand loyalty, which acted as a barrier to entry for potential new entrants to the market. Many rival firms dedicated considerable resources to brand building and advertising. Finally, because of the extremely slim profit margins that existed in the industry, it was critical for companies to have excellent financial management and inventory management skills to control cash flow, reduce debt, and keep costs low.[13]

MAJOR RIVALS IN THE US FAMILY CLOTHING STORE INDUSTRY

With the exception of national chains, the US family clothing stores industry was highly fragmented and was made up of thousands of small local or regional retailers that individually held very small market shares. However, the four largest national chains accounted for about 39.4 percent of the total market share in 2009. The top four US family clothing stores industry performers were (1) the TJX Companies Inc., with a 13.4 percent market share (up from 11.5 percent in 2006); (2) Gap Inc., with a 15 percent market share (down from 18.6 percent in 2006); (3) Ross Stores Inc., with a 6.9 percent market share (up from 4.0 percent in 2006); and (4) Abercrombie & Fitch, with a 4.1 percent market share (steady since 2006 but up from 3.8 percent in 2005). American Eagle Outfitters was also a notable rival in the industry, with an estimated market share in 2009 of about 1 percent.

TJX Companies

TJX Companies was the leading off-price retailer of clothing and home fashions in the United States in 2010. The company owned and operated 890 T. J. Maxx discount stores, which carried family clothing, women's footwear and apparel, home fashion, beauty items, and jewelry and accessories. T. J. Maxx priced its products at 20–60 percent below department and specialty store pricing. Similarly, TJX operated 813 Marshall's, which was a discount department store chain carrying family clothing, a full line of family footwear, women's apparel, men's apparel, home fashions, and toys. The company also operated 323 HomeGoods off-price home decor stores and 150 A. J. Wright deep-discount family clothing and home fashion stores. In Canada, TJX owned and operated 208 Winners family clothing stores and 79 HomeSense stores. Winners' merchandise mix was similar to that of T. J. Maxx, and HomeSense's was similar to HomeGoods'. In 2008, the company launched Stylesense in Canada, which was an off-price footwear retailer. There were no plans to expand the number of Stylesense stores until the concept was more fully developed.

In 1994, the company opened T. K. Maxx stores in the United Kingdom and had become the seventh-largest UK fashion retailer, with 263 stores, and it was the only major off-price retailer in Europe in 2010. The company expanded T. K. Maxx to Germany in 2007 and Poland in 2009. TJX also operated 14 HomeSense stores in the United Kingdom in 2010. In 2009, TJX's Canadian and European stores accounted for 10.7 percent and 10.9 percent of total revenues, respectively. For the fiscal year ending January 31, 2010, TJX's comparable-store sales in Canada increased by 3 percent, comparable-store sales in Europe increased by 5 percent, and comparable-store sales at T. J. Maxx and Marshall's stores improved by 7 percent. Comparable-store sales at HomeGoods and A. J. Wright increased by 9 percent during fiscal 2009. Comparable-store sales for all TJX stores for the first quarter of 2010 increased by 9 percent when compared to the same period in 2009. A summary of TJX's financial performance for fiscal 2008 and 2009 is presented in Exhibit 4.

[13]Ibid.

EXHIBIT 4   Financial Summary for TJX Companies, Fiscal 2009–Fiscal 2010 ($ thousands except per share amounts)

	52 Weeks Ended January 30, 2010	53 Weeks Ended January 31, 2009
Net sales	$20,288,444	$18,999,505
Cost of sales, including buying and occupancy costs	14,968,429	14,429,185
Selling, general, and administrative expenses	3,328,944	3,135,589
Provision (credit) for Computer Intrusion related costs	—	(30,500)
Interest expense, net	39,509	14,291
Income from continuing operations before provision for income taxes	1,951,562	1,450,940
Provision for income taxes	737,990	536,054
Income from continuing operations	1,213,572	914,886
Income (loss) from discontinued operations, net of income taxes	—	(34,269)
Net income	$ 1,213,572	$ 880,617
Diluted earnings per share:		
Income from continuing operations	$2.84	$2.08
Net income	$2.84	$2.00

Source: TJX Companies, press release, February 24, 2010.

Ross Stores

Ross Stores was the second-largest off-price retailer in the United States, with fiscal 2009 revenues of $7.2 billion. As of January 30, 2010, the company operated a chain of 953 Ross Dress for Less stores in 27 states and Guam—up from 904 stores in 2008. Ross Dress for Less offered name-brand apparel and designer apparel at everyday low prices that were 20 to 60 percent off regular department store prices. In addition, the company operated 52 dd's DISCOUNTS locations in California, Florida, Texas, and Arizona. The dd's DIS-COUNTS stores featured a moderately priced assortment of first-quality, in-season, name-brand fashion apparel, accessories, and footwear for the entire family at everyday savings of 20 to 70 percent off moderate department and discount store regular prices. For the fiscal year 2009, ending January 30, 2010, Ross Stores posted record earnings of $442.8 million on revenues of nearly $7.2 billion. Its comparable-store sales were 6 percent greater than in fiscal 2008. The company's comparable store sales for the first quarter of fiscal 2010 were 10 percent greater than the same period in fiscal 2009. A summary of Ross Stores' financial performance for fiscal 2008 and fiscal 2009 are presented in Exhibit 5.

Abercrombie & Fitch

Abercrombie & Fitch (A&F) was a specialty retailer selling upscale, premium-priced casual clothing for men, women, and children. At year-end 2009, A&F operated approximately 1,096 stores in the United States, Canada, and Europe, including 340 Abercrombie & Fitch stores, 205 abercrombie kids stores, 507 Hollister stores, and 16 Gilly Hicks stores. All A&F store brands also operated Internet retailing sites through which consumers could purchase its apparel items. The company also operated 6 Abercrombie & Fitch stores, 4 abercrombie kids stores, and 18 Hollister stores internationally. Both Abercrombie & Fitch and aber-crombie kids stores developed images and product lines that were inspired by East Coast Ivy League and preparatory schools, while Hollister drew on the Southern California culture for its image and product line. Gilly Hicks was an Australian-themed chain specializing in un-derwear, swimwear, and casual wear for young women. In 2009, the company discontinued its Ruehl clothing stores business, which had incurred losses of $23.4 million in 2007, $35.9 million in 2008, and $78.7 million in 2009. The closure of the Ruehl clothing stores business resulted in a $56.1 million pretax exit charge against 2009 earnings. The company's Ruehl-branded stores had been launched in 2004 with higher price points than its other stores and

EXHIBIT 5   Financial Summary for Ross Stores, Fiscal 2009–Fiscal 2010 ($ thousands except per share amounts)

	Twelve Months Ended	
	January 30, 2010	January 31, 2009
Sales	$7,184,213	$6,486,139
Costs and expenses		
Costs of goods sold	5,327,278	4,956,576
Selling, general and administrative	1,130,813	1,034,357
Interest expense (income), net	7,593	(157)
Total costs and expenses	6,465,684	5,990,776
Earnings before taxes	718,529	495,363
Provision for taxes on earnings	275,772	189,922
Net earnings	$ 442,757	$ 305,441
Earnings per share		
Basic	$ 3.60	$ 2.36
Diluted	$ 3.54	$ 2.33
Weighted average shares outstanding (000)		
Basic	122,887	129,235
Diluted	125,014	131,315

Source: Ross Stores, press release, March 18, 2010.

were intended to appeal to young professionals. Between 2010 and 2011, the company planned to open new flagship Abercrombie & Fitch stores in Fukuoka, Japan; Copenhagen, Denmark; and Paris, France, and 30 new Hollister stores in Europe and Asia. A comparison of the financial performance of Abercrombie & Fitch's store brands between 2007 and 2009 is presented in Exhibit 6. A summary of the company's consolidated financial performance for 2009 and 2010 is presented in Exhibit 7.

American Eagle Outfitters

American Eagle Outfitters (AEO) operated 938 stores in the United States and Canada. AEO stores carried trendy, affordable priced casual wear appealing to 15- to 25-year-olds.

EXHIBIT 6   Financial Comparison of Abercrombie & Fitch Store Brands, 2007–2009 ($ thousands except per share amounts)

	2009	2008	2007
Net sales	$2,928,626	$3,484,058	$3,699,656
Abercrombie & Fitch	1,272,287	1,531,480	1,638,929
abercrombie kids	343,164	420,518	471,045
Hollister	1,287,241	1,514,204	1,589,452
Gilly Hicks	25,934	17,856	230
Increase (decrease) in net sales from prior year	(16)%	(6)%	13%
Abercrombie & Fitch	(17)	(7)	8
abercrombie kids	(18)	(11)	16
Hollister	(15)	(5)	17
Gilly Hicks	45	NM	NM
Decrease in comparable store sales	(23)%	(13)%	(1)%
Abercrombie & Fitch	(19)	(8)	0
abercrombie kids	(23)	(19)	0
Hollister	(27)	(17)	(2)

Source: Abercrombie & Frtch, 2009 10-K report.

EXHIBIT 7   Financial Summary for Abercrombie & Fitch, 2008–2009 ($ thousands except per share amounts)

	2009	% of Net Sales	2008	% of Net Sales
Net sales	$2,928,626	100.0%	$3,484,058	100.0%
Cost of goods sold	1,045,028	35.7%	1,152,963	33.1%
Gross profit	1,883,598	64.3%	2,331,095	66.9%
Total stores and distribution expense	1,425,950	48.7%	1,436,363	41.2%
Total marketing, general and administrative expense	353,269	12.1%	405,248	11.6%
Other operating income, net	(13,533)	−0.5%	(8,778)	−0.3%
Operating income	117,912	4.0%	498,262	14.3%
Interest income, net	(1,598)	−0.1%	(11,382)	−0.3%
Income from continuing				
Operation before income taxes	119,510	4.1%	509,644	14.6%
Income tax expense for continuing operations	40,557	1.4%	201,475	5.8%
Net income from continuing operations	78,953	2.7%	308,169	8.8%
Net loss from discontinued operations (net of taxes)	(78,699)	−2.7%	(35,914)	−1.0%
Net income	$ 254	0.0%	$ 272,255	7.8%
Net income per share from continuing operations:				
Basic	$ 0.90		$ 3.55	
Diluted	$ 0.89		$ 3.45	
Net loss per share from discontinued operations:				
Basic	$(0.90)		$(0.41)	
Diluted	$(0.89)		$(0.40)	
Total net income per share:				
Basic	$ 0.00		$ 3.14	
Diluted	$ 0.00		$ 3.05	
Weighted-average shares outstanding (000s):				
Basic	87,874		86,816	
Diluted	88,609		89,291	

Source: Abercrombie & Fitch, press release, February 16, 2010.

The company also operated 138 stores under the brand name aerie in the United States and Canada; aerie stores sold underwear and leisure wear for young women. Apparel sold in both American Eagle Outfitters and aerie stores was also available for purchase online at www.ae.com. The company's 77kids by American Eagle brand of clothing for children was available online only at www.ae.com and www.77kids.com. The company had operated 28 Martin + Osa stores, which carried apparel items similar to those sold in American Eagle Outfitters stores but focused on the 30+ age demographic. AEO closed all Martin + Osa stores in March 2010 after the brand lost $44 million in fiscal 2009.

Even though recession had contributed to an overall comparable-store sales decline of 10 percent in 2008 and 4 percent in 2009, the company's new aerie stores experienced a 25 percent improvement in comparable-store sales between 2008 and 2009. In addition, the company planned to open seven brick-and-mortar 77kids stores in 2010. A summary of AEO's financial performance for 2008 and 2009 is presented in Exhibit 8.

Competition from Other Clothing Sector Industries

Consumers purchased apparel not only from family clothing stores but also from sellers competing in the department store industry, big-box store industry, men's clothing store industry, women's clothing store industry, and children's and infant's clothing store industry. Department store companies such as The Federated Group, Sears, and JCPenney as well as big-box mass merchandisers such as Target and Walmart brought competitive pressure on

EXHIBIT 8   Financial Summary for American Eagle Outfitters, 2008–2009 ($ thousands except per share amounts)

	For the Fiscal Year Ending	
	January 30, 2010	January 31, 2009
Summary of Operations		
Net sales	$2,990,520	$ 2,988,866
Comparable store sales (decrease) increase	(4)%	(10)%
Gross profit	$1,158,049	$ 1,174,101
Gross profit as a percentage of net sales	38.7%	39.3%
Operating income	$ 238,393	$ 302,140
Operating income as a percentage of net sales	8.0%	10.1%
Income from continuing operations	$ 169,022	$ 179,061
Income from continuing operations as a percentage of net sales	5.7%	6.0%
Per Share Results		
Income from continuing operations per common share—basic	$ 0.82	$ 0.87
Income from continuing operations per common share—diluted	$ 0.81	$ 0.86
Weighted average common shares outstanding (000s)—basic	206,171	205,169
Weighted average common shares outstanding (000s)—diluted	209,512	207,582

Source: American Eagle Outfitters, 2009 annual report.

family clothing stores. In addition, consumers who did not need to try on an article of clothing frequently turned to the Internet to find closeouts or other discounts that might not be available locally. Internet retailing sites also allowed customers who were loyal to a particular brand to purchase desired items even if the retailer did not have a store nearby. Subsequently, most major brick-and-mortar apparel retailers had expanded into Internet retailing as well.

TURNAROUND STRATEGIES AT GAP

With Gap's same-store sales beginning a long-term decline in 2000, the company's first turnaround strategy began with Mickey Drexler's replacement by Paul Pressler as CEO in 2002. Pressler had spent 15 years with the Walt Disney Company before coming to Gap and began his turnaround with a redesign of the company's websites and online presence. A completely new e-commerce platform was developed for Gap.com, BananaRepublic.com, and OldNavy.com, with all three websites redesigned to provide greater functionality and a more convenient shopping experience. The *New York Times* reported that Gap's redesigned websites were "among the best e-commerce sites in retail."[14]

In an effort to expand Gap's brand offerings to women older than 35 years, Pressler created the Forth & Towne chain of branded clothing stores in 2005 with the first stores opening in Chicago and New York. However, the concept was short lived, with mixed reviews on the attractiveness and fit of the clothes—some customers and analysts loved them, whereas others hated them. It was generally recognized that the company ineffectively launched and marketed the chain. Gap ended up closing all of its Forth & Towne stores in June 2007 following Pressler's departure from the company. Some analysts and customers complained that the concept had not been given a chance. Pressler's turnaround strategy also included the 2006 launch of Piperlime.com—an online shoe store offering men, women, and children an assortment of third-party brands.

[14]Gap, 2005 annual report.

Under Pressler's leadership, the company also focused on reducing debt, which had reached nearly $2.9 billion in fiscal 2002. Pressler and the company's chief financial managers had successfully reduced the company's outstanding long-term indebtedness to $513 million by the end of fiscal 2005 and had eliminated all long-term debt by the end of fiscal 2007. The elimination of debt allowed Gap to consistently increase dividend payments to shareholders from $0.09 per share in 2002 to $0.32 per share in 2007. In addition, the company executed share repurchase plans that reduced outstanding shares from 887 million shares outstanding in 2002 to 794 million shares outstanding in 2007. However, despite Pressler's success in strengthening the company's balance sheets, many analysts believed that Pressler had made excessive cuts in expenditures related to design, product development, and marketing. Also, decisions to cut costs in the supply chain led to slowed product-to-market cycle times, which made the company less able to respond to fashion changes.

Analysts also believed that Gap was hindered in the marketplace by constant disagreements between research and design personnel that led to delayed decision making and eventual unwise compromises to merely get something on store shelves. With a lack of interesting new lines and products, Gap's revenues and earnings began to decline after peaking in fiscal 2004 at $16.2 billion and $1.15 billion, respectively. As the company's revenues began to decline, Pressler began to lose key executives who were frustrated with his approach and lack of understanding of the apparel industry.

The company's weakening financial and strategic performance led to Pressler's replacement by Glenn Murphy in the summer of 2007. Murphy came to Gap with more than 20 years of retail experience in the areas of food, health and beauty, and books. His turnaround strategy for Gap focused on improving the appeal of the company's product lines and expanding its business internationally. During Murphy's first year as CEO, Gap opened franchised stores in 11 countries, including Saudi Arabia, Bahrain, Indonesia, United Arab Emirates, Kuwait, Qatar, and South Korea. Murphy also opened franchised Banana Republic stores in nine countries during his first year as CEO. By 2008, more than 100 Gap franchised stores were in operation, with additional stores opening in Greece, Russia, Israel, Jordan, Mexico, and Romania in 2008 and 2009. New franchised Banana Republic stores opened in the United Kingdom, Saudi Arabia, Turkey, and the Philippines. The company also expanded its Gap and Banana Republic factory outlet stores to Canada in 2008. Murphy also diversified the company's apparel store variety with the $150 million acquisition of Athleta in 2008. Athleta was a direct marketer of women's athletic apparel, swimwear, and athletic-inspired leisure wear.

Murphy continued many of the cost-cutting measures of his predecessor but found it necessary to allocate resources to restore Gap brands' reputation for style and quality. One of Murphy's first and most important moves was to bring in Patrick Robinson as Gap's design chief. Robinson was well-known in apparel design circles, having worked for Anne Klein, Giorgio Armani, Perry Ellis, and Paco Rabanne. Robinson believed that what ailed the company was targeting a customer who was too young (18–24 years old), producing poor-quality clothes, and trying to imitate foreign newcomers Uniqlo (Japan), H&M (Sweden), and Zara (Spain), all of which emphasized "fast fashion," or rapid-fire mini-trends. Robinson commented that he was determined to get Gap off the "trend treadmill" and bring back the classics that had established the brand in its heyday.[15]

By the fall of 2008, some Wall Street analysts were hailing Murphy and Robinson's efforts as being in the right direction. Analysts saw the company's improved merchandise, clearer focus on the 25- to 35-year-old demographic, stronger leadership team, and additional cost-cutting initiatives as strengths of the turnaround strategy. However, the company's revenues and comparable-store sales had not seen a great deal of improvement through

[15]Jane Porter, "A Fashion Guy Gets Gap Back to Basics," *BusinessWeek*, August 18, 2008, p. 56.

year-end 2009. There was some debate concerning to what extent the lingering recession was impeding a financial turnaround of the company.

GAP IN 2010

Store Operations

Gap owned and operated more than 3,100 Gap, Banana Republic, and Old Navy stores world-wide in 2010. This number also included a number of Gap Outlet stores. Store locations outside the United States included Canada, the United Kingdom, France, Ireland, and Japan. In addition to company-owned stores, the company had franchising agreements to operate Gap and Banana Republic stores in Bahrain, Indonesia, Kuwait, Malaysia, the Philippines, Oman, Qatar, Saudi Arabia, Singapore, South Korea, Turkey, the United Arab Emirates, Greece, Romania, Bulgaria, Cyprus, Mexico, Egypt, Jordan, and Croatia. In February 2009, the company announced plans to open stores in Israel under the Gap and Banana Republic brands through an agreement with Elbit Trade and Retail Ltd.

The seasonality of the business required that the company carry a significant amount of inventory, especially before the beginning of a peak selling season. Replenishment inventory was kept not in the stores but at distribution centers from which it could be quickly shipped to stores. The company reviewed its inventories regularly to identify slow-moving merchandise and determine markdown amounts necessary to clear merchandise.[16] One of Pressler's most significant achievements as CEO was the reduction of Gap's inventory carrying costs.

Information Systems and Technology

Gap's information technology systems were critical to maintaining proper inventory and supporting its Internet retailing efforts. The company's website was attractive and easy to navigate for customers wanting to view new styles or purchase products online. Gap had contracted with IBM to operate aspects of its information technology infrastructure, including support for its mainframe computer, servers, network and data center, store operations systems, help desk, customer service support, and some disaster recovery. In January 2009, the company implemented a sophisticated software package for managing the real estate throughout its operations. The software allowed the company to monitor its real estate workflow and forecast the financial impact of real estate decisions, including those of consolidating or expanding or remodeling store locations. In the fall of 2009, in time for the holiday season, the company also successfully transitioned its order processing to a new system acquired from Kiva Systems. The company said that the system would allow its e-commerce division, Gap Inc. Direct, to process orders faster and with greater accuracy. The company planned to leverage its investment in its Kiva Systems software as it expanded its Internet retailing internationally in 2010.

Brand and Product Development

Gap controlled all aspects of brand development from design to distribution in-house. Most of its products were manufactured by approximately 79 independent vendors located in 60 countries. Approximately 3 percent of the company's products were produced domestically, with the remainder produced outside the United States. The company also offered products designed and manufactured by branded third parties for the company's online shoe store, Piperlime.

---

[16]Gap, 2007 annual report.

Gap also initiated a number of collaborations with celebrity designers and other companies to develop products.

- In June 2009, the company announced collaboration with designer Stella McCartney to create a collection for GapKids and babyGap that would be sold in select GapKids and babyGap stores in the United States, Canada, the United Kingdom, France, and Ireland and online in the United States.
- Also in 2009, the company entered into a partnership with the Paris boutique Merci, to create a Merci Gap store in Paris. The store would feature a number of products sourced from all over the world as well as Gap T-shirts with Merci graphics.
- In February 2010, Collective Brands, the parent company of the shoe retailer Keds, announced that it would create an alliance with Gap to create classically inspired lines of sneakers. The collection was expected to be in stores by fall 2010.[17]
- In May 2010, Gap's Banana Republic division announced that it had teamed up with Chan Lau, a renowned jewelry designer, to develop a collection of limited-edition bracelets.

Marketing

Gap allocated considerable resources to store design, customer service, and advertising. The company's primary advertising media included print ads in major metropolitan newspapers, Sunday magazines, and magazines emphasizing lifestyle and fashion. The company also placed ads in various outdoor and indoor venues using transit posters, exterior bus panels, billboards, and mall kiosks. Gap also spent significantly on television and radio advertising with highly recognizable ads. In the fall of 2009, the company introduced an ad campaign for its flagship Gap division that included a Facebook page, video clips, a realistic online fashion show on a virtual catwalk, and an application for the iPhone called the StyleMixer.

The company also hosted a nationwide "simultaneous acoustic concert" in its stores across the country to commemorate its 40th anniversary on August 21, 2009. "Music has always been an integral part of Gap—from musicians participating in our ad campaigns to musicians performing in our stores, to the way music is infused into the very soul of Gap," said Ivy Ross, Gap's executive vice president of marketing.[18] During the 2009 holiday retail season, the company put on a multi-city road tour of street performances featuring Gap's Cheer Squad and Drumline, a group of 12 professional dancers and drummers.

The company also donated to arts-related organizations in an effort to boost its image in urban art-oriented communities. A number of art benefit events were planned, including the sponsorship of the Metropolitan Museum of Art's May 2010 exhibition titled *American Woman: A Celebration of Fashion's Role in Defining the Modern Woman*. Working with award-winning designers for the gala, the company sponsored the creation of eight original gowns, which were worn by celebrities from fashion, music, film, television, and Broadway. The company also collaborated with a number of artists in a celebration of the San Francisco Museum of Modern Art's 75th anniversary in 2010.

Corporate Citizenship and Social Responsibility

In March 2010, Gap was recognized for a fourth consecutive year as one of the world's most ethical companies by the Ethisphere Institute. Also in 2010, Gap had been recognized

[17]Bee-Shyuan Chang, "Gap and Keds to Collaborate on Collection of Sneakers," *StyleList*, February 19, 2010.
[18]"First Time in Exchange History Traders Wear Jeans on NYSE Trading Floor," *Business Wire*, August 21, 2009.

for the fifth time by *Corporate Responsibility Magazine* on its list of "100 Best Corporate Citizens." The company was ranked ninth on the overall list and first among retailers. Gap had achieved such recognition by focusing on corporate citizenship activities such as improving factory conditions and standards for suppliers, investing in various communities and charities, environmental stewardship, and developing diversity and enrichment programs for employees. The company had developed its own Code of Vendor Conduct (COVC), by which it managed its relationships with its vendors. The code was designed to ensure that workers employed by vendors were paid fairly, did not work excessively long hours, and worked in a safe and healthy environment. Exhibit 9 lists selected Gap's social responsibility policies.

The company also supported a number of nonprofit organizations and sponsored various charitable events, including the following:

- In July 2009, Gap joined up with Grammy Award winner John Legend to create a (RED) ZONE seating section for the artist's August 13, 2009, concert at Madison Square Garden in New York City. Sales of tickets from the zone would go to benefit HIV/AIDS treatment programs in Africa.

- In November 2009, Gap announced its Give and Get campaign. Participants in the program were able to donate 5 percent of the purchase price of Gap products to a number of charities, including the Leukemia and Lymphoma Society, during the holiday season.[19]

- Also in November 2009, Gap's Piperlime shoe division unveiled its Holiday Gift List, featuring shopping lists from celebrities Brooke Shields, Rachel Bilson, Rashida Jones, and Kristen Bell. Ten percent of proceeds from items on the celebrities' lists were slotted to go to the Art of Elysium, a nonprofit organization that helps children through music and the arts.[20]

- In March 2010, Cotton Incorporated announced that it would be working with Gap to launch its Cotton: From Blue to Green denim drive. The drive encouraged consumers to bring their used denim clothing to Gap stores; the used items would then be recycled to provide cotton fiber insulation for 540 homes. Consumers who brought in their used denims were given a 30 percent discount on a new pair of Gap jeans.[21]

International Operations

In 2009, international revenues accounted for 18 percent of Gap's total company revenues. The company operated stores in the United States, Canada, the United Kingdom, France, Ireland, and Japan. The company also had entered into franchise agreements with third parties that operated more than 130 franchise stores selling Gap apparel in 20 countries throughout Asia, Europe, Latin America, and the Middle East. Some of the company's international plans included the following:

- *Expansion into China.* The company announced that it planned to open its first Gap store in China during 2010.

- *Online business expansion.* Gap expected to launch online businesses in both Canada and the United Kingdom in 2010.

- *Italy.* In February 2010, Gap announced that it would be opening its first Italian stores in Milan, and an outlet store in Rome was scheduled for a 2011 opening.

[19]"GAP Inc. Give and Get Campaign Benefits Leukemia and Lymphoma Society," *States News Service*, November 6, 2009.

[20]"Piperlime Unveils Celebrity Holiday Favorites," *PR Newswire*, November 24, 2009.

[21]"Cotton Incorporated Partners with Gap for Nationwide 'Cotton: From Blue to Green®' Denim Drive," *PR Newswire*, March 4, 2010.

EXHIBIT 9   Selected Social Responsibility Policies at Gap, Inc., 2009

Working with Factories

Because we don't own the factories where our clothes are made, we regularly inspect them to ensure that working conditions meet our standards. But our efforts dont stop there. We recognize that we have a responsibility to work in partnership with factories, as well as other apparel companies and concerned organizations, to improve working conditions across the industry. Together, we are striving to make garment factories around the world safe and fair places to work. Gap Inc. has more than 80 full-time employees around the world who are dedicated to improving the lives of factory workers. In 2007, our Vendor Compliance Officers conducted approximately 4,000 inspections in more than 2,000 garment factories around the world.[22]

Improving our Practices

Through our membership in the Ethical Trading Initiative (ETI), we started working with Women Working Worldwide (WWW), a non-governmental organization, to better understand how our purchasing practices can impact working conditions and how we can improve. WWW met with our employees, factory management and workers to understand our planning and production process and its impact on factories.

Partnerships

Today, we're partnering with many organizations around the world to address industry-wide issues. Our initiatives include helping workers better understand their rights, training factory supervisors how to lead more effectively and encouraging governments to strengthen enforcement of their own labor and environmental laws. Our partners include labor and human rights groups, internationally based non-governmental organizations (NGOs), trade unions and universities.

Our Team

Our Social Responsibility Team represents approximately 25 nationalities and speaks as many languages. Most members are from the region or country they work in.

Source: Gap, http://www.gapinc.com/public/SocialResponsibility/socialres.shtml, accessed March 16, 2009.

- *Thailand.* Minor International plc, a leading distributor of fashion goods, opened its first store in Thailand, selling Gap clothes, in March 2010. The company planned to open three more Gap stores in Bangkok.
- *Australia.* In March 2010, Gap signed a franchise agreement with Brand Republic Pty. Ltd. for exclusive rights to operate Gap brand stores in Australia.

GAP'S FINANCIAL PERFORMANCE IN 2010

The year 2009 had been a difficult one for Gap, and its brands as sales continued to decline across all of it chains—see Exhibits 10 and 11. Poor economic conditions in the United States likely contributed to the company's lackluster performance, but improving sales across the retail sector during the first quarter of 2010 were expected to help boost Gap's performance. However, the first-quarter improvement in same-store sales proved to be short-lived, as US consumer confidence dropped by 10 points between May and June 2010. Lynn Franco, the director of the Conference Board Consumer Research Center, suggested that "until the pace of job growth picks up, consumer confidence is not likely to pick up."[23]

[22]Gap, www.gapinc.com/public/documents/SR_India_Fact_Sheet_Update.pdf, accessed March 16, 2009. In response to allegations in 2007 that the company used factories employing child labor to make product for its GapKids brand, the company, on June 12, 2008, announced enhanced monitoring activities of suppliers and canceled the product made by the "unauthorized makeshift factory in India."

[23]Quoted in "The Conference Board Consumer Confidence Index Drops Sharply," Conference Board press release, June 29, 2010.

EXHIBIT 10   Gap Sales by Quarter and Division, Fiscal 2006–Fiscal 2009 ($ millions)

Fiscal Year 2009 Ending January 30, 2010

	Q1	Q2	Q3	Q4	FY2009
Gap North America	$ 834	$ 878	$ 987	$1,100	$ 3,799
Banana Republic North America	475	516	541	664	2,196
Old Navy North America	1,180	1,240	1,300	1,600	5,320
International*	369	361	378	514	1,622
Other**	267	224	298	329	1,110
Total Gap Inc.	$3,125	$3,219	$3,504	$4,207	$ 14,04

Fiscal Year 2008 Ending January 31, 2009

	Q1	Q2	Q3	Q4	FY2008
Gap North America	$1,052	$1,058	$1,161	$1,231	$ 4,502
Banana Republic North America	571	629	603	709	2,512
Old Navy North America	1,353	1,390	1,363	1,601	5,707
International*	398	412	413	505	1,728
Other**	10	10	21	36	77
Total Gap Inc.	$3,384	$3,499	$3,561	$4,082	$14,526

Fiscal Year 2007 Ending February 2, 2008

	Q1	Q2	Q3	Q4	FY2007
Gap North America	$1,086	$1,079	$1,224	$1,429	$ 4,818
Banana Republic North America	559	623	643	809	2,634
Old Navy North America	1,546	1,603	1,598	1,918	6,665
International*	353	373	379	510	1,615
Other**	5	7	10	9	31
Total Gap Inc.	$3,549	$3,685	$3,854	$4,675	$15,763

Fiscal Year 2006 Ending February 3, 2007

	Q1	Q2	Q3	Q4	FY2006
Gap North America	$1,121	$1,155	$1,282	$1,576	$ 5,134
Banana Republic North America	518	571	590	808	2,487
Old Navy North America	1,503	1,649	1,644	2,033	6,829
International*	296	339	335	496	1,466
Other**	1	—	—	6	7
Total Gap Inc.	$3,439	$3,714	$3,851	$4,919	$15,923

Note: Prior periods subject to adjustments for rounding purposes. Annual amounts agree to 10-K.
* Includes wholesale business and franchise business beginning September 2006.
** Other includes Piperlime.com beginning October 2006, Athleta beginning September 2008, and Business Direct which ended in July 2006.

Source: Gap, http://www.gapinc.com/public/investors/inv_Fittcials.shtml, accessed June 7, 2010.

In June 2010, Gap's chief financial officer, Sabrina Simmons, reported, "In May, we continued to deliver on our overarching goal of driving sales growth."[24] May's net sales were up 2 percent, reaching $1.05 billion versus the previous year's May sales of $1.03 billion. Company-wide year-to-date sales for the first quarter of 2010 were also reported up 5 percent, to $4.38 billion versus sales over the same period of 2009 $4.16 billion.[25] Despite the positive news, not all Gap's brands had fared equally well. While Banana Republic

[24]Gap, , accessed June 5, 2010.
[25]Ibid.

EXHIBIT 11   Gap Sales by Brand, Region, and Reportable Segment, Fiscal 2006–Fiscal 2009 ($ millions)

Fiscal Year 2009 (Ending January 30, 2010)	GAP	Old Navy	Banana Republic	Other	Total	Percentage of Net Sales
United States*	$3,508	$4,949	$2,034	$ —	$10,491	74%
Canada	312	386	162	—	860	6
Europe	683	—	24	36	743	5
Asia	774	—	106	48	928	7
Other regions	—	—	—	57	57	—
Total stores segment	$5,277	$5,335	$2,326	$141	$13,079	92
Direct reportable segment**	324	473	134	187	1,118	8
Total	$5,601	$5,808	$2,460	$328	$14,197	100%

Fiscal Year 2008 (Ending January 31, 2009)	GAP	Old Navy	Banana Republic	Other	Total	Percentage of Net Sales
United States*	$3,840	$4,840	$2,221	$ —	$10,901	75%
Canada	329	392	146	—	867	6
Europe	724	—	23	33	780	6
Asia	732	—	101	47	880	6
Other regions	—	—	—	68	68	—
Total stores segment	$5,625	$5,232	$2,491	$148	$13,496	$93
Direct reportable segment**	333	475	145	77	1,030	7
Total	$5,958	$5,707	$2,636	$225	$14,526	100%

Fiscal Year 2007 (Ending Febraury 2, 2008)	GAP	Old Navy	Banana Republic	Other	Total	Percentage of Net Sales
United States*	$4,146	$5,776	$2,351	$ —	$12,273	78%
Canada	364	461	147	—	972	6
Europe	822	—	—	5	827	5
Asia	613	—	89	36	738	5
Other regions	—	—	—	50	50	—
Total stores reportable segment	$5,945	$6,237	$2,587	$ 91	$14,860	94
Direct reportable segment**	308	428	136	31	903	6
Total	$6,253	$6,665	$2,723	$122	$15,763	100%

Fiscal Year 2006 (Ending Febraury 3, 2007)	GAP	Old Navy	Banana Republic	Other	Total	Percentage of Net Sales
United States*	$4,494	$6,042	$2,251	$ —	$12,787	80%
Canada	379	442	119	—	940	6
Europe	792	—	—	1	793	5
Asia	581	—	61	7	649	4
Other regions	—	—	—	24	24	—
Total stores reportable segment	$6,246	$6,484	$2,431	$ 32	$15,193	95
Direct reportable segment**	261	345	117	7	730	5
Total	$6,507	$6,829	$2,548	$ 39	$15,923	100%

*Includes United States and Puerto Rico.
**Results of online business. Includes Athleta beginning September 2008.
***Other includes wholesale business, franchise business, Piperlime, and, beginning September 2008, Athleta.

Source: Gap, 2008 annual report, p. 63, and 2009 annual report, pp. 65–66.

North America, Old Navy, and the company's international stores reported gains in sales compared to losses in the previous year, Gap North America, the flagship division of the company, continued to lose same-store sales, although the losses slowed to 2 percent compared to the previous year's losses of 11 percent. While Wall Street analysts were generally positive about the company's prospects, many questions about the potential success of the turnaround strategy remained.

5

Harley-Davidson, Inc.— Motorcycle Division

J. Paul Peter *University of Wisconsin–Madison*

Harley-Davidson, Inc., is a diversified company with corporate headquarters at 3700 Juneau Avenue, Milwaukee, Wisconsin. Its three major business segments include (1) motorcycles and related products, (2) transportation vehicles including both recreational and commercial vehicles, and (3) defense and other businesses. In 1990, the company experienced another record year of growth. In the *Business Week 1,000* ranking of the top U.S. companies, Harley-Davidson, Inc., with a market value of $515 million, moved from the 973rd to the 865th largest U.S. company. Richard F. Teerlink, president and chief executive officer of the company, offered the following introduction to the company's 1990 annual report:

> Fellow Shareholder: I am again pleased to announce a record year at Harley-Davidson, Inc. in terms of revenues, profits and earnings. I'm especially proud this year because we were able to deliver very impressive results despite the fact that 1990—the third and fourth quarters, especially—was tough on most American manufacturers.
>
> Revenues for 1990 totaled $864.6 million, an increase of 9.3 percent over 1989. Net income was $37.8 million, a 14.8 percent increase and net earnings per share increased 11.0 percent to $2.12. Since 1987, revenues, net income, and net earnings per share have increased 33.8, 78.3, and 29.3 percent, respectively. Considering where we were as recently as five years ago, these are tremendous results.

Indeed, these were tremendous results given that the company is the only U.S. motorcycle manufacturer still in business, although there were once more than 140 competitors. In addition, the company had tremendous difficulties surviving the 1970s and early '80s and few analysts thought it would survive. In fact, the company would have gone bankrupt in 1985 had it not gotten refinancing with only days to spare.

COMPANY BACKGROUND AND OPERATIONS

Harley-Davidson was established in 1903 and had a virtual monopoly on the heavyweight motorcycle market by the 1960s.[1] In the early '60s Japanese manufacturers entered the marketplace with lightweight motorcycles that did not directly compete with Harley-Davidson. The influx of the Japanese products backed by huge marketing programs caused the demand for motorcycles to expand rapidly.

Recognizing the potential for profitability in the motorcycle market, American Machine and Foundry (AMF, Inc.) purchased Harley-Davidson in 1969. AMF almost tripled production to 75,000 units annually over a four-year period to meet the increases in demand. Unfortunately, product quality deteriorated significantly, as over half the cycles came off the assembly line missing parts and dealers had to fix them up in order to make sales. Little money was invested in improving design or engineering. The motorcycles leaked oil, vibrated, and could not match the excellent performance of the Japanese products. While hard-core motorcycle enthusiasts were willing to fix up their Harleys and modify them for better performance, new motorcycle buyers had neither the devotion nor skill to do so. If Harley-Davidson was to remain in business, it desperately needed to improve quality and update its engine designs. Japanese manufacturers also moved into the heavyweight motorcycle market and began selling Harley look-alike motorcycles. Yamaha was the first company to do so and was soon followed by the three other major Japanese manufacturers, Honda, Suzuki, and Kawasaki. Their products looked so similar to Harley's that it was difficult to tell the difference without reading the name on the gas tank. The Japanese companies also copied the style of the Harley advertisements. As one Harley executive put it, "We weren't flattered."

In late 1975, AMF appointed Vaughn Beals in charge of Harley-Davidson. He set up a quality control and inspection program that began to eliminate the worst of the production problems. However, the cost of the program was high. For example, the company had to spend about $1,000 extra per bike to get the first 100 into shape for dealers to sell at around $4,000. Beals along with other senior managers began to develop a long-range product strategy—the first time the company had looked 10 years ahead. They recognized the need to upgrade the quality and performance of their products to compete with the faster, high-performance Japanese bikes. However, they also recognized that such changes would require years to accomplish and a huge capital investment.

In order to stay in business while the necessary changes in design and production were being accomplished, the executives turned to William G. Davidson, Harley's styling vice president. Known as "Willie G." and a grandson of one of the company founders, he frequently mingled with bikers, and with his beard, black leather, and jeans was well accepted by them. Willie G. understood Harley customers and stated that:

> They really know what they want on their bikes: the kind of instrumentation, the style of bars, the cosmetics of the engine, the look of the exhaust pipes, and so on. Every little piece on a Harley is exposed, and it has to look just right. A tube curve or the shape of a timing case can generate enthusiasm or be a total turnoff. It's almost like being in the fashion business.[2]

Willie G. designed a number of new models by combining components from existing models. These included the Super Glide, the Electra Glide, the Wide Glide, and the Low Rider. Each model was successful and other Harley executives credit Davidson's skill with

---

[1] This section is based on "How Harley Beat Back the Japanese," *Fortune,* September 25, 1989, pp. 155–64.

[2] Ibid., p. 156.

saving the company. One senior executive said of Willie G., "The guy is an artistic genius. In the five years before we could bring new engines on-stream, he performed miracles with decals and paint. A line here and a line there and we'd have a new model. It's what enabled us to survive."

Still, Harley-Davidson was losing market share to its Japanese competitors, who continued to pour new bikes into the heavyweight market. By 1980, AMF was losing interest in investing in the recreational market and decided to focus its effort on its industrial product lines. Since AMF could not find a buyer for Harley-Davidson, it sold the company to 13 senior Harley executives in an $81.5 million leveraged buyout financed by Citicorp on June 16, 1981.

In 1982 things turned worse than ever for Harley-Davidson. The overall demand for motorcycles dropped dramatically, and Harley's market share of this smaller market also continued to drop. The company had a large inventory of unsold products and could not continue in business with its level of production and expenses. Production was cut drastically, and more than 1,800 of the 4,000 employees were let go.

The Japanese manufacturers continued producing and exporting to the United States at rates well above what the market could endure. Harley-Davidson was able to prove to the International Trade Commission (ITC) that there was an 18-month finished-goods inventory of Japanese motorcycles that fell well below fair market value and asked for protection. The ITC can offer protection to a U.S. industry being threatened by a foreign competitor. In 1983, President Reagan increased the tariffs on large Japanese motorcycles from 4.4 percent to 49.4 percent, but these would decline each year and be effective for only five years. While this did decrease the imports somewhat and gave Harley some protection, Japanese manufacturers found ways to evade most of the tariffs, for example, by assembling more of their heavyweight bikes in their U.S. plants. Harley-Davidson's market share in the 1983 heavyweight motorcycle market slipped to 23 percent, the lowest ever, although it did earn a slight profit. By 1984, it had sales of $294 million and earned $2.9 million; it has continued to increase sales and profits through the early 1990s.

Manufacturing Changes

From the late 1970s, Harley-Davidson executives recognized that the only way to achieve the quality of Japanese motorcycles was to adopt many of the manufacturing techniques they used. The manufacturing systems changes that were instituted included a just-in-time manufacturing program and a statistical operator control system.[3]

The just-in-time manufacturing program was renamed MAN, which stood for Materials As Needed. When the program was discussed with managers and employees at the York, Pennsylvania, manufacturing facility, many of them reacted in disbelief. The York plant already had a modern computer-based control system with overhead conveyors and high-rise parts store and the new system would replace all of this with push carts! However, the MAN system eliminated the mountains of costly parts inventory and handling systems, speeded up set up time, and could solve other manufacturing problems. For example, parts at the York facility were made in large batches for long production runs. They were stored until needed and then loaded on a 3.5 mile conveyor that rattled endlessly around the plant. In some cases, parts couldn't be found, or when they were, they were rusted or damaged. In other cases, there had been engineering changes since the parts were made and they simply no longer fit. The MAN system consisted of containers that traveled between the place where the parts were made and where they were to be used. The containers served as a

---

[3]This section is based on Thomas Gelb, "Overhauling Corporate Engine Drivers Winning Strategy," *Journal of Business Strategy,* November/December 1989, pp. 8–12.

signal at each end to either "feed me" or "empty me." This system is credited with reducing work-in-process inventory by $22 million.

The statistical operator control (SOC) system allows continuous process improvements to reduce costs. The system involves teaching machine operators to use simple statistics to analyze measurements taken from parts to determine dimensional accuracy and quality. The system helps identify problems that occur during production early enough that they can be corrected before many parts are produced.

Human Resource Changes

In designing the new manufacturing processes, Harley executives recognized the importance of employee involvement.[4] In 1978, the company was among the first in the United States to institute a companywide employee involvement program. Harley-Davidson was the second U.S. company to begin a quality circles program, which permits employees to contribute their ideas, solve problems, and improve the efficiency and quality of their work. Prior to these changes, engineers would figure out how to improve the manufacturing process and then tell operating employees what changes they needed to make. Naturally, the engineering plans were not flawless but the operating employees would not lift a finger to help solve the problems and would simply blame the engineers for screwing up again.

The changes in manufacturing and human resource strategy were credited with a 36 percent reduction in warranty costs, a 46 percent increase in defect-free vehicles received by dealers since 1982, inventory turnover up 500 percent, and productivity per employee up 50 percent.

Marketing Changes

By 1983, Harley executives recognized that they had become too internally oriented and needed to pay greater attention to customers.[5] They recognized that they would not be able to compete effectively with the Japanese manufacturers by offering a complete product line of motorcycles but rather would have to find a niche and defend it successfully. They decided to focus all of their efforts on the superheavyweight motorcycle market (850cc or greater) and adopted a "close-to-the-customer" philosophy. This involved several unique marketing strategies. First, Harley executives actively sought out and discussed motorcycle improvement issues with customers. Second, it started the Harley Owner Group (HOG) to bring together Harley riders and company management in informal settings to expand the social atmosphere of motorcycling. The club is factory sponsored and is open to all Harley owners. It sponsors national rallies and local events and gives customers a reason to ride a Harley and involves them in a social group whose main activities revolve around the product.

Third, it began a Demo Ride program in which fleets of new Harleys were taken to motorcycle events and rallies and licensed motorcyclists were encouraged to ride them. This program was felt to be critical for convincing potential new customers that Harley-Davidson motorcycles were of excellent quality and not the rattling, leaking bikes of the 1970s. The program was renamed SuperRide and $3 million was committed to it. A series of TV commercials was purchased to invite bikers to come to any of Harley's over 600 dealers for a ride on a new Harley. Over three weekends, 90,000 rides were given to 40,000 people, half of whom owned other brands. While sales from the program did not immediately cover costs, many of the riders came back a year or two later and purchased a Harley.

Fourth, the company invited several manufacturing publications to visit the plant and publish articles on quality improvement programs. These articles reached the manufacturing trade audience and the national media as well. Finally, recognizing that many dealers

---

[4]Ibid.
[5]Ibid.

viewed their business as a hobby and did not know how to sell, the company increased its sales force by 50 percent to give sales representatives more time to train dealers in how to sell Harleys.

Financial Changes

Although Harley-Davidson was improving its quality, reducing its breakeven point, catching up with competitors in the superheavyweight market, and marketing more aggressively, Citicorp was concerned about the economy and what would happen to Harley-Davidson when the tariffs on Japanese bikes were lifted in 1988.[6] The bank decided it wanted to recover its loans and quit being a source of funds for the company. After a number of negotiations, Citicorp took a $10 million write-off which might have facilitated Harley obtaining new financing. However, other bankers felt that the company must have been in really bad shape if Citicorp took a write-off and refused financial assistance. While lawyers were drawing up a bankruptcy plan, Harley executives continued to seek refinancing. Finally, several banks did agree to pay off Citicorp and refinance the company with $49.5 million.

Harley-Davidson went public with a stock sale on the American Stock Exchange in 1986. The company hoped to raise an additional $65 million and obtained over $90 million with the sale of common stock and high-yielding bonds. It then was in an excellent cash position and purchased Holiday Rambler Corporation, at that time the largest privately held recreational vehicle company in the United States. Holiday Rambler is similar to Harley-Davidson in that it is a niche marketer that produces premium-priced products for customers whose lives revolve around their recreational activities. In 1987 the company moved to the New York Stock Exchange and made two additional stock market offerings. Selected financial data for Harley-Davidson is contained in Exhibits 1 through 4.

By 1987, Harley-Davidson was doing so well that it asked to have the tariffs on Japanese bikes removed a year ahead of schedule. On its 85th birthday in 1988, the company held a huge motorcycle rally involving over 40,000 motorcyclists from as far away as San Francisco and Orlando, Florida. All attenders were asked to donate $10 to the Muscular Dystrophy Association and Harley memorabilia was auctioned off. The event raised over $500,000 for charity. The final ceremonies included over 24,000 bikers whose demonstration of product loyalty is unrivaled for any other product in the world.

MOTORCYCLE DIVISION—EARLY 1990

Exhibit 5 shows the motorcycle division's growth in unit sales. In 1990, Harley-Davidson dominated the superheavyweight motorcycle market with a 62.3 percent share while Honda had 16.2 percent, Yamaha had 7.2 percent, Kawasaki had 6.7 percent, Suzuki had 5.1 percent, and BMW had 2.5 percent. Net sales for the division were $595.3 million with parts and accessories accounting for $110 million of this figure. Production could not keep up with demand for Harley-Davidson motorcycles, although a $23 million paint center at the York, Pennsylvania plant was nearing completion and would increase production to 300 bikes per day.[7]

Approximately 31 percent of Harley-Davidson's 1990 motorcycle sales were overseas. The company worked hard at developing a number of international markets. For example, anticipating the consolidation of Western European economies in 1992, a European parts and accessories warehouse was established in Frankfurt, Germany, in 1990. After

---

[6]Ibid.

[7]Harley-Davidson, Inc., Annual Report 1990, p. 12.

EXHIBIT 1   Harley-Davidson, Inc., Selected Financial Data (in thousands, except share and per share amounts)

	1990	1989	1988	1987	1986
Income statement data:					
Net sales	$864,600	$790,967	$709,360	$645,966	$295,322
Cost of goods sold	635,551	596,940	533,448	487,205	219,167
Gross profit	229,049	194,027	175,912	158,761	76,155
Selling, administrative, and engineering	145,674	127,606	111,582	104,672	60,059
Income from operations	83,375	66,421	64,330	54,089	16,096
Other income (expense):					
Interest expense, net	(9,701)	(14,322)	(18,463)	(21,092)	(8,373)
Lawsuit judgment	(7,200)	—	—	—	—
Other	(3,857)	910	165	(2,143)	(388)
	(20,758)	(13,412)	(18,298)	(23,235)	(8,761)
Income from continuing operations before income taxes and extraordinary items	62,617	53,009	46,032	30,854	7,335
Provision for income taxes	24,309	20,399	18,863	13,181	3,028
Income from continuing operations before extraordinary items	38,308	32,610	27,169	17,673	4,307
Discontinued operation, net of tax	—	3,590	(13)	—	—
Income before extraordinary items	38,308	36,200	27,156	17,673	4,307
Extraordinary items	(478)	(3,258)	(3,244)	3,542	564
Net income	$ 37,830	$ 32,942	$ 23,912	$ 21,215	$ 4,871
Weighted average common shares outstanding	17,787,788	17,274,120	15,912,624	12,990,466	10,470,460
Per common share:					
Income from continuing operations	$ 2.15	$ 1.89	$ 1.70	$ 1.36	$ 0.41
Discontinued operation	—	0.21	—	—	—
Extraordinary items	(.03)	(.19)	(.20)	0.28	0.05
Net income	$ 2.12	$ 1.91	$ 1.50	$ 1.64	$ 0.46
Balance sheet data:					
Working capital	$ 50,152	$ 51,313	$ 74,904	$ 64,222	$ 38,552
Total assets	407,467	378,929	401,114	380,872	328,499
Short-term debt, including current maturities of long-term debt	23,859	26,932	33,229	28,335	18,090
Long-term debt, less current maturities	48,339	74,795	135,176	178,762	191,594
Total debt	72,198	101,727	168,405	207,097	209,684
Stockholders' equity	198,775	156,247	121,648	62,913	26,159

In December 1986, the company acquired Holiday Rambler Corporation. Holiday Rambler Corporation's results of operations are not included in the income statement data for 1986.

Source: Harley-Davidson, Inc., Annual Report 1990, p. 29.

entering a joint venture in 1989 with a Japanese distributor, the company bought out all rights for distribution in Japan in 1990. Revenue from international operations grew from $40.9 million in 1986 to $175.8 million in 1990.

Product Line

For 1991, Harley-Davidson offered a line of 20 motorcycles shown in Exhibit 6. Other than the XLH Sportster 883 and XLH Sportster 883 Hugger, which had chain drives, all models were belt driven; all models had a five-speed transmission. Three of the Sportster models had an

EXHIBIT 2   Harley-Davidson, Inc., Consolidated Statement of Income (in thousands except per share amounts)

Years Ended December 31	1990	1989	1988
Net sales	$864,600	$790,967	$709,360
Operating costs and expenses:			
Cost of goods sold	635,551	596,940	533,448
Selling, administrative, and engineering	145,674	127,606	111,582
	781,225	724,546	645,030
Income from operations	83,375	66,421	64,330
Interest income	1,736	3,634	4,149
Interest expense	(11,437)	(17,956)	(22,612)
Lawsuit judgment	(7,200)	—	—
Other-net	(3,857)	910	165
Income from continuing operations before provision for income taxes and extraordinary items	62,617	53,009	46,032
Provision for income taxes	24,309	20,399	18,863
Income from continuing operations before extraordinary time	32,610	27,169	38,308
Discontinued operation, net of tax:			
Income (loss) from discontinued operation	—	154	(13)
Gain on disposal of discontinued operation	—	3,436	—
Income before extraordinary items	38,308	36,200	27,156
Extraordinary items:			
Loss on debt repurchases, net of taxes	(478)	(1,434)	(1,468)
Additional cost of 1983 AMF settlement, net of taxes	—	(1,824)	(1,776)
Net income	$ 37,830	$ 32,942	$ 23,912
Earnings per common share:			
Income from continuing operations	$ 2.15	$ 1.89	$ 1.70
Discontinued operation	—	.21	—
Extraordinary items	(.03)	(.19)	(.20)
Net income	$ 2.12	$ 1.91	$ 1.50

Source: Harley-Davidson, Inc., Annual Report 1990, p. 34.

883cc engine and one had a 1200cc engine; all of the remaining models had a 1340cc engine. The first five models listed in Exhibit 6 were touring models while the remaining bikes were standard and cruising types. All of the models exhibited impressive painting and classic styling attributes visually reminiscent of Harley-Davidson motorcycles from the 1950s and 1960s.

Motorcycle magazine articles commonly were favorable toward Harley-Davidson products but pointed out weaknesses in various models. For example, a review of the XLH Sportster 1200 in the December 1990 edition of *Cycle* reported that

> But Harley undeniably has its corporate finger on the pulse of Sportster owners, and knows what they want. All of the complaints—poor suspension, high-effort brakes, awkward riding position, short fuel range, engine vibration, and poor seat—have echoed through the halls of 3700 Juneau Ave. for more than a decade, yet have had seemingly little effect on XL sales. H-D sold 24,000 Sportsters over the past two years, and these complaints have been common knowledge to anyone who's cared enough to listen.[8]

The article, however, was very complimentary of the newly designed engine and new five-speed transmission and concluded that "This is the best Sportster ever to roll down an assembly line."

A review of the same model in *Cycle World's 1991 Motorcycle Buyer's Guide* pointed out a number of the same problems but concluded,

[8]"Harley-Davidson 1200 Sportster," *Cycle,* December 1990, p. 90.

EXHIBIT 3   Harley-Davidson, Inc., Consolidated Balance Sheet (in thousands except share amounts)

December 31	1990	1989
ASSETS		
Current assets:		
Cash and cash equivalents	$ 14,001	$ 39,076
Accounts receivable, net of allowance for doubtful accounts	51,897	45,565
Inventories	109,878	87,540
Deferred income taxes	14,447	9,682
Prepaid expenses	6,460	5,811
Total current assets	196,683	187,674
Property, plant and equipment, net	136,052	115,700
Goodwill	63,082	66,190
Other assets	11,650	9,365
	$407,467	$378,929
LIABILITIES AND STOCKHOLDERS' EQUITY		
Current liabilities:		
Notes payable	$ 22,351	$ 22,789
Current maturities of long-term debt	1,508	4,143
Accounts payable	50,412	40,095
Accrued expenses and other liabilities	72,260	69,334
Total current liabilities	146,531	136,361
Long-term debt	48,339	74,795
Other long-term liabilities	9,194	5,273
Deferred income taxes	4,628	6,253
Commitments and contingencies (Note 6)		
Stockholders' equity:		
Series A Junior Participating preferred stock, 1,000,000 shares authorized, none issued	—	—
Common stock, 18,310,000 and 9,155,000 shares issued in 1990 and 1989, respectively	183	92
Additional paid-in capital	87,115	79,681
Retained earnings	115,093	77,352
Cumulative foreign currency translation adjustment	995	508
	203,386	157,633
Less:		
Treasury stock (539,694 and 447,091 shares in 1990 and 1989, respectively), at cost	(771)	(112)
Unearned compensation	(3,840)	(1,274)
Total stockholders' equity	198,775	156,247
	$407,467	$378,929

Source: Harley-Davidson, Inc., Annual Report 1990, p. 33.

Yet the bike's appeal is undeniable. A stab at the starter button rumbles it into instant life, and as the engine settles into its characteristically syncopated idle, the bike is transformed into one of the best platforms anywhere from which to Just Cruise. And that means everything from cruising your immediate neighborhood to cruising (with appropriate gas and rest stops) into the next state.

This the bike is more than willing to do, with its premium tires and seemingly bullet-proof reliability. The important thing is to not ask the Sportster 1200 to be something it isn't. What it is, is a Sportster, much as Sportsters always have been.

This is merely the best one yet.[9]

[9]"Harley-Davidson Sportster 1200—Improving on Tradition," *Cycle World 1991 Motorcycle Buyer's Guide,* April–May 1991, p. 27.

EXHIBIT 4   Harley-Davidson, Inc., Business Segments and Foreign Operations

A. Business Segments (in thousands)

	1990	1989	1988
Net sales:			
Motorcycles and related products	$595,319	$495,961	$397,774
Transportation vehicles	240,573	273,961	303,969
Defense and other businesses	28,708	21,045	7,617
	$864,000	$790,967	$709,360
Income from operations:			
Motorcycles and related products	$ 87,844	$ 60,917	$ 49,688
Transportation vehicles	825	12,791	20,495
Defense and other businesses	2,375	2,236	755
General corporate expenses	(7,699)	(9,523)	(6,608)
	83,375	66,421	64,330
Interest expense, net	(9,701)	(14,322)	(18,463)
Other	(11,057)	910	165
Income from continuing operations before provision for income taxes and extraordinary items	$ 62,617	$ 53,009	$ 46,032

	Motorcycles and Related Products	Transportation Vehicles	Defense and Other Businesses	Corporate	Consolidated
1988					
Identifiable assets	$180,727	$215,592	$2,863	$1,932	$401,114
Depreciation and amortization	10,601	6,958	3	396	17,958
Net capital expenditures	14,121	6,693	66	29	20,909
1989					
Identifiable assets	192,087	176,813	7,018	3,011	378,929
Depreciation and amortization	9,786	7,282	1,125	1,814	20,007
Net capital expenditures	18,705	3,524	1,190	200	23,619
1990					
Identifiable assets	220,656	177,498	7,163	2,150	407,467
Depreciation and amortization	13,722	6,925	1,166	618	22,431
Net capital expenditures	34,099	2,547	1,257	490	38,393

There were no sales between business segments for the years ended December 31, 1990, 1989, and 1988.

B. Foreign Operations

	1990	1989	1988
Assets	$25,853	$18,065	$ 6,557
Liabilities	17,717	15,814	3,761
Net sales	82,811	39,653	22,061
Net income	5,555	2,281	1,941

Export sales of domestic subsidiaries to nonaffiliated customers were $93.0 million, $75.4 million, and $56.8 million in 1990, 1989, and 1988, respectively.

Source: Harley-Davidson, Inc., Annual Report 1990, p. 43.

EXHIBIT 5

Harley-Davidson
Motorcycle Unit Sales
1983–1990

Source: Adapted from
Harley-Davidson, Inc.,
Annual Report 1990, p. 20.

Year	Total Units	Domestic Units	Exports Units	Export Percentage
1990	62,458	43,138	19,320	30.9
1989	58,925	43,637	15,288	25.9
1988	50,517	38,941	11,576	22.9
1987	43,315	34,729	8,586	19.8
1986	36,735	29,910	6,825	18.6
1985	34,815	29,196	5,619	16.1
1984	39,224	33,141	6,083	15.5
1983	35,885	31,140	4,745	13.2

EXHIBIT 6

Harley-Davidson,
Inc., 1991 Product
Line and Suggested
Retail Prices

Source: Adapted from *Cycle
World 1991 Motorcycle
Buyer's Guide*, pp. 76–82.

Model	Suggested Retail Price
FLTC Tour Glide Ultra Classic	$13,895
FLHTC Electra Glide Ultra Classic	$13,895
FLTC Tour Glide Classic	$11,745
FLHTC Electra Glide Classic	$11,745
FLHS Electra Glide Sport	$10,200
FXDB Sturgis	$11,520
FLSTC Heritage Softail Classic	$11,495
FLSTF Fat Boy	$11,245
FXSTS Springer Softail	$11,335
FXSTC Softail Custom	$10,895
FXLR Low Rider Custom	$10,295
FXRT Sport Glide	$10,595
FXRS Low Rider Convertible	$10,445
FXRS SP Low Rider Sport Edition	$10,295
FXRS Low Rider	$10,195
FXR Super Glide	$ 8,995
XLH Sportster 1200	$ 6,095
XLH Sportster 883 Deluxe	$ 5,395
XLH Sportster 883 Hugger	$ 4,800
XLH Sportster 883	$ 4,395

Pricing

The suggested retail prices for 1991 Harley-Davidson motorcycles are also shown in Exhibit 6. These products were premium-priced although the low-end XLH Sportster 883 and XLH Sportster 883 Hugger were less so in order that new motorcyclists could buy them and then trade up at a later time to larger, more expensive models. In fact, in 1987 and 1988, the company offered to take any Sportster sold in trade on a bigger Harley-Davidson at a later time.

The prices for Harleys can be compared with competitive products.[10] For example, the three 1991 Honda Gold Wing touring models with larger 1520cc engines had suggested retail prices of $8,998, $11,998 and $13,998. A Harley look-alike, the Kawasaki Vulcan 88, had a 1470cc engine and a suggested retail selling price of $6,599; a Kawasaki Voyager XII with a 1196cc engine had a suggested retail selling price of $9,099. Another Harley look-alike, the Suzuki Intruder 1400, had a 1360cc engine and a suggested retail selling price of

---

[10]All prices are taken from the same reference as footnote 9.

$6,599. The Yamaha Virago 1100, another Harley look-alike, had a 1063cc engine and also had a suggested retail selling price of $6,599.

Promotional Activities

Kathleen Demitros, vice president of marketing for the Motorcycle Division, discussed a problem in designing advertising for Harley-Davidson motorcycles:

> One of the problems was that we had such a hard-core image out there that it was turning off a lot of people, even though people basically approved of Harley-Davidson. We had to find a way to balance our image more, without turning it into "white bread" and making it bland. Our goal was to get as close to our Harley riders as possible and communicate with them very personally.[11]

In addition to print advertising in general magazines, and Harley's own quarterly magazine, called *Enthusiast,* Harley has its own catalogs with full color pictures and descriptions of each model and discussions of Harley-Davidson products. For example, following is an excerpt from the 1991 Harley-Davidson catalog:

> To the average citizen, it's a motorcycle. To the average motorcyclist, it's a Harley. To the Harley owner, it's something else entirely, something special. Once you've got your Harley, it's much more than a piece of machinery or a way to get around. In a sense, it actually owns you. It occupies you even when you're not riding it. It's part of your life. And while you might not ever be able to explain it to anyone who doesn't know, you know; the trip certainly doesn't end after the road does. Different? Most wouldn't have it any other way.

In 1990 the Harley Owner Group had 650 chapters and 134,000 members with expected growth in 1991 of 15 percent and an additional 55 chapters.[12] In addition to national, regional, and state rallies and other events, meetings between HOG members and Harley management continued to provide suggestions for product improvements. HOG groups have "adopted" various scenic highways and have taken responsibility for their upkeep. In the 10 years Harley-Davidson and its owner groups have been involved, they have raised over $8.6 million for the Muscular Dystrophy Association.

Dealer Improvements

Several years earlier Harley-Davidson instituted a Designer Store program to improve the appearance, image, and merchandising of its products at the retail level. By the end of 1990, more than 310 of the company's 851 domestic and international motorcycle dealerships had completed major store renovation projects or had agreed to do them in 1991. Some dealers reported receiving full return on the renovation investment within 12 to 18 months due to increased sales brought about by a more inviting shopping environment.

Market Information

The traditional U.S. motorcyclist is an 18- to 24-year-old male.[13] Since 1980, the number of men in this age group has declined from 42.4 million to 35.3 million. By 2000 the number is expected to be only slightly higher, at 36.1 million. Women are buying motorcycles in increasing numbers, and sales to them have doubled. However, they still account for only 6 percent of the total motorcycles purchased. Motorcycle manufacturers have responded to this market, however, by designing bikes that are lower slung and easier for

---

[11]Kate Fitzgerald, "Kathleen Demitros Helps Spark Comeback at Harley-Davidson," *Advertising Age,* January 8, 1990, p. 3.

[12]This discussion is based on Harley-Davidson, Inc., Annual Report 1990, pp. 15–26.

[13]This discussion is based on Doron P. Levin, "Motorcycle Makers Shift Tactics," *The New York Times,* September 16, 1989.

EXHIBIT 7

U.S. Motorcycle
Market Shares for
Major Manufacturers

Source: R. L. Polk & Co., as
reported in "That 'Vroom!'
You Hear Is Honda
Motorcycles," *Business-
Week,* September 3, 1990,
p. 74.

Company	1985	1987	1989
Honda	58.5	50.8	28.9
Yamaha	15.5	19.8	27.7
Kawasaki	10.2	10.2	15.6
Suzuki	9.9	11.6	14.2
Harley-Davidson	4.0	6.3	13.9

women to ride. The Harley-Davidson XLH Sportster 883 Hugger was designed in part for this market.

The sale of motorcycles, including three- and four-wheel off-road vehicles, peaked in 1984 at 1,310,240 units. Five years later sales had dropped to 483,005 units. Sales dropped in all categories, although dirt bikes had the largest sales losses. Sales of larger motorcycles, which tend to be purchased by older buyers for use on highways, represented 12.2 percent of sales in 1984 but increased to 21.3 percent of sales five years later.

As less-affluent young men have drifted away from motorcycling, the sport has been taken up by professionals and businesspeople in their 40s and 50s. Likely, the late Malcolm S. Forbes, motorcycle enthusiast and wealthy magazine publisher, influenced this market which is older, more conservative, and often rides long distances with their spouses on luxury vehicles.

There is some evidence that many motorcycle owners do not use their bikes very often, some only for a ride or two in the summer. Although the number of fatal accidents involving motorcycles declined 9 percent in a recent year, this decrease was likely because of decreased usage. The Insurance Institute for Highway Safety reported that in a crash, a person was 17 times more likely to die on a motorcycle than in a car.

Competition

Exhibit 7 shows changes in overall market share percentages for the five major competitors in the U.S. motorcycle market.[14] Honda clearly lost the greatest share and its sales decreased from $1.1 billion in fiscal 1985 to $230 million in fiscal 1990. However, motorcycle sales represent less than 1 percent of Honda's worldwide revenues.

Honda's plan to battle its sagging sales involved the introduction of more expensive, technologically advanced bikes. However, with an increase in the value of the yen to the dollar from 250 in 1987 to 120 by 1988, all Japanese competitors had to raise prices. Honda had to raise its prices even more to cover its expensive new models and became less price competitive. In fact, nearly 600 Honda motorcycle dealers went out of business since 1985, leaving the company with 1,200 dealers in North America. Honda's Maryville, Ohio, plant had so much excess capacity that executives considered transforming much of it to production of auto parts.

Honda's 1990 strategy included cutting back prices and a $75 million advertising campaign to reintroduce the "wholesome" angle of cycling to reach new market segments. Promotional emphasis was also given to encouraging Americans to use motorcycles for commuting as an alternative to cars as is done in Europe and the Far East. High levels of air pollution, increased traffic, and rising fuel costs supported Honda's strategy. The advertising campaign was oriented less to selling individual products than to selling the idea that motorcycling is fun. Honda also offered free rides in shopping malls, sponsored races, and paid for Honda buyers to be trained at Motorcycle Safety Centers throughout the country.

[14]This discussion is based on "That 'Vroom!' You Hear Is Honda Motorcycles," *BusinessWeek,* September 3, 1990, pp. 74, 76.

In 1991, Honda's motorcycle product line included 25 models with displacements from 49 to 1520cc's including sportbikes, touring, cruisers, standards, and dual purpose types. It also included four models of four-wheel all terrain vehicles (ATVs). Kawasaki's line included 23 motorcycle models in a variety of types and 4 four-wheel models. Suzuki offered 24 models of motorcycles and 8 four-wheel models. Yamaha offered 25 motorcycle models and 7 four-wheel models. Other smaller competitors in the U.S. market included ATK, BMW, Ducati, Husqvarna, KTM, and Moto Guzzi.

The Future

Rich Teerlink and the other Harley executives have much to be proud of in bringing back the company to a profitable position. However, they must also plan for the future, a future that is uncertain and fraught with problems. For example, the company faces much larger, well-financed competitors in the industry. The company faces increasing legislation on motorcycle helmet use and noise abatement laws that could decrease industry sales.

The company clearly recognizes the fact that the motorcycle industry has contracted greatly since the mid-1980s. It faces the problem of judging how much to increase supply of Harley-Davidson motorcycles given that it is a mature product whose future is uncertain. It faces decisions concerning how much should be invested in such an uncertain market and what marketing approaches are the most appropriate given this situation.

Case

6

PepsiCo's Diversification Strategy in 2008

John E. Gamble *University of South Alabama*

PepsiCo was the world's largest snack and beverage company, with 2007 net revenues of approximately $39.5 billion. The company's portfolio of businesses in 2008 included Frito-Lay salty snacks, Quaker Chewy granola bars, Pepsi soft drink products, Tropicana orange juice, Lipton Brisk tea, Gatorade, Propel, SoBe, Quaker Oatmeal, Cap'n Crunch, Aquafina, Rice-A-Roni, Aunt Jemima pancake mix, and many other regularly consumed products. Gatorade, Propel, Rice-A-Roni, Aunt Jemima, and Quaker Oats products had been added to PepsiCo's arsenal of brands through the $13.9 billion acquisition of Quaker Oats in 2001. The acquisition was the final component of a major portfolio restructuring initiative that began in 1997. Since the restructuring, the company had increased revenues and net income at annual rates of 7 percent and 12 percent, respectively. A summary of PepsiCo's financial performance is shown in Exhibit 1.

Through 2007, the company's top managers were focused on sustaining the impressive performance that had been achieved since its restructuring through strategies keyed to product innovation, close relationships with distribution allies, international expansion, and strategic acquisitions. Newly introduced products such as Gatorade G2, Tiger Woods signature sports drinks, and Quaker Simple Harvest multigrain hot cereal had accounted for 15–20 percent of all new growth in recent years. New product innovations that addressed consumer health and wellness concerns were the greatest contributors to the company's growth, with PepsiCo's better-for-you and good-for-you products accounting for 16 percent of its 2007 snack sales in North America, 70 percent of net beverage revenues in North America during 2007, and more than 50 percent of its 2007 sales of Quaker Oats products in North America. The company also increased the percentage of healthy snacks in markets outside North America since consumers in most developed countries wished to reduce their consumption of saturated fats, cholesterol, trans fats, and simple carbohydrates.

EXHIBIT 1   Financial Summary for PepsiCo Inc., 1998–2007 ($ in millions, except per share amounts)

	2007	2006	2005	2004	2003	2002	2001	2000	1999	1998
Net revenue	$39,474	$35,137	$32,562	$29,261	$26,971	$25,112	$23,512	$20,438	$20,367	$22,348
Net income	5,599	5,065	4,078	4,212	3,568	3,000	2,400	2,183	2,050	1,993
Income per common share—basic, continuing operations	$ 3.38	$ 3.00	$ 2.43	$ 2.45	$ 2.07	$ 1.69	$ 1.35	$ 1.51	$ 1.40	$ 1.35
Cash dividends declared per common share	$ 1.42	$ 1.16	$ 1.01	$ 0.85	$ 0.63	$ 0.60	$ 0.58	$ 0.56	$ 0.54	$ 0.52
Total assets	$34,628	$29,930	$31,727	$27,987	$25,327	$23,474	$21,695	$18,339	$17,551	$22,660
Long-term debt	4,203	2,550	2,313	2,397	1,702	2,187	2,651	2,346	2,812	4,028

Source: PepsiCo 10-Ks, various years.

The company's Power of One retailer alliance strategy had been in effect for more than 10 years and was continuing to help boost PepsiCo's volume and identify new product formulations desired by consumers. Under the Power of One strategy, PepsiCo marketers and retailers collaborated in stores and during offsite summits to devise tactics to increase consumers' tendency to purchase more than one product offered by PepsiCo during a store visit. In addition, some of PepsiCo's most successful new products had been recommended by retailers.

PepsiCo's international sales had grown by 22 percent during 2007, but the company had many additional opportunities to increase sales in markets outside North America. The company held large market shares in many international markets for beverages and salty snacks, but it had been relatively unsuccessful in making Quaker branded products available outside the United States. In 2006, 75 percent of Quaker Oats' international sales of $500 million was accounted for by just six countries. In addition, PepsiCo's international operations were much less profitable than its businesses operating in North America. While the operating profit margins of PepsiCo's international division had ranged from 13.4 to 15.6 percent between 2004 and 2007, operating profit margins for its Frito-Lay and North American beverage business ranged from 21.3 percent to 25 percent during the same time. Quaker Foods' sales of Cap'n Crunch, Life cereal, Quaker oatmeal, Chewy granola bars, Aunt Jemima, and Rice-A-Roni produced the highest profit margins among all PepsiCo brands, with operating profits exceeding 30 percent each year between 2004 and 2007.

PepsiCo management developed a new organizational structure in 2008 to address the low relative profitability of its international operations and to produce even faster growth in international markets. The new structure that would place all brands sold in the United Kingdom, Europe, Asia, the Middle East, and Africa into a common division was expected to aid the company in its ability to capture strategic fits between its various brands and products. It was also quite possible that PepsiCo management needed to consider restructuring its lineup of snack and beverage businesses to improve overall profitability and reverse the downturn in its stock price that began in 2008. Exhibit 2 tracks PepsiCo's market performance between 1998 and October 2008.

EXHIBIT 2 Monthly Performance of PepsiCo Inc.'s Stock Price, 1998 to March 2008

(a) Trend in PepsiCo, Inc.'s Common Stock Price

(b) Performance of PepsiCo, Inc.'s Stock Price versus the S&P 500 Index

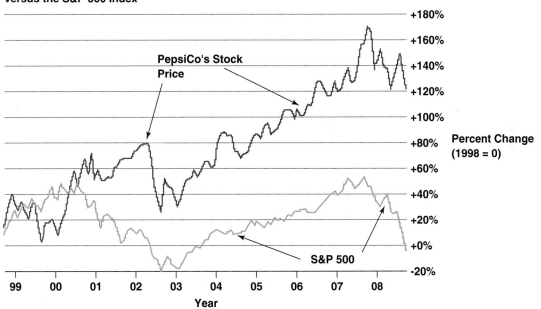

COMPANY HISTORY

PepsiCo Inc. was established in 1965 when Pepsi-Cola and Frito-Lay shareholders agreed to a merger between the salty snack icon and soft drink giant. The new company was founded with annual revenues of $510 million and such well-known brands as Pepsi-Cola, Mountain Dew, Fritos, Lay's, Cheetos, Ruffles, and Rold Gold. PepsiCo's roots can be traced to 1898, when New Bern, North Carolina, pharmacist Caleb Bradham created the formula for a carbonated beverage he named Pepsi-Cola. The company's salty-snack business began in 1932 when Elmer Doolin of San Antonio, Texas, began manufacturing and marketing Fritos corn chips and Herman Lay started a potato chip distribution business in Nashville, Tennessee. In 1961, Doolin and Lay agreed to a merger between their businesses to establish the Frito-Lay Company.

During its first five years as a snack and beverage company, PepsiCo introduced new products such as Doritos and Funyuns; entered markets in Japan and Eastern Europe; and opened, on an average, one new snack food plant per year. By 1971, PepsiCo had more than doubled its revenues to reach $1 billion. The company began to pursue growth through acquisitions outside snacks and beverages as early as 1968, but its 1977 acquisition of Pizza Hut significantly shaped the strategic direction of PepsiCo for the next 20 years. The acquisitions of Taco Bell in 1978 and Kentucky Fried Chicken in 1986 created a business portfolio described by Wayne Calloway (PepsiCo's CEO between 1986 and 1996) as a balanced three-legged stool. Calloway believed the combination of snack foods, soft drinks, and fast food offered considerable cost-sharing and skills-transfer opportunities, and he routinely shifted managers between the company's three divisions as part of the company's management development efforts.

PepsiCo also strengthened its portfolio of snack foods and beverages during the 1980s and 1990s with acquisitions of Mug root beer, 7UP International, Smartfood ready-to-eat popcorn, Walker's Crisps (UK), Smith's Crisps (UK), Mexican cookie company, Gamesa, and SunChips. Calloway also added quick-service restaurants Hot-n-Now in 1990, California Pizza Kitchens in 1992, and East Side Mario's, D'Angelo Sandwich Shops, and Chevy's Mexican Restaurants in 1993. The company expanded beyond carbonated beverages with a 1992 agreement with Ocean Spray to distribute single-serving juices, the introduction of Lipton ready-to-drink teas in 1993, and the introduction of Aquafina bottled water and Frappuccino ready-to-drink coffees in 1994.

By 1996, it had become clear to PepsiCo management that the potential strategic-fit benefits existing between restaurants and PepsiCo's core beverage and snack businesses were difficult to capture. In addition, any synergistic benefits achieved were more than offset by the fast-food industry's fierce price competition and low profit margins. In 1997, CEO Roger Enrico spun off the company's restaurants as an independent, publicly traded company to focus PepsiCo on food and beverages. Soon after the spin-off of PepsiCo's fast-food restaurants was completed, Enrico acquired Cracker Jack, Tropicana, Smith's Snack-food Company in Australia, SoBe teas and alternative beverages, Tasali Snack Foods (the leader in the Saudi Arabian salty snack market), and the Quaker Oats Company.

The Quaker Oats Acquisition

At $13.9 billion, Quaker Oats was PepsiCo's largest acquisition and gave it the number one brand of oatmeal in the United States, with a 60+ percent category share; the leading brand of rice cakes and granola snack bars; and other well-known grocery brands such as Cap'n Crunch, Rice-A-Roni, and Aunt Jemima. However, Quaker's most valuable asset in its arsenal of brands was Gatorade.

Gatorade was developed by University of Florida researchers in 1965 but was not marketed commercially until the formula was sold to Stokely–Van Camp in 1967. When

Quaker Oats acquired the brand from Stokely–Van Camp in 1983, Gatorade gradually made a transformation from a regionally distributed product with annual sales of $90 million to a $2 billion powerhouse. Gatorade was able to increase sales by more than 10 percent annually during the 1990s, with no new entrant to the isotonic beverage category posing a serious threat to the brand's dominance. PepsiCo, Coca-Cola, France's Danone Group, and Swiss food giant Nestlé all were attracted to Gatorade because of its commanding market share and because of the expected growth in the isotonic sports beverage category. PepsiCo became the successful bidder for Quaker Oats and Gatorade with an agreement struck in December 2000 but would not receive U.S. Federal Trade Commission (FTC) approval until August 2001. The FTC's primary concern over the merger was that Gatorade's inclusion in PepsiCo's portfolio of snacks and beverages might give the company too much leverage in negotiations with convenience stores and ultimately force smaller snack food and beverage companies out of convenience store channels. In its approval of the merger, the FTC stipulated that Gatorade could not be jointly distributed with PepsiCo's soft drinks for 10 years.

Acquisitions after 2001

After the completion of the Quaker Oats acquisition in August 2001, the company focused on integration of Quaker Oats' food, snack, and beverage brands into the PepsiCo portfolio. The company made a number of "tuck-in" acquisitions of small, fast-growing food and beverage companies in the United States and internationally to broaden its portfolio of brands. Tuck-in acquisitions in 2006 included Stacy's bagel and pita chips, Izze carbonated beverages, Duyvis nuts (Netherlands), and Star Foods (Poland). Acquisitions made during 2007 included Naked Juice fruit beverages, Sandora juices (Ukraine), Bluebird snacks (New Zealand), Penelopa nuts and seeds (Bulgaria), and Lucky snacks (Brazil). The company also entered into a joint venture with the Strauss Group in 2007 to market Sabra, the top-selling and fastest-growing brand of hummus in the United States and Canada.

PepsiCo's acquisitions in 2007 totaled $1.3 billion, whereas the company had made acquisitions totaling $522 million in 2006 and $1.1 billion in 2005. The combination of acquisitions and the strength of PepsiCo's core snacks and beverages business allowed the company's revenues to increase from approximately $20 billion in 2000 to more than $39.5 billion in 2007. Exhibit 3 presents PepsiCo's consolidated statements of income for 2005–2007. The company's balance sheets for 2005–2007 are provided in Exhibit 4. The company's calculation of management operating cash flow for 2004–2007 is shown in Exhibit 5.

EXHIBIT 3
PepsiCo Inc.'s Consolidated Statements of Income, 2005–2007 ($ in millions, except per share amounts)

Source: PepsiCo Inc., 2007 10-K report.

	2007	2006	2005
Net revenue	$39,474	$35,137	$32,562
Cost of sales	18,038	15,762	14,176
Selling, general, and administrative expenses	14,208	12,774	12,314
Amortization of intangible assets	58	162	150
Operating profit	7,170	6,439	5,922
Bottling equity income	560	616	557
Interest expense	(224)	(239)	(256)
Interest income	125	173	159
Income before income taxes	7,631	6,989	6,382
Provision for income taxes	1,973	1,347	2,304
Net income	$ 5,658	$ 5,642	$ 4,078
Net income per common share—basic	$ 3.48	$ 3.42	$ 2.43
Net income per common share—diluted	$ 3.41	$ 3.34	$ 2.39

EXHIBIT 4   PepsiCo Inc.'s Consolidated Balance Sheets, 2005–2007 ($ in millions, except per share amounts)

	December 29, 2007	December 30, 2006	December 31, 2005
ASSETS			
Current assets			
Cash and cash equivalents	$ 910	$ 1,651	$ 1,716
Short-term investments	1,571	1,171	3,166
Accounts and notes receivable, net	4,389	3,725	3,261
Inventories	2,290	1,926	1,693
Prepaid expenses and other current assets	991	657	618
Total current assets	$10,151	$ 9,130	$10,454
Property, plant and equipment, net	11,228	9,687	8,681
Amortizable intangible assets, net	796	637	530
Goodwill	5,169	4,594	4,088
Other nonamortizable intangible assets	1,248	1,212	1,086
Nonamortizable intangible assets	6,417	5,806	5,174
Investments in noncontrolled affiliates	4,354	3,690	3,485
Other assets	1,682	980	3,403
Total assets	$34,628	$29,930	$31,727
LIABILITIES AND SHAREHOLDERS' EQUITY			
Current liabilities			
Short-term obligations	—	$ 274	$ 2,889
Accounts payable and other current liabilities	7,602	6,496	5,971
Income taxes payable	151	90	546
Total current liabilities	7,753	6,860	9,406
Long-term debt obligations	4,203	2,550	2,313
Other liabilities	4,792	4,624	4,323
Deferred income taxes	646	528	1,434
Total liabilities	$17,394	$14,562	$17,476
Commitments and contingencies			
Preferred stock, no par value	41	41	41
Repurchased preferred stock	(132)	(120)	(110)
Common shareholders' equity			
Common stock, par value 1⅔¢ per share (issued 1,782 shares)	30	30	30
Capital in excess of par value	450	584	614
Retained earnings	28,184	24,837	21,116
Accumulated other comprehensive loss	(952)	(2,246)	(1,053)
	27,712	23,205	20,707
Less: repurchased common stock, at cost (144 and 126 shares, respectively)	(10,387)	(7,758)	(6,387)
Total common shareholders' equity	$17,325	$15,447	$14,320
Total liabilities and shareholders' equity	$34,628	$29,930	$31,727

Source: PepsiCo Inc., 2007 10-K report.

BUILDING SHAREHOLDER VALUE IN 2008

Three people had held the position of CEO since the company began its portfolio restructuring in 1997. Even though Roger Enrico was the chief architect of the business lineup as it stood in 2007, his successor, Steve Reinemund, and the company's CEO in 2007, Indra Nooyi, were both critically involved in the restructuring. Nooyi joined PepsiCo in 1994 and

EXHIBIT 5

Net Cash Provided by
PepsiCo's Operating
Activities, 2004–2007
($ in millions)

Source: PepsiCo Inc., 2007
10-K report.

	2007	2006	2005	2004
Net cash provided by operating activities	$6,934	$6,084	$5,852	$5,054
Capital spending	(2,430)	(2,068)	(1,736)	(1,387)
Sales of property, plant and equipment	47	49	88	38
Management operating cash flow	$4,551	$4,065	$4,204	$3,705

developed a reputation as a tough negotiator who engineered the 1997 spin-off of Pepsi's restaurants, spearheaded the 1998 acquisition of Tropicana, and played a critical role in the 1999 initial public offering of Pepsi's bottling operations. After being promoted to chief financial officer, Nooyi was also highly involved in the 2001 acquisition of Quaker Oats. Nooyi was selected as the company's CEO upon Reinemund's retirement in October 2006. Nooyi had emigrated to the United States in 1978 to attend Yale's Graduate School of Business and worked with Boston Consulting Group, Motorola, and Asea Brown Boveri before arriving at PepsiCo in 1994.

In 2008, PepsiCo's corporate strategy had diversified the company into salty and sweet snacks, soft drinks, orange juice, bottled water, ready-to-drink teas and coffees, purified and functional waters, isotonic beverages, hot and ready-to-eat breakfast cereals, grain-based products, and breakfast condiments. Most PepsiCo brands had achieved number one or number two positions in their respective food and beverage categories through strategies keyed to product innovation, close relationships with distribution allies, international expansion, and strategic acquisitions. A relatively new element of PepsiCo's corporate strategy was product reformulations to make snack foods and beverages less unhealthy. The company believed that its efforts to develop "good-for-you" or "better-for-you" products would create growth opportunities from the intersection of business and public interests.

The company was organized into four business divisions, which all followed the corporation's general strategic approach. Frito-Lay North America manufactured, marketed, and distributed such snack foods as Lay's potato chips, Doritos tortilla chips, Cheetos cheese snacks, Fritos corn chips, Quaker Chewy granola bars, Grandma's cookies, and Smartfood popcorn. The PepsiCo Beverages North America beverage business manufactured, marketed, and sold beverage concentrates, fountain syrups, and finished goods under such brands as Pepsi, Gatorade, Tropicana, Lipton, Dole, and SoBe. PepsiCo International manufactured, marketed, and sold snacks and beverages in approximately 200 countries outside the United States. Quaker Foods North America manufactured and marketed cereals, rice and pasta dishes, and other food items that were sold in supermarkets. A full listing of Frito-Lay snacks, PepsiCo beverages, and Quaker Oats products is presented in Exhibit 6. Selected financial information for PepsiCo's four divisions is presented in Exhibit 7.

Frito-Lay North America

In 2007, Frito-Lay brands accounted for 29 percent of the PepsiCo's total revenues and 36 percent of the company's operating profits. Frito-Lay also accounted for more than 70 percent of the salty snack food industry's total sales in the United States, which had grown at low single-digit rates annually since 2000 to reach $15.9 billion in 2008. Three key trends that were shaping the industry were convenience, a growing awareness of nutritional content of snack foods, and indulgent snacking. A product manager for a regional snack producer explained, "Many consumers want to reward themselves with great-tasting, gourmet flavors and styles. . . . The indulgent theme carries into seasonings as well. Overall, upscale, restaurant-influenced flavor trends are emerging to fill consumers' desires to escape from the norm and taste snacks from a wider, often global, palate."[1] Most manufacturers had

[1]As quoted in "Snack Attack," *Private Label Buyer,* August 2006, p. 26.

EXHIBIT 6   PepsiCo Inc.'s Snack, Beverage, and Quaker Oats Brands, 2008

Frito-Lay Brands

- Lay's potato chips
- Maui Style potato chips
- Ruffles potato chips
- Doritos tortilla chips
- Tostitos tortilla chips
- Santitas tortilla chips
- Fritos corn chips
- Cheetos cheese flavored snacks
- Rold Gold pretzels and snack mix
- Funyuns onion flavored rings
- Go Snacks
- SunChips multigrain snacks
- Sabritones puffed wheat snacks
- Cracker Jack candy-coated popcorn
- Chester's popcorn
- Grandma's cookies
- Munchos potato crisps
- Smartfood popcorn
- Baken-ets fried pork skins
- Oberto meat snacks
- Rustler's meat snacks
- Churrumais fried corn strips
- Frito-Lay nuts
- Frito-Lay, Ruffles, Fritos, and Tostitos dips and salsas
- Frito-Lay, Doritos, and Cheetos snack crackers
- Fritos, Tostitos, Ruffles, and Doritos snack kits
- Hickory Sticks
- Hostess Potato
- Lay's Stax potato crisps
- Miss Vickie's potato chips
- Munchies snack mix
- Stacy's pita chips
- Flat Earth Fruit and Vegetable Chips
- Sabra hummus

OUTSIDE NORTH AMERICA

- Bocabits wheat snacks
- Crujitos corn snacks
- Fandangos corn snacks
- Hamka's snacks
- Niknaks cheese snacks
- Quavers potato snacks
- Sabritas potato chips
- Smiths potato chips
- Walkers potato crisps

PepsiCo Beverage Brands

- Pepsi-Cola
- Mountain Dew
- Mountain Dew AMP energy drink
- Mug root beer
- Sierra Mist
- Slice
- Lipton Brisk (partnership)
- Lipton Iced Tea (partnership)
- Dole juices and juice drinks (license)
- FruitWorks juice drinks
- Aquafina purified drinking water
- Frappuccino ready-to-drink coffee (partnership)
- Starbucks DoubleShot (partnership)
- SoBe juice drinks, dairy, and teas
- SoBe energy drinks (No Fear and Adrenaline Rush)
- Gatorade
- Propel
- Tropicana
- Tropicana Twister
- Tropicana Smoothie
- Izze soft drinks
- Naked Juice

OUTSIDE NORTH AMERICA

- Mirinda
- 7UP
- Pepsi
- Kas
- Teem
- Manzanita Sol
- Paso de los Toros
- Fruko
- Evervess
- Yedigun
- Shani
- Fiesta
- D&G (license)
- Mandarin (license)
- Radical Fruit
- Tropicana Touche de Lait
- Alvalle gazpacho fruit juices and vegetable juices
- Tropicana Season's Best juices and juice drinks
- Loóza juices and nectars
- Copella juices

Quaker Oats Brands

- Quaker Oatmeal
- Cap'n Crunch cereal
- Life cereal
- Quaker 100% Natural cereal
- Quaker Squares cereal
- Quisp cereal
- King Vitaman cereal
- Quaker Oh's! Cereal
- Mother's cereal
- Quaker grits
- Quaker Oatmeal-to-Go
- Aunt Jemima mixes & syrups
- Quaker rice cakes
- Quaker rice snacks (Quakes)
- Quaker Chewy granola bars
- Quaker Dipps granola bars
- Rice-A-Roni side dishes
- PastaRoni side dishes
- Near East side dishes
- Puffed Wheat
- Harvest Crunch cereal
- Quaker Baking Mixes
- Spudz snacks
- Crisp'ums baked crisps
- Quaker Fruit & Oatmeal bars
- Quaker Fruit & Oatmeal Bites
- Quaker Fruit and Oatmeal Toastables
- Quaker Soy Crisps
- Quaker Bakeries

OUTSIDE NORTH AMERICA

- FrescAvena beverage powder
- Toddy chocolate powder
- Toddynho chocolate drink
- Coqueiro canned fish
- Sugar Puffs cereal
- Puffed Wheat
- Cruesli cereal
- Hot Oat Crunch cereal
- Quaker Oatso Simple hot cereal
- Scott's Porage Oats
- Scott's So Easy Oats
- Quaker bagged cereals
- Quaker Mais Sabor
- Quaker Oats
- Quaker oat flour
- Quaker Meu Mingau

(*continued*)

EXHIBIT 6 PepsiCo Inc.'s Snack, Beverage, and Quaker Oats Brands, 2008 *(concluded)*

Frito-Lay Brands	PepsiCo Beverage Brands	Quaker Oats Brands
• Gamesa cookies	• Frui'Vita juices	• Quaker cereal bars
• Doritos Dippas	• Sandora juices	• Quaker Oatbran
• Sonric's sweet snacks		• Corn goods
• Wotsits corn snacks		• Magico chocolate powder
• Red Rock Deli		• Quaker Vitaly Cookies
• Kurkure		• 3 Minutos Mixed Cereal
• Smiths Sensations		• Quaker Mágica
• Cheetos Shots		• Quaker Mágica con Soja
• Quavers Snacks		• Quaker Pastas
• Bluebird Snacks		• Quaker Frut
• Duyvis Nuts		
• Lucky snacks		
• Penelopa nuts and seeds		

Source: Pepsico.com.

EXHIBIT 7 Selected Financial Data for PepsiCo Inc.'s Business Segments, 2004–2007 ($ in millions)

	2007	2006	2005	2004
NET REVENUES				
Frito-Lay North America	$11,586	$10,844	$10,322	$ 9,560
PepsiCo Beverages North America	10,230	9,565	9,146	8,313
Pepsi International	15,798	12,959	11,376	9,862
Quaker Foods North America	1,860	1,769	1,718	1,526
Total division	39,474	35,137	32,562	29,261
Corporate	—	—	—	—
Total	$39,474	$35,137	$32,562	$29,261
OPERATING PROFIT				
Frito-Lay North America	$ 2,845	$ 2,615	$ 2,529	$ 2,389
PepsiCo Beverages North America	2,188	2,055	2,037	1,911
Pepsi International	2,322	2,016	1,661	1,323
Quarker Foods North America	568	554	537	475
Total division	7,923	7,240	6,764	6,098
Corporate	(753)	(738)	(780)	(689)
Total	$ 7,170	$ 6,502	$ 5,984	$ 5,409
CAPITAL EXPENDITURES				
Frito-Lay North America	$ 624	$ 499	$ 512	$ 469
PepsiCo Beverages North America	430	492	320	265
Pepsi International	1,108	835	667	537
Quaker Foods North America	41	31	31	33
Total division	2,203	1,857	1,530	1,304
Corporate	227	211	206	83
Total	$ 2,430	$ 2,068	$ 1,736	$ 1,387

(continued)

EXHIBIT 7   Selected Financial Data for PepsiCo Inc.'s Business Segments, 2004–2007 ($ in millions)   *(concluded)*

	2007	2006	2005	2004
TOTAL ASSETS				
Frito-Lay North America	$ 6,270	$ 5,969	$ 5,948	$ 5,476
PepsiCo Beverages North America	7,130	6,567	6,316	6,048
Pepsi International	14,747	11,274	9,983	8,921
Quaker Foods North America	1,002	1,003	989	978
Total division	29,149	25,110	23,482	21,423
Corporate	2,124	1,739	5,331	3,569
Investments in bottling affiliates	3,355	3,378	3,160	2,995
Total	$34,628	$29,930	$31,727	$27,987
DEPRECIATION AND OTHER AMORTIZATION				
Frito-Lay North America	$ 437	$ 432	$ 419	$ 420
PepsiCo Beverages North America	302	282	264	258
Pepsi International	564	478	420	382
Quaker Foods North America	34	33	34	36
Total division	1,337	1,225	1,137	1,096
Corporate	31	19	21	21
Total	$ 1,368	$ 1,244	$ 1,158	$ 1,117
AMORTIZATION OF OTHER INTANGIBLE ASSETS				
Frito-Lay North America	$ 9	$ 9	$ 3	$ 3
PepsiCo Beverages North America	11	77	76	75
Pepsi International	38	76	71	68
Quaker Foods North America	—	—	—	1
Total division	58	162	150	147
Corporate	—	—	—	—
Total	$ 58	$ 162	$ 150	$ 147

Source: PepsiCo Inc., 2007 10-K report.

developed new flavors of salty snacks such as jalapeno and cheddar tortilla chips and pepper jack potato chips to attract the interest of indulgent snackers. Manufacturers had also begun using healthier oils when processing chips and had expanded lines of baked and natural salty snacks to satisfy the demands of health-conscious consumers. Snacks packaged in smaller bags also addressed overeating concerns and were additionally convenient to take along on an outing. In 2008, Frito-Lay owned the top-selling chip brand in each U.S. salty snack category and held more than a two-to-one lead over the next largest snack food maker in the United States. The following table presents shares of the U.S. convenience food market for leading manufacturers in 2006. Convenience foods included both salty and sweet snacks such as chips, pretzels, ready-to-eat popcorn, crackers, dips, snack nuts and seeds, candy bars, and cookies.

Frito-Lay North America's (FLNA) revenues increased 7 percent during 2007 as a result of double-digit growth in sales of SunChips, Quaker rice cakes, and multipacks of other products. FLNA's better-for-you and good-for-you snacks also grew at double-digit rates during 2007 and represented 16 percent of the division's total revenue. In 2008, improving the performance of the division's core salty brands and further developing health and wellness products were key strategic initiatives. The company had eliminated trans fats from all Lay's, Fritos, Ruffles, Cheetos, Tostitos, and Doritos varieties and was looking for further innovations to make its salty snacks more healthy. The company had introduced Lay's Classic potato chips, which were cooked in sunflower oil and retained Lay's traditional flavor

Manufacturer	Market Share
PepsiCo	21%
Kraft Foods	12
Hershey	9
Kellogg	6
Master Foods	5
General Mills	2
Procter & Gamble	1
Private label	7
Others	37
Total	100%

Note: The share information shown above excludes data from certain retailers such as Wal-Mart that do not report data to Information Resources Inc. and ACNielsen Corporation.

Source: PepsiCo Inc., 2006 10-K report.

but contained 50 percent less saturated fat. The company had also developed new multi-grain and flour tortilla Tostitos varieties that appealed to indulgent snackers and were healthier than traditional Tostitos. Other new indulgent Doritos flavors included Fiery Habanero and Blazin' Buffalo & Ranch. FLNA had also expanded the number of flavors of SunChips to sustain the brand's double-digit growth. New SunChips flavors included Garden Salsa and Cinnamon Crunch. SunChips were also introduced in 100-calorie mini-packs and 20-bag multipacks.

PepsiCo's 2006 acquisition of Flat Earth fruit and vegetable snacks offered an opportunity for the company to exploit consumers' desires for healthier snacks and address a deficiency in most diets. Americans, on average, consumed only about 50 percent of the U.S. Department of Agriculture's recommended daily diet of fruits and vegetables. Flat Earth's baked vegetable crisps (Farmland Cheddar, Tangy Tomato Ranch, Garlic & Herb Field) and baked fruit crisps (Peach Mango Paradise, Apple Cinnamon Grove, and Wild Berry Patch) were launched in 2007. Other good-for-you snacks included Stacy's pita chips, which was also acquired in 2006, and Quaker Chewy granola bars. In 2008, Stacy's pita chips came in 15 varieties, including Multigrain, Soy Thin Sticky Bun, Cinnamon Sugar, Whole Wheat, and Texarkana Hot. Quaker Chewy granola bars had achieved a number two rank in the segment, with a 25 percent market share in 2006. Some of the success of Quaker Chewy granola products was related to product innovations such as reduced-calorie oatmeal-and-raisin bars. PepsiCo Beverages North America also distributed Quaker rice cakes, which had added chocolate-drizzled and multigrain varieties in 2007.

PepsiCo Beverages North America

PepsiCo was the largest seller of liquid refreshments in the United States, with a 26 percent share of the market in 2006. Coca-Cola was the second largest nonalcoholic beverage producer, with a 23 percent market share. Cadbury-Schweppes and Nestlé were the third and fourth largest beverage sellers in 2006, with market shares of 10 percent and 8 percent, respectively. Like Frito-Lay, PepsiCo's beverage business contributed greatly to the corporation's overall profitability and free cash flows. In 2007, PepsiCo Beverages North America (PBNA) accounted for 28 percent of the corporation's total revenues and 31 percent of its profits. Revenues for PBNA had increased by 7 percent annually between 2006 and 2007 as the company broadened its line of noncarbonated beverages like Gatorade, Tropicana fruit juices, Lipton ready-to-drink tea, Propel, Aquafina, Dole fruit drinks, Starbucks cold coffee drinks, and SoBe. Carbonated soft drinks were the most-consumed type of beverage in the United States, with a 48 percent of share of the total beverage market, but carbonated soft

EXHIBIT 8   Volume Size and Share of the U.S. Liquid Refreshment Beverage Market by Segment, 2005–2007

Beverage Category	Volume by Beverage Category (Millions of Gallons)			Volume Share		
	2005	2006	2007	2005	2006	2007
Carbonated soft drinks	15,271.6	15,103.6	14,707.4	52.9%	50.1%	48.1%
Bottled water*	7,537.1	8,253.1	8,822.4	26.1	27.4	28.9
Fruit beverages	4,119.0	4,020.1	3,899.5	14.3	13.3	12.8
Isotonic sports drinks	1,207.5	1,322.0	1,355.1	4.2	4.4	4.4
Ready-to-drink tea	555.9	760.9	875.1	1.9	2.5	2.9
Flavored and enhanced water	—	418.5	546.5	—	1.4	1.8
Energy drinks	152.5	242.7	302.6	0.5	0.8	1.0
Ready-to-drink coffee	38.9	44.5	45.1	0.1	0.1	0.1
Total	28,882.5	30,165.8	30,553.7	100.0%	100.0%	100.0%

*Excludes flavored and enhanced water after 2005.
Source: Beverage Marketing Corporation.

drink volume declined by 2.6 percent in 2007 as consumers searched for healthier beverage choices. In contrast, flavored and enhanced water products grew by 30.6 percent, energy drinks grew by 24.7 percent, ready-to-drink tea grew by 15 percent, and bottled water grew by 6.9 percent between 2006 and 2007. The size and volume share of the U.S. beverage industry by beverage category for 2005 through 2007 is presented in Exhibit 8.

PepsiCo's Carbonated Soft Drinks Business

During the mid-1990s, it looked as if Coca-Cola would dominate the soft drink industry, with every Pepsi-Cola brand except Mountain Dew losing market share to Coca-Cola's brands. Coca-Cola's CEO at the time, Roberto Goizueta, had stated that the company's strategic intent was to control 50 percent of the U.S. cola market by 2000 and seemed convinced PepsiCo could do little to stop the industry leader. Goizueta summed up his lack of concern about Pepsi as a key rival in an October 28, 1996, *Fortune* article entitled "How Coke Is Kicking Pepsi's Can" by saying, "As they've become less relevant, I don't need to look at them very much anymore."

PepsiCo's management engineered a comeback in the late 1990s and early 2000s by launching new brands like Sierra Mist and focusing on strategies to improve local distribution. Among Pepsi's most successful strategies to build volume and share in soft drinks was its "Power of One" strategy, which attempted to achieve the synergistic benefits of a combined Pepsi-Cola and Frito-Lay envisioned by shareholders of the two companies in 1965. The Power of One strategy called for supermarkets to place Pepsi and Frito-Lay products side by side on shelves. In 2006, PepsiCo added "Innovation Summits" to its Power of One program whereby retailers could share their views on consumer shopping and eating habits. PepsiCo used the information gleaned from the summits in developing new products like SoBe Life Water and Lay's potato chips cooked in sunflower oil. The summits, which continued into 2007, also helped identify PepsiCo supply chain inefficiencies that affected retailers. PepsiCo managers and retailers collaborated during one Innovation Summit to develop new shipping procedures that reduced stock-outs in retailers' stores.

PepsiCo's primary focus in soft drink innovation was directed toward improving the nutritional properties of soft drinks. The company was attempting to develop new types of sweeteners that would lower the calorie content of nondiet drinks. The company also hoped its 2006 acquisition of Izze lightly carbonated sparkling fruit drinks would prove popular with health-conscious consumers. Tava was an additional calorie-free, caffeine-free, better-for-you carbonated beverage that PBNA launched in the United States in 2007. Even though PepsiCo strengthened its position in the U.S. carbonated soft drink industry, its 31.1 percent market share during 2007 was considerably less than Coca-Cola's 2007 market share of 41.6 percent.

PepsiCo's Noncarbonated Beverage Brands

Although carbonated beverages made up the largest percentage of PBNA's total beverage volume, much of the division's growth was attributable to the success of its noncarbonated beverages. In 2007, total revenue for the division increased by 7 percent, which was driven by a 5 percent increase in noncarbonated beverages and the contribution of new acquisitions. Carbonated soft drink volume declined by 3 percent during 2007.

Aquafina was the number one brand of bottled water in the United States and grew by 6.9 percent between 2006 and 2007. Bottled water was a particularly attractive segment for PepsiCo since bottled water consumption in the United States had increased from 4.6 billion gallons in 1999 to 8.8 billion gallons in 2007. PepsiCo's Frappuccino ready-to-drink (RTD) coffee and Lipton RTD teas made it the leader in the RTD tea and RTD coffee categories as well. The RTD tea category grew by 15 percent between 2006 and 2007, while RTD coffees grew by just over 1 percent during 2007. PepsiCo's SoBe Essential Energy and SoBe Adrenaline Rush drinks held a negligible share of the energy drink market, with Red Bull accounting for 40 percent of industry sales in 2007. Red Bull was produced and marketed by the privately held Red Bull GmbH, of Austria. Hansen Natural Corporation's Monster energy drink and Coca-Cola's Full Throttle energy drink accounted for approximately 30 percent of industry sales in 2007.

In 2008, PBNA's Propel Fitness Water was the leading brand of functional water. In 2006, the company had also introduced SoBe Life Water and functional versions of Aquafina. The product lines for its water business were developed around customer type and lifestyle. Propel was a flavor- and vitamin-enriched water marketed to physically active consumers, while Life Water was a vitamin-enhanced water marketed to image-driven consumers. The company targeted mainstream water consumers with unflavored Aquafina, Aquafina FlavorSplash (offered in four flavors), and Aquafina Sparkling (a zero-calorie, lightly carbonated citrus- or berry-flavored water). Aquafina Alive, launched in 2007, included vitamins and natural fruit juices. The company's strategy involved offering a continuum of healthy beverages from unflavored Aquafina to nutrient-rich Gatorade. In 2007, Gatorade, Propel, and Aquafina were all number one in their categories, with market shares of 76 percent, 40 percent, and approximately 15 percent, respectively.

Gatorade's volume had grown by 21 percent in 2005 and by 12 percent in 2006 to reach sales of over $3 billion. Gatorade's impressive growth had come about through the introduction of new flavors and formulations such as the lower-calorie G2 and the Tiger Woods signature Gatorade sub-brand. Volume growth was also attributable to new container sizes and designs, new multipacks, world-class advertising, and added points of distribution. Analysts believed that Gatorade could achieve even stronger performance once the U.S. Federal Trade Commission's 10-year prohibition on bundled beverage contracts with retailers and joint Gatorade/soft drink distribution came to an end. Gatorade's broker-distribution system also allowed Tropicana and Lipton RTD teas to double sales volume between the 2001 acquisition of Quaker Oats and year-end 2006. PepsiCo's 39.5 percent market share in RTD teas in 2007 was nearly four times greater than the 10.7 percent share held by Coca-Cola's Nestea RTD tea. Tropicana was the number one brand in the $3 billion orange juice industry, with an approximate 30 percent market share in 2007. Coca-Cola's Minute Maid brand of orange juice held a 25 percent market share in 2007. The combined sales of PBNA's better-for-you and good-for-you beverages made up 70 percent of the division's net revenue in both 2006 and 2007.

PepsiCo International

All PepsiCo snacks, beverages, and food items sold outside North America were included in the company's PepsiCo International division. International snack volume grew by 9 percent in 2007, with double-digit growth in emerging markets such as Russia, the Middle East, and Turkey. Beverage volume in international markets increased by 8 percent during 2007, with the fastest growth occurring in the Middle East, China, and Pakistan. Volume gains, along with acquisitions in Europe, the Middle East, Africa, New Zealand, and Brazil, allowed the division's revenues and operating profits to increase by 22 percent and 15 percent, respectively, between 2006 and 2007. PepsiCo's 2007 acquisitions in international markets were expected to boost 2008 revenues by more than $1 billion.

PepsiCo's Sale of Beverages in International Markets

PepsiCo also found that it could grow international sales through its Power of One strategy. A PepsiCo executive explained how the company's soft drink business could gain shelf space through the strength of Frito-Lay's brands: "You go to Chile, where Frito-Lay has over 90 percent of the market, but Pepsi is in lousy shape. Frito-Lay can help Pepsi change that."[2] PepsiCo's market share in carbonated soft drinks in its strongest international markets during 2006 is presented in the following table:

Country/Region	PepsiCo's Carbonated Soft Drink Market Share
Middle East	75% +
India	49
Thailand	49
Egypt	47
Venezuela	42
Nigeria	38
China	36
Russia	24

Source: PepsiCo Investor Presentation by Mike White, CEO PepsiCo International, 2006.

PepsiCo International management believed further opportunities in other international markets existed. In 2007, the average consumption of carbonated soft drinks in the United States was 60 servings per month, while the average consumption of carbonated soft drinks in other developed countries was 23 servings per month and in developing countries was 6 servings per month. The company also saw a vast opportunity for sales growth in the $70 billion market for noncarbonated beverages in international markets. In 2006, PepsiCo International recorded less than $1 billion in noncarbonated beverage sales outside North America. The company was rapidly rolling out Tropicana to international markets and had acquired two international juice brands to capture a larger share of the $37 billion international markets for juice drinks. Also, PepsiCo was making Gatorade available in more international markets to capture a share of the $5 billion isotonic sports drink market outside the United States. Sales of Gatorade in Latin America more than doubled between 2001 and 2006, giving the sports drink a 72 percent market share in the entire Latin American region in 2006. PepsiCo International was also moving into new markets with Lipton RTD tea, gaining a share of the $15 billion international RTD tea market. In 2007, Gatorade was available in 42 international markets, Tropicana was in 27 country markets outside North

[2]"PepsiCo's New Formula," *BusinessWeek Online,* April 10, 2000.

America, and Lipton was sold in 27 international markets. Tropicana was the number one juice brand in Europe and had achieved a 100 percent increase in sales in the region between 2001 and 2006. By 2012, PepsiCo planned to launch Gatorade in 15 additional country markets, Tropicana in 20 new markets, and Lipton in 5 new international markets.

PepsiCo had moved somewhat slowly into international bottled water markets, with its most notable effort occurring in Mexico. In 2002, PepsiCo's bottling operations acquired Mexico's largest Pepsi bottler, Pepsi-Gemex SA de CV, for $1.26 billion. Gemex not only bottled and distributed Pepsi soft drinks in Mexico but was also Mexico's number one producer of purified water. After its acquisition of Gemex, PepsiCo shifted its international expansion efforts to bringing Aquafina to selected emerging markets in Eastern Europe, the Middle East, and Asia. In 2006, Aquafina was the number one brand of bottled water in Russia and Vietnam, and the number two brand in Kuwait.

PepsiCo's Sales of Snack Foods in International Markets

Frito-Lay was the largest snack chip company in the world, with sales of approximately $7 billion outside the United States and a 40+ percent share of the international salty snack industry in 2006. Frito-Lay held commanding shares of the market for salty snacks in many country markets. The following table presents PepsiCo's salty snack market share in selected countries in 2006:

Country	PepsiCo's Salty Snack Market Share
Mexico	75%
Holland	59
South Africa	57
Australia	55
Brazil	46
India	46
United Kingdom	44
Russia	43
Spain	41
China	16

Source: PepsiCo Investor Presentation by Mike White, CEO PepsiCo International, 2006.

PepsiCo management believed international markets offered the company's greatest opportunity for growth since per capita consumption of snacks in the United States averaged 6.6 servings per month, while per capita consumption in other developed countries averaged 4.0 servings per month and per capita consumption in developing countries averaged 0.4 servings per month. PepsiCo executives expected that, by 2010, China and Brazil would be the two largest international markets for snacks. The United Kingdom was projected to be the third largest international market for snacks, while developing markets Mexico and Russia would be the fourth and fifth largest international markets, respectively.

Developing an understanding of consumer taste preferences was a key to expanding into international markets. Taste preferences for salty snacks were more similar from country to country than many other food items, which allowed PepsiCo to make only modest modifications to its snacks in most countries. For example, classic varieties of Lay's, Doritos, and Cheetos snacks were sold in Latin America. However, the company supplemented its global brands with varieties spiced to local preferences such as the seaweed-flavored Atesanas chips sold in Thailand and Lay's White Mushroom potato chips sold in Russia. In addition, consumer characteristics in the United States that had forced snack food makers to adopt better-for-you or good-for-you snacks applied in most other developed countries as well. In 2007, PepsiCo was eliminating trans fats from its snacks and expanding the nutritional credentials of its snacks sold in Europe, since demand for health and wellness products in Europe was growing by 10–13 percent per year. The annual revenue growth for core salty snacks in Europe was growing at a modest 4–6 percent per year. Among PepsiCo's fastest-growing snacks in the United Kingdom was Walker's baked potato chips, which had 70 percent less saturated fat and 25 percent less salt than regular Walker's chips. Walker's baked potato chips was named Britain's best new product of 2007 by *Marketing Week* magazine.

International Sales of Quaker Oats Products

PepsiCo International also manufactured and distributed Quaker Oats oatmeal and cereal in international markets. In 2006, 75 percent of Quaker Oats' international sales of $500 million was accounted for by just six countries. The United Kingdom was Quakers largest market outside the United States, where it held more than a 50 percent market share in oatmeal. The company had launched new oatmeal products in the United Kingdom, including Organic Oats, OatSo Simple microwaveable oatmeal and oatmeal bars, and Oat Granola and Oat Muesli cereals. PepsiCo also added new varieties of Quaker oatmeal products in Latin America to double the brand's sales in the region. Exhibit 9 presents a breakdown of PepsiCo's net revenues and long-lived assets by geographic region.

Quaker Foods North America

Quaker Oats produced, marketed, and distributed hot and ready-to-eat cereals, pancake mixes and syrups, and rice and pasta side dishes in the United States and Canada. The division recorded sales of approximately $1.8 billion in 2007. Sales volume of Quaker Foods products increased by 2 percent during 2007, with Quaker Oatmeal, Life cereal, and Cap'n Crunch cereal volumes increasing at mid-single-digit rates. Sales of Aunt Jemima syrup and pancake mix declined slightly, while sales of Rice-A-Roni and PastaRoni kits declined at a double-digit rate during 2007. Quaker Oats was the star product of the division, with a 58 percent market share in North America in 2006. Rice-A-Roni held a 33 percent market share in the rice and pasta side dish segment of the consumer food industry. Quaker Foods was the third largest ready-to-eat cereal maker, with a 14 percent market share in 2005. In 2005, Kellogg's held a 30 percent share of the $6 billion ready-to-eat cereal market and

EXHIBIT 9
PepsiCo Inc.'s U.S. and International Sales and Long-Lived Assets, 2004–2006 ($ in millions)

Source: PepsiCo Inc., 2006 10-K report.

	2007	2006	2005	2004
NET REVENUES				
United States	$21,978	$20,788	$19,937	$18,329
Mexico	3,498	3,228	3,095	2,724
United Kingdom	1,987	1,839	1,821	1,692
Canada	1,961	1,702	1,509	1,309
All other countries	10,050	7,580	6,200	5,207
Total	$39,474	$35,137	$32,562	$29,261
LONG-LIVED ASSETS				
United States	$12,498	$11,515	$10,723	$10,212
Mexico	1,067	996	902	878
United Kingdom	2,090	1,995	1,715	1,896
Canada	699	589	582	548
All other countries	6,441	4,725	3,948	3,339
Total	$22,795	$19,820	$17,870	$16,873

General Mills held a 26 percent market share. Quaker grits and Aunt Jemima pancake mix and syrup competed in mature categories, and all enjoyed market leading positions. More than half of Quaker Foods' 2007 revenues were generated by better-for-you and good-for-you products.

Value Chain Alignment Between PepsiCo Brands and Products

PepsiCo's management team was dedicated to capturing strategic fit benefits within the business lineup throughout the value chain. The company's procurement activities were coordinated globally to achieve the greatest possible economies of scale, and best practices were routinely transferred between its 230 plants, 3,600 distribution systems, and 120,000 service routes around the world. PepsiCo also shared marketed research information to better enable each division to develop new products likely to be hits with consumers and coordinated its Power of One activities across product lines.

PepsiCo management had a proven ability to capture strategic fits between the operations of new acquisitions and its other businesses. The Quaker Oats integration produced a number of noteworthy successes, including $160 million in cost savings resulting from corporate-wide procurement of product ingredients and packaging materials and an estimated $40 million in cost savings attributed to the joint distribution of Quaker snacks and Frito-Lay products. Also, the combination of Gatorade and Tropicana hot fill operations saved an estimated $120 million annually by 2005.

PEPSICO'S STRATEGIC REALIGNMENT IN 2008

For the most part, PepsiCo's strategies seemed to be firing on all cylinders in 2007. PepsiCo's chief managers expected the company's lineup of snack, beverage, and grocery items to generate operating cash flows sufficient to reinvest in its core businesses, provide cash dividends to shareholders, fund an $8 billion share buyback plan, and pursue acquisitions that would provide attractive returns. Nevertheless, the low relative profit margins of PepsiCo's international businesses created the need for a new organizational structure that might better exploit strategic fits between the company's international operations.

Beginning in 2008, PepsiCo's former Frito-Lay North America, Quaker Foods North America and all of its food and snack businesses in Latin America would be combined into a common PepsiCo Americas Foods division. The Latin American beverage businesses would be pulled from the PepsiCo International division and combined with PepsiCo Beverages North America to form the PepsiCo Americas Beverages division. PepsiCo International would include all of the company's snack and beverage businesses outside of North America and Latin America. The new three-division structure would include six reporting segments: Frito-Lay North America, Quaker Foods North America, Latin American Foods, PepsiCo Americas Beverages, United Kingdom & Europe, and Middle East, Africa & Asia. Some food and beverage industry analysts had speculated that corporate strategy changes might also be required to improve the profitability of PepsiCo's international operations and to help restore share price appreciation. Possible actions might include a reprioritization of internal uses of cash, new acquisitions, further efforts to capture strategic fits existing between the company's various businesses, or the divestiture of businesses with poor prospects of future growth and minimal strategic fit with PepsiCo's other businesses.

7

Expresso Espresso

Calvin M. Bacon, Jr. *University of South Alabama*

"DAVID, WHATSUP?" Todd Sylvester bellowed as a regular customer entered. He believed the need to feel recognized and loved was part of the human condition and considered it part of his mission to provide those feelings. To make the customers feel welcome, Todd made a point of knowing their names and recognizing them as they came through the door. Years ago, when he drove a school bus through the same tollbooth every day, he made a point of knowing the tollbooth operators' names. Every day as he paid his toll, he gave them the biggest smile he could muster, greeted them by name, and wished them a happy day. "There is a real deprivation of joy in society. I think it is important to provide comfort and help people feel good," Todd noted.

Expresso Espresso coffee shop opened in March 2006 across the street from the University of South Alabama (South) in Mobile. The shop targeted the university's 13,000 students as well as the staff and faculty. Although the business had only been open for 12 weeks and was still operating at a loss, Todd, the owner, was already making plans to expand into the city's midtown area. He believed that the culture and values he instilled in the company would make it successful anywhere, and he believed growth was imperative to achieve his long-term goals. Todd wanted to use his first shop to prove the business concept so he could begin expanding as soon as possible.

Although he was optimistic about the business, he was worried about the changing dynamics of the coffee shop industry in the Mobile Bay area. Several other new shops were either in the planning or construction stage, and he wondered what impact those shops might have on Expresso. Moreover, he was concerned about the strategic position his shop would have once the dust settled from all the expansion. In addition, Todd was not sure if his marketing efforts would increase sales soon enough to avoid a financial hardship for his family. He and his wife, Angelle, had taken a $100,000 equity loan on their home to provide start-up funds for the new business. Exhibits 1 and 2 present income and profit and loss statements.

Copyright © 2007 by the *Case Research Journal* and Calvin M. Bacon, Jr.

The author is grateful to Todd Sylvester for his cooperation in preparing this case, to Robin Hayes for transcribing the interviews, and to the reviewers of the *Case Research Journal* who gave invaluable advice and suggestions for improving the case. This case is intended to stimulate class discussion rather than to illustrate the effective or ineffective handling of a managerial situation. All events and individuals in this case are real. I disguised the name of the company for competitive reasons and consolidated the financial statements to facilitate student analysis.

THE ENTREPRENEUR

Todd was born in Boston and raised in Connecticut. Upon graduating from high school, he entered Franciscan University in Ohio and majored in divinity with the intention of becoming a priest. Before his second year, he changed majors to theology. After graduating from college and getting married, Todd took a job at an electronics store while he waited for Angelle to graduate. Although the store offered him a management position, he turned it down because he felt it would be too much strain on his marriage. Within a year, he accepted a teaching job in Louisiana. There, he supplemented his income by driving a school bus.

While teaching, he became an active singer and recorded a couple of tapes. His music reached Nashville, where a recording company signed him to a contract. Soon Todd went on tour and became the small company's biggest act. However, one day while he was driving across the country in his tour bus, he realized that he was spending lots of time away from his family, and he noticed that he was the only person on the bus who was not divorced. He abruptly notified the record company that he was quitting.

Fortunately, Todd was able to begin working in his parents' business, Cool Wraps. The Connecticut-based company produced specialty CD cases. Todd was glad to get a position as the operations manager, but he was disillusioned. He observed that, "We had millions of dollars in sales, but it was all done over the phone—no personal contact, no shaking hands. So, to me it just wasn't human enough. Anyone can sit at a desk and crunch numbers. We couldn't even develop a relationship with the buyers because every two months they had different employees."

The experience at Cool Wraps helped Todd realize that he loved being with people and wanted to put his people skills to use. As a result, he decided to take an offer to become the youth minister in Mobile and move his family there. He and Angelle had eight children, and she spent her time home-schooling them. They had been in Mobile nine years when they started the business.

MOTIVATION FOR STARTING THE BUSINESS

Having come from an entrepreneurial family Todd had considered opening a business for years. He had thought about a pizza restaurant because people could socialize there, but he was afraid that the concept might be too complicated. Finally, Todd and Angelle chose to open a coffee shop primarily because they saw it as a good family business, a place where their kids could work and learn certain life lessons they viewed as important. The Sylvesters envisioned their kids growing up and going off to college at the university across the street. Regardless of their children's future career directions, the Sylvesters wanted them to have business and management skills. In Todd's words:

I want them to know how business works. To give you an example, we charge a dollar fifty for a muffin that costs us fifty cents. So when my son, Stephen, saw that, he thought it was great to make a dollar a muffin, but I told him that we certainly do not. The bakery case breaks even and doesn't make us any money. I explained that when you grab the muffin, you're using wax paper and a paper bag and a napkin and sometimes they want butter that we don't charge for. The labor costs us and the lights are on. Also, you throw away muffins when they are not fresh, and they're not free. Then my son said we need to charge more for the muffins. I explained that we can't charge more because the market has pretty much set that price. If you can go down the road, no one is going to pay more for a muffin. Now when my son comes in, he realizes that when he gets a drink for himself, that drink is not free.

FIGURE 1
Todd Sylvester with
His Daughter, Mary
Catherine

THE VISION AND CORE VALUES

Todd wanted a place where customers could find comfort. He relished the fact that some customers would visit a few times a week as a treat. Some would come in, sit down in one of the four black leather chairs placed about the store, and read while they sipped mocha lattes and frappes. Some customers drank one of Expresso Espresso's frothy delights instead of having dessert, and some would actually take their shoes off and relax as if they were at home. Todd saw this as "creating an environment of comfort."

Todd placed such an emphasis on comfort, that it was a major consideration when developing the business. The owner wanted customers to feel at home, even selecting the color scheme and furniture for the warm feeling they invoked. He wanted the interior to draw the customers in. Once in, Todd wanted them to linger. If students wanted to use the free Wi-Fi Internet connection, or if professors wanted to come in to grade papers, they had no pressure to buy anything.

THE SPECIALTY COFFEE INDUSTRY

The specialty coffee industry had seen steady growth for years, and the trend was expected to continue until at least 2015.[1] Of the various segments within the specialty coffee industry, most of the growth was attributable to beverage retailers (cafes and kiosks). In 1979, there were approximately 250 specialty coffee retailers. The number quadrupled by 1989 to approximately 1,000 outlets, and it exploded to roughly 15,000 by 2002. Nationally, specialty coffee sales totaled over $10 billion in 2005 (see Table 1).

For specialty coffee beverage services, including coffee, espresso, tea, chai, and granita, (see Exhibit 5) the leading drinks in 2004 were espresso-based beverages with average

[1]"Specialty Coffee," *Encyclopedia of Emerging Industries.* Online Edition, Thomson Gale, 2005, http://galenet.galegroup.com/servlet/BCRC.

TABLE 1   Specialty Coffee Industry Locations and Sales for 2005

Segment	Description	Locations	Average Sales	Total Sales (in $ millions)
Cafes	Beverage retailer with seating	13,900	$550,000	$ 7,650
Kiosks	Beverage retailer without seating	3,300	$300,000	990
Carts	Mobile beverage retailers	2,500	$140,000	350
Roasters	Roasting on premise	1,700	$925,000	1,570
Total				$10,560

Source: Ferguson, "Specialty Coffee Retail in the USA 2005," Specialty Coffee Association of America, 2006.

sales of $50,395 per store.[2] The second best selling drinks were drip-brewed coffee beverages at $33,336 per store, and third were cold and iced coffee beverages with an average of $22,061 per store.

By May 2006, Starbucks Corporation was the premier coffee retailer in the United States. Industry analysts generally credited it for popularizing specialty coffee and legitimizing higher drink prices. Starbucks sold specialty coffee, food items, coffee-related equipment, and teas in about 37 countries.[3] The company, headquartered in Seattle, had roughly 115,000 employees and 2005 revenues of over $6.3 billion. Starbucks was changing its menu to add more food, and it was doubling the number of outlets selling hot breakfast sandwiches. The firm expected revenues to grow 20 percent per year and to increase its dominating 40 percent market share. Starbucks had strong profits and cash flow that it planned to use to open company-owned and licensed stores domestically and abroad.

Diedrich Coffee, Inc., roasted and sold various brands of coffee through company-owned retail stores and through distributors, restaurants, mail order, and specialty stores. Diedrich was headquartered in Irvine, California, and had 2005 revenues of more than $52.5 million with growth from 2004 of about 3 percent.[4] Its brands included Diedrich Coffee, Gloria Jean's, and Coffee People. Located in 33 states and 15 foreign countries, the firm operated 50 retail stores and franchised more than 420 others. Diedrich had been a small family business with three locations until 1992 when it began expansion through acquisitions of other coffeehouses in Houston, Denver, and San Diego.

Caribou Coffee Co., Inc., went public in October 2005 and reported sales of $191 million in 2005.[5] The company expected the $67.7 million the IPO raised to fund growth of the 360-store chain.[6] By the end of 2005, the firm expected to add 40 new outlets and another 130 in 2006. While the company owned almost all of the current stores, management expected to franchise about 10 percent of the new stores. The company expected 6–7 percent in further growth to come from existing stores, largely due to the introduction of its Bou Gourmet brand of food products, which expanded and upgraded its previous food offerings.

Coffee Beanery was a coffee shop franchise with over 200 franchisees by the end of 2005.[7] During 2006, industry analysts expected about 40 new stores to open[8] with much of

[2]Laura Everage, Specialty Coffee Research Results I, *Gourmet Retailer* 26, no. 5 (May 2005).

[3]"Starbucks Corporation Company Profile," Datamonitor, PLC, www.datamonitor.com, May 2006.

[4]"Diedrich Coffee, Inc., Company Profile," Datamonitor, PLC, www.datamonitor.com, February 2006.

[5]Caribou Coffee Company, Inc., Annual Report, Brooklyn Center, Minnesota, March 31, 2006.

[6]Carolyn Walkup, "IPO-enriched Caribou Coffee Brews Plans to Gain Ground on Starbucks," *Nation's Restaurant News,* November 28, 2005.

[7]"About Us," Coffee Beanery, http://www.coffeebeanery.com/company/default.htm, 2005.

[8]Walkup, "IPO-enriched Caribou Coffee."

TABLE 2

Common-Size Income Statement (Snack and Nonalcoholic Beverage Bars)

Net sales	100.0
Operating expenses	91.6
Operating profit	8.4
All other expenses	3.8
Profit before taxes	4.7

Source: RMA Annual Statement Studies, 2006.

this growth coming from existing franchisees in China, South Korea, and the Middle East. At the beginning of 2006, the private company was testing a co-branding concept with the Cinnabon bakery chain.

Peet's Coffee & Tea claimed the title "grandfather of specialty coffee" because it could trace its roots to Alfred Peet who opened his first store in 1966. The company roasted its beans "European Style" from processes developed by the family business in Holland. By January 2006, the company operated 111 retail stores in six states and had revenues of $175 million.[9] Peet's sold coffee, coffee-based beverages, teas, pastries, and other related items, with an emphasis on freshness. In 1997, the company made the decision to increase distribution channels and currently distributes coffee beans through company-owned stores, direct sales, restaurants, specialty groceries, and gourmet food stores. (Common-size income statement for snack and nonalcoholic beverage bars is shown in Table 2.)

There were two trends in the specialty coffee industry. First, although convenience had been a key success factor within the industry for many years, specialty coffee retailers were adding new stores in suburban locations. Locating within buyers' communities not only provided convenience but also gave them places to meet friends and neighbors.

Second, while industry observers traditionally viewed specialty coffee as served by coffee shops and kiosks, large restaurants were trying to find ways to capitalize on the specialty coffee industry growth.[10] McDonald's, Krispy Kreme, and Dunkin' Donuts were modifying their menus to feature more upscale coffee. In February 2006, McDonald's introduced a new premium roast coffee that it priced 40 cents above the price of $1.19 for the previous large size and about 30 cents less than Starbucks. Analysts credited the premium roast coffee offered by McDonald's with increasing sales 5.2 percent.[11] At the same time, Starbucks was changing its menu to add more food. Between 2005 and 2006, the company doubled the number of outlets selling hot breakfast sandwiches from 300 to 600 stores.[12]

THE SPECIALTY COFFEE MARKET

According to the National Coffee Association, 54 percent of adults in America consumed coffee daily with over 18 percent buying specialty coffee beverages.[13] Specialty coffee buyers were generally more affluent, well educated, and worked in urban areas.[14] Research indicated that individuals with college degrees purchased almost 50 percent more specialty

[9]Peet's Coffee & Tea, Inc., Annual Report, 2005. Peets Coffee & Tea, Inc., Berkeley, California.

[10]Elizabeth Fuhrman, "Brew Wars," *Beverage Industry,* March, 2006.

[11]"Coffee Culture: Making a Great Cup o' Joe," *The Breakfast Journal,* August 7, 2006.

[12]Fuhrman, "Brew Wars."

[13]"Coffee Culture."

[14]"Specialty Coffee."

FIGURE 2
Expresso Espresso
Seating Area

coffee than those without college degrees. The link to education was even greater for people with some postgraduate education. In addition to education, households with two working parents and kids were more likely to purchase specialty coffee. According to the Specialty Coffee Association of America, the market for specialty coffee was "an educated urban resident with the disposable income to spend on fine coffee."

Three factors heavily influenced purchasing decisions. About 70 percent of coffee drinkers thought the most important coffeehouse characteristic was coffee quality and convenient location.[15] The next most important was friendly and knowledgeable staff with a 40 percent response. The third most important characteristic was variety with 35 percent. The least important factor was price.

EXPRESSO ESPRESSO MARKETING

Target Market

Because of the store location, Expresso Espresso necessarily targeted college students, staff, and faculty. Students at South Alabama were older than those at most four-year universities and Todd theorized that the older students would have more disposable income. According to him, the street in front of the store had between 24,000 and 27,000 cars a day, and these potential customers had a median income of about $45,000.

While talking with one of the business professors from the university, Todd asked how he might get more information about what the target market really wanted. The professor offered to allow the students in one of his classes to conduct a survey to find out more. Todd eagerly agreed. The survey was not scientific, as it was intended to be a demonstration of surveying methods. However, the professor shared the survey information with Todd anyway. The results of the survey are in Exhibit 8.

[15]G. Ferguson, Specialty Coffee Retail in the USA 2005, Specialty Coffee Association of America, 2006.

Products

Todd tried to remain a "purist" in developing his products. He did not brew drip coffee and then leave it sitting around in warming pots. In fact, he did not offer drip-brewed coffee at all although it cost substantially less to make. Instead, he preferred to make each drink fresh from espresso. If a customer asked for coffee, the barista would offer an Americano instead. An Americano was an espresso with water added. It did not taste the same as drip-brewed coffee, and Todd considered it better. Expresso's menu offered traditional European-style coffee drinks. Todd stated that, "Some people come in and they want a Snickerdoodle, which is half chocolate and half caramel. We don't put it up on the menu because if you write it up there, people are going to be like, what's a Snickerdoodle? It's too complicated."

Although he wanted a European-style shop, occasionally he bent to customer demand. One customer wanted iced tea. He really did not want to offer iced tea, but the customer was a close friend so he relented. It turned out to be a lot more popular than he expected. The other product pressure he got was from Starbucks. "You have Starbucks that just came out with a new green tea cappuccino. So we've already had people come and ask if we have a green tea blend," Todd said with amazement. He continued, "We will have to add it because they are selling so well over there. Just like before the holiday season, Starbucks comes out with the spiced cappuccino, the pumpkin cappuccino, and the eggnog cappuccino. We're going to have to have them. Even though I'll be pumping a bunch of sugar into people because that is what they are. I will try to make it as best I can. They set the market." Todd was trying to be sensitive to what his customers wanted, but he was concerned that if all he did was copy Starbucks, he would not be able to differentiate his business. Somehow, he sensed that he should not just make Starbucks drinks. However, he was not sure what alternatives he had.

In addition to traditional coffee drinks, the shop also sold teas, smoothies, and a limited variety of pastries (see Table 3 and Exhibit 3). No sandwiches or soups were available. The display case usually had some muffins, lemon bars, cookies, and brownies on hand. Prices for pastries that Todd bought from a nearby grocery store ranged from $.75 to $1.50. Todd was not keen on the idea of selling food. He thought the waste and overall cost of food was excessive. Although he kept a few food items, he did not expect to make a profit on them. In addition, the store offered other retail items such as T-shirts and coffee mugs with humorous coffee-related sayings on them. The idea was to get people smiling when thinking about Expresso Espresso.

Prices

When deciding on prices, Todd went around town looking at everyone else's prices (see Exhibit 4). He made sure that his were 10 percent lower than any competitor. He believed

TABLE 3
Expresso Espresso's Sales By Type (5/14/2006–5/20/2006)

Source: Expresso Espresso POS data.

Type	Amount	Tickets
Hot drinks	$ 605.95	552
Iced drinks	254.58	206
Iced blended drinks	415.74	236
Add-ons	40.38	91
Baked goods	81.56	80
Retail items	96.85	16
Total	$1,651.84	1,271

that having a low price was important in attracting new customers. He also considered it important to show that he was providing a good value.

Promotion

Some coffee shops used a "buyer card" to promote customer loyalty and to give the perception of offering more value. Commonly shops gave the customer a free coffee after they bought nine cups, which was similar to a 10 percent discount if you bought enough coffee. Todd considered it more of a "psychological tool" rather than a true discount. Buyer cards were often lost before customers used them, and he thought asking the customer to keep track of the card was a hassle. To Todd, pricing products at 10 percent less was a more direct and honest approach to serving the customer. He commented, "When people say 'Hey, do you have a buyer's card?' I'll say 'Hey, our prices are already 10 percent lower than everybody so I am giving you the discount now.'" Although he felt his approach was more honest, he was not sure it was the best approach. "Now, I don't know if that is generating more sales," he said. "I don't know if it is working against me, quite frankly, but I just feel personally—not that I'm some high moralist in the business world—but I feel like if I have 300 customers a day, I don't want to rip off 100."

Other promotions included a mix of media. Expresso Espresso advertised on 92-ZEW, a local radio station that Todd believed had a strong student audience. In addition, the company placed ads in the campus newspaper and distributed flyers at apartment complexes surrounding the campus. Flyers typically showed the menu and contained a 10 percent off coupon. The coupons were good for one day only. It was as close to a "grand opening" as the store had. According to Todd, Expresso Espresso used a "soft opening" approach. It could still have a grand opening, but most of the students would not be on campus until the fall semester began.

One idea that Todd considered for promoting the shop was having live music. He thought that local musicians would make Expresso Espresso a destination rather than simply a convenience. He expected that many people would drive across the Mobile Bay just

FIGURE 3
The Food Case

FIGURE 4
Product Display

to see popular performers. He intended to begin having bands play on Friday and Saturday nights during the summer. There would be no cover charge; the store would simply make money from the drink sales. News of the performers would be by word of mouth. It was not clear where the band would play. The only reasonable space was in front of the product display case shown in Figure 4.

Publicity

Todd wanted to run the store differently from other coffee shops. He did not like the idea that employees might argue over the shifts because some shifts may get better tips. He also wanted to make sure the business could help others. He decided to create a policy whereby he would give away all tips. A huge coffee cup sat on the front counter with a sign indicating the charity of the week. At the end of each week, Todd would collect whatever people chose to give and pass it on to a good cause (see Figure 5 and Table 4). In just a few weeks, the business had given thousands to other organizations. The local paper considered this approach so novel that it ran an article on the practice. However, Todd did not think it was a big deal, "I don't think it is a new concept. A lot of restaurants will have jars that are specifically for someone—saying so and so has leukemia and people will drop money in." The primary difference was that Todd's approach was more organized. He selected a different recipient each week and prominently placed the cup and sign so that customers were more aware. It was part of the comfort concept of the store. Customers had the opportunity to help others as they treated themselves. This not only benefited the community but also had considerable "feel-good" value for those participating.

FIGURE 5
The Tip Cup

Tips this week go to:

St. Mary's Home

Competitors

The nearest competitor was Satori Coffee House, an eclectic coffee house that also sold music and alcohol (see Mobile Area Map in Exhibit 10). It was located about a half mile east on Old Shell Road, the same street as Expresso Espresso, in an old residence converted into commercial property. None of the furniture matched, and dark, moody paint colored the walls. In general, Satori attracted an "edgier" crowd than other competitors. Occasionally, Satori offered live bands. It levied a cover charge to pay the band and generated a profit from selling drinks to the listeners.

Todd considered Carpe Diem to be a competitor although it was about two miles east of Expresso Espresso. It catered more to the students and teachers at Springhill College which was also on Old Shell Road. The shop was also a favorite of students from nearby St. Paul's High School. Like Satori, Carpe Diem did not have a drive-through window, and was a house that had been converted into a coffee shop. Unlike Satori, the atmosphere was a bit

TABLE 4
Tip Charities (Year
to Date)

Source: Expresso Espresso
company records.

Recipient	Amount
St. Mary's Home	$ 165.01
American Cancer Society	165.01
2B Choices for Women	315.18
Ronald McDonald House	107.95
Little Sisters of the Poor	226.32
Penelope House	185.45
St. Jude's Children's Hospital	223.01
Home of Grace	266.72
Camp Rap-A-Hope	242.85
Habitat for Humanity	193.96
Total	$2,004.44

more "wholesome." It was rather busy when school was in session, and often the parking lot was full. Carpe Diem was the only coffee shop that roasted its own coffee on-site, and the company was the sole supplier of roasted beans to Expresso. The company provided the high-quality Arabica beans that Todd insisted on using.

Another competing coffee shop was the Daily Grind, which was in the cafeteria on campus at the University of South Alabama and operated by contract by the same company that ran the cafeteria. The facility was well kept and within convenient walking distance from most administration and classroom buildings. If students wanted to, they could read a free copy of the local newspaper or study in the cafeteria while waiting for their next class. Overall, the Daily Grind did not offer the cozy atmosphere of the other shops. It participated in the "Proudly Serving Starbucks Coffee" program.

Some patrons preferred Beaners, a franchise operation, because of its convenient location on Airport Boulevard, its gourmet coffee, and its unique atmosphere. It was in the end unit of a shopping center and provided tables outside for customers to enjoy the sunshine while they drank their coffee. Sometime people commented on Beaners' self-serve option. Customers could get coffee from the self-serve line and pay for it by placing their money in an "Honor Box." The system made customers feel the company trusted them and made it possible for customers to customize their coffee and still get fast service. Beaners was about a one-mile drive from Expresso.

Although Todd did not necessarily view them as "competitors," some local churches had opened coffee shops in town. Warm Heart Café and The Mug were both on Grelot Road close to the new Starbucks location. These shops did not have the look or feel of Starbucks, and mostly they catered to church members and their friends. The churches supported the shops financially so they did not have to make a profit. Some attributes of various Mobile coffee shops are provided in Table 5.

Perhaps the competitor that worried Todd the most was Starbucks. Starbucks had a freestanding store on Airport Boulevard—the busiest road in Mobile, a shop on Schillinger Road, and a shop in the Mobile County Government building downtown. It also had licensed stores in the Barnes and Noble by the interstate and in the new Target in the developing west side of town. Starbucks had started building four new freestanding stores—one by the mall, one by I-65, one on Airport Boulevard across from Beaners, and one on Grelot Road across from Warm Heart Café. Baldwin County, which was in the Mobile metropolitan statistical area, only had three coffee shops, but Starbucks had recently announced a new store on one of the busiest streets in the county.

As if that were not enough competition from Starbucks, the company had announced plans to build a drive-through store on Old Shell Road about 400 feet east of Expresso Espresso. One of Todd's biggest concerns was the ability of Mobile to support so many coffee shops. The warm, humid climate did not seem to match the typical city for coffee shops. Exhibit 6 shows coffee shop densities for the top coffee-shop cities. In addition, Todd was concerned that Starbucks would take customers from Expresso's drive-through window.

TABLE 5
Attributes of Mobile Coffee Shops

Source: Case researcher observation of coffee shops.

	Expresso Espresso	Carpe Diem	Satori	Daily Grind	Starbucks	Beaners
Seating Space	Moderate	High	High	Extra High	Low	High
Food Variety	Low	Moderate	High	Low	Moderate	Moderate
Drive-Through	Yes	No	No	No	Yes	No

OPERATIONS

Quality

Although Todd wanted patrons to feel comfortable, he also understood the importance of convenience and speed especially when individuals were getting coffee before going to work. He placed a priority on making orders quickly for the drive-through. The acceptable standard was to complete the order within 45 seconds. To give employees feedback, Todd often set a timer when customers placed their orders. Completing orders fast might not seem like a big deal to McDonald's or Krispy Kreme, but it was a bit more challenging for Expresso Espresso because all of the drinks were made to order. Before they made any coffee drink, baristas had to fill the espresso maker, tamp it, brew it, and pour it. These steps took more time than other restaurants but provided the consistent, high-quality drinks that Todd insisted on serving.

While there was a sensor that beeped to let baristas know when a drive-though customer was present, Todd often would be heard yelling, "DRIVE-THROUGH" to give the baristas advance warning and to reinforce the importance of fast service. Todd knew that the drive-through not only gave the store a differentiating factor but also contributed about 40 percent of its total revenues.

Costs

Quality was an important factor for Expresso Espresso. As a result, some of its costs were higher than those of competitors. Todd stated, "I don't compromise with making coffee. Like my espresso blend. It is not cheap because it is so good. You can get much cheaper." Other ingredients also are on the high end. "Most of my flavored syrups have reasonable costs, but my chocolate, caramel, and white chocolate syrups are from a high-end company in San Francisco, and they are very expensive. But they are so good! Any person can taste the difference. I refuse to compromise. I refuse to use powders. I hate the grittiness."

Another example of the cost/quality trade-off made by the company was the way it produced drinks. There were actually no coffee machines in the store; the staff made all

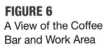

FIGURE 6
A View of the Coffee
Bar and Work Area

TABLE 6
Expresso Espresso's
Sales By Hour
(5/14/2006–5/20/2006)

Source: Expresso Espresso
POS data.

Time	Amount	Tickets
6:00–6:59 A.M.	$ 20.00	7
7:00–7:59 A.M.	131.95	39
8:00–8:59 A.M.	108.25	32
9:00–9:59 A.M.	98.05	31
10:00–10:59 A.M.	126.50	36
11:00–11:59 A.M.	60.65	17
12:00–12:59 P.M.	101.75	25
1:00–1:59 P.M.	50.65	15
2:00–2:59 P.M.	122.25	36
3:00–3:59 P.M.	117.70	32
4:00–4:59 P.M.	108.10	30
5:00–5:59 P.M.	54.40	17
6:00–6:59 P.M.	58.15	16
7:00–7:59 P.M.	130.00	27
8:00–8:59 P.M.	213.15	61
9:00–9:59 P.M.	114.20	32
10:00–10:59 P.M.	53.00	17

coffee drinks from espresso. If a customer wanted a simple coffee, then the baristas made an Americano, a drink with two shots of espresso diluted in water. As for the espresso machines, Todd had to choose between a standard machine and a super-automatic machine as used by Starbucks. The super-automatic machines were faster and baristas needed less training to operate them. However, Todd believed manual machines produced a higher quality drink, although operating them required close monitoring. He observed, "With us, we're adjusting our grind all day long. The first thing I do when I come in is to ask the baristas how they are 'pulling.' What that means is: Are you timing them? Are you getting the essence of the coffee out? Does the coffee have a consistent taste? Is the espresso bitter?" Because manual machines were slower, and because the company made all coffee drinks from espresso, Expresso Espresso had installed two of them in the barista work area.

Operating Hours

Normal store hours were Monday–Friday, 6:30 A.M. to 11:00 P.M.; Saturday, 7:30 A.M. to 11:00 P.M.; and Sunday, 4:00 P.M. to 11:00 P.M. Expresso Espresso usually had two employees running the store. This provided plenty of help during the busy periods, but resulted in overstaffing during the slow times of the day (see Table 6). During the first few months after opening, the store had two days that were so busy Todd had to call in extra help. Both days were during spring semester final exams (see April 26 and 29 in Exhibit 7). During finals week, customers tended to linger more than usual. In fact, the store had to ask customers to leave when it closed at 11:00 P.M. No restaurant served specialty coffee past 11:00 P.M.; the best alternative was a nearby Waffle House.

MANAGEMENT AND ORGANIZATION

Todd was the only manager of the business. This caused some stress on his time because his primary job was youth minister of a local church. He worked in the shop on his days off, Tuesdays and Saturdays, and on some evenings. To supplement Todd's efforts, certain employees had the responsibility of opening and closing the shop. Todd did not think of himself as a manager. To him he was simply the one who trained employees to become baristas, and it was their job to work as good team members and to become self-managed. He believed that if people knew what to do, you just did not have to watch over them. Todd enjoyed developing people more than working with numbers. To assist him with the financials, he hired a bookkeeper to come in once a month. This was a big help because Todd did not want to spend his time on the books.

In general, employees were very happy working at Expresso Espresso. Because Todd had worked as a youth minister for nine years, he had a rich pool of high school and college students from which he could hire. He believed his employees were the cream of the crop—he could pick and choose from people he knew very well. In return, the employees were very loyal. He paid them a bit above minimum wage, but they often left higher-paying jobs to work for Todd. Expresso had higher operating costs, due in part to the fact that the company donated tips rather than giving them to employees. Other coffee shops used tips to supplement wages to reach the minimum wage requirements.

Todd did not believe in being what he called a "tyrannical boss." He created a family environment and even allowed employees to chat with their friends who came in while the baristas worked. Employees enjoyed the workplace so much they often hung out at the shop during their off-hours. Occasionally, when employees were off the clock, they would pitch in to help if needed. They felt a strong sense of responsibility to the company and to the other employees. In addition to nonfamily staff, Expresso Espresso also employed two of the Sylvesters' children.

THE NEW LOCATION

Todd wanted to find a midtown location where the target market would be young professionals. He wanted more space for seating and sufficient parking, which was at a premium in that area of Mobile. In addition, he expected the new store to have a kitchen that could support making items like breakfast foods and sandwiches. There was such a building about a mile east of the mall on Airport Boulevard; the owner was selling it for $500,000. It had a place where he could add a drive-through window. Todd planned to purchase the building so that he would get the full benefit from the upgrades he would make. The new store would allow customers to grab breakfast and an espresso drink on the way to work, and with a kitchen available, Todd could prepare food at the new store to send to the first store. Exhibit 9 presents start-up costs for the new location.

DECISION TIME

Although Todd was proud of the organization he had created, he knew that he needed to make some decisions about the future of his company. He felt he had developed a warm, friendly place for people to relax and socialize, but he was not sure what to do about the threat of Starbucks moving in and stealing his customers. Todd faced several nagging questions: Was the company positioned properly in the local specialty coffee industry? How high would sales need to go to reach profitability? What would he need to do to be successful? Todd was confident about the company's success but just was not sure of the best combination to get there quickly.

EXHIBIT 1   Expresso Espresso, Inc., Profit and Loss, 2006

	February	March	April	May
Sales		$ 9,162.86	$ 10,970.67	$ 11,891.41
Cost of goods sold		6,821.18	6,128.68	6,897.02
Gross profit		2,341.68	4,841.93	4,994.39
Operating expenses				
Advertising	—	—	1,064.50	1,177.00
Automobile expenses	—	—	70.91	214.40
Credit card expenses	62.71	127.59	186.05	389.21
Contributions	—	315.18	—	—
Depreciation	—	122.05	122.05	122.05
Gift cards	—	—	—	685.00
Licenses and taxes	—	243.00	21.16	8.51
Postage	24.73	39.00	41.00	26.33
Professional fees	—	300.00	—	—
Rent	1,727.00	1,727.00	1,727.00	1,727.00
Repairs	8,109.45	3,243.76	1,091.64	655.62
Janitorial supplies	73.20	514.48	214.62	107.84
Miscellaneous	—	—	—	1,483.33
Office supplies	149.65	—	235.36	20.51
Telephone	47.93	64.86	243.59	367.83
Utilities	189.52	301.02	390.97	448.41
Payroll	1,330.59	5,054.49	5,322.36	5,011.89
Total operating expenses	$ 11,714.78	$ 12,052.43	$ 10,731.21	$ 12,444.93
Net income	$−11,714.78	$−9,710.75	$−5,889.28	$−7,450.54

Source: Expresso Espresso company records.

Note: Expresso Espresso was an S Corporation.

EXHIBIT 2 Expresso Espresso, Inc., Ending Balance Sheet, 2006

	February 28	March 31	April 30	May 31
ASSETS				
Current assets				
Cash	$ 5,187.49	$ 5,678.65	$ 5,788.33	$ 4,781.93
Accounts receivable	—	336.36	885.42	1,072.72
Other current assets	917.79	1,835.57	1,115.39	2,343.92
Total current assets	6,105.28	7,850.58	7,789.14	8,198.57
Fixed assets				
Fixtures, furniture, equipment	25,473.08	25,473.08	25,473.08	25,473.08
Accumulated depreciation	—	544.87	1,089.74	1,634.61
Total fixed assets	25,473.08	26,017.95	26,562.82	23,838.47
Total assets	$ 31,578.36	$ 33,868.53	$ 34,351.96	$ 32,037.04
LIABILITIES AND EQUITY				
Liabilities				
Current liabilities				
Payroll payable	$ —	$ 101.81	$ 276.54	$ 362.87
Sales tax payable	—	856.96	998.95	1,189.43
Total current liabilities	—	958.77	1,275.49	1,552.30
Total long-term liabilities	—	—	—	—
Total liabilities	$ —	$ 958.77	$ 1,275.49	$ 1,552.30
Equity				
Owner's contribution	$ 43,293.14	$ 54,335.29	$ 60,391.28	$ 65,250.09
Retained earnings	—	−11,714.78	−21,425.53	−27,314.81
Net income	−11,714.78	−9,710.75	−5,889.28	−7,450.54
Total equity	$ 31,578.36	$ 32,909.76	$ 33,076.47	$ 30,484.74
TOTAL LIABILITIES AND EQUITY	$ 31,578.36	$ 33,868.53	$ 34,351.96	$ 32,037.04

Source: Expresso Espresso company records.

EXHIBIT 3 Expresso Espresso Menu

HOT DRINKS (espresso with hot steamed milk, some foam)	Small (12 oz.)	Medium (16 oz.)	Large (20 oz.)
Cafe Latte	$1.95	$2.50	$2.95
Vanilla Latte	2.25	2.75	3.25
Carmel Latte	2.25	2.75	3.25
Mocha Latte	2.25	2.75	3.25
Mocha Bianca (white chocolate Mocha)	2.50	3.00	3.50
Raspberry Mocha	2.50	3.00	3.50
Italian Style real Cappuccino (espresso with hot, mostly foamy milk)	1.95	2.50	—
Espresso (strong black "real taste" coffee, served in a small 1.5 oz. cup)	1.75	2.00	—
Hot Chocolate	1.75	2.00	2.50
Americano	1.25	1.50	1.75
Add a shot of espresso: add 50 cents			
Any drink made with soy or half and half: add 50 cents			

ICED DRINKS	Small (16 oz.)	Medium (20 oz.)	Large (24 oz.)
Iced Latte	$1.95	$2.50	$2.95
Iced Vanilla Latte	2.25	2.75	3.25
Iced Carmel Latte	2.25	2.75	3.25
Iced Raspberry Mocha (or any other flavor)	2.50	3.00	3.50
Iced Chai Latte	2.25	2.75	3.25
Iced Tea (Lemon Blossom, Wild Raspberry, Ruby Mist, Mango Passionfruit)	1.25	1.50	1.75

ICED BLENDED DRINKS	Small (16 oz.)	Medium (20 oz.)	Large (24 oz.)
Vanilla Frappe (a delightful blend of espresso and vanilla cream)	$3.25	$3.60	$3.95
Carmel Frappe	3.25	3.60	3.95
Mocha Frappe	3.25	3.60	3.95
Smoothies (Strawberry, Four Berry, Mango Tropics, Pineapple Paradise)			
Flavors: Vanilla, Almond, Hazelnut, Raspberry, Carmel, Irish Cream, Butterscotch, Peppermint	3.35	3.60	3.95

Source: Expresso Espresso menu.

EXHIBIT 4 Price Comparison among Several Mobile Coffee Shops

	Beaners	Carpe Diem	Daily Grind	Expresso Espresso	Satori	Starbucks
HOT DRINKS						
Espresso (small)	$1.69	$1.80	$1.45	$1.75	$1.75	$1.75
Cappuccino	3.09	3.05	3.10	2.50	2.50	3.20
Latte	3.09	2.85	3.10	2.50	3.00	3.20
Mocha	3.49	3.15	3.30	3.00	3.25	3.50
Hot Chocolate	3.29	2.50	3.00	2.00	2.75	2.60
Americano	2.06	1.80	2.15	1.50	2.00	2.15
Coffee	1.49	1.59	1.60	none	1.69	1.70
Chai Latte	3.30	3.10	3.10	2.75	3.00	3.30
Hot Tea	1.69	1.21	1.65	1.50	1.30	1.70
ICED DRINKS						
Latte	3.59	2.95	3.50	2.50	3.25	3.20
Vanilla Latte	3.49	3.20	3.50	2.75	3.25	3.50
Iced Tea	1.69	1.30	none	1.50	1.30	1.70
BLENDED DRINKS						
Frappe	4.39	3.60	3.50	3.60	3.50	3.80
Smoothies	4.39	3.60	none	3.60	3.75	none

Source: Case researcher observation of coffee shops. All medium size except where indicated.

EXHIBIT 5
Typical Coffee
Beverages in Coffee
Shops

Source: Adapted from
http://www.espressotec.com
and http://www
.coffeeandteawarehouse
.com.

Beverage	Description
Americano	A single shot of espresso with 6 to 8 ounces of hot water
Caffe Latte	A single shot of espresso with steamed milk (about 1:3 ratio)
Caffe au Lait	A 1:1 mixture of coffee and steamed milk
Cappucino	Equal parts espresso and steamed milk with milk froth on top
Cafe Breva	A cappuccino made with half-and-half instead of whole milk
Cafe Macchiato	A shot of espresso topped off with steamed milk
Cafe Mocha	A cappuccino or caffe latte with chocolate syrup
Espresso Breve	A single shot of espresso with heated half-and-half added
Espresso Con Panna	A shot of espresso with whipped cream
Espresso Mocha	An espresso with steamed milk and chocolate syrup
Espresso Romano	An espresso served with a twist of lemon
Iced Cappuccino	A double espresso with cold milk (1:1 ratio) over ice
Iced Latte	A double espresso with cold milk (1:3 ratio) over ice
Granita	An espresso that has been frozen and crushed
Macchiato	A single espresso topped with a dollop of frothed milk
Nienta	Decaffeinated cappuccino with nonfat milk

EXHIBIT 6
Coffee Shop
Densities

Top Ten Cities For Coffee Restaurants per Capita

MSA*	MSA Population	Units	Units per 10,000 Population
Anchorage, AK	274,398	77	2.8
Seattle, WA	2,494,976	628	2.5
San Francisco, CA	1,682,362	373	2.2
Bellingham, WA	179,262	37	2.1
Portland, OR	2,064,660	419	2.0
Bremerton, WA	241,570	45	1.9
Boulder, CO	302,622	55	1.8
Olympia, WA	225,373	40	1.8
San Luis Obispo, CA	254,929	41	1.6
Santa Rosa, CA	468,852	72	1.5

Source: "Anchorage Alaska Tops the List of Most Coffee Shops Per Capita in the U.S." NPD Press Release, The NPD Group, March 14, 2005, http://www.npd.com.
*Metropolitan Statistical Area

Top Ten Cities for Number of Coffee Restaurants

MSA*	MSA Population	Units	Units per 10,000 Population
Los Angeles, CA	9,980,242	801	0.8
Seattle, WA	2,494,976	628	2.5
Chicago, IL	8,558,311	568	0.7
New York, NY	9,434,917	525	0.6
Portland, OR	2,064,660	419	2.0
Minneapolis, MN	3,117,850	384	1.2
Washington, DC	5,326,702	379	0.7
San Francisco, CA	1,682,362	373	2.2
San Diego, CA	2,966,163	344	1.2
Orange County, CA	2,991,264	326	1.1

Source: "Anchorage Alaska Tops the List of Most Coffee Shops Per Capita in the U.S." NPD Press Release, The NPD Group, March 14, 2005, http://www.npd.com.
*Metropolitan Statistical Area

Mobile Area Population

Geographical Area	Population
City of Mobile	198,983
Mobile County	410,500
Baldwin County	158,944
Metropolitan Statistical Area	569,524

Source: Mobile Area Chamber of Commerce, viewed September 15, 2006, http://www.mobilechamber.com/faq.asp.

EXHIBIT 7
Daily Sales
for April 2006

Source: Expresso Espresso
POS data.

	Day	Sales	Tax	Total	Tickets
1	Saturday	$261.49	$26.41	$287.89	84
2	Sunday	157.35	15.77	173.12	47
3	Monday	313.84	31.47	345.31	94
4	Tuesday	351.65	35.14	386.78	106
5	Wednesday	361.56	36.41	397.97	122
6	Thursday	228.40	22.93	251.32	70
7	Friday	449.52	45.13	494.65	119
8	Saturday	396.53	39.94	436.47	103
9	Sunday	151.89	15.28	167.17	40
10	Monday	318.98	32.21	351.19	106
11	Tuesday	312.77	31.54	344.31	98
12	Wednesday	331.67	33.21	364.88	101
13	Thursday	359.72	35.86	395.58	97
14	Friday	319.68	32.09	351.77	86
15	Saturday	250.81	25.08	275.89	74
16	Sunday	—	—	—	—
17	Monday	301.61	30.43	332.04	105
18	Tuesday	355.96	35.69	391.65	105
19	Wednesday	418.29	41.88	460.16	104
20	Thursday	417.63	41.86	459.49	127
21	Friday	295.66	29.79	325.45	76
22	Saturday	314.26	31.67	345.93	93
23	Sunday	121.80	12.25	134.05	36
24	Monday	416.13	41.97	458.09	126
25	Tuesday	354.94	35.71	390.65	116
26	Wednesday	472.94	47.28	520.22	133
27	Thursday	446.57	44.54	491.11	128
28	Friday	402.29	40.24	442.52	114
29	Saturday	780.93	76.33	857.26	169
30	Sunday	306.79	30.90	337.69	86

EXHIBIT 8
Partial Student
Survey Results

FAVORITE COFFEE SHOP	
Barney's	4
Beaners	5
Carpe Diem	9
Daily Grind	2
Expresso Espresso	10
Joe Mugs	2
Satori	5
Starbucks	53
Other	3
None	31
Total	124

AVERAGE DRINK PRICE	
Cappuccino	4.23
Coffee	1.99
Espresso	3.64
Frappuccino	3.71
Latte	3.49
Tea	2.00
Other	2.99
Average	3.24

IMPORTANCE OF FEATURES	
Product Quality	4.52
Convenient Location	4.16
Product Variety	3.86
Low Price	3.85
Drive-Through	3.10
Self-Service	2.85
Food	2.76
Wi-Fi Internet	2.77
Frequent Buyer Card	2.71
Live Entertainment	2.16

FAVORITE COFFEE SHOP DRINK	
Frappuccino	35
Coffee	17
Cappuccino	16
Latte	13
Tea	13
Other	27

EXHIBIT 9
Some Projected
Start-up Expenses for
Expresso Espresso's
New Location

EQUIPMENT	
Espresso machines/Bunn brewing equipment/grinders	$ 4,000
Two-door refrigerator (used)	1,500
Two-door freezer (used)	1,800
Blenders	1,800
Convection oven	2,900
Under counter commercial dishwasher	3,000
Three compartment sink and prep tables	800
Tables and chairs (most used)	2,700
Refrigerated glass display case for desserts (used)	1,500
Two refrigerators for other cold beverages (used)	1,400
Total	**$21,400**

CONSTRUCTION	
Drive-through window installation	$ 4,500
Architect costs/permits/contractor	7,000
Counters and counter tops including retail shelves	2,800
Cups/saucers/disposable stock	1,000
T-Shirts/light retail items (mugs)	600
Alarm system	500
Video surveillance system	1,500
POS computers and software	4,000
Office computer and software/office supplies	2,500
Sign on building	1,200
Sign at street	1,700
Total	**$27,300**

EXHIBIT 10 Mobile Area Map

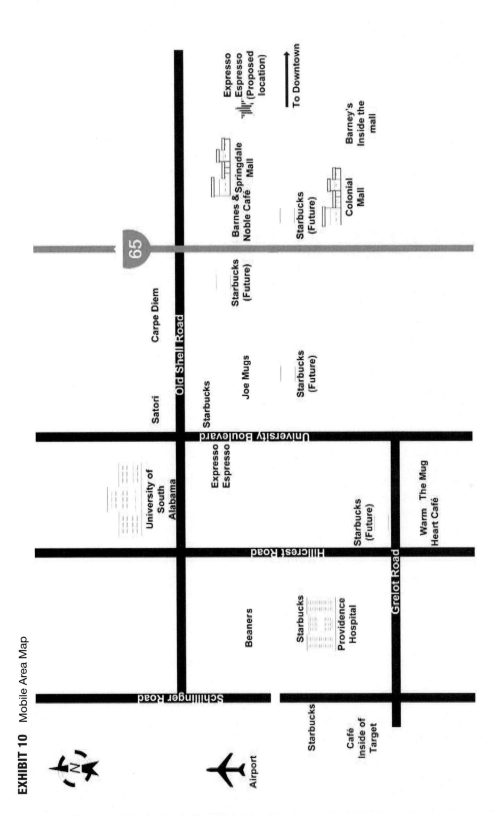

Case

8

Respironics, Incorporated: Take a Deep Breath

Janet L. Rovenpor *Manhattan College*
Armand Gilinsky, Jr. *Sonoma State University*

> I ask people at parties, "If we could come up with an elegant way to eliminate snoring, would you pay $100 so your bed partner doesn't snore anymore?" So far I have gotten 100 percent "yes" on that question.[1]
>
> —John Miclot, CEO, Respironics, Inc.

On August 30, 2006, John Miclot, President and CEO of Respironics, rang the opening bell at the NASDAQ in Times Square to commemorate the 30th anniversary of the company's founding. Standing next to him was Gerald McGinnis, the entrepreneur who had started Respironics with $13,000 in capital raised from angel investors. From a small, one-product company that made surgical masks for the delivery of anesthesia, Respironics had evolved into a designer, manufacturer and marketer of medical devices for the treatment of sleep and respiratory disorders. Headquartered in Murrysville, Pennsylvania, Respironics manufactured and marketed continuous positive airway pressure systems (CPAPs) and masks to treat obstructive sleep apnea (OSA) to customers in over 131 countries.

Besides passing an important milestone in its history, Respironics had exceeded the $1 billion mark in revenues for the first time for the fiscal year that ended on June 30.

This case was developed for the sole purpose of providing material for class discussion. It is not intended to illustrate either effective or ineffective handling of a managerial situation.

The authors wish to thank Joseph Bourgart, vice president of strategic planning and business development, and Daniel Bevevino, chief financial officer, for their valuable insights, during personal interviews, into Respironics' history and strategies. They also thank Dr. Lew G. Brown, editor, and three anonymous reviewers for their helpful comments and suggestions in the refinement of this case.

[1]From interviews with John Miclot, in R. Grilliot, "Tapping into the Problem Sleeper Market," *HomeCare Magazine* 28 (7) (July 2005): 30.

EXHIBIT 1   Global Sleep Therapy Equipment Market Share Chart

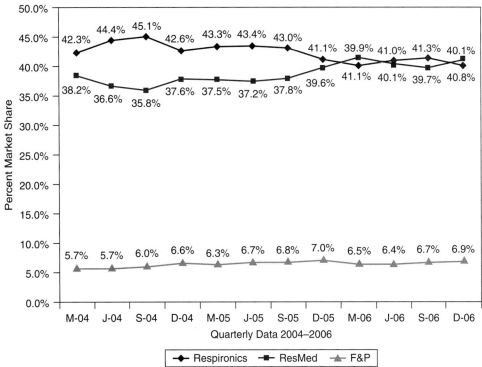

Source: Michael S. Matson, Senior Analyst, Medical Device Equity Research, *Sleep FQ307 Review & Medtrade Summary* (April 30, 2007), Wachovia Capital Markets, LLC.
Note: Other industry competitors, together, held between 12.0–13.9 percent market share across the same quarters.

The company had nearly $260 million in cash and marketable securities on hand to pursue new market opportunities. Yet, as Miclot celebrated this anniversary and pondered future avenues for growth, many challenges lay ahead. Respironics' stock price had fluctuated, reaching a high of $42.95 per share on October 4, 2005, sinking to a low of $32.66 per share on May 24, 2006, and standing at $36.67 per share on August 30, 2006. In the past fiscal year, it had recalled 172,000 humidifiers at a cost of $5 million. Respironics' share of the domestic sleep therapy equipment market was slipping too, from 51.8 percent in 2004, to 48.5 percent in 2005, and to 45.4 percent in 2006. In the global sleep therapy equipment market, Respironics was locked in a tight two-way battle for market share with a formidable rival, ResMed, Incorporated (Exhibit 1, Exhibit 2, and Exhibit 3).

Becky Quick, a CNBC anchor, had asked John Miclot about ResMed just before the opening bell at the NASDAQ: "You know, you are not the only player in this area. ResMed (RMD) is also one of your competitors. They have seen even stronger revenue growth. How are you fighting off the competition here?" Miclot replied: "Well, our company has continued to innovate this therapy. Recently we introduced some new technology called C-Flex which reduces pressure on exhalation and makes a patient more comfortable. You know, we broke the billion dollar mark and have forecasted to grow mid teens top line and our earnings per share of 17 to 18 percent in FY '07. So we feel like we have got a very, very bright future."[2]

Meanwhile, unknown to the public, another drama was unfolding. John Miclot had received a message from his office. Ivo Lurvink, the chief executive of Philips Consumer

[2]"Respironics—Pres. & CEO Interview," CNBC/Dow Jones Business Video Transcripts (August 30, 2006).

EXHIBIT 2
Domestic Sleep
Therapy Equipment
Market Share Chart

Source: Michael S. Matson,
Senior Analyst, Medical
Device Equity Research,
*Sleep FQ307 Review &
Medtrade Summary* (April 30,
2007), Wachovia Capital
Markets, LLC.

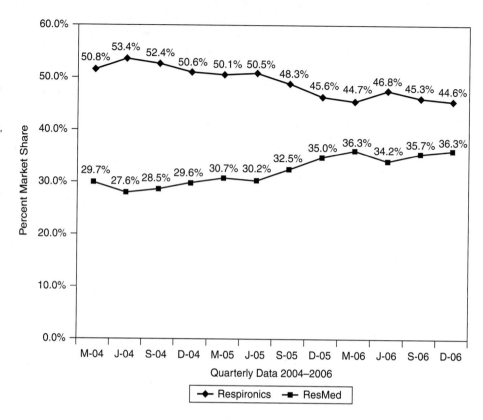

EXHIBIT 3
International Sleep
Therapy Equipment
Market Share Chart

Source: Michael S. Matson,
Senior Analyst, Medical
Device Equity Research,
*Sleep FQ307 Review &
Medtrade Summary* (April 30,
2007), Wachovia Capital
Markets, LLC.
Note: O. U.S.: Outside of
the U.S.

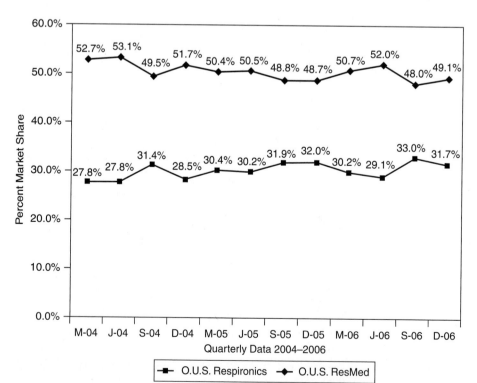

Healthcare Solutions, a unit of Royal Philips Electronics NV (Philips), wanted to arrange a meeting "to discuss matters of mutual business interest between Philips and Respironics."[3] Miclot knew what that meant. Philips, a Dutch conglomerate, had been rumored for some time to be seeking to purchase selected U.S.-based medical equipment manufacturers to bolster market expansion of its Medical Systems division. Philips group sales in fiscal year 2006 had been 27.0 million Euros. Its medical systems division, which comprised both professional and consumer health care products, posted fiscal year 2006 sales of 6.7 million Euros, having grown from 21 percent of Philips' portfolio in 2005 to 27 percent in 2006.

Perhaps Philips' interest in Respironics was friendly; perhaps it was not. During the past two years, Miclot had been approached by third parties on several occasions and his answer had always been the same—Respironics wanted to remain an independent company and was not interested in a business combination or acquisition.[4] Miclot wondered how he should respond now. He would need to discuss this development with his management team, and in the event of a bid, convene Respironics' board of directors.

COMPANY HISTORY

Gerald McGinnis, an inventor, founded Respironics in 1976. When a fire destroyed Respironics' sole manufacturing facility in western Pennsylvania, McGinnis, who had business associates in Hong Kong, moved manufacturing offshore to China. McGinnis was replaced as CEO of Respironics by Dennis Meteney in 1994. McGinnis continued as the company's chairman of the board and advanced technology officer. Apria Healthcare demoted Respironics' status from primary to secondary supplier in 1996, resulting in a loss of sales in fiscal 1997. In that year, Respironics became mired in a patent infringement lawsuit filed by ResMed.

Respironics acquired Healthdyne Technologies, Incorporated for approximately $337 million in stock and $38 million in assumed debt in 1998. Healthdyne manufactured monitoring devices for newborns and therapeutic devices for sleep apnea and other respiratory disorders. It had been "put in play" by Invacare (a manufacturer of wheelchairs) which had launched a hostile takeover bid offering $15 a share. Respironics viewed Healthdyne as an excellent strategic fit, so it stepped in as a "white knight." The result was a "merger of equals" with the goal of combining Respironics' internal product development capabilities with Healthdyne's expertise in product development, licensing and product acquisition.[5] The merger put additional stress on the business, whose revenues were declining because new Medicare guidelines restricted who could use certain types of ventilators.

On July 29, 1999, Respironics announced a major restructuring. CEO Meteny was asked to resign. James Liken, a Respironics board member and health care consultant, became the new CEO. Board members had concluded that the company needed a leader with strong sales and marketing skills who could better relate to health care professionals, salespeople, and customers.[6] John Miclot, a senior vice president of sales and marketing at Healthdyne, was appointed president of Respironics' largest division, the Homecare Group. He was soon promoted into a newly created position, Chief Strategic Officer. Craig Reynolds, the

---

[3]"Offer to Purchase" (January 3, 2008), Exhibit (a) (1) (A), Form SC TO-T. Retrieved from EDGAR.

[4]"Solicitation/Recommendation Statement under Section 14(d) (4) of the Securities Exchange Act of 1934" (January 3, 2008), Form SC 14D9. Retrieved from EDGAR.

[5]"Respironics to acquire Healthdyne Technologies for 2.2 times revenue," *Weekly Corporate Growth Report* 970 (November 17, 1997): 9332.

[6]J. E. Robinet, "Positive step for company and me,' says ousted CEO," *Pittsburgh Business Times* 19 (5) (August 27, 1999): 1.

CEO of Healthdyne at the time of the acquisition, was appointed to the newly created position of chief operating officer.

Liken inherited a company that, in his words, was "mentally flat" and "very bureaucratic."[7] He believed that Respironics had excellent engineering talent but had lost touch with its customers. Liken launched educational programs for customers and physicians. He held motivational talks with employees and delineated behavioral expectations. He gave managers the autonomy to implement strategies on their own. He also set up systems to evaluate progress on a continual basis, allocated resources to maximize shareholder value, and hired and retained the best employees.[8]

Forty-four-year-old John Miclot succeeded Liken as CEO in October 2003. Miclot believed that Respironics had the ability to extend its core competencies beyond the diagnosis and treatment of OSA to discover cures for insomnia, restless leg syndrome, and circadian rhythm disorders. It could develop medical devices to treat asthma and end-of-life diseases (e.g., emphysema and chronic bronchitis). Miclot was concerned that too much of the company's business relied on sales of sleep therapy devices. If the fundamental market dynamics changed, the entire company would be at risk.[9]

On April 22, 2006, Respironics named Harvard Medical School professor of sleep medicine, Dr. David P. White, as its chief medical officer. At the age of 56, White felt he had ten years or so of "kick" left in him to redefine the sleep industry.[10] As he commented, "CPAPs have gotten better, quieter and smaller, but it's basically the same therapy. I think it would be exciting to change the paradigm and do something that ends up changing how we address breathing abnormalities."[11]

In fiscal year 2006, Respironics reported revenues of $1.046 billion, making it the fifth straight year that sales had grown by at least 15 percent.[12] Its fiscal 2006 net income was $99.9 million (or $1.36 a share) compared to fiscal 2005 net income of $84.4 million (or $1.17 a share). Frost & Sullivan, a global growth consulting company, gave Respironics two awards for market leadership—one in the sleep diagnostic device market and one in the positive airway pressure devices market. Respironics' Alice sleep diagnostic platform was described as being "by far one of the most popular and reliable sleep diagnostic systems ever introduced."[13] A research analyst at Frost & Sullivan praised Respironics' Flow Generator for OSA patients as representing the "gold standard in respiratory care."[14]

ORGANIZATIONAL STRUCTURE AND CULTURE

Respironics' basic organizational structure consisted of three groups, each with its own separate business units (see Exhibit 4). Two groups, the Sleep and Home Respiratory Group and the Hospital Group, reflected the location of a patient's diagnosis and treatment—in a

[7]P. Gaynor, "Murrysville, Pa., firm prospers making products to help people sleep better," *Knight Ridder Tribune Business News* (December 18, 2003): 1.

[8]T. Carbasho, "Manufacturer of the year award: Large-size category—Respironics, putting customers first," *Pittsburgh Business Times*, 23 (20) (December 5, 2003): S10.

[9]M. Moran, "Meet HME's new billion dollar baby," *HME News* 12 (9) (September, 2006): 1.

[10]J. Andrews, "The doctor is in, David White, M.D., assumes clinical controls at Respironics," *HME News* 12 (7) (July, 2006): 1.

[11]Ibid.

[12]C. Snowbeck, "Respironics revenues top $1 billion," *Knight Ridder Tribune Business News* (July 28, 2006): 1.

[13]"Frost & Sullivan recognizes Respironics' leadership in the highly demanding sleep diagnostic devices market," *PR Newswire US* (June 6, 2006).

[14]"Frost & Sullivan lauds Respironics' market leadership in the U.S. positive airway pressure therapy devices markets," *PR Newswire US* (August, 2006).

EXHIBIT 4   Respironics' Overall Structure

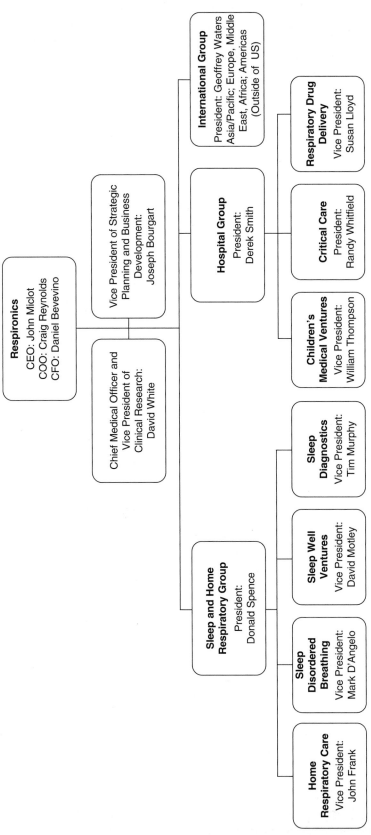

Source: Interview with Joseph Bourgart, vice president of strategic planning and business development (December 2006).

sleep center or at home on the one hand, or in a hospital, on the other hand. Both groups had their own domestic sales forces. Sleep area sales representatives called on operators of sleep clinics (to sell sleep diagnostics equipment and services) and on durable medical equipment (DME) distributors (to sell CPAPs, surgical masks, ventilators, and oxygen concentrators). Hospital Group sales forces visited pulmonologists,[15] who managed intensive care units in hospitals, and marketed ventilators. The International Group was organized into three distinct geographic regions: Asia and the Pacific; Europe, the Middle East and Africa; the Americas (e.g., Canada and South America). Sales associates sold sleep and ventilator products in over 25 different countries.

Miclot spoke about Respironics' organizational structure: ". . . we've really created a bunch of little businesses underneath the broader organization, and that allows you to create entrepreneurship around the organization, even when you're performing well."[16]

Respironics' vision was "to be the worldwide leader at anticipating needs and providing valued solutions to the sleep and respiratory markets." It developed a set of core competencies to support its vision and organizational structure (see Exhibit 5). The three competencies were: "teaming," "market foresight" and "learning agility."

EXHIBIT 5

Respironics' Vision, Key Competencies and Core Practices

Source: Company documents.

VISION:

To be the worldwide leader at anticipating needs and providing valued solutions to the sleep and respiratory markets.

KEY COMPETENCIES:

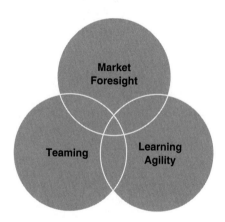

CORE PRACTICES:

- Focus on driving the success of our customers.
- Innovate valued solutions around the needs of our customers and the markets we serve; if in doubt, ask our customers.
- Drive quality, cost and speed as a competitive advantage.
- Hire the best people; retain the best people; accept no less.
- Lead, energize and empower everyone to make decisions, accept responsibility and get things done.
- Create clear simple methods to accomplish objectives; eliminate bureaucracy.
- Evaluate plans and progress continuously; enhance what is working and change what is not.
- Allocate resources relentlessly to achieve our objectives, maximize shareholder value and assure social responsibility.

[15]A pulmonologist is a physician who specializes in the lungs.

[16]R. Marano, "Market maker," *Smart Business Pittsburgh* 12 (9) (January 1, 2006): 25.

Respironics employed 4,700 employees worldwide in 2006. It provided employees with medical and dental benefits, wellness programs and fitness centers, educational reimbursement, savings bonds, stock options, and shares and access to a credit union. Some employees were allowed to telecommute from home.[17] The company cared about the health and well-being of its employees. A walk in the hallways of its Murrysville headquarters revealed an informational flyer, part of a series, about the health benefits of herbs and spices. Ginger, for example, was good for nausea, vomiting, and headaches. The flyer suggested that employees take advantage of the nice spring weather and walk outside during breaks to soak up vitamin D from the sun. It reminded employees to drink one-half of their body weight in ounces of water every day.

FINANCE AND ACCOUNTING

Whereas the functions of sales/marketing and research/development were decentralized and managed by the heads of the different business units and groups, all finance-related functions (i.e., billing and payments), were centralized at Respironics' Murrysville headquarters. Information management was totally integrated for Respironics' global operations, with SAP enterprise business software. The CFO received daily, monthly and quarterly reports so that he could react quickly to an aberration.

Daniel Bevevino, the CFO, oversaw three activities: (a) conducting financial audits and ensuring compliance with different laws and regulations, including Sarbanes-Oxley and the tax code; (b) completing transaction-oriented processes, including billing clients, collecting payments, and handling cash receipts; (c) supporting value-added business processes that could involve investments in new projects and acquisitions of other businesses.

Bevevino described Respironics' acquisition screening processes as follows: "An acquisition candidate must first represent a strategic fit for the company. The target company also has to demonstrate financial fit. We would calculate net present value, years to pay back, dilution, and accretion. Case studies featuring acquisitions and other contemporary business issues are used to provide our managers with relevant leadership training."

RESEARCH AND DEVELOPMENT

As a rule of thumb, new products, including major enhancements to existing ones, were to account for 40–50 percent of sales in every two-year period. An internal company Web site enabled design team members, consisting of engineers, manufacturing people, clinical staff, quality staff, document control staff, marketing employees, and purchasing agents, to communicate with one another. All the documents associated with a project were posted as PDF files and were updated on a regular basis so that teams could identify and solve problems early on.[18]

Respironics invested approximately 6 percent of its annual revenues in R&D ($60 million in 2005 and $65 million in 2006). Joseph Bourgart, vice president of strategic planning and business development, believed these R&D investments were appropriate and that companies making respiratory devices should target the 5–7 percent range. Companies with high-tech products (e.g., pacemakers and pharmaceutical products) required higher R&D spends as a percentage of sales, while companies with low-tech products (e.g., band-aids and surgical gowns) had correspondingly lower R&D requirements.

---

[17]"Respironics. Inc.," *Plunkett's Health Care Industry Almanac* (2004).
[18]P. E. Teague, "Home-Grown websites," *Design News* 60 (6) (April 18, 2005): 12.

Respironics also supported other types of research activities. In 2006, it gave $1.5 million to its foundation, formed for scientific, educational and charitable purposes and used to promote awareness of and research into the medical consequences of sleep and respiratory problems.[19] Respironics sponsored empirical articles and reviews for a 2005 special issue, "Behavioral Issues in Adherence to CPAP Therapy," in *Behavioral Sleep Medicine*.

MANUFACTURING AND ASSEMBLY

Respironics' manufacturing facilities were located in Murrysville, Pennsylvania; Atlanta, Georgia; Carlsbad, California; Wallingford, Connecticut; Shenzhen and Hong Kong, China; and Subic Bay, the Philippines. The company was in the process of establishing centers of excellence in manufacturing at each of its locations. Depending on the type of product being made, different facility layouts, material storage and handling processes, and manufacturing techniques were required. It made sense, therefore, to set up facilities to handle homogeneous processes. They would be highly specialized and employees would gain experience with one type of process. Respironics planned, for example, to move the assembling of its high volume, disposable products (i.e., masks) to the Asian-Pacific. It would continue to make its high volume, electro-mechanical devices in Murrysville.

The facility in Murrysville used demand flow technology (DFT) to assemble electro-mechanical devices (e.g., CPAPs, hospital ventilators and life support equipment) and patient interface/Children's Medical Venture products (e.g., masks). Sleep devices were assembled in three, eight-hour shifts; the evening shift was added in 2005 to enable additional testing. The other products were assembled in two, eight-hour shifts.[20]

DFT meant that employees made products only based on orders received. They stored necessary components in a few bins near the line of workstations. Suppliers, who were alerted when one of the bins was depleted, replenished them. Line operators were trained in the jobs on either side of their own station so that they could "flex" to assist their neighbors when required to keep the production moving. Lines were designed so that multiple products could pass along them.[21] After Respironics implemented DFT in 1998, unit volume increased by 400 percent and component inventory was reduced by 60–70 percent.[22]

QUALITY ASSURANCE

If the on/off button on a vacuum cleaner malfunctioned, the worst that could happen was that the carpet did not get cleaned. If a respirator or ventilator failed, a patient's life could be at risk. Respironics worked to ensure that its products were of the highest quality. It, for example, improved the process in which adhesives were used in the manufacture of a manual resuscitator. In 1995, it used a system from EFD, Inc. to apply the adhesive in precise, repeated amounts; to use fixtures to hold parts during gluing and assembly; to alert assembly workers that the adhesive was in place. The adhesive was clear so a powdered colorant visible under UV light was added and a black light was mounted at the dispensing station.

---

[19]Respironics, 10–K.

[20]Special thanks are given to Mr. Steve Buccilli, After Market Support Team Leader, who contributed to this section and gave one of the case authors a guided tour of the Murrysville manufacturing facility on May 24, 2007.

[21]P. Baker, "The future is flow," *Works Management* (1999): 52–54.

[22]"Respironics. Breathe Easy," *Manufacturing in Action* (February, 2003). Retrieved May 25, 2007, from http://www.themanufacturer.com/us/profile/944/Respironics?PHPSESSID=1b8093.

A soft purple tint assured assemblers that the adhesive had been applied as each cycle was completed.[23] Similar solutions were implemented as part of the imbedded quality assurance steps integrated into the company's current production lines. Customized test fixtures were put into use to assure quality levels were achieved and to minimize the number of units that ultimately were rejected upon inspection.

Quality assurance inspectors met across product lines to discuss quality issues. Assemblers were given training in QCDSM (quality, cost, delivery, safety, and morale)—each of which held equal importance to a job well done. Assemblers were able to rotate to different stations during the week. This reduced carpal tunnel injuries, enhanced quality, improved cross functionality and developed different skills among operators.

Respironics voluntarily recalled several of its products in recent years. In 2006, for example, it recalled 172,000 humidifiers that had been in use for three to five years at a cost of $5 million. Respironics hired a firm to handle the collection and replacement of the units. The third party was responsible for contacting the patients and collecting the humidifiers. The process had to be handled with sensitivity since the medical equipment distributors wanted to maintain control over their rosters of customers.

SUPPLY CHAIN MANAGEMENT

Respironics bought components from many different suppliers. In 2004, Electronic Product Integration Company (EPIC) used a *kanban* system to deliver printed circuit boards (PCBs) to Respironics' Murrysville assembly facility on an as needed basis. Respironics had three bins for PCBs, each of which held 1,672 boards. As soon as it depleted a bin, it faxed EPIC to start filling another one. EPIC kept two full bins. When it received notice, EPIC shipped a bin and started to fill a new one. Between them, they never had more than five days' worth of PCB inventory.[24]

Sometimes, it was hard to purchase certain items—especially relays, IR components and flow sensors—needed for medical devices. These were much in demand by firms in other industries, especially toy manufacturers. When quantities were low, suppliers might have preferred to sell their components to toy and electronics manufacturers. Respironics' procurement agents were quick to step in, explain the importance of its medical devices for patients and thereby appeal to the supplier's sense of social responsibility.

SLEEP AND RESPIRATORY MARKETS

Sleep, or the lack of it, had become an important issue by the beginning of the third millennium. According to the popular press, the two most brilliant inventions of 2006 were: sleep-inducing toothpaste and a head-nodding alarm to avert sleep while driving.[25] Individuals slept when they shouldn't (e.g., when driving a truck, operating equipment, or participating in military action) and couldn't sleep when they should (e.g., at night or after traveling across time zones). A poll conducted for the National Sleep Foundation revealed that three-quarters of adults said that they frequently had a sleep problem (e.g., snoring or waking during the night).[26] According to the U.S. Surgeon General, sleep deprivation and

[23]"Built-in quality," *Appliance Manufacturer* 43 (12) (December, 1995): 20.

[24]B. Roberts, "Just in time just makes sense," *Electronic Business* 30 (6) (June, 2004): 12.

[25]D. Eatock and A. Horowitz, "Endpaper," *The New York Times Magazine* (December 10, 2006): 108.

[26]"Mergers & acquisitions; Sleep and respiratory company acquires Mini-Mitter," *World Disease Weekly* (May 3, 2005): 1118.

related disorders cost the nation $16 billion in annual health care expenses and $50 billion in lost productivity.[27]

There was a growing perception among the public that oxygen concentrators and ventilators were not used solely to treat a patient who was critically ill or in a coma. They were available to people of all ages, from premature infants to adults who were unable to breathe normally.[28] If Christopher Reeve, the actor who played Superman, needed a portable ventilator, then anyone might need one at some point in their lives. According to Medtech Insight, over $1.3 billion was spent on ventilators, oxygen therapy systems, and airway management accessories in 2004 in the U.S.; sales were expected to reach more than $1.9 billion by the year 2010 (a compound annual rate of 6.3 percent).[29]

Diagnosis and Treatment of Sleep-Related Disorders

The International Classification of Diseases (ICD) provided descriptions of over 80 recognized sleep disorders.[30] Individuals commonly reported that they suffered from minor problems, such as jet lag and snoring, to more severe problems, such as insomnia and sleep apnea.

Sleep Apnea

Individuals with narrow upper airways or poor muscle tone were prone to temporary collapses of the upper airway during sleep, called "apneas," and to near closures of the upper airway, called "hypopneas." These breathing irregularities resulted in a lowering of blood oxygen concentration, causing the central nervous system to react to the lack of oxygen or increased carbon dioxide and signaling the body to respond. Typically, the individual subconsciously was aroused from sleep, causing the throat muscles to contract, opening the airway. After a few gasping breaths, or snores, blood oxygen levels increased and the individual resumed a deeper sleep until the cycle repeated itself. Sufferers of OSA typically experienced ten or more such cycles per hour. While these awakenings greatly impaired the quality of sleep, the individual was not normally aware of these disruptions. They could, however, lead to excessive daytime sleepiness, reduced cognitive functioning, depression, and irritability.[31]

Sleep apnea could be a contributing factor in an individual's death. The disorder received public attention when retired NFL football player Reggie White died in 2004 at the age of 43. He suffered from respiratory diseases that included OSA. A study by ResMed and Sleep Tech found that football players were almost five times more likely to test positive for OSA than similarly aged adults; sleep apnea was associated with large body masses.[32] A strong association was also discovered between OSA and a number of cardiovascular diseases.[33] A recent study found that OSA increased an individual's risk of

[27]D. Lazarus, "Sleep: Can't get enough of it," *San Francisco Chronicle* (March 1, 2006). Retrieved January 2, 2007, from http://www.sfgate.com/cgi-bin/article.cgi?file=/chronicle/archive/2006/03/01/BUGLTHFG8O50.DTL.

[28]P. Kurtzweil, "When machines do the breathing," *FDA Consumer* 33 (5) (September/October, 1999): 22–25.

[29]"U.S. Markets for Ventilators, Oxygen Therapy Systems, and Airway Management Accessories" (October, 2005). Retrieved December 29, 2006, from http://www.medtechinsight.com/ReportA366.html.

[30]"Managing sleep disorders," *Practitioner* (April 25, 2006): 226.

[31]F. N. Kjelsberg, E. A. Ruud, and K. Stavem, "Predictors of symptoms of anxiety and depression in obstructive sleep apnea," *Sleep Medicine* 6 (4) (July, 2005): 341–346.

[32]J. Gundersen, "OSA linked to death of NFL veteran," *HME News* 11 (2) (February, 2005): 43–44.

[33]A. Quershi, R. D. Ballard, and H. S. Nelson, "Obstructive sleep apnea," *Journal of Allergy and Clinical Immunology* 112 (4) (October, 2003): 643–651.

EXHIBIT 6   Photographs of Masks and CPAP Machines for Sleep Apnea

   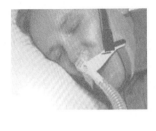

Source: www.respironics.com.

having a heart attack or dying by 30 percent over a period of four to five years.[34] Another study found that patients with OSA were twice as likely as people without OSA to have a car crash and three to five times as likely to have a serious crash involving personal injury.[35]

To receive a diagnosis of OSA, a patient might visit a general practitioner who would refer the patient to a clinical sleep lab. The patient would participate in an overnight sleep study in which he/she was connected through electrodes placed on the head, chin, alongside the eyes, nostrils and legs to equipment that measured brain waves, eye movements, muscle relaxation, airflow, and leg twitching. Other devices monitored the level of oxygen in the blood and air movement in the chest. A polysomnography recorded the number of abnormal respiratory episodes that occurred during the night.

To treat severe cases of OSA, sufferers could undergo uvulopalatopharyngoplasty (UPPP) surgery to remove excess tissue from the upper airway, to streamline the shape of the airway, or to implant a device to support the soft palate. In mandibular advancement surgery, a patient's lower jaw was moved forward to widen his or her airway. UPPP was expensive, painful and had less than a 50 percent success rate, Bourgart noted.

A non-invasive alternative, involving the use of continuous positive airway pressure devices (CPAP), was also available. An individual slept with a nasal interface connected to a small portable airflow generator that delivered room air at a positive pressure. He or she breathed in air from the flow generator and breathed out through an exhaust port in the interface. Continuous air pressure applied in this manner acted as a "pneumatic splint" to keep the upper airway open and unobstructed (see Exhibit 6 for photographs of masks and CPAPs). CPAP was not a cure for OSA, and needed to be used on a nightly basis. Patient compliance in using these devices on a regular, uninterrupted basis proved to be a major factor in the efficacy of CPAP treatment.[36]

Simple Snoring

Snoring occurred when the airway at the back of the throat constricted and caused air to be inhaled at increased velocity and pressure. The tissue at the back of the mouth vibrated, creating noise.[37] There were over 800 patented anti-snoring devices.[38] They ranged from nasal strips, special pillows, and dental appliances to a therapeutic ring that applied acupressure

[34]"Heart disease; Sleep apnea increases risk of heart attack or death by 30 percent," *Cardiovascular Business Week* (June 5, 2007): 114.

[35]"Sleep apnea; Sleep apnea patients have greatly increased risk of severe car crashes," *Biotech Week* (June 6, 2007): 153.

[36]H. Engleman, and M. R. Wild, "Improving CPAP use by patients with the sleep apnea/hypopnea syndrome (SAHS)," *Sleep Medicine Reviews* 7 (1) (February, 2003): 81–99.

[37]"Device available to control snoring," *Journal Record* (February 17, 1993).

[38]J. M. Farrell, "Pinkie ring claims to relieve snoring," *Chicago Tribune* (May 23, 2006): 7.

points and an electrical device that produced unpleasant stimuli when the patient snored. Surgery could be performed to correct a deviated nasal septum or to remove nasal polyps, enlarged adenoids and/or tonsils. That solved the problem for some patients. For others, snoring could be a symptom of OSA. They would go through the same diagnostic and treatment process as for sleep apnea. Chronic snorers could elect UPPP surgery or CPAP therapy.

Insomnia

Insomnia referred to the difficulty in initiating and maintaining sleep.[39] Short-term insomnia was attributed to stress, jet lag, drugs, or an unfamiliar sleep environment; long-term insomnia was related to hereditary factors and resulted from an underlying psychiatric or medical condition (e.g., post-traumatic stress disorder, chemical imbalances in the brain, or anatomical differences in the nervous system).[40]

Stimulus control therapy encouraged insomniacs to go to bed only when sleepy and wake up at the same set time every morning. Cognitive behavioral therapy encouraged individuals to talk with a trained psychologist; relaxation techniques taught individuals yoga and meditation; and light therapy suggested that individuals avoid bright lights at night. Finally, some insomniacs were prescribed sleeping pills.

Diagnosis and Treatment of Respiratory Disorders

As the baby boomers (those persons born between 1946 and 1964) aged and were eager to maintain active lifestyles, breathing devices needed to be portable and highly reliable. Ventilators had become substantially more sophisticated than the iron lungs that were first introduced in the 1920s. Noninvasive, positive pressure ventilators enabled an exchange of gases through facial or nasal masks that were attached to an oxygen concentrator. Bilevel positive airway pressure (bilevel PAP) ventilators responded to a patient's own airflow rates and cycles; they were designed to deliver two different levels of positive pressure; the amount of pressure during inspiration was set higher and the amount of pressure delivered to keep the airway open during expiration was set lower.[41]

The advantages of BiPAP ventilators were that the patient could talk, swallow and move around. The disadvantages were pressure sores, nasal dryness, eye irritation and air leaks.[42] Other ways of delivering ventilation were through volume ventilators, pressure-controlled ventilators or continuous positive airway pressure (CPAP) devices.[43]

Ventilators were used when patients suffered from neuromuscular disorders (e.g., Lou Gehrig's disease and spinal muscular atrophy), respiratory diseases (e.g., chronic obstructive pulmonary disease or COPD, cystic fibrosis and severe pneumonia), and bone disorders (severe curvature of the spine and deformities of the chest wall).[44]

COMPETITION

Respironics' primary competitors in the sleep disorder market were California-based ResMed, Inc. and New Zealand-based Fisher & Paykel Healthcare Corp. Ltd (see Exhibit 7, Exhibit 8, and Exhibit 9 for comparative financial data).

[39]"Managing sleep disorders" (2006), op. cit.

[40]"Managing sleep disorders" (2006), op. cit.

[41]L. M. Tamburri, "Assisting your patient's breathing with noninvasive ventilation," *Nursing* 28 (10) (October, 1998): 1–3.

[42]N. O'Neill, "Improving ventilation in children using bilevel positive airway pressure," *Pediatric Nursing* 24 (4) (July/August, 1998): 377–382.

[43]R. E. Hillberg, and D. C. Johnson, "Noninvasive ventilation," *The New England Journal of Medicine* 337 (24) (December 11, 1997): 1746–1752.

[44]Kurtzweil (1999), op. cit.

EXHIBIT 7 Comparative Income Statements, Fiscal Years 2003–2006

(all amounts in U.S. $000 except per share amounts)	F&P Healthcare				ResMed				Respironics			
	2003	2004	2005	2006	2003	2004	2005	2006	2003	2004	2005	2006
INCOME STATEMENTS												
Net Revenues from Cont. Ops.	103,063	132,056	162,599	199,556	273,570	339,338	425,505	606,996	629,817	759,550	911,497	1,046,141
Cost of Sales	33,412	38,468	66,324	83,645	100,483	122,602	150,645	230,101	310,385	356,625	413,215	473,263
Gross Profit	69,651	93,588	96,275	115,911	173,087	216,736	274,860	376,895	319,432	402,925	498,282	572,878
Operating Expenses												
Selling, General and Admin.	27,411	36,350	45,543	56,293	85,313	104,706	135,703	200,168	200,031	247,972	305,836	355,918
Research and Development	5,704	8,675	10,947	11,956	20,534	26,169	35,282	37,216	24,047	29,478	45,625	58,966
Donations to Foundations	0	0	0	0	0	500	500	760	0	2,844	3,000	1,500
Restructuring and/or Acquisition-Related Expenses	0	0	0	0	0	0	5,152	1,124	19,825	19,475	9,908	6,888
Amortization of Acquired Intangible Assets	0	0	0	0	0	0	870	6,327	0	0	0	0
Total Operating Expenses	33,115	45,025	56,490	68,249	105,847	131,375	177,507	245,595	243,903	299,769	364,369	423,272
Operating Profit	36,536	48,563	39,785	47,662	67,240	85,861	97,353	131,300	75,529	103,156	133,913	149,606
Interest and Other Net Income (loss)	18,458	1,180	22,102	24,301	(133)	(693)	(727)	2,094	(639)	2,078	1,806	9,616
Income (loss) before Tax	54,994	49,743	61,887	71,963	67,127	84,668	96,626	133,394	74,890	105,234	135,719	159,222
Less: Provision for Income Tax	18,941	16,125	20,383	23,743	21,398	27,384	31,841	45,183	28,309	40,214	51,363	59,329
Net Income	36,053	33,618	41,504	48,220	45,729	57,284	64,785	88,211	46,581	65,020	84,356	99,893
Weighted Avg. Shs. Out.-Basic (000)	511,837	512,120	508,687	508,382	66,108	67,388	68,644	72,307	67,170	68,754	70,896	72,311
Weighted Avg. Shs. Out.-Diluted (000)	519,802	524,113	523,841	524,847	68,878	70,250	74,942	77,162	68,688	70,619	72,255	73,570
Year End Shares Outstanding (000)	512,184	511,285	508,635	509,332	66,742	67,717	70,001	75,670	67,914	69,967	71,699	72,740
Net Income per Share-Basic	$0.07	$0.07	$0.08	$0.09	$0.69	$0.85	$0.94	$1.22	$0.69	$0.95	$1.19	$1.38
Net Income per Share-Diluted	$0.07	$0.06	$0.08	$0.09	$0.66	$0.82	$0.86	$1.14	$0.68	$0.92	$1.17	$1.36
Total Number of Employees	767	900	1,096	1,276	1,464	1,520	1,927	2,500	2,700	3,000	3,900	4,700

Sources: Fisher & Paykel Healthcare *Annual Reports, 2002–2006*; data for ResMed and Respironics from *Mergent Online*, accessed April 26, 2007.
Notes: (1) Fisher & Paykel Healthcare (F&P), fiscal year ending March 31; (2) ResMed (RMD) and Respironics (RESP) fiscal years ending June 30.

EXHIBIT 8 Comparative Balance Sheets, Fiscal Years 2003–2006

(All amounts in U.S. $000) For the year ending	F&P Healthcare March 31				ResMed June 30				Respironics June 30			
	2003	2004	2005	2006	2003	2004	2005	2006	2003	2004	2005	2006
ASSETS												
Cash and Marketable Securities	26,623	30,993	23,405	18,035	121,024	140,928	142,185	219,544	95,900	192,446	234,632	259,513
Short-term Investment Accounts												
Receivable, Net of Doubtful Accounts	32,495	32,012	34,480	34,746	56,694	67,242	103,951	138,147	128,127	140,634	153,479	187,502
Inventories	12,036	15,683	19,520	22,858	49,386	55,797	89,107	116,194	83,986	85,539	96,315	124,149
Prepaid Expenses and Other	198	206	316	224	6,500	6,821	9,737	9,763	7,890	8,621	11,931	19,197
Deferred Income Tax	2,330	917	2,907	3,302	8,301	7,041	15,230	26,636	24,112	25,373	39,767	45,893
Total Current Assets	73,682	79,811	80,628	79,164	241,905	277,829	360,210	510,284	340,015	452,613	536,124	642,092
Property, Plant and Equipment, Net	39,354	46,604	52,359	81,032	104,687	147,268	174,168	245,376	98,680	111,057	127,376	137,943
Other Assets	10,786	16,984	10,079	6,664	7,098	8,173	58,662	55,949	34,592	37,466	48,319	55,981
Patents, Net	972	1,454	1,504	1,424	3,745	4,814						
Goodwill	1,203	1,173	894	651	102,160	106,075	181,106	195,612	108,909	110,003	166,627	181,362
TOTAL ASSETS	125,997	146,026	145,464	168,934	459,595	544,159	774,146	1,007,221	582,196	711,139	878,446	1,017,378
LIABILITIES AND SHAREHOLDERS' EQUITY												
Accounts Payable, Trade	4,779	7,042	9,521	12,110	19,368	18,574	34,416	45,045	40,531	52,789	57,474	70,667
Accrued Expenses and Other Current Liabilities	13,268	12,782	12,921	15,686	31,215	42,017	68,700	79,086	68,389	88,255	126,242	122,173
Current Portion of Long-Term Debt	1,102	—	1,152	11,580	—	—	115,435	4,869	18,308	10,536	17,411	18,201
Total Current Liabilities	19,149	19,824	23,594	39,375	50,583	60,591	218,551	129,000	127,229	151,581	201,128	211,041
Long-Term Debt	209	1,471	340	336			58,934	116,212	16,513	26,897	29,241	26,756
Other Non-Current Liabilities	435	167	243	381	122,579	122,069	22,596	23,861	11,585	13,608	20,432	15,131
TOTAL LIABILITIES	19,793	21,462	24,177	40,092	173,162	182,660	300,081	269,073	155,327	192,086	250,801	252,928
SHAREHOLDERS' EQUITY												
Common Stock	134	135	140	303	375	385	787	797				
Additional Paid-In Capital	107,317	127,138	123,555	128,997	107,432	132,875	180,005	353,464	226,885	249,595	278,765	315,857
Retained Earnings					160,372	217,656	282,441	370,652	241,474	310,510	389,534	489,233
Less: Treasury Stock					-11,415	-30,440	-41,405	-41,405	-41,864	-41,437	-41,440	-41,439
Foreign Currency Translation Adjust.	-1,113	-2,574	-2,268	-155	29,901	41,267	52,884	55,134				
Unrealized Gains (Loss) on Securities	—	—	—	—	9	6	0	0	—	—	—	—
Total Shareholders' Equity	106,204	124,564	121,287	128,842	286,433	361,499	474,065	738,148	426,869	519,053	627,646	764,448
TOTAL LIABILITIES AND SHAREHOLDERS' EQUITY	125,997	146,026	145,464	168,934	459,595	544,159	774,146	1,007,221	582,196	711,139	878,446	1,017,378

Sources: Fisher & Paykel Healthcare *Annual Reports, 2002–2006*; data for ResMed and Respironics from *Mergent Online*, accessed April 26, 2007.

EXHIBIT 9
Revenues by Region,
Fiscal Years
2003–2006

Sources: Fisher & Paykel
Healthcare *Annual Reports,
2002–2006;* data for
ResMed and Respironics
from *Mergent Online,*
accessed April 26, 2007.

Notes: (1) Fisher & Paykel
Healthcare (F&P), fiscal year
ending 3/31; (2) ResMed
(RMD) and Respironics
(RESP) fiscal years ending
6/30; (3) Respironics 2003
revenues for the Americas
included only Latin America.

	2003	2004	2005	2006
RESMED				
GEOGRAPHIC ANALYSIS ($000)				
USA	$124,375	$159,283	$210,495	$320,941
Germany	51,992	67,253	72,824	96,436
Australia	6,972	10,293	14,160	18,709
France	27,745	34,629	47,537	59,402
Rest of World	62,486	67,880	80,489	111,508
Total	$273,570	$339,338	$425,505	$606,996
FISHER & PAYKEL HEALTHCARE				
GEOGRAPHIC ANALYSIS ($000)				
North America	$50,071	$57,722	$70,522	$93,997
Europe	28,938	39,594	50,826	57,548
Asia Pacific	20,402	29,294	33,914	37,847
Rest of World	3,652	5,446	7,337	10,164
Total	$103,063	$132,056	$162,599	$199,556
RESPIRONICS				
GEOGRAPHIC ANALYSIS ($000)				
USA	$467,943	$547,224	$625,211	$724,781
Europe, Africa and Middle East	74,441	95,001	143,375	163,292
Americas	9,272	31,309	37,425	44,544
Far East/Asia Pacific	78,161	86,016	105,486	113,524
Total	$629,817	$759,550	$911,497	$1,046,141

Joseph Bourgart, vice president of strategic planning, said, "Respironics is committed to finding solutions to all sleep and respiratory disorders. It will pursue any type of effective treatment—including medical devices, surgical procedures, pharmaceutical products, or some optimal combination of one or more of these therapies. It will provide the best possible products through any means possible—organic growth, licensing arrangements, strategic alliances, or by acquiring existing companies with unique technologies." As Bourgart believed, "continued diversification into the diagnosis and treatment of sleep disorders beyond OSA will have a profound effect on the value of the company in the long run."

At the same time, Bourgart acknowledged that Respironics' primary competitors had viable strategic plans and that only time would tell which approach would lead to ultimate success. ResMed, an early entrant in the market for medical devices to treat OSA, had taken a clinical perspective and was committed to extending its solid CPAP technology platform to treat different diseases and different stages of disease. Fisher & Paykel, which had been part of a large New Zealand-based appliance manufacturer before it was spun off in 2001, had built a solid foundation in humidification. To this, it added infant care products (e.g., warmers) and lower end, lower cost CPAP devices.

In the respiratory market, Respironics competed with Tyco Healthcare Group (a division of Tyco International Ltd.) and Invacare Corp.

ResMed

ResMed was founded as ResCare in 1989 after Peter Farrell led a management buyout of Baxter Healthcare's respiratory technology unit. Farrell, 63, was ResMed's CEO from its inception to 2007. ResCare initially developed the SULLIVAN nasal CPAP systems (named after inventor Colin Sullivan) in Australia. In 1991 it introduced the Bubble Mask and the APD2 portable CPAP device. Three years later, ResCare began marketing its first VPAP, which applied different air pressures for inhalation and exhalation, in the U.S. In 1995, the company went public, changing its name to ResMed (its former name was already taken by another medical company).

Farrell believed that the SDB market would continue to grow in the future due to increasing awareness of OSA; improved understanding of the role of SDB treatment in the management of cardiac, neurological, metabolic and related disorders; and an increase in home-based diagnosis. Even in the U.S., market penetration had reached only 10–12 percent; the company was simply "lacing" its "shoes before the marathon."[45] Tremendous opportunities were to be found in selling medical devices to the 83 percent of hypertension patients who also had SDB, to the 80 percent of type two diabetics who also had SDB, and to the 80 percent of long haul truckers who suffered from OSA.

In the words of Farrell:

> If you took a poll of people that use our products and competitors' products, you would find that we are the number-one choice. . . . If you look at what the signs and symptoms of sleep-disordered breathing are, it covers every medical silo. We know it does cause heart disease and it causes stroke. We know it causes gastroesophageal reflux, and we know it causes cognitive dysfunction, morning headaches, nocturia, (getting up a lot at night to take a pee) and so forth. I agree that there are other products in the marketplace, but branding is important. Respironics' base is bigger in the U.S. than ours. Outside, we are twice as big as they are in the sleep business: our growth rate was twice their growth rate in the U.S. That's a huge difference. They've got a big chunk of their business in Japan. We go through a distributor there; they are direct. That [also] has a big impact. We will have opportunities in Canada and Latin America and India and China. But again, we have got to take care of business in Europe before we start pushing the boat too far out, too quickly. We think that there are plenty of opportunities because of our position in the sleep and breathing marketplace.[46]

ResMed relied on clinical literature to tell it where the market was headed. In the case, for example, of type two diabetes, early data suggested that CPAPs could help patients control their glucose levels. If diabetics did not get a good night's sleep, their leptin and ghrelin levels[47] were thrown off, they lost control over their appetites, their energy levels were low and, therefore, they overate. CPAPs could help diabetics sleep better at night so this cycle of events did not occur. ResMed's strategy was to work with endocrinologists and officers of the International Diabetes Federation, invite them to Sydney, show them the clinical literature, and let them draw their own conclusions. If the data were convincing, the endocrinologists would recommend sleep therapy to their patients. ResMed could then go to diabetes educators "to drive volume into the marketplace and help treat these disorders."[48]

ResMed's R&D and manufacturing facilities were located in Sydney, Australia. A $43.8 million expansion was underway at the Sydney plant, and its completion was expected in the second half of 2006.[49] About 13 percent of its workforce was devoted to research and development activities. In fiscal year 2006, ResMed invested $37.2 million, or 6.1 percent of revenues, in R&D. ResMed's innovation and worldwide distribution prowess set it apart from rivals, according to one industry analyst.[50] As of 2006, ResMed employed 2,500

[45]"ResMed Inc. at Wachovia Securities CEO Summit-Final," *Fair Disclosure Wire* (June 28, 2007).

[46]"Q4 2005 ResMed Inc. earnings conference call," *Fair Disclosure* Wire (August 22, 2005).

[47]Leptin and ghrelin are two hormones that affect food intake and energy balance.

[48]"ResMed Inc. at Wachovia" (2007), op. cit.

[49]T. Somers, "Poway, Calif.-based maker of sleep apnea expects to continue growth trend," *Knight Ridder Tribune Business News* (December 30, 2005): 1.

[50]J. Stralow, "ResMed," Morningstar Ratings (April 18, 2006).

people and sold products in 68 countries through a combination of wholly owned subsidiaries and independent distributors.

Fisher & Paykel Health Care

Across the globe in New Zealand, Fisher & Paykel Healthcare (F&P) designed, manufactured, and marketed heated humidification products and systems for use in respiratory care and the treatment of OSA. It invested 5.4 percent of revenues (almost $12 million) in research and development in 2006. F&P also manufactured and marketed patient warming and neonatal care products, infant resuscitators, and infant CPAP systems, designed to improve infant respiratory function. Five new respiratory mask products were added to its OSA therapy line in 2005.[51] The company's products were sold in more than 90 countries, exposing the company to considerable exchange rate risk.

Fisher & Paykel employed 1,276 people as of March 31, 2006. The company was engaged in an NZ$60 million project (about U.S.$38.5 million based on exchange rates as of May 4, 2006) to double the size of its factory in East Tamaki, Auckland, New Zealand, in order to bolster its position as a low-cost producer and provide more space for OSA product manufacturing and R&D.[52]

In 2003, severe acute respiratory syndrome (SARS) had boosted F&P's profits by millions. On November 17, 2005, Fisher & Paykel announced that it stood to make another windfall should avian (bird) flu become a human-to-human pandemic. Chief executive Michael Daniell said, "We are increasing inventory and putting measures in place to ensure we can help out."[53] One analyst, who declined to be identified, quipped, "It could be good for the [company's] stock [price] and bad for the world."[54]

Tyco Healthcare Group

Tyco Healthcare Group was one of the world's largest manufacturers of disposable medical devices and the largest producer of generic Acetaminophen. It generated over $9 billion in sales for its parent (one-fourth of Tyco's total revenues). Tyco Healthcare had three divisions: medical devices and supplies, pharmaceutical, and retail products. The medical devices and supplies division manufactured wound care dressings, needles, medical imaging equipment, life support systems, and ventilators.

In August 2006, Tyco Healthcare acquired an equity interest in Airox, a French company that manufactured and marketed home respiratory ventilation systems. It announced plans to acquire the entire company for a total purchase price of approximately $108 million.[55] Tyco Healthcare was thus poised to strengthen its position in the respiratory market, though at the same time, its parent company, Tyco International, had already made plans to spin it off (along with two other business units) by the end of 2007.

Invacare

Invacare was the leading manufacturer of wheelchairs worldwide. It also made respiratory devices and other medical equipment products for the home and the extended care markets. Based on an estimated $177 million in revenues from sales of respiratory products world wide in 2005, Invacare had achieved considerable market share for oxygen therapy

---

[51]G. Bond, "F&P adds to its range of masks," *New Zealand Herald* (September 26, 2005).

[52]G. Bond, "Good night's sleep boosts F&P health," *New Zealand Herald* (November 18, 2005).

[53]S. Louisson, "F&P Healthcare poised to make windfall if birdflu hits humans," *New Zealand Press Association* (November 17, 2005).

[54]Ibid.

[55]"Mergers and acquisitions: Tyco Healthcare to acquire interest in ventilator maker Airox, expand respiratory products," *Managed Care Weekly Digest* (August 28, 2006): 81.

products. Its line of HomeFill oxygen systems became very popular. Invacare had a presence in the sleep therapy market as well. Invacare had been particularly troublesome for Respironics going back to the days when it launched its unsuccessful, hostile takeover for Healthdyne Technologies.

In 1999, Invacare introduced a CPAP device called Polaris, using licensed ResMed technology. In 2004, Invacare received FDA approval to sell the Polaris EX with SoftX technology and announced its intention to capture 10 percent of the sleep market in three years.[56] That same year, Respironics filed a patent infringement lawsuit against Invacare, claiming that the SoftX technology was a copy of its C-Flex technology that Respironics had introduced in 2003. Invacare countersued, complaining that Respironics engaged in monopolistic behaviors. A federal trial court dismissed Invacare's antitrust lawsuit in November 2006.

Invacare wasn't about to give up on the sleep apnea market. In September 2006, it had become the exclusive distributor for AEIOMed's products (which included a modular, light-weight CPAP and a nasal pillow interface).[57]

RESPIRONICS' STRATEGIES

Sleep and Respiratory Products

Respironics made progress in developing diagnostic tools and solutions for other sleep disorders. Market research had helped it identify different types of "problem sleepers."[58] "Pill dislikers" refused to take medication because they did not want to become dependent on a drug for sleep or they were taking an antibiotic or antidepressant and were afraid of dangerous drug interactions. For them, a mechanical device would work. "Pill likers" would get a prescription for Ambien or Sonata. "Solution seekers" tried to self-treat—using devices that blocked out noises, taking herbal remedies and experimenting with special positioning cushions (sleeping on one's side could alleviate snoring).[59] They would do anything to get a good night's sleep, except see a doctor. "Solution avoiders" did not seek treatment for their sleep disorders and accepted the fact that they were just poor sleepers.

Respironics' Sleep Well Ventures business unit was started in 2004 with six employees and with the goal of selling products directly to consumers without a doctor's prescription. It introduced its first product, a dental appliance to help people with mild to moderate OSA stop snoring, in 2005. In the same year, Respironics acquired the Mini Mitter Company for $10.5 million in cash, with future payments based on operating performance over the following two-year period. This acquisition resulted in the addition of two new products to Respironics' portfolio: (1) an Actiwatch, worn on a patient's wrist, and used by sleep researchers and sleep lab technicians to monitor insomnia; and (2) VitalSense, used to measure core and dermal body temperatures that, in turn, affected sleep-wake cycles.[60]

Respironics also made ventilator-related products. Its global hospital ventilation sales were $130 million in 2006 (up 15 percent from 2005). It made the Vision Ventilator to provide noninvasive ventilation to patients for use in hospitals and sub-acute care facilities. It developed a Cadence Self-Breathing technology, in which a tracheostomy tube attached to

---

[56]J. Sullivan, "Invacare stirs and issues a wake-up call," *HME News* 10 (6) (June, 2004): 45–46.

[57]M. Moran, "Invacare jumps in 'with both feet,' " *HME News* 12 (9) (September, 2006): 97–98.

[58]"Respironics, Inc. at Bank of America Health Care Conference—Final," *Fair Disclosure Wire* (May 30, 2007).

[59]R. Grilliot, "Tapping into the problem sleeper market," *HomeCare Magazine* 28 (7) (July, 2005): 30.

[60]"Mergers & acquisitions, Sleep and respiratory company acquires Mini-Mitter," *Medical Devices & Surgical Technology Week* (May 8, 2005): 305.

a catheter was inserted into a patient's carina (located in between the bronchial tubes of the lungs), instead of his/her trachea. The tube was then connected to an oxygen concentrator. This "minimally invasive" technique enabled a COPD patient to speak.

In 2006, Respironics acquired the Oxy Tec Medical Corporation (Oxy Tec) for $10.4 million in cash (including transaction costs), with provisions for up to $30 million of additional payments to be made based on its operating performance in future years. Oxy Tec had developed an innovative portable oxygen concentrator, the Oxy Tec 900, which could provide ambulatory oxygen patients with greater mobility. The Oxy Tec 900, renamed the EverGo, weighed nine pounds and could pump oxygen for eight hours. Respironics hoped that the new product would help it increase its market share in the oxygen business. Historically, its five-liter Millennium concentrator had lower market share than rival products from Invacare and AirSep.[61]

Respiratory Drug Delivery

Respironics began to acquire technologies and form partnerships so that it could offer medication, not just oxygen, to patients through their respiratory systems. Delivery of drugs through a patient's airways was effective because it improved the speed at which medications worked and decreased the doses needed.

In 2004, Respironics acquired Profile Therapeutics for approximately $44.6 million. Profile used adaptive aerosol delivery (AAD) technology to deliver the antibiotic, Promixin, to patients suffering from cystic fibrosis. Respironics also was granted the right to market and distribute Aerogen's aerosolized delivery of therapies via its ventilators (for critical care) on a non-exclusive basis. In 2006, Respironics entered a licensing agreement with CoTherix Inc. so that its portable, battery-operated, third-generation AAD device, the I-neb system, could be used to deliver Ventavis to patients with pulmonary arterial hypertension.

Children's Medical Products

Respironics' Children's Medical Ventures (ChMV) provided products and services for premature infants in neonatal intensive care units. The lungs were the last organ that developed in human beings. Infants had special needs when they born before their lungs were fully mature. Respironics' expertise in products for infants dated back to its 1998 acquisition of Healthdyne Technologies. Before starting Healthdyne, Parker Petit, an engineer, had suffered a personal tragedy. His infant son had died of sudden infant death syndrome (SIDS) in June 1970. Working with three other engineers during his spare time, he developed a machine that monitored the breathing and heart beat of an infant at risk for SIDS. Petit left his job at an aerospace company and founded Healthdyne.[62] Respironics continued to manufacture devices that monitored vital signs. Its Smart Monitor sounded an alarm when an infant stopped breathing and recorded the episodes so that physicians could study them further.

Through a series of acquisitions, Respironics expanded its infant care product line. In 2002, it acquired Novametrix, which had operated ChMV for two years (Novametrix acquired ChMV in 1999). Novametrix made such products as the Soothie pacifier and diapers for preemies. Respironics opted to retain the ChMV name. In 2006, Respironics acquired Omni Therm Inc., which made a line of warming products.[63] Respironics offered a simulation program for hospital workers—Preemie for a Day—so that they could experience what it was like to live in a neonatal intensive care unit. Administrators and nurses became aware of

[61]J. Sullivan, "They're no one-trick pony: Respironics expands O2 biz," *HME News* 12 (7) (July, 2006): 39–40.

[62]M. E. Kanell, "Home-grown firm born of tragedy," *The Atlanta Constitution* (March 28, 1997): H2.

[63]C. Snowbeck, "Products for babies help Respironics keep growing," *Knight Ridder Tribune Business News* (June 29, 2006): 1.

inappropriate behaviors. When, for example, they placed a clipboard on top of an incubator it "vibrated and disturbed its tiny occupant," Bourgart said. For older children with asthma, Respironics introduced a bilingual coloring and activity book, "Tucker Tackles Asthma," to teach them how to use a nebulizer.

International Markets

The incidence of sleep disorders and respiratory diseases were similar, if not sometimes higher, in countries across the world. Each country stood on its own and offered unique opportunities and challenges.[64] Despite its large population, electro-mechanical devices (e.g., CPAPs) were not very popular in China because only a fraction of homes could accommodate them. So, instead, Respironics sold its non-invasive ventilators with masks to hospitals in China. There were 12,500 hospitals in China and 70 percent of them did not even have a single ventilator.[65]

In France, Respironics successfully sold its portable sleep diagnostic tool, Stardust. Worn on the chest, the device recorded physiological data while the patient slept in the comfort of his/her own home. There was no channel to market this product in the U.S. because patients and clinicians could not get medical reimbursement. It was argued that unattended home studies did not provide valid information for the diagnosis of a patient's conditions. Logistically, there were concerns regarding whether or not the patients would return the units to the distributors. Approval of home studies by the Centers for Medicare and Medicaid Services (CMS), however, could result in faster diagnosis and treatment of OSA sufferers; the wait for clinical sleep lab studies could be long. Respironics' strategy was to be prepared in case reimbursement policies changed in the future.

Until the early 2000s, the Japanese government did not recognize sleep apnea as a medical condition for health insurance reimbursement. To prepare the groundwork for future sales, Respironics established a school for sleep, home and respiratory therapy in Tokyo. It trained physicians in how to diagnose and treat sleep apnea; it also helped them start up their own sleep labs.[66] Respironics had to make sure its products met strict regulatory requirements regarding noise, power consumption and size (since homes were small). It faced competition from many home grown manufacturers of airflow generators and oxygen concentrators. Tanita Corporation, a Japanese electronic scale maker, for example, recently announced that it had developed an SPL Monitor, placed under a mattress or futon, which recorded a person's pulse, breathing rate, number of tosses and turns during sleep, how long it took to fall asleep and how frequently the person woke up after sleep. At the same time, there were only a handful of medical equipment distributors. Respironics responded by acquiring Fuji RC Co. Ltd, a provider of home care and hospital products and services for respiratory impaired patients in Japan.

In 2006, Respironics acquired Normed AS in Norway and Spiropharma AS in Denmark in order to establish a direct presence in Scandinavian markets. It also expanded vertically by acquiring distributors in the UK, Italy, Switzerland, Finland, and Australia.

THE FUTURE

After the anniversary celebration in Times Square and already two months into fiscal year 2007, John Miclot was worried about the future of the company and his management team. Towards the end of the 2006 fiscal year, he had asked his team to identify opportunities for

---

[64]Personal interviews with Joseph Bourgart and Daniel Bevevino, May 24, 2007.

[65]"Respironics, Inc. Analyst Meeting-Final," *Fair Disclosure Wire* (February 1, 2007).

[66]Ibid.

Respironics. Among the options on the table at that time were purchasing intellectual property, taking equity positions in related businesses, or seeking companies to acquire outright.

Based on Respironics' rising cash balances, perhaps as many as two to three new investments could be identified for fiscal 2007. On the short list might be RespCare, Inc., a startup, which had just introduced an inexpensive hybrid CPAP mask system, and Restore Medical, another startup, which had invented an implant procedure to reduce vibrations that caused snoring. Aspire Medical, a small, privately held medical device company, was conducting clinical trials of an implantable device to treat tongue-based breathing obstructions.

Yet now, Respironics was perhaps itself on the short list of Royal Philips Electronics! Maybe that was what Respironics needed, help from a larger company, so that it could retain its position as the global market share leader for OSA treatments. Or, perhaps, Respironics should fight to remain independent and make a bold move—such as borrowing sufficient additional funds—to acquire a major competitor in the sleep therapy equipment market. That could be either ResMed or F&P. In any event, it was time for John Miclot to meet Ivo Lurvink from Philips Consumer Healthcare Solutions to see exactly what he wanted.

Case

9

Research In Motion— Entering a New Era

Sofy Carayannopoulos *Wilfrid Laurier University*

In the summer of 2007, as Jim Balsillie, co-CEO of Research In Motion (RIM), sat down at his desk in the Waterloo, Ontario, headquarters, a news headline caught his eye: "Apple's iPhone to hit stores, jolt mobile industry."[1] Other coverage described it as a "BlackBerry killer" that would challenge RIM's primacy in the **enterprise*** market.

Balsillie believed the iPhone was "one more entrant into an already very busy space," but the launch of this product had analysts debating RIM's choices and its future. The technology was converging, competition was intensifying, and large competitors were starting to target RIM's enterprise market. Balsillie viewed developing a strategy in these conditions as being similar to white water rafting. His objective was to get "every last dollar [he could] possibly get" in sales, but he had to constantly watch for "rocks" in the water ahead, and position the company to avoid them.

In order to grow, RIM had expanded its focus from the enterprise market to the mainstream consumer market with two new products—the BlackBerry "Pearl," and the BlackBerry "Curve." Although some analysts thought this was a wise move because RIM would otherwise be a "dominant player in the relatively small enterprise market,"[2] others believed that RIM should continue to place primary emphasis on the enterprise market.[3] Entering the consumer market exposed RIM to strong pricing pressure, as it would be competing against large companies such as Nokia and Motorola.

Copyright © 2007 by the *Case Research Journal* and Sofy Carayannopoulos. The author gratefully acknowledges the support and guidance provided by the editor, Dr. Lew Brown, and the helpful suggestions of three anonymous reviewers. This case was prepared solely to provide material for discussion. Certain names and other identifying information may have been disguised to protect confidentiality. Research In Motion does not necessarily confirm the accuracy or endorse the opinions expressed by the author in this case.

*See glossary for definitions of all words in bold font.

[1]Scott Hillis, "Apple's iPhone to Hit Stores, Jolt Mobile Industry," *Reuters* (June 27, 2007), http://www.canada.com/.

[2]Simon Avery, "With Pearl, the World's RIM's Oyster," *Globe and Mail Update* (October 13, 2006), http://www.theglobeandmail.com.

[3]Jonathan Richards, "RIM: iPhone Is No Threat to BlackBerry," *Times Online* (March 5, 2007), http://business.timesonline.co.uk.

Balsillie allowed his gaze to wander to the autographed Aerosmith guitar that hung on his wall—a souvenir of a company party celebrating RIM's 20th anniversary. The analysts were right about the competitive and technological environment changing. Balsillie thought about what RIM had to do to maximize sales, avoid "rocks," and make sure it was well-positioned for the future.

RIM'S EXTERNAL ENVIRONMENT

Market

The global wireless market had approximately 2.7 billion wireless subscribers in 2006 and analysts expected it to surpass 3 billion by the end of 2007, with China, India, Japan, Russia, and the United States showing the fastest subscriber growth.[4]

Users of mobile communication devices consisted of the mainstream consumer who purchased the device for personal use, the prosumer who used the device for business and some personal use, and the enterprise, which purchased the product for employees' business use.

In order of declining preference, mainstream consumers used their devices for voice communication, listening to music, browsing the Internet, and e-mail (see Exhibit 1 for a detailed breakdown). Among nonbusiness consumers in Japan and Korea, text messaging accounted for 30 percent of the data revenue collected by service providers. The remainder was from multimedia applications, browser traffic, and other infotainment applications. The opposite was

EXHIBIT 1   Relative Importance Score for Different Functions to Be Included in Most Frequently Used Mobile Device

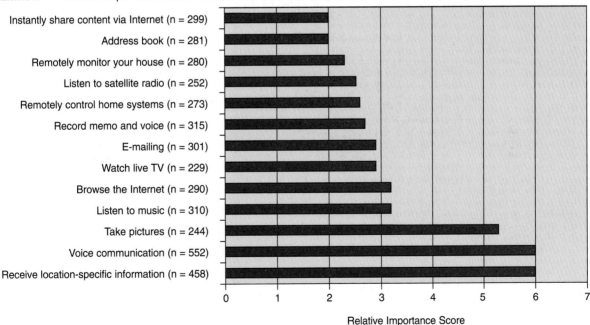

Source: Yuanzhe Cai, "Mobile Entertainment Platforms and Services," Parks and Associates, July 2005, http://www.parksassociates.com/research/reports/tocs/2005/multi-mobile_entertainment.htm.

n = number of respondents out of 1,919 owners of mobile devices surveyed that indicated interest in or use of a particular function

Relative Importance Score = how important a function is to the user on a scale of 0–7 (0 = not important, 7 = extremely important)

[4]Chetan Sharma, "Global Wireless Data Market Update 2006," http://www.chetansharma.com/worlddatatrends2006.htm.

true in Europe with approximately 70–80 percent of the data revenue coming from messaging. For North America, the data revenue from non-messaging applications was approximately 20 percent.[5] A U.S. Census report published in the second quarter of 2006 showed that 34.6 million subscribers had accessed the Internet through their wireless devices in June 2006, most frequently accessing e-mail and weather sites.[6]

The mainstream consumer valued attractive devices that were easy to use, graphical, and small.[7] It was the most price sensitive of the three segments, sometimes causing device price drops of 6 to 7 percent per quarter.[8] A survey of American consumers in 2007 found that, on an average, they were willing to pay US$99 for a regular cellphone and US$199 for a smartphone with a two-year contract,[9] although they tended to seek out cellular telephones that could support the additional functions desired. An important subset of the consumer segment was the group that wanted phones with the lowest price and functionality. This segment was particularly prominent in the world's emerging phone markets such as India and China, and it would be a major driver behind future handset market growth.[10]

In the enterprise segment, the purchase decision involved the information technology (IT) department, which researched, approved, paid for, and supported devices for the enterprise's employees. In some cases, the user had no choice but to use a device chosen by IT. Employees used the devices primarily for e-mail and data communication, access to the enterprise network and data, personal organizer functions, and voice communication. IT departments' primary considerations in product selection were security, reliability, and data integration between the mobile device and the enterprise. The ability of the IT department to control the device to ensure the security of confidential enterprise information was also very important. Consequently, this segment tended to prefer personal digital assistant (PDA)-type devices, although with the changing technology, it was moving toward converged mobile devices that provided all but entertainment-oriented features.

The prosumer segment was difficult to distinguish from the other two as it used the product for both business and personal use. A prosumer could be an enterprise employee who had either purchased the device independently to increase his/her productivity, or had purchased a device approved, supported, and subsidized by the employer. The prosumer could also be an independent entrepreneur such as the Argentinean milk farmers who used their BlackBerry to coordinate pick-up and delivery of produce. This segment was most likely to use the devices for voice communications, personal organizer functions, and data storage and access, but also wanted the flexibility of using some entertainment applications. Prosumers valued reliability, the availability of business applications, and multi-functionality so that they needed fewer devices. This segment was consequently very likely to purchase a converged mobile device. Prosumers were somewhat more sensitive to the price and appearance of the device than those in the enterprise segment, but not as much as mainstream consumers.

[5]Chetan Sharma, "Worldwide Wireless Data Trends—Mid-Year Update 2006," http://www.chetansharma.com/midyearupdateww06.htm.

[6]Telephia, "Mobile Internet Population Jumps to 34.6 Million, with E-mail, Weather, and Sports Websites Securing the Highest Reach, According to Telephia" (August 16, 2006), http://www.telephia.com/html/insights.html.

[7]Matt Walcoff, "BlackBerry Ripe for Change?" *Kitchener Waterloo Save & Sell* (September 1, 2006): 1, 5.

[8]Richards, "RIM: iPhone Is No Threat."

[9]Kurt Scherf, Michael Cai, and John Barret, "The iPhone: A Consumer Perspective," Parks Associates (2007): 1.

[10]ABI Research, "High Growth Handset Market Faces Low-Cost Dilemma" (June 8, 2006), http://linuxdevices.com/new/NS5105024528.html.

Although the three market segments had different priorities with respect to the devices, the technology of these devices was converging. Cellular telephones could now act as personal organizers, receive e-mail, and access the Internet, and PDAs could do the same. The most recent generation of products was "smartphones," or converged mobile devices. These were cellular telephones with **multimedia** and computer functionality. Smartphone features tended to include, but were not limited to, Internet access, e-mail access, personal organizer, music, television and/or video, and camera. The price of handheld devices depended upon the features offered and performance. Consumers could purchase cellular telephones with simple organizer and text-messaging features for under $100. Smartphones could cost as much as $600. Manufacturers believed that they would be able to maintain higher prices and margins on smartphones due to their features and functions, but recognized that low-cost devices would generate more sales volume.

As demand for multiple functions on all types of devices was increasing, manufacturers were focusing on enhancing their products' software capabilities, in addition to hardware features, in order to differentiate them. They were placing a stronger emphasis on adding more support for software development tools for outside software developers and convincing third-party software suppliers to develop specialized applications for their devices.

Demand for products in all segments was high and growing (see Exhibit 2). The PDA market was 13.88 million units in 2006 and analysts predicted it would reach 16.6 million units by 2011. Analysts also predicted the annual worldwide demand for cellular telephones would reach 1.24 billion units by 2008. Although the smartphone segment represented a small portion of the cellular telephone market, analysts estimated that the smartphone segment of the handset market would grow from worldwide sales of 46.55 million units in 2005 to 164 million units in 2010 with global shipments reaching 1 billion by 2012.[11] Many organizations were implementing enterprise applications, especially in North America.[12]

EXHIBIT 2A
Worldwide Market for PDAs and Smartphones

Source: "Smartphones to Outsell PDAs by 5:1 in 2006," *eTForecasts,* March 28, 2006, http://www.etforecasts.com/pr/pr0306.htm.

Unit Sales (millions)	2000	2003	2005	2006	2008	2010	2011
PDA Sales	11.43	12.75	13.51	13.88	14.82	15.97	16.60
Smartphone Sales	0.31	7.40	46.55	69.23	114.60	163.80	190.00

EXHIBIT 2B
Worldwide PDA Market by Vendor, 2004–2006 (Thousands of Units)

Source: Gartner Dataquest, February 14, 2006; October 9, 2006.

Company	Market Share (percent)		
	2006	2005	2004
Research In Motion	20.0	21.4	17.4
Palm	11.1	18.6	29.8
Hewlett-Packard	9.7	15.2	21.3
Nokia	Not applicable	6.8	2.0
T-Mobile	8.0	5.5	1.5
Others	Not applicable	32.5	28.0

Note: Totals do not include smartphones, but include wireless PDAs, such as the iPAQ 6315 and Nokia 9300.

[11]Symbian, "Fast Facts" (2007), http://www.symbian.com/about/fastfacts/fastfacts.html.
[12]Sharma, "Global Wireless Data."

EXHIBIT 2C

Top Five Converged
Mobile Device
Vendors, 2005–2006
(Units)

Source: IDC Worldwide
Quarterly Mobile Phone
Tracker, February 2007.

Vendor	Market Share (percent)		
	2006	2005	Share Growth
Nokia	48.1	50.3	35.8%
Research In Motion	7.5	7.2	46.3%
Panasonic	6.2	9.7	–9.1%
Motorola	6.1	4.2	104.2%
NEC	6.0	9.7	–12.7%
Others	26.2	18.9	97.2%
Total	**100.0**	**100.0**	**42.0**

EXHIBIT 2D

Mobile Phone
Forecast, 2005–2008

Source: M. Hoffman and
J. Baxter, "Wireless
Equipment—Mobile Phone
Industry Still Seeking
Balance," *Cowan and
Company,* April 13, 2007.

Market Overview	2005	2006	2007	2008
Market demand (million units)	856.9	1,019.6	1,149.5	1,240.0
Replacement units (million units)	420.4	580.3	711.5	823.9
Replacement % of annual sales	49.0%	57.0%	62.0%	66.0%
Global subscriptions (million)	2,172.6	2,611.9	3,049.9	3,466.0
Net new subscriptions (million)	436.5	439.3	438.0	416.1
Handsets by Region (million units)				
North America	137.3	152.6	165.7	153.8
Latin America	109.3	120.9	138.8	147.0
Western Europe	162.6	184.7	192.8	201.2
EMEA	183.9	211.6	268.5	299.2
Asia Pacific	252.6	359.0	398.7	421.6
Total Unit Sell-in	845.8	1,028.7	1,164.6	1,222.8
Handsets (million units) and Market Share (%) by Vendor				
Nokia	264.8	347.5	431.7	445.2
	31.3%	33.8%	37.1%	36.4%
Motorola	146.0	217.4	204.0	226.4
	17.3%	21.1%	17.5%	18.5%
Samsung	102.1	118.0	131.0	140.2
	12.1%	11.5%	11.2%	11.5%
Sony Ericsson	51.1	74.8	96.8	99.8
	6.0%	7.3%	8.3%	8.2%
LG	55.6	64.6	68.9	72.3
	6.6%	6.3%	5.9%	5.9%
BenQ-Siemens	36.8	23.0	6.5	0.0
	4.4%	2.2%	0.6%	0.0%
Others	189.4	183.5	225.8	238.8
	22.4%	17.8%	19.4%	19.5%
Total	845.8	1,028.7	1,164.6	1,222.8

Analysts predicted that by 2010 North American businesses would be spending over $10 billion annually on wireless enterprise data services,[13] and shipments of enterprise converged mobile devices would reach 63 million units.[14]

[13]StrategyAnalytics, "Mobile Email Revenues Set to Surpass SMS in $10 Billion North American Wireless Enterprise Market" (October 3, 2006), http://www.strategyanalytics.net/default.aspx?mod= PressReleaseViewer&a0=3088.

[14]Sharma, "Global Wireless Data."

Network Providers (also known as Carriers or Operators)

Analysts ranked network providers based on the number of subscribers, and revenues. However, the two metrics did not always agree, partly because revenues were a function of both frequency of use and the nature of the use. Data transmission generated greater revenues per use than voice communications. See Exhibit 3 for details on the data revenues and subscribers of the largest network providers.

The relationship between device manufacturers and network providers was one of mutual dependence. Device manufacturers needed networks on which their products could function—the better the networks, the more likely that products would perform well and satisfy consumers. The network providers also promoted and distributed their devices. The network providers needed the devices to attract subscribers to their networks and encourage network usage. Providers attracted subscribers by signing agreements with device manufacturers to promote mobile devices that could run on their networks—the more appealing and better performing the devices and the larger the coverage of the network, the more likely it was that customers would subscribe to a particular network.

To attract and "lock in" subscribers, most providers offered multi-year contracts that had high early cancellation fees, often packaged with reduced prices on mobile devices. One of the key areas of concern for providers was commoditization and the loss of subscribers who were attracted to other providers offering better performing or more interesting devices. The item of interest and value to the consumer was the device rather than the carrier or the network. One significant barrier to switching providers was that the subscriber would not be able to keep the same cellphone number (known as "number portability"). This was a particularly significant deterrent to switching providers for prosumers because their cellphone number was often a business contact. However, starting in 2001, countries around the world began enacting legislation requiring providers to allow number portability.

Network technology was continuing to evolve—networks allowed voice and data transmission, but providers were investing in new networks that would support multimedia

EXHIBIT 3

Top Wireless Carrier Revenues and Subscribers

Source: Chetan Sharma, "Global Wireless Data Market Update 2006," http://www.chetansharma.com/worlddatatrends2006.htm.

Carrier	Revenues FY 2006 (US$ billions)
NTT DoCoMo	10.75
China Mobile	6.90
KDDI	6.50
Verizon Wireless	4.30
AT&T Wireless	4.10
Sprint Nextel	4.00
SK Telecom	2.90
Vodafone Japan	2.70
02 UK	2.10
China Unicom	2.10

Carrier	Subscribers (millions)
China Mobile	301.0
Vodafone (Verizon in U.S.)	200.0
China Unicom	142.0
America Movil	125.0
Telefonica	102.0
SingTel	100.0
T-Mobile	106.0
Orange (France Telecom)	97.6

messaging (MMS) such as pictures or video clips and would allow faster and better access to data and Internet resources. Given the sizable investments that providers were making for upgraded networks, they were eager for new devices that would attract subscribers and encourage consumers to use data.

Competition

The competitive landscape was crowded, with multiple companies fully committed to usurping RIM's leading position in the wireless handheld market (see Exhibit 4 for an overview of hardware and software competitors, and Exhibit 2 for worldwide market shares of some of these companies).

Cellphone manufacturers such as Nokia and Motorola had entered the wireless data market by leveraging their dominant positions in the cellphone industry. These companies had global brand equity, strong financial resources, experience in wireless communications, and network carrier partnerships around the world. They were already offering "cost-optimized" handsets (basic cellphones offered at very low prices) in emerging regions to increase their market share. Nokia and Motorola had 37.1 percent and 17.5 percent market shares, respectively, of the worldwide handset market. Motorola had the reputation as a leader in launching "must-have" handsets. However, these cellphone manufacturers still had limited experience in data transmission, and some, like Nokia, had chosen to partner with other firms to embed e-mail functionality in their products. Traditional computer/notebook manufacturers, including Hewlett-Packard (HP) and Dell, had also turned their attention to this market. These manufacturers had very limited experience in mobile telephones, but significant experience in computing.

In late 2006 and early 2007, Samsung and Apple had entered the PDA/smartphone market with competing devices. Samsung's "BlackJack" was a device that included a complete **QWERTY** keyboard, camera, **push** e-mail enabled by Good Technology, organization functions, Web-browsing, and viewing of video content. The BlackJack was wider and longer than the BlackBerry Pearl, and only 1 mm thinner. AT&T offered it at US$499.99. Some users, however, had criticized its keyboard as being too small and poorly designed.

Apple's iPhone dimensions were 4.5 by 2.4 by .46 inches, and users controlled it entirely through a large touch-screen. It had e-mail, camera, could play music and videos, and browse the Internet. Analysts described it as an attractive and user-friendly device that put multimedia first and productivity second. Early reviews were mixed. Although many users loved the sleek appearance, some were disappointed that, although the iPhone allowed users to view entire Web pages as they would on a computer screen, downloading was slow due to the slow speed of AT&T's network. It also did not have some important business features such as Microsoft Office/Exchange or third-generation capabilities, which would enable both voice and non-voice data exchange and downloading over the Internet. The iPhone offered limited security for e-mail and other data.[15] Its price was US$500–600, depending on memory capacity, and required a two-year contract from AT&T priced between $60 and $100 per month.

Like RIM, Apple had negotiated a portion of monthly network subscriber fees in addition to hardware sales. However, unlike almost all other mobile device producers, Apple was selling the iPhone directly to end users in Apple stores as well as through AT&T. Furthermore, subscribers had to go to Apple's iTunes music store to activate their phones rather than the network carrier. Balsillie believed this was a dangerous strategy as it exposed network providers to the risk of becoming even more of a commodity, and they might react by promoting competing products to reduce Apple's power. Nevertheless, the consumer

---

[15]Arik Hesseldahl, "Not Everyone Wants an iPhone," *Business Week Online* (June 29, 2007), http://www.businessweek.com/print/technology/content/jun2007/tc20070628_831343.htm.

EXHIBIT 4   Competitive Analysis, Hardware and Software Companies

Hardware Companies

Company	Device	Partnerships	Advantages	Limitations	Financials* (US$ millions)

Nokia	Nokia E61	• RIM: BlackBerry Connect Licensing Program
		• 48 percent ownership of Symbian OS
		• Visto and Good Technology for software
			• World's largest cellphone maker
			• Financial strength and stability
			• Strong brand equity
			• In-house manufacturing and design
			• Competing device is slimmer with higher resolution and more easily customized software
				• Less experience and knowledge of wireless data devices
				• Competing device:
				  -Relatively new product
				  -Inferior keyboard ergonomics
					Rev. = 41,590
					EBITDA = 6,420
					56,896 employees

Motorola	Moto Q	• RIM: BlackBerry Connect Licensing Program
		• Microsoft for software, Kodak for mobile imaging
			• World's second largest cellphone maker
			• Financial strength and stability
			• Competing device:
			  -Thinnest and lightest handset
			  -QWERTY keyboard
				• Reputation for inferior design and execution
				• Less experience and knowledge of wireless data devices
				• Competing device is unproven, with "glitchy" software
					Rev. = 36,840
					EBITDA = 4,890
					69,000 employees

Palm	Treo 650	• RIM: BlackBerry Connect Licensing Program
		• Microsoft for software
		• Acquired Handspring
			• Recognized brand for PDA-type devices
			• Competing device:
			  -Touch screen with higher resolution
			  -MP3 player and camera
			  -More customizable, e.g., loading memory cards
				• Company has undergone tumultuous re-structuring, with name changes and spin-offs
				• Founders left company
				• Competing device is heavier and larger, has reliability issues (missed messages)
					Rev. = 1,410
					EBITDA = 107
					1,103 employees

HP	iPAQ hw6515	• Powered by Samsung	• World's leader in notebooks, with strategic shift in focus to grow handheld devices business • Global company with significant financial resources • Competing device has GPS and camera	• Relatively unknown wireless data devices with reputation for poor performance and reliability • Small customer base for handheld devices • Competing device has poor audio quality	Rev. = 87,900 EBITDA = 7,640 150,000 employees
Samsung	Blackjack	• Good Technology e-mail capabilities	• Global company with recognized brand for audio/video equipment and home appliances • Wide array of cellular telephone models	• Inferior keyboard ergonomics • Bulkier than Pearl	Rev. = 56,720 NIBT = 8,757 123,000 employees

(continued)

EXHIBIT 4 Competitive Analysis, Hardware and Software Companies *(continued)*

Hardware Companies *(continued)*

Company	Device	Partnerships	Advantages	Limitations	Financials* (US$ millions)
Apple	iPhone	• HP • Intel	• Recognized brand for innovative and interesting computer designs and multimedia devices • Global company with strong innovative and marketing capabilities	• Less experience and knowledge of communication and business communication devices • Not 3G capable • Doesn't have Microsoft Exchange capabilities • Concerns regarding e-mail security	Rev. = 19,300 EBITDA = 2,424 17,787 employees
Dell	Axim X51v	• Powered by Good Technology	• Global presence • Financial strength and stability • Competing device has a touch screen	• Relatively unknown wireless data device • Small customer base for handheld devices • Competing device lacks QWERTY keyboard and has poor battery life	Rev. = 55,910 EBITDA = 4,840 65,200 employees

Software Companies

Company	Platform	Partnerships	Advantages	Limitations	Financials* (US$ millions)
Good Technology	GoodLink Enterprise	• Supports Dell, HP, Nokia, Motorola, Palm, and Symbol	• Software sits on virtually all smart-phone platforms except Blackberry's operating system • Supports industry standards: Windows Mobile platforms	• Compatible only with servers running Microsoft's Exchange software, compared to RIM which can also handle Lotus Notes • Outstanding lawsuits with Visto	Privately held corporation Estimated revenue in 2003 = $25 160 employees (2003)
Microsoft Corp.	Microsoft Exchange Server, and Windows Mobile	• Supports Motorola and Palm	• World leader in software applications • Financial strength and stability	• Lacks interest and experience in wireless data communication	Revenue = 39,800 EBITDA = 15,400 71,000 employees
Danger Inc.	The Hiptop	• Support manufacturer Sharp Corp. and smaller technology providers	• Provides end-to-end platform including backend infrastructure	• Small customer base	Privately held corporation Estimated revenue in 2003 = $24 110 employees (2004)

(continued)

EXHIBIT 4 Competitive Analysis, Hardware and Software Companies *(concluded)*

Software Companies *(continued)*

Company	Platform	Partnerships	Advantages	Limitations	Financials* (US$ millions)
Visto Corp.	Visto Mobile 5.5	• Supports Nokia, Motorola, SonyEricsson, Sony, Microsoft, Palm, Symbian, Sony, and Kyocera	• Unlike RIM, mobile e-mail service does not require specialized hardware • Partnerships with several technology companies • Holds twenty-five patents, fifty-seven pending	• Compatible only with servers running Microsoft's Exchange software	Privately held corporation Estimated revenue in 2002 = $10 80 employees (2003)
PalmSource (Palm)	Palm OS	• Supports Aceeca, Fossil, Garmin, Kyocera, Lenovo, Palm, Samsung, Song, and Symbol • Partnership with RIM -Jointly developing a software solution that enables Blackberry connectivity to the Palm OS -Technology distribution agreement allowing RIM to license a BlackBerry Connect offering to Palm Powered licensees	• Leading operating system powering next-generation mobile devices -65 percent share in U.S., and 51 percent market share worldwide -Customer base: more than thirty-nine million mobile phones, handhelds, and other mobile devices	• Company has undergone tumultuous re-structuring, with multiple name changes, spin-offs, and acquisitions	Revenue = 17.9 EBITDA = 4.0 1,103 employees

Source: Case writer analysis based on information found in Tom Astle's "Competitive Update," *Merrill Lynch Global Securities Research*, January 13, 2003, company Web sites, Mergent Online, and sources listed on the references page.

*Financials reflect most recent year-end data available unless otherwise indicated.

enthusiasm for the iPhone and speculation that up to 25 percent of cellphone users who bought the iPhone on its release would be switching from another network provider had caused other providers including Orange, T-Mobile, and Vodafone to aggressively bid for European iPhone rights.[16]

Because RIM's product offering also comprised software licensing, its competitive environment included software companies such as Good Technologies, Microsoft, and Danger, Inc. The software these companies produced functioned on virtually any device, thereby increasing an enterprise's flexibility in selecting its own providers, handheld devices, networks, and platforms. Some analysts considered Microsoft one of the greatest competitive threats on the software horizon, if it decided to dedicate resources to the wireless communication market. However, Microsoft Mobile was one of the weak points in Motorola's Moto Q, and Palm's Treo 650 devices due to "glitchy" operation and reliability issues.

Palm, Inc. offered both the handheld device and accompanying software. Despite its recognized brand and product, internal restructuring had negatively affected Palm's growth. Between 2001 and 2005, there had been a series of spin-offs, acquisitions, and name changes. In late 2001/early 2002 the company split into two operational businesses—one focusing on developing and marketing the Palm Operating System (Palm OS), which it licensed to other PDA and device manufacturers, and one focused on its PDAs, which it sold to consumers. The restructuring aimed to improve Palm's ability to cater to its many licensees and developers and to address the complex and sometimes contradictory demands of its businesses. In its fourth-quarter fiscal 2007 results, its revenues were down in comparison to fiscal 2006. It also expected to see sales of its Treo smartphone stall due to the launch of the iPhone.[17]

RESEARCH IN MOTION

History

Mike Lazaridis and Douglas Fregin founded RIM in 1984. In 1992, Jim Balsillie sank a substantial portion of his savings into RIM and joined the company as co-CEO. Fregin became a director and vice-president of operations, and Lazaridis became president and co-CEO. Balsillie and Lazaridis worked as a team with Lazaridis concentrating on the technology and Balsillie focusing on expanding the business. From its inception, RIM focused on developing hardware and software for wireless data communication. It developed a capability in producing wireless two-way data communication devices that were small, lightweight, and energy-efficient.

The BlackBerry Bursts onto the Market

In January 1999, RIM launched BlackBerry—a product that combined hardware, software, and service to provide wireless e-mail messaging. Messages sent to a user's e-mail address were automatically forwarded ("**pushed**") to the BlackBerry handheld (see Exhibit 5). The user was notified of their arrival and could read and reply to them quickly. This represented a significant performance improvement, because with all other e-mail systems the user had to connect with a network to see if he/she had an e-mail and "pull" or retrieve the e-mail to his/her device.

The BlackBerry hardware and software were easy to use, even by those unaccustomed to handling their own e-mails. The product was roughly the size of a pager, and had a small

---

[16]Philip Elmer-DeWitt, "Apple iPhone: It Stoppeth One of Four," *Apple 2.0* (July 13, 2007), http://blogs.business2.com/apple/2007/07/apple-iphone-it.html.
[17]Hillis, "Apple's iPhone to Hit Stores."

EXHIBIT 5
How the BlackBerry
Works

Source: Research In Motion.

1. Someone sends an e-mail to your e-mail address.
2. E-mail arrives at your desktop PC.
3. BlackBerry Enterprise Server (or desktop version) encrypts and forwards the message.
4. E-mail is forwarded to the handheld via the Internet to BlackBerry Operations Centre—Centre then forwards onto designated wireless network.
5. The handheld receives and decrypts the e-mail. User responds to e-mail using the keyboard on the BlackBerry handheld.

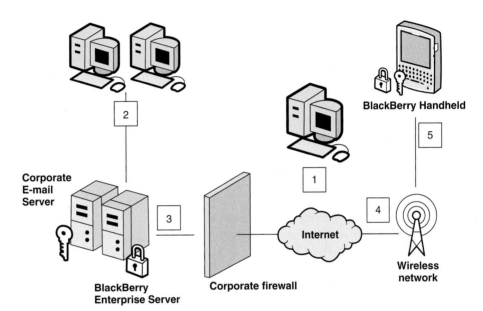

QWERTY keyboard that the user would type on using his/her thumbs. Extensive testing confirmed its ease of use. It ran on one AA battery that required replacement approximately once every two weeks. All of these elements represented significant technological and functional improvements over all other wireless products. Lazaridis also incorporated advanced **encryption software** in the BlackBerry that met Intel's security benchmark. Intel was RIM's chip supplier, but more importantly, meeting its security needs represented a significant source of product differentiation.

The BlackBerry solution enabled mobile users to manage e-mail while away from the office just as e-mail was increasing in popularity and wireless products were achieving wider acceptance. The only substitutes for the product at the time were laptops and a bulkier, slower device made by Motorola. Although Nokia and Motorola were both making advances in wireless communication, they focused on voice rather than data because it represented a larger market at the time. Personal digital assistants, such as the PalmPilot, focused on increasing functionality and memory, but did not have the technological capabilities for wireless communication. RIM targeted corporations and their employees, particularly those handling time-sensitive information such as financial services. It believed that corporations were more likely to find value in its product and more likely than individual consumers to purchase it.

RIM offered two versions of the product—a BlackBerry Enterprise Server (BES) and a non-server version of the BlackBerry. The non-server version routed the e-mails from the user's desktop computer to the BlackBerry handheld. The BES version worked with the corporation's e-mail system to redirect e-mail through the **corporate mail server.** This software allowed centralized administration of the BlackBerry by IT departments, and increased the e-mail security. The BES was designed to work with the most popular e-mail systems, which at the time were Microsoft Exchange and Lotus Domino.

RIM launched the non-server version first so that it could provide free trials to CEOs such as Jack Welsh, CEO of GE, without needing the approval or cooperation of the IT departments. Most IT departments resisted the idea of implementing new products, such as the BlackBerry, as they often complicated an already complex environment. It was a successful strategy, as almost everyone who tried the product chose to keep it, and many adopted it throughout their enterprises.

A final component of the BlackBerry solution was its own Operations Centre, through which it routed all wireless data to and from wireless networks. The Operations Centre involved a significant investment in hardware and software but helped ensure e-mail security and reliable and efficient data transmission. The efficiency and performance created by the Operations Centre meant RIM's users experienced better and more secure data transmission with a data plan that cost the same or less than that of other vendors. It also gave enterprises the ability to run their BlackBerrys on multiple networks without additional costs or software. It represented an additional source of revenue for RIM, as it charged a monthly service fee for each BlackBerry subscriber. The fee was included in the monthly fees charged by the network operators and paid by the operators to RIM. Similar operations centers were employed by Motorola and Visto.

By 2002, BlackBerry had become a proprietary brand that companies asked for by name. Users found it so addictive that Andy Grove of Intel coined the nickname "Crackberry." BlackBerry had become a popular and sometimes indispensable solution in such organizations as the U.S. House of Representatives and the military. It had even made its way into pop culture with product placement in popular movies and television shows. Analysts estimated that by fourth quarter of 2006, BlackBerry devices accounted for roughly 20 percent of all sales of personal digital assistants, and handled 59 percent of corporate wireless e-mail traffic.[18]

In May 2006, RIM initiated a trade-up program for the BlackBerry, which allowed existing customers to upgrade an older device to the newest BlackBerry model at a discount. The company did this to retain customers by encouraging them to upgrade to newer BlackBerry models rather than switching to a competitor's device. Balsillie believed this program also provided a strong signal to consumers that RIM was committed to innovation and to keeping pace with technological advances.

RESEARCH IN MOTION IN 2007

Financial Performance

Revenue for fiscal 2007 was US$3.04 billion, up 50 percent from US$2.07 billion the year before (see Exhibit 6 for financial statements). RIM's handhelds accounted for approximately 73 percent of revenue. OEM radios and other sources accounted for 3 percent, while service and software licenses and development accounted for 18.4 percent and 5.7 percent of revenue, respectively. The approximate contribution margin[19] for each category was hardware—43 percent, and service and software—90 percent. Service revenues from enterprise subscribers were approximately $7 to $10 per month per subscriber, and $3 to $5 per consumer or prosumer subscriber.

---

[18]Ian Austen, "RIM Is Counting on Customers," *clnet NEWS.com* (September 18, 2006), http://news.com.

[19]These margins are provided to further the case and enable analysis. They are based on industry averages and conversations with RIM employees, and may not reflect RIM's actual contribution margins.

EXHIBIT 6 Research In Motion Financial Results

CONSOLIDATED STATEMENTS OF OPERATIONS (US$, THOUSANDS)

	For the Year Ended			
	March 3 2007	March 4 2006	February 6 2005	February 28 2004
Revenue	$3,037,103	$2,065,845	$1,350,447	$594,616
Cost of sales	1,378,301	925,215	635,914	323,365
Gross margin	1,657,802	1,140,630	714,533	271,251
Expenses				
R&D, net of government funding	236,173	157,629	101,180	62,638
Selling and administration	537,922	311,420	190,730	108,492
Amortization	76,879	49,951	35,941	27,911
Litigation and related expenses		201,791	352,628	35,187
Total expenses	850,974	720,791	680,479	234,228
Income from operations	806,828	419,839	34,054	37,023
Investment income	52,117	66,218	37,107	10,606
Provision for income taxes	227,373	103,979	−142,226	−4,200
Net income	631,572	382,078	213,387	51,839

REVENUE BREAKDOWN

	Fiscal 2007		Fiscal 2006		Fiscal 2005		Fiscal 2004	
Devices sold	6,400,000		4,043,000		2,444,000		920,000	
Average selling price	$336		$356		$382		$373	
Revenues								
Devices	$2,215,951	73.0%	$1,439,674	69.7%	$933,989	69.2%	$343,200	57.7%
Service*	560,116	18.4%	383,021	18.5%	235,015	17.4%	171,200	28.8%
Software	173,187	5.7%	156,556	7.6%	131,811	9.8%	47,400	8.0%
Other	87,849	2.9%	86,594	4.2%	49,632	3.6%	32,816	5.5%
Total	$3,037,103		$2,065,845		$1,350,447		$594,616	

*Service refers to one of the three RIM components in its BlackBerry solution (hardware and software being the other two). Service revenue is a charge of approximately US$8 per user per month charged to network operators for handling e-mail through the Operations Centre. The service charge for the "Pearl" was approximately $3.

RESEARCH IN MOTION LIMITED CONSOLIDATED BALANCE SHEETS (US$, THOUSANDS) (AUDITED)

	March 3 2007	March 4 2006	February 26 2005	February 28 2004
ASSETS				
Current				
Cash and cash equivalents	$ 677,144	$ 459,540	$ 610,354	$1,156,419
Short-term investments	310,082	175,553	315,495	—
Trade receivables	572,637	315,278	227,750	95,213
Other receivables	40,174	31,861	13,125	12,149
Inventory	255,907	134,523	92,489	42,836
Restricted cash	—	—	111,987	36,261
Other current assets	41,697	45,035	22,857	12,527
Deferred tax asset	21,624	94,789	150,200	—
	1,919,265	1,256,579	1,544,248	1,355,405
Long-term portfolio investments	425,652	614,309	753,868	339,285
Capital assets	487,579	326,313	210,112	147,709
Goodwill and other intangible assets	256,453	114,955	112,766	94,378
Total assets	$3,088,949	$2,312,156	$2,620,994	$1,936,777

(*continued*)

EXHIBIT 6   Research In Motion Financial Results   *(concluded)*

	March 3 2007	March 4 2006	February 26 2005	February 28 2004
LIABILITIES				
Current				
Accounts payable and accrued liabilities	$ 417,899	$ 239,866	$ 155,597	$ 106,108
Accrued litigation and related expenses	—	—	455,610	84,392
Income taxes payable	99,958	17,584	3,149	1,684
Deferred revenue	28,447	20,968	16,235	16,498
Current portion of long-term debt	271	262	223	193
	546,575	278,680	630,814	208,875
Long-term debt	6,342	6,851	6,504	6,240
Deferred income tax liability	52,532	27,858	—	—
	605,449	313,389	637,318	215,115
Shareholders' equity				
Capital stock	2,099,696	1,852,713	1,892,266	1,829,388
Retained earnings	359,227	148,028	94,181	(119,206)
Paid-in capital	36,093	—	—	—
Acc. other comprehensive income	(11,516)	(1,974)	(2,771)	(11,480)
Total shareholders' equity	2,483,500	1,998,767	1,983,676	1,721,662
Total liabilities and shareholders' equity	$3,088,949	$2,312,156	$2,620,994	$1,936,777

Gross margin for the year was 54.6 percent, down slightly from the previous year's due to the increased percentage of revenue coming from smartphones such as their "Pearl." These consumer-oriented products had lower average selling prices than the devices targeting enterprise users. Nevertheless, the gross margin improved from fiscal 2005 and fiscal 2004 due to economies of scale and reductions in material costs. Service margins had also improved due to cost efficiencies caused by the increase in the BlackBerry subscriber account base. Operating expenses as a percentage of revenue increased slightly from the previous year due to increased investments in hardware and software development; new marketing programs associated with the launch of the consumer-oriented products; and higher administrative expenses in the second half of the year (see Exhibit 6 for detailed financials). RIM's cash and marketable securities were approximately US$635 million—a relatively strong cash position compared to such rivals as Palm (see Exhibit 7 for a financial comparison of RIM and some of its competitors).

Products

BlackBerry Wireless Devices

Each year RIM launched new BlackBerry models with a range of features, services, and prices, targeting enterprise users. Generally, basic features included e-mail, wireless Internet browsing, organizer applications, short message servicing (SMS), instant messaging, corporate data access, and paging. Recent models had added telephone capabilities and cameras, although RIM still offered some models without cameras. One of RIM's most recent innovations was its SureType keyboard technology. This technology allowed RIM to fit a full **QWERTY** keyboard on a smaller device by putting two letters on some of the keys. Users could "double tap" to select the letter of their choice, or allow the SureType technology to predict the word being typed by referencing its expandable 35,000-word vocabulary. This innovation addressed the concern of customers who resisted using the BlackBerry device as a phone because they felt its size made its use look awkward.

EXHIBIT 7   Financial Comparison of RIM and Competitors

(as of most recent annual financials at July, 2007. US$, millions)

	Current Ratio	Debt/ Equity	Cash	Revenues/ Growth over previous two years	ROE	Gross Margin	ROA and Asset Turnover	Marketing, Selling, and Admin. (% of revenue)	R&D (% of revenue)
RIM	3.51	.20	$ 677	$3,037	32.60%	$ 1,658	20.44%	$ 538	$ 236
				47.0% $(t_0 - t_{-1})$		54.60%	0.98	17.70%	7.80%
				53.0% $(t_{-1} - t_{-2})$					
Apple	2.24	.72	$6,392	$19,315	19.90%	$ 5,598	11.56%	$2,433	$ 712
				38.6% $(t_0 - t_{-1})$		29.00%	1.12	12.60%	3.70%
				68.2% $(t_{-1} - t_{-2})$					
Motorola	2.01	.23	$3,212	$42,879	19.00%	$12,727	8.45%	$4,504	$3,680
				16.4% $(t_0 - t_{-1})$		29.70%	1.11	10.50%	10.00%
				17.6% $(t_{-1} - t_{-2})$					
Nokia	1.83	.01	$2,024	$56,262	36.20%	$19,019	19.04%	$5,757	$5,332
				20.3% $(t_0 - t_{-1})$		33.80%	1.82	10.23%	9.50%
				16.4% $(t_{-1} - t_{-2})$					
Palm	1.95	.46	$ 65	$1,561	5.31%	$ 575	3.64%	$ 308	$ 136
				−1.0% $(t_0 - t_{-1})$		36.86%	1.01	19.70%	9.00%
				24.0% $(t_{-1} - t_{-2})$					

Source: Mergent Online.

Two of RIM's most recent products were the BlackBerry "Pearl" (BlackBerry 8100), introduced in September 2006, and the BlackBerry "Curve" (BlackBerry 8300), launched in May 2007 (see Exhibit 8). Lazaridis stated that these products were responses to consumers who wanted other features, such as multimedia. The "Curve" measured 4.2 by 2.4 by 0.6 inches,

EXHIBIT 8   Current Products

BLACKBERRY PEARL 8100

Size:
width: 5 cm/1.97"
height: 10.7 cm/4.2"
depth: 1.4 cm/.57"
weight: 87.88 grams/ 3.1 ounces

BLACKBERRY CURVE 8300

Size:
width: 6 cm/2.4"
height: 10.7 cm/4.2"
depth: 1.52 cm/.6"
weight: 110.6 grams/ 3.9 ounces

weighed approximately 3.9 ounces, and was RIM's smallest and lightest full-QWERTY keyboard smartphone. It extended previous BlackBerry offerings by offering a two-mega pixel camera and software and Internet features such as TeleNav maps that would allow a user to find addresses and obtain directions. It was available for US$200 through AT&T with a two-year calling plan that began at US$30 per month.

The Pearl smartphone targeted mainstream consumers and prosumers. It weighed 3.1 ounces, and was roughly the size of a large cellular telephone (4.2 by 1.97 by .57 inches). It incorporated e-mail, messaging, Web browsing, and a 1.3 mega pixel camera with three zoom levels and built-in flash. It also served as a multimedia player with stereo headset for MP3 and AAC music files, and it had expandable memory. It was sleek, available in three colors (black, white, and red) and used RIM's SureType technology. Upon launch the BlackBerry Pearl was available from T-Mobile in the United States at US$200, and Rogers Wireless Communications Inc. in Canada for CDN$250. AT&T and other providers in North America, as well as Europe, Asia and Latin America, launched the product by the end of 2006.

The Pearl had taken three years to bring to market. In 2003, RIM had recognized that many BlackBerry owners avoided using their devices as cellphones because they appeared awkward, and some resisted them because they were bulky. Although adding features such as a camera and MP3 player was easy, creating a small attractive product that did not compromise the BlackBerry reputation for simple and reliable e-mail required significant research and design efforts. Furthermore, Lazaridis insisted that the BlackBerry Pearl was not built as a budget version of the corporate devices—it was designed using the full BlackBerry platform. Balsillie described it as follows:

> It's the "Triple Crown"—it's the no-compromise smartphone for features, it's the no-compromise style phone for style purposes, and it's the no-compromise BlackBerry. So many of these things in the world have been addressed with fundamental compromises—people want more features, but don't want to give up the features they already have.

There was a great deal of speculation about how the BlackBerry Pearl would affect RIM. According to national retailers of cellphones and other wireless devices, the Pearl was selling well, and was attracting non-enterprise buyers between the ages of 19 and 37 who had never before shown any interest in owning a BlackBerry device.[20] Some analysts believed the move into the consumer market would boost RIM's revenue growth and sales volume.[21] Others were concerned that RIM's presence in the consumer market, where it had less than a 1 percent market share, would put it in direct competition with large multinationals such as Nokia and Motorola.

Furthermore, there was speculation that the new products would diminish RIM's image as an enterprise device manufacturer, which was one reason RIM had consciously avoided the consumer market. The inclusion of cameras and multimedia could also pose security issues for IT managers who would then be reluctant to adopt the BlackBerrys. RIM responded by assuring IT managers that they could disable cameras and multimedia features. There was also concern because other companies' attempts to market similar devices had resulted in limited success due to performance challenges and the cost of wireless Internet access, which was approximately US$40 per month.

Mainstream consumers who were users of the BlackBerry made comments like, "I used to change devices once a month because nothing worked well enough. Now I wouldn't consider changing my BlackBerry—its phone works great, and it perfectly synchronizes all of my information with my computer wirelessly and immediately." On the other hand, early

---

[20]Avery, "With Pearl."
[21]Austen, "RIM Is Counting."

purchasers of the iPhone commented, "I love my iPhone. When I show it to my friends at work who have BlackBerrys, the jealousy and interest are tangible."

BlackBerry products were sold through supply agreements with network operators. These operators marketed the products, bundled with voice and data packages, to subscribers. By the end of fiscal 2007, RIM had agreements with over 270 network operators in 110 countries, including those with some of the highest wireless data revenues in the world: NTT DoCoMo, Verizon, Vodafone, and Cingular. RIM signed over 100 new carrier agreements with operators in fiscal 2006, which further increased its geographic reach in Europe, Asia-Pacific, Africa, and Latin America. RIM had signed an agreement in May 2006 with China Mobile to offer service to BlackBerry devices and to make the devices themselves available at a later date.

However, reports showed that a growing gap existed between the number of devices shipped and the number of new wireless accounts. For example, in the quarter ending March 4, 2006, RIM reported shipping 1.12 million BlackBerry devices, while only 625,000 BlackBerry subscribers signed up for service, representing a difference of about 495,000. In the previous three quarters, the differences were 475,000, 335,000 and 248,000 respectively. These gaps indicated that RIM's BlackBerry shipments weren't selling through to end users as rapidly as they had previously. Some analysts were saying that they believed the market for business subscribers was approaching saturation.

BlackBerry Subscribers

RIM had approximately nine million subscribers by June 2007, having added approximately one million subscribers since end of fiscal 2007 on March 3, 2007.[22] RIM had been doubling its subscriber base each year over the previous four years. It had 4.9 million subscribers at the end of fiscal 2006, as compared with 2.4 million (2005), one million (2004) and 500,000 (2003). More than 100,000 organizations had installed the BlackBerry Enterprise Server, and RIM had successfully expanded its target market to include the prosumer and individual consumer. At the end of fiscal 2007, over 27 percent of BlackBerry subscribers were non-enterprise users.

Although North America represented RIM's largest market, its subscriber account base had expanded to over 110 countries by end of fiscal year 2007. International customers outside North America accounted for approximately 28 percent of BlackBerry subscribers and 35 percent of overall revenues. Most of the company's international growth was in major European markets and Asia. Outside Europe, RIM's geographic expansion into the Pacific Rim included a plan to continue market penetration in Australia, India, Singapore, and Hong Kong.

Software

All BlackBerry models emphasized security. RIM had been awarded the FIPS 140-2 Validation by the U.S. National Institute of Standards and Technology for its encryption technology and was seeking similar types of validation in Europe, Australia, and New Zealand. This certification validated the high level of security that the BlackBerry products offered and was an important and often mandatory purchasing criterion for many organizations, including the government sector and the military. Lazaridis also insisted that new versions of the BES continued to provide IT departments with features that increased manageability, security, and centralized control of BlackBerry wireless handheld devices, such as the ability to remotely shut off devices that were lost, and the ability to disable multimedia features.

---

[22]Subscribers included users of BlackBerry handheld devices as well as BlackBerry-enabled devices such as some Nokia cellular telephones.

RIM's latest version of its BES software allowed the BlackBerry to be integrated with Microsoft Exchange, Lotus Domino, and Novell Group Wise, ensuring its compatibility with the most popular e-mail programs and making it easier for users of these e-mail programs to use the BlackBerry.

Software Development Tools

RIM continued to offer the BlackBerry Developer Zone, software development kits, and other tools for creating applications for BlackBerry wireless handhelds. RIM recognized that independent software developers were constantly looking for opportunities to modify their existing programs to run on popular devices, as well as developing new and unique applications. RIM BlackBerry Developer Zone allowed developers to create specialized wireless applications that would increase the value of the BlackBerry for users through programs specifically designed for their needs. Enterprise customers and Independent Software Vendors (ISVs) could easily and quickly develop applications that leveraged the unique features of BlackBerry.

The BlackBerry Java Development Environment was a fully integrated development environment and simulation tool for creating applications for BlackBerry handhelds. Java, and its subset of programs known as J2ME, was the most popular software development environment. It enabled the development of new applications for space-constrained devices such as cellphones. By implementing Java as the application development software, RIM was making its devices available as platforms for new applications created by a large and growing developer community that included over three million software developers. One example of a specialized application that increased the Blackberry's value in the health care industry was software that allowed diabetic patients and caregivers to automatically monitor a diabetic patient's activities and health conditions.

Licensing

In addition to its integrated solutions and service, RIM had begun licensing individual components of its products in 2002. The BlackBerry Connect Licensing Program enabled mobile devices from a variety of leading manufacturers to take advantage of BlackBerry "push" technology by allowing them to equip their devices with BlackBerry built-in e-mail and organizer applications. RIM's management believed this would allow consumers to benefit from RIM's technology on a device they were already familiar with and would provide the market with a broader choice of devices. It would also mean providers and corporations would not be forced to choose between their existing or strategic devices and BlackBerry.

Through this program, RIM licensed its **push** technology to mobile phone manufacturers such as Nokia in 2002, and Sony Ericsson in 2004. More recently, RIM licensed its "push" technology to Palm's Treo 650 in October 2005, and signed agreements with Motorola and Samsung in 2006. By end of fiscal 2007, there were 50 BlackBerry enabled devices. In addition to licensing revenue, this program also generated service revenue for RIM as the e-mail for the BlackBerry devices was routed through RIM's Operations Centre.

Manufacturing

RIM originally manufactured all of its products in-house because it wanted to ensure tight control over quality, and believed it benefited from the integration of manufacturing with research and development. However, in 2005 with demand growing globally, RIM began an outsourcing relationship with Elcoteq Network Corporation for the manufacture of certain devices in Europe and Mexico. At the end of fiscal 2006, RIM began expansion of its manufacturing facility in Waterloo, which had a production capacity of five million devices per year, with the goal of doubling its existing 122,000 square foot facility. It would use the expanded facility for incremental production, materials storage, and colocation of some dispersed manufacturing operations.

Organization

Research and Development

RIM was continuing to focus on the development of next-generation handhelds, along with ongoing development of the BlackBerry platform/solution. The company had made notable increases in R&D expenditures over the years, increasing spending from US$62.6 million in 2004 to almost US$235 million in 2007. Approximately 2,100 employees (34 percent) of RIM's employees focused on research and development activities. To encourage innovation, RIM had created an Inventor's Banquet to honor those employees who had applied for patents, and rewarded the creators of key patents with substantial cash awards. By end of fiscal 2006, RIM held over 650 patents.

Lazaridis also insisted on a strong focus on quality testing. RIM tested its products extensively before releasing them. He commented, "We have a saying here at RIM. It is 'doing your math.' Our culture is to double-check, check twice, and ask customers before we undertake changes."

In fiscal 2007, RIM acquired Ascendent Systems, a San Jose, California, company which was a provider of enterprise voice mobility solutions. It purchased Ascendent because its expertise would enable RIM to enhance the voice capabilities and features of its products. The intention was to provide enterprises with the same integration between desk and mobile telephones that RIM already provided with e-mail. For example, the user's BlackBerry could become a secure extension of a user's desk phone so that the user could be reached through one telephone number whether in the office or not, consolidation and access to a single voice mailbox, conference-calling capabilities, and even four- or five-digit extension dialing. Corporations with multiple locations, or large numbers of employees who spent a significant time away from their desks but needed to be accessible by telephone would find these features valuable.

RIM was also leveraging the expertise of SlipStream, a 60-person company based in Waterloo that it acquired in 2006. SlipStream's expertise in efficiently transferring data through the Internet would increase the performance of Internet browsing on BlackBerry devices. SlipStream's capabilities could also potentially enable other multimedia functions on BlackBerry devices such as on-the-go video conferencing.

Culture, Control, and Human Resources

Management described RIM as a creative, energetic workplace that was fun but focused on success. The company had an employee turnover rate of less than 1 percent, and a reputation among the local universities as a coveted employer. Some examples of corporate events that RIM organized to keep its young image and culture were the celebration of achievements with concert performances by Barenaked Ladies and Aerosmith and the shutdown of the company for half days for each release of the *Star Wars* movies. Even meeting rooms were identified by names based on themes such as *Lord of the Rings* ("Frodo Room," "Samwise Room") or famous Canadian hockey players ("Wayne Gretzky Room," "Bobby Orr Room") rather than numbers.

Although RIM had grown from 1,850 employees in 2003 and 4,700 in 2006 to approximately 6,250 employees in 2007, Balsillie did not believe becoming bureaucratic and rigid was inevitable.

> If you value what's important and invest in culture, then the natural rigor mortis can be counteracted. With the go-to-market activities, we've evolved into business units that still give you projects that you can sink your teeth into. Two hundred go-to-market people meet once a

week, and everyone will take a minute to talk about what they're doing. They see how they're interdependent and how each part is trusting the other and counting on it. Other parts of the organization like engineering naturally are project oriented. Mike does similar meetings with engineers, and there are lots of interdisciplinary meetings. There's ownership, latitude, and creativity, but it's still a synthesized and integrated experience so people still care and commit to it but recognize it's part of a bigger system.

With respect to control and structure, Balsillie believed organization charts were anachronistic and only useful insofar as outlining basic authority and reporting relationships (see Exhibit 9 for an organization chart). He described RIM's internal communication as more fluid than hierarchical. He also rejected the idea of formal controls as necessary to monitor work efforts.

Formal controls create a way to hide because you can hide in the system—there are teams and groups and the transparency and collaboration make it pretty hard to be a renegade. . . . If you play a team sport you can't have five people doing their own thing—there is a system and an element of structure but a good system has lots of decision-making and creativity on the court. . . . These are smart people—you don't want to tell them what to do—as long as it resonates with their belief system, they will do it.

He did admit, however, that although visibility, transparency, and collaboration were important elements in the organization's success, his own visibility had declined and he was seeing less of everything due to the company's increased size and his responsibilities.

Strategy

Balsillie described RIM's approach to strategy as similar to white-water rafting. He and Lazaridis both believed that focusing on the fundamentals and identifying imperatives rather than setting specific expectations for the future was the right approach to ensuring success. Balsillie described their approach to strategy as follows:

The way you become a good white water rafter is fundamentally managing well what is in front of you now, and positioning for the next step—to go beyond that is useless and it takes you away from doing what you have before you now because there are too many contingent events and too much uncertainty to predict. If you focus on the fundamentals, the totality is better—if you look at it and say 'I want 10 percent more sales, what do I have to do?' I think you're coming at it backwards. How many sales do I want? Every last dollar I can possibly get.

Balsillie described the strategic decision-making process as, "anything but ad hoc—it was deliberate, specific, and highly integrative." It involved consultation and collaboration with top management and relevant areas of the organization. He stated that this was important to him and Lazaridis not only so that they were making the best decision possible, but also so that all areas of the organization could understand what was being done and why, recognize the importance of their role in it, and ensure that they could be more adaptive to changing conditions.

EXAMINING CHOICES AS COMPETITION CHANGES

Balsillie smiled when he thought how flattering it was that a new product like the iPhone was described as a "BlackBerry killer." It signaled that RIM's products were the ones to beat. However, he recognized that the industry was changing—competitors were increasing and moving into RIM's enterprise market, and the technology was converging. His objective was to get every last sales dollar he could for RIM, and be well-positioned to avoid "rocks" down the road. The analysts' debate about which market RIM should emphasize was in the back of his mind as he considered RIM's situation.

EXHIBIT 9   Research In Motion's Organization Chart

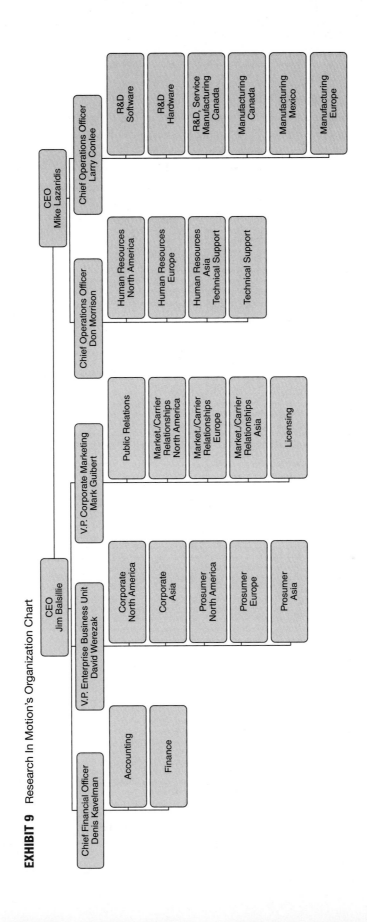

GLOSSARY

Corporate mail server: A corporate mail server is a software application on a dedicated corporate computer that receives incoming e-mails and forwards outgoing e-mails for delivery. It is similar to a virtual mailroom in a company.

Encryption: Encryption software translates data into a secret code that is unreadable until it is "decrypted." Encryption is the most effective way to achieve data security.

Enterprise: a business—the enterprise market refers to the market segment where the entire company adopts a product. The devices are approved and installed by the organization; installation, support, and control is managed by the organization's information technology (IT) department.

Multimedia: a combination of media such as text, audio, video, graphics, and interactive features that can be used to inform or entertain the user (i.e., a video game or a television program).

Push: Push e-mail means that an e-mail message is automatically redirected to the user's handheld device, and the user is notified of its arrival. This is in contrast to "pull" e-mail systems where the user must connect with and retrieve e-mail manually.

QWERTY: The QWERTY keyboard is the standard keyboard letter configuration that allows users to benefit from the familiarity of letter locations and type faster and with less frustration than on a telephone touchpad.

Case

10

Dell Inc. in 2008:
Can It Overtake
Hewlett-Packard as
the Worldwide Leader
in Personal
Computers?

Arthur A. Thompson, Jr. *University of Alabama*
John E. Gamble *University of South Alabama*

In 1984, at the age of 19, Michael Dell invested $1,000 of his own money and founded Dell Computer with a simple vision and business concept—that personal computers (PCs) could be built to order and sold directly to customers. Michael Dell believed his approach to the PC business had two advantages: (1) bypassing distributors and retail dealers eliminated the markups of resellers, and (2) building to order greatly reduced the costs and risks associated with carrying large stocks of parts, components, and finished goods. Between 1986 and 1993, the company worked to refine its strategy, build an adequate infrastructure, and establish market credibility against better-known rivals. In the mid-to-late 1990s, Dell's strategy started to click into full gear. By 2003, Dell's sell-direct and build-to-order business model and strategy had provided the company with the most efficient procurement, manufacturing, and distribution capabilities in the global PC industry and given Dell a substantial cost and profit margin advantage over rival PC vendors.

During 2004–2005, Dell overtook Hewlett-Packard (HP) to become the global market leader in PCs. But Dell's global leadership proved short-lived; HP, energized by a new CEO who engineered a revitalized strategy, dramatically closed the gap on Dell in 2006 and regained the global market share lead by a fairly wide margin in 2007—winning an 18.8 percent global share versus Dell's 14.9 percent. In the United States, Dell also struggled to fend off a resurgent HP during 2006–2007. Whereas Dell had a commanding 33.6 percent share of PC sales in the United States in 2005, comfortably ahead of HP (19.5 percent) and far outdistancing Apple, Acer, Toshiba, Gateway, and Lenovo/IBM, Dell's U.S. share had slipped to 28.0 percent by the end of 2007, while HP's share was up to 23.9 percent. Exhibit 1 shows the shifting domestic and global sales and market share rankings in PCs during 1998–2007.

Since the late 1990s, Dell had also been driving for industry leadership in servers. In the mid-to-late 1990s, a big fraction of the servers sold were proprietary machines running on customized Unix operating systems and carrying price tags ranging from $30,000 to $1 million or more. But a seismic shift in server technology, coupled with growing cost-consciousness on the part of server users, produced a radical shift away from more costly, proprietary, Unix-based servers during 1999–2004 to low-cost x86 machines that were based on standardized components and technology, ran on either Windows or Linux operating systems, and carried price tags below $10,000. Servers with these characteristics fit Dell's strategy and capabilities perfectly, and the company seized on the opportunity to use its considerable resources and capabilities in making low-cost, standard-technology PCs to go after the market for low- and mid-range x86 servers in a big way. During 2004–2007, Dell reigned as the number one domestic seller of x86 servers for Windows and Linux (based on unit volume), with just over a 30 percent market share (up from about 3–4 percent in the mid-1990s). Dell ranked number two in the world in x86 server shipments during this same period, with market shares in the 24–26 percent range, which put it in position to contend with HP for global market leadership.

In addition, Dell was making market inroads in other product categories. Its sales of data storage devices had grown to nearly $2.5 billion annually, aided by a strategic alliance with EMC, a leader in data storage. In 2001–2002, Dell began selling low-cost, data-routing switches—a product category where Cisco Systems was the dominant global leader. Starting in 2003, Dell began marketing Dell-branded printers and printer cartridges, product categories that provided global leader HP with the lion's share of its profits; as of 2008, Dell's sales of printers and printer supplies was believed to exceed $3 billion. Also in 2003, Dell began selling flat-screen LCD TVs and retail-store systems, including electronic cash registers, specialized software, services, and peripherals required to link retail-store checkout lanes to corporate information systems. Dell's MP3 player, the Dell DJ, was number two behind the Apple iPod. Dell added plasma screen TVs to its TV product line in 2004. Since the late 1990s, Dell had been marketing CD and DVD drives, printers, scanners, modems, monitors, digital cameras, memory cards, data storage devices, and speakers made by a variety of manufacturers.

So far, Dell's foray into new products and businesses had, in most cases, proved to be profitable—for a time, Dell sold handheld PC devices, an MP3 player (called the Dell DJ) that competed against the Apple iPod, and big-screen TVs, but these products were abandoned when profits proved elusive. According to Michael Dell, "We believe that all our businesses should make money. If a business doesn't make money, if you can't figure out how to make money in that business, you shouldn't be in that business."[1] Dell products were sold in more than 170 countries, but sales in 60 countries accounted for about 95 percent of total revenues.

---

[1]As quoted in "Dell Puts Happy Customers First," *Nikkei Weekly,* December 16, 2002.

EXHIBIT 1 U.S. and Global Market Shares of Leading PC Vendors, 1998–2007

A. U.S. Market Shares of the Leading PC Vendors, 1998–2005

2003 Rank	Vendor	2007 Shipments (in 000s)	2007 Market Share	2006 Shipments (in 000s)	2006 Market Share	2005 Shipments (in 000s)	2005 Market Share	2004 Shipments (in 000s)	2004 Market Share	2002 Shipments (in 000s)	2002 Market Share	2000 Shipments (in 000s)	2000 Market Share	1998 Shipments (in 000s)	1998 Market Share
1	Dell	19,645	28.0%	20,472	31.2%	21,466	33.6%	19,296	33.7%	13,324	27.9%	9,645	19.7%	4,799	13.2%
2	Hewlett-Packard[1]	16,759	23.9	11,600	21.5	12,456	19.5	11,600	20.3	8,052	16.8	5,630	11.5	2,832	7.8
	Compaq[1]	—		—		—				—	—	7,761	15.9	6,052	16.7
3	Apple	4,081	5.8	3,109	4.7	2,555	4.0	1,935	3.3	1,693	3.5	n.a.	n.a.	n.a.	n.a.
4	Acer[2]	3,860	5.5	1,421	2.2	n.a.	n.a.	n.a.	n.a.	n.a.	n.a.	n.a.	n.a.	n.a.	n.a.
5	Toshiba	3,509	5.0	2,843	4.3	2,327	3.6	2,945	5.1	2,725	5.7	4,237	8.7	3,039	8.4
	Gateway	—		n.a.	n.a.	n.a.	n.a.	n.a.	n.a.	n.a.	n.a.	n.a.	n.a.	n.a.	n.a.
	Lenovo/IBM[3]	n.a.	n.a.	n.a.	n.a.	n.a.	n.a.	2,932	5.0	2,531	5.3	2,668	5.5	2,983	8.2
	Others	22,235	31.7	23,350	35.7	25,070	39.2	24,425	33.6	19,514	40.8	18,959	38.8	16,549	45.6
	All vendors	70,088	100.0%	65,481	100.0%	63,874	100.0%	57,256	100.0%	47,839	100.0%	48,900	100.0%	36,254	100.0%

B. Worldwide Market Shares of the Leading PC Vendors, 1998–2007[4]

2003 Rank	Vendor	2007 Shipments (in 000s)	2007 Market Share	2006 Shipments (in 000s)	2006 Market Share	2005 Shipments (in 000s)	2005 Market Share	2004 Shipments (in 000s)	2004 Market Share	2002 Shipments (in 000s)	2002 Market Share	2000 Shipments (in 000s)	2000 Market Share	1998 Shipments (in 000s)	1998 Market Share
1	Hewlett-Packard[1]	50,526	18.8%	38,838	16.5%	32,575	15.7%	28,063	15.8%	18,432	13.6	10,327	7.4	5,743	6.3
2	Dell	39,993	14.9%	39,094	16.6	37,755	18.2	31,771	17.9	20,672	15.2%	14,801	10.6%	7,770	8.5%
—	Compaq[1]	—		—		—				—	—	17,399	12.5	13,266	14.5
3	Acer[2]	21,206	7.9	13,594	5.8	9,845	4.7	6,461	3.6	n.a.	n.a.	n.a.	n.a.	n.a.	n.a.
4	Lenovo/IBM[3]	20,224	7.5	16,609	7.1	12,979	6.2	10,492	5.9	8,292	6.2	9,308	6.7	7,946	8.7
5	Toshiba	10,936	4.1	9,292	3.9	7,234	3.5	n.a.	n.a.	n.a.	n.a.	n.a.	n.a.	n.a.	n.a.
	Others	126,075	46.9	117,971	50.1	107,450	51.7	100,693	52.7	73,237	54.9	80,640	58	50,741	55.5
	All Vendors	268,960	100.0%	235,397	100.0%	207,837	100.0%	177,480	100.0%	133,466	100.0%	139,057	100.0%	91,442	100.0%

n.a. = not available; sales and market shares for these companies in the years where n.a. appears are included in the "Others" category because the company was not in the top five in shipments or market share.

[1]Compaq was acquired by Hewlett-Packard in May 2002. The 2002 data for Hewlett-Packard include both Compaq-branded and Hewlett-Packard-branded PCs for the last three quarters of 2002 plus only Hewlett-Packard-branded PCs for Q1 2002. Compaq's worldwide PC shipments during Q1 2002 were 3,367,000; its U.S. PC shipments during Q1 2002 were 1,280,000 units. Compaq's line of PCs were later rebranded and absorbed into Hewlett-Packard PC offerings.

[2]Acer acquired Gateway in 2007. Data for Acer include shipments for Gateway starting in Q4 2007, and only Acer data for prior periods.

[3]Lenovo, a Chinese computer company, completed the acquisition of IBM's PC business in the second quarter of 2005 (the deal was made in December 2004). The numbers for Lenovo/IBM for 1998–2004 reflect sales of IBM branded PCs only; the numbers for 2005–2007 reflect their combined sales beginning in the second quarter of 2005. In 2007, Lenovo rebranded all IBM PCs as Lenovo.

[4]The worldwide market share data includes branded shipments only and excludes sales of units carrying the brands of other PC producers and marketers; shipments of Compaq PCs for last three quarters of 2002 are included in 2002 figures for Hewlett-Packard due to HP's acquisition of Compaq.

Source: International Data Corporation.

COMPANY BACKGROUND

At age 12, Michael Dell was running a mail order stamp-trading business, complete with a national catalog, and grossing $2,000 a month. At 16 he was selling subscriptions to the *Houston Post,* and at 17 he bought his first BMW with the money he had earned. He enrolled at the University of Texas in 1983 as a premed student (his parents wanted him to become a doctor), but he soon became immersed in computers and started selling PC components out of his college dormitory room. He bought random-access memory (RAM) chips and disk drives for IBM PCs at cost from IBM dealers, who at the time often had excess supplies on hand because they were required to order large monthly quotas from IBM. Dell resold the components through newspaper ads (and later through ads in national computer magazines) at 10–15 percent below the regular retail price.

By April 1984, sales were running about $80,000 per month. Dell decided to drop out of college and form a company, PCs Ltd., to sell both PC components and PCs under the brand name PCs Limited. He obtained his PCs by buying retailers' surplus stocks at cost, then powering them up with graphics cards, hard disks, and memory before reselling them. His strategy was to sell directly to end users; by eliminating the retail markup, Dell's new company was able to sell IBM clones (machines that copied the functioning of IBM PCs using the same or similar components) about 40 percent below the price of IBM's best-selling PCs. The discounting strategy was successful, attracting price-conscious buyers and generating rapid revenue growth. By 1985, the company was assembling its own PC designs with a few people working on six-foot tables. The company had 40 employees, and Michael Dell worked 18-hour days, often sleeping on a cot in his office. By the end of fiscal 1986, sales had reached $33 million.

During the next several years, however, PCs Limited was hampered by growing pains—specifically, a lack of money, people, and resources. Michael Dell sought to refine the company's business model; add needed production capacity; and build a bigger, deeper management staff and corporate infrastructure while at the same time keeping costs low. The company was renamed Dell Computer in 1987, and the first international offices were opened that same year. In 1988, Dell added a sales force to serve large customers, began selling to government agencies, and became a public company—raising $34.2 million in its first offering of common stock. Sales to large customers quickly became the dominant part of Dell's business. By 1990, Dell Computer had sales of $388 million, a market share of 2–3 percent, and an R&D staff of more than 150 people. Michael Dell's vision was for Dell Computer to become one of the top three PC companies.

Thinking its direct sales business would not grow fast enough, in 1990–93, the company began distributing its computer products through Soft Warehouse Superstores (now Comp-USA), Staples (a leading office products chain), Wal-Mart, Sam's Club, and Price Club (which merged with Costco in 1993). Dell also sold PCs through Best Buy stores in 16 states and through Xerox in 19 Latin American countries. But when the company learned how thin its margins were in selling through such distribution channels, it realized it had made a mistake and withdrew from selling to retailers and other intermediaries in 1994 to refocus on direct sales. At the time, sales through retailers accounted for only about 2 percent of Dell's revenues.

In 1993, further problems emerged: Dell reportedly lost $38 million in risky foreign-currency hedging, quality difficulties arose with certain PC lines made by the company's contract manufacturers, profit margins declined, and buyers were turned off by the company's laptop PC models. To get laptop sales back on track, the company took a charge of $40 million to write off its laptop line and suspended sales of laptops until it could get redesigned models into the marketplace.

Because of higher costs and unacceptably low profit margins in selling to individuals and households, Dell did not pursue the consumer market aggressively until sales to individuals at the company's Internet site took off in 1996 and 1997. It became clear that PC-savvy individuals, who were buying their second and third computers, wanted powerful computers with multiple features; did not need much technical support; and liked the convenience of buying direct from Dell, ordering a PC configured exactly to their liking, and having it delivered to their door within a matter of days. In early 1997, Dell created an internal sales and marketing group dedicated to serving the individual consumer segment and introduced a product line designed especially for home and personal use.

By late 1997, Dell had become a low-cost leader among PC vendors by wringing greater and greater efficiency out of its direct sales and build-to-order business model. Since then, the company had continued driving hard to reduce its costs by closely partnering with key suppliers to drive costs out of its supply chain and by incorporating e-commerce technology and use of the Internet into its everyday business practices. Throughout 2002–2007, Dell was widely regarded as the lowest-cost producer among all the leading vendors of PCs and servers worldwide. Moreover, its products were highly regarded; in 2007, Dell products received more than 400 awards relating to design, quality, and innovation—this was the largest number of product awards for a single year in the company's history.

In its 2008 fiscal year, Dell posted revenues of $61.1 billion and profits of nearly $3.0 billion. It ranked number 34 on *Fortune*'s list of the 500 largest U.S. corporations for 2007. In 2008, Dell had approximately 88,200 employees worldwide, up from 16,000 at year-end 1997; more than 66 percent of Dell's employees were located in countries outside the United States, and this percentage was growing. The company's headquarters and main office complex was in Round Rock, Texas (an Austin suburb). Its name had been changed from Dell Computer to Dell Inc. in 2003 to reflect the company's growing business base outside of PCs. Exhibits 2 and 3 provide information about Dell's financial performance and geographic operations.

Michael Dell

In the company's early days Michael Dell hung around mostly with the company's engineers. He was so shy that some employees thought he was stuck up because he never talked to them. But people who worked with him closely described him as a likable young man who was slow to warm up to strangers.[2] He was a terrible public speaker and wasn't good at running meetings. But Lee Walker, a 51-year-old venture capitalist brought in by Michael Dell to provide much-needed managerial and financial experience during the company's organization-building years, became Michael Dell's mentor, built up his confidence, and was instrumental in turning him into a polished executive.[3] Walker served as the company's president and chief operating officer from 1986 to 1990; he had a fatherly image, knew everyone by name, and played a key role in implementing Michael Dell's marketing ideas. Under Walker's tutelage, Michael Dell became intimately familiar with all parts of the business, overcame his shyness, learned to control his ego, and turned into a charismatic leader with an instinct for motivating people and winning their loyalty and respect.

When Walker had to leave the company in 1990 for health reasons, Dell turned to Morton Meyerson, former CEO and president of Electronic Data Systems, for advice and guidance on how to transform Dell Computer from a fast-growing medium-sized company into a billion-dollar enterprise. Though sometimes given to displays of impatience, Michael Dell usually spoke in a quiet reflective manner and came across as a person with maturity

---

[2]"Michael Dell: On Managing Growth," *MIS Week,* September 5, 1988, p. 1.
[3]"The Education of Michael Dell," *BusinessWeek,* March 22, 1993, p. 86.

EXHIBIT 2 Selected Financial Statement Data for Dell Inc., Fiscal Years 2000–2008 ($ in millions, except per share data)

	Fiscal Year Ended								
	February 1, 2008	February 2, 2007	February 3, 2006	January 28, 2005	January 30, 2004	February 1, 2002	January 28, 2000		

RESULTS OF OPERATIONS

	February 1, 2008	February 2, 2007	February 3, 2006	January 28, 2005	January 30, 2004	February 1, 2002	January 28, 2000
Net revenue	$61,133	$57,420	$55,788	$49,121	$41,327	$31,168	$25,265
Cost of revenue	49,462	47,904	45,897	40,103	33,764	25,661	20,047
Gross margin	11,671	9,516	9,891	9,018	7,563	5,507	5,218
Gross profit margin	19.1%	16.6%	17.7%	18.4%	18.3%	17.7%	20.7%
Operating expenses:							
Selling, general and administrative[a]	7,538	5,948	5,051	4,352	3,604	2,784	2,387
Research, development and engineering[b]	693	498	458	460	434	452	374
Special charges	—	—	—	—	—	482	194
Total operating expenses	8,231	6,446	5,509	4,812	4,038	3,718	2,955
Total operating expenses as a % of net revenues	13.5%	11.2%	9.9%	9.8%	9.8%	10.4%[c]	10.9%[c]
Operating income	3,440	3,070	4,382	4,206	3,525	1,789	2,263
Operating profit margin	5.6%	5.3%	7.9%	8.6%	8.5%	5.7%	9.0%
Investment and other income (loss), net	387	275	26	197	186	(58)	188
Income before income taxes, extraordinary loss, and cumulative effect of change in accounting principle	3,827	3,345	4,608	4,403	3,711	1,731	2,451
Provision for income taxes	880	762	1,006	1,385	1,086	485	785
Net income	$ 2,947	$ 2,583	$ 3,602	$ 3,018	$ 2,625	$ 1,246	$ 1,666
Net profit margin	4.8%	5.8%	6.5%	6.1%	6.4%	4.0%	6.6%
Earnings per common share: Basic	$1.33	$1.15	$1.50	$1.20	$1.02	$0.48	$0.66
Diluted	$1.31	$1.14	$1.47	$1.18	$1.01	$0.46	$0.61
Weighted average shares outstanding: Basic	2,223	2,255	2,403	2,509	2,565	2,602	2,536
Diluted	2,247	2,271	2,449	2,568	2,619	2,726	2,728

CASH FLOW AND BALANCE-SHEET DATA

	February 1, 2008	February 2, 2007	February 3, 2006	January 28, 2005	January 30, 2004	February 1, 2002	January 28, 2000
Net cash provided by operating activities	$ 3,949	$ 3,969	$ 4,751	$ 5,821	$ 3,670	$ 3,797	$ 3,926
Cash, cash equivalents, and short-term investments	7,972	10,298	9,070	9,807	11,922	8,287	6,853
Total assets	27,561	25,635	23,252	23,215	19,311	13,535	11,560
Long-term debt	362	569	625	505	505	520	508
Total stockholders' equity	3,735	4,328	4,047	6,485	6,280	4,694	5,308

[a]Includes stock-based compensation expenses for fiscal years 2007 and 2008, pursuant to Statement of Financial Accounting Standards No. 123.
[b]Includes one-time in-process research and development charges of $83 million related to companies acquired by Dell during fiscal 2008.
[c]Excluding special charges.
Sources: Dell Inc., 10-K reports, 2002, 2005–2008.

EXHIBIT 3   Dell's Geographic Area Performance, Fiscal Years 2000–2008 ($ in millions)

	February 1, 2008	February 2, 2007	February 3, 2006	January 28, 2005	January 30, 2004	February 1, 2002	January 28, 2000
NET REVENUES							
Americas							
Business	$31,144	$29,311	$28,365	$25,289	$21,824	$17,275	$15,160
U.S. consumer	6,244	7,069	7,960	7,614	6,696	4,485	2,719
Total Americas	37,368	36,380	36,325	32,903	28,520	21,760	17,879
Europe/Middle East/Africa	15,267	13,682	12,887	10,753	8,472	6,429	5,590
Asia-Pacific/ Japan	8,498	7,358	6,576	5,465	4,335	2,979	1,796
Total net revenues	$61,133	$57,420	$55,788	$49,121	$41,444	$31,168	$25,265
OPERATING INCOME							
Americas							
Business	$ 2,549	$ 2,388	$ 2,956	$ 2,534	$ 2,229	$ 1,482	$ 1,800
U.S. consumer	(59)	135	452	414	373	260	204
Total Americas	2,490	2,523	3,408	2,948	2,602	1,742	2,004
Europe/Middle East/Africa	1,009	583	871	815	614	377	359
Asia-Pacific/ Japan	471	332	524	443	309	152	94
Special charges	(530)	(368)	(421)	—	—	(482)	(194)
Total operating income	$ 3,440	$ 3,070	$ 4,382	$ 4,206	$ 3,525	$ 1,789	$ 2,263

Sources: Dell Inc., 10-K reports, 2002, 2005 and 2008; financial data posted at www.dell.com (accessed May 6, 2008).

and seasoned judgment far beyond his age. His prowess was based more on an astute combination of technical knowledge and marketing know-how than on being a technological wizard. In 1992, at the age of 27, Michael Dell became the youngest CEO ever to head a Fortune 500 company; he was a billionaire at the age of 31.

By the late 1990s, Michael Dell had become one of the most respected executives in the PC industry. Journalists had described him as "the quintessential American entrepreneur" and "the most innovative guy for marketing computers." He was a much-sought-after speaker at industry and company conferences. His views and opinions about the future of PCs, the Internet, and e-commerce practices carried considerable weight both in the PC industry and among executives worldwide. Once pudgy and bespectacled, in early 2008, 43-year-old Michael Dell was physically fit, considered good-looking, wore contact lenses, ate only health foods, and lived in a three-story 33,000-square-foot home on a 60-acre estate in Austin, Texas, with his wife and four children. In 2008, he owned about 10 percent of Dell's common stock, worth about $4.3 billion.

Michael Dell was considered a very accessible CEO and a role model for young executives because he had done what many of them were trying to do. He delegated authority to subordinates, believing that the best results came from "turning loose talented people who can be relied upon to do what they're supposed to do." Business associates viewed Michael Dell as an aggressive personality, an extremely competitive risk taker who had always played close to the edge. He spent about 30 percent of his time traveling to company operations and meeting with customers. In a typical year, he would make two or three trips to Europe and two trips to Asia.

In mid-2004, Michael Dell, who had been the company's first and only CEO, transferred his title of CEO to Kevin Rollins, the company's president and chief operating officer. Dell remained as chairman of the board. Dell and Rollins had run the company for the past seven years under a shared leadership structure. The changes were primarily ones of title, not of roles or responsibilities. But when the company's performance stalled in 2006, Kevin Rollins was relieved of his responsibilities and Michael Dell reassumed the title of CEO (and continued in the role of chairman of the company's board of directors).

DELL'S STRATEGY AND BUSINESS MODEL

In orchestrating Dell Inc.'s rise to global prominence, company executives had come to believe strongly that four tenets were the key to delivering superior customer value:[4]

1. Selling direct to customers is the most efficient way to market the company's products because it eliminates wholesale and retail dealers that impede Dell's understanding of customer needs and expectations and that add unnecessary time and cost.

2. Allowing customers to purchase custom-built products and custom-tailored services is the most effective way to meet customer needs.

3. A highly efficient supply chain and manufacturing organization, grounded in the use of standardized technologies and selling direct, paves the way for a low-cost structure where cost savings can be passed along to customers in the form of lower prices.

4. Dell can deliver added value to customers by (1) researching all the technological options, (2) trying to determine which ones are "optimal" in the sense of delivering the best combination of performance and efficiency, and (3) being accountable to customers for helping them obtain the highest return on their investment in IT products and services. In almost all cases, non-proprietary, standardized technologies deliver the best value to customers.

With top management holding firmly to these tenets, Dell's strategy during the 2002–2007 period had seven core elements: (1) making build-to-order manufacturing progressively more cost-efficient, (2) partnering closely with suppliers to squeeze cost savings out of the supply chain, (3) using direct sales techniques to gain customers, (4) expanding into additional products and services to capture a bigger share of customers' IT spending, (5) providing good customer service and technical support, (6) keeping R&D and engineering activities focused squarely on better meeting the needs of customers, and (7) using standardized technologies in all product offerings.

The business model on which the strategy was predicated was straightforward: Continuously search for ways to reduce costs—the company's latest initiative was to reduce costs by $3 billion in 2008. Use the company's strong capabilities in supply chain management, low-cost manufacturing, and direct sales to grow sales and market share in both the PC and server segments and expand into product categories where Dell could provide added value to its customers in the form of lower prices. The standard pattern for entering new product categories was to identify an IT product with good margins, figure out how to build it (or else have it built by others) cheaply enough to be able to significantly underprice competitive products; market the new product to Dell's steadily growing customer base, and watch the market share points, incremental revenues, and incremental profits pile up.

[4]Dell's 2005 10-K report, pp. 1–2.

Cost-Efficient Build-to-Order Manufacturing

Dell built the vast majority of its computers, workstations, and servers to order; only a small fraction was produced for inventory and shipped to wholesale or retail partners. Dell customers could order custom-equipped servers and workstations according to the needs of their applications. Desktop and laptop customers ordered whatever configuration of microprocessor speed, random-access memory, hard disk capacity, CD or DVD drives, fax/modem/wireless capabilities, graphics cards, monitor size, speakers, and other accessories they preferred. The orders were directed to the nearest factory. In 2008, Dell had assembly plants in Austin, Texas; Nashville, Tennessee; Winston-Salem, North Carolina; Limerick, Ireland; Xiamen, China; Penang, Malaysia; Hortolândia, Brazil; Chennai, India; and Lodz, Poland. In March 2008, the company announced that its desktop assembly plant in Austin, Texas, would be closed. The Winston-Salem plant was Dell's largest when it opened in 2005 and had the capacity to assemble 15,000 to 20,000 desktops per day—it could turn out a new PC every five seconds. Dell shipped about 140,000 products daily—about 1 every second. PCs, workstations, and servers were assembled at all locations; assembly of lower-volume products was concentrated in a more limited number of locations. All plants used much the same production systems and procedures. Typically, a plant had the capability to build and deliver a customer's order in three to five business days; however, the Winston-Salem plant could in most cases deliver orders to customers on the eastern coast of the United States in one to three business days. Dell believed in building its assembly plants close to customers because the labor costs to assemble a PC were about $10 whereas the logistics costs to move parts and ship a finished PC were about $40.[5]

Ongoing Improvements in Assembly Efficiency

Until 1997, Dell operated its assembly lines in traditional fashion, with each worker performing a single operation. An order form accompanied each metal chassis across the production floor; drives, chips, and ancillary items were installed to match customer specifications. As a partly assembled PC arrived at a new workstation, the operator, standing beside a tall steel rack with drawers full of components, was instructed what to do by little red and green lights flashing beside the drawers. When the operator was finished, the component drawers were automatically replenished from the other side and the PC chassis glided down the line to the next workstation. However, Dell had reorganized its plants in 1997, shifting to "cell manufacturing" techniques whereby a team of workers operating at a group workstation (or cell) assembled an entire PC according to customer specifications. The shift to cell manufacturing reduced Dell's assembly times by 75 percent and doubled productivity per square foot of assembly space. Assembled computers were first tested and then loaded with the desired software, shipped, and typically delivered five to six business days after the order was placed.

Later, the cell manufacturing approach was gradually abandoned in favor of an even more efficient assembly-line approach that allowed workers to turn out close to 800 desktop PCs per hour on three assembly lines that took half the floor space of the cell manufacturing process, where production had run about 120 units per hour. Here the gains in assembly efficiency were achieved partly by redesigning the PCs to permit easier and faster assembly, partly by making innovations in the assembly process, and partly by reducing (by 50 percent) the number of times a computer was touched by workers during assembly and shipping. In 2005, it took about 66 minutes to assemble and test a PC. Moreover, just-in-time inventory practices that left pallets of parts sitting around everywhere had been tweaked to just-in-the-nick-of-time delivery by suppliers of the exact parts needed every couple of hours; double-decker conveyor belts moved parts and components to designated

[5]Remarks by Kevin Rollins in a speech at Peking University, November 2, 2005, and posted at www.dell.com.

assembly points. Newly assembled PCs were routed on conveyors to shipping, where they were boxed and shipped to customers the same day.

Dell's new 750,000-square-foot plant in Winston-Salem featured a production layout that allowed computers to be tested as its components and software were installed. This "instantaneous build and test" operation permitted team members to identify and correct any problems on the spot rather than waiting until the PC was fully assembled. Workers at all Dell plants competed with one another to come up with more efficient assembly methods. Cost-saving assembly innovations pioneered in one Dell plant were quickly implemented worldwide.

Dell's latest cost-saving initiative was to move away from 100 percent configure-to-customer-order assembly to a mixture of fixed configurations (for components that rarely varied from order to order) and flexible configurations (for components that were subject to strong and varying customer preferences—like hard drive size, screen displays, amount of memory, graphics cards, type of microprocessor, and version of Windows operating system).

Dell was regarded as a world-class manufacturing innovator and a pioneer in how to mass-produce a customized product—its methods were routinely studied in business schools worldwide. Several of Dell's PC rivals—most notably Hewlett-Packard—had given up on trying to produce their own PCs as cheaply as Dell and shifted to outsourcing their PCs from contract manufacturers who specialized in PC assembly and often assembled a variety of PC brands. Dell management believed that its in-house manufacturing delivered about a 6 percent cost advantage versus outsourcing. Dell's build-to-order strategy meant that the company had only a tiny stock of finished goods inventories in-house and that, unlike competitors using the traditional value chain model, it did not have to wait for resellers to clear out their own inventories before it could push new models into the marketplace—resellers typically operated with 30 to 60 days inventory of prebuilt models (see Exhibit 4). Equally important was the fact that customers who bought from Dell got the satisfaction of having their computers customized to their particular liking and pocketbook.

Quality Control

All assembly plants had the capability to run testing and quality control processes on components, parts, and subassemblies obtained from suppliers, as well as on the finished products Dell assembled. Suppliers were urged to participate in a quality certification program that committed them to achieving defined quality specifications. Quality control activities were undertaken at various stages in the assembly process. In addition, Dell's quality control program included testing of completed units after assembly, ongoing production reliability audits, failure tracking for early identification of production and component problems associated with new models shipped to customers, and information obtained from customers through service and technical support programs. All of the company's plants had been certified as meeting ISO 9001:2000 standards. But while Dell's quality control program was first-rate, it was not perfect; in fiscal year 2008, Dell incurred special warranty cost charges of $307 million to service or replace certain desktop models that included a vendor part that failed to perform to specifications.

Partnerships with Suppliers

Michael Dell believed that it made much better sense for the company to partner with reputable suppliers of PC parts and components than to integrate backward and get into parts and components manufacturing on its own. He explained why:

> If you've got a race with 20 players all vying to make the fastest graphics chip in the world, do you want to be the twenty-first horse, or do you want to evaluate the field of 20 and pick the best one?[6]

---

[6]As quoted in Joan Magretta, "The Power of Virtual Integration: An Interview with Dell Computer's Michael Dell," *Harvard Business Review*, March–April 1998, p. 74.

EXHIBIT 4 Comparative Value Chain Models of PC Vendors

Traditional Build-to-Stock Value Chain Used by Hewlett Packard, IBM/Lenovo, Apple, Sony, Toshiba, and Most Others

| Manufacture and delivery of PC parts and components by suppliers | Assembly of PCs as needed to fill orders from distributors and retailers | Sales and marketing activities of PC vendors to build a brand image and establish a network of resellers | Sales and marketing activities of resellers | Purchases by PC users | Service and support activities provided to PC users by resellers (and some PC vendors) |

Dell's Build-to-Order, Sell-Direct Value Chain

| Manufacture and delivery of PC parts and components by supply partners | Custom assembly of PCs as orders are received from PC buyers | Sales and marketing activities of PC vendor to build brand image and secure orders from PC buyers | Purchases by PC users | Service and support activities provided to PC users by Dell or contract providers |

Close collaboration and real-time data sharing to drive down costs of supply chain activities, minimize inventories, keep assembly costs low, and respond quickly to changes in the make-up of customer orders

Dell management evaluated the various makers of each component; picked the best one or two as suppliers; and then stuck with them as long as they maintained their leadership in technology, performance, quality, and cost. Management believed that long-term partnerships with reputable suppliers had at least five advantages. First, using name-brand processors, disk drives, modems, speakers, and multimedia components enhanced the quality and performance of Dell's PCs. Because of varying performance among different brands of components, the brand of the components was quite important to customers concerned about performance and reliability. Second, because Dell partnered with suppliers for the long term and because it committed to purchase a specified percentage of its requirements from each supplier, Dell was assured of getting the volume of components it needed on a timely basis even when overall market demand for a particular component temporarily exceeded the overall market supply. Third, Dell's long-run commitment to its suppliers made it feasible for suppliers to locate their plants or distribution centers within a few miles of Dell assembly plants, putting them in position to make deliveries daily or every few hours, as needed. Dell supplied data on inventories and replenishment needs to its suppliers at least once a day—hourly in the case of components being delivered several times daily from nearby sources.

Fourth, long-term supply partnerships facilitated having some of the supplier's engineers assigned to Dell's product design teams and being treated as part of Dell. When new products were launched, suppliers' engineers were stationed in Dell's plants; if early buyers called with a problem related to design, further assembly and shipments were halted while the supplier's engineers and Dell personnel corrected the flaw on the spot.[7] Fifth, long-term partnerships enlisted greater cooperation on the part of suppliers to seek new ways to drive costs out of the supply chain. Dell openly shared its daily production schedules, sales forecasts, and new model introduction plans with vendors. Dell also did a three-year plan with each of its key suppliers and worked with suppliers to minimize the number of different stock-keeping units of parts and components in its products and to identify ways to drive costs down.

Commitment to Just-in-Time Inventory Practices

Dell's just-in-time inventory emphasis yielded major cost advantages and shortened the time it took for Dell to get new generations of its computer models into the marketplace. New advances were coming so fast in certain computer parts and components (particularly microprocessors, disk drives, and wireless devices) that any given item in inventory was obsolete in a matter of months, sometimes quicker. Moreover, rapid-fire reductions in the prices of components were not unusual—for example, Intel regularly cut the prices on its older chips when it introduced newer chips, and it introduced new chip generations about every three months. In 2003–2004, component costs declined an average of 0.5 percent weekly.[8] Michael Dell explained the competitive and economic advantages of minimal component inventories:

> If I've got 11 days of inventory and my competitor has 80 and Intel comes out with a new chip, that means I'm going to get to market 69 days sooner. In the computer industry, inventory can be a pretty massive risk because if the cost of materials is going down 50 percent a year and you have two or three months of inventory versus 11 days, you've got a big cost disadvantage. And you're vulnerable to product transitions, when you can get stuck with obsolete inventory.[9]

For a growing number of parts and components, Dell's close partnership with suppliers was allowing it to operate with no more than two hours of inventory.

In fiscal year 1995, Dell averaged an inventory turn cycle of 32 days. By the end of fiscal 1997 (January 1997), the average was down to 13 days. In fiscal 1998, Dell's inventory averaged 7 days, which compared very favorably with a 14-day average at Gateway, a 23-day average at then industry leader Compaq, and the estimated industrywide average of over 50 days. In fiscal years 1999 and 2000, Dell operated with an average of 6 days' supply of production materials in inventory; the average dropped to 5 days' supply in fiscal year 2001, 4 days' supply in 2002, and 2.7 to 4 days' supply in fiscal years 2003–2007.

Dell's Direct Sales Strategy and Marketing Efforts

With thousands of phone, fax, and Internet orders daily and ongoing field sales force contact with customers, the company kept its finger on the market pulse, quickly detecting shifts in sales trends, design problems, and quality glitches. If the company got more than a few of the same complaints, the information was relayed immediately to design engineers who checked out the problem. When design flaws or components defects were found, the factory was notified and the problem corrected within a few days. Management believed Dell's ability to respond quickly gave it a significant advantage over PC makers that operated on the basis of large production runs of variously configured and equipped PCs and

---

[7]Ibid., p. 75.

[8]Speech by Michael Dell at University of Toronto, September 21, 2004, www.dell.com (accessed December 15, 2004).

[9]Ibid., p. 76.

sold them through retail channels. Dell saw its direct sales approach as a totally customer-driven system, with the flexibility to transition quickly to new generations of components and PC models.

Web Site Strategy

Dell's Web site was one of the world's highest volume Internet commerce sites, with nearly 500 million unique visitors, well over 1 billion visits, and close to 10 billion page requests annually. Dell began Internet sales at its Web site in 1995, almost overnight achieving sales of $1 million a day. Sales at its Web site reached $5 million daily in 1998, $35 million daily in 2000, and $60 million a day in 2004. By early 2003, over 50 percent of Dell's sales were Web-enabled—and the percentage trended upward through 2007. The revenues generated at the Web site were greater than those generated at Yahoo, Google, eBay, and Amazon combined.[10]

At the company's Web site, prospective buyers could review Dell's entire product line in detail, configure and price customized PCs, place orders, and track orders from manufacturing through shipping. The closing rate on sales at Dell's Web site was 20 percent higher than that on sales inquiries received via telephone. Management believed that enhancing www.dell.com to shrink transaction and order fulfillment times, increase accuracy, and provide more personalized content resulted in a higher degree of "e-loyalty" than traditional attributes like price and product selection.

Dell's Customer-Based Sales and Marketing Focus

Whereas many technology companies organized their sales and marketing efforts around product lines, Dell was organized around customer groups. Dell had placed managers in charge of developing sales and service programs appropriate to the needs and expectations of each customer group. Until the early 1990s, Dell operated with sales and service programs aimed at just two market segments—high-volume corporate and governmental buyers and low-volume business and individual buyers. But as sales took off in 1995–1997, these segments were subdivided into finer, more homogeneous categories that by 2000 included global enterprise accounts, large and midsize companies (over 400 employees), small companies (under 400 employees), health care businesses (over 400 employees), federal government agencies, state and local government agencies, educational institutions, and individual consumers. Many of these customer segments were further subdivided—for instance, in education, there were separate sales and marketing programs for K–12 schools; higher education institutions; and personal-use purchases by faculty, staff, and students.

Dell had a field sales force that called on large business and institutional customers throughout the world. Dell's largest global enterprise accounts were assigned their own dedicated sales force—for example, Dell had a sales force of 150 people dedicated to meeting the needs of General Electric's facilities and personnel scattered across the world. Individuals and small businesses could place orders by telephone or at Dell's Web site. Dell had call centers in the United States, Canada, Europe, and Asia with toll-free lines; customers could talk with a sales representative about specific models, get information faxed or mailed to them, place an order, and pay by credit card. The Asian and European call centers were equipped with technology that routed calls from a particular country to a particular call center. Thus, for example, a customer calling from Lisbon, Portugal, was automatically directed to a Portuguese-speaking sales rep at the call center in Montpelier, France.

However, in some countries Dell's sell-direct-to-customers strategy put it at a disadvantage in appealing to small business customers and individual consumers, since most of these customers were reluctant to place orders by phone or over the Internet. Rivals in

---

[10]Remarks by Michael Dell, Gartner Symposium, Orlando, FL, October 20, 2005, www.dell.com.

Japan and China who marketed PCs through retailers and other resellers were outselling Dell in the small business and household segments. According to an executive at Lenovo, one of Dell's biggest rivals in China, "It takes two years of a person's savings to buy a PC in China. And when two years of savings is at stake, the whole family wants to come out to a store to touch and try the machine."[11] To address the reluctance of households to buy direct from Dell, the head of Dell's consumer PC sales group in Japan installed 34 kiosks in leading electronics stores around Japan, allowing shoppers to test Dell computers, ask questions of staff, and place orders—close to half the sales were to people who did not know about Dell prior to visiting the kiosk. The kiosks proved quite popular and were instrumental in boosting Dell's share of PC sales to consumers in Japan.

Inspired by the success of kiosks in Japan, in 2002, Dell began installing Dell Direct Store kiosks in a variety of U.S. retail settings as a hands-on complement to Internet and phone sales. The kiosk stores showcased Dell's newest notebook and desktop computers, plasma and LCD TVs, printers, and music players. The kiosks did not carry inventory, but customers could talk face-to-face with a knowledgeable Dell sales representative, inspect Dell's products, and order them on the Internet while at the kiosk. The kiosks were considered a success in getting consumers to try Dell products. More kiosks were added and, by December 2005, Dell had 145 Dell Direct Store kiosks in 20 states, within reach of more than 50 percent of the U.S. population.

Supplementing the Direct Sales Strategy with Sales at the Retail Stores of Select Partners

In fiscal 2006, Dell's share of PC sales to U.S. households dropped to 25.6 percent from 29.3 percent the prior year. In 2007, its share of the home or consumer market in the United States dropped even more precipitously, to 18.9 percent (see Exhibit 5). Sales to households weakened in other parts of the world market as well. The declines were partly due (1) to Hewlett-Packard's aggressive and successful efforts (mainly, lower pricing and better feature sets) to gain market share at Dell's expense and (2) to surging U.S. sales of Apple's PC models (see Exhibit 1), buoyed chiefly by consumer infatuation with Apple's iPod models and its new iPhone. Dell management responded to the unexpected and unprecedented falloff in sales to households by backing off on its almost 100 percent commitment to selling direct and forging partnerships with such retailers as Wal-Mart, Staples, and Best Buy to begin offering select Dell PCs in retail stores. Similar initiatives to begin selling through retailers were taken in other parts of the world market. In Latin America, Dell forged retailing partnerships with Wal-Mart and Pontofrio. Dell's retailing partners in Europe, the Middle East, and Africa included Carphone Warehouse, Carrefour, Tesco, and DSGi. In China, Japan, and other parts of the Asia-Pacific region, Dell began selling its PCs at the stores of Gome (the leading consumer electronics retailer in China), Suning, Hontu, HiMart, Courts, Croma, Officeworks (104 stores in Australia), and Bic Camera. By mid-2008, Dell had its products available in 12,000 retail stores worldwide and planned to grow this number considerably.

So far, Dell management was pleased with the initial results of its shift to using retail stores as a way to supplement online and telephone sales to consumers and small businesses.

Expansion into New Products

In recent years, Dell had expanded its product offerings to include data storage hardware, switches, handheld PCs, printers, and printer cartridges, and software products in an effort to diversify its revenue stream and use its competitive capabilities in PCs and servers to

---

[11]Quoted in Neel Chowdhury, "Dell Cracks China," *Fortune,* June 21, 1999, p. 121.

EXHIBIT 5   Trends in Dell's Market Shares in PCs and x86 Servers, 1994–2007

Market Segment	Dell's Market Share								
	2007	2006	2005	2004	2002	2000	1998	1996	1994
Worldwide share by geographic area	14.9%	17.2%	18.2%	17.7%	14.9%	10.5%	8.0%	4.1%	2.7%
United States	29.3	31.3	33.6	33.1	28.0	18.4	12.0	6.4	4.2
Europe/Middle East/Africa	11.0	12.2	12.5	11.5	9.6	7.8	7.0	3.8	2.4
Asia-Pacific	8.9	8.8	8.2	7.0	4.8	3.4	2.4	1.3	0.3
Japan	14.0	14.2	12.3	11.3	7.7	4.0	3.0	1.6	1.1
Worldwide share by product									
Desktop PCs	15.0%	17.2%	18.2%	18.0%	14.8%	10.1%	7.8%	4.3%	3.0%
Notebook PCs	14.2	16.4	17.3	16.2	14.4	11.3	8.5	3.4	1.1
x86 Servers	25.0	25.6	26.3	24.8	21.7	15.4	9.7	3.4	3.1
U.S. segment share	29.3%	31.3%	33.1%	33.1%	28.0%	18.4%	12.0%	6.4%	4.2%
Education	40.7	43.8	44.6	44.3	34.9	26.2	11.0	3.9	1.1
Government	37.7	33.2	36.0	32.9	33.7	22.9	14.6	6.5	7.1
Home	18.9	25.6	29.3	29.7	22.7	6.5	3.5	2.1	1.2
Large business	43.3	43.7	43.3	44.2	39.9	31.3	21.6	11.2	6.9
Small/medium business	29.1	27.0	29.2	28.5	24.2	22.6	14.3	7.9	5.4

Source: Information posted at www.dell.com (accessed May 6, 2008).

pursue growth opportunities. Michael Dell explained why Dell had decided to expand into products and services that complemented its sales of PCs and servers:

> We tend to look at what is the next big opportunity all the time. We can't take on too many of these at once, because it kind of overloads the system. But we believe fundamentally that if you think about the whole market, it's about an $800 billion market, all areas of technology over time go through a process of standardization or commoditization. And we try to look at those, anticipate what's happening, and develop strategies that will allow us to get into those markets. In the server market in 1995 we had a 2 percent market share, today we have over a 30 percent share, we're number 1 in the U.S. How did that happen? Well, first of all it happened because we started to have a high market share for desktops and notebooks. Then customers said, oh yes, we know Dell, those are the guys who have really good desktops and notebooks. So they have servers, yes, we'll test those, we'll test them around the periphery, maybe not in the most critical applications at first, but we'll test them here. [Then they discover] these are really good and Dell provides great support . . . and I think to some extent we've benefited from the fact that our competitors have underestimated the importance of value, and the power of the relationship and the service that we can create with the customer.
>
> And, also, as a product tends to standardize there's not an elimination of the requirement for custom services, there's a reduction of it. So by offering some services, but not the services of the traditional proprietary computer company, we've been able to increase our share. And, in fact, what tends to happen is customers embrace the standards, because they know that's going to save them costs. Let me give you an example . . . about a year ago we entered into the data networking market. So we have Ethernet switches, layer 2 switches. So if you have PCs and servers, you need switches; every PC attaches to a switch, every server attaches to a switch. It's a pretty easy sale, switches go along with computer systems. We looked at this market and were able to come up with products that are priced about $2\frac{1}{2}$ times less than the market leader today, Cisco, and as a result the business has grown very, very

quickly. We shipped 1.8 million switch ports in a period of about a year, when most people would have said that's not going to work and come up with all kinds of reasons why we can't succeed.[12]

As Dell's sales of data-routing switches accelerated in 2001–2002 and Dell management mulled over whether to expand into other networking products and Internet gear, Cisco elected to discontinue supplying its switches to Dell for resale as of October 2002. Dell's family of PowerConnect switches—simple commodity like products generally referred to as layer 2 switches in the industry—were about 75 percent cheaper than those made by Cisco as of 2005.

Senior Dell executives saw external storage devices as a growth opportunity because the company's corporate and institutional customers were making increasing use of high-speed data storage and retrieval devices. Dell's PowerVault line of storage products had data protection and recovery features that made it easy for customers to add and manage storage and simplify consolidation. The PowerVault products used standardized technology and components (which were considerably cheaper than customized ones), allowing Dell to underprice rivals and drive down storage costs for its customers by about 50 percent. Dell's competitors in storage devices included Hewlett-Packard and IBM.

Some observers saw Dell's 2003 entry into the printer market as a calculated effort to go after Hewlett-Packard's biggest and most profitable business segment and believed the Dell offensive was deliberately timed to throw a wrench into HP's efforts to resolve the many challenges of successfully merging its operations with those of Compaq. One of the reasons Dell had entered the market for servers back in 1995 was that Compaq Computer, then its biggest rival in PCs, had been using its lucrative profits on server sales to subsidize charging lower prices on Compaq computers and thus be more price-competitive against Dell's PCs—at the time Compaq was losing money on its desktop and notebook PC business. According to Michael Dell:

> Compaq had this enormous profit pool that they were using to fight against us in the desktop and notebook business. That was not an acceptable situation. Our product teams knew that the servers weren't that complicated or expensive to produce, and customers were being charged unfair prices.[13]

Dell management believed that in 2000–2002 HP was doing much the same thing in printers and printer products, where it had a dominant market share worldwide and generated about 75 percent of its operating profits. Dell believed that HP was using its big margins on printer products to subsidize selling its PCs at prices comparable to Dell's, even though Dell had costs that were about 8 percent lower than HP's. HP's PC operations were either in the red or barely in the black during most of 2000–2003, while Dell consistently had profit margins of 8 percent or more on PCs. Dell management believed the company's entry into the printer market would add value for its customers. Michael Dell explained:

> We think we can drive down the entire cost of owning and using printing products. If you look at any other market Dell has gone into, we have been able to significantly save money for customers. We know we can do that in printers; we have looked at the supply chain all the way through its various cycles and we know there are inefficiencies there. I think the price of the total offering when we include the printer and the supplies . . . can come down quite considerably.[14]

[12]Remarks by Michael Dell, Gartner Fall Symposium, Orlando, FL, October 9, 2002, www.dell.com.

[13]Remarks by Michael Dell at the University of Toronto, September 21, 2004, www.dell.com.

[14]Quoted in the *Financial Times* Global News Wire, October 10, 2002.

When Dell announced it had contracted with Lexmark to make printers and printer and toner cartridges for sale under the Dell label beginning in 2003, HP immediately discontinued supplying HP printers to Dell for resale at Dell's Web site. Dell had been selling Lexmark printers for two years and, since 2000, had resold about 4 million printers made by such vendors as HP, Lexmark, and other vendors to its customers. Lexmark designed and made critical parts for its printers but used offshore contract manufacturers for assembly. Gross profit margins on printers (sales minus cost of goods sold) were said to be in single digits in 2002–2004, but the gross margins on printer supplies were in the 50–60 percent range—brand-name ink cartridges for printers typically ran $25 to $35. As of fall 2005, Dell had sold more than 10 million printers and had an estimated 20 percent of the market for color network lasers and color inkjet printers in the United States.[15]

Dell executives believed the company's entry and market success in printer products had put added competitive pressure on Hewlett-Packard in the printer market and was partly responsible for HP's share of the printer market worldwide slipping from just under 50 percent to around 46 percent in 2004. To further keep the pricing pressure on HP in 2003, Dell had priced its storage and networking products below comparable HP products.

Exhibit 6 shows a breakdown of Dell's sales by product category. Exhibit 7 shows Dell's average revenues per unit sold for fiscal years 1998–2008. The declines were driven by

EXHIBIT 6   Dell's Revenues by Product Category, 2006–2008

	2008		**2007**		**2006**	
Product Category	**Revenues (in billions)**	**% of Total Revenues**	**Revenues (in billions)**	**% of Total Revenues**	**Revenues (in billions)**	**% of Total Revenues**
Desktop PCs	$19.6	32.1%	$19.8	34.5%	$21.6	38.7%
Mobility products (laptop PCs and workstations)	17.4	28.5	15.5	27.0	14.4	25.8
Software and peripherals (printers, monitors, TVs, projectors, ink and toner cartridges)	9.9	16.2	9.0	15.7	8.3	14.9
Servers and networking hardware	6.5	10.6	5.8	10.1	5.4	9.8
Consulting and enhanced services	5.3	8.8	5.1	8.9	4.2	7.5
Storage products	2.4	3.9	2.3	4.0	1.9	3.4
Totals	$61.1	100.1%	$57.4	100.2%	$55.8	100.1%

Source: Dell's 10-K report, fiscal 2008, p. 90.

EXHIBIT 7

Trend in Dell's Approximate Average Revenue per Unit Sold, Fiscal Years 1998–2008

Source: Company financial records and company postings at www.dell.com (accessed May 3, 2008).

Fiscal Year	**Dell's Approximate Average Revenue per Unit Sold**
1998	$2,600
2000	2,250
2001	2,050
2002	1,700
2003	1,640
2004	1,590
2005	1,560
2006	1,500
2007	1,510
2008	1,540

[15]Remarks by Michael Dell, Gartner Symposium, Orlando, FL, October 20, 2005, www.dell.com.

steadily falling costs for components, Dell's ability to improve productivity and take costs out of its value chain, and Dell's strategy of passing along cost savings to its customers and trying to deliver more value to customers than its rivals did. However, the tiny increases in average revenues per unit in the past two fiscal years reflected slowing declines in components prices, a shift in the PC sales mix away from desktops to laptops (which carried higher price tags and thus yielded greater average revenues per unit sold), and Dell's more restrained pricing (to protect its operating and net profit margins from further erosion). In fiscal 2007–2008, unlike prior years, Dell had difficulty in lowering unit costs; out-of-proportion increases in operating expenses (see Exhibit 2) made it infeasible for Dell to cut prices and still preserve its operating profit margins. Top executives opted to maintain prices to keep the company's already lower operating profit margins from going down any further (see Exhibit 2); this left Dell vulnerable to HP's strategic offensive to regain sales and market share—an offensive that featured prices for HP products that were more in line with what Dell was charging.

Customer Service and Technical Support

Service became a feature of Dell's strategy in 1986 when the company began providing a year's free on-site service with most of its PCs after users complained about having to ship their PCs back to Austin for repairs. Dell began offering PC buyers the option of buying contracts for on-site repair services for a defined period (usually one to four years). Dell contracted with local service providers to handle customer requests for repairs; on-site service was provided on a four-hour basis to large customers and on a next-day basis to small customers. Dell generally contracted with third-party providers to make the necessary on-site service calls. Customers notified Dell when they had problems; such notices triggered two electronic dispatches—one to ship replacement parts from Dell's factory to the customer, and one to notify the contract service provider to prepare to make the needed repairs as soon as the parts arrived.[16] Bad parts were returned so that Dell could determine what went wrong and how to prevent such problems from happening again (problems relating to faulty components or flawed components design were promptly passed along to the relevant supplier for correction). If business or institutional customers preferred to work with their own service provider, Dell supplied the provider of choice with the training and spare parts needed to service the customers' equipment.

Later, Dell began offering contracts for CompleteCare accidental damage service. In 2006, Dell began using an online diagnostics tool called DellConnect to troubleshoot and resolve problems with a customer's computer while the customer was connected to Dell's Web site. In 2007, Dell launched a corporate blog called Direct2Dell, a customer idea engine called IdeaStorm, and several online community forums for the purpose of better listening to and engaging with customers. Dell's online training programs featured more than 1,200 courses for consumer, business, and IT professionals. Over 50 percent of Dell's technical support and customer service activities were conducted via the Internet. Customers could also request technical support via a toll-free phone number and e-mail; Dell received more than 8 million phone calls and 500,000 to 600,000 e-mail messages annually requesting service and support.

Dell had 25 customer service centers worldwide in 2008 that were primarily engaged in handling technical support, requests for repairs, and other issues and inquiries. In a move to trim rising technical support and customer service costs in 2004–2005, Dell opted to move a large portion of its support services to countries where labor costs were low. But according to Dell's president of global services and chief information officer, "We did it way

---

[16]Kevin Rollins, "Using Information to Speed Execution," *Harvard Business Review*, March–April 1998, p. 81.

too quickly—we didn't move process management disciplines with it as effectively as we should have, and we wound up making some mistakes with the services experience."[17] The outcome was a sharp rise in customer complaints, especially among small business and individual customers who were most affected—a number of irritated Dell customers went so far as to post their horror stories at Web sites like IhateDell.net, and the resulting media publicity tarnished Dell's reputation for customer service among these buyers. To correct the service problems, Dell had moved many of its service centers back to countries where big numbers of its customers were located. Service processes were standardized worldwide, and best practices from all over the world were built into the standards. Dell's goal was to reach 90 percent customer satisfaction—where customers rated their service experience with Dell as "top notch" or "very satisfied"—as quickly as possible. In early 2008, Dell's customer satisfaction ratings were at 92 percent for Asia, at 90 percent in the Europe/Middle East/Africa region, and in the 80 percent range for the Americas (these ratings included all services for small, medium, and large customers).[18]

Premier Pages

Dell had developed customized, password-protected Web sites called Premier Pages for more than 50,000 corporate, governmental, and institutional customers worldwide. These Premier Pages gave customers' personnel online access to information about all Dell products and configurations the company had purchased or that were currently authorized for purchase. Employees could use Premier Pages to (1) obtain customer-specific pricing for whatever machines and options the employee wanted to consider, (2) place an order online that would be routed electronically to higher-level managers for approval and then on to Dell for assembly and delivery, and (3) seek advanced help desk support. Customers could also search and sort all invoices and obtain purchase histories. These features eliminated paper invoices, cut ordering time, and reduced the internal labor customers needed to staff corporate purchasing and accounting functions. Customer use of Premier Pages had boosted the productivity of Dell salespeople assigned to these accounts by 50 percent. Dell was providing Premier Page service to additional customers annually and adding more features to further improve functionality.

Product Design Services

One of Dell's latest services for large customers was making special-purpose products for such customers as Internet search providers, social networking sites, and big video content sites that might need 10,000 or more units to accommodate its requirements. Such customers did not want to pay for a general-purpose product with components or performance features it did not need. So Dell created a group that had the capability to provide a big user with thousands of units of a product stripped of unnecessary features and equipped with whatever processor, memory, and disk drive suited the customer's needs. Dell personnel would visit with the customer, ascertain the customer's needs and preferences, provide a prototype within three weeks for evaluation and testing, make any additional changes within another two weeks for further testing and evaluation, and then be in volume production by the thousands of units within another three or four weeks—altogether about a nine-week design-to-production/delivery cycle.

Value-Added Services for Customers with Large IT Operations

Dell kept close track of the purchases of its large global customers, country by country and department by department—and customers themselves found this purchase information valuable. Dell's sales and support personnel used their knowledge about a particular

---

[17]As quoted in Don Tennant, "Dell Exec Addresses Service Woes in Run-up to IT-as-a-Service Launch," *Computerworld,* March 17, 2008, www.computerworld.com (accessed May 12, 2008).

[18]Ibid.

customer's needs to help that customer plan PC purchases, to configure the customer's PC networks, and to provide value-added services. For example, for its large customers Dell loaded software and placed ID tags on newly ordered PCs at the factory, thereby eliminating the need for the customer's IT personnel to unpack the PC, deliver it to an employee's desk, hook it up, place asset tags on the PC, and load the needed software—a process that could take several hours and cost $200–$300.[19] While Dell charged an extra $15 or $20 for the software-loading and asset-tagging services, the savings to customers were still considerable—one large customer reported savings of $500,000 annually from this service.[20]

In 2007 and early 2008, Dell spent about $2 billion to make a series of software-related acquisitions that gave it an altogether new value-added capability:

1. Everdream Corporation—Everdream was a leading provider of Software as a Service (SaaS) solutions, with operations in California and North Carolina. This acquisition enabled Dell to extend its capabilities to use the Internet to remotely manage global delivery of software solutions from servers, storage devices, and printers to desktop PCs, laptops, and other end-user devices. Dell management believed that remote-service management of software products would help business customers of all sizes simplify their IT infrastructure—a value-added outcome that Dell was aggressively pursuing. Terms of the acquisition were not disclosed.

2. SilverBack Technologies Inc.—Silverback was a privately owned, Massachusetts-based company that had a delivery platform to remotely manage and monitor SaaS products. Such a platform was essential to Dell's strategy of simplifying customers' IT infrastructures by providing their personnel with desirable software applications on an as-needed basis via the Internet. Terms of the acquisition were not disclosed.

3. MessageOne Inc.—Acquired for $155 million, MessageOne was an industry leader in SaaS-enabled continuous e-mail service, e-mail archiving, and disaster recovery of e-mail messages. The MessageOne acquisition further enhanced Dell's strategy to use SaaS applications and remote software management tools to deliver configure-to-order IT services to commercial customers over the Internet.

4. EqualLogic—This company, acquired for $1.4 billion, was a leading provider of high-performance storage area network (SAN) solutions that made storing and processing data easier and cheaper. EqualLogic's technological capabilities allowed Dell to offer its customers a secure data storage solution that used the customer's existing IT infrastructure, could be installed in minutes, managed itself, and was easily expanded as needs increased.

5. ASAP Software—ASAP, acquired at a cost of $340 million, was a leading software solutions and licensing services provider, with expertise in software licensing and the management of IT assets. The ASAP acquisition expanded Dell's lineup of software offerings from 200 to 2,000.

6. The Networked Storage Company—Networked Storage was a leading IT consulting group that specialized in transitioning customers to proven, simplified, cost-efficient data storage solutions. Dell management saw this acquisition as an important element in its strategy to build the capability to offer Dell customers simple, cost-effective ways to manage their IT infrastructures. Terms of the acquisition were not disclosed.

Dell management saw all six acquisitions as greatly strengthening the company's capabilities to provide an altogether new value-added service to customers with sizable IT operations, all of whom were finding the tasks of managing and maintaining an IT infrastructure to be increasingly complex and costly. Executives at Dell believed that

[19]Magretta, "The Power of Virtual Integration," p. 79.
[20]"Michael Dell Rocks," *Fortune*, May 11, 1998, p. 61.

having greater capability than rivals to offer commercial customers simple, cost-effective ways to manage their IT operations would give Dell added competitiveness in marketing its lineup of product offerings to commercial enterprises worldwide. While Dell already was the sales leader in PCs sold to corporations and businesses in North America and Europe, extending its lead in these regions and growing sales and market share in the remaining parts of the world could make a material contribution not only to growing Dell's overall business but also to overtaking Hewlett-Packard as the global leader in PCs.

Enhanced Services and Support for Large Enterprises

Corporate customers paid Dell fees to provide on-site service and help with migrating to new information technologies. Service revenues had climbed from $1.7 billion in 2002 to about $5.3 billion in fiscal 2008. This portion of Dell's business was split between what Michael Dell called close-to-the-box services and management/professional services. Dell estimated that close-to-the-box support services for Dell products represented about a $50 billion market as of 2005, whereas the market for management/professional services (IT life-cycle services, deployment of new technology, and solutions for greater IT productivity) in 2005 was about $90 billion. The market for IT consulting and services was forecast to be in the $850–$900 billion range in 2011. For the most part, IT consulting services were becoming more standardized, driven primarily by growing hardware and software standardization, reduction in on-site service requirements (partly because of online diagnostic and support tools, growing ease of repair and maintenance, increased customer knowledge, and increased remote management capabilities), and declines in the skills and know-how that were required to perform service tasks on standardized equipment and install new, more standardized systems.

Dell's strategy in enhanced services, like its strategy in hardware products, was to bring down the cost of IT-related services for its large enterprise customers and free customers from "overpriced relationships" with such vendors as IBM, Sun Microsystems, and Hewlett-Packard that typically charged premium prices ($250 per hour) and realized hefty profits for their efforts.[21] According to Michael Dell, customers who bought the services being provided by Dell saved 40 to 50 percent over what they would have paid other providers of IT services.

The caliber of technical support and customer service that Dell provided to its large enterprise customers was highly regarded (despite the problems sometimes experienced by small businesses and individuals). In a 2005 survey of IT executives by *CIO* magazine, Dell was rated number one among leading vendors for providing "impeccable customer service" to large enterprises.

Providing Online Shoppers with Customer Reviews of Dell Products

Users of Dell products were encouraged to provide Dell with a review of their experiences with the products they had purchased. As part of the review process, customers were asked to provide a rating of the product using a 5-point scale that ran from 1 (poor) to 5 (excellent). Shoppers browsing through Dell's product offerings could view the average customer rating score for each product directly on the screen where the product details were displayed and could click on an adjacent link to read the accompanying reviews. In 2008, about 50,000 customer reviews of Dell products were posted and available for inspection.

Listening to Customers

In addition to using its sales and support mechanisms to stay close to customers, Dell periodically held regional forums that gave senior Dell personnel opportunities to listen to the company's biggest and most influential customers and discuss their emerging needs and

---

[21]Quoted in Kathryn Jones, "The Dell Way," *Business 2.0,* February 2003.

expectations. The meeting agenda frequently included a presentation by Michael Dell, plus presentations by Dell's senior technologists on the direction of the latest technological developments and what the flow of technology really meant for customers, presentations on what new and upgraded products Dell was planning to introduce, and breakout sessions on topics of current interest.

In February 2007, Dell began inviting customers to post their ideas for improving its products and services at a section of its Web site called IdeaStorm. As of April 2008, customers had posted more than 8,900 ideas, 45 of which had been implemented. Michael Dell believed that the Internet and the speed with which people worldwide were able to connect to the Internet via a growing number of devices had forever redefined what it means to listen to customers:

> Listening used to mean commissioning a customer survey. Now it means engaging directly with customers and critics and using those relationships to create a smarter business. Tapping into the ideas of our customers is like having an open source R&D lab.[22]

Customer-Driven Research and Development and Standardized Technology

Dell's R&D focus was to track and test new developments in components and software, ascertain which ones would prove most useful and cost-effective for customers, and then design them into Dell products. Management's philosophy was that it was Dell's job on behalf of its customers to sort out all the new technology coming into the marketplace and design products having the features, options, and solutions that were the most relevant for customers. Studies conducted by Dell's R&D personnel indicated that, over time, products incorporating standardized technology delivered about twice the performance per dollar of cost as products based on proprietary technology.

At the University of Buffalo, for example, Dell had installed a 5.6 teraflop cluster of about 2,000 Dell servers containing 4,000 microprocessors that constituted one of the most powerful supercomputers in the world and gave researchers the computing power needed to help decode the human genome. The cluster of servers, which were the same as those Dell sold to many other customers, had been installed in about 60 days at a cost of a few million dollars—far less than the cost of another vendor's supercomputer that used proprietary technology. Energy giant Amerada Hess Corporation (now known as Hess Corporation), attracted by Dell's use of standardized and upgradable parts and components, installed a cluster of several hundred Dell workstations and allocated about $300,000 a year to upgrade and maintain it; the cluster replaced an IBM supercomputer that cost $1.5 million a year to lease and operate.

Dell's R&D unit also studied and implemented ways to control quality and to streamline the assembly process. In 2008, Dell had a portfolio of 1,954 U.S. patents and another 2,196 patent applications were pending. Dell's R&D group included about 4,000 engineers, and its annual budget for research, development, and engineering was in the $430–$500 million range before jumping to more than $600 million in fiscal 2008 (see Exhibit 2).

Other Elements of Dell's Business Strategy

Dell's strategy had three other elements that complemented its core strategy: entry into the white-box segment of the PC industry, advertising, and continuous pursuit of cost reduction initiatives.

---

[22]Company press release, April 6, 2008.

Dell's Entry into the White-Box PC Segment

In 2002, Dell announced it would begin making so-called white-box (i.e., unbranded) PCs for resale under the private labels of retailers. PC dealers that supplied white-box PCs to small businesses and price-conscious individuals under the dealer's own brand name accounted for about one-third of total PC sales and about 50 percent of sales to small businesses. According to one industry analyst, "Increasingly, Dell's biggest competitor these days isn't big brand-name companies like IBM or HP; it's white-box vendors." Dell's thinking in entering the white-box PC segment was that it was cheaper to reach many small businesses through the white-box dealers that already served them than by using its own sales force and support groups to sell and service businesses with fewer than 100 employees. Dell believed that its low-cost supply chain and assembly capabilities would allow it to build generic machines cheaper than white-box resellers could buy components and assemble a customized machine. Management forecast that Dell would achieve $380 million in sales of white-box PCs in 2003 and would generate profit margins equal to those on Dell-branded PCs. Some industry analysts were skeptical of Dell's move into white-box PCs because they expected white-box dealers to be reluctant to buy their PCs from a company that had a history of taking their clients. Others believed this was a test effort by Dell to develop the capabilities to take on white-box dealers in Asia and especially in China, where the sellers of generic PCs were particularly strong.

Advertising

Michael Dell was a firm believer in the power of advertising and frequently espoused its importance in the company's strategy. He insisted that the company's ads be communicative and forceful, not soft and fuzzy. The company regularly had prominent ads describing its products and prices in such leading computer publications as *PC Magazine* and *PC World,* as well as in *USA Today,* the *Wall Street Journal,* and other business publications. From time to time, the company ran ads on TV to promote its products to consumers and small businesses. Catalogs of about 25–30 pages describing Dell's latest desktop and laptop PCs, along with its printers and other offerings, were periodically mailed to consumers who had bought Dell products. Other marketing initiatives included printing newspaper inserts and sending newsletters and promotional pieces to customers via the Internet.

Continuous Pursuit of Cost-Reduction Initiatives

Michael Dell had long been an ardent advocate of relentless efforts to improve efficiency and keeps costs as low as feasible. But during Kevin Rollins's tenure as CEO, Dell's cost edge over rivals had narrowed, and the company's profit margins had slipped as well (partly because fierce price competition was driving down the prices of many products that Dell sold faster than Dell was able to lower its costs per unit)—Exhibit 7 shows the downward trend in the average revenue Dell received from each unit sold. When he reassumed his role as CEO in 2007, Michael Dell announced that tighter controls over operating expenses would be implemented immediately and that management would begin an in-depth exploration of ways for improving Dell's cost-competitiveness, organizing operations more efficiently, and boosting profitability and cash flows. In May 2007, Dell announced an initiative to reduce the global workforce headcount by 10 percent, or 8,800 people. By March 2008, a net of 3,200 jobs had been eliminated. However, the company had actually hired 2,100 more people to staff frontline operations and customer-facing activities; the net reduction of 3,200 people was achieved by cutting 5,300 personnel engaged in performing what Dell called non-frontline activities. The result was to increase the number of Dell employees engaged in frontline and customer-facing activities from 54 percent to 57 percent.

In March 2008, Dell executives announced that over the next three years the company would seek to achieve annualized savings of $3 billion via productivity improvements and cost-reduction efforts across all the company's value chain—design, supply chain logistics, materials, manufacturing, and other operating activities. Management reaffirmed its commitment to reducing the global employee headcount by 8,800 and achieving the related labor-cost savings. At the same time, Dell also put programs in place to reignite the company's revenue growth in five focus areas: global consumer products, sales to large enterprise customers, laptop computers, sales to small and medium enterprises, and sales in emerging countries.

THE INFORMATION TECHNOLOGY MARKETPLACE IN 2008

Analysts expected the worldwide IT industry to grow from $1.2 trillion in 2007 to $1.5 trillion in 2010, a compound growth rate of about 7.7 percent. Of that projected 2010 total, about $560 billion was expected to be for hardware (PCs, servers, storage devices, networking equipment, and printers and peripherals); $327 billion for software; and $613 billion for services. From 1980 to 2000, IT spending had grown at an average annual rate of 12 percent; thereafter, it had flattened—to a 1 percent decline in 2001, a 2.3 percent decline in 2002, a single-digit increase in 2003—then rose more briskly at rates in the 5–10 percent range in 2004, 2005, 2006, and 2007. The slowdown in IT spending in 2001–2007 compared to earlier years reflected a combination of factors: sluggish economic growth in many countries in 2001–2003; overinvestment in IT in the 1995–1999 period; declining unit prices for many IT products (especially PCs and servers); and a growing preference for lower-priced, standard-component hardware that was good enough to perform a variety of functions using off-the-shelf Windows or Linux operating systems (as opposed to relying on proprietary hardware and customized Unix software). The selling points that appealed most to IT customers were standardization, flexibility, modularity, simplicity, economy of use, and value.

There were several driving forces contributing to increased global spending for information technology products and services starting in 2004.[23] One was the explosion of digital information and content. According to Forrester Research, the world's data doubled approximately every three years, a phenomenon that was expected to produce more than a sixfold increase in data between 2003 and 2010. A second force was the rapid expansion of search engine activity, e-mail, text messages, social networking Web sites like MySpace and Facebook, blogs, and online video and images; these fed the worldwide demand for digital devices to create, store, share, and print the mushrooming volume of digital information and content. The third force was the rapidly growing demand for information technology products and services in emerging markets around the world—like Brazil, Russia, China, India, and several other countries in Southeast Asia and Eastern Europe—where over half of the world's population resided. At the same time, several other complicating factors were at work. Much of the growing volume of content lacked authentication and proper security, plus the content was increasingly global and mobile. And consumer expectations were changing—people wanted instantaneous access to content regardless of what kind of device they were using or where they happened to be, and their tolerance for complexity was low. All of these aspects of the global IT marketplace created huge opportunities for IT providers and huge challenges for IT users.

Exhibit 8 shows actual and projected PC sales for 1980–2012 as compiled by industry researcher International Data Corporation (IDC). According to Gartner Research, the billionth PC was shipped sometime in July 2002; of the billion PCs sold, an estimated

---

[23]Much of this paragraph was developed by the case authors from information in Hewlett-Packard's 2007 annual report.

EXHIBIT 8
Worldwide Shipments
of PCs, Actual and
Forecast, 1980–2012
(in millions)

Source: International Data
Corporation.

Year	PCs Shipped
1980	1
1985	11
1990	24
1995	58
2000	139
2001	133
2002	136
2003	153
2004	177
2005	208
2006	235
2007	269
2008*	302
2009*	335
2010*	368
2011*	398
2012*	426

*Forecast.

550 million were still in use. Forrester Research estimated that the numbers of PCs in use worldwide would exceed 1 billion by the end of 2008 (up from 575 million in 2004) and would approach 1.3 billion by 2011 and 2.0 billion by 2016. With a world population of more than 6 billion, most industry participants believed there was ample opportunity for further growth in the PC market. Growth potential for PCs was particularly strong in Russia, China, India, several other Asian countries, and portions of Latin America (especially Brazil and Mexico). At the same time, forecasters expected full global buildout of the Internet to continue, which would require the installation of millions of servers.

HOW DELL'S STRATEGY PUT COMPETITIVE PRESSURE ON RIVALS

When the personal computer industry first began to take shape in the early 1980s, the founding companies manufactured many of the components themselves—disk drives, memory chips, graphics chips, microprocessors, motherboards, and software. Subscribing to a philosophy that mandated in-house development of key components, they built expertise in a variety of PC-related technologies and created organizational units to produce components as well as handle final assembly. While certain noncritical items were typically outsourced, if a computer maker was not at least partially vertically integrated and did not produce some components for its PCs, then it was not taken seriously as a manufacturer. But as the industry grew, technology advanced quickly in so many directions on so many parts and components that the early personal computer manufacturers could not keep pace as experts on all fronts. There were too many technologies and manufacturing intricacies to master for a vertically integrated manufacturer to keep its products on the cutting edge.

As a consequence, companies emerged that specialized in making particular components. Specialists could marshal enough R&D capability and resources to either lead the technological developments in their area of specialization or else quickly match the advances made by their competitors. Moreover, specialist firms could mass-produce the component and supply it to several computer manufacturers far cheaper than any one manufacturer could fund the needed component R&D and then make only whatever smaller volume of components it needed for assembling its own brand of PCs. Thus, in the early 1990s, such computer makers as Compaq Computer, IBM, Hewlett-Packard, Sony, Toshiba, and Fujitsu-Siemens began to abandon vertical integration in favor of a strategy of outsourcing most components from specialists and concentrating on efficient assembly and marketing their brand of computers. They adopted the build-to-stock value chain model shown in the top section of Exhibit 4. It featured arm's-length transactions between specialist suppliers, manufacturer/assemblers, distributors and retailers, and end users. However, a few others, most notably Dell and Gateway, employed a shorter value chain model, selling directly to customers and eliminating the time and costs associated with distributing through independent resellers. Building to order avoided (1) having to keep many differently equipped models on retailers' shelves to fill buyer requests for one or another configuration of options and components, and (2) having to clear out slow-selling models at a discount before introducing new generations of PCs—for instance, Hewlett-Packard's retail dealers had an average of 43 days of HP products in stock as of October 2004. Direct sales eliminated retailer costs and markups; retail dealer margins were typically in the range of 4–10 percent.

Because of Dell's success in using its business model and strategy to become the low-cost leader, most other PC makers had tried to emulate various aspects of Dell's strategy, but with only limited success. Nearly all vendors were trying to cut days of inventory out of their supply chains and reduce their costs of goods sold and operating expenses to levels that would make them more cost-competitive with Dell. In an effort to cut their assembly costs, several others (including HP) had begun outsourcing assembly to contract manufacturers and refocusing their internal efforts on product design and marketing. Virtually all PC vendors were trying to minimize the amount of finished goods in dealer/distributor inventories and shorten the time it took to replenish dealer stocks. Collaboration with contract manufacturers was increasing to develop the capabilities to build and deliver PCs equipped to customer specifications within 7 to 14 days, but these efforts were hampered by the use of Asia-based contract manufacturers—delivering built-to-order PCs to North American and European customers within a two-week time frame required the use of costly air freight from assembly plants in Asia.

While most PC vendors would have liked to adopt Dell's sell-direct strategy for at least some of their sales, they confronted big channel conflict problems: if they started to push direct sales hard, they would almost certainly alienate the independent dealers on whom they depended for the bulk of their sales and service to customers. Dealers saw sell-direct efforts on the part of a manufacturer whose brand they represented as a move to cannibalize their business and to compete against them. However, Dell's success in gaining large enterprise customers with its direct sales force had forced growing numbers of PC vendors to supplement the efforts of their independent dealers with direct sales and service efforts of their own. During 2003–2007, several of Dell's rivals were selling 15 to 25 percent of their products direct.

HEWLETT-PACKARD: DELL'S CHIEF RIVAL IN PCS AND X86 SERVERS

In one of the most contentious and controversial acquisitions in U.S. history, Hewlett-Packard shareholders in early 2002 voted by a narrow margin to approve the company's acquisition of Compaq Computer, the world's second largest full-service global computing company (behind IBM), with 2001 revenues of $33.6 billion and a net loss of $785 million. Compaq had passed IBM to become the world leader in PCs in 1995 and remained in first place until it was overtaken by Dell in late 1999. Compaq had acquired Tandem Computer in 1997 and Digital Equipment Corporation in 1998 to give it capabilities, products, and service offerings that allowed it to compete in every sector of the computer industry—PCs, servers, workstations, mainframes, peripherals, and such services as business and e-commerce solutions, hardware and software support, systems integration, and technology consulting.[24] In 2000, Compaq spent $370 million to acquire certain assets of Inacom Corporation that management believed would help Compaq reduce inventories, speed cycle time, and enhance its capabilities to do business with customers via the Internet. Nonetheless, at the time of its acquisition by HP, Compaq was struggling to compete successfully in all of the many product and service arenas where it operated.

Carly Fiorina, who became HP's CEO in 1999, explained why the acquisition of Compaq was strategically sound:[25]

> With Compaq, we become No. 1 in Windows, No. 1 in Linux and No. 1 in Unix. . . . With Compaq, we become the No. 1 player in storage, and the leader in the fastest growing segment of the storage market—storage area networks. With Compaq, we double our service and support capacity in the area of mission-critical infrastructure design, outsourcing and support. . . . Let's talk about PCs. . . . Compaq has been able to improve their turns in that business from 23 turns of inventory per year to 62—100 percent improvement year over year—and they are coming close to doing as well as Dell does. They've reduced operating expenses by $130 million, improved gross margins by three points, reduced channel inventory by more than $800 million. They ship about 70 percent of their commercial volume through their direct channel, comparable to Dell. We will combine our successful retail PC business model with their commercial business model and achieve much more together than we could alone. With Compaq, we will double the size of our sales force to 15,000 strong. We will build our R&D budget to more than $4 billion a year, and add important capabilities to HP Labs. We will become the No. 1 player in a whole host of countries around the world—HP operates in more than 160 countries, with well over 60 percent of our revenues coming from outside the U.S. The new HP will be the No. 1 player in the consumer and small- and medium-business segments. . . . We have estimated cost synergies of $2.5 billion by 2004. . . . It is a rare opportunity when a technology company can advance its market position substantially and reduce its cost structure substantially at the same time. And this is possible because Compaq and HP are in the same businesses, pursuing the same strategies, in the same markets, with complementary capabilities.

However, going into 2005 the jury was still out on whether HP's acquisition of Compaq was the success that Carly Fiorina had claimed it would be. The company's only real bright spot was its $24 billion crown jewel printer business, which still reigned as the unchallenged world leader. But the rest of HP's businesses (PCs, servers, storage devices, digital cameras, calculators, and IT services) were underachievers. Its PC and server businesses were struggling, losing money in most quarters and barely breaking even in others—and HP was definitely losing ground to Dell in PCs and low-priced servers. In servers, HP was being squeezed on the low end by Dell's low prices and on the high end by strong competition from IBM. According to most observers, IBM overshadowed HP in corporate computing—high-end servers and IT services. HP had been able to grow revenues in data storage and technical support services, but profit margins and total operating profits were declining. While HP had successfully cut annual operating costs by $3.5 billion—beating the $2.5 billion target set at the time of the Compaq acquisition, the company had missed its earnings forecasts in 7 of the past 20 quarters.

With HP's stock price stuck in the $18–$23 price range, impatient investors in 2004 began clamoring for the company to break itself up and create two separate companies, one for its printer business and one for all the rest of the businesses. While HP's board of directors had looked at breaking the company into smaller pieces, Carly Fiorina was

[24]"Can Compaq Catch Up?" *BusinessWeek,* May 3, 1999, p. 163.

[25]Company press release and speech posted at www.hp.com, accessed December 11, 2004.

steadfastly opposed, arguing that HP's broad product/business lineup paid off in the form of added sales and lower costs. But in February 2005, shortly after HP released disappointing financials for 2004 (the company's earnings per share total of $1.16 in 2004 was substantially below the earnings per share total of $1.80 reported in 2000), Carly Fiorina resigned her post as HP's CEO amid mounting differences between herself and members of HP's board of directors about what actions were needed to revive HP's earnings.

Mark Hurd, president and CEO of NCR (formerly National Cash Register Systems), was brought in to replace Fiorina, effective April 1, 2005; Hurd had been at NCR for 25 years in a variety of management positions and was regarded as a no-nonsense executive who underpromised and overdelivered on results.[26] Hurd immediately sought to bolster HP's competitiveness and financial performance by bringing in new managers and attacking bloated costs. In his first seven months as CEO, the results were encouraging. HP posted revenues of $86.7 billion and net profits of $2.4 billion for the fiscal year ending October 31, 2005. HP had the number one ranking worldwide for server shipments (a position it had held for 14 consecutive quarters) and disk storage systems, plus it was the world leader in server revenues for Unix, Windows, and Linux systems. During the first seven months that Hurd was HP's CEO, the company's stock price rose about 25 percent.

With Hurd at the helm, Hewlett-Packard continued to gain traction in the marketplace in the next two fiscal years. For example, HP's sales of laptop computers increased 47 percent in fiscal 2007 and its PC business in China nearly doubled, making China HP's third biggest market for PCs. The company posted revenues of $91.7 billion in fiscal 2006 and $104.3 billion in fiscal 2007. Earnings climbed from $2.4 billion in 2005 to $6.2 billion in 2006 (equal to a diluted earnings per share of $2.18) and to $7.3 billion in 2007 (equal to a diluted earning per share of $2.68). By late fall 2007, HP's stock price was more than double what it had been during Carly Fiorina's last days as CEO. The company's 2007 share of the estimated $1.2 trillion global IT market was almost 9 percent. It was the global leader in both PCs and x86 servers running on Windows and Linux operating systems. About 67 percent of HP's sales were outside the United States. In May 2008, HP announced that it was expecting fiscal 2008 revenues of about $114 billion and a diluted earnings per share in the range of $3.30 to $3.34. Exhibit 9 shows the performance of Hewlett-Packard's four major business groups for fiscal years 2001–2007.

HP's strategy in PCs and servers differed from Dell's in two important respects:

1. Although HP had a direct sales force that sold direct to large enterprises and select other customers, a very sizable share of HP's sales of PCs were made through distributors, retailers, and other channels. These included:

   - Retailers that sold HP products to the public through their own physical or Internet stores.

   - Resellers that sold HP products and services, frequently with their own value-added products or services, to targeted customer groups.

   - Distribution partners that supplied HP products to smaller resellers with which HP had no direct relationships.

   - Independent distributors that sold HP products into geographic areas or customer segments in which HP had little or no presence.

   - Independent software vendors that often assisted HP in selling HP computers, servers, and other products/services to their software clients.

   - Systems integrators that helped large enterprises design and implement custom IT solutions and often recommended that these enterprises purchase HP products when such products were needed to put a customized IT solution in place.

[26]Louise Lee and Peter Burrows, "What's Dogging Dell's Stock," *BusinessWeek,* September 5, 2005, p. 90.

EXHIBIT 9   Performance of Hewlett-Packard's Four Major Business Groups, Fiscal Years 2001–2007 ($ in billions)

Fiscal Years Ending October 31	Printing and Imaging	Personal Computing Systems	Enterprise Systems and Software	HP Services
2007				
Net revenue	$28,465	$36,409	$21,094	$16,646
Operating income	4,315	1,939	2,327	1,829
2006				
Net revenue	$26,786	$29,169	$18,609	$15,617
Operating income	3,978	1,152	1,531	1,507
2005				
Net revenue	$25,155	$26,741	$17,878	$15,536
Operating income	3,413	657	751	1,151
2004				
Net revenue	$24,199	$24,622	$16,074	$13,778
Operating income	3,847	210	28	1,263
2003				
Net revenue	$22,569	$21,210	$15,367	$12,357
Operating income (loss)	3,596	22	(48)	1,362
2002*				
Net revenue	$20,358	$21,895	$11,105	$12,326
Operating income (loss)	3,365	(372)	(656)	1,369
2001*				
Net revenue	$19,602	$26,710	$20,205	$12,802
Operating income (loss)	2,103	(728)	(579)	1,617

*Results for 2001 and 2002 represent the combined results of both HP and Compaq Computer.

Source: Company 10-K reports 2003, 2004, and 2007.

Much of HP's global market clout in PCs and servers came from having the world's biggest and most diverse network of distribution partners. The percentage of PCs and servers sold by its direct sales force and by its various channel partners varied substantially by geographic region and country, partly because customer buying patterns and different regional market conditions made it useful for HP to tailor its sales, marketing, and distribution accordingly.

2. While in-house personnel designed the company's PCs and x86 servers, the vast majority were assembled by contract manufacturers located in various parts of the world. Big-volume orders from large enterprise customers were assembled to each customer's particular specifications. The remaining units were assembled and shipped to HP's retail and distribution partners; these were configured in a variety of ways (different microprocessor speeds, hard drive sizes, display sizes, memory size, and so on) that HP and its resellers thought would be attractive to customers and then assembled in large productions runs to maximize manufacturing efficiencies.

During 2005–2007, after replacing a number of HP's senior executives, Mark Hurd engineered several strategic moves to strengthen HP's competitiveness and ability to deliver better financial performance to shareholders:

• Top executives charged each HP business with identifying and implementing opportunities to boost efficiency and lower costs per unit. Every aspect of the company's supply chain and internal cost structure was scrutinized for ways to become more efficient and reduce costs. The costs of each value chain component—from real estate to procurement to IT to marketing—were examined so that managers could know costs by business group, region, country, site, product, and employee; these levels of cost analysis were then used to scrutinize how each expense supported HP's strategy and whether there were opportunities for cost savings. Corporate overheads were trimmed, negotiations with suppliers were conducted to be sure that HP was getting the best terms and best prices on its purchases, steps were taken to trim HP's workforce by about 15,000 people worldwide, the organizational structure was streamlined resulting in three layers of management being removed, and the company's very complicated IT operations were simplified and the expenses reduced—the objective was to engineer HP's IT architecture and operations to be the world's best showcase for the company's technology. In 2008, HP began trimming the number of sites worldwide at which it conducted activities by 25 percent. The resulting improvements in operating expenses paved the way for HP to price its products more competitively against those of Dell and other rivals.

- Company personnel began working more closely with large enterprise customers to find ways to simplify their experience with information technology.
- A number of new products and services were introduced.
- HP spent close to $7 billion to acquire more than a dozen software, technology, and service companies that management believed would add significant capabilities and technology to HP's portfolio and help fuel revenue growth.
- The company prepared to capitalize on three big growth opportunities that top management saw emerging over the next four or five years: (1) next-generation data center architecture; (2) growing consumer interest in always-ready, always-on mobile computing; and (3) digital printing. Mark Hurd believed that HP had important strengths in all three of these high-growth market arenas but needed to be more adept in getting new products into the marketplace. He directed company personnel to develop a better "go-to-market" model and to arm the sales force with the tools needed to "get quotes and proposals in front of customers as fast as anybody on the planet." HP added 1,000 people to its sales force in 2007 to expand its coverage of key accounts and geographic markets; an additional 1,000 salespeople were added through acquisitions.

Soon after becoming CEO in 2005, Mark Hurd concluded that HP needed to beef up its IT services business in order to go head-to-head against IBM, the unquestioned worldwide leader in IT services; IBM had 2007 revenues of about $54 billion and an estimated 7.2 percent global share of a $748 billion market. Hurd took a major step in that direction in May 2008, making his first really big strategic move as HP's CEO by cutting a deal to acquire Electronic Data Systems (EDS) for a cash price of $13.25 billion. According to Gartner (one of the world's leading technology research firms), EDS had IT service revenues of $22.1 billion in 2007, equal to a global share of 3.0 percent—ahead of HP with revenues of $17.3 billion and a 2.3 percent share (see Exhibit 10 for the sales and market shares of the world's top six IT service providers). While a combined HP/EDS would have IT service revenues of more than $49 billion and market share of 5.3 percent—sufficient for a strong second place in the global market—industry observers were not enamored with the ability of HP/EDS to compete with IBM for high-end, high-profit buyers of IT services. IBM's profit margin in IT services was almost double EDS's 6 percent profit margin, partly because IBM catered to the needs of high-end customers and partly because IBM had about 74,000 employees in India, where wages for IT professionals were considerably lower—only 27,000 of EDS's 140,000 employees were in India.

EDS, founded in 1962, was best known for its capabilities in running clients' mainframe systems, operating help desks to support personal computer users, developing and running business software for its clients, and handling such automated IT processes as billing and

EXHIBIT 10

Estimated Sales and Market Shares of the World's Six Leading Providers of Information Technology Services, 2007

Source: Gartner, as reported in Justin Scheck and Ben Worthen, "Hewlett-Packard Takes Aim at IBM," *Wall Street Journal,* May 14, 2008, p. B1.

Company	2007 Revenues (in billions)	Market Share
IBM	$ 54.1	7.2%
Electronic Data Systems (EDS)	22.1	3.0
Accenture	20.6	2.8
Fujitsu	18.6	2.5
Hewlett-Packard	17.3*	2.3
Computer Sciences Corp. (CSC)	16.3	2.2
All others	599.0	80.0
Totals	$748.0	100.0%

*Gartner's $17.3 billion number for HP's 2007 revenues in IT services exceeds the $16.6 billion reported by HP in its 2007 10-K report and shown in Exhibit 9.

payments for clients.[27] In contrast, HP's IT service business revolved around managing infrastructure—such as back-office server systems—for its large enterprises. There was relatively little overlap between the customer bases of the two companies. HP executives believed there was plenty of opportunity to cut costs at EDS and that there were clear revenue-boosting opportunities, such as expanding sales of managed printing services. Even so, HP's shareholders were unenthusiastic about the EDS acquisition—HP's stock price fell more than $10 per share in the two days following news of the acquisition but recovered $2.50 of the drop within a week.

DELL'S FUTURE PROSPECTS

In a February 2003 article in *Business 2.0,* Michael Dell said, "The best way to describe us now is as a broad computer systems and services company. We have a pretty simple system. The most important thing is to satisfy our customers. The second most important thing is to be profitable. If we don't do the first one well, the second one won't happen."[28] For the most part, Michael Dell was not particularly concerned about the efforts of competitors to copy many aspects of Dell's build-to-order, sell-direct strategy. He explained why on at least two occasions:

> The competition started copying us seven years ago. That's when we were a $1 billion business. . . . And they haven't made much progress to be honest with you. The learning curve for them is difficult. It's like going from baseball to soccer.[29]
>
> I think a lot of people have analyzed our business model, a lot of people have written about it and tried to understand it. This is an $18\frac{1}{2}$-year process. . . . It comes from many, many cycles of learning. . . . It's very, very different than designing products to be built to stock. . . . Our whole company is oriented around a very different way of operating. . . . I don't, for any second, believe that they are not trying to catch up. But it is also safe to assume that Dell is not staying in the same place.[30]

---

[27]Justin Scheck and Ben Worthen, "Hewlett-Packard Takes Aim at IBM," *Wall Street Journal,* May 14, 2008, p. B1.

[28]Business 2.0, February 2003, www.business2.com.

[29]Comments made to students at the University of North Carolina and reported in the *Raleigh News & Observer,* November 16, 1999.

[30]Remarks by Michael Dell, Gartner Fall Symposium, Orlando, FL, October 9, 2002, www.dell.com.

On other occasions, Michael Dell spoke about the size of the company's future opportunities:

> When technologies begin to standardize or commoditize, the game starts to change. Markets open up to be volume markets and this is very much where Dell has made its mark—first in the PC market in desktops and notebooks and then in the server market and the storage market and services and data networking. We continue to expand the array of products that we sell, the array of services and, of course, expand on a geographic basis. The way we think about it is that there are all of these various technologies out there. . . . What we have been able to do is build a business system that takes those technological ingredients, translates them into products and services and gets them to the customer more efficiently than any company around.[31]
>
> There are enormous opportunities for us to grow across multiple dimensions in terms of products, with servers, storage, printing and services representing a huge realm of expansion for us. There's geographic expansion and market share expansion back in the core business. The primary focus for us is picking those opportunities, seizing on them, and making sure we have the talent and the leadership growing inside the company to support all that growth. And there's also a network effect here. As we grow our product lines and enter new markets, we see a faster ability to gain share in new markets versus ones we've previously entered.[32]
>
> A great portion of our growth will come from key markets outside the U.S. We have about 10 percent market share outside the United States, so there's definitely room to grow. We'll grow in the enterprise with servers, storage, and services. Our growth will come from new areas like printing. And, quite frankly, those are really enough. There are other things that I could mention, other things we do, but those opportunities I mentioned can drive us to $80 billion and beyond.[33]

That Dell had ample growth opportunities was indisputable—in 2007, it only had a minuscule 2 percent share of the $1.2 trillion global market for IT products and services. Exhibit 11 shows Dell's principal competitors in each of the industry's major product categories and its estimated 2007 market shares in each category.

In 2008, despite near-term prospects of sluggish economic growth in the United States and perhaps elsewhere, Michael Dell remained enthusiastic about the unrivaled opportunity for the company's business given that the number of people online globally (via PCs, cell phones, and other devices with Internet connectivity) was expected to increase from just over 1 billion in 2008 to over 2 billion by 2011:

> The world is witnessing the most exciting and promising period for technology ever seen. We call it the "Connected Era." The second billion people coming online, many from the world's fast growing and emerging economies, expect a different technology experience to the first. The Internet has unleashed billions of new conversations and made it possible for people to connect in new ways. The emergence of this connected era is arguably the most influential single trend remodeling the world today.[34]

In May 2008, the latest sales and market share data indicated that Dell might be closing the gap on Hewlett-Packard and on the verge of mounting another run at being the global leader in PC sales. Exhibit 12 shows the sales and market shares of the world's top five PC vendors in the first quarter of 2008 as compared to the fourth quarter of 2007. Moreover, Dell's senior executives believed that their aggressive moves to reduce costs would help restore profit margins, given that there seemed to be some modest relief from having to contend with eroding average revenues per unit sold (see Exhibit 7).

---

[31]Remarks by Michael Dell, MIT Sloan School of Management, September 26, 2002, www.dell.com.
[32]Remarks by Michael Dell, University of Toronto, September 21, 2004, www.dell.com.
[33]Remarks by Michael Dell, Gartner Symposium, Orlando FL, October 20, 2005, www.dell.com.
[34]Remarks by Michael Dell to reporters in Dubai, company press release, April 6, 2008.

EXHIBIT 11 Dell's Principal Competitors and Dell's Estimated Market Shares by Product Category, 2007

Product Category	Dell's Principal Competitors	Estimated Size of Worldwide Market, 2007	Dell's Estimated Worldwide Share, 2007
PCs	Hewlett-Packard (maker of both Compaq and HP brands); Lenovo, Apple, Acer, Toshiba, Sony, Fujitsu-Siemens (in Europe and Japan)	$375 billion	~15%
Servers	Hewlett-Packard, IBM, Sun Microsystems, Fujitsu	$60 billion	~11%
Data storage devices	Hewlett-Packard, IBM, EMC, Hitachi	$48 billion	~5%
Networking switches and related equipment	Cisco Systems, Broadcom, Enterasys, Nortel, 3Com, Airespace, Proxim	~$65 billion	~2%
Printers and printer cartridges	Hewlett-Packard, Lexmark, Canon, Epson	~$50 billion	~5%
Services	Accenture, IBM, Hewlett-Packard, Fujitsu, EDS, many others	$748 billion	<1%

Source: Compiled by the case authors from a variety of sources, including International Data Corporation, www.dell.com, and *The Wall Street Journal*, May 14, 2008, p. B1.

EXHIBIT 12 Worldwide Unit Sales and Market Shares of Top Five PC Manufacturers, First Quarter 2008 versus Fourth Quarter 2007

Rank	Company	Q1, 2008 Shipments	Market Share	Q4, 2007 Shipments	Market Share	Percentage Growth in Shipments
1	Hewlett-Packard	13,251,000	19.1%	11,291,000	18.6%	17.4%
2	Dell	10,913,000	15.7%	8,971,000	14.8%	21.6%
3	Acer*	6,914,000	9.9%	4,164,000	6.9%	66.0%
4	Lenovo	4,814,000	6.9%	3,980,000	6.6%	21.0%
5	Toshiba	3,069,000	4.4%	2,544,000	4.2%	20.6%
	All Others	30,537,000	43.9%	29,674,000	48.9%	2.9%
	Total	69,498,000	100.0%	60,624,000	100.0%	14.6%

*Figures for Acer include shipments of Gateway, which was acquired by Acer in 2007.

Source: International Data Corporation, as per posting at www.dell.com (accessed May 12, 2008).

However, by late Fall 2008, Dell's prospects for overtaking HP were looking more bleak. Global recessionary forces had caused a significant slowdown in global IT spending during 2008 and even larger cutbacks were being forecast for at least the first half of 2009 in light of the global financial crisis that emerged in Fall 2008. Still, HP reported a 5 percent increase in revenues for its 2008 fourth quarter ending October 31 (excluding the effect of its recent acquisition of EDS) versus the year earlier 2007 fourth quarter and a 2008 fourth quarter earnings increase of 4 percent; moreover HP was forecasting that fiscal 2009 revenues would be in the $127.5 to $130 billion range, up from $118.4 billion in 2008. Dell's sales revenues in the third quarter of 2008 were 3 percent below those in the 2007 third quarter on unit-shipment growth of 3 percent; Dell's third quarter 2008 net profits were down 5 percent.

The Wall Street Journal reported in September 2008 that Dell was trying to sell its worldwide network of computer factories in an effort to reduce production costs; the apparent plan was to enter into agreements with contract manufacturers to produce its PCs.

While Dell had for many years been the industry leader in lean manufacturing approaches and cost-efficient build-to-order production methods and was still the low-cost leader in producing desktop PCs, it had fallen behind contract manufacturers in producing notebook PCs cost efficiently—and there was a pronounced shift among individual consumers to purchase laptop PCs instead of desktops. Laptop PCs were more complex and labor-intensive to assemble than were desktops. To help contain the assembly costs of laptops, Dell had already begun having Asian contract manufacturers partially assemble its laptops; these partly assembled laptop units were then shipped to Dell's own plants where assembly was completed. Because each laptop was produced at two factories, Dell referred to its assembly of laptops as a "two-two" system. But the two-touch system was more costly than simply having a contract manufacturer in Asia perform the entire assembly. Hence, Dell's interest in abandoning in-house production altogether and shifting to 100 percent outsourcing.

As of late November 2008, Dell had found no buyers for its plants. But the company had nonetheless begun outsourcing the full assembly of some laptop models to contract manufacturers (such as Taiwan's Foxconn Group) to eliminate the extra costs of the two-touch system, and it had made significant progress in cutting operating expenses elsewhere—operating expenses were 12.1 percent of revenues in the 2008 third quarter versus 12.8 percent in the 2007 third quarter. There were some other positives. In the 2008 third quarter, Dell's Global Consumer business posted a 10 percent revenue gain on a 32 percent increase in unit shipments—Dell's revenue growth was double the industry average and the profitability of this business was the highest in 13 quarters. Dell consumer products won 41 awards in the 2008 third quarter—the Inspiron Mini 9 notebook was selected as one of *Time Magazine*'s "Best Inventions of 2008" and as one of CNET's "10 Most Cutting Edge Products of 2008."

Section 6

Developing Marketing Plans

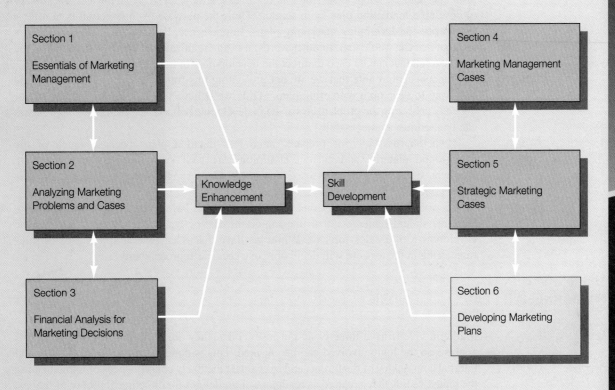

Section 1
Essentials of Marketing Management

Section 2
Analyzing Marketing Problems and Cases

Section 3
Financial Analysis for Marketing Decisions

Knowledge Enhancement

Skill Development

Section 4
Marketing Management Cases

Section 5
Strategic Marketing Cases

Section 6
Developing Marketing Plans

Imagine this scenario. After receiving your bachelor's or master's degree in marketing, you are hired by a major consumer goods company. Because you've done well in school, you are confident that you have a lot of marketing knowledge and a lot to offer to the firm. You're highly motivated and are looking forward to a successful career.

After just a few days of work you are called in for a conference with the vice president of marketing. The vice president welcomes you and tells you how glad the firm is that you have joined them. The vice president also says that, because you have done so well in your marketing courses and have had such recent training, he wants you to work on a special project.

He tells you that the company has a new product, which is to be introduced in a few months. He also says, confidentially, that recent new product introductions by the company haven't been too successful. Suggesting that the recent problems are probably because the company has not been doing a very good job of developing marketing plans, the vice president tells you not to look at marketing plans for the company's other products.

Your assignment, then, is to develop a marketing plan for the proposed product in the next six weeks. The vice president explains that a good job here will lead to rapid advancement in the company. You thank the vice president for the assignment and promise that you'll do your best.

How would you feel when you returned to your desk? Surely, you'd be flattered that you had been given this opportunity and be eager to do a good job. However, how confident are you that you could develop a quality marketing plan? Would you even know where to begin?

We suspect that many of you, even those who have an excellent knowledge of marketing principles and are adept at solving marketing cases, may not yet have the skills necessary to develop a marketing plan from scratch. Thus, the purpose of this section is to offer a framework for developing marketing plans. In one sense, this section is no more than a summary of the whole text. In other words, it is an organizational framework based on the text material that can be used to direct the development of marketing plans.

Students should note that we are not presenting this framework and discussion as the only way to develop a marketing plan. While we believe this is a useful framework for logically analyzing the problems involved in developing a marketing plan, other approaches can be used just as successfully.

Often, successful firms prepare much less detailed plans because much of the background material and current conditions are well known to everyone involved. However, our review of plans used in various firms suggests that something like this framework is not uncommon.

We would like to mention one other qualification before beginning our discussion. Students should remember that one important part of the marketing plan involves the development of a sales forecast. While we have discussed several approaches to sales forecasting in the text, we will detail only one specific approach here.

A MARKETING PLAN FRAMEWORK

Marketing plans have three basic purposes. First, they are used as a tangible record of analysis so the logic involved can be checked. This is done to ensure the feasibility and internal consistency of the project and to evaluate the likely consequences of implementing the plan. Second, they are used as roadmaps or guidelines for directing appropriate actions. A marketing plan is designed to be the best available scenario and rationale for directing the firm's efforts for a particular product or brand. Third, they are used as tools to obtain funding for implementation. This funding may come from internal or external sources. For

FIGURE 1
A Marketing Plan
Format

- Title page.
- Executive summary.
- Table of contents.
- Introduction.
- Situational analysis.
- Marketing planning.
- Implementation and control of the marketing plan.
- Summary.
- Appendix: Financial analysis.
- References.

example, a brand manager may have to present a marketing plan to senior executives in a firm to get a budget request filled. This would be an internal source. Similarly, proposals for funding from investors or business loans from banks often require a marketing plan. These would be external sources.

Figure 1 presents a format for preparing marketing plans. Each of the 10 elements will be briefly discussed. We will refer to previous chapters and sections in this text and to other sources where additional information can be obtained when a marketing plan is being prepared. We also will offer additional information for focusing particular sections of the plan as well as for developing financial analysis.

Title Page

The *title page* should contain the following information: (1) the name of the product or brand for which the marketing plan has been prepared—for example, Marketing Plan for Little Friskies Dog Food; (2) the period for which the plan is designed—for example, 2010–2012; (3) the person(s) and position(s) of those submitting the plan—for example, submitted by Amy Lewis, brand manager; (4) the persons, group, or agency to whom the plan is being submitted—for example, submitted to Lauren Ellis, product group manager; and (5) the date of submission of the plan—for example, June 30, 2010.

While preparing the title page is a simple task, remember that it is the first thing readers see. Thus, a title page that is poorly laid out, is smudged, or contains misspelled words can lead to the inference that the project was developed hurriedly and with little attention to detail. As with the rest of the project, appearances are important and affect what people think about the plan.

Executive Summary

The *executive summary* is a two- to three-page summary of the contents of the report. Its purpose is to provide a quick summary of the marketing plan for executives who need to be informed about the plan but are typically not directly involved in plan approval. For instance, senior executives for firms with a broad product line may not have time to read the entire plan but need an overview to keep informed about operations.

The executive summary should include a brief introduction, the major aspects of the marketing plan, and a budget statement. This is not the place to go into detail about each and every aspect of the marketing plan. Rather, it should focus on the major market opportunity and the key elements of the marketing plan that are designed to capitalize on this opportunity.

It is also useful to state specifically how much money is required to implement the plan. In an ongoing firm, many costs can be estimated from historical data or from discussions with other executives in charge of specific functional areas. However, in many situations (such as a class project), sufficient information is not always available to give exact costs for every aspect of production, promotion, and distribution. In these cases, include a rough estimate of total marketing costs of the plan. In many ongoing firms, marketing cost elements are concentrated in the areas of promotion and marketing research, and these figures are integrated with those from other functional areas as parts of the overall business plan.

Table of Contents

The *table of contents* is a listing of everything contained in the plan and where it is located in the report. Reports that contain a variety of charts and figures may also have a table of exhibits listing their titles and page numbers within the report.

In addition to using the table of contents as a place to find specific information, readers may also review it to see if each section of the report is logically sequenced. For example, situational analysis logically precedes marketing planning as an activity, and this ordering makes sense in presenting the plan.

Introduction

The types of information and amount of detail reported in the *introduction* depend in part on whether the plan is being designed for a new or existing product or brand. If the product is new, the introduction should explain the product concept and the reasons it is expected to be successful. Basically, this part of the report should make the new idea sound attractive to management or investors. In addition, it is useful to offer estimates of expected sales, costs, and return on investment.

If the marketing plan is for an existing brand in an ongoing firm, it is common to begin the report with a brief history of the brand. The major focus here is on the brand's performance in the last three to five years. It is useful to prepare graphs of the brand's performance that show its sales, profits, and market share for previous years and to explain the reasons for any major changes. These exhibits can also be extended to include predicted changes in these variables given the new marketing plan. A brief discussion of the overall strategy followed in previous years also provides understanding of how much change is being proposed in the new marketing plan.

Also useful in the introduction is to offer a precise statement of the purpose of the report as well as a roadmap of the report. In other words, tell readers what this report is, how it is organized, and what will be covered in the following sections.

Situational Analysis

The *situational analysis* is not unlike the analysis discussed in Chapter 1 and Section 2 of this text. The focus remains on the most critical and relevant environmental conditions (or changes in them) that affect the success or failure of the proposed plan. While any aspect of the economic, social, political, legal, or cooperative environment might deserve considerable attention, there is seldom if ever a marketing plan in which the competitive environment does not require considerable discussion. In fact, the competitive environment may be set off as a separate section called *industry analysis*. The strengths and weaknesses of major competitors, their relative market shares, and the success of various competitive strategies are critical elements of the situation analysis.

Marketing Planning

Marketing planning is, of course, a critical section of the report. As previously noted, it includes three major elements: marketing objectives, target markets, and the marketing mix.

Marketing Objectives

Marketing objectives are often stated in plans in terms of the percentage of particular outcomes that are to be achieved: for example, 80 percent awareness of the brand in particular markets, increase in trial rate by 30 percent, distribution coverage of 60 percent, or increase in total

Understanding an industry and the actions of competitors is critical to developing successful marketing plans. Below is a list of some questions to consider when performing competitive analysis. Thinking about these questions can aid the marketing planner in developing better marketing strategies.

1. Which firms compete in this industry and what is their financial position and marketing capability?
2. What are the relative market shares of various brands?
3. How many brands and models does each firm offer?
4. What marketing strategies have the market leaders employed?
5. Which brands have gained and which have lost market share in recent years, and what factors have led to these changes?
6. Are new competitors likely to enter the market?
7. How quickly do competitive firms react to changes in the market?
8. From which firms or brands might we be able to take market share?
9. What are the particular strengths and weaknesses of competitors in the industry?
10. How do we compare with other firms in the industry in terms of financial strength and marketing skills?

market share by 3 percent over the life of the plan. Similarly, objectives may be stated in terms of sales units or dollars or increases in these. Of course, the reasons for selection of the particular objectives and rationale are important points to explain.

Target Markets

The *target markets* discussion explains the customer base and rationale or justification for it. An approach to developing appropriate target markets is contained in Chapter 5 of this text.

This section also includes relevant discussion of changes or important issues in consumer or organizational buyer behavior: for example, what benefits consumers are seeking in this products class, what benefits does the particular brand offer, or what purchasing trends are shaping the market for this product. Discussions of consumer and organizational buyer behavior are contained in Chapters 3 and 4 of this text.

Marketing Mix

The *marketing mix* discussion explains in detail the selected strategy consisting of product, promotion, distribution, and price, and the rationale for it. Also, if marketing research has been done on these elements or is planned, it can be discussed in this section.

Product   The *product* section details a description of the product or brand, its packaging, and its attributes. Product life-cycle considerations should be mentioned if they affect the proposed plan.

Of critical importance in this discussion is the competitive advantage of the product or brand. Here it must be carefully considered whether the brand really does anything better than the competition or is purchased primarily on the basis of brand equity or value. For example, many brands of toothpaste have fluoride, yet Crest has the largest market share primarily through promoting this attribute of its brand. Thus, does Crest do anything more than other toothpastes, or is it Crest's image that accounts for sales?

Discussion of product-related issues is contained in Chapters 6 and 7, and services are discussed in Chapter 12 of this text. For discussion of marketing plans for products marketed globally, see Chapter 13.

Promotion   The *promotion* discussion consists of a description and justification of the planned promotion mix. It is useful to explain the theme of the promotion and to include some examples of potential ads as well as the nature of the sales force if one is to be used. For mass-marketed consumer goods, promotion costs can be large and need to be considered explicitly in the marketing plan.

Discussion of promotion-related issues is contained in Chapters 8 and 9 of this text. Secondary sources, such as *Standard Rate and Data, Simmons Media/Market Service, Starch Advertising Readership Service,* and the *Nielsen Television Index,* provide useful information for selecting, budgeting, and justifying media and other promotional decisions.

Distribution   The *distribution* discussion describes and justifies the appropriate channel or channels for the product. This includes types of intermediaries and specifically who they will be. Other important issues concern the level of market coverage desired, cost, and control considerations. In many cases, the channels of distribution used by the firm, as well as competitive firms, are well established. For example, General Motors and Ford distribute their automobiles through independent dealer networks. Thus, unless there is a compelling reason to change channels, the traditional channel will often be the appropriate alternative. However, serious consideration may have to be given to methods of obtaining channel support, for example, trade deals to obtain sufficient shelf space.

Discussion of distribution-related issues is contained in Chapter 10 of this text. Useful retail distribution information can be found in the *Nielsen Retail Index* and the *Audits and Surveys National Total-Market Index.*

Price   The pricing discussion starts with a specific statement of the price of the product. Depending on what type of channel is used, manufacturer price, wholesale price, and suggested retail price need to be listed and justified. In addition, special deals or trade discounts that are to be employed must be considered in terms of their effect on the firm's selling price.

Discussion of price-related issues is contained in Chapter 11. In addition to a variety of other useful information, the *Nielsen Retail Index* provides information on wholesale and retail prices.

Marketing Research   For any aspect of marketing planning, there may be a need for marketing research. If such research is to be performed, it is important to justify it and explain its costs and benefits. Such costs should also be included in the financial analysis.

If marketing research has already been conducted as part of the marketing plan, it can be reported as needed to justify various decisions that were reached. To illustrate, if research found that two out of three consumers like the taste of a new formula Coke, this information would likely be included in the product portion of the report. However, the details of the research could be placed here in the marketing research section. Discussion of marketing research is contained in Chapter 2.

Implementation and Control of the Marketing Plan

This section contains a discussion and justification of how the marketing plan will be implemented and controlled. It also explains who will be in charge of monitoring and changing the plan should unanticipated events occur and how the success or failure of the plan will be measured. Success or failure of the plan is typically measured by a comparison of the results of implementing the plan with the stated objectives.

For a marketing plan developed within an ongoing firm, this section can be quite explicit, because procedures for implementing plans may be well established. However, for a classroom project, the key issues to be considered are the persons responsible for implementing the plan, a timetable for sequencing the tasks, and a method of measuring and evaluating the success or failure of the plan.

For the direction-setting purpose of objectives to be fulfilled, objectives need to meet five specifications:

1. An objective should relate to a single, specific topic. (It should not be stated in the form of a vague abstraction or a pious platitude—"we want to be a leader in our industry" or "our objective is to be more aggressive marketers.")
2. An objective should relate to a result, not to an activity to be performed. (The objective is the result of the activity, not the performance of the activity.)
3. An objective should be measurable (stated in quantitative terms whenever feasible).
4. An objective should contain a time deadline for its achievement.
5. An objective should be challenging but achievable.

Consider the following examples:

1. Poor: Our objective is to maximize profits.
   Remarks: How much is "maximum"? The statement is not subject to measurement. What criterion or yardstick will management use to determine if and when actual profits are equal to maximum profits? No deadline is specified.
   Better: Our total profit target in 2015 is $1 million.
2. Poor: Our objective is to increase sales revenue and unit volume.
   Remarks: How much? Also, because the statement relates to two topics, it may be inconsistent. Increasing unit volume may require a price cut, and if demand is price inelastic, sales revenue would fall as unit volume rises. No time frame for achievement is indicated.
   Better: Our objective this calendar year is to increase sales revenues from $30 million to $35 million; we expect this to be accomplished by selling 1 million units at an average price of $35.
3. Poor: Our objective in 2015 is to boost advertising expenditures by 15 percent.
   Remarks: Advertising is an activity, not a result. The advertising objective should be stated in terms of what result the extra advertising is intended to produce.
   Better: Our objective is to boost our market share from 8 percent to 10 percent in 2015 with the help of a 15 percent increase in advertising expenditures.
4. Poor: Our objective is to be a pioneer in research and development and to be the technological leader in the industry.
   Remarks: Very sweeping and perhaps overly ambitious; implies trying to march in too many directions at once if the industry is one with a wide range of technological frontiers. More a platitude than an action commitment to a specific result.
   Better: During the 2010–2020 decade, our objective is to continue as a leader in introducing new technologies and new devices that will allow buyers of electrically powered equipment to conserve on electric energy usage.
5. Poor: Our objective is to be the most profitable company in our industry.
   Remarks: Not specific enough by what measures of profit—total dollars, or earnings per share, or unit profit margin, or return on equity investment, or all of these? Also, because the objective concerns how well other companies will perform, the objective, while challenging, may not be achievable.
   Better: We will strive to remain atop the industry in terms of rate of return on equity investment by earning a 25 percent after-tax return on equity investment in 2015.

Knowledge of consumers is paramount to developing successful marketing plans. Below is a list of questions that are useful to consider when analyzing consumers. For some of the questions, secondary sources of information or primary marketing research can be employed to aid in decision making. However, a number of them require the analyst to do some serious thinking about the relationship between brands of the product and various consumer groups to better understand the market.

1. How many people purchase and use this product in general?
2. How many people purchase and use each brand of the product?
3. Is there an opportunity to reach nonusers of the product with a unique marketing strategy?
4. What does the product do for consumers functionally and how does this vary by brand?
5. What does the product do for consumers in a social or psychological sense and how does this vary by brand?
6. Where do consumers currently purchase various brands of the product?
7. How much are consumers willing to pay for specific brands and is price a determining factor for purchase?
8. What is the market profile of the heavy user of this product and what percentage of the total market are heavy users?
9. What media reach these consumers?
10. On average, how often is this product purchased?
11. How important is brand equity for consumers of this product?
12. Why do consumers purchase particular brands?
13. How brand loyal are consumers of this product?

Summary

This *summary* need not be much different than the executive summary stated at the beginning of the document. However, it is usually a bit longer, more detailed, and states more fully the case for financing the plan.

Appendix—Financial Analysis

Financial analysis is a very important part of any marketing plan. While a complete business plan often includes extensive financial analysis, such as a complete cost breakdown and estimated return on investment, marketing planners frequently do not have complete accounting data for computing these figures. For example, decisions concerning how much overhead is to be apportioned to the product are not usually made solely by marketing personnel. However, the marketing plan should contain at least a sales forecast and estimates of relevant marketing costs.

Sales Forecast

As noted, there are a variety of ways to develop sales forecasts. Regardless of the method, however, they all involve trying to predict the future as accurately as possible. It is, of course, necessary to justify the logic for the forecasted figures, rather than offer them with no support.

One basic approach to developing a sales forecast is outlined in Figure 2. This approach begins by estimating the total number of persons in the selected target market. This estimate comes from the market segmentation analysis and may include information from test

FIGURE 2
A Basic Approach to
Sales Forecasting

Total number of people in target markets (a)		a
Annual number of purchases per person (b)	$\times$	b
Total potential market (c)	$=$	c
Total potential market (c)		c
Percent of total market coverage (d)	$\times$	d
Total available market (e)	$=$	e
Total available market (e)		e
Expected market share (f)	$\times$	f
Sales forecast (in units) (g)	$=$	g
Sales forecast (in units) (g)		g
Price (h)	$\times$	h
Sales forecast (in dollars) (i)	$=$	i

marketing and from secondary sources, such as *Statistical Abstracts of the United States.* For example, suppose a company is marketing a solar-powered watch that is designed not only to tell time but also to take the pulse of the wearer. The product is targeted at joggers and others interested in aerobic exercise. By reviewing the literature on these activities, the marketing planner, John Murphy, finds that the average estimate of this market on a national level is 60 million persons and is growing by 4 million persons per year. Thus, John might conclude that the total number of people in the target market for next year is 64 million. If he has not further limited the product's target market and has no other information, John might use this number as a basis for starting the forecast analysis.

The second estimate John needs is the annual number of purchases per person in the product's target market. This estimate could be quite large for such products as breakfast cereal or less than one (annual purchase per person) for such products as automobiles. For watches, the estimate is likely to be much less than one since people are likely to buy a new watch only every few years. Thus, John might estimate the annual number of purchases per person in the target market to be .25. Of course, as a careful marketing planner, John would probably carefully research this market to refine this estimate. In any event, multiplying these two numbers gives John an estimate of the *total potential market,* in this case, 64 million times .25 equals 16 million. In other words, if next year alone John's company could sell a watch to every jogger or aerobic exerciser who is buying a watch, the company could expect sales to be 16 million units.

Of course, the firm cannot expect to sell every jogger a watch for several reasons. First, it is unlikely to obtain 100 percent market coverage in the first year, if ever. Even major consumer goods companies selling convenience goods seldom reach the entire market in the first year and many never achieve even 90 percent distribution. Given the nature of the product and depending on the distribution alternative, John's company might be doing quite well to average 50 percent market coverage in the first year. If John's plans call for this kind of coverage, his estimate of the total available market would be 16 million times .5, which equals 8 million.

A second reason John's plans would not call for dominating the market is that his company does not have the only product available or wanted by this target market. Many of the people who will purchase such a watch will purchase a competitive brand. He must, therefore, estimate the product's likely market share. Of all the estimates made in developing a sales forecast, this one is critical because it is a reflection of the entire marketing plan. Important factors to consider in developing this estimate include (1) competitive market shares and likely marketing strategies; (2) competitive retaliation should the product do well; (3) competitive advantage of the product, such as lower price; (4) promotion mix and budget relative to competitors; and (5) market shares obtained by similar products in the introductory year.

Below is a brief list of questions about the marketing planning section of the report. Answering them honestly and recognizing both the strengths and weaknesses of the marketing plan should help improve it.

1. What key assumptions were made in developing the marketing plan?
2. How badly will the product's market position be hurt if these assumptions turn out to be incorrect?
3. How good is the marketing research?
4. Is the marketing plan consistent? For example, if the plan is to seek a prestige position in the market, is the product priced, promoted, and distributed to create this image?
5. Is the marketing plan feasible? For example, are the financial and other resources (such as a distribution network) available to implement it?
6. How will the marketing plan affect profits and market share, and is it consistent with corporate objectives?
7. Will implementing the marketing plan result in competitive retaliation that will end up hurting the firm?
8. Is the marketing mix designed to reach and attract new customers or increase usage among existing users or both?
9. Will the marketing mix help to develop brand-loyal consumers?
10. Will the marketing plan not only be successful in the short run but also contribute to a profitable long-run position?

Overall, suppose John estimates the product's market share to be 5 percent, because other competitive products have beat his company to the market and because the company's competitive advantage is only a slightly more stylish watch. In this case, the sales forecast for year one would be 8 million times .05, which equals 400,000 units. If the manufacturer's selling price was $50, then the sales forecast in dollars would be 400,000 times $50, which equals $20 million.

This approach can also be used to extend the sales forecast for any number of years. Typically, estimates of most of the figures change from year to year, depending on changes in market size, distribution coverage, and expected market shares. The value of this approach is that it forces an analyst to carefully consider and justify each of the estimates offered, rather than simply pulling numbers out of the air.

Estimates of Marketing Costs

A complete delineation of all costs, apportionment of overhead, and other accounting tasks are usually performed by other departments within a firm. All of this information, including expected return on investment from implementing the marketing plan, is part of the overall business plan.

However, the marketing plan should at least contain estimates of major marketing costs. These include such things as advertising, sales force training and compensation, channel development, and marketing research. Estimates may also be included for product development and package design.

For some marketing costs, reasonable estimates are available from sources such as *Standard Rate and Data*. However, some cost figures, such as marketing research, might be obtained from asking various marketing experts for the estimated price of proposed research. Other

Implementation and control of a marketing plan require careful scheduling and attention to detail. While some firms have standard procedures for dealing with many of the questions raised below, thinking through each of the questions should help improve the efficiency of even these firms in this stage of the process.

1. Who is responsible for implementing and controlling the marketing plan?
2. What tasks must be performed to implement the marketing plan?
3. What are the deadlines for implementing the various tasks and how critical are specific deadlines?
4. Has sufficient time been scheduled to implement the various tasks?
5. How long will it take to get the planned market coverage?
6. How will the success or failure of the plan be determined?
7. How long will it take to get the desired results from the plan?
8. How long will the plan be in effect before changes will be made to improve it based on more current information?
9. If an ad agency or other firms are involved in implementing the plan, how much responsibility and authority will they have?
10. How frequently will the progress of the plan be monitored?

types of marketing costs might be estimated from financial statements of firms in the industry. For example, Morris's *Annual Statement Studies* offers percentage breakdowns of various income statement information by industry. These might be used to estimate the percentage of the sales-forecast figure that would likely be spent in a particular cost category.

References

The *references* section contains the sources of any secondary information that was used in developing the marketing plan. This information might include company reports and memos, statements of company objectives, and articles or books used for information or support of the marketing plan.

References should be listed alphabetically using a consistent format. One way of preparing references is to use the same approach as is used in marketing journals. For example, the format used for references in *Journal of Marketing* articles is usually acceptable.

CONCLUSION

Suppose you're now sitting at your desk faced with the task of developing a marketing plan for a new product. Do you believe that you might have the skills to develop a marketing plan? Of course, your ability to develop a quality plan will depend on your learning experiences during your course work and the amount of practice you've had; for example, if you developed a promotion plan in your advertising course, it is likely that you could do a better job on the promotion phase of the marketing plan. Similarly, your experiences in analyzing cases should have sharpened your skills at recognizing problems and developing solutions to them. But inexperience (or experience) aside, hopefully you now feel that you understand the process of developing a marketing plan. You at least know where to start, where to seek information, how to structure the plan, and some of the critical issues that require analysis.

Additional Resources

Cohen, William A. *The Marketing Plan*. 5th ed. New York: John Wiley, 2006.

Cravens, David W., and Nigel F. Piercy. *Strategic Marketing*. 9th ed. Burr Ridge, IL: McGraw-Hill/Irwin, 2009.

Hiebing, Roman G., and Scott W. Cooper. *The One-Day Marketing Plan: Organizing and Completing a Plan That Works*. 3rd ed. Burr Ridge, IL: McGraw-Hill, 2004.

Hiebing, Roman G., and Scott W. Cooper. *The Successful Marketing Plan*. Burr Ridge, IL: McGraw-Hill, 2003.

Kerin, Roger A., Steven W. Hartley, and William Rudelius. *Marketing*. 9th ed. Burr Ridge, IL: McGraw-Hill/Irwin, 2009, pp. 54–67.

Lehmann, Donald R., and Russell S. Winer. *Analysis for Marketing Planning*. 7th ed. Burr Ridge, IL: McGraw-Hill/Irwin, 2008.

Walker, Orville C., Jr., John Mullins, and Harper W. Boyd, Jr. *Marketing Strategy: A Decision Focused Approach*. 6th ed. Burr Ridge, IL: McGraw-Hill/Irwin, 2008.

Notes

SECTION 1

Chapter 1

1. See Reinhard Angelmar and Christian Pinson, "The Meaning of Marketing," *Philosophy of Science,* June 1975, pp. 208–14.

2. Approved by the American Marketing Association, 2007.

3. Much of this section is based on J. H. Donnelly, Jr., J. L. Gibson, and J. M. Ivancevich, *Fundamentals of Management,* 9th ed. (Burr Ridge, IL: McGraw-Hill/Irwin, 1998), chap. 7.

4. The process may differ depending on the type of organization or management approach, or both. For certain types of organizations, one strategic plan will be sufficient. Some manufacturers with similar product lines or limited product lines will develop only one strategic plan. However, organizations with widely diversified product lines and widely diversified markets may develop strategic plans for units or divisions. These plans usually are combined into a master strategic plan.

5. For a discussion of this topic, see Gerald E. Ledford, Jr., Jon R. Wendenhof, and James T. Strahely, "Realizing a Corporate Philosophy," *Organizational Dynamics,* Winter 1995, pp. 4–19; and Stephan Cummings and John Davies, "Mission, Vision, Fusion," *Long Range Planning,* December 1994, pp. 147–50.

6. Philip Kotler and Gary Armstrong, *Principles of Marketing,* 6th ed. (Englewood Cliffs, NJ: Prentice Hall, 1994), Chap. 2.

7. Philip Kotler, *Marketing Management: Analysis, Planning, Implementation and Control,* 8th ed. (Englewood Cliffs, NJ: Prentice Hall, 1994), chap. 3.

8. Norton Paley, "A Sign of Intelligence," *Sales & Marketing Management,* March 1995, pp. 30–31.

9. Peter Drucker, *Management: Tasks, Responsibilities, Practices* (NY: Harper & Row, 1974), pp. 77–89; Kotler, *Marketing Management,* chap. 3.

10. Much of the following discussion is based on Drucker, *Management,* pp. 79–87.

11. Noel B. Zabriskie and Alan B. Huellmantel, "Marketing Research as a Strategic Tool," *Long Range Planning,* February 1994, pp. 107–18.

12. Originally discussed in the classic H. Igor Ansoff, *Corporate Strategy* (NY: McGraw-Hill, 1965).

13. For complete coverage of this topic, see Michael E. Porter, *Competitive Advantage: Creating and Sustaining Superior Performance* (NY: The Free Press, 1985).

Material in this section is based upon discussions contained in Steven J. Skinner, *Marketing,* 2nd ed. (Boston: Houghton Mifflin Co., 1994), pp. 48–50; and Thomas A. Bateman and Carl P. Zeithaml, *Management Function & Strategy,* 2nd ed. (Burr Ridge, IL: McGraw-Hill/Irwin, 1993), pp. 152–53.

14. For a complete discussion of this topic, see Michael Treacy and Fred Wiersema, *The Discipline of Market Leaders* (Reading, MA: Addison-Wesley, 1995); and Michael Treacy and Fred Wiersema, "How Market Leaders Keep Their Edge," *Fortune,* February 6, 1995, pp. 88–98.

15. Philip Kotler, *Marketing Management,* p. 13.

16. For a discussion of this issue and other mistakes marketers frequently make, see Kevin J. Clancy and Robert S. Shulman, "Breaking the Mold," *Sales & Marketing Management,* January 1994, pp. 82–84.

17. George S. Day and David B. Montgomery, "Diagnosing the Experience Curve," *Journal of Marketing,* Spring 1983, pp. 44–58.

18. P. Rajan Varadarajan, Terry Clark, and William M. Pride, "Controlling the Uncontrollable: Managing Your Market Environment," *Sloan Management Review,* Winter 1992, pp. 39–47.

19. Reed E. Nelson, "Is There Strategy in Brazil?" *Business Horizons,* July–August 1992, pp. 15–23.

20. Peter S. Davis and Patrick L. Schill, "Addressing the Contingent Effects of Business Unit Strategic Orientation on the Relationship between Organizational Context and Business Unit Performance," *Journal of Business Research,* 1993, pp. 183–200.

21. J. Scott Armstrong and Roderick J. Brodie, "Effects of Portfolio Planning Methods on Decision Making: Experimental Results," *International Journal of Research in Marketing,* January 1994, pp. 73–84.

22. Michel Roberts, "Times Change but Do Business Strategies?" *Journal of Business Strategy,* March–April 1993, pp. 12–15.

23. Donald L. McCabe and V. K. Narayanan, "The Life Cycle of the PIMS and BCG Models," *Industrial Marketing Management,* November 1991, pp. 347–52.

Chapter 2

1. Based on Peter D. Bennett, ed., *Dictionary of Marketing Terms,* 2nd ed. (Chicago: American Marketing Association, 1995), p. 77.

2. Gilbert A. Churchill, Jr., and J. Paul Peter, *Marketing: Creating Value for Customers*, 2nd ed. (Burr Ridge, IL: McGraw-Hill/Irwin, 1998), p. 116.

3. For a discussion of some general problems in marketing research, see Alan G. Sawyer and J. Paul Peter, "The Significance of Statistical Significance Testing in Marketing Research," *Journal of Marketing Research*, May 1983, pp. 122–33.

4. This section is based on Churchill and Peter, *Marketing*, pp. 114–16.

Chapter 3

1. Richard P. Coleman, "The Continuing Significance of Social Class to Marketing," *Journal of Consumer Research*, December 1983, pp. 265–80.

2. See William O. Bearden and Michael J. Etzel, "Reference Group Influence on Product and Brand Purchase Decisions," *Journal of Consumer Research*, September 1982, pp. 183–94; and Terry L. Childers and Akshay R. Rao, "The Influence of Familial and Peer-Based Reference Groups on Consumer Decisions," *Journal of Consumer Research*, September 1992, pp. 198–211.

3. See Rosann L. Spiro, "Persuasion in Family Decision Making," *Journal of Consumer Research*, March 1983, pp. 393–402.

4. See Janet Wagner and Sherman Hanna, "The Effectiveness of Family Life Cycle Variables in Consumer Expenditure Research," *Journal of Consumer Research*, December 1983, pp. 281–91. Also see Charles M. Schanninger and William D. Danko, "A Conceptual and Empirical Comparison of Alternative Household Life Cycle Models," *Journal of Consumer Research*, March 1993, pp. 580–94.

5. Russell W. Belk, "Situational Variables and Consumer Behavior," *Journal of Consumer Research*, December 1975, pp. 156–64. Also see Jacob Hornik, "Situational Effects on the Consumption of Time," *Journal of Marketing*, Fall 1982, pp. 44–55; C. Whan Park, Easwer S. Iyer, and Daniel C. Smith, "The Effects of Situational Factors on In-Store Grocery Shopping Behavior: The Role of Store Environment and Time Available for Shopping," *Journal of Consumer Research*, March 1989, pp. 422–33; and Mary Jo Bitner, "Servicescapes: The Impact of Physical Surroundings on Customers and Employees," *Journal of Marketing*, April 1992, pp. 57–71.

6. J. Paul Peter and Jerry C. Olson, *Consumer Behavior and Marketing Strategy*, 9th ed. (Burr Ridge, IL: McGraw-Hill/Irwin, 2010), chap. 4.

7. A. H. Maslow, *Motivation and Personality* (NY: Harper & Row, 1954); also see James F. Engel, Roger D. Blackwell, and Paul W. Miniard, *Consumer Behavior*, 8th ed. (Fort Worth, TX: Dryden Press, 1995), chap. 5, for further discussion of need recognition.

8. For a detailed review of research on external search, see Sharon E. Beatty and Scott M. Smith, "External Search Effort: An Investigation across Several Product Categories," *Journal of Consumer Research*, June 1987, pp. 83–95. Also see Narasimhan Srinivasan and Brian T. Ratchford, "An Empirical Test of a Model of External Search for Automobiles," *Journal of Consumer Research*, September 1991, pp. 233–42; and Julie L. Ozanne, Merrie Brucks, and Dhruv Grewal, "A Study of Information Search Behavior during the Categorization of New Products," *Journal of Consumer Research*, March 1992, pp. 452–63.

9. For further discussion of information processing, see J. Paul Peter and Jerry C. Olson, *Consumer Behavior and Marketing Strategy*, 8th ed. (Burr Ridge, IL: McGraw-Hill/Irwin, 2008), chap. 3.

10. For a summary of research on attitude modeling, see Blair H. Sheppard, Jon Hartwick, and Paul R. Warshaw, "The Theory of Reasoned Action: A Meta-Analysis of Past Research with Recommendations for Modification and Future Research," *Journal of Consumer Research*, December 1988, pp. 325–43.

11. For further discussion of postpurchase feelings, see Richard L. Oliver, "Cognitive, Affective, and Attribute Bases of the Satisfaction Response," *Journal of Consumer Research*, December 1993, pp. 418–30; and Haim Mano and Richard L. Oliver, "Assessing the Dimensionality and Structure of the Consumption Experience: Evaluation, Feeling, and Satisfaction," *Journal of Consumer Research*, December 1993, pp. 451–66.

Chapter 4

1. This discussion is based on Gilbert A. Churchill, Jr., and J. Paul Peter, *Marketing: Creating Value for Customers*, 2nd ed. (Burr Ridge, IL: McGraw-Hill/Irwin, 1998), pp. 182–84. Also see Michele D. Bunn, "Taxonomy of Buying Decision Approaches," *Journal of Marketing*, January 1993, pp. 38–56.

2. This discussion is based on Eric N. Berkowitz, Roger A. Kerin, Steven W. Hartley, and William Rudelius, *Marketing*, 8th ed. (Burr Ridge, IL: McGraw-Hill/Irwin, 2006), p. 157.

3. For research on influence strategies in organizational buying, see Gary L. Frazier and Raymond Rody, "The Use of Influence Strategies in Interfirm Relationships in Industrial Product Channels," *Journal of Marketing*, January 1991, pp. 52–69; and Julia M. Bristor, "Influence Strategies in Organizational Buying," *Journal of Business-to-Business Marketing*, 1993, pp. 63–98.

4. For research on the role of organizational climate in industrial buying, see William J. Qualls and Christopher P. Puto, "Organizational Climate and Decision Framing: An Integrated Approach to Analyzing Industrial Buying Decisions," *Journal of Marketing Research*, May 1989, pp. 179–92.

Chapter 5

1. Russell I. Haley, "Benefit Segmentation: A Decision-Oriented Research Tool," *Journal of Marketing,* July 1968, pp. 30–35; Russell I. Haley, "Benefit Segmentation—20 Years Later," *Journal of Consumer Marketing,* 1983, pp. 5–13; and Russell I. Haley, "Benefit Segments: Backwards and Forwards," *Journal of Advertising Research,* February–March 1984, pp. 19–25.

2. Roger J. Calantone and Alan G. Sawyer, "The Stability of Benefit Segments," *Journal of Marketing Research,* August 1978, pp. 395–404; also see James R. Merrill and William A. Weeks, "Predicting and Identifying Benefit Segments in the Elderly Market," in *AMA Educator's Proceedings,* eds. Patrick Murphy et al. (Chicago: American Marketing Association, 1983), pp. 399–403; Wagner A. Kamakura, "A Least Squares Procedure for Benefit Segmentation with Conjoint Experiments," *Journal of Marketing Research,* May 1988, pp. 157–67; and Michel Wedel and Jan-Benedict E. M. Steenkamp, "A Clusterwise Regression Method for Simultaneous Fuzzy Market Structuring and Benefit Segmentation," *Journal of Marketing Research,* November 1991, pp. 385–96.

3. John L. Lastovicka, John P. Murry, Jr., and Eric Joachimsthaler, "Evaluating the Measurement Validity of Lifestyle Typologies with Qualitative Measures and Multiplicative Factoring," *Journal of Marketing Research,* February 1990, pp. 11–23.

4. This discussion is taken from J. Paul Peter and Jerry C. Olson, *Consumer Behavior and Marketing Strategy,* 9th ed. (Burr Ridge, IL: McGraw-Hill/Irwin, 2010), pp. 367–372.

5. Ibid., pp. 379–381.

6. See Al Ries and Jack Trout, *Positioning: The Battle for Your Mind* (NY: Warner Books, 1981); and Al Ries and Jack Trout, *Marketing Warfare* (NY: McGraw-Hill, 1986).

Chapter 6

1. Material for this section is based on discussions contained in Louis E. Boone and David L. Kurtz, *Contemporary Marketing,* 8th ed. (Fort Worth, TX: Dryden, 1995), Chap. 2; Gilbert A. Churchill, Jr., and J. Paul Peter, *Marketing: Creating Value for Customers* (Burr Ridge, IL: McGraw-Hill/Irwin, 1995), chap. 1, p. 634; James H. Donnelly, James L. Gibson, and John M. Ivancevich, *Fundamentals of Management,* 9th ed. (Burr Ridge, IL: McGraw-Hill/Irwin, 1995), p. 501; Joseph M. Juran, "Made in the U.S.A.: A Renaissance in Quality," *Harvard Business Review,* July–August 1993, pp. 42–47, 50; and Valerie A. Zeithaml, "Consumer Perceptions of Price, Quality, and Value: A Means End Model and Synthesis of Evidence," *Journal of Marketing,* April 1988, pp. 35–48.

2. For a discussion on this topic, see Andrew J. Bergman, "What the Marketing Professional Needs to Know about ISO 9000 Series Registration," *Industrial Marketing Management,* 1994, pp. 367–70.

3. The material for this section comes from Glenn L. Urban and Steven H. Star, *Advanced Marketing Strategy* (Englewood Cliffs, NJ: Prentice Hall, 1991), Chap. 16.

4. For a detailed discussion of this topic, see Anne Perkins, "Product Variety beyond Black," *Harvard Business Review,* November–December 1994, pp. 13–14; and "Perspectives: The Logic of Product-Line Extensions," *Harvard Business Review,* November–December 1994, pp. 53–62.

5. Mats Urde, "Brand Orientation—A Strategy for Survival," *Journal of Consumer Marketing,* 1994, pp. 18–32.

6. James Lowry, "Survey Finds Most Powerful Brands," *Advertising Age,* July 11, 1988, p. 31.

7. Peter H. Farquhar, "Strategic Challenges for Branding," *Marketing Management,* 1994, pp. 8–15.

8. Peter D. Bennett, ed., *Dictionary of Marketing Terms,* 2nd ed. (Chicago: American Marketing Association, 1995), p. 27.

9. Terance Shimp, *Promotion Management and Marketing Communications,* 2nd ed. (Hinsdale, IL: Dryden Press, 1990), p. 67.

10. David A. Aaker and Kevin Lane Keller, "Consumer Evaluations of Brand Extensions," *Journal of Marketing,* January 1990, pp. 27–41.

11. Ibid.

12. For a detailed discussion of brand equity, see David Aaker, *Managing Brand Equity* (New York and London: Free Press, 1991).

13. For a complete discussion of this topic, see Geoffrey L. Gordon, Roger J. Calantone, and C. A. Di Benedetto, "Brand Equity in the Business-to-Business Sector: An Exploratory Study," *Journal of Product & Brand Management,* 1993, pp. 4–16.

14. Jeffrey D. Zbar, "Industry Trends Hold Private-Label Promise," *Advertising Age,* April 3, 1995, p. 31.

15. Karen Benezra, "Frito Bets 'Reduced' Pitch Is in the Chips," *Brandweek,* January 23, 1995, p. 18.

16. Thomas Hine, "Why We Buy," *Worth,* May 1995, pp. 80–83.

17. For a discussion of problems related to this issue, see Geoffrey L. Gordon, Roger J. Calantone, and C. Anthony Di Benedetto, "Mature Markets and Revitalization Strategies: An American Fable," *Business Horizons,* May–June 1991, pp. 39–50.

18. Barry L. Bayus, "Are Product Life Cycles Really Getting Shorter?" *Journal of Product Innovation Management,* September 1994, pp. 300–308.

19. The discussion on benchmarking is based on Stanley Brown, "Don't Innovate—Imitate," *Sales & Marketing Management,* January 1995, pp. 24–25; Charles

Goldwasser, "Benchmarking: People Make the Process," *Management Review,* June 1995, pp. 39–43; and L. S. Pryor and S. J. Katz, "How Benchmarking Goes Wrong (and How to Do It Right)," *Planning Review,* January–February 1993, pp. 6–14.

Chapter 7

1. "Face Value: The Mass Production of Ideas, and Other Impossibilities," *The Economist,* March 18, 1995, p. 72.

2. Greg Erickson, "New Package Makes a New Product Complete," *Marketing News,* May 8, 1995, p. 10.

3. Zina Mouhkheiber, "Oversleeping," *Forbes,* June 15, 1995, pp. 78–79.

4. See C. Merle Crawford and Anthony Di Benedetto, *New Products Management,* 10th ed. (Burr Ridge, IL: McGraw-Hill/Irwin 2011), p. 14.

5. H. Igor Ansoff, *Corporate Strategy* (NY: McGraw-Hill, 1965), pp. 109–10.

6. Richard Stroup, "Growing in a Crowded Market Requires Old and New Strategies," *Brandweek,* August 22, 1994, p. 19.

7. These two examples came from Justin Martin, "Ignore Your Customers," *Fortune,* May 1, 1995, pp. 121–26.

8. "Where Do They Get All Those Ideas?" *Machine Design,* January 26, 1995, p. 40.

9. This section is based on Daryl McKee, "An Organizational Learning Approach to Product Innovation," *Journal of Product Innovation Management,* September 1992, pp. 232–45.

10. The discussion on risk is from Thomas D. Kuczmarski and Arthur G. Middlebrooks, "Innovation Risk and Reward," *Sales & Marketing Management,* February 1993, pp. 44–51.

11. For a more complete discussion on the advantages and disadvantages of strategic alliances, see Richard N. Cardozo, Shannon H. Shipp, and Kenneth J. Roering, "Proactive Strategic Partnerships: A New Business Markets Strategy," *Journal of Business and Industrial Marketing,* Winter 1992, pp. 51–63; and Frank K. Sonnenberg, "Partnering: Entering the Age of Cooperation," *Journal of Business Strategy,* May/June 1992, pp. 49–52.

12. James Quinn, "Managing Innovation: Controlled Chaos," *Harvard Business Review,* May–June 1985, pp. 73–84; and Hirotaka Takeuchi and Ikujiro Nonaka, "The New New Product Development Game," *Harvard Business Review,* January–February 1986, pp. 137–46.

13. For a discussion of this issue, see Eric M. Olson, Orville C. Walker, Jr., and Robert W. Ruekert, "Organizing for Effective New Product Development: The Moderating Role of Product Innovativeness," *Journal of Marketing,* January 1995, pp. 48–62; and Christopher

Meyer, "How the Right Measures Help Teams Excel," *Harvard Business Review,* May–June 1994, pp. 95–97.

14. For a detailed discussion on these stages, see Karl T. Ulrich and Steven D. Eppinger, *Product Design and Development* (NY: McGraw-Hill, 1995); and Glen Rifken, "Product Development: Emphatic Design Helps Understand Users Better," *Harvard Business Review,* March–April 1994, pp. 10–11.

15. Patricia W. Meyers and Gerald A. Athaide, "Strategic Mutual Learning between Producing and Buying Firms during Product Innovation," *Journal of Product Innovation Management,* September 1991, pp. 155–69.

16. For a discussion of this issue, see Christina Brown and James Lattin, "Investigating the Relationship between Time in Market and Pioneering Advantage," *Management Science,* October 1994, pp. 1361–69; Robin Peterson, "Forecasting for New Product Introduction," *Journal of Business Forecasting,* Fall 1994, pp. 21–23; and Tracy Carlson, "The Race Is On," *Brandweek,* May 9, 1994, pp. 22–27.

17. For a discussion of reasons why products fail, see Betsy Spellman, "Big Talk, Little Dollars," *Brandweek,* January 23, 1995, pp. 21–29.

Chapter 8

1. This discussion is adapted from material contained in Gilbert A. Churchill, Jr., and J. Paul Peter, *Marketing: Creating Value for Customers,* 2nd ed. (Burr Ridge, IL: McGraw-Hill/Irwin, 1998), chap. 18.

2. Material for this section is largely based on the discussion of advertising tasks and objectives contained in William Arens and Courtland Bovèe, *Contemporary Advertising,* 5th ed. (Burr Ridge, IL: McGraw-Hill/Irwin, 1994), chap. 7.

3. For more comprehensive coverage of this topic, see George E. Belch and Michael A. Belch, *Advertising and Promotion: An Integrated Marketing Communications Perspective,* 7th ed. (Burr Ridge, IL: McGraw-Hill/Irwin, 2007), chap. 12.

4. For a fuller explanation of the pros and cons associated with push marketing strategies, see Betsy Spellman, "Trade Promotion Redefined," *Brandweek,* March 13, 1995, pp. 25–34; and John McManus, "'Lost' Money Redefined as 'Found' Money Won't Connect the Disconnects," *Brandweek,* March 25, 1995, p. 16.

5. This discussion is based on Donald R. Glover, "Distributor Attitudes toward Manufacturer-Sponsored Promotions," *Industrial Marketing Management,* August 1991, pp. 241–49.

6. For a discussion of this topic, see Murray Raphel, "Frequent Shopper Clubs: Supermarkets' Newest Weapon," *Direct Marketing,* May 1995, pp. 18–20; Richard G. Barlow, "Five Mistakes of Frequency Marketing,"

Direct Marketing, March 1995, pp. 16–17; and Alice Cuneo, "Savvy Frequent-Buyer Plans Build on a Loyal Base," *Advertising Age,* March 20, 1995, pp. S10–11.

Chapter 9

1. Warren Keegan, Sandra Moriarty, and Thomas Duncan, *Marketing,* 2nd ed. (Englewood Cliffs, NJ: Prentice Hall, 1994), p. 654.

2. Material for this discussion came from Ronald B. Marks, *Personal Selling: An Interactive Approach,* 5th ed. (Boston, MA: Allyn and Bacon, 1994), pp. 12–13.

3. Material for the discussion of objectives is adapted from Joel R. Evans and Barry Berman, *Marketing,* 6th ed. (NY: Macmillan, 1994), pp. 640–42.

4. Unless otherwise noted, the discussion on the relationship-building process is based largely on material contained in Barton A. Weitz, Stephen B. Castleberry, and John F. Tanner, Jr., *Selling: Building Partnerships,* 3rd ed. (Burr Ridge, IL: McGraw-Hill/Irwin, 1998); and Rolph Anderson, *Essentials of Personal Selling: The New Professionalism* (Englewood Cliffs, NJ: Prentice Hall, 1995). For an in-depth discussion of this topic, readers should consult these references.

5. The discussion of aftermarketing is based on the work of Terry Vavra, *Aftermarketing: How to Keep Customers for Life through Relationship Marketing* (Burr Ridge, IL: McGraw-Hill, 1995).

6. Ibid.

7. The discussion on national account management is from James S. Boles, Bruce K. Pilling, and George W. Goodwyn, "Revitalizing Your National Account Marketing Program," *Journal of Business & Industrial Marketing,* no. 1 (1994), pp. 24–33.

8. Based on a survey by the National Industrial Conference Board: "Forecasting Sales," *Studies in Business Policy,* no. 106.

9. Much of the discussion in this section is based on material contained in Gilbert A. Churchill, Jr., Neil M. Ford, and Orville C. Walker, Jr., *Sales Force Management,* 4th ed. (Burr Ridge, IL: McGraw-Hill/Irwin, 1993); and William J. Stanton, Richard H. Buskirk, and Rosann L. Spiro, *Management of a Sales Force,* 9th ed. (Burr Ridge, IL: McGraw-Hill/Irwin, 1995), pp. 319–20.

10. For a complete discussion of the skills and policies successful sales leaders use in motivating salespeople, see David W. Cravens, Thomas N. Ingram, Raymond W. LaForge, and Clifford E. Young, "Hallmarks of Effective Sales Organizations," *Marketing Management,* Winter 1992, pp. 57–66; Thomas R. Wortruba, John S. Mactie, and Jerome A. Colletti, "Effective Sales Force Recognition Programs," *Industrial Marketing Management,* February 1991, pp. 9–15; and Ken Blanchard, "Reward Salespeople Creatively," *Personal Selling Power,* March 1992, p. 24.

Chapter 10

1. Peter D. Bennett, *Dictionary of Marketing Terms,* 2nd ed. (Chicago: American Marketing Association, 1995), p. 242.

2. For further discussion of relationship marketing, see Jan B. Heide, "Interorganizational Governance in Marketing Channels," *Journal of Marketing,* January 1994, pp. 71–85; Robert M. Morgan and Shelby D. Hunt, "The Commitment-Trust Theory of Relationship Marketing," *Journal of Marketing,* July 1994, pp. 20–38; and Manohar U. Kalwani and Narakesari Narayandas, "Long-Term Manufacturer-Supplier Relationships: Do They Pay Off for the Supplier Firm?" *Journal of Marketing,* January 1995, pp. 1–16.

3. This section is based on Donald J. Bowersox and M. Bixby Cooper, *Strategic Marketing Channel Management* (NY: McGraw-Hill, 1992), pp. 104–7; Bert Rosenbloom, *Marketing Channels: A Management View,* 4th ed. (Hinsdale, IL: Dryden Press), pp. 440–65; and Roger A. Kerin, Eric N. Berkowitz, Steven W. Hartley, and William Rudelius, *Marketing,* 8th ed. (Burr Ridge, IL: McGraw-Hill/Irwin, 2006), pp. 405–407.

4. This section is based on Gilbert A. Churchill, Jr., and J. Paul Peter, *Marketing: Creating Value for Customers,* 2nd ed. (Burr Ridge, IL: McGraw-Hill/Irwin, 1998), pp. 392–98.

5. This classification is based on Michael Levy and Barton A. Weitz, *Retailing Management,* 8th ed. (Burr Ridge, IL: McGraw-Hill/Irwin, 2012), p. 10.

6. Ibid., Chapter 3.

7. For an excellent discussion of electronic exchange, see David W. Stewart and Qin Zhao, "Internet Marketing, Business Models, and Public Policy," *Journal of Public Policy & Marketing,* Fall 2000, pp. 287–96.

Chapter 11

1. Kent B. Monroe, "Buyers' Subjective Perceptions of Price," *Journal of Marketing Research,* February 1973, pp. 70–80; also see Donald R. Lichtenstein and Scot Burton, "The Relationship between Perceived and Objective Price—Quality," *Journal of Marketing Research,* November 1989, pp. 429–43.

2. For research concerning the effects of price and several other marketing variables on perceived product quality, see Akshay R. Rao and Kent B. Monroe, "The Effect of Price, Brand Name, and Store Name on Buyers' Perceptions of Product Quality: An Integrative Review," *Journal of Marketing Research,* August 1989, pp. 351–57; and William B. Dodds, Kent B. Monroe, and Dhruv Grewal, "Effects of Price, Brand, and Store Evaluations on Buyers' Product Evaluations," *Journal of Marketing Research,* August 1991, pp. 307–19.

3. For further discussion of price elasticity, see Stephen J. Hoch, Byung-Do Kim, Alan L. Montgomery, and Peter Rosi, "Determinants of Store-Level Price Elasticity," *Journal of Marketing Research,* February 1995, pp. 17–29.

4. For further discussion of legal issues involved in pricing, see Louis W. Stern and Thomas L. Eovaldi, *Legal Aspects of Marketing Strategy* (Englewood Cliffs, NJ: Prentice Hall, 1984), chap. 5.

5. For more detailed discussions, see Frederick E. Webster, *Marketing for Managers* (NY: Harper & Row, 1974), pp. 178–79; also see Thomas T. Nagle and Reed K. Holden, *The Strategy and Tactics of Pricing* (Englewood Cliffs, NJ: Prentice Hall, 1995); and Kent B. Monroe, *Pricing: Making Profitable Decisions,* 3rd ed. (Burr Ridge, IL: McGraw-Hill/Irwin, 2003).

Chapter 12

1. Much of the material for this introduction came from Ronald Henkoff, "Service Is Everybody's Business," *Fortune,* June 27, 1994, pp. 48–60; and Tim R. Smith, "The Tenth District's Expanding Service Sector," *Economic Review,* Third Quarter 1994, pp. 55–66.

2. Peter D. Bennett, ed., *Dictionary of Marketing Terms,* 2nd ed. (Chicago: American Marketing Association, 1995), p. 261.

3. The material in this section draws from research performed by Leonard L. Berry, Valerie A. Zeithaml, and A. Parasuraman, "Quality Counts in Services, Too," *Business Horizons,* May–June 1985, pp. 44–52; A. Parasuraman, Valerie A. Zeithaml, and Leonard L. Berry, "A Conceptual Model of Service Quality and Its Implications for Future Research," *Journal of Marketing,* Fall 1985, pp. 41–50; Leonard L. Berry, A. Parasuraman, and Valerie A. Zeithaml, "The Service-Quality Puzzle," *Business Horizons,* September–October 1988, pp. 35–43; Stephen W. Brown and Teresa A. Swartz, "A Gap Analysis of Professional Service Quality," *Journal of Marketing,* April 1989, pp. 92–98; Leonard L. Berry, Valerie A. Zeithaml, and A. Parasuraman, "Five Imperatives for Improving Service Quality," *Sloan Management Review,* Summer 1990, pp. 29–38; A. Parasuraman, Leonard L. Berry, and Valerie A. Zeithaml, "Understanding Customer Expectations of Service," *Sloan Management Review,* Spring 1991, pp. 39–48; and Leonard L. Berry, *On Great Service: A Framework for Action* (NY: Free Press, 1995).

4. Rick Berry, "Define Service Quality So You Can Deliver It," *Best's Review,* March 1995, p. 68.

5. Material for this section is drawn from John T. Mentzer, Carol C. Bienstock, and Kenneth B. Kahn, "Benchmarking Satisfaction," *Marketing Management,* Summer 1995, pp. 41–46; and Alan Dutka, *AMA Handbook for Customer Satisfaction: A Complete Guide to Research, Planning and Implementation* (Lincolnwood, IL: NTC Books, 1994). For detailed information on this topic, readers are advised to consult these sources.

6. Much of the material for this section was taken from Karl Albrecht and Ron Zemke, *Service America* (Burr Ridge, IL: McGraw-Hill/Irwin, 1985); and Ron Zemke and Dick Schaaf, *The Service Edge 101: Companies That Profit from Customer Care* (NY: New American Library, 1989).

7. Chip R. Bell and Kristen Anderson, "Selecting Super Service People," *HR Magazine,* February 1992, pp. 52–54.

8. James A. Schlesinger and James L. Heskett, "Breaking the Cycle of Failure in Services," *Sloan Management Review,* Spring 1991, pp. 17–28.

9. Leonard L. Berry and A. Parasuraman, "Services Marketing Starts from Within," *Marketing Management,* Winter 1992, pp. 25–34.

10. Ibid.

11. Leonard L. Berry and A. Parasuraman, "Prescriptions for a Service Quality Revolution in America," *Organizational Dynamics,* Spring 1992, pp. 5–15.

12. Bob O'Neal, "World-Class Service," *Executive Excellence,* September 1994, pp. 11–12.

13. This example is from David E. Bowen and Edward E. Lawler III, "The Empowerment of Service Workers: What, Why, How, and When," *Sloan Management Review,* Spring 1992, pp. 31–39.

14. Howard Schlossberg, "Study: U.S. Firms Lag in Using Customer Satisfaction Data," *Marketing News,* June 1992, p. 14.

15. Andrew E. Serwer, "The Competition Heats Up in Online Banking," *Fortune,* June 26, 1995, pp. 18–19.

16. John Labate, "Chronimed," *Fortune,* February 20, 1995, p. 118.

17. Elaine Underwood, "Airlines Continue Flight to E-Ticketing," *Brandweek,* May 8, 1995, p. 3.

18. Peter L. Ostrowski, Terrence V. O'Brien, and Geoffrey L. Gordon, "Determinants of Service Quality in the Commercial Airline Industry: Differences between Business and Leisure Travelers," *Journal of Travel & Tourism Marketing* 3, no. 1 (1994), pp. 19–47.

Chapter 13

1. Jason Vogel, "Chicken Diplomacy," *Financial World,* March 14, 1995, pp. 46–49.

2. For a full explanation on cultural differences, see Rose Knotts, "Cross-Cultural Management: Transformations and Adaptations," *Business Horizons,* January–February 1989, pp. 29–33.

3. Claudia Penteado, "Pepsi's Brazil Blitz," *Advertising Age,* January 16, 1995, p. 12.

4. Karen Benezra, "Fritos 'Round the World,'" *Brandweek,* March 27, 1995, pp. 32, 35.

5. Material for this section is from Craig Mellow, "Russia: Making Cash from Chaos," *Fortune,* April 17, 1995, pp. 145–51; and Peter Galuszka, "And You Think You've Got Tax Problems," *Business Week,* May 29, 1995, p. 50.

6. Mir Magbool Alam Khan, "Enormity Tempts Marketers to Make a Passage to India," *Advertising Age International,* May 15, 1995, p. 112.

7. This section was taken from James F. Bolt, "Global Competitors: Some Criteria for Success," *Business Horizons,* January–February 1988, pp. 34–41.

8. This section is based on George S. Yip, Pierre M. Loewe, and Michael Y. Yoshino, "How to Take Your Company to the Global Market," *Columbia Journal of World Business,* Winter 1988, pp. 37–48.

9. Ibid.

10. The introductory material on foreign research is based on Michael R. Czintoka, "Take a Shortcut to Low-Cost Global Research," *Marketing News,* March 13, 1995, p. 3.

11. Donald B. Pittenger, "Gathering Foreign Demographics Is No Easy Task," *Marketing News,* January 8, 1990, pp. 23, 25.

12. This discussion is based on John Burnett, *Promotion Management* (Boston: Houghton-Mifflin Co., 1993), chap. 19.

13. The material for this section on market entry and growth approaches is based on Philip R. Cateora, *International Marketing,* 8th ed. (Burr Ridge, IL: McGraw-Hill/Irwin, 1993), pp. 325–34; Charles W. L. Hill, *International Business: Competing in the Global Marketplace* (Burr Ridge, IL: McGraw-Hill/Irwin, 1994), pp. 402–8; and William M. Pride and O. C. Ferrell, *Marketing: Concepts and Strategy,* 9th ed. (Boston: Houghton-Mifflin Co., 1995), pp. 111–14.

14. Bruce A. Walters, Steve Peters, and Gregory G. Dess, "Strategic Alliances and Joint Ventures: Making Them Work," *Business Horizons,* July–August 1994, pp. 5–10.

15. Material in this section is based on Subhash C. Jain, "Standardization of International Marketing Strategy: Some Research Hypotheses," *Journal of Marketing,* January 1989, pp. 70–79.

SECTION 2

1. Michael E. Porter, *Competitive Strategy* (NY: Free Press, 1980). Also see Michael E. Porter, *Competitive Advantage: Creating and Sustaining Superior Performance* (NY: Free Press, 1985); and Michael E. Porter, *The Competitive Advantage of Nations* (NY: Free Press, 1990).

SECTION 3

1. For methods of estimating the cost of capital, see Charles P. Jones, *Introduction to Financial Management* (Burr Ridge, IL: McGraw-Hill/Irwin, 1992), chap. 14.

2. See Eugene F. Brigham, *Fundamentals of Financial Management* (Hinsdale, IL: Dryden Press, 1986).

3. It is useful to use average inventory rather than a single end-of-year estimate if monthly data are available.

4. For a discussion of ratio analysis for retailing, see Michael Levy and Barton A. Weitz, *Retailing Management* (Burr Ridge, IL: McGraw-Hill/Irwin, 2007), chap. 5.

Index

SUBJECT INDEX